Egypt

Virginia Maxwell

Mary Fitzpatrick, Siona Jenkins, Anthony Sattin

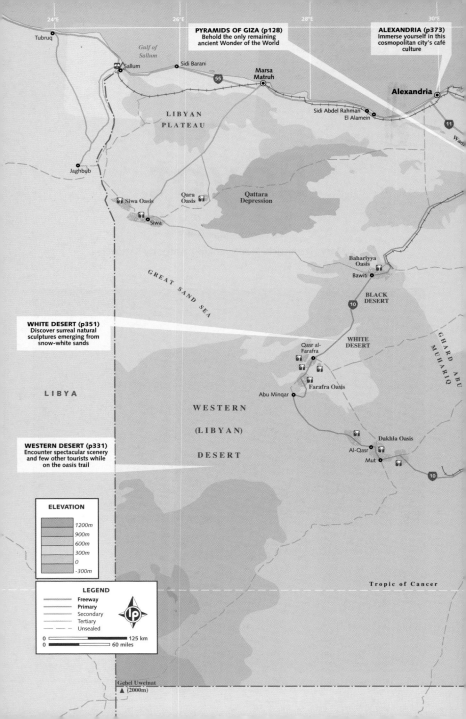

PYRAMIDS OF GIZA (p128)
Behold the only remaining
ancient Wonder of the World

ALEXANDRIA (p373)
Immerse yourself in this
cosmopolitan city's café
culture

Tubruq

Gulf of
Sallum

Sallum

Sidi Barani

Marsa
Matruh

55

Alexandria

Sidi Abdel Rahman
El Alamein

11

Wadi

LIBYAN
PLATEAU

Jaghbub

Siwa Oasis

Qara
Oasis

Qattara
Depression

Siwa

Bahariyya
Oasis

Bawiti

BLACK
DESERT

10

WHITE DESERT (p351)
Discover surreal natural
sculptures emerging from
snow-white sands

GREAT SAND SEA

WHITE
DESERT

GHARD ABU
MUHARIQ

LIBYA

Qasr al-
Farafra

Farafra Oasis

Abu Minqar

WESTERN

(LIBYAN)

DESERT

Dakhla Oasis

Al-Qasr

Mut

10

WESTERN DESERT (p331)
Encounter spectacular scenery
and few other tourists while
on the oasis trail

ELEVATION

1200m
900m
600m
300m
0
-300m

Tropic of Cancer

LEGEND
Freeway
Primary
Secondary
Tertiary
Unsealed

LP

0   125 km
0   60 miles

Gebel Uweinat
▲ (2000m)

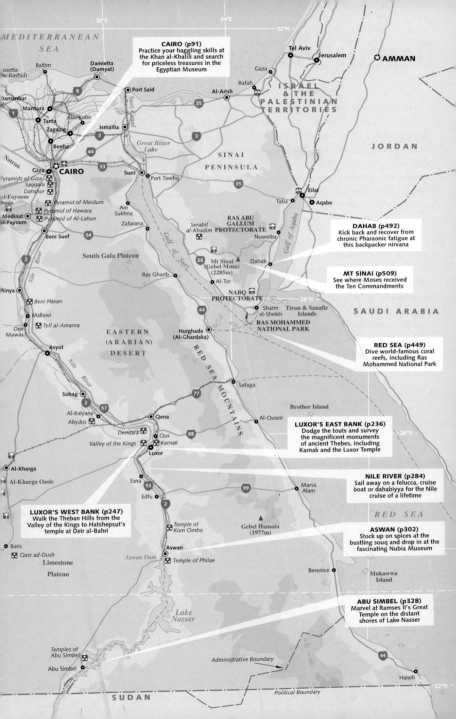

CAIRO (p91)
Practice your haggling skills at the Khan al-Khalili and search for priceless treasures in the Egyptian Museum

DAHAB (p492)
Kick back and recover from chronic Pharaonic fatigue at this backpacker nirvana

MT SINAI (p509)
See where Moses received the Ten Commandments

RED SEA (p449)
Dive world-famous coral reefs, including Ras Mohammed National Park

LUXOR'S EAST BANK (p236)
Dodge the touts and survey the magnificent monuments of ancient Thebes, including Karnak and the Luxor Temple

NILE RIVER (p284)
Sail away on a felucca, cruise boat or dahabiyya for the Nile cruise of a lifetime

LUXOR'S WEST BANK (p247)
Walk the Theban Hills from the Valley of the Kings to Hatshepsut's temple at Deir al-Bahri

ASWAN (p302)
Stock up on spices at the bustling souq and drop in at the fascinating Nubia Museum

ABU SIMBEL (p328)
Marvel at Ramses II's Great Temple on the distant shores of Lake Nasser

Destination Egypt

A land of magnificent World Heritage sites and a thousand tourist clichés, Egypt was enticing visitors millennia before Mr Cook sailed his first steamers up the Nile. It was in Egypt that the Holy Family sheltered, Alexander conquered and Mark Anthony flirted. Napoleon stopped long enough to pilfer a few obelisks, the Ottomans paused to prop up the great and barbarous pasha Mohammed Ali and the British stayed around to get the train system running and furnish every spare nook of the British Museum. And all this was long, long after Menes united the two states of Upper and Lower Egypt and set the stage for the greatest civilisation the world has ever known.

Lingering over coffee in one of Alexandria's cosmopolitan cafés or sipping a calming glass of *shai* (tea) after a frenzied shopping episode in Cairo's Khan al-Khalili are activities as popular today as they were back when 19th-century tourists started to arrive en masse. Magnificent monuments are everywhere – the pointed perfection of the pyramids, graceful minarets of Cairo's skyline and majestic tombs and temples of Luxor are just a few of the wonders that generations of visitors have admired during their city sojourns, jaunts up and down the Nile and expeditions through spectacularly stark desert landscapes. Their journey completed, they are inevitably left with the same exhilarating realisation: that Howard Carter's discovery of Tutankhamun's tomb did a lot more than raise the boy pharaoh's previously negligible profile and set off a craze for Egyptology in the Western world – it confirmed once and for all that Egypt's discoveries are ongoing and its treasures, limitless.

City Life

Leap into the chaos of Cairo (p91)

IZZET KERIBAR

Kick up a gear when the sun goes down and enjoy Cairo's nightlife (p156)

BRETT SHEARER

MARCO DI LAURO/GETTY IMAGES

Catch a sea breeze on the Corniche, Alexandria (p373)

OTHER HIGHLIGHTS

- Relax in one of Alexandria's gracefully fading period cafés (p394)
- Wander among the port-city bustle and belle époque architecture of Port Said (p411)

Pharaonic Treasures

Run the gauntlet of stony stares down the avenue of ram-headed sphinxes (p243) at Karnak

Face off against the Colossi of Memnon (p250) on Luxor's West Bank

OTHER HIGHLIGHTS

- Take a shine to the young pharaoh's treasure at the Egyptian Museum's Tutankhamun Galleries (p173)
- Marvel at Ramses II's awe-inspiring tribute to himself, the Great Temple at Abu Simbel (p328)
- Go royal-spotting in the Royal Mummy Room (p172) at the Egyptian Museum

The Temple of Hatshepsut (p262) rises out of the desert plain at Deir al-Bahri

IZZET KERIBAR

The spectacular temples of Karnak (p242) are littered with obelisks, pylons and statues

JOHN ELK III

Be overwhelmed with reliefs at the Temple of Hatshepsut (p262), Deir al-Bahri

Zoser's Step Pyramid (p182), the world's earliest stone monument, still stands tall

JOHN ELK III

Diving the Red Sea

MARK WEBSTER

Discover the spectacular coral-reef ecosystems at
Ras Mohammed National Park (p453)

Get deep and meaningful at the
Red Sea's Brother islands (p456)

CASEY & ASTRID WITTE MAHANEY

MARK WEBSTER

Meet the locals at dive sites off Sharm
el-Sheikh (p453)

OTHER HIGHLIGHTS

- Combine diving and Bedouin culture in a camel/
  dive safari (p459) from Dahab
- Explore the famous wreck of the British warship
  The Thistlegorm (p454)
- Sail between remote dive sites on a live-aboard
  dive safari (p456)

Cruising the Nile

Sail away on a felucca cruise (p287), Luxor

CHERYL CONLON

JOHN ELK III

Cruisers dock where sacred crocodiles used to bask
in front of the Temple of Kom Ombo (p300)

Pay your respects at Edfu's Temple of
Horus (p298), a major cruising destination

LEE FOSTER

OTHER HIGHLIGHTS

- Sail in style on a dahabiyya (p287), the Rolls Royce of the Nile
- Reel in a whopper on a fishing/sightseeing cruise (p291) on Lake Nasser
- Bring a picnic on a felucca ride (p137) in Cairo

Deserts & Oases

Make the most of the wide open spaces of the Western Desert (p331)

Duck down an alley in Balat (p346), Dakhla Oasis

Find out how the locals beat the heat in the Western Desert (p331)

OTHER HIGHLIGHTS

- Go shape-spotting amid the surreal, snow-white rock formations of the White Desert (p351)
- Take a moonlit soak on the edge of the desert in one of the western oases' hot springs (p364)
- Follow ancient trade routes across the rugged Eastern Desert (p444)

Siwa Oasis (p359) appears out of the
desert like a mirage

Remnants of an ancient past still linger in
Siwa Oasis (p359)

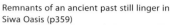

Trek into the stark interior of the Sinai Peninsula on a camel trek (p495)

Islamic Cairo

Haggle your heart out in the Khan al-Khalili (p112)

IZZET KERIBAR

The Madrassa and Mausoleum of Barquq (p115) is one of three great Mamluk complexes in Bein al-Qasreen

PATRICK HORTON

Enter an ancient centre of learning, Al-Azhar Mosque (p111)

ARIADNE VAN ZANDBERGEN

OTHER HIGHLIGHTS

- Drink in the atmosphere at Fishawi's Coffeehouse (p154), one of Egypt's oldest and most famous coffeehouses
- Step into a Mahfouz novel with an Islamic Cairo walking tour (p138)
- Discover 18th-century sophistication at the merchant's house Beit el-Suhaymi (p114)

Contents

Regional Map Contents

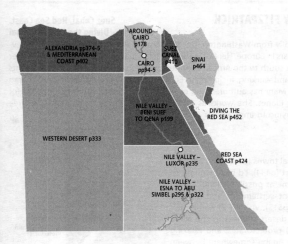

The Authors

VIRGINIA MAXWELL

**Coordinating Author,
Cairo, Around Cairo, Egyptian Museum**

After working for many years as a publishing manager at Lonely Planet's Melbourne headquarters, Virginia decided she'd be happier writing guidebooks than commissioning them. Since then she's authored Lonely Planet's *Istanbul* city guide and covered Lebanon, Syria and the United Arab Emirates for other titles. Virginia is also the author of the Egypt chapter of the *Middle East* guidebook. With partner Peter and young son Max she's explored most corners of the Middle East, including multiple visits to the Land of the Pharaohs.

My Favourite Trip

South is up in Egypt, and there's nothing quite like making one's way from Cairo (p91) to Aswan (p302) and spending a few days languishing where the Nile is most picturesque. Rested, I then make my way even further south into Nubia – the ultimate reward being half a day visiting Ramses II's magnificent monument to himself, Abu Simbel (p328). After this, a week or so staying on Luxor's West Bank (p233) is a must – there's just so much to do in this town of monuments and magic. Then I take the train all the way back to Alexandria (p373), home to historic cafés, great coffee and sumptuous seafood feasts.

Alexandria
CAIRO
Luxor
Aswan
Abu Simbel

MARY FITZPATRICK

**Suez Canal, Red Sea Coast,
Diving the Red Sea, Sinai**

Originally from Washington, DC, Mary set off after graduate studies for several years in Europe. Her fascination with languages and cultures soon led her further south to the African continent, where she has spent extended stints living and working, including in Egypt and various countries in sub-Saharan Africa. Mary has authored and coauthored numerous other guidebooks for Lonely Planet. She works as a full-time travel writer, and spends her free time trying to improve her Arabic.

My Favourite Trip

After a quick foray around the canal towns (p409), and a longer detour south to the Eastern Desert (p444), I'd head straight to Sinai, where I'd spend as much time as possible hiking around Mt Sinai (p510), exploring ancient settlements and pilgrimage routes around Wadi Feiran (p513), visiting St Katherine's Monastery (p508), taking in the desert stillness in the Nabq (p492) or Ras Abu Gallum (p499) protectorates, and relaxing on the beaches along the Gulf of Aqaba somewhere between Nuweiba (p500) and Taba (p507). With any time remaining, I'd head south to Ras Mohammed National Park (p468) to enjoy the underwater magnificence.

Port Said
Suez Canal
Ismailia
Sinai Peninsula
Suez
Mt Sinai;
St Katherine's Monastery
Taba
Nuweiba
Ras Abu Gallum Protectorate
Wadi Feiran
Nabq Protectorate
Eastern Desert
Ras Mohammed National Park

SIONA JENKINS
Nile Valley chapters, Cruising the Nile

After spending her teenage years visiting her parents in Saudi Arabia, Siona decided there was more to the Middle East than oil and veils. Armed with a degree in Islamic history, she arrived in Cairo in 1989 with hopes of mastering Arabic, but soon ditched plans for a PhD in favour of living in the megalopolis and speaking colloquial Egyptian. She worked as a freelance journalist and helped to produce documentary films. Now based in London, she is introducing her baby daughter to the joys of travel. Siona has worked on three previous editions of *Egypt* and wrote Lonely Planet's Egyptian Arabic phrasebook.

My Favourite Trip

It may be a cliché, but the Nile Valley seems timeless, and a daytime train ride is the best way to see it. Heading south from Cairo, clustered villages evoke an ancient way of life, satellite dishes notwithstanding. Nothing quite beats the ruined grandeur of Luxor's monuments (p233). I love biking around the West Bank, chatting with villagers and lingering in temples. An early train to Aswan (p302) lets you stop at the temples of Esna (p295), Edfu (p297) and Kom Ombo (p300) en route. The Nile dominates Aswan, and there is no better way to appreciate the river than to take a cruise from here on Lake Nasser (p291), ending up at Abu Simbel's awesome temples (p328).

ANTHONY SATTIN
Western Desert, Alexandria & the Mediterranean Coast

Anthony has spent much of his life living in, travelling around or writing about Egypt. He is the author of several acclaimed books including *The Pharaoh's Shadow,* in which he searched for surviving ancient Egyptian culture, and most recently *The Gates of Africa.* He is a regular contributor to the *Sunday Times* and has made TV and radio documentaries about Egypt. Described by a British newspaper as 'a cross between Indiana Jones and a John Buchan hero', he divides his time between London, Cairo and the further reaches of the Nile.

My Favourite Trip

I love travelling along the Nile and for years that's just about all I did. But the past few years I have been spending more and more time away from the Nile, in the desert and oases. One of my favourite trips (and I can narrow it down no more than that) is in and around Siwa (p359), which manages to combine the scenic and remote with the historically significant. But I also love driving the desert circuit, particularly from Bahariyya (p353) through the White Desert (p351) to Farafra (p348) and on to Dakhla (p341). Expect to see me somewhere between Siwa and Bahariyya as soon as the new road is opened.

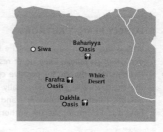

CONTRIBUTING AUTHOR

Dr Joann Fletcher Fascinated with Egypt since she was a small child, Joann Fletcher's first visit to the country in 1981 only confirmed her decision to make it her career. A degree in Egyptology was followed by a PhD in the same subject, and as a research fellow at the University of York she undertakes scientific research on everything from royal mummies to ancient perfumes. She is the Egyptologist for several UK museums, and designed the UK's first nationally available Egyptology qualification. Having excavated at a number of sites in Egypt, including the Valley of the Kings, Joann regularly appears on TV, contributes to the BBC's online history service and has written eight books to date. When in Egypt she stays with her Egyptian family on Luxor's West Bank, or otherwise is at home on the Yorkshire coast or in Normandy.

Getting Started

Exploring Egypt is easy. Most of the tourist hotspots are well connected by cheap buses, and many are also linked by train and plane. Accommodation is plentiful, particularly in the budget and top-end categories, and decent eateries are thick on the ground in every corner of the country except the oases. Unlike some other parts of the Middle East, enjoying a beer, meeting the locals and accessing the Internet are all things that can be taken for granted. Predeparture planning will usually guarantee your accommodation of choice, but on the whole it's not necessary – unless you're on a tight timetable, it's usually more enjoyable to leave your itinerary in the lap of the gods. After all, there are a lot of them to call on…

WHEN TO GO

The best time to visit Egypt depends on where you want to go. Generally speaking, winter (December to February) is the tourist high season and summer (June to August) is the low season in all parts of the country except on the coasts, and to a lesser degree in Cairo. Hotel prices reflect this.

Weather-wise, June to August is unbearable almost anywhere south of Cairo, especially around Luxor and Aswan, where daytime temperatures soar up to 40°C. Summer in Cairo is almost as hot, and the combination of heat, dust, pollution, noise and crush makes walking the city streets a real test of endurance. On the other hand, a scorching sun might be exactly what's wanted for a week or two of slow roasting on the beaches of southern Sinai, the Alexandrian coast or the Red Sea – just be prepared to fight for hotel rooms with locals on their summer holidays and Gulf Arabs escaping the even greater heat in their home countries. When visiting somewhere such as Luxor, winter is easily the most comfortable time. Cairo isn't quite as pleasant, with often overcast skies and chilly evenings, while up on the Mediterranean coast Alexandria is subject to frequent downpours resulting in flooded, muddy streets. Even Sinai's beaches are a little too chilly for sunbathing in January. The happiest compromise for an all-Egypt trip is to visit in spring (March to May) or autumn (September to November).

Most of Egypt's religious and state holidays (for dates see p529) last only one or two days at most and should not seriously disrupt any travel plans. Buses, though, may be fully booked around the two *eid*s (Islamic feasts) and on Sham an-Nessim. Ramadan, the Muslim month of fasting, is seriously disruptive. During daylight hours many cafés and restaurants

See Climate Charts (p522) for more information.

DON'T LEAVE HOME WITHOUT...

There is very little that you might need that you won't be able to find in Egypt. That said, you may not have the same degree of choice as at home. So bring sunglasses, a torch (flashlight), sunscreen (anything above factor eight is hard to find in Egypt) and a hat. If you're a light sleeper you may also want to bring earplugs – bus rides are rarely quiet, Cairo is a very noisy city and throughout the country dawn is accompanied by the amplified voice of the muezzin calling the faithful to prayer. If you are visiting during winter a sweater is necessary for evenings, especially in desert areas. Although most toiletries can be found in city pharmacies and supermarkets, certain items can be difficult to get. When you do find them they can be expensive, too. This is certainly the case with contact-lens solution, roll-on mosquito repellent, tampons and contraceptives (local condoms have a distressingly high failure rate).

Finally, make sure you check travel advisories (see p526) for a current security update.

are closed, while bars cease business completely for the duration. Offices also operate at reduced and very erratic hours.

COSTS & MONEY

By international standards Egypt is still fairly cheap. It is possible to get by on E£50 (US$9) a day or maybe less if you are willing to stick to the cheapest hotels (you can get a bed for as little as E£10), eat the staple snacks of *fuul* and *ta'amiyya,* use the cheapest local transport and limit yourself to one historical site per day. At the other end of the scale, Cairo has plenty of accommodation charging upwards of E£580 a night, and some of the better restaurants will set you back E£170 (US$30) per person or more.

Taking a middle route, if you stay in a modest hotel with a fan and private bathroom, eat in low-key restaurants frequented by locals (allowing for the occasional splurge), and aim to see a couple of sites each day, you'll be looking at between E£120 (US$20) and E£170 (US$30) a day.

Getting around the country is cheap: the 10-hour train ride between Cairo and Luxor can cost as little as E£35 in 2nd class.

The major expense is going to be the entry fees to tourist sites. Foreigners are seen as dollars on legs, so places where they flock tend to be pricey. A complete visit to the Giza Pyramids costs E£300 in admission charges (E£155 for students), and if you want to see the mummies at the Egyptian Museum, the adult combined fee is E£140.

A service charge of between 10% and 15% is applied in most upmarket restaurants and hotels, to which VAT and municipal taxes are also added. In other words, the price you are quoted at a hotel or read on a menu could be almost 25% higher when it comes to paying the bill.

TRAVEL LITERATURE

Surprisingly little travel literature has appeared in recent times concerning Egypt. However, a great many entertaining 19th-century accounts continue to be reprinted.

In an Antique Land by Amitav Ghosh is a wonderfully observant account of the author's lengthy stay in a Delta village; it's entertaining, educational and one of the few travel books that is not patronising towards its subject.

The Pharaoh's Shadow by Anthony Sattin is travel lit with a twist. Sattin searches for 'survivals' of Pharaonic traditions and practices in the Egypt of today, encountering along the way magicians, snake catchers, mystics and sceptics. A fascinating read. Also by Anthony Sattin, *Florence Nightingale's Letters from Egypt* tell of the five-month trip that the famous 'Lady with the Lamp' took through Egypt in the winter of 1849–50. The book is packed with 19th-century images of Egypt.

The Blue Nile and *The White Nile* by Alan Moorhead form a two-volume *tour de force* describing the search for sources of the Nile.

Flaubert in Egypt: A Sensibility on Tour, translated and edited by Francis Steegmuller, includes choice excerpts from Flaubert's diary as he made his way up the Nile. Detailed descriptions of Upper Egyptian dancing girls and prostitutes spice up his accounts of ancient sites.

A Thousand Miles Up the Nile by Amelia Edwards is a travel classic describing a 19th-century journey from Cairo to Abu Simbel and back on a dahabiyya.

Letters from Egypt by Lucie Duff Gordon is the journal of a solo woman traveller who lived in Luxor for seven years from 1862 to 1869.

Travels With a Tangerine: A Journey in the Footnotes of Ibn Battutah by Tim Mackintosh-Smith sees the modern-day author following the route taken by the medieval adventurer; three great chapters are set in Egypt.

HOW MUCH?

Meal in a cheap restaurant E£10 to E£15

Meal in a good restaurant E£40 to E£100

Glass of tea E£2

Short taxi hop E£4

Average museum admission E£30

See also Lonely Planet Index, inside front cover.

TOP TENS

Films Set in Egypt

In recent years extortionate taxes levied on foreign film companies have kept the cameras away (that's actually Tunisia standing in for Egypt in *The English Patient* and *Raiders of the Lost Ark*, Arizona in *Stargate*, and CGI in the remake of *The Mummy*). But even if they haven't been shot on location, there are plenty of films that evoke the country and its colourful history splendidly. All make great pre-departure viewing.

- *The Ten Commandments* (1923 & 1956)
- *Cleopatra* (1963)
- *Death on the Nile* (1978)
- *The English Patient* (1996)
- *The Mummy* (1932 & 1999)

- *Raiders of the Lost Ark* (1981)
- *Valley of the Kings* (1954)
- *Sphinx* (1981)
- *The Spy Who Loved Me* (1977)
- *Land of the Pharaohs* (1955)

Great Reads

With a vivid history encompassing pyramid builders (human or otherwise), horror caliphs, the enchantment of *The Thousand and One Nights* and colonial high jinks and romance, there's no lack of colourful Egyptian subject matter to base a story on. For more on Egyptian literature, see p69.

- *The Alexandria Quartet* by Lawrence Durrell
- *Beer at the Snooker Club* by Waguih Ghali
- *The Levant Trilogy* by Olivia Manning
- *Cairo: The City Victorious* by Max Rodenbeck
- *The Cairo Trilogy* by Naguib Mahfouz

- *Zayni Barakat* by Gamal al-Ghitani
- *The Yacoubian Building* by Alaa Al Aswany
- *The Map of Love* by Ahdaf Soueif
- *Moon Tiger* by Penelope Lively
- *Point Zero* by Nawal el-Sadawi

Museums & Galleries

With 5000 years of history, you can figure that Egypt has no shortage of exhibits for its museums.

- Egyptian Museum (p167), Cairo
- Gayer-Anderson Museum (p121), Cairo
- Graeco-Roman Museum (p379), Alexandria
- Museum of Islamic Art p118), Cairo
- Luxor Museum (p236), Luxor

- Museum of Modern Egyptian Art (p124), Cairo
- Mummification Museum (p240), Luxor
- Mr & Mrs Mahmoud Khalil Museum (p125), Cairo
- Nubia Museum (p305), Aswan
- Alexandria National Museum (p381), Alexandria

INTERNET RESOURCES

Al-Ahram Weekly (http://weekly.ahram.org.eg) Electronic version of the weekly English-language newspaper. Almost the whole paper is online and the archives are fully searchable and free to access.

Cairo Magazine (www.cairomagazine.com) Electronic version of the weekly English-language magazine covering life in the Big Mango.

Egypt: The Complete Guide (www.touregypt.net) The official site of Egypt's Ministry of Tourism is updated reasonably regularly with magazine-type features, news and a huge range of resources and links.

Lonely Planet (www.lonelyplanet.com) Includes summaries on travelling to Egypt, the Thorn Tree bulletin board, travel news and links to the most useful travel resources on the Web.

Red Sea Guide & Search Engine (www.red-sea.com) This site does exactly what the name suggests: provides heaps of travel tips and water-sports information and links.

State Information Service (www.sis.gov.eg) A huge amount of information on tourism, geography and culture, plus a great many useful links, all courtesy of the Egyptian State Information Service.

Itineraries
CLASSIC ROUTES

WHISTLE-STOP NILE TOUR   One Week / Cairo to Abu Simbel

On a punishing schedule, one week is just enough time to see the bare highlights of this magnificent country. Fly into **Cairo** (p91). Two days in the capital allow you to take in the astounding **Pyramids of Giza** (p128) and seek out the treasures in the **Egyptian Museum** (p167), as well making an evening visit to the **Khan al-Khalili** (p112), the city's grand bazaar.

Catch the overnight train to **Luxor** (p233; book this as soon as you arrive in Cairo to be sure of a berth), arriving early in the morning – the perfect time to head over to the **West Bank** (p247) to see the monuments of the ancient necropolis of Thebes. In two days you can visit the major sights, including **Medinat Habu** (p269), **Deir al-Bahri** (temple of Hatshepsut; (p262) and the **Valley of the Kings** (p251). Spend afternoons or evenings on the East Bank at **Karnak** (p242) and **Luxor Temple** (p240).

Jump on a morning train to **Aswan** (p302; five hours) and you'll be able to spend a relaxing afternoon sailing on a felucca on the Nile.

At a push the next day you could go to **Abu Simbel** (p328) to visit the grandest of all Pharaonic monuments, before hightailing it by train back to Cairo.

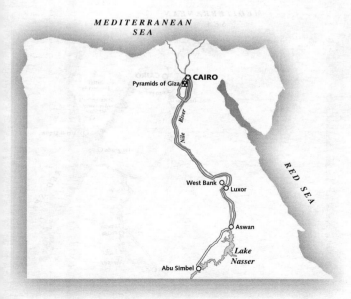

The 1020km Whistle-Stop Nile Tour will race you through Egypt's major attractions, teasing you with a brief taste of the country's flavours.

FORTNIGHT JAUNT   Two Weeks / Cairo to Mt Sinai

A fortnight is an ideal amount of time in which to explore the country's ancient and modern facets.

Start with three days in **Cairo** (p91). Spend your first day touring the area's huge collection of monuments in proper chronological order, starting at **Saqqara** (p181), moving on to **Dahshur** (p187), and finally visiting the **Pyramids of Giza** (p128), a wonder of the ancient world.

Spend your second day at the **Egyptian Museum** (p167) marvelling at the antiquities and relics, of which there are more than 100,000. On day three explore the twisting alleyways and splendid mosques of the medieval quarters of **Islamic Cairo** (p110). Take your time and spend a moment or two relaxing in one of the area's fabulous *ahwas* (coffeehouses).

Train it straight down to **Aswan** (p302), from where you can organise a day tour to see both **Abu Simbel** (p328) and the island temple of Isis at **Philae** (p319). Then move into relaxation mode with two nights on a **felucca** (p287) sailing up to **Edfu** (p297), site of a fine Ptolemaic-era temple.

From here you can move on to **Luxor** (p233), where two or three days can be spent looking around the Pharaonic sights before catching a bus across the Eastern Desert to the resort town of **Hurghada** (p428), where you can catch a ferry to **Sharm el-Sheikh** (p470) in southern Sinai. Around here you can delight in the underwater world before visiting the Greek Orthodox **St Katherine's Monastery** (p508) and climbing to the top of **Mt Sinai** (p510), which is revered by Muslims, Christians and Jews.

Two weeks – a perfect time frame in which to experience the ancient and modern elements described in our 1500km Fortnight Jaunt.

TRAVELLING AT A STEADY PACE   One Month / Cairo to Sinai

In a month you could cover most of Egypt's main sights, but you'd still have to travel at a steady pace.

Spend four or five days in and around **Cairo** (p91) doing all the things described in the Whistle-Stop Nile Tour and Fortnight Jaunt itineraries, but also spend some time in **Coptic Cairo** (p107), the oldest part of modern-day Cairo and the Christian heartland of the city. You could also explore the narrow and history-rich streets of Islamic Cairo by taking in a fascinating **walking tour** (p138).

Next on your journey, take an early train north to Alexandria's Sidi Gaber station and transfer directly to a bus for **Siwa Oasis** (p359), one of Egypt's most idyllic spots. After a couple of days hanging out in this tranquil haven, backtrack along the Mediterranean coast to **Alexandria** (p373) and spend a couple of days in its wonderful cafés and museums.

Take the sleeping train to **Aswan** (p302), where you should spend a few days, including a full day devoted to making the trip to **Abu Simbel** (p328) and back. Then on to **Luxor** (p233), where you'll need at least five days before heading east to **Hurghada** (p428) on the coast. After an overnight stop, catch the ferry across the Red Sea. You'll have another six or so days to explore **Sinai** (p462), home to **Mt Sinai** (p509), the **Coloured Canyon** (p502), and the laid-back beachside town of **Dahab** (p492).

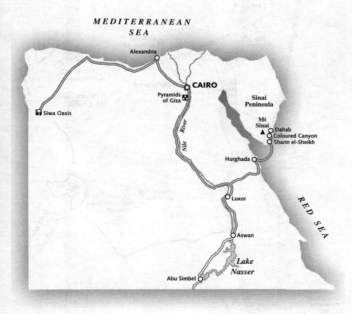

In a month you could comfortably cover 2190km and familiarise yourself with sites and attractions as diverse as city and oasis.

ROADS LESS TRAVELLED

CITY LIFE
One Week / Cairo

Organised tours are increasingly skipping Cairo in favour of the antiquities of Upper Egypt and the beaches of the Red Sea and Sinai, but for anybody interested in living culture, the capital of the Arab world is a blast. Spend a week here and you won't regret a minute.

Dive in at the deep end by exploring the **Khan al-Khalili** (p112) and the northern part of **Islamic Cairo**, perhaps following the walking tour of **Mahfouz's Cairo** (p138), then winding down at **Fishawi's Coffeehouse** (p154).

On day two roam **Downtown** (p101), lunching at **At-Tabie ad-Dumyati** (p146) or one of the other budget eateries, later taxiing to **Zamalek** (p124) for boutique hopping and an afternoon drink at the **Marriott Garden Café** (p155). Enjoy some **belly-dancing** (p158) in the evening.

Day three, hit the **Pyramids of Giza** (p128) in the morning and the **Egyptian Museum** (p167) in the afternoon.

On day four travel back to Islamic Cairo for the **Citadel** (p119), the **Mosque of Ibn Tulun** (p121) and the marvellous **Gayer-Anderson Museum** (p121). Relax in the late afternoon with a **felucca cruise** (p137).

On your fifth day take the metro down to **Old Cairo** (p107) and the **Nilometer** (p107), returning to central Cairo for lunch. Cross the Nile and walk down to the **Mr & Mrs Mahmoud Khalil Museum** (p125).

Any extra time can be invested in a day trip or even an overnight stay in **Alexandria** (p373).

Our City Life trip will introduce you to Cairo for a week of rich culture, where you'll enjoy museums, monuments, coffeehouses and felucca rides.

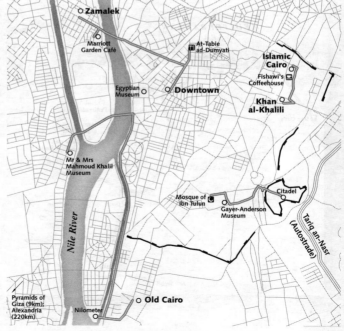

DESERT & OASES   Two weeks / Al-Kharga Oasis to Siwa

Taking inspiration from films such as *Lawrence of Arabia* or *The English Patient,* would-be desert rovers could disregard the country's many Pharaonic monuments for a couple of weeks in favour of getting sand happy in the amazing **Western Desert** (p331).

Begin your journey by taking a Nile Valley bus from Luxor to **Al-Kharga Oasis** (p334), the southernmost and least attractive oasis in the Western Oases loop. It's worth a day for exploring the **Al-Kharga Museum of Antiquities** (p336) and the profusion of Graeco-Roman temples, tombs and other interesting ruins.

From Al-Kharga Oasis make your way north to **Dakhla Oasis** (p341) for the experience of seeing the fascinating hivelike mud-walled settlements of **Balat** (p346) and **Al-Qasr** (p347), and on north again to **Farafra Oasis** (p348) and then **Bahariyya Oasis** (p353). Either of these latter two oases is the place to organise trips out into the stunning **White Desert** (p351), with its strangely shaped rock formations.

Real desert addicts can then negotiate a fee (E£500 to E£600) to strike due west across several hundred kilometres of open desert to **Siwa Oasis** (p359). (The alternative is to travel by bus back to Cairo, change for Alexandria and change again for Siwa – more than a day's travel.) Perched on the edge of the **Great Sand Sea** (p371), Siwa, renowned for its dates and olives, is the base for some of the most stunning yet accessible sandscapes in Egypt, although you will need to hire cars and drivers to reach these areas.

For two weeks and 1440km of breathtaking sites and adventures, shun the cities in favour of getting swept up in deserts. Also take time to chill out and cool down in the stunning oases.

TAILORED TRIPS

THE ANCIENT EGYPT TRAIL

If you're interested in the Pharaonic era, it greatly adds to the experience to tour Egypt in a chronological fashion. Start in **Cairo** (p91), making **Saqqara** (p181) the first port of call to view the **Step Pyramid of Zoser** (p182), the prototype of all pyramids to come. Travel to **Dahshur** (p187) to view the failed Bent Pyramid before returning to Giza to see the final article in the **Great Pyramid of Khufu** (p132). Visit the **Egyptian Museum** (p167) in Cairo, but try restraining your enthusiasm to the Old Kingdom galleries only.

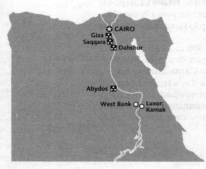

Travel to **Luxor** (p233), leaving the Old Kingdom behind and moving into the era of the Middle and New Kingdoms. The temple complex of **Karnak** (p242), constructed over 1500 years, offers a history lesson set in stone. Then cross to the West Bank and explore the **Valley of the Kings** (p251), viewing the tombs in chronological order to witness the development of tomb painting.

Visit **Medinat Habu** (p269) for the most complete expression of the Pharaonic golden age. Travel north by taxi or train (tourist police permitting) to Al-Balyana for **Abydos** (p226) and the sublime **Temple of Seti I**. Return to Cairo and revisit the **Egyptian Museum** again, this time to see the Middle and New Kingdom galleries.

SINAI – BEDOUIN, BEACHES & THE TEN COMMANDMENTS

Head first to **St Katherine's Monastery** (p508). The monastery is a must for the complete biblical experience; it has the burning bush, a famous Byzantine church and a stunning icon collection. Arrange a hike with a Bedouin guide through the spectacular **St Katherine Protectorate** (p513). Then, take a sleeping bag up **Mt Sinai** (p509), where Moses received the Ten Commandments, and set your alarm in order to catch the spectacular sunrise.

Relax on a beach to recover from your mountain-climbing exertions. If you prefer small resorts, **Dahab** (p492) is the place to arrange camels for

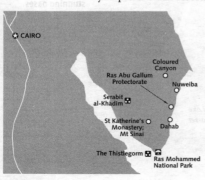

diving or snorkelling trips to nearby reefs, such as those at the **Ras Abu Gallum Protectorate** (p499). A trip to **Ras Mohammed National Park** (p468), home to some of the world's most spectacular reefs, is a must. Serious divers can arrange trips to more remote reefs or to the world-famous **Thistlegorm** (p454) wreck.

Back on dry land, there are plenty of Bedouin in Dahab or **Nuweiba** (p500) who can arrange camel or jeep treks to such natural wonders as the **Coloured Canyon** (p502). On your way back to Cairo allow for a detour to the impressively remote temple remains at **Serabit al-Khadim** (p468), where the ancient Egyptians mined turquoise.

Snapshot

Half a century on from the great Nasser-led revolution, and 25 years since Hosni Mubarak and his wife Suzanne first set up house in the presidential palace, Egypt is in a pretty bad state. Unemployment is rife (some analysts put it as high as 25%, though the government bandies around the rather unbelievable figure of 9.9%), the economy is of the basket-case variety and terrorist attacks are starting to occur with worrying regularity. Once home to the all-powerful pharaohs, the country has largely been reduced to being a dependent state of the USA, reliant on the US$1.3 billion in military aid and US$600 million in economic assistance it receives each year from the superpower. Perhaps not surprisingly, America is starting to attach some conditions to its generosity, the most significant of which was its recent openly articulated pressure on Mr Mubarak to introduce multicandidate presidential elections to the country.

The president bowed to the inevitable, announcing that an election would be held in September 2005. While pro-democracy supporters welcomed his action, most Egyptians shrugged their shoulders and waited for the disclaimer. This came in the form of a rule that all independent candidates standing in the election were required to have the backing of at least 65 members of the lower house of parliament, which is overwhelmingly dominated by the president's National Democratic Party. As a result, a small and pretty lacklustre field of opposition candidates lined up on the day. To no-one's surprise, President Mubarak was returned to office with 89% of the vote.

Subsequent parliamentary elections in November 2005 saw Muslim Brotherhood–aligned independent candidates winning an extraordinary 88 seats in the national parliament (six times the number they had previously held), making the Brotherhood a major player on the national political scene despite its officially illegal status.

The elections highlighted Egypt's lousy human-rights record. In the lead-up to the presidential campaign, Ayman Nour, leader of the popular Ghad (Tomorrow) party, was thrown into jail on what most Egyptians assumed to be trumped-up charges. Opposition rallies around the country were violently dispersed and opposition supporters alleged that they were abused after being taken into custody by police. Human-rights violations were even more apparent during the parliamentary elections, when government supporters in some parts of the country physically prevented supporters of Muslim Brotherhood–aligned independent candidates from entering polling booths. Ensuing confrontations between the two camps resulted in some deaths.

Groups such as Amnesty International and Human Rights Watch wouldn't have been at all surprised at these goings on – their annual reports excoriate Egypt year after year, asserting that the media and judiciary are allowed no real independence and that police regularly abuse their legislative right to unlimited powers of search and arrest. Other criticisms are that Egyptian police regularly torture and ill-treat prisoners in detention; that the Cairo police force has been involved in a long-running campaign of entrapment and harassment of homosexual men; that child labour is common within the lucrative national cotton industry; and that scores of members of Islamist opposition groups are regularly imprisoned without charge or trial.

FAST FACTS

Population: 74.9 million

Population growth rate: 2%

Inflation: 3.1%

GDP: US$267.4 billion

Main exports: Petroleum, petroleum products, cotton

Average annual income: US$1390

Average male life expectancy: 67 years

Average female life expectancy: 72 years

Male literacy rate: 68.3%

Female literacy rate: 46.9%

In the lead-up to the elections, two bombs in Sharm el-Sheikh in July 2005 killed 64 people. The government – deeply concerned that further terrorist action would impact badly on the country's vitally important tourist industry, which brings 8.1 million visitors and US$6.6 billion into the country every year – cracked down even harder on Islamist opposition groups (which it saw as the prime suspects) as a result.

The list of woes continues. Only 11 members of the national parliament are female (a mere 2.4% of the total), and women and girls face systematic discrimination under personal-status and other laws. And the environment is under constant threat, with oil pollution in waterways, overpopulation, air pollution and soil salinity being of serious concern.

The only good news on the horizon is that an economically liberal cabinet was elected in 2004, leading to the International Monetary Fund (IMF) and World Bank making some encouraging noises about the country's potential for future economic improvement. If this occurs, young Egyptians may be able to look to the future with confidence, and towards democracy and the upholding of human rights as their due. The country's well-wishers (of which there are many) can only hope that this will be the case.

History

The history of Egypt has always been linked to the Nile River. Back in prehistory the savanna lands of the Sahara began to dry up, forcing the region's nomadic populations to gradually migrate towards the river. Its ever-fertile banks gave birth to the world's first nation-state. It also spawned some of the most important achievements in human history, since Egypt was the place where writing was invented, the first stone monuments erected and an entire culture set in place that would remain largely unchanged for thousands of years. All of this was made possible by the regular rhythms of the river and, in contrast to the vast areas of barren desert known as *deshret* (red land), the narrow banks of the Nile were known as *kemet* (black land), after the rich silt deposited by the annual floods.

Ever since the earliest known communities settled its valley, the Nile River has inspired and controlled the religious, economic, social and political life of the Egyptians. For many centuries the narrow, elongated layout of the country's fertile lands hampered the fusion of those early settlements, which held fast to their local independence. But with the river providing a highway for commercial traffic and communication, those barriers were eventually broken. The small kingdoms developed into two important states: Upper Egypt comprised the long thin valley, from its furthest navigable reaches at Aswan north to the Delta (or to the future site of Cairo); Lower Egypt consisted of the flat, marshy Delta itself.

The unification of these two states by Narmer (also known as Menes), in around 3100 BC, set the scene for the greatest era of ancient Egyptian civilisation. Known as the Dynastic Period, a span of some 3000 years saw more than 30 royal dynasties. Towards the end of the Dynastic Period, Egypt was ruled by a series of foreign invaders from Libya, Nubia and Persia (among others), marking the start of a long period of foreign rule that was only to end with the revolution of 1952.

The 5000 years from the time of Narmer can be divided roughly into seven periods:

- Pharaonic Egypt 3100–332 BC
- Alexander & the Ptolemaic Era 332 BC–30 BC
- Roman Rule 30 BC–AD 638
- Arab Conquest 640–1517
- Ottoman Turkish Rule 1517–1882
- British Occupation 1882–1952
- Independent Egypt 1952–present

PHARAONIC EGYPT

The unification that occurred under the rule of Narmer is the subject of one of the Egyptian Museum's oldest Pharaonic artefacts, the Narmer Palette (p169), but little is known of the immediate successors of this enigmatic pharaoh except that, attributed with divine ancestry, they promoted the development of a highly stratified society, patronised the

The British Museum Dictionary of Ancient Egypt by I Shaw and P Nicholson gives an authoritative overview of ancient Egypt.

J Baines and J Malek's Atlas of Ancient Egypt, B Manley's The Penguin Historical Atlas of Ancient Egypt and BJ Kemp's Anatomy of a Civilisation are all great Egypt resources.

c 250,000 BC	c 4500–3100 BC
Earliest human traces in Egypt	Local cultures appear in the Nile Valley

arts and built many temples and public works. Their capital, founded by Narmer, was Memphis (p179). Memphis lay 24km south of what is now modern Cairo, a site that at that time marked the meeting point of Upper and Lower Egypt. The city survived for three and a half millennia as the cradle of Pharaonic civilisation, where writing and administration, art and architecture were nurtured and developed.

Though little of the greatest ancient Egyptian city remains, we can get an idea of the size and importance of Memphis by the remarkable funerary complexes that were created for its pharaohs. Foremost of these is the necropolis of Saqqara, which spread over 7km and had as its centrepiece a stepped pyramid, the earliest of the many pyramids to follow. Dating from about 2650 BC, the Step Pyramid (p182), built for the pharaoh Zoser, was not only a striking testimony to his power and the prosperity of the period but also a marker for the start of a whole new trend.

For more comprehensive information on this period, see the Pharaonic Egypt special section (p47).

The Old Kingdom & First Intermediate Period

For the next 500 years after the rule of Zoser (2667–2648 BC), a period which Egyptologists refer to as the Old Kingdom (2686–2181 BC), the power of Egypt's pharaohs would seem to have greatly increased, judging by the scale and ambition of their monuments. Most of these drew direct inspiration from Zoser's imposing structure, earning this period its other name, 'the Age of the Pyramids'.

First came Sneferu (2613–2589), the most prolific of the pyramid builders, who presided over the raising of the Bent and Red (North) Pyramids at Dahshur (p187), near Saqqara, and possibly of the Pyramid of Meidum (p191), in Al-Fayoum. His son, Khufu (Cheops), and grandson, Khafre (Chephren), were responsible for the two largest of the Pyramids at Giza (p128). Khufu (2589–2566) took the throne when the Old Kingdom was reaching the apex of its prosperity and culture and, if his colossal pyramid is any indication, he must have been one of the greatest of all the pharaohs. Its sheer size and mathematical precision is not only a monument to the extraordinary development of Egyptian architecture, it also suggests through the enormous labour and discipline involved that the era of Khufu saw the emergence, for the first time in human history, of an organisational principle.

As the centuries passed and the 5th dynasty (c 2494–2345 BC) began, there were changes in the power and rule of the pharaohs. One of the first indications of this was the comparatively small pyramids built at Abu Sir (p180), 12km south of Giza. The pharaohs had begun to delegate power to various high officials and nobles in the vast bureaucracies they had created, so they were not quite the absolute monarchs their predecessors were and did not have the same resources for the construction of immense funerary monuments.

Control became even more diffuse during the 6th dynasty (2345–2181 BC), before the fall of the Old Kingdom resulted in the formation of a number of small local principalities. During the 7th and 8th dynasties (2181–2125 BC) a second rival capital was established at Heracleopolis, near present-day Beni Suef, while the south was controlled by rulers of

Wonderful illustrations by Ian Andrew, Nick Harris and Helen Ward make *Egyptology* – a fictional journal of Emily Sands' 1926 journey to Egypt – one of the most stunning children's books ever produced.

The Great Pyramid of Khufu (built in 2570 BC) remained the tallest artificial structure in the world until the building of the Eiffel Tower in 1889.

The Ancient Egyptian Child by Joann Fletcher is a boxed set of a book and facsimiles of objects that children might have possessed in ancient Egypt.

3100 BC	2650–2323 BC
Memphis founded as the capital of a united Upper Egypt and Lower Egypt	Era of the great pyramid builders at Giza and Saqqara

the 11th dynasty (2125–1985 BC) based at Thebes (now Luxor). Both power bases had their own private armies, and small wooden models of the Egyptian and Nubian troops employed in Asyut at this time are on display in Cairo's Egyptian Museum (p167).

The anarchy and civil war of the First Intermediate Period (2181–2055 BC) only ended when the Thebans finally defeated the pharaohs of Heracleopolis and made Thebes the capital. Under Montuhotep II (2055–2004 BC) the north and south were again united under the leadership of a single pharaoh, marking the beginning of what Egyptologists refer to as the Middle Kingdom (2055–1650 BC).

The Middle Kingdom & Second Intermediate Period

The return to political order was marked by another spurt of tomb and temple building. The Middle Kingdom pharaohs saw their country thrive. The art of this time is regarded as the 'classical' period of Egyptian culture and the rulers built extensively throughout the land, erecting their pyramids at Dahshur, Hawara and Al-Lahun, all of which, though semi-ruined, remain standing in the vicinity of Al-Fayoum Oasis (p192). At the same time, the boundaries of Egyptian rule were also pushed southwards into the land of Nubia, where the pharaohs built huge mud-brick fortresses (now submerged beneath Lake Nasser) to maintain control of the region. The pharaohs centralised their government by replacing provincial governors with a vast bureaucracy of officials, many of them 'Asiatics' from Palestine who had settled peacefully and had been absorbed into Egyptian society. By gradually infiltrating the government this way the Asiatics were able to take advantage of the instability caused by the 70 or so short-lived pharaohs of the 13th and 14th dynasties (1795–1650 BC) and eventually took the throne around 1650 BC.

These new rulers were known as the Hyksos, a corruption of *hekaw-khasut* (meaning 'rulers of foreign lands'), and they were to provide the full stop to the Middle Kingdom. Yet the south was never fully conquered and Thebes remained a bastion of resistance throughout a century of Hyksos rule (which marks what's known as the Second Intermediate Period). By 1550 BC the Theban warlords once again triumphed to reunite their country and drive the Hyksos out, following this with vigorous campaigning as far as the Euphrates and down into Nubia. This marks the beginning of the New Kingdom (1550–1069 BC) and a lineage of power that would continue more or less unbroken for almost 500 years.

The New Kingdom & Third Intermediate Period

Beginning with Ahmose (1550–1525 BC), more than 30 monarchs from three successive dynasties ruled through what is commonly regarded as the golden age of the pharaohs. Most of the incredible monuments at Luxor date from the period of the New Kingdom. Thebes was the religious and political centre of the kingdom, while the age-old capital of Memphis took care of practical affairs such as administration. For this new age came a new god, and Amun-Ra became Egypt's state god. He was a composite of a Theban god, Amun, and the great sun god of Heliopolis, Ra. Great temples were built in his honour, particularly at Karnak (p242), and Karnak soon became the religious capital and power

The Penguin Guide to Ancient Egypt by William J Murnane is one of the best overall books on the life and monuments of the Pharaonic period, with illustrations and descriptions of the major temples and tombs.

The Complete Pyramids: Solving the Ancient Mysteries by Mark Lehner and Richard H Wilkinson is a readable reference to the famous threesome of Giza and the other 70-plus triangular-sided funerary monuments besides.

The best source for accurate plans of the Theban tombs can be found in Reeves and Wilkinson's 1996 book *The Complete Valley of the Kings*, supplemented by Siliotti's *Guide to the Valley of the Kings*.

2125–1650 BC	1650–1550 BC
Thebes is the seat of religious power in Egypt	Hyskos rule marks what's known as the Second Intermediate Period

CHRONOLOGY OF THE PHARAOHS

This is not a complete listing but it does include the most significant rulers mentioned throughout this book.

EARLY DYNASTIC PERIOD

1st dynasty including:	**3100–2890 BC**
Narmer (Menes)	c 3100 BC
2nd dynasty	**2890–2686 BC**

OLD KINGDOM

3rd dynasty including:	**2686–2613 BC**
Zoser	2667–2648 BC
Sekhemket	2648–2640 BC
4th dynasty including:	**2613–2494 BC**
Sneferu	2613–2589 BC
Khufu (Cheops)	2589–2566 BC
Djedefra	2566–2558 BC
Khafre (Chephren)	2558–2532 BC
Menkaure (Mycerinus)	2532–2503 BC
Shepseskaf	2503–2498 BC
5th dynasty including:	**2494–2345 BC**
Userkaf	2494–2487 BC
Sahure	2487–2475 BC
Neferirkare	2475–2455 BC
Shepseskare	2455–2448 BC
Raneferef	2448–2445 BC
Nyuserra	2445–2421 BC
Unas	2375–2345 BC
6th dynasty including:	**2345–2181 BC**
Teti	2345–2323 BC
Pepi I	2321–2287 BC
Pepi II	2278–2184 BC
7th–8th dynasties	**2181–2125 BC**

FIRST INTERMEDIATE PERIOD

9th–10th dynasties	**2160–2025 BC**

MIDDLE KINGDOM

11th dynasty including:	**2055–1985 BC**
Montuhotep II	2055–2004 BC
Montuhotep III	2004–1992 BC

1550–1186 BC	**1352–1336 BC**
18th- and 19th-dynasty pharaohs expand rule into Nubia and Syria-Palestine	Akhenaten briefly establishes a new monotheism and a short-lived capital at Akhetaten

12th dynasty	**1985–1795 BC**
including:	
Amenemhat I	1985–1955 BC
Sesostris I	1965–1920 BC
Amenemhat II	1922–1878 BC
Sesostris II	1880–1874 BC
Sesostris III	1874–1855 BC
Amenemhat III	1855–1808 BC
Amenemhat IV	1808–1799 BC

13th–14th dynasties	**1795–1650 BC**

SECOND INTERMEDIATE PERIOD

15th–17th dynasties	**1650–1550 BC**

NEW KINGDOM

18th dynasty	**1550–1290 BC**
including:	
Ahmose	1550–1525 BC
Amenhotep I	1525–1504 BC
Tuthmosis I	1504–1492 BC
Tuthmosis II	1492–1479 BC
Tuthmosis III	1479–1425 BC
Hatshepsut	1473–1458 BC
Amenhotep II	1427–1400 BC
Tuthmosis IV	1400–1390 BC
Amenhotep III	1390–1352 BC
Akhenaten	1352–1336 BC
Tutankhamun	1336–1327 BC
Horemheb	1323–1295 BC

19th dynasty	**1295–1186 BC**
including:	
Ramses I	1295–1294 BC
Seti I	1294–1279 BC
Ramses II	1279–1213 BC
Seti II	1200–1194 BC

20th dynasty	**1186–1069 BC**
including:	
Ramses III	1184–1153 BC

THIRD INTERMEDIATE PERIOD

21st dynasty	**1069–945 BC**
including:	
Psusennes I	1039–991 BC

1327 BC	**945–715 BC**
The death of Tutankhamun	Libyans capture parts of the Delta and rule as the 22nd and 23rd Dynasties

base, swelling in size as the empire expanded. Each successive pharaoh of the 18th and 19th dynasties added a room, hall or pylon, replete with intricately carved hieroglyph inscriptions.

Significant expansion of the empire began during the reign of Tuthmosis I, when he grabbed Upper Nubia (now part of Sudan). On his death, he was also the first pharaoh to be entombed in the Valley of the Kings on the West Bank across from Thebes, although the Theban area had been in use as a necropolis since the end of the Old Kingdom (Montuhotep II, first ruler of the Middle Kingdom, had already built an impressive funerary temple at Deir al-Bahri; p262).

The daughter of Tuthmosis I was Hatshepsut (1473–1458 BC), the most famous of the female pharaohs. She had a spectacular funerary temple built for herself next to and dwarfing that of Montuhotep II.

Hatshepsut was married to her half-brother Tuthmosis II and, on his death, his child by a minor wife was to become pharaoh. As Tuthmosis III was still young when his father died, Hatshepsut became regent and later crowned herself pharaoh, sharing the regency with Tuthmosis III. Tuthmosis III became the sole ruler in around 1458 BC and was Egypt's greatest conqueror, expanding the empire beyond Syria and into western Asia. His son and successor Amenhotep II (1427–1400 BC) shared his warlike nature, unlike the next pharaoh, Tuthmosis IV (1400–1390 BC). His policy of diplomacy was inherited by his son Amenhotep III (1390–1352 BC), whose long, peaceful reign marks the zenith of ancient Egyptian power. The resulting prosperity made possible a huge building programme, including Luxor Temple and the pharaoh's enormous funerary temple, of which the Colossi of Memnon (p250) are just about all that remains.

While Amenhotep III is regarded as the most splendid of Egypt's pharaohs, astutely managing to reduce the power of the priests of Amun, his son and successor Amenhotep IV (1352–1336 BC) irreversibly changed the course of Egyptian history with his disastrous policies. Alienating the priests completely, he abandoned the traditional gods and also closed down their temples, diverting all their revenues to the crown, while at the same time losing his grip on the empire. He also changed his name to Akhenaten, which means 'one who is beneficial to the Aten' – the sun disc – which Akhenaten raised to the status of Egypt's main god. The so-called 'heretic pharaoh' also spurned Thebes and, along with his powerful wife Nefertiti, moved further north to establish a new but short-lived capital called Akhetaten (Horizon of the Aten) at Tell al-Amarna (p218) near Minya.

After Akhenaten's death his successor, who many now believe to be Nefertiti, returned to Thebes and prepared the throne for Akhenaten's son, Tutankhaten. Changing his name to Tutankhamun (and known today chiefly for the discovery of his treasure-filled tomb in 1922), he restored the old gods along with their temples while the Aten was phased out. The memory of Akhenaten's rule (known today as 'the Amarna Period' after the site of the new capital) was finally obliterated by the next generation of pharaohs.

For the next few centuries, Egypt was ruled by military men such as Horemheb (1323–1295 BC), Seti I (1294–1279 BC) and Ramses II

The trilogy of *The Mummy* (1999), *The Mummy Returns* (2001) and *The Scorpion King* (2002) was written by Stephen Sommers. The films feature fabulous art direction and far-fetched plots set in ancient and early-20th-century Egypt.

Joann Fletcher's *Egypt's Sun King* is an intimate life study of one of the greatest pharaohs, Amenhotep III, builder of the Luxor Temple. The writing is lively with great details, accompanied by well-chosen illustrations.

The clothing identified among the treasures of Tutankhamun's tomb ranges from gold-encrusted tunics to neatly folded underwear, several pairs of socks and 47 pairs of flip-flop type sandals.

(1279–1213 BC). Keen to establish their Pharaonic credentials, they built massive monuments at Abydos, Abu Simbel and Thebes, greatly expanding Amun-Ra's temple at Karnak. They also waged war to reclaim Egypt's empire abroad and fought against the Hittites and Libyans to successfully defend Egypt's borders.

Following the reign of the last of the great warrior-pharaohs – Ramses III (1184–1153 BC), builder of Medinat Habu (p269) at Thebes – the glory days were finally over and Egypt's fortunes began to decline. As the empire shrank, it was subject to attack from outsiders until the north was occupied piecemeal when Libyans captured parts of the Delta and ruled as the 22nd and 23rd dynasties from 945 BC to 715 BC. The Kushites moved up through Nubia to occupy much of southern Egypt, forming the 25th dynasty (747–656 BC), which in turn ended after the Assyrian invasions in 671 BC and 669 BC. The Persians ruled Egypt for more than a century (525–404 BC) until the native dynasties reasserted themselves for the last time between 404 BC and 343 BC; after this Persia once again took over. Yet this second Persian period was short lived and after only 10 years they and their entire empire were taken over by Alexander the Great of Macedonia in his conquest of the ancient world.

ALEXANDER & THE PTOLEMAIC ERA

Due to the unpopularity of Persian rule, the Egyptians greeted Alexander (332–323 BC) as a liberator. He was crowned pharaoh by the priests of Memphis before choosing to found a new city on the Mediterranean coast, named for himself. His creation of Alexandria opened up Egypt to the rest of the world, changing its outlook forever from conservative to cosmopolitan. Although Alexandria soon eclipsed both Memphis and Thebes in its importance, Alexander never lived to see the city he had founded, although his body was eventually buried there by his Ptolemaic successors. (For a history of the city of Alexandria see p373.)

At Alexander's death one of his generals, Ptolemy, took over and founded a highly successful dynasty that lasted three centuries (305–30 BC). Although they were Macedonian Greeks, the Ptolemies would come to assimilate much of Egypt's heritage, adopting Pharaonic dress, reworking Egyptian gods into a new Graeco-Egyptian pantheon and, most visibly, adopting Pharaonic building styles: the temples of Dendara (p229), Edfu (p297), Esna (p295), Kom Ombo (p300) and Philae (p319) all date from the time of the Ptolemies.

The Ptolemies made Alexandria the greatest city of the ancient world in terms of both wealth and scholarship, and they did everything in their power to hold out against the growing power of Rome.

The last of their line, Cleopatra VII (*the* Cleopatra of asp, Liz Taylor and great eyeliner fame) was a brilliant politician who kept Egypt independent by allying herself with Julius Caesar, whom she married and gave a son. After his assassination she married Marc Antony (with whom she had three more children), and their combined forces were a serious threat to Caesar's nephew Octavian who now wielded power in Rome. After their naval forces were defeated in 31 BC at the Battle of Actium, Antony committed suicide. Rather than face capture, Cleopatra followed suit.

Ramses: The Son of Light by Christian Jacq is the first of a five-volume popular hagiography of the famous pharaoh. The prose is simplistic, but Jacq is an Egyptologist so the basics are accurate.

City of the Horizon, City of Dreams, City of the Dead by Anton Gill is a highly readable mystery trilogy set in the turmoil of post-Akhenaten Egypt.

Cleopatra (1963) is the best known of several screen adaptations of the Ptolemaic queen's life, and best remembered for the on-set affair between Richard Burton and Liz Taylor.

30 BC–AD 640	AD 640
Roman-Byzantine rule in Egypt	An Arab army under Amr ibn al-As enters Egypt, establishes a base at Babylon

ROMAN RULE

Taking the title Augustus Caesar and becoming the first emperor of Rome, Octavian also had himself portrayed as pharaoh in Egypt, although he and his successors ruled from Rome through governors. They did little to develop the country, which served largely as the granary of the Roman Empire, but they established trading posts down the Red Sea coast and out across the Western (Libyan) Desert to link up with their territories in Cyrenaica (now Libya). They also established a fortress on the site of a Pharaonic river crossing near Memphis, 10km east of the Pyramids. Controlling the access to the upper Nile, the fortress of Babylon-in-Egypt (p179), as it became known, grew to become a busy port and major frontier stronghold.

To ensure their rule of the native population, the Romans continued to build temples in a Pharaonic style, worship Egyptian gods and keep Egyptian traditions such as mummification. When Christianity arrived in Egypt in AD 40 with the preachings of St Mark, the Romans regarded the new religion as a potential threat, and although Christians were persecuted the religion nevertheless flourished. When the Romans finally accepted Christianity as their official religion in AD 323, they went on to close down 'pagan' temples all across the empire in AD 394. As the last hieroglyphic inscription was carved at the Temple of Philae on 24 August AD 394, ancient Egyptian culture finally died.

Yet soon Egyptian Christianity, known as Coptic Christianity, ran into trouble with the church in Rome, since its Monophysitic doctrine held that Christ was divine, rather than both human and divine. The Egyptians were therefore declared heretical and expelled from the rest of the Christian world.

Within Egypt the Roman overlords continued to persecute the local population. This oppressive state of affairs came to an end in AD 640 with the arrival of an army of mounted warriors riding out of the deserts of the Arabian Peninsula.

> What was and what is are described and ruminated over by the archaeologists leading the ongoing harbour explorations in *Alexandria Rediscovered* by Jean-Yves Empreur.

ARAB CONQUEST

Led by the general Amr ibn al-As, the Arab conquest brought Islam to Egypt. By AD 642 the new rulers had established a base immediately north of the walls of the Roman fortress of Babylon. This encampment, called Fustat, was the precursor of the city of Cairo. From this point on, the history of Egypt becomes largely synonymous with the history of Cairo.

From the arrival of Islam onwards, all of Egypt's existing historical capitals (Memphis, Thebes, Alexandria) were allowed to decline and, in a relatively short space of time, all became thinly populated backwaters. Their monuments served as quarries for the stone needed for the walls, palaces and religious buildings of the new Islamic capital.

Like Christianity before it, Islam, though still in its infancy, was already subject to splinter factions and dynasties. In AD 658 the Umayyads, an Arab dynasty based in Damascus, became rulers, or caliphs, of the whole Muslim world, including Egypt. They were supplanted by the Abbasids of Baghdad, whose influence also extended to the lands of the Nile from AD 750. Neither caliphate made much of a physical mark on Egypt, a

> The site of Luxor Temple has been a place of worship for the last 3500 years. Today the Mosque of Abu al-Haggag is situated high above the great court.

Ahmed ibn Tulun arrives as a governor for the Abbasid caliph in Baghdad and establishes his own dynasty

Shiite Fatimid general Jawhar lays the foundations of Al-Qahira (Cairo)

distant province far removed from the seats of power. The exception was when an ambitious governor sent from Baghdad made the country his independent fief, adorning it with great palaces (now long gone) and a splendid mosque named for himself, the Mosque of Ibn Tulun (p121), which still stands. Sweeping changes came with the next rulers, the Fatimids, a dynasty that came out of North Africa to establish a countercaliphate to the Abbasids. They conquered Egypt in AD 969 and made Cairo their capital.

Like Alexander and the invading Arab army before them, the Fatimids chose not to base their authority in any existing city. Instead they marked out territory to the north of Fustat. The fortified walled city they built formed the core of Al-Qahira (the Victorious), a name later corrupted by European merchants to Cairo. The Fatimids, though, were not popular rulers. They held themselves aloof from the country's indigenous Egyptian citizens, whom they kept outside the city walls. The division was made even greater by the fact that the Fatimids were Shiites, a brand of Islam at odds with the traditional orthodox Sunnism of Egypt and the eastern Mediterranean.

Around this time the Christians of Western Europe took up arms against the 'heathen' armies in occupation of the holy sites of the Bible. Their prime goal was to wrest Jerusalem from the Muslims, and this they achieved in 1099. By 1168, having bloodily rampaged through Palestine, the Crusaders advanced into Egypt. They got as far as the Delta before they were driven off by the Seljuks of Damascus, a powerful warrior dynasty to whom the Fatimids had appealed for help. The Seljuks were Sunni Muslims and once in Cairo they promptly deposed the Shiite dynasty they had come to aid and sent the Fatimids into exile.

The restorer of Sunni rule and the new overlord of Cairo was Salah ad-Din al-Ayyoub (known to the Crusaders, and later to the West, as Saladin), who established a new dynasty, the Ayyubids (1171–1250). A soldier foremost, Saladin made his mark on Cairo by looping it with a great defensive wall and by establishing the Citadel (p119) that still dominates the city's eastern skyline. The Ayyubid line ran to only four rulers before a vicious bout of scheming and betrayals resulted in the seizure of power by a group of former mercenaries, the Mamluks.

The Mamluks

A Turkish slave-soldier class, the Mamluks' (1250–1517) military service had been rewarded by Saladin with gifts of land. They were organised in a quasi-feudal manner, with groups of Mamluks each attached to their own ruler or emir. The purchase of new young slaves maintained the groups. There was no system of hereditary lineage, instead it was rule by the strongest. Rare was the sultan who died of old age.

Natural born soldiers, the military prowess of the Mamluks led to a series of successful campaigns that gave Egypt control of all of Palestine and Syria. At the same time, while renowned for their savagery, the Mamluks also endowed Cairo with the most exquisite architectural constructions and, during their 267-year reign, the city was the intellectual and cultural centre of the Islamic world. The contradictions in the constitution of the Mamluks are typified in the figure of Sultan Qaitbey, who was bought

Coptic Egypt by Christian Cannuyer tells the story from the earliest preachings by Mark the Evangelist in 1st-century-AD Alexandria to 21st-century Christianity in Egypt.

The sixth Fatimid caliph Hakim banned women's shoes as a means of keeping them indoors.

Cairo: The City Victorious by Max Rodenbeck is the single best read on the convoluted and picturesque thousand-year history of the Egyptian capital.

1171	1250
Saladin restores Sunni rule to Egypt and establishes the Ayyubid dynasty	The Mamluk slave warriors seize control of Cairo

as a slave-boy by one sultan and witnessed the brief reigns of nine more before he himself clawed his way to the throne. As sultan he rapaciously taxed all his subjects and dealt out vicious punishments with his own hands, once tearing out the eyes and tongue of a court chemist who had failed to transform lead into gold. Yet Qaitbey marked his ruthless sultanship with some of Cairo's most beautiful monuments, notably his mosque, which stands in the Northern Cemetery (p123).

The funding for the Mamluks' great buildings came from trade. A canal existed that connected the Red Sea with the Nile at Cairo, and thus the Mediterranean, forming a vital link in the busy commercial route between Europe and India and the Orient. In the 14th and 15th centuries, the Mamluks, in partnership with Venice, virtually controlled east–west trade and grew fabulously rich off it.

The end of these fabled days came in the closing years of the 15th century when Vasco da Gama discovered the sea route around the Cape of Good Hope, freeing European merchants from the heavy taxes raked in by Cairo and Venice. At around the same time the Ottoman Turks of Constantinople were emerging as a mighty new empire looking to unify the Muslim world, a goal that included the conquest of Egypt. In 1516 the Mamluks, under the command of their penultimate sultan Al-Ghouri, were obliged to meet the Turkish threat. The battle, which took place at Aleppo in Syria, resulted in complete defeat for the Mamluks. In January of the following year the Turkish sultan Selim I entered Cairo.

OTTOMAN TURKISH RULE

Egypt's days as a great imperial centre were at an end. Under the Ottoman Turks the country was once again, as it had been under the Romans, reduced to the level of a far-flung province. What trading revenues there were went back to Constantinople (Istanbul), as did the taxes that were squeezed from the local population.

Although the Mamluk sultanate had been abolished, the Mamluks themselves lived on in the form of lords known as beys and maintained considerable power. Over time the Turkish hold on Egypt became weaker as the Ottoman Empire went into decline. In 1796 one of the Mamluk beys was confident enough to take on the Turkish garrison in Cairo, defeat them and dispatch the Ottoman governor back to Constantinople. But the Mamluks' reemergence was short lived. Within two years they were unseated again, not by the Turks but by a new force in Egypt: Europeans, in the form of Napoleon Bonaparte and the French army.

Napoleon & Description de l'Egypte

Napoleon and his musket-armed forces blew apart the sword-wielding Mamluk cavalry, supposedly as a show of support for the Ottoman sultanate. In reality, Napoleon wanted to strike a blow at Britain, with whom the French were at war, by gaining control of the land and sea routes to the British colony of India.

The diminutive general established a French-style government, revamped the tax system, implemented public works projects and introduced new crops and a new system of weights and measures. Napoleon was also accompanied by 167 scholars and artists who were set to work

Zayni Barakat by Gamal al-Ghitani is full of intrigue, back stabbing and general Machiavellian goings-on in the twilight of Mamluk-era Cairo.

Many of the tales recounted each night by Sherezade in The Thousand and One Nights (Anonymous) are set in Mamluk-era Egypt, particularly in Cairo.

Favoured punishments employed by the Mamluks included al-tawsit, in which the victim was cut in half at the belly, and al-khazuq (impaling).

Turkish sultan Selim I enters Cairo, executing the last Mamluk sultan and initiating almost 300 years of rule from Istanbul

Napoleon invades; the British destroy the French fleet at Abu Qir and within three years the French are gone

making a complete study of Egypt's monuments, crafts, arts, flora and fauna, and of its society and people. The resulting work was published as the 24-volume *Description de l'Egypte;* it's still in print today, albeit in a radically slimmed-down, one-volume edition.

Anthropological efforts aside, Napoleon's Egyptian adventure seemed doomed from the beginning. Less than a month after he arrived, the British navy, under Admiral Nelson, appeared off the coast of Alexandria and destroyed the French fleet. Then the Ottoman sultan sent an army which, though trounced by the French, put paid to any pretence that the French were in Egypt with the complicity of Constantinople. Relations between the occupied and occupier deteriorated rapidly and uprisings in the capital could only be quashed by shelling that left 3000 Egyptians dead.

Sitting on a powder keg in Cairo with the British and Turks allying in Syria, the French forces readily agreed to an armistice and in 1801 departed the way they had come, via Alexandria.

Mohammed Ali

Although brief, the French occupation had significantly weakened Egyptian political stability. Turkish rule was reinstated but it was tenuous and masked great internal strife. A lieutenant in an Albanian contingent of the Ottoman army named Mohammed Ali took advantage of the melee. Within five years of the departure of the French he had fought and intrigued his way to become the pasha (governor) of Egypt, nominally the vassal of Constantinople but in practice looking on the country as his own.

The sultan in Constantinople was too weak to challenge this usurpation and the only possible threat to Mohammed Ali's power could have come from the Mamluk beys. Any danger here was swiftly and viciously snuffed out by a deadly dinner invitation. On 1 March 1811 Mohammed Ali had 500 Mamluk leaders attend a grand day of feasting and revelry at the Citadel in honour of his son's imminent departure for Mecca. When the feasting was over the Mamluks mounted their lavishly decorated horses and were led in procession down the narrow, high-sided defile below what's now the Police Museum towards the Bab al-Azab. But as they approached, the great gates were swung closed before them. Gunfire rained down from above. After the fusillades, Mohammed Ali's soldiers waded in with swords and axes to finish the job. Not one Mamluk escaped alive.

Although Mohammed Ali's means of achieving his ends could be barbarous, his reign is pivotal in the history of Egypt, as under his uncompromising rule the country underwent a transition from medieval-style feudalism to something approaching industrialisation. Mohammed Ali is credited with introducing a public education system and with planting Egypt's fields with the valuable cash crop, cotton. On his death, Mohammed Ali's preoccupations were taken up by his heirs, who continued the work of implementing reforms and social projects, foremost of which were the establishment of the railway system, factories and a telegraph and postal system that was one of the first in the world. Egypt's fledgling cotton industry boomed as production in the USA was disrupted by civil

At the Battle of the Pyramids Napoleon's forces took just 45 minutes to rout the Mamluk army, killing 1000 for the loss of just 29 of their own men.

Zarafa by Michael Allin is the charming story of a giraffe sent as gift in 1826 from the ruler of Egypt to the king of France. It overlies a study of the meeting between Age of Enlightenment Europe and Egypt.

1805	1869
Albanian mercenary Mohammed Ali claws his way to become ruler of Egypt	Khedive Ismail presides over the inauguration of the Suez Canal

war, and revenues were directed into ever-grander schemes. Grandest of all was the Suez Canal, which opened in 1869 to great fanfare and an audience composed of most of the crowned heads of Europe.

The opera *Aida* was originally commissioned for the opening ceremony of the Suez Canal.

Egypt was attracting increasing numbers of foreign tourists. As early as 1869 Thomas Cook had begun leading organised tours down the Nile. Cairo had gained a large foreign population that was involved in running businesses and conducting trade and the place almost had the character of a gold-rush town. The pickings were particularly rich for the European bankers who, with the connivance of their governments, bestowed lavish loans upon the Egyptian khedive (viceroy) Ismail for his grandiose schemes. They advanced the kind of money Egypt could never conceivably repay, at insatiable rates of interest, providing a convenient excuse for Britain to intervene in 1882 and announce that until such time as Egypt could repay its debts, it was taking control.

BRITISH OCCUPATION

The British allowed the heirs of Mohammed Ali to remain on the throne but all real power was concentrated in the hands of the British agent. It has been written that the British viewed their role in Egypt as a stern sort of paternalism, acting for a country that couldn't look after itself, but, more honestly, at the heart of the matter was the desire to ensure the security of the Suez Canal for continued British use. And while the British introduced a form of Egyptian legislative assembly and many local landowners benefited from the improved administration, the bottom line was that this was occupation by might. In this were sown the seeds of a national movement toward independence.

Famed as an American icon, the monument now known as the Statue of Liberty was originally intended to stand at the mouth of the Suez Canal.

The Egyptians' desire for self-determination was strengthened by the Allies' use of the country as a glorified barracks during WWI. Popular national sentiments were articulated by riots in 1919 and, more eloquently, by the likes of Saad Zaghloul, the most brilliant of an emerging breed of young Egyptian politicians, who said of the British, 'I have no quarrel with them personally but I want to see an independent Egypt.'

As a young Egyptian officer during WWII, Anwar Sadat was imprisoned by the British for conspiring with German spies.

As a sop to the independence movement, the British allowed the formation of a nationalist political party, called the Wafd (Delegation), and granted Egypt its sovereignty. But this was an empty gesture; King Fuad enjoyed little popularity among his people and the British kept tight hold of the reins. Moreover, they came in ever-greater numbers with the outbreak of WWII. The war wasn't all bad news for the Egyptians, certainly not for the shopkeepers and businessmen who saw thousands of Allied soldiers pouring into the towns and cities with money to burn on 48-hour leave from the desert.

There was a vocal element that saw the Germans as potential liberators. Students held rallies in support of Rommel, and in the Egyptian army a small cabal of officers, which included future presidents Nasser and Sadat, plotted to aid the German general's advance on their city.

Rommel pushed the Allied forces back almost to Alexandria, which had the British hurriedly burning documents in such quantity that the skies over Cairo turned dark with the ash, but the Germans did not break through. Instead, the British were to remain for almost 10 more years until a day of flames was to drive them out for good.

1882	1902
British occupation of Egypt begins	Inauguration of the Egyptian Museum on what is now Midan Tahrir in Cairo

EGYPTOMANIA

In the decades following Napoleon's doomed expedition and the wonders portrayed in *Description de l'Egypte*, Egypt attracted attention like no place ever before. During the 1820s, '30s and '40s the country was visited by a stream of adventurers and intrepid early travellers, including Mark Twain, Gustave Flaubert, Florence Nightingale and Richard Burton, translator of *The Thousand and One Nights*. The resulting accounts and journals were eagerly devoured by Western audiences enraptured by tales of temples in the sand, veiled harems and the bare-breasted women of the slave markets.

Artists too found Egypt a rich source of material and several made the journey to set up their easels in backstreets and before temples to record images little changed since the medieval days of the Mamluks. The most prolific was a Scot, David Roberts, who produced an immense body of work from Egypt and the Holy Lands that ensured him a fortune in his lifetime.

As a result of this import of fantastic images and texts, the world was swept by Egyptomania. Sphinxes and Pharaonic motifs adorned architecture from Melbourne to Chicago, operas were written around ancient Egyptian themes, and towns and cities in the 'New World' of America were even christened with names from the Old: Memphis, Tennessee and Cairo, Illinois.

The appetite for all things Egyptian didn't halt with words and images. The imperial powers had to have antiquities. Intent on modernising Egypt through emulating and forging relationships with the great powers of the industrial age, Mohammed Ali, ruler of Egypt, readily gave away the obelisks that now adorn the Place de la Concorde in Paris, London's Embankment and Central Park in New York.

While some antiquities were presented as gifts, the core of the great collections of Egyptian antiquities at the British Museum in London, the Louvre in Paris, Germany's Berlin Museum and the Metropolitan Museum in New York were being built up with pieces hauled back as booty by wealthy traveller-collectors and treasure hunters. The most famous, an Italian circus strongman named Giovanni Belzoni, supplied the British with a huge bust of Ramses II looted from the Ramesseum; the bust now rests in the British Museum. The same museum also houses the famed Rosetta Stone, originally discovered by the French but claimed by the British as spoils of war.

For many years now there have been requests from the Egyptian government for the return of key pieces, including the Rosetta Stone, a bust of Nefertiti held by the Berlin Museum and some statues of Hatshepsut held in New York. But although the Western fascination with 'Oriental' Egypt has long since abated, the chances of these treasures being returned are very slight.

INDEPENDENT EGYPT

On 26 January 1952, 'Black Saturday', Cairo was set on fire. After years of demonstrations, strikes and riots against foreign rule, the storming by the British of a rebellious Egyptian police station in the Suez Canal zone provided a spark that ignited the capital. Shops and businesses owned or frequented by foreigners were torched by mobs and all the landmarks of 70 years of British rule were reduced to charred ruins within a day.

The British must have realised that, as far as they were concerned, Egypt was ungovernable, so when just a few weeks later a group of young army officers seized power in a coup it was accepted as a *fait accompli*. On 26 July 1952 the Egyptian puppet-king Farouk, descendant of the Albanian Mohammed Ali, departed Alexandria harbour on the royal yacht, leaving Egypt to be ruled by Egyptians for the first time since the pharaohs.

Colonel Gamal Abdel Nasser, leader of the revolutionary Free Officers, ascended to power and was confirmed as president in elections held in

1922	1952
Howard Carter discovers the tomb of Tutankhamun	Cairo burns in rioting; a coup against the monarchy and foreign rule results in independence and the birth of the Republic of Egypt

1956. With the aim of returning Egypt to the long put-upon Egyptian peasantry, in an echo of the events of Russia in 1917, the country's landowners were dispossessed and their assets nationalised. This applied equally, if not more so, to foreigners, so while the country's huge foreign community was not forced to go, they nevertheless began to hurriedly sell up and stream out of the country.

In the year of his inauguration, Nasser successfully faced down Britain and France over the Suez Canal and the colonial legacy was finally and dramatically shaken off in full world view. To finance the building of a great dam that would control the flooding of the Nile, Nasser had announced his intention to nationalise the Suez Canal. The military attempt by the two former occupiers of Egypt to seize the waterway resulted in diplomatic embarrassment and undignified retreat, leaving Nasser the hero of the developing world, a sort of Robin Hood and Ramses rolled into one.

War & Peace with Israel

Little more than 10 years later, the brave new Egypt came crashing down. On 5 June 1967 Israel wiped out Egypt's air force in a surprise attack. With it went the confidence and credibility of Nasser and his nation.

Relations with Israel had been hostile ever since its founding in 1948. Egypt had sent soldiers to aid the Palestinians in fighting the newly proclaimed Jewish state and ended up on the losing side. Since that time, the Arabs had kept up a barrage of anti-Zionist rhetoric. Although privately Nasser acknowledged that the Arabs would probably lose another war against Israel, for public consumption he gave rabble-rousing speeches about liberating Palestine. But he was a skilled orator and by early 1967 the mood engendered throughout the Arab world by these speeches was beginning to catch up with him. Soon other Arab leaders started to accuse him of cowardice and of hiding behind the UN troops stationed in Sinai since the Suez Crisis. Nasser responded by ordering the peacekeepers out and blockading the Strait of Tiran, effectively closing the southern Israeli port of Eilat. He gave Israel reassurances that he wasn't going to attack but meanwhile massed his forces east of Suez. Israel struck first.

When the shooting stopped six days later Israel controlled all of the Sinai Peninsula and had closed the Suez Canal (which didn't reopen for another eight years). A humiliated Nasser offered to resign, but in a spontaneous outpouring of support, the Egyptian people wouldn't accept this move and he remained in office. However, it was to be for only another three years; abruptly in November 1970, the president died of a heart attack.

Anwar Sadat, Egypt's second president, instigated a complete about-face; where Nasser looked to the USSR for his inspiration, Sadat looked to the US. Out went socialist principles, in came capitalist opportunism. After a decade and a half of keeping a low profile, the wealthy resurfaced and were joined by a large, new, moneyed middle class grown rich on the back of Sadat's much-touted *al-infitah* (open door policy). Sadat also believed that to truly revitalise Egypt's economy he would have to deal with Israel. But first he needed bargaining power, a basis for negotiations.

On 6 October 1973, the Jewish holiday of Yom Kippur, Egypt launched a surprise attack across the Suez Canal. Its army beat back the much better

Ancient Egypt: the Great Discoveries by Nicholas Reeves is a chronology of 200 years of marvellous finds, from the Rosetta Stone (1799) to the Valley of the Golden Mummies (1999).

1967	1970
Egypt participates in the Six Day War against Israel and is on the losing side	Gamal Abdel Nasser, leader of Egypt since 1954, dies of a heart attack and is replaced by Anwar Sadat

armed Israelis and although these initial gains were later reversed, Egypt's national pride was restored. Sadat's negotiating strategy had succeeded.

In November 1977 Sadat travelled to Jerusalem to begin negotiating a peace treaty with Israel, a process that ended in 1978 with the cosigning of the Camp David Agreement. Israel agreed to withdraw from Sinai while Egypt recognised Israel's right to exist. This was a complete abandonment of Nasser's pan-Arabist principles and Sadat's peace was viewed by the Arab world as a betrayal. It cost Sadat his life: on 6 October 1981, as he observed a parade in commemoration of the 1973 War, one of his soldiers broke from the marching ranks and sprayed the presidential stand with gunfire. Sadat was killed instantly.

Mubarak & the Rise of the Islamist Movement

Sadat's assassin was a member of one of the Islamist groups in Egypt loosely described as 'Muslim fundamentalists'. Mass roundups of Islamists and suspected Islamists were carried out based on the orders of Sadat's successor Hosni Mubarak, a former air-force general and vice president.

Less flamboyant than Sadat and less charismatic than Nasser, Mubarak has often been criticised as being both unimaginative and indecisive. Nevertheless, he managed to carry out a balancing act on several fronts, abroad and at home. To the irritation of more hard-line states such as Syria and Libya, Mubarak was able to rehabilitate Egypt in the eyes of the Arab world without abandoning the treaty with Israel. For almost a decade he also managed to keep the lid on the Islamist extremists, but in the early 1990s the lid blew off.

Despite their use of religious symbolism the Islamists essentially form a political movement that has grown out of harsh socioeconomic conditions. In the 1980s discontent had been brewing among the poorer sections of society. Government promises had failed to keep up with the population explosion and a generation of youths was without jobs and living in squalid, overcrowded housing with little or no hope for the future. With a repressive political system that allowed little chance to legitimately voice opposition, the only hope lay with Islamic parties such as the Muslim Brotherhood and their calls for change. Denied recognition by the state as a legal political entity, the Islamists turned to force. There were frequent attempts on the life of the president and his ministers and clashes with the security forces. The matter escalated from a domestic issue to a matter of international concern when the Islamists began to target one of the state's most vulnerable and valuable sources of income: tourists.

Several groups of foreign tourists were shot at, bombed or otherwise assaulted throughout the 1990s, most horrifically in 1997 with the sickening one-two of the fire-bomb attack on a tour bus outside the Egyptian Museum in Cairo, followed a few weeks later by the massacre of holidaymakers at the Temple of Hatshepsut in Luxor by members of the Gama'a al-Islamiyya (Islamic Group), a Muslim Brotherhood splinter group.

The massacre destroyed grass-roots support for militants and the Muslim Brotherhood declared a ceasefire the following year. Things were relatively quiet until October 2004, when bombs at Taba, on the border with Israel, and the nearby Ras Shaytan camp, killed 34 and signalled the start of an unsettled 12 months.

'Mubarak was able to rehabilitate Egypt in the eyes of the Arab world'

1977	1981
Publication of 1st edition of Lonely Planet's *Egypt & the Sudan*	President Sadat is assassinated while watching a parade; he is replaced by Hosni Mubarak

In 2005 President Mubarak bowed to growing international pressure to bring the country's political system in line with Western-style democracy, and proposed a constitutional amendment (subsequently approved by parliament and ratified at a national referendum) that aimed to introduce direct and competitive presidential elections. While some pundits saw this as a step in the right direction, others saw it as a sham, particularly as popular opposition groups such as the Muslim Brotherhood were still banned and other independent candidates were required to have the backing of at least 65 members of the overwhelmingly National Democratic Party (NDP) dominated lower house of parliament. When the Kifaya! (Enough!) coalition of opposition groups loudly voiced its unhappiness with these restrictions, security forces cracked down. Ayman Nour, the leader of the popular Ghad (Tomorrow) party, was thrown into jail on what many thought were trumped-up charges and opposition rallies around the country were violently dispersed. At this stage the banned Muslim Brotherhood began holding its own rallies and there were two isolated terrorist incidents in Cairo aimed at foreign tourists, both carried out by members of the same pro-Islamist family. Soon after, three bombs at the popular beach resort of Sharm el-Sheikh claimed the lives of 64 people, most of them Egyptian. Various groups claimed responsibility, tourism took an immediate hit and Egyptians braced themselves for the possibility of further terrorist incursions and domestic unrest.

The result of the presidential election was predictable: President Mubarak was victorious, with 89% of the vote, though with a turnout of just 23% of the 32 million registered voters. No surprise, then, that opposition parties and candidates (including Ayman Nour) alleged that the vote had been rigged and that the result was invalid.

They were even more concerned when subsequent parliamentary elections in November 2005 were marred by widespread allegations that progovernment supporters had physically prevented some voters from entering polling booths and voting for Brotherhood-aligned independent candidates. Even after these intimidation tactics, the Muslim Brotherhood independents managed to win an extraordinary 88 seats in the national parliament (six times the number that they had previously held), making the Brotherhood a major player on the national political scene despite its officially illegal status.

Egypt Today

Despite the ever-present – though slim – threat of an Islamist uprising, the major challenge facing President Mubarak's government as this book goes to print isn't associated with an election backlash, with religious extremism or with global terrorism. Nor is it related to the constant international and opposition denunciations of press censorship and other infringements on human rights in Egypt. The biggest threat to the NDP's hold on power is the irrefutable fact that Egypt is in serious economic crisis, and has been for many years. The national economy is best described as a basket case, and when the ever-burgeoning growth in population, rise in unemployment and decline in tourism arrivals resulting from the July 2005 Sharm el-Sheikh bombs are considered, a prosperous national future look increasingly unlikely.

No God but God: Egypt and the Triumph of Islam by Genevieve Abdo is one of the best books on the Egyptian Islamist movement. It examines the movement as a response to a general increase in Muslim piety and the ineptitude of governance in the post-Nasser era.

A History of Egypt by PJ Vatiokis is the best one-volume history available, although it's a decidedly modern history with a focus on the 19th and 20th centuries.

1988	2005
Naguib Mafouz wins the Nobel Prize for Literature	President Mubarak commences his fifth term (25th year) in office after winning a highly controversial presidential election

Pharaonic Egypt Dr Joann Fletcher

Despite its rather clichéd image, there is so much more to ancient Egypt than temples, tombs and Tutankhamun. As the world's first nation-state, predating the civilisations of Greece and Rome by several millennia, Egypt was responsible for some of the most important achievements in human history – it was the place where writing was invented, the first stone monuments erected and an entire culture set in place which remained largely unchanged for thousands of years.

Dr Joann Fletcher is an Egyptologist, a writer, and a consultant to museums and the media. For more biographical information, see p18.

All this was made possible by the Nile River, which brought life to this virtually rainless land. In contrast to the vast barren 'red land' of desert which the Egyptians called *deshret*, the narrow river banks were known as *kemet* (the 'black land'), named after the rich silt deposited by the river's annual floods. The abundant harvests grown in this rich earth were then gathered as taxes by a highly organised bureaucracy working on behalf of the king (pharaoh). They redirected this wealth to run the administration and to fund ambitious building projects designed to enhance royal status. Although such structures have come to symbolise ancient Egypt, the survival of so many pyramids, temples and tombs have created a misleading impression of the Egyptians as a morbid bunch obsessed with religion and death, when they simply loved life so much that they went to enormous lengths to ensure it continued for eternity.

The depth of this conviction suffused every aspect of the ancient Egyptians' lives, and gave their culture its incredible coherence and conservatism. They believed they had their gods to take care of them, and each pharaoh was regarded as the gods' representative on earth, ruling by divine approval. Absolute

The Tomb of Nerfertari one of five wives of Ramses II and perhaps his favourite, in Luxor.

PHOTO BY LEANNE LOGAN

monarchy was integral to Egyptian culture, and the country's history was shaped around the lengths of each pharaoh's reign. Thirty royal dynasties ruled over a 3000-year period, now divided into the Old, Middle and New Kingdoms separated by intermittent periods of unrest (Intermediate periods) when the country split into north (Lower Egypt) and south (Upper Egypt).

When this split finally became permanent at the end of the New Kingdom (around 1069 BC), foreign powers were gradually able to take control of the government. Yet even then, Egyptian culture was so deeply rooted that the successive invaders could not escape its influence, and Libyans, Nubians and Persians all came to adopt traditional Egyptian ways. The Greeks were so impressed with the ancient culture that they regarded Egypt as the 'cradle of civilisation', and even the occupying Romans adopted the country's ancient gods ands traditions. It was only at the end of the 4th century AD, when the Roman Empire adopted Christianity, that ancient Egypt finally died; their gods were taken from them, their temples were closed down, and all knowledge of the 'pagan' hieroglyphs that transmitted their culture was lost for some 1400 years.

PHARAONIC WHO'S WHO

Egypt's Pharaonic history is based on the regnal years of each king, or pharaoh, a word derived from *per-aa* (great house), meaning palace. Among the many hundreds of pharaohs who ruled Egypt over a 3000 year period, the following are some of the names found most frequently around the ancient sites.

Narmer c 3100 BC First king of a united Egypt after he conquered the north (Lower) Egypt, Narmer from southern (Upper) Egypt is portrayed as victorious on the famous Narmer Palette in the Egyptian Museum. He is perhaps to be identified with the semimythical King Menes, founder of Egypt's ancient capital city Memphis. See also p31, p31, p169 & p179.

Zoser (Djoser) c 2667–2648 BC As second king of the 3rd Dynasty, Zoser was buried in Egypt's first pyramid, the world's oldest monumental stone building, designed by the architect Imhotep. Zoser's statue in the foyer of the Egyptian Museum shows a long-haired king with a slight moustache, dressed in a tight-fitting robe and striped nemes headcloth. See also p32, p169 & p182.

Sneferu c 2613–2589 BC The first king of the 4th Dynasty, and held in the highest esteem by later generations, Sneferu was Egypt's greatest pyramid builder. Responsible for four such structures, his final resting place, the Red (Northern) Pyramid at Dahshur, was Egypt's first true pyramid and a model for the more famous pyramids at Giza. See also p32, p187 & p191.

Khufu (Cheops) c 2589–2566 BC As Sneferu's son and successor, Khufu was second king of the 4th Dynasty. Best known for Egypt's largest pyramid, the Great Pyramid at Giza, his only surviving likeness is Egypt's smallest royal sculpture, a 7.5cm-high figurine in the Egyptian Museum. The gold furniture of his mother Hetepheres is also in the museum. See also p32, p132 & p170.

Khafre (Khephren, Chephren) c 2558–2532 BC Khafre was a younger son of Khufu who succeeded his half-brother to become fourth king of the 4th Dynasty. He built the second of Giza's famous pyramids and although he is best known as the model for the face of the Great Sphinx, his diorite statue in the Egyptian Museum is equally stunning. See also p32, p133 & p170.

Menkaure (Mycerinus) c 2532–2503 BC As the son of Khafre and fifth king of the 4th Dynasty, Menkaure built the smallest of Giza's three huge pyramids. He is also well represented by a series of superb sculptures in the Egyptian Museum which show him with the goddess Hathor and deities representing various regions (nomes) of Egypt. See also p133 & p169.

Pepi II c 2278–2184 BC As fifth king of the 6th Dynasty, Pepi II was a child at his accession; his delight with a dancing pygmy was recorded in the Aswan tomb of his official Harkhuf. As one of the world's longest-reigning monarchs (96 years), Pepi contributed to the decline of the Pyramid Age. See also p187 & p310.

Montuhotep II c 2055–2004 BC As overlord of Thebes, Montuhotep II reunited Egypt and his reign began the Middle Kingdom. He was the first king to build a funerary temple at Deir al-Bahri, in which he was buried with five of his wives and a daughter, with further wives and courtiers buried in the surrounding area. See also p32, p170 & p262.

Sesostris III (Senwosret, Senusret) c 1874–1855 BC The fifth king of the 12th Dynasty, Sesostris III reorganised the administration by taking power from the provincial governors (nomarchs). He strengthened Egypt's frontiers and occupied Nubia with a chain of fortresses, and is recognisable by the stern, 'careworn' faces of his statues. His female relatives were buried with spectacular jewellery. See also p187.

Amenhotep I c 1525–1504 BC As second king of the 18th Dynasty, Amenhotep I ruled for a time with his mother Ahmose-Nofretari. They founded the village of Deir el-Medina for the workers who built the tombs in the Valley of the Kings, and Amenhotep I may have been the first king to be buried there. See also p172 & p247.

Hatshepsut c 1473–1458 BC As the most famous of Egypt's female pharaohs, Hatshepsut took power at the death of her brother-husband Tuthmosis II and initially ruled jointly with her nephew-stepson Tuthmosis III. After taking complete control, she undertook ambitious building schemes, including obelisks at Karnak Temple and her own spectacular funerary temple at Deir al-Bahri. See also p33, p171, p246 & p262.

Tuthmosis III c 1479–1425 BC As sixth king of the 18th Dynasty, Tuthmosis III ('the Napoleon of ancient Egypt') expanded Egypt's empire with a series of foreign campaigns into Syria. He built

Although the Narmer Palette is in many ways Egypt's earliest historical document, it is also a giant piece of cosmetic equipment, designed as a surface on which to prepare eye make-up.

Sneferu was a great inspiration to later pharaohs. Excavations at Dahshur have revealed that incense was still being offered to Sneferu's memory 2000 years after his death.

Among the wives of Tuthmosis III were three Syrians, whose joint tomb at Thebes, found in 1916, was filled with gold necklaces, crowns and bracelets, drinking vessels, mirrors and even pots of face cream.

extensively at Karnak, added a chapel at Deir al-Bahri and his tomb was the first in the Valley of the Kings to be decorated. See also p33, p171, p245 & p259.

Amenhotep III c 1390–1352 BC As ninth king of the 18th Dynasty, Amenhotep III's reign marks the zenith of Egypt's culture and power. Creator of Luxor Temple and the largest ever funerary temple marked by the Colossi of Memnon, his many innovations, including Aten worship, are usually credited to his son and successor Amenhotep IV (later 'Akhenaten'). See also p33, p169, p236 & p250.

Akhenaten (Amenhotep IV) c 1352–1336 BC Changing his name from Amenhotep to distance himself from the state god Amun, Akhenaten and his wife Nefertiti relocated the royal capital to Amarna. While many still regard him as a monotheist and benign revolutionary, the evidence suggests he was a dictator whose reforms were political rather than religious. See also p33, p171, p218 & p236.

Nefertiti c 1338–1336 BC (?) Famous for her painted bust in Berlin, Nefertiti ruled with her husband Akhenaten, and while the identity of his successor remains controversial, this may have been Nefertiti herself, using the throne name 'Smenkhkare'. Equally controversial is the suggested identification of her mummy in tomb KV 35 in the Valley of the Kings. See also p33, p171, p218 & p236.

Tutankhamun c 1336–1327 BC As the 11th king of the 18th Dynasty, Tutankhamun's fame is based on the great quantities of treasure discovered in his tomb in 1922. Most likely the son of Akhenaten by minor wife Kiya, Tutankhamun reopened the traditional temples and restored Egypt's fortunes after the disastrous reign of his father. See also p33, p236 & p255.

Horemheb c 1323–1295 BC As a military general, Horemheb restored Egypt's empire under Tutankhamun and after the brief reign of Ay eventually became king himself. Married to Nefertiti's sister Mutnodjmet, his tomb at Saqqara was abandoned in favour of a royal burial in a superbly decorated tomb in the Valley of the Kings. See also p33 & p258.

Seti I c 1294–1279 BC The second king of the 19th Dynasty, Seti I continued to consolidate Egypt's empire with foreign campaigns. Best known for building Karnak's Hypostyle Hall, a superb temple at Abydos and a huge tomb in the Valley of the Kings, his mummy in the Egyptian Museum is one of the best preserved examples. See also p33, p172, p226, p245 & p260.

Ramses II c 1279–1213 BC As son and successor of Seti I, Ramses II fought the Hittites at the Battle of Kadesh and built temples including Abu Simbel and the Ramesseum, once adorned with the statue that inspired poet PB Shelley's 'Ozymandias'. The vast tomb of his children was rediscovered in the Valley of the Kings in 1995. See also p33, p171, p172, p179, p228, p254, p256, p326 & p328.

Ramses III c 1184–1153 BC As second king of the 20th Dynasty, Ramses III was the last of the warrior kings, repelling several attempted invasions portrayed in scenes at his funerary temple Medinat Habu. Buried in a finely decorated tomb in Valley of the Kings, his mummy was the inspiration for Boris Karloff's The Mummy. See also p33 & p269.

Taharka 690–664 BC As fourth king of the 25th Dynasty, Taharka was one of Egypt's Nubian pharaohs and his daughter Amenirdis II high priestess at Karnak where Taharka undertook building work. A fine sculpted head of the king is in Aswan's Nubian Museum, and he was buried in a pyramid at Nuri in southern Nubia. See also p243.

Alexander the Great 332–323 BC During his conquest of the Persian Empire, the Macedonian king Alexander invaded Egypt in 332 BC. Crowned pharaoh at Memphis, he founded Alexandria, visited Amun's temple at Siwa Oasis to confirm his divinity and after his untimely death in Babylon in 323 BC his mummy was eventually buried in Alexandria. See also p37, p172, p240, p360 & p373.

Ptolemy I 305–285 BC As Alexander's general and rumoured half-brother, Ptolemy seized Egypt at Alexander's death and established the Ptolemaic line of pharaohs. Ruling in traditional style for 300 years, they made Alexandria the greatest capital of the ancient world and built many of the temples standing today, including Edfu, Philae and Dendera. See also p37 & p373.

Cleopatra VII 51–30 BC As the 19th ruler of the Ptolemaic dynasty, Cleopatra VII ruled with her brothers Ptolemy XIII then Ptolemy XIV before taking power herself. A brilliant politician who restored Egypt's former glories, she married Julius Caesar then Mark Antony, whose defeat at Actium in 31 BC led to the couple's suicide. See also p37, p230, p373 & p379.

Regarded as the most magnificent of the pharaohs, Amenhotep III seems to have appreciated literature, judging by the discovery of small glazed bookplates bearing his name.

Nefertiti had a taste for beer. She is shown drinking in several tomb scenes at Amarna, and even had her own brewery at the site, which produced a quick-fermenting brew.

Although synonymous with ancient Egypt, Cleopatra VII was actually Greek by descent, one of the Ptolemaic dynasty of pharaohs who originated from Macedonia where Cleopatra was a popular royal name.

EVERYDAY LIFE

With ancient Egypt's history focussed on its royals, the part played by the rest of the ancient population is frequently ignored. The great emphasis on written history also excludes the 99% of the ancient population who were unable to write, and it can often seem as if the only people who lived in ancient Egypt were pharaohs, priests and scribes.

The silent majority are often dismissed as little more than illiterate peasants, although these were the very people who built the monuments and produced the wealth on which the culture was based.

Fortunately Egypt's climate, at least, is democratic, and has preserved the remains of people throughout society, from the mummies of the wealthy in their grand tombs to the remains of the poorest individuals buried in hollows in the sand. The worldly goods buried with them for use in the afterlife can give valuable details about everyday life and how it was lived, be it in the bustling, cosmopolitan capital Memphis or in the small rural settlements scattered along the banks of the Nile.

Domestic Life

In Egypt's dry climate, houses were traditionally built of mud brick, whether they were the back-to-back homes of workers or the sprawling palaces of the royals. The main differences were the number of rooms and the quality of fixtures and fittings. The villas of the wealthy often incorporated walled gardens with stone drainage systems for small pools, and some even had en-suite bathroom facilities – look out for the limestone toilet seat found at Amarna and now hanging in the Egyptian Museum in Cairo.

Just like the mud-brick houses in rural Egypt today, ancient homes were warm in winter and cool in summer. Small, high-set windows reduced the sun's heat but allowed breezes to blow through, and stairs gave access to the flat roof where the family could relax or sleep.

Often whitewashed on the outside to deflect the heat, interiors were usually painted in bright colours, the walls and floors of wealthier homes further enhanced with gilding and inlaid tiles. Although the furniture of most homes would have been quite sparse – little more than a mud-brick bench, a couple of stools and a few sleeping mats – the wealthy could afford beautiful furniture, including inlaid chairs and footstools, storage chests, beds with linen sheets and feather-stuffed cushions. Most homes also had small shrines for household deities and busts of family ancestors, and a small raised area seems to have been reserved for women in childbirth.

The home was very much a female domain. The most common title for women of all social classes was *nebet per* (lady of the house), emphasising their control over most aspects of domestic life. Although there is little evidence of marriage ceremonies, monogamy was standard practice for the majority, with divorce and remarriage relatively common and initiated by either sex. With the same legal rights as men, women were responsible for running the home, and although there were male launderers, cleaners and cooks, it was mainly women who cared for the children, cleaned the house, made clothing and prepared food in small open-air kitchens adjoining the home.

The staple food was bread, produced in many varieties, including the dense calorie-laden loaves mass-produced for those working on government building schemes. Onions, leeks, garlic and pulses were eaten in great quantities along with dates, figs, pomegranates and grapes. Grapes were also used, along with honey, as sweeteners. Spices, herbs, nuts and

Chickens, described as miraculous birds which 'give birth every day', were first imported from Syria around 1450 BC.

Wine jars were sometimes inscribed with the intended purpose of their contents, from 'offering wine' or 'wine for taxes' to 'wine for merry-making'.

Eugen Strouhal's *Life in Ancient Egypt* (Cambridge University Press, 1992) is one of the most informative and best illustrated books dealing with domestic life. Drawing on the author's medical expertise, the chapter on health and medicine is particularly good.

seeds were also added to food, along with oil extracted from native plants and imported almonds and olives. Although cows provided milk for drinking and making butter and cheese, meat was only eaten regularly by the wealthy and by priests allowed to eat temple offerings once the gods had been satisfied. This was mostly beef, although sheep, goats and pigs were also eaten, as were game and wild fowl. Fish was generally dried and salted, and because of its importance in workers' diets, a fish-processing plant existed at the pyramid builders' settlement at Giza.

Although the wealthy enjoyed wine (with the best produced in the vineyards of the Delta and western oases, or imported from Syria), the standard beverage was rather soupy barley beer, which was drunk throughout society by everyone, including children. The ancient Egyptians' secret to a contented life is summed up by the words of one of their poems: 'it is good to drink beer with happy hearts, when one is clothed in clean robes'.

Public Life/At Work

The majority of ancient Egyptians were farmers, whose lives were based around the annual cycle of the Nile. This formed the basis of their calendar with its three seasons – *akhet* (inundation), *peret* (spring planting) and *shemu* (summer harvest). As the flood waters covering the valley floor receded by October, farmers planted their crops in the silt left behind, using irrigation canals to distribute the flood waters where needed and to water their crops until harvest time in April.

Agriculture was so fundamental to life in both this world and the next that it was one of the main themes in tomb scenes. The standard repertoire of ploughing, sowing and reaping is often interspersed with officials checking field boundaries or calculating the grain to be paid as tax in this pre-coinage economy. The officials are often accompanied by scribes busily recording all transactions, with hieroglyphs first developed c 3250 BC as a means of recording produce.

A huge civil service of scribes worked on the king's behalf to record taxes and organise workers, and in a society where less than 1% were

> Struggling with their hieroglyphs, student scribes were advised to 'Love writing and shun dancing, make friends with the scroll and palette, for they bring more joy than wine!'

> A contract from AD 206 states that Isadora the castanet dancer and two other women hired to perform at a six-day festival received 36 drachmae a day, well above the average wage.

HEALTH

With average life expectancy around 35 years, the ancient Egyptians took health care seriously, and used a blend of medicine and magic to treat problems caused mainly by the environment. Wind-blown sand damaged eyes, teeth and lungs; snakes and scorpions were a common danger; parasitic worms lurked in infected water; and flies spread diseases. Medicines prescribed for such problems were largely plant- or mineral-based, and included honey (now known to be an effective antibacterial) and 'bread in mouldy condition' – as described in the ancient medical texts – which provided a source of penicillin.

By 2650 BC there were dentists and doctors, with specialists in surgery, gynaecology, osteopathy and even veterinary practice trained in the temple medical schools. The pyramid builders' town at Giza had medical facilities capable of treating fractures and performing successful surgical amputations.

Magic was also used to combat illness or injury, and spells were recited and amulets worn to promote recovery. Most popular was the *wedjat*-eye of Horus, representing health and completeness, while amulets of the household deities Bes and Taweret were worn during the difficult time of childbirth. Mixtures of honey, sour milk and crocodile dung were recommended as contraceptives, and pregnancy tests involving barley were used to foretell the sex of the unborn child. Magic was also used extensively during childhood, with the great mother goddess Isis and her son Horus often referred to in spells to cure a variety of childhood ailments.

The BBC History Online article 'From Warrior Women to Female Pharaohs: Careers for Women in Ancient Egypt' looks at what was available for women outside the home. Go to www.bbc.co.uk/history /ancient/egyptians /women_01.shtml

literate, scribes were regarded as wise and were much admired. Taught to read and write in the schools attached to temples where written texts were stored and studied, the great majority of scribes were male, although some women are also shown with documents and literacy would have been necessary to undertake roles they are known to have held, including overseer, steward, teacher, doctor, high priestess, vizier and even pharaoh on at least six occasions.

Closely related to the scribe's profession were the artists and sculptors who produced the stunning artefacts synonymous with ancient Egypt. From colossal statues to delicate jewellery, all were fashioned using simple tools and natural materials.

Building stone was hewn by teams of labourers supplemented by prisoners, with granite obtained from Aswan, sandstone from Gebel Silsila, alabaster from Hatnub near Amarna and limestone from Tura near modern Cairo. Gold came from mines in the Eastern Desert and Nubia, and both copper and turquoise were mined in the Sinai. With such precious commodities being transported large distances, trade routes and border areas were patrolled by guards, police (known as *medjay*) and the army, when not out on campaign.

Men also plied their trade as potters, carpenters, builders, metalworkers, jewellers, weavers, fishermen and butchers, with many of these professions handed down from father to son (especially well portrayed in the tomb scenes of Rekhmire (see Tombs of Sennofer & Rekhmire, p265). There were also itinerant workers such as barbers, dancers and midwives, and those employed for their skills as magicians. Men worked alongside women as servants in wealthy homes, performing standard household duties, and thousands of people were employed in the temples which formed the heart of every settlement as a combination of town hall, college, library and medical centre. As well as a hierarchy of priests and priestesses, temples employed their own scribes, butchers, gardeners, florists, perfume makers, musicians and dancers, many of whom worked on a part-time basis.

Hair colour had great significance for the Egyptians, and in a largely dark-haired population, redheads were regarded as dangerous and described as 'followers of Seth', the god of chaos.

Clothing, Hairstyles & Jewellery

Personal appearance was clearly important to the Egyptians, with wigs, jewellery, cosmetics and perfumes worn by men and women alike. Garments were generally linen, made from the flax plant before the intro-

OILS, PERFUMES & COSMETICS

Most Egyptians seem to have bathed regularly and used moisturising oils to protect their skin from the drying effects of the sun. These oils were sometimes perfumed with flowers, herbs and spices, and Egyptian perfumes were famous throughout the ancient world for their strength and quality. Perfume ingredients are listed in ancient texts, along with recipes for face creams and beauty preparations, and cosmetics were also used to enhance the appearance. Responsible for the familiar elongated eye shape, eye-paint also had a practical use, acting like sunglasses by reducing the glare of bright sunlight and explaining why builders are shown having their eyes made up during work. Both green malachite and black galena (kohl) were used in crushed form, mixed with water or oil and stored ready for use in small pots. Red ochre prepared in similar fashion was used by women to shade their lips and cheeks. Some Egyptians were also trained to apply cosmetics and perform manicures and pedicures.

Although most people kept their cosmetic equipment in small baskets or boxes, the wealthy had beautifully decorated chests with multiple compartments, pull-out drawers and polished metal mirrors with which they could inspect their carefully designed appearance.

duction of cotton in Ptolemaic times. Status was reflected in the fineness and quantity of the linen, but as it was expensive, surviving clothes show frequent patching and darning. Laundry marks are also found; male launderers were employed by the wealthy, and even a few ancient laundry lists have survived, listing the types of garments they had to wash in the course of their work.

The most common garment was the loincloth, worn like underpants beneath other clothes. Men also wore a linen kilt, sometimes pleated, and both men and women wore the bag-tunic made from a rectangle of linen folded in half and sewn up each side. The most common female garments were dresses, most wrapped sari-like around the body, although there were also V neck designs cut to shape, and detachable sleeves for easy cleaning.

Linen leggings have also been found, as well as socks with a gap between the toes for wearing with sandals made of vegetable fibre or leather. Royal footwear also featured gold sequins, embroidery and beading, with enemies painted on the soles to be crushed underfoot.

Plain headscarves were worn to protect the head from the sun or during messy work; the striped headcloth *(nemes)* was only worn by the king, who also had numerous crowns and diadems for ceremonial occasions.

Jewellery was worn by men and women throughout society for both aesthetic and magical purposes. It was made of various materials, from gold to glazed pottery, and included collars, necklaces, hair ornaments, bracelets, anklets, belts, earrings and finger rings.

Wigs and hair extensions were also popular and date back to c 3400 BC, as does the hair dye henna *(Lawsonia inermis)*. Many people shaved or cropped their hair for cleanliness and to prevent head lice (which have even been found in the hair of pharaohs). The clergy had to shave their heads for ritual purity, and children's heads were partially shaved to leave only a side lock of hair as a symbol of their youth.

Amun

Anubis

Aten

GODS & GODDESSES

Initially representing aspects of the natural world, Egypt's gods and goddesses grew more complex through time. As they began to blend together and adopt each other's characteristics, they can often be difficult to identify, although their distinctive headgear and clothing can provide clues as to who they are. The following brief descriptions should help travellers spot at least a few of the many hundreds who appear on monuments and in museums.

Bes

Amun The local god of Thebes (Luxor) who absorbed the war god Montu and fertility god Min and combined with the sun god to create Amun-Ra, King of the Gods. He is generally portrayed as a man with a double-plumed crown and sometimes the horns of his sacred ram.

Anubis God of mummification, patron of embalmers and guardian of cemeteries, Anubis is generally depicted as a black jackal or a jackal-headed man.

Apophis The huge snake embodying darkness and chaos was the enemy of the sun god Ra and tried to destroy him every night and prevent him reaching the dawn.

Hapy

Aten The solar disc whose rays end in outstretched hands, first appearing c 1900 BC and becoming chief deity during the Amarna Period c 1360–c 1335 BC.

Atum Creator god of Heliopolis who rose from the primeval waters and ejaculated (or sneezed depending on the myth) to create gods and humans. Generally depicted as a man wearing the double crown, Atum represented the setting sun.

Bastet Cat goddess whose cult centre was Bubastis; ferocious when defending her father Ra the sun god, she was often shown as a friendly deity, personified by the domestic cat.

Bes Grotesque yet benign dwarf god fond of music and dancing; he kept evil from the home and protected women in childbirth by waving his knife and sticking out his tongue.

Hathor

Horus

Isis

Khepri

Nut

Osiris

Geb God of the earth generally depicted as a green man lying beneath his sister-wife Nut the sky goddess, supported by their father Shu, god of air.

Hapy God of the Nile flood and the plump embodiment of fertility shown as an androgynous figure with a headdress of aquatic plants.

Hathor Goddess of love and pleasure represented as a cow or a woman with a crown of horns and sun's disc in her guise as the sun god's daughter. Patron of music and dancing whose cult centre was Dendara, she is known as 'she of the beautiful hair' and 'lady of drunkenness'.

Horus Falcon god of the sky and son of Isis and Osiris, he avenged his father to rule on earth and was personified by the ruling king. He can appear as a falcon or a man with a falcon's head, and his eye *(wedjat)* was a powerful amulet.

Isis Goddess of magic and protector of her brother-husband Osiris and their son Horus, she and her sister Nephthys also protected the dead. As symbolic mother of the king she appears as a woman with a throne-shaped crown, or sometimes has Hathor's cow horns.

Khepri God of the rising sun represented by the scarab beetle, whose habit of rolling balls of dirt was likened to the sun's journey across the sky.

Khnum Ram-headed god who created life on a potter's wheel; he also controlled the waters of the Nile flood from his cave at Elephantine and his cult centre was Esna.

Khons Young god of the moon and son of Amun and Mut. He is generally depicted in human form wearing a crescent moon crown and the 'sidelock of youth' hairstyle.

Maat Goddess of cosmic order, truth and justice, depicted as a woman wearing an ostrich feather on her head, or sometimes by the feather alone.

Mut Amun's consort and one of the symbolic mothers of the king; her name means both 'mother' and 'vulture' and she is generally shown as woman with a vulture headdress.

Nekhbet Vulture goddess of Upper Egypt worshipped at el-Kab; she often appears with her sister-goddess Wadjet the cobra, protecting the pharaoh.

Nut Sky goddess usually portrayed as a woman whose star-spangled body arches across tomb and temple ceilings. She swallows the sun each evening to give birth to it each morning.

Osiris God of regeneration portrayed in human form and worshipped mainly at Abydos. As the first mummy created, he was magically revived by Isis to produce their son Horus, who took over the earthly kingship while Osiris became ruler of the underworld and symbol of eternal life.

Ptah Creator god of Memphis who thought the world into being. He is patron of craftsmen, wears a skullcap and usually clutches a tall sceptre (resembling a 1950s microphone).

Ra Supreme sun god generally shown as a man with a falcon's head topped by a sun disc, although he can take many forms (eg Aten, Khepri) and other gods merge with him to enhance their powers (eg Amun-Ra, Ra-Atum). Ra travelled through the skies in a boat, sinking down into the underworld each night before re-emerging at dawn to bring light.

Sekhmet Lioness goddess of Memphis whose name means 'the powerful one'. As a daughter of sun god Ra she was capable of great destruction and was bringer of pestilence; her priests functioned as doctors.

Seth God of chaos personified by a mythological, composite animal. After murdering his brother Osiris he was defeated by Horus, and his great physical strength was harnessed to defend Ra in the underworld.

Sobek Crocodile god representing Pharaonic might, he was worshipped at Kom Ombo and the Fayuum.

Taweret Hippopotamus goddess who often appears upright to scare evil from the home and protect women in childbirth.

Thoth God of wisdom and writing, and patron of scribes. He is portrayed as an ibis or baboon and his cult centre was Hermopolis.

TEMPLES

Although many gods had their own cult centres, they were also worshipped at temples throughout Egypt. Built on sites considered sacred, existing temples were added to by successive pharaohs to demonstrate their piety. This is best seen at the enormous complex of Karnak (p242), the culmination of 2000 years of reconstruction.

Surrounded by huge enclosure walls of mud brick, the stone temples within were regarded as houses of the gods where daily rituals were performed on behalf of the king. As the intermediary between gods and humans, the king was high priest of every temple, although in practice these powers were delegated to each temple's high priest.

As well as the temples housing the gods (cult temples), there were also funerary (mortuary) temples where each pharaoh was worshipped after death. Eventually sited away from their tombs for security reasons, the best examples are on Luxor's West Bank, where pharaohs buried in the Valley of the Kings had huge funerary temples built closer to the river. These include Ramses III's temple at Medinat Habu, Amenhotep III's once-vast temple marked by the Colossi of Memnon and the best known example built by Hatshepsut into the cliffs of Deir al-Bahri.

Ra

TOMBS & MUMMIFICATION
Tombs
Initially, tombs were created to differentiate the burials of the elite from the majority, whose bodies continued to be placed directly into the desert sand. By around 3100 BC the mound of sand heaped over a grave was replaced by a more permanent structure of mud brick, whose characteristic bench-shape is known as a mastaba after the Arabic word for bench.

As stone replaced mud brick, the addition of further levels to increase height created the pyramid, the first built at Saqqara for King Zoser (see Zoser's Funerary Complex on p182). Its stepped sides soon evolved into the familiar smooth-sided structure, with the Pyramids of Giza (p128) the most famous examples.

Sekhmet

Pyramids are generally surrounded by the mastaba tombs of officials (see Cemeteries on p134, Tomb of Akhethotep & Ptahhotep on p185, Mastaba of Ti on p185, Tombs of Mereruka & Ankhmahor on p186) wanting burial close to their king in order to share in an afterlife which was still the prerogative of royalty. It was only when the power of the monarchy broke down at the end of the Old Kingdom that the afterlife became increasingly accessible to those outside the royal family, and as officials became increasingly independent they began to opt for burial in their home towns. With little room for grand superstructures along many of the narrow stretches beside the Nile, an alternative type of tomb developed, cut tunnel-fashion into the cliffs which border the river. Most were built on the west bank, the traditional place of burial where the sun was seen to sink down into the underworld each evening.

Sobek

These simple rock-cut tombs consisting of a single chamber gradually developed into more elaborate structures complete with an open courtyard, offering a chapel and entrance façade carved out of the rock, with a shaft leading down into a burial chamber (see Tomb of Kheti on p204, Tomb of Baqet on p204, Tomb of Khnumhotep on p204, Tombs of the Nobles on p310).

The most impressive rock-cut tombs were those built for the kings of the New Kingdom (1550–1069 BC), who relocated the royal burial ground south to the religious capital Thebes (modern Luxor) to a remote desert valley on the west bank, now known as the Valley of the Kings (see p251). With new evidence suggesting the first tomb (KV 39) here may have been built by Amenhotep I, the tomb of his successor Tuthmosis I was built by royal architect Ineni, whose biographical inscription states that he supervised its construction alone, 'with no-one seeing, no-one hearing'. In a radical departure from tradition, the offering chapels that

Taweret

Thoth

The subterranean chambers beneath Zoser's pyramid were decorated with bright turquoise-blue tiles, some of which can be seen in the upper rooms of the Egyptian Museum.

were once part of the tomb's layout were now replaced by funerary (mortuary) temples built some distance away to preserve the tomb's secret location.

The tombs themselves were designed with a long corridor descending to a network of chambers decorated with scenes to help the deceased reach the next world. Many of these were extracts from the Book of the Dead, the modern term for works including The Book of Amduat (literally, 'that which is in the underworld'), the Book of Gates and The Litany of Ra. These describe the sun god's nightly journey through the darkness of the underworld, the realm of Osiris, with each hour of the night regarded as a separate region guarded by demigods. In order for Ra and the dead souls who accompanied him to pass through on their way to rebirth at dawn, it was essential that they knew the demigods' names in order to get past them. Since knowledge was power in the Egyptian afterlife, the funerary texts give 'Knowledge of the power of those in the underworld, knowledge of the hidden forces, knowing each hour and each god, knowing the gates where the great god must pass and knowing how the powerful can be destroyed'.

Mummification

Although mummification was used by many ancient cultures across the world, the Egyptians were the ultimate practitioners of this highly complex procedure, which they refined over 4000 years.

Current research is starting to reveal that the Egyptians were experimenting with mummification as early as 4300 BC, almost a thousand years earlier than previously believed.

Their preservation of the dead can be traced back to the very earliest times, when bodies were simply buried in the desert away from the limited areas of cultivation. In direct contact with the sand, the hot, dry conditions allowed body fluids to drain away while preserving the skin, hair and nails intact. Accidentally uncovering such bodies must have had a profound effect upon those able to recognise people who had died years before.

As society developed, those who would once have been buried in a hole in the ground demanded tombs befitting their status. But as the bodies were no longer in direct contact with the sand, they rapidly decomposed. An alternative means of preservation was therefore required. After a long process of experimentation, and a good deal of trial and error, the Egyptians seem to have finally cracked it around 2600 BC when they started to remove the internal organs, where putrefaction begins.

As the process became increasingly elaborate, all the organs were removed except the kidneys, which were hard to reach, and the heart, considered as the source of intelligence. The brain was removed by inserting a metal probe up the nose and whisking until it had liquefied sufficiently to be drained down the nose. All the rest – lungs, liver, stomach and intestines – were removed through an opening cut in the left flank. Then the body and its separate organs were covered with natron salt (a combination of sodium carbonate and sodium bicarbonate) and left to dry out for 40 days, after which they were washed, purified and anointed with a range of oils, spices and resins. All were then wrapped in layers of linen, with the appropriate amulets set in place over the various parts of the body as priests recited the necessary incantations.

One of the most common souvenirs of a trip to Egypt in the 19th century was a mummy, either whole or in bits – heads and hands were particularly popular as they fitted easily into luggage.

With each of the internal organs placed inside its own burial container (one of four Canopic jars), the wrapped body with its funerary mask was placed inside its coffin. It was then ready for the funeral procession to the tomb, where the vital Opening of the Mouth ceremony reanimated the soul and restored its senses. Offerings could then be given and the deceased wished 'a thousand of every good and pure thing for your soul and all kinds of offerings'.

The Egyptians also used their mummification skills to preserve animals, both much-loved pets and creatures presented in huge numbers as votive offerings to the gods with which they were associated. Everything from huge bulls to tiny shrews were mummified, with cats, hawks and ibis preserved in their millions by Graeco-Roman times.

ART IN LIFE & DEATH

Ancient Egyptian art is instantly recognisable, and its distinctive style remained largely unchanged for more than three millennia. With its basic characteristics already in place at the beginning of the Pharaonic period c 3100 BC, the motif of the king smiting his enemies on the Narmer Palette (see Room 43 – Atrium on p169) was still used in Roman times.

Despite being described in modern terms as 'works of art', the reasons for the production of art in ancient Egypt are still very much misunderstood. Whereas most cultures create art for purely decorative purposes, Egyptian art was primarily functional. This idea is best conveyed when gazing at the most famous and perhaps most beautiful of all Egyptian images, Tutankhamun's death mask (see Room 3 on p175), which was quite literally made to be buried in a hole in the ground.

The majority of artefacts were produced for religious and funerary purposes, and despite their breathtaking beauty would have been hidden away from public gaze, either within a temple's dark interior or, like Tut's mask, buried in a tomb with the dead. This only makes the objects – and those who made them – even more remarkable. Artists regarded the things they made as pieces of equipment to do a job rather than works of art to be displayed and admired, and only once or twice in 3000 years did an artist actually sign their work.

This concept also explains the appearance of carved and painted wall scenes, whose deceptively simple appearance and lack of perspective reinforces their functional purpose. The Egyptians believed it was essential that the things they portrayed had every relevant feature shown as clearly as possible. Then when they were magically reanimated through the correct rituals they would be able to function as effectively as possible, protecting and sustaining the unseen spirits of both the gods and the dead.

Figures needed a clear outline, with a profile of nose and mouth to let them breathe, and the eye shown whole as if seen from the front, to allow the figure to see. This explains why eyes were often painted on the sides of coffins to allow the dead to see out, and why hieroglyphs such as snakes or enemy figures were sometimes shown in two halves to prevent them causing damage when re-activated.

The vast quantities of food and drink offered in temples and tombs were duplicated on surrounding walls to ensure a constant supply for eternity. The offerings are shown piled up in layers, sometimes appearing to float in suspension if the artist took this practice too far. In the same way, objects otherwise hidden from view if portrayed realistically appear to balance on top of the boxes which actually contained them.

While working within such restrictive conventions, the ancient artists still managed to capture a feeling of vitality. Inspired by the natural world around them, they selected images to reflect the concept of life and rebirth, as embodied by the scarab beetles and tilapia fish thought capable of self-generation. Since images were also believed to be able to transmit the life-force they contained, fluttering birds, gambolling cattle and the speeding quarry of huntsmen were all favourite motifs. The life-giving properties of plants are also much in evidence, with wheat, grapes, onions and figs stacked side by side with the flowers the Egyptians loved

The textiles used to wrap mummies are often described as 'bandages', although all kinds of recycled linen was used for the purpose, from old shirts to boat sails.

Many of the treasures found in the tomb of Tutankhamun bear the names of his predecessors Akhenaten and the mysterious 'Smenkhkare', and apparently buried with Tutankhamun simply to get rid of all trace of this unpopular family.

The ancient Egyptians were very good at faking certain materials, with wooden pots painted to resemble costly stone and painted linen used for priestly vestments instead of real panther skin.

so much. Particularly common are the lotus (water lily) and papyrus, the heraldic symbols of Upper and Lower Egypt often shown entwined to symbolise a kingdom united.

Colour was also used as a means of reinforcing an object's function, with bright primary shades achieved with natural pigments selected for their specific qualities. Egypt was represented politically by the White Crown of Upper Egypt and the Red Crown of Lower Egypt, fitted together in the dual crown to represent the two lands brought together. The country could also be represented in environmental terms by the colours red and black, the red desert wastes of *deshret* contrasting with the fertile black land of *kemet*. For the Egyptians, black was the colour of life, which also explains the choice of black in representations of Osiris, god of fertility and resurrection in contrast to the redness associated with his brother Seth, god of chaos. Colour does not indicate ethnic origins however, since Osiris is also shown with green skin, the colour of vegetation and new life. Some of his fellow gods are blue to echo the ethereal blue of the sky, and the golden-yellow of the sun is regularly employed for its protective qualities. Even human figures were initially represented with different coloured skin tones, the red-brown of men contrasting with the paler, yellowed tones of women, and although this has been interpreted as indicating that men spent most of the time working outdoors whereas women led a more sheltered existence, changes in artistic convention meant everyone was eventually shown with the same red-brown skin tone.

The choice of material was also an important way of enhancing an object's purpose. Sculptors worked in a variety of different mediums, with stone often chosen for its colour – white limestone and alabaster (calcite), golden sandstone, green schist (slate), brown quartzite and both black and red granite. Smaller items could be made of red or yellow jasper, orange carnelian or blue lapis-lazuli, metals such as copper, gold or silver, or less costly materials such as wood or highly-glazed blue faïence pottery.

All these materials were used to produce a wide range of statuary for temples and tombs, from 20m-high stone colossi to gold figurines a few centimetres tall. Regardless of their dimensions, each figure was thought capable of containing the spirit of the individual they represented – useful insurance should anything happen to the mummy. Amulets and jewellery were another means of ensuring the security of the dead, and while their beauty would enhance the appearance of the living, each piece was also carefully designed as a protective talisman or a means of communicating status. Even when creating such small-scale masterpieces, the same principles employed in larger-scale works of art applied, and little of the work that the ancient craftsmen produced was either accidental or frivolous.

There was also a standard repertoire of funerary scenes, from the colourful images that adorn the walls of tombs to the highly detailed vignettes illuminating funerary texts. Every single image, whether carved on stone or painted on papyrus, was designed to serve and protect the deceased on their journey into the afterlife.

Initially the afterlife was restricted to royalty, and the texts meant to guide the pharaohs towards eternity were inscribed on the walls of their burial chambers. Since the rulers of the Old Kingdom were buried in pyramids, the accompanying funerary writings are known as the Pyramid Texts (see Pyramid & Causeway of Unas on p183, Pyramid of Teti on p186, South Saqqara on p187).

In the hope of sharing in the royal afterlife, Old Kingdom officials built their tombs close to the pyramids until the pharaohs lost power at the end of the Old Kingdom. No longer reliant on the pharaoh's favour, the of-

The first recorded workers' strike in history occurred in 1152 BC when royal tomb builders refused to go back to work because their supplies of moisturising oil had not been delivered.

Among the very few named artists known from ancient Egypt, Men worked as a sculptor for Amenhotep III while his son Bek worked for Amenhotep's son and successor Akhenaten, claiming he was 'the apprentice whom his majesty himself taught'.

ficials began to use the royal funerary texts for themselves, and inscribed on their coffins they are known as Coffin Texts – a Middle Kingdom version of the earlier Pyramid Texts, adapted for nonroyal use.

This 'democratisation' of the afterlife evolved even further when the Coffin Texts were literally brought out in paperback, inscribed on papyrus and made available to the masses during the New Kingdom. Referred to by the modern term The Book of the Dead, the Egyptians knew this as The Book of Coming Forth by Day, with sections entitled 'Spell for not dying a second time', 'Spell not to rot and not to do work in the land of the dead' and 'Spell for not having your magic taken away'. The texts also give various visions of paradise, from joining the sun god Ra in his journey across the sky, joining Osiris in the underworld or rising up to become one of the Imperishable Stars, the variety of final destinations reflecting the ancient Egyptians' multifaceted belief system. These spells and instructions acted as a kind of guidebook to the afterlife, with some of the texts accompanied by maps, and images of some of the gods and demons that would be encountered en route together with the correct way to address them.

The same scenes were also portrayed on tomb walls; the New Kingdom royal tombs in the Valley of the Kings (p251) are decorated with highly formal scenes showing pharaoh in the company of the gods and all the forces of darkness defeated. Since pharaoh was always pharaoh, even in death, there was no room for the informality and scenes of daily life that can be found in the tombs of lesser mortals (see Tombs of the Nobles on p264).

> Since it was thought that images of living things could reanimate in the afterlife, the nose and mouth of unpopular figures were often defaced to prevent them inhaling the breath of life needed to live again in the next world.

This explains the big difference between the formal scenes in royal tombs and the much more relaxed, almost eclectic nature of nonroyal tomb scenes, which feature everything from eating and drinking to dancing and hairdressing. Yet even here these apparently random scenes of daily life carry the same message found throughout Egyptian art – the eternal continuity of life and the triumph of order over chaos. As the king is shown smiting the enemy and restoring peace to the land, his subjects contribute to this continual battle of opposites in which order must always triumph for life to continue.

In one of the most common nonroyal tomb scenes, the tomb owner hunts on the river (see Tombs of Menna & Nakht on p264). Although generally interpreted on a simplistic level as the deceased enjoying a day out boating with his family, the scene is far more complex than it first appears. The tomb owner, shown in a central position in the prime of life, strikes a formal pose as he restores order amid the chaos of nature all around him. In his task he is supported by the female members of his family, from his small daughter to the wife standing serenely beside him. Dressed far too impractically for a hunting trip on the river, his wife wears an outfit more in keeping with a priestess of Hathor, goddess of love and sensual pleasure. Yet Hathor is also the protector of the dead, and capable of great violence as defender of her father, the sun god Ra, in his eternal struggle against the chaotic forces of darkness.

> The eyes of cats in tomb scenes were occasionally painted with gold leaf, giving them a realistic reflective quality in the darkness of the tomb and linking them to the sun god's protective powers.

Some versions of this riverside hunting scene also feature a cat? Often described as a kind of 'retriever' (whoever heard of a retriever cat?), the cat is one of the creatures who was believed to defend the sun god on his nightly journey through the underworld. Similarly, the river's teeming fish were regarded as pilots for the sun god's boat and were themselves potent symbols of rebirth. Even the abundant lotus flowers are significant since the lotus, whose petals open each morning, is the flower that symbolised rebirth. Once the coded meaning of ancient Egyptian art is understood, such previously silent images almost scream out the idea of 'life'.

Another common tomb scene is the banquet at which guests enjoy generous quantities of food and drink (see Tombs of Menna & Nakht p264, Tombs of Sennofer & Rekhmire on p265). Although no doubt reflecting some of the pleasures the deceased had enjoyed in life, the food portrayed was also meant to sustain their souls, as would the accompanying scenes of bountiful harvests which would ensure supplies never ran out. Even the music and dance performed at these banquets indicate much more than a party in full swing – the lively proceedings were another way of reviving the deceased by awakening their senses.

The culmination of this idea can be found in the all-important Opening of the Mouth ceremony, performed by the deceased's heir, either the next king or the eldest son. The ceremony was designed to reanimate the soul (ka) which could then go on to enjoy eternal life once all its senses had been restored. Noise and movement were believed to reactivate hearing and sight, while the sense of smell was restored with incense and flowers. The essential offerings of food and drink then sustained the soul that resided within the mummy as it was finally laid to rest inside the tomb.

HIEROGLYPHS

Hieroglyphs, meaning 'sacred carvings' in Greek, are the pictorial script used by the ancient Egyptians. First developed as a means of recording produce, recent discoveries at Abydos dating to around 3250 BC make this the earliest form of writing yet found, even predating that of Mesopotamia.

The impact of hieroglyphs on Egyptian culture cannot be overestimated, as they provided the means by which the state took shape. They were used by a civil service of scribes working on the king's behalf to collect taxes and organise vast workforces, and with literacy running at less than 1%, scribes were considered wise and part of society's elite.

Within a few centuries, day-to-day transactions were undertaken in a shorthand version of hieroglyphs known as hieratic, whereas hieroglyphs remained the perfect medium for monumental inscriptions. They were in constant use for over three and a half thousand years until the last example was carved at Philae temple on 24 August AD 394. Covering every available tomb and temple surface, hieroglyphs were regarded as 'the words of the Thoth', the ibis-headed god of writing and patron deity of scribes, who, like the scribes, is often shown holding a reed pen and ink palette.

The small figures of humans, animals, birds and symbols that populate the script were believed to infuse each scene with divine power. In fact certain signs were considered so potent they were shown in two halves to prevent them causing havoc should they magically reanimate. Yet the ancient Egyptians also liked a joke, and their language was often onomatopoeic – for example, the word for cat was *miw* after the noise it makes, and the word for wine was *irp*, after the noise made by those who drank it.

Evolving from a handful of basic signs, more than 6000 hieroglyphs have been identified, although less than a thousand were in general use. Although they may at first appear deceptively simple, the signs themselves operate on several different levels and can best be understood if divided into three categories – logograms (ideograms), determinatives and phonograms. While logograms represent the thing they depict (eg the sun sign meaning 'sun'), and determinatives are simply placed at the ends of words to reinforce their meaning (eg the sun sign in the verb 'to shine'), phonograms are less straightforward and are the signs which represent either one, two or three consonants. The 26 signs usually described in simple terms as 'the hieroglyphic alphabet' are the single consonant signs (eg the owl pronounced 'm', the zig-zag water sign 'n'). Another 100 or so

For a straightforward approach to ancient Egypt's artistic legacy, Cyril Aldred's *Egyptian Art* (Thames & Hudson, 1985) remains hard to beat, while a useful guide to the way hieroglyphs were used in art is provided by Richard Wilkinson's *Reading Egyptian Art: A Hieroglyphic Guide to Ancient Egyptian Painting and Sculpture* (Thames & Hudson, 1994).

Fond of word play, the Egyptians often incorporated hieroglyphs into their designs to spell out names or phrases – the basket, beetle and sun disc featured in some of Tutankhamun's jewellery, for example, spells out his throne name 'neb–kheperu-re'.

signs are biconsonantal (eg the bowl sign read as 'nb'), and a further 50 are triconsonantal signs (eg 'nfr' meaning good, perfect or beautiful).

Unfortunately there are no actual vowels as such, and the absence of any punctuation can also prove tricky, especially since the signs can be arranged either vertically to be read down or horizontally to be read left to right or right to left, depending which way the symbols face.

Although they can seem incredibly complex, the majority of hieroglyphic inscriptions are simply endless repetitions of the names and titles of the pharaohs and gods, surrounded by protective symbols. Names were of tremendous importance to the Egyptians and as vital to an individual's existence as their soul (ka), and it was sincerely believed that 'to speak the name of the dead is to make them live'. The loss of one's name meant permanent obliteration from history, and those unfortunate enough to incur official censure included commoners and pharaohs alike. At times it even happened to the gods themselves, a fate which befell the state god Amun during the reign of the 'heretic' pharaoh Akhenaten, who in turn suffered the same fate together with his god Aten when Amun was later restored.

In order to prevent this kind of obliteration, names were sometimes carved so deeply into the rock it is possible to place an outstretched hand right inside each hieroglyph, as is the case of Ramses III's name and titles at his funerary temple of Medinat Habu.

Royal names were also followed by epithets such as 'life, prosperity, health', comparable to the way in which the name of the Prophet Mohammed is always followed by the phrase 'peace be upon him'. For further protection, royal names were written inside a rectangular fortress wall known as a *serekh*, which later developed into the more familiar oval-shaped cartouche (the French word for cartridge).

Although each pharaoh had five names, cartouches were used to enclose the two most important ones, the 'prenomen' or 'King of Upper and Lower Egypt' name assumed at the coronation and written with a bee and a sedge plant, and the 'nomen', or 'Son of Ra' name which was given at birth, written with a goose and a sun sign.

As an example Amenhotep III is known by his nomen or Son of Ra name 'Amun-hotep' (meaning Amun is content), although his prenomen or King of Upper and Lower Egypt name, was Neb-maat-Re (meaning Ra, lord of truth). His grandson had the most famous of all Egyptian names, Tut-ankh-amun, which literally translates as 'the living image of Amun', yet he had originally been named Tut-ankh-aten, meaning 'the living image of the Aten', a change in name which reflects the shifting politics of the time.

Gods were also incorporated into the names of ordinary people, and as well as Amunhotep, there was Rahotep, (the sun god Ra is content) and Ptahhotep, (the creator god Ptah is content). By changing 'hotep' (meaning 'content') to 'mose' (meaning 'born of'), the names Amenmose, Ramose and Ptahmose meant that these men were 'born of' these gods.

In similar fashion, goddesses featured in women's names. Hathor, goddess of love, beauty and pleasure was a particular favourite, with names such as Sithathor ('daughter of Hathor'). Standard names could also be feminised by the simple addition of 't', so Nefer, 'good', 'beautiful' or 'perfect', becomes Nefert, which could be further embellished with the addition of a verb, as in the case of the famous name Nefertiti, 'goodness/beauty/perfection has come'.

Others were known by their place of origin, such as Panehesy, 'the Nubian', or could be named after flora and fauna – Miwt (cat), Debet (hippopotamus) and Seshen (lotus), which is still in use today as the name Susan.

PHARAONIC CARTOUCHES

Ramses II (Usermaatre Setepenre)

Amenhotep III (Nebmaatre)

Tuthmosis III (Menkheperre)

Hatshepsut (Maatkare)

PHARAONIC GLOSSARY

akh – usually translated as 'transfigured spirit', produced when the ka (soul) and ba (spirit) united after the deceased was judged worthy enough to enter the afterlife

Ammut – composite monster of the underworld who was part crocodile, part lion, part hippo and ate the hearts of the unworthy dead, her name means 'The Devourer'

ba – usually translated as 'spirit', which appeared after death as a human-headed bird, able to fly to and from the tomb and into the afterlife

Book of the Dead – modern term for the collection of ancient funerary texts designed to guide the dead through the afterlife, developed at the beginning of the New Kingdom and partly based on the earlier Pyramid Texts and Coffin Texts

Canopic jars – containers usually made of limestone or calcite to store the preserved entrails (stomach, liver, lungs and intestines) of mummified individuals

cartouche – the protective oval shape (the name derived from the French word for cartridge), which surrounded the names of kings and queens and occasionally gods

cenotaph – a memorial structure set up in memory of a deceased king or queen, separate from their tomb or funerary temple

Coffin Texts – funerary texts developed from the earlier Pyramid Texts which were then written on coffins during the Middle Kingdom

coregency – a period of joint rule by two pharaohs, usually father and son

cult temple – the standard religious building(s) designed to house the spirits of the gods and accessible only to the priesthood, usually located on the Nile's east bank

deshret – 'red land', referring to barren desert

djed pillar – the symbolic backbone of Osiris, bestowing strength and stability and often worn as an amulet

false door – the means by which the soul of the deceased could enter and leave the world of the living to accept funerary offerings brought to their tomb

funerary (mortuary) temple – the religious structures where the souls of dead pharaohs were commemorated and sustained with offerings, usually built on the Nile's west bank

Heb-Sed festival – the jubilee ceremony of royal renewal and rejuvenation, which kings usually celebrated after 30 years' rule

Heb-Sed race – part of the Heb-Sed festival when kings undertook physical feats such as running to demonstrate their prowess and fitness to rule

hieratic – ancient shorthand version of hieroglyphs used for day-to-day transactions by scribes

hieroglyphs – Greek for 'sacred carvings', referring to ancient Egypt's formal picture writing used mainly for tomb and temple walls

hypostyle hall – imposing section of temple characterised by densely packed monumental columns

ka – usually translated as 'soul', this was a person's 'double', which was created with them at birth and which lived on after death, sustained by offerings left by the living

kemet – 'black land' referring to the fertile areas along the Nile's banks

king lists – chronological lists of each king's names kept as a means of recording history

lotus (water lily) – the heraldic plant of Upper (southern) Egypt

mammisi – the Birth House attached to certain Late Period and Graeco-Roman temples and associated with the goddesses Isis and Hathor

mastaba – Arabic word for bench, used to describe the mud-brick tomb structures built over subterranean burial chambers and from which pyramids developed

name – an essential part of each individual given at birth, and spoken after their death to allow them to live again in the afterlife

naos – sanctuary containing the god's statue, generally located in the centre of ancient temples

natron – mixture of sodium carbonate and sodium bicarbonate used to dry out the body during mummification and used by the living to clean linen, teeth and skin

nemes – the yellow-and-blue striped headcloth worn by kings, the most famous example found on Tutankhamun's golden death mask

nomarch – local governor of each of Egypt's 42 nomes

nome – Greek term for Egypt's 42 provinces, 22 in Upper Egypt and later 20 added in Lower Egypt

Temple rituals included the burning or smashing of wax or clay figurines of anyone who threatened divine order, from enemies of the state to enemies of the sun god.

obelisk – monolithic stone pillar tapering to a pyramidal top that was often gilded to reflect sunlight around temples and usually set in pairs

Opening of the Mouth ceremony – the culmination of the funeral, performed on the mummy of the deceased by their heir or funerary priest using spells and implements to restore their senses

Opet festival – annual celebration held at Luxor Temple to restore the powers of pharaoh at a secret meeting with the god Amun

papyrus – the heraldic plant of Lower (northern) Egypt whose reedlike stem was sliced and layered to create paperlike sheets for writing

pharaoh – term for an Egyptian king derived from the ancient Egyptian word for palace, *per-aa*, meaning great house

pylon – monumental gateway with sloping sides forming the entrance to temples

Pyramid Texts – funerary texts inscribed on the walls of late Old Kingdom pyramids and restricted to royalty

sacred animals – living creatures thought to represent certain gods, eg the crocodile (identified with Sobek), the cat (identified with Bastet), and often mummified at death

sarcophagus – derived from the Greek for 'flesh-eating' and referring to the large stone coffins used to house the mummy and its wooden coffin(s)

scarab – the sacred dung beetle believed to propel the sun's disc through the sky in the same way the beetle pushes a ball of dung across the floor

Serapeum – vast network of underground catacombs at Saqqara in which the Apis bulls were buried, later associated with the Ptolemaic god Serapis

serdab – from the Arabic word for cellar, a small room in a mastaba tomb containing a statue of the deceased to which offerings were presented

shabti (or ushabti) – small servant figurines placed in burials designed to undertake any manual work in the afterlife on behalf of the deceased

shadow – an essential part of each individual, the shadow was believed to offer protection, based on the importance of shade in an extremely hot climate

sidelock of youth – characteristic hairstyle of children and certain priests in which the head is shaved and a single lock of hair allowed to grow

solar barque – the boat in which the sun god Ra sailed through the heavens, with actual examples buried close to certain pyramids for use by the spirits of the pharaohs

Uraeus – an image of the cobra goddess Wadjet worn at the brow of royalty to symbolically protect them by spitting fire into the eyes of their enemies

Weighing of the Heart (The Judgement of Osiris) – the heart of the deceased was weighed against the feather of Maat with Osiris as judge; if light and free of sin they were allowed to spend eternity as an *akh*, but if their heart was heavy with sin it was eaten by Ammut and they were damned forever

Although cats were considered sacred, X-ray examinations have revealed that some at least were killed to order by strangulation prior to their mummification for use as votive offerings.

By Roman times Isis had become the most important of all Egypt's gods and by the 1st century AD her worship had even spread as far as London.

The Culture

THE NATIONAL PSYCHE

If there's one characteristic that links the majority of Egyptians, from the university professor in Alexandria to the shoeshine boy in Luxor, it's an immense pride in simply being Egyptian. Locals you encounter may express their wistful dreams of going to 'Amrika' and ask visitors' help in securing a visa to travel overseas, but that's purely for the opportunities that living in the West presents to earn money. You can be sure that their hearts will remain rooted firmly in Misr (local parlance for 'Egypt'). It's hard sometimes to see where that pride could come from given the pervasive poverty, low literacy levels, high unemployment, housing shortages, infrastructure shortfalls and myriad other pitfalls and complications that dog daily life. But aiding every Egyptian in the daily struggle is every other Egyptian. There's a sense that everybody's in it together. Large extended families and close-knit neighbourhoods act as social support groups, strangers fall easily into conversation with each other, and whatever goes wrong, somebody always knows someone somewhere who can fix it.

Religion also cushions life's blows. Islam permeates Egyptian life. It's manifested not in a strictly authoritarian manner as in Saudi Arabia – Egyptians love enjoying themselves too much for that – but it's there at an almost subconscious level. Ask after someone's health and the answer is *'Alhamdulallah'*, (Fine. Praise to God). Arrange to meet tomorrow and it's *'in sha'Allah'*, (God willing). Then, if your appointee fails to turn up, God obviously didn't mean it to be. And when all else fails there's humour. Egyptians are renowned for it. Jokes and wisecracks are the parlance of life. Comedy is the staple of the local cinema industry and backbone of TV scheduling. The stock character is the little guy who through wit and a sharp tongue always manages to prick pomposity and triumph over the odds. Laughter lubricates the wheels of social exchange and one of the most enjoyable aspects of travel in Egypt is how much can be negotiated with a smile.

Fifty per cent of Egyptians live or work within 150km of Cairo.

LIFESTYLE

There's no simple definition of Egyptian society. On the one hand there's traditional conservatism, reinforced by poverty, in which the diet is one of *fuul*, *ta'amiyya* and vegetables; women wear the long, black, all-concealing *abeyya* and men wear the gownlike *galabiyya;* cousins marry cousins; going to Alexandria constitutes the trip of a lifetime; and all is 'God's will'. On the other hand, there are sections of society whose members order out from McDonald's; whose daughters wear slinky black numbers and flirt outrageously; who think nothing of regular trips to the USA; and who never set foot in a mosque until the day they're laid out in one.

On their return from a women's suffrage conference in Rome in 1923, pioneer Arab feminists Huda Sharawi and Saiza Nabarawi threw away their *abeyya*s at Ramses Railway Station in Cairo; many in the crowd of women who had come to welcome them home followed suit.

The bulk of the Egyptian populace falls somewhere between these two extremes. The typical urban family lives in an overcrowded suburb in a six-floor breeze-block apartment building with cracking walls and dodgy plumbing. If they're lucky they may own a small car (Fiat or Lada), which will be 10 or more years old. Otherwise the husband will take the metro to work or, more likely, fight for a handhold on one of the city's sardine-can buses. He may well be a university graduate (about 40,000 people graduate each year), although a degree is no longer any guarantee

---

BACKHAND ECONOMY – THE ART OF BAKSHEESH

Tipping in Egypt is called baksheesh, but it's more than just a reward for services rendered. Salaries and wages in Egypt are much lower than in Western countries, so baksheesh is an essential means of supplementing income. It's far from a custom exclusively reserved for foreigners. Egyptians have to constantly dole out the baksheesh too – to park their cars, receive their mail, ensure they get fresh produce at the grocers and to be shown to their seat at the cinema.

For travellers who are not used to continual tipping, demands for baksheesh for doing anything from opening doors to pointing out the obvious in museums can be quite irritating. But it is the accepted way in Egypt. Just use your discretion, always remembering that more things warrant baksheesh here than anywhere in the West.

In hotels and restaurants, a 12% service charge is included at the bottom of the bill, but the money goes into the till; it's necessary therefore to leave an additional tip for the waiter. Services such as opening a door, delivering room service or carrying your bags warrant at least E£1. A guard who shows you something off the beaten track at an ancient site or an attendant at a mosque who looks after your shoes should receive a couple of pounds. Baksheesh is not necessary when asking for directions.

We suggest carrying lots of small change with you (trust us – you'll need it!) and also to keep it separate from bigger bills; flashing your cash will lead to demands for greater baksheesh.

---

of a job. He may also be one of the million-plus paper-pushing civil servants, earning a pittance to while away each day in an undemanding job. This at least allows him to slip away from work early each afternoon to borrow his cousin's taxi for a few hours to bring in some much-needed supplementary income. His wife remains at home cooking, looking after the three or more children, and swapping visits with his mother, her mother and various other family members.

Meanwhile life in rural Egypt, where just over half the country's population lives, is undergoing a transformation. The population density on the agricultural land of the Nile Valley, on which most cities and villages are built, is one of the highest in the world. What little land remains is divided into small plots (averaging just 0.6 hectares) that do not support even a medium-sized family. As much as 50% of the rural population no longer makes its living off the land. For those who do, the small size of their plots prevents the mechanisation needed to increase yields and they increasingly rely on animal husbandry or are forced to look for other ways of surviving. So the fellah you see working his field is probably spending his afternoons working as a labourer or selling cigarettes from a homemade kiosk in an effort to make ends meet.

The countryside remains the repository of traditional culture and values. Large families are still the norm, particularly in Upper Egypt, and extended families still live together. High rates of female illiteracy are standard. Whether all this will change with the steady diet of urban Cairene values and Western soap operas currently beamed into village cafés and farmhouses each night remains to be seen.

Hakmet Abu Zeid became the first woman in the Egyptian cabinet in 1962, assuming the post of social affairs minister.

POPULATION

Although the latest census results show that Egypt's population growth rate is falling, the number of citizens continues to increase by around one million every nine months. The Nile Valley is in danger of becoming a single sprawling city. Greater Cairo alone is home to nearly 20 million people. Parts of the city continue to house the world's highest density of people per kilometre. The strain placed on the city's decaying infrastructure is enormous and more than it can cope with.

A Diverse Culture

Most Egyptians will proudly tell you that they are descendants of the ancient Egyptians, and while there is a strand of truth in this, any Pharaonic blood still flowing in modern veins has been seriously diluted. The country has weathered invasions of Libyans, Persians, Greeks, Romans and, most significantly, the 4000 Arab horsemen who invaded in AD 640. Following the Arab conquest, there was significant Arab migration and intermarriage with the indigenous population. The Mamluks, rulers of Egypt between the 13th and 16th centuries, were of Turkish and Circassian origins, and then there were the Ottoman Turks, rulers and occupiers from 1517 until the latter years of the 18th century.

Beside the Egyptians, there are a handful of separate indigenous groups with ancient roots. The ancestors of Egypt's Bedouins migrated from the Arabian Peninsula. They settled the Western and Eastern Deserts and Sinai. The number of Bedouin in Egypt these days is around 500,000, but their nomadic way of existence is under threat as the interests of the rest of the country increasingly intrude on their once-isolated domains (see p499). In the Western Desert, particularly in and around Siwa Oasis, are a small number of Berbers who have retained much of their own identity. They are quite easily distinguished from other Egyptians by, for instance, the dress of the women – usually the *meliyya* (head-to-toe garment with slits for the eyes). Although many speak Arabic, they have preserved their own language. In the south are the tall, dark-skinned Nubians. They originate from Nubia, the region between Aswan in southern Egypt and Khartoum in Sudan, an area that almost completely disappeared in the 1970s when the High Dam was created and the subsequent build-up of water behind it drowned their traditional lands.

Though women received the vote in 1956, restrictive personal-status laws prohibited a woman leaving her husband's house without his permission or a court order up until 1979.

MEDIA

According to a survey by the Egyptian Radio and TV Union, 54% of Egyptians watch five or more hours of TV a day.

As in the West the media is big business in Egypt. The biggest daily newspapers, which include *Al-Akbar*, the biggest seller with a circulation of around one million, *Al-Ahram*, the oldest daily in the Arab world (founded in 1877) and *Al-Gomhurriya*, set up by the military regime following the 1952 coup, are all progovernment or 'nationalist'. Ranged against them is an array of independents, including the weekly opposition publications *Al-Arabi* and the Islamist *Al-Ahrar*, as well as the business-slanted *Al-Alam al-Yom*. Although there are red lines not to be crossed (no criticism of the military, no presidential sleaze, nothing detrimental to 'national unity'), editors are given a degree of licence to publish what they will – which they do, often irrespective of whether a story happens to be true or not.

Illiteracy of around 50% means TV is the medium with the most penetration. In addition to the state channels (whose most popular output is Arabic films and home-grown soap operas), Egypt has its own satellite channels (ArabSat, NileSat 101, NileSat 202) including a couple of private operations (Al-Mehwar and Dream), both set up by well-known, politically connected businessmen. Quality of programming has markedly improved in recent years, forced to evolve by competition from other Arab and foreign channels such as CNN, Al-Jezira and even transmissions from the old enemy to the north, Israel, whose channels many Egyptians furtively tune to for the better quality US-made soaps and comedies.

RELIGION

About 90% of Egypt's population is Muslim. Islam prevails in Egyptian life at a low-key, almost unconscious level. Few pray the specified five times a day, but almost all men heed the amplified call of the muezzin (mosque official) each Friday noon, when the crowds from the mosques block streets and footpaths. The 10% of Egypt that isn't Muslim is Coptic Christian. The two communities enjoy a more-or-less easy coexistence, although flare-ups in Minya and Alexandria in 2005 seemed to herald the introduction of tensions in this historically peaceful relationship.

Islam

Islam is the predominant religion of Egypt. It shares its roots with Judaism and Christianity. Adam, Abraham (Ibrahim), Noah, Moses and Jesus are all accepted as Muslim prophets, although Jesus is not recognised as the son of God. Muslim teachings correspond closely to the Torah (the foundation book of Judaism) and the Christian Gospels. The essence of Islam is the Quran and the Prophet Mohammed, who was the last and truest prophet to deliver messages from Allah to the people.

Islam was founded in the early 7th century by Mohammed, who was born around AD 570 in Mecca. Mohammed received his first divine message at about the age of 40. The revelations continued for the rest of his life and were transcribed to become the holy Quran. To this day not one dot of the Quran has been changed, making it, Muslims claim, the direct word of Allah.

Mohammed started preaching in AD 613, three years after the first revelation, but could only attract a few dozen followers. Having attacked the ways of Meccan life, especially the worship of a wealth of idols, he made many enemies. In AD 622 he and his followers retreated to Medina, an oasis town some 360km from Mecca. This Hejira, or migration, marks the start of the Muslim calendar.

Mohammed died in AD 632 but the new religion continued its rapid spread, reaching all of Arabia by AD 634 and Egypt in AD 642.

Islam means 'submission' and this principle is visible in the daily life of Muslims. The faith is expressed by observance of the five so-called pillars of Islam:

■ Publicly declare that 'there is no God but Allah and Mohammed is his Prophet'.
■ Pray five times a day: at sunrise, noon, midafternoon, sunset and night.
■ Give zakat (alms) for the propagation of Islam and to help the needy.
■ Fast during daylight hours during the month of Ramadan.
■ Complete the haj, the pilgrimage to Mecca.

The first pillar is accomplished through prayer, which is the second pillar and an essential part of the daily life of a believer. Five times a day the muezzins bellow out the call to prayer through speakers on top of the minarets. It is perfectly permissible to pray at home or elsewhere; only the noon prayer on Friday should be conducted in the mosque. It is preferred that women pray at home. (For information about Islamic holidays and festivals, see p529.)

The fourth pillar, Ramadan, is the ninth month of the Muslim calendar, when all believers fast during the day. Pious Muslims do not allow anything to pass their lips in daylight hours. Although many Muslims do not follow the injunctions to the letter, most conform to some extent. However, the impact of the fasting is often lessened by a shift in waking hours: many only get up in the afternoon when there are just a few hours of fasting left to observe. They then feast through the night until sunrise.

'The impact of the fasting is often lessened by a shift in waking hours'

The combination of abstinence and lack of sleep means that tempers are often short during Ramadan.

Although there are no public holidays until Eid al-Fitr, it is difficult to get anything done during Ramadan because of erratic hours. Almost everything closes in the afternoon or has shorter daytime hours; this does not apply to businesses that cater mostly to foreign tourists, but some restaurants and hotels may be closed for the entire month. Although non-Muslims are not expected to fast it is considered impolite to eat or drink in public during fasting hours. The evening meal during Ramadan, called *iftar* (breaking the fast), is always a celebration. In some parts of town tables are laid out in the street as charitable acts by the wealthy to provide food for the less fortunate. Evenings are imbued with a party atmosphere and there's plenty of street entertainment, often through until sunrise.

The ultimate Islamic authority in Egypt is the Sheikh of Al-Azhar, a position currently held by Mohammed Sayyed Tantawi. It is the role of the supreme sheikh to define the official Islamic line on any particular matter from organ donations to heavy metal music.

Coptic Christianity

Egyptian Christians are known as Copts. The term is the Western form of the Arabic *qibt,* derived from the Greek *aegyptios* (Egyptian).

'The first Christian monks, St Anthony and St Pachomius, were Copts'

Before the arrival of Islam, Christianity was the predominant religion in Egypt. St Mark, companion of the apostles Paul and Peter, began preaching Christianity in Egypt around AD 40 and although it did not become the official religion of the country until the 4th century, Egypt was one of the first countries to embrace the new faith.

Egyptian Christians split from the Orthodox Church of the Eastern (or Byzantine) Empire, of which Egypt was then a part, after the main body of the church described Christ as both human and divine. Dioscurus, the patriarch of Alexandria, refused to accept this description. He embraced the theory that Christ is totally absorbed by his divinity and that it is blasphemous to consider him human.

The Coptic Church is ruled by a patriarch (presently Pope Shenouda), other members of the religious hierarchy and an ecclesiastical council of laypeople. It has a long history of monasticism and can justly claim that the first Christian monks, St Anthony and St Pachomius, were Copts. The Coptic language is still used in religious ceremonies, sometimes in conjunction with Arabic for the benefit of the congregation. It has its origins in several Egyptian hieroglyphs and Ancient Greek. Today the Coptic language is based on the Greek alphabet with an additional seven characters taken from hieroglyphs.

The Copts have long provided something of an educated elite in Egypt, filling many important government and bureaucratic posts, and they've always been an economically powerful minority.

Other Creeds

Other Christian denominations are represented in Egypt, each by a few thousand adherents. In total, there are about one million members of other Christian groups. Among Catholics, apart from Roman Catholics of the Latin rite, the whole gamut of the fragmented Middle Eastern rites is represented, including the Armenian, Syrian, Chaldean, Maronite and Melkite rites. The Anglican communion comes under the Episcopal Church in Jerusalem. The Armenian Apostolic Church has 10,000 members, and the Greek Orthodox Church is based in Alexandria.

Egypt was home to a significant number of Jews but, from an all-time peak of 80,000 in the early 20th century, they now number no more than 200. Historical sources record that there were 7000 Jews living in Cairo as far back as 1168 and in Mamluk times there was a Jewish quarter, Haret al-Yahud, in the vicinity of the Al-Azhar Mosque. The first 40 years of the 20th century constituted something of a golden age for Egyptian Jews as their numbers expanded and they came to play a bigger role in society and the affairs of state.

The reversal began with the creation of Israel in 1948. Not long after, the exodus received further impetus with the nationalisation that followed Gamal Abdel-Nasser's seizure of power. In the present climate of media-led anti-Israeli hysteria, mention of the 'J' word in connection with Egypt is virtually taboo, but there is incontrovertible evidence of the Jewish presence in Cairo's Ben Ezra and Shar Hashamaim Synagogues, and in synagogues in Alexandria and Minya.

ARTS

To the Arab world, Egypt (or more specifically Cairo) is a powerhouse of film, TV, music and theatre. While little of this culture has had any impact on the West, a great many Egyptian actors and singers are superstars and revered cultural icons to Arabic-speakers around the world.

Literature

Awarded the Nobel Prize for Literature in 1988, Naguib Mahfouz can claim to have single-handedly shaped the nature of Arabic literature in the 20th century. Born in 1911 in Cairo's Islamic quarter, Mahfouz began writing when he was 17. His first efforts were influenced by European models, but over the course of his career he developed a voice that was uniquely Arab and drew its inspiration from the talk in the coffeehouses and the dialect of Cairo's streets. In 1994 he was the victim of a knife attack that left him partially paralysed. The attack was a response to a book that Mahfouz had written, which was a thinly disguised allegory of the life of the great religious leaders including Mohammed. Islamists consider it blasphemous.

On the strength of what's available in English, it's easy to view Egyptian literature as beginning and ending with Mahfouz, but he's only the best known of a canon of respected writers. Others include Taha Hussein, a blind author and intellectual who spent much of his life in trouble with whichever establishment happened to be in power; the Alexandrian Tewfiq Hakim; and Yousef Idris, a writer of powerful short stories. Unfortunately, none of these authors has gained the international attention they deserve and they're only published in English by the American University in Cairo Press, a small Cairo-based academic publishing house that publishes an impressive line-up of Egyptian novelists as well as a large (and quite excellent) nonfiction list.

Egypt's women writers are enjoying more international success than the men. Nawal al-Saadawi's fictional work *Woman at Point Zero* has been published, at last count, in 28 languages. An outspoken critic on behalf of women, she is marginalised at home – her nonfiction book *The Hidden Face of Eve*, which considers the role of women in the Arab world, is banned in Egypt and for many years Saadawi was forced to stay out of the country after Islamists issued death threats against her. She's now one of the few female Egyptian members of parliament. Those interested in learning more about her fascinating and brave life should read her autobiography *Walking Through Fire*, which was published in 2002.

Shahhat: An Egyptian by Richard Critchfield has become an anthropology classic, even though much of its content was recently debunked as a copy of a 1930s ethnographic study. So long as you keep this in mind it's still a good read, especially if you're spending time on Luxor's West Bank.

Salwa Bakr is another writer who tackles taboo subjects such as sexual prejudice and social inequality. All of this is a world away from Egypt's current best-known cultural export, Ahdaf Soueif. Though Egyptian, born and brought up in Cairo, she's something of an anomaly in that she writes in English. She lives and is published in London, where she's part of the UK literary scene. So far, most of her work has yet to appear in Arabic. Her absolutely wonderful 1999 novel *The Map of Love* was short-listed for the UK's most prestigious literary prize, the Booker. Her other novels are *Aisha, Sandpiper* and *In the Eye of the Sun.*

The most controversial novel to hit the Egyptian literary scene in recent years is Sonallah Ibrahim's *Zaat*, a scathing piece of satire on contemporary Egyptian life. Ibrahim became a cause célèbre in 2003 when he declined to accept the country's most prestigious literary prize, the Arab Novel Conference Award, which was being presented by the Egyptian Ministry of Culture and the Egyptian Supreme Council for Culture. Ibrahim labelled the award 'worthless'.

If you're new to Egyptian writers then the following is a short list of must-read books, all of which are (or have been) available in English-language translations.

EGYPTIAN CLASSICS

Beer at the Snooker Club by Waguih Ghali is a fantastic novel of youthful angst set against a backdrop of revolutionary Egypt and literary London. It's the Egyptian *Catcher in the Rye.*

The Cairo Trilogy by Naguib Mahfouz is usually considered Mahfouz' masterpiece; this generational saga of family life is rich in colour and detail and earned comparisons with Dickens and Zola.

Yousef Idris is best known for his short stories, but the novel *City of Love and Ashes* is set in January 1952 as Cairo struggles free of British occupation.

The Harafish by Naguib Mahfouz would be our desert-island choice if we were allowed only one work by Mahfouz. This is written in an episodic, almost folkloric style that owes much to the tradition of *The Thousand and One Nights.*

Albert Cossery is an Egyptian but has resided in Paris since 1945; his novels are widely available in French, less so in English, not at all in Arabic. His novel *Proud Beggars* is worth a read.

Zayni Barakat by Gamal al-Ghitani is a drama set in Cairo during the waning years of the Mamluk era. It was made into an extremely successful local TV drama in the early 1990s.

EGYPTIAN CONTEMPORARY

The 2002 blockbuster *The Yacoubian Building* by Alaa Al Aswany is a bleak and utterly compelling snapshot of contemporary Cairo and Egypt seen through the stories of the occupants of a Downtown building. The world's best-ever-selling novel in Arabic, it is reminiscent (though not at all derivative) of the novels of Rohinton Mistry. If you read only one contemporary Egyptian novel before or during your visit, make it this one.

Inmates in a women's prison exchange life stories in the short novel *The Golden Chariot* by Salwa Bakr. It's surprisingly upbeat, funny and even bawdy.

No One Sleeps in Alexandria by Ibrahim Abdel Meguid is an antidote to the mythical Alexandria of Lawrence Durrell. It portrays the city in the same period as the *Quartet* but as viewed by two poor Egyptians.

In *Khul-Khaal: Five Egyptian Women Tell their Stories* by Nayra Atiya (ed), five women from different backgrounds speak out. It's an often harrowing but revealing portrait of women's lives in Egypt, although it could use an update in light of the effect of Islamism on Egyptian society.

Author Alaa Al-Aswany (*The Yacoubian Building*) is a professional dentist whose first office was located in the real-life Yacoubian Building, which is on Sharia Suleiman Basha in Downtown Cairo.

HOLY HOMEGROWN HEROES, BATMAN!

Cairo-based AK Comics launched the Middle East's first homegrown superhero comic books in February 2004. The superheroes include Zein, a mild-mannered philosophy professor who is the last in an ancient line of pharaohs and battles arch-villain Anubis; Jalila, a female scientist whose superpowers are the result of being irradiated during a terrorist attack; Aya, a motorbike-riding 'Princess of Darkness' who has been forced into secretly fighting crime as a result of her mother being framed for her father's murder; and Rakan, a wild warrior who battles wizards, beasts and armies of crusaders.

The Tent by Miral al-Tahawy is a bleak but beautiful tale of the slow descent into madness of a crippled Bedouin girl.

Love in Exile by Bahaa Taher is a meditation on the themes of exile, disillusionment, failed dreams and the redemptive power of love. Taher was born in Egypt in 1935 but lived for many years in Switzerland, and is one of the most outspoken figures within the local literary scene. The novel may be too mannered for some readers' tastes.

WESTERN NOVELS OF EGYPT

The Alexandria Quartet by Lawrence Durrell is essential reading perhaps, but to visit Alexandria looking for the city of the *Quartet* is a bit like heading to London hoping to run into Mary Poppins.

Baby Love by Louisa Young is a smart, hip novel that shimmies between Shepherd's Bush in London and the West Bank of Luxor, as an ex-belly dancer, now single mother, skirts romance and a violent past.

City of Gold by Len Deighton is a thriller set in wartime Cairo, elevated by solid research. The period detail is fantastic and brings the city to life.

Death on the Nile by Agatha Christie draws on Christie's experiences of a winter in Upper Egypt. An absolute must if you're booked on a cruise.

Although the well-known film of the same name bears little resemblance to the novel, Michael Ondaatje's *The English Patient* – a story of love and destiny in WWII – remains a beautifully written, poetic novel.

The Face in the Cemetery by Michael Pearce is the latest in an ever-expanding series of lightweight historical mystery novels featuring the 'Mamur Zapt', Cairo's chief of police. A bit like Tintin but without the pictures.

Egypt during the war serves as the setting for the trials and traumas of a dislikable bunch of expats in *The Levant Trilogy* by Olivia Manning. It has some fabulous descriptions of life in Cairo during WWII, and was filmed by the BBC as *Fortunes of War* starring Kenneth Branagh and Emma Thompson.

Moon Tiger by Penelope Lively is an award-winning romance, technically accomplished, very moving in parts, with events that occurred in Cairo during WWII at its heart.

The Photographer's Wife by Robert Sole is one of three historical romances by this French journalist set in late-19th-century Egypt. They're slow going but it's worth persevering for the fine period detail and emotive stories.

Crocodile on the Sandbank is the first of a bestselling series of crime fiction novels by American Egyptologist, Elizabeth Peters. Lightweight but highly entertaining, it and its successors recount the various adventures of Amelia Peabody Emerson, a feisty archaeologist and amateur sleuth

The American University in Cairo Press was established in 1960 and now has over 600 English-language titles in print, including a highly regarded list of translated contemporary Egyptian novels.

excavating in Egypt at the start of the 20th century. Peters has researched her period well and writes ripping, albeit totally improbable, yarns.

Cinema

EGYPTIAN CINEMA

In the halcyon years of the 1940s and 1950s Cairo's film studios turned out more than 100 movies annually, filling cinemas throughout the Arab world. These days, only about 20 films are made each year. The chief reason for the decline, according to the producers, is excessive government taxation and restrictive censorship. Asked what sort of things they censor, one film industry figure replied, 'Sex, politics, religion – that's all'. However, at least one Cairo film critic has suggested that another reason for the demise of local film is that so much of what is made is trash. The ingredients of the typical Egyptian film are shallow plot lines, farcical slapstick humour, over-the-top acting and perhaps a little belly dancing.

One director who consistently stands apart from the mainstream detritus is Yousef Chahine. Born in 1926, he directed 37 films before officially retiring in a career that defies classification. Accorded messiahlike status by critics in Egypt (though he's not a huge hit with the general public), he has been called Egypt's Fellini and was honoured at Cannes in 1997 with a lifetime achievement award. Chahine's films are also some of the very few Egyptian productions that are subtitled into English or French, and they regularly do the rounds of international film festivals. His most recent works are 1999's *Al-Akhar* (The Other), 1997's *Al-Masir* (Destiny) and, from 1994, *Al-Muhagir* (The Emigrant), effectively banned in Egypt because of Islamist claims that it portrays scenes from the life of the Prophet. Others to look out for are *Al-Widaa Bonaparte* (Adieu Bonaparte), a historical drama about the French occupation, and *Iskandariyya Ley?* (Alexandria Why?), an autobiographical meditation on the city of Chahine's birth.

EGYPT IN WESTERN CINEMA

The meticulously painted backdrops of 1998's animated *Prince of Egypt* aside, Egypt hasn't been seen much at the cinema in recent years. True, a large part of the Oscar-sweeping *The English Patient* (1996) was set in the Western Desert and Cairo, but this was silver-screen trickery, achieved with scenic doubles – the Egyptian locations were filmed in Tunisia and, in the case of some interiors, Venice. The same goes for *The Mummy* (1999), *The Mummy Returns* (2001) and *The Scorpion King* (2002), all of which used Morocco and computer graphics to stand in for Egypt. (The original 1932 version, however, with Boris Karloff, does feature footage shot at Cairo's Egyptian Museum.)

It's not that Egypt is unphotogenic – quite the opposite. Its deserts, temples and colourful bazaars appear beguilingly seductive on a wide screen. So much so, that the country experienced a surge in tourism in the wake of *The English Patient,* despite the best attempts of the Tunisian tourist authority to set the record straight. But extortionate taxes levied on foreign film companies keep the cameras away. It wasn't always so, and the 1970s and 1980s, in particular, resulted in a number of films on location in Egypt, most of which you should still be able to find at the local video library.

The Awakening (1980) is a lame, ineffective horror film about an ancient Egyptian queen possessing modern souls, loosely based on Bram Stoker's *The Jewel of the Seven Stars*.

The father and son team of screenwriter Wahis Hamed and director Marwan Hamed are adapting Alaa Al Aswany's bestselling *The Yacoubian Building* into a feature film. The US$3 million budget is one of the largest ever seen in Egypt.

During the 1950s the Egyptian film industry was the third largest in the world after Hollywood and Bombay.

Agatha Christie's whodunit, *Death on the Nile* (1978), has Poirot investigating the murder of an heiress on board a Nile cruiser. Gorgeous scenery but the real mystery is how the boat manages to sail from Aswan down to Karnak in Luxor and back up to Abu Simbel all in the same day.

Five Graves to Cairo (1943) is a wartime espionage thriller directed by Billy Wilder *(Some Like It Hot)* featuring a British corporal holed up in a Nazi-controlled hotel in the Western Desert.

The Aussie film *Gallipoli* (1981) is about the fateful WWI battle with an extended middle section devoted to the young soldiers' training in Egypt in the shadow of the Pyramids.

In the classic wartime thriller *Ice Cold in Alex* (1958), a British ambulance officer and crew flee Rommel's forces across the Western Desert and dream of an ice-cold beer in a little bar in Alexandria.

Ruby Cairo (1992), one of the last Hollywood productions to brave the bureaucracy, is the limp tale of a wife who tracks down her missing-presumed-dead husband to a hideaway in Egypt. The real star of the film is Cairo, where no cliché is left unshown, including camels, pyramids and feluccas.

Sphinx (1980), adapted from a bestselling novel by Robin Cook *(Coma)*, is a tale about antiquities smuggling shot entirely in Cairo and Luxor, but from which no-one emerges with any credit, except the location scout.

In *The Spy Who Loved Me* (1977) the Pyramids, Islamic Cairo and Karnak provide glamorous backdrops for the campy, smirking antics of Roger Moore as James Bond.

Music

There's no getting away from music in Egypt. Taking a taxi, shopping or just walking the streets – these routines of daily life are played out to a constant musical accompaniment blasted from tinny cassette players. The music you hear can be broadly divided into two categories: classical and pop. In the south of the country you'll also encounter more regional music types.

Amr Diab's *Nour El Ain* (Minds Eye) is the highest selling album ever released by an Arabic artist.

CLASSICAL

Classical Arabic music peaked in the 1940s and '50s. These were the golden days of a rushing tide of nationalism and then, later, of Nasser's rule when Cairo was the virile heart of the Arab-speaking world. Its singers were icons and through radio their impassioned words captured and inflamed the spirits of listeners from Algiers to Baghdad. Chief icon of all was Umm Kolthum, the most famous Arab singer of the 20th century. Her protracted love songs and *qasa'id* (long poems) were the very expression of the Arab world's collective identity. Egypt's love affair with Umm Kolthum was such that on the afternoon of the first Thursday of each month, streets would become deserted as the whole country sat beside a radio to listen to her regular live-broadcast performance.

She had her male counterparts in Abdel Halim Hafez and Farid al-Attrache but they never attracted anything like the devotion accorded to 'As-Sitt' (the Lady). She sang well into the mid-1970s, and when she died in 1975 her death caused havoc, with millions of grieving Egyptians pouring onto the streets of Cairo.

Her cassettes still sell as well now as any platinum pop and her presence is strongly felt in the media, including a radio station that broadcasts four hours of her music daily. An Umm Kolthum Museum (p107) also opened in Cairo in 2002. Her appeal hasn't been purely confined to the Arab world.

RECOMMENDED LISTENING

Together, the following tapes/CDs give a pretty good taster of what Egyptian music is about. Some of these are available internationally on CD.

'Aho' by Hakim 'Hey People' – a loud, anthemic shout rooted in a traditional *shaabi* sound.

'Layli Nahari ' by Amr Diab The latest catchy album from the Egyptian heart-throb skyrocketed to the top of the charts across the Arab world. Highly sing-along-able.

'Khosara' by Abdel Halim Hafez The riff from this song was apparently ripped off by US rapper Jay-Z for his track 'Big Pimpin'.

'Inta Omri' by Umm Kolthum One hour long and an absolute classic. Also try *Fakharuni* and *Al-Atlal*.

'Lo Laki' by Ali Hameida Pivotal The 1988 track that set the formula for much of the Egyptian pop to follow.

'Al-Darb fil Iraq' by Shaaban Abdel Rahim A former ironing man and the *shaabi*est of *shaabi* singers, hugely popular for singing the words that few others in the spotlight would dare say.

'Nagham al-Hawa' by Warda Algerian by birth but an honorary Cairene by residency. This double CD includes one of her best songs, 'Batwanes Beek'.

'Fi'lshq al-Banat' by Mohammed Mounir Latest album by the thinking-person's pop star, a Nubian who fuses traditional Arabic music with jazz. His lyrics are admired above all others.

'Zakhma' by Ahmed Adawiyya Social comment (the title means 'crowded') from the 1970s when Adawiyya's irreverent sound was at the peak of its popularity.

POP

As Egypt experienced a population boom and the mean age decreased, a gap in popular culture developed, which the memory of the greats couldn't fill. Enter Ahmed Adawiyya, who did for Arabic music what punk did to popular music in the West. Throwing out traditional melodies and melodramas, his backstreet, streetwise and, to some, politically subversive songs captured the spirit of the times and dominated popular culture throughout the 1970s.

Adawiyya set the blueprint for a new kind of music known as *al-jeel* (the generation), characterised by a clattering, hand-clapping rhythm overlaid with synthesised twirling and a catchy, repetitive vocal. Highly formulaic, poorly recorded and mass-produced on cheap cassettes, this form of Egyptian pop was always tacky and highly disposable. That's changing fast as in recent years the Cairo sound is getting ever more chic and slickly produced as the big-name artists look towards the international market. Head of the pack is Amr Diab, the foremost purveyor of Western-style pop who is often described as the Arab world's Ricky Martin.

Adawiyya's legacy also spawned something called *shaabi* (from the word for popular), which is considered the real music of the working class; it's much cruder than *al-jeel* and its lyrics are often satirical or politically provocative. The acceptable face of *shaabi* is TV-friendly Hakim, whose albums regularly sell around the million mark.

The majority of current big sellers in Cairo cassette shops hail from Lebanon, Syria, Tunisia and even Iraq. The consolation is that Egypt still provides the best backing musicians, songwriters and production facilities in the Arab world, not to mention the biggest audiences.

Pop star Amr Diab recently starred in a Pepsi Middle East commercial with an all-star cast including Jennifer Lopez, Beyoncé and David Beckham.

Dance

BELLY DANCING

Tomb paintings in Egypt prove that the tradition of formalised dancing goes back as far as the pharaohs. During medieval times dancing became institutionalised in the form of the *ghawazee*, a cast of dancers who travelled with storytellers and poets and performed publicly or for hire, rather like the troubadours of medieval Europe. Performances were often segregated, with women dancers either performing for other women or appearing before men veiled.

The arrival of 19th-century European travellers irrevocably changed this tradition. Religious authorities, outraged that Muslim women were performing for 'infidel' men, pressured the government to impose heavy taxes on the dancers. When high prices failed to stop Western thrill seekers, the dancers were banished from Cairo. Cut off from their clientele, many turned to prostitution to survive. For intrepid male travellers, this only increased the lure and they went out of their way to fulfil their erotic fantasies. Visitors such as French author Gustave Flaubert, who travelled through Egypt in 1849 and wrote *Flaubert in Egypt,* supplied lurid accounts of their experiences, titillating Victorian Europeans and helping to cement the less-than-respectable reputation of Egyptian dance:

> They both wore the same costume – baggy trousers and embroidered jacket, their eyes painted with kohl. The jacket goes down to the abdomen, whereas the trousers, held by an enormous cashmere belt folded over several times, begin approximately at the pubis, so that the stomach, the small of the back and the beginning of the buttocks are naked, seen through a bit of black gauze held in place by the upper and lower garments. The gauze ripples on the hips like a transparent wave with every movement they make.
>
> *Gustave Flaubert*

And that was just the men.

Belly dancing began to gain credibility and popularity in Egypt with the advent of cinema, when dancers were lifted out of nightclubs and put on the screen before mass audiences. The cinema imbued belly dancing with glamour and made household names of a handful of dancers. It also borrowed liberally from Hollywood, adopting Tinseltown's fanciful costumes of hip-hugging bikini bottoms, sequined bras and swathes of diaphanous veils.

Also imported from the Western movie industry was the modern phenomenon of the belly dancer as a superstar capable of commanding Hollywood-style fees for an appearance. Dancers such as Samia Gamal and Tahia Carioca, who became the stars of black-and-white films of the 1930s and '40s, can still be seen today as the old films are endlessly rerun on Egyptian TV. Such is the present-day earning power of the top dancers that in 1997 a series of court cases was able to haul in E£900 million in back taxes from 12 of the country's top artists.

Despite its long history, belly dancing is still not considered completely respectable and, according to many aficionados, is slowly dying out. In the early 1990s, Islamist conservatives patrolled weddings in poor areas of Cairo and forcibly prevented women from dancing or singing, cutting off a vital source of income for lower-echelon performers. In an attempt to placate the religious right, the government joined in and declared that bare midriffs, cleavage and thighs were out. At the same time a number of high-profile entertainers donned the veil and retired, denouncing their former profession as sinful. Since then, bellies have once more been bared but the industry has not recovered.

One of Egypt's most famous belly dancers, Soheir el-Babli, renounced show business and adopted the Islamic veil in 1993, setting off a wave of religiously motivated resignations among the country's belly-dance artists.

OTHER DANCE

Belly dancing (or raqs sharqi, purist terminology for the same thing) is an exclusively female pursuit, but there is also a male dance performed with wooden staves. Called *tahtib,* it looks something like a stylised,

SISTERS ARE DANCIN' IT FOR THEMSELVES *Louisa Young*

'Why did you make the heroine of your novels a belly dancer?' I get asked with some regularity. 'Because she gets to hang out in low dives and swanky hotels, wear fabulous outfits and consider the historical background to a woman's power over her own body, from Salome to contemporary prostitution, via Flaubert and sexual tourism in the developing world,' I reply.

It's easy to forget, when you're being dragged up onto a tiny nightclub stage by a strapping Ukrainian lass in a sequinned bikini, that belly dancing is older than the hills, deeply private and an icon of postfeminism. Men and foreigners tend to see it as a sexual show but for many Arab women – and an increasing number of Western women – it is a personal activity incorporating identity, history and community alongside fun, exercise and girl-bonding.

The Babylonian goddess Ishtar, when she went down to the underworld to get her dead husband Tammuz back, danced with her seven veils at each of the seven entrances. Ancient Egyptian wall paintings, the Bible, Greek legend and *The Thousand and One Nights* are full of women dancing by and for themselves and each other. Salome's dance for Herod – the seven veils again – was so powerful because she was bringing into public what normally only happened in the women's quarters.

Arab domestic dancing nowadays tends to involve tea, cakes, female friends and relations, little girls and old ladies, a scarf around the hips and a lot of laughter and gossip. Western versions, particularly in the US and Germany, are the bastard children of aerobics classes, women's groups, New Age Goddess awareness, and the perennial female weakness for fancy underwear and showing off in it. Belly dancing is extremely good exercise – for the back, the figure, stamina, sex life. It's also good for the soul – it's an art, and requires the distilled concentration, self-respect and 'heart' necessary to art.

Louisa Young is the author of Baby Love, Desiring Cairo *and* Tree of Pearls.

slow-motion martial art. It can be seen at *moulids* (religious festivals) in Upper Egypt and is often part of the folkloric shows on the five-star hotel circuit.

Sufi dancing in its true form isn't dancing but a form of worship. The Sufis are adherents of a Muslim mystic order who spin and whirl to attain a trancelike state of devotion. There's a Sufi troupe that performs regularly in Islamic Cairo (p158).

Painting

While Egypt has produced one or two outstanding painters, contemporary art is very much in the doldrums. The problem stems from the Egyptian art school system, where a student's success largely depends on their ability to emulate the artistic styles favoured or practised by their professors. Not surprisingly, some of the most interesting work comes from artists with no formal training at all. Such artists are often shunned by the state-run galleries but there are several private exhibition spaces that are happy to show nonconformist work. Anyone seriously interested in contemporary art should visit the Mashrabia or Townhouse galleries (p136) in Cairo.

For an overview of 20th-century Egyptian art, make sure you drop into the impressive Museum of Modern Egyptian Art (see p124) in the Gezira Exhibition Grounds. In particular look out for the work of Abdel Hady al-Gazzar, who painted Egypt as a kind of colourful but slightly freakish circus, and the rich, warm and strikingly beautiful works by Alexandrian Mahmoud Said. Said's masterpiece, *Al Madina* (The City) has pride of place in the museum's ground-floor exhibition. Said also has a museum devoted to his work in his home city of Alexandria (p387).

For more information see Liliane Karnouk's *Modern Egyptian Art 1910–2003*, or pick up Fatma Ismail's *29 Artists in the Museum of Egyptian Modern Art.*

Architecture

Early in the 21st century, architecture in Egypt is in a sad state – in fact, according to one published survey the highest rate of depression in 2000 in Egypt was among architects. Beside Cairo's Opera House (p124) and Alexandria's Bibliotheca Alexandrina (p386) – both foreign designs – the country possesses few buildings of architectural worth that postdate the 1950s. The only exceptions are works by the influential Hassan Fathy, author of the seminal work *Architecture for the Poor* and designer of utopian projects such as New Gurna (p270) on Luxor's West Bank; and the Fathy-influenced practice of Rami el-Dahan and Soheir Farid, responsible for the pavilion at the new Al-Azhar Park in Cairo (see the boxed text, p118), as well as a number of tourist hotels on the Red Sea and Sinai coasts.

This sad state of affairs wasn't always so. Cairo and Alexandria possess a splendid legacy of late-19th- and early-20th-century apartment blocks, villas and public buildings. Even more splendid is the capital's fantastic legacy of medieval architecture. Starting with the Mosque of Amr ibn al-As (p109) in AD 642, the earliest existing Islamic structure in Cairo, it's possible to trace the development of Muslim architecture through more than 1000 years of history.

For the first 300 years of Arab rule (a period known as Early Islamic) there was no uniform style and the few buildings in Cairo that remain from this period vary in inspiration: the Mosque of Ibn Tulun (p121), for example, has its stylistic precedents in Iraq. A common architectural vocabulary only began to develop with the Fatimids who were the first to introduce the use of the dome and the keel arch, the pointed arch that has come to typify Islamic architecture. The Fatimids also introduced the use of heavy stone masonry, where previously mud brick and stucco had been the main building materials.

'Under the influence of the Mamluks, Islamic architecture quickly became sophisticated'

Under the influence of the Mamluks, Islamic architecture quickly became sophisticated and expressive. During their time in power, the Mamluks extended the existing repertoire of buildings to include not only mosques, walls and gates but also the *madrassa* (Quranic school), *khanqah* (Sufi monastery) and mausoleum complexes. These buildings, especially in the latter part of the Mamluk era, are often characterised by the banding of red and white stonework (a technique known as *ablaq*) and by the elaborate stalactite carvings *(muqarnas)* and patterns around the windows and in the recessed portals. The Mamluks were also responsible for the transformation of the minaret from a squat, stubby, often square tower, into the slender cylindrical structure typical of Cairo. Decorative stone carving also reached its zenith, best seen on the myriad domes on the city skyline. As the masons' skills developed patterns progressed from simple zigzags to geometric star patterns, to floral designs.

The Mamluks were eventually defeated by the Ottoman Turks who ruled out of Constantinople (Istanbul) and Cairo became a provincial capital. Most of the city's Ottoman buildings are therefore small practical structures, plus a handful of mosques, instantly recognisable by their slim, pencil-shaped minarets.

Environment

THE LAND

The Nile Valley is home to most Egyptians, with some 90% of the population confined to the narrow carpet of fertile land bordering the great river. To the south the river is hemmed in by mountains and the agricultural plain is narrow, but as the river flows north the land becomes flatter and the valley widens to between 20km and 30km.

To the east of the valley is the Eastern Desert (also known as the Arabian Desert), a barren plateau bounded on its eastern edge by a high ridge of mountains that rises to more than 2000m and extends for about 800km. To the west is the Western Desert (also known as the Libyan Desert), which officially comprises two-thirds of the land surface of Egypt; if you ignore the political boundaries on the map it stretches right across the top of North Africa under its better-known and highly evocative name of the Sahara. Though it suffers extremes of temperature and can appear barren and forbidding, the desert is not completely devoid of life. A series of wind-sculpted depressions allow water to come to the surface, thereby creating a string of cultivatable oases.

Cairo also demarcates Egyptian geography. It lies roughly at the point where the Nile splits into several tributaries and the valley becomes a 200km-wide delta, a vast green fan of fertile countryside running into the Mediterranean Sea. Burdened with the task of providing for the entire country, this Delta region ranks among the world's most intensely cultivated lands. Everything north of Cairo is known as 'Lower Egypt', while everything to the south is loosely known as 'Upper Egypt'. It must be the only country in the world where south is up!

To the east, across the Suez Canal, is the triangular wedge of Sinai. A geological extension of the Eastern Desert, terrain here slopes from the high mountain ridges, which include Mt Sinai and Gebel Katarina, the highest mountain in Egypt at 2642m, in the south, to desert coastal plains and lagoons in the north.

WILDLIFE

Egypt is about 94% desert. Such a figure conjures up images of vast, barren wastelands where nothing can live, and while there are areas that are extremely arid and incapable of supporting life, there are also plenty of desert regions where fragile ecosystems have adapted over millennia to extremely hostile conditions. For more information on desert flora, see the boxed text on p465.

Animals

Egypt is home to about a hundred type of mammals. There are still a few exotic species about, but the most common critters are house mice, black and brown rats, and bats. You'll be lucky to see anything other than camels, donkeys and, to a lesser extent, domesticated horses and buffalo.

Egypt's deserts were once sanctuaries for an amazing variety of larger mammals, such as the leopard, cheetah, oryx, aardwolf (which feeds on termites), striped hyena and caracal (a desert lynx with long black ear tufts). Unfortunately, all of these have been brought to the brink of extinction through hunting. In fact, there's only one known family of cheetah still alive in Egypt, and many years have passed since a leopard was sighted. Other creatures such as the sand cat (the soles of their feet

Egypt From the Air by Guido Alberto Rossi has stunning bird's-eye views of the Egyptian landscape.

Egypt has four of the world's five officially identified types of sand dunes, including the *seif* (sword) dunes, so named because they resemble the blades of curved Arab swords.

Natural Selections: A Year of Egypt's Wildlife, written and illustrated by Richard Hoath and published locally by the American University in Cairo Press, is a passionate account of the birds, animals, insects and marine creatures that make Egypt their home.

are covered in fur to aid hunting), the fennec fox (the world's smallest vulpine) and the Nubian ibex (the males of this species have long, back-swept horns) are very occasionally sighted.

There are three types of gazelle in Egypt: the Arabian, Dorcas and white. The first species is thought to be extinct, and there are only individual sightings of the other two groups these days, despite the fact that herds of Dorcas gazelle were, up until 30 or so years ago, common features of the desert landscape.

The zorilla, a kind of weasel, lives in the Gebel Elba region, while in Sinai you may see rock hyrax: small creatures about the size of a large rabbit, which live in large groups and are extremely sociable.

Less loveable are the 34 species of snake in Egypt. The best known is the cobra, which featured on the headdress of the ancient pharaohs. Another well-known species is the horned viper, a thickset snake that has horns over its eyes. There are also plenty of scorpions, although they're largely nocturnal and rarely seen. Be careful if you're lifting up stones, as they like to burrow into cool spots.

> The Egyptian tortoise, native to the Mediterranean coastal desert, is one of the world's smallest tortoises; most males are less than 9cm long.

BIRDS

About 430 bird species have been sighted in Egypt, of which about one-third actually breed in Egypt, while most of the others are passage migrants or winter visitors. Each year an estimated one to two million large birds migrate via certain routes from Europe to Africa through Egypt. Most large birds, including flamingo, stork, crane, heron and all large birds of prey, are protected under Egyptian law.

The most ubiquitous birds are the house sparrow and the hooded crow; one of the most distinctive is the hoopoe. This cinnamon-toned

> www.birdingegypt.com is the website of Birding Egypt, the Egyptian birding community. It lists top birding sites, rarities and travel tips.

RESPONSIBLE TRAVEL

Tourism is vital to the Egyptian economy and the country would be in a mess without it, but at the same time, millions of visitors a year can't help but add to the ecological and environmental overload. As long as outsiders have been stumbling upon or searching for the wonders of ancient Egypt, they have also been crawling all over them, chipping bits off or leaving their own contributions engraved in the stones. This is no longer sustainable. The organised menace of mass tourism threatens to destroy the very monuments that visitors come to see. At sites such as the Valley of the Kings, thousands of visitors a day mill about in cramped tombs designed for one occupant. The deterioration of the painted wall reliefs alarms archaeologists whose calls for limits on the numbers of visitors have largely fallen on deaf ears. Even the Pyramids, which have so far survived 4500 years, are suffering. Cracks have begun to appear in inner chambers and, in this case, authorities have been forced to limit visitors and to close the great structures periodically to give them some rest and recuperation. It can only be a matter of time before similar measures are enforced elsewhere.

In the meantime, it's up to you, the traveller, to behave responsibly. Don't be tempted to baksheesh guards so you can use your flash in tombs. Don't clamber over toppled pillars and statues. Don't touch painted reliefs. It's all just common sense.

The same goes with adventuring off-road in protected areas such as Ras Mohammed. True, you're in the middle of nowhere and who's going to know anyway? But it's illegal to drive off the beaten tracks and the fragile desert environment needs you to enforce this law.

Few places in Egypt are likely to win a tidy-town award: inadequate waste disposal and little regard for the environmental issues that are popular in the West produces some ugly sights. But some of the refuse – plastic mineral water bottles for instance – is actually recycled, so don't be too quick to point an accusing finger at the Egyptians. More than one traveller has reported being disgusted by the garbage left behind by visitors climbing Mt Sinai. Try not to add to it.

bird has a head shaped like a hammer and, when excited, extends its crest. Hoopoes are often seen hunting for insects in gardens in central Cairo, though they're more common in the countryside.

For information on bird watching in Egypt, see p520.

MARINE LIFE

See Marine Life (p450) in the Diving the Red Sea chapter for details on Egypt's marine life.

Plants

The lotus that symbolises ancient Egypt can be found, albeit rarely, in the Delta area, but the papyrus reed, depicted in ancient art as vast swamps where the pharaohs hunted hippos, has been lost. Except for one clump found in 1968 in Wadi Natrun, papyrus can only be found in botanical gardens.

More than a hundred varieties of grass thrive in areas where there is water, and the date palm is to be seen in virtually every cultivatable area. Along with tamarisk and acacia, the imported jacaranda and poinciana (red and orange flowers) have come to mark Egyptian summers with their vivid colours. You'll also see a water hyacinth, known as the 'Nile rose', choking parts of the Nile and many canals.

NATIONAL PARKS

Egypt currently has 23 'protected areas', although just what the status of 'protected area' means varies wildly. Take for instance the Nile Islands Protected Area, which runs all the way from Cairo to Aswan: nobody is clear which islands are included and most are inhabited and cultivated without restriction. Other sites are closed to the public while some, such as Ras Mohammed National Park (p468) in the Red Sea, are popular tourist destinations that have received international plaudits for their eco smarts.

The problem, as always, is a lack of funding. The Egyptian Environmental Affairs Agency (EEAA) has neither the high-level support nor the resources needed to provide effective management of the protectorates. Some help has arrived through foreign donorship and assistance: the Italians at Wadi Rayyan; the EU at St Katherine; and the US Agency for International Development (Usaid) at the Red Sea coast and islands.

Egypt has a number of notable national parks:

Lake Qarun Protected Area (p192) Scenic oasis lake important for wintering water birds.

Nabq Protected Area (p492) Southern Sinai coastal strip with the most northerly mangrove swamp in the world, plus gazelles.

Ras Mohammed National Park (p468) Spectacular reefs with sheer cliffs of coral; marine life; a haven for migrating white storks in autumn.

Siwa Reserve (p359) Three separate areas of natural springs, palm groves, salt lakes and endangered Dorcas gazelles.

St Katherine Protectorate (boxed text, p513) Mountains rich in plant and animal life including Nubian ibex and rock hyrax.

Wadi Rayyan (p193) Uninhabited Saharan oasis with endangered wildlife.

White Desert (p351) White chalk monoliths, fossils and rock formations.

Zerenike Protectorate (p515) A lagoon on Lake Bardawil in northern Sinai that is busy with migrating water birds and has sea turtles on a nearby beach.

ENVIRONMENTAL ISSUES

Ill-planned touristic development remains one of the biggest threats to Egypt's environment, particularly along the Red Sea coast and in Sinai. With the construction of a new airport halfway between Al-Quseir and

UNDER A BLACK CLOUD

Cairo is close to claiming the dubious title of the world's most polluted city. Airborne smoke, soot, dust, and liquid droplets from fuel combustion constantly exceed World Health Organisation (WHO) standards (up to 259 ug/m3 when the international standard is 50), leading to skyrocketing instances of emphysema, asthma and cancer among the city's population. A startling feature article by Ursula Lindsey published in a March 2005 edition of *Cairo* magazine asserted that as many as 20,000 Cairenes die each year of pollution-related disease and that close to half a million contract pollution-related respiratory diseases every year.

The government blames the city's pollution on its dry, sandy climate, which leads, it says, to a thick dust rarely cleared by rain. Not surprisingly, it doesn't like to comment on contributing factors such as the increase in dirty industry (a direct result of government economic initiatives) and Cairo's ever-burgeoning population, a result of people moving to the city from rural areas in search of work.

Cars are, of course, a major offender. Some estimates place over two million cars in the greater Cairo area, and it's clear that this number is increasing every year. Very few run on unleaded petrol; most are poorly maintained diesel-run Fiats and Peugeots that spew out dangerous fumes.

Though factories are officially required to undertake environmental impact assessments and the government lays out a system of incentives and penalties designed to encourage industrial polluters to clean up their acts, few have done so and the government is doing little to prosecute offenders. Neither is it enforcing laws designed to have emission levels of vehicles tested. Organisations such as Usaid are trying to turn the situation around, funding initiatives such as the US$200-million Cairo Air Improvement project, but to date these welcome initiatives are making little impact.

The seriousness of the situation is particularly apparent each October and November, when the infamous 'black cloud' appears over the city. A dense layer of smog that is variously blamed on thermal inversion, rice straw burning in the Delta, automobile exhaust, burning garbage and industrial pollution, it is a vivid reminder of an increasingly serious environmental problem.

Marsa Alam, a frenzy of development has been unleashed along this coastline, endangering the fragile coral that marks reefs along its length.

In Sinai, the coast north of Nuweiba is already the site of a building boom and a wall of half-finished and extremely ugly resorts connects the town to the border crossing of Taba. Whether the businesspeople investing here will make good on their promises to protect the reefs around the area remains to be seen. Given their past record there is little reason to believe them.

Now that the Ministry of Tourism is actively promoting the Western Desert and the oases as a tourist destination, this is another area under threat from environmental damage. A boom in adventure tourism in this remote place is already leaving its mark on the landscape.

Solid waste disposal is also an enormous problem. Cairo, for instance, produces more than 12,500 tons of garbage per day and disposes of this by open burning, contributing to the city's dreadful air-pollution problem.

Fortunately, there have been some positive developments. A National Parks office (see boxed text, p431) has opened in Hurghada and it is hoping to rein in some of the more grandiose development plans in the Marsa Alam area. And new 'green' guidelines for running hotels are being trialled under a joint US-Egyptian Red Sea Sustainable Tourism Initiative (RSSTI). Recommendations focus on energy use, water conservation, and handling and disposal of waste, including simple measures such as installing foot-pedal taps at sinks that make it harder to leave water running.

Finally, Egypt now has a growing number of high-profile ecolodges (including the fabulous Basata in Sinai (p506) and Adrére Amellal at Siwa (boxed text, p367) that may be the harbingers of a new, environmentally responsible trend in Egyptian tourism. We can only hope that this is the case.

Food & Drink

The reputation of Egyptian cuisine takes a constant battering, largely because it's compared with regional heavyweights such as those of Lebanon, Turkey and Iran. This is unfortunate, because the food here is good, honest peasant fare that packs an occasional – and sensational – knockout punch.

STAPLES & SPECIALITIES

Mezze

Most of the Mamluk monuments in Cairo were built with profits from the international spice trade.

Largely vegetable based and always bursting with colour and flavour, mezze aren't strictly Egyptian (many hail from the Levant), but they have been customised here in a more limited and economical form. They're the perfect start to any meal, and it's usually perfectly acceptable for diners to order an entire meal from the mezze list and forego the mains.

Bread

'Aish (bread) is the most important staple of the national diet. Usually made with a combination of plain and wholemeal flour with sufficient leavening to form a pocket and soft crust, it's cooked over an open flame. Locals use it in lieu of cutlery to scoop up dips and rip it into pieces to wrap around morsels of meat. Shammy, a version made with plain flour only, is the usual wrapping for ta'amiyya (see Quick Eats p86).

Duqqa (Arabic for 'to pound') is an ancient mixture of spices used as a condiment in Egyptian kitchens. It combines dry roasted cumin, coriander, sesame and nigella seeds, as well as salt, pepper, nuts and mint. Egyptians dip bread anointed with olive oil into it and gobble it as a snack.

Salads

Simplicity is the key to Egyptian salads, with crunchy fresh ingredients (including herbs) often tossed in oil and vinegar and eaten with relish as a mezze or as an accompaniment to a meat or fish main. Two salads are found on menus throughout the country: oriental salad, a colourful mix of chopped tomatoes, cucumber, onion and pepper; and the Middle East's signature salad, tabbouleh (bulgur wheat, parsley and tomato, with a sprinkling of sesame seeds, lemon and garlic). Less common, but equally delicious, is a salad made of boiled beetroot with a tangy oil and vinegar dressing.

Vegetables & Soups

In Egypt, there's none of the silly Western fixation with preparing vegetables that are out of season – here tomatoes are eaten when they're almost bursting out of their skins with sweet juices, corn is picked when it's

---

TRAVEL YOUR TASTEBUDS

- Fatta – dish involving rice and bread soaked in a garlicky-vinegary sauce with lamb or chicken, which is then oven cooked in a tāgen (clay pot). Very heavy; after eating retire to a chaise lounge.

- Mahshi kurumb – these rice and meat stuffed cabbage leaves are decadently delightful when correctly cooked with plenty of dill and lots of sinful semna (clarified butter).

- Molokhiyya – a soup made from mallow. Properly prepared with rabbit broth and plenty of garlic, it's quite delicious.

- Hamam mahshi – smaller than European pigeons and usually stuffed with fireek (green wheat) and rice, this dish is served at all traditional restaurants but can be fiddly to eat. Beware the plentiful little bones.

golden and plentiful, and cucumbers are munched when they're crunchy and sweet. There are a number of vegetables that are particular to Middle Eastern cuisine, including *molokhiyya*, a green leafy vegetable known in the West as mallow. Here it's made into a slimy and surprisingly sexy soup with a glutinous texture and earthy flavour. Usually served as an accompaniment to roast chicken, it inspires an almost religious devotion among locals.

Vegetable soups are extremely popular, as are soups made with pulses. *Shourba ads* (lentil soup) is made with red or yellow lentils and is always served with wedges of lemon on the side. *Fuul nabbed* (broad bean soup) is almost as popular.

Meats

Kofta and kebab are two of the most popular dishes in Egypt. *Kofta,* spiced ground meat peppered with spices and shaped into balls, is skewered and grilled. It is the signature element of the Egyptian favourite *daoud basha,* meatballs cooked with pine nuts and tomato sauce in a *tāgen* (a clay pot; also used to describe a stew cooked in one of these pots). Kebab is skewered and flame-grilled chunks of meat, normally lamb (the chicken equivalent is called *shish tawouq*). The meat usually comes on a bed of *badounis* (parsley) and may be served in upmarket restaurants with grilled tomatoes and onions; otherwise you eat it with bread, salad and tahini.

Firekh (chicken) roasted on a spit is a common dish and, in restaurants, is ordered by the half. *Hamam* (pigeon) is also extremely popular. It's also served as a *tāgen* with onions, tomatoes and rice or cracked wheat.

Seafood

When in Alexandria, Suez Canal and Sinai, you'll undoubtedly join the locals in falling hook, line and sinker for the marvellous array of fresh seafood on offer. Local favourites are *kalamaari* (squid); *balti,* which is about 15cm long, flattish and grey with a light belly; and the larger, tastier *bouri* (mullet). You'll also commonly find sea bass, bluefish, sole, *subeit* or *gambari* (shrimp) on restaurant menus. The most popular ways to cook fish are to bake it (sometimes in salt), grill it over coals or fry it in olive oil.

Desserts & Sweets

If you have a sweet tooth, be prepared to put it to good use on your travels in Egypt. The prince of local puds is undoubtedly *muhalabiyya*, a blancmange-like concoction made with ground rice, milk, sugar and rose or orange water and topped with chopped pistachios and almonds. Almost as popular are *ruz bi laban* (rice pudding) and *omm ali* (layers of pastry filled with nuts and raisins, soaked in cream and milk, and baked in the oven). Seasonal fresh fruit is just as commonly served, and provides a refreshing finale to any meal.

Best of all are the pastries, including *kunafa,* a vermicelli-like pastry over a vanilla base soaked in syrup that is often associated with feasts and is always eaten at Ramadan. The most famous of all pastries is baklava, made from delicate filo drenched in honey or syrup. Variations on baklava are flavoured with fresh nuts or stuffed with wickedly rich clotted cream *(eishta)*.

DRINKS
Tea & Coffee

Drinking *shai* (tea) is the signature pastime of the country, and it is seen as strange and decidedly antisocial not to swig the tannin-laden beverage

The crazed Fatimid sultan Hakim so hated *molokhiyya* that he had the soup banned from Cairo.

A New Book of Middle Eastern Food by Egyptian-born Claudia Roden brought the cuisines of the region to the attention of Western cooks when it was released in 1968. It's still an essential reference, as fascinating for its cultural insights as for its great recipes.

The popular Egyptian dessert of *omm ali* is said to have been introduced into the country by Miss O'Malley, an Irish mistress of Khedive Ismail.

THAT HUBBLY BUBBLY FEELING

The *sheesha* (water pipe) is a tradition, an indulgence and a slightly naughty habit all wrapped into the one gloriously fragrant and relaxing package. A feature of coffee houses from Alexandria to Aswan, it's a pastime that's as addictive as it is magical. Consider yourselves warned.

When you order a water pipe you'll need to specify the type of tobacco and molasses mix you would like. Most people opt for tobacco soaked in apple juice *(tufah)*, but it's also possible to order strawberry, melon, cherry or mixed fruit flavours. Some purists order their tobacco un-adulterated, but in doing this they miss out on the wonderfully sweet and fragrant aroma that makes the experience so memorable. Once you've specified your flavour, a decorated bulbous glass pipe filled with water will be brought to your table, hot coals will be placed in it to get it started and you will be given a disposable plastic mouthpiece to slip over the pipe's stem. Just draw back and you're off. The only secret to a good smoke is to take a puff every now and again to keep the coals hot; when they start to lose their heat the waiter (or dedicated water pipe-minder) will replace them. Bliss!

at regular intervals throughout the day. *Shai* will either come in the form of a teabag plonked in a cup or glass of hot water (Lipton is the usual brand) or a strong brew of the local leaves (the brew of choice is El Arosa). It is always served sweet; to moderate this, order it *sukar shwaiyya*, with 'a little sugar'. If you don't want any sugar, ask for *min ghayr sukar*. Far more refreshing, when it's in season, is *shai* served with mint leaves: ask for *shai na'na'*. Be warned that you'll risk severe embarrassment if you ask for milk anywhere but in tourist hotels and restaurants. In these places, ask for *b'laban*.

Surprisingly, Turkish and Arabic coffee *(ahwa)* aren't widely con-sumed in the region; instant coffee (always called *neskaf*) is far more common. If you do find the real stuff, it's likely to be a thick and powerful Turkish-style brew that's served in small cups and drunk in a couple of short sips. As with tea, you have to specify how much sugar you want: *ahwa mazboot* comes with a moderate amount of sugar but is still fairly sweet; if you don't want any sugar ask for *ahwa saada*.

Beer & Wine

For beer in Egypt just say 'Stella'. It's been brewed and bottled in Cairo now for more than 100 years. A yeasty and highly drinkable lager, it has a taste that varies enormously by batch. Since 1998, the standard Stella has been supplemented by sister brews including Stella Meister (a light lager) and Stella Premium. Most locals just stick to the unfussy basic brew – it's the cheapest (around E£8 in restaurants) and as long as it's cold, it's not bad. Since the late 1990s there's been a worthy competitor on the market called Saqqara, which is brewed at Al-Gouna on the Red Sea Coast.

There's a growing viticulture industry around Alexandria, but the product is pretty unimpressive; Grand de Marquise is by far the best of a lacklustre bunch, producing an Antipodean-style red and a Chablis-style white. Obelisk is a newcomer to the scene and has a quaffable cabernet sauvignon, a pinot blanc and a dodgy rosé. The country's oldest winery Gianaclis produces three decidedly headache-inducing tipples: a dry red known as Omar Khayyam, a rosé called Rubis D'Egypte and a gasoline-like dry white called Cru des Ptolémées.

These wines average between E£80 and E£120 per bottle in restaurants throughout the country. Imported wines are both hard to find and pro-hibitively expensive.

Among the most popular drinks for New Kingdom (1550–1069 BC) royalty was sweet beer, known as *sermet* and wine, known as *irep* after the noise made after overindulging. Some of the wine jars from this period are even inscribed 'offering wine', 'wine for a happy return' and 'wine for merry-making'.

Water

Don't even *think* of drinking from the tap in Egypt. Cheap bottled water is readily available in even the smallest towns.

Other Drinks

Over the hot summer months many *ahwa*-goers forgo their regular teas and coffees for cooler drinks such as the crimson-hued, iced *karkadai*, a wonderfully refreshing drink boiled up from hibiscus leaves; *limoon* (lemon juice); or *zabaadi* (yogurt beaten with cold water and salt). In winter many prefer *sahlab*, a warm drink made with semolina powder, milk and chopped nuts; or *yansoon*, a medicinal-tasting aniseed drink.

Juice stands are recognisable by the hanging bags of netted fruit (and carrots) that adorn their façades and are an absolute godsend on a hot summer's day. Standard juices *(asiir)* include banana *(moz)*, guava *(guafa)*, lemon *(limoon)*, mango *(manga)*, orange *(bortuaan)*, pomegranate *(rumman)*, strawberry *(farawla)*, and sugar cane *(asab)*. A glass costs between 50pt to E£1.50 depending on the fruit used.

Did you know that the delicious drink *karkadai*, made from boiling hibiscus leaves, is famous for 'strengthening the blood' (lowering blood pressure).

CELEBRATIONS

Egyptians love nothing more than a celebration, and food plays an important role when it comes to giving thanks for a birth, celebrating an engagement or marriage, bringing in a harvest or marking a significant religious holiday.

The most important religious feasts occur during Ramadan, the Muslim holy month. *Iftar*, the evening meal prepared to break the fast, is a special feast calling for substantial soups, chicken and meat dishes, and other delicacies. It's often enjoyed communally in the street or in large, specially erected tents.

Family celebrations are always accompanied by a flurry of baking. *Ataif* (pancakes dipped in syrup) are eaten on the day of a betrothal and biscuits known as *kahk bi loz* (almond bracelets) are favourites at wedding parties. The birth of a son is marked by serving an aromatic rice pudding with aniseed called *meghlie*. *Moulids* (see p528) also involve copious eating of sweet pastries.

The Complete Middle East Cookbook by Tess Mallos is full of easy-to-follow recipes and devotes an entire chapter to the cuisine of Egypt.

WHERE & WHEN TO EAT & DRINK

In Egypt, one rule stands firm: the best food is always served in private homes. If you are fortunate enough to be invited to share a home-cooked meal, make sure you take up the offer. You may find the experience strange, though, as usually your hosts will not sit and eat with you. Instead, they'll seat you in solitary splendour, serve the best the house has to offer and then join you for a tea after the meal. Guests should always take a gift. A nicely wrapped box of pastries is the usual offering. Wine should only be taken if you know that your hosts drink it.

The only place we'd recommend branching out and trying other regional cuisines is Cairo, where we have no hesitation in highly recommending eateries such as the excellent Thai and Lebanese restaurants at the Semiramis InterContinental Hotel. Otherwise, look for where the locals are eating. In Alexandria, for instance, you should follow their lead and dine out in the local seafood restaurants – they're some of the best in the region.

When you do eat out, you'll find that locals usually dine at a later hour than is the norm in the West; it's usual to see diners arrive at a restaurant at 10pm or even later in the big cities, particularly in summer. They also dine in large family groups, order up big, smoke like chimneys and linger over their meals. The main meal of the day is usually lunch, which is enjoyed at around 2pm. See p521 for restaurants' and cafés' business hours. Tipping is expected in almost every eatery and restaurant and 10% is the norm.

Egyptian Cooking: A Practical Guide by Samia Abdennour is published by the American University Press and readily available in Egypt.

The coffeehouse or *ahwa* (the Arabic word means both coffee and the place in which it's drunk) is one of the great Egyptian social institutions. Typically just a collection of cheap tin-plate-topped tables and wooden chairs in a sawdust-strewn room open to the street, the *ahwa* is a relaxed and unfussy place where the average Joe, or Ahmed, will hang out for part of each day whiling away the hours reading the papers, meeting friends or sipping tea. The hubbub of conversation is usually accompanied by the incessant clacking of slammed *domina* (dominoes) and *towla* (backgammon) pieces, and the burbling of smokers drawing heavily on their *sheesha*s, the cumbersome water pipes. Traditionally *ahwa*-going has been something of an all-male preserve, and older men at that, but in recent years *sheesha* smoking has become almost fashionable. It's now common to see young, mixed-sex groups of Egyptians in *ahwa*s, especially in Cairo and Alexandria.

Quick Eats

Forget the bland international snack food served up by the global chains: once you've sampled the joys of Egyptian street food you'll never again be able to face dining under the golden arches or with the colonel.

The national stars of the snack-food line up are *fuul* and *ta'amiyya*, and they are both things of joy when served and eaten fresh. *Fuul*, an unassuming peasant dish of slow-cooked fava beans cooked with garlic and garnished with parsley, olive oil, lemon, salt, black pepper and cumin, is the national dish. It's absolutely delicious stuffed into *shammy* and eaten as a sandwich. *Ta'amiyya* (better known outside Cairo as felafel) is mashed broad beans and spices rolled into balls and deep fried. The piping hot balls are then stuffed into a pocket of *shammy* that's been smeared with tahini and then the whole thing is topped with fresh salad (those with sensitive tummies may want to pass as the salad is often washed in tap water, which can be a recipe for disaster), or sometimes with bright pink pickled vegetables known as *torshi*. Delicious!

The earliest physical evidence of an international spice trade is found in the wall reliefs of the Temple of Hatshepsut in Luxor, Egypt.

The better takeaway joints and sit-down restaurants offer variations on the *fuul* and *ta'amiyya* theme serving them with hard-boiled egg, garlic, butter, mincemeat or *basturma* (a cold sliced meat cured with fenugreek).

Almost as popular as *fuul* and *ta'amiyya* is *shwarma*, the local equivalent of the Greek *gyros* sandwich or the Turkish döner kebap; strips are sliced from a vertical spit of compressed lamb or chicken, sizzled on a hot plate with chopped tomatoes and garnish, and then stuffed into a *shammy*.

OUR FAVOURITE EATERIES

- Qadoura (p393) in Alexandria. The best seafood in the country.
- Sabaya (p148) in Cairo. Lebanese food as impressive as any served in Beirut.
- Oasis Café (p277) in Luxor. Sophisticated décor and great food in the heart of town.
- Al-Fanar (p489) in Sharm el-Sheikh. The best pizza in Egypt, with views to match.
- Andrea (p149) in Cairo. Unpretentious and delicious in equal portion.

You should also look out for shops sporting large metal tureens in the window: these specialise in the vegetarian delight *kushari*, a delicate mix of noodles, rice, black lentils and dried onions, served with an accompanying tomato sauce that's sometimes fiery with chilli.

The local variation of the pizza is *fiteer*, which has a thin, flaky pastry base. Try it topped with salty haloumi cheese, or even with a mixture of sugar-dusted fruit.

Picturesque as some of them are, avoid the street carts trundled around by vendors. These guys sell anything from sandwiches to milk puddings but the food has often been out in the sun all day long, not to mention exposed to fumes, dust and all manner of insect life.

VEGETARIANS & VEGANS

Though it's quite usual for the people of the Middle East to eat vegetarian meals, the concept of vegetarianism is quite foreign. Say you're a vegan, and they will either look mystified or assume that you're 'fessing up' to some sort of socially aberrant behaviour.

Fortunately, it's not difficult to order vegetable-based dishes. You'll find that you eat loads of mezze and salads, *fuul, kushari, ta'amiyya*, the occasional omelette or oven-baked vegetable *tāgen*s with okra (ladies' fingers) and eggplant.

The main source of inadvertent meat eating is meat stock, which is often used to make otherwise vegetarian *tāgen*s and soups. Your hosts may not even consider such stock to be meat, so they will reassure you that the dish is vegetarian. Be vigilant.

EATING WITH KIDS

It's usual for Egyptians to eat out as a family group, and you'll often see children and teenagers dining with their parents and friends in restaurants until the early hours. Waiters are uniformly accepting of children, and they will usually go out of their way to make them feel welcome (offerings of fried potato chips being a tried and true method). Best of all, the cuisine of the region is very child-friendly, being simple yet varied.

Letting the youngest members of the party choose from the mezze dishes is a good idea, kebabs (particularly *shish tawouq*) are perennial favourites and roast chicken is usually a safe bet, especially when put into fresh bread to make a sandwich. And of course the snack foods tend to go down a treat, particularly *fiteer, kushari* and *ta'amiyya*. Fresh juice and soft drinks are almost always available to quench junior's thirst, too.

Some places have high chairs, but they're in the minority. Kid's menus are usually only seen at Western-style hotel restaurants.

For more information on travelling with children, see p521.

HABITS & CUSTOMS

Egyptians eat a standard three meals a day. When it comes to breakfast, Kellogg's have yet to make inroads – for much of the populace the morning meal consists of bread and cheese, maybe olives or a fried egg at home, or a fuul sandwich on the run. Lunch is the day's main meal, taken from 2pm onwards, but more likely around 3pm or 4pm when dad's home from work and the kids are back from school. Whatever's served, the women of the house (usually the mother) will probably have spent most of her day in the kitchen preparing it, it'll be hot and there'll probably be plenty to go around. Whatever's left over is usually served up again later in the evening as supper.

The common name of the famous Spice Bazaar in Istanbul is the *Mısír Çarşísı* (Egyptian Market), commemorating the fact that Egypt was once the centre of the world's spice trade.

To ask 'Do you have any vegetarian dishes?' say *Andak akla nabateeyya?* For 'I'm vegetarian' say *Ana nabaatee* (if you are male) or *Ana nabateeyya* (if you are female).

Apricots on the Nile: A Memoir by Collette Rossant brings to life a young girl's childhood in 1930s and '40s Cairo. The story is accompanied by several recipes.

DOS & DON'TS

■ Remember to always remove your shoes before sitting down on a rug or carpet to eat or drink tea.

■ Avoid putting your left hand into a communal dish if you're eating Bedouin style.

■ Be sure to leave the dining area and go outside or to the toilet before blowing your nose in a restaurant.

■ Make sure you refrain from eating, drinking or smoking in public during the daytime in the holy month of Ramadan (international hotels are an exception to this rule).

■ Always sit at the dinner table next to a person of the same sex unless your host(ess) suggests otherwise.

EAT YOUR WORDS

Following are some phrases to help you order successfully. For pronunciation guidelines, see p561.

Useful Phrases

Table for (five), please.	ta·ra·*bay*·za li (*kham*·sa) low sa·*maHt*
May we see the menu?	*mum*·kin ni·*shoof* il mi·*nay*?
Is service included in the bill?	il Hi·*saab* shaa·mil il *khid*·ma?
I'm vegetarian.	a·na na·*baa*·tee (male speaker)/ a·na na·ba·*tee*·ya (female speaker)
Do you have any vegetarian dishes?	'an·dak *ak*·la na·ba·*tee*·ya?
I can't eat dairy products.	ma ba·*kulsh* il al·*baan*
Please bring us the bill.	low sa·*maHt* hat·*li*·na il Hi·*saab*

Menu Decoder

MEZZE

Note that because of the imprecise nature of transliterating Arabic into English, spellings will vary; for example, what we give as *kibbeh* may appear variously as 'kibba', kibby or even gibeh.

baba ghanoug (*ba*·ba gha·*noug*) – a lumpy paste of mashed eggplant mixed with tomato and onion and sometimes, in season, pomegranate; done well, it has a delicious smoky taste

besara (be·*sā*·ra) – puree of broad beans served as a dip

hummus (*Hum*·mus) – cooked chickpeas ground into a paste and mixed with tahini, garlic and lemon; this is available in every restaurant and at its best it should be thick and creamy

kibbeh (*kib*·beh) – minced lamb, bulgur wheat and pine seeds shaped into a patty and deep-fried

kibbeh nayeh (*kib*·beh *nay*·eh) – ground lamb and cracked wheat served raw like steak tartare

kibda (*kib*·da) – liver, often chicken liver *(kibda firekh),* usually sautéed in lemon or garlic; done correctly it should have an almost pâté-like consistency

labneh (*lab*·neh) – a cheesy yogurt paste, which is often heavily flavoured with garlic or sometimes, even better, with mint

loubieh (*lou*·bieh) – French bean salad with tomatoes, onions and garlic

mahshi (*maH*·shi) – mincemeat, rice, onions, parsley and herbs stuffed into vine leaves (in summer), cabbage (in winter), peppers, courgettes or white and black aubergines; the mixture is baked and is delicious when just cooked and hot, but less so when cold

mokh (mokh) – brains served crumbed and deep fried or whole, garnished with salad

muhalabiyya (mu·hal·a·*biy*·ya) – blancmange-like concoction made with ground rice, milk, sugar and rose or orange water and topped with chopped pistachios and almonds

muttabel (mut·*ta*·bel) – similar to *baba ghanoug* but the blended eggplant is mixed with tahini, yogurt and olive oil to achieve a creamier consistency

sanbusak (san·*boo*·sak) – pastry filled with salty white cheese or spicy minced meat with pine kernels

shanklish (shank·*leesh*) – a salad of small pieces of crumbled, tangy, eye-wateringly strong cheese mixed with chopped onion and tomato

tabbouleh (tab·*bou*·leh) – a salad of bulgur wheat, parsley and tomato, with a sprinkling of sesame seeds, lemon and garlic

tahina/tahini (ta·*Hee*·na/ta·*Hee*·nee) – paste made of sesame seeds and served as dip

wara einab (*wa*·ra' *ai*·nab) – stuffed vine leaves, served both hot and cold

MAIN COURSES

fasoolyeh (fa·*sool*·yeh) – a green-bean stew

hamam (Ham·*aam*) – pigeon, usually baked or grilled and served stuffed with rice and spices; it's also served as a stew, known as *tāgen*, cooked in a deep clay pot

kebab (ke·*baab*) – skewered chunks of meat (usually lamb) cooked over a flame grill

kofta (*kof*·ta) – mincemeat and spices grilled on a skewer

shish tawouq (shish ta·*wouq*) – kebab with pieces of marinated, spiced chicken instead of lamb

DESSERTS

asabeeh (a·*sā*·beeh) – rolled filo pastry filled with pistachio, pine and cashew nuts and honey; otherwise known as 'lady's fingers'

baklava (*ba*·kla·wa) – generic term for any layered, flaky pastry with nuts, drenched in honey

barazak (*ba*·ra·zak) – flat, circular cookies sprinkled with sesame seeds; very crisp and light

isfinjiyya (is·fin·*jiy*·ya) – coconut slice

kunafa (ku·*naa*·fa) – vermicelli-like strands of cooked batter over a creamy sweet cheese base baked in syrup

mushabbak (mu·*shab*·bak) – lace-shaped pastry drenched in syrup

zalabiyya (za·la·*beey*·ya) – pastries dipped in rose-water

Food Glossary

BASICS

ah·wa	coffeehouse
kub·*baa*·ya	glass
makh·baz	bakery
ma'·*la*'·a	spoon
shō·ka	fork
ma·t'am	restaurant
me·*nai*	menu
si·*kee*·na	knife
ta·ba'	plate

COOKING TERMS

fil·*forn*	baked
ma'·li	fried
mas·*loo*'	boiled

DRINKS

ah·wa	coffee
bee·ra	beer
la·ban	milk
li·*moon*	lemonade
may·ya	water
may·ya ma'·dan·*eey*·ya	mineral water
shai	tea

FRUIT & VEGETABLES

a·na·*naas*	pineapple
ar·na·*beet*	cauliflower

ba'-*doo*-nis	parsley
bam-ya	okra
ba-sal	onion
ba-*tā*-tis	potatoes
bat-*teekh*	watermelon
bi-*sil*-la	peas
bur-tu'-*ān*	orange
fa-*raw*-la	strawberry
ga-*waa*-fa	guava
ga-zar	carrot
'i-nab	grapes
man-ga	mango
mooz	banana
oo-tah/ta-*mā*-tim	tomato
tom	garlic
tor-shi	pickled veg
tuf-*faaH*	apple

MEAT

fir-*aakh*	chicken
kib-da	liver
laH-ma	meat
laH-ma *dā*-ni	lamb

OTHER DISHES & CONDIMENTS

'a-sal	honey
bayd	eggs
fil-fil	pepper
gib-na	cheese
mal-H	salt
sa-*lā*-ta	salad
suk-kar	sugar
talg	ice
za-*baa*-di	yogurt
zib-da	butter

STAPLES

'ai-sh	bread
ruz	rice

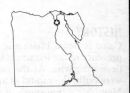

Cairo

Cairo can be hard work, but boy she's worth it. Her millions of children live in the shadow of the Pyramids, along the banks of the Nile, among the mausoleums of the dead and on the edges of her voracious urban sprawl. All have their complaints about pollution, traffic and overcrowding, but none of them would dream of living elsewhere. This is, after all, Egypt's greatest city, the 'Mother of the World'.

Here the past effortlessly coexists with the present. The backstreets and tenements of Islamic Cairo have changed little since medieval times, but the affluent suburbs claiming the desert around the city are brand spanking new, featuring high-tech malls and ersatz Tuscan villas. Throughout the city, locals relax over *sheeshas* (water pipes) and listen to scratchy recordings of Umm Kolthum in centuries-old *ahwas* (coffeehouses), while others sip cappuccino and watch the latest music videos from Lebanon in European-style cafés.

Many travellers are initially overwhelmed by Cairo's aggressive assault on the senses, but after a few days exploring the fascinating fabric of the city, they inevitably do as the locals do: forgive its faults and fall victim to its manifold charms. Tutankhamun's treasure, the perfectly pointed Pyramids and the labyrinthine Khan al-Khalili are obvious – and wonderful – diversions for the visitor, but you'll soon find it's the everyday rituals of life in Cairo that are most enticing. Once you've dodged the gladiatorial traffic a few times, promenaded along the Corniche and grown attuned to the multitudinous calls to prayer, you'll forget that you're filthy and exhausted and throw yourself willingly into the mayhem.

HIGHLIGHTS

- Visit the **Pyramids of Giza** (p128), one of the ancient Seven Wonders of the World
- Overdose on artefacts at the truly extraordinary **Egyptian Museum** (p167)
- Stroll through the labyrinthine lanes and boulevards of **Islamic Cairo** (p110), the city's medieval and symbolic heart
- Hang with the locals over *shai* (tea) and *sheesha* (water pipe) in an **ahwa** (p154)
- Watch Dina, Soraya or one of their belly-dancing sisters wow the audience at a **Cairene nightclub** (p158)

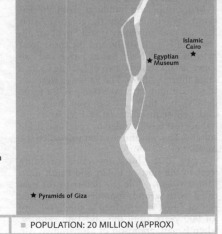

Islamic Cairo ★

★ Egyptian Museum

★ Pyramids of Giza

■ TELEPHONE CODE: ☎ 02   ■ POPULATION: 20 MILLION (APPROX)

HISTORY

Cairo is not a Pharaonic city, though the presence of the Pyramids leads many to believe otherwise. At the time the Pyramids were built, the capital of ancient Egypt was Memphis, 22km south of the Giza Plateau.

The core foundations of the city of Cairo were laid in AD 969 by the Fatimid dynasty, but the city's history goes further back than that. There was an important ancient religious centre at On (modern-day Heliopolis). The Romans built a fortress at the port of On, which they called Babylon, while Amr ibn al-As, the general who conquered Egypt for Islam in AD 642, established the city of Fustat nearby. Fustat's huge wealth was drawn from Egypt's excessively rich soil and the taxes imposed on the heavy Nile traffic. Descriptions left by 10th-century travellers tell of public gardens, street lighting and buildings up to 14 storeys high. Yet in the 10th century, when the Fatimids marched in from modern-day Tunisia, they spurned Fustat and instead set about building a new city.

The area for the new city, the story goes, was pegged out, and labourers were waiting for a signal from the astrologers to commence digging. The signal was to be the ringing of bells attached to the ropes marking off the construction area, but a raven landed on the rope and set the bells ringing prematurely. The planet Mars (Al-Qahir, 'the Victorious') was in the ascendant, so the Fatimid caliph decided to call the city Al-Qahira, which Europeans corrupted to Cairo.

Many imposing buildings from the Fatimid city remain today: the great Al-Azhar Mosque and university is still Egypt's main centre of Islamic study, and the three great gates of Bab an-Nasr, Bab al-Futuh and Bab Zuweila still straddle two of Islamic Cairo's main thoroughfares. The Fatimids were not to remain long in power (see p31 for more details), but their city survived them and, under subsequent dynasties, became a capital of great wealth, ruled by cruel and fickle sultans. This was the city that was called the Mother of the World.

Cairo finally burst its walls, spreading west to the port of Bulaq and south onto Rhoda island, while the desert to the east filled with grand funerary monuments. But at heart it remained a medieval city for 900 years, until the mid-19th century, when Ismail, grandson of Mohammed Ali,

decided it was time for change. During his 16-year reign (1863–79), Ismail did more than anyone since the Fatimids to alter the city's appearance.

Before the 1860s the future site of modern central Cairo was a swampy plain subject to the annual flooding of the Nile. When the French-educated Ismail came to power, he was determined to remake his capital into a city of European standing. This could only be done by dismissing what had gone before and starting afresh. For 10 years the former marsh became one vast building site as Ismail invited architects from Belgium, France and Italy to design and build a new European-style Cairo beside the old Islamic city.

Since the revolution of 1952 the population of Cairo has grown spectacularly, and urban planners have been struggling to keep pace. In the 1960s and 1970s the previously sparsely populated west bank of the Nile was concreted over with new suburbs. In more recent times, even the rocky Muqattam Hills – which had traditionally halted the city's eastward spread – have been leap-frogged, and the desert is now a vast, messy construction site for a series of government-planned satellite cities and what are called informal (unsanctioned) settlements.

ORIENTATION

Finding your way around Cairo's ever-growing sprawl is not as difficult as it may at first seem. Midan Tahrir is the centre. The Downtown area lies northeast of Tahrir, centred on Midan Talaat Harb. Downtown is a noisy, busy commercial district where you'll find cheap eating places and budget accommodation. Midan Ramses, location of the city's main train station, marks the northernmost extent of Downtown. Beyond are teeming middle- and working-class suburbs such as Shubra, perhaps the true soul of modern-day Cairo.

Back in the city centre and heading east, Downtown ends at Midan Ataba and Islamic Cairo takes over. This is the medieval heart of the city, still very much alive today. At its centre is the great bazaar of Khan al-Khalili and the Al-Azhar Mosque and university. Eastwards, beyond Islamic Cairo, are the Northern and Southern Cemeteries, vast necropolises now inhabited by both the living and the dead.

South of Midan Tahrir, the curving tree-lined streets of Garden City are prime embassy territory. Once past Garden City you are out of central Cairo and into a succession of ramshackle neighbourhoods loosely termed Old Cairo, the site of Roman Babylon and Arab Fustat. Buried in here is the small, walled enclave of Coptic Cairo, a feature on many tourist agendas. Beyond that is the relatively green residential suburb of Ma'adi, where many expat families live.

West of all these districts is the Nile, obstructed by two sizable islands. The more central of these, connected directly to Downtown by three bridges, is Gezira, home to the Cairo Tower and the Cairo Opera House. The northern half of Gezira is an affluent, leafy suburb called Zamalek, historically favoured by the city's European residents and home to many embassies. The southern island is known as Rhoda, although its northern part goes by the name of Manial.

The west bank of the Nile is less historic and much more residential than areas along the east bank. The primary districts from north to south are Mohandiseen, Agouza, Doqqi and Giza. Much of it is heavy on concrete, light on charm. Giza covers by far the largest area of the four, stretching either side of a 20km-long road that ends at the foot of the Pyramids.

Maps

The American University in Cairo Press publishes *Cairo Maps: The Practical Guide* (E£30), a book-sized but lightweight collection of 40 street maps, with index.

THE CAIRO CONUNDRUM

Cairo has always inspired a love/hate response in its residents and visitors. Take the prominent Egyptian author and activist Nawal El Saadawi, who says of it in her autobiography *Walking Through Fire*: 'It is a city that I love and hate. The moment I arrive there from a journey abroad, I want to leave again. The moment I am ready to depart, have climbed into the plane, I feel like jumping out and running back.'

Once you've spent some time here, you'll know exactly how she feels.

INFORMATION
Bookshops

American University in Cairo (AUC) Bookshop
Downtown (Map pp102-3; ☎ 797 5370; Sharia Mohammed Mahmoud; ☾ 9am-6pm Sat-Thu); Zamalek (Map pp126-7; ☎ 739 7045; 16 Sharia Mohammed ibn Thakeb; ☾ 10am-7pm Sat-Thu, 1-7pm Fri) The best English-language bookshop in Egypt, with stacks of material on the politics, sociology and history of Cairo, Egypt and the Middle East. It also has plenty of guidebooks and some fiction. The Zamalek branch is smaller than the main Downtown branch.

Anglo-Egyptian Bookshop (Map pp102-3; ☎ 391 4337; 165 Sharia Mohammed Farid, Downtown; ☾ 9am-1.30pm & 4.30-8pm Mon-Sat) Excellent selection of books on Egypt and the Middle East.

Diwan (Map pp126-7; ☎ 736 2578; 159 Sharia 26th of July, Zamalek; ☾ 9am-11.30pm) This fabulous English- and French-language bookshop has its own café as well as a wide range of novels, guidebooks, music, kids' books and coffee-table books.

Lehnert & Landrock (Map pp102-3; ☎ 392 7606; 44 Sharia Sherif, Downtown; ☾ 9.30am-2pm & 4-7.30pm Mon-Fri, Sat morning) This is a good place to find maps, books about Cairo and Egypt (some secondhand), old postcards and reprints of old photographs. It also has a convenient branch opposite the Egyptian Museum.

Zamalek Bookshop (Map pp126-7; ☎ 736 9197; 19 Sharia Shagaret ad-Durr, Zamalek; ☾ 9am-8pm Mon-Sat) This narrow shop is filled to the brim with stationery, newspapers, magazines and books. It has a large range of English-language crime fiction, airport-style novels and books about Egypt.

SECONDHAND BOOKS

Ezbekiyya Book Market (Map pp102-3) On the north-east side of the Ezbekiyya Gardens, reached from Midan Ataba in central Cairo. Many of its 40 to 50 stalls (cabins, actually) carry secondhand English-language books and magazines. There are some treasures, but half the stock is piled knee high on the floor, and much of the rest is shelved with spines to the wall, so browsing is something of a chore.

L'Orientale (Map pp102-3; ☎ 576 2440; www.orientale cairo.com; Shop 757, Basement, Nile Hilton Shopping Mall, Corniche el-Nil, Downtown; ☾ 10am-8pm Mon-Sat, 10am-5pm Sun) Great shop for rare (and pricey) old books on Egypt and the Middle East, as well as original David Roberts lithographs (E£3500 to E£5000), old maps and engravings.

NEWSSTANDS

Cairo's best newsstands are across from each other on the corners of Sharia 26th of July and Hassan Sabry/Brazil in Zamalek

CAIRO

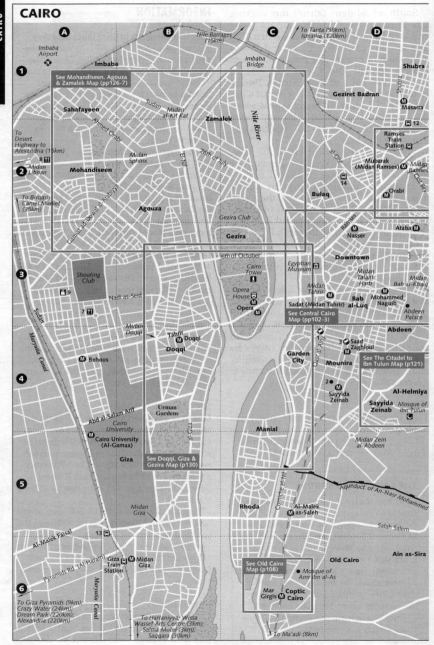

CAIRO

To Nile Barrages (15km)

Imbaba Airport

Imbaba

Imbaba Bridge

To Tanta (58km); Ismailia (120km)

Shubra

Geziret Badran

Shubra

Masarra

12

See Mohandiseen, Agouza & Zamalek Map (pp126-7)

Sahafayeen

Sudan

Midan al-Kit Kat

Zamalek

Nile River

Ramses Train Station

Ahmed Orabi

26th of July

al-Gisr

Mubarak (Midan Ramses)

Midan Ramses

To Desert Highway to Alexandria (15km)

8

Midan Sphinx

El-Nil

14

Orabi

Midan Libnan

Mohandiseen

Gamat ad-Dowal al-Arabiya

Agouza

Bulaq

Ramses

Nasser

Ataba

To Birqash Camel Market (35km)

Gezira Club

Gezira

6th of October

Cairo Tower

Egyptian Museum

Downtown

Midan Talaat Harb

Midan Bab al-Khalq

Shooting Club

Nadi as-Seid

Opera House

Opera

Midan Tahrir

Sadat (Midan Tahrir)

Bab al-Luq

Mohammed Naguib

Abdeen Palace

9

7

Sudan

Maryutia Canal

Midan Doqqi

Tahrir

Doqqi

Doqqi

See Central Cairo Map (pp102-3)

Behoos

Garden City

Qasr al-Aini

Saad Zaghloul

Abdeen

3

Mounira

See The Citadel to Ibn Tulun Map (p121)

Abd al-Salam Arif

Urman Gardens

al-Giza

Manial

Sayyida Zeinab

2

Al-Helmiya

Sayyida Zeinab

Mosque of Ibn Tulun

Cairo University (Al-Gamaa)

Giza

See Doqqi, Giza & Gezira Map (p130)

Midan Zein al-Abdeen

Aqueduct of An-Nasr Mohammed

Midan Giza

Rhoda

Comiche El-Nil

Al-Malek as-Saleh

Salah Salem

Al-Malek Falsal

13

Ain as-Sira

Pyramids Rd (Al-Haram)

Giza Train Station

Midan Giza

See Old Cairo Map (p108)

Old Cairo

Mosque of Amr ibn al-As

Maryutia Canal

To Giza Pyramids (9km); Crazy Water (24km); Dream Park (220km); Alexandria (220km)

Mar Girgis

Coptic Cairo

To Harraniyya; Wissa Wassef Arts Centre (3km); Salma Motel (3km); Saqqara (30km)

To Ma'adi (8km)

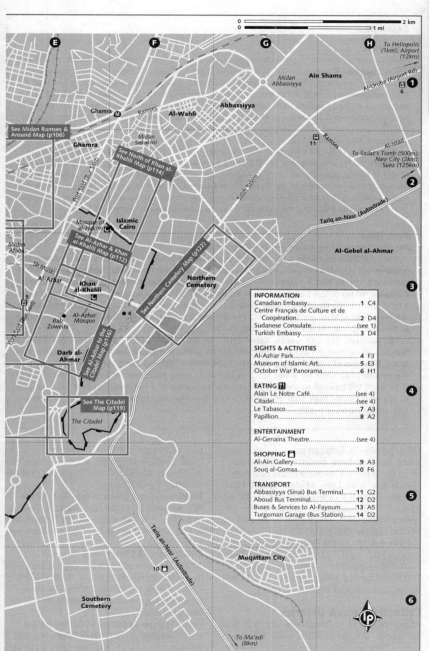

INFORMATION
Canadian Embassy	1	C4
Centre Français de Culture et de Coopération	2	D4
Sudanese Consulate	(see 1)	
Turkish Embassy	3	D4

SIGHTS & ACTIVITIES
Al-Azhar Park	4	F3
Museum of Islamic Art	5	E3
October War Panorama	6	H1

EATING
Alain Le Notre Café	(see 4)	
Citadel	(see 4)	
Le Tabasco	7	A3
Papillion	8	A2

ENTERTAINMENT
Al-Genaina Theatre	(see 4)	

SHOPPING
Al-Ain Gallery	9	A3
Souq al-Gomaa	10	F6

TRANSPORT
Abbassiyya (Sinai) Bus Terminal	11	G2
Aboud Bus Terminal	12	D2
Buses & Services to Al-Fayoum	13	A5
Turgoman Garage (Bus Station)	14	D2

CAIRO IN...

Two Days

Start day one by braving the crowds and spending the morning viewing the magnificent exhibits at the **Egyptian Museum** (p100). When you've reached Pharaonic overload, leave the museum and wander around the Downtown area, stopping to grab a cheap and delicious lunch at **At-Tabie ad-Dumyati** (p146). In the afternoon, make your way to the historic **Khan al-Khalili** (p112) and practice your haggling skills with the cheerful stall owners. While there, don't forget to have a mint tea and a *sheesha* at **Fishawi's** (p154). Return Downtown to eat a simple but delicious Levantine meal at the long-running **Greek Club** (p147) or dine like a pasha at Zamalek's glamorous **Abu el-Sid** (p152).

On day two make an early start and hire a taxi for the day to take you to **Dahshur** (p187), **Memphis** (p179) and **Saqqara** (p181). Bring a picnic to eat at the foot of the **Step Pyramid** (p182) or have a late outdoor lunch at **Andrea's** (p149). In the afternoon visit the only remaining Ancient Wonder of the World, the **Pyramids of Giza** (p128). After this, return to central Cairo and rent a **felucca** (p137) for a relaxing sunset cruise. Then it's on to the fabulous **Sabaya** (p148) at the Semiramis InterContinental Hotel for a mezze-laden Lebanese dinner.

Four Days

For days one and two, follow the Two Days itinerary.

Start day three by taking a taxi to the **Mosque of Ibn Tulun** (p121) and the **Gayer-Anderson Museum** (p121) in Islamic Cairo. Indulge in a bit of shopping at **Khan Misr Touloun** (p159) before catching a taxi to Midan Hussein to visit the historic **Al-Azhar Mosque** (p111) and **Al-Ghouri Complex** (p116) before popping into **Al-Khatoun** (p159) to buy a stylish souvenir or two. Have a light lunch at the **Mahfouz Coffee Shop** (p150) in the Khan al-Khalili and afterwards follow the **Walking Tour** of Mahfouz' Cairo (p138). For dinner join the city's glitterati at the ultra-fashionable **El Morocco** (p149) on the Blue Nile Boat in Gezira.

On your last day visit **Coptic Cairo** (p107) in the morning and catch a river bus back to Maspero. Walk over the 6th of October Bridge to Gezira and check out the excellent collection at the **Museum of Modern Egyptian Art** (p124) before strolling along the banks of the Nile to the suburb of Zamalek for a late lunch at one of its many cafés and restaurants. After a rest at your hotel, bid farewell to the city by having a late dinner and watching the best belly dancers in the world shake their stuff at one of Cairo's upmarket **nightclubs** (p158) or at the wonderfully sleazy **Palmyra** (p158).

(Map pp126–7). You can get just about anything (except bare breasts and buttocks) from these guys. Downtown, the best newsstands are found on Midan Talaat Harb outside Groppi's café (Map pp102–3); on Mohammed Mahmoud opposite the entrance to the AUC (Map pp102–3); and on Midan Tahrir (Map pp102–3). Elsewhere, the bookshops at the Nile Hilton's garden court (Map pp102–3), in the Cairo Marriott (Map pp126–7) and the Semiramis InterContinental (Map pp102–3) are best for periodicals and papers.

Cultural Centres & Libraries

Many of these cultural centres will ask for some ID (preferably your passport) before they will allow you to enter. For de-

tails of events at cultural centres check the local English-language press, particularly *Al-Ahram Weekly*, *Cairo* magazine and the monthly *Egypt Today*.

American Cultural Center (Map pp102–3; ☎ 794 9601; www.usembassy.egnet.net; 5 Sharia Latin America, Garden City; ⏰ 8.30am-4.30pm Sun-Thu) Part of the US embassy complex. There's an American studies centre and a good library.

British Council & Library Agouza (Map pp126-7; ☎ 300 1666; www.britishcouncil.org.eg; 192 Sharia el-Nil; ⏰ 9am-9pm); Heliopolis (Map p136; ☎ 452 3395/7; 4 Sharia el-Minia, off Sharia Nazih Khalifa) The British Council organises performances, exhibitions and talks and has a useful library.

Centre Français de Culture et de Coopération Mounira (Map pp94-5; ☎ 794 7679; 1 Sharia Madrassat al-Huquq al-Fransiyya; ⏰ 8am-7pm); Heliopolis (☎ 417

4824; 5 Sharia Chafik al-Dib, Ard al-Golf; ⊗ 10am-10pm Sun-Thu) This centre regularly puts on films, lectures and exhibitions, opens its libraries to the public and screens French-language news from the satellite TV station TV5. The Mounira branch also runs French- and Arabic-language courses.

Egyptian Centre for International Cultural Cooperation (Map pp126-7; ☎ 736 5410; 11 Sharia Shagaret ad-Durr, Zamalek; ⊗ 10am-3pm & 4-9pm Sat-Thu) The centre organises musical concerts of Egyptian composers and performers, and exhibitions, as well as good classical and colloquial Arabic classes.

Goethe Institut (Map pp102-3; ☎ 575 9877; 5 Sharia al-Bustan, Downtown; ⊗ library 1-7pm Mon-Thu, 8am-noon Fri) The Goethe presents seminars and lectures in German on Egyptology and other topics. It also hosts visiting music groups, special art exhibitions and film screenings. The library has more than 15,000 (mainly German) titles.

Great Cairo Library (Map pp126-7; ☎ 736 2280; 15 Sharia Mohammed Mazhar, Zamalek; ⊗ 9am-4pm Sat-Thu) This is the city's best public library, stocked with a fantastic collection of art, science and other reference books, mainly in English. It also has English-language magazines for browsing. You'll need to show your passport to enter.

Instituto Cervantes (☎ 337 1962; www.elcairo .cervantes.es; 20 Sharia Boulos Hanna, Doqqi; ⊗ 9am-4pm Sun-Thu) Spanish language and cultural institute.

Istituto Italiano di Cultura (Map pp126-7; ☎ 735 8791; 3 Sharia Sheikh al-Marsafy, Zamalek; ⊗ library 10am-1pm Sun-Thu) The centre has a busy programme of films and lectures (sometimes in English), hosts art exhibitions and has a library.

Netherlands–Flemish Institute (Map pp126-7; ☎ 738 2527; 1 Sharia Mahmoud Azmy, Zamalek; ⊗ 9am-2pm Mon-Fri) This centre hosts art exhibitions and is well known in the Cairo expatriate community for its high-quality weekly lectures, delivered on a wide variety of topics and usually in English.

Emergency

In the case of an accident or injury, call the As-Salam International Hospital (p98). For details on lost credit cards, see p531. For anything more serious, contact your embassy (see p526).

Ambulance (☎ 123)
Fire service (☎ 180)
Police (☎ 122)

The **tourist police office** (Map pp102-3; ☎ 395 9116; emergency 126) is on the 1st floor of a building in the alley just left of the main tourist office. This should be your first port of call for minor emergencies, including theft.

Internet Access

There are Internet cafés scattered throughout town. The following are some of the most conveniently located.

4U Internet Café (Map pp102-3; ☎ 575 9304; 1st fl, 8 Midan Talaat Harb, Downtown; per hr E£5; ⊗ 24hr) Under the Lialy Hostel.

Five St@rs Net (Map pp102-3; ☎ 574 7881; 1st fl, 8 Midan Talaat Harb, Downtown; ⊗ 24hr) Next to 4U Internet Café and offers an almost identical service for the same price, the only difference is that it doesn't burn CDs.

Hany Internet Cafe (Map pp102-3; ☎ 395 1985; 16 Sharia Abdel Khalek Sarwat, Downtown; per hr E£3; ⊗ 24hr) In front of El-Tahrir Kushari.

Internet@Cafe (Map pp126-7; 25 Sharia Ismail Mohammed, Zamalek; per hr E£5; ⊗ 9am-1am)

Internet Egypt (Map pp102-3; per hr E£10; Basement, Nile Hilton Mall, Corniche el-Nil, Downtown; ⊗ 9am-midnight) Offers a 20% student discount.

Sigma Net (Map pp126-7; ☎ 738 0516; Sharia Gezirat al-Wusta, Zamalek; per hr E£8; ⊗ 24hr) Opposite the Flamenco Hotel. Offers very fast connections and a comfortable air-con setup.

Internet Resources

Cairo Magazine (www.cairomagazine.com) Website of the newish weekly English-language print magazine covering the city. Runs news stories, features and interesting reviews.

Egyptian Gazette (www.egy.com) Nothing to do with the newspaper of that name, but a great website by the Egyptian social historian and journalist Samir Raafat. It includes articles on architecture, events and people in 19th- and 20th-century Cairo and has an interesting section on the history of the city's Jewish community.

Guardians (www.guardians.net) Great site covering the Giza, Dahshur and Saqqara pyramid sites. Has photos, interesting articles about recent discoveries, and the official Giza Plateau site of Dr Zahi Hawass, the Secretary General of the Supreme Council of Antiquities.

Views from Cairo (www.cairolive.com) Online magazine with views on Cairo's cultural events, political developments and general news. It has a useful kids' section.

Virtual Cairo (www.cairotourist.com) Travel guide with virtual tours of Pharaonic, Coptic, Islamic and modern Cairo, weather reports and hotel listings.

Yallabina (www.yallabina.com) Excellent site devoted to the Big Mango's nightlife: listings, openings, restaurant and bar reviews, and a regularly updated events calendar.

Media

The weekly English-language *Cairo* magazine was launched in March 2005 and is available from city newsstands for E£7. It includes listings, news articles and feature stories about the city. The monthly *Egypt Today* (E£12) magazine includes Cairo listings, as do the flimsy daily *Egyptian Gazette* (50pt) and the more substantial *Al-Ahram Weekly* (E£1).

Medical Services
HOSPITALS

Many of Cairo's hospitals suffer from antiquated equipment and a cavalier attitude to hygiene, but there are several exceptions. Your embassy should be able to recommend doctors and hospitals. Other options:

Anglo–American Hospital (Map p130; ☎ 735 6162/5; Sharia Hadayek al-Zuhreyya, Gezira) West of the Cairo Tower.

As-Salam International Hospital Ma'adi (☎ 524 0250, emergency 524 0077; Corniche el-Nil); Mohandiseen (Map pp126-7; ☎ 303 0502; 3 Sharia Syria)

PHARMACIES

In Egyptian pharmacies almost any medicine can be obtained without prescription. The following pharmacies operate 24 hours, have English speaking staff and will deliver to your hotel room.

Al-Ezaby Heliopolis (☎ 415 3409, 414 8467); Mohandiseen (☎ 304 1847); Ma'adi (☎ 364 6325)

Ali & Ali Downtown (☎ 365 3880); Mohandiseen (☎ 302 1421)

New Victoria Pharmacy (☎ 735 1628; Zamalek)

Seif Pharmacy (☎ 794 1732; Downtown)

Money

For general information about money, foreign exchange bureaux and transferring funds, see p531. For banking hours, see p521. The Banque Misr branches located at the Nile Hilton, Helnan Shepheard's and Mena House Oberoi hotels are open 24 hours. Hotel branches of the big banks are happy to change your cash, but rates are slightly better at independent exchange bureaux, of which there are several along Sharia Adly in Downtown or on Sharia 26th of July in Zamalek. These tend to be open from 10am to 8pm Saturday to Thursday.

American Express (☎ 24hr helpline 569 3299; www .americanexpress.com.eg; ☒ 8.30am-5pm Sat-Thu); Airport (☎ 291 0645); Downtown (Map pp102-3; ☎ 574 7991; 15 Sharia Qasr el-Nil); Downtown (Map pp102-3; ☎ 578 5001/2; Nile Hilton, 1113 Corniche el-Nil); Giza (Map p130; ☎ 567 2288/99; Nile Tower Bldg, 21-23 Sharia Al-Giza); Heliopolis (☎ 418 2144; 11 Midan Almaza) All offices will hold mail for cardholders and give cash advances on gold and platinum cards. There is an American

Express Bank in Gezira (Map pp126–7) that has an ATM but no cardholder services.

Diners Club (Map pp102-3; ☎ 578 3355; Nile Hilton, Midan Tahrir, Downtown)

Thomas Cook (☎ emergency hotline 010 140 1367; ☒ 8am-4.30pm Sat-Thu); Downtown (Map pp102-3; ☎ 574 3776; 17 Sharia Mahmoud Bassiouni); Garden City (Map pp102-3; ☎ 795 8544; Semiramis InterContinental, Corniche el-Nil); Heliopolis (Map p136; ☎ 417 3511; 7 Sharia Baghdad, Korba); Ma'adi (☎ 359 1419; Station Sq); Mohandiseen (Map pp126-7; ☎ 346 7187; 10 Sharia 26th of July)

ATMS

ATMs are located on all major streets, in shopping malls and in the foyers of five-star hotels. The only part of town where they're hard to find is in Islamic Cairo – the most convenient machine in this part of town is below the Al-Hussein Hotel (Map p112) in the Khan al-Khalili.

Post

Express Mail Service (EMS; Map pp102-3; ☎ 390 5874; fax 390 4250; ☒ 8am-7pm Thu-Sat) Opposite the poste restante office. Most post offices also have an EMS counter.

Main post office (Map pp102-3; Midan Ataba; ☒ 7am-7pm Sat-Thu, 7am-noon Fri & public holidays)

Poste restante (Map pp102-3; ☒ 8am-6pm Sat-Thu, 10am-noon Fri & public holidays) Down the side street to the right of the main post office. Mail is usually held for three weeks. It's divided into three sections: letters, small packages and large packages. You'll need to take your passport.

Post traffic centre (Map p106; Midan Ramses; ☒ 8.30am-3pm Sat-Thu) The only place to send packages abroad. Bring your passport. Packages will probably be inspected, so leave them unsealed. Someone will wrap the parcel for you (officially E£1.50 per metre of paper plus E£1.60 for sealing). Be prepared for a bureaucratic, time-consuming experience.

Zamalek post office (Map pp126-7; Sharia Brazil; ☒ 8am-3pm Sat-Thu)

Telephone & Fax

Card phones Menatel card phones are all over the city, although the practice of placing them on street corners (or streets, for that matter) can make it hard to hear and be heard.

Faxes These can be sent to/from the Telephone centrales on Midan Tahrir, Sharia Adly and Sharia Alfy. You can also send and receive them from EMS main office in Ataba (see above).

Telephone centrales Downtown (Map pp102-3; fax 578 0979; 13 Midan Tahrir; ☒ 24hr); Downtown (Map pp102-

3; fax 393 3903; 8 Sharia Adly; 24hr); Downtown (Map pp102-3; fax 589 7635; Sharia Alfy; 24hr); Downtown (Map pp102-3; Sharia Ramses; 24hr); Zamalek (Map pp126-7; Sharia 26th of July) The branch on Sharia Alfy is next to the Windsor Hotel. The Sharia Ramses branch is opposite Sharia Tawfiqiyya.

Tourist Information

Cairo International Airport tourist office Terminal I (☎ 291 4255 ext 2223; 24hr); Terminal II (☎ 291 4255; 24hr)

Main tourist office (Map pp102-3; ☎ 391 3454; 5 Sharia Adly; 8.30am-7pm) Staff here seem totally uninterested in supplying tourist information. It's not worth a visit.

Pyramids tourist office (Map p129; ☎ 385 0259; Pyramids Rd; 9am-5pm) Opposite Oberoi Mena House.

Ramses Station tourist office (Map p163; ☎ 579 0767; 9am-7pm) Next to the Abela Sleeping Car office.

Travel Agencies

The streets around Midan Tahrir teem with travel agencies, but don't expect any amazing deals. Instead, you should watch out for dodgy operators (see right). Amex and Thomas Cook (see opposite) offer a reliable service. Other recommendations:

Abercrombie & Kent (☎ 393 6272; www.abercrombiekent.com; 10th fl, Bustan Commercial Centre, Bab al-Louq, Downtown) The premier company for upmarket travel. Has its own fleet of cruise ships and excellent guides.

Egypt Panorama Tours (☎ 359 0200; www.eptours .com; 4 Road 79, Ma'adi; 9am-5pm) Opposite Ma'adi metro station, this is one of the best and most reputable agencies in town, though it's a long way from Downtown. Fortunately, it will book tickets, tours and hotel rooms over the phone and courier the tickets/vouchers to you for a US$20 booking and courier fee. Staff speak excellent English and are extremely efficient. It's good for cheap air fares, four- and five-star hotel room deals (usually 40% to 50% off rack rates) and tours within Egypt and around the Mediterranean region. The surcharge for credit-card payment is 3%.

Misr Travel (☎ 482 6850, information, 682 3822); Downtown (Map pp102-3); Abbassiyya (Misr Travel Tower, Midan Abbassiyya) The official Egyptian government travel agency.

Travco (☎ 736 2042, 737 0488; www.travco-eg.com; 13 Sharia Mahmoud Azmi, Zamalek) The highly regarded Zamalek branch of a large Egypt-wide travel group.

Visa Extensions

All visa business is carried out at the **Mogamma** (Map pp102-3; Midan Tahrir, Downtown; 8am-1.30pm Sat-Wed), a 14-storey Egypto-Stalinist monolith. Foreigners go up to the 1st floor, turn right and proceed straight down the corridor ahead. Go to window 12 for a form, fill it out and then buy stamps from window 43 before returning to window 12 and submitting your form with the stamps, one photograph, and photocopies of the photo and visa pages of your passport (photos and photocopies can be organised on the ground floor). The visa will be processed overnight and be available for collection from 9am the next day.

DANGERS & ANNOYANCES

You can walk almost wherever you like in Cairo, at any time of day or night, as long as you are properly dressed and a little streetwise. That said, single women should still be careful when walking alone at night.

Theft

Theft is not a big problem, but it pays to be safe. We regularly receive letters from readers who have had personal items stolen from locked hotel rooms and even from hotel safes, so think about keeping money and valuables on you or locked in a suitcase. Pickpockets are rare, but do sometimes operate in crowded spots such as the Khan al-Khalili, the Birqash camel market, the metro and on buses. If anything does get stolen go straight to the tourist police (p97).

Scams

Scams in Cairo are so numerous that there's no way we can list them all here. They are roughly divided into three types: hotel scams (see p141), overcharging on tours to other parts of Egypt and shopping scams.

The worst scams currently afflicting Cairo are associated with tours. If you are planning to travel to other parts of Egypt, you are almost always better off making your own way there and brokering arrangements for tours or onward travel on the ground rather than doing this in Cairo. Though there are some reputable tour agencies here (see left), they are outnumbered by dodgy operators, many of whom have forged partnerships with the city's hotels. We can't emphasise enough that it's NOT a good idea to book travel arrangements through Cairo hotels – you will inevitably pay considerably over the odds to cover their commission on the transaction. Also be wary of travel agencies in the Downtown area. Many of these places rent out office space to unscrupulous types who will charge you over the odds (and then some) for any arrangements they make. If you return to make a complaint, the agencies will deny any accountability, saying that you booked through a freelance agent whose only association with the company is that he rents some of its office space. And finally: never, *ever* book a tour through a tout you meet on the street or in a souvenir or papyrus shop.

Cairo shopping scams are almost as prevalent as those associated with tours. One long-running shopping scam occurs around the Egyptian Museum: a charming chap approaches foreigners and asks if they are looking for the museum entrance or the bus to the Pyramids. If the answer is yes, he asserts that it's prayer time/lunchtime/any-inventive-reason time and that the museum is temporarily closed and the bus isn't running for an hour. Then he suggests that while they're waiting, they may be interested in going to the nearby 'Government Bazaar', which happens to be having its annual sale on that day. Needless to say, there's a sale every day, it's not much of a sale at all, the bazaar isn't government run and he'll collect a commission on anything you purchase…

Other shopping scams include the old 'two for five pounds' hard sell (when you go to pay, the stallholder will say that he meant five *British* pounds) and the dried-banana-leaf-instead-of-papyrus con.

When you're in Downtown or Islamic Cairo, locals may start walking next to you, offering help or chatting. Invariably these are hustlers or touts who want to direct you into shops where they will earn a hefty commission on everything you buy. They can be persistent, but telling them you just want to walk and know where you are going, with a joke thrown in to keep everything amicable, will save you a lot of hassle.

Mosques are now free of charge but you sometimes get a stream of people asking for *baksheesh* (alms, tip), so be firm and don't pay more than you want to (E£5 per monument is reasonable).

Finally, be aware that fake International Student Identity Cards (ISIC) are sold by scam artists in Downtown. For more information on ISIC cards see p533.

SIGHTS

Cairo's sights are spread all over the city, so it makes sense to do things in one area before moving on to the next. You'll need half a day at the Egyptian Museum; after being awed by the magnificent and enormous collection, many visitors opt for a return visit on a subsequent day. The Khan al-Khalili and most of the mosques and Islamic monuments are in Islamic Cairo, and you'll need at least a full day or a few visits to appreciate them. For Coptic Cairo you'll need a half a day and for the Pyramids and tombs of Giza, Saqqara and Dahshur make sure you put aside a whole extra day.

Central Cairo

Midan Tahrir and Midan Talaat Harb are the chaotic centrepoints of central Cairo. Crossing from one side of these car-choked squares to the other is a true Egyptian baptism by fire – once you've made it across in one piece, you'll be ready to take on anything the country can dish out, bypassing the most persistent tout or the filthiest street with supreme confidence. This part of town is where you'll find the Egyptian Museum, as well as an amazing variety of shops, budget hotels and eateries. Its once-elegant Empire-style office and apartment buildings are now crumbling, but they still have bags of character and a strong whiff of their former glamour. These days they house everything from budget hotels to tiny factories and their rooftops are home to untold numbers of people and pigeons. It's a wonderful part of town to explore – just be prepared for total sensory overload after a few hours spent within its boundaries.

MIDAN TAHRIR & AROUND

Midan Tahrir (Liberation Sq) is the fulcrum of modern-day Cairo. Many of Downtown's main roads converge here, often resulting in serious traffic and pedestrian jams. But the square is one of the few central spaces that isn't hemmed in by buildings or choked by overpasses, making it an excellent spot to have a look around and orient yourself.

One of the most distinctive buildings to use as a location aid is the **Nile Hilton** (p144), the blue-and-white slab that stands between Midan Tahrir and the Nile. When it was built in 1959 it was the first modern hotel in Cairo, replacing a former British Army barracks. Due north of the Nile Hilton is the terracotta-red neoclassical bulk of the **Egyptian Museum** (p167), while south is the **Arab League Building** (Map pp102–3), the occasional gathering place of the leaders from the Arab world.

Continuing around Midan Tahrir anticlockwise, the big white building is Cairo's monstrous, Kafkaesque monument to bureaucracy, the **Mogamma** (Map pp102–3), which is home to 18,000 semisomnolent civil servants – this is where you come for visa extensions (see p99). If the Mogamma is a symbol of Egypt's recent Soviet-inspired past, then the next building around, across four-lane Qasr al-Ainy, is a beacon for the private initiative–led future: the **American University in Cairo** (AUC; Map pp102–3) is the university of choice for the sons and daughters of Cairo's moneyed classes. Its campus has an attractive courtyard and a good bookshop (see p93). Entrance (ID required, your passport will do) is via the gate on Sharia Mohammed Mahmoud, opposite the enterprisingly sited McDonald's.

About 50m north of the AUC is the **Ali Baba Cafeteria** (Map pp102–3), closed at the time of research, which once was a regular morning stop for Nobel Prize–winning author Naguib Mahfouz. It was here that the 1994 knife attack that almost killed him occurred. The buildings around Midan Tahrir then break for Sharia Tahrir, which leads 250m east to a busy square (Midan Falaki) with the **Souq Mansour** to one side. Continuing east brings you to Midan al-Gomhuriyya (Square of the Republic), a scraggly grass square skirted by speeding traffic. The great building to the east, dominating the square, is the Abdeen Palace, former residence of the rulers of Egypt.

Abdeen Palace

Designed by the French architect Rosseau and begun in 1863, the **Abdeen Palace** (Qasr Abdeen; Map pp102–3; ☎ 391 0042; Midan Qasr Abdin; adult/student E£10/E£5; ☯ 9am-3pm Sat-Thu) was one of the centrepieces of Khedive Ismail's plan to modernise Cairo. He wanted it finished for the 1869 opening of the Suez Canal, hoping to impress visiting foreign dignitaries, but its 500 rooms were not completed until 1874. It then served as the royal residence until the abolition of the monarchy in 1952, when Abdeen became the presidential palace. President Mubarak prefers to live in the Uruba Palace in Heliopolis but still uses Abdeen for official occasions. One section, though not the glitzy royal chambers, is open to the public; its halls are filled with a vast array of weaponry, ranging from ceremonial daggers to howitzers.

DOWNTOWN

The commercial heart of Cairo is Downtown, packed with glitzy shops and thousands of small businesses. The two main streets, Sharia Talaat Harb and Sharia Qasr el-Nil, intersect at Midan Talaat Harb, which is marked by a statue of *tarboosh*-touting Mr Harb, founder of the National Bank. On the square is **Groppi's** (p153), in its heyday one of the most celebrated patisseries this side of the Mediterranean, the venue of ritzy society functions and concert dances. The only hint of glitter remaining today is in the beautiful mosaics around the doorway.

Just south of the square, on Sharia Talaat Harb, **Café Riche** (p147) was once a hang-out for Egyptian writers and intellectuals. It's claimed that Nasser met with his cronies here while planning the Revolution of 1952.

North of the square, shops along Sharia Qasr el-Nil sell a drag queen's dream of footwear. The street itself boasts some particularly fine architecture, notably the **Italian Insurance building** (Map pp102–3), on the corner of Qasr el-Nil and Sharia Sherifeen, and the **Cosmopolitan Hotel** (p143), hidden away just a block to the south of Qasr el-Nil. The area around the hotel and the neighbouring **Cairo Stock Exchange** has been pedestrianised, so you can take extra note of the turn-of-the-century architecture. Sharia Talaat Harb is also graced by **Cinema Metro** (Map pp102–3), a great 1930s movie palace: when it first opened, with *Gone with the Wind*, it boasted a Ford showroom and a diner.

One block east of Cinema Metro, along Sharia Adly, is the **Shar Hashamaim Synagogue** (Map pp102–3). Resembling a set from *Tomb Raider*, it is testament to Cairo's once-thriving Jewish community. The synagogue can be visited on Saturday, the Jewish holy day of Shabbat, when the caretaker opens up on the chance that there'll be somebody coming by to pray. Also on Sharia Adly is the faded **Groppi Garden** (p153), a café that was a favoured relaxation spot for Allied troops in WWII and was immortalised in

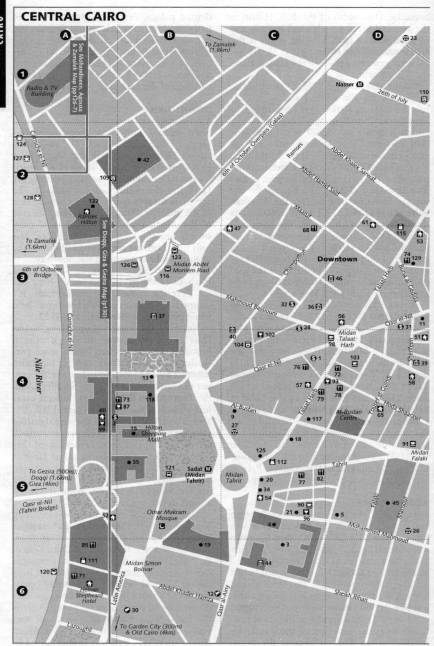

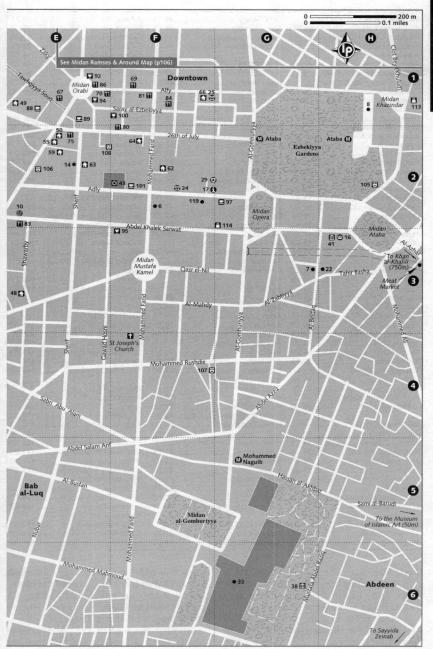

CAIRO

Olivia Manning's *The Levant Trilogy* as '...a garden of indulgences where the Levantine ladies came to eye the staff officers who treated it as a home away from home'.

A block north of Adly is Sharia 26th of July, named for the date of abdication of Egypt's last king, Farouk. The street's major

attraction, as far as Cairenes are concerned, is **El-Abd Bakery** (see p147), packed out morning to midnight with locals jostling for cakes, sweets and delicious pastries (there's also a branch on Sharia Talaat Harb).

Another block north, the pedestrianised Sharia Saray al-Ezbekiyya is the street for kebabs and café-terraces, while the equally car-free Sharia Alfy is Downtown's night-life centre, with several seedy bars, some dubious belly-dancing joints and a 24-hour eating place in the **Akher Sa'a** (p147). The nearby **Tawfiqiyya Souq** (Map pp102–3) is a late-night fruit-and-vegetable market with cheap eating places and good coffeehouses in the surrounding alleyways.

Heading east along Sharia 26th of July leads to the **Ezbekiyya Gardens** (Map pp102–3), now mainly closed to the public. The famous Shepheard's Hotel was once located opposite here – it occupied a mansion that had once been Napoleon's Cairo base and was the preferred accommodation of the British colonial classes for a century, until it was destroyed by Black Saturday rioters in 1952. Next to the gardens is Midan Opera, named for the opera house that burnt down in 1971, but now more notable for a multi-storey car park. Beyond the car park, to the east, is Midan Ataba.

MIDAN ATABA

Here, 'modern European' Cairo runs up against the old medieval Cairo of Saladin (Salah ad-Din), the Mamluks and the Ottomans. It seems like one big bazaar, with all its traders and hawkers. In the south-west corner, the domed **main post office** (Map pp102–3) has a pretty courtyard and an attached **Postal Museum** (Map pp102-3; ☎ 391 0011; 2nd fl, Midan Ataba; admission free; ⏱ 9am-1pm Sat-Thu), whose collection tells the history of Egypt's postal service.

On the opposite side of Midan Ataba, behind the big white **Puppet Theatre**, is the **Ezbekiyya Book Market** (p93). To the north beyond that is Midan Khazindar, which has **Sednaoui Department Store** (Map pp102–3), one of Cairo's prime early-20th-century department stores. Now state-owned and full of tat, the three-storey glass-atrium interior remains glorious. Running north from Khazindar is Sharia Clot Bey (also known as Sharia Khulud) named after a French physician, Antoine Clot, who introduced Western ideas about public health into Mohammed Ali's Egypt. Ironically, the street later became the diseased heart of Cairo's red-light district, known as 'Birka'; an area of brothels, peepshows and pornographic cabarets. These days it's a shabby but charming street with stone arcades over the pavements sheltering dozens of sepia-toned coffeehouses and eating places. It eventually emerges onto Midan Ramses.

MIDAN RAMSES & AROUND

The northern gateway into central Cairo, Midan Ramses (Map p106) is a byword for bedlam. The city's main north–south access collides with overpasses and numerous arterial roads to swamp the square with an unchoreographed slew of minibuses, buses, taxis and cars. Commuters swarm from the train station to add to the melee.

In the middle of it all stands a Pharaonic-style **Colossus of Ramses II** (Map p106). This is a copy of a statue discovered near Giza. The original was erected here in 1955 but later removed to save it from damaging exhaust emissions.

Mahattat Ramses (Ramses Station; Map p106) is an attractive marriage of Islamic style and industrial-age engineering. At its eastern end it houses the **Egyptian National Railways Museum** (Map p106; ☎ 576 3793; Midan Ramses; admission E£10, Fri & public holidays E£20; ⏱ 8.30am-1pm Tue-Sun) with a beautiful collection of old locomotives, including one built for Empress Eugénie on the occasion of the opening of the Suez Canal.

On the south side of the square is Cairo's pre-eminent orientation aid, the **Al-Fath Mosque** (Map p106). Completed in the early 1990s, the mosque's minaret is visible from just about anywhere in central and Islamic Cairo.

GARDEN CITY & RHODA

Garden City was developed in the early 1900s along the lines of an English garden suburb. Its curving, tree-lined streets were designed to inspire tranquillity, while its proximity to the UK embassy was no doubt intended to create a sense of security. Many of the enclave's elegant villas have fallen prey to quick-buck developers, but enough grand architecture and palm, rubber and mango trees survive to make a walk through the streets still worthwhile. Alternatively, it's a pleasant – though often noisy – walk south along the Nile from the salmon-pink Semiramis InterContinental Hotel.

It will take only 20 minutes to walk from the Semiramis InterContinental down the Corniche until you hit the small Manial Bridge. Crossing this, you will come to

CAIRO

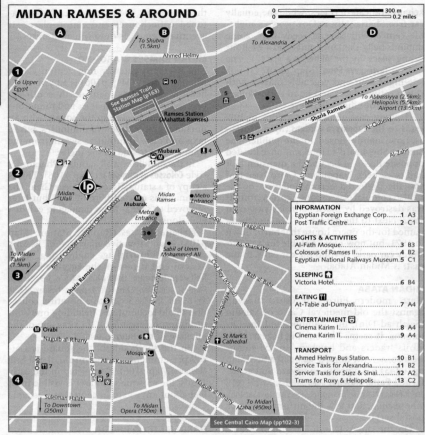

MIDAN RAMSES & AROUND

0 _____ 300 m
0 _____ 0.2 miles

To Shubra (1.5km)

Ahmed Helmy

To Alexandria

To Upper Egypt

Shubra

See Ramses Train Station Map (p163)

Ramses Station (Mahattat Ramses)

Metro

To Abbassiyya (2.5km); Heliopolis (5.5km); Airport (13.5km)

Sharia Ramses

Al-Qubeisi

As-Sabliya

Mubarak

Al-Zahir

Qasr al-Ubira

12

Midan Ulali

Mubarak

Midan Ramses

Metro Entrance

Metro Entrance

Karmel Sidqi

Seif ad-Din Mahraby

(Faggala)

INFORMATION
Egyptian Foreign Exchange Corp.......1 A3
Post Traffic Centre...............................2 C1

SIGHTS & ACTIVITIES
Al-Fath Mosque....................................3 B3
Colossus of Ramses II...........................4 B2
Egyptian National Railways Museum...5 C1

SLEEPING
Victoria Hotel.......................................6 B4

EATING
At-Tabie ad-Dumyati............................7 A4

ENTERTAINMENT
Cinema Karim I.....................................8 A4
Cinema Karim II....................................9 A4

TRANSPORT
Ahmed Helmy Bus Station..................10 B1
Service Taxis for Alexandria...............11 B2
Service Taxis for Suez & Sinai............12 A2
Trams for Roxy & Heliopolis..............13 C2

6th of October overpass Sharia Galaa

To Midan Tahrir (1.5km)

Sharia Ramses

Al-Gomhuriyya

Sabil of Umm Mohammed Ali

As-Shankaby

Clot Bey (Khulid)

Bab al-Bahr

Al-Kineesa al-Marqusiyya

Orabi

Naguib al-Rihany

Emad ad-Din

Ali al-Kassar

Orabi

Mosque

St Mark's Cathedral

Al-Qablit

Naguib al-Rihany

Suleiman Halabi

To Downtown (250m)

To Midan Opera (150m)

To Midan Ataba (450m)

See Central Cairo Map (pp102-3)

Sharia al-Saray and one of Cairo's least visited and most eccentric tourist sites, the **Manial Palace Museum** (Mathaf al-Manial; Map p130; ☎ 368 7495; Sharia al-Saray, Manial; adult/student E£10/5; ⏱ 9am-4pm, 9am-3pm during Ramadan). The palace was built in the early part of the 20th century as a residence for Prince Mohammed Ali Tawfiq, the uncle of King Farouk, Egypt's last monarch. Apparently the prince couldn't decide which architectural style he preferred, so he went for the lot: Ottoman, Moorish, Persian and European rococo. Today the palace houses an assortment of collections in five buildings, including a Hunting Museum housing Farouk's huge horde of dusty stuffed hunting trophies – not recommended for animal lovers. The main palace has large

rooms filled with authentic furniture, while the prince's private museum displays some of his manuscripts, clothing, silver objects, furniture, writing implements and other items dating from medieval times to the 19th century. Stroll through the beautiful gardens afterwards, planted with rare tropical plants and marvellous palms collected by the prince on his travels. If you don't want to walk to the museum, a taxi from Midan Tahrir should cost E£3.

A 15-minute walk south along the eastern side of the island takes you to the southern tip of the island, home to the Monastirli Palace, the Umm Kolthum Museum and a Nilometer. From there, it's an easy walk on to Old Cairo.

Monastirli Palace & Umm Kolthum Museum

Set in a peaceful Nileside garden, the **Monastirli Palace** (Map p108) was built in 1851 for the Monastirli family. Part of the palace is now an elegant venue for concerts, while the other part was turned into the **Umm Kolthum Museum** (Map p108; ☎ 363 1467; Sharia al-Malek as-Salih, Rhoda; admission E£6; ⊗ 10am-5pm). The small museum displays photographs and personal effects – including sunglasses and good-luck scarves – of the most famous of all Arab singing divas, Umm Kolthum. A short film shows some of the key moments of her life, from the early beginnings when she performed disguised as a Bedouin boy, to her magnetic performances that brought Cairo to a standstill on the first Thursday of each month, and her funeral that brought millions onto the streets.

Nilometer

Built in AD 861, the **Nilometer** (Map p108; Sharia al-Malek as-Salih, Rhoda) was designed to measure the rise and fall of the Nile, and thus predict the fortunes of the annual harvest. If the Nile rose to 16 cubits (a cubit is about the length of a forearm) the harvest was likely to be good, giving people reason to celebrate, though also to fear the higher taxes that came with abundance. The conical dome was added in a 19th-century restoration. The measuring device, a graduated column, sits well below the level of the Nile in a paved area at the bottom of a flight of steps.

Old Cairo

Broadly speaking, Old Cairo (Map p108; in Egyptian, Misr al-Qadima, with a glottal-stop 'Q') incorporates the entire area south of Garden City down to the quarter known to foreigners as Coptic Cairo. Most people visiting this area head straight to the latter. From there, you can also visit the Mosque of Amr ibn al-As.

In this very traditional part of Cairo appropriate dress is essential. Visitors of either sex wearing shorts or with bare shoulders will not be allowed into churches or mosques. The best time to visit is on a Sunday, when Cairene Copts visit en masse; if you want a quiet wander among the monuments, avoid Friday and Sunday. The churches do not charge admission fees, but most have donation boxes.

The easiest way of getting to Old Cairo is by metro – Mar Girgis station is right outside the Coptic Cairo compound. The ride costs 50pt from Midan Tahrir and trains run every few minutes. There are buses running between Tahrir and Old Cairo but they are incredibly crowded. The bus trip back to Tahrir isn't as bad because you can get on at the terminal, beside the Mosque of Amr ibn al-As, before the bus fills up. Another – and probably the most pleasant – option is to take the river bus from Maspero to its last stop at Misr al-Qadima in Old Cairo. The service runs from 7am to 3pm and costs 50pt.

COPTIC CAIRO

Coptic Cairo (Map p108) is the heartland of Egypt's Coptic community, a haven of tranquillity and peace that is rich in history. Archaeologists claim that there was a small Nileside settlement on this site as far back as the 6th century BC. Early in the 2nd century AD the Romans established a fortress here, called Babylon-in-Egypt. The name Babylon is most likely a Roman corruption of 'Per-hapi-en-on' (Estate of the Nile God at On), a Pharaonic name for what was the former port of On (ancient Heliopolis).

Babylon has always been a stronghold of Christianity and at one time there were more than 20 churches clustered within less than 1 sq km, although just a handful survive today. They are linked by narrow cobbled alleyways running between high stone walls: the place feels quite similar to parts of Jerusalem's Old City. That might not be mere coincidence, because when Jews were exiled from their holy city in AD 70, some found refuge in Egypt; the country's oldest synagogue, **Ben Ezra Synagogue**, is here in Coptic Cairo. There are two entrances to the Coptic compound: a sunken staircase beside the footbridge over the metro gives access to most churches and the synagogue, while the main entrance is used for visiting the Coptic Museum and Hanging Church. The area has suffered both from water levels raised by the Aswan Dam and from the 1992 earthquake, but when ongoing restoration works are finished, the two parts of the compound should be reconnected.

Roman Towers

You'll find the main entrance to the Coptic compound between the remains of the two

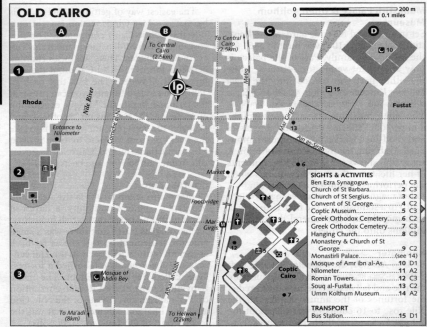

OLD CAIRO

SIGHTS & ACTIVITIES
Ben Ezra Synagogue	1 C3
Church of St Barbara	2 C3
Church of St Sergius	3 C2
Convent of St George	4 C2
Coptic Museum	5 C3
Greek Orthodox Cemetery	6 C2
Greek Orthodox Cemetery	7 C3
Hanging Church	8 C3
Monastery & Church of St George	9 C2
Monastirli Palace	(see 14)
Mosque of Amr ibn al-As	10 D1
Nilometer	11 A2
Roman Towers	12 C3
Souq al-Fustat	13 C3
Umm Kolthum Museum	14 A2

TRANSPORT
Bus Station	15 D1

round **towers** (Map p108) of Babylon's western gate. Built in AD 98 by Emperor Trajan, these were part of riverfront fortifications: at the time, the Nile would have lapped right up against them. Excavations around the southern tower have revealed part of the ancient quay, several metres below street level. The Greek Orthodox **Monastery** and **Church of St George** sit on top of the northern tower.

Coptic Museum

This **museum** (Map p108; ☎ 363 9742; www.coptic museum.gov.eg; Sharia Mar Girgis; adult/student E£16/8; ☺ 9am-5pm), founded in 1908, houses Coptic art from Graeco-Roman times to the Islamic era in a collection drawn from Cairo, the desert monasteries and Nubia. In recent years it has undergone a major restoration programme, and parts of the collection have been closed to the public. By the time this book goes to print, the full collection should be on show. Exhibits include textiles, frescoes, stonework, woodwork, manuscripts, glass and ceramics. There's a pleasant enclosed garden and a small café.

Hanging Church

Dedicated to the Virgin Mary, the **Hanging Church** (Map p108; Kineeset al-Muallaqa; Sharia Mar Girgis; ☺ Coptic mass 8-11am Fri, 9-11am Sun), which is still in use, is called the Hanging or Suspended Church as it is built on top of the Water Gate of Roman Babylon. Steep stairs lead from the forecourt to a 19th-century façade topped by twin bell towers. Beyond is a small inner courtyard, usually filled with sellers of taped liturgies and videos of the Coptic pope, Shenouda III.

The interior of this 9th-century (some say 7th-century) church, renovated many times throughout the centuries, has three barrel-vaulted, wooden-roofed aisles. Ivory-inlaid screens hide the three *haikals* (altar areas), but in front of them, raised on 13 slender pillars that represent Christ and his disciples, is a fine pulpit used only on Palm Sunday. One of the pillars, darker than the rest, is said to symbolise Judas. In the baptistry, off to the right, a panel has been cut out of the floor revealing the Water Gate below. From here there is a good view of one of the gate's twin towers.

Monastery & Church of St George

Back on Sharia Mar Girgis, the first doorway north of the main entrance leads to the Greek Orthodox **Monastery** and **Church of St George** (Map p108). St George (Mar Girgis), is one of the region's most popular Christian saints. A Palestinian conscript in the Roman army, he was executed in AD 303 for resisting Emperor Diocletian's decree forbidding the practice of Christianity. There has been a church dedicated to him in Coptic Cairo since the 10th century, but this particular one dates from 1909. The interior has been gutted by fires, but the stained glass windows remain bright and colourful. The neighbouring monastery is closed to visitors. On St George's Day (April 23), the Coptic *moulid* (religious festival) of Mar Girgis is held here.

Convent of St George

Down a sunken staircase by the footbridge, along the alleyway, the first doorway on your left leads into the courtyard of the **Convent of St George** (Map p108). The convent is closed to visitors, but you can step down into the main hall and the chapel. Inside the latter is a beautiful wooden door, almost 8m high, behind which is a small room still occasionally used for the chain-wrapping ritual that symbolises the persecution of St George during the Roman occupation. Occasionally, visitors wishing to be blessed are wrapped in chains by the resident nuns, who then intone the requisite prayers. Usually, though, the nuns will merely offer to show you a chain that they claim to have been used to bind early martyrs.

Churches of St Sergius & St Barbara

To get to the **Church of St Sergius** (Abu Serga; Map p108; ⌚ 8am-4pm) walk down the lane that the Convent of St George is on, following it around to the right and then take a left for the church entrance. This is the oldest church inside the walls, with 3rd- and 4th-century pillars, although the earliest known written reference to it dates from the 9th century. It is said to be built over a cave where Joseph, Mary and the newly born infant Jesus sheltered after fleeing to Egypt to escape persecution from King Herod of Judea, who had embarked upon a 'massacre of the first born'. The cave (now a crypt) in question is reached by descending steps to the right of the altar, but it's been flooded for some time now. Every year, on 1 June, a special mass is held here to commemorate the event.

Further along the alley brings you to Ben Ezra Synagogue on the right and, on the left, to the **Church of St Barbara** (Sitt Barbara; Map p108), who was beaten to death by her father for trying to convert him to Christianity. Her relics supposedly rest in a small chapel to the left of the nave.

Beyond the church an iron gate on the right leads to the large, peaceful **Greek Orthodox cemetery** (Map p108). Women who are on their own should be careful here – we've heard reports of flashers lurking among the gravestones.

Ben Ezra Synagogue

Egypt's oldest synagogue, **Ben Ezra Synagogue** (Map p108; admission free, donations welcome) dates from the 9th century, but occupies the shell of a 4th-century Christian church. In the 12th century the synagogue was restored by Abraham Ben Ezra, rabbi of Jerusalem, hence its name. Tradition marks this as the spot where the prophet Jeremiah gathered the Jews in the 6th century after Nebuchadnezzar had destroyed the Jerusalem temple. The adjacent spring is supposed to mark the place where the pharaoh's daughter found Moses in the reeds, and where Mary drew water to wash Jesus. More recently, a cache of more than 250,000 documents, known as the Geniza, has revealed details of the life of the Jewish community around here from the 11th to 13th centuries.

MOSQUE OF AMR IBN AL-AS

What little has survived of the original structure of the **Mosque of Amr ibn al-As** (Map p108; Sharia Sidi Hasan al-Anwar, Masr Qadima) is all that remains of the first mosque built in Egypt. It was constructed in AD 642 by Amr ibn al-As, who conquered Egypt for Islam, on the site where he first pitched his tent. The original structure is said to have been made of palm trunks thatched with leaves, but it expanded to its current size in AD 827. The mosque has been continuously reworked since then. The oldest part is to the right of the sanctuary, but there's little of interest to see inside, although of the 200 or so columns supporting the ceiling no two are said to be the same.

Further along the same street, towards the churches of Coptic Cairo, is the **Souq al-Fustat** (Map p108; 8am-4pm), a domed covered market with excellent crafts shops and workshops.

Islamic Cairo

Islamic Cairo can almost feel like another world. As you head east from Midan Ataba you'll feel almost like Alice passing through her looking glass, with the familiar trappings of the modern world being replaced by the chaos and curiosities of a completely different nature and era.

The term 'Islamic Cairo' is something of a misnomer, as this area is no more or less Islamic than other parts of the city. The name pays testament to the fact that the area is home to the city's most important mosque and its most sacred shrine, but it could equally stem from the profusion of minarets on the skyline – a visual indicator of the area's overwhelming atmosphere of piety and its profusion of wonderful mosque architecture. Worried that tourists will be put off visiting by the 'Islamic' tag, the Egyptian government refers to the area as 'Fatimid Cairo' and its Ministry of Culture has embarked upon an ambitious, costly and painstakingly slow restoration programme. Some conservation architects are concerned that many of the buildings are being rebuilt rather than restored, and that the area will change from being an architecturally significant and intact precinct with a vibrant human presence to a lifeless heritage theme park. There are also concerns that beautifully restored buildings such as the Wikala al-Bazara are not being given creative reuses and are quickly sliding back into disrepair. While there does seem to be some truth behind these accusations, it's also true to say that some parts of Islamic Cairo are being wonderfully reinvigorated as a result of all of this attention; the recent opening of the Al-Azhar Park in the district of Darb al-Ahmar being a perfect example.

The best way to explore here is to spend a couple of days wandering through the neighbourhood's narrow streets and twisting alleyways. Passing splendid geometric mosques and great medieval façades, you'll have to compete for right of way with Suzuki vans, overburdened donkeys

---

ISLAMIC CAIRO HIGHLIGHTS

- Visit the keystone of Islam in Egypt, the **Al-Azhar Mosque** (opposite), which has been a mosque and university for over 1000 years

- See the **Mosque of Ibn Tulun** (p121), one of Egypt's oldest and a marvel of simplicity, and check out the nearby **Gayer-Anderson Museum** (p121), a quirky set for Hollywood adventures

- Find out just how elegant and sophisticated life in 18th-century Cairo could be at the magnificent **Beit el-Suhaymi** (p114)

- Do as locals have done for centuries – relax over a *sheesha* and mint tea at **Fishawi's Coffeehouse** (p154) after a heavy bargaining session with the smooth-talking merchants of the Khan al-Khalili

- Bring Naguib Mahfouz's *Cairo Trilogy* to life by following the **walking tour** of Islamic Cairo on p138

---

and merchants pushing barrows laden with everything from mattresses to marrows. Here the sweet aromas of turmeric, basil and cumin mix with the stink of livestock, petrol and sewage – the real smell of the city. The effect can be disorientating and the casual visitor can lose not just a sense of direction but also a sense of time. Of all Cairo's neighbourhoods, this is undoubtedly the most fascinating.

VISITING ISLAMIC CAIRO

With more than 800 listed monuments and few signposts or other concessions to the visitor, Islamic Cairo can be a fairly daunting place. We've divided it into seven segments, most with their own map and each making for a half-day outing.

Al-Azhar & Khan al-Khalili (opposite) The geographical and symbolic heart of ancient Cairo.

North of Khan al-Khalili (p113) A monument-studded walk to the Northern Gates.

Al-Azhar to the Citadel (p116) Through the Darb al-Ahmar district to Mohammed Ali's seat of power.

Museum of Islamic Art (p118) One of the world's finest collections of Islamic Art.

The Citadel (p119) Home to Egypt's rulers for 700 years.

The Citadel to Ibn Tulun (p120) Two magnificent mosques and the city's quirkiest museum.
Northern Cemetery (p122) Cairo's famous City of the Dead.

This part of Cairo is very traditional and appropriate dress is necessary – legs and shoulders should be covered, otherwise custodians may refuse entry to mosques. Shoes must be removed before entering prayer halls, so bring footwear that can be easily slipped off, but that is robust enough to survive rutted, rubble-strewn alleys. Caretakers at most mosques and museums expect tips, so bring plenty of change – E£2 to E£5 should be sufficient at each place.

Bear in mind that opening times can be fluid; caretakers are usually around from 9am until early evening, but may follow their own whims. Most mosques are closed to visitors during prayer times.

To prepare, check out the fifth edition of *Islamic Monuments in Cairo: The Practical Guide* by Caroline Williams, published by AUC Press (E£75), or *Historic Cairo: A Walk through the Islamic City*, by British architect Jim Antoniou and also published by AUC Press (E£75). Those serious about their architecture may like to splurge E£300 on Nicholas Warner's recently published *The Monuments of Historic Cairo: A Map and Descriptive Catalogue*, which features 31 maps and a full descriptive catalogue. Published by AUC Press, it was funded by Usaid and the Egyptian Antiquities Project of the American Research Centre in Egypt. The website at www.cim.gov.eg also has some information about the area.

GETTING TO ISLAMIC CAIRO
Islamic Cairo covers a vast area, but the heart of it is Al-Azhar and Khan al-Khalili, both easily reached from Downtown. By foot, head for Midan Ataba then bear east under the elevated motorway along Sharia al-Azhar, or walk up Sharia al-Muski. Alternatively you can hail a taxi and ask for 'Al-Hussein' – the name of the *midan* and the mosque at the mouth of the Khan al-Khalili bazaar (expect to pay E£5 from Downtown). Most of the places in the following pages can be reached from Al-Hussein, although for the Citadel and Mosque of Ibn Tulun it may be easier to take a taxi (about E£5 from Downtown) to the Citadel entrance.

AL-AZHAR & KHAN AL-KHALILI
By far the best place to become acquainted with Islamic Cairo is the area around the Al-Azhar Mosque and the great bazaar, Khan al-Khalili (Map p112), which panders perfectly to Western preconceptions of the Orient.

Al-Azhar Mosque
Founded in AD 970 as the centrepiece of newly created Fatimid Cairo, the **Al-Azhar Mosque** (Gami' al-Azhar; Map p112; Sharia al-Azhar; admission free, baksheesh often requested; 24hr) is one of Cairo's earliest mosques and its sheikh is the highest theological authority for Egyptian Muslims. Its university was established in AD 988, and claims to be the world's oldest surviving educational institution (a claim disputed by the Kairaouine Mosque and University in Fez, Morocco). At one time the mosque itself was one of the world's pre-eminent centres of learning, drawing scholars from Europe and across the Arab world. Students are now taught in various campuses around the country.

The mosque is a harmonious blend of architectural styles, the result of frequent enlargements over a thousand years. The central courtyard is the earliest part, while from south to north, the three minarets date from the 14th, 15th and 16th centuries; the latter, with its double finial, was added by Sultan al-Ghouri, whose mosque and mausoleum complex stands nearby. The tomb chamber, through a doorway on the left just inside the entrance, has a beautiful *mihrab* (a niche indicating the direction of Mecca) and should not be missed.

Midan Hussein
The square between the two highly venerated mosques of Al-Azhar and Sayyidna al-Hussein was one of the focal points of medieval Cairo and remains an important space at feast times, particularly on Ramadan evenings, and during the *moulids* (see the boxed text p528) of Al-Hussein and An-Nabi Mohammed. At these times the *midan* is crowded with people, bright lights and loud music. The partying goes on until the early hours of the morning. At other times the square is still a popular meeting place, and the *ahwas* with outdoor seating at the entrance to the khan are often full of locals and tourists.

One of the most sacred Islamic sites in Egypt, the **Mosque of Sayyidna al-Hussein** (Map p112) is the reputed burial place of the head of Al-Hussein, grandson of the Prophet. Due to the importance of this holy relic, non-Muslims are not allowed inside the mosque. Most of the current building dates from about 1870 and is of little interest to travellers, except for the beautiful 14th-century stucco panels on the minaret. The area around the mosque is considered sacred; bread sold here is believed to have a special *baraka* (blessing) and alcohol is banned.

Khan al-Khalili

Jaundiced travellers often dismiss the **Khan al-Khalili** (Map p112) as a tourist trap; there's

no ignoring the fact that it's a favoured stop of tour buses and has all the associated annoyances (touts and tat) that come with them. But it's worth remembering that Cairenes have plied their trades here since the founding of the Khan in the 14th century – the buying and selling didn't begin with the arrival of the first tour group. Today the market still plays an important role in the day-to-day commercial life of thousands of locals.

An immense conglomeration of markets and shops open from early morning to sundown (though some stalls are closed on Friday and most are closed on Sunday), it's possible to find everything from blankets and soap powder to books of magic spells

AL-AZHAR & KHAN AL-KHALILI

0   100 m
0   0.05 miles

SIGHTS & ACTIVITIES	
Al-Azhar Mosque	1 C4
Madrassa & Mausoleum of Qalaun	2 A1
Mausoleum of Al-Ghouri	3 A4
Mosque of Sayyidna al-Hussein	4 C1
Mosque-Madrassa of Al-Ghouri	5 A4
Wikala of Al-Ghouri	6 B4

SLEEPING	
Al-Hussein Hotel	7 C2

EATING	
Al-Halwagy	8 B3
Egyptian Pancake House	9 B3
Gad	10 B4
Khan el-Khalil Restaurant & Mahfouz Coffee Shop	11 B2

DRINKING	
Fishawi's Coffeehouse	12 C2

MARKET AREA	
Antiques	D
Bedouin Dresses/Jewellery (Hareem Khan)	N
Belly-Dancing Costumes	C
Brasswork	E
Carpets & Rugs	H
Coppersmiths	B
Cotton & Cloth	J
Gold & Silver	A
Muski Glass	I
Perfumes	G
Semiprecious Stones	L
Spices	F
Stationery	K
Tailors	M

Madrassa & Mausoleum of As-Salih Ayyub

Wikalat Haramein

Khan al-Khalili

Sabil-Kuttab of Ahmed Pasha

Al-Gamaliyya

An-Nahaseen

Medieval Gates

Al-Muizz li-Din Allah

Stairs to Upper Level (Brasswork & Bedouin Rugs)

Midan Hussein

Mosque of Al-Mutahhar

Al-Muski

Mosque of Al-Ashraf Barsbey

Midaq Alley

To Northern Cemetery (800m)

To Al-Azhar University

Subway

To Midan Ataba; Downtown (750m)

Al-Azhar

Footbridge

To Bab Zuweila (350m); Citadel (1.2km)

Mosque of Abu Dahab

To Haret al-Fahhamin (100m)

To Beit Zeinab al-Khatoun (100m)

Fruit-& Vegetable Market

To Northern Gates (400m)

and precious stones here – not forgetting, of course, the ubiquitous stuffed-toy camels and alabaster pyramids. Apart from the clumsy 'Hey mister, look for free' touts, the merchants of Khan al-Khalili are some of the greatest smooth-talkers you will ever meet. Almost anything can be bought in the Khan and if one merchant doesn't have what you're looking for, he'll happily find somebody who does (for information on what's sold where within Khan al-Khalili, see the Market Areas key on Map p112).

There are few specific things to see in the Khan but **Fishawi's Coffeehouse** (Map p112; ☾ 24hr except during Ramadan), in an alley one block west of Midan Hussein, is an absolute must. Hung with huge mirrors and packed day and night, it claims to have been open continuously for the last 200 years, except perhaps on mornings during Ramadan when everyone is fasting. Entertainment comes in the form of roaming salesmen, women and children who hawk wallets, carved canes, *sheesha*-style cigarette holders, pistol-shaped cigarette lighters and packet after packet after packet of tissues.

Sharia al-Muski

A congested but fabulous market street, Sharia al-Muski (Map p112) runs parallel to Sharia al-Azhar from Midan Hussein to Midan Ataba. It is less overtly 'Oriental' than Khan al-Khalili but usually more vivid and boisterous.

NORTH OF KHAN AL-KHALILI

From Midan Hussein walk up Sharia al-Gamaliyya, the road that leads up along the western side of the Mosque of Sayyidna al-Hussein. Stick to it as it doglegs left and enters the district known as Gamaliyya. **Sharia al-Gamaliyya** (Map p114) was the second-most important of medieval Cairo's thoroughfares. Today it looks more like a back alley, barely squeezing between the buildings. These buildings include some fine clusters of Mamluk-era mosques, *madrassas* and caravanserais, many of them being restored and thus partly obscured by forests of crude wooden scaffolding.

Easily identified by its blindingly white new stone, the 1408 **Mosque of Gamal ad-Din** (Map p114) is one monument that has received the somewhat overzealous attentions of restorers. It's raised above a row of shops,

the rent from which was intended for the mosque's upkeep. Next door is the **Wikala al-Bazara** (Map p114; Sharia al-Tombakshiyya; adult/student E£10/5; ☾ 10am-5pm). A *wikala* (also called a caravanserai) is a medieval merchants' hostel; traders slept in the upper rooms while the ground-floor rooms around the courtyard were used for storing goods and stabling animals. The gates of the *wikala* were locked at night to protect the merchandise. In Ottoman times Cairo had more than 360 *wikalas* but now less than 20 remain. The Wikala al-Bazara lay in ruins for many years but it is now open to the public, almost completely rebuilt from scratch and sadly empty.

Diagonally opposite the *wikala* is the Mamluk **Mosque & Mausoleum of Sultan Beybars al-Gashankir**, which features a particularly impressive vaulted wooden ceiling in the mausoleum. The caretaker will take you up the minaret if you offer some *baksheesh*.

Northern Walls & Gates

The square-towered **Bab an-Nasr** (Gate of Victory; Map p114) and the rounded **Bab al-Futuh** (Gate of Conquests; Map p114) were built in 1087 as the two main northern entrances to the walled Fatimid city of Al-Qahira. Walk along the outside and you'll see what a hugely imposing bit of military architecture the whole thing is. In the past visitors were able to get access to the top of the walls and explore inside the gates via the roof of the neighbouring Mosque of al-Hakim, but this hasn't been possible for quite a while, as a lengthy restoration project is underway here. Perhaps once restoration work has finished in the vicinity the walls may be open again and you can look for the inscriptions above the doorways that read 'Tour Lascalle' and 'Tour Milhaud', evidence that Napoleon's troops were once garrisoned here during the French occupation. You'll also be able to find carved animals and Pharaonic figures, evidence that stone for Al-Qahira's fortifications was scavenged from the ruins of ancient Memphis.

Mosque of Al-Hakim

Al-Hakim became the sixth Fatimid ruler of Egypt at the age of 11. His tutor nicknamed him 'Little Lizard' because of his frightening looks and behaviour. Hakim later took his revenge by having the tutor murdered. During his 24-year reign, those nearest to him lived in constant fear for their lives. A victorious general rushing unannounced into the royal apartments was confronted by a bloodied Hakim standing over a disembowelled page boy. The general was beheaded.

Hakim took a great interest in the affairs of his people and would patrol the streets on a donkey called Moon. Most notoriously, he punished dishonest merchants by having them dealt with by a well-endowed black servant. His death was as bizarre as his life. On one of his solitary nocturnal jaunts on Moon up onto the Muqattam Hills, Hakim simply disappeared; his body was never found. To one of his followers, a man called Al-Darizy, this was proof of Hakim's divine nature. From this seed Al-Darizy founded the sect of the Druze that continues to this day.

Completed in 1013, the **Mosque of Al-Hakim** (Map p114) is one of Cairo's older mosques but it was rarely used as a place of worship. Instead it functioned as a Crusaders' prison, a stable, a warehouse, a boys' school and, most fittingly of all, considering the behaviour of its notorious founder, as a madhouse. The two stone minarets are the earliest surviving minarets in the city. The mosque is now used by an Ismailia group. It's not particularly interesting architecturally, and has some of the pushiest attendants in all Cairo – don't let them bully you into giving them more *baksheesh* than you feel is appropriate.

Sharia al-Muizz li-Din Allah

Al-Muizz li-Din (as it's often shortened to), which takes its name from the Fatimid caliph who conquered Cairo in AD 969, is the former grand thoroughfare of medieval Cairo. It was the city's main shopping street and a 15th-century description tells us that storytellers and entertainers, as well as stalls serving cooked food, were to be found along its length. The garlic and onion market, beside the Mosque of Al-Hakim, was a slave market until the middle of the 19th century.

Heading south, the produce gives way to a variety of small places selling *sheesha*s, braziers and big pear-shaped cooking pots. On the right, about 200m south, is the **Mosque of Suleiman Silahdar** (Map p114), built comparatively late in 1839, during the reign of Mohammed Ali and distinguished by its thin, Turkish-inspired minaret.

Beit el-Suhaymi

Tucked down a small whitewashed alley off Sharia al-Muizz li-Din Allah, **Beit el-Suhaymi** (Map p114; Darb al-Asfar; admission E£20; 🕒 9am-5pm) is Islamic Cairo's finest example of the traditional family mansion built throughout the city from Mamluk times to the 19th century. The façade of the *beit* (house) is typi-

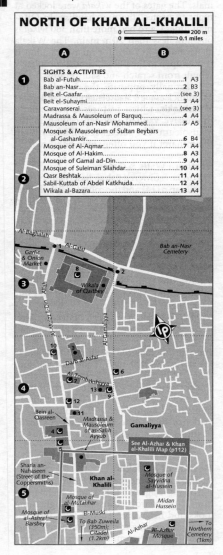

NORTH OF KHAN AL-KHALILI

0 ─────── 200 m
0 ─────── 0.1 miles

cally plain on the street, but once through the tunnel-like entrance you emerge into a beautiful inner courtyard. Guests are received in an impressive *qa'a* (reception room) off the courtyard, graced with a polychrome marble fountain inset in the floor and a high, painted wooden ceiling. Upstairs are the family quarters: wooden-lattice windows, known as *mashrabiyya*, allowed the women to observe the goings on below without being seen. The rooms were kept cool by *malqaf* (angled wind catchers on the roof) that direct the prevailing northerly breezes down into the building. Next door are an adjoining 18th-century **caravanserai** and another, equally attractive, house – the **Beit el-Gaafar**. The admission fee may seem a little steep but if you only shell out for one Islamic monument, this should be it. Make sure you ask for an official ticket.

Back on Sharia al-Muizz li-Din Allah, just 50m south of the junction with Darb al-Asfar, is the petite **Mosque of Al-Aqmar** (Map p114). Built in 1125 by one of the last Fatimid caliphs, it is the oldest stone-façaded mosque in Egypt. Several features appear here that were to become part of the mosque builders' essential vocabulary, including stalactite carving and the ribbing in the hooded arch.

Sabil-Kuttab of Abdel Katkhuda

Further along the street, where the road splits, is the **Sabil-Kuttab of Abdel Katkhuda** (Map p114), a public drinking fountain and a Quranic school. Building a *sabil-kuttab* was one way to atone for sins, as it provided the two things commended by the Prophet: water for the thirsty and spiritual enlightenment for the ignorant. This one was built in 1744 by an emir notorious for his debauched behaviour. It has some nice ceramic work inside, so it's worth trying to find the caretaker who has the key. He often sits in the **Qasr Beshtak** (Beshtak Palace; Map p114) down the little alley that runs to the east, then through the archway at the bottom. The palace is a rare example of 14th-century domestic architecture, originally five floors high, now largely ruined but with splendid rooftop views.

Bein al-Qasreen

The part of Al-Muizz li-Din immediately south of the Sabil-Kuttab of Abdel Katkhuda is known as **Bein al-Qasreen** (Between the Palaces), a reminder of two great palace complexes that flanked the street during the Fatimid era. The palaces fell into ruin and were replaced by the works of subsequent rulers. Today three great abutting Mamluk complexes line the west of the street, providing one of Cairo's most impressive assemblies of minarets, domes and towering façades.

Northernmost of the three is the **Madrassa & Mausoleum of Barquq** (Map p114). Barquq seized power in 1382 when Egypt was reeling from plague and famine; his madrassa was completed four years later. Enter through the bold black-and-white marble portal into a vaulted passageway. To the right the inner court has a colourful ceiling supported by four porphyry Pharaonic columns. Although this is called the Mausoleum of Barquq, only his daughter is buried in the splendid domed tomb chamber; the sultan rests in the Northern Cemetery (see p123).

South of Barquq's complex is the **Mausoleum of An-Nasir Mohammed** (Map p114), built in 1304 by the son of Qalaun. The Gothic doorway was plundered from a church in Acre (now Akko, Israel) when An-Nasir and his Mamluk army ended Crusader domination there in 1290. More foreign influence is discernible in the fine stucco on the minaret, which is North African in style. Buried in the mausoleum (on the right as you enter but usually kept locked) is An-Nasir's favourite son; the sultan himself is buried next door in the mausoleum of his father, Qalaun.

Both of these complexes can be visited in return for some *baksheesh*. Look for the caretakers at the entry doors.

The third and most splendid of the complexes is the **Madrassa & Mausoleum of Qalaun** (Map p112), which was closed for restoration at the time of research. The earliest of the trio, the Qalaun complex was completed in just 13 months in 1279. The mausoleum, on the right, is a particularly beautiful assemblage of inlaid stone and stucco, patterned with stars and floral motifs and lit by stained-glass windows. The complex also includes a *maristan* (hospital), which Qalaun had ordered built because he had been impressed by a *maristan* in Damascus, where he had been cured of colic. The Arab traveller and historian Ibn Battuta, who visited Cairo in 1325, recorded that Qalaun's hospital contained 'an innumerable quantity of appliances and medicaments'. He also recorded that Quran reciters would sit by the mausoleum day and night chanting a requiem for the dead within. In those days the tombs were guarded by eunuchs – we doubt the tradition will be continued when the complex reopens.

Bein al-Qasreen to the City Centre

Want to buy a minaret top? South of Bein al-Qasreen, the monuments give way to a string of shops filled with pots and pans and crescent-shaped finials, hence its more popular name: Sharia an-Nahaseen (Street of the Coppersmiths). After a short stretch, copper gives way to gold, signifying that you have re-entered the precincts of Khan al-Khalili. At the junction with Sharia al-Muski, beside the two mosques, a left turn leads back to Midan Hussein, while heading right will eventually take you to Midan Ataba (1km); straight ahead is Sharia al-Azhar, the best place to find a taxi.

AL-AZHAR TO THE CITADEL

South of Sharia al-Azhar, Sharia al-Muizz li-Din Allah continues as a busy market street running 400m down to the twin-minareted gate of **Bab Zuweila** (Map p116). From there two routes lead to the Madrassa of Sultan Hassan – east along Sharia Ahmed Mahir Pasha, or south through Sharia al-Khayamiyya (Street of the Tentmakers). Either way, it's a long (at least 40 minutes), very dusty but interesting walk to the main entrance of the Citadel.

Ottoman Houses

Leaving the Al-Azhar Mosque, turn left and then left again to reach an alley squeezed between the southern wall of the mosque and a row of tiny shops housed in the vaults of a 15th-century merchants' building. At the top of this road lies **Beit Zeinab al-Khatoun** (House of Zeinab Khatoun; Map p116; ☎ 735 7001; Sharia al-Sheikh Mohammed Abdo; admission E£10; ☑ 8am-6pm), a restored Ottoman-era house with a rooftop affording superb views of the surrounding minaret-studded skyline. Across a small and very peaceful garden (a welcome retreat from the surrounding mayhem) is **Beit al-Harrawi** (Harrawi House; Map p116; ☎ 510 4174; admission E£10; ☑ 8am-6pm), another fine 18th-century mansion, but too sparse inside to really warrant the admission charge. It is sometimes used as a

concert venue and houses the Arabic Oud House; you may hear rehearsals. Between the two houses is **Al-Khatoun** (p159), one of the city's most stylish homewares shops.

Al-Ghouri Complex (Al-Ghouriyya)

The grand **Mosque-Madrassa of Al-Ghouri** (Map p112; admission free), with its red-chequered

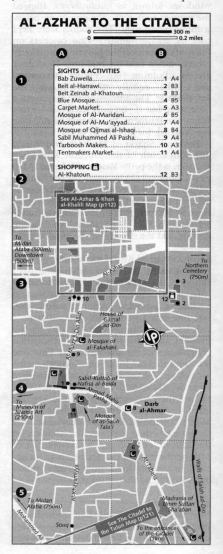

AL-AZHAR TO THE CITADEL

0   300 m
0   0.2 miles

SIGHTS & ACTIVITIES
Bab Zuweila	1 A4
Beit al-Harrawi	2 B3
Beit Zeinab al-Khatoun	3 B3
Blue Mosque	4 B5
Carpet Market	5 A3
Mosque of Al-Maridani	6 B5
Mosque of Al-Mu'ayyad	7 A4
Mosque of Qijmas al-Ishaqi	8 B4
Sabil Muhammed Ali Pasha	9 A4
Tarboosh Makers	10 A3
Tentmakers Market	11 A4

SHOPPING
Al-Khatoun	12 B3

minaret, and the elegant **Mausoleum of Al-Ghouri** (Map p112) face each other across the *souq* on the south side of Sharia al-Azhar. Together they form an exquisite monument to the end of the Mamluk era. Qansuh al-Ghouri, the penultimate Mamluk sultan, ruled for 16 years. Then, at the age of 78, he rode to Syria at the head of his army to do battle with the Ottoman Turks. The head of the defeated Al-Ghouri was sent to Constantinople, but his body was never recovered. His mausoleum (dating from 1505) contains the body of Tumanbey, his short-lived successor, hanged by the Turks at Bab Zuweila. The mausoleum, which has been under restoration for a number of years, should reopen as a cultural centre soon after this book is released. The beautifully restored mosque is open to visitors and it's possible to climb the minaret. Also part of the complex, the **Wikala of Al-Ghouri** (Map p112; ☎ 511 0472; admission E£6; ⏰ 9am-5pm Sat-Thu), 300m east, is another of the doomed sultan's legacies. Similar to the Wikala Al-Bazara (see p113), but more sympathetically restored, the upper rooms serve as artists' ateliers while the former stables are showrooms and craft shops. The courtyard serves as an occasional theatre and concert hall.

Carpet & Clothes Market
Al-Ghouriyya, the stretch of Sharia al-Muizz li-Din Allah between the mosque-madrassa and the Mausoleum of Al-Ghouri, used to be known as Cairo's 'Silk Market', a place where carpets were sold. The passageways behind the mosque-madrassa (slip down the side or enter from Sharia al-Azhar) are still filled with **carpet sellers** (Map p116), whose wares are now made of wool or synthetics. South of Al-Ghouriyya, Sharia al-Muizz li-Din Allah becomes a busy market street given over to household goods and cheap clothing. On the right, less than 50m south of Al-Ghouriyya are two of Cairo's last **tarboosh (fez) makers** (Map p116), who shape hats on heavy brass presses. Once worn by every respectable *effendi* (gentleman), *tarboosh*es are now mainly bought by hotels and tourist restaurants. They sell for between E£10 and E£45. A bit further down on the left is the charming Ottoman-style **Sabil Muhammed Ali Pasha** (Map p116), a drinking fountain built in 1820 and restored in recent years. The fountain introduced a completely new

architectural style to Cairo, featuring gilded window grilles and calligraphic panels in Ottoman Turkish. Unfortunately, it is currently closed to the public.

Bab Zuweila
Built at the same time as the northern gates (10th century), the beautiful gate of **Bab Zuweila** (Map p116) is the only remaining southern gate of the old medieval city of Al-Qahira. Until the late 19th century it was still closed each evening. The area in front of the gate was one of the main public gathering places in Mamluk times. It was also the site of executions, a popular form of street theatre, with some victims being executed by being sawn in half or crucified.

The two splendid minarets atop the gate belong to the neighbouring **Mosque of Al-Mu'ayyad** (Map p116). It is usually possible to climb the minarets (reached through the mosque) to see one of the best available views of the city.

Sharia al-Khayamiyya
The 'Street of the Tentmakers', **Sharia al-Khayamiyya** (Map p116), takes its name from the artisans who produced the bright fabrics formerly used by the caravans. Nowadays these fabrics are used for the ceremonial tents that are set up for funerals, wakes, weddings and feasts. They also make appliqué wall hangings and bedspreads, and print original patterns for tablecloths.

About a kilometre to the south beyond the interesting covered **tentmakers market** (Map p116), Sharia al-Khayamiyya intersects with Sharia Mohammed Ali; a left turn here will take you to the great Mosque-Madrassa of Sultan Hassan and to the Citadel, but the Darb al-Ahmar route is more interesting.

Darb al-Ahmar
This district was the heart of 14th- and 15th-century Cairo and is named after its main thoroughfare, the historic **Darb al-Ahmar** (Red Rd; Map p116), which is now officially titled Sharia Ahmad Mahir Pasha. In the district's heyday Cairo had a population of about 250,000, most of whom lived outside the city walls in tightly packed residential districts of narrow, twisting streets and dark cul-de-sacs. As the walled inner city of Al-Qahira was completely built-up, patrons of new mosques,

RUBBISH TO ROSES

Cairo is one of the world's most crowded cities, and finding green spaces within its choked boundaries is as difficult as acquiring real papyrus in its souvenir shops. So when the Historic Cities Support Programme (run by the Aga Khan Trust for Culture) announced in the early 1990s that it intended to fund an ambitious project to clear an enormous mound of centuries of accumulated rubbish on the Darassa Hills and construct a 30-hectare urban park in its place, Cairenes were understandably excited.

The major component of a costly and ambitious project to conserve and revitalise the historic Darb al-Ahmar district and improve the quality of life of its community, **Al-Azhar Park** (Map pp94–5) is a triumph of thoughtful urban planning, inspired architecture and sensible environmental management – a rare mix indeed in this muddled megalopolis. Work took over a decade and started with the grading of the site and the construction of three enormous underground water tanks and a pumping station to bolster Cairo's water supply. The water tanks, which were funded by Usaid, were incorporated into the park's master plan by the Cairo-based concept designers, Sites International, and the Boston-based landscape architects, Sasaki Associates. During the regrading of the site, 1.3km of Ayyubid-era city wall was uncovered; its conservation and incorporation into the master plan for the park became an important part of the project.

The former rubbish heap now sports lush formal and informal plantings, a small lake, a central palm court, water channels, informal pathways, a children's playground and fruit orchards – all designed to reference classical Islamic gardens. A restaurant and gallery building on the park's northern hill boasts spectacular 360-degree views of the city and a design referencing surrounding historic buildings. Its Egyptian architects, Rami el-Dahan and Soheir Farid, have clearly been inspired by the architecture of the Darb al-Ahmar district and have used vaulted ceilings and delicate archways to wonderful effect. The park's other building, a lakeside pavilion, is a modern interpretation of classical Islamic pavilions designed by French architect, Serge Santelli.

Entrance to the park is free, which makes a visit here a very tempting alternative to coughing up E£35 to visit the nearby and vastly over-rated Citadel, particularly as the views here are just as impressive.

grand palaces and religious institutions were forced to build outside the city gates; most of the structures around here date from the late Mamluk era. One of the best examples of architecture from this period is the 1481 **Mosque of Qijmas al-Ishaqi** (Map p116). Don't be deceived by the plain exterior: inside there are beautiful stained-glass windows, inlaid marble floors and stucco walls.

About 150m further on the right, the 1339 **Mosque of Al-Maridani** (Map p116) incorporates architectural elements from several periods: eight granite columns were taken from a Pharaonic monument; the arches contain Roman, Christian and Islamic designs; and the Ottomans added a fountain and wooden housing. Trees in the courtyard, attractive *mashrabiyya* screening and a lack of visitors make this a peaceful place to stop.

The **Blue Mosque** (Map p116), more correctly known as the Mosque of Aqsunqur, gets its popular name from the combination of blue-grey marble on the exterior and the flowery tiling inside. The mosque was built in 1347, though the tiles, imported from Syria, were not added until 1652. The minaret affords an excellent view of the Citadel, while over to the east, just behind the mosque, you can see the remains of Saladin's city walls. The caretaker will escort you up in exchange for some *baksheesh*.

MUSEUM OF ISLAMIC ART

Overshadowed by the crowd-pulling Egyptian Museum, the **Museum of Islamic Art** (Map pp94-5; ☎ 390 1520; Sharia Bur Said) contains one of the world's finest collections of Islamic applied art but has traditionally received few visitors.

At the time of research the museum was closed for restoration – it is scheduled to reopen some time in 2006. When it does, you can expect to see displays such as woodwork (including some nice coffered ceilings and gorgeous *mashrabiyya* work), inlaid brass work and Mamluk weaponry. There should also be pottery and glass, carved marble fountains, and beautifully illuminated manuscripts and ornate Qurans formerly owned by King Farouk.

The museum is 750m southeast of Midan Ataba, straight down Sharia Mohammed Ali (also called Sharia al-Qala'a). Midan Tahrir is 1.5km west along Sharia Sami al-Barudi (passing the Mohammed Naguib metro station en route). A taxi to or from Downtown should cost around E£4.

THE CITADEL

Sprawling over a limestone spur on the eastern edge of the city, the **Citadel** (Al-Qala'a; Map p119; ☎ 512 1735; Midan al-Qala'a; adult/student E£35/20; ☑ Citadel 8am-5pm Oct-May, 8am-6pm Jun-Sep, museums 8.30am-4.30pm, mosques closed during Friday prayers) was home to Egypt's rulers for 700 years. Their legacy is a collection of three very different mosques, several palaces (housing some underwhelming museums) and a couple of terraces with views over the city. The admission includes entry to all the museums within the Citadel. Though this is one of the most popular tourist attractions in Cairo (particularly for Egyptians), it is relatively unimpressive and decidedly overpriced.

Saladin began building the Citadel in 1176 to fortify the city against the Crusaders, then rampaging through Palestine. Following their overthrow of Saladin's Ayyubid dynasty, the Mamluks extended the Citadel, adding sumptuous palaces and harems. Under the Ottomans (1517–1798) the fortress was further enlarged westwards and a new main gate, the Bab al-Azab, was added, while the Mamluk palaces were allowed to deteriorate. Even so, when Napoleon's French expedition took control of the Citadel in 1798, the emperor's savants regarded these buildings as some of the finest Islamic monuments in Cairo. This didn't stop Mohammed Ali – who rose to power when the French left – from demolishing them. The only Mamluk structure left standing was a single mosque, used as a stable. Mohammed Ali completely remodelled the rest of the Citadel and crowned it with the Turkish-style mosque that currently dominates Cairo's eastern skyline.

After Mohammed Ali's grandson Ismail moved his residence to the Abdeen Palace (p101), the Citadel became a military

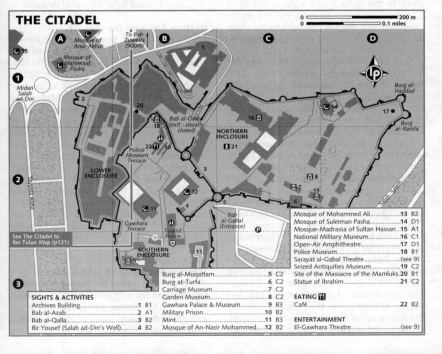

garrison. The British army was barracked here during WWII and Egyptian soldiers still have a small foothold, although most of the Citadel has now been given over to tourists.

Mosque of Mohammed Ali

The fortress – and indeed, the skyline of Cairo – is dominated by the **Mosque of Mohammed Ali** (Map p119). Modelled along classic Turkish lines, it took 18 years to build (1830–48) although the domes subsequently had to be rebuilt. Perhaps the most evocative description of it is in Olivia Manning's *The Levant Trilogy*: 'Above them Mohammed Ali's alabaster mosque, uniquely white in this sand-coloured city, sat with minarets pricked, like a fat, white, watchful cat'.

Manning is not alone in not taking the mosque as seriously as Mohammed Ali intended. It has never found much favour with writers, who have criticised it for being unimaginative, lacking in grace and resembling a great toad. Beyond criticism, the mosque's patron lies in the marble tomb on the right as you enter. Note the chintzy clock in the central courtyard, a gift from King Louis-Philippe of France in thanks for the Pharaonic obelisk that adorns the Place de la Concorde in Paris. It was damaged on delivery and has yet to be repaired.

Dwarfed by Mohammed Ali's mosque, but possibly more interesting, is the 1318 **Mosque of An-Nasir Mohammed** (Map p119), the Citadel's sole surviving Mamluk structure. The interior is a little sparse because the Ottoman sultan Selim I had it stripped of its marble, but the twisted finials of the minarets are interesting for their covering of glazed tiles, something rarely seen in Egypt.

Facing the entrance of the Mosque of An-Nasir Mohammed, a mock-Gothic gateway leads to a grand terrace. On a clear day (unfortunately rare) this has superb views across Islamic Cairo to the tower blocks of Downtown and across to the Pyramids at Giza – it's best seen at sunset. There's also an overpriced and ordinary café here.

The **Police Museum** (Map p119), at the northern end of the terrace, has a flyblown collection that includes a strange 'Assassination Room'. Immediately below the Police Museum, in the Citadel's Lower Enclosure (closed to the public), the steep-sided roadway leading to the Bab al-Azab

was the site of the infamous massacre of the Mamluks (see p41).

South of Mohammed Ali's mosque is another terrace with good views. Beyond the terrace, the dull **Gawhara Palace & Museum** (Map p119) lamely attempts to evoke 19th-century court life.

Northern Enclosure

Entrance to the Northern Enclosure is via the 16th-century Bab al-Qalla, which faces the side of the Mosque of An-Nasir Mohammed. Here you'll find Mohammed Ali's one-time Harem Palace, which is now home to the wonderfully kitsch **National Military Museum** (Map p119). The top floor houses an excellent scale model of the Citadel.

East of the lawns a narrow road leads to a rather sparse area dotted with a few small, low buildings, one of which is the **Carriage Museum** (Map p119) containing a small collection of 19th-century horse-drawn carriages that might occupy five minutes of your time. Devotees of Islamic architecture might appreciate the 1528 **Mosque of Suleiman Pasha** (Map p119), a beautiful Ottoman-era structure topped by a cluster of domes.

Getting To/From the Citadel

It's an unpleasant 3km walk from Downtown to the Citadel. From Midan Ataba go straight down Sharia al-Qala'a and its continuation, Sharia Mohammed Ali, to Midan Salah ad-Din; from Midan Tahrir the best route is via Midan al-Falaki to Midan Bab al-Khalq and then down Mohammed Ali. A taxi will cost E£5. By public transport, bus 174 from Midan Ramses passes by the Citadel as does bus 173, which starts and terminates at Midan Falaki. Bus 905 operates between the Citadel and the Pyramids. Buses 57 and 951 go to Midan Ataba and the 54 minibus travels to Midan Tahrir. Note that all these services stop at Midan Salah ad-Din in front of the Citadel, a 15-minute walk or short taxi ride (E£1) to the entrance on Sharia Salah Salem.

THE CITADEL TO IBN TULUN
Mosque-Madrassa of Sultan Hassan

The great structure of the **Mosque-Madrassa of Sultan Hassan** (Map p119; Midan Salah ad-Din; admission free; ☺ 8am-5pm Oct-May, 8am-6pm Jun-Sep) is regarded as the finest piece of early-Mamluk architecture in Cairo. It was built between

THE CITADEL TO IBN TULUN

0   400 m
0   0.2 miles

SIGHTS & ACTIVITIES		DRINKING 🍷	
Gayer-Anderson Museum..........**1** C2		Zahrat al-Midan............................**6** A2	
Madrassa of Sunqur Sa'adi.....**2** C1			
Mevlevi Theatre....................(see 2)		SHOPPING 🛍	
Mosque of Ar-Rifai................**3** D1		Khan Misr Touloun.....................**7** C2	
Mosque of Ibn Tulun.............**4** B2			
Sayyida Zeinab Cultural Park....**5** B2			

To Midan Tahrir (1km)

See Al-Azhar to the Citadel Map (p116)

To Bab Zuweila (750m)

See The Citadel Map (p119)

Midan Salah ad-Din

Citadel

To Southern Cemetery (500m)

1356 and 1363 by the troubled Sultan Hassan, who took the throne at the age of 13, was deposed and reinstated no less than three times and was assassinated shortly before the mosque was completed. Tragedy also shadowed the construction when one of the minarets collapsed, killing 300 or so onlookers. In later years the mosque was substantially damaged by warring Mamluk factions and was shelled when Napoleon attempted to subdue an uprising against French occupation. What survives is still impressive. Beyond the striking, recessed entrance, a dark passage leads through into a square courtyard whose soaring walls are punctured by four arched recesses, known as *iwans*. In these *iwans* the four main schools of Sunni Islam were taught. At the rear of the eastern *iwan* is an especially beautiful *mihrab*, flanked by stolen Crusader columns. To the right, a bronze door leads to the sultan's mausoleum.

Opposite the grand mosque, constructed on a similarly monumental scale, is the mock-Mamluk **Mosque of Ar-Rifai** (Map p121). Construction began in 1867 and finished in 1912. Members of modern Egypt's royal family, including Khedive Ismail and King Farouk, are buried inside, as is the last shah of Iran. The tombs of the royals lie to the left of the entrance (*baksheesh* required).

Mosque of Ibn Tulun

Walking west along busy Sharia as-Saliba you'll come to the wonderful **Mosque of Ibn Tulun** (Map p121; Sharia ibn Tulun; ☾ 8am-6pm), built between AD 876 and 879 by Ibn Tulun, who was sent to rule Cairo in the 9th century by the Abbasid caliph of Baghdad. The city's oldest intact, functioning Islamic monument, it's also one of its most beautiful. True to his origins, Ibn Tulun drew inspiration from his homeland, particularly the ancient Mosque of Samarra (Iraq). Ibn Tulun also added some innovations of his own; according to architectural historians, this is the first structure to use the pointed arch – a good 200 years before the European Gothic arch. Constructed entirely of mud brick and timber, the mosque covers 2.5 hectares in area, large enough for the whole community to assemble for Friday prayers.

After wandering around the massive courtyard you can climb the spiral minaret. This is reached from the outer, moat-like courtyard, originally created to keep the secular city at a distance, but at one time filled with shops and stalls. The mosque's grandeur and geometric simplicity are best appreciated from the top of the minaret, which also has magnificent views of the Citadel and across Cairo.

Gayer-Anderson Museum

Reached through a gateway to the south of the main entrance of the mosque, this quirky **museum** (Beit al-Kritliyya, the House of the Cretan Woman; ☎ 364 7822; www.gawp.org; Sharia ibn Tulun; adult/student E£30/15, video E£20; ☾ 8am-4pm Sat-Thu, 8am-noon & 1-4pm Fri) gets its current name from

CAIRO

a British major, John Gayer-Anderson, an army doctor who restored and furnished the two adjoining 16th-century houses between 1935 and 1942, filling them with antiquities, artworks and Oriental artefacts acquired on his travels in the region. The houses and their contents were bequeathed by Gayer-Anderson to Egypt (he died in 1945) and have been lovingly restored by a British mission. The puzzle of rooms is decorated in a variety of styles: the Persian room has exquisite tiling, the Damascus room has lacquer and gold, and the Queen Ann Room has ornate furniture and a silver tea set. The enchanting *mashrabiyya* gallery looks down onto a magnificent *qa'a* which has a central marble fountain, decorated ceiling beams and carpet-covered alcoves. The rooftop terrace has been lovingly restored and features a visually arresting display of *mashrabiyya* screens. When you enter, you may find the houses familiar – the museum was used as a location in the James Bond film *The Spy Who Loved Me*.

Across the street, the **Khan Misr Touloun** (see p159) is a good handicrafts emporium. The area is filled with many smaller monuments, including the **Madrassa of Sunqur Sa'adi** (Map p121). Here, behind a green door (with an Italian Institute sign), the beautifully restored, circular, wooden **Mevlevi Theatre** (Map p121) was formerly used by whirling dervishes.

NORTHERN CEMETERY

The Northern Cemetery (Map p122) is the more interesting half of a vast necropolis known popularly as the City of the Dead. The lurid, arcade-game name refers to the fact that the cemeteries are not only resting places for Cairo's dead, but for the living too. Some estimates put the number of living Cairenes here at 50,000; others at 10 times this number. As Max Rodenbeck notes in *Cairo: the City Victorious*, some of the tomb dwellers, especially the paid guardians and their families, have lived here for generations. Others, forced by low income into the bleak shanty suburbs on the outskirts of the city and wanting to come back to the city centre, have moved in more recently. Visitors keen on viewing the cemetery's splendid funerary architecture and mosques can feel uncomfortable walking here because of the quasi-residential and

clearly poverty-stricken atmosphere; provided you behave respectfully, dress appropriately, don't flaunt costly jewellery or electronic devices and leave before nightfall you will be OK. For additional security, women may want to wear a headscarf. On Fridays and public holidays visitors flock here to picnic and pay their respects to the

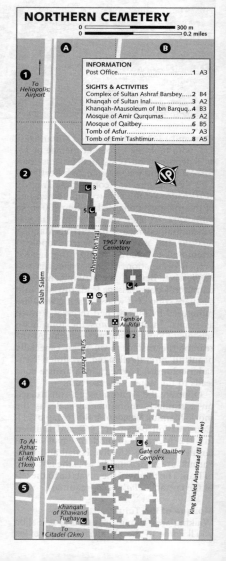

NORTHERN CEMETERY

INFORMATION	
Post Office	1 A3

SIGHTS & ACTIVITIES	
Complex of Sultan Ashraf Barsbey	2 B4
Khanqah of Sultan Inal	3 A2
Khanqah-Mausoleum of Ibn Barquq	4 B3
Mosque of Amir Qurqumas	5 A2
Mosque of Qaitbey	6 B5
Tomb of Asfur	7 A3
Tomb of Emir Tashtimur	8 A5

dead – this is undoubtedly the best time to visit.

The cemetery began as an area of desert outside the city walls that offered Mamluk sultans and emirs the sort of building space that was unavailable inside the densely packed city. The vast mausoleum complexes they built were more than just tombs, they were also meant as places for entertaining. This is part of an Egyptian tradition that has its roots in Pharaonic times, when people would picnic among the graves. Even the humblest of family tombs were designed to include a room where visitors could stay overnight. The dead hoped they would be remembered; the city's homeless saw their tombs as free accommodation. This was happening as far back as the 14th century, leading to the situation today where the living and dead coexist. In some tomb-houses, cenotaphs serve as tables and washing is strung between headstones. The municipality has installed water, gas and electricity and there's a local police station and even a post office. Despite this, there's a push to move these tomb dwellers out – with the authorities yet to be able to provide a solution as to where they will be relocated.

The easiest way to reach the Northern Cemetery is to walk east from Al-Hussein along Sharia al-Azhar. As you break the top of the hill, bear right, under the overpass and straight on along the dusty road between the tombs. Follow this road to the left then right. You'll pass by the large, crumbling, domed **Tomb of Emir Tashtimur** (Map p122) on your left. About 100m further on, a narrow lane goes off to the left passing under a stone archway. This archway is the gate to the former compound of Qaitbey, whose splendid mosque is immediately ahead.

Mosque of Qaitbey

Sultan Qaitbey, a prolific builder, was the last Mamluk leader with any real power in Egypt. He ruled for 28 years and, though he was as ruthless as any Mamluk sultan, he was also something of an aesthete. His **mosque** (Map p122), completed in 1474 and depicted on the E£1 note, is widely agreed to mark the pinnacle of Islamic building in Cairo. The façade has bold stripes and the interior has four iwans around a central court lit by large, lattice-screened windows. Featuring loads of marble, it's one

of the most pleasant places in Cairo to sit for a while and relax. The adjacent tomb chamber contains the cenotaphs of Qaitbey and his two sisters, as well as two stones that supposedly bear the footprints of the Prophet. The true glory, however, is above, where the dome was carved with interlaced star and floral designs; its intricacy and delicacy were never surpassed in Cairo or anywhere else in the Islamic world – climb the minaret for the best view.

Other Monuments

From Qaitbey cross the square and continue north. The cemetery has a villagelike feel with small shops, cafés and street sellers, and sandy paths pecked by chickens and nosed around by goats. After about 250m the street widens and on the right a stone wall encloses a large area of rubble-strewn ground that was formerly the **Complex of Sultan Ashraf Barsbey** (Map p122). Though not as sophisticated as the one topping the Mosque of Qaitbey, the dome here is carved with a beautiful star pattern. Inside there is some fine marble flooring and a beautiful minbar (pulpit) inlaid with ivory. The guard will let you in for baksheesh (ask the ever-present children if he's not around).

Two hundred metres further north is the **Khanqah-Mausoleum of Ibn Barquq** (Map p122). Ibn means 'son of', and this is the mausoleum of Farag, son of Barquq, whose great madrassa and mausoleum stand on Bein al-Qasreen (see p115). Completed in 1411 the khanqah (Sufi monastery) is an imposing fortresslike building with high, sheer façades and twin minarets and domes. In the courtyard, small monastic cells lead off the arcades. There's a tomb chamber under each dome, one for women, one for men, both have beautiful painted ceilings and look great. It's also possible to get up onto the roof and climb the minarets.

Northern Cemetery to Al-Hussein

Two large adjacent complexes are northwest of the Khanqah-Mausoleum of Ibn Barquq: the 1507 **Mosque of Amir Qurqumas** (Map p122) and the 1456 **Khanqah of Sultan Inal** (Map p122). Both have been the subject of extensive restoration work by a Polish team, but neither is open to the public just yet.

Rather than just retracing your steps from Ibn Barquq, walk straight ahead from the

CAIRO

entrance, passing the post office on your left, until you come to a small, elongated mausoleum, the **Tomb of Asfur** (Map p122); turn left immediately after this and a straight walk of 1km down Sharia Sultan Ahmed will bring you back to the road leading to the underpass.

Zamalek & Gezira

Uninhabited until the mid-19th century, Gezira (Arabic for 'island') was a narrow strip of alluvial land rising up out of the Nile. Following the creation of the modern-day Downtown on the river's east bank, Khedive Ismail had a great palace built on the island and had much of it landscaped as a vast royal garden. During the land-development boom of the early 20th century, the palace grounds were sold off and built upon, while the palace was converted into a hotel (now incorporated into the Cairo Marriott).

The island today is divided into the southern part of Gezira, largely green and leafy, and the northern, upmarket residential district of Zamalek.

ZAMALEK

Occupying the northern part of the island, Zamalek (Map pp126–7) is an attractive residential district with a Continental tinge. It has few tourist sites but it's a pleasant place to wander around and an even better place to eat, drink and shop.

The main street, Sharia 26th of July, cuts from east to west across the island. The junction of Sharia Hassan Sabry and Sharia Brazil is the focal point of the area. There's good shopping around here and two of the city's best newsstands are located at the crossroads. Just a couple of doors east of Hassan Sabry on Sharia 26th of July is **Simonds** (see p154), one of the city's oldest European-style cafés.

Further east along Sharia 26th of July, towards the bridge to Bulaq, are the excellent bookshop **Diwan** (p93) and café **Cilantro** (p153). A few doors down from Cilantro is the **Centre of Arts** (see p137), housed in a European-style villa built in the early 20th century by an aristocratic Egyptian family. There are usually several different exhibitions on here, so it's worth dropping in.

Immediately south of Sharia 26th of July, overlooking the Nile, is the salmon-pink

Cairo Marriott (see p146). It has a good bakery (see p153), some good restaurants (see p152) and an attractive garden where you can enjoy a coffee, beer or glass of wine. Behind the Marriott, a beautiful neo-Islamic villa dating from the 1920s houses the **Gezira Centre of Arts** (Map pp126–7; ☎ 737 3298; 1 Sharia Sheikh al-Marsafy, Zamalek; adult/student E£25/12; ☒ 10am-1.30pm & 5.30-9pm Sat-Thu). Besides the permanent exhibition of Islamic ceramics, several galleries host temporary exhibitions of art. There's also an attractive sculpture garden here.

GEZIRA

Gezira (Map p130) is best approached across Qasr el-Nil Bridge from Midan Tahrir. This brings you to **Midan Saad Zaghloul**, presided over by the statue of a tarbooshed Saad Zaghloul, a nationalist leader of the 1930s. North of the *midan* on the banks of the Nile you'll find two well-maintained and magnificently planted **formal gardens** (Map p130; admission E£10), both of which have outdoor cafés where local families and young couples partake of tea and *sheesha*. Below the gardens is a popular **pedestrian corniche** (admission E£2) that is one of the most popular open spaces in the whole of Cairo.

Immediately west of Midan Saad Zaghloul are the well-groomed **Gezira Exhibition Grounds** (Map p130), dominated by the **Cairo Opera House** (☎ information 739 8144; www.operahouse.gov.eg). Built in 1988, the building is a modern take on traditional Islamic design and was a gift from the Japanese. See p157 for details of performances.

Across from the opera house, the **Museum of Modern Egyptian Art** (Map p130; ☎ 736 6665; www.modernartmuseum.gov.eg; admission free; ☒ 10am-1pm & 5-9pm Tue-Sun) houses an impressive collection of 20th- and 21st-century Egyptian art, including Mahmoud Said's masterpiece *Al Madina* (*The City*, 1937). The ground floor is home to the museum's high-profile 'Art Today' exhibition, which showcases works by 95 artists produced from 1975 to the present day. Look out for Mahmoud Mokhtar's bronze statue *Bride of the Nile*, and Ragheb Ayyad's wonderful canvas *Dating* (1978). The museum reopened in March 2005 after a long renovation, and at the time of research it hadn't confirmed its opening hours and whether an admission charge would be introduced. It has a pleasant café and a gift shop selling an excellent array of postcards and posters.

Two other galleries in the grounds at the rear of the Cairo Opera House host temporary art exhibitions and occasional performances: the **Hanager Arts Centre** (Map p130; ☎ 735 6861; 🕒 10am-10pm Tue-Sun), and the **Palace of Arts** (Map p130; ☎ 737 0603, 736 7627; www.fineart.gov.eg; 🕒 10am-1.30pm & 5.30-10pm Sat-Thu).

If you're leaving the Gezira Exhibition Grounds from the rear entrance near the Galaa Bridge, you will see a modest gate across the road, which leads to the **Mahmoud Mokhtar Museum** (Map p130; ☎ 735 2519; 🕒 10am-1pm & 5-9pm Tue-Thu & Sat-Sun, 9am-noon Fri). Mahmoud Mokhtar (1891–1934) was the sculptor laureate of independent Egypt; he was responsible for Saad Zaghloul on the nearby *midan* and for the *Mother of Egypt* statue outside the entrance to the Giza Zoo. The gallery building was designed by Egyptian architect Ramses Wissa Wassef (1911–1974).

North of the Cairo Opera House and south of the Al-Zuhreya Gardens is the **Cairo Tower** (Burg Misr; Map p130; ☎ 735 7187; Sharia Hadayek al-Zuhreya; admission E£50, children under 6 free, video E£20; 🕒 8am-midnight). Completed in 1961 and resembling a 185m-high wickerwork tube, the tower was apparently built as a thumb to the nose at the Americans, who had given Nasser the money used for its construction to buy US arms. After the Pyramids the tower is the city's most famous landmark. The 360-degree views from the top are excellent; clearest in the early morning or late afternoon. There's an expensive revolving restaurant on top serving dodgy-looking food (lunch or dinner plus entrance E£95), as well as a cheaper cafeteria. You might be greeted with quite a long queue at dusk.

Mohandiseen, Agouza & Doqqi

A map of Cairo in Baedecker's 1929 guide to Egypt shows nothing on the Nile's west bank other than a hospital and the road to the Pyramids. The hospital is still there, set back from the Corniche in Agouza, but it's now hemmed in on all sides by mid-rise buildings that shot up during the 1960s and 1970s when Mohandiseen, Agouza and Doqqi were created to house Egypt's emerging professional classes. The three districts remain middle-class bastions, home largely to families who made good during the years of Sadat's open-door policy. Unless you happen to find concrete and traffic stimulating, the main attractions here are some good restaurants (see p151).

What little history there is here floats on the river in the form of the **houseboats** moored off Sharia el-Nil just north of Zamalek Bridge in Agouza (Map pp126–7). Known as *dahabiyya*s, these floating two-storey wooden structures once lined the Nile all the way from Giza to Imbaba. During the 1930s they were something of a tourist attraction and some boats were converted into casinos, music halls and bordellos. Many of the survivors continue to be rented out.

AGRICULTURAL MUSEUM

It may sound dull, but the **Agricultural Museum** (Map p130; ☎ 761 6785; Sharia Wizaret al-Ziraa, Doqqi; admission 10pt; 🕒 9am-1pm Tue-Sun) is quite fascinating and verges on the bizarre. The displays tell you all you've ever wanted to know about agriculture in Egypt, from Pharaonic times onwards, and range from Roman loaves and giant plastic fruits to glass cases packed with stuffed birds and a Pharaonic-era mummified bull from Memphis. The easiest way to get here is to catch the metro to Doqqi station.

MR & MRS MAHMOUD KHALIL MUSEUM

Mohammed Mahmoud Khalil was a noted politician during the 1940s, but his legacy to the arts is more long lasting, for he amassed one of the Middle East's finest collections of 19th- and 20th-century European art. The wonderful **Mr & Mrs Mahmoud Khalil Museum** (Map p130; ☎ 338 9720; www.mkm.gov.eg; 1 Sharia Kafour, Doqqi; admission with ID card or passport only, adult/student E£25/12; 🕒 10am-5.30pm Tue-Sun, 10am-3pm holidays) includes sculptures by Rodin and a rich selection of French works by the likes of Delacroix, Gauguin, Toulouse-Lautrec, Manet, Monet and Pissarro. There are also some Rubens, Sisleys and a Picasso. The paintings are housed in a temperature-controlled villa, the former home of Khalil, which was later taken over by President Sadat. It's just a few minutes' walk south of the Cairo Sheraton.

CAIRO

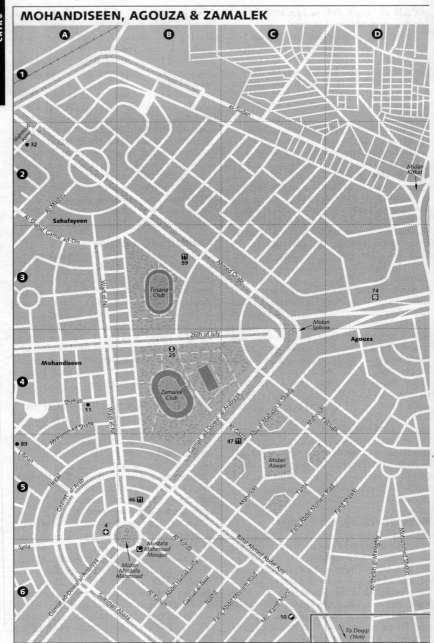

MOHANDISEEN, AGOUZA & ZAMALEK

as-Sudan

Midan Kitkat

Mahmoud Azmy

● 32

Al-Mahni

Al-Shahid Gamal ad-Din

Sahafayeen

Wadi el-Nil

Tirsana Club

Ahmed Orabi

59

74

Midan Sphinx

Agouza

26th of July

25

Mohandiseen

Zamalek Club

Shehab

11

Mohammed Shafik

Gamal ad-Dowal al-Arabiya

Al-Gazira

Abu al-Mahasin al-Shazly

Mahrouki

Falouza

47

Midan Aswan

● 89

Libnan

Gezirret al-Arab

Hegaz

46

Mahrouki

Tana

Farid Abdel Moniem Riad

Farid Shawki

Syria

4

Mustafa Mahmoud Mosque

Al-Ashab

Batal Ahmed Abdel Aziz

Al-Sheikh al-Mararghi

Mohammed Shahin

Midan Mustafa Mahmoud

Gamal ad-Dowal al-Arabiya

Suleiman Abaza

Al-Kurum

Abdel Hamid Loffy

Gamal al-Nasr

Nakhil

Farid Abdel Moniem Riad

Mo. Kamil Mursi

10

To Doqqi (1km)

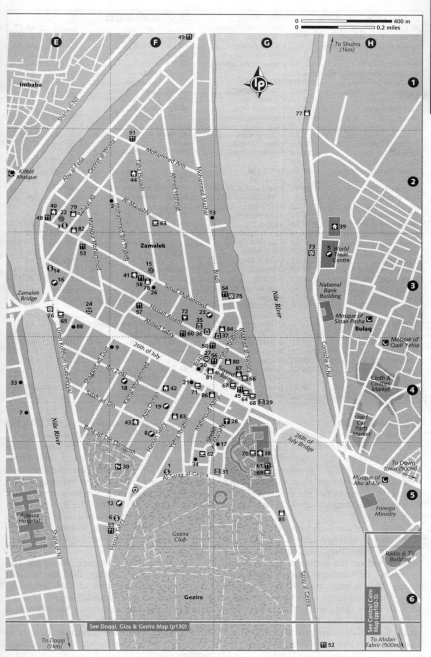

Pyramids Of Giza

The sole survivor of the Seven Wonders of the World, the Pyramids of Giza still live up to more than 4000 years of hype. Their extraordinary shape, geometry and age render them somehow alien constructions; they seem to rise out of the desert and pose the ever-fascinating question, 'How were we built, and why?'.

Centuries of research have given us parts of the answer to this double-barrelled question. We know they were massive tombs constructed on the orders of the pharaohs by teams of workers tens-of-thousands strong. This is supported by the discovery of a pyramid-builders' settlement, complete with areas for large-scale food production and medical facilities. Ongoing excavations on the Giza Plateau are providing more and more evidence that the workers were not the

slaves of Hollywood tradition, but a highly organised workforce of Egyptian farmers. During the season of the inundation, when the annual Nile flood covered their fields and made farm work impossible, the same farmers could have been redeployed by the highly structured bureaucracy to work on the pharaoh's tomb. The Pyramids can almost be seen as an ancient job-creation scheme, with the flood waters also making it easier to transport building stone to the site.

Despite all the evidence, there are still those who won't accept that the ancient Egyptians were capable of such astonishing achievements. Pyramidologists – for the study of the vast structures has become a 'science' in its own right – point to the carving and placement of the stones, precise to the millimetre, and argue the cosmological significance of the structures' dimensions as evidence that the Pyramids were variously constructed by angels, the devil or visitors from another planet. It's easy to laugh at such seemingly out-there ideas, but visit the Giza Plateau and you'll immediately see why so many people believe such awesome structures could only have unearthly origins.

THE PYRAMIDS AS FUNERARY COMPLEX

It was neither an obsession with death, nor a fear of it, that led the ancient Egyptians to build such incredible mausoleums as the pyramids. Rather it was their belief in eternal life and their desire to be at one with the cosmos. The pharaoh was the son of the gods and also their intermediary. His role was to conduct the gods' powers to his people. Set between the earth and the sky to connect the worlds mortal and divine, he was therefore honoured in life and worshipped in death. The pyramid was a fitting tomb for such an individual. A funerary temple attached to each pyramid allowed the pharaoh to be worshipped long after

his death, with daily rounds of offerings to sustain his soul. A long covered causeway connected the funerary temple to a 'valley temple' built on the quayside where the annual flood waters would reach each season (there's a superb model of the Abu Sir pyramids illustrating all this on the 1st floor of the Egyptian Museum). The whole complex also provided a constant visible reminder of the eternal power of the gods and at the same time the absolute power of the pharaoh for whom it was built.

PRACTICALITIES

It can be a bit of a shock to visit the **Giza Plateau** (Map p129; adult/student E£60/30; ☼ 7am-7.30pm) and realise that the sandy mound that's home to the pyramids is actually plonked in the middle of the congested city suburb of Giza. There are currently two entrances: the main entrance is via a continuation of Pyramids Rd (Sharia al-Haram) at the foot of the Great Pyramid of Khufu and the secondary entrance is via the village of Nazlet as-Samaan, below the Sphinx. Most independent visitors enter from Sharia

THE GIZA PLATEAU

0   0.5 km
0   0.3 miles

INFORMATION
Giza Tourist Office...................1 C1

SIGHTS & ACTIVITIES
Eastern Cemetery.......................2 C2
Great Pyramid of Khufu (Cheops)..3 C2
Khafre's Funerary Temple............4 C3
Khafre's Valley Temple................5 D3
Mena House Golf Course.............6 C1
Menkaure's Funerary Temple.......7 B3
Menkaure's Valley Temple...........8 C3
Pyramid of Khafre (Chephren)....9 B3
Pyramid of Menkaure
  (Mycerinus).........................10 B3
Pyramid of Queen Hetepheres...11 C2
Queens' Pyramids....................12 C2
Queens' Pyramids....................13 B3
Solar Barque Museum...............14 C2
Solar Barque Pits.....................15 C2
Sound-&-Light Auditorium.........16 D3
Sound-&-Light Ticket Office.......17 D3
Sphinx..................................18 C3
Stables..................................19 C1
Ticket Box for Great Pyramid.....20 C2
Ticket Box for Pyramids of Khafre
  & Menkaure..........................21 B2
Ticket Office...........................22 C1
Ticket Office...........................23 D3
Tomb of Khentkawes................24 C3
Tomb of Seshemnufer IV...........25 C2
Western Cemetery....................26 B2

SLEEPING 🏠
Oberoi Mena House..................27 C1

To Peace II;
Felfela (300m)

Mena
House
Oberoi

Pyramids Rd (Al-Haram)

Desert Highway
to Alexandria
(215km)

To Andrea's (1.2km);
Kerdassa (4km);
Midan Giza (9km);
Central Cairo (12km)

EATING 🍴
Khan El-Khalili ....(see 27)
Moghul Room.................(see 27)

DRINKING 🍸
Coffee Shop.........................28 D3

TRANSPORT
355/357 Bus Stop.................29 C1

↓ Entry

Causeway

Nazlet
as-Samaan

To Abu Sir,
Kerdassa,
Saqqara Rd
(5km)

↓ Entry

Causeway

Causeway

Coach
Park

To Horse
Stables

CAIRO

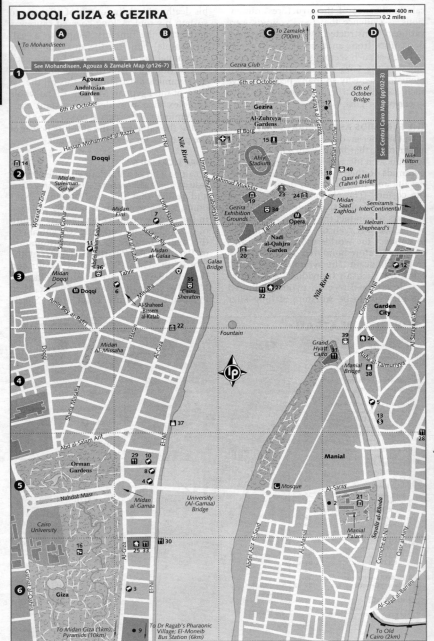

DOQQI, GIZA & GEZIRA

INFORMATION		Manial Palace Museum	21 D5	Spice	(see 26)
Anglo-American Hospital	1 C2	Mr & Mrs Mahmoud Khalil		TGI Friday's	(see 30)
Egyptian Student Travel Servises	2 D5	Museum	22 B3		
French Embassy	3 B6	Museum of Modern Egyptian		DRINKING	
Israeli Embassy	4 B5	Art	23 C2	Revolving Restaurant Lounge	(see 31)
Italian Embassy	5 D4	Palace of Arts	24 C2		
Jordanian Embassy	6 B3			ENTERTAINMENT	
Kenyan Embassy	7 B2	SLEEPING		Cairo Opera House	34 C2
Lebanese Embassy	8 B5	Four Seasons at the First		Cairo Sheraton Cinema	35 B3
Nile Tower Building	9 B6	Residence	25 B6	Casablanca Club	(see 35)
Saudi Arabian Embassy	10 B5	Four Seasons Nile Plaza	26 D4	Cinema Tahrir	36 A3
Syrian Embassy	11 A3	Sofitel El Gezirah	27 C3	Good News Grand Hyatt	(see 31)
UK Embassy	12 D3				
Western Union	13 D4	EATING		SHOPPING	
		Abou Shakra	28 D5	Dr Ragab's Papyrus Institute	37 B4
SIGHTS & ACTIVITIES		Aqua	(see 26)	First Residence Mall	(see 33)
Agricultural Museum	14 A2	El-Mashrabia	29 B5	Nagada	38 D4
Cairo Tower	15 C2	Fish Market	30 B6	Nomad	(see 31)
Cairo Zoo	16 A6	Hard Rock Café	31 D4		
Formal Garden	17 D1	Kebabgy	32 C3	TRANSPORT	
Formal Garden	18 D2	La Gourmandise	33 B6	Dok Dok Felucca Point	39 D4
Hanager Arts Centre	19 C2	Revolving Restaurant	(see 31)	EgyptAir	(see 35)
Mahmoud Mokhtar Museum	20 C3	Seasons Restaurant	(see 25)	Felucca Mooring Point	40 D2

al-Haram, and this is where the bus and minibus from Downtown stop. Follow the road up from the roundabout towards the pyramids and firmly ignore anyone who tries to distract you from going that way (see below). Continue along the tarmacked road, climbing up to the temporary ticket office (a hut) to your right. Work is currently underway to fence the plateau, and when this is completed there will only be one entrance, via a new visitors centre on the Cairo–Al-Fayoum road. No officials are willing to confirm when this visitors centre will open (this *is* Egypt, after all).

There are extra entry charges for each of the three pyramids and the solar barque. Before visiting, you may want to look at www .guardians.net/hawass, the official website of Dr Zahi Hawass, secretary general of the Supreme Council of Antiquities and director of the Giza Pyramids Excavation.

Note that climbing the Pyramids, a must for European visitors in the 19th and 20th centuries, is dangerous and is now strictly forbidden.

THE HASSLE
Since the time of Mark Twain (who visited in 1866), and even before, tourists at the Pyramids have 'suffered torture that no pen can describe from the hungry appeals for baksheesh that gleamed from Arab eyes'. As writer Tony Horwitz comments in *Baghdad Without a Map*, it's difficult to gaze in awe at these ancient wonders with modern

Egypt tugging so persistently at your sleeve. Zahi Hawass has been working hard to keep the plateau clear of touts, camel drivers and other hustlers, and the good news is that, with the help of the police, he seems to be succeeding.

Nowadays most of the hassle happens before you arrive and after visiting the plateau. If you come by taxi or minibus, 'friendly' young men hanging around on Pyramids Rd might try to convince your driver in Arabic to bring you to their shop or stable in Nazlet as-Samaan. They might also tell you not to go straight along the road, as described above, or suggest that they can get you into the Pyramids area without a ticket. Ignore everyone until you get to the ticket office.

CAMELS & HORSES
In the past the area in front of the Pyramids resembled a chaotic, smelly paddock full of milling horses and camels, whose owners had a fine old time reeling in the tourists. The authorities, under the Giza Plateau Conservation Project, have moved most animals away from the monuments. A sign next to the ticket office announces the official prices for riding a donkey (E£10 per hour), a camel (E£25 per hour), a horse (E£25 per hour) or a horse cart (E£30 per hour). This said, away from the eyes of the tourist police things do still happen: you may still be asked to pay a ridiculous amount; you may be forced off

your mount some way from the agreed place; and women may find the camel- or horse-owner trying to climb up behind them. Do not allow this to happen. At the first sign of trouble, insist on talking to the tourist police (located near the tourist office), who will settle the matter.

If you want to ride, hiring a horse from one of the stables is a far better option than taking one at the Pyramids. Once you're mounted, you will be off on your own in the desert with the Pyramids as a background. The best stables in Nazlet as-Samaan, the village near the Sphinx, are **MG** (☎ 358 3832) and **AA** (☎ 385 0531), near the coach park. Both stables look after their horses; if they know that you're an experienced rider you might get a better mount. Expect to pay around E£25 per hour and keep your Pyramids site ticket or you'll be charged E£20 to enter the desert. While you used to be able to take a horse out at any time day or night – moonlight rides around the Pyramids were a big favourite with the city's expat community – under new regulations, riding in the area is only permitted between 6am and sunset.

GREAT PYRAMID OF KHUFU (CHEOPS)
The oldest pyramid in Giza and the largest in Egypt, the **Great Pyramid of Khufu** (Map p129; adult/student E£150/75) stood 146m high when it was completed in around 2570 BC. After 46 centuries its height has been reduced by 9m. About 2.3 million limestone blocks, reckoned to weigh on average about 2.5 tonnes each, were used in the construction.

Note that only Egyptian pounds are accepted at the ticket office. The extortionately priced tickets are limited to 300 per day – 150 in the morning and 150 in the afternoon. These go on sale at 8am and 1pm at the dedicated ticket box in front and slightly to the east (city side) of the pyramid and you'll need to queue ahead of time, especially on Wednesdays and Thursdays, when tour groups from the Red Sea visit Cairo for the day and block book tickets. Cameras are not allowed into the pyramid – you must surrender them to the guards at the entrance, who will ask for *baksheesh* before returning them – E£1 will be sufficient.

Although there is not much to see inside the pyramid, the experience of climbing

through the ancient structure is unforgettable, though completely impossible if you suffer even the tiniest degree of claustrophobia. The elderly and unfit should not attempt the climb, as it is very steep.

The entrance, on the north face, leads to a descending passage that ends in an unfinished tomb (usually closed) about 100m along and 30m below the pyramid. Before this, about 20m from the entrance, there is an ascending passage, 1.3m high and 1m wide. After some 40m, this opens into the Great Gallery, an impressive area 47m long and 8.5m high. There is also a smaller horizontal passage leading into the so-called Queen's Chamber.

As you ascend the Great Gallery to the King's Chamber, notice how precisely its blocks were fitted together at the top. The walls of the main tomb chamber, just over 5m wide and 10m long, were built of red granite blocks. The roof consists of nine huge slabs of granite, which weigh more than 400 tonnes. Above these, four more slabs are separated by gaps designed to distribute the enormous weight away from the chamber. There is good ventilation here, as the chamber was designed so that fresh air would flow in from twin shafts in the north and south walls.

Climbing the outside of the Great Pyramid was, for centuries, a popular adventure despite the fact that every year a few people fell to their death. Scaling the pyramid is now forbidden.

On the eastern side of the pyramid, three small structures some 20m high resemble pyramid-shaped piles of rubble. These are the Queens' Pyramids, the tombs of Khufu's wives and sisters.

SOLAR BARQUE MUSEUM
South of the Great Pyramid is the fascinating **Solar Barque Museum** (Map p129; adult/student E£35/20; ☺ 9am-4pm Oct-May, 9am-5pm Jun-Sep). Five long pits near the Great Pyramid of Khufu once contained the pharaoh's solar barques (boats), which may have been used to bring the mummy of the dead pharaoh across the Nile to the valley temple, from where it was brought up the causeway and into the tomb chamber. The barques were then buried around the pyramid to provide transport for the pharaoh in the next world.

One of these ancient cedar-wood vessels, possibly the oldest boat in existence, was unearthed in 1954. It was carefully restored from 1200 pieces of wood and encased in a glass museum to protect it from damage from the elements. Visitors to the museum

---

WHAT THEY SAID ABOUT THE PYRAMIDS

We will also mention the Pyramids…that idle and foolish exhibition of royal wealth. For the cause by most assigned for their construction is an intention on the part of those kings to exhaust their treasures, rather than leave them to successors or plotting rivals, or to keep the people from idleness.

Pliny the Elder, c AD 50

Soldiers, forty centuries of history look down upon you from these Pyramids.

Napoleon, readying his forces for battle at Giza, 1798

Khafre's Pyramid seems to me inordinately huge and completely sheer; it's like a cliff, like a thing of nature, a mountain – as though it had been created just as it is, and with something terrible about it as if it were going to crush you.

Gustave Flaubert, 1849

The Pyramids looked as if they would wear out the air, boring holes in it all day long.

Florence Nightingale, 1850

The Pyramids were a quarter of a mile away; it felt odd to be living at such close quarters with anything quite so famous – it was like having the Prince of Wales at the next table in a restaurant; one kept pretending not to notice, while all the time glancing furtively to see if they were still there.

Evelyn Waugh at the Mena House Hotel, 1929

I discovered that the marvels of the Pyramids at Gizeh and the Sphinx had been degraded into commodities for an enormous tourist trade.

Cecil Beaton, 1942

Very big. Very old.

camel owner, 1999

---

must help this process by donning protective footwear to keep sand out.

There are plans to move the boat to the nearby Great Museum of Egypt when it opens some time after 2009.

PYRAMID OF KHAFRE (CHEPHREN)

Southwest of the Great Pyramid, the **Pyramid of Khafre** (Map p129; adult/student E£30/15) seems larger than that of his father, Khufu. At 136m high, it's not, but appears that way because it stands on higher ground and its peak is still capped with a limestone casing. Originally all three pyramids were totally encased with a polished white limestone casing. They would have gleamed like giant crystals. Over the centuries, this limestone has been stripped away and used to build palaces and mosques, exposing the softer inner-core stones to the elements.

The chambers and passageways of this particular pyramid are less elaborate than those in the Great Pyramid, but are almost as claustrophobic. The entrance descends into a passage and then across to the burial chamber, which still contains Khafre's large granite sarcophagus. Tickets are obtained from the ticket office in front of the pyramid.

Back outside, to the east of the pyramid, are the substantial remains of **Khafre's funerary temple** and the flagged flooring of the causeway that provided access from the Nile to the tomb.

PYRAMID OF MENKAURE (MYCERINUS)

At 62m (originally 66.5m), the **Pyramid of Menkaure** (Map p129; adult/student E£25/15) is the smallest of the great trio. A deep gash in the north face is the result of an attempt by Saladin's son Malek Abdel Aziz to dismantle the pyramid in AD 1186. He gave up after eight months having achieved little. Inside, a hall descends from the entrance into a passageway, which in turn leads into a small chamber and a group of rooms. There is nothing noteworthy about the interior, but at the very least you can have the thrill of exploring a seldom-visited site. Tickets are obtained from the ticket office in front of the Pyramid of Khafre.

Outside the pyramid you'll see the excavated remains of **Menkaure's funerary temple** and, further east, the ruins of his **valley temple** still lying beneath the sand.

THE SPHINX

Legends and superstitions abound about the **Sphinx** (Map p129), and the mystery surrounding its long-forgotten purpose is almost as intriguing as its appearance. On seeing it for the first time, many visitors agree with the sentiments of English playwright Alan Bennett, who noted in his diary that seeing the Sphinx is like meeting a TV personality in the flesh – always smaller than had been imagined.

Known in Arabic as Abu al-Hol (Father of Terror), the feline man was called the Sphinx by the ancient Greeks because it resembled the mythical winged monster with a woman's head and lion's body who set riddles and killed anyone unable to answer them.

The Sphinx was carved from the natural bedrock at the bottom of the causeway to the Pyramid of Khafre; a recent geological and archaeological survey has shown that it was most likely carved during this particular pharaoh's reign and it probably portrays his features, framed by the striped *nemes* headcloth only worn by royal personages.

As is clear from the accounts of early Arab travellers, the nose was hammered off sometime between the 11th and 15th centuries, although some still like to blame Napoleon for the deed. Part of the fallen beard was carted off by 19th-century adventurers and is now on display in the British Museum in London.

These days the Sphinx has problems that are potentially greater than its ordnance-inflicted injuries. The monument is suffering the stone equivalent of cancer and is being eaten away from the inside. Experts don't know the exact cause, but pollution and rising ground water are the likeliest diagnoses. A succession of restoration attempts were made throughout the 20th century, several of which unfortunately sped up the decay rather than halting it. The Sphinx's shiny white paws are the result of the most recent effort.

Just below the Sphinx there's an expensive **café** (tea E£10, fresh juice E£15), which boasts an outdoor terrace and truly amazing view. It's just outside the site, but as long as you have your ticket, the guards will let you leave and come back in again after your break.

TOMB OF KHENTKAWES

This rarely visited but imposing structure (Map p129), opposite the Great Pyramid and south of Khafre's causeway, is the tomb of Menkaure's powerful daughter. The tomb is a rectangular building cut into a small hill. A corridor at the back of the chapel room leads down to the burial chambers, but the descent can be hazardous.

CEMETERIES

Private cemeteries with several rows of tombs are organised around the Pyramids in a grid pattern. Most tombs are closed to the public, but those of Qar, Idu and Queen Meresankh III, in the **eastern cemetery** (Map p129), are accessible, although it's sometimes difficult to find the guard who has the keys.

The Tomb of Iasen, in the **western cemetery** (Map p129), contains interesting inscriptions and wall paintings that offer a glimpse of daily life during the Old Kingdom. The recently opened **tomb of Seshemnufer IV** (Map p129), just south of the Great Pyramid, has vivid hunting scenes on the wall.

SOUND-&-LIGHT SHOW

The Sphinx narrates this show, which is a little cheesy, though worth attending to see the Pyramids by starlight. Every night there are two or three **sound-and-light shows** (☎ 386 3469; www.sound-light.egypt.com; adult/child 7-12 years E£60/30; ✆ 6.30pm, 7.30pm & 8.30pm winter, 8.30pm, 9.30pm & 10.30pm summer). Though there's officially no student discount, you may be able to negotiate one. Schedules were as follows at the time of writing, but you can see the website for the latest details:

Day	Show 1	Show 2	Show 3
Monday	English	French	Spanish
Tuesday	English	Italian	French
Wednesday	English	French	German
Thursday	Japanese	English	Arabic
Friday	English	French	
Saturday	English	Spanish	Italian
Sunday	German	French	Russian

GETTING THERE & AWAY

Bus 355/357 runs from Heliopolis to the Pyramids via Midan Tahrir every 20 minutes. It picks up from the road (not the island) under the overpass at Midan Abdel Moniem Riad. There's no sign so you'll have to ask a local where to stand. Be alert, as the bus won't automatically stop and you'll have to flag it down. It can sometimes also be flagged down from the side of the road near the northwestern metro stairs on Midan Tahrir. See the map on pp102–3 for the exact position. The bus is white, and has a 'CTA' sign on its side. A ticket costs E£2 and the trip takes 45 minutes.

Alternatively, you can take a microbus from Midan Abdel Moniem Riad bus station. These depart from near the Ramses Hilton hotel – there are no signs, just ask for 'Haram' and somebody will point you to the right line of vehicles. The fare is E£1 and you'll be dropped off about 500m short of the Oberoi Mena House hotel (which is also where buses 355 and 357 terminate).

Expect to pay about E£20 one way for a taxi. You can avoid the city-centre traffic by taking the metro to the Giza stop (50pt) at the foot of Pyramids Rd. From there, a taxi to the Pyramids should cost only E£5.

Returning to Cairo, taxis leave from outside the Mena House Oberoi hotel. They'll try for E£40, so you'll need to bargain hard.

Around the Pyramids
KERDASSA

Many of the scarves, *galabiyyas* (full-length robes worn by men), rugs and weavings sold in the bazaars and shops of Cairo are made in this touristy village near Giza. There is one main market street along which you'll find all of the above. You will also find a hideous collection of stuffed gazelles, jackals, rabbits and their friends because Kerdassa is almost as well known for its illegal trade in wildlife as it is for crafts. The Egyptian Environmental Affairs Agency periodically raids the bazaar to try to halt this.

To get to Kerdassa head down Pyramids Rd, turn right at the Maryutia Canal, and follow the road for about 5km to the village. The minibus from Midan Tahrir to the Pyramids begins and ends its trips at the junction of the canal and Pyramids Rd, and a local microbus does the stretch along the canal for 50pt. You can also get bus 116 from Midan Giza all the way to Kerdassa, the trip takes 20 minutes and costs 50pt.

Heliopolis

It's only a suburb of Cairo, but were it to stand alone as a town in its own right, Heliopolis (Misr al-Gedida or 'New Cairo'; Map p136) would be considered one of the gems of North Africa. The modern district was conceived in the early years of the 20th century as a 'garden city' in the desert, home to the colonial officials who ruled Egypt. The architectural style is a European fantasy of the Orient set in stone. Since the 1950s, however, overcrowding in Cairo has caught up with this not-so-distant neighbour and the desert has been covered with middle-income high-rises. Ranks of apartment buildings festooned with satellite-TV dishes now greatly outnumber the graceful old villas. Although there are no major sites as such, Heliopolis has a relaxed, almost Mediterranean air and is a pleasant place for an evening's wandering, with a couple of interesting bars, good designer shops and loads of cafés and restaurants.

The main street is Sharia al-Ahram, on which stands the **Uruba Palace** (Map p136), formerly the Heliopolis Palace Hotel but now occupied by the office of the Egyptian president. From the palace, at the first intersection with the splendid Sharia Ibrahim Laqqany (detour left for some fantastic architecture), is the open-air cafeteria **Amphitrion** (Map p136); this café is as old as Heliopolis itself and was a popular watering hole for Allied soldiers during WWI and WWII. It's a good place to relax and people-watch on a balmy evening.

Further along the street, the **Basilica** is a miniature version of Istanbul's famous Aya Sofya, known as the 'jelly mould' by local expats. This is where Baron Empain, the Belgian industrialist who founded Heliopolis, is buried. South on Sharia al-Uruba (Airport Rd), you'll see the extraordinary **Baron's Palace** (Qasr al-Baron), a Hindu-style temple modelled on the temples of Angkor Wat in Cambodia. It has been allowed to fall into ruin, and while a rich collection of sandstone Buddhas, geishas, elephants and serpents still adorns the exterior, the interior has been gutted. Entry is not permitted but if you tip the *bawwab* (doorman), who lives in a shack on the grounds, he might let you walk around the outside.

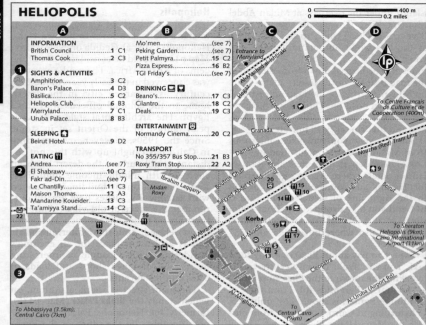

HELIOPOLIS

INFORMATION
British Council.................1 C1
Thomas Cook.................2 C3

SIGHTS & ACTIVITIES
Amphitrion...................3 C2
Baron's Palace...............4 D3
Basilica......................5 C2
Heliopolis Club..............6 B3
Merryland....................7 C1
Uruba Palace.................8 B3

SLEEPING
Beirut Hotel..................9 D2

EATING
Andrea.....................(see 7)
El Shabrawy.................10 C2
Fakr ad-Din................(see 7)
Le Chantilly.................11 C3
Maison Thomas..............12 A3
Mandarine Koueider..........13 C2
Ta'amiyya Stand.............14 C2

Mo'men....................(see 7)
Peking Garden.............(see 7)
Petit Palmyra..............15 C2
Pizza Express..............16 B2
TGI Friday's...............(see 7)

DRINKING
Beano's....................17 C3
Cilantro....................18 C3
Deals......................19 C3

ENTERTAINMENT
Normandy Cinema...........20 C2

TRANSPORT
No 355/357 Bus Stop.......21 B3
Roxy Tram Stop.............22 A2

OCTOBER WAR PANORAMA

Built with help from North Korean artists, the **October War Panorama** (Map pp94-5; ☎ 402 2317; Sharia al-Uruba, Heliopolis; admission E£10; ☺ shows 9.30am, 11am, 12.20pm, 6pm & 7.30pm Wed-Mon), a memorial to the 1973 'victory' over Israel, is an extraordinary propaganda effort. Contained within the purpose-built cylindrical structure is a large combined 3D mural and diorama depicting the breaching of the Bar Lev Line on the Suez Canal by Egyptian forces and the initial retreats by the Israelis. A stirring commentary (in Arabic only) recounts the heroic victories, but is short on detail on the successful Israeli counterattacks that pushed the Egyptians back before both sides accepted a UN-brokered cease-fire. Sinai was eventually liberated by negotiation six years later. The exhibition is located about 2km south of the Baron's Palace, on the same main road; walk or get a taxi.

GETTING THERE & AWAY

The best way to get to Heliopolis is by airport bus 356 from Midan Abdel Moniem

Riad, behind the Egyptian Museum (see Map pp102-3). The ride takes between 30 to 45 minutes. Get off outside the Heliopolis Club (the first stop after reaching the street with tram tracks – look out for a Pizza Express on the left). The fare is E£2 and buses usually run every 20 minutes. Alternatively a tram (25pt, 30 to 40 minutes) runs from just north of Midan Ramses (see Map p106). You should get off where it branches into two lines, just before Midan Roxy.

ACTIVITIES

For more details of activities around town, check *Al-Ahram Weekly*, the weekly *Cairo* magazine or the monthly *Egypt Today* magazine.

Art Galleries

Cairo has loads of art galleries where local and foreign artists exhibit. The city's cultural centres (see p96) often mount interesting exhibitions. Check out:

Atelier du Caire (Map pp102-3; ☎ 574 6730; 2 Sharia Karim al-Dawla, Downtown; ☺ 10am-1pm & 5-11pm

Sat-Thu) Off Sharia Mahmoud Bassiouni, this is an exhibition space for Egyptian contemporary artists.

Centre of Arts (Map pp126-7; ☎ 735 8211; 1 Sharia Maahad al-Swissry, Zamalek; ☒ 10am-1.30pm & 5-9pm Sat-Thu) Official Ministry of Culture exhibition halls housed in a grand villa on the banks of the Nile.

Karim Francis Art Gallery Downtown (Map pp102-3; ☎ 391 6357; 1 Sharia el-Sherifein; ☒ 2-9pm Sat-Thu); Zamalek (Map pp126-7; ☎ 736 2183; www.karimfrancis .com; 3rd fl, Baehler's Mansions, 157 Sharia 26th of July; ☒ 4-11pm Tue-Sun)

Khan al-Maghraby Gallery (☎ 735 3349; 18 Sharia Mansour Mohamed, Zamalek; ☒ 10.30am-9pm Mon-Sat)

Mashrabia Gallery for Contemporary Art (Map pp102-3; ☎ 578 4494; 8 Sharia Champollion, Downtown; ☒ 11am-8pm Sat-Thu) This attractive gallery just off Midan Tahrir has a strong stable of local artists.

Picasso Gallery (Map pp126-7; ☎ 736 7544; 30 Sharia Hassan Assem, Zamalek; ☒ 10am-9pm Mon-Sat) International and local contemporary artists.

Safar Khan Gallery (Map pp126-7; ☎ 735 3314; www.safarkhan.com; 6 Sharia Brazil, Zamalek; ☒ 10am-1.30pm & 5-8.30pm Mon-Sat)

Sawy Cultural Centre (Culture Wheel; Map pp126-7; ☎ 736 6178; www.culturewheel.com; Sharia 26th of July, Zamalek; ☒ 9am-9pm)

Sony Gallery (Map pp102-3; ☎ 794 2964; AUC Campus, Sharia Sheikh Rihan, Downtown; ☒ 9am-noon Sun-Thu) This gallery frequently has excellent photographic exhibitions.

Townhouse Gallery of Contemporary Art (Map pp102-3; ☎ 576 8086; 10 Sharia Nabrawy, Downtown; ☒ 10am-2pm & 6-9pm Sat-Wed, 6-9pm Fri) Occupying three floors of an old 'townhouse', off Sharia Champollion, this is Cairo's most cutting-edge gallery. It shows two or three exhibitions at any one time, screens art films and has a small sales space selling art and books.

Zamalek Art Gallery (Map pp126-7; ☎ 735 1240; www.zamalekartgallery.com; 11 Sharia Brazil, Zamalek; ☒ 10.30am-9pm Sat-Thu) An attractive, light-filled space showing contemporary Egyptian artists.

Belly-Dancing Lessons

The most famous belly-dancing teacher in Cairo (and, indeed, the whole of Egypt) is **Mme Raqia Hassan** (☎ 748 2338; raqiahassan@hotmail .com). Many of the country's best dancers have learned their craft from Mme Hassan, and she still gives private lessons in her home. Though most of her students are serious dancers, she's never been known to turn away a beginner.

The general reluctance to accept belly dance as a true art form means that official schools do not exist. Instead, some of

the city's gyms and health clubs organise group courses – try **Horizon** (☎ 012 222 6227) in Mohandiseen.

Felucca Rides

Feluccas, the ancient broad-sail boats that are seen everywhere on the Nile, can be hired by the hour from several places along the Corniche. One of the most pleasant things to do on a warm day is to go out on a felucca with a supply of beer and a small picnic just as sunset approaches. One of the best spots for hiring is the Dok Dok landing stage (Map p130) on the Corniche at Garden City just north of the Royal Nile Tower. A boat and captain should cost about E£25 to E£30 per hour irrespective of the number of people on board. This, of course, is subject to haggling. Other felucca mooring points are at the southeast end of Gezira just north of the Qasr el-Nil Bridge (Map p130), opposite the Helnan Shepheard's hotel (Map pp102–3), where captains tend to be more voracious in their demands for money, and in Ma'adi just north of the Felfela restaurant.

Golf

Run by the hotel, the **Mena House Golf Course** (Map p129; ☎ 383 3222; www.oberoihotels.com; Pyramids Rd, Giza; green fee E£150 plus club rental E£55; ☒ 7am-sunset), beneath the pyramids, is always busy on Friday and Saturday, so your best option is to tee off midweek.

Horse Riding

A horse ride out by the Pyramids can be a great way to escape the clamour of Cairo. For details, see p131.

Pool & Snooker

Pool and snooker are popular in Cairo. Most venues are in the wealthier suburbs away from the city centre, such as Ma'adi and Medinat Nasr. The most central venue is on the top floor of the **Ramses Hilton Mall** (Map pp102-3; ☎ 577 7444; Downtown; ☒ 2pm-4am), which has snooker and pool halls. In Ma'adi, the popular **Cuba Cabana** (☎ 378 3300; 28 Road 7, Ma'adi; min charge E£20; ☒ 8am-2am; ☒) offers pool tables, Cuban food and *sheesha*s. It doesn't sell alcohol.

Swimming

Finding a place to cool off can be difficult in Cairo. Most Cairenes who can afford it

CAIRO

go to swim in sporting clubs, which do not admit nonmembers. Some hotels will allow day use for nonguests, but at a price. Best options:

Cairo Marriott (Map pp126-7; ☎ 735 8888; Sharia Saray al-Gezira, Zamalek; day use E£111) A good pool in a garden setting. The fee includes the use of the gym and sauna.

Le Meridien Pyramids (☎ 383 0383; Al-Rimayah Sq, Giza; per day E£80) This hotel near the pyramids has a great pool area. There's a heated pool with waterfalls, a children's pool and massage pools.

Oberoi Mena House (Map p129; Pyramids Rd, Giza; pool use only per day E£80, pool cabin per day US$85) The best pool setting in Cairo, with fantastic Pyramid views. You can swim from 9am to sunset and there's a poolside café.

If you're a serious lap swimmer, try the **Ash-Shams Sporting Club** (admission E£20) next to the Concorde As-Salaam Hotel in Heliopolis. It has a heated, Olympic-sized pool.

WALKING TOUR

Islamic Cairo is a world in itself and first-time visitors can be daunted by its narrow alleys, hives of activity, its smells and sounds. It is one place where it can be instructive to get lost. A good preparation is offered by the works of Nobel laureate Naguib Mahfouz (see p69), who set some of his masterpieces in the area. This walk is an introduction both to his work and to the Islamic monuments in the area. It covers a distance of about 2km and should take two to three hours to cover, not including time spent in ahwas.

Mahfouz was born in Gamaliyya, and although his family moved to Abbassiyya during his childhood, in his writing he did not really leave. He returned often and loved the ahwas in the area, where he most probably picked up a lot of characters for his books. One of his favourites was **Fisha-wi's Coffeehouse** (**1**; see p154) where he met fellow writers in the small interior room. It's a good place to start the walk, lingering over a mint shai (tea) and perhaps getting into the mood while reading a few chapters of one of his novels.

Leaving Fishawi's, walk north to the very end of the alley, turning left and then right before passing under the great tunnel-like arched gateway that leads into **Midan Beit al-Qadi (2)**. This was formerly a garden of a Mamluk palace, of which the huge five-

arched arcade on the south side is all that remains. Off the midan's northeast corner is a tiny alleyway, **Darb Qirmiz (3)**, where Mahfouz was born in 1912 and lived during his childhood. The influence of this neighbourhood dominates his early books, such as Khan al-Khalili (still not translated into English) and Hikayet Haretna (Tales of Our Quarter, published in English as Fountain and Tomb), which begins with the narrator as a child telling how much he enjoys playing 'in the small square between the archway and the takiyya'. In his later, more experimental novels, such as Children of the Alley and Harafish, Mahfouz focussed on the microcosm of one alley and its inhabitants, with a largely unknown and infinite world beyond it.

WALK FACTS

Start Fishawi's Coffeehouse
Finish Zuqaq al-Midaq
Distance 2km
Duration two to three hours

At the top of the alley turn left and head west along Darb at-Tablawi. **Qasr Beshtak** (**4**; p115), on the left at the end of the alley, has great views over the area from its top floor and leads onto the busy Bein al-Qasreen. This historic main thoroughfare gives its name to the first volume in Mahfouz' *Cairo Trilogy*, published in English as *Between the Palaces*. The family of the trilogy's main character, Us-Said, live within sight of the **Sabil-Kuttab of Abdel Kathkuda** (**5**; p115), in front of which you should now be standing.

The other two titles in the trilogy are also rooted in local geography: *As-Sukkariya* (Sugar Street) is down near Bab Zuweila, while *Qasr as-Shuq* (Palace of Desire) is the name of a street just east of Sharia al-Gamaliyya.

From here you can head to the imposing *madrassa* and mausoleum complexes on the west side of Bein al-Qasreen. Then walk due south through the coppersmiths and gold bazaars, across Al-Muski, past a couple of spice shops, and take the next left: just 10m or so along here is a tiny stepped alley running up to your left that terminates in three stubby dead ends. This is **Zuqaq al-Midaq** (**6**; Midaq Alley), the title of perhaps Mahfouz' best-known work, and a good introduction to the author and this part of Cairo.

In *Midaq Alley* Mahfouz focuses on a mixed bunch of fictional characters who inhabit this small cul-de-sac. The story was filmed in Mexico as *El Callejon de los Milagros* (1994), starring Salma Hayek. Such is the alley's fame that the street sign is kept in the coffeehouse at the foot of the steps and is produced only on payment of *baksheesh*.

From here, retrace your steps to Sharia an-Nahaseen, at the end of which you can get a taxi out, or better head eastwards along Sharia al-Muski and end up in Fishawi's for another mint *shai* (tea) and a few more chapters.

CAIRO FOR CHILDREN

Cairo can be exhausting for children, but there is much they will enjoy. If you have a few days in the city it may be worth buying *Cairo, the Family Guide* by Lesley Lababidi and Dr Lisa Sabbany (AUC Press, E£60). Just be aware that it hasn't been revised since 2003. Most children will

enjoy pretending to be a pirate on a Nile felucca (p137), gawking at the treasures of Tutankhamun in the Egyptian Museum (p167), investigating the Pyramids at Giza and Dahshur (p128) and strolling around the Khan al-Khalili (p112). There are also a number of child-oriented activities and theme parks that are worth considering.

The long-running **Cairo Puppet Theatre** (Map pp102-3; ☎ 591 0954; admission E£5; ⏱ 6.30-8.15pm Thu, 10.30am-1pm Fri & Sun) is opposite Ezbekiyya Gardens in Downtown. The shows are in Arabic, but are colourful and animated enough to entertain non-Arabic speakers. Great fun for all the family.

Fun Planet (Map pp126-7; Arkadia Mall, Corniche el-Nil, Bulaq; first three games E£10, each subsequent game E£3-5; ⏱ 3-11pm Sat-Thu & 1-11pm Fri), an indoor amusement centre in Cairo's most popular shopping mall, offers loads of rides and games and will appeal to teenagers.

The **National Circus** (Map pp126-7; ☎ 347 0612; Sharia el-Nil, Agouza, near the Zamalek Bridge; admission E£30-50; ⏱ box office 11am-10pm, performances 9.30pm-midnight) is a traditional circus with clowns, Russian acrobats, trapezists, animals (including lions and tigers) and lots of glitter. You'll usually find it here during the cooler months – it tours the country at other times of the year.

Children can feed the animals at the **Cairo Zoo** (Guineenat al-Haywanet; Map p130; ☎ 570 8895; Midan al-Gamaa, Giza; admission 25pt; ⏱ 9am-4pm) for 25pt per feeding.

The aqua park **Crazy Water** (☎ 781 4564; admission children 3-10 E£25, children 10 & older E£35-45; ⏱ 10am-10pm) has half a dozen or more water slides, a wave pool, a kiddies' pool, and a playground area with sand, slides and tunnels. To get there, drive 15km from the intersection of the Giza road and Cairo–Alexandria road, then turn left on the route to 6th of October City.

Also on the city's outskirts, **Dream Park** (☎ 840 0887; www.dreamparkegypt.com; Oasis Rd, 6th of October City; ⏱ 4pm-midnight Sat-Thu, noon-9pm Fri) was designed by the company that built Disneyworld in Florida. It offers 32 rides, a shopping mall and a food court.

The cheesy theme park, **Dr Ragab's Pharaonic Village** (☎ 571 8675; www.touregypt.net/village; 3 Sharia al-Bahr al-Azam, Corniche, Giza; adult E£79-159, child under 5 free, child 5-10 20% discount; ⏱ 9am-6pm Sep-Jun, 9am-9pm Jul-Aug), offers a child-friendly glimpse of what life in ancient Egypt would have been like. There's a boat trip, actors in Pharaonic costumes, a multilingual commentary and a playground. One-hour trips on the Nile on the village's yacht *Nefertari* cost an additional US$6. The admission fee varies according to the package you choose. You'll need a taxi to get there.

Fagnoon Art School (☎ 815 1014, 012 214 7136; Saqqara Rd, Sabil Umm Hashim; per day E£25; ☒ 10am-7pm) is a wonderful art centre run by artist Mohammed Allam in the fields between Giza and Saqqara. Children can slosh paint around, model clay, work with wrought iron, print and paint on textiles or hammer together some wood in a farm-type setting, all in the shadow of the Saqqara step pyramid. Expect to pay about E£30 for canvases and other materials. You can bring your own food and drink, although *fiteer* (pancake/pizza), coffee and water are usually on sale. To get here, take a microbus from the Pyramids Rd 12.5km in the direction of Saqqara and asked to be dropped off at Sabil Umm Hashim.

Commonly known as the 'Fish Garden', the pleasant **Gabalaya Park & Aquarium** (Map pp126-7; Sharia Umm Kolthum, Zamalek; admission 50pt; ☒ 9am-3.30pm) has landscaped gardens with aquariums set in rocks. It's a great central spot to escape the crowds, and small children will love looking at the fish.

Suzanne Mubarak Children's Museum (☎ 642 4246; 34 Sharia Bakr Al-Seddiq, Heliopolis; ☒ 9am-2.30pm) is an interactive educational museum about the history and geography of Egypt set in a large garden. There's also a children's arts and activity centre (admission E£5).

A vast garden off Sharia Bur Said, **Sayyida Zeinab Cultural Park** (Map p121; ☎ 391 5220; Sharia Qadri, Sayyida Zeinab; admission free; ☒ 10am-5pm Mon-Thu, Sat & Sun) has been specially landscaped for children. It's extremely popular with local families and has a playground and loads of space to run around in. Two passport photos are required for admission.

In Islamic Cairo, the recently opened **Al-Azhar Park** (Map pp94-5; admission free; ☒ 10am-10pm) is home to one of the few children's playgrounds in the central city.

In times of crisis (ie, when only bribery will help), try **Top II Toys** (Zamalek Map pp126-7; ☎ 736 3741; 13 Sharia Brazil; ☒ 10am-11pm; Doqqi ☎ 748 3524; 40 Sharia Mosadek; ☒ 10am-11pm) or **Toys R Us** (Map pp126-7; ☎ 578 0820; Ground fl, Arkadia Mall, Bulaq).

TOURS

Innumerable companies and individuals offer tours of sights within and around Cairo. We recommend Salah Muhammad's **Noga Tours** (☎ 205 7908, 012 313 8446; www.first24hours.com), as he employs excellent English-speaking guides, Egyptologists and drivers. His vehicles are also properly maintained. Mohamed Anwar's specialised **museum tours** (☎ 012 340 7724) also have a good reputation.

If you want to hire a taxi for the day and dispense with a guide, the friendly **Fathy el-Menesy** (☎ 259 3218, 012 278 1572) owns a well-maintained Peugeot and speaks English. Otherwise, ask at your hotel. To give an idea of cost, the Berlin Hotel can organise a taxi to visit Dahshur, Memphis and Saqqara for E£40 per person; Fathy el-Menesy charges between E£200 and E£250 for a full day; and Noga Tours charges US$22.50 (plus entry fees) per person for a full-day trip to the Giza Pyramids, Memphis and Saqqara. Its half-day tour of Dahshur costs US$18.99 (plus entry fees) per person.

FESTIVALS & EVENTS

For general information on festivals and public holidays see p527.

Arabic Music Festival Held at the Cairo Opera House in November.

Belly-dance festival (www.nilegroup.net) Held at the Mena House Oberoi hotel in June. Check the website for details.

Cairo International Film Festival (www.cairofilm fest.com) Held at the Cairo Opera House in November/December.

Moulid an-Nabi Birthday of Prophet Mohammed. The area around Midan Hussein is the venue for several days of riotous celebrations, Sufi *zikrs* (long sessions of dancing, chanting and swaying carried out to achieve oneness with God) and processions of sheikhs.

Moulids Festivals celebrating the birthday of a local saint or holy person. The big *moulids* in Cairo are Sayyidna al-Hussein, Sayyida Zeinab and Imam ash-Shafi. They are wonderful celebrations if you are not afraid of rowdy crowds (see the boxed text on p528). Ask a local for the right dates as they vary from year to year.

Ramadan Ninth month of the lunar Islamic calendar. Everything slows down during Ramadan. Shops and offices open later and close earlier and just before sunset the streets empty as everyone goes home to break the fast. The nights, particularly in Islamic Cairo, are buzzing until the early morning hours.

Sham an-Nassim First Monday after Coptic Easter. Literally meaning 'sniffing the breeze' (ie to welcome spring), it's a Coptic holiday but is celebrated by all Cairenes, who picnic at places such as the zoo, on riverbanks, traffic islands, parks and the Pyramids.

SLEEPING

If you're on a budget, you're best off staying in Downtown. Most of the city's hostels and cheap hotels are located on or around Sharia Talaat Harb on the upper floors of old, usually decrepit, apartment blocks. Rooms tend to be large, but can be musty and are often sparsely furnished. Most have fans rather than air-con (though this is starting to change) and can be unbearably hot in summer; many have balconies and windows overlooking noisy main streets, so request a rear room if you're a light sleeper. Plumbing often seems to date from the Pharaonic era, and you shouldn't assume that the hot water systems are reliable. Still, you will truly be staying in the heart of Cairo here, and cheap eateries and the city's major tourist attractions are close by.

The best sleeping location in town is the green and leafy suburb of Zamalek at the northern end of Gezira Island. This is where many of Cairo's best restaurants, shops, bars and coffee shops are located, and most of the city's sights are only a short taxi ride away. It's also much quieter than Downtown. There are a few good-quality midrange choices here and a couple of excellent top-end places; unfortunately, budget options are almost nonexistent.

The city's top-end hotels tend to be located along the Nile in Bulaq, Garden City, Zamalek, Gezira and Giza. The Cairo Hilton, Semiramis Intercontinental and Cairo Marriott have the best positions in town. Though Mena House Oberoi and the Four Seasons First Residence are world-class hotels, they suffer from supremely inconvenient locations and are not ideal if you want more out of your stay than an indulgent few days by the hotel pool.

Be aware that prices are often negotiable and you should consider the listed room rates as estimates. You can pay less or more depending on your bargaining skills.

CAIRO HOTEL SCAMS

On arrival at the airport, you may be approached by a man or woman with an official-looking badge that says 'Ministry of Tourism' or something similar. These people are not government tourism officials, they are hotel touts, and they have more tricks up their sleeves than they do scruples. For instance, they'll often ask if you've booked a hotel. If you have, they'll offer to call the hotel to make sure that a room is waiting for you. Of course, they don't call the hotel – they call a friend who pretends to be the hotel and says that there is no booking and that his establishment is full. Concerned, the tout will offer to find you an alternative…

Other scams include telling you that the hotel you're heading for is closed/very expensive/horrible/a brothel and suggesting a 'better' place, for which they earn a commission, which will then be added to your bill. Many taxi drivers will also try it on too. The most innovative scam is when these touts ask you your name and where you're staying under the pretence of striking up a casual conversation. After a chat (often on the airport bus), they say goodbye and aren't seen again. What they next do is call a friend, who goes and stands outside the hotel you've booked. When you arrive, he or she will ask 'Are you…?', using the name you volunteered back at the airport. When you answer in the affirmative, you'll be told that the hotel has been flooded/closed by the police/totally booked out and that the owners have organised a room for you elsewhere.

Do not be swayed by anyone who tries to dissuade you from going to the hotel of your choice. Hotels do not open and close with any great frequency in Cairo, and if it's listed in this book it is very unlikely to have gone out of business by the time you arrive. Some taxi drivers will stall by telling you that they don't know where your hotel is. In that case tell them to let you out at Midan Talaat Harb – from here it's a short walk to almost all the budget hotels.

When checking in, never pay in advance for your room. If reception does ask for cash up front that should set warning bells ringing that there's something dodgy about the place – no decent hotel would ever make such a request. We've had letters from readers asked to stump up for two nights on arrival and then when they've decided to check out after one night (because of grotty toilets, no hot water, whatever), they've been unable to get a refund.

CAIRO

Bulaq

Conrad Cairo (Map pp126–7; ☎ 580 8000; Conrad@ conradcairo.com.eg; 1191 Corniche el-Nil; s/d from US$250; ✗ ✗ ⌨ ⌨) This attractive hotel, opened in 1999, is popular with business travellers but tourists might find it a little devoid of life thanks to a location (Nileside) a long walk north of the city centre. It has excellent restaurants, a health club and a number of pools (including a kids' pool). All rooms have Nile views.

Downtown
BUDGET

Hotel Luna (Map pp102–3; ☎ 396 1020; www.hotel lunacairo.com; 5th fl, 27 Sharia Talaat Harb; s/d E£60/80, with private bathroom E£80/100; ✗ ⌨) The Luna is one of the best budget hotels in Egypt. Its large rooms have crisp, clean linen and air-con; seven have private bathrooms and the others have hand basins. Shared bathrooms are so clean they gleam. There's a sitting area near reception where you can relax, and free use of the kitchen. Guests staying four or more nights get a free airport pick-up. Fantastic.

Lialy Hostel (Map pp102–3; ☎ 575 2802; www .lialyhostel.com; 3rd fl, 8 Midan Talaat Harb; dm/s/d E£25/50/60, s/d with air-con E£70/80; ✗) One of the friendliest hostels in the city, the Lialy's position on Midan Talaat Harb puts it right in the thick of the action. Eleven

---

THE AUTHOR'S CHOICE

Talisman Hotel (Map pp102–3; ☎ 393 9431; talisman_hoteldecharme@yahoo.fr; 5th fl, 39 Sharia Talaat Harb; s/d/ste US$80/95/120; ✗ ⌨) This exquisite boutique hotel is straight out of the pages of *The 1001 Nights*. Rooms are individually decorated and sumptuously equipped; common areas are equally impressive, featuring antique furniture, *objets d'art* and rugs. The suites are quite simply works of art. It's not often that we give hotels a 10 out of 10 score, but for value, style and comfort that's what the Talisman deserves. Reservations are essential. To find it, turn off Sharia Talaat Harb into the alley opposite the A L'Americaine Coffee Shop and enter the first building entrance on the right, where you'll see a sign for the New Minerva Hotel. The Talisman uses the lift on the left-hand-side of the foyer.

---

rooms share three bathrooms; everything is clean but the hot water sometimes runs out. Some rooms have double beds and air-con. There's a small collection of books to read, a large breakfast room with satellite TV, and free use of the kitchen. Also fantastic.

King Tut Hostel (Map pp102–3; ☎ 391 7897; King _Tut_hostel@hotmail.com; 8th fl, 37 Sharia Talaat Harb; s/d E£40/60, s/d with air-con & TV E£45/80; ✗ ⌨) One of a number of recent additions to the Cairo hostel scene, the King Tut has freshly painted rooms with comfortable beds; nine have air-con and two have satellite TV. All share spotless bathrooms. There's an attractive lounge with cushions, brass tables and satellite TV. Nearly as fantastic.

Meramees Hotel (Map pp102–3; ☎ 396 2318; 32 Sharia Sabri Abu 'Alam; dm/s/d E£17/35/50, d with private bathroom E£75) It's been around for a while, but the Meramees is maintaining its standards of cleanliness and comfort. Rooms share bathrooms and come with fans – the downstairs singles are particularly nice. There's free use of the kitchen, free tea and coffee, and free airport pick-up for guests staying three or more nights.

Sara Inn (Map pp102–3; ☎ 392 2940; www.sara innhostel.2ya.com; 7th fl, 21 Sharia Yousef al-Guindi; dm E£25, s E£25-50, d E£40-60, d with private bathroom & air-con E£120; ✗ ⌨) This new place has a range of rooms, the best of which have air-con, private bathrooms and a hefty price tag. Though lacking both character and enough shared bathrooms, it's quiet and clean.

Pension Roma (Map pp102–3; ☎ 391 1088; fax 579 6243; 4th fl, 169 Sharia Mohammed Farid; s/d E£37/69, with private shower E£40/78) Staying here is like sleeping over at your Grandma's house – it's charmingly old fashioned. Positives are the helpful staff, large rooms and elegant lounge area; negatives include the uncomfortable beds, miserly breakfast and lack of air-con. Book ahead.

Samar Palace Hotel (Map pp102–3; ☎ 390 1093; samar-palace-hotel@yahoo.com; 3rd fl, Sharia Magharipi; s/d E£35/65; d with private bathroom & air-con E£75; ✗) A hotel rather than a hostel, this place has recently been refurbished and is worth considering. It's popular with Egyptians and Gulf Arabs, who clearly appreciate the comfortable rooms and lounge area with satellite TV. Breakfast (E£5) is served on the roof terrace. It's down a laneway off Sharia 26th of July, directly over an *ahwa*.

Richmond Hotel (Map pp102-3; ☎ 393 9358; amarichmond@hotmail.com; 5th fl, 41 Sharia Sherif; s/d E£30/60; 🖳) Bright turquoise and orange walls provide a cheerful note at this friendly place. Of the 17 large rooms on offer, seven come with king-sized beds. Shared bathrooms are worn but clean. Guests can use the kitchen and there's a lounge with satellite TV.

Ismailia House Hotel (Map pp102-3; ☎ 796 3122; ismahouse@hotmail.com; 8th fl, 1 Midan Tahrir; dm E£16-17, s E£22-27, d E£48-50, d with private bathroom E£60-65; 🖳) Listed here predominantly due to its fabulous views over the *midan* and to the Nile, this long-running hostel has rooms that could benefit from a good scrub. Ask for rooms 805, 810 or 820, all of which come with balcony and amazing views. There's a pleasant lounge with satellite TV.

Berlin Hotel (Map pp102-3; ☎ 395 7502; berlin hotelcairo@hotmail.com; 4th fl, 2 Sharia Shawarby; s/d E£77/97; 🌂 🖳) This small place just off Qasr el-Nil is pricey for what it offers, but is worth considering because of its very helpful and knowledgeable manager, Hisham Youssif. Rooms come with comfortable beds, air-con and shower cubicles. When we last visited, the hotel was being renovated and a new breakfast room/lounge was on its way.

New Minerva Hotel (Map pp102-3; ☎ 392 3273; new-minerva@yahoo.com; 6th fl, 39 Sharia Talaat Harb; 🖳) This very friendly place has large rooms with parquet floors and high ceilings. The seven rooms are freshly painted, have fans and share two bathrooms. Ask to see the room before you make a decision to stay here, as some are noisy and one has no natural light. There's a funky – if slightly claustrophobic – foyer with turquoise walls and a tiger-skin rug, and a small kitchen for guest use. It's in the first building on the right when you enter the alley opposite the A L'Americaine Coffee Shop.

Claridge Hotel (Map pp102-3; ☎ 010 108 3049; pupils994@hotmail.com; 41 Sharia Talaat Harb; s/d with fan E£40/75, s/d with air-con E£60/95; 🌂 🖳) After the visual assault provided by lurid lime-green walls in the corridor, the 40 rooms in this sprawling place seem very bland. Four rooms have air-con and all have reasonably clean private bathrooms. Beds are hard but ceiling fans work. Sixteen rooms have balconies facing noisy Sharia Talaat Harb. There's a cafeteria with satellite TV. It's a bit pricey for what it offers.

MIDRANGE

Victoria Hotel (Map p106; ☎ 589 2290; info@victoria .com.eg; 66 Sharia Gomhuriyya; s/d US$28/37; 🌂 🖳) It's a shame the Victoria's location isn't better. Near Ramses Station, it offers large rooms with comfortable beds, satellite TV and private bathroom. Though lacking atmosphere, it offers four-star amenities for two-star prices and that's a pretty attractive proposition.

Arabesque Hotel (Map pp102-3; ☎ 579 9679; arab esque_hotel@yahoo.com; 11 Sharia Ramses; s/d E£60/80, with private bathroom & air-con E£100/150; 🌂) Midrange hotels are thin on the ground in Cairo, so the Arabesque is destined to do well. Rooms have a bland fit-out but are comfortable and clean; avoid those at the front, which overlook one of the city's busiest and noisiest motorways. The lounge has great views over the Nile, comfortable seating and a satellite TV.

Windsor Hotel (Map pp102-3; ☎ 591 5277; www .windsorcairo.com; 19 Sharia Alfy; s/d with shower & hand basin US$30/38, with private bathroom US$37/46, deluxe US$47/57; 🌂 🖳) This ageing edifice was the British Officers' Club before 1952 and retains a colonial air. Rooms have more atmosphere than comfort, though all come with air-con. The large deluxe rooms also have satellite TV. Run by the same family since 1962, the hotel's main drawcards are the friendly staff and the charming lounge bar.

Odeon Palace Hotel (Map pp102-3; ☎ 577 6637; mervat@odeonpalace.com; 6 Sharia Abdel Hamid Said; s/d with private bathroom US$40.50/50.50; 🌂) Though this comfortable hotel just off Sharia Talaat Harb is lacking character, its spotless rooms are comfortable and come complete with private bathroom, satellite TV and air-con, making them a good deal for the price. Staff members are helpful and its 24-hour rooftop bar is popular with night owls.

Carlton Hotel (Map pp102-3; ☎ 575 5022; carl tonhotelcairo@yahoo.com; 21 Sharia 26th of July; s/d half board US$18/27; 🌂 🖳) The rooms at this old-fashioned place near Cinema Rivoli are reasonably priced, but vary enormously in size and degree of dilapidation. We suggest that you request one of the recently renovated rooms with air-con, satellite TV and private bathroom. There's a restaurant, a coffee-house and a welcoming rooftop cafeteria where you can enjoy a cold beer.

Cosmopolitan Hotel (Map pp102-3; ☎ 392 384; fax 393 3531; 1 Sharia ibn Taalab; s/d with private bathroom

US$44/55; ✷) In a tranquil backstreet in the heart of Downtown, this grand Art Nouveau building has a fabulous location and entry staircase, but its rooms are less impressive. Though all are clean and come with private bathroom, many are poorly maintained. In our experience service veers from overly attentive (read tip-hungry) to surly. And steer right away from the restaurant – we were served bread that had been recycled from a previous guest's breakfast (think a bite missing and jam already applied).

Lotus Hotel (Map pp102-3; ☎ 575 0966; www.lotus hotel.com; 12 Sharia Talaat Harb; s/d E£65/92, with private bathroom E£95/124; ✷) We've only included the Lotus in our listings because of the dearth of decent midrange alternatives around town. Falling into ever-increasing disrepair, its slightly grubby rooms have high ceilings and parquet floors. Beds are uncomfortable and there are no fans. Shared bathrooms are clean, but don't provide soap or toilet paper and there is only hot water at certain times. The hotel is reached via an elevator at the end of the arcade opposite the Felfela Takeaway.

TOP END

Nile Hilton (Map pp102-3; ☎ 578 0444; www.hilton .com; 1113 Corniche el-Nil; s/d from US$120, with Nile views US$140; ✷ ☐ ☑) Cairo's oldest five-star hotel is still a fine place to stay courtesy of the best location in the city, off Midan Tahrir beside the Egyptian Museum. Standard rooms have a fussy pinkish décor – it's worth upgrading to the stylish executive rooms with their Nile-view balconies. There are a number of special-needs rooms and the hotel's secluded pool is one of the best in town.

Garden City

BUDGET

Garden City House Hotel (Map pp102-3; ☎ 542 0600; www.gardencity.plus.com; 23 Sharia Kamal ad-Din Salah; s E£55, d E£81-95, s/d with private bathroom E£73/106; ✷) A long-time favourite among Egyptologists and Middle Eastern scholars, this pension at the back of the Semiramis InterContinental is now more popular with students from the nearby AUC. It's noisy and nothing posh, but many people love it and keep coming back because of its homely feel and close proximity to the river and Egyptian Mu-

seum. Some rooms have a Nile view. Aircon rooms cost an extra E£12.50 per night.

TOP END

Semiramis InterContinental (Map pp102-3; ☎ 795 7171; www.cairo.intercontinental.com; Corniche el-Nil; s/d US$263/290, with Nile views US$290/326; ✷ ✷ ☐ ☑) The Semiramis benefits from a great riverside location just off Midan Tahrir, close to the Egyptian Museum. Rooms are large and feature five-star amenities; many have balconies and Nile views. The glitzy foyer is a popular Cairo meeting place, and its 1st-floor restaurants are the best in the city. In all, it's an excellent choice. Book ahead, because the place is inevitably full of tourists from the Gulf. Breakfast costs US$16.

Four Seasons at Nile Plaza (Map p130; ☎ 791 7000; 1089 Corniche el-Nil; s/d from US$310; ✷ ✷ ☐ ☑) It's not quite as posh as its First Residence sister in Giza, but the Four Seasons Nile Plaza has a much better location and is within walking distance of the Egyptian Museum and the Cairo Opera House. Facilities are excellent, as are the hotel restaurants. The building has been designed to be wheelchair-accessible. Rooms overlook the Nile, the Citadel, Zamalek or the hotel's pool area and the cost varies accordingly. The room price doesn't include breakfast.

Gezira

Sofitel El Gezirah (Map p130; ☎ 737 3737; H5307-SL@ accor.com; Sharia al-Orman; s US$100-185, d US$120-185; ✷ ✷ ☐ ☑) This ugly cylindrical tower is on the very southern tip of Gezira island and offers superb views from both its rooms and its excellent riverside restaurants and bars. The foyer is looking a bit worn but rooms are in the process of being renovated and are large, comfortable and well equipped. Breakfast costs US$10.

Giza

TOP END

Four Seasons at the First Residence (Map p130; ☎ 573 1212; www.fourseasons.com; 35 Sharia al-Giza; r from US$310; ✷ ✷ ☐ ☑) This luxe hotel is part of the exclusive First Residence Complex, the city's most expensive real estate, and is the first choice of stars, sheikhs and heads of state when they hit Cairo. The location opposite the Cairo Zoo is miles from everywhere, but if you want the best service in Cairo, superb food and total luxury, then this is the place to stay. Rooms either overlook the Nile or the Zoo and distant Pyramids. Check out the hotel's extensive collection of contemporary Egyptian art; it's one of the best in the country. Room prices don't include breakfast.

Oberoi Mena House (Map p129; ☎ 383 3222; www .oberoihotels.com; Pyramids Rd; r garden wing US$186-273, s palace wing US$199-252, d palace wing US$236-372; ✗ ▢ ▣) Staying in a pyramid-view room in Mena House's palace wing is truly a once-in-a-lifetime experience. This former royal hunting lodge in the shadow of the pyramids was built in 1869 and converted into a sumptuous luxury hotel in 1880. The interior of the palace wing is opulent and Oriental in equal measure, but rooms in the garden wing are stock-standard five-star models built in the late 20th century and not worth their price tag. Leisure facilities are excellent: there's a large swimming pool in a lush garden setting, tennis courts, a golf course and a gym. Breakfast costs E£58 to E£75.

Harraniyya

Salma Motel (☎ 381 5210, 010 145 7316; Saqqara Rd, Harraniyya; camping per person E£20) The only camping option in Cairo is miles from the centre and next to an unbelievably filthy and mosquito-infested canal, close to the Wissa Wassef Art Centre. It's sometimes used by overland tour companies. Breakfast costs E£20 per person. To get here, look for the blue 'Harraniyya' sign off the Saqqara Rd. There are no minibuses along the Maryutia Canal, so you'll need to take a taxi from the Pyramids Rd.

Heliopolis
MIDRANGE
Beirut Hotel (Map p136; ☎ 291 1092; www.beirut hotels.eg.com; 56 Sharia Beirut; s/d with private bathroom US$60/72; ✗ ▢) This shabby place is worth considering only because it's one of the only midrange choices in the Heliopolis area. Rooms are bland but reasonably clean; all have bathrooms, satellite TV and air-conditioning. Those at the front on the higher floors have a nice view of the cathedral. There's a sleazy-looking bar, a restaurant and a totally tragic disco. Breakfast costs US$4.50.

TOP END
Sheraton Heliopolis (☎ 267 7730; www.sheraton.com /heliopolis; Airport Rd, Heliopolis; cabana r US$169-189,

standard r US$153-297; ✗ ✗ ▢ ▣) A sprawling resort close to the airport, the Sheraton has an excellent pool area with kids' pool and playground, a health club and tennis courts. Its foyer chandeliers are bigger than any seen in Vegas and it boasts an array of restaurants, included the highly regarded Shahenshah, which serves up delicate Iranian dishes. The cheapest rooms are the poolside cabanas but the best rooms are in the huge white block; these feature work desks with ADSL connections, coffee and tea making facilities, king-sized beds and large bathrooms. Breakfast costs US$13.

Islamic Cairo
Al-Hussein Hotel (Map p112; ☎ 591 8089; Midan Hussein; s/d with private bathroom E£70/90, with air-con & private bathroom E£85/105; ✗) This is just about the only option if you want to stay in the heart of the Khan al-Khalili area (we'd advise against doing so). Rooms are pretty grim and the call to prayer at dawn is relentless, but the views over Cairo's minarets are great and it's good for people-watching in the square below. There's a top-floor restaurant, but no alcohol is served.

Zamalek
BUDGET
Mayfair Hotel (Map pp126-7; ☎ 735 7315; www .mayfaircairo.com; 9 Sharia Aziz Osman; s/d E£60/75, with private bathroom E£80/95; ✗ ▢) This rundown place is on the 2nd floor of a grand Art Deco apartment block in a quiet and leafy residential street just a minute away from bustling Sharia 26th of July. Rooms have high ceilings and noisy air-con units, those that share bathrooms are in a separate and unpleasantly musty wing. All are pretty grubby and have an institutional feel. Breakfast and drinks are served on a pleasant shady balcony overlooking the street.

MIDRANGE
Hotel Longchamps (Map pp126-7; ☎ 735 2311; www .hotellongchamps.com; 5th fl, 21 Sharia Ismail Mohammed; s US$42-46, d US$56-62; ✗ ✗) This place is probably the best midrange option in Cairo. Pristine rooms feature extremely comfortable beds, private bathrooms and satellite TV; it's worth paying a bit extra to get an executive room with balcony and bathtub. There's a generous breakfast buffet, restaurant (alcohol served) and a blissfully peaceful rear

balcony where guests can relax with a tea. Owner Hebba Bakri is an excellent host.

President Hotel (Map pp126-7; ☎ 735 0718; pres hotl@thewayout.net; 22 Sharia Taha Hussein; s/d US$70/55; ☒ 🖳) The President's in-house 'Le Bec Sucré' patisserie is one of the best in the city, and breakfasts are a highlight of any stay. The mouldy bathrooms provide the downside. Rooms come with three-star accoutrements, including satellite TV.

Pension Zamalek (Map pp126-7; ☎ 735 9318; pensionzamalek@msn.com; 6 Sharia Salah ad-Din; s/d E£90/150; ☒) You'll feel as if you've moved in with the owner's family if you stay at this clean and quiet pension. In a quiet and leafy location in Zamalek, it has 14 shabby rooms (four with air-con, extra E£25) and shared bathrooms. There's a discount for long stays.

Horus House Hotel (Map pp126-7; ☎ 736 0694; www .horushousehotel.4t.com; 4th fl, 21 Sharia Ismail Mohammed; s/d US$52/70; ☒) On the floor underneath the Longchamps and nowhere near as impressive, this old-fashioned and slightly overpriced place offers rooms with bland décor, satellite TV and clean bathrooms. The rooms are arranged along a labyrinthine corridor; some look out onto brick walls whereas others have attractive views. The best are the large rooms (numbers 103, 104 and 105) off the breakfast room. There's a lounge with a sunny outdoor balcony, as well as a bar.

TOP END

Cairo Marriott (Map pp126-7; ☎ 735 8888; www.mar riott.com/CAIEG; Sharia Saray al-Gezira; s/d from US$157; ☒ ☒ 🖳 ☒) Despite the addition of two very modern towers that house all the rooms, this is one of the few historic hotels left in the city. It has a popular garden café, great pool, loads of restaurants, large rooms with all the mod cons and a health club. Breakfast costs an extra US$16.

Flamenco Hotel (Map pp126-7; ☎ 735 0815; www .flamencohotels.com; 2 Sharia Gezirat al-Wusta; standard s/d US$90/108; superior s/d US$100/126; ☒ ☒ 🖳) A popular business hotel, the Flamenco occupies a relatively peaceful spot on the Nile and offers rooms that are comfortable and well equipped. There's a 24-hour business centre and most large 'superior' rooms have Internet connection (E£60 per day) and balconies with Nile views. All this plus good service, a lounge bar, restaurant and patisserie means that you'll usually need to book ahead to score a room. A 25% discount applies in May and June.

EATING

Cairo has the best and most sophisticated restaurants in Egypt, many of which serve world-class cuisine, boast magical Nile views and are frequented by the city's affluent elite. These venues often require a bit of dressing up as wealthy Cairenes, never knowingly underdressed, go to these venues to see and to be seen.

At the other end of the eating spectrum are the many quick-eat joints scattered around the city. Fast-food chains are mushrooming in Cairo quicker than you can say 'Big Mac and fries' and there are now over 30 international franchises, among them a Pizza Hut/KFC within swiping distance of the Sphinx's paws. But the city's signature fast foods have nothing to do with bland foods and Westernised marketing; instead cheap and tasty *kushari*, *fuul* (fava bean paste) and *ta'amiyya* rule the local fast-food roost. Downtown Cairo has a particularly good selection, especially around the AUC on Sharia Mahmoud Mohammed and Sharia Saray al-Gezira.

Bulaq

Villa d'Este (Map pp126-7; ☎ 580 8440; Conrad Cairo, 1191 Corniche el-Nil; dishes E£30-85; ☒ ☒) Cairo's top Italian restaurant has a formal dress code, a resident violin player and an old-fashioned feel. The food, mainly from northern Italy, is exquisite and beautifully presented – desserts are to die for.

Downtown

Forget fine dining. This is predominantly cheap and cheerful territory, with a few eateries with strong nostalgic overtones.

BUDGET

At-Tabie ad-Dumyati Downtown (Map p106; ☎ 575 4211; 31 Sharia Orabi; dishes E£2-8; ☒ 7am-1am); Mohandiseen (Map pp126-7; ☎ 304 1123; 17 Sharia Gamiat ad-Dowal al-Arabiyya; ☒ 7am-1am) About 200m north of Midan Orabi, this highly recommended place offers the best cheap meals in Cairo. Your choice of four salads from a large array costs E£3.25 and a small plate of *shwarma* costs £5.75. A fresh juice is E£2.50. You can sit down or take away. There's also a branch (Map pp102-3) in the food court of the Talaat Harb Complex.

Akher Sa'a (Map pp102-3; 8 Sharia Alfy; meals E£3-4; 24hr) A frantically busy *fuul* and *ta'amiyya* takeaway joint with a no-frills cafeteria next door, Akher Sa'a has a limited menu but its food is fresh and good. The *ta'amiyya* is particularly tasty.

Gad (Map pp102-3; ☎ 576 3583; 13 Sharia 26th of July; 9am-2am;) This fast-food eatery is usually packed to the rafters with a constant stream of young Cairenes sampling its fresh and well-priced food. The *fiteer* with Greek cheese (E£9.50) is scrumptious and the quarter chicken with rice and salad (E£10) is both tasty and very good value. You can sit upstairs or take away from the streetfront counters. There are branches throughout the city, including opposite the Khan al-Khalili (Map p112).

Abu Tarek (Map pp102-3; 40 Sharia Champollion; small/large kushari E£3/4; 8am-midnight) This phenomenally popular *kushari* joint has been serving up the noodly stuff to locals for nearly as long as touts have been working the Ramses train station. Though you may have to queue, it's worth it.

Sayed Hanafy (Map pp102-3; Midan Orabi; small/medium/large kushari E£2/3/4; 24hr) Though relatively new, this tiny place is building a big and well-deserved reputation for its excellent *kushari*.

International Public Meal Kushari (Map pp102-3; 4 Sharia Emad ad-Din; kushari E£2-3; 10am-midnight) The grand chandeliers, etched mirrors and marble walls of this Cairo institution stand in bizarre contrast with its sawdust-strewn floor and Formica-topped tables. The quality of the *kushari* is only average, but the waiters are friendly and service is fast.

Fatatri at-Tahrir (Map pp102-3; 166 Sharia Tahrir; dishes E£8-16; 7am-1am) This small restaurant serves sweet or savoury *fiteers*.

At-Tahrir (Map pp102-3; 19 Sharia Abdel Khalek Sarwat; small/medium/large kushari E£2/3/4) Another long-standing *kushari* joint serving up decent nosh for dirt-cheap prices. There's a second branch on Sharia Tahrir.

The **Felfela takeaway** (Map pp102-3; Sharia Talaat Harb) and **Abu Samra** (Map pp102-3; Tawfiqiyya Souq) sell excellent *ta'amiyya* sandwiches.

MIDRANGE
Greek Club (Map pp102-3; ☎ 575 0822; 3 Sharia Mahmoud Bassiouni; mains E£9-16; 7am-2am) With its great neo-classical interior, soaring ceilings and outdoor terrace, this Cairene institu-

---

THE AUTHOR'S CHOICE

El-Abd Bakery (Map pp102-3; 35 Sharia Talaat Harb; 8am-midnight) Cairo's most famous patisserie is always bursting at the seams with crowds of locals ordering its honey-drenched Oriental sweets and pastries, luridly coloured ice cream and wicked-looking European-style cakes. You'll need to fight to get to the counter and make your choice, after which you should pay the cashier and return to the counter to collect your takeaway parcel of pastries. There's another branch on the corner of Sharia 16th of July and Sharia Sherif.

---

tion oozes faded charm. There's no menu, but the waiter will reel off the dishes of the day, which are likely to include well-cooked Levantine choices such as *shish tawouq* (marinated chicken on skewers, E£30) and excellent Greek salad (E£15). A Stella costs E£10. You'll find it above the Groppi Patisserie (the entrance is on the side street).

Estoril (Map pp102-3; ☎ 574 3102; 12 Talaat Harb; mezze E£6, mains E£29-56;) Tucked down an alley next to the Amex office, this eatery has been serving up traditional Egyptian and French dishes since 1959. It claims to offer its diners an intro into 'the esoteric Cairene's world of art, literature, journalism and the rest' and though we're not sure it delivers on this, it's a great place to linger over a beer and a few mezze dishes.

Felfela Restaurant (Map pp102-3; ☎ 392 2833; 15 Sharia Hoda Shaarawi; mezze E£2-5, mains E£12-35; 8am-midnight;) Perpetually packed with tourists, coach parties and locals, Felfela deserves its popularity. A bizarre jungle theme rules when it comes to the décor, but the food is straight-down-the-line Egyptian and consistently good, especially the mezze and grilled chicken. A Stella costs E£12.

Café Riche (Map pp102-3; ☎ 392 9793; 17 Sharia Talaat Harb; dishes E£12-25; 8am-midnight;) This Cairene institution was being renovated when we visited. Once the favoured drinking spot of Cairo's intelligentsia, in recent years it's been a reliable and atmospheric spot to enjoy a meal and a glass of wine.

Alfy Bey (Map pp102-3; ☎ 577 4999; 3 Sharia Alfy; mains E£10-32; 1pm-1am) In business since 1938, Alfi Bey describes itself as a 'traditional

CAIRO

restaurant' and offers a rare Downtown dining experience: old-fashioned décor, age-old waiters and basic, somewhat stodgy food. The *plat du jour* costs E£30 and usually includes dolma, mixed vegetables, rice and some type of roast or grilled meat. Other dishes include kebabs, grilled chicken and stuffed pigeon. No alcohol is served (tea E£2).

Da Mario (Map pp102-3; ☎ 578 0444; Nile Hilton, 1113 Corniche el-Nil; pastas & pizzas E£25-45; ☺ noon-1.30am; ✗ ✗) The Hilton's Italian restaurant is a great spot to recover after a full-on morning at the Egyptian Museum. It serves decent pizzas, salads and home-made pastas.

SELF-CATERING

For fresh fruit and vegetables try **Tawfiqiyya Souq** (Map pp102-3; Sharia Talaat Harb) or **Souq Mansour** (Map pp102-3; off Midan Falaki). Tawfiqiyya Souq is open late at night and has a larger range of produce, including fruit, vegetables, bakeries and numerous *ba'al*s, the all-purpose grocers where you can stock up on things such as bread, cheese and yogurt. For Western-style bread try the **Nile Hilton Deli** (Map pp102-3; ☺ 8am-11pm). For pastries and sweets head for El-Abd Bakery (p147).

Garden City

MIDRANGE

Abou Shakra Garden City (Map p130; ☎ 531 6111; 69 Sharia Qasr al-Ainy; ☺ 9am-2am; ✗ ✗); Ma'adi (☎ 703 1333; 74 Sharia el-Nasr; ✗ ✗); Mohandiseen (Map pp126-7; 7 Sharia Gamiat ad-Dowal al-Arabiyya; ✗ ✗) Abou Shakra is where to come for a skewer or two. It's been serving up its kebab-and-kofta plates (E£28) and *shwarma* sandwiches (E£6 to E£12) at this main branch since 1947 and locals love it to bits. There's a takeaway at the front and a dining room behind it. Believe it or not, on Fridays an Imam reading from the Quran is posted next to the toilets. No alcohol is served.

Hard Rock Café (Map p130; ☎ 532 1277; Grand Hyatt Hotel, Corniche el-Nil; dishes E£25-40; ☺ noon-4am; ✗ ✗) Like its twins around the globe, this concept café/nightclub serves up burgers, rock paraphernalia and T-shirts (you can buy fake ones in the Khan al-Khalili) to a young crowd. The Nile view is great.

TOP END

Sabaya (Map pp102-3; ☎ 795 7171; Semiramis Inter-Continental, Corniche el-Nil; mezze E£12-25, mains E£40-70; ☺ 7.30pm-1am; ✗) Sabaya is sleek, stylish and utterly seductive. The contemporary Lebanese food could hold its head high in Beirut, the service is impeccable, the wine list is well priced and the surrounds are extremely attractive. The mezze are out of this world, particularly the *kibbeh nayye* (ground lamb and cracked wheat served raw) and cheese *sambousik* (pastries). A bottle of Chateau Marquise costs a reasonable E£130. The only quibble we have is that the ghastly music from the hotel foyer can sometimes intrude. Highly recommended.

Bird Cage (Map pp102-3; ☎ 795 7171; Semiramis InterContinental, Corniche el-Nil; mains E£40-80; ☺ noon-1am; ✗) Cairo's best Thai restaurant has contemplative décor featuring wooden floors, water features and starkly stylish table settings. The menu includes knockout dishes such as *koong sai mai* (deep fried marinated shrimps with Thai herbs wrapped in *kunafa*, E£80), *pla pow* (grilled marinated sea bass fillet wrapped in banana leaves, E£53) and *paneang ped yang* (roasted duck breast with thick red curry sauce, E£48). All are delicious. There's a good-value three-course degustation menu (E£105) and a four-course 'bento-box' lunch special (E£93) that includes sensational ice cream for dessert.

Revolving Restaurant (Map p130; ☎ 365 1234; 41st fl, Grand Hyatt Cairo, Corniche el-Nil; mains E£50-80; ☺ 7pm-1am; ✗ ✗) If you fancy a view with your meal, this über-pricey place offers 360-degree views of Cairo and an excellent international menu. You'll need to book and dress up to the nines.

Aqua (Map p130; ☎ 791 6876; Four Seasons Nile Plaza, 1089 Corniche el-Nil; ☺ 7pm-1am; ✗ ✗) The promise of 'an aquatic experience' may sound a bit fishy, but all is forgiven when the offerings from the sushi bar and the excellent Pacific Rim dishes from the kitchen are sampled. Nile views just enhance the package. It's pricey and trendy in equal measure, so you'll need to dress up and ensure that your credit card has leverage.

Spice (Map p130; ☎ 791 6888; Four Seasons Nile Plaza, 1089 Corniche el-Nil; ✗ ✗) Also at the Four Seasons Nile Plaza, this Cantonese restaurant is highly regarded and has a Nile view.

Asia House (Map pp102-3; ☎ 792 1000; Helnan Shepheard Hotel, Corniche el-Nil; ☺ noon-3.30pm & 7pm-midnight; ✗ ✗) One of the few places in Cairo serving top-quality tandoori dishes,

Asia House's menu travels from China to the subcontinent and back. The wood and stained-glass interior won't be to everyone's taste, but the food is pretty good (albeit pricey).

Gezira

TOP END

Kebabgy (Map p130; ☎ 739 8295; Sofitel El Gezirah; mezze E£13-33, kebabs E£50-56) The bestselling novel *The Yacoubian Building* (by Alaa al-Aswany) has a scene set at this Nileside restaurant when loathsome businessman Hagg Azzam and corrupt politician Kamal el-Fouli strike a dodgy deal – a scene close to reality, for the outdoor terrace here is one of the most popular places for Cairo's political and business elite to meet. The mezze are only of average quality but the kebabs, which are cooked over charcoal and served with freshly baked *baladi* bread, are excellent. A Stella costs E£17 and a glass of wine E£25. Go for dinner, when you don't have to see how dirty the Nile is.

El Morocco (Map pp126-7; ☎ 735 3314; Blue Nile Boat, Saraya al-Gezira; mezze E£15-38, mains E£39-49; ⌚ 9pm-4am; ✗) Fantastic Moroccan food is served in sumptuous surrounds at this perennially popular nightspot. The pigeon *bastilla* (pie, E£49) is fragrant and delicious and the lamb *tagine* (savoury stew) with prunes (E£43) will transport you to Marrakesh as soon as you taste it. A bottle of Grand Marquise costs E£118, which is surprisingly reasonable considering the amount of gold jewellery adorning the regulars. Book ahead and dress to kill.

Dar El Amar (Map pp126-7; ☎ 735 3114; Blue Nile Boat, Saraya al-Gezira; mezze E£10-36, grills E£27-47; ⌚ noon-3am) The challenge at this popular Lebanese floating restaurant is to draw your eyes away from the Nile views long enough to make a choice from the 53 mezze on offer. Unlike many other eateries on the river, prices are reasonable and you don't have to be wearing designer glad rags to score a table. A Stella costs E£21.

Giza & Pyramids Road

There are a number of good eateries in this part of Cairo, but it's debatable whether they're all worth the trip from town. Andrea's, El-Mashrabia, Seasons Restaurant and Fish Market certainly are.

BUDGET & MIDRANGE

Andrea's (☎ 381 0938; 59-60 Qanaat Maryoutia, Saqqara; set menu E£45; ⌚ 10am-9pm) This garden restaurant 1.5km north of Pyramids Rd is justly famous for its spit-roasted chicken served with salad, hummus and freshly baked bread – there's little else on the menu. Weather permitting, seating is in a large garden with playground equipment and a swimming pool – kids love it to bits and parents inevitably enjoy relaxing over the excellent food and cold Stella (E£15). Be warned that mosquitoes can be vicious, so douse yourself in repellent beforehand. A taxi from central Cairo should cost about E£20; E£5 from the Pyramids/Mena House area.

La Gourmandise (Map p130; ☎ 569 2557; Ground fl, First Mall complex, 35 Sharia al-Giza; ⌚ 10am-11pm; ✗ ✗) One of the city's most popular French patisseries, this ground-floor café in one of the city's glitziest malls comes complete with tuxedoed waiters, a profusion of potted palms and a grand piano. It serves good-quality Mediterranean dishes that are perfect for lunch.

If you want a cheap but good-quality eatery within walking distance of the Pyramids, try the Giza branch of **Felfela** (☎ 383 0234; 27 Cairo–Alexandria rd; ⌚ 8am-2am; ✗) or the popular Peace II Seafood Restaurant. Both are beloved by tour groups but also patronised by locals. You'll find them on the main road off the roundabout in front of the Mena House Oberoi hotel (Cairo side).

TOP END

Seasons Restaurant (Map p130; ☎ 573 1212; Four Seasons First Residence Hotel, 35 Sharia al-Giza; dishes E£50-120; ⌚ 11.30am-1am; ✗ ✗) The kitchen at Seasons – one of Cairo's most expensive restaurants – is known for its use of quality ingredients and its Italian-influenced food. The elegant dining room, wonderful flower arrangements, live jazz and excellent service are more Manhattan than Cairo, although the Nile views will always remind you where you are. The perfect spot for an all-out splurge.

Fish Market (Map p130; ☎ 570 9693; Americana Boat, 26 Sharia el-Nil; dishes E£25-50; ⌚ noon-2am; ✗ ✗) After selecting some of the finest and freshest seafood in town from the large display counter here, most guests tuck into delicious mezze while their fish is simply but expertly cooked. With its wonderful Nile views (particularly at night), laid-back feel and efficient service, this place is a real gem.

TGI Friday's (Map p130; ☎ 570 9690; ☺ noon–2am; ☒ ☒) The lower deck on the same boat is home to the all-American TGI Friday's, which is very popular with Egyptian families on weekends.

Moghul Room (Map p129; ☎ 383 3222; Oberoi Mena House, Pyramids Rd; mains E£55–110; ☺ 7.30–11.45pm Sat–Thu, 12.30–2.45pm & 7.30–11.45pm Fri; ☒ ☒) Cairo's best Indian restaurant specialises in mild North Indian–style curries and kebabs, with an emphasis on tandoori dishes. Though it's a long taxi ride from Downtown, the opulent décor, good food and live sitar music make the trip worthwhile. There's a wide range of vegetarian options (from E£35 to E£40) and an extensive (and pricey) wine list.

El-Mashrabia (Map p130; ☎ 748 2801; 4 Sharia Ahmed Nessim; mains E£12–25; ☺ noon–1am) Excellent Egyptian food is served at this intimate eatery. Meat lovers will be in seventh heaven (the kofta and tagines are particularly good), but vegetarians should steer clear. It's opposite the Orman Gardens. No alcohol is served.

Khan El Khalili (Map p129; ☎ 383 3222; Oberoi Mena House, Pyramids Rd; ☺ 24hr; ☒ ☒) The funky 1960s Arabesque interior of this hotel restaurant is more impressive than the food. Brass tables, marble floor and floor-to-ceiling windows overlooking the Great Pyramid star; dishes such as fish and chips (E£68), penne arrabbiata (E£39) and molokhiyya bil merakh (stewed leaf soup with chicken, E£65) are the somewhat bland supporting acts. A Stella costs E£19.

Heliopolis
BUDGET
El Shabrawy (Map p136; ☎ 258 6954; Sharia Ibrahimy; dishes E£4–15; ☺ 8am–2am) This extremely cheap and popular fuul and ta'amiyya place is one of the best cheap restaurants in the city. It serves up unusual dishes such as egg-fried cauliflower and agah (a cross between a puffed-up omelette and a giant ta'amiyya), and is almost totally vegetarian. It's signed in Arabic only – look for the red awning. The ta'amiyya stand (Map p136) on the opposite side of the street is also very popular.

MIDRANGE
Petit Palmyra (Map p136; ☎ 417 1720; 24 Sharia al-Ahram; mezze E£8–14, mains E£14–36; ☺ 11am–2am; ☒) The type of place your elderly parents would like, Petit Palmyra has a calming beige interior complete with comfortable chairs and stiffly starched serviettes. The menu serves up Egyptian-Levantine staples such as stuffed pigeon, and has a few European dishes as well (penne puttanesca E£14). A bottle of Grand Marquise will set you back E£110, but is probably a necessary accompaniment to the live piano music that is performed from 9pm each night.

Le Chantilly (Map p136; ☎ 415 5620; 11 Sharia Baghdad, Korba; ☺ 7am–1am; ☒ ☒) This Swiss-run place features a chalet-style décor and even serves up cheese (E£61) and meat (E£65) fondue. Fortunately, the waiters don't yodel. There's a wide range of pastas (E£22 to E£40) and soups (E£7) on the menu, as well as alcohol and great freshly baked bread.

Merryland (Map p136), north of central Heliopolis, is a large garden entertainment centre with a disco, nightclub, kiddies' rides and places to eat, including a branch of Andrea, TGI Friday's, Peking Garden and Mo'men, a popular Western-style fast food eatery. It's also home to the excellent Fakhr ad-Din Lebanese restaurant.

Islamic Cairo
There are plenty of fast-food stands and joints around Midan Hussein but the quality of the restaurants in this part of town is generally poor.

BUDGET
Egyptian Pancake House (Map p112; Midan Hussein; dishes E£10–15; ☺ 24hr) This popular place serves up made-to-order fiteer topped with your choice of cheese, egg, tomato, olives and ground meat. For dessert, choose your toppings from raisins, coconut and icing sugar.

Al-Halwagy (Map p112; ☎ 591 7055; Midan Hussein; dishes E£10–25; ☺ 24hr) Just along from the Pancake House, this good ta'amiyya, fuul and salad place has been around for nearly a century. You can eat at pavement tables or secrete yourself upstairs.

MIDRANGE
Khan el-Khalil Restaurant & Mahfouz Coffee Shop (Map p112; ☎ 590 3788; 5 Sikket el-Baddistan; snacks E£9–20, mains E£30–50; ☺ 10am–2am; ☒) After wan-

dering the souq and dealing with its touts there's nothing better than sheltering for a while in the luxurious Moorish-style interiors of this restaurant and adjoining café. It's also home to the only clean toilets in the *khan*. The only upmarket restaurant in the area, it's run by the Oberoi group and serves good, safe Egyptian–Levantine dishes to wealthy Egyptians and foreign tour groups. The café is a perfect if extremely pricey place to enjoy a tea (E£7) or Stella (E£8) and *sheesha* (E£6); it also serves mezze (E£9.50 to E£14) and sandwiches (E£12 to E£20). Look for the wooden door onto the lane.

Citadel (Map pp94-5; ☎ 510 7378; Al-Azhar Park; ☽ noon-1am; ✗ ☒) This new Oriental grill is located in the gorgeous setting of Cairo's newest park.

Alain Le Notre Café (Map pp94-5; ☽ 2pm-1am) Near Citadel, this place is a popular ice-cream stop.

Mohandiseen & Doqqi

These grey concrete suburbs look bland and flavourless, but it's possible to find some excellent restaurants among their plethora of fast-food outlets.

BUDGET

Al-Omdah (Map pp126-7; ☎ 346 2701; 6 Sharia al-Ghazza, Mohandiseen; dishes E£8-30; ☽ noon-2am; ✗ ☒) Cheap but succulent grilled meats such as kofta (minced meat and spices grilled on a skewer), kebab and *shish tawouq* are served with spicy pickles and salads at this ever-popular place. You can also score fast-food favourites such as *kushari* (E£4 to E£6) and *fiteer*. The next-door vegetarian branch features a good salad bar and serves up honest vegetable dishes. No alcohol is served at either.

MIDRANGE

Papillion (Map pp94-5; ☎ 347 1672; Tersana Shopping Centre, Sharia 26th of July, Mohandiseen; mains E£45-70; ☽ 11am-1am; ☒) Rapidly acquiring the reputation of being Cairo's second-best Lebanese restaurant (after Sabaya), Papillion offers excellent mezze dishes (try the goat-milk *labneh* and vine leaf dolma) and delectable grills (we reckon it serves the best *shish tawouq* in the city). It also home delivers.

Samakmak (Map pp126-7; ☎ 302 7308; 24 Ahmed Orabi, Mohandiseen; dishes E£25-55; ☽ 10am-4am) The noisy Cairo branch of the respected Alex-

andrian fish restaurant has an extremely odd setting on a paved terrace between two apartment blocks off a busy road. It's worth a visit, though, for its excellent, reasonably priced seafood. Choose what you want from the display and tell the waiters how you want it cooked; it will come to the table accompanied by salads and rice. No alcohol is served.

Cairo Jazz Club (Map pp126-7; ☎ 345 9939; www .cairojazzclub.com; 197 Sharia 26th of July, Agouza; ☽ noon-3am; ☒) This popular nightclub also does a good weekend brunch.

Le Tabasco (Map pp94-5; ☎ 359 1222; 45 Road 7, Ma'adi; minimum charge E£40; ☽ 1pm-2am) One of the city's most popular and glamorous bar/restaurants, Le Tabasco's menu is truly international, ranging from the Mediterranean to Mexico. Reservations are needed and be aware that the music gets loud later in the evening. There's also a branch of Abu el-Sid (see p152) here.

Zamalek

Zamalek has some of Cairo's best and most stylish restaurants. Cheap dining is not one of the island's fortes, but there are a few possibilities, including the Baraka *shwarma* stand on Sharia Brazil, and the popular Dido's Al Dente.

BUDGET

Didos Al Dente Zamalek (Map pp126-7; ☎ 735 9117; 26 Sharia Bahgat Ali; pasta E£5-19; ☒); Ma'adi (☎ 520 2255; 1 Road 270, off Sharia el-Nasr; ☽ 10am-2am) A pasta joint popular with students from the nearby AUC, Didos comes pretty close to living up to its claim of making the best pasta in town. It's tiny, so be prepared to wait on the street for a table. Neither branch serves alcohol.

MIDRANGE

Hana Korean Restaurant (Map pp126-7; ☎ 738 2972; 21 Sharia Aziz Abaza; mains E£20-40; ☒) You'll feel as if you're in Seoul when you eat at this bustling Zamalek restaurant. The *kimchi* (fermented chilli peppers and vegetables) packs a tremendous punch, the fried dumplings (E£8) are excellent, the BBQ beef is tender and the Stella (E£12) is ice cold – we can't ask more than that. Perhaps the best endorsement is provided by Cairo's Korean expats, whose constant presence pays testament to the authenticity of the food.

Maison Thomas Zamalek (Map pp126-7; ☎ 735 7057; 157 Sharia 26th of July; pizzas E£22-35, sandwiches E£16-26; ⏰ 24hr; ☒); Heliopolis (Map p136; ☎ 419 2914; 114 Sharia al-Mirghani; ⏰ 24hr); Ma'adi (☎ 524 3800; 1 Sharia Abd el-Waheb; ⏰ 24hr) Is this the best pizza in Cairo? Many locals think it is, and can be seen lining up to perch on the high stools and grab a quick pizza or sandwich fix. You can eat in or take away (alcohol is served only with takeaway).

L'Aubergine (Map pp126-7; ☎ 738 0080; 5 Sharia Sayyed al-Bakry, Zamalek; mains E£16-30; ⏰ noon-2am; ☒) This stylish Western-style bistro serves up a wide range of dishes, lots of which are vegetarian. The menu includes blue cheese gnocchi (E£23), aubergine moussaka (E£22) and fennel with parmesan au gratin (E£16). Its upstairs bar (Stella E£14) is popular, and often has a DJ.

Andrea Zamalek (Map pp126-7; ☎ 737 0523/5; 3 Sharia Abu al-Feda; mains E£20-45; ⏰ 1pm-1am; ☒) Ma'adi (☎ 524 7300; Corniche el-Ma'adi; ⏰ 11am-midnight) Not to be confused with the similarly named (and excellent) chicken restaurant in Saqqara, this Greek/Egyptian place occupies an enviable position on the Nile and has a welcoming terrace where you can eat simple but tasty dishes, listen to the in-house DJ and enjoy a *sheesha*.

Deals (Map pp126-7; ☎ 736 0502; 2 Sharia Maahad al-Swissry; dishes E£24-35; ⏰ 4pm-2am) Although primarily a bar, Deals serves decent burgers, chilli con carne, calamari and large salads, as well as daily specials. As bar food goes, it's good and inexpensive. Get there before 8pm to stand a chance of finding table space.

La Piazza (Map pp126-7; ☎ 736 2961; 3rd fl, Four Corners, 4 Sharia Hassan Sabry; pasta E£20-30, mains E£34-50; ⏰ 12.30pm-12.30am; ☒ ☒) Part of a complex of restaurants under the collective title Four Corners, La Piazza is decorated to resemble a gazebo – think cane furniture, floral-motif stained glass and candy-cane colours. It won't be to everyone's taste, but it's a good place for lunch and casual dinners, offering soups (E£9 to E£14), club sandwiches (E£31), chicken Caesar salad (E£22) and pastas (E£26 to E£41). There are a number of vegetarian dishes. A glass of wine costs E£30 and a Stella E£12.

Five Bells (Map pp126-7; ☎ 735 8980; 13 Sharia Ismail Mohammed; ⏰ 12.30-1.30pm; ☒) This old-fashioned place has one of the few outdoor courtyards in Zamalek and is a pleasant

spot for a summer dinner. Food is uninspired but quite edible international fare, with pastas, grills and fondue featuring on the menu. It's a bit pricey, but the cute cherub fountain compensates.

Peking Zamalek (Map pp126-7; ☎ 736 6167; entrees E£8-31, mains E£17-45; ⏰ noon-1am); Downtown (Map pp102-3; ☎ 591 2381; 14 Sharia Saray al-Ezbekiyya; ☒ ☒) This dimly lit and attractively decorated basement bar/restaurant serves up adequate Cantonese dishes and Beijing-style claypot specials. It also offers what it calls 'Peking barbeques' of beef, chicken or seafood (E£31 to E£45). A Stella Premium costs E£16. There are branches in Heliopolis and in Ma'adi. Check your bill carefully. It also home delivers.

TOP END

Abu el-Sid Zamalek (Map pp126-7; ☎ 735 9640; 157 Sharia 26th of July; mezze E£6-24, mains E£20-50; ⏰ noon-2am; ☒); Ma'adi (☎ 380 5050; 45 Sharia 45) A sumptuous Orientalist fantasy of a restaurant/bar, Abu el-Sid serves traditional Egyptian food to wannabe pashas amid hanging lamps, large cushions and brass tables. This is a great place to try famous Egyptian dishes such as chicken with *molokhiyya* (E£32) or stuffed pigeon (E£20), followed by a *sheesha* and coffee. A beer costs E£20. Both branches are extremely popular, so make sure you book ahead.

Justine's (Map pp126-7; ☎ 736 2961; 3rd fl, Four Corners, 4 Hassan Sabry; mains E£45-85; ⏰ 1-4pm & 8-11pm; ☒ ☒) Resembling a discreet gentleman's club, with panoramic views over the lush gardens of the Gezira Club, Justine's is the perfect place for a romantic dinner or important business meeting. Comfortable leather furniture, subdued lighting and pristine napery set a classy tone that the food more than lives up to. This is one of the best places in town to enjoy beef dishes such as roasted tenderloin with green peppercorn sauce (E£86) or quality seafood concoctions (roasted salmon served with leek and red wine sauce, E£84). There's an impressive and well priced wine list.

Torii (Map pp126-7; ☎ 739 4691; Cairo Marriott; sushi per piece E£10-35, sashimi per serve E£30-49, noodles E£53-88; ⏰ noon-midnight; ☒) The theatrical interior of this upmarket Japanese restaurant comes complete with a wooden sushi bar, Japanese sushi chefs, arty flower arrangements and a ceiling illuminated with hundreds of twinkling lights. It claims to be 'the gateway to sushi and self discovery', and while we can't confirm the latter we certainly enjoyed the former. Service is exemplary. A Stella costs E£19.

La Bodega (Map pp126-7; ☎ 735 6761; Baehler's Mansions, 1st fl, 157 Sharia 26th of July; mains E£29-50; ✆ 7pm-1am) La Bodega's extremely attractive interior can't compensate for its disappointing menu. Asian-inspired dishes feature, but just don't make the grade – when we visited, the chicken with cabbage was bland and the spicy beef was overcooked. Limit your visit to a drink in the fabulous cocktail lounge or extremely popular bar. A glass of wine costs E£20.

JW's Steakhouse (Map pp126-7; ☎ 736 2961; Cairo Marriott Hotel; ✆ 1-4pm & 6.30pm-midnight; ✖ 🐾) JW's is more Texan than the Alamo, with juicy steaks and a rodeo interior. Expats adore it, and regularly order up big from the classic menu and extensive wine list.

Chin Chin (Map pp126-7; ☎ 737 2119; 3rd fl, Four Corners, 4 Sharia Hassan Sabry; mains E£35-70; ✆ 7.30-11.30pm; ✖ 🐾) This Chinese stalwart is a great place to bring the family. The friendly and efficient waiters serve up good-quality basics such as spring rolls, stir fries and egg noodles.

SELF-CATERING

Marriott Bakery (Map pp126-7; ☎ 735 8888; Cairo Marriott, Sharia Saray al-Gezira; caffe latte E£14; ✆ 6.30am-10pm) This place sells excellent European-style bread.

Sekem (Map pp126-7; ☎ 738 2724; Sharia Ahmed Sabry) Off Sharia Brazil, Sekem is Cairo's only health food store, selling a small selection of organic products.

Alpha Market (Map pp126-7; Sharia Abu al-Feda) Has everything, including both local and imported foods.

Mandarine Koueider (Map pp126-7; ☎ 735 5010; 17 Sharia Shagaret ad-Durr; per scoop E£2.75; ✆ 9am-11pm) Cairenes regularly cross town for a fix of the delectable ice cream at Mandarine Koueider. There are other branches in Heliopolis (Map p136) and Ma'adi.

Several shops on Sharia 26th of July sell good-quality fruit and vegetables. Pork products such as prosciutto and ham are available from the deli counter at Maison Thomas (opposite) and there's a 24-hour Metro Supermarket (Map pp126–7) branch on Sharia Ismail Mohammed.

DRINKING

Most of Cairo's bars and pubs are in hotels, on the island of Zamalek or on boats moored along the island. Downtown has some dark, cheap drinking dens, which are pretty seedy, and can be fun, but are certainly not recommended for women on their own. Muslims are not supposed to drink alcohol, so it is only served indoors or on the terraces of five-star hotels. During Ramadan alcohol is only served to foreigners.

Cafés & Patisseries

The following are all European-style places, not to be confused with *ahwas*, the Egyptian coffeehouses (see p154) where food is not available.

DOWNTOWN

Groppi's (Map pp102-3; Midan Talaat Harb; ✆ 7am-midnight) This was once the place to take tea and cake, but that was a long time ago. Now the offerings are poor and overpriced (there's a minimum charge of E£19 per person, which gives you a tea or coffee and two slices of plastic-looking gateau), and the tearoom reeks of cheap tobacco. For nostalgia buffs only.

Groppi Garden (Map pp102-3; ☎ 361 1946; Sharia Adly; ✆ 7am-midnight) Same uninteresting pastries as the other Groppi, but the garden terrace here is a pleasant and relatively peaceful place for a pricey cup of tea.

La Chesa (Map pp102-3; ☎ 393 9360; 21 Sharia Adly; ✆ 7am-midnight) This air-conditioned coffee shop serves Illy coffee, Swiss pastries and light meals.

GARDEN CITY

Cilantro (Map pp102-3; ☎ 792 4571; 31 Sharia Mohammed Mahmoud; ✆ 9am-2am) This popular and stylish café is located opposite the AUC. Small and extremely clean, it serves up excellent Italian-style coffee (regular cappuccino E£6) and Twinings tea (E£4.50), and has open fridges displaying packaged sandwiches, cakes and salads (E£5.50 to E£14), which you can eat in or take away. The brownies (E£3.50) are particularly delicious. There are other, equally impressive, branches in Zamalek (Map pp126–7), Ma'adi, Giza and Heliopolis (Map p136). Most of these branches offer free wireless access.

ZAMALEK

Simonds (Map pp126-7; ☎ 735 9436; 112 Sharia 26th of July, Zamalek; ☾ 7am-10pm) The barista here looks as if he's been frothing cappuccino (E£5) for over half a century and the croissants (E£2.50) are as good as any served up in Paris. Claiming a rickety stool at the bar is a great Cairene breakfast tradition.

Beano's Zamalek (Map pp126-7; ☎ 736 2388; 8 Midan Sheikh al-Marsafy; ☾ 8am-midnight); Downtown (Map pp102-3; ☎ 792 2328; 49 Sharia el-Falaky, off Sharia Mohammed Mahmoud; ☾ 8am-midnight) This branch of an extremely popular chain serves good coffee (large cappuccino E£9), fresh juice (E£6) and a range of snacks (sandwiches E£13 to E£18) to scores of young Cairenes who come to catch up on the gossip, use the wireless Internet provided and listen to music videos. There's another branch in Heliopolis (Map p136).

Café Tabasco (Map pp126-7; ☎ 735 8465; 18B Sharia al-Marashly; cappuccino E£7; ☾ 7am-3am; ✖) This comfortable basement café resembles someone's lounge room. It's a great spot to spend an hour or so browsing the magazine collection and drinking coffee. The food (baguette sandwiches E£12 to E£14, pizzas E£16 to E£22) is generally forgettable, though the breakfast (omelette E£12, pancakes E£14) has a fair few devotees among the expat set.

Coffee Roastery (Map pp126-7; ☎ 738 0936; 140 Sharia 26th of July; espresso E£4, cappuccino E£5.75; ☾ 24hr) Its fast-food menu, blaring music videos and young staff make this Hard Rock café–style eatery an extremely popular meeting place for groups of young locals. The coffee, served in 30 different ways, is surprisingly good. Don't bother with the food.

Marriott Bakery (Map pp126-7; ☎ 735 8888; Cairo Marriott, Sharia Saray al-Gezira; caffe latte E£14; ☾ 6.30am-10pm) You can order a decent but mighty pricey Italian-style coffee here (Illy beans) and enjoy it with a sandwich (E£6.50 to E£16) or cake (E£5.50 to E£9).

Ahwas

Cairo has thousands of *ahwa*s where you can while away the hours over a glass of *shai*, a *sheesha* and a few games of *towla* (backgammon). Smoking *sheesha*s also used to be strictly for men, but it is not at all unusual to see girls and women smoking, even at the regular *ahwa*s. Most *ahwa*s are open from 8am to 2am. *Domina* (dominoes), *towla* and

occasionally cards are the standard games, although chess is sometimes played.

Ashara (Map pp102-3; cnr Sharia Talaat Harb & Sharia 26th of July, Downtown) A bright, clean place behind the Grand Hotel that's a favourite stop on the itinerary of the city's wandering hawkers.

Fishawi's Coffeehouse (Map p112; in alley off Midan Hussein, Khan al-Khalili; ☾ 24hr except in Ramadan) One of the oldest *ahwa*s in the city, and certainly the most famous, Fishawi's (signed El Fishawy) is still a great place to watch the world go by. Despite being swamped by foreign tourists and equally wide-eyed out-of-town Egyptians, it is a regular *ahwa*, serving up *shai* (E£3) and *sheesha* (E£4.50) to stallholders and shoppers alike. It's especially alluring in the early hours of the morning. Note that it closes from 3am till about 5pm during Ramadan.

Ash-Shams (Map pp102-3; Downtown) Decorated with gilt stucco and kitschy faux-classical paintings, this colourful *ahwa*, in the courtyard alleyway between Sharia 26th of July and Tawfiqiyya Souq in Downtown, is busy with people from the nearby market and travellers from neighbouring hotels. Check your bill before paying.

Mahran (Map pp102-3; ☎ 576 2487; Downtown) This is a friendly neighbourhood *ahwa* situated under a tree in an alley off Sharia Mahmoud Bassiouni in Downtown. Women are welcome.

Kawkab ash-Sharq (Map pp102-3; ☎ 575 1111; 11 Sharia Saray al-Ezbekiyya, Downtown; ☾ 24hr) Dedicated to the 'Star of the Orient', the Egyptian singer Umm Kolthum, this café is popular with couples and families who come to listen to her music and admire her portraits.

Zahret al-Bustan (Map pp102-3; Sharia Talaat Harb, Downtown) Formerly the haunt of intellectuals, journalists and writers, this coffeehouse behind Café Riche has become a favourite with backpackers and students from the nearby AUC. With hustlers too, so keep your wits about you.

Once the *ahwa* was the only place you could puff on a *sheesha*, but it is now so fashionable that you can indulge the habit at glam hotel café terraces including the 1st-floor, Nile-view café at the **Semiramis InterContinental** (Map pp102-3; ☎ 795 7171; Corniche el-Nil, Downtown; ☾ 8pm-1am summer); the Helnan Shepheard Hotel's **Narjila Café** (Map pp102-3; ☎ 792 1000; Corniche el-Nil, Garden City; minimum charge

E£15; ⓨ 11am-late); the Hilton's courtyard **Abu Aly Café** (Map pp102-3; ☎ 578 0444; Nile Hilton, 1113 Corniche el-Nil, Downtown; minimum charge E£15; ⓨ 10am-1.30am); and the Kaab Aaly terrace bar (see right). You can also order a *sheesha* in trendy restaurants such as Abu el-Sid (see p152). For a game of cards, head to **Cafeteria Horreyya** (Map pp102-3; Midan Falaki, Bab al-Luq) or **Zahret al-Midan** (Map p121; cnr Midan Sayyida Zeinab & Sharia Abdel Meguid, Garden City).

Bars
LOCAL BARS
If you want to see Cairo's underbelly, there are a few Downtown bars serving beer and (mainly) local spirits. Be warned that they're all fairly unwelcoming: none are suitable for women on their own and the toilets are pretty foul. A Stella will set you back around E£7.50 at most of these joints.

Cafeteria Horreyya (Map pp102-3; Midan Falaki, Bab al-Luq) Primarily a coffeehouse, the Horreya also serves the cheapest Stella in town (E£5.50).

Cafeteria Port Tawfiq (Map pp102-3; Midan Orabi, Downtown) Dark and slightly more inviting than the rest in this neighbourhood.

Cairo (Map pp102-3; ☎ 574 1479; 3 Sharia Saray al-Ezbekiyya, Downtown; ⓨ 24hr) Walk through the restaurant to the 1st-floor bar. The beer is not always icy, but the atmosphere is slightly sleazy and fun.

Cap d'Or (Map pp102-3; Sharia Abdel Khalek Sarwat, Downtown) Quite run down, but nonetheless possibly the best of central Cairo's local bars. The staff and regulars are quite used to seeing foreigners.

Cafeteria Stella (Map pp102-3; cnr Sharia Hoda Shaarawi & Sharia Talaat Harb, Downtown; ⓨ until midnight) A spit'n'sawdust–style place with lots of small tables and a depressing air.

WESTERN-STYLE BARS
As is the case in any other busy city, bars open and close and go in and out of favour. The best place to go boozing (if you have the cash) is Zamalek, where several stylish bars are within staggering distance of each other.

White/Zen (Map pp126-7; ☎ 012 230 4404; 25 Sharia Hassan Assem, Zamalek; ⓨ 6pm-3am; ✖) An über-glam bar that serves fusion cuisine and sushi, White/Zen has a DJ and sells two Heinekens for the price of one at its Wednesday happy hour.

La Bodega (Map pp126-7; ☎ 735 6761; 157 Sharia 26th of July, Zamalek; ⓨ noon-2am; ✖) A swish lounge bar, which is part of La Bodega restaurant (see p153). You need to dress to impress here and drinks are pricey, but you'll get to watch Cairo's nouveaux rich at play, which is always fun.

Kaab Aaly (Map pp102-3; ☎ 578 0444; Nile Hilton, 1113 Corniche el-Nil, Downtown; ⓨ 9am-2am; ✖) Formerly named High Heels (Kaab Aaly is the Arabic translation), this place is where local fashion victims come to strut their stuff. Occupying one of the hotel's Nileside outdoor terraces, it's a great place to enjoy a few drinks before kicking off to a nearby nightclub. Its popular dining area has a decent Lebanese menu (mains E£35) and there's also a fresh juice bar.

Sand Bar (Map pp126-7; ☎ 736 3558; 13A Sharia al-Marashly, Zamalek; ⓨ 4pm-3am; ✖) A newcomer to the local drinking scene, this stylish place is more laid-back than most. You don't need to dress to impress, which is a welcome change in this part of town.

Marriott Garden Café (Map pp126-7; ☎ 735 8888; Cairo Marriott, Sharia Saray al-Gezira, Zamalek; ⓨ 6.30am-10pm) The Marriott's garden terrace is one of the most comfortable spots in town to relax over a drink. Big cane chairs, a lack of the thick cigarette smoke so ubiquitous in the city's other drinking dens, and good-quality wine and beer make it deservedly popular. You can eat here, too. The only downside is that it's pricey.

Le Tabasco Ma'adi (Map pp94-5; ☎ 359 1222; 45 Road 7; minimum charge E£40; ⓨ 1pm-2am; ✖); Doqqi (☎ 336 5583; 8 Midan Amman; ⓨ 1pm-2am; ✖) Loud and smoky, Le Tabasco serves up drinks, good music and fun in equal measure. Designer outfits are *de rigueur*.

L'Aubergine (Map pp126-7; ☎ 738 0080; 5 Sharia Sayyed al-Bakry, Zamalek; mains E£16-30; ⓨ noon-2am; ✖) The 1st floor of this popular restaurant is home to a popular bar that is always packed with AUC types. Tuesday is 'Retro Night' – it's up to you whether this should be taken as a warning or not.

Abu el-Sid (Map pp126-7; ☎ 735 9640; 157 Sharia 26th of July, Zamalek; mezze E£6-24, mains E£20-50; ⓨ noon-2am; ✖) Though predominantly a restaurant (see p152), the bar here is a great spot to indulge in a *sheesha* and expensive drink (beer E£20). You'll need to frock up to get past the doormen.

Deals (Map pp126-7; ☎ 736 0502; 2 Sharia Sayyed al-Bakry, off Sharia 26th of July, Zamalek; ☾ 6pm-2am) A small cellar bar that gets too smoky and packed for comfort late in the evening and at weekends, Deals is pleasant enough at quieter times. There are other branches in Mohandiseen and Heliopolis (Map p136).

Odeon Palace Hotel (Map pp102-3; ☎ 577 6637; 6 Sharia Abdel Hamid Said, Downtown; ☾ 24hr; ✗) This rooftop bar is favoured by Cairo's heavy-drinking theatre and cinema clique. A Stella costs E£10.

Sangria (Map pp126-7; ☎ 579 6511; Casino ash-Shaggara, Corniche el-Nil, Bulaq; ☾ 1pm-3am; ✗) Opposite the World Trade Centre, the Sangria has great Nile views. The Far Eastern–inspired décor and hip music adds to the ambience. There's a minimum charge of E£50.

Hard Rock Café (Map p130; ☎ 532 1281; Grand Hyatt Cairo, Corniche el-Nil, Garden City; ☾ noon-4am; ✗ ✗) Exactly what you'd expect from the global chain.

Windsor Bar (Map pp102-3; ☎ 591 5277; 19 Sharia Alfy, Downtown; ☾ 6pm-1am; ✗) The bar at the Windsor Hotel is a one-off, with colonial-era décor, grand old waiters and a loyal crowd of elderly drinkers. Solo women will feel quite comfortable here. A Stella costs E£11.

Revolving Restaurant Lounge (Map p130; ☎ 365 1234; 41st fl, Grand Hyatt Cairo, Corniche el-Nil, Garden City; minimum charge E£35; ☾ 3pm-2am; ✗ ✗) Cheesy, yes, but there's a lot to be said for comfortable seats and knock-out views. There's a pianist and you'll need to frock up.

Red Onion (☎ 520 0240; 27A Road 276, New Ma'adi; ☾ 12.20pm-1.30am; ✗ ✗) A popular haunt of the city's expat community, Red Onion is a decent spot to grab a beer and some basic pub grub.

ENTERTAINMENT

Western-style clubs, cinemas that screen English-language films and five-star nightclubs with floorshows abound in Cairo. Theatre is mainly in Arabic, and is thus not very accessible to travellers.

Nightclubs

There are nightclubs in most of the city's five-star hotels, on some Nile houseboats and in a few upmarket restaurants, but most of these are Gulf-style temples of glitz or Hard Rock Café–style venues that are more hoedown than get down. The 'in'

places change from week to week, but there are a few perennials.

Absolute (Map pp126-7; ☎ 579 6512; Corniche el-Nil, Bulaq; minimum charge E£50; ☾ 1pm-3am) If you can get past the door bitches (and we use the expression with feeling), you'll have a good time here. There's a big dance floor, a good DJ and a delicious sushi menu. Bookings are advisable.

Rive Gauche (Map pp126-7; ☎ 012 210 0129; 21 Sharia Maahad al-Swissry, Zamalek). Above the faded Zamalek Hotel, this newly refurbished club has a large dance floor and different DJs each night. There's also a very pleasant outdoor terrace to get your breath after some boogieing. With less attitude than many other venues around town, it's a great spot to party.

Latex (Map pp102-3; ☎ 578 0444, 578 0666 ext 285/214; Nile Hilton, 1113 Corniche el-Nil, Downtown; ☾ 10pm-5am) One of Cairo's most enduring disco venues (formerly called Jackie's), this was the venue *de jour* when we last hit town. It's famous for its theme nights, including Arabic fusion (Tuesday), house (Friday) and R&B/soul (Saturday). The door policy calls for mixed groups only (to prevent groups of ogling males), but groups of women are generally allowed in.

El Morocco (Map pp126-7; ☎ 735 3114, ext 100; Blue Nile Boat, 9A Saraya al-Gezira; ☾ 9pm-4am) Cairo's gilded 20- and 30-somethings love this Moroccan restaurant/nightclub to bits and if you can air kiss and pout you'll feel right at home. There's a different DJ every night of the week except Sunday.

Hard Rock Café (Map p130; ☎ 532 1277; Grand Hyatt Hotel, Corniche el-Nil, Garden City; ☾ noon-4am) Differs from the other venues mentioned here in that burgers are more evident than Botox. There's a DJ, live music and the dreaded karaoke.

Exit (Map pp102-3; ☎ 391 8127; Atlas Hotel, 2 Sharia Mohammed Rushdie, Downtown; ☾ 8pm-3am) A cheap and perennially popular venue that spins everything from African beats to rap to pop.

Cinemas

For details of what's showing, check the listings section of *Al-Ahram Weekly* or *Cairo* magazine. Tickets typically cost around E£25, and can be cheaper at daytime sessions. The following places regularly screen English-language films:

Cairo Sheraton Cinema (Map p130; ☎ 760 6081; Cairo Sheraton, Midan al-Galaa, Doqqi) The closest Cairo has to an art-house cinema. Sessions at 1pm, 4pm, 7pm and 10pm, with extra sessions at 12.30pm on Thursday and Friday.

Cinema Karim I & II (Map p106; ☎ 592 4830; 15 Sharia Emad ad-Din, Downtown) A refurbished cinema that typically screens action movies. Cheap tickets make it popular with young Egyptian males – it's not a place for unaccompanied women. The entrance to Karim II is around the corner. Sessions at 10am, 10.30am, 12.30pm, 1.30pm, 3.30pm, 6.30pm, 9.30pm and 12.30am.

Cinema Metro (Map pp102–3; ☎ 393 7061; 35 Talaat Harb, Downtown) Once Cairo's finest, now one of its scruffiest. Sessions at 11am, 1pm, 4pm, 7pm, 10pm and 1am.

Cinema Tahrir (Map p130; ☎ 335 4726; 112 Sharia Tahrir, Doqqi) Comfortable, modern cinema where single females shouldn't receive hassle.

City Centre (☎ 010 667 5096; 3 Sharia Makram Ebeid, Nasr City) Sessions at 11.30am, 1.15pm, 4.15pm, 7.15pm, 10.15pm, 1am.

Cosmos (☎ 574 2177; 12 Sharia Emad el-Din, Downtown) Five screens.

Family (☎ 524 8100, 524 8200; Othman Buildings, next to Ma'adi Hospital, Ma'adi)

Galaxy (☎ 532 5745; 67 Sharia Abdel-Aziz al-Seoud, Manial) Six screens. Sessions at 10.30am, 1.30pm, 4pm, 7pm,10pm and 1am.

Good News Grand Hyatt (Map p130; ☎ 365 1234, 365 4448; Grand Hyatt Annex, Nile Corniche, Garden City) Three screens. Sessions at 10.20am, 1pm, 4pm, 7pm, 10pm and 1am.

Nile City (☎ 461 9101/2/3; Northern Tower, Nile Corniche)

Normandy Cinema I & II (Map p136; ☎ 258 0254; 31 Sharia al-Ahram, Heliopolis) Open-air screenings in summer.

Ramses Hilton I & II (Map pp102–3; ☎ 574 7435; 7th fl, Ramses Hilton Mall, Midan Abdel Moniem Riad, Downtown) Two relatively new, well maintained screens; II is a bit small. Sessions at 10.30am, 1.30pm, 6.30pm, 9.30pm and midnight.

Rivoli (Map pp102–3; ☎ 575 5053/95 Sharia 26th of July, Downtown) Five screens.

Stars City (☎ 480 2013/4; Stars Centre, Nasr City) Thirteen screens. Sessions at 10.50am, 1.30pm, 3.30pm, 6.30pm, 9.30pm and 12.30am.

A number of the city's cultural centres and universities screen experimental and retrospective film programmes.

American University in Cairo (Map pp102–3; ☎ 797 6373; Main Campus, Sharia Sheikh Rihan, Garden City)

Centre Français de Culture et de Coopération Heliopolis (☎ 417 4824; 5 Sharia Chafik al-Dib, Ard al-Golf; ☾ 10am-10pm Sun-Thu); Mounira (Map pp94–5; ☎ 794 7679; 1 Sharia Madrassat al-Huquq al-Fransiyya; ☾ 8am-7pm)

Egyptian Centre for International Cultural Co-operation (Map pp126–7; ☎ 736 5419; 11 Sharia Shagaret Al Dorr, Zamalek)

Sawy Cultural Centre (Culture Wheel; Map pp126–7; ☎ 736 6178; www.culturewheel.com; Sharia 26th of July, Zamalek)

Townhouse Gallery of Contemporary Art (Map pp102–3; ☎ 576 8086; 10 Sharia Nabrawy, Downtown; ☾ 10am-2pm & 6-9pm Sat-Wed, 6-9pm Fri)

Live Music & Theatre

Cairo Opera House (Map p130; ☎ 739 8144; www.operahouse.gov.eg; Gezira Exhibition Grounds, Gezira) The Cairo Opera House has five auditoria. Performances by the Cairo Opera and the Cairo Symphony Orchestra tend to be held in its Main Hall and there's a varied programme of recitals, theatre and dance from Egypt and the rest of the world in its Small Hall, Gomhouria Theatre and Arab Music Institute. Occasional performances are staged in the open-air theatre. Jacket and tie are required by males for Main Hall performances (travellers have been known to borrow them from staff). Programmes are available at the information window (to the right of the main entrance) and performances are listed in the 'ET Calendar' in *Egypt Today*.

American University in Cairo Theatre (Map pp102–3; ☎ 794 2964; Midan Tahrir, Garden City) There are regular music recitals and plays of varying quality at the Ewart Hall, the Wallace Theatre and Falaki Studio Theatre at the AUC. Events are advertised on boards at the campus entrance on Sharia Mohammed Mahmoud, in the 'ET Calendar' in *Egypt Today* and in the *Egyptian Gazette*.

Other live-music venues:

Cairo Jazz Club (Map pp126–7; ☎ 345 9939; www.cairojazzclub.com; 197 Sharia 26th of July, Agouza; ☾ noon-3am) Modern Egyptian folk, electronica, Oriental fusion, traditional. Two bars.

After Eight (Map pp102–3; ☎ 574 0855; 6 Sharia Qasr el-Nil, Downtown; minimum charge Fri-Wed E£60, Thu E£90; ☾ 8pm-2am) Jazz, swing, folk and rock.

Jazz Up (Map pp102–3; ☎ 578 0444; Nile Hilton, 1113 Corniche el-Nil, Downtown; ☾ 11am-2am) This pricey bar features live music and theme nights (salsa, Latino, '60s and '70s).

Sawy Cultural Center (Culture Wheel; Map pp126–7; ☎ 736 6178; www.culturewheel.com; Sharia 26th of July, Zamalek) Musical poetry, rock, classical Arabic and Nubian.

Occasional performances are staged in the open-air Al-Genaina Theatre (Map pp94–5) at the new Al-Azhar Park in Islamic Cairo. Check the 'ET Calendar' in *Egypt Today* or the *Egyptian Gazette* for details.

Dance

BELLY DANCING

If you only see one belly dancer in your life, it had better be in Cairo, the art form's true home. These days the best belly dancers perform at Cairo's five-star hotels. Shows typically begin at around midnight, although the star dancer might not take to the stage until 2am or later. Admissions are steep; expect to shell out upwards of E£150. This will include food, but not drinks. At the other end of the scale, you can watch belly dancing for just a few pounds at several places Downtown and along Pyramids Rd (watch out for expensive rip-offs). These places cater mainly to Egyptians, rather than oil-rich Gulf Arabs who make up much of the five-star audiences. They're fairly seedy and most of the dancers have the appearance and grace of amateur wrestlers, but it can be fun, especially when inebriated patrons join in, as they invariably do.

Haroun al-Rashid Nightclub (Map pp102-3; ☎ 795 7171; Corniche el-Nil, Downtown; ⏱ 11pm-3.30am Tue-Sun) At the Semiramis InterContinental Hotel, this is where the famous Dina undulates.

Casablanca Club (Map p130; ☎ 336 9700; Midan al-Galaa, Doqqi; ⏱ 7pm-4am) Located in the Cairo Sheraton where Soraya is the star.

Nile Pharaoh Dinner Cruises (☎ 570 1000; cruise E£155; ⏱ 7.15pm, 8pm, 10pm & 10.30pm daily) A touristy but quite enjoyable option is to join the package tourists on one of the Nile cruises that are operated by the Mena House Oberoi hotel. These feature a floorshow with belly dancer and Egyptian singer. The meal is buffet-style international cuisine and the cruise takes two hours, from Giza to Downtown and back. Bookings are essential.

Palmyra (Map pp102-3; admission E£5.50; off Sharia 26th of July, Downtown ⏱ 10pm-4am) The best of the 'other end of the scale' is Palmyra, a cavernous, dilapidated 1950s dancehall in an alley off Sharia 26th of July. It has a full Arab musical contingent, belly dancers who get better the more money is thrown at them, and an occasional singer or acrobat. The Stella here costs a very reasonable

E£11, but the *sheesha*s are expensive (E£20 for apple). There's a minimum charge of E£35, which basically covers the entrance fee, a beer and a *sheesha*.

SUFI DANCING

Al-Tannoura Egyptian Heritage Dance Troupe (☎ 512 1735; admission free; ⏱ 7pm winter, 8pm summer Mon, Wed & Sat) There are regular displays of Sufi dancing by this troupe at the El-Gawhara Theatre at the Citadel (see p119). Go to the exit gate rather than the main entrance gate of the Citadel and be there at least one hour before the performance.

SHOPPING

Cairo is one big bazaar and anything from anywhere in Egypt is for sale here.

Antiques

Noubi Tapis & Antiquaire (Map pp126-7; ☎ 735 3233; 106-126 Sharia 26th of July, Zamalek; ⏱ 10am-10pm) An elephant sculpture guards the entrance to this corner shop, which is chock full of quality antique rugs, glass, postcards, china and books.

Belly-Dance Costumes

For belly-dance costumes try **Mahmoud abd el Ghaffar** (☎ 589 7443) and **Yasser Bellydance** (☎ 786 5966; yasserbelly@hotmail.com) in the Khan al-Khalili.

Books, Tapes & CDs

Cairo bookshops are listed under Information (see p93). For CDs (local and international) try the following:

Cinderella (Map pp126-7; ☎ 579 2082 ext 1164; Arkadia Mall, Corniche el-Nil, Downtown)

Diwan (Map pp126-7; ☎ 736 2578; 159 Sharia 26th of July, Zamalek; ⏱ 9am-11.30pm)

Vibe (Map pp126-7; ☎ 736 0502; 2 Sharia Sayed al-Bakry, Zamalek)

Carpets & Rugs

Unlike Morocco, Turkey or Iran, Egypt has no rich tradition of 'Oriental' carpet weaving. What you can find, however, are brown-and-beige striped, hard-wearing camel-hair rugs of Bedouin origin. The biggest selection is to be found in the Haret al-Fahhamin, a tight squeeze of alleys behind the Mosque of Al-Ghouri, across the road from Khan al-Khalili in Islamic Cairo. Some of the places mentioned in the Handicrafts section also carry Bedouin rugs. The village of Kerdassa (see p135) is almost entirely devoted to the red-and-white Bedouin rugs.

Wissa Wassef Art Centre (☎ 385 0746; Saqqara Rd, Harraniyya; ⏰ 9am-7pm) Four kilometres south of the Pyramids, next to the Maryutia Canal on the road to Saqqara, the Wissa Wassef Art Centre specialises in distinctive woollen rugs and wall hangings depicting rural and folkloric scenes. The attractive complex comprises a museum, workshops and sales galleries. Wissa Wassef rugs are now very much imitated and you can buy similar ones at most souvenir shops, but you'll find the greatest choice here. To get here, take a microbus or taxi from Pyramids Rd in the direction of Saqqara and get off when you see the blue 'Harraniyya' sign. The centre is by the canal on the western side of the road and the workshop is closed on Fridays.

Clothes

Mix & Match Zamalek (Map pp126-7; ☎ 736 4640; 11 Sharia Brazil, Zamalek; ⏰ 10am-8pm); Zamalek (Map pp126-7; 11 Sharia Hassan Sabry) Local designer Madame Shahira creates fetching seasonal collections for women in wool, silk and cotton. Well-made, stylish and reasonably priced, the range is also noteworthy for its particular focus on larger sizes.

Mobaco Cottons (Map pp102-3; ☎ 797 1823; Semiramis InterContinental Hotel, Corniche el-Nil, Downtown) Egypt has always been known for its cotton products, and Mobaco is the most popular of the local chain stores offering reasonably priced, decent-quality cotton clothes for men, women and children. There are stores throughout the city, including at the Nile Hilton and Ramses Hilton Mall.

Handicrafts & Homewares

Cairo has some excellent small handicraft galleries and boutiques selling items made in villages and oases all over Egypt.

Al-Ain Gallery (Map pp94-5; ☎ 349 3940; 73 Sharia al-Hussein, Doqqi; ⏰ 10am-9pm) Established in 1981, this gallery is known for intricate 'Oriental' metalwork lamps by internationally renowned designer Randa Fahmy and its gorgeous items of traditional jewellery fashioned by her sister Azza. The gallery is closed Fri mornings.

Beit Sherif (Map pp126-7; ☎ 736 5689; 3A Sharia Bahgat Ali, Zamalek; ⏰ 11am-9pm) Zaki Sherif is responsible for the décor of some of Cai-

ro's trendiest bars. Here he recreates his Ottoman dreams, mixing old furniture and *objets d'art* with his own designs and artfully displaying the result on three floors of an attractive old house. The glass-and-brass light shades (E£550) are lovely, as are the richly embroidered cushions.

Egypt Crafts Center/Fair Trade Egypt (Map pp126-7; ☎ 736 5123; www.fairtradeegypt.com; Apt 8, 1st fl, 27 Sharia Yehia Ibrahim, Zamalek; ⏰ 9am-8pm Sat-Thu, 10am-6pm Fri) This is a fair-trade shop, with crafts produced in income-generating projects throughout Egypt. Items for sale include Bedouin rugs from Sinai and the northern Western Desert, cotton handwoven by the Coptic community in Upper Egypt, pottery from Al-Fayoum, beaded jewellery from Aswan and silk weaving from Naqada, near Qena. The cotton bedcovers and silk/cotton shawls are particularly lovely. Prices are competitive.

Khan Misr Touloun (Map p121; ☎ 365 2227; ⏰ 10am-5pm Mon-Fri) This shop opposite the Mosque of Ibn Tulun is stacked with a desirable jumble of crafts from all over Egypt, including wooden chests, jewellery, pottery, glass work, puppets, scarves, shawls and woven clothing. There are also gorgeous dolls (E£180) that make wonderful gifts for little ones. All goods carry price tags.

Al-Khatoun (Map p116; ☎ 514 7164; www.al khatoun.com; 3 Sharia Mohammed Abduh, Islamic Cairo; ⏰ 11am-9pm) Sharing a small and peaceful garden square with the Beit al-Harrawi and the Beit Zeinab al-Khatoun, this gorgeous store stocks an ever-changing array of contemporary and very chic light-fittings, alabaster pots, linen, jewellery, clothes and shawls. All are designed and made in Egypt. Prices are clearly marked.

Loft (Map pp126-7; ☎ 736 6931; www.loftegypt .com; 12 Sharia Sayyed al-Bakry, Zamalek; ⏰ 10am-10pm Mon-Sat) This eccentric store stocks curiosities, furniture, trays, frames and lights.

Makan (Map pp126-7; ☎ 738 2632; 4 Sharia Ismail Mohammed, Zamalek; ⏰ 10am-11pm) This place advertises itself as providing 'Contemporary Egyptian Interiors'. The attractive stock includes furniture, *objets d'art*, cushions, rich embroidered and appliquéd fabrics, lightfittings (check out the lights made from old tambourines), paintings copied from tombs and great candelabra.

Nagada (Map p130; ☎ 792 3249; 3rd fl, 8 Sharia Dar al-Shifa, Garden City) Beautiful hand-woven silk/cotton textiles and clothes from Na-gada (about 28km north of Luxor) are sold here, as well as gorgeous hand-made pottery from Al-Fayoum, lamps and jewellery. If you can't find anything that fits, it will measure and make clothes to order (10-day turnaround).

Nomad (Map pp126-7; ☎ 736 1917; 1st fl, 14 Saray al-Gezira, Zamalek; ☺ 10am-7pm) This well-hidden gem of a place specialises in jewellery and traditional Bedouin crafts and costumes, particularly from Siwa. Standout items include appliquéd tablecloths and cushion covers, dresses made in the oases, woven baskets from Upper Egypt and chunky Yemeni silver jewellery. It's well worth a look. To find it, go past the Egyptian Water Works office to the first floor and ring the bell. There are smaller branches in the Cairo Marriott (Map pp126–7), Grand Hyatt (Map p130) and Nile Hilton (Map pp102–3) hotels.

Oum El Dounia (Map pp102-3; ☎ 393 8273; 1st fl, 3 Sharia Talaat Harb, Downtown; ☺ 10am-7pm) A new store in the centre of town, Oum El Dounia sells a small but attractive range of locally made glassware, Bedouin jewellery, cotton clothes, bags, embroidered shawls and light fittings. It also stocks a small range of maps, postcards and English- and French-language books about Cairo and Egypt. All stock is clearly priced and you can use a credit card for purchases over E£100.

Senouhi (Map pp102-3; ☎ 391 0955; 5th fl, 54 Sharia Abdel Khalek Sarwat, Downtown; ☺ 10am-5pm Mon-Fri, 10am-1pm Sat) Madame Layla's grotto-like apartment is full of textiles, antiques, jewellery and paintings collected over many years, as well as some fine crafts she promotes.

Tukul Craft Shop Zamalek (Map pp126-7; ☎ 736 8391; www.refuge-egypt.org/tukul; All Saints Anglican Cathedral, Sheikh al-Marsafy, Zamalek; ☺ 9am-4.30pm Mon-Thu & Sat, 11am-3pm Fri & Sun); Ma'adi (☎ 525 0348; 18 Road 162) This charity store next to the Marriott Hotel was established in 1988 and sells an attractive range of cotton bags, aprons, tablecloths and teatowels silkscreen printed with original designs by displaced Sudanese refugees. The Ma'adi store is just opposite the metro station .

Jewellery

Egypt's gold and silver shops are concentrated in the centre of Khan al-Khalili. Jewellery is sold by weight, with a little extra added for workmanship. The day's gold prices are listed in the *Egyptian Gazette*. The most popular souvenirs are gold or silver cartouches with your name engraved in hieroglyphs. The following shops sell something a bit different.

Al-Ain Gallery (Map pp94-5; ☎ 349 3940; 73 Sharia al-Hussein, Doqqi; ☺ 10am-9pm) The work of Azza Fahmy is for sale here. The Gallery closes on Friday mornings.

Hareem Khan (Map p112; ☎ 593 1581; 6 Sharia al-Haramatiya, Khan al-Khalili) Small shop selling colourful Bedouin jewellery, both original and reproduction, at good prices.

Both Nomad (left) and Oum El Dounia (left) sell interesting, chunky Bedouin silver.

Shopping Malls

Shopping malls are popping up all over Cairo, particularly in the suburbs. Young middle-class Cairenes like to hang out in the food courts or atriums, meeting their friends and eyeing up the opposite sex.

Arkadia Mall (Map pp126-7; Corniche el-Nil, Bulaq) The biggest mall in town, with bars and a top-floor amusement arcade that are always full of young people. Its 500 shops stock international brands, sportswear, clothing, toys and shoes, and there is a good food court.

First Residence Mall (Map p130; First Residence Complex, 35 Sharia al-Giza, Giza) Cairo's most exclusive shopping mall features international designers and upmarket local gear.

Ramses Hilton Mall (Map pp102-3; Midan Abdel Moniem Riad, Downtown) Middle class–family oriented, this mall has lots of casual clothing, shoes, jewellery and homewares shops. The centre's top floor houses a cinema, a popular branch of McDonald's and a billiards/snooker hall.

Talaat Harb Complex (Map pp102-3; Sharia Talaat Harb, Downtown) Very popular with young Cairenes for its cheap food court, casual clothing and shoes.

Souqs & Markets

Bulaq Market (north of Sharia 26th of July, Bulaq) Sells textiles, secondhand clothing, car parts and military surplus.

Khan al-Khalili (Map p112; ☺ Mon-Sat) The Cairo shopping experience par excellence. As well as tacky souvenirs, you'll also find copperware, blown glass, gold and silver, clothing, fabrics, Bedouin dresses, semiprecious stones, perfume, spices, belly-dancing costumes, antiques and all manner of other nonessentials. See the map for an indication of what's sold where, or just stroll about and be surprised by what turns up around the corner.

Sharia al-Muski (Map p112; Islamic Cairo) A wonderful street market selling outrageous underwear, cheap shoes, plastic toys, wedding dresses, bucket-sized bras and haberdashery.

Souq al-Gomaa (Friday Market; Map pp94-5; Islamic Cairo; �) 6am-noon Fri) Just south of the Citadel, Souq al-Gomaa sells the oddest mix covering everything from bric-a-brac to animals. You'll need a taxi to get there.

Souvenirs

Khan al-Khalili (Map p112; ☉ Mon-Sat) The Khan al-Khalili is full of incredible kitsch, but there are also some worthwhile items. Backgammon boards, as used in Egyptian coffeehouses, start at around E£25 for something quite plain, considerably more for mother-of-pearl inlay. If you have enjoyed smoking a *sheesha*, you could buy your own – though you'll need to also stock up on the special tobacco and the small clay pots that it is stuffed into. Small jewellery boxes inlaid with mother-of-pearl are also pretty and very inexpensive. Painted papyrus at Khan al-Khalili is as cheap as you'll find anywhere, usually because you are buying painted banana leaves.

Dr Ragab's Papyrus Institute (Map p130; ☎ 336 7212; Sharia el-Nil, Doqqi) For the real thing, visit Dr Ragab's which is between the Cairo Sheraton and University Bridge.

Spices

Spices are a good buy, particularly coriander (*kuzbara*), cumin (*kamoon*), chilli (*shatta*), black pepper (*filfil iswad*) and hibiscus (*karkadeh*). Watch out for a popular scam involving selling high-priced saffron that tastes of little more than dust. The following are specialist spice sellers, usually with fixed prices.

Abd ar-Rahman Harraz (☎ 512 6349; 1 Midan Bab al-Khalq, Islamic Cairo) The sheikh of herbalist and medicinal plants, near the Museum of Islamic Art, has kitchen spices and more.

Attara Ahl al-Beit (Map pp126-7; ☎ 735 4955; Sharia Shagaret ad-Durr, Zamalek) Excellent spice shop with very friendly service.

GETTING THERE & AWAY
Air

For international airfare details see p539; for domestic flights, see p545. For information on airline offices in Cairo see p539.

CAIRO INTERNATIONAL AIRPORT

For information on the airport see p164. For flight information call ☎ 291 4255/66/77.

EGYPTAIR OFFICES

EgyptAir Airport (☎ 290 9787); Doqqi (Map p130; ☎ 761 3278 Cairo Sheraton, Midan el-Galaa); Downtown (☎ 391 4501; Midan Opera, Sharia el-Gomhoureya); Downtown (Map pp102-3; ☎ 393 2836; cnr Sharia Talaat Harb & Sharia al-Bustan); Downtown (Map pp102-3; ☎ 392 7649; 6 Sharia Adly); Downtown (Map pp102-3; ☎ 577 2410; Nile Hilton, 1113 Corniche el-Nil)

Bus

Cairo's main bus station is **Turgoman Garage** (Mo'af Turgoman; Map pp94-5; Sharia al-Gisr, Bulaq), 1km northwest of the intersection of Sharias Galaa and 26th of July. It's too far to walk from Downtown and the only way to get there is by taxi (E£5). The station was being redeveloped at the time of research, so its confusing split into two sections will soon be a thing of the past. All companies operating services from Turgoman have their own ticket cabin. It is advisable to advance-book most tickets, particularly for popular routes such as Sinai, Alexandria and Marsa Matruh in summer. There are no student discounts on the buses.

There are three other bus stations:

Al-Mazar is near the airport (a taxi will cost E£30). International services depart from here and most other services stop here en route out of Cairo.

Abbassiyya (Map pp94-5; Sharia Ramses, Abbassiyya) is where all of the services from Sinai arrive (confusingly, these leave from Turgoman). To get to Abbassiyya you will need to take bus 983 or 948 or minibus 32 from the station at Midan Abdel Moniem Riad. A taxi to/from Downtown should cost around E£15.

El-Moneib is the small station where buses from Al-Fayoum terminate. The station is located on the Giza Corniche after Sharia al-Bahr al-Aazam and just past Dr Ragab's Pharaonic Village. A taxi will cost E£20 from Downtown.

AROUND EGYPT

Alexandria & the Mediterranean Coast

Services leave from Turgoman and from Aboud Bus Terminal (Map pp94–5), 3km north of Ramses Station. From Turgoman, **West Delta Bus Co** (☎ 576 5582) travels to Alexandria (E£16, 2½ hours) on the hour between 5am and 1am. Services to Marsa Matruh (E£32 to E£40, 5½ hours) leave at 6.45am, 8.15am, 1.15pm and 9.30pm.

Al-Fayoum

Buses and service taxis for Al-Fayoum (E£5, one hour) leave from Ahmed Helmy station (Map p106), behind Cairo's Ramses train station, stopping en route at El-Moneib station in Giza. Fares on Thursdays are E£1 more expensive. The buses stop en route at Midan el-Remaya after the Pyramids Rd and just before the Giza–Fayoum road.

Sinai

All Sinai buses leave from Turgoman, but return to Abbassiyya, stopping at Al-Mazar en route.

East Delta Bus Co (☎ 574 2814) has services running to Sharm el-Sheikh (E£55 to E£65, seven hours) at 6.30am, 7.15am, 10am, 1pm, 3pm, 5pm, 7pm, 11pm, 11.30pm, midnight and 12.15am. The 7.15am, 1pm, 5pm and 12.15am services go on to Dahab (E£62 to E£75, nine hours).

There are three daily buses to Nuweiba (E£55 to E£75, eight hours) and Taba (E£55 to E£75, nine hours), leaving at 6.30am, 9.30am and 10.15pm. A daily service to St Katherine's Monastery leaves at 10.30am (E£37, 7½ hours).

Superjet (☎ 579 8181) has services to Sharm el-Sheikh (E£68) at 7.30am, 3.15pm and 11.15pm.

Suez Canal

All Suez buses depart from Turgoman Garage. East Delta Bus Co travels to Ismailia (E£7.25, 2½ hours) and Suez (E£7.25, 1½ hours) every 30 minutes between 6am and 8pm. Buses to Port Said (E£16, three hours) leave every 30 minutes between 6am and 9.30am and then every hour until 9.30pm.

Luxor & Aswan

Upper Egypt Travel (☎ 576 0261) buses depart from Turgoman. There's one daily service to Luxor (E£85, 10 to 11 hours) at 9pm and one

service to Aswan (E£85, 14 hours) at 5pm. You're much better off getting the train.

Red Sea

Superjet (☎ 579 8181) departs from Turgoman to Hurghada (E£57 to E£60, 6½ hours) at 7.30am, 2.30pm and 11.15pm. Upper Egypt Travel services to Hurghada (E£55) depart at 7.30am, 9am, noon, 3pm, 10pm and 11.30pm. The 9am and 10pm services go on to Safaga (E£65, 7½ hours).

There are Upper Egypt Travel services running to Al-Quseir (E£70, nine hours) at 1.30pm, 6.30pm, 9pm and 11pm. The 1.30pm, 6.30pm and 11pm services go on to Marsa Alam (E£80, 12 hours).

Western Oases

All Western Oases buses leave from Turgoman. Note that to get to Siwa you must take a bus to Alexandria or Marsa Matruh, and then another onwards. For journeys to the oases take food and water as sometimes these buses don't stop anywhere useful for breaks.

There are two Upper Egypt Bus Co services per day to Bahariyya (E£20, five hours), Farafra (E£40, eight hours) and Dakhla (E£50 to E£55, 10 to 12 hours) at 7am and 6pm. Two extra services travel to Dakhla via Asyut and Al-Kharga (E£50), leaving at 9.30pm and 10pm.

INTERNATIONAL

For information about buses to Libya, Israel and Jordan see p541.

Service Taxi

Most service taxis depart from lots around Ramses Station and Midan Ulali (see Map p106). Delta and Suez services leave from just north of Ulali, to the right of Sharia Shubra, running to destinations including Suez (E£7.50, one hour), Ismailia (E£8, 1½ hours) and Port Said (E£14, two hours).

Service taxis for Alexandria (E£12, 2½ to 3 hours) leave from in front of Ramses Station.

Train

Ramses station (Mahattat Ramses; Map p106; ☎ 575 3555; Midan Ramses) is Cairo's main train station. It has a **left luggage office** (Map p163; per piece per day E£2.50; ⏰ 24hr), a **post office** (Map p163; ⏰ 8am-8pm), ATMs, a pharmacy and a **tourist information office** (Map p163; ⏰ 9am-7pm).

RAMSES TRAIN STATION

For general details about the types of trains and tickets available, including student discounts, see p546.

ALEXANDRIA

The best trains running between Cairo and Alexandria are the air-conditioned *Turbini* (1st/2nd class E£36/28, two hours). Second class in this train is about as good as 1st class in most others. They depart from Cairo at 8am, 2pm and 7pm. The next best trains are the *Espani* (Spanish) services, which cost the same as the *Turbini* and leave at 9am, noon, 6pm and 10.30pm stopping at Benha, Tanta and Damanhur en route. Slower trains known as the *Francese* (French, 1st/2nd class E£26/16, three hours) leave at 6am, 8.30am, 11am, 3.10pm, 4pm and 8pm. Student discounts are available on all tickets.

LUXOR & ASWAN

Go to the **Abela Egypt Sleeping Train Ticket Office** (Map p163; ☎ 574 9274; www.sleepingtrains .com; ☺ 8.30am-9pm) to organise a seat on the excellent overnight wagons-lit service to Upper Egypt. You'll find the office next to the tourist information office, near the station's main entrance. Tickets for same-day travel must be purchased before 6pm, although in the high season (from about October to April) you may need to book several days in advance. Bookings can also be made through travel agencies – if you want to pay by credit card you'll need to do

this as tickets purchased at the station must be paid for in US dollars or euros (cash only). The closest place to access US dollars or euros is the Egyptian Foreign Exchange Corp office on Sharia Emad ad-Din, a 10-minute walk from the station.

The sleeping car service departs at 8pm daily, arriving in Luxor at 5.05am the next morning (the perfect hour to head off sightseeing) and in Aswan at 8.15am. It costs US$53 per person one way in a double cabin; US$74 in a single cabin. Children four to nine years of age pay US$40. There are no student discounts. If you wish to get off at Luxor and continue to Aswan a few days later this must be specified when booking. The price includes an aeroplane-style dinner and breakfast.

Aside from the sleeping train, foreigners can only travel to Luxor and Aswan on train 980, departing Cairo daily at 7am; train 996, departing at 10pm; and train 1902, departing at 12.30am. To Luxor, 1st/2nd class fares on the night trains are E£67/45, and E£62/40 on the morning train. To Aswan they're E£81/47 on the night train, E£77/43 on the morning train. The trip to Luxor takes 10 hours; to Aswan it's around 13. Student discounts are available on tickets for both classes.

Tickets on these services can be bought from the ticket office beside platform 11, which is on the other side of the tracks from the main hall. You must buy your tickets at least a couple of days in advance.

SUEZ CANAL

Trains to Port Said (2nd class E£20) and Ismailia (E£14) leave at 8.45am, 11.30am, 2.30pm, 7pm and 10pm. Going by bus is a far better option.

GETTING AROUND

Overcrowded buses and minibuses are the most common form of transport for the majority of Cairenes, but for anyone with the means and a preference for comfort and less delay, taxis are the only option. Taxis are usually at hand and, by Western standards, are very cheap, although the fare can mount up if you travel any distance – to Heliopolis, say, or Ma'adi – in which case the bus or metro are a better alternative. It's also wise to avoid taking taxis between about 2.30pm and 4pm (that's supposing that you can find one free at this time of day) when everyone slinks off home and the roads are even more congested than usual.

To/From the Airport

Cairo International Airport Terminal 1 (☎ 265 5000); Terminal 2 (☎ 265 2222) is on the northeastern fringes of Heliopolis, 20km northeast of the city centre. There are four terminals in all, but two terminals about 3km apart handle most passenger traffic: Terminal 1 services EgyptAir's international and domestic flights and Terminal 2 services all international airlines except Saudi Arabian Airlines. You'll find ATMs and exchange booths in the arrivals halls.

BUS

Don't believe anyone who tells you that there is no bus to the city centre – there are two, plus a minibus.

Air-con bus 356 (E£2, plus E£1 per large luggage item, one hour) runs at 20-minute intervals from 7am to midnight between Midan Abdel Moniem Riad (behind the Egyptian Museum) in central Cairo and both terminals of the airport. There is a far less comfortable 24-hour service on bus 400 (50pt), which leaves from the same place. Note that between the hours of midnight and 6am, this bus only stops at Terminal 1.

Minibus 27 (50pt) runs the same route from 6am till midnight.

If you arrive at Terminal 1 you'll see the bus parking area to the side of the arrivals hall. If you arrive at Terminal 2, walk out of the arrivals hall, cross the road, go down the stairs/escalator, cross through the car park and wait on the opposite side of the street at the end of the car park to flag the bus down. There's no marked stop.

TAXI

The going rate for a taxi from the airport to central Cairo is around E£45 to E£60. (Heading to the airport from the centre, there are more taxis around so you can afford to bargain harder – you shouldn't pay more than E£35.) It's generally better to get away from the arrivals hall and all the touts before starting to bargain with anyone, as walking away often tends to bring the price down. A good place to get the best price is the car park. Triple-check the agreed fare,

as there is an irritating tendency for drivers to nod at what you say and hit you with an out-of-the-world fare later on. If you don't want to bargain and would prefer a clean and comfortable ride, head for the limousine counter, where you can organise a car at a fixed price of E£60 to E£85 (you can occasionally broker a cheaper deal in the car park). There's a lot to be said for this option, particularly after a long international flight.

In the traffic-free early hours of the morning (when so many flights seem to arrive), the journey to central Cairo takes 20 minutes. At busier times of the day it can take an hour.

Bus & Minibus

Cairo's main local bus and minibus stations are at Midan Abdel Moniem Riad, behind the Egyptian Museum, where services leave for just about everywhere in the city (see Map pp102–3).

Car

Driving in Cairo is not for the faint-hearted. It's like the chariot race in *Ben Hur*, only with ageing Peugeots and Fiats. The roads are always crowded – the city's rush hour begins at about 8am each morning and doesn't slacken until around midnight. Lane markings are ignored as Cairo drivers treat other vehicles like obstacles on a slalom – a favourite manoeuvre is to sweep across multiple lanes of traffic to make a turn on the opposite side of the carriageway. Brakes are scorned in favour of the horn. Traffic lights are discretionary unless enforced by a policeman, who is equally likely to wave you through a red light and halt you on green. Driving at night is particularly hazardous as some drivers use their headlights exclusively for flashing oncoming vehicles.

But in spite of appearances, Cairo drivers have their own road rules: they look out for each other and are extremely tolerant of the type of driving that elsewhere might provoke road rage. Things only tend to go awry when an inexperienced driver is thrown into the mix – something anyone considering driving here should bear in mind.

For more information about cars and driving in Egypt see p547.

HIRE

If you are crazy enough to want to battle Cairo's traffic, there are a number of car rental agencies in the city, including the big three – Avis, Hertz and Budget.

Avis Airport (☎ 291 4288); Nile Hilton (Map pp102-3; ☎ 579 2400; www.avisegypt.com; Corniche el-Nil, Downtown)

Budget Airport (☎ 265 2395); Zamalek (Map pp126-7; ☎ 340 0070; 5 Sharia Makrizy)

Europcar Airport (☎ 265 2395); Mohandiseen (Map pp126-7; ☎ 347 4712; Sharia Libnan)

Hertz Airport (☎ 265 2430); Ramses Hilton (Map pp102-3; ☎ 575 8914; www.hertzegypt.com; Corniche el-Nil, Downtown)

The rates of these big guns match international charges and finding a cheap deal with local dealers is virtually impossible. You are much better off organising cheap car hire via the web before you arrive in Egypt. Of the locals, **Max Rent A Car** (☎ 303 5630; maxrent@max.com.eg; 22 Sharia el-Kods el-Sherif, Mohandiseen; ☒ 9am-5pm Sun-Thu) has a good reputation.

Metro

The metro is startlingly efficient and the stations are cleaner than many of Cairo's other public places. It's also extremely inexpensive and, outside rush hours (7am to 9am and 3pm to 6pm), not too crowded. Two lines were in operation at the time of writing: the 32-station main line stretches for 43km from the southern suburb of Helwan up to Al-Marg; the second line connects Shubra with Giza, stopping at the Cairo Opera House en route. There are

USEFUL METRO STATIONS

Attaba The closest stop to the Khan al-Khalili.

Gezira/Opera Connects with the Cairo Opera House.

Mar Girgis In the middle of Coptic Cairo.

Mohammed Naguib Close to the Abdeen Palace and Museum of Islamic Art.

Mubarak Beneath Midan Ramses and Ramses Railway Station.

Nasser Near the top (north) end of Sharia Talaat Harb.

Sadat Beneath Midan Tahrir, close to the Egyptian Museum.

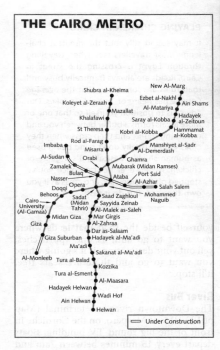

THE CAIRO METRO

New Al-Marg
Shubra al-Kheima
Koleyet al-Zeraah   Ezbet al-Nakhl   Ain Shams
Mazallat   Al-Mataryia
Khalafawi   Saray al-Kobba   Hadayek al-Zeitoun
St Theresa   Kobri al-Kobba   Hammamat al-Kobba
Imbaba   Rod al-Farag   Manshiyet al-Sadr
Misarra   Al-Demerdash
Al-Sudan   Orabi
Zamalek   Ghamra
Bulaq   Mubarak (Midan Ramses)
Nasser   Port Said
Doqqi   Opera   Ataba   Al-Azhar
Behoos   Sadat   Saad Zaghloul   Salah Salem
Cairo   (Midan   Sayyida Zeinab   Mohammed
University   Tahrir)   Al-Malek as-Saleh   Naguib
(Al-Gamaa)   Midan Giza   Mar Girgis
Giza   Al-Zahraa
Giza Suburban   Dar as-Salaam
Ma'adi   Hadayek al-Ma'adi
Al-Monleeb   Tura al-Balad   Sakanat al-Ma'adi
Tura al-Esment   Kozzika
Hadayek Helwan   Al-Maasara
Ain Helwan   Wadi Hof
Helwan

⇐ ⇒ Under Construction

plans to extend this line at least one stop from Giza. A planned third line will cross the city east to west linking Islamic Cairo with Zamalek and Mohandiseen. See the Cairo Metro map on p165.

Metro stations are easily identified by signs with a big red 'M' in a blue star. Tickets cost 50pt to ride up to nine stops, 70pt for up to 16 stops, 90pt for up to 22 stops, E£1.20 for up to 28 stops and E£1.50 to ride the length of the line. Trains run from around 6am until 11.30pm.

The first (and sometimes second) carriage on each train is reserved for women only. Women who want to ride in this carriage should make sure they're standing near where the front part of the train will stop, as trains don't hang around long in the station.

Microbus

Increasingly Cairenes use private microbuses rather than public minibuses to get around. No destinations are marked (which can make them hard to use unless you know their routes). To catch a 'micro', position

PLAYING CHICKEN IN CAIRO

It may sound silly, but the greatest challenge most travellers face when travelling through Egypt is crossing the street in Cairo. Roads are always frantically busy and road rules are something that the average Cairene has heard of, but only in jokes. Our advice is to position yourself so that one or more locals forms a buffer between you and oncoming traffic, and then cross when they cross – they usually don't mind being used as human shields. Basically, it's a game of chicken. Never, ever hesitate once you've stepped off the sidewalk, and cross as if you own the road. But do it fast!

yourself beside the road that leads where you want to go and, as one approaches, yell out your destination. If it's going where you want to go and there are seats free, it'll stop.

River Bus

The Downtown river-bus terminal (Map pp102–3) is at Maspero, on the Corniche in front of the big round TV building. Boats depart every 15 minutes between 7am and 3pm for Doqqi, and from 7am to 10pm for Manial, Giza and Misr al-Qadima (Old Cairo). The trip takes 50 minutes and the fare is 50pt. There's also a service between Zamalek and Imbaba (E£25pt).

Taxi

If a destination is too far to walk, the easiest way of getting there is to take a taxi.

They're cheap enough to make buses, with all their attendant hassles, redundant. Use the following table as a rough guide as to what you should be paying for a taxi ride around Cairo. If you decide to hire a taxi for a longer period, you'll be up for between E£15 and E£25 per hour, depending on your bargaining skills. Note that it's best to hail a Peugeot 504 rather than one of the diabolically unroadworthy Fiats. Following are some sample fares from Downtown:

Destination	Fare (E£)
Abbassiyya Garage	15
Airport	30-35
	(45-60 airport to Downtown)
Heliopolis	10-15
Khan al-Khalili	5
Midan Ramses	3
The Citadel	5
The Pyramids	20
Turgoman Garage	5
Zamalek	5

For information on taxi etiquette see p550.

Tram

Most of Cairo's trams (known to Cairenes, confusingly, as 'metros') have been phased out. One useful survivor connects central Cairo with Heliopolis (25pt, 30 to 45 minutes). This runs from just north of Midan Ramses (see Map p106) up to Midan Roxy on the southern edge of Heliopolis (see Map p136), at which point the line divides into three – Nouzha, Al-Mirghani and Abdel Aziz Fahmy.

Egyptian Museum

More than 120,000 relics and antiquities from almost every period of ancient Egyptian history are housed in the Egyptian Museum in Cairo.

The nucleus of this collection was first gathered under one roof in Bulaq in 1858 by Auguste Mariette, the French archaeologist who had founded the Egyptian Antiquities Service. In 1878 the Bulaq Museum was flooded and many artefacts were destroyed or stolen. The remaining objects were transferred in 1890 to an annexe of the palace of Ismail Pasha at Giza, where they stayed until the current museum was built in 1902. Since then the number of exhibits in the museum has completely outgrown the available space and the place is virtually bursting at the seams. A persistent urban legend in Cairo has it that the building's storerooms are piled so high with uncatalogued artefacts that archaeologists will have to excavate their contents when and if the planned 2009 move to a new US$500 million 'Grand Museum of Egypt', close to the Pyramids in Giza, takes place. The move will see up to 100,000 items from the museum's collection (including some of the main exhibits) relocated into a purpose-built facility featuring a stunning design and state-of-the-art climate control (something sorely lacking in the current building).

Beyond arranging the exhibits chronologically from the Old Kingdom to the Roman Empire, little has been done in the current building to present any sort of context for the collection or to highlight pieces that are of particular significance or beauty. In fact. displays have not been reorganised since the museum's foundation a century ago. Labelling is poor or nonexistent and most displays are in old wood-and-glass cases with no direct lighting. Fortunately, this is slowly starting to change, with fibre optic lighting and clearly marked labels being introduced. Security and lighting systems were installed following a sensational attempted robbery in 1996, when the authorities belatedly realised that bars on the windows and a dog making the rounds after closing were insufficient protection for the museum's priceless contents. Despite all this, the museum's eccentricity is part of its charm, and you'll find that accidentally stumbling across treasures in its sometimes-musty rooms is half the fun.

Despite the enormous international fanfare surrounding the design for the planned Grand Museum of Egypt, the Egyptian government has yet to raise or allocate the estimated US$500 million needed for its construction.

The design for the planned Grand Museum of Egypt features a spectacular alabaster façade that will be illuminated at night.

PRACTICALITIES

With so much to see in the **Egyptian Museum** (Map p168; ☎ 575 4319; www.egyptian museum.gov.eg; Midan Tahrir, Downtown; adult/student E£60/30; ⌚ 9am-6.45pm), trying to get around everything in one go is liable to induce chronic 'Pharaonic phatigue'. The best strategy is to make at least two visits, maybe tackling one floor at a time. Unfortunately, there's no best time to visit as the museum is heaving with visitors throughout the day, although late afternoons can be a little quieter.

There are several queues to brave before entering, which in winter (the peak season) often start to form an hour before opening time. The fourfold admission procedure is as painfully slow as it sounds:

- queue to pass through a metal detector and have your bags X-rayed

- queue at the booth on the right as you enter to buy a ticket and at the booth on the left to leave possessions at the cloak room
- queue at the automatic ticket barriers to enter the building
- queue to pass through a second metal detector and have your bags searched again.

Note that the ghoulish **Royal Mummy Room** (adult/student E£80/40, tickets inside the museum; ☾ 9am-6.15pm) closes before the rest of the museum.

Visitors cannot take cameras or videos into the museum (these must be checked into the cloak room before you enter the museum). Official guides can take you around for about E£50 per hour.

HIGHLIGHTS OF THE EGYPTIAN MUSEUM

The following is our list of the top 10 must-see exhibits, for which you need at least a half-day, but preferably a little more.

Tutankhamun Galleries (1st fl; p173)
Old Kingdom Rooms (ground fl, rooms 42, 37 & 32; p170)
Amarna Room (ground fl, room 3; p171)
Royal Tombs of Tanis (1st fl, room 2; p175)
Royal Mummy Room (1st fl, room 56; p172)
Graeco-Roman Mummies (1st fl, room 14; p176)
Yuya and Thuyu Rooms (1st fl, room 43; p176)
Ancient Egyptian Jewellery (1st fl, room 4; p175)
Animal Mummies (1st fl, rooms 53 & 54; p176)
Pharaonic Technology (1st fl, room 34; p176)

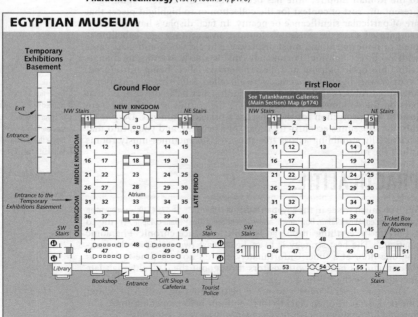

MUSEUM TOUR: GROUND FLOOR

Before entering the museum, wander through the garden; to your left lies the **tomb of Mariette** (1821–81), with a statue of the man, arms folded, shaded under a spreading tree. Mariette's tomb is also adorned with an **arc of busts** of other famous Egyptologists including Champollion, who cracked the code of hieroglyphs; Maspero, Mariette's successor as director of the Egyptian Antiquities Service; and Lepsius, the pre-eminent 19th-century German Egyptologist. Further left, around the corner at the side of the building, is an entrance to the basement. This leads to a space that hosts **temporary exhibitions** covering Pharaonic and Greco-Roman subject matter. Make sure you check to see what's on.

The ground floor of the museum is laid out roughly chronologically in a clockwise fashion starting at the entrance hall. Room numbers are marked on the map (Map p168).

ROOM 48 – EARLY DYNASTIC PERIOD

In glass cabinet No 16 is the near-life-size limestone seated **statue of Zoser (Djoser)**, the 3rd-dynasty pharaoh, whose chief architect Imhotep designed the revolutionary Step Pyramid at Saqqara. He wears a tight-fitting robe and striped headcloth over a huge wig. With a thin moustache and false beard, the original inlaid eyes may have been gouged out in ancient times, but the figure is still impressive. The statue was discovered in 1924 in its *serdab* (cellar) in the northeastern corner of the pyramid and is the oldest statue of its kind in the museum.

ROOM 43 – ATRIUM

The central atrium feels like a warehouse, filled with a disordered miscellany of large and small Egyptological finds. In central cabinet No 8, the double-sided **Narmer Palette** is one of the museum's most significant artefacts, although you'd never know it from the way it's presented. Dating from around 3100 BC it depicts Pharaoh Narmer (also known as Menes) wearing the crown of Upper Egypt on one side of the palette, and the crown of Lower Egypt on the other side, representing the first uniting of Upper and Lower Egypt under one ruler. This is the event Egyptologists take as the start of ancient Egyptian civilisation. Here begins over 3000 years of Pharaonic history, encompassing 170 or more rulers presiding over 30 dynasties, during which time almost every exhibit in this building was fashioned. The Narmer Palette is the keystone of the Egyptian Museum.

At the far end of the atrium is a representation of all that the successors of Narmer would achieve in the form of a huge **colossus of Amenhotep III and Tiy**, his wife, with their small daughters at their feet. This particular pharaoh's lengthy reign (1390–1352 BC) represented the zenith of ancient Egypt's power and prestige. His rule was marked by great architectural achievements, including the Luxor Temple and his own temple on the West Bank. This was possibly the greatest ever built in Egypt, although the only significant remains are the two lone guardians, known as the Colossi of Memnon.

ROOMS 47 & 46 – OLD KINGDOM

Look for the three matching **black schist triads** that depict the pharaoh Menkaure (Mycerinus), builder of the smallest of the three Pyramids of Giza, flanked either side by a female figure. The figure to the pharaoh's

The Egyptian Government established the Service des Antiques de l'Egypte in 1835 to halt the plundering of archaeological sites and to arrange the exhibition of all the artefacts it owned. Its most enduring legacy is this museum.

right is the goddess Hathor, while each of the figures on his left represents a nome (district) of Egypt, the name of which is given by the symbol above their head. These triads (plus one other that is not held by this museum) were discovered at the pharaoh's valley temple, just east of his pyramid at Giza.

ROOMS 42, 37 & 32 – MASTERPIECES OF THE OLD KINGDOM

In the centre of Room 42 is one of the museum's masterpieces, a smooth, black, dioritic, larger than life-size **statue of Khafre (Chephren)**. The builder of the second pyramid at Giza sits on a lion throne, which has the wings of the falcon god Horus wrapped around his head. From the number of statueless bases discovered, archaeologists believe that this is just one of 23 such pieces that originally lined the hall of the pharaoh's valley temple on the Giza Plateau.

Slightly to the left in front of Khafre, the stunning **wooden statue of Ka-Aper** (No 40) was carved out of a single piece of sycamore (except for the arms). He's amazingly lifelike, especially the eyes, which, set in copper lids, have whites of opaque quartz and corneas of rock crystal that have been drilled and filled with black paste to form the pupils. When this statue was excavated at Saqqara in 1860, local workmen named him Sheikh al-Balad (Headman), for his resemblance to their own headman. Also in Room 42 sits the **Seated Scribe** (No 44), a painted limestone figure, his hand poised as if he's waiting to take dictation and the inlaid eyes set in an asymmetrical face giving him a very vivid appearance.

Room 37 is entered via Room 36; it contains finds from the Giza Plateau **tomb of Queen Hetepheres**, including a carrying chair, bed, bed canopy and a jewellery box. Although her mummy was never found, the remains of her internal organs are still inside her Canopic chest. A glass cabinet holds a ministatue of her son Khufu, found at Abydos. Ironically, at just 8cm or so high, it's the only surviving representation of the builder of Egypt's largest pyramid.

Room 32 is dominated by the beautiful **statues of the royal couple, Rahotep and Nofret** (No 27), son and daughter-in-law of Sneferu, builder of the Bent and the Red Pyramids at Dahshur. Almost life-sized with well-preserved painted surfaces, the limestone sculptures' simple lines make them seem almost contemporary, despite having been around for a staggering 4600 years.

Another highlight here, displayed in a cabinet off to the left, is the 'chief of the royal wardrobe' **Seneb** and his family (No 39). Seneb is a dwarf who sits cross-legged, his two children strategically placed where his legs would otherwise have been. His full-size wife Senetites places her arms protectively and affectionately around his shoulders. The happy couple and their two kids have been used in recent Egyptian family planning campaigns.

The panel known as the **Meidum Geese** (No 138) is part of a wall painting from a mud-brick mastaba at Meidum, near the oasis of Al-Fayoum (see p188). Painted around 2600 BC, the pigments remain vivid and the degree of realism (while still retaining a distinct Pharaonic style) is astonishing – ornithologists have had no trouble identifying the bird types.

ROOM 26 – MONTUHOTEP II

The seated statue in the corridor on your right after leaving Room 32, with black skin (representing fertility and rebirth) and the red crown of Lower Egypt, is **Montuhotep II** (No 136), first ruler of the Middle Kingdom period. This statue was discovered by Howard Carter under the forecourt

The Treasures of the Egyptian Museum, edited by Francesco Tiradritti, is an excellent reference published by the American University in Cairo Press. Available in most of Cairo's English-language bookshops and at the museum bookshop, it features 416 pages of stunning colour photographs and costs E£300.

of the pharaoh's temple at Deir al-Bahri in Thebes in 1900, when the ground gave way under his horse – a surprisingly recurrent means of discovery in the annals of Egyptology.

ROOMS 21 & 16 – SPHINXES

These **grey-granite sphinxes** are very different from the great enigmatic Sphinx at Giza – they look more like the Lion Man from *The Wizard of Oz*, with a fleshy human face surrounded by a great shaggy mane and big ears. Sculpted for Pharaoh Amenemhat III (1855–1808 BC) during the 12th dynasty, they were later relocated to the Delta city of Tanis (see p197).

ROOM 12 – HATHOR SHRINE

The centrepiece of this room is a remarkably well-preserved **sandstone chapel**, from Tuthmosis III's temple at Deir al-Bahri. Its vaulted roof is painted with reliefs of Tuthmosis III, his wife Meritre and two princesses, making offerings to Hathor. The life-size cow statue suckles Tuthmosis III's son and successor Amenhotep II, who also stands beneath her chin.

Hatshepsut, who was coregent for part of Tuthmosis III's reign, eventually had herself crowned as pharaoh. Her life-sized **pink granite statue** stands to the left of the chapel. Although she wears a pharaoh's headdress and a false beard, the statue has definite feminine characteristics. The large reddish-painted limestone head in the corridor outside this room is also of Hatshepsut and this piece once belonged to one of her huge Osiris-type statues that adorned the pillared façade of her great temple at Deir al-Bahri.

ROOM 3 – AMARNA ROOM

Akhenaten (1352–1336 BC) was the 'heretic pharaoh' who closed temples of the traditional state god Amun and promoted the sun god Aten in his place. A quick glance around the room will show that artistic styles changed as drastically as the state religion during his 17-year tenure. Compare these great torsos with their strangely bulbous bellies, hips and thighs, their elongated faces, and thick, Mick Jagger–like lips, with the sleek, hard-edged Middle Kingdom sculpture that you've just seen.

Perhaps most striking of all is the **unfinished head of Nefertiti** (No 161), wife of Akhenaten. Worked in light brown quartzite, it's an incredibly delicate and sensitive portrait and shows the queen to have been extremely beautiful – unlike some of the relief figures of her elsewhere in the room, in which she appears with exactly the same strange features as her husband.

ROOM 10 – RAMSES II

At the foot of the northeast stairs is a fabulous large, **grey-granite representation of Ramses II**, builder of the Ramesseum and Abu Simbel. But here in this statue he is tenderly depicted as a child with his finger in his mouth nestled against the breast of a great falcon, in this case the Canaanite god Horus.

ROOM 34 – GRAECO-ROMAN ROOM

There's not always an explanation or context for the fascinating pieces in this room, but the assimilation by Egypt's Greek, then Roman, overlords of the indigenous Pharaonic style is evident in many of the exhibits. Perhaps this is most obvious in the **stelae** on the back wall, and on the large **sandstone panel** on the right-hand wall that is inscribed in three

www.ancientegypt.co.uk is a fabulous website hosted by the British Museum that has loads of interactive online games and information about ancient Egypt for children. It is guaranteed to keep aspiring Egyptologists occupied for hours.

languages: in hieroglyphics (the Egyptian literary language); demotic (the popular script) and Greek (the official language of the then rulers). This trilingual stone is similar in nature to the more famous Rosetta stone (see p401), which is now housed in London's British Museum (a cast replica stands near the museum entrance in Room 48). Also, notice the **bust** situated immediately to the left as you enter this room: a typically Greek face with curly beard and locks, but wearing a Pharaonic-style headdress.

ROOMS 50 & 51 – ALEXANDER THE GREAT

On the official museum plan this area is labelled 'Alexander the Great' but currently there's nothing here that relates directly to the Macedonian conqueror who became pharaoh. However, there is a beautiful small marble **statuette of the Greek goddess Aphrodite**, found in Alexandria and carved at the end of the 1st century BC. The Egyptians identified her with Isis.

MUSEUM TOUR: FIRST FLOOR

The Illustrated Guide to the Egyptian Museum in Cairo is written by Zahi Hawass, the secretary-general of Egypt's Supreme Council of Antiquities, and published by the excellent American University in Cairo Press. Available all over the city, it costs E£150 and features colour photographs and useful itineraries.

Exhibits here are grouped thematically and can be viewed in any order, but assuming that you've come up the southeast stairs, we'll enter the Tutankhamun Galleries at Room 45. This way, you'll experience the pieces in roughly the same order that they were laid out in the tomb (a poster on the wall outside Room 45 illustrates the tomb and treasures as they were found). But if you are fascinated by mummies, then some of the most amazing ones are on display in the Royal Mummy Room, best visited before entering the Tutankhamun Galleries.

ROOM 56 – ROYAL MUMMY ROOM

The Royal Mummy Room houses the remains of 11 of Egypt's most illustrious pharaohs and queens from the 17th to 21st dynasties, 1650 to 945 BC. They lie in individual glass showcases (kept at a constant 22°C) in a sombre, dimly lit environment reminiscent of a tomb. Talking above a hushed whisper is forbidden (somewhat counterproductively, a guard will bellow 'silence' if you do) and tour guides are not meant to enter, making it a peaceful haven. Of course, this being Egypt, rules are made to be broken and silence and a lack of guides shouldn't be assumed.

Displaying dead royalty has proved highly controversial in the past, with the late President Anwar Sadat taking the Royal Mummies off display in 1979 for political reasons, but the subsequent reappearance of 11 of the better looking mummies in 1994 has done wonders for tourism figures. The extra admission charge is steep, but well worth it if you have any interest in mummies or in ancient Egypt's great rulers. Parents should be aware that the mummies can be a frightening sight for young children.

Take time to study the faces of some of the room's celebrated inmates, beginning with the brave Theban king **Seqenre II** who died violently, possibly during struggles to reunite the country at the end of the Second Intermediate Period (1650–1550 BC). His wounds are still visible beneath his curly hair and his twisted arms reflect the violence of his death. The perfectly wrapped mummies of **Amenhotep I** and **Queen Meryetamun** show how all royal mummies would once have looked, while Hatshepsut's brother-husband **Tuthmosis II** lies close by, as does **Tuthmosis IV** with his beautifully styled hair – he was the first king to have his ears pierced. Here too is **Seti I**, often described as the best-preserved royal mummy, although his son **Ram-**

ses II, in the middle of the room, might argue with that, his haughty profile revealing the family's characteristic nose shape and his hair touched up in old age with a yellow henna rinse. Ramses II's 13th son and successor **Merneptah** has a distinctly white appearance caused by the mummification process, while the small raised spots visible on the face of **Ramses V** may have been caused by smallpox. In the centre of the room lie **Queen Nodjmet** (c 1064 BC), wife of the priest-king Herihor, with artificial stone eyes, false eyebrows, a wig and well-packed cheeks, and **Queen Henttawy** (c 1025 BC), daughter of King Smendes and wife of the priest-king Pinudjem I. Although her cheeks had burst apart due to overpacking during the mummification process, her appearance now owes as much to modern restoration techniques as it does to the skills of the ancient embalmers, although like many ancient Egyptians she also owes a lot to her hairdresser and wears a wig of black string dressed in tight spiral curls.

TUTANKHAMUN GALLERIES

The treasure of the young and comparatively insignificant New Kingdom pharaoh Tutankhamun outshines everything else in the museum. The tomb and treasures of this pharaoh, who ruled for only nine years during the 14th century BC (1336–1327 BC), were discovered in 1922 by English archaeologist Howard Carter. Its well-hidden location in the Valley of the Kings, below the much grander but ransacked tomb of Ramses VI, had long prevented its discovery (see Tomb of Tutankhamun, p255). Many archaeologists now believe that up to 80% of these extraordinary treasures were made for Tutankhamun's predecessors, Akhenaten and Smenkhkare – some still carry the names of the original owners. Perhaps with Tutankhamun's death, everything connected with the Amarna Period was simply chucked in with him to be buried away and forgotten.

About 1700 items are spread throughout a series of rooms, and although the gold shines brightest, it is the other, less grand objects that give an insight into the pharaoh's life.

Room 45

Flanking the doorway as you enter are two life-size **statues of Tutankhamun**, which were found in the tomb antechamber; a large black-and-white photo on the wall shows them *in situ*. Made of wood, they were coated in bitumen – the black skin, identified with Osiris and the rich, black river silt, symbolised fertility and rebirth.

Room 40

Note **Tutankhamun's wig box** of dark wood, with strips of blue and orange inlay, the wooden mushroom-shaped support inside once holding the king's short curly wig.

Rooms 35 & 30

The highlight here is the **pharaoh's lion throne** (No 179). Covered with sheet gold and inlaid with glass and semiprecious stones, the wooden throne is supported by spindly lions. The colourful tableau on the back of the chair depicts Ankhesenamun applying perfume to husband Tutankhamun, under the rays of the sun (Aten), the worship of which was a hangover from his father and predecessor, Akhenaten, whose throne this may also once have been (there is evidence of remodelling of both the figures and the names). Their robes are modelled in beaten silver and their hair is fashioned from glass paste.

Despite the magnificence of his burial artefacts, Tutankhamun only ruled Egypt for nine years and made little impression in the annals of its history.

The many **golden statues** were placed in the tomb to help the pharaoh on his journey in the afterlife. They include a series of 28 gilded wooden deities, meant to protect the pharaoh, and 413 shabti (only a selection of these symbolic servants are here) who would perform, on behalf of the pharaoh, any labours required of him in the afterlife.

Room 20

This room contains exquisite **alabaster jars** and **vessels**.

Room 15

Intricately rigged **model barques** (boats), to be used by the pharaoh on his voyage through the afterlife, are displayed here.

Rooms 10 & 9

The northern end of this gallery is filled with the pharaoh's three elaborate **funerary couches**, one supported by two figures of the cow-goddess Mehetweret; one by two figures of the goddess of the underworld Ammut, 'the devourer' who ate the hearts of the damned; and the third by two lionesses. Their exact purpose is unknown. The huge **bouquet** of persea and olive leaves in Room 10, near the top of the stairs, was originally propped up beside the two black and gold guardian statues in Room 45.

The alabaster chest contains four **Canopic jars**, the stoppers of which are in the form of Tutankhamun's head. Inside these jars were placed the four miniature gold coffins exhibited in Room 3 that, in turn, contained the pharaoh's internal organs. The chest and its gory contents was then placed inside the golden Canopic shrine with the four gilded goddesses: Isis, Neith, Nephthys and Selket, all portrayed with protective outstretched arms.

Most people walk right past Tutankhamun's amazing **wardrobe** in Room 9. The pharaoh was buried with a whole range of clothing, including sumptuous tunics covered in gold discs and beading, ritual robes of 'fake fur', a large supply of neatly folded underwear and even socks to be worn with flip-flop type sandals, 47 pairs of which were buried with him. From these and other objects, the Tutankhamun Textile Project has worked out that Tutankhamun's vital statistics were 31in chest, 29in waist and 43in hips.

Moisturising oils were very popular; even troops were anointed with perfumes as a mark of honour. One Spartan king stormed out of a banquet when his fellow Egyptian guests had overdone the perfume. He thought them decadent and effeminate.

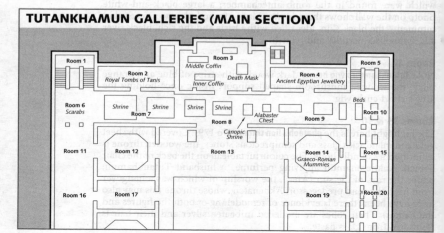

TUTANKHAMUN GALLERIES (MAIN SECTION)

MYTH BUSTING

In January 2005 the National Geographic Society arranged for 1700 CT scans of the mummy of Tutankhamun to be taken at his tomb in Luxor's Valley of the Kings. The scans were then given to three teams of researchers (from Paris, New York and Egypt) who used them to model busts showing what the boy king might have looked like on the day of his death 3300 years ago. Unveiling the startlingly similar-looking busts to a packed international press conference, Zahi Hawass, secretary-general of Egypt's Supreme Council of Antiquities, stated that the scans had shown that Tut was healthy and well fed at the time of his death and that there was no evidence of foul play, contradicting the oft-repeated theory that he had been murdered at the behest of Ay, the commoner who ruled Egypt as regent while Tut was growing up. The scans showed that one of Tut's legs had been fractured shortly before his death, leading to conjecture that this had led to infection or a fat embolism that eventually killed him.

Rooms 8 & 7

These galleries just barely accommodate the four huge **gilded wooden shrines** that fitted one inside the other like a set of Russian dolls, encasing at their centre the sarcophagi of the boy pharaoh.

Room 3

This is the room that everybody wants to see and at peak times you'll have to queue. The central exhibit is Tutankhamun's astonishing **death mask**. Made of solid gold and weighing 11kg, the mask covered the head of the mummy, where it lay inside a series of three sarcophagi. The mask is an idealised portrait of the young pharaoh; the eyes are fashioned from obsidian and quartz, while the outlines of the eyes and the eyebrows are delineated with lapis lazuli.

No less wondrous are the two **golden sarcophagi**. These are the inner two sarcophagi – the outermost coffin, along with the mummified remains of Tutankhamun, remains in place in his tomb in the Valley of the Kings. The smallest coffin is, like the mask, cast in solid gold and inlaid in the same fashion. It weighs 110kg. The slightly larger coffin is made of gilded wood.

ROOM 4 – ANCIENT EGYPTIAN JEWELLERY

One of two galleries opened in 1998, this room exhibits finds from across the country. The stunning jewellery collection includes belts, inlaid beadwork, necklaces, semiprecious stones and bracelets. Most beautiful of all is a **diadem of Queen Sit-Hathor-Yunet**, a golden headband with a rearing cobra inset with semiprecious stones. As well as the Pharaonic cache there are finds from the Graeco-Roman period from the Western Oases and Red Sea areas including bracelets, another diadem and agate bowls.

ROOM 2 – ROYAL TOMBS OF TANIS

The second of the new galleries, this room contains a glittering collection of gold- and silver-encrusted objects from six intact 21st- and 22nd-dynasty tombs that were found at the Delta site of Tanis (p197). Unearthed by the French in 1939, the tombs' discovery rivalled Carter's finding of Tutankhamun's tomb, but news of the discovery was overshadowed by the outbreak of WWII. The gold **death mask of Psusennes I** (1039–991 BC) is on display here along with his silver inner coffin, and another silver coffin with the head of a falcon belonging to the pharaoh Shoshenq II (c 890 BC).

Cosmetics played an important role in the daily life of both women and men; the tomb builders of Deir al-Medina are shown having their eye paint applied during working hours as protection against glare and various eye diseases.

ROOM 14 – GRAECO-ROMAN MUMMIES

This room contains a small sample of the stunning portraits found on Graeco-Roman mummies, popularly known as the **Fayoum Portraits** (see the boxed text, p191). These faces were painted onto wooden panels that were then placed over the mummies' embalmed faces; some were even painted directly onto the shrouds themselves. The display is dusty and badly lit, but these portraits still manage to express the personalities of their subjects more successfully than the stylised elegance of most other ancient Egyptian art.

ROOM 34 – PHARAONIC TECHNOLOGY

For gadget buffs, this room contains a great number of everyday objects that helped support ancient Egypt's great leap out of prehistory. Some are still in use in Egypt today. **Pharaonic boomerangs** were apparently used for hunting birds.

ROOM 43 – YUYA & THUYU ROOMS

Before Tutankhamun, the discovery of the tomb of Yuya and Thuyu (the parents of Queen Tiy, and Tutankhamun's great-grandparents) was the most spectacular find in Egyptian archaeology. The tomb was discovered virtually intact in the Valley of the Kings in 1905 and contained a vast number of treasures, including five ornate sarcophagi and the remarkably well-preserved mummies of the two commoners who became royal in-laws. Among many other items on display are such essentials for the hereafter as beds and sandals, as well as the fabulous gilded **death mask of Thuyu**.

ROOM 48 – PYRAMID MODEL

An excellent large-scale model of one of the Abu Sir pyramids perfectly illustrates the typical pyramid complex with its valley temple, high-walled causeway, mortuary temple and minisatellite pyramid – well worth studying before a trip to Giza. Case No 82 contains the much copied blue faïence **hippopotamus** from the Middle Kingdom.

ROOM 53 – ANIMAL MUMMIES

Animal cults proliferated in ancient Egypt, as the battered and dust-covered mummified cats, dogs, crocodiles, birds, rams and jackals in Room 53 suggest.

ROOM 37 – MODEL ARMIES

Discovered in the Asyut tomb of the governor Meseheti and dating from about 2000 BC (11th dynasty), these are two sets of 40 **wooden warriors** marching in phalanxes. The darker soldiers (No 72) are Nubian archers from the south of the kingdom, each wearing brightly coloured kilts of varying design, while the lighter-skinned soldiers (No 73) are Egyptian pikemen.

ROOMS 32 & 27 – MIDDLE KINGDOM MODELS

These sensational lifelike models were mostly found in the tomb of Meketre, an 11th-dynasty chancellor in Thebes, and together constitute a fascinating portrait of daily life in Egypt almost 4000 years ago. They include fishing boats, a slaughterhouse, a carpentry workshop, a loom and a model of Meketre's house (with fig trees in the garden). Most spectacular is the 1.5m-wide scene of Meketre sitting with his sons, four scribes and various others, counting cattle.

www.egyptianmuseum
.gov.eg is the Egyptian
Museum's own website.
It has a games section
where you can play with
falling lotuses, work with
hieroglyphs and complete
a Tutankhamun puzzle.

www.animalmummies
.com is an interesting
website about the
Egyptian Museum's
animal mummies that
encourages you to adopt
one and help pay for a
climate-controlled room
and special cases to
conserve the poor beasts.

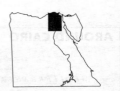

Around Cairo

Held hostage by Cairo's endless charms, too few travellers escape into the surrounding countryside. This is a shame, because the city is circled by ancient sites that are begging to be explored. Within a short drive of the city limits lie some of the oldest, most important and certainly most impressive ancient sites in Egypt. Memphis may retain little to suggest that it was once the mighty capital of Old Kingdom Egypt, but the vast necropolis of Saqqara with the Step Pyramid at its centre pays eloquent visual testimony to the power of the early pharaohs, as does nearby Abu Sir. With Dahshur, home to the stunning Red and Bent pyramids, these sites offer a fabulous day-trip opportunity.

Further south, the lush semioasis of Al-Fayoum is home to rarely visited ancient monuments, a picturesque lake with abundant wildlife and a spectacular desert rich in fossils.

North of the city, the Nile Delta hides more ancient sites amid sprawling villages and green fields. The shortest – and certainly dustiest – trip into this region is to the noisy Birqash camel market, where Sudanese traders dispose of the last of their camels. The most enjoyable trip is with a boatload of Cairenes who are kicking up their heels en route to the Cairene equivalent of Coney Island or Blackpool, the Nile Barrages.

Away from the Nile, the fortresslike monasteries of Wadi Natrun sit on the edge of the desert, luring urban Copts to follow in the pilgrimage footsteps of their ancestors.

Apart from the history of the region, it's great to swap Cairo's overwhelming urbanity for the serenity of the countryside, with its luscious green fields and palm groves that end abruptly at the edges of the vast desert.

HIGHLIGHTS

- Explore the half-buried ruins at **Saqqara** (p181) in the peaceful solitude of the desert
- Marvel at the **pyramids of Dahshur** (p187), the older and smaller cousins of the Pyramids of Giza
- Take a music-filled boat ride to the **Nile Barrages** (p196)
- Visit **Birqash camel market** (p193) for a wild contrast with Cairo city life
- Meet the astonishing monks of the desert monasteries of **Wadi Natrun** (p194)

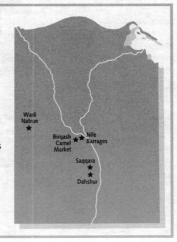

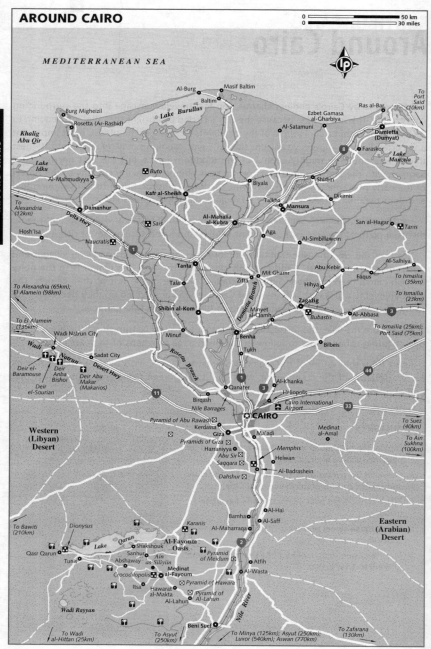

AROUND CAIRO

MEDITERRANEAN SEA

To Port Said (10km)

To Alexandria (12km)

To Alexandria (65km); El Alamein (98km)

To El Alamein (135km)

Khalig Abu Qir

Lake Idku

Lake Burullus

Al-Burg
Masif Baltim
Baltim
Burg Migheizil
Rosetta (Ar-Rashid)
Al-Satamuni
Ezbet Gamasa al-Gharbiya
Ras al-Bar
Damietta (Dumyat)
Faraskor
Lake Manzela

Al-Mahmudiyya
Buto
Blyala
Shirbin
Dikirnis

Hosh'Isa
Damanhur
Delta Hwy
Kafr al-Sheikh
Talkha
Mansura

Naucratis
Sais
Al-Mahalla al-Kubra
Aga
Al-Simbillawein
San al-Hagar
Tanis

Tanta
Mit Ghamr
Abu Kebir
Fáqus
Al-Salhiya

Tala
Zifta
Hihya
Zagazig
Al-Abbasa

Shibin al-Kom
Minyet al-Qamh
Bubastis

To Ismailia (35km)
To Ismailia (23km)
To Ismailia (25km); Port Said (75km)

Minuf
Benha
Bilbeis
Tukh

Wadi Natrun City
Sadat City
Desert Hwy

Rosetta Branch
Damietta Branch

Wadi Natrun
Deir el-Baramouse
Deir Anba Bishoi
Deir el-Sourian
Deir Abu Makar (Makarios)

Birqash
Nile Barrages
Qanater
Al-Khanka
Heliopolis

Western (Libyan) Desert

Pyramid of Abu Rawash
Kerdassa
Giza
Pyramids of Giza
Harraniyya
Abu Sir
Saqqara
Dahshur

Cairo International Airport

CAIRO
Ma'adi
Memphis
Helwan
Al-Badrashein

Medinat al-Amal

To Suez (40km)
To Ain Sukhna (100km)

Bamha
Al-Hai
Al-Saff

To Bawiti (210km)

Dionysus
Lake Qarun
Karanis
Al-Maharraqa

Qasr Qarun
Tunis
Shakshouk
Sanhur
Abshaway
Ain as-Siliyin
Al-Fayoum Oasis
Pyramid of Meidum
Atfih

Crocodilopolis
Medinat al-Fayoum
Itsa
Hawarat al-Makta
Pyramid of Hawara
Pyramid of Al-Lahun
Al-Lahun
Al-Wasta

Wadi Rayyan

To Wadi al-Hittan (25km)
To Asyut (250km)
Beni Suef
To Minya (125km); Asyut (250km); Luxor (540km); Aswan (770km)
To Zafarana (130km)

Eastern (Arabian) Desert

Nile River

0   50 km
0   30 miles

SOUTH OF CAIRO

The great Pyramids of Giza are just three of approximately 90 ancient pyramids spread along the Nile. Most pyramids are concentrated just south of Cairo, from the pyramid fields of Abu Sir, the must-see Step Pyramid at Saqqara and the magnificent Red and Bent Pyramids of Dahshur, all the way to the oasis of Al-Fayoum. These monuments predate the better-known temples of Luxor and Upper Egypt by hundreds of years, and represent the formative steps of art and architecture that reached fruition at Abydos, Karnak and in the Valley of the Kings.

MEMPHIS

☎ 02

The legendary pharaoh Narmer, also known as Menes, is credited with unifying the two lands of Upper and Lower Egypt around 3100 BC. He founded his new capital symbolically on the spot where the Nile Delta met the valley, in Memphis. For most of the Pharaonic period Memphis was the capital of Egypt; later, Thebes (now Luxor) became its ceremonial capital. Originally called Ineb-hedj, meaning 'White walls', the modern name derives from Men-nefer, meaning 'Established and beautiful'. Indeed, the city was filled with palaces, gardens and temples, making it one of the greatest cities of the ancient world. In the 5th century BC, long after its period of power, Greek historian and traveller Herodotus still described Memphis as 'a prosperous city and cosmopolitan centre'. Its importance was reflected in the size of its cemetery on the west bank of the Nile, an area replete with royal pyramids, private tombs and the necropolises of sacred animals. This cemetery on the edge of the desert, centred at Saqqara, runs for 35km, from Dahshur in the south to Giza in the north.

Even after Thebes became the new capital during the New Kingdom, Memphis remained Egypt's second city; it was finally abandoned only after the first Muslim invasions in the 7th century AD. Centuries of builders quarrying for stone, of annual floods and of antiquity hunters have succeeded where even the mighty Persians failed: Memphis has almost completely vanished. Even the enormous temple of the creator god, Ptah, is little more than a few sparse ruins frequently waterlogged due to the high water table. The foundations of other ancient buildings have long since been ploughed under. All of which means that today there are few clues as to Memphis' former grandeur and importance; in fact, it's difficult to imagine that any sort of settlement once stood here.

Memphis' **museum** (Mit Rahina; adult/student E£25/15, parking E£5; ⏱ 8am-4pm Oct-Apr, to 5pm May-Sep, to 3pm Ramadan), most of which is open-air, is built around a magnificent fallen colossal limestone statue of Ramses II. This is displayed in a somewhat tatty pavilion, but the rest of the collection, including an alabaster sphinx of the New Kingdom, two statues of Ramses II that originally adorned Nubian temples, and the huge travertine beds on which the sacred Apis bulls were mummified before being placed in the Serapeum at Saqqara, are in the sculpture garden. Every piece on display is either of Ramses II or Amenhotep III.

Getting There & Away

The tiny village of Memphis is 24km south of Cairo and 3km from Saqqara. While it is worth visiting as part of a tour of Saqqara, only those seriously into Egyptology would want to trek down here by public transport; others might be disappointed by the little that remains of the mighty city. Getting to Memphis is a pain in the neck and a lengthy process. The cheapest way is to take a crowded 3rd-class train from Cairo's Ramses Station to Al-Badrashein village (the trip usually takes about 40 minutes), then walk for about half an hour, catch a Saqqara microbus and ask to be dropped off at Memphis. Unless

---

SEEING THE SITES

Many visitors to Cairo choose to spend a day getting out of the city and visiting Memphis, Saqqara and Dahshur. The best way to do this is to go on a small tour or hire a private taxi to take you around the sites, which are connected by a road that runs south from Giza along the edge of the fields. A taxi will cost E£120 to E£140 per day (around seven hours) and day tours range from E£40 to E£130 per person plus entry fees. See p140 for more details.

AROUND CAIRO

you have plenty of time, enjoy discomfort or have overspent, we recommend taking a tour or hiring a taxi for a day instead. See the boxed text, p179, for more details.

PYRAMIDS OF ABU SIR

Lying at the edge of the desert and surrounded by sand dunes, the **pyramids of Abu Sir** (Saqqara rd) form the necropolis of the 5th dynasty. Most of the remains have not withstood the ravages of time as well as their bigger, older brethren at Giza. These pyramids are slumped and lack geometric precision. For a long time few visitors bothered to visit Abu Sir, and although the site was officially 'opened' at the beginning of 1999 with the construction of a visitors centre/gatehouse, in reality most visitors have been denied entry. On our last attempt, we were told 'soon, soon', so it seems the situation is poised to change.

There are four pyramid complexes here and although the Pyramid of Sahure is in ruins, its funerary complex is the most complete of the four.

Pyramid of Sahure

Sahure (2487–2475 BC) was the first of the 5th-dynasty pharaohs to be buried at Abu Sir, but his pyramid, originally 50m high, is now badly damaged. The entrance corridor is only half a metre high and slopes down to a small room. You then walk through a 75m-long corridor before crawling 2m on your stomach, through Pharaonic dust and spider webs, to reach the burial chamber. The better-preserved remains of Sahure's funerary temple complex stand east of the pyramid. This must have been an impressive temple, with black basalt-paved floors, red granite date-palm columns and walls decorated with 10,000 sq metres of superbly detailed reliefs (some of this is now in the museums of Cairo and Berlin). It was connected by a 235m-long causeway to the valley temple, built at the edge of the cultivation and bordered by water. From the pyramid, on a clear day, you can see some 10 other pyramids stretching out to the horizon.

Pyramid of Nyuserra

The most dilapidated of the finished pyramids at Abu Sir belonged to Nyuserra (2445–2421 BC). Originally some 50m high, this pyramid has been heavily quarried. Nyuserra

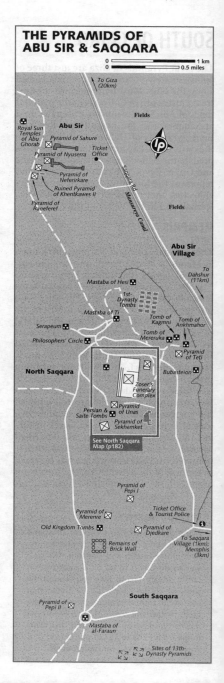

THE PYRAMIDS OF
ABU SIR & SAQQARA

0 —————— 1 km
0 —————— 0.5 miles

To Giza
(20km)

Fields

Abu Sir

Royal Sun
Temples
of Abu
Ghorab

Pyramid of Sahure

Ticket
Office

Pyramid of Nyuserra

Pyramid of
Neferirkare

Ruined Pyramid
of Khentkawes II

Pyramid of
Raneferef

Fields

Abu Sir
Village

To
Dahshur
(11km)

Mastaba of Hesi

1st-
Dynasty
Tombs

Mastaba of Ti

Serapeum

Tomb of
Kagmni

Tomb of
Ankhmahor

Tomb of
Mereruka

Philosophers' Circle

Pyramid
of Teti

North Saqqara

Bubasteion

Zoser's
Funerary
Complex

Persian &
Saite Tombs

Pyramid
of Unas

Pyramid of
Sekhemket

See North Saqqara
Map (p182)

Pyramid of
Pepi I

Ticket Office
& Tourist Police

Pyramid of
Merenre

Old Kingdom Tombs

Pyramid of
Djedkare

To Saqqara
Village (1km);
Memphis
(3km)

Remains of
Brick Wall

South Saqqara

Pyramid of
Pepi II

Mastaba of
al-Faraun

Sites of 13th-
Dynasty Pyramids

reused his father Neferirkare's valley temple and then redirected the causeway to lead not to his father's pyramid, but to his own.

Pyramid of Neferirkare

The Pyramid of Neferirkare (2475–2455 BC), the third pharaoh of the 5th dynasty and Sahure's brother, resembles the Step Pyramid at Saqqara. This, however, is only the core: the original outer casing has been stripped away, reducing the pyramid from its original planned height of 72m to today's 45m. Neferirkare's causeway and valley temple were appropriated by his son and successor Nyuserra. In the early 20th century in Neferirkare's funerary temple, archaeologists found the so-called Abu Sir Papyri, a highly important archive of Old Kingdom documents written in hieratic, a shorthand form of hieroglyphs. They relate to the cult of the pharaohs buried at the site, recording important details of ritual ceremonies, temple equipment, priests' work rotas and the temple accounts.

South of Neferirkare's pyramid lies the badly ruined **Pyramid of Queen Khentkawes II**, wife of Neferirkare and mother of both Raneferef and Nyuserra. In her nearby funerary temple, Czech archaeologists discovered another set of papyrus archive documents. Two virtually destroyed pyramids to the south of the queen's pyramid may have belonged to the queens of Nyuserra.

Pyramid of Raneferef

On a diagonal, just west of Neferirkare's pyramid, are the remains of the unfinished Pyramid of Raneferef (also known as Neferefre), who reigned for seven years before Nyuserra. Work was so little advanced at the time of his death that the tomb was only completed as a mastaba. In the adjoining mud-brick cult building, Czech archaeologists have found fragments of statuary, including a superb limestone figurine of Raneferef protected by Horus (now in Cairo's Egyptian Museum, p167), along with papyrus fragments relating to the Abu Sir temple archives.

Royal Sun Temples of Abu Ghorab

Just northwest of the Abu Sir pyramids lies the site of Abu Ghorab, with two royal sun temples dedicated to the worship of Ra, the sun god of Heliopolis. The Abu Sir Papyri describe six such temples, but only two, built for Pharaohs Userkaf and Nyuserra, have been discovered. Both follow the traditional plan of a valley temple, a causeway and a large stone enclosure. This enclosure contained a large limestone obelisk: Nyuserra's stood some 37m tall on a 20m-high base. In front of the obelisk, the enormous alabaster altar can still be seen. Made in the form of a solar disc flanked by four 'hotep' signs, the hieroglyphic sign for 'offerings' and 'satisfied', the altar itself reads as 'The sun god Ra is satisfied'. Although it can easily be reached from Abu Sir, this enigmatic site is rarely visited.

Getting There & Away

Some distance off the main Saqqara road, there's no way to reach Abu Sir by public transport. The best way to visit is as part of an organised tour, in a taxi or by car. The other option is to ride a horse or camel from Giza to Saqqara and visit Abu Sir on the way.

SAQQARA

Saqqara, the huge cemetery of ancient Memphis, was an active burial ground for more than 3500 years. The necropolis is situated high above the Nile Valley's cultivation area, covering a 7km stretch of the Western Desert. Deceased pharaohs and their families, administrators, generals and sacred animals were all interred here.

Old Kingdom pharaohs were buried within Saqqara's 11 major pyramids, but their subjects were buried in the hundreds of smaller tombs in the great necropolis. Most of Saqqara, except for the Step Pyramid, was buried in sand until the mid-19th century, when the great French Egyptologist Auguste Mariette uncovered the Serapeum. Since then, it has been a gradual process of rediscovery: the Step Pyramid's massive funerary complex was not discovered until 1924 and it is still being restored. French architect Jean-Philippe Lauer, who began work here in 1926, was involved in its restoration for an incredible 75 years until his death in 2001.

A visit to Saqqara deserves half a day. Because of its size, it seems that other visitors are few and far between, apart from the organised tour groups who rush through in the mornings. As a result, here on the edge of the desert you'll find a peaceful quality rarely found at other ancient sites in Egypt.

The main monuments are in the area around the Step Pyramid, known as **North Saqqara** (adult/student E£35/20, parking E£2-5; ☺ 8am-4pm Oct-Apr, to 5pm May-Sep, to 3pm Ramadan). Until South Saqqara and Abu Sir are once again opened to the public, you'll have to limit your visit to this area. There's no resthouse at the site, and only a few vendors selling soft drinks and water. Before setting off, check at the ticket office to see which monuments are open – this constantly changes.

Zoser's Funerary Complex

STEP PYRAMID

Imhotep, the pharaoh's chief architect (later deified), built the 2650 BC **Step Pyramid** (Map p182) for Zoser. It is Egypt's (and the world's) earliest stone monument and its significance cannot be overstated. Previously tombs and temples were made of perishable materials – royal tombs were underground rooms topped with mud-brick mastabas. Imhotep developed the mastaba into a pyramid *and* built it in hewn stone. From this flowed Egypt's later architectural achievements.

The pyramid was transformed from mastaba into pyramid through six separate stages of construction and alteration. With each stage, the builders gained confidence in their use of the new medium and mastered the techniques required to move, place and secure the huge blocks. This first pyramid rose in six steps to a height of 60m and was encased in fine white limestone.

The Step Pyramid is surrounded by a vast funerary complex, enclosed by a 1645m-long panelled limestone wall, covering 15 hectares. Part of the enclosure wall survives today at a height of about 5m, and a section near the entrance was restored to its original 10m height. Fourteen false doors, formerly of wood but now carved from stone and painted to resemble real wood, hinges and sockets, allowed the pharaoh's ka, or attendant spirit, to come and go at will. The complex is entered on the southeastern corner, via a vestibule and along a colonnaded corridor into the broad hypostyle hall. The 40 pillars in the corridor are the original 'bundle columns', ribbed to resemble a bundle of palm or papyrus stems. The walls have been restored, but the protective ceiling is modern concrete. The roof of the hypostyle hall is supported

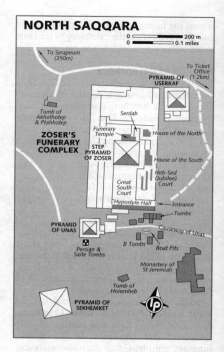

NORTH SAQQARA

by four impressive columns and there's a large, false, half-open ka door.

GREAT SOUTH COURT

The hypostyle hall leads into the **great south court** (Map p182), a huge open area flanking the south side of the pyramid, with a section of wall featuring a frieze of cobras. The cobra, or uraeus, represented the goddess Wadjet, a fire-spitting agent of destruction and protector of the pharaoh. It was a symbol of Egyptian royalty, and a rearing cobra always appeared on the brow of a pharaoh's headdress or crown.

Near the base of the pyramid is an altar and in the centre of the court are two stone B-shaped boundary markers, which delineated the ritual race the pharaoh had to run, a literal demonstration of his fitness to rule. The race was part of the Jubilee Festival, or Heb-Sed, which usually occurred after 30 years' reign and involved the pharaoh's symbolic rejuvenation and the recognition of his supremacy by officials from all over Egypt. The construction of Heb-Sed features within Zoser's funerary complex was

---

SAQQARA HALF-DAY ITINERARY

Enter through the hypostyle hall and gaze on the **Step Pyramid**, the world's oldest pyramid. Run the rejuvenation race in Zoser's **Heb-Sed Court**, wonder at the ancient graffiti in the **Houses of the North and South** and stare into Zoser's stone eyes in the eerie **Serdab** (cellar). Walk anticlockwise around the Step Pyramid, visit the mastaba tomb of 5th-dynasty father and son **Akhethotep** and **Ptahhotep**, with its beautiful painted reliefs of animals, battle scenes and the two men receiving offerings, then head south towards the causeway of Unas.

Moving away from the Step Pyramid, descend 25m into the **Pyramid of Teti** to see the famous Pyramid Texts inside, and then pop into the nearby tombs of **Mereruka** and **Ankhmahor**. You'll be able to watch members of a Polish archaeological mission at work restoring reliefs in Mereruka. To complete your visit, move on to the most wonderful tomb of all, the **Mastaba of Ti**, with its fascinating tomb reliefs of daily life in the Old Kingdom that show people trading, building ships, milking cows and rescuing their livestock from crocodiles.

---

therefore intended to perpetuate his revitalisation for eternity.

The buildings on the eastern side of the pyramid are also connected with the royal jubilee, and include the **Heb-Sed (Jubilee) Court**. Buildings on the east side of the court represent the shrines of Lower Egypt, and those on the west represent Upper Egypt. All were designed to house the spirits of Egypt's gods when they gathered to witness the rebirth of the pharaoh during his jubilee rituals.

North of the Heb-Sed Court are the **House of the South** and **House of the North**, representing the two main shrines of Upper and Lower Egypt and symbolising the unity of the country. The heraldic plants of the two regions were chosen to decorate the column capitals: papyrus in the north, lotus in the south.

The House of the South also features one of the earliest examples of tourist graffiti. In the 47th year of Ramses II's reign, nearly 1500 years after Zoser's death, Hadnakhte, a treasury scribe, recorded his admiration for Zoser while 'on a pleasure trip west of Memphis' in about 1232 BC. His hieratic script, written in black ink, is preserved behind Perspex just inside the building's entrance.

SERDAB

A stone structure right in front of the pyramid, the **serdab** (Map p182) contains a slightly tilted wooden box with two holes drilled into its north face. Look through these and you'll have the eerie experience of coming face to face with Zoser himself. Inside is a near-life-size, lifelike painted statue of the long-dead pharaoh, gazing stonily out towards the stars, although this one is only a copy (the original is in Cairo's Egyptian Museum, p169).

The original entrance to the Step Pyramid is directly behind the *serdab*, and leads down to a maze of subterranean tunnels and chambers quarried for almost 6km through the rock. The pharaoh's burial chamber is vaulted in granite. Some chambers are decorated with reliefs of the jubilee race and feature some exquisite blue faïence tile decoration. Although the interior of the pyramid is unsafe and closed to the public, part of the blue-tiled decoration can be seen in the Egyptian Museum.

Pyramid of Userkaf

Northeast of the funerary complex is the **Pyramid of Userkaf** (Map p182), which is closed to the public. Although the removal of its limestone casing has left little more than a mound of rubble, it once rose to a height of 49m. Its funerary temple was once decorated with the most exquisite naturalistic relief carvings, judging from one of the few remaining fragments showing birds by the river, now in the Egyptian Museum.

Pyramid & Causeway of Unas

What appears to be another big mound of rubble, this time to the southwest of Zoser's funerary complex, is actually the 2375–2345 BC **Pyramid of Unas** (Map p182), the last pharaoh of the 5th dynasty. Built only 300 years after the inspired creation of the Step Pyramid, and after the perfection of the Pyramids of Giza, this unassuming pile of loose blocks and debris once stood 43m high. Although it looks nothing special from the outside, the interior marked the beginning of a significant development in funerary practices. For the first time, the royal burial chamber was decorated, its ceiling adorned with stars and its white alabaster-lined walls inscribed with beautiful blue hieroglyphs. These are the funerary inscriptions now known as the Pyramid Texts, comprising 283 separate 'spells' chosen by Unas to protect his soul. The inscriptions include rituals, prayers and hymns, as well as lists of items, such as the food and clothing Unas would require in the afterlife. Unfortunately, deterioration of the interior led to the pyramid's permanent closure in 1998.

The 750m-long causeway running from the east side of Unas' pyramid to his valley temple (now marked by little more than a couple of stone columns at the side of the road leading up to the site) was originally roofed and decorated with a great range of painted relief scenes, including a startling image of people starving, now preserved in the Louvre in Paris.

The two 45m-long boat pits of Unas lie immediately south of the causeway, while on either side of the causeway are numerous tombs; more than 200 have been excavated. Of the several better-preserved examples usually open to visitors are the tombs of one of Unas' queens, Nebet, and that of Princess Idut, who was possibly his daughter. There are also several brightly painted tombs of prominent 5th- and 6th-dynasty officials. These include the Tomb of Mehu, the vizier (minister) and the Tomb of Nefer, the supervisor of singers.

B TOMBS

Several beautiful **tombs** (Map p182), not quite as impressive as the tombs north of the Step Pyramid, have been cleared in the area east of the Pyramid of Unas. These include the joint Tomb of Niankhkhnum and Khnumhotep, overseers of the royal manicurists to Pharaoh Nyuserra; the Tomb of Neferherenptah, the overseer of the royal hairdressers, which is also known as the Bird Tomb on account of its superbly drawn bird-hunting scene; and the Tomb of Irukaptah, overseer of the royal butchers, the appropriate scenes in which support its title of the Butchers' Tomb. None are currently open to the public.

SAITE & PERSIAN TOMBS

Around the sides of the Pyramid of Unas are several large shaft **tombs** (Map p182) of the Saite (664–525 BC) and Persian (525–404 BC) eras. These are some of the deepest tombs in Egypt, the depth intended to prevent grave robbers. Here, as with just about everywhere else in Egypt, the precaution failed. To the north of the pyramid is the enormous tomb shaft of the Saite general Amun-Tefnakht. On the south side of the pyramid is a group of three Persian tombs; the entrance is covered by a small wooden hut to which a guard in the area has the key. If you don't have your own torch he'll lead you down a 25m-deep winding staircase to the vaulted tombs of three officials: the admiral Djenhebu to the west, chief royal physician Psamtik in the centre and Psamtik's son, Pediese, to the east. The sheer size of the tombs and the great stone sarcophagi within, combined with their sophisticated decoration, demonstrate that the technical achievements of the later part of Egyptian history were equal to those of earlier times.

Monastery of St Jeremiah

Uphill from the causeway of Unas, southeast of the boat pits, are the half-buried remains of this **monastery** (Map p182), dating from the 5th century AD. Little is left of the structure, ransacked by invading Arabs in AD 950. More recently, the wall paintings and carvings were removed to the Coptic Museum in Cairo (p108). The area around here is a favourite picnic spot with Cairenes.

Pyramid of Sekhemket

Closed to the public because of its dangerous condition, the **unfinished pyramid** (Map p182) of Zoser's successor Sekhemket (2648–2640 BC) is a short distance west of the ruined monastery. The project was abandoned for unknown reasons when the great limestone enclosure wall was only 3m high, but the architects had already constructed the underground chambers in the rock beneath the pyramid, together with the deep shaft of the south tomb. An unused travertine sarcophagus was found in the sealed burial chamber, and a quantity of gold, jewellery and a child's body in the south tomb. Recent surveys have also revealed another mysterious large complex to the west of Sekhemket's enclosure, but this remains unexcavated.

Tomb of Akhethotep & Ptahhotep

Akhethotep and his son Ptahhotep were senior royal officials during the reigns of Djedkare (2414–2375 BC) and Unas at the end of the 5th dynasty. Akhethotep was vizier, judge, supervisor of pyramid cities and supervisor of priests. Most of his titles were inherited by his son, Ptahhotep, along with his **tomb** (Map p182) – the joint mastaba has two burial chambers, two chapels and a pillared hall.

The painted reliefs in Ptahhotep's section are particularly beautiful and portray a wide range of animals, from lions and hedgehogs to the domesticated cattle and fowl that were brought as offerings to the deceased. Ptahhotep himself is portrayed resplendent in a panther-skin robe inhaling perfume from a jar. Further on he is having his wig fitted, his feet massaged and his fingers manicured (some Egyptologists prefer to interpret this detail as Ptahhotep inspecting an important document, which would be in keeping with his official status).

Philosophers' Circle

Nearby is a sad-looking group of **Greek statues** (Map p180) arranged in a semicircle and sheltered by a spectacularly ugly concrete shelter. This is the remnant of a collection of philosophers and poets set up as a wayside shrine by Ptolemy I (305–285 BC) as part of his patronage of learning. From left to right are Plato (he's standing), Heraclitus (seated), Thales (standing), Protagoras (seated), Homer (seated), Hesiod (seated), Demetrius of Phalerum (standing against a bust of Serapis) and Pindar (seated).

Serapeum

An eerie site lit by tiny lanterns, the **Serapeum** (Map p180) was one of the highlights of visiting Saqqara, but has been closed for a few years.

The sacred Apis bulls were by far the most important of the cult animals entombed at Saqqara. The Apis, it was believed, was an incarnation of Ptah, the god of Memphis, and was the calf of a cow struck by lightning from heaven. Once divinely impregnated, the cow could never again give birth and

her calf was kept in the Temple of Ptah at Memphis and worshipped as a god. The Apis was always portrayed as black, with a distinctive white diamond on its forehead, the image of a vulture on its back and a scarab-shaped mark on its tongue. When it died, the bull was mummified on one of the large travertine embalming tables discovered at Memphis, then carried in a stately procession to the subterranean galleries of the Serapeum at Saqqara, and placed in a huge stone sarcophagus.

The first Apis burial took place in the reign of Amenhotep III (1390–1352 BC), and the practice continued until 30 BC. The enormous granite and limestone coffins could weigh up to 80 tonnes each. Until the mid-19th century, the existence of the sacred Apis tombs was known only from classical references. But having found a half-buried sphinx at Saqqara, and using the description given by the Greek historian Strabo in 24 BC, in 1851 Auguste Mariette uncovered the avenue leading to the Serapeum. Only one Apis sarcophagus was found intact.

Mastaba of Ti

Northeast of the Philosophers' Circle is the **Mastaba of Ti** (Map p180), discovered by Mariette in 1865. It is perhaps the grandest and most detailed private tomb at Saqqara and one of our main sources of knowledge about life in Old Kingdom Egypt. Its owner, Ti, was overseer of the Abu Sir pyramids and sun temples (among other things) during the 5th dynasty. The superb quality of his tomb is in keeping with his nickname, Ti the Rich. Like Zoser, a life-size statue of the deceased stands in a *serdab* in the tomb's offering hall (as with Zoser's, the original is in the Egyptian Museum). Ti's wife, Neferhetpes, was priestess and 'royal acquaintance'. Together with their two sons, Demedj (overseer of the duck pond) and Ti (inspector of royal manicurists), the couple appear throughout the tomb alongside detailed scenes of daily life. As men and women are seen working on the land, preparing food, fishing, building boats, dancing, trading and avoiding crocodiles, their images are accompanied by chattering hieroglyphic dialogue, all no doubt familiar to Ti during his career as a royal overseer: 'Hurry up, the herdsman's coming', 'Don't make so much noise!', 'Pay up – it's cheap!'.

Pyramid of Teti

The avenue of sphinxes excavated by Mariette in the 1850s has again been hidden by desert sands, but it once extended to the much earlier **Pyramid of Teti** (Map p180). Teti (2345–2323 BC) was the first pharaoh of the 6th dynasty and his pyramid was built in step form and cased in limestone. Unfortunately, the pyramid was robbed for its treasure and its stone, and only a mound remains. The interior has fared better and is similar to that of the Pyramid of Unas (p183), in plan and also for its walls, inscribed with Pyramid Texts. Within the intact burial chamber, Teti's basalt sarcophagus is well preserved and represents the first instance of a sarcophagus with inscriptions on it.

Tombs of Mereruka & Ankhmahor

Near the Pyramid of Teti is the **mastaba** (Map p180) of his highest official, Mereruka, vizier and overseer of priests. It's the largest Old Kingdom courtier's tomb, with 32 chambers covering an area of 1000 sq metres. The 17 chambers on the eastern side belong to Mereruka, including a magnificent six-columned offering hall featuring a life-size statue of Mereruka appearing to walk right out of the wall to receive the offerings brought to him. Other rooms are reserved for Mereruka's wife, Princess Seshseshat (Teti's daughter), and their eldest son, Meriteti (whose name means 'Beloved of Teti'). Much of the tomb's decoration is similar to that of the Mastaba of Ti, with an even greater number of animals portrayed – look out for the wide-mouthed, sharp-tusked hippos as you enter – along with a charming scene of domestic bliss as husband and wife are seated on a bed and Seshseshat plays them music on her harp. The tomb is currently being restored by a team of Polish archaeologists, and it's possible to watch them while they are working.

Further east, the **tomb** (Map p180) of the 6th-dynasty vizier and palace overseer Ankhmahor contains more interesting scenes of daily life. Most unusual here are images of surgical procedures, earning the tomb its alternative title, the Doctor's Tomb. As two boys are circumcised the hieroglyphic caption says, 'Hold him firmly so he does not fall'! At the time of research, the tomb was closed to the public.

LOOKING GOOD FOR ETERNITY Dr Joann Fletcher

When visiting temples and tombs, the endless scenes of pharaohs – standing sideways, presenting a never-ending line of gods with the same old offerings – can start to get a bit much. Look closer, however, and these scenes can reveal a few surprises.

As the little figures on the wall strike their eternal poses, a keen eye can find anything from pharaohs ploughing fields to small girls pulling at each other's hair. A whole range of activities that we consider modern can be found among the most ancient scenes, including hairdressing, perfumery, manicures and even massage – the treasury overseer Ptahhotep (p185) certainly enjoyed his comforts and is seen inhaling deeply from a jar of perfume, while his feet are massaged and fingers manicured. There are similar scenes elsewhere at Saqqara, with a group of men in the Tomb of Ankhmahor (above) enjoying both manicures and pedicures.

With the title 'overseer of royal hairdressers and wigmakers' commonly held by the highest officials in the land, hairdressing scenes can also be found in the most unexpected places. Not only does Ptahhotep have his wig fitted by his menservants, similar hairdressing scenes can even be found on coffins, as on the limestone sarcophagus of 11th-dynasty Queen Kawit (in the Egyptian Museum, p167), which shows her wig being deftly styled.

Among its wealth of scenes, the Theban Tomb of Rekhmire (p265) shows a banquet at which the female harpist sings, 'Put perfume on the hair of the goddess Maat'. And then in the Deir al-Medina tomb of the workman Peshedu (p267), his family tree contains relatives whose hair denotes their seniority, the eldest shown with the whitest hair as opposed to with wrinkles.

As in many representations of ancient Egyptians, black eye make-up is worn by both male and female, adult and child. As well as its aesthetic value, it was also used as a means of reducing the glare of the sun – think ancient sunglasses. Even manual workers wore it: the Deir al-Medina Tomb of Ipy (p267) once contained a scene in which men building the royal tombs were having eye paint applied while they worked. Difficult to imagine on a building site today!

ONGOING EXCAVATIONS

If you thought major Egyptological discoveries were a thing of the past, think again. In early 2005 Egyptian archaeologists working alongside the Pyramid of Teti unearthed a 2300-year-old unidentified mummy buried in sand at the bottom of a 6m shaft. The perfectly preserved mummy was wearing a golden mask and was encased in a wooden sarcophagus covered in brightly coloured images of gods and goddesses. Describing the find, Dr Zahi Hawass, secretary-general of Egypt's Supreme Council of Antiquities, said 'We have revealed what may be the most beautiful mummy ever found in Egypt.'

South Saqqara

Currently off-limits to visitors, the monuments of South Saqqara include the **Mastaba of Al-Faraun** (Map p180), or Pharaoh's Bench, an unusual funerary complex belonging to the last 4th-dynasty pharaoh, the short-lived Shepseskaf (2503–2498 BC). Shepseskaf was the son of Menkaure, builder of Giza's third great pyramid. But Shepseskaf failed to emulate his father: inside an enclosure once covering 700 sq metres, his rectangular tomb was built of limestone blocks and originally covered by a further layer of fine, white limestone and a lower course or lower layer of red granite. Inside the tomb, a 21m-long corridor slopes down to storage rooms and a vaulted burial chamber.

A short distance northwest of the mastaba is the 2278–2184 BC **Pyramid of Pepi II** (Map p180), whose 94-year reign at the end of the 6th dynasty appears to have been the longest in Egyptian history. Despite his longevity, Pepi II's 52m-high pyramid was of the same modest proportions as those of his predecessor, Pepi I. Although the exterior is little more than a mound of rubble, the interior is decorated with more passages from the Pyramid Texts.

Getting There & Away

Saqqara is about 25km south of Cairo and is best visited in a taxi, combined with a visit to Memphis and Dahshur. See the boxed text, p179, for more details. Competent riders can hire a horse or camel for the day in Giza and make the three-hour ride to Saqqara. See p131.

If you're coming from Cairo or Giza and are determined to do it on your own, you have several options, including the time-consuming and hassle-rich combination of train, bus and foot via Al-Badrashein. One of the cheapest options is to take a bus or minibus (50pt) to the Pyramids Rd and get off at the Saqqara road stop. From there, take a microbus to the turn-off to the Saqqara site (Haram Saqqara; don't ask for Saqqara village as you'll end up in the wrong place). You'll then probably have to walk 1.5km to the ticket office.

Getting Around

It's easy to walk around North Saqqara. It's also possible to hire a camel, horse or donkey from near the Serapeum to take you on a circuit of the site for between E£10 and E£20. You'll need to pay more the further into the desert away from North Saqqara you go.

DAHSHUR

About 10km south of Saqqara, in a quiet bit of desert, **Dahshur** (adult/student E£20/10; ☯ 8am-4pm Oct-Apr, to 5pm May-Sep, to 3pm Ramadan) is an impressive 3.5km-long field of 4th- and 12th-dynasty pyramids. The site was an off-limits military zone until mid-1996 and the Bent Pyramid and its surrounds is still a militarised zone, meaning that it can only be admired at a distance.

Fortunately, the wonderful Red Pyramid is open to visitors. Many cluey travellers are choosing to visit Dahshur instead of the Giza Plateau for three reasons: the pyramid is just as impressive as its counterparts at Giza, the site is much more peaceful and the entry fee here is significantly cheaper.

There were originally 11 pyramids at Dahshur, although only the two Old Kingdom ones (the Bent and Red Pyramids) remain intact. Of the three Middle Kingdom pyramid complexes built by Amenemhat II (1922–1878 BC), Sesostris III (1874–1855 BC) and his son Amenemhat III (1855–1808 BC), only the oddly shaped **Black Pyramid** of Amenemhat III is worth a look. The towerlike structure appears to have completely collapsed due to the pilfering of its limestone outer casing in medieval times, but the mud-brick remains contain a maze of corridors and rooms designed to deceive tomb robbers. Thieves did manage to penetrate the burial chambers, but left behind a number of precious funerary artefacts, discovered in 1993.

Pharaoh Sneferu (2613–2589 BC), father of Khufu and founder of the 4th dynasty, built Egypt's first true pyramid here, the Red Pyramid. He also built an earlier version, the Bent Pyramid. These two pyramids were the same height. They are also the equal third-largest pyramids in Egypt, after the two largest at Giza. Before founding the necropolis at Dahshur, Sneferu began the Pyramid of Meidum (p191).

Bent Pyramid

Experimenting with ways to create a true, smooth-sided pyramid, Sneferu's architects began with the same steep angle and inward-leaning courses of stone they used to create step pyramids. When this began to show signs of stress and instability around halfway up its eventual 105m height, they had little choice but to reduce the angle from 54 degrees to 43 degrees and begin to lay the stones in horizontal layers. This explains why the structure has the unusual shape that gives it its name. Most of its outer casing is still intact, and inside (closed to visitors) are two burial chambers, the highest of which retains its original ancient scaffolding of great cedar beams to counteract internal instability. There is a small subsidiary pyramid to the south and the remains of a small funerary temple to the east. About halfway towards the cultivation to the east are the ruins of Sneferu's valley temple, which yielded some interesting reliefs.

Red Pyramid

The world's oldest true pyramid is the North Pyramid, which is better known as the Red Pyramid. It derives its name from the red tones of its weathered limestone, after the better-quality white limestone casing was removed, or perhaps from the red graffiti and construction marks scribbled on its masonry in ancient times. Having learnt from their experiences building the Bent Pyramid, the same architects carried on where they had left off, building the Red Pyramid at the same 43-degree angle as the Bent Pyramid's more gently inclining upper section. The entrance – via 125 extremely

steep stone steps and a 63m-long passage – takes you down to two antechambers with stunning 12m-high corbelled ceilings and a 15m-high corbelled burial chamber in which fragmentary human remains, possibly of Sneferu himself, were found.

Getting There & Away

The simplest way to visit Dahshur is as part of a tour including Saqqara and Memphis, or to hire a taxi and driver for the day, visiting Memphis and Saqqara on the way. See the boxed text, p179, for more details.

AL-FAYOUM OASIS

☎ 084

Approximately 100km southwest of Cairo, Al-Fayoum is a large semioasis, about 70km wide and 60km long. Home to more than two million people, it is an extremely fertile basin watered by the Nile via hundreds of capillary canals.

The Al-Fayoum region was once filled by Lake Qarun. During the 12th-dynasty reigns of Sesostris III and his son Amenemhat III a series of canals were dug, linking the lake to the Nile. Amenemhat also drained marshes in an early effort at land reclamation. Later the Nile was diverted to the agricultural land. The lake was constantly filled, but at 45m below sea level, it has suffered from increasing salinity.

The oasis was a favourite holiday spot for 13th-dynasty pharaohs, who built palaces in the area. The Greeks, who believed the crocodiles in Lake Qarun were sacred, called the area Crocodilopolis and built a temple in honour of Sobek, the crocodile-headed god. During Ptolemaic and Roman times pilgrims came from across the ancient world to feed the sacred beasts.

These days the region is famous for its lush fields of vegetables and sugar cane, its groves of citrus fruits, nuts and olives. The lake, canals and vegetation support a wide variety of birdlife. All of the oasis' canals are drained for maintenance from January to early February, exposing the loads of rubbish that have been chucked into them over the preceding year. There isn't a lot to do here, but a couple of the archaeological sites (particularly Qasr Qarun and the Pyramid of Meidum) are worth a visit, the lake is attractive and the scenery around Wadi Rayyan, just beyond Al-Fayoum, is gorgeous.

Given that the oasis is so spread out, you really need your own transport. If you hire a taxi for a day in Cairo to bring you down here and chauffeur you around, expect to pay a minimum of E£200. Alternatively, get a bus to Medinat al-Fayoum from Giza, and hire a taxi locally (E£50 to E£70 for half a day).

At the Governorate Building in Medinat al-Fayoum, the genial Mohamed Kamal el Din at the **Fayoum Tourism Authority** (☎ 634 2313, 010 543 4726; F_tourism73@hotmail.com) can organise guides to take travellers around the oasis's sites. From Al-Fayoum, you'll be looking at a cost of around E£300 for a guide and taxi for the day, which should allow you to visit the Pyramid of Meidum, Lake Qarun and Wadi Rayyan.

For more information on the oasis, access a copy of *The Fayoum: History and Guide* by R Neil Hewison (American University in Cairo Press, E£50). For information on ecotourism initiatives and tours in the area, contact Nina Prochazka, the program manager of **North South Consultants Exchange** (☎ 02-735 1045; nina@nsce-inter.com; 27 Sharia Yahia Ibrahim, Zamalek, Cairo).

Medinat al-Fayoum

After visiting Medinat al-Fayoum (Town of the Fayoum) we had a recurring – and terrifying – nightmare about being forced to live there permanently in order to pay penance for past sins. The town is an unhappy mix of concrete, horn-happy drivers, choking fumes and dust, crowded streets and more than 500,000 people. It's one of the ugliest places in the whole of Egypt, with an unfriendly atmosphere and no tourist attractions of note. We suggest avoiding it if at all possible.

ORIENTATION & INFORMATION

The filthy Bahr Yusuf canal acts as the city's main artery and most commercial activities take place along it. There are a number of **banks** (☾ 8.30am-2pm Sun-Thu), two of which have ATMs. The town doesn't yet have any conveniently located Internet cafés. The **main tourist office** (Sharia Saad Zaghloul; ☾ 8am-3pm) is in the town's Governorate Building, but there's also a **tourist information booth** (Midan Qarun; ☾ 8am-3pm) situated next to the water wheels; unfortunately this isn't always open.

AROUND CAIRO

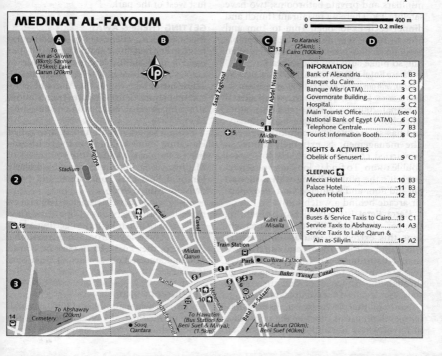

MEDINAT AL-FAYOUM

0   400 m
0   0.2 miles

To Ain as-Siliyiin (8km); Sanhur (15km); Lake Qarun (20km)

To Karanis (25km); Cairo (100km)

Stadium

Midan Misalla

Kubri al-Misalla

Midan Qarun

Train Station

Park • Cultural Palace

Bahr Yusuf Canal

Ramla

To Abshaway (20km)

Cemetery

Souq Qantara

To Hawatim (Bus Station for Beni Suef & Minya) (1.5km)

To Al-Lahun (20km); Beni Suef (40km)

INFORMATION	
Bank of Alexandria	1 B3
Banque du Caire	2 C3
Banque Misr (ATM)	3 C3
Governorate Building	4 C1
Hospital	5 C2
Main Tourist Office	(see 4)
National Bank of Egypt (ATM)	6 C3
Telephone Centrale	7 B3
Tourist Information Booth	8 C3

SIGHTS & ACTIVITIES	
Obelisk of Senusert	9 C1

SLEEPING	
Mecca Hotel	10 B3
Palace Hotel	11 B3
Queen Hotel	12 B2

TRANSPORT	
Buses & Service Taxis to Cairo	13 C1
Service Taxis to Abshaway	14 A3
Service Taxis to Lake Qarun & Ain as-Siliyiin	15 A2

The Fayoum **tourist police booth** (☎ 634 7298) is also near the water wheels.

The bus and taxi stations are a short hike from the centre.

SIGHTS

As far as sights go, there's the **Obelisk of Senusert**, which you'll pass coming in from Cairo at the centre of a roundabout to the northeast of town. Although it looks lost among the cars and buses, it's supposedly the only obelisk in Egypt with a rounded top, and it also features a cleft in which a golden statue of Ra was placed, reflecting the sun's rays in the four directions of the wind.

The **Governorate Building** on Sharia Saad Zaghloul houses a small and unimpressive display on the history and fauna of the oasis.

SLEEPING & EATING

If you have to spend the night in town, there are a few options.

Queen Hotel (☎ 634 6819; fax 634 6233; Sharia Minshaat Lutfallah; s/d E£150/180; ✷) The Queen is undoubtedly the most comfortable option in town. The clean spacious rooms have minibars and private bathrooms; two have satellite TV. There's a restaurant (lunch and dinner each E£40; open 1pm to 4pm and 5pm to 10pm) serving bland but acceptable food; no alcohol is served. The hotel is often full, so make sure you book ahead.

Palace Hotel (☎ 631 1222, 631 3277; Bahr Yusef; s/d E£25/40, with private bathroom E£40/50, with private bathroom & air-con E£50/65; ✷) On the south side of the canal, 200m west of the park, this rather worn hotel is clean, though slightly musty, and has spectacularly uncomfortable beds. The management is extremely pious, so unmarried couples are unlikely to score a double room. To find it, look up from street level; it's the pink building with a sign on the 2nd floor and is entered via a tiled open-air arcade behind a watch kiosk.

Mecca Hotel (s/d E£15/25) For something cheaper, the Palace Hotel's management runs this extremely spartan hotel, where you'll find cell-like rooms and waterlogged shared bathrooms. To find it, look for a yellow sign with red Arabic writing and go through the brown door and up a stone staircase. It doesn't serve breakfast.

None of the places to eat deserve recommendation (this must be the only place in Egypt where it's impossible to score an

edible *ta'amiyya* – mashed, deep-fried fava beans). There are several very basic cafés and assorted eateries on the canalside road just west of the park.

GETTING THERE & AWAY

Buses to Cairo (E£5, two to three hours) leave every half-hour from 7am until 7pm from a new station on the west side of Gamal Abdel Nasser Rd (the Cairo road). These buses take you to the Ahmed Helmy station behind Cairo's Ramses train station, stopping en route at Al-Monieb station on Midan Giza.

From a separate station in an area called Hawatim, about 1.5km from the tourist office in the centre and to the southwest of Medinat al-Fayoum, buses leave regularly for Beni Suef (E£2, one hour) and twice daily for Minya (E£7).

Filthy trains leave Medinat al-Fayoum en route to Cairo every day at 5pm (3rd class E£2). You're much better off getting a bus.

Service taxis leave from the bus stations. To Cairo, they cost E£5 to Giza or E£6 to Midan Ramses. You can get to Beni Suef for E£2.

GETTING AROUND

Green-and-white minibuses (25pt) cover all areas of Medinat al-Fayoum between the western and eastern bus stations.

PORTRAITS OF THE PAST

Al-Fayoum may not be famous for much these days, but it was here that caches of what are some of the world's earliest portraits were found. These extraordinarily lifelike representations, known as the 'Fayoum Portraits', were painted on wooden panels and put over the faces of the mummies, or painted directly onto linen shrouds covering the corpses. This fusion of ancient Egyptian and Graeco-Roman funerary practices laid the foundation for the Western tradition of realistic portraiture.

Dating from between 30 BC and AD 395, the paintings were executed in a technique involving a heated mixture of pigment and wax. Remarkable for the skill of the anonymous artists who painted them, the realistic and eerily modern-looking faces bridge the centuries. The haunting images are made all the more poignant by their youth (some are only babies) – a reflection of the high mortality rates at the time.

More than a thousand of these portraits have been found, not just in Al-Fayoum but also throughout Egypt. They now reside in numerous museums around the world, including the Egyptian Museum in Cairo (see p176).

Karanis

At the edge of the oasis depression, 25km north of Medinat al-Fayoum on the road to Cairo, Ptolemy II's 3rd-century-BC mercenaries lived in a town called Karanis. You can see the remains of their **bathhouse** among the ruins. Of the two **Graeco-Roman temples** (adult/student E£16/8; ☾ 8am-4pm) in the southern part of the town, the larger one (1st century BC) was dedicated to two local crocodile gods, Pnepheros and Petesouchos. There are inscriptions dating from the reigns of the Roman emperors Nero, Claudius and Vespasian. Some of the painted portraits found here are now in the Egyptian Museum in Cairo.

The nearby **Museum of Kom Aushim** (Mathaf Kom Aushim; ☎ 650 1825; Cairo rd; adult/student E£16/8; ☾ 8am-4pm) has good displays of Old and Middle Kingdom objects, including sacred wooden boats, Canopic jars, and wooden and ceramic statuettes entombed to serve the deceased in the afterlife. Items from the Graeco-Roman period and later history are exhibited on the 1st floor.

To get here, catch one of the Cairo-bound buses from Medinat al-Fayoum (E£5).

Pyramid of Meidum

About 32km to the northeast of Medinat al-Fayoum and 45km north of Beni Suef is the ruin of the first true pyramid attempted by the ancient Egyptians. The **Pyramid of Meidum** (adult/student E£16/8; ☾ 8am-4pm) is impressive as it rises abruptly from the rubble. It began as an eight-stepped structure; the steps were then filled in and the outer casing was added, forming the first true pyramid shell. But there were serious design flaws and some time after completion (possibly as late as the last few centuries BC) the pyramid's own weight caused the sides to collapse, leaving just the core that stands today.

Pharaoh Huni (2637–2613 BC) started the pyramid but his son Sneferu was responsible for the actual building. His architects obviously learnt from the mistakes that had been made at Meidum, because they then went on to build the more successful Bent and Red Pyramids at Dahshur (p187).

The guard at the nearby house will unlock the entrance of the pyramid, from where steps lead 75m down to the empty burial chamber. Near the pyramid are the large mastaba tombs of some of Sneferu's family and officials, including his son Rahotep and wife Nofret. The superb statues found in this Meidum tomb are in Cairo's Egyptian Museum.

GETTING THERE & AWAY

It's easier to reach the pyramid from Beni Suef, about 45km to the south, than from Medinat al-Fayoum. Get a pick-up (E£1, 45 minutes) from Beni Suef to Al-Wasta, and then another to Meidum village (50pt), from where you'll have to walk a couple of kilometres, unless you can get a ride.

Alternatively, you could get one of the service taxis or buses running between Beni Suef and Cairo and ask to be dropped off at the Meidum turn-off, from where you still have about 6km to go. The reverse of this is probably the easiest way to get back to Beni

Suef (or to Cairo for that matter) – just flag down a service taxi, but be prepared to wait.

Pyramid of Hawara

About 8km to the southeast of Medinat al-Fayoum, off the Beni Suef road, stands the dilapidated mud-brick **Pyramid of Hawara** (adult/student E£16/8; ☺ 8am-4pm). This is the second pyramid of Amenemhat III; his other is the towerlike Black Pyramid at Dahshur (p187). Originally covered with white limestone casing, only the mud-brick core remains. It has been suggested that like Pharaoh Sneferu 800 years before him, Amenemhat III built a second pyramid at a gentler angle after his first at Dahshur showed signs of instability. The interior reveals several technical developments – corridors were blocked using a series of huge stone portcullises; the burial chamber is carved from a single piece of quartzite; and after the pharaoh's burial, the chamber was sealed by an ingenious device using sand to lower the roof block into place.

The funerary complex is nothing but rubble; even the once-famous temple has been quarried. Herodotus described the temple (300m by 250m) as a 3000-room labyrinth that surpassed even the Pyramids of Giza. Strabo claimed it had as many rooms as there were provinces, so that all the pharaoh's subjects could be represented by their local officials in the presentation of offerings.

The Greeks and Romans used the area as a cemetery: the dead were mummified in an Egyptian way, but the mummies' wrappings incorporated a portrait-style face (see the boxed text, p191). Widespread excavations left little more than pieces of mummy cloth and human bones sticking up through the mounds of rubble. It hasn't been possible to enter the pyramid since 1882.

Buses between Beni Suef and Medinat al-Fayoum pass through Hawarat al-Makta, a short walk to the pyramid.

Pyramid of Al-Lahun

About 10km southeast of Hawara, on the Nile side of the narrow fertile passage that connects Al-Fayoum to the Nile, are the ruins of this mud-brick **pyramid** (adult/student E£16/8; ☺ 8am-4pm), which was once cased in limestone. Built by Pharaoh Sesostris II (1880–1874 BC), ancient tomb robbers stripped it of all its treasures, except for an amazing solid-

gold uraeus, now displayed in the Jewellery Room (room 4) of the Egyptian Museum in Cairo. From the top of the pyramid, there is a great view of the surrounding area.

This pyramid is definitely off the beaten track. Hitch from Beni Suef or Medinat al-Fayoum, or take the local bus between the two cities to the village of Al-Lahun; it's then a 2km walk to the site.

Lake Qarun

Marketed as 'the world's most ancient lake', this is a pleasant enough spot where there is really nothing to do but sit at a lakeside café or hire a boat for about E£5 an hour.

The four-star **Auberge du Lac** (☎ 657 2001/2; fax 657 2003; Lake Qarun; s/d US$74/96; ✷ ✸) was for a long time the only accommodation on the lake, but others are now under construction. World leaders met at the original hotel on this site after WWI to decide on the borders of the Middle East. It later served as King Farouk's private hunting lodge. These days it is often taken over by hunting groups out for ducks and geese and by Cairenes families looking for some fresh air, making it a less-than-restful proposition. Rooms are extremely worn and ridiculously overpriced for what they offer; those on the 2nd floor have a lake view and ground-floor ones look over the straggly garden. Another option is the characterless but reasonably comfortable **Panorama Shakshouk** (☎ 670 1314; fax 670 1757; s/d US$31/38; ✷), a newish three-star development.

To get here, take a pick-up (50pt) from Sanhur to Shakshouk. When you see the lake, look out for the *auberge*. There's a restaurant complete with lakeside position and dodgem cars just down from the *auberge*, near the junction with the road from Medinat al-Fayoum.

Qasr Qarun

The ruins of ancient Dionysus, once the starting point for caravans to the Western Desert oasis of Bahariyya, are near the village of Qasr Qarun at the western end of Lake Qarun.

The **Ptolemaic temple** (adult/student E£16/8; ☺ 8am-4pm), built in 4 BC and dedicated to Sobek, the crocodile-headed god of Al-Fayoum, is just off to the left of the road shortly before the village. You can go down to the underground chambers (beware of snakes), and up to the roof for a view of the desert, the sparse remains of Ptolemaic and Roman settlements, and the oasis.

Getting here is a bit of an ordeal, considering the relatively small distances involved. From Medinat al-Fayoum, take a service taxi or pick-up to the town of Abshaway (75pt, one hour) and change for Qasr Qarun (75pt, one hour). Some pick-ups ply the road south of the lake to Qasr Qarun, but they are not to be relied upon.

WADI RAYYAN

In the 1960s Egyptian authorities created three lakes in the Wadi Rayyan depression, southwest of Lake Qarun, to hold excess water from agricultural drainage. The lakes were intended to be the first step in an ambitious land-reclamation project, but all has not gone to plan: one of the lakes has dried up, the other two are increasingly brackish. One lake drains into the other at a spot rather grandly called 'the Waterfalls'.

Now a protected area, **Wadi Rayyan** (admission E£5, vehicle E£5) has become a major nesting ground for birds and a popular weekend picnic spot for Cairenes. There are a couple of small cafés, a camp site near the Waterfalls and even a hut in which it's possible to bed down overnight, although you need permission in advance from the tourist police in Medinat al-Fayoum and from the protected areas manager in Shakshouk if you plan to do this.

The road in from Lake Qarun is spectacular; the thin black belt of Tarmac snakes along the sides of sand hills. Avoid Fridays and national holidays if you're hoping for peace.

Getting There & Away

There is no public transport to get to Wadi Rayyan so you'll either need your own vehicle or have to hire a taxi (from Medinat al-Fayoum expect to pay about E£100 for a half-day; from Cairo it will cost about E£200 for a full day). To get to Wadi Rayyan, follow the road to the end of Lake Qarun and take the wide asphalt road to the left just after you see the mud-brick domes of the village of Tunis (a rural retreat for Cairo's artists and Westernised intelligentsia) on a ridge to your left. An asphalt road leads right to the lake. The entrance fee is payable at a toll booth on the edge of the protected area.

WADI AL-HITTAN

Some 55km further south into the desert at Wadi al-Hittan (Whale Valley) are the fossilised skeletons of primitive whales that have been lying here for about 40 million years. To get here is something of an expedition and requires at least two 4WDs, one to help haul the other out in the event of getting stuck in the sand. Ask at Wadi Rayyan for directions.

NORTHWEST OF CAIRO

The Cairo–Alexandria Desert Hwy, the fastest and most direct road between the country's two major cities, roughly separates the green fields of the Delta and the harsh sands of the desert. Previously desolate, the highway has made possible the development of several new satellite towns, including 6th of October City and Sadat City, designed to ease the population pressure on Cairo. Increasingly large swathes of the area's prairie-type expanses have also been greened to create farms and golfing resorts. For the curious who have access to a car, such places are worth visiting for a glimpse into Egypt's vision of the future. For an insight into desert life of the past, opt for Wadi Natrun or the Birqash camel market. Both are accessible by public transport or by taxi from Cairo.

BIRQASH CAMEL MARKET

Egypt's largest camel market, **Birqash camel market** (souq al-gamaal; admission E£5; ⏰ 6am-noon) is held at Birqash, 35km northwest of Cairo. It is most lively between 7am and 10am on Fridays. Until 1995 the market was held in Cairo's western suburb of Imbaba, but when land became too precious for camels, one of Cairo's age-old institutions was relocated to the edge of the Western Desert. Beware of the ticket officers who will try to get you to cough up £20 as an admission fee – the official ticket price is E£5.

It is an easy half-day trip (one to 1½ hours) from Cairo, and one hour in the hot and dusty market is usually enough for most travellers. Like all Egypt's animal markets, it's not for animal-lovers or the fainthearted. Hundreds of camels are sold here every day, most having been brought up the Forty Days Rd from western Sudan to just north of Abu Simbel by camel herders and from there to the market in Daraw (see p302). Unsold camels are then hobbled and crammed into trucks for the 24-hour drive to Birqash. By the time they arrive, many are emaciated, fit only for the knacker's yard. Traders stand no nonsense and camels that get out of line are beaten relentlessly.

In addition to those from Sudan, there are camels from various parts of Egypt (including Sinai, the west and the south) and sometimes from as far away as Somalia. They are traded for cash or other livestock, such as goats, sheep and horses, and sold for farm work or slaughter. If you're interested in buying a camel, smaller ones cost about E£2000, bigger beasts sometimes as much as E£5000. Negotiations tend to take place early in the day; by early afternoon, the market is quite subdued.

When here, watch out for pickpockets. Women should dress conservatively – the market is very much a man's scene, with the only female presence other than the occasional traveller being the local tea lady. When you arrive, pick a strategic spot and settle in to watch the negotiations. The best area is around the middle of the lot; there aren't as many camels at the entrance and at the very back, and it's noticeably scruffier there.

Getting There & Away

Using public transport, the cheapest way involves getting yourself to the site of the old camel market at Imbaba, from where microbuses filled with traders and potential buyers shuttle back and forth to Birqash. To get to the old camel market, take a minibus from Midan Abdel Moniem Riad or Midan Ramses to Imbaba (E£1), or one to Midan Libnan (in Mohandiseen) from where you can catch a connecting microbus. Easier still, take a taxi from central Cairo all the way to the old site (about E£10); Imbaba airport (matar Imbaba) is the closest landmark. Once at Imbaba, ask a local to show you where to get the microbus (E£1) to Birqash. From Imbaba, the road winds through fields dotted with date palms, dusty villages, orange orchards and patches of encroaching urban sprawl before climbing the desert escarpment to the market. Microbuses from Birqash back to Imbaba leave when full: depending on the time of the day, you could wait up to two hours or so.

Alternatively, on Fridays the **New Sun Hotel** (Map pp102-3; ☎ 02-578 1786; newsunhotel@yahoo .com; 9th fl, 2 Sharia Talaat Harb, Downtown, Cairo) organises a minibus that leaves from the hotel at 7.30am and returns around noon. The charge is E£40 per person (minimum five people), nonguests are welcome and you must book a day or two in advance.

The easiest way to get to and from the market is to hire a private taxi for the morning. This will cost somewhere between E£70 and E£120, depending on your bargaining skills.

WADI NATRUN

Wadi Natrun, about 100km northwest of Cairo, was of great importance to ancient Egyptians, for this was where they found natron, used in the mummification process. Natron comes from large deposits of sodium carbonate that are left when the valley's salt lakes dry up every summer; those deposits have been more recently used on a larger scale by the chemical industry. The valley is now also strongly connected with the Coptic Church.

A visit to the monasteries of Wadi Natrun reveals clues as to the survival of the Coptic Church, for the desert has long been the protector of the faith. It was there that thousands of Christians retreated to escape Roman persecution in the 4th century AD. They lived in caves, or built monasteries, and developed the monastic tradition that was later adopted by European Christians.

The focal point of the monasteries was the church, around which were built a well, storerooms, a dining hall, kitchen, bakery and the monks' cells. These isolated, unprotected communities were fortified after destructive raids in AD 817 by Arab tribes on their way to conquer North Africa. Of the 60 monasteries once scattered over the valley, only four remain. But the religious life they helped protect is thriving. The Coptic pope is still chosen from among the Wadi Natrun monks, and monasticism is experiencing a revival, with young professional Copts once again donning robes and embroidered hoods to live within these ancient walls in the desert. Some monks still retreat into caves in the surrounding countryside for weeks and months at a time.

Besides their solitude and serenity, the monasteries are worth visiting for the

Coptic art they contain, particularly Deir el-Sourian. Each monastery has different opening times, with some closed completely during the three annual fasting periods (Lents) at Easter, Christmas and in August. Before going, it is worth checking with their Cairo residences that visits are possible.

As a general rule, you can visit all of the monasteries without prior notice; the only exception being Deir Abu Makar (Makarios). Males wishing to stay overnight (women are not allowed) need written permission from the monasteries' Cairo residences:

Deir Anba Bishoi (☎ 02-591 4448)
Deir el-Baramouse (☎ 02-592 2775)
Deir el-Sourian (☎ 02-592 9658)

Deir Anba Bishoi

St Bishoi founded two monasteries in Wadi Natrun: this one (which bears his name) and neighbouring Deir el-Sourian. **Deir Anba Bishoi** (daily incl during Lents) is built around a church that contains the saint's body, said to be perfectly preserved in its sealed, tube-like container. Each year on 17 July, the tube is carried in procession around the church; according to the monks, the bearers clearly feel the weight of a whole body. The church contains the cell where St Bishoi tied his hair to the ceiling to stop him sleeping during prayers.

There's a lovely internal garden with an impressive vegetable patch, an enormous new cathedral and an interesting fortified keep that you enter via a drawbridge. This contains a well, kitchens, two churches and storerooms that can hold provisions for a year. On the roof, trap doors open to small cells that acted as makeshift tombs for those who died during frequent sieges. The rooftop is a splendid place to watch the desert sunset.

Deir el-Sourian

About 500m northwest of Deir Anba Bishoi, **Deir el-Sourian** (Monastery of the Syrians; daily, 3-6pm Fri, 9am-6pm Sat & Sun during Lents) is named after wandering Syrian monks who bought the monastery from the Copts in the 8th century, and is the most picturesquely situated of the monasteries. Since the 16th century it has been solely occupied by Coptic monks. Its Church of the Virgin was built around a 4th-century cave that had been occupied by St Bishoi and is worth visiting for its superb series of 11th-century wall paintings.

Deir Abu Makar (Makarios)

Nearly 20km southeast of Deir Anba Bishoi, **Deir Makarios** (daily but only by prior arrangement, closed during Lents) was founded around the cell where St Makarios spent his last 20 or so years. Structurally it suffered more than other monasteries at the hands of raiding Bedouin, but it is famous as most of the Coptic popes over the centuries have been selected from among its monks. It is the last resting place of many of those popes and also contains the remains of the 49 Martyrs, a group of monks killed by Bedouin in AD 444. It is understandably the most secluded of the monasteries, so permission to visit must be requested in advance by phoning ☎ 048-260 0471/2.

Deir el-Baramouse

Until recently, when a good road was built to Deir Anba Bishoi to the southeast, **Deir el-Baramouse** (Fri-Sun, closed during Lents) was the most isolated of the Wadi Natrun monasteries. These days 110 monks live here. There are six churches (most relatively modern) and a restored medieval fortress (not open to the public) within its compound. There are remnants of 13th-century wall frescoes in its oldest church, the Church of the Virgin Mary.

When you arrive, make your way to the information office; one of the monks will then show you around.

Getting There & Away

You can catch a West Delta Co bus to the filthy and extremely ugly small town functioning as the gateway to the monasteries that goes by the grandiloquent name of Wadi Natrun City. These leave from Cairo's Turgoman Garage (p161) every 30 minutes between 6am and 10pm and cost E£5. From the bus lot at Wadi Natrun City, you'll have to negotiate with a taxi driver to take you around the monasteries. Expect to pay around E£20 per hour. On Fridays and Sundays, when the monasteries are crowded with pious Copts, you can easily pick up a lift. The last bus back to Cairo leaves at 6pm.

A taxi from Cairo should cost about E£150 to E£200 there and back, including a couple of hours driving around the monasteries. If you have your own vehicle and you're coming from Cairo, take the Pyramids Rd and turn onto the Cairo–Alexandria Desert Hwy (usually just called the Desert Hwy). After about 95km (just after the rest house and petrol station) turn left into the wadi, drive another 4km or so to Wadi Natrun City and continue on, following the signs pointing to the monasteries.

THE NILE DELTA

If you have the time, it's worth the effort (and it is an effort) to explore the lush, fan-shaped Delta of Egypt between Cairo and Alexandria. Here the Nile divides into two branches that enter the Mediterranean at the old ports of Damietta and Rosetta. The Delta is also laced with waterways and is reputedly one of the most fertile and, un-surprisingly, most cultivated regions in the world.

The Delta region played just as important a part as Upper Egypt in the early history of the country, but few archaeological remains record this. While the desert and dryness of the south helped preserve its Pharaonic sites, the amazing fertility of the Delta region had the opposite effect. Over the centuries, as the ancient cities, temples and palaces of the Delta fell into ruin, they were literally ploughed into oblivion by the fellaheen (farmers). The attraction of this area, therefore, is the chance to encounter communities rarely visited by foreigners, where you can gain insight into the Egyptian farmer's way of life. If you do intend spending any time in this region, we strongly recommend reading Amitav Ghosh's excellent *In An Antique Land,* an account of the author's lengthy stay in a Delta village.

Service taxis and buses crisscross the region from town to town but if you want to really explore this incredibly green countryside you'll have to hire a car. Theoretically, you're not supposed to leave the main roads, but in the unlikely event of being hassled by the police you can always say that you're lost.

NILE BARRAGES

It's great fun taking a ride on one of the ramshackle river buses that ply the Nile between Cairo and Qanater (Arabic for 'Barrages'), 16km to the north of the city where the Nile splits in two. The trip, which takes 90 minutes each way, is best taken on Fridays or public holidays, when large groups of young people and smaller family parties pack the boats and the tawdry but highly atmospheric funfair and public gardens at Qanater. On the boats, Arabic pop blares and the younger passengers sing along, clap their hands, dance and decorously flirt. It's an immensely enjoyable half-day jaunt – particularly when the sun is out and the sky is clear.

The barrages were begun in the early 19th century. The series of basins and locks, on both main branches of the Nile and the two side canals, guaranteed a year-round flow of water into the Delta region and led to a great increase in cotton production.

The Damietta Barrage consists of 71 sluices stretching 521m across the river; the Rosetta Barrage is 438m long with 61 sluices. The area between the two is 1km and filled with straggly gardens, riverside cafés and souvenir stands. The Cairene equivalent of Coney Island or Blackpool, it's particularly popular with young males, whose pastime of choice is to hire motor scooters and bikes and ride them at break-neck speed up and down the promenade, dodging indignant pedestrians and scaring the saddles off the poor horses pulling *calèches* (horse-drawn carriages) full of families up and down the Corniche.

The best way to reach the barrages is to take a privately run river bus (E£6 return) from the water-taxi station in front of the Radio and TV Building (Maspero station), just north of the Ramses Hilton in central Cairo. The less-popular government-run boat leaves from the same spot but costs E£10 return.

ZAGAZIG & BUBASTIS

Just outside the 19th-century town of Zaga-zig are the ruins of Bubastis, one of Egypt's most ancient cities. There's not much to see in Zagazig itself, but as it's only 80km northeast of Cairo it's an easy day trip to the ruins. The train heading for Port Said takes about 1½ hours to get here; these leave Cairo's Ramses Station (p162) at 8.45am, 11.30am, 2.30pm, 7pm and 10pm. Ticket costs for adult/student are E£20/15 (2nd class only).

The great deity of the ancient city of Bubastis was the elegant cat goddess Bastet. Festivals held in her honour are said to have attracted more than 700,000 revellers who sang, danced, feasted, consumed great quantities of wine and offered sacrifices to the goddess. The temple was begun by the great pyramid-builders Khufu and Khafre during the 4th dynasty, and pharaohs of subsequent dynasties made their additions over about 17 centuries. An architectural gem once raised above the city, the temple is now just a pile of rubble. More interesting is the cat cemetery 200m down the road: the series of underground galleries, where many bronze statues of cats were found, is great to explore.

TANIS

Just outside the village of San al-Hagar, 70km northeast of Zagazig, are the partly excavated ruins of the ancient city of Tanis, spread over 4 sq km. For several centuries Tanis (ancient name Djanet) was one of the largest cities in the Delta and became a site of great importance after the end of the New Kingdom, especially during the Late Period (747–332 BC). (It's also where Indiana Jones discovered the 'Lost Ark'.)

Although many of the blocks and statues found here date from the Old and Middle Kingdoms, they had been brought here from other sites for reuse by later kings. The earliest buildings at Tanis actually date from the reign of Psusennes I (1039–991 BC), who surrounded the temple of Amun with a great enclosure wall. His successors added a temple to Mut, Khons and the Asiatic goddess Astarte, together with a sacred lake, and temple building continued until Ptolemaic times.

Tanis is most famous for its royal tombs, created by the kings of the 21st dynasty after the Valley of the Kings was abandoned at the end of the New Kingdom (c 1070 BC). In 1939 the French discovered six royal tombs here, including that of Psusennes I and several of his successors. Although the tombs themselves might seem relatively unimpressive today, they once contained some of the most spectacular treasure ever found in Egypt – gold and silver coffins, mummy masks and jewellery which can now be seen in the Egyptian Museum (p175).

TANTA

The largest city in the Delta, Tanta is 90km from Cairo and 110km from Alexandria. Its main mosque is dedicated to Sayyed Ahmed al-Badawi, a Moroccan Sufi who fought the Crusaders in the 13th century. The city remains a centre for Sufism. The *moulid* (religious festival) held in honour of Sayyed Ahmed al-Badawi follows the October cotton harvest and is one of the biggest in Egypt, drawing crowds of over a million.

While there are no actual structural remains in this area of the western Delta, there are the sites of three ancient cities. Northwest of Tanta, on the east bank of the Rosetta branch of the Nile is **Sais**, Egypt's 26th-dynasty capital. Sacred to Neith, goddess of war and hunting and protector of embalmed bodies, Sais dates back to the start of Egyptian history and once had palaces, temples and royal tombs.

West of Tanta, more than halfway along the road to Damanhur, is **Naucratis**, given to the Greeks to settle during the 7th century BC. The city of **Buto**, northeast of Damanhur and northwest of Tanta, was the cult centre of Wadjet, the cobra goddess of Lower Egypt, always represented on a pharaoh's crown as a uraeus.

Superjet buses to Tanta (E£6.50) leave Turgoman Garage (p161) every hour between 7am and 7pm.

Nile Valley:
Beni Suef to Qena

He who rides the sea of the Nile must have sails woven of patience.

Egyptian Proverb

Heading south from Cairo, lush green fields flank the Nile and are framed by the desert beyond. Mud-brick houses are clustered amid the fields and crops are grown using age-old techniques. Farmers still practise flood irrigation and occasionally you can catch a glimpse of a *sakia* (water wheel), being turned by a blindfolded donkey, or a *shadouf,* the archaic implement for lifting water. The land is worked by hand, often using tools modelled on ancient designs, and it is tempting to imagine that the landscape of ancient Egypt did not look much different.

The large provincial capitals that punctuate the fields are less picturesque, however, and have little to offer most visitors. But on the fringes of the fertile farmland lie fascinating remains from the area's ancient past. From the lavishly painted tombs of provincial rulers to the remains of the doomed city of Akhetaten, these seldom-visited sites are evocative reminders of the distant past. Further south lies Abydos, one of Ancient Egypt's most sacred burial grounds, where Pharaoh Seti I built his cenotaph, one of the most beautiful surviving New Kingdom monuments. Close to modern-day Qena is Dendara, one of the most intact temple complexes to survive to modern times.

Sadly, despite its treasures, this area's turbulent recent past (this was where Islamist militants carried out many of their operations in the 1990s) means that security remains heavy and individual travel is difficult.

HIGHLIGHTS

- Admire lithe dancing girls and muscular wrestlers in the finely painted **tombs of Baqet** and **Kheti** (p204) in Beni Hasan

- Wander among the desolate remains of **Tell al-Amarna** (p219), ancient Egypt's Sun City, capital of the heretic Akhenaten's brave new world

- Gaze upon some of ancient Egypt's finest temple reliefs at the **Temple of Seti I** (p226) in Abydos

- Marvel at one of the best-preserved temple complexes in Egypt in Dendara's magnificent **Temple of Hathor** (p229)

★ Beni Hasan
★ Tell al-Amarna
★ Abydos   ★ Dendara

History

For the ancient Egyptians, Upper Egypt began south of Memphis, closest to present-day Saqqara. The area between Beni Suef and Qena was divided into 15 nomes or provinces. Each had its own capital, an administrative centre that was a local hub of commerce and wealth. Provincial governors and notables built their tombs on the desert edge. Abydos, close to modern Sohag, was the predominant religious centre in the region. Egypt's earliest rulers were interred here and it flourished well into the Christian era.

During the New Kingdom, the pharaoh Akhenaten turned his back on the Theban priesthood and created a new capital in one of the few places in Egypt not already associated with a known deity. The short-lived city, Akhetaten (near modern Mallawi), was a brief glimpse of prominence for the area.

Christianity arrived early in Upper Egypt. Sectarian splits in Alexandria and the popularity of the monastic tradition established by St Anthony in the Eastern Desert encouraged priests to settle in the provinces. The many churches and monasteries that remain in the area are a testament to the strength of the Christian tradition here.

Throughout the medieval period, much of the area remained a backwater, although Asyut flourished as a trading post linking the Western Desert with the Nile through the Darb al-Arba'een caravan route.

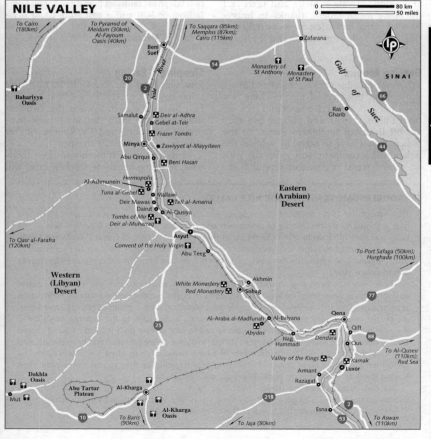

NILE VALLEY

0 —— 80 km
0 —— 50 miles

Today the region is poor and neglected by the state. Agriculture is the mainstay of the economy but, labour-intensive as it may be, it cannot employ all of the area's burgeoning population and the lack of any real industrial base south of Cairo has caused severe economic hardship, particularly for young people. Resentment at their lack of hope exploded into violence in the 1990s, when religious militants fought the government in a bid to create an Islamic state. The violence petered out but the poverty remains.

Getting There & Away

Trains are your best option for getting in and out of this part of the country. There are frequent services heading both north and south. Private vehicles and taxis end up being inconvenient, thanks to heavy-handed police measures; for more information see the following section and the boxed text, below.

Getting Around

Wherever possible stick to trains and buses throughout this part of Egypt. There is a good network of service taxis and pick-up taxis linking towns and villages but they are off limits to foreigners thanks to the police. If you have to travel by vehicle, the police will accompany you, generally with an armed truck in front of you and an-

other behind. Irritatingly, they will change vehicles at each of the many checkpoints along the way, slowing down your journey considerably (see below).

BENI SUEF

☎ 082 / pop 3.8 million

Beni Suef is a provincial capital located 120km south of Cairo. There's little here to capture the traveller's interest; it is close to the Pyramid of Meidum (p191) and the oasis area of Al-Fayoum (p188) but both places can be just as easily visited from Cairo. There's a small **museum** (adult/student E£10/5; ☾ 9am-4pm), next to the governorate building, which displays artefacts found in the area.

Should you find yourself here, there are two **telephone centrales** (train station & Sharia Safiyya Zaghloul; ☾ 24hr) and a **post office** (Sharia Safiyya Zaghloul; ☾ 8.30am-2.30pm Sat-Thu). There is also a **Bank of Alexandria** (just off Midan al-Gomhuriyya; ☾ 9am-2pm Sun-Thu).

Sleeping & Eating

Semiramis Hotel (☎ 232 2092; fax 232 6017; Sharia Safiyya Zaghloul; s/d/tr E£60.25/79.50/88.50; 🅿) The best place to stay in town is this two-star hotel near the train station. Rooms have private bathrooms and TV. Rooms without air-con are about E£20 cheaper.

There's not much to choose from food-wise. A filling kebab or chicken meal will

---

TROUBLESOME TRAVEL IN THE NILE VALLEY

Throughout the 1990s northern Upper Egypt was the centre of an Islamist insurgency that saw over a thousand deaths, mostly of policemen and Islamists. Tourists who travelled here in the early and mid-1990s were often caught up in this violence, victims of Gama'a al-Islamiyya militants who wanted to target the government by crippling the tourism industry. Not surprisingly, tourism ground to a halt. The few foreigners who did venture here were accompanied by heavily armed police guards.

There have not been any attacks on foreigners in the area since the late 1990s and travel advisories have been lifted by Western embassies in Egypt but the police continue to insist on accompanying tourists everywhere. Not only does travelling with a group of heavily armed men mean that you are very restricted in your movements, it also adds to the expense of your trip if you're on a tight budget because you are forced to hire private taxis instead of using shared taxis or microbuses. Many travellers resent such an intrusive police presence and have complained that it destroys their visit. One reader wrote of a long-awaited trip to Abydos that was ruined by policemen pushing a large group of tourists to stay together as they toured the temple, then forcing them to leave after an hour. 'Don't go' was his advice.

Our trips around northern Upper Egypt have been equally frustrating, and until the police lighten up our advice is to go only if you have a very strong desire to see the area's sights.

For more information on the 'curse of the convoys', see p548.

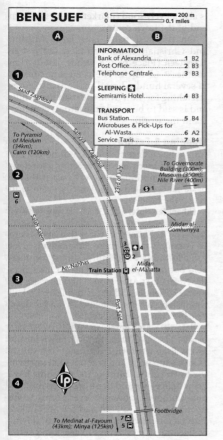

BENI SUEF

0 ————— 200 m
0 ————— 0.1 miles

INFORMATION
Bank of Alexandria..................1 B2
Post Office.............................2 B3
Telephone Centrale..................3 B3

SLEEPING
Semiramis Hotel.....................4 B3

TRANSPORT
Bus Station...........................5 B4
Microbuses & Pick-Ups for
Al-Wasta.............................6 A2
Service Taxis........................7 B4

To Pyramid
of Meidum
(34km);
Cairo (120km)

Saad Zaghloul

Safiyya Zaghloul

Saha Salem

An-Nahhas

Port Said

To Governorate
Building (300m);
Museum (350m);
Nile River (400m)

Midan al-
Gomhuriyya

Midan
el-Mahatta

Train Station

Footbridge

To Medinat al-Fayoum
(43km); Minya (125km)

There are frequent train connections
north to Cairo and Giza, and south to
Minya. There are also (slow) trains to Al-
Fayoum.

GEBEL AT-TEIR & FRAZER TOMBS

The main feature of the small Christian
hamlet of Gebel at-Teir, 93km south of
Beni Suef, is **Deir al-Adhra** (Monastery of the
Virgin). Established as a church/monastery
in the 4th century AD by the Roman empress Helena, it was built on one of the sites
where the Holy Family supposedly rested
while fleeing Palestine. Gebel at-Teir and
its church are perched on a hill 130m above
the east bank of the Nile.

The village can be reached much more
quickly from Minya, about 20km to the
south, than from Beni Suef. If the police
allow it, get a service taxi or microbus for
between E£2 and E£5 from Minya to Samalut and from there take a pick-up to the
Nile boat landing (50pt), where you can
take the car ferry for E£1 or the felucca for
the same price. On the other side is a pick-
up going to Deir al-Adhra, but you may
find yourself paying extra to get it moving,
as not many passengers go that way. When
you arrive, ask for the *kineesa* (church) and
someone will appear with the keys and give
you a short tour. There are some interesting
400-year-old icons inside.

About 5km south of Gebel at-Teir are
the **Frazer Tombs**, which date back to the
5th and 6th dynasties. These Old Kingdom tombs are hewn into the desert cliff
on the east bank of the Nile and overlook
the plain and fields. The four tombs are
very simple, containing eroded statues and
carved hieroglyphs but no colourful scenes.
If you're attracted to places where other
tourists rarely go, these are for you.

MINYA

☎ 086 / pop 261,872

It is called the 'Bride of Upper Egypt' (Arous
as-Sa'id), as Minya more or less marks the
divide between Upper and Lower Egypt.
A semi-industrial provincial capital 245km
south of Cairo, it is a centre for sugar processing and the manufacture of soap and
perfume. In the 1990s it also acquired the
unfortunate reputation of being a centre for
Islamist opposition to the government. Because so many of the 'troubles' were based

cost you about E£25 at Semiramis Hotel,
or you'll find kushari places and *fuul* (fava
bean paste) and *ta'amiyya* stands around
the train station.

Getting There & Away

The bus station is along the main road,
south of town. Buses run from about 6am
to 6pm to Turgoman Garage in Cairo.
There are also frequent buses to Minya and
Al-Fayoum.

Beni Suef is also a departure point for the
trek across the desert to the Monastery of
St Anthony (p425), which is about 150km
east, near the Gulf of Suez. There is a daily
bus to Zafarana (E£20, three hours), the
closest Red Sea town to the monastery.

in the countryside around here, Minya became something of an armed fortress, with nervous policemen patrolling in tanks and personnel carriers. This heavy police presence remains today, even though the threat of violence has abated. This is a shame because Minya's centre is pleasant, with a long corniche along the Nile and some great, if shabby, early-20th-century buildings that testify to its former prosperity as a centre of the cotton industry. Unfortunately the police insist on accompanying foreigners around and their heavy-handedness makes it unpleasant to wander about freely.

Information

EMERGENCY
Tourist police (☎ 236 4527; Amarat el-Gama'a)

MEDICAL SERVICES
Mustashfa Gama'a (University Hospital; ☎ 236 6743, 234 2505; Sharia Corniche el-Nil)
Public Hospital (☎ 236 4098; Sharia Corniche el-Nil) Near the bridge.

MONEY
Banque Misr (Midan as-Sa'a; ⏱ 8.30am-2pm Sun-Thu)
National Bank of Egypt (Sharia al-Gomhuriyya; ⏱ 9am-2pm Sun-Thu) ATM.
Western Union (☎ 236 4905; Sharia al-Gomhuriyya; ⏱ 9am-7pm Sat-Thu)

POST
Main post office (⏱ 8.30am-2pm Sat-Thu) Off Sharia Corniche el-Nil.

TELEPHONE
Telephone centrale (⏱ 24hr) At the train station.

TOURIST INFORMATION
Tourist office Sharia Corniche el-Nil (☎ 236 0150; ⏱ 9am-3pm); train station (☎ 234 2044; ⏱ supposedly 24hr but rarely staffed)

VISA EXTENSIONS
Passport office (☎ 236 4193; 2nd fl, post office; ⏱ 8.30am-2pm Sat-Thu) Off Sharia Corniche el-Nil.

Sights & Activities
Although Minya is a pleasant place, the town itself doesn't have that much to see. Other than the interesting architecture in the town centre, there's the tree-lined corniche along the Nile, which is a relaxing place for a ride in a *hantour* (horse-drawn carriage). There

is also a lively souq (market) at the southern end of the town centre.

On the east bank is a large Muslim and Christian cemetery called **Zawiyyet al-Mayyiteen** (Place of the Dead), about 7km southeast of town. The cemetery consists of several hundred mud-brick mausoleums stretching for 4km from the road to the hills and is said to be one of the largest cemeteries in the world.

Sleeping & Eating
Minya has a decent selection of hotels, but these days many are not accepting foreigners. Eating options are few. Apart from the basic places listed here, your best bet is to eat in the hotels.

Ekhenaten Hotel (☎ 236 5917/8; www.kingakhen aton.8m.com; Corniche el-Nil; s/d with Nile view E£68/88; ❄) The only hotel in town that appears to be booming, the 48-room Ekhenaten is great value for money and Minya's most comfortable option if your budget won't stretch to the Nefertiti & Aton Hotel. Staff here are extremely friendly and eager to please and all rooms have air-con, satellite TV and fridges. The breakfast is buffet style.

Nefertiti & Aton Hotel (☎ 233 1515; fax 232 6467; Corniche el-Nil; s/d US$60/80; ❄ ⓡ) Known locally as the Etap (its former incarnation), this is Minya's top hotel and is about 1km north of the town centre. Most of its 96 rooms have great Nile views and there are three restaurants (although only one ever seems to be open), two bars, a pool and a tennis court. The facilities are looking distinctly down-at-heel these days thanks to a lack of guests, but it remains friendly and comfortable.

Ibn Khassib Hotel (☎ 364 535; 5 Sharia Ragheb; s/d E£36/43, with air-con E£48/60; ❄) On a side street near the train station, the Ibn Khassib has 18 gloomy rooms, most with high ceilings and faux Victorian furniture. Room sizes vary considerably so check before agreeing to anything. There's a restaurant and bar with beer and a billiard area.

Palace Hotel (☎ 324 021; Midan Tahrir; s/d E£15/20, with private bathroom E£25/35) Fabulous high ceilings, hand-painted Pharaonic murals and time-warp atmosphere make this a great budget hotel. The owners are reluctant to accept foreigners but it's worth trying to get them to make an exception. The huge Nefertiti mural and ancient posters alone make it worth a visit.

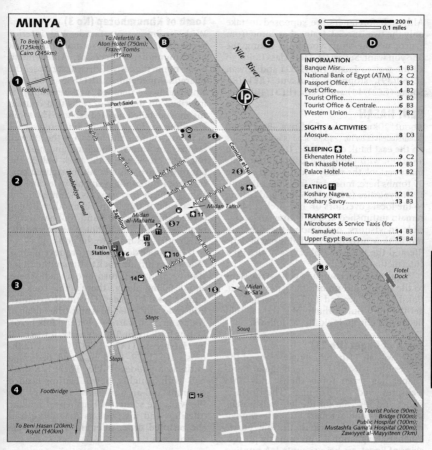

MINYA

INFORMATION
Banque Misr.....................................1 B3
National Bank of Egypt (ATM)....2 C2
Passport Office................................3 B2
Post Office......................................4 B2
Tourist Office.................................5 B2
Tourist Office & Centrale...............6 B3
Western Union...............................7 B2

SIGHTS & ACTIVITIES
Mosque..8 D3

SLEEPING
Ekhenaten Hotel............................9 C2
Ibn Khassib Hotel........................10 B3
Palace Hotel.................................11 B2

EATING
Koshary Nagwa.............................12 B2
Koshary Savoy..............................13 B3

TRANSPORT
Microbuses & Service Taxis (for
Samalut)..................................14 B3
Upper Egypt Bus Co....................15 B4

Koshary Savoy (Midan al-Mahatta; dishes E£2-15) is a busy corner *ahwa* (coffeehouse) with a restaurant attached. Kushari, shwarma (meat sliced off a spit and stuffed in a pocket of pita-type bread with chopped tomatoes and garnish), and *ta'amiyya* are all on offer. You can eat in or takeaway. Just down the street is **Koshary Nagwa** (Sharia al-Gomhuriyya; dishes E£2-12) serving similar good, basic Egyptian fare.

Getting There & Away

BUS

Upper Egypt Bus Co (☎ 236 3721; Sharia Saad Zaghloul) has frequent services to Cairo (E£15 to E£20, four hours) from 6am to 4pm. There is a morning bus through to Alexandria

(E£30). Buses also depart for Beni Suef (E£8, one to two hours) every 20 to 40 minutes.

SERVICE TAXI

At present the police forbid foreigners from using service taxis.

TRAIN

Trains to Cairo (three to four hours) have only 1st- and 2nd-class carriages and leave at 5.55am, 6.30am, 8.50am, 4.30pm (which goes on to Alexandria) and 6.50pm. Tickets in 1st-class range from E£30 to E£40, in 2nd-class from E£27 to E£29.

Trains heading south leave fairly frequently, with the fastest trains departing Minya between around 11pm and 1am.

Although foreigners are supposed to take only the two 'special' trains that come from Cairo, no-one stops you from taking the one you want. Seven 1st-/2nd-class trains go all the way to Luxor (E£49/32) and Aswan (E£60/39), stopping at Asyut (E£13/8), Sohag (E£21/13) and Qena (E£31/19).

BENI HASAN

About 20km south of Minya, **Beni Hasan** (adult/student E£20/10; 8am-5pm) is a necropolis on the east bank of the Nile. It has a superb location, with the tombs cut into the cliffs that overlook the valley and the river. Of the 39 tombs here, most date from the 11th and 12th dynasties (2125–1795 BC) and belong to the local governors or 'nomarchs'. Many remain unfinished and only four are accessible to visitors, but among the funerary motifs they provide a vivid glimpse of daily life and the political upheavals of the First Intermediate Period.

A guard will accompany you up the steps to the tombs and unlock the gates for you. Baksheesh of around E£5 is expected. To get the most out of the tombs, they should be viewed chronologically, as follows.

Tomb of Baqet (No 15)

Baqet was an 11th-dynasty governor of the Oryx nome (district). His rectangular tomb chapel has seven tomb shafts and some well-preserved wall paintings. They include Baqet and his wife on the left wall watching weavers and acrobats – mostly women in diaphanous dresses in flexible poses. Further along, animals, presumably possessions of Baqet, are being counted. A hunting scene in the desert shows mythical creatures among the gazelles. The back wall has clear depictions of wrestlers in moves that are still used today. The right wall shows scenes from daily life, with potters, metalworkers and a flax harvest, among others.

Tomb of Kheti (No 17)

Son of Baqet, Kheti was, like his father, governor of the Oryx nome. His tomb chapel was supported by six lotus columns and its scenes include hunting by the river and in the desert, linen production, playing board games, metalwork, wrestling, acrobatics and dancing, farming, warfare, funerary offerings, and barbers at work (on the wall left of the entrance).

Tomb of Khnumhotep (No 3)

With its impressive façade and interior decoration, this tomb is second only to that of Khnumhotep's successor, Amenemhat. Governor in the early 12th dynasty under the pharaoh Amenemhat III (1855–1808 BC), Khnumhotep's detailed 'autobiography' is inscribed on the base of walls that contain the most detailed painted scenes. The tomb is famous for its rich, finely rendered scenes of plants, animals and birds. On the left wall farmers are shown ploughing and harvesting their crops, while the back wall to the left of the shrine is a beautiful stylised portrayal of Khnumhotep and his wife catching fish and birds in a papyrus swamp. On the other side of the shrine is another fishing scene, while the right-hand wall has scenes of priests with Khnumhotep's wife and the lavish offerings made to the gods.

If the police don't deter (or prevent) you, follow the cliffside track to the southeast for about 1.5km, then turn into a wadi where, about 500m along, there's the rock-cut temple **Speos Artemidos** (Grotto of Artemis), known locally as Istabl Antar (the Stable of Antar, an Arab warrior-poet and folk hero). Dating back to the 18th dynasty, it was built by Hatshepsut (1473–1458 BC) and Tuthmosis III (1479–1425 BC) and dedicated to the lion-goddess Pakht. There is a small hall with roughly hewn Hathor-headed columns and an unfinished sanctuary. On the walls are scenes of Hatshepsut making offerings and inscriptions describing how she restored order after the Hyksos were overthrown.

Tomb of Amenemhat (No 2)

Amenemhat was a 12th-dynasty governor of Oryx; his tomb is the largest and possibly the best at Beni Hasan. Entered through a columned doorway, it contains beautifully executed scenes of farming, hunting, manufacturing and offerings to the deceased, who can also be seen with his dogs. As well as the fine paintings, the tomb has a long, faded text in which Amenemhat addresses the visitors to his chapel: 'You who love life and hate death, say: Thousands of bread and beer, thousands of cattle and wild fowl for the ka of the hereditary prince…the Great Chief of the Oryx Nome…'

(Continued on page 217)

DONALD C. & PRISCILLA ALEXANDER EASTMAN

The pyramids of Khufu and Khafre, Pyramids of Giza (p128)

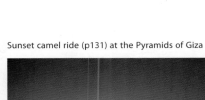

Sunset camel ride (p131) at the Pyramids of Giza

CASEY & ASTRID WITTE MAHANEY

CHRIS MELLOR

The Sphinx (p134), Giza

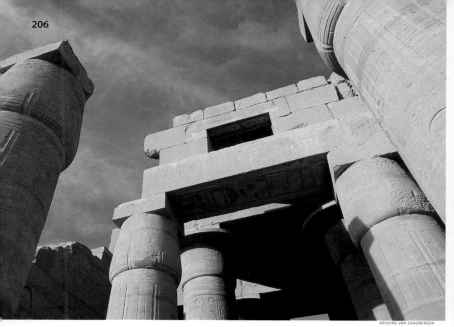

ARIADNE VAN ZANDBERGEN

Great hypostyle hall at the Temple of Ramses II, the Ramesseum (p265), Luxor

ANDERS BLOMQVIST

Tutankhamun's death mask
(p175), Egyptian Museum, Cairo

The avenue of the sphinxes, Luxor Temple (p240)

JOHN

Painted wooden chest, Tutankhamun Galleries (p173),
Egyptian Museum, Cairo

ANDERS BLOMQVIST

ARIADNE VAN ZANDBERGEN
Detail of the Temple of
Hatshepsut (p262), Deir al-Bahri

Interior of the Egyptian Museum (p167), Cairo

ANDERS BLOMQVIST

© APL/CORBIS/ROB HOW

Dome of the Planetarium (p386) at the Bibliotheca Alexandrina, Alexandria

SIMON FOALE

Moat at the Bibliotheca Alexandrina (p386), Alexandria

Mosque of Mohammed
Ali (p120), Islamic Cairo

SARA-JANE CLELAND

Madrassa and Mausoleum of Barquq (p115),
Islamic Cairo

Domes and minarets of the Mosque of Abu Abbas
al-Mursi (p384), Alexandria

The Northern Cemetery (City of the Dead; p122), Islamic Cairo

210

The Khan al-Khalili (p112), Islamic Cairo

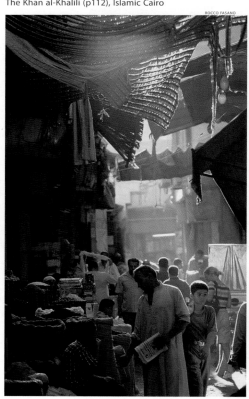

ROCCO FASANO

MARY L PEACHIN

Spice bazaar (p161), Cairo

Street vendor, Islamic Cairo (p110)

SARA-JANE CLEL

Backgammon in a period café (p394), Alexandria

Fishawi's Coffeehouse (p154), Khan al-Khalili, Islamic Cairo

Man smoking *sheesha* (p154), Cairo

212

WILL SALTER

Hieroglyphs on a tomb wall, Valley of the
Kings (p251), Luxor

Bas-relief of Ramses III, Medinat Habu
(p269), Luxor

ARIADNE VAN ZANDBERGEN

ARIADNE VAN ZANDBERGEN

Carving detail, Luxor Temple (p240)

Hieroglyphs at the Temple of Kom Ombo (p300)

LOU

Mural, Edfu (p297)

Mural, Esna (p295)

Urban advertising, Cairo (p91)

Weavers, Kerdassa (p135)

DONALD C. & PRISCILLA ALEXANDER EASTMAN

Ornate headdress, a traditional
Siwan craft (p369)

JULIET COOMBE

LEE FOSTER

Henna tattoo (p308)

Hat seller, Edfu (p297)

JULIET CO

LOU JONES

Man at hypostyle hall, Temples of Karnak (p242), Luxor

GREG ELMS

Obelisk, Valley of the Kings
(p251), Luxor

The Temple of Isis (p319), Philae (Agilkia Island)

JOHN ELK III

Passageway, Al-Qasr, Dakhla Oasis (p341)

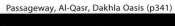

JOHN ELK III

JOHN ELK III

Fortress of Shali (p362), Siwa

Mosque of Ibn Tulun (p121), Islamic Cairo

IZZET K

(Continued from page 204)

Many of the wall paintings show the cattle, beer and fowl as offerings, in addition to a voyage to Abydos and a painted false door. The destroyed statues in the shrine were of Amenemhat sitting between his wife and his mother.

Getting There & Away

About the only way to get to Beni Hasan these days is in a private taxi with an accompanying phalanx of policemen. The taxi will charge about E£50 from Minya, depending on your bargaining skills and how long you stay at the site. Should you manage to avoid the excessive security, get a microbus to Abu Qirqus. There you take a pick-up to the river. At the river you'll find an office, where return boat tickets cost E£6 if there are less than eight people, E£8 if you're by yourself. The price drops to E£2 per person if there are eight or more passengers.

MALLAWI

Mallawi is situated 48km south of Minya and is famous in Egypt for being the home town of President Sadat's assassin (see p44), Khalid al-Islambouli. A centre of foment and armed rebellion throughout the 1990s, the town is a tense place, with a heavy police presence, resentful populace and blighted economy. There's little for visitors to see, even if the overzealous police allow a stop. Should this change, there's a small **museum** (admission E£5; ⏰ 9am-2pm Sat-Tue & Thu, to noon Fri) housing a collection of artefacts from Tuna al-Gebel and Hermopolis. Food is limited to basic *fuul* and *ta'amiyya* places and trucker restaurants along the main road beside the Ibrahimiyya Canal. There are no hotels.

Getting There & Away

At present you can only travel here with a police escort in a private taxi or your own vehicle. Should this change, all buses to or from Minya and Asyut stop here. Only the very slow 2nd- and 3rd-class trains stop at the station, which is on the east bank of the Ibrahimiyya Canal.

HERMOPOLIS

Hermopolis, 8km north of Mallawi near the town of Al-Ashmunein, is the site of the ancient city of Khmun, capital of the 15th Upper Egyptian nome and cult centre of Thoth, god of wisdom and writing. The Greeks identified Thoth with their god Hermes and so referred to his city by its now more familiar name, 'Hermopolis'.

Little remains of this ancient city. The most striking ruins are two colossal quartzite figures of Thoth set up by Amenhotep III (1390–1352 BC), with the god represented as a baboon rather than his more familiar ibis-headed figure. The other main ruins are a Middle Kingdom temple gateway, a pylon of Ramses II built from stone plundered from nearby Tell al-Amarna and the extensive ruins of a Coptic basilica adapted from an earlier Ptolemaic temple on the site.

Getting There & Away

If the police escort continues to be mandatory, you will have to take a private taxi to Hermopolis from Minya. Expect to pay about E£60, depending on how long you take. If the situation changes, you can take a local microbus or service taxi from Mallawi to the village of Al-Ashmunein; the turn-off to the site is 1km from the main road. From the junction you can either walk the short distance to Hermopolis or coax your driver to go a bit further.

TUNA AL-GEBEL

The necropolis of Hermopolis was **Tuna al-Gebel** (admission E£20; ⏰ 8am-5pm). It bordered Akhetaten, the short-lived capital of the pharaoh Akhenaten (see p218). The area's oldest monument is one of 14 stelae that marked the boundary of the royal city; in this case the western perimeter of the city's farmlands and associated villages. Like the rest, the large stone stele is inscribed with Akhenaten's vow never to expand his city beyond these boundaries, nor to be buried anywhere else. To the left stand two damaged statues of the pharaoh and his wife Nefertiti holding offering tables, on the sides of which are inscribed the figures of three of their daughters.

To the south of the stele, which is located about 5km past the village of Tuna al-Gebel, are the **catacombs** and tombs of the residents and sacred animals of Hermopolis. The most interesting things to see are the dark catacomb galleries that once held millions (literally) of mummified ibis, the 'living image of Thoth', together with

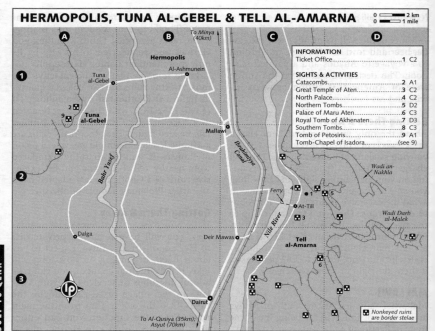

HERMOPOLIS, TUNA AL-GEBEL & TELL AL-AMARNA

INFORMATION
Ticket Office...1 C2

SIGHTS & ACTIVITIES
Catacombs..2 A1
Great Temple of Aten.............................3 C2
North Palace...4 C2
Northern Tombs......................................5 D2
Palace of Maru Aten...............................6 C3
Royal Tomb of Akhenaten......................7 D3
Southern Tombs......................................8 C3
Tomb of Petosiris....................................9 A1
Tomb-Chapel of Isadora...................(see 9)

a smaller number of mummified baboons.
Most of the animals have been destroyed
by robbers, and in fact only one of the baboons was found fully intact by archaeologists. Most of the mummification was done
in the Ptolemaic and Roman periods. The
subterranean cemetery extends for at least
3km – Egyptologists suspect it may stretch
all the way to Hermopolis. You definitely
need a torch if you're going to explore the
galleries.

There's also the interesting **Tomb of Petosiris**, dedicated to a high priest of Thoth
who was alive just before the arrival of Alexander the Great (c 340 BC). It was built
in the form of a small temple with wonderful coloured reliefs of traditional Egyptian
scenes such as farming and the deceased
being given offerings, but all done in Greek
style with the figures wearing Greek dress.
Ancient graffiti, thought to be of pilgrims,
covers many of the walls.

In a two-storey building behind the Tomb
of Petosiris is the **Tomb-Chapel of Isadora**. Isadora was a wealthy woman who drowned in
the Nile during the rule of Antoninus Pius

(AD 138–161), and whose tomb became the
centre of a cult. Her **mummy** is extremely well
preserved, with her teeth, hair and finger-
nails clearly visible. You'll need to give the
guard baksheesh to see her.

Getting There & Away
Tuna al-Gebel is 7km west of Hermopolis.
The very few tourists who come here these
days are usually escorted by police from
Minya. Make sure you check with the tourist office in Minya (p202) that it is open
before you set out.

There's a fair amount of traffic between
the Hermopolis junction and the village, so
you could flag down a pick-up truck, but as
you'll probably be there with the police, you
will have to take a taxi (E£50 to E£75).

TELL AL-AMARNA
The scant remains of this once-glorious
city, 12km southeast of Mallawi, are a little disappointing when compared with its
fascinating, albeit brief, history.

In the 14th century BC, the pharaoh
Akhenaten (1352–1336 BC) and his queen

Nefertiti (1388–1336 BC) left the gods and temples of Karnak to establish a new city and a new religion. Here the pharaoh, his queen and their followers worshipped Aten, god of the sun disc.

The city, in the area now known as Tell al-Amarna, was built on the east bank of the Nile on a beautiful yet solitary crescent-shaped plain, which extends about 12km from north to south. Except for the side bounded by the river, the palaces, temples and residences of the city were surrounded by high cliffs, broken here and there by wadis. The royal couple named their city Akhetaten (Horizon of the Aten), and it was the capital of Egypt for about 14 years.

It was abandoned for all time after Akhenaten's death, when his successor (believed by some Egyptologists to be Nefertiti ruling as pharaoh) relocated to Thebes and restored the worship of traditional gods. As the priests of Karnak regained their religious control, they desecrated the temples of Aten and did their best to obliterate all record of the heretic pharaoh. Akhenaten's son (by a minor wife) and successor Tutankhaten, or Tutankhamun (1336–1327 BC) as he became known, re-established the cult of Amun at Thebes, bringing to an end what is known as the 'Amarna Period'. Akhetaten fell into ruin, and the stones of its palaces and temples were used for buildings in Hermopolis and other cities.

Tell al-Amarna Necropolis

Two groups of cliff tombs, about 8km apart, make up the **Tell al-Amarna necropolis** (adult/student E£20/10; ⏰ 8am-4pm Oct-May, to 5pm Jun-Sep), which features colourful wall paintings of life during the Aten revolution. Remains of temples and private or administrative buildings are scattered about a wide area.

You have three options to cross the Nile: the local passenger launch (50pt), the car ferry (50pt) or the blue tourist boat (E£5 return for one or two people; E£1.25 each for three or more). Tickets for the latter are bought from the ticket office on the east bank; you cross the river before paying for your ticket.

There is a bus that can take you on a tour around the site. For the southern tombs expect to pay a total of E£35 for one to eight people, or E£5 each for more than eight. It takes about 35 minutes to arrive at the south-ern tombs via the Great Temple of Aten. A two-hour bus tour around the northern tombs and the palace is E£8; for three or more people you each pay E£3.75.

In all, there are 25 tombs cut into the base of the cliffs, numbered from one to six in the north, and seven to 25 in the south. Those worth visiting are described here.

TOMB OF HUYA (NO 1)

Huya was the steward of Akhenaten's mother, Queen Tiy. The tomb contains two wonderful relief scenes either side of the entrance that show Tiy wining and dining with her son and his family. Over the door to the inner room is a scene with Tiy and her husband Amenhotep III and their son and daughter-in-law. Akhenaten also takes his mother to see a small temple he has built for her, and then he is shown together with Nefertiti in a carrying chair.

TOMB OF MERYRE II (NO 2)

Meryre was superintendent of Nefertiti's household, and his tomb includes a scene of Nefertiti pouring wine for Akhenaten. Together with the Tomb of Huya, this is the most distant of the northern tombs and guides are often keen to skip them. They have a point – unless you are really interested in Amarna reliefs, you could give this a miss.

TOMB OF AHMOSE (NO 3)

Ahmose's title was 'Fan-bearer on the King's Right Hand'. Much of his tomb is unfin-ished with the initial ink outlines still to be seen. The royal couple drive their chariot to the Aten temple, followed by their armed guards – whose modern counterparts never seem very far away at Tell al-Amarna.

TOMB OF MERYRE I (NO 4)

High priest of the Aten, Meryre is shown being carried by his friends to receive re-wards from the royal couple, who are also shown going to the temple driving their own chariots accompanied by Meryre. A fascinating detail close to the Aten disc, to the right of the doorway into the columned hall, is the depiction of a rainbow.

TOMB OF PANEHESY (NO 6)

Panehesy was chief servant of the Aten in Akhetaten, and his tomb retains the decorated façade most of the others have lost. Inside, the scenes repeatedly show the royal family, again Nefertiti driving her own chariot, and on the right side of the entrance passage there is even Nefertiti's sister Mutnodjmet, later married to Pharaoh Horemheb, together with her two dwarf servants. There are also two unfinished burial chambers intended for Panehesy and his family.

TOMB OF MAHU (NO 9)
This southern tomb is one of the best preserved, and the wall paintings provide interesting details of Mahu's duties as Akhenaten's chief of police, including taking prisoners to the vizier (minister), checking supplies and visiting the temple.

TOMB OF AY (NO 25)
This is the finest tomb at Tell al-Amarna. Although Ay's titles were simply 'God's Father' and 'Fan-bearer on the King's Right Hand', his wife Tiyi was Nefertiti's wet nurse and the couple may have been related to Queen Tiy's family. Scenes include Ay and Tiyi worshipping the sun and Ay receiving rewards from the royal family, including red leather riding gloves. Ay wasn't buried here; after he became pharaoh (1327–1323 BC, following Tutankhamun) he was buried in the west valley beside the Valley of the Kings (p261) at Thebes.

ROYAL TOMB OF AKHENATEN
Akhenaten's own **tomb** (adult/student E£20/10) is in a ravine about 13km up the Royal Valley (Wadi Darb al-Malek), the valley that divides the north and south sections of the cliffs and where the sun was seen to rise each dawn. The journey to the tomb is very bumpy, although the bleak valley with its tumbleweed and occasional sandstorm is incredibly atmospheric, as is the little-visited tomb. Recently restored and reopened to the public, very little remains of the tantalising wall reliefs that show Akhenaten and his family worshipping Aten. A raised rectangular outline in the burial chamber once held the pharaoh's sarcophagus (now hidden away in the gardens of the Egyptian Museum in Cairo). Yet it seems that Akhenaten himself was not buried here, and although there have been endless theories about his final resting place, the whereabouts of his remains are a mystery.

Getting There & Away
If police are escorting you, you'll have to take a taxi from either Asyut or Minya. Expect to pay about E£50 to E£60 for a return trip. If you've somehow evaded the police, you can get to Tell al-Amarna from Mallawi, by taking a service taxi or a covered pick-up.

AL-QUSIYA
Located about 8km southwest of the small rural town of Al-Qusiya, 35km south of Mallawi, is the Coptic complex of Deir al-Muharraq (Burnt Monastery). About 7km further northwest, on an escarpment at the edge of the desert, lie the Tombs of Mir. There are no hotels in Al-Qusiya, but there's a large guesthouse just outside the pseudo-medieval crenellated walls of Deir al-Muharraq and the monks sometimes allow groups of travellers to stay there (but not usually individuals). In any event, both sites can be visited in an easy day trip from Minya or Asyut.

Sights
DEIR AL-MUHARRAQ
The 100 or so monks who reside in Deir al-Muharraq claim that Mary and Jesus inhabited a cave on this site for six months and 10 days after fleeing from Herod into Egypt – their longest stay at any of the numerous places where they are said to have rested during that flight. For 10 days every year (usually 18 to 28 June), thousands of pilgrims attend feasts to celebrate the consecration of the **Church of Al-Adhra** (Church of the Virgin) that was built over the cave. Coptic Christians believe Al-Adhra to be one of the first churches in the world. Remember to remove your shoes before entering.

The religious significance of this place is, they say, given in the Old Testament:

> In that day there will be an altar to the Lord in the midst of the land of Egypt, and a pillar to the Lord at its border. It will be a sign and a witness to the Lord of Host in the land of Egypt; when they cry to the Lord because of oppressors he will send them a saviour, and will defend and deliver them. And the Lord will make himself known to the Egyptians; and the Egyptians will

know the Lord in that day and worship with sacrifice and burnt offering, and they will make vows to the Lord and perform them.

Isaiah 19:19-21

Next to Al-Adhra is a **square tower**, a 5th-century structure built for the monks to use as added protection in case of attack. It has four floors, an old sundial on an outer wall, and a church inside.

The **Church of St George** (or Mar Girgis), built in 1880, is behind Al-Adhra and is decorated with paintings of the 12 apostles and other religious scenes. Again, be sure to take off your shoes.

You will usually be escorted around the monastery (there is no fee but donations are appreciated) and will finish with a brief visit to the new church built in 1940 and the nearby gift shop, and sometimes with a cool drink in the monastery's reception room.

TOMBS OF MIR

The necropolis of the governors of Cusae, or the **Tombs of Mir** (adult/student E£20/10) as they're also known, were dug into the barren escarpment during the Old and Middle Kingdoms. Nine of the tombs are decorated and open to the public; six others were never finished and remain unexcavated.

Tomb No 1 and the adjoining tomb No 2 are inscribed with 720 Pharaonic deities, but during early Christian times the Copts used the tombs as cells and many faces and names of the gods were destroyed. In tomb No 4 you can still see the original grid drawn on the wall to assist the artist in designing the layout of the tomb art. Tomb No 3 features a cow giving birth.

Getting There & Away

If you're not with the police, the Asyut to Minya bus will drop you at Al-Qusiya, about 50 minutes from Asyut. From Al-Qusiya you may be able to get a local microbus to the monastery, or the police may take you there themselves.

Few vehicles from Al-Qusiya go out to the Tombs of Mir, so you'll have to hire a taxi to take you there. Expect to pay E£15 to E£25, depending on your bargaining skills and how long you spend there. Ideally, you could combine this with a visit to the monastery.

ASYUT

☎ 088

Asyut, 375km south of Cairo, was settled during Pharaonic times on a broad fertile plain bordering the west bank of the Nile. In ancient times the town was named Zowty and was capital of the 13th nome of Upper Egypt. An important trading post, it was the end of the line for the Darb al-Arba'een (Forty Days Rd), one of Africa's great desert caravan routes that led from Sudan via Al-Kharga Oasis (see p337). For centuries one of the main commodities traded here was slaves, and as recently as 150 years ago the town had the largest slave market in Egypt.

However, this long history has been erased by the modern Assiutis, leaving an ugly agglomeration of high-rises that resemble an Eastern European new town rather than an ancient Egyptian entrepôt.

In the late 1980s Asyut was one of the earliest centres of Islamist fomentation. Although the town has been quiet for several years, the police continue to maintain a visible presence and you are likely to find yourself with a police escort whether you want it or not. With few sights and your freedom to wander curtailed, there's little to keep most visitors here.

Information

EMERGENCY

Ambulance (☎ 123)
Tourist police (☎ 232 3328; Sharia Farouk Kidwani)

MEDICAL SERVICES

Gama'a Hospital (☎ 232 2574; University of Asyut)

MONEY

Bank of Alexandria (Midan al-Bank; ☯ 9am-2pm & 6-8pm Sun-Thu)
Banque du Caire (Sharia Saad Zaghloul; ☯ 9am-2pm Sun-Thu)
Banque Misr (Midan al-Bank; ☯ 9am-2pm Sun-Thu) ATM.

POST

Main post office (Sharia Nahda; ☯ 8.30am-2.30pm Sat-Thu)

TELEPHONE

Telephone centrale (Sharia Nahda; ☯ 24hr)

TOURIST INFORMATION

Tourist office (☎ 231 0010; 1st fl, Governorate Bldg, Sharia al-Thawra; ☯ 8.30am-2pm Sat-Thu)

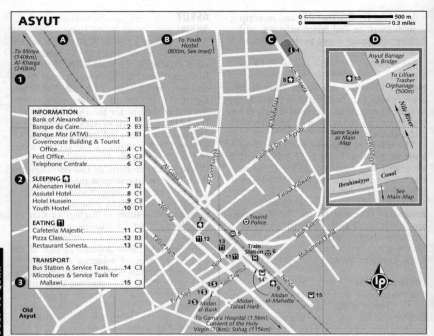

ASYUT

INFORMATION
Bank of Alexandria..................1 B3
Banque du Caire.....................2 B3
Banque Misr (ATM)................3 B3
Governorate Building & Tourist
Office...............................4 C1
Post Office...........................5 C3
Telephone Centrale................6 C3

SLEEPING
Akhenaten Hotel....................7 B2
Assiutel Hotel........................8 C1
Hotel Hussein.......................9 C3
Youth Hostel.......................10 D1

EATING
Cafeteria Majestic.................11 C3
Pizza Class..........................12 B3
Restaurant Sonesta..............13 C3

TRANSPORT
Bus Station & Service Taxis......14 C3
Microbuses & Service Taxis for
Mallawi..........................15 C3

Sights

Banana Island (Gezirat al-Moz), at the end of Sharia Salah Salem, is a shady, pleasant place to picnic. You'll have to bargain with a felucca captain for the ride across.

At the northern edge of town is the 19th-century **Asyut barrage**, built across the Nile to regulate the flow of water into the Ibrahimiyya Canal and assist in the irrigation of the valley as far north as Beni Suef; it also serves as a bridge across the Nile. The barrage is considered to have strategic importance and taking photographs is forbidden, so keep your camera in your bag.

On the east bank, about 200m to the right after you've crossed the barrage, is the **Lillian Trasher Orphanage**. American-born Lillian Trasher came to Egypt in 1910 at the age of 23 and the following year she founded an orphanage in Asyut. Trasher never left, dying in her adopted country in 1961. The orphanage is something of a symbol of Christian charity in a city with a heavy concentration of Copts, and welcomes interested visitors. Donations are appreciated. Microbuses will take you close to

it from the centre of town for 50pt; a taxi will cost E£4. Ask for 'Malga Trasher'.

CONVENT OF THE HOLY VIRGIN

About 10km southwest of Asyut, in an area known as Dirunka, is the Convent of the Holy Virgin, built near a cave where Coptic Christians believe the Holy Family sought refuge during their flight into Egypt. Some 50 nuns and monks live at the convent, which is built into a cliff about 120m above the valley. One of the monks will happily show you around. During the Moulid (Festival) of the Virgin (7 to 22 August), tens of thousands of pilgrims descend on the place and there are daily parades with portraits of Mary and Jesus carried around.

Sleeping

As a large provincial centre, Asyut has a reasonable selection of hotels. Eating poses more of a problem, with few options outside the hotels, although there is a decent selection of takeaways around the train station.

Assiutel Hotel (☎ 231 2121; fax 231 2122; Sharia ath-Thawra; s/d E£89/110; ☒) Overlooking the

Nile, this three-star hotel is the best place in town and has comfortable rooms with satellite TV, fridge and private bathroom. It also has one of Asyut's only bars.

Youth Hostel (☎ 232 4846; Lux Houses, 503 Sharia al-Walidiyya; dm E£8.25) The youth hostel, with its entrance off a side street, is the best cheap option in town. Staff are friendly and eager to help but avoid visiting during Egyptian college breaks, when it gets very crowded.

Akhenaten Hotel (☎ 233 7723; fax 233 1600; Sharia Mohammed Tawfiq Khashba; s/d E£40/50; ❄) Rooms here are gloomy but clean and comfortable with private bathroom, TV and friendly staff.

Hotel Hussein (☎ 233 8437; fax 235 2599; Sharia Mohammed Farid; s/d E£45/60) Conveniently located overlooking the bus station, the Hussein is noisy but comfortable enough to spend a few hours waiting to make a getaway.

Groups and individuals who wish to stay at the Convent of the Holy Virgin are welcome at the basic **rest house** (dm E£8-10; reception ⏱ 6am-6pm), just outside the convent's main gate. No food is available there.

Eating

Most hotels have their own restaurants – the best is at the Assiutel. At the cheaper end of the scale, the restaurant at the Akhenaten Hotel does an escalope as well as good pizza and soup. Beer is also served. Cafeteria Majestic, opposite the train station, has decent food and there are the usual *fuul* and *ta'amiyya* stands around.

Pizza Class (Sharia 26th July; dishes E£2-12) On a busy street corner, the bright and cheerful Pizza Class serves excellent sweet and savoury *fiteer* (Egyptian pizza).

Restaurant Sonesta (☎ 234 2778; Sharia Nour; dishes E£5-15) A reasonable option in a city with little to offer on the culinary front. Serves the usual chicken and kebab in addition to a small selection of mezze.

Getting There & Away

Asyut is a major hub for all forms of transport but the police will encourage you to take the train.

BUS

Upper Egypt Bus Co (☎ 233 0460; Midan al-Mahatta) has hourly buses to Cairo (E£25, five to six hours) between 7.45am and 1.30am. There are services to Alexandria (E£32 to E£35,

10 hours) at 7am and 7pm. There are daily departures to Qena (E£13, three hours) and Sohag (E£5, one hour).

If you are heading out to the oases, there are eight daily buses to Al-Kharga (E£8, two to three hours) between 8am and 10pm, four of which go on to Dakhla (E£13, five hours).

To the coast, there is a service to Hurghada (E£25, five to six hours) at 9am and one to Sharm el-Sheikh (E£60, 14 hours) at 3pm.

SERVICE TAXI

Service taxis congregate around the bus station, but most drivers will only accept foreigners and act as private taxis at the insistence of the police.

TRAIN

Frequent trains arrive and depart for destinations north and south of Asyut. There are several trains throughout the day to Cairo (1st/2nd class E£33/19, four to five hours) and Minya (E£13/8, one hour). There are about 10 daily trains south to Luxor (E£40/26, five to six hours) and Aswan (E£48/32, eight to nine hours). All stop in Sohag (E£19/15, one to two hours) and Qena (E£30/21, three to four hours).

SOHAG

☎ 093 pop / 221,543

The city of Sohag, 115km south of Asyut, is the administrative centre for the governorate of the same name and one of the major Coptic Christian areas of Upper Egypt. The main reason to visit is to see the White and Red Monasteries just outside Sohag, and the town of Akhmin across the river. However, the police presence here is even stronger than in Asyut and Minya and travellers are discouraged from staying. If the police know you're in town they'll insist on escorting you everywhere and you'll probably be banned from leaving your hotel after dark. It's usually better to visit the sights as a day trip from Luxor.

There's no tourist office but you can change cash or travellers cheques at the **Bank of Alexandria** (Sharia al-Gomhuriyya; ⏱ 9am-2pm & 6-8pm Sun-Thu) or the **Banque du Caire** (Sharia al-Gomhuriyya; ⏱ 9am-2pm Sun-Thu). There is also a **post office** (Sharia al-Gomhuriyya; ⏱ 8.30am-2.30pm Sat-Thu).

Sights

WHITE & RED MONASTERIES

Twelve kilometres northwest of Sohag, the **White Monastery** (Deir al-Abyad; ⊙ 8am-8pm) was built in AD 400 by the Coptic saint Shenouda, with chunks of white limestone from a Pharaonic temple. It once supported a community of 2000 monks; today there are just four. Its fortress walls still stand, but most of the interior is in ruins. Nevertheless, it is easy to make out the plan of the church of St Shenouda inside the enclosure walls. Made of brick and measuring 75m by 35m, it follows a basilica plan, with a nave, two side aisles and a triple apse. A dome on the sanctuary is decorated with the Dormition of the Virgin. In the centre of the sanctuary, Christ Pantocrator was painted on the dome. In the centre of the church, 19 columns, taken from an earlier structure, separate the side chapels from the nave.

The **Red Monastery** (Deir al-Ahmar; ⊙ 8am-8pm), 4km southeast of Deir al-Abyad, is hidden at the rear of a village; you'll need to ask for directions. It was founded by Besa, a disciple of Shenouda who, according to legend, was a thief who converted to Christianity. He built this monastery and dedicated it to St Bishoi. It is thought to date from the 4th century AD, although the earliest inscription found here is from 1301. There are two chapels on the grounds, Santa Maria Chapel and St Bishoi Chapel. Be sure to see the remains of a 10th-century fresco in a frame on a side altar in St Bishoi Chapel – it contains a 1000-year-old icon. There are interesting, though fading, frescoes on the walls, unusual pillars and old wooden peg locks on the doors.

To get to the monasteries you'll have to take a taxi (about E£20 there and back) unless you're visiting some time during the first two weeks of July, when you can catch a bus for about E£1 with the thousands of other pilgrims.

AKHMIN

On the east bank of the Nile lies the town of Akhmin, known as Ipu to the ancient Egyptians. Built on the ruins of an older predynastic settlement, it was dedicated to

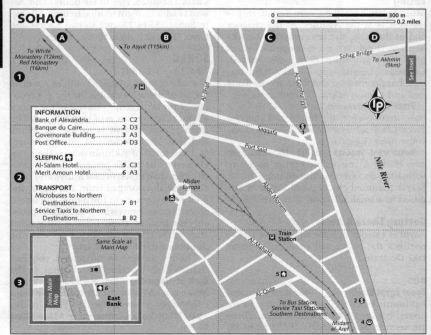

Min, a fertility god often represented by a giant phallus, equated with Pan by the Greeks (who later called the town Panopolis). Links to this ancient past were uncovered in 1982 when excavations to build a new school in the centre of town led to the discovery of the 11m-high **statue of Meret Amun** (adult/student E£12/6; ☾ 8am-4pm Oct-Apr, to 5pm May-Sep). This is the tallest statue of an ancient queen to have been discovered in Egypt. Meret Amun (Beloved of the God Amun) was one of the daughters of Ramses II and wife of Amenhotep. She was also a priestess of the Temple of Min. Little is left of the temple itself, and the statue of Meret Amun now stands in a huge excavation pit among the houses in the middle of town. As the statue is so tall, you can get a good view of its rapidly fading colours without even entering the site.

Akhmin is also famed for its unique woven carpets and textiles. Opposite the statue of Meret Amun is a tiny post office and, across the road from this, a small **weaving factory**. It's the house with the green door; just knock to be led through to the showroom where you can buy hand-woven silk and cotton textiles straight from the bolt or packets of ready-made tablecloths and serviettes. Ask to see the men and boys who make the products at work – you'll hear the 25 looms clattering away before you climb the stairs.

Should the police have missed you, a microbus from Sohag to Akhmin costs 50pt and takes 15 minutes.

Sleeping & Eating

There are only two hotels that will accept foreigners in Sohag, probably because of the hassle with the police.

Merit Amoun Hotel (☎ 460 1985; fax 460 3222; East Bank; s/d E£59/85.50; ✷) This big three-star hotel on the east bank offers the most comfortable accommodation in town.

Al-Salam Hotel (☎ 233 3317; Sharia al-Mahatta; s/d E£25/35, with private bathroom E£35/55) Close to the train station, the Al-Salam can be noisy, but it's one of the few clean budget options that will accept foreigners.

There's not much choice in the way of food in Sohag. As well as the usual fruit and vegetable stands, there are a few kushari, *fuul* and *ta'amiyya* places near the train station. If you follow Sharia al-Mahatta south

of the train station (left as you exit) to a big square, Midan el-Aref, and cross this, there is a kebab/roast chicken restaurant. There is also a restaurant at the Merit Amoun Hotel.

Getting There & Away

BUS

Should the police allow you to take the bus, **Upper Egypt Bus Co** (☎ 233 2021; near Midan el-Aref) has frequent services to Cairo (E£25, seven hours) between 7.30am and 12pm. There is one service a day to Hurghada (8.30am, E£20, five hours), going via Qena (E£6, three hours). Change at Qena for buses to Luxor and Aswan. Buses to Asyut (E£6, two hours) depart at 6am and noon.

SERVICE TAXI

There are several service taxi stations in Sohag but, as in other Upper Egyptian towns, you're likely to be forced by the police to hire a private taxi. Should they lighten up, cars to northern destinations can be found north of the train station on Midan Europa. Service taxis for Qena leave from the southern depot, which is on the main road south, just after a canal.

TRAIN

Trains north and south stop reasonably frequently at Sohag. The 1st-/2nd-class fare to Asyut is E£12/7. The train to Al-Balyana generally makes a lot of stops (E£2.50 in 3rd class only).

AL-BALYANA

☎ 093

The only reason to go to this town is to visit the village of **Al-Araba al-Madfuna**, 10km away. There you'll find the necropolis of Abydos and the magnificent Temple of Seti I, one of the most beautiful monuments in Egypt. The police here tend to be somewhat heavy-handed in their efforts to protect you and if you haven't been escorted thus far, you'll certainly pick up some policemen here.

Should you need to change money, there's a tiny Banque Misr kiosk at the entrance to Abydos, which usually opens when groups of tourists arrive.

As you're unlikely to be able to stay in Al-Balyana, you will be limited to travelling here on a day trip, best done from Luxor (see p271).

Abydos

As the traditional burial ground of the god Osiris, **Abydos** (ancient name Ibdju; adult/student E£30/15; ⏰ 8am-4pm Oct-Apr, to 5pm May-Sep) was *the* place to be buried in ancient Egypt. It was used as a necropolis from predynastic to Christian times (c 4000 BC–AD 600), an incredible time span of more than 4500 years of constant use. The area now known as Umm al-Qa'ab (Mother of Pots), named for the piles of ancient debris that litter the site, is Egypt's earliest royal burial ground and contains the mastaba tombs of the first pharaohs of Egypt, including that of the third pharaoh of the 1st dynasty, Djer (c 3000 BC). By the Middle Kingdom his tomb had become identified as the tomb of Osiris himself.

Abydos maintained its importance for so many centuries because of the cult of Osiris, god of the dead. The area was a natural shrine for the worship of this ruler of the netherworld because, according to mythology, it was here that the head of Osiris was buried after his brother Seth had murdered him (see opposite). The temple at Abydos was the most important shrine to Osiris and a place of pilgrimage that most Egyptians would try to visit in their lifetime (much as Muslims try to get to Mecca today). If they didn't manage it they would be buried with small boats to enable their souls to make the journey after death.

Should you want more information, there's a booklet on sale at the Osiris Park Camp shop for E£10. There's also *Abydos – The Holy City in Ancient Egypt* written by a fascinating woman by the name of Dorothy Eady, better known to many as 'Omm Sety'. She was an English woman who believed she was a temple priestess and lover of Seti I, and for 35 years, until her death in 1981, she lived at Abydos. *The Search for Omm Sety* by Jonathan Cott is a biography of her life there.

TEMPLE OF SETI I

The first structure you'll see at Abydos is one of Egypt's most beautiful temples, also known as the Cenotaph or Great Temple of Seti I, which, after a certain amount of restoration work, is also one of the most

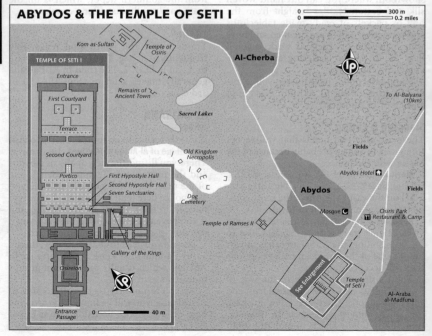

ABYDOS & THE TEMPLE OF SETI I

0 ——————— 300 m
0 ——————— 0.2 miles

TEMPLE OF SETI I

- Entrance
- First Courtyard
- Terrace
- Second Courtyard
- Portico
- First Hypostyle Hall
- Second Hypostyle Hall
- Seven Sanctuaries
- Gallery of the Kings
- Osireion
- Entrance Passage

0 ——— 40 m

Kom as-Sultan
Temple of Osiris
Al-Cherba
Remains of Ancient Town
Sacred Lakes
Old Kingdom Necropolis
Dog Cemetery
Temple of Ramses II
Sacred Lakes
Fields
Abydos Hotel
Abydos
Fields
Mosque
Osiris Park Restaurant & Camp
To Al-Balyana (10km)
See Enlargement
Temple of Seti I
Al-Araba al-Madfuna

complete. This great limestone structure, which unusually is L-shaped rather than rectangular, was dedicated to the six major gods – Osiris, Isis and Horus, Amun-Ra, Ra-Horakhty and Ptah – and also to Seti I (1294–1279 BC) himself. In the aftermath of the Amarna Period, it is almost as if Seti was trying to appease as many of the traditional gods as possible. As you roam through Seti's dark halls and sanctuaries a definite air of mystery, an almost tangible impression of ancient pomp and circumstance, surrounds you.

The temple is entered through a largely destroyed **pylon** and two **courtyards**, built by Ramses II, Seti I's son, who is depicted on the portico killing Asiatics and worshipping Osiris. Beyond is the **first hypostyle hall**, also completed by Ramses after his father's death. Reliefs depict the pharaoh making offerings to the gods and preparing the temple building.

The **second hypostyle hall**, with 24 sandstone papyrus columns, was the last part of the temple to have been decorated by Seti, although he died before the work was completed. The reliefs that were finished are stunning. Particularly outstanding is a scene on the rear right-hand wall showing Seti standing in front of a shrine to Osiris,

upon which sits the god himself. Standing in front of him are the goddesses Maat, Renpet, Isis, Nephthys and Amentet.

At the rear of this second hypostyle hall there are separate **sanctuaries** for each of the seven gods (right to left: Horus, Isis, Osiris, Amun-Ra, Ra-Horakhty, Ptah and Seti), which once held their statues. The sanctuary of Osiris is especially imposing and opens out at the back to extend across the width of the temple, with two columned halls and two sets of three further sanctuaries dedicated to Osiris, his wife and child, Isis and Horus, and the ever-present Seti.

Passing through to the left of the seven sanctuaries, the corridor known as '**Gallery of the Kings**' is carved with the figures of Seti with his eldest son, the future Ramses II, and a long list of the pharaohs who preceded them. Such valuable historical evidence not only provided early Egyptologists with a means of unravelling Egypt's long history, but is graphic evidence for the way in which the ancient Egyptians used to rewrite their history. Try to find the names of the female pharaoh Hatshepsut, or the so-called heretic Akhenaten and you'll draw a blank; they simply aren't there – removed from the records as if they had never existed. It seems that Seti and

THE CULT OF OSIRIS

The most familiar of all ancient Egypt's myths is the story of Isis and Osiris, preserved in the writings of the Greek historian Plutarch (c AD 46–126) following a visit to Egypt. According to Plutarch, Osiris and his sister-wife Isis had once ruled on earth, bringing great peace and prosperity to their kingdom. Seething with jealousy at their success, their evil brother Seth invited Osiris to a banquet and tricked him into trying out a coffin he had made. Once Osiris was inside, Seth sealed up the coffin and threw it into the Nile, drowning his brother. Following the murder, the distraught Isis retrieved her brother-husband's body, only to have it seized back by Seth who dismembered it, scattering the pieces far and wide. But Isis refused to give up, and taking the form of a kite she took to the skies with her sister Nephthys to search for the separate body parts. They then buried each piece wherever they found it, which explains why there are so many places that claim to be Osiris' tomb.

The traditional Egyptian version of the story differs slightly from Plutarch's. In it Isis collected the parts of Osiris and reassembled them to create the first mummy, helped by Anubis, god of embalming. Then, using her immense magic, she restored Osiris to life – so successfully that she conceived their son Horus, a miraculous act in which she quite literally created new life from death. Raised to avenge his father, Horus defeated Seth and became the living ruler on earth, represented by each pharaoh, while his resurrected father ruled as Lord of the Afterlife. A much-loved god, Osiris represented salvation after death, a concept that was very important to the life-loving ancient Egyptians, who wanted to make sure that they would continue to exist in the hereafter. So popular was Osiris that people even had their name prefaced with his to show that they would be with him in his kingdom.

his hard-line successors simply would not tolerate any more 'unusual' goings-on and from this time on the kingship would be run along the most orthodox lines.

THE OSIREION

Directly behind Seti's temple is the Osireion, a weird, wonderful building interpreted as a cenotaph to Osiris. It was originally thought to be an Old Kingdom structure on account of the great blocks of granite used in its construction, and although now dated to Seti's reign (and completed by his grandson Merneptah), its design is said to be based on the rock-cut tombs in the Valley of the Kings. At the centre of its columned 'burial chamber', which lies at a lower level than Seti's temple, is a dummy sarcophagus originally surrounded by water. It's surrounded by water today as the Osireion is permanently submerged by the rising water table. If you want to visit be prepared to wade. This, together with the collapse of the roof, makes inspection of the funerary and ritual texts carved on its walls hazardous.

TEMPLE OF RAMSES II

Just northwest of Seti I's temple is the smaller and less well-preserved structure built by Seti's son, Ramses II (1279–1213 BC). Although taking the more standard rectangular plan of a traditional temple, there are sanctuaries for each of the gods Ramses considered important, including Osiris, Amun-Ra, Thoth, Min, the deified Seti I and, of course, Ramses himself. Although the roof is missing, the reliefs again retain a significant amount of their colour, clearly seen on figures of priests, offering bearers and the pharaoh anointing the gods' statues. You may have to get the guard to unlock the gate.

Sleeping & Eating

You are unlikely to be allowed to stay in Al-Balyana, given the nervousness of the local police. Should the situation change, there are a few hotels and some cafés and food stands around the town.

Abydos Hotel (☎ 494 0102; s/d E£120/200; ✕) The only potential accommodation option is this hotel, 200m before Osiris Park on the way to the Temple of Seti I. The rooms are comfortable enough, but overpriced and not worth the hassle of staying here.

Osiris Park Restaurant (Abydos Temple) Right in front of the temple, and aimed at tour groups, this is the only option at the temple. The food is overpriced and consists mostly of snacks. It's best to bring your own from elsewhere.

Getting There & Away

The most common way of getting to Al-Balyana is by tour bus or private taxi in the 8am convoy from Luxor (see p282). You can also catch a train from Luxor at 9.15am (1st/2nd class E£16/13, three hours). A return trip by taxi from the station to the temple costs about E£25 to E£30. Expect a police escort. There is a train back to Luxor at 5pm (3rd class only, E£5). Occasionally the police will stick you on the bus of a tour group going to Luxor with an armed police escort.

KING LISTS Dr Joann Fletcher

The ancient Egyptians constructed their history around their kings, with each regnal year used as a means of dating. Instead of using a continuous year-by-year sequence, events were recorded as happening in a specific year of a specific king, so at each king's accession they started at year 1 until the king died, then began again with year 1 of the next king.

So it was vital to have reliable records listing each reign, and although a number of so-called king lists have survived and can be seen in Cairo's Egyptian Museum, the Louvre in Paris and the British Museum, the only one remaining in its original location was created by Seti I in his Abydos Temple. With an emphasis on the royal ancestors, Seti names 75 of his predecessors beginning with the semimythical Menes (usually regarded as Narmer), yet in typical Egyptian fashion he rewrites history by excluding those considered 'unsuitable', from the foreign Hyksos kings of the Second Intermediate Period and the female pharaoh Hatshepsut to the Amarna kings: Amenhotep III is immediately followed by Horemheb, and thus Akhenaten, Smenkhkare, Tutankhamun and Ay are simply erased from the record.

QENA

☎ 096 / pop 201,996

Qena, a provincial capital 91km east of Al-
Balyana and 62km north of Luxor, is at the
intersection of the main Nile road and the
road running across the desert to the Red
Sea towns of Port Safaga and Hurghada.
A scruffy market town and provincial capital, Qena has little to recommend it to the
visitor. Unless you're on your way to or
from the Red Sea and don't have a through
connection, the only reason to stop is to
visit the spectacular temple complex at
Dendara, located just outside the town,
although this is best done as a day trip
from Luxor. The town has two service taxi
stations quite a long way apart from one
another, one for northern destinations
and places across the Nile, the other for
southern destinations. Again, you will be
met by policemen here and escorted to the
temple and then put on the first train to
Luxor. If you need money, there is a **Bank
of Alexandria** (off Sharia Luxor; ⌚ 8.30am-2pm & 6-
8pm Sun-Thu) and a **Banque du Caire** (Sharia Luxor;
⌚ 9am-2.30pm Sun-Thu) in town.

Dendara

Although built at the very end of the Pharaonic period, the wonderfully preserved
Temple of Hathor (adult/student E£30/15; ⌚ 7am-
6pm) at her cult site of Dendara is a sight to
behold. Its main building is virtually intact,
with a great stone roof and columns, dark
chambers, underground crypts and twisting
stairways all carved with hieroglyphs.

Dendara itself was an important administrative and religious centre as early as
the 6th dynasty (c 2320 BC), when it also
served as an important burial ground.
Montuhotep II of the 11th dynasty built
a small limestone chapel here (now in the
Egyptian Museum), although the great temple that dominates the site was begun in
the 30th dynasty, with much of the building undertaken by the Ptolemies and completed during the Roman period. Yet it was
almost certainly built on the site of earlier
versions in which the goddess Hathor had
been worshipped since the Old Kingdom.

Hathor was the goddess of love and sensual pleasures, patron of music and dancing, and as 'Lady of the West' was protector

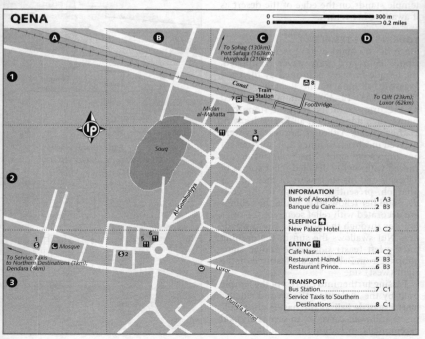

of the dead. The Greeks also associated Hathor with their goddess Aphrodite. Like most Egyptian deities Hathor was known by a range of titles, including 'the golden one', 'she of the beautiful hair' and 'lady of drunkenness', representing the joyful intoxication involved in her worship. She is generally represented as a woman, a cow, or a woman with a headdress of cow's horns and sun disc between to highlight her role as the daughter of the sun-god Ra. Yet she was also a maternal figure and as wife of Horus was often portrayed as the divine mother of the reigning pharaoh, who was identified with the god. In a statue from Deir al-Bahri in Luxor she even appears in the form of a cow suckling Amenhotep II (1427–1400 BC). Confusingly, she shared many of these attributes with the goddess Isis, who was also described as the mother of the king. In the end Isis essentially overshadowed Hathor as an über-mother when the legend of Isis and Osiris expanded to include the birth of Horus.

Dendara was the ritual location where Hathor gave birth to Horus' child, and her temple stands on the edge of the desert as if awaiting her return.

TOURING THE TEMPLE

Since the standard pylon gateway and entrance courtyard were never completed, the temple frontage is formed by the **outer hypostyle hall** built by the Roman emperor Tiberius (AD 14–37). Visitors are greeted by the first six of its 24 great stone columns, each adorned on all four sides with Hathor's head. Although her features were defaced in Christian times they still present an impressive sight. The walls inside are carved with highly detailed relief scenes of Tiberius and his successors in their role as pharaoh, presenting offerings to the goddess and her fellow gods, while the ceilings are decorated with relief scenes of the sun's journey through the heavens. The sky goddess Nut swallows the sun in the evening on the left (east) side while zodiac signs adopted from Babylonia are featured on the right (west) side.

Passing further into the rest of the temple built by the Ptolemies, the second smaller **inner hypostyle hall** again has Hathor columns and walls carved with scenes of royal ceremonials, including the founding of the temple. But notice the 'blank' cartouches that reveal much about the political instability of late Ptolemaic times – with such a rapid turnover of pharaohs, the stonemasons seem to have been reluctant to carve the names of those who might not be in the job for long. Things reached an all-time low in 80 BC when Ptolemy XI murdered his more popular wife Berenice III (who was also his stepmother) after only 19 days of corule, whereupon the outraged citizens of Alexandria dragged the pharaoh from his palace and killed him in revenge.

To either side of the inner hypostyle hall are six small chambers; the fourth chamber on the right side gives access to the western stairway up to the roof.

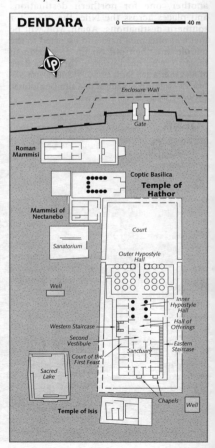

Beyond lies the **Hall of Offerings** that leads to the **sanctuary**, the most holy part of the temple that originally contained the statue of the goddess herself as portrayed on the sanctuary's wall reliefs. A further Hathor statue was stored in the crypt beneath her temple, and brought out each year for the New Year Festival (in ancient times this fell on 19 July). It was carried into the Hall of Offerings with the statues of her fellow gods, then all were then taken into the raised shrine inside the small open-air court known as 'the Court of the First Feast' just to the right (west) of the Hall of Offerings. After further ceremonials beneath the huge figure of Nut giving birth to the sun on the shrine's ceiling, the statues were then taken up to the roof via the western staircase, decorated with carvings of a procession of priests walking up the stairs. Placed inside the open-air kiosk on the southwestern corner of the roof, they were then left to await the first reviving rays of the sun-god Ra on New Year's Day. Once ceremonies were over, the statues were taken back down via the eastern staircase, with its carved priests appropriately walking downstairs.

The theme of reviving the gods continues opposite the kiosk on the northwestern corner of the roof and duplicated on the northeastern corner, where two suites of rooms are dedicated to the revival of Osiris. Relief scenes show the means by which the god was restored by the power of his sister-wife, Isis, and in the centre room of the northeastern suite is the famous 'Dendara Zodiac', or at least a plaster cast, since the original is now in the Louvre in Paris. Views of the surrounding countryside from the roof are magnificent. The graffiti on the edge of the temple was left by Napoleon's commander Desaix, and other French soldiers, in 1799.

The **exterior walls** of the temple feature lion-headed gargoyles to cope with the very occasional rainfall and are decorated along their length with highly detailed relief scenes of Ptolemaic pharaohs and their Roman successors paying homage to the gods. The most interesting scene of all can be found on the rear (south) wall, where none other than the great Cleopatra stands with Ptolemy XV, aka Caesarion, her son by Julius Caesar.

Facing this back wall is a small **temple of Isis** built by Cleopatra's great rival Octavian once he was the Emperor Augustus. Walking back toward the front of the Hathor temple on the west side, notice the now palm-filled Sacred Lake and the smaller well to its north that supplied the temple's water. To the north of the well lie the mudbrick walls of the **sanatorium**, where the ill would seek a cure through the healing abilities of Hathor.

Finally there are the two **mammisi** (Coptic for 'birth house'), the first built by the 30th-dynasty Egyptian pharaoh Nectanebo I (380–362 BC) and decorated by the Ptolemies, and the one nearest the temple wall built by the Romans and decorated by the emperor Trajan (AD 98–117). Such buildings were used as places to celebrate divine birth, both of the young gods and of the pharaoh himself as son of the gods. Between the *mammisi* is a **Coptic basilica**, built in the 5th century AD. It functioned as a church when Christianity took over from the old religion.

Dendara is 4km southwest of Qena on the west side of the Nile. As elsewhere, the police here are heavy-handed and these days almost everyone arrives here from Luxor in convoy (see the boxed text, p282). If you hire a taxi from Luxor for the trip, it will cost you about E£150 to E£200 return. There is also a day cruise to Dendara from Luxor (see p271). If you arrive in Qena by train, you can find taxis near the station. Reckon on E£20 to E£30 for the return trip. Expect a police escort.

Sleeping & Eating

Even if the police don't send you packing, Qena is not a place to spend the night. The choices are limited and it is close enough to Luxor for commuting. If you must stay, there are few possibilities.

New Palace Hotel (☎ 532 2509; near Sharia al-Gomhuriyya; s/d E£70/80; ✷) Slightly improved since our last visit, with the addition of aircon and better private bathrooms, the New Palace is behind the Mobil petrol station.

The food scene in town is about as dismal as the hotel choice. There are several *fuul*, kushari and *ta'amiyya* places along Sharia al-Gomhuriyya. Other than that you are limited to several fairly similar cheap restaurants.

Cafe Nasr (Sharia al-Gomhuriyya; dishes E£2-6), a workers' café serving cheap food including spinach, tahini, salads (which should be avoided) and tea. **Restaurant Hamdi** (Sharia Luxor; dishes E£7-15) features full meals of soup, chicken, kofta and vegetables, while **Restaurant Prince** (Sharia al-Gomhuriyya; dishes E£5-15) serves yet more chicken and kofta.

Getting There & Away
BUS
Upper Egypt Bus Co (☎ 532 5068; Midan al-Mahatta) is in front of the train station. However, buses not originating or terminating here pass along the main road and drop (and might pick up) passengers at the bridge over the canal. Three buses to Cairo (E£30, nine hours) leave at 6.30pm, 8pm and 9pm. These head up the Nile Valley, not stopping at any towns along the way. Two 'Pullman' services leave at 7pm and 10.30pm for Cairo (E£40 to E£50) stopping in Hurghada (E£20) and Suez (E£40).

Buses leave for Luxor (E£3 to E£5, one hour) and Aswan (E£12, four hours) at 7am (originating in Hurghada), 1.30pm, 7pm and 1.30am.

SERVICE TAXI
The police are likely to limit your transportation choices, but in case this changes, service taxis to destinations north of Qena leave from a T-junction 1km outside town. For destinations to the south of Qena, such as Luxor, service taxis leave from the taxi station on the other side of the canal from the train station.

TRAIN
All main north–south trains stop at Qena. There are 1st-/2nd-class air-con trains to Luxor (E£15/12, 40 minutes) and trains to Al-Balyana (2nd/3rd class E£10/4, two hours), if you want to visit Abydos.

Getting Around
There is a local microbus that shuttles from town to the northern service taxi station. Depending on the police, you can pick it up near the train station or, if you're coming from the south, at the canal bridge near the southern service taxi station. It costs 50pt.

Nile Valley: Luxor

Royal Thebes,
Egyptian treasure-house of countless wealth,
Who boasts her hundred gates, through each of which,
With horse and car, two hundred warriors march.

Homer, The Iliad, *Book IX*

Luxor is a place like no other on earth, where the grandeur of ancient Thebes sits comfortably alongside a bustling Upper Egyptian town. With the Nile flowing between the modern town and the former necropolis, and the enigmatic Theban escarpment dominating the landscape, its historic beauty is still breathtaking. The sheer size and number of its wonderfully preserved monuments have made Luxor Egypt's greatest attraction after the Pyramids. From the temples of Karnak and Luxor on its East Bank across to the temples of Deir al-Bahri and Medinat Habu, the Colossi of Memnon and the Valley of the Kings on its West Bank, there's an embarrassment of riches to be found here. Small wonder that the area is often described as the world's largest open-air museum.

For millennia Luxor's monuments have drawn travellers but the advent of mass tourism means that greater numbers pass through the area than ever before. Surrounded by coachloads of tourists as they are herded through tombs and temples at a furious pace, individuals often feel lost amid a sea of jostling groups. But with a little planning and flexibility the crowds can be avoided, and the magic of the Theban landscape and its unparalleled archaeological heritage can be enjoyed in peace.

NILE VALLEY: LUXOR

HIGHLIGHTS

- Lose yourself in a stone papyrus forest in the **great hypostyle hall** (p245) at Karnak
- See how ancient rulers tried to defy mortality – and thieves – with spectacular tombs in the **Valley of the Kings** (p251)
- Marvel at the architectural feat of the mountainside temple built by one of Egypt's rare woman rulers at **Deir al-Bahri** (p262)
- Wander among pharaohs and Theban treasures at **Luxor Museum** (p236)
- Witness the grisly fate of ancient prisoners of war on the walls of the best-preserved Theban temple, **Medinat Habu** (p269)

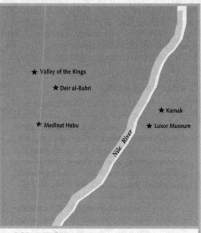

★ Valley of the Kings
★ Deir al-Bahri
★ Karnak
★ Medinat Habu
★ Luxor Museum

Nile River

■ TELEPHONE CODE: ☎ 095   ■ POPULATION: 199,885

HISTORY

Predynastic remains indicate that the Luxor area has been inhabited for at least 6000 years, although it did not reach its apogee until the time of the New Kingdom (1550–1069 BC). Following the collapse of centralised authority at the end of the Old Kingdom, Egypt fragmented into a series of local power bases. During the chaos of the First Intermediate Period (2181–2055 BC), the small southern village of Thebes (ancient name Waset) eventually became strong enough to overpower the northern capital Heracleopolis under the capable leadership of Montuhotep II (2055–2004 BC).

After reuniting the country and moving the capital to Thebes, Montuhotep initiated a series of great building works, including a temple to Thebes' local god Amun at his cult centre of Karnak and his own royal funerary temple complex at Deir al-Bahri. Although the 12th-dynasty pharaohs moved their capital back north, Thebes remained the capital of the south (Upper Egypt) and never lost its place as Egypt's ceremonial capital, a counterbalance to the administrative capital at Memphis.

Following a Second Intermediate Period (1650–1550 BC) Thebes once again emerged as the unifying power. Its ruling family drove out the foreign Hyksos pharaohs in the north, laying the foundations of Egypt's empire and all the glories of the New Kingdom (1550–1069 BC). For 500 years Thebes was at its peak, a great city with a population of many thousands, and it was during this time that most of its great monuments were constructed.

The decline of Pharaonic rule was mirrored by Luxor's gradual slide into insignificance. Mud-brick settlements clung to the once mighty Theban temples, their stone walls the only protection against marauding tribespeople from the desert. Remains of these communities can still be seen at sites such as Medinat Habu on the West Bank. In early Christian times a number of monasteries and churches were built, many in the remains of Pharaonic shrines. Visitors today can see crosses carved into temple walls and traces of where monks and priests tried to scratch out reliefs of Pharaonic gods.

As Christian rule gave way to Islamic, the area fell into obscurity and the only reminder of its glorious past was the name given to it by its Arab rulers: Al-Uqsur (The Palaces). By the time European travellers arrived here in the 18th century, Luxor was little more than a large Upper Egyptian village, known more for its 12th-century saint, Abu al-Haggag, than for its half-buried temples and tombs.

The growth of Egyptomania changed that. The arrival of Napoleon in 1798 and the publication of the *Description de l'Egypte* by his savants piqued interest in Egypt. European exhibitions of mummies, jewellery and other spectacular funerary artefacts from Theban tombs (often found by plundering adventurers rather than enquiring scholars) made Luxor an increasingly sought-after destination. By 1869, when Thomas Cook brought his first group of tourists to Egypt, Luxor was one of the highlights. Mass tourism had arrived and Luxor regained its place on the world map.

ORIENTATION

What most visitors today know as Luxor is actually three separate areas: the town of Luxor itself, the village of Karnak located a couple of kilometres to the northeast, and the monuments and necropolis of ancient Thebes on the West Bank of the Nile.

In Luxor town (Map pp238–9) there are four main thoroughfares: Sharia al-Mahatta, Sharia al-Karnak, the Corniche el-Nil (also referred to as 'the Corniche') and Sharia Televizyon, a bustling area around which many of the town's cheap hotels are clustered.

On the West Bank (Map p248) the village of Al-Gezira, close to the ferry landing, is becoming a hub of shops, midrange hotels

---

WHAT'S IN A NAME?

Ramses II may have called his glittering capital Waset, but when the Greeks arrived here they took the conqueror's prerogative and changed the name to Thebes, possibly after a Greek city of the same name. By the time the conquering Arabs arrived, the ancient grandeur was ruined but still impressive, prompting them to call the area Al-Uqsur (The Palaces) – rendered 'Luxor' in English.

Today Luxor is often used to describe the modern town, and Thebes the ruins of the ancient capital on the West Bank.

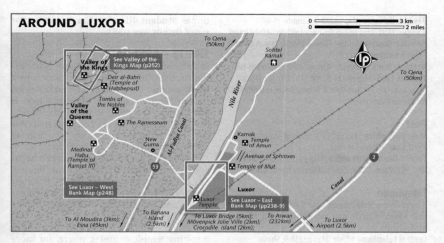

and restaurants. Further west is the village of Gurna, strung out among the tombs and temples at the edge of the desert.

INFORMATION
Bookshops
Luxor has two excellent English-language bookshops. The larger hotels, such as the Mercure and the Sheraton, also have bookshops. There are newsstands in front of Aboudi Bookshop and on the Corniche outside the Old Winter Palace Hotel.

AA Gaddis Bookshop (Map pp238-9; ☎ 237 0753; Corniche el-Nil; ☺ 9am-10pm Mon-Sat) Between Old and New Winter Palace Hotels. Extensive selection of books on Egypt.

Aboudi Bookshop (Map pp238-9; ☎ 237 3390; Tourist Bazaar, Corniche el-Nil; ☺ 9am-10pm) Excellent selection of guidebooks, maps, postcards and fiction.

Emergency
Ambulance (☎ 123)
Police (Map pp238-9; ☎ 237 2350; cnr Sharias Karnak & al-Matafy)
Tourist police (Map pp238-9; ☎ 237 6620; Corniche el-Nil) Next to the tourist office.

Internet Access
You can find Internet access everywhere in Luxor, including in many hotels. Prices range from E£4 to E£10 per hour.

EAST BANK
Aboudi Bookshop (Map pp238-9; ☎ 237 3390; Corniche el-Nil; ☺ 9am-10pm)

Al-Azhar Internet Café (Map pp238-9; ☎ 238 0595; Sharia St Joseph; ☺ 9am-11pm)
GBC Internet (Map pp238-9; ☎ 236 5519; lower level, Corniche el-Nil; ☺ 9.30am-6pm) In front of the Winter Palace Hotel.
Heroes Internet (Map pp238-9; Sharia Televizyon; ☺ 24hr)
Rainbow Internet (Map pp238-9; ☎ 238 7938; 19 Sharia Yousef Hassan; ☺ 9am-11pm)

WEST BANK
Nile Centre (Map p248; ☎ 231 3482; Gezira; ☺ 9am-midnight)
Technology Access Community Center (TACC; Map p248; ☎ 231 2275; www.taccluxor.egnet.net; ferry landing, Gezira; ☺ 8.30am-9pm)

Medical Services
General Hospital (Map pp238-9; ☎ 237 2025, 382 698; Corniche el-Nil) As a last resort.
International Hospital (☎ 238 7192/3/4; Sharia Televizyon) The best place in town.

Money
Most major Egyptian banks have branches in Luxor. Unless otherwise noted, usual opening hours are 8.30am to 2pm and 5pm to 6pm, Sunday to Thursday. ATMs can be found all over town, including at most banks and most five-star hotels.

American Express (Map pp238-9; ☎ 237 8333; Corniche el-Nil; ☺ 9am-4.30pm) Beside entrance to Old Winter Palace Hotel.
Bank of Alexandria (Map pp238-9; Corniche el-Nil) Near Hotel Mercure.

Banque du Caire (Map pp238-9; Corniche el-Nil)
Banque Misr (Map pp238-9; Sharia Labib Habashi) Around the corner from the Mercure. There is another branch on Sharia Televizyon.
National Bank of Egypt (Map pp238-9; Corniche el-Nil)
Thomas Cook (Map pp238-9; ☎ 237 2196; fax 376 502; Corniche el-Nil; ☺ 8am-2pm & 3-8pm) Below entrance to Old Winter Palace Hotel.

Post
Main post office (Map pp238-9; Sharia al-Mahatta; ☺ 8.30am-2.30pm Sat-Thu)
Tourist Bazaar post office (Map pp238-9; Corniche el-Nil; ☺ 8.30am-2.30pm Sat-Thu) Next to tourist office.

Telephone
There are cardphones scattered throughout the town. Cards are available from kiosks and shops.
Central telephone office (Map pp238-9; Sharia al-Karnak; ☺ 24hr)
Telephone office (Map pp238-9; Corniche el-Nil; ☺ 8am-8pm) Below entrance to Old Winter Palace Hotel.
Vodaphone (Map pp238-9; ☎ 235 5872; cnr Sharia Televizyon & Sharia Medina el Manawarra; ☺ 10am-10pm Sun-Thu, 2-10pm Fri) For tourist SIM cards.

Tourist Information
Main tourist office (Map pp238-9; ☎ 237 2215; fax 237 3922; Tourist Bazaar, Corniche el-Nil; ☺ 8am-8pm)
Train station office (Map pp238-9; ☎ 237 0259; ☺ 8am-8pm)

Visa Extensions
Passport office (Map pp238-9; ☎ 238 0885; Sharia Khaled ibn al-Walid; ☺ 8am-8pm Sat-Thu, 2-8pm for information only)

DANGERS & ANNOYANCES
For all its long experience with tourists, the town of Luxor has the dubious distinction of being the hassle capital of Egypt and our readers frequently write about their frustration with the town. We agree. The tourist office is sympathetic but claims it is unable to do anything without a written report. It may seem absurd to write a letter about a tout who was rude but if you can do so, it might have an effect. Luxor's tourist officials will be grateful for your help.

If you are looking for student cards in Luxor, make sure you get to the correct office; one office issues ISE (International Student & Youth Exchange) cards, which provide fewer discounts than the Interna-

tional Student Identity Card (ISIC). For more details, see p534.

SIGHTS – EAST BANK
In spite of its illustrious past and its booming tourism-driven economy, Luxor's East Bank retains its provincial market-town flavour. Easily walkable when the heat is not intense, the town is where the hotels, bars and restaurants are concentrated. But the wide boulevards quickly give way to narrow backstreets and a rural feel.

Against such a backdrop the area's heritage is all the more striking. Luxor Temple, around which the town is built, is an elegant architectural masterpiece, its courtyards and sanctuaries dedicated to the Theban gods.

Further down the Nile is Karnak, an awe-inspiring temple complex where, for more than 1500 years, pharaohs vied for the gods' attention by outdoing each other's architectural feats.

Complementing the monuments are two excellent museums. Luxor Museum has a fascinating collection of artefacts discovered in this antiquities-rich area, while the Mummification Museum displays animal and human mummies and explains in gory detail how the ancient Egyptians perfected the embalming process.

Luxor Museum
About halfway between the Luxor and Karnak Temples, the great little **Luxor Museum** (Map pp238-9; ☎ 238 0269; Corniche el-Nil; adult/student E£55/30; ☺ 9am-1pm & 4-9pm Oct-Apr, 9am-1pm & 5-10pm May-Sep) has a well-chosen collection of relics from the end of the Old Kingdom right through to the Mamluk period, mostly gathered from the Theban temples and necropolis. A new wing, built to house the mummy some believe to be Ramses I, examines Egyptian power at its New Kingdom apogee.

The main entrance to the museum is via the new wing, on the right-hand side of the façade. You are first ushered into a small cinema playing a specially commissioned National Geographic documentary, *Egypt's Army in the Golden Age*. Well-produced and worth sticking around for (it's on a loop so if you come part way through, you can stay and watch it again) it provides excellent background to the exhibits inside, many of which relate in some way to Egypt's military prowess at the height of its power. Among them are examples of weapons and shields and a beautifully made wooden chariot from Tutankhamun's tomb.

The highlight of the new wing – and the real reason for its construction – is the presence of two **royal mummies**, Ahmose I (founder of the 18th dynasty), and the mummy some believe to be Ramses I (founder of the 19th dynasty and father of Seti I and grandfather of Ramses II). The mummy of Ahmose I was part of the famous cache of royal mummies discovered in the 19th century (see p263) and the two mummies are displayed in darkened rooms without their wrappings – a compelling if slightly gruesome sight.

On the upper floor the military theme is diluted with scenes from daily life in the New Kingdom. **Multimedia displays** show workers harvesting papyrus and processing it into sheets to be used for writing. Young boys are shown learning to read and write hieroglyphs beside a display of a scribe's implements and an architect's tools.

Returning to the ground floor, a doorway links the new wing to the original part of the museum. In the ground floor gallery are two outstanding pieces: a finely carved **statue of Tuthmosis III** from the Temple of Karnak (No 61) and an alabaster group **figure of Amenhotep III** protected by the great crocodile god Sobek (No 107), found at the site of the Temple of Sobek at Dahamsah in 1967 at the bottom of a canal.

Moving up via the ramp to the 1st floor, you come to face a seated **granite figure** of the legendary scribe Amenhotep (No 117), son of Hapu, the great official eventually deified in Ptolemaic times and who, as overseer of all the pharaoh's works under Amenhotep III (1390–1352 BC), was responsible for many of Thebes' greatest buildings.

One of the most interesting exhibits is the **Wall of Akhenaten**, a series of small sandstone blocks named *talalat* or 'threes' by workmen, probably because their height and length was about three hand lengths. The blocks were part of Amenhotep IV's contribution to the Temples of Karnak before he changed his name to Akhenaten and left Thebes for Tell al-Amarna. After his death his buildings were demolished and these blocks were used to fill the inside of Karnak's ninth pylon, where about 40,000 were found in the late 1960s. Now partially reassembled here, they show Akhenaten, his wife Nefertiti and scenes of temple life. They are among relatively few examples of decoration from a Temple of Aten.

Further highlights on the 2nd floor are treasures from Tutankhamun's tomb, including shabti (servant) figures, model boats, sandals, arrows and a series of gilded bronze rosettes from his funeral pall.

A ramp back down to the ground floor leaves you close to the exit and beside a black-and-gold wooden head of the cow deity Mehit-Weret, an aspect of the goddess Hathor, which was also found in Tutankhamun's tomb.

THE LONG WAY HOME

Egypt's antiquities authority found the cache of royal mummies in 1881 (see p263) but over the previous decade its original discoverers, the Abdel Rassoul family, made a tidy sum by selling its contents. Mummies, coffins, sumptuous jewellery and other artefacts made their way to Europe and North America, and many ended up in museums. One of the mummies spirited out of the country at some time languished in a small museum in Niagara Falls, Canada until the late 1990s, when the crossed arms and excellent state of the body were recognized by an Egyptologist as signs of a possible royal personage. When the museum closed in 1999, the mummy was acquired by the Michael Carlos Museum in Atlanta. Once there CT scans, X-rays, radiocarbon dating and computer imaging were used in an attempt to identify the mystery royal. Although the results were inconclusive, with some suggesting the mummy is in fact dated later than the Ramesside period, an uncanny resemblance to the mummified faces of Seti I and Ramses II was seized upon by some Egyptologists as proof that this was the missing mummy of Ramses I.

As a gesture of goodwill, the museum returned the mummy to Egypt in 2003, where he was welcomed home with songs and ceremonies. Later he was taken to Luxor where, as befitting a pharaoh in his afterlife, he made the final stage of his journey under sail.

LUXOR – EAST BANK

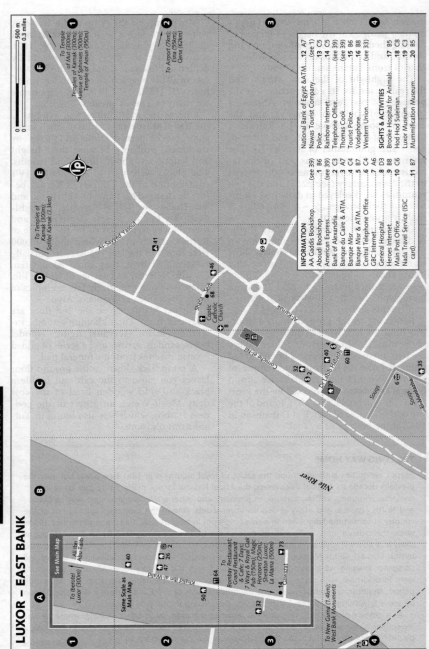

INFORMATION	
AA Gaddis Bookshop	(see 39)
Aboudi Bookshop	1 B6
American Express	(see 39)
Bank of Alexandria	2 C3
Banque du Caire & ATM	3 A7
Banque Misr	4 C4
Banque Misr & ATM	5 B7
Central Telephone Office	6 C4
GBC Internet	7 A6
General Hospital	8 D3
Heroes Internet	9 B8
Main Post Office	10 C6
Nada Travel Service (ISIC card)	11 B7
National Bank of Egypt &ATM	12 A7
Nawas Tourist Company	(see 1)
Police	13 C5
Rainbow Internet	14 C5
Telephone Office	(see 39)
Thomas Cook	15 B6
Tourist Police	16 B8
Vodaphone	(see 33)
Western Union	

SIGHTS & ACTIVITIES	
Brooke Hospital for Animals	17 B5
Hod Hod Suleiman	18 C8
Luxor Museum	19 C3
Mummification Museum	20 B5

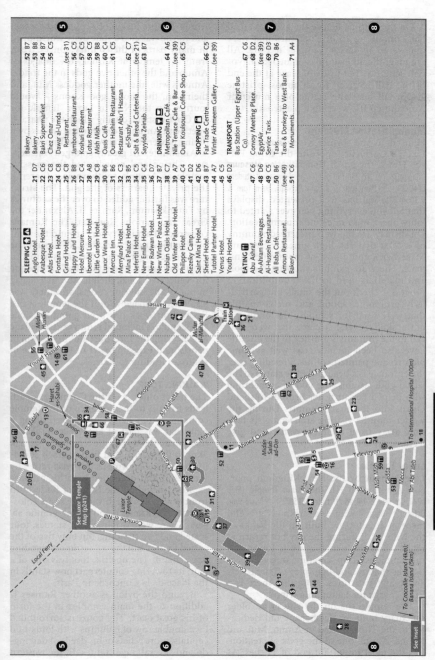

SLEEPING

Anglo Hotel	21 D7
Arabesque Hotel	22 C6
Atlas Hotel	23 C8
Fontana Hotel	24 C8
Grand Hotel	25 C8
Happy Land Hotel	26 B8
Hotel Mercure	27 C4
Iberotel Luxor Hotel	28 A8
Little Garden Hotel	29 C8
Luxor Wena Hotel	30 B6
Mercure Inn	31 B6
Merryland Hotel	32 C3
Mina Palace Hotel	33 B5
Neferiti Hotel	34 C5
New Emilio Hotel	35 C4
New Radwan Hotel	36 D7
New Winter Palace Hotel	37 B7
Nubian Oasis Hotel	38 B7
Old Winter Palace Hotel	39 A7
Philippe Hotel	40 C4
Rezeiky Camp	41 D2
Saint Mina Hotel	42 D6
Sherief Hotel	43 B7
Tutotel Partner Hotel	44 A7
Venus Hotel	45 C5
Youth Hostel	46 D2

EATING

Abu Ashraf	47 C6
Al-Ahram Beverages	48 D6
Al-Hussein Restaurant	49 C5
Ali Baba Café	50 B6
Amoun Restaurant	(see 49)
Bakery	51 C6

Bakery	52 B7
Bakery	53 B8
Bakri Supermarket	54 B7
Chez Omar	55 C5
Dawar al-Umda Restaurant	(see 31)
Jamboree Restaurant	56 C5
Koshari Elzaeem	57 C5
Lotus Restaurant	58 C5
Mish Mish	59 B8
Oasis Café	60 C4
Oum Hashim Restaurant	61 C5
Restaurant Abu'l Hassan el-Shazly	62 C7
Salt & Bread Cafeteria	(see 21)
Sayyida Zeinab	63 B7

DRINKING

Metropolitan Café	64 A6
Nile Terrace Cafe & Bar	(see 39)
Oum Koulsoum Coffee Shop	65 C5

SHOPPING

Fair Trade Centre	66 C5
Winter Akhmeen Gallery	(see 39)

TRANSPORT

Bus Station (Upper Egypt Bus Co)	67 C6
Convoy Meeting Place	68 D2
EgyptAir	(see 39)
Service Taxis	69 D3
Taxis	70 B6
Taxis & Donkeys to West Bank Monuments	71 A4

On the left just before the exit is a small hall containing 16 of 22 statues that were uncovered in Luxor Temple in 1989. All are magnificent examples of ancient Egyptian sculpture but pride of place at the end of the hall is given to an almost pristine 2.45m-tall quartzite statue of a muscular Amenhotep III, wearing a pleated kilt.

Mummification Museum

Housed in the former visitors centre on Luxor's Corniche, opposite the Mina Palace Hotel, the small **Mummification Museum** (Map pp238-9; ☎ 238 1501; Corniche el-Nil; adult/student E£40/20; ⏱ 9am-1pm & 4-9pm Oct-Apr, 9am-1pm & 5-10pm May-Sep) has well-presented displays that tell you everything you ever wanted to know about mummies and mummification. On display are the well-preserved mummy of a 21st-dynasty high priest of Amun, Maserharti, and a host of mummified animals. There are exhibits showing the tools and materials used in the mummification process – check out the small, but particularly gruesome, spoon and metal spatula that were used for scraping the brain out of the skull. Several artefacts that were crucial to the mummy's journey to the afterlife have also been included, as well as some picturesque painted coffins. Presiding over the entrance is a beautiful little statue of the jackal god, Anubis, the god of embalming who helped Isis turn her brother-husband Osiris into the first mummy. During the winter months visiting archaeologists take time away from their excavations to give lectures on Saturdays at 7pm.

Luxor Temple

Largely built by the New Kingdom pharaoh Amenhotep III, the **Luxor Temple** (Map p241; Corniche el-Nil; adult/student E£50/25; ⏱ 6am-9pm Oct-Apr, to 10pm May-Sep) is a strikingly graceful piece of architecture built on the banks of the Nile. Visit during the day but return at night when the temperature is lower and the temple is lit up, creating an eerie spectacle as shadow and light play off the reliefs and many structures. Note that there is a E£20 charge for taking in a tripod.

The temple sits on the site of an older sanctuary built by Hatshepsut and dedicated to the Theban triad of Amun, Mut and Khons. Amun, one of the gods of creation, was the most important god of Thebes. As Amun-Ra, the fusion of Amun and the sun god Ra, he was also a state deity worshipped in many parts of the country. Once a year, from his temple at Karnak, the images of Amun and the other two gods in the triad – Amun's wife, the mother goddess Mut, and their son, the moon god Khons – would journey up the Nile to Luxor Temple for the Opet Festival, during which the pharaoh 'met' with Amun in order to restore his own divine powers and reinvigorate himself.

Amenhotep III greatly enlarged Hatshepsut's shrine and rededicated the massive temple as Amun's southern *ipet* (harem), the private quarters of the god. The structure was further added to over the centuries by Tutankhamun, Ramses II, Alexander the Great and various Romans. The Romans constructed a military fort around the temple that the Arabs later called Al-Uqsur (The Palaces), giving modern Luxor its name. In the 14th century the Arabs built a mosque for venerated local sheikh Abu al-Haggag in one of the interior courts, and there was also once a village within the temple walls. Excavation work has been going on since 1885, and has included removing the village and clearing the forecourt and first pylon of debris, and exposing part of the avenue of sphinxes leading to Karnak.

WALKING TOUR

The ticket office is on the Corniche; a path leads from it to the entrance of the temple complex. From here you proceed along a path that was part of an **avenue of sphinxes** that ran all the way to the temples at Karnak 3km to the north. You find yourself standing before the enormous **first pylon** raised by Ramses II and decorated with his military exploits, including the Battle of Kadesh. In front of this 24m-high wall are some colossal **statues of Ramses II** and a pink granite **obelisk**. There were originally six statues, four seated and two standing, but only two of the seated figures and the westernmost standing one remain. The obelisk, too, was one of a pair; its towering counterpart now stands in the Place de la Concorde in Paris.

Beyond the pylon is another Ramses II addition to the main complex in the form of his **great court**. The court is surrounded by a double row of columns with lotus-bud capitals, more reliefs of his deeds of derring-do and several huge statues. In the western corner of the court is the earlier triple-barque shrine built by Hatshepsut and her successor Tuthmosis III for Amun, Mut and Khons when the gods' statues were brought from Karnak during the annual Opet Festival. On the southeastern side is the 14th-century **Mosque of Abu al-Haggag**, dedicated to a local sheikh and holy man. The mosque entrance is reached from Sharia al-Karnak, outside the temple precinct.

Beyond the court are 14 papyrus columns forming the **colonnade of Amenhotep III**. The walls behind the splendid columns were decorated during the reign of the young pharaoh Tutankhamun and celebrate the return to Theban orthodoxy following the wayward reign of the previous pharaoh,

Akhenaten. The Opet Festival is depicted in lively detail, with the pharaoh, nobility and common people joining the triumphal procession. Look out for the drummers and acrobats doing back bends.

The colonnade leads into the **court of Amenhotep III**, which is open to the sun. It was once enclosed on three sides by double rows of towering columns, the best preserved of which, with their architraves extant, are those on the eastern and western sides.

The **hypostyle hall**, on the southern side of the court, is the first inner room of the temple proper and features four rows of eight columns each. Beyond are the main rooms of the **Temple of Amun**, the central chamber of which was once stuccoed over by the

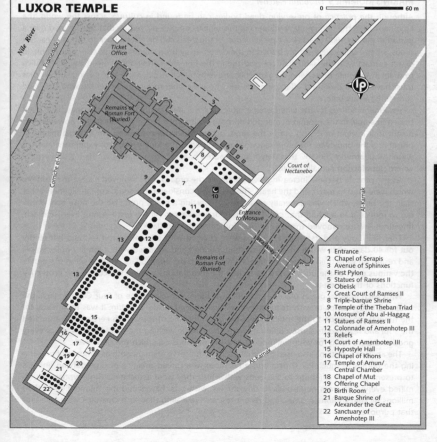

LUXOR TEMPLE

0   60 m

1 Entrance
2 Chapel of Serapis
3 Avenue of Sphinxes
4 First Pylon
5 Statues of Ramses II
6 Obelisk
7 Great Court of Ramses II
8 Triple-barque Shrine
9 Temple of the Theban Triad
10 Mosque of Abu al-Haggag
11 Statues of Ramses II
12 Colonnade of Amenhotep III
13 Reliefs
14 Court of Amenhotep III
15 Hypostyle Hall
16 Chapel of Khons
17 Temple of Amun/
   Central Chamber
18 Chapel of Mut
19 Offering Chapel
20 Birth Room
21 Barque Shrine of
   Alexander the Great
22 Sanctuary of
   Amenhotep III

NILE VALLEY: LUXOR

Romans in the 3rd century AD and used as a cult sanctuary. Through this chamber, either side of which are chapels dedicated to Mut and Khons, is an **offering chapel** with four columns.

Amenhotep III's **birth room** scenes seem to have been inspired by earlier scenes at Hatshepsut's temple. You can even see the moment of conception when the fingers of the god touch those of the queen and 'his dew filled her body', according to the accompanying hieroglyphic caption.

Alexander the Great rebuilt the **barque shrine**, beyond the offering chapel, adding to it reliefs of himself portrayed in traditional Egyptian regalia in his role as pharaoh. The **sanctuary of Amenhotep III** is the last chamber; it still has the remains of the stone base on which Amun's statue stood, and although it was once the most sacred part of the temple, the busy street that now runs directly behind it makes it less atmospheric.

Temples of Karnak

More than a temple, **Karnak** (Map p235; Sharia al-Karnak; adult/student E£60/30, tripod E£20; ⏱ 6am-5.30pm Oct-Apr, to 6pm May-Sep) is a spectacular complex of sanctuaries, kiosks, pylons and obelisks dedicated to the Theban gods and the greater glory of the pharaohs. Everything here is on a gigantic scale: the site measures about 1.5km by 800m, large enough to

---

MAKING MUMMIES Dr Joann Fletcher

Although the practice of preserving dead bodies can be found in cultures across the world, the Egyptians were the ultimate practitioners of this highly complex procedure that they refined over a period of almost 4000 years. Their preservation of the dead can be traced back to the very earliest times, when bodies were simply buried in the desert away from the limited areas of cultivation. In direct contact with the sand that covered them, the hot, dry conditions allowed the body fluids to drain away while preserving the skin, hair and nails intact. Accidentally uncovering such bodies must have had a profound effect upon those who were able to recognise people who had died sometimes years before.

As burial practices for the elite became more sophisticated, people who would once have been buried in a hole in the ground demanded purpose-built tombs befitting their status; however, this meant that instead of drying out in the sand, bodies rapidly decomposed. An artificial means of preserving the body was therefore required, and so began the long process of experimentation. It wasn't until around 2600 BC that they finally cracked it, and began to remove the internal organs where putrefaction actually begins.

As the process became increasingly elaborate, all the organs were removed except the kidneys, which were hard to reach, and the heart. The heart was considered the source of intelligence rather than the brain, which was generally removed by inserting a metal probe up the nose and whisking to reduce it to a liquid that could be easily drained away. All the rest – lungs, liver, stomach, intestines – were removed through an opening cut in the left flank.

Then the body and its separate organs were covered with piles of natron salt and left to dry out for 40 days, after which they were washed, purified and anointed with a range of oils, spices and resins. All were then wrapped in layers of linen, with the appropriate amulets set in place over the various parts of the body as priests recited the incantations needed to activate the protective functions of the amulets.

With each internal organ placed inside its own burial container (one of four Canopic jars), the wrapped body complete with its funerary mask was placed inside its coffin. It was then ready for the funeral procession to the tomb, where the vital Opening of the Mouth ceremony reanimated the soul and restored its senses; offerings were given, while wishing the dead 'a thousand of every good and pure thing for your soul and all kinds of offerings on which the gods live'.

The ancient Egyptians also used mummification to preserve animals, both as a means of preserving the bodies of much-loved pets and a far more widespread practice of mummifying animals to present as votive offerings to the gods with which they were associated. The Egyptians mummified everything from huge bulls to tiny shrews, with cats, hawks and ibis mummified in their millions by Graeco-Roman times, and recent research revealing that such creatures were killed for that purpose.

contain about 10 cathedrals, while the first pylon is twice the size of the one at Luxor Temple. The Amun Temple Enclosure alone measures some 260,000 sq metres. During the reign of Ramses III, 80,000 people worked in or for the temple, giving us an idea of its economic, as well as spiritual, significance. Built, added to, dismantled, restored, enlarged and decorated over nearly 1500 years, Karnak was the most important place of worship in Egypt during the height of Theban power and was called Ipet-Isut, meaning 'The Most Perfect of Places'.

Trying to describe this immense monument has vexed travellers for centuries. As Amelia Edwards, the 19th-century writer and artist who journeyed up the Nile, succinctly put it:

> It is a place that has been much written about and often painted; but of which no writing and no art can convey more than a dwarfed and pallid impression … The scale is too vast; the effect too tremendous; the sense of one's own dumbness, and littleness, and incapacity, too complete and crushing.

At the centre of this remarkable place is the enormous **Amun Temple Enclosure** (Map pp244–5), sometimes referred to as the Precinct of Amun, and dominated by the great Temple of Amun and containing a large sacred lake. This was the main place of worship of the Theban triad (Amun, Mut and Khons), and contains the famous hypostyle hall, a spectacular forest of giant papyrus-shaped columns.

Flanking the Amun Temple Enclosure on the southern side is the Mut Temple Enclosure, which was once linked to the main temple by an avenue of ram-headed sphinxes. To the north is the Montu Temple Enclosure, which honoured the local Theban war god. A paved avenue of human-headed sphinxes from Euergetes' Gate on the southern side of the Mut Temple Enclosure once linked Karnak with Luxor Temple. Only a small section of this sacred way, where it leaves the great Temple of Amun and enters the forecourt of his southern *ipet*, has been excavated. The rest of the 3km avenue lies beneath the town and roads of modern Luxor – bits of it are visible in places among the buildings.

Although the original sanctuary of the great Temple of Amun was built during the Middle Kingdom period, when the Theban pharaohs first came to prominence, the rest of the temples, pylons, courts, columns and reliefs were the work of New Kingdom rulers and their successors. The further into the complex you venture the further back in time you go.

The oldest parts of the complex are the White Chapel of Senusret (Sesostris I, 1965–1920 BC) and the 12th-dynasty foundations of what became the most sacred part of the great Temple of Amun, the sacred barque sanctuary and central court of Amun (behind the sixth pylon). The limestone fragments of the demolished pavilion, or chapel, were recovered from the foundations of the third pylon, built five centuries after Sesostris' reign, and expertly reconstructed in the open-air museum to the north of the great court.

The major additions to the complex were constructed by pharaohs of the 18th to 20th dynasties, between 1570 and 1090 BC. The pharaohs of the later dynasties extended and rebuilt the complex, and the Ptolemies and early Christians also left their mark on it.

Wandering through this gigantic complex is one of the highlights of any visit to Egypt and more than one visit helps you make sense of the sometimes overwhelming jumble of ancient remains. As almost every pharaoh left his or her mark here, you can get a crash course in the evolution of ancient Egyptian artistic and architectural styles.

AMUN TEMPLE ENCLOSURE – MAIN AXIS

From the entrance you pass down the processional **avenue of ram-headed sphinxes** (Map pp244–5) that originally flanked a canal connecting the temple to the Nile; this opened out into a rectangular dock that now lies beneath the present-day wooden entrance bridge. These lead to the massive unfinished **first pylon**, most likely built by Nectanebo I of the 30th dynasty. You used to be able to climb the stairs on your left to the top of the pylon's north tower, from where there is an amazing view of Karnak and the surrounding country but the stairs were closed off after a tourist fell from it and died. Anyway, as the pylon is home to hundreds of bats, it is not an inviting place.

Great Court

You emerge from the first pylon into the Great Court (Map pp244–5), the largest area of the Karnak complex. To the left is the **Temple of Seti II**, dedicated to the Theban triad. The three small chapels held the sacred barques of Mut, Amun and Khons during the lead up to the Opet Festival.

The north and south walls of the court are lined with columns with papyrus-bud capitals. The south wall is intersected by **Temple of Ramses III**, a glorified trio of barque shrines or chapels for the Theban triad built in the form of a miniature temple. Obligatory scenes of the pharaoh as glorious conqueror adorn the pylon of this 60m-long temple

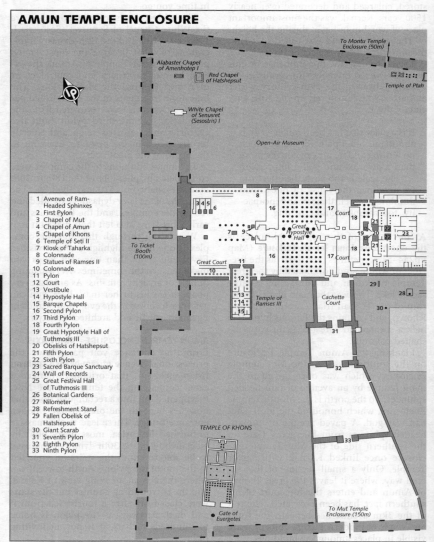

AMUN TEMPLE ENCLOSURE

To Montu Temple Enclosure (50m)

Alabaster Chapel of Amenhotep I

Red Chapel of Hatshepsut

Temple of Ptah

White Chapel of Senusret (Sesostris) I

Open-Air Museum

1 Avenue of Ram-Headed Sphinxes
2 First Pylon
3 Chapel of Mut
4 Chapel of Amun
5 Chapel of Khons
6 Temple of Seti II
7 Kiosk of Taharka
8 Colonnade
9 Statues of Ramses II
10 Colonnade
11 Pylon
12 Court
13 Vestibule
14 Hypostyle Hall
15 Barque Chapels
16 Second Pylon
17 Third Pylon
18 Fourth Pylon
19 Great Hypostyle Hall of Tuthmosis III
20 Obelisks of Hatshepsut
21 Fifth Pylon
22 Sixth Pylon
23 Sacred Barque Sanctuary
24 Wall of Records
25 Great Festival Hall of Tuthmosis III
26 Botanical Gardens
27 Nilometer
28 Refreshment Stand
29 Fallen Obelisk of Hatshepsut
30 Giant Scarab
31 Seventh Pylon
32 Eighth Pylon
33 Ninth Pylon

To Ticket Booth (100m)

Great Court

Great Hypostyle Hall

Court

Court

Temple of Ramses III

Cachette Court

TEMPLE OF KHONS

Gate of Euergetes

To Mut Temple Enclosure (150m)

that also features an open court, a vestibule with four columns, a hypostyle hall of eight columns and three barque chapels.

In the centre of the Great Court was the **Kiosk of Taharka**. A 25th-dynasty Nubian pharaoh, Taharka built this open-sided pavilion of 10 columns, each rising 21m and topped with papyrus-form capitals. Only

one of the columns remains, together with an alabaster altar.

The **second pylon** was originally built by Horemheb, an 18th-dynasty general who later became the last pharaoh of his dynasty. Ramses I and II added their names and deeds to the pylon above that of Horemheb. Ramses II also raised two colossal pink granite statues of himself on either side of the entrance.

Great Hypostyle Hall

Beyond the second pylon is the awesome great hypostyle hall (Map pp244–5). It was planned by Amenhotep III and built by Seti I, who decorated the northern half in delicate raised relief. Ramses II added the rest of the (sunken) relief work. Covering 6000 sq metres – area enough to contain both Rome's St Peter's and London's St Paul's Cathedral, the hall is an unforgettable forest of 134 towering papyrus-shaped stone pillars. Originally, the whole would have been brightly painted and roofed, making it pretty dark. It is impossible to get an overall idea of this court; there is nothing to do but stand and stare up at the dizzying spectacle.

Between the **third pylon**, built by Amenhotep III, and the **fourth pylon**, raised by Tuthmosis I, is a narrow court. Tuthmosis I raised a pair of obelisks in front of the fourth pylon, which was the entrance to the temple proper during his reign. Only one is still standing.

Inner Temple

Beyond the fourth pylon is the oldest preserved part of the complex, its 14 columns suggesting it was originally a small hypostyle hall (Map pp244–5). It was constructed by Tuthmosis III in his attempt to eradicate or hide all signs of the reign of Hatshepsut, who was appointed regent when Tuthmosis III's father died (Tuthmosis III was too young to rule at that stage), and who later had herself appointed as pharaoh. In this hall, around the two magnificent **obelisks of Hatshepsut**, Tuthmosis III built a 25m-high sandstone structure. The upper shaft of one of the obelisks, which Hatshepsut raised to the glory of her 'father' Amun, lies on the ground by the sacred lake (p246); the other obelisk still stands, reclaimed from the sandstone, in front of the fifth pylon. It is the tallest obelisk in Egypt, standing 29.2m high; the tip was originally covered in electrum (a commonly used alloy of gold and silver).

NILE VALLEY: LUXOR

The **fifth pylon** was constructed by Tuthmosis I, with little space between it and the now ruined **sixth pylon** (built at a later date). The latter, the smallest pylon at Karnak, was raised by Tuthmosis III, who is also responsible for the two pink granite columns in the vestibule beyond, on which the emblems of Egypt are carved in high relief – the water lily (lotus) of Upper Egypt on the north pillar and the papyrus of Lower Egypt on the south. Nearby are two huge statues of Amun and his female counterpart Amunet, which date from the reign of Tutankhamun.

The original **sacred barque sanctuary** of Tuthmosis III was replaced by a granite one, built by Alexander the Great (332–323 BC); its well-preserved painted relief scenes were undertaken by his successor and half-brother Philip Arrhidaeus (323–317 BC).

Tuthmosis III's reputation as a great hero and empire builder is set in stone in the relief work on what is known as the **Wall of Records** on the northern side of the central court. Though unrelenting in his bid for power, he had a penchant for being fair in his treatment of the people he conquered. This wall was a running tally of the organised tribute he exacted in honour of Amun from his subjugated lands.

Great Festival Hall of Tuthmosis III

This is an unusual structure (Map pp244–5) with its uniquely carved stone columns imitating tent poles, perhaps a reference to the pharaoh's life under canvas on his frequent military expeditions abroad. The columned vestibule that lies beyond, generally referred to as the **Botanical Gardens**, has relief scenes of strange flora and fauna that 'his majesty encountered in the lands of Syria and Palestine' and brought back to Egypt.

For the many people not allowed inside the temple's sacred enclosure, Tuthmosis III built a small chapel onto the back of the temple wall behind his festival hall, at either side of which can be seen the enormous bases for two of Hatshepsut's obelisks that once stood here. Beyond this, further to the southeast, Ramses II built a similar chapel, the **Temple of the Hearing Ear**, again with a base for a single obelisk standing 32.2m tall and which Ramses usurped from Tuthmosis III. Removed from Karnak on the orders of the Emperor Constantine (AD 306–337) and bound for Constantinople,

the obelisk was redirected to Rome to stand in the Circus Maximus; it was re-erected in 1588 on the orders of Pope Sixtus V where it now stands, in front of the church of St John (Giovanni) Lateran.

Against the northern enclosure wall of the Amun Temple Enclosure is the well-preserved cult **Temple of Ptah**, started by Tuthmosis III and finished by the Ptolemies and Romans. Access to the inner chambers is through a series of five doorways, which lead to two of the temple's original statues. The headless figure of Ptah, the creator god of Memphis, is in the middle chapel behind a locked door – the custodian will unlock it for the usual remittance. To his left is the eerily beautiful black granite statue of his goddess-wife Sekhmet (the spreader of terror), bare-breasted and lioness-headed.

AMUN TEMPLE ENCLOSURE – SOUTHERN AXIS

The secondary axis of the Amun Temple Enclosure (Map pp244–5) runs south from the third and fourth pylons. It is basically a processional way, bounded on the eastern and western sides by walls, and sectioned off by a number of pylons that create a series of courts. Just before the **seventh pylon**, built by Tuthmosis III, is the **cachette court**, so named because of the hundreds of stone and thousands of bronze statues discovered there during excavation work in 1903. Although most of the statues were sent to the Egyptian Museum in Cairo, seven of the statues of pharaohs from this cachette stand in front of the pylon. Nearby are the remains of two colossal statues of Tuthmosis III.

The well-preserved **eighth pylon**, built by Queen Hatshepsut, is the oldest part of the north–south axis of the temple. Four of the original six colossi are still standing, the most complete being the one of Amenhotep I.

The **ninth** and **10th pylons** were built by Horemheb, who used some of the stones of a demolished temple that had been built to the east by Akhenaten (before he decamped to Tell al-Amarna), some of which are now displayed in Luxor Museum (p236).

East of the seventh and eighth pylons is the **sacred lake** (Map pp244–5), where, according to Herodotus, the priests of Amun bathed twice daily and nightly for ritual purity. On the northwestern side of the lake is the top half of **Hatshepsut's fallen obelisk** and a huge **stone statue of a scarab beetle** dedicated by Amenhotep III to Khepri, god of the rising sun and an aspect of the Aten sun disc.

There are the ruins of about 20 other chapels within the main enclosure. In a fairly good state of repair in the southwestern corner is the **Temple of Khons**, god of the moon, and son of Amun and Mut. The pylon faces Euergetes's Gate and the avenue of sphinxes leading to Luxor Temple, and provides access to a small hypostyle hall and ruined sanctuary. The temple was started by Ramses III, and added to by other Ramessids and later the Ptolemies.

MUT TEMPLE ENCLOSURE

From the 10th pylon an avenue of sphinxes leads to the partly excavated southern enclosure – the Precinct of Mut (Map p235). The badly ruined Temple of Mut was built by Amenhotep III and consists of a sanctuary, a hypostyle hall and two courts. Amenhotep also set up an enormous number of black granite statues of the lioness goddess Sekhmet, Mut's northern counterpart. There were more than 700 of these statues and it has been suggested that they formed some sort of calendar, with two for every day of the year, receiving offerings each morning and evening.

MONTU TEMPLE ENCLOSURE

A gate, usually locked, on the wall near the Temple of Ptah (in the Amun Temple Enclosure) leads to the Montu Temple Enclosure. Montu, the falcon-headed warrior god, was one of the original deities of Thebes. The main temple was built by Amenhotep III and modified by others. The complex is very dilapidated.

OPEN-AIR MUSEUM

Off to the left of the first court, set among three chapels, is Karnak's **open-air museum** (Map pp244-5; tickets at main ticket office; adult/student E£20/10; ⏱ 6am-5.30pm). The well-preserved chapels include the **White Chapel of Senusret** (sometimes called Sesostris), one of the oldest monuments in Karnak, which has beautiful Middle Kingdom reliefs; the **Red Chapel of Hatshepsut**, with red quartzite blocks that were reassembled in 2000; and the **Alabaster Chapel of Amenhotep I**. The museum also contains a collection of the statuary found throughout the temple complex.

SOUND-&-LIGHT SHOW

Karnak's highly kitsch **sound-and-light show** (Map pp244-5; ☎ 237 2241; www.sound-light.egypt.com; adult/student E£55/44, video E£35 ⏱ 6.30pm, 7.45pm, 9pm & 10.15pm winter, 8pm, 9.15pm, 10.30pm & 11.45pm summer) is a 1½-hour, Hollywood-style extravaganza that recounts the history of Thebes and the lives of the many pharaohs who built here in honour of Amun. The overly dramatic text and booming music are only made bearable by the specially lit night-time walk through the temple.

The following schedule was correct at the time of writing but check before heading there.

Day	Show 1	Show 2	Show 3	Show 4
Monday	English	French	Spanish	-
Tuesday	Japanese	English	French	-
Wednesday	German	English	French	-
Thursday	English	French	Arabic	-
Friday	English	French	Spanish	-
Saturday	French	English	Italian	-
Sunday	German	English	Italian	French

SIGHTS – WEST BANK

Leaving behind the din and hassle of Luxor and heading away from the Nile towards the desert, you meet with one of the most striking vistas in Egypt. As you pass through the lush green fields, desert mountains dotted with brightly coloured houses loom ahead. Drawing closer you begin to make out gaping black holes among the houses and giant sandstone forms on the edge of the cultivation below. These are the tombs and temples of the necropolis of ancient Thebes, where magnificent monuments were raised to honour the cults of pharaohs and where queens, royal children, nobles, priests, artisans and even workers built tombs that ranged in the quality of their design and décor from the spectacular to the ordinary.

From the New Kingdom onwards, the necropolis also supported a large living population. In an attempt to protect the valuable tombs from robbers, the artisans, labourers, temple priests and guards devoted their lives to the construction and maintenance of this city of the dead. They perfected the techniques of tomb building, decoration and concealment, and passed the secrets down through their families.

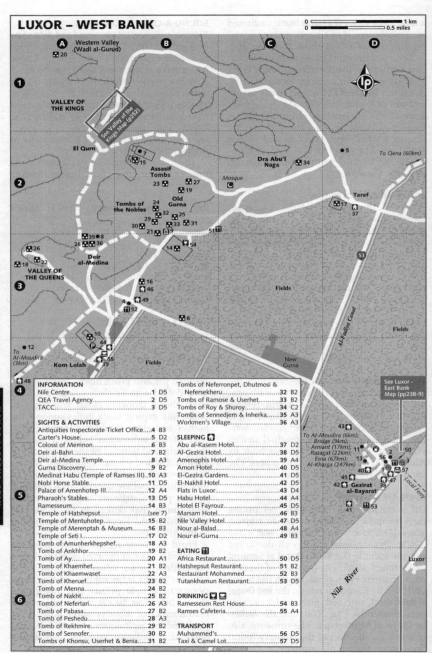

LUXOR – WEST BANK

0 — 1 km
0 — 0.5 miles

TACKLING THE WEST BANK

Because of the heat and desolate mountain landscape around most of the archaeological remains on the West Bank, a series of early morning visits – ideally between sunrise and 1pm – is the best way to see its many sites. Unfortunately, everybody else has the same idea. Still, you'll have your afternoons free to loll beside a pool or have a siesta and you can visit Luxor and Karnak temples, or one of the museums, in the evening. This is our advice for getting the most out of your time on the West Bank:

Keep tomb viewing time to a minimum: most tombs are small and claustrophobic, and your breath helps destroy their ancient pigments. Twenty minutes is ample time for most.

Don't push yourself: no matter how limited your time, cramming in too much will leave you unable to distinguish a sarcophagus from a scarab.

Take breaks: sipping a cold drink beside a temple can be as sublime an experience as seeing your first tomb. Medinat Habu is the choice locale.

With all this in mind, here are some itineraries for those with limited time. The one- and two-day plans need a brisk pace and assume you have some sort of a vehicle.

One day Go via the Colossi of Memnon on the way to the Valley of the Kings. See some tombs, then spend an hour at Deir al-Bahri and an hour at Medinat Habu. If you have energy left, allow an hour to see two tombs at either the Valley of the Queens or the Tombs of the Nobles.

Two days The above at a slower pace, adding the temple of Merneptah and its fascinating museum, and another set of tombs.

Three days Spread out the previous offerings; take the mountain path from the Valley of the Kings to Deir al-Bahri; check out the Ramesseum.

Four days or more Take things at a leisurely pace; add the tombs at Deir al-Medina. See some of the other Tombs of the Nobles. While there, pop in to Gurna Discovery to see the area's modern history. Revisit the Valley of the Kings. Take a sunset horse or camel ride. Drink tea with villagers.

Magnificent funerary temples were built on the plains, where the illusion of the pharaoh's immortality could be perpetuated by the devotions of his priests and subjects, while the pharaoh's body and worldly wealth were laid in splendidly decorated secret tombs excavated in the hills.

Nowadays, ancient and modern coexist on the West Bank of Luxor. Until a generation ago, villagers used tombs to shelter from the extremes of the desert climate. Some even derived their livelihood from trafficking the ancient artefacts that they found there. Today their houses are built among the tomb entrances, and their income still depends on their Pharaonic ancestor – but now from the legal trade in trinkets, alabaster and tour-guiding.

Information
WHAT TO BRING
You need to bring a torch (flashlight) and, more importantly, plenty of water, though it is available at many of the sites. Also bring plenty of small change for baksheesh.

Tomb and temple guards rely on tips to augment their pathetic salaries. E£2 will be enough for them to either leave you in peace, or to open a door or reflect light on a particularly beautiful painting.

TICKETS
Tickets for most monuments are only available from the **Antiquities Inspectorate ticket office** (Map p248; 3km inland from ferry landing; ⏰ 6am-4pm, to 5pm Jun-Sep). The exceptions are Deir el-Bahri, the Assassif tombs, the tombs of the Valley of the Kings and the Valley of the Queens. All sites are officially open from 7am to 5pm October to May (though you can often get in from 6am) and from 6am to 7pm June to September. The exception is the Tomb of Nefertari which, when open to the public, has its own hours (see p267).

Photography is not permitted in any tombs and guards may confiscate film or memory cards.

Tickets are valid only for the day of purchase and no refunds are given. They are priced (adult/student) as follows:

Assasif Tombs (Kheruef & Ankhor) E£20/10
Assasif Tombs (Pabasa) E£20/10
Deir al-Medina Temple & Tombs (except Peshedu) E£20/10
Medinat Habu (Temple of Ramses III) E£30/15
Ramesseum E£30/15
Temple of Merneptah E£20/10
Temple of Seti I E£30/15
Tomb of Ay (Western Valley) E£20/10
Tomb of Peshedu (Deir al-Medina) E£10/5
Tombs of the Nobles (Neferronpet, Dhutmosi & Nefersekheru) E£20/10
Tombs of the Nobles (Khonsu, Userhet & Benia) E£12/6
Tombs of the Nobles (Menna & Nakht) E£20/10
Tombs of the Nobles (Ramose, Userhet & Khaemhet) E£20/10
Tombs of the Nobles (Sennofer & Rekhmire) E£20/10
Dra Abu'l Naga (Roy & Shuroy) E£20/10

Colossi of Memnon

The massive pair of statues known as the Colossi of Memnon (Map p248) are the first monuments that tourists see when they arrive on the West Bank. Rising about 18m from the plain, the enthroned, faceless statues have kept a lonely vigil on the changing landscape, and are the remains of what was once the largest complex on the West Bank. It was built by Amenhotep III as his funerary temple, and some experts have recently discovered that it covered a larger area than Karnak. It was also filled with hundreds of statues (including the huge dyad of Amenhotep III and Tiy that now dominates the central court of the Egyptian Museum in Cairo), most of which were later dragged off by other pharaohs. A stele, also now in the Egyptian Museum, describes the temple as being built from 'white sandstone, with gold throughout, a floor covered with silver, and doors covered with electrum'. Other statues and fragments of wall reliefs can be seen at the nearby Temple of Merneptah.

The reason for the temple's complete disappearance is that it sat on the flood plain of the Nile and the annual inundation of water that used to occur has eroded away almost all traces of the building over the centuries.

Though smaller parts of the temple remain and more is being uncovered by excavation, the colossi are the only large-scale elements to have survived. They were among the great tourist attractions of Egypt during Graeco-Roman times because the Greeks believed they were actually statues of the

legendary Memnon, a king of Ethiopia and son of the dawn goddess Eos, who was slain by Achilles during the Trojan War.

The northern statue attracted the most attention because each sunrise it would emit a haunting, musical sound the Greeks believed was the voice of Memnon greeting his mother. Eos in turn would weep tears of dew for the untimely death of her beautiful son.

The strange phenomenon of the famous vocal statue was probably produced by the combined effect of a simple change in temperature and the fact that the upper part of the colossus was severely damaged by an earthquake in 27 BC. As the heat of the morning sun baked the dew-soaked stone, sand particles would break off and resonate inside the cracks in the structure. After Septimus Severus (193–211 AD) repaired the statue in the 3rd century AD, Memnon's plaintive greeting was heard no more.

The colossi are just off the road, before you reach the Antiquities Inspectorate ticket office, and are usually being snapped and filmed by an army of tourists. There is a new archaeological project at the site, intended to open up what remains behind the colossi.

Temple of Merneptah

Just beside the Marsam Hotel, between the ticket office and the Ramesseum, lies the remains of the **Temple of Merneptah** (Map p248; adult/student E£20/10). Merneptah was one of Ramses II's sons. He succeeded his father in 1213 BC and ruled for 10 years. Little remains of the temple itself, although an important stele was found here in the 19th century. Called the 'Israel Stele' it is the first Egyptian text to mention the Israelites (which Merneptah claimed to have defeated). It now sits in the Egyptian Museum in Cairo.

The Swiss Institute in Egypt's exhaustive research here uncovered the temple's original structure and unearthed a number of statues. A fascinating history of the site and its excavation can be found in the small **museum** beside the entrance. As well as clear diagrams and explanations of the temple plan, the museum contains a number of statues and fragments of coloured wall decoration. Heading here first will help make sense of the temple itself, of which little remains beyond the foundations. Grouped together in a covered storage area at the temple's western edge are statues recovered from the site, including parts of 12 jackal-headed sphinxes, some of which retain their original colours. Merneptah pilfered these, and many other statues and large stone blocks, from the nearby Temple of Amenhotep III. He even usurped statues of the earlier pharaoh, scratching out the latter's cartouche and replacing it with his own. Remains of the reliefs of Merneptah with various gods that once stood atop the temple pylons are kept in covered rooms in the centre of the temple (ask the caretaker to unlock them). Diagrams show how they would have fitted together and give an idea of their impressive scale.

Temple of Seti I

Seti I (1294–1279 BC), the second pharaoh of the 19th dynasty, continued his predecessor Horemheb's policies to restore Egypt's fortunes following the Amarna Period. His military campaigns re-established control abroad and won back much of the empire, and he undertook an ambitious building programme at home, creating a superbly

decorated temple at Abydos and building Karnak's hypostyle hall at Thebes. He constructed a huge rock-cut tomb for himself in the Valley of the Kings, as well as this associated funerary **temple** (Map p248), but unfortunately died before the latter was finished. It was completed by his son Ramses II.

Surrounded by a reconstructed fortresslike enclosure wall, the temple unfortunately has not stood the test of time, largely because it was used as a quarry by locals until the 18th century. But although the first two pylons and courts are in ruins the ninecolumned portico is well preserved. Its walls, and those of the hypostyle court beyond it, contain some superbly executed reliefs that are among the finest examples of New Kingdom art. Off the hypostyle are six shrines and to the south is a small chapel dedicated to Seti's father, Ramses I, who died before he could build his own mortuary temple.

Carter's House

Surrounded by a lush garden on what is otherwise a barren hill, where the road from Deir al-Bahri to the Valley of the Kings meets the road from Seti's temple, stands the domed house where Howard Carter lived during his search for Tutankhamun's tomb. There are discussions about turning it into a West Bank conservation centre. In the meantime it languishes.

Valley of the Kings

Once called the Great Place or the Place of Truth, the canyon now known as the **Valley of the Kings** (Map p252; adult/student for three tombs E£70/35) is a place of death, where nothing grows on its scorching cliffs. It is a majestic domain of the pharaohs who once lay there in great sarcophagi, awaiting immortality. The isolated valley, behind Deir al-Bahri, is dominated by the pyramid-shaped mountain peak of Al-Qurn (The Horn). It consists of the east and west valleys; the former contains most of the royal burial sites.

It seems the ancient Egyptians chose the remote ravine as the final resting place for their royalty for both symbolic and practical reasons. Thebes had been the site of royal burials as far back as the First Intermediate Period (2181–2055 BC), when at least three 11th-dynasty rulers built their tombs near the modern village of Taref, northeast of what was to become the Theban necropolis.

NILE VALLEY: LUXOR

But it was not until the 18th dynasty that the valley behind the symbolic pyramid of Al-Qurn was chosen for royal burials. The site was isolated, relatively easy to guard and, when seen from the Theban plain, appears to be the site of the setting sun, associated with the afterlife by ancient Egyptians. Egyptologists are still unsure which pharaoh was first buried here. Although many still consider Tuthmosis I (c 1504–1492 BC) the most likely candidate, recent re-examination of the uninscribed and undecorated tomb KV 39, the highest tomb in the valley, suggests Amenhotep I may have been buried here first, in 1504 BC. As this pharaoh also established the village of Deir el-Medina where those who built the Valley's tombs lived, this would certainly make sense.

In all, some 62 tombs have been excavated in the valley, although not all belong to pharaohs. Not all the tombs are open to the public and there are always several that are closed for renovation. At the time of writing the following were open: Ramses I, Ramses IV, Ramses VII, Ramses IX, Merneptah, Tawosret/Sethnakt, Seti II, Tuthmosis III, Tuthmosis IV and Montuhirkhopshef, but check with the ticket office for the latest list. Each tomb has a number that represents the order in which it was discovered. KV (short for Kings Valley) 1 belongs to Ramses VII; it has been open since Greek and Roman times, and was mentioned in the *Description de l'Egypte,* dating from the late 18th century. KV 62 – Tutankhamun's famous tomb, which was discovered by Howard Carter in 1922 – remains the most recent discovery.

Newly erected signs and maps make navigating the site far easier than before. Tomb plans and history have also been upgraded to help visitors better understand what they're seeing. More changes are afoot in the valley: Dr Kent Weeks and his Theban Mapping Project are developing a site management plan to improve the experience of visitors and improve protection of the tombs themselves. It's worth having your own torch to illuminate badly lit areas.

The road into the Valley of the Kings is a gradual, dry, hot climb, so be prepared if you are riding a bicycle. There is usually a rest house before the entrance to the valley where you can buy mineral water, soft drinks and meals but at the time of writing this was being moved and was closed. There is a

tuf-tuf – a noisy tractor dressed up to look like a train – which ferries visitors between the entrance and the tombs (it can be hot during summer). The ride costs E£1.

Most of the tombs described here are usually open to visitors and are listed in the order that they are found when entering the site. If you want to avoid the inevitable crowds that tour buses bring to the tombs, head for those outside the entrance area.

The Tomb of Tutankhamun (KV 62) has been deemed worth a ticket on its own (adult/student E£100/50) and this can be bought at a second ticket office where the *tuf-tuf* arrives. The tomb of Ay (KV 23) also has its own ticket (E£20/10), available from the main ticket office.

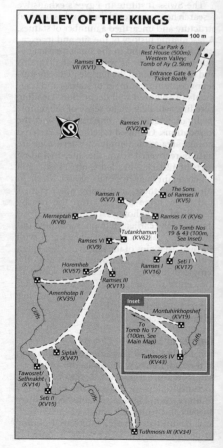

VALLEY OF THE KINGS

0   100 m

To Car Park & Rest House (500m); Western Valley; Tomb of Ay (2.5km)

Entrance Gate & Ticket Booth

Ramses VII (KV1)

Ramses IV (KV2)

Ramses II (KV7)

The Sons of Ramses II (KV5)

Merneptah (KV8)

Ramses IX (KV6)

Tutankhamun (KV62)

To Tomb Nos 19 & 43 (100m, See Inset)

Ramses VI (KV9)

Ramses I (KV16)

Seti I (KV17)

Horemheb (KV57)

Ramses III (KV11)

Amenhotep II (KV35)

Cliffs

Inset

Montuhirkhopshef (KV19)

To Tomb No 17 (100m, See Main Map)

Tuthmosis IV (KV43)

Cliffs

Siptah (KV47)

Tawosret/ Sethnakht (KV14)

Seti II (KV15)

Cliffs

Tuthmosis III (KV34)

TOMB OF RAMSES VII (KV 1)

Up a small wadi near the main entrance is the small, unfinished tomb of Ramses VII (1136–1129 BC; Map p252). Only 44.3 metres long, it consists of a corridor, a burial chamber and an unfinished third chamber. Its truncated length is the result of Ramses' sudden death in the seventh year of his reign. His architects hastily widened what was to have been the tomb's second corridor, making it a burial chamber, and the pharaoh was laid to rest in a pit covered with a sarcophagus lid. Niches for Canopic jars are carved into the pit's sides, a feature unique to this tomb. Walls on the corridor leading to the chamber

---

TOMB BUILDING   *Dr Joann Fletcher*

Tombs were initially created to differentiate the burials of the elite from the majority of people whose bodies continued to be placed directly into the desert. By about 3100 BC the mound of sand heaped over these elite graves was replaced by a more permanent structure of mud brick, whose characteristic bench shape is known as a 'mastaba' after the Arabic word for bench.

As stone replaced mud-brick, the addition of further levels to increase height gave birth to the pyramid, whose first incarnation at Saqqara is also the world's oldest monumental structure. Its stepped sides soon evolved into the more familiar smooth-sided structure, of which the Pyramids of Giza are the most famous examples.

It was only when the power of the monarchy broke down at the end of the Old Kingdom that the afterlife became increasingly accessible to those outside the royal family, and as officials became increasingly independent they began to opt for burial in their home towns. Yet the narrow stretches of fertile land make up much of the Nile Valley generally left little room for grand superstructures, so an alternative type of tomb developed, cut tunnel-fashion into the cliffs that border the valley and which also proved more resilient against robbery. Most were also built on the west side of the river, the traditional place of burial where the sun was seen to sink down into the underworld each evening.

These simple rock-cut tombs consisting of a single chamber gradually developed into more elaborate structures complete with an open courtyard, offering chapel, and entrance façade carved out of the rock with a shaft leading down into an undecorated burial chamber.

The most impressive rock-cut tombs were those built for the pharaohs of the New Kingdom (1550–1069 BC), who relocated the royal burial ground south to the remote desert valley now known as the Valley of the Kings. New evidence suggests that the first tomb in the valley may have been built for Amenhotep I (KV 39). The tomb intended for his successor, Tuthmosis I (KV 20), demonstrated a radical departure from tradition: the offering chapel that was once part of the tomb's layout was built as a separate structure some distance away in an attempt to preserve the tomb's secret location. The tombs themselves were designed to resemble the underworld, with a long, inclined rock-hewn corridor descending into either an antechamber or a series of sometimes pillared halls, and ending in the burial chamber.

The tomb builders lived in their own village of Deir al-Medina and worked in relays. The ancient week was 10 days (eight days on, two days off) and the men tended to spend the nights of their working week at a small camp located on the pass leading from Deir al-Medina to the eastern part of the Valley of the Kings. Then they spent their two days off at home with their families.

Once the tomb walls were created, decoration could then be added; this dealt almost exclusively with the afterlife and the pharaoh's existence in it. Many of the colourful paintings and reliefs are extracts from ancient theological compositions, now known as 'books', and were incorporated in the tomb to assist the deceased into the next life. Texts were taken from the Book of the Dead, the collective modern name for a range of works, all of which deal with the sun god's nightly journey through the darkness of the underworld, the realm of Osiris and home of the dead.

The Egyptians believed that the underworld was traversed each night by Ra, and it was the aim of the dead to secure passage on his sacred barque to travel with him for eternity. Since knowledge was power in the Egyptian afterlife, the texts give 'Knowledge of the power of those in the underworld and knowledge of their actions, knowing the sacred rituals of Ra, knowing the hours and the gods and the gates and paths where the great god passes'.

are decorated with fairly well preserved excerpts from the Book of the Caverns and the Opening of the Mouth ritual, while the burial chamber is decorated with passages from the Book of the Earth. Although it has only recently reopened to the public, the Greek, demotic, Coptic and 19th-century graffiti show that it has been open since antiquity – at one stage it was even inhabited by Coptic hermits.

TOMB OF RAMSES IV (KV 2)

This is the second tomb (Map p252) on the right as you enter the Valley of the Kings. Its whereabouts were already known by Ptolemaic times, as is evident from the graffiti on the walls dating back to 278 BC. Ramses IV (1153–1147 BC) died before the tomb was completed and its pillared hall had to be hastily turned into a burial chamber. While it's not one of the finest tombs – many of the paintings in the burial chamber have deteriorated – it has a striking painting of the goddess Nut, stretched across the blue ceiling, and is the only tomb in the valley to contain the text of the Book of Nut. The red granite sarcophagus, though empty, is one of the largest in the valley. The discovery of an ancient plan of the tomb on papyrus (now in the Turin Museum) shows the sarcophagus was originally enclosed by four large shrines similar to those in Tutankhamun's tomb (opposite). Following the robbery of the tomb in antiquity, the mummy of Ramses IV was one of those reburied in the Tomb of Amenhotep II (KV 35), and is now in the Egyptian Museum in Cairo.

TOMB OF RAMSES IX (KV 6)

Opposite Ramses II, the Tomb of Ramses IX (1126–1108 BC; Map p252) has the widest entrance of any royal tomb in the valley and consists of a long sloping corridor, a large antechamber decorated with animals, serpents and demons – most taken from the Book of the Dead – then a pillared hall and short hallway before the burial chamber. Just before the staircase down to the burial chamber are the cartouche symbols of Ramses IX; flanking the doorway of this room are two striking figures of Iunmutef, representing a funerary priest and dressed in priestly panther-skin robes with his hair set in a ceremonial sidelock. The walls of the burial chamber feature the Book of Amduat, the Book of

Caverns and the Book of the Earth; the Book of the Heavens is represented on the ceiling. Although unfinished it was the last tomb in the valley to have so much of its decoration completed. Archaeologists believe that plastering and painting were incomplete when Ramses IX died and that much of the decoration was hastily completed. Nonetheless, its accessibility and reasonably well-preserved painting make it the most visited tomb in the valley. This tomb, which has stood open since antiquity, was thoroughly ransacked in ancient times. A number of wooden statues of the pharaoh and the gods were salvaged and taken to the British Museum in the 19th century, although the pharaoh's mummy had already been removed in antiquity and reburied as part of the Deir al-Bahri cache.

TOMB OF RAMSES II (KV 7)

As befits the burial place of one of Egypt's longest reigning pharaohs (67 years, from 1279 to 1213 BC), KV 7 (Map p252) is one of the biggest tombs in the valley. However, the location of its entrance at a low point in the valley left it vulnerable to flash floods – archaeologists estimate that it has flooded at least seven times since it was built. This has destroyed much of what must have been spectacular decoration. Based on the decorative scheme in his father Seti I's superb tomb, the walls of Ramses' tomb would once have been just as brightly coloured, the wall scenes featuring the Litany of Ra, Book of Gates, the Book of the Dead and other sacred texts, most of which have been identified by fragments found in debris inside the tomb. The tomb plan also has some interesting features, including a number of side chambers off the burial chamber. In one is a statue of Osiris similar to one found by Dr Kent Weeks in KV 5 (see p256) giving him yet more evidence for his theory that KV5 belongs to the many sons of Ramses.

Excavations have shown that Ramses II, following his father Seti, had his sarcophagus made from alabaster, although his mummy was eventually buried in a wooden coffin in the Deir al-Bahri tomb cache; it's now in the Egyptian Museum in Cairo.

TOMB OF MERNEPTAH (KV 8)

Because Ramses II lived for so long, 12 of his sons died before he did, so it was his

13th son Merneptah (1213–1203 BC) who finally succeeded him in his 60s. His tomb (Map p252) has been open since antiquity and has its share of classical graffiti. Although there is flood damage on the lower portions of the walls of the long tunnel-like tomb, the upper parts have well-preserved reliefs. As you enter the first long corridor, on the left is a striking relief of Merneptah with the god Ra-Horakhty followed by the Litany of Ra. Further down, the corridors are decorated with the Book of the Dead, the Book of Gates and the Book of Amduat. There is also some Greek and Coptic graffiti on the top portion of the wall. The third corridor is decorated with scenes from the Book of Amduat, the ceiling painted blue with gold stars. Beyond a shaft is a false burial chamber with two pillars decorated with the Book of Gates. Although much of the decoration in the burial chamber has faded, it remains an impressive room, with a sunken floor and brick niches on the front and rear walls.

The pharaoh was originally buried inside four stone sarcophagi, three of granite (the lid of the second still *in situ*, with an effigy of Merneptah on top) and the fourth, innermost, sarcophagus of alabaster. In a rare mistake by ancient Egyptian engineers, the outer sarcophagus did not fit through the tomb entrance and its gates had to be hacked away. Merneptah's mummy was removed in antiquity and was found in Amenhotep II's tomb (KV 35); it's now displayed in the Egyptian Museum. One of his granite sarcophagi was taken from the tomb and reused by the later pharaoh Psusennes 1 in 991 BC for his own treasure-filled burial in Tanis, and is now on display in the ground floor atrium of the Egyptian Museum in Cairo.

TOMB OF TUTANKHAMUN (KV 62)
The story of the celebrated discovery of the most famous tomb in the Valley of the Kings and the fabulous treasures it contained, far outshines its actual appearance.

TOMB PLANNING

Although each of the tombs in the valley is unique, most follow a basic plan that developed over time. In the 18th dynasty (1550–1295 BC) the typical tomb was built on a north–south axis (often symbolic since many did not correspond to real north and south) and had four passages in which steps alternated with sloping ramps. Each passage symbolised a stage on the journey to the afterlife. The passages led into a small chamber with a well or pit, called the 'Hall of Waiting', which led into a pillared hall called the 'Chariot Hall'. From here another passage, at right angles to the first four, led into the burial chamber. This change in axis may have had a symbolic meaning, possibly reflecting winding waterways in the afterlife, or simply a function of the topography. Another feature of the earliest tombs is the oval shape of the burial chambers. Some Egyptologists theorise that the shape reflects the royal cartouche. Others say that the way in which the painted scenes appear on the curving burial chamber walls represents the sun's passage through the sky.

During the 19th dynasty (1295–1186 BC) the bent axis began to straighten and eventually it switched to east–west orientation, although the sarcophagus was set at right angles, maintaining a symbolic north–south axis. The descent of the passages became less steep and as time passed an antechamber, which may have been a false burial chamber, was added to the first pillared hall. Wooden doors were added to close off passages and rooms (previously mortar had been used to seal off sections of tombs).

By the 20th dynasty (1186–1069 BC) the tomb axis had straightened and the structure was simplified. Tombs also became smaller in area, although the proportions were expanded so that the height and width of corridors and chambers increased. The east–west orientation of the tomb itself was echoed by the sarcophagus; its head was now placed at the back of the tomb and the pharaoh spent eternity facing the rising sun in the symbolic east.

The tombs were decorated with texts from the Book of the Dead and with colourful scenes to help guide the pharaoh on his or her journey through the afterlife. In the 18th dynasty only the burial chamber was decorated but by the 19th dynasty the entire tomb became a riot of colour. Time, floods and the breath of thousands of tourists have dulled many of these exquisite works of art but even visiting the most damaged tombs can be a wonderful experience.

Tutankhamun's tomb (Map p252) is neither large nor impressive and bears all the signs of a rather hasty completion and inglorious burial. For years archaeologists believed that if Tutankhamun was buried in the valley, his tomb would contain little of interest. The son of Akhenaten by a minor wife, he ruled relatively briefly (1336–1327 BC) and died young, with no great battles or buildings to his credit.

The Egyptologist Howard Carter set out believing he would find the young pharaoh buried among his ancestors with his treasures intact. Carter slaved away for six seasons in the valley, excavating thousands of tonnes of sand and rubble from possible sites, until even his wealthy patron, Lord Carnarvon, tired of the obsession.

With his funding about to be cut off Carter made one last attempt at the only unexplored area that was left, which was covered by workers' huts just under the already excavated Tomb of Ramses VI.

The first step was found on 4 November 1922, and on 5 November the rest of the steps and a sealed doorway came to light. Carter wired Lord Carnarvon to join him in Egypt immediately for the opening of what he believed was the completely intact Tomb of Tutankhamun.

The discovery proved sceptics wrong, and the tomb's priceless cache of Pharaonic treasures, which, although it had been partially robbed twice in antiquity, vindicated Carter's dream beyond even his wildest imaginings. Four chambers were found

THE GREATEST FIND SINCE TUTANKHAMUN

In May 1995 American archaeologist Dr Kent Weeks announced to the world his discovery of the largest tomb ever to be unearthed in Egypt. Believed to be the burial place of the many sons of Ramses II – one of Egypt's most prolific pharaohs in terms of producing both offspring and monuments – it was immediately hailed as the greatest find since that of Tutankhamun. Or, as one London newspaper put it: 'The Mummy of all Tombs'.

The story of the tomb's discovery starts in 1987 when the Egyptian Antiquities Organisation announced plans to level a hillside at the entrance to the Valley of the Kings in order to expand the paved car park. Having spent years mapping the entire Theban necropolis for his Theban Mapping Project, Weeks was familiar with the area and knew that there was a tomb entrance hidden somewhere in the hill. Howard Carter had uncovered it earlier in the 20th century and partly cleared it in his search for Tutankhamun's tomb. Robbed in antiquity then filled with debris from flash floods it appeared to have been destroyed and Carter soon dismissed it as insignificant. The entrance was once again lost under rubble. From 1960 to 1990 tour buses parked beside it, their vibrations adding to the damage of millennia.

After moving mountains of rubble, Weeks finally located the entrance to the tomb, known only as KV 5. Together with his wife, Susan, and a small team of workers, he then set about clearing the entrance chambers. Remnants of pottery, fragments of sarcophagi and, more importantly, wall decorations led Weeks to believe it was the Tomb of the Sons of Ramses II.

However, it wasn't until 1995 that Weeks unearthed a doorway leading to an incredible 121 chambers and corridors, making the tomb many times larger and more complex than any other found in Egypt. Clearing the debris from this unique and enormous tomb is a painstaking and dangerous task. Not only does every bucketful have to be sifted for fragments of pottery, bones and reliefs, but major engineering work has to be done to shore up the tomb's structure. Despite the slow progress, Weeks has found the remains of six males that he contends are the sons of Ramses II. So far representations of 20 others have been found in the fragmentary reliefs, indicating that they too are likely to have been buried here.

Much of the tomb still lies tantalisingly off limits to investigation thanks to the tonnes of debris jammed inside its rooms and corridors. Weeks speculates that it has many as 150 chambers. So far he has confirmed the existence of 125 but exploration remains painfully slow. He believes it will take at least another decade to study the tomb, which means it will be at least that long before it opens to the public. For the next few years they will have to content themselves with reading *The Lost Tomb*, Week's fascinating account of the KV 5's discovery, or following his team's progress on their excellent website at www.thebanmappingproject.com.

crammed with furniture, statues, chariots, musical instruments, weapons, boxes, jars and food – even the later discovery that many had been stuffed haphazardly into the wrong boxes by necropolis officials 'tidying up' after the ancient robberies does not detract from their dazzling wealth. Most are now in the Egyptian Museum in Cairo (a few items remain in Luxor Museum).

People often try to imagine what tombs belonging to the great pharaohs must have contained given that Tutankhamun was a relatively minor pharaoh. However, Tutankhamun's burial was in no way typical of other pharaohs'. As the last of the unpopular Amarna royal line, his tomb was used as a 'dumping ground' for much of their regalia, and some of it is still inscribed with the names of his father Akhenaten and the mysterious Smenkhkare, who some Egyptologists believe was Nefertiti ruling as pharaoh.

Although little remains to help visualise the huge quantities of treasure Carter found here, the fact that Tutankhamun still lies in his tomb gives the place a special atmosphere. His mummy once again lies inside its gilded wooden coffin, the outermost of the three wooden coffins in which it was originally buried. The coffin rests within a carved, red quartzite sarcophagus, the corners of which are defended by the outstretched wings of protective goddesses. The burial chamber walls are decorated by chubby figures of Tutankhamun before the gods, painted against a yellow-gold background. The wall at the foot end of the sarcophagus shows scenes of the pharaoh's funeral; the 12 squatting apes from the Book of Amduat, representing the 12 hours of the night, are featured on the opposite wall.

TOMB OF RAMSES VI (KV 9)

The intactness of Tutankhamun's tomb is largely thanks to the existence of this tomb (Map p252). Tons of rock chippings thrown outside during its construction completely covered the tomb of Tutankhamun, which lay below it, keeping Tut's tomb safe until its discovery in 1922. The tomb was actually begun for the ephemeral Ramses V (1147–1143 BC) and continued by Ramses VI (1143–1136 BC), with both pharaohs apparently buried here; the names and titles of Ramses V still appear in the first half of the tomb. Following the tomb's ransacking a

mere 20 years after burial, the mummies of both Ramses V and Ramses VI were moved to Amenhotep II's tomb where they were found in 1898 and taken to Cairo.

Although the tomb's plastering was not finished, its fine decoration is well preserved, with an emphasis on astronomical scenes and texts. Extracts from the Book of Gates and the Book of Caverns cover the entrance corridor. These continue into the midsection of the tomb and well room, with the addition of the Book of the Heavens. Nearer the burial chamber the walls are decorated with extracts from the Book of Amduat. The burial chamber is beautifully decorated, although only part of the sarcophagus remains. On the ceiling is a superb double image of Nut framing the books of the day and the night. This nocturnal landscape in black and gold shows the sky goddess swallowing the sun each evening to give birth to it each morning in an endless cycle of new life designed to revive the souls of the dead pharaohs. The walls of the chamber are filled with images of Ramses VI with various deities, as well as scenes from the Book of the Earth, which show the sun god's journey through the night. Multiple registers show the god's progress through the hours of the night, the gods who help him and the forces of darkness trying to stop him reaching the dawn; look out for the decapitated, kneeling figures of the sun god's enemies around the base of the chamber walls and the black-coloured executioners who turn the decapitated bodies upside down to render them as helpless as possible. On the beautifully decorated right wall of the burial chamber also try to pick out the ithyphallic figure (the one with a noticeable erection); the lines and symbols surrounding him represent a water clock. Plenty of Greek graffiti can also be made out on the upper portions of the chamber's right and left walls; much of it is thought to date back to c AD 150.

TOMB OF RAMSES III (KV 11)

Ramses III (1184–1153 BC) was the last of Egypt's warrior pharaohs; he built an impressive funerary temple at Medinat Habu and has one of the longest tombs in the Valley of the Kings. The tomb (Map p252) was originally started by Sethnakht (1186–1184 BC), who abandoned it when the tomb builders mistakenly cut through into the earlier, adjacent Tomb of Amenmesse. By changing the corridor's course to the right, Ramses III carried on to create a huge tomb 125m long, much of it still beautifully decorated with colourful painted sunken reliefs featuring the traditional ritual texts (Litany of Ra, Book of Gates etc) and Ramses before the gods. There are also, quite uniquely, a collection of secular scenes shown in a series of small side rooms in the first part of the entrance corridor. Look out for registers of foreign tribute such as highly detailed pottery imported from the Aegean, the royal armoury, boats and, in the last of these side chambers, the blind harpists that gave the tomb one of its alternative names: 'Tomb of the Harpers'.

In the chamber beyond is the aborted tunnel where the ancient builders ran into the neighbouring tomb. From here, the axis of the tomb shifts to the west and a corridor decorated with the Book of Amduat leads to a pillared hall with walls decorated with scenes from the Book of Gates. There is also ancient graffiti on the rear right pillar describing the reburial of the pharaoh during the 21st dynasty (1069–945 BC). The side chamber off the hall shows Ramses in the presence of various gods. The remainder of the tomb is only partially excavated and structurally weak.

Ramses III's sarcophagus is in the Louvre in Paris, its detailed lid is in the Fitzwilliam Museum in Cambridge and his mummy – found in the Deir al-Bahri cache – was the model for Boris Karloff's character in the 1930s film *The Mummy*. The mummy is now in Cairo's Egyptian Museum.

TOMB OF HOREMHEB (KV 57)
This tomb (Map p252) was discovered in 1908, still filled with ransacked pieces of the royal funerary equipment, including a number of wooden figurines that were taken to the Egyptian Museum in Cairo. Horemheb (1323–1295 BC), a general and military strongman under Tutankhamun and his successor Ay, succeeded in ridding Egypt of the remnants of the Amarna period and is generally seen as an administrative reformer who brought stability to the country after the turmoil of Akhenaten's reign. Although he had already built a lavish tomb in Saqqara, he abandoned it for his tomb in

the Valley of the Kings. It is known for its steep descent and burial chamber that was left in various stages of decoration, giving Egyptologists a fascinating glimpse into the process of tomb decoration.

From the entrance, a steep flight of steps and an equally steep passage leads to a well shaft decorated with superb figures of Horemheb before the gods. Notice Hathor's blue-and-black striped wig and the lotus crown of the young god Nefertum, all executed against a grey-blue background. This leads to an undecorated pillared hall, and an antechamber beyond decorated with more painted figures of the pharaoh and gods. The six-pillared burial chamber decorated with part of the Book of Gates remains partially unfinished, showing how the decoration was applied by following a grid system in red ink over which the figures were drawn in black prior to their carving and painting. The pharaoh's empty red granite sarcophagus carved with protective figures of goddesses with outstretched wings remains in the tomb; his missing mummy has not been identified among those in the two major caches of royal mummies.

TOMB OF AMENHOTEP II (KV 35)
One of the deepest structures in the valley, this tomb (Map p252) has more than 90 steps that take you down to a modern gangway built over a deep pit designed to protect the inner, lower chambers from both thieves (which it failed to do) and the water from flash floods.

Stars cover the entire ceiling in the huge burial chamber and the walls feature, as if on a giant painted scroll, text from the Book of Amduat. While most figures are of the same stick-like proportions as in the tomb of Amenhotep's father and predecessor Tuthmosis III, this is the first royal tomb in the valley to also show figures of more rounded proportions, as on the pillars in the burial chamber showing the pharaoh before Osiris, Hathor and Anubis. The burial chamber is also unique for its double level; the top level was filled with pillars, the bottom contained the sarcophagus.

Although thieves breached the tomb in antiquity and made off with valuable funerary items, Amenhotep's mummy was restored by the priests, put back in his sarcophagus, and no fewer than 13 other royal mummies reburied with him. When the tomb was excavated by the French in 1898, archaeologists were amazed to find not only Amenhotep II (1427–1400 BC) still in his sarcophagus (with a garland of flowers around his neck), but an unidentified mummy lying on a model boat in the first pillared hall, and 12 other bodies hidden in two side rooms. In the first chamber lay the mummies of Tuthmosis IV, Amenhotep III, Merneptah, Ramses IV, V and VI, Seti II, Siptah and a royal woman some believe to be the female pharaoh Tawosret. All of these were taken to the Egyptian Museum; three other mummies in the next side chamber – two women and a boy – were left behind and walled up. The identification in the 1970s of the elder of the two women as Queen Tiy, mother of Akhenaten, was not universally accepted. The mummies were re-examined in 2002 and again in 2003 by a British-Egyptian team and their suggested identification of the younger woman as Nefertiti has also been highly controversial.

TOMB OF TUTHMOSIS III (KV 34)

Hidden in the hills between high limestone cliffs and reached only via a steep staircase that crosses an even steeper ravine, this tomb (Map p252) demonstrates the lengths to which the ancient pharaohs went to thwart the cunning of the ancient thieves.

Tuthmosis III (1479–1425 BC), an innovator in many fields whose military exploits and stature has earned him the name 'the Napoleon of ancient Egypt', was one of the first to build his tomb in the Valley of the Kings. As secrecy was his utmost concern, he chose the most inaccessible spot and designed his burial place with a series of passages at haphazard angles and a deep shaft to mislead or catch potential robbers – all to no avail – and to protect the inner, lower chambers from from flash floods.

The shaft, now traversed by a narrow gangway, leads to an antechamber supported by two pillars, the walls of which are adorned with a list of over 700 gods and demigods. As the earliest tomb in the valley to be painted, the walls appear to be simply giant versions of funerary papyri, with scenes populated by stick men. The burial chamber has curved walls and is oval in shape; it contains the pharaoh's quartzite sarcophagus that is

carved in the shape of a cartouche. An exact replica of the chamber was produced by an Anglo-Spanish company and is the highlight of 'The Quest for Immortality' exhibition that will be touring the United States and Europe until 2007.

Tuthmosis' mummy, which shows he was a short man of around 1.5m, was one of those found in the Deir al-Bahri cache and is now in the Egyptian Museum in Cairo.

TOMB OF SIPTAH (KV 47)

Discovered in 1905, Siptah's (1194–1188 BC) tomb (Map p252) was never completed but the upper corridors are nonetheless covered in fine paintings. Like the builders of Ramses III's tomb, workmen struck an adjacent tomb when digging out the rock, but fortunately they were already in the burial chamber and didn't have to make significant changes to the tomb axis. You can see the stone blocks used to repair the mistake on the left-hand side of the corridor outside the burial chamber.

The tomb's entrance is decorated with the sun disc and figures of Maat, the goddess of truth, kneel on each side of the doorway. The corridor beyond features colourful scenes from the Litany of Ra with an elaborately dressed Siptah before various gods, including Ra-Horakhty (an aspect of the sun god Ra combined with Horakhty, a form of Horus the sky god). There are further scenes from the Book of Amduat, and figures of Anubis, after which the tomb remains undecorated. Although the tomb contents were smashed in antiquity, Siptah's mummy was found in Amenhotep II's tomb, and it clearly shows the pharaoh's left leg to be shorter than his right, his left foot severely deformed; Siptah had probably suffered from either cerebral palsy or polio.

TOMB OF TAWOSRET/SETHNAKHT (KV 14)

Tawosret was wife of Seti II and after his successor Siptah died she took power herself (1188–1186 BC). Egyptologists think she began the tomb (Map p252) for herself and Seti II – there are signs of an abandoned attempt at adding another burial chamber adjacent to her own – but their burials were removed by her successor, the equally short-lived Sethnakht (1186–1184 BC), who completed the tomb by adding, unusually for the Valley of the Kings, a second burial chamber where he himself was buried. The change of ownership can be seen in the tomb's decoration; the upper corridors show the queen, accompanied by her stepson Siptah, in the presence of the gods. Siptah's cartouche was later replaced by Seti II's. However, in the lower corridors and burial chambers images of Tawosret have been plastered over by images or cartouches of Sethnakht.

The tomb has been open since antiquity and although the decoration has worn off in some parts, the colour and state of the burial chambers remains good. Both have astronomical ceiling decorations and images of the Tawosret and Sethnakht with the gods, as well as scenes from the Book of Gates, Book of Caverns and Book of Amduat. The final scene from the Book of Caverns adorning Tawosret's burial chamber is particularly impressive, showing the sun god as a ram-headed figure stretching out his wings to emerge from the darkness of the underworld. Although confusion surrounds the fate of both Tawosret and Sethnakht's mummies, two anonymous bodies found in the Amenhotep II cache may be theirs; the female mummy identified by some as Tawosret has the most fabulous upswept hairstyle of crisply set curls.

TOMB OF SETI II (KV 15)

Adjacent to Tawosret/Sethnakht's tomb is a smaller tomb (Map p252) where it seems Sethnakht buried Seti II (1200-1194 BC) after turfing him out of KV 14. Open since ancient times judging by the 50-plus examples of classical graffiti, the tomb's entrance area has some finely carved relief scenes, although the rest was quickly finished off in paint alone. The walls have extracts from the Litany of Ra, the Book of Gates and the Book of Amduat and, unusually, on the walls of the well room, images of the type of funerary objects used in pharaohs' tombs, such as golden statuettes of the pharaoh within a shrine (just like the actual examples found in Tutankhamun's tomb, which are now in the Egyptian Museum in Cairo). The sky goddess Nut stretches out across the ceiling of the burial chamber. Seti II's mummy was found in the Amenhotep II tomb cache. During the 1920s, Seti II's tomb was used by Carter and his team as a conservation laboratory and photographic studio during their clearance of Tutankhamun's tomb.

TOMB OF RAMSES I (KV 16)

Although this tomb (Map p252) belongs to the founder of the 19th dynasty, it is a very simple affair because Ramses I only ruled for a year (1295–1294 BC). Ramses I, originally called Paramessu, was a military officer who became vizier under Horemheb, and in the absence of an heir was chosen as Horemheb's successor. His tomb has the shortest entrance corridor of all the royal resting places in the valley, leading to a single, almost square, burial chamber, containing the pharaoh's open pink granite sarcophagus. The chamber is the only part of the tomb that is decorated and the decoration, although of superb quality, is very similar to that in Horemheb's tomb (KV 57). It features extracts from the Book of Gates, as well as scenes of the pharaoh in the presence of the gods, eg the pharaoh kneeling between the jackal-headed 'Soul of Nekhen' and the falcon-headed 'Soul of Pe', symbolising Upper and Lower Egypt. For information on the long journey of the mummy some think is Ramses I from here to North America and back again, see the boxed text The Long Way Home (p237).

TOMB OF SETI I (NO 17)

As befits such an important pharaoh, Seti I (1294–1279 BC), son and heir of Ramses I, has one of the longest (137m) and most beautiful tombs (Map p252) in the valley. Its discovery by Giovanni Belzoni in 1817 generated almost the same interest as the discovery of Tutankhamun's tomb a century later. As the first royal tomb to be decorated throughout, its raised, painted relief scenes are similar to those found in the pharaoh's beautifully decorated temple at Abydos (p226) and the quality of the work is superb. Two of its painted reliefs showing Seti with Hathor are now in the Louvre in Paris and Florence's Archaeological Museum, while Seti's alabaster sarcophagus was brought to London. The British Museum refused to pay Belzoni's asking price, so it went to a private collector, Sir John Soane, and it can still be seen in the basement of his London house-turned-museum. Seti's mummy was found in the Deir al-Bahri mummy cache, and is now in the Egyptian Museum.

Despite the pilfering, this is in many people's opinion the most beautifully decorated tomb in the valley. The first part of the pharaoh's burial chamber is decorated with texts from the Litany of Ra, and the Book of Amduat, with the Book of Gates featured in the first pillared hall. The walls of the burial chamber are adorned with the Book of Gates, the Book of Amduat and the Book of the Divine Cow, while the ceiling, with its innovative vaulted construction, depicts vivid astronomical scenes featuring the various constellations.

At the time of writing, this tomb was closed for restoration (ongoing since 1991).

TOMB OF MONTUHIRKHOPSHEF (KV 19)

The Tomb (Map p252) of Ramses IX's son, whose name translates as 'The Arm of Montu is Strong', is located high up in the valley's eastern wall and seems to have been originally constructed for an earlier prince. It is small and unfinished but has fine paintings and few visitors. Its entrance corridor is adorned with life-size reliefs of various gods, including Osiris, Ptah, Thoth and Khonsu, receiving offerings from the young prince, who is shown in all his finery, wearing exquisitely pleated fine linen robes and a blue-and-gold 'sidelock of youth' attached to his black wig – not to mention his gorgeous make-up (as worn by both men and women in ancient Egypt).

TOMB OF TUTHMOSIS IV (KV 43)

The tomb (Map p252) of Tuthmosis IV (1400–1390 BC) is one of the largest and deepest tombs constructed during the 18th dynasty. It is also the first in which paint was applied over a yellow background, beginning a tradition that was continued in many tombs, although like all other 18th-dynasty royal tombs, only parts of the tomb were ever meant to be decorated. Discovered in 1903 by Howard Carter (who less than 20 years later would find the tomb of Tuthmosis IV's great-grandson Tutankhamun), it is above the Tomb of Montuhirkhopshef and accessed by a separate path. Two long flights of steps lead down and around to the burial chamber where there's an enormous sarcophagus covered in hieroglyphs. The walls of the well shaft and antechamber are decorated with painted scenes of Tuthmosis before the gods, and the figures of the goddess Hathor are particularly fetching in a range of beautiful dresses with beaded designs. On the left (south) wall of the antechamber there

is a patch of ancient Egyptian graffiti dating to 1315 BC, written by government official Maya and his assistant Djehutymose and referring to their inspection and restoration of Tuthmosis IV's burial on the orders of Horemheb following the first wave of robbery in the eighth year of Horemheb's reign, some 67 years after Tuthmosis IV died.

After the tomb was ransacked a second time it was decided it would be safer to rebury Tuthmosis' mummy in the tomb of his father Amenhotep II (KV 35). Tuthmosis' mummy is now displayed in the Egyptian Museum in Cairo, and shows him to be the first pharaoh to have had his ears pierced.

TOMB OF AY (KV 23)

Although he succeeded Tutankhamun, Ay's brief reign from 1327 to 1323 BC tends to be associated with the earlier Amarna period and Akhenaten (some Egyptologists have suggested he could have been the father of Akhenaten's wife Nefertiti). Ay abandoned a grandiose tomb in Amarna (see p220) and took over another in the West Valley. The West Valley also played an important part in the Amarna story, as it was chosen as a new burial ground by Amenhotep III for his own enormous tomb (KV 22, part way up the valley). His son and successor Akhenaten began his own tomb here too, until he changed his plans and relocated the royal capital to Amarna, where he was eventually buried. When Tutankhamun returned the court to Thebes (Luxor), it seems he too planned to be buried in the West Valley, until his early death saw his successor Ay 'switch' tombs. Tutankhamun was buried in a tomb (KV 62) in the traditional section of the Valley of the Kings, while Ay himself took over the tomb Tutankhamun had begun at the head of the West Valley. The tomb (Map p248) is accessed by a dirt road leading off from the car park at the Valley of the Kings that winds for almost 2km up a desolate valley past sheer rock cliffs. Recapturing the atmosphere (and silence) once found in the neighbouring Valley of the Kings makes it worth the visit.

Although only the burial chamber is decorated, it is noted for its scenes of Ay hippopotamus hunting and fishing in the marshes (scenes usually found in the tombs of nobles not royalty) and for a wall featuring 12 baboons, representing the 12 hours of the night, after which the West Valley or Wadi al-Gurud (Valley of the Monkeys) is named. This is so similar to the decoration in Tutankhamun's tomb that archaeologists suspect that the same artists worked on both tombs. Although Ay's mummy has never been identified, his smashed up sarcophagus has been restored for tourists.

If you're travelling by bicycle, note that it is not feasible to cycle up here without a sturdy mountain bike.

Walk to Deir al-Bahri

The steep walk out of the valley and over the surrounding mountains to Hatshepsut's mortuary temple below guarantees some of the best views in Egypt. Begin by climbing the steep hill opposite the tomb of Seti I. Best to ask a guard to set you in the right direction; there are no signs here or anywhere else along the route and the main path is sometimes blocked by restoration work. As you start to ascend the path, souvenir hawkers will offer to guide you for a tip; if you decide to go with them, steel yourself for their constant efforts to sell you tourist tat as you go. Once you reach the ridge, follow the path to the left and continue left when the path forks. Following the path round the ridge you'll pass a police post on your left and eventually you'll see Deir al-Bahri down the sheer cliff to your right. Stick to the path that follows the ridge, ignoring the steep trail that plunges down the cliff face. Once you've almost completed a full circle you will find yourself at the ticket office to the temple.

The walk takes about 50 minutes through an amazing lunar-surface-type landscape, but be warned that it is very steep in parts. You should take a hat, water and some decent walking shoes. In summer you should start this hike as early as possible to avoid the intense heat. If you tire on the ascent there are sometimes donkeys available to carry you to the top.

Deir al-Bahri

Rising out of the desert plain, in a series of terraces, the **Temple of Hatshepsut** (Map p262; adult/student E£30/15; ☾ 6am-4.30pm Oct-Apr, to 5pm May-Sep) merges with the sheer limestone cliffs of the eastern face of the Theban cliffs as if Nature herself had built this extraordinary monument.

The partly rock-cut, partly freestanding structure is one of the finest monuments of ancient Egypt, although its original appearance, surrounded by a variety of exotic trees and plants and garden beds and approached by a grand sphinx-lined causeway, must have been even more spectacular.

Excavations began in 1891, although it wasn't completely excavated until 1896 and it is still in the process of being restored.

Unfortunately, the temple has been vandalised over the centuries. Akhenaten removed all references to Amun, before taking his court off to Tell al-Amarna; and the early Christians who took it over as a monastery (hence the name Deir al-Bahri or 'Monastery of the North') also defaced the pagan reliefs. Hatshepsut's successors scratched out her name where they could.

The daughter of Tuthmosis I, Hatshepsut was married to her half-brother Tuthmosis II, whose son by a minor wife was to be his successor. As Tuthmosis III was still young when his father Tuthmosis II died, Hatshepsut was made regent. With the political support of the Amun priesthood, she ruled

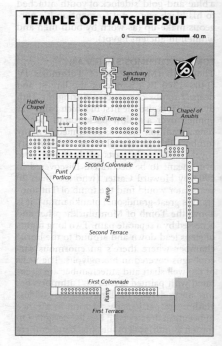

TEMPLE OF HATSHEPSUT

0 ————————— 40 m

Sanctuary of Amun

Hathor Chapel

Third Terrace

Chapel of Anubis

Second Colonnade

Punt Portico

Ramp

Second Terrace

First Colonnade

Ramp

First Terrace

MUMMY FIND

In 1881 the greatest mummy find in history was made just south of Deir al-Bahri in tomb No 320. After objects belonging to pharaohs that had not yet been discovered began showing up in the marketplace the authorities realised someone had found, and was plundering, an unknown tomb – or tombs.

Gurna residents lived, as they do now, amongst the tombs and were immediately suspected of involvement. One family in particular, the Abdel Rassouls, had a long history of tomb robbing but protested its innocence. After a family squabble one aggrieved Abdel Rassoul broke ranks and took officials to the source of the family discovery: a massive shaft containing the mummies of 40 pharaohs, queens and nobles.

It seems that 21st-dynasty priests realised that the bodies of their pharaohs would never be safe from violation in their own tombs, no matter what precautions were taken, so they moved them after 934 BC to this communal grave, which was originally the family vault of the high priest Pinudjem II. The mummies included those of Amenhotep I, Tuthmosis I, II and III, Seti I and Ramses II and III, many of which are now on display at the Egyptian Museum in Cairo.

Their removal from the tomb and procession down to the Nile, from where they were taken by barge to Cairo, was accompanied by the eerie sound of black-clad village women ululating to give a royal send-off to the remains. The episode makes for one of the most stunning scenes in Shadi Abdel Salam's 1975 epic *The Mummy (Al-Mumia)*, one of the best films made in Egypt.

as pharaoh for 15 years (from 1473 to 1458 BC), and for Egypt it was a time of peace and internal growth. In certain reliefs, she is shown in the regalia of a pharaoh, including a false beard; in other scenes she is clearly female. Her depiction as male in some scenes was likely a case of conforming with accepted decorum. After her death in 1458 BC Tuthmosis III became the sole ruler.

The temple's 37m-wide causeway leads onto the three huge terraced courts, each approached by ramps and separated by colonnades. The renowned delicate relief work of the lower terrace features scenes of birds being caught in nets, and the transportation from the Aswan quarries to Thebes of a pair of obelisks commissioned by Hatshepsut.

The large **central court** contains the best-preserved reliefs. Here Hatshepsut recorded her divine birth and, in the **Punt Portico** to the left of the entrance, told the story of an expedition to the Land of Punt to collect myrrh trees needed for the incense used in temple ceremonies. There are two chapels at either end of the colonnade. At the northern end the colourful reliefs in the **Chapel of Anubis** show the corulers, Hatshepsut and Tuthmosis III (with the female pharaoh's image disfigured), in the presence of Anubis, Ra-Horakhty and Hathor. In the **Hathor Chapel** each of the 12 columns is topped by the goddess' image. You can see (if you have a torch) an untouched figure of Hat-

shepsut worshipping Hathor in the guise of a cow. On the northern side there is a faded relief of Hatshepsut's soldiers in naval dress in the goddess' honour.

The third terrace has been restored by a Polish-Egyptian team and recently opened to the public. You can see the pink granite doorway leading into the Sanctuary of Amun, which is hewn out of the cliff.

On the south side of Hatshepsut's temple lie the remains of the **Temple of Montuhotep**, built for the founder of the 11th dynasty and one of the oldest temples so far discovered in Thebes, and the **Temple of Tuthmosis III**, Hatshepsut's successor. Both are in ruins.

Assasif Tombs

This group of tombs, located between Deir al-Bahri and the Tombs of the Nobles, dates back to the 18th dynasty and is under excavation by archaeologists. Of the many tombs here, several may be open to the public including the **Tombs of Kheruef & Ankhor** (Map p248; ⏰ 6am-4.30pm Oct-Apr, to 5pm May-Sep), tickets at Deir el-Bahri ticket office, and the **Tomb of Pabasa** (Map p248). The tombs portray scenes of daily life rather than the heavy ritual in the royal tombs.

Dra Abu'l Naga

In the desert cliffs north of Deir el-Bahri lies yet another necropolis, **Dra Abu'l Naga** (Map p248). Hidden in the barren rock are 114 tombs of rulers and officials, most dating from the 17th dynasty to the late period (about 1550–500 BC). The area has been extensively plundered but two tombs escaped with their paintings more or less intact.

Roy was a royal scribe and steward of Horemheb. His **tomb** (No 234; Map p248) is small but on the east wall are some well-preserved agricultural themes. The southern wall shows Roy and his wife making offerings to the gods. Inside a niche at the back of the tomb a stele shows a barque of Ra with baboons.

A few metres away, the T-shaped **tomb of Shuroy** (No 13; Map p248) contains some finely executed, but in places heavily damaged, paintings. In the small first chamber are scenes of Shuroy and his wife making offerings to the gods. In the tiny second chamber, a funeral procession is led by a child mourner, while on the opposite side a sumptuous banquet is laid out for eternity.

Tombs of the Nobles

The **tombs** (Map p248) in this area are some of the best, but least visited, attractions on the West Bank. Nestled in the foothills and among the houses of the old village of Gurna (Sheikh Abd al-Gurna) are more than 400 tombs that date from the 6th dynasty to the Graeco-Roman period.

Of the hundred or so tombs here that have something of interest, 15 are highly recommended. They have been numbered and divided into five groups, each requiring a separate ticket (see p249).

Some of the tombs have no signs, so you'll need to ask the locals or look out for the modern stone walls built around the entrances to some of the tombs.

TOMBS OF KHONSU, USERHET & BENIA (NOS 31, 51 & 343)

Khonsu was high priest of Tuthmosis III's funerary cult, and lived during the reign of Ramses II, when the dead pharaoh was still honoured. Inside his colourful tomb (Map p248) there is a scene of Khonsu offering flowers to Montuhotep II, who had been dead about 800 years but who was still honoured. The gods Osiris and Anubis are also honoured, and priests with shaved heads are shown carrying the barque of the war. Scenes inside his tomb include a boat carrying the dead to Abydos and, before the final shrine, Khonsu offering incense to

Osiris and Anubis. The ceiling is adorned with images of birds and eggs.

The Tomb of Benia, just behind that of Khonsu, is more colourful than its neighbour. Benia was a child of the royal nursery during the 18th dynasty. At the end of the tomb, there's a ka (spirit or double) statue of Benia flanked by his parents. Statues such as these are typical of tombs in this area, but the faces of this trio have been destroyed.

The Tomb of Userhet (not to be confused with Userhet No 56) was closed at the time of writing.

TOMBS OF MENNA & NAKHT (NOS 52 & 69)

Situated close to the Tombs of Khonsu, Userhet and Benia, the beautiful and highly colourful wall paintings in the Tombs of Menna and Nakht (Map p248) emphasise rural life in 18th-dynasty Egypt. Menna was an estate inspector and Nakht was an astronomer of Amun. Their finely detailed tombs show scenes of farming, hunting, fishing and feasting. The Tomb of Nakht has a small museum area in its first chamber. Although this tomb is so small that only a handful of visitors can squeeze in at a time, the walls have some of the best-known examples of Egyptian tomb paintings, including some familiar scenes such as that of the three musicians, which shows up on a million souvenir T-shirts, posters, postcards and papyrus paintings.

TOMBS OF RAMOSE, USERHET & KHAEMHET (NOS 55, 56 & 57)

The Tomb of Ramose (Map p248), who was a governor of Thebes during the reigns of Amenhotep III and Akhenaten in the 18th dynasty, is fascinating. It's one of the few monuments dating from that time, when the cult power of the priests of Karnak was usurped by the Aten. Exquisite paintings and low reliefs grace the walls, showing scenes from the reigns of both pharaohs and the transition between the two forms of religious worship. The reliefs of Ramose, his wife and other relatives are extraordinarily lifelike and clearly show their affectionate relationships. The tomb was never actually finished and Ramose's fate is unknown. He may have fallen from royal favour or deserted Thebes to follow the rebel pharaoh Akhenaten to his new city at Tell al-Amarna.

The Tomb of Userhet, who was one of Amenhotep II's royal scribes, is next to Ramose's. Its distinctive features are the wall paintings depicting daily life in ancient Egypt. Userhet is shown presenting gifts to Amenhotep II; there's a barber cutting hair on another wall; other scenes include men making wine and people hunting gazelles from a chariot.

The third tomb belongs to Khaemhet, Amenhotep III's royal inspector of the granaries and court scribe. The scenes on the walls show Khaemhet offering sacrifices; the pharaoh depicted as a sphinx; the funeral ritual of Osiris; and images of daily country life as well as official business.

TOMBS OF SENNOFER & REKHMIRE (NOS 96 & 100)

Prince Sennofer of Thebes worked for Amenhotep II as a supervisor of the gardens of the Temple of Amun. The most interesting parts of his tomb (Map p248) are deep underground in the main chamber. The ceiling there is covered with clear paintings of grapes and vines, while most of the vivid scenes on the surrounding walls and columns depict Sennofer with his sister. The guard usually has a kerosene lamp, but bring a torch just in case.

The Tomb of Rekhmire, who was a governor during the reigns of Tuthmosis III and Amenhotep II, is one of the best preserved in the area. In the first chamber, to the extreme left, are scenes of Rekhmire receiving gifts from foreign lands. The panther and giraffe are gifts from Nubia; the elephant, horses and chariot from Syria; and the expensive vases from Crete and the Aegean Islands. Beyond this is the unusual chapel. The west wall shows Rekhmire inspecting the production of metals, bricks, jewellery, leather, furniture and statuary, while the east wall shows banquet scenes, complete with lyrics (the female harpist sings 'Put perfume on the hair of the goddess Maat').

TOMBS OF NEFERRONPET, DHUTMOSI & NEFERSEKHERU (NOS 178, 295 & 296)

This trio of tombs (Map p248) is not far from the Tombs of Khonsu, Userhet and Benia. Neferronpet, commonly known as Kenro, was an official scribe of the treasury. Discovered in 1915, the highlight of this brightly painted tomb is a scene showing Kenro overseeing the weighing of gold at the treasury. Next door, the Tomb of Nefersekheru is equally rich in yellow hues and, like Kenro's tomb, features a ceiling painted with a riot of geometric designs. From this long tomb, a small passage leads into the Tomb of Dhutmosi, which is in poor condition.

Qurna Discovery

Within Gurna, in a restored 1920s mudbrick house beside the Tomb of Ramose, is **Qurna Discovery** (Map p248; www.qurna.org; admission free but donations appreciated; 🕑 8am-noon & 2-5pm Wed-Mon), a fascinating permanent exhibition of drawings of the village by early-19th-century British artist Robert Hay. His finely detailed works depict ancient mudbrick structures that are now lost and, of course, the famous tomb houses, all showing a life that has all but disappeared in the past 50 years. One constant, however, is that Gurnawis were, even in the 1820s, working as labourers for archaeologists.

Built around his works is a compelling description of Gurna's modern history, highlighting the interplay between the village and tourism for over a century. The exhibition also addresses the current problems facing the Gurnawis and suggests alternative solutions to their relocation.

The Ramesseum

This is yet another monument raised by Ramses II to the ultimate glory of himself. The massive **temple** (Map p266) was built to impress his priests, his subjects, his successors and the gods, so that he, the great warrior pharaoh, could live forever. Many of his other works were rather crudely constructed but in this, his funerary temple, he demanded perfection so that it would stand as an eternal testimony to his greatness.

Of course, it has done no such thing. It's mostly in ruins, despite extensive restoration – a fact that would no doubt disappoint Ramses II. He dared all those who questioned his greatness in future centuries to gaze on the magnificence of his monuments in order to understand his power over life and death. The scattered remains of the colossal statue of the pharaoh and the ruins of his temple prompted the English poet Shelley to cut this presumptuous pharaoh down to size in his poem 'Ozymandias', by using the undeniable fact of

Ramses' mortality to ridicule his aspirations to immortality.

> I met a traveller from an antique land
> Who said: Two vast and trunkless legs of stone
> Stand in the desert...Near them, on the sand,
> Half sunk, a shattered visage lies, whose frown,
> And wrinkled lip, and sneer of cold command,
> Tell that its sculptor well those passions read
> Which yet survive, stamped on these life-less things,
> The hand that mocked them, and the heart that fed:
> And on the pedestal these words appear:
> 'My name is Ozymandias, king of kings:
> Look on my works, ye Mighty, and despair!'
> Nothing beside remains. Round the decay

Of that colossal wreck, boundless and bare
The lone and level sands stretch far away.

Although more elaborate than other temples, the fairly orthodox layout of the Ramesseum, with its two courts, hypostyle hall, sanctuary, accompanying chambers and storerooms, is uncommon in that the usual rectangular floor plan was altered to incorporate an older, smaller temple – that of Ramses' mother, Tuya – off to one side.

The **first** and **second pylons** measure more than 60m across and feature reliefs of Ramses' military exploits. Through the first pylon are the ruins of the huge **first court**, including the double colonnade that fronted the royal palace.

Near the western stairs is part of the **Colossus of Ramses II**, the Ozymandias of Shelley's poem, lying somewhat forlornly on the ground. When it stood, it was 17.5m tall. The head of another granite statue of Ramses, one of a pair, lies in the **second court**. Twenty-nine of the original 48 columns of the **great**

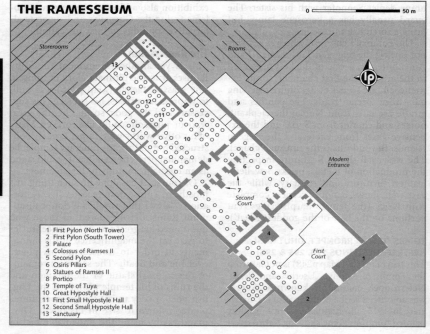

THE RAMESSEUM

0 — 50 m

1 First Pylon (North Tower)
2 First Pylon (South Tower)
3 Palace
4 Colossus of Ramses II
5 Second Pylon
6 Osiris Pillars
7 Statues of Ramses II
8 Portico
9 Temple of Tuya
10 Great Hypostyle Hall
11 First Small Hypostyle Hall
12 Second Small Hypostyle Hall
13 Sanctuary

Storerooms

Rooms

Modern Entrance

Second Court

First Court

hypostyle hall are still standing. In the smaller hall behind it, the roof, which features astronomical hieroglyphs, is still in place.

There is a rest house/restaurant next to the temple that is called, not surprisingly, Ramesseum Rest House. It is a great place to relax and have a cool drink or something to eat. You can leave your bike here while exploring the surroundings.

Deir al-Medina

About 1km off the road to the Valley of the Queens and up a short, steep paved road is **Deir al-Medina** (Monastery of the Town; Map p248), named after a temple that was occupied by early Christian monks. Near the temple is the ruined settlement, the Workmen's Village. Many of the workers and artists who created the royal tombs lived and were buried here. Some of the small tombs here have exquisite reliefs, making it worth a visit.

TEMPLE

The small Ptolemaic-era temple of Deir al-Medina is set just north of the Workmen's Village, along a rocky track. Measuring only 10m x 15m, it was built between 221 and 116 BC, the last of a series of earlier temples built on the same site. It was dedicated to Hathor, the goddess of pleasure and love, and to Maat, the goddess of truth and personification of cosmic order.

WORKMEN'S VILLAGE

Archaeologists have been excavating this settlement (Map p248) for most of this century and at least 70 houses have been uncovered. Some tombs in the village's terraced necropolis are now open to the public.

The beautifully adorned **Tomb of Inherka** (No 359) belonged to a 19th-dynasty servant who worked in the so-called Place of Truth – the Valley of the Kings. The tomb has only one chamber, but the wall paintings are magnificent. One of the most famous scenes shows a cat (representing the sun god Ra) killing a snake (representing the evil serpent Apophis) under a sacred tree; it's on the left of burial chamber. There are also beautiful domestic scenes of Inherka with his wife and children. Right next to it is the **Tomb of Sennedjem** (No 1), a stunningly decorated 20th-dynasty tomb that contains two small chambers and some equally exquisite paintings. Sennedjem was

an artist who lived during the reigns of Seti I and Ramses II and it seems he ensured his own tomb was as finely decorated as those of his Pharaonic masters. Due to the popularity and small size of both these tombs, only 10 people at a time are allowed inside; it's likely you'll find yourself in a queue.

While you wait, take a look at the 19th-dynasty **Tomb of Peshedu** (No 3) just up the slope from the other two tombs. Peshedu was another servant in the Place of Truth and can be seen in the burial chamber praying under a palm tree beside a lake. Close by is the **Tomb of Ipy** (No 217), a sculptor during the reign of Ramses II. Here scenes of everyday life eclipse the usual emphasis on ritual, with scenes of farming and hunting, and a depiction of Ipy's house in its flower- and fruit-filled garden (see the boxed text, p186).

Valley of the Queens

There are at least 75 tombs in the **Valley of the Queens** (Biban al-Harim; Map p248; adult/student E£30/15). They belonged to queens of the 19th and 20th dynasties and other members of the royal families, including princesses and the Ramessid princes. Only three were open at the time of writing.

TOMB OF NEFERTARI (NO 66)

Hailed as the finest tomb in the Theban necropolis – and in all of Egypt for that matter – the **Tomb of Nefertari** (Map p268; admission upon reopening E£100; ☉ 6am-4.30pm winter, to 5pm summer) was first opened to the public in November 1995 and was solidly booked until it closed in 2003. When we visited it was closed to the public and the Supreme Council of Antiquities gave no indication of when it will reopen. But if and when it does, tickets are likely to be limited to 150 per day as they were prior to its closure. Only 10 people are allowed in at any one time for a maximum of 15 minutes, and photography is strictly prohibited. You may be required to wear shoe covers and nose masks.

Nefertari was one of the five wives of Ramses II, the New Kingdom pharaoh known for his colossal monuments of self-celebration. However, the tomb he created for his favourite queen is a shrine to her beauty and, without doubt, an exquisite labour of love. Every centimetre of the walls in the tomb's three chambers and connecting

TOMB OF NEFERTARI

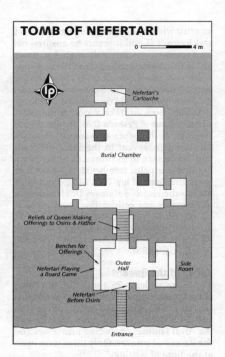

0   4 m

Nefertari's Cartouche

Burial Chamber

Reliefs of Queen Making Offerings to Osiris & Hathor

Benches for Offerings

Nefertari Playing a Board Game

Outer Hall

Side Room

Nefertari Before Osiris

Entrance

corridors is adorned with colourful scenes of Nefertari in the company of the gods and with associated text from the Book of the Dead nearby. Invariably, the 'Most Beautiful of Them', as Nefertari was known, is depicted wearing a divinely transparent white gown and a golden headdress featuring two long feathers extending from the back of a vulture. The ceiling of the tomb is festooned with golden stars.

Some of the best scenes in the tomb are in the side room off to your right at the bottom of the first set of stairs. In one panel here, the queen is shown with her arms outstretched next to the mummiform body of Osiris. At the top of the second staircase, which leads to the burial chamber, is another of the tomb's highlights – Nefertari offering two bowls of milk to Hathor.

Like most of the tombs in the Valley of the Kings, this one had been plundered by the time it was discovered by archaeologists. Only a few fragments of the queen's pink granite sarcophagus remained. Of her mummified body, only traces of her knees were left.

TOMB OF AMUNHERKHEPSHEF (NO 55)

Until the opening of Nefertari's tomb, the Tomb of Amunherkhepshef (Map p248) was the valley's showpiece, with beautiful, well-preserved reliefs. Amunherkhepshef was the son of Ramses III and was about 10 years old when he died. On the left (south) wall of the tomb's vestibule, Ramses is portrayed holding the prince's hand and introducing him to the various gods that would help him on his journey to the afterlife. Amunherkhepshef can be seen wearing a kilt and sandals, with the sidelock of hair typical of young boys. Reliefs also show Ramses leading his son to Anubis, the jackal-headed god of the dead, who then takes the young prince forward on his journey to the afterlife.

The mummified five-month-old fetus on display in a glass case in the tomb is the subject of many an inventive story. It was actually found by Italian excavators in a valley to the south of the Valley of the Queens.

TOMB OF KHAEMWASET (NO 44)

One of Ramses III's many sons, Khaemwaset died young, although Egyptologists have little information about his age or cause of death. His tomb (Map p248) is filled with well-preserved, brightly coloured reliefs. Like that of his brother Amunherkhepshef, Khaemwaset's tomb follows a linear plan, with an entrance leading into a long vestibulelike corridor, followed by a burial chamber leading into a smaller room at the tomb's rear. The vestibule has an astronomical ceiling above walls showing Ramses III in full ceremonial dress, followed by his son wearing a tunic and the sidelock of hair signifying his youth. The reliefs show Khaemwaset in the presence of the gods and scenes from the Book of the Dead. In the vestibule and the burial chamber, his father leads him on his way, while in a small chamber on the tomb's north side the prince faces the gods alone.

TOMB OF TITI (NO 52)

Egyptologists are not sure which Ramesside pharaoh Titi was married to but in her tomb she is referred to as the royal wife, royal mother and royal daughter. The tomb (Map p248) consists of a corridor leading to a square chapel, off which is the burial chamber and two other small rooms. The paintings are faded but you can still make out a winged Maat kneeling on the left-hand side of the corridor, and the queen before Toth, Ptah and the four sons of Horus opposite. Inside the burial chamber are a series of animal guardians: a jackal and lion, two monkeys and a monkey with a bow.

MEDINAT HABU

Second in size only to the temple complex at Karnak, the magnificent temple complex of **Medinat Habu** (Map p269) is one of the most underrated sites on the West Bank. With the Theban mountains as a backdrop and the sleepy village of Kom Lolah in front, it is a wonderful place to spend a few hours.

The site was one of the first places in Thebes to be closely associated with the local god Amun. Although the complex is most famous for the funerary temple built by Ramses III, Hatshepsut and Tuthmosis III also constructed buildings here. They were later added to and altered by a succession of rulers through to the Ptolemies. At Medinat Habu's height there were temples, storage rooms, workshops, administrative buildings and accommodation for priests and officials. It was the centre of the economic life of Thebes for centuries and was still inhabited as late as the 9th century AD, when a plague was thought to have decimated the town. You can still see the mud-brick remains of the medieval town that gave the site its name (medina means 'town' or 'city') on top of the enclosure walls.

The original **Temple of Amun**, which was built by Hatshepsut and Tuthmosis III, was later completely overshadowed by the enormous **Funerary Temple of Ramses III**, the dominant feature of Medinat Habu.

Ramses III was inspired in the construction of his shrine by the Ramesseum of his illustrious forebear, Ramses II. His own temple and the smaller one dedicated to Amun are both enclosed within the massive outer walls of the complex.

Also just inside, to the left of the gate, are the **Tomb Chapels of the Divine Adorers**, which were built for the principal priestesses of Amun. Outside the eastern gate, one of only two entrances, was a landing quay for a canal that once connected Medinat Habu with the Nile.

You enter the site through the unique **Syrian Gate**, a large two-storey building modelled after an Asiatic fortress. If you follow the wall to the left you will find a staircase leading to the upper floors. There's not much to see in the rooms but you get some great views over the village in front of the temple and across the fields to the south.

The well-preserved **first pylon** marks the front of the temple proper. Ramses III is portrayed in its reliefs as the victor in several wars. Most famous are the fine **reliefs** of his victory over the Libyans (who you can recognise by their long robes, sidelocks and beards). There is also a gruesome scene of scribes tallying the number of enemies killed by counting severed hands and genitals.

To the left of the **first court** are the remains of the **Pharaoh's Palace**; the three rooms at the rear were for the royal harem. There is

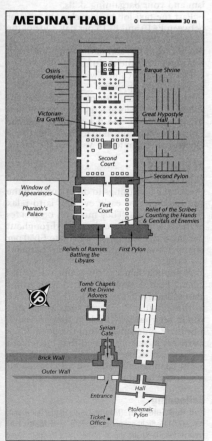

MEDINAT HABU

0 —————— 30 m

- Osiris Complex
- Barque Shrine
- Victorian-Era Graffiti
- Great Hypostyle Hall
- Second Court
- Second Pylon
- Window of Appearances
- Pharaoh's Palace
- First Court
- Relief of the Scribes Counting the Hands & Genitals of Enemies
- Reliefs of Ramses Battling the Libyans
- First Pylon
- Tomb Chapels of the Divine Adorers
- Syrian Gate
- Brick Wall
- Outer Wall
- Entrance
- Hall
- Ptolemaic Pylon
- Ticket Office

a window between the first court and the Pharaoh's Palace known as the **Window of Appearances**, which allowed the pharaoh to show himself to his subjects.

The reliefs of the **second pylon** feature Ramses III presenting prisoners of war to Amun and his vulture-goddess wife, Mut. Colonnades and reliefs surround the **second court**, depicting various religious ceremonies.

If you have time to wander about the extensive ruins around the funerary temple you will see the remains of an early Christian basilica as well as a small sacred lake.

New Gurna

For architecture buffs, Hassan Fathy's mudbrick architectural masterpiece, **New Gurna** (Map p248), lies just past the railway track on the main road from the ferry to the ticket office. It was built to rehouse the inhabitants of Old Gurna, whom the authorities have been trying to remove from their mountainside homes since the 1930s. The majority stayed put, however, with even Fathy himself admitting that his vision was a failure as a social engineering experiment. He blamed the authorities' disdain for the Gurnawis rather than any flaw in his own vision.

But while it may have been a sociological failure, architecturally the buildings were stunning, with his signature domes and vaults, thick mud-brick walls and natural ventilation. Eventually they filled up thanks to the burgeoning local population. But, sadly, many of the domed mudbrick houses have been replaced with crude concrete boxes – Fathy did not plan his buildings to allow for extensions to accommodate growing extended families. However, the beautiful mud-brick mosque and theatre still survive, and you can still see the venerable architect's own house. Just ask for someone from the Abu al-Haggag family and they will show you around.

Getting There & Around

Most tourists cross to the West Bank by bus or taxi via the bridge, about 7km south of town. But the river remains the quickest way to go. The *baladi* (municipal) ferry costs E£1 for foreigners (10pt for locals) and leaves from a dock in front of Luxor Temple. Alternatively, small motor launches (locally called *lunches*) leave from wherever they can find customers and will take you

across for E£5 or for E£1 per person if there are more than five in your group.

On the West Bank, the taxi lot is up the hill from the ferry landing. Voices call out the destinations of pick-up truck taxis. If you listen for Gurna you'll be on the right road to the ticket office (25pt). Pick-ups run back and forth between the villages, so you can always flag one down and find your way to one of the sites, although you might have to walk from the main road to the entrance. If you want to have an entire pick-up for yourself, it'll cost E£5. The driver will likely stick to his normal route.

To hire a private taxi for the day, expect to pay between E£100 and E£150 per day, depending on the season, the state of tourism and your bargaining skills.

Past the taxi lot are bicycles for rent for between E£10 and E£15 per day. One of the best selections is at Muhammed's, just up the hill from the taxi park at the first track forking left off the main road.

Donkeys and camels with guides can also be rented; see opposite.

To give you an idea of the distances involved, from the local ferry landing it is 3km straight ahead to the ticket office, past the Colossi of Memnon; 4km to the Valley of the Queens; and 8km to the Valley of the Kings.

ACTIVITIES
Felucca Rides

One of the best things to do in Luxor in the late afternoon or early evening is to relax aboard a felucca. They moor on both sides of the Nile and cruise the river throughout the day. Prices range from E£30 to E£50 per boat per hour, depending on your bargaining skills.

A popular felucca trip is upriver to Banana Island, a tiny isle dotted with palms about 5km from Luxor. The trip takes two to three hours. Plan it in such a way that you're on your way back in time to watch a brilliant Nile sunset from the boat. Some travellers have complained that the felucca captain has added money for 'admission' to the island; make sure you are clear about what is included in the price you agree.

Ballooning

Hod Hod Suleiman (Map pp238-9; Sharia Televizyon; ☎ 237 0116; flight per person US$250) and **Magic Horizons** (Sharia Khalid ibn al-Walid; ☎ 236 5060; www

.magic-horizon.com; adult/child E£700/350) offer early morning balloon flights over Luxor's West Bank. When the air is clear, the view over the monuments and the desert mountains is amazing. Changing winds mean that the trips are subject to cancellation at the last minute. The flight includes a champagne breakfast and some folkloric dancing.

Donkey, Horse & Camel Rides

Almost all the smaller hotels organise donkey treks around the West Bank. These trips, which start at around 7am (sometimes 5am) and finish near lunchtime, cost a minimum of about E£55 per person.

If you want to see the Nile from the back of a camel, the boys at the local ferry dock on the West Bank ask E£45 for an hour. Some of the bigger hotels offer camel trips, which include visits to nearby villages for a cup of tea.

A sunset ride in the desert is an unforgettable experience. **Pharaoh's Stables** (Map p248; ☎ 231 0015; ⏱ 7am-sunset) and **Nobi Horse Stables** (Map p248; ☎ 231 0024, 010 504 8558; ⏱ 7am-sunset) have horses, camels and donkeys. Some of the horses are healthier than others so choose your mount carefully. Both stables ask between E£20 and E£25 for an hour's ride. They also offer guided camel rides (E£20 per hour) and donkey rides (E£15 per hour).

Swimming

After a hot morning of tombs and temples, a dip in a pool can seem like heaven. Most of the bigger hotels and some of the budget places have swimming pools. The St Joseph, Karnak, Windsor, New Emilio and Arabesque Hotels have small rooftop pools that you can use for E£10. Rezeiky Camp's slightly larger pool is also E£10. The Sheraton pool sits on a secluded Nileside spot and charges E£50 for day use.

TOURS

The ever-increasing travel restrictions for foreigners and the constant bargaining and hassle involved in even a simple transaction can make independent travel challenging, so you may want to visit sites on a day tour. American Express and Thomas Cook (see p235) offer an array of tours. Prices range from around US$20 to US$50 per person for a half-day.

Jolleys Travel & Tours (Map pp238-9; ☎ 010 183 8894; ⏱ 9am-10pm) This reputable company, located next to the Old Winter Palace, also runs day trips to the main sites.

Nada Travel Service (NTS; Map pp238-9; ☎ 238 2163; elnada91@hotmail.com; Petra Travel Agency Bldg, Sharia Ahmed Oraby; ⏱ 8am-11pm) Near the Luxor Temple. Deals with lots of young travellers and is where you go to organise ISIC student cards. It's more geared to long-range travel than day trips around Luxor.

Nawas Tourist Company (Map pp238-9; ☎ 237 0701; magednawas@yahoo.com; ⏱ 10am-2pm & 5-9pm) Located behind the tourist office, this company also has a good reputation. As well as organising day trips, it sells ferry tickets from Hurghada to Sharm el-Sheikh and day cruises to Dendara.

QEA Travel Agency (Map p248; ☎ 231 1667; www .questfortheegyptianadventure.com; Al-Gezira) The British/ Egyptian-run place is a newly opened agency based on the West Bank. It runs tailor-made tours in and around Luxor, as well as further afield on the Red Sea or in the Western Desert. A percentage of its profits go towards charitable projects in Egypt.

Most of the small budget hotels aggressively promote their own tours. Some of these are better than others and there have been complaints by a number of travellers that they ended up seeing little more than papyrus shops and alabaster factories from a sweaty car with no air-conditioning. If you do decide to take one of these tours, expect to pay about E£50 to E£75 per person.

The Iberotel Luxor Hotel (p277) organises day cruises on its Lotus Boat to Dendara for E£260 per adult and E£130 per child, including lunch, guide and admission fees. Trips to Abydos are less frequent but go for about E£350 per person.

FESTIVALS & EVENTS

The town's biggest traditional festival is the **Moulid of Abu al-Haggag**. One of Egypt's largest *moulids* (religious festivals), it is held in honour of Luxor's patron sheikh, Yousef Abu al-Haggag, a 12th-century Iraqi who settled in Luxor. The *moulid* takes place around the Mosque of Abu al-Haggag, the town's oldest mosque, which is actually on top of the northeastern corner of Luxor Temple. It's a raucous five-day event that takes place in the third week before Ramadan. See p272 for details of other *moulids*.

In February each year a **marathon** is held on the West Bank. It begins at Deir al-Bahri

MOULIDS AROUND LUXOR

At a moulid (a festival celebrating the birthday of a local saint) you can hear real Saidi music, see traditional stick dancing (tahtib) or watch mirmah, where riders on Arabian horses gallop to and fro in what looks like stylised jousting.

There are a number of moulids in the Luxor area, most of them smaller and more manageable than the Moulid of Abu al-Haggag, which draws hundreds of thousands of visitors. Most happen in Sha'aban, the month immediately before Ramadan.

Abu'l Gumsan, named after a religious man who died in 1984, is a small moulid that takes place on 27 Sha'aban near the West Bank village of Taref, just south of the road to the Valley of the Kings. Sheikh Musa and Abu al-Jud both take place in the sprawling village of Karnak. Other local moulids include Sheikh Hamid on 1 Sha'aban and Sheikh Hussein a couple of days later.

One of the only accessible Christian moulids is Mar Girgis (St George), which takes place at the monastery of the same name and has its climax on 11 November, although the celebrations go on for most of the week before. The monastery is at the village of Razagat. Although this area is officially forbidden to foreigners, service taxis ferrying the hundreds of people attending the moulid will often avoid the checkpoint on the main road and go via a desert track.

Women attending moulids should dress very conservatively and, if possible, be accompanied by a man. Readers have complained of groping and harassment, and if possible women should avoid large crowds.

Ask at the tourist office for exact dates.

and loops around the main antiquities sites before ending back where it began. Contact the tourist office for information.

SLEEPING

Luxor has a wide range of hotels for all budgets. Whether to stay on the East or West Bank depends on whether you prefer peace and quiet (the West Bank) or want to be able to walk to hotels, shops and restaurants (the East Bank).

Budget

Luxor has a good selection of budget places. Many boast both roof gardens and washing machines.

Avoid the hotel touts who pounce on you as you get off the train or bus – they get a 25% to 40% commission for bringing you in, which is added to your bill.

EAST BANK

Nefertiti Hotel (Map pp238-9; ☎ 237 2386; www.nefertitihotel.com; btwn Sharia al-Karnak & Sharia as-Souq; s/d E£40/60; ☒) Rooms are simple and spotlessly clean, with small private bathrooms and air-con: midrange facilities at budget prices. The roof terrace has views of the West Bank and the top-floor lounge has satellite TV and a pool table. It's no wonder that the Nefertiti gets consistently good reviews from our readers. Recommended.

Happy Land Hotel (Map pp238-9; ☎ 237 1828; www.luxorhappyland.com; Sharia Qamr; dm with air-con E£12.50, s/d E£15/21, with private bathroom, fridge & air-con E£45/50; ☒ ⌨) Competition among Luxor's budget hotels is fierce, and the Happy Land comes out on top almost every time. The rooms here are spotless, and about half have private bathrooms and air-conditioning. Toilet paper, soap and mosquito coils are provided. Bikes can be rented for E£10 per day and laundry facilities are free. All this is presided over by the jovial Mr Ibrahim.

Nubian Oasis Hotel (Map pp238-9; ☎ 292 9445; Sharia Mohammed Farid; dm E£10, s/d E£10/20, with air-con E£20/35) Renamed (this used to be The Oasis Hotel) and revamped, the Nubian Oasis is making a big effort to win the budget hotel sweepstakes. All 24 rooms are clean and come with private bathrooms; 18 also have air-conditioning and some have double beds and satellite TV. The included breakfast is generous and there is free use of two kitchens and a washing machine. Hot and cold drinks (including Stella for E£6) are available on the roof terrace and bicycles can be hired for E£6 per day. An excellent new edition to the Luxor scene.

Sherief Hotel (Map pp238-9; ☎ 237 0757; sheriefhotel@yahoo.co.uk; Sharia Badr; s/d E£25/50, s/d with private bathroom E£40/60; ☒ ⌨) A homey place on the west side of Sharia Televizyon, the Sherief is under new ownership and is trying hard. Of the 15 rooms, six have their own bathroom and four have air-con. There is a mural-filled downstairs restaurant and sunny roof terrace, and staff are friendly, but the rooms need a lick of paint. Still not a bad option.

Grand Hotel (Map pp238-9; ☎ 238 2905; off Sharia Mohammed Farid; s/d E£8/12, with fan E£10/15) The Grand is clean and welcoming with a small (if overly cluttered) rooftop terrace with great views and decent shared bathrooms with hot water. The owner, a local school-teacher named Nobi, is very friendly and keeps a room off the lobby where people can leave their belongings after checking out if they have a long wait for their train or bus. Bikes can be hired for E£9 per day. All this is let down by the quality of the rooms, which are in need of renovation.

Fontana Hotel (Map pp238-9; ☎ 238 0663; off Sharia Televizyon; s/d E£15/20, with private bathroom E£25/40; ✷) An old stalwart of the budget hotel scene, this 25-room hotel has clean rooms, a washing machine for guest use, a rooftop terrace and a kitchen. Shared bathrooms are large and clean, and toilet paper and towels are provided. The problem is the shifty attitude of the staff, which spoils what would otherwise be a decent place.

Mina Palace Hotel (Map pp238-9; ☎ 237 2074; fax 238 2194; Corniche el-Nil; s/d E£80/100; ✷) Right on the Corniche in front of the Mummification Museum – which is about the only spot where cruise boats cannot moor – the Mina Palace offers five-star views at bargain-basement prices. The two corner rooms have unparalleled views of both the West Bank and the avenue of sphinxes at Luxor Temple. All rooms could use a coat of paint but have satellite TV, comfortable beds and very clean bathrooms. There's a roof terrace where you can enjoy a beer while watching the sun setting over the Nile.

Merryland Hotel (Map pp238-9; ☎ 238 1746; s/d E£50/80; ✷ ▯) Large but quiet and well located close to Luxor Museum, off Sharia Labib Habashi, the Merryland has been around for years but its prices haven't changed much, making it a bargain for a three-star hotel. The clean, slightly dark rooms all come with satellite TV, private bathrooms and small balconies. The roof terrace has a bar, breakfast area and great views over to the West Bank.

Venus Hotel (Map pp238-9; ☎ 237 2625; Sharia Yousef Hassan; s/d E£25/30, with air-con E£35/45; ✷) Although popular with budget groups, the Venus' 25 rooms, all with private bathrooms, are looking distinctly shabby these days. Those overlooking the street can also be noisy. There is large restaurant/bar with satellite TV, and a 6th-floor terrace where you can down a cold Stella for E£7. Breakfast is E£5

Saint Mina Hotel (Map pp238-9; ☎ 237 5409; fax 237 6568; off Sharia Ramses; s/d E£30/35, with private bathroom E£35/50; ✷) A friendly, family-run hotel, the St Mina doesn't have the aura of hustle that plagues so many of Luxor's budget hotels. Its 20 rooms are clean, with air-con or fans. Prices drop considerably in summer.

Atlas Hotel (Map pp238-9; ☎ 237 3514; fax 236 5000; off Sharia Ahmed Orabi; s/d with fan E£20/25; d with air-con E£35; ✷) Difficult to find, with 40 shabby but clean rooms (all with private bathrooms), the Atlas is rarely full – something to keep in mind if you have no luck elsewhere. Staff are a bit sleepy, apart from the manager, who calls himself Ali Baba. Definitely not a first choice hostelry but a decent back-up option. Breakfast is E£5.

Anglo Hotel (Map pp238-9; ☎ 238 1679; fax 238 1679; Midan al-Mahatta; s/d E£30/35; ✷) Badly located for light sleepers, the Anglo is right next to the train station, and therefore noisy, but the large rooms are clean and well maintained, with air-con, private bathrooms and telephones. Despite being an excellent deal, it is often empty, perhaps because of the less-than inspiring management.

Youth Hostel (Map pp238-9; ☎ 237 2139; fax 237 0539; off Sharia al-Karnak; members E£10.10, nonmembers E£11.10) With a minimum of three beds in each room and bathrooms that could use a refit, prices should be lower given everything else on offer in the town. It is also beside a school, which means lots of early-morning noise. You can do better. Breakfast is E£3.

Rezeiky Camp (Map pp238-9; ☎ 381 334; www .rezeikycamp.com.eg; Sharia al-Karnak; camp site per person E£10, vehicle E£10, s/d $15/23; ✷ ▯ ▨) Rezeiky Camp is the only place to pitch a tent in town, but it is pleasant enough with a pool on your doorstep. There is a large garden with a restaurant and bar, and Internet access. The motel-style rooms are not nice enough to make up for the inconvenient location, but the place is popular with overland groups, so call ahead to make sure there is space.

WEST BANK

Marsam Hotel (Map p248; ☎ 237 2403, 231 1603; marsam@africamail.com; Gurna; s/d E£45/90, with private bathroom E£65/130) Also known as Sheikh Ali Hotel, this is the best budget place in the vicinity – although prices have risen sharply since our last edition. It has 27 simple but spotless rooms (four with bathrooms), with ceiling fans and traditional palm-reed beds. It was originally built for American archaeologists in the 1920s. In the 1960s it became a retreat for Egyptian artists (*marsam* means 'a place for drawing' in Arabic), and you can still see the odd sculpture in the shady courtyard. Atmospheric and quiet, it is an old favourite with archaeologists, so it can be difficult to get rooms during the dig season (generally January to March), but it is well worth giving it a try.

Al-Gezira Hotel (Map p248; ☎/fax 310 034; www .el-gezira.com; Al-Gezira; s/d E£60/80; ✷) An excellent budget hotel that is often full, the Al-Gezira is a bargain, despite the need for a coat of paint in some of the rooms. But all are pristine, with comfortable beds, private bathrooms and air-con. Management and staff are friendly and efficient, and the upstairs rooftop restaurant has great Nile views as well as cold beer (E£8) and traditional Egyptian food. The only downside is the adjacent mosquito-infested canal.

Habu Hotel (Map p248; ☎ 237 2477; Kom Lolah; s/d E£25/40) If you like character in a hotel, the Habu is for you. It's a mud-brick warren of small, vaulted rooms and has stunning views over the entrance to Medinat Habu temple complex and the mountains beyond. Go for one of the three domed 1st-floor terrace rooms, which are practically in the forecourt of Medinat Habu and have a large terrace with palm-reed furniture. The downstairs restaurant has dusty ceiling fans and great old tourist posters. The downside? The less welcome saggy beds, mosquitos, somnolent staff and waterlogged bathrooms.

Abu al-Kasem Hotel (Map p248; ☎ 231 3248; At-Taref; s/d E£35/50) Out of the way near the Temple of Seti I on Sharia Wadi al-Melouk, Abu al-Kasem has 20 tired but basically clean rooms with private bathrooms. During the dig season, Polish archaeologists often take over several rooms, otherwise it is generally empty, due as much to the inconvenient location as to the general need of a renovation. The owners, the Abu al-Kasem family, are friendly enough but this is really only worth considering if others are full.

Midrange

Luxor has a wide and very varied selection of midrange hotels. At the top are the small mud-brick character hotels on the West Bank, followed by slick chain-run places in town. There are also some excellent bargains in this category, with good facilities at rock-bottom rates.

EAST BANK

Little Garden Hotel (Map pp238-9; ☎ 238 9038; www .littlegardenhotel.com; Sharia Radwan; s/d US$18/24; ✷) Don't let the location put you off: this little hotel is an excellent new addition to Luxor's midrange options. The owner worked in hotel management in Germany and it shows with the friendly but professional staff, 24-hour room service, cotton mattresses, air-con, satellite TV and spanking new private bathrooms. There is also a small garden courtyard and a rooftop restaurant serving Oriental foods and *sheesha* (water pipe) but no alcohol. Students can get a 10% discount.

Tutotel Partner Hotel (Map pp238-9; ☎ 237 7990; tutotel@partner-hotels.com; Sharia Salah ad-Din; s/d US$20/27; ✷ ▣) Under new management, this three-star hotel has four-star facilities and a convenient location between the Corniche and Sharia Televizyon. The 79 rooms, most with Nile views, have comfy beds, satellite TV, air-con and minibars. There is also a rooftop pool with a Jacuzzi, three restaurants and one of Luxor's few discos.

St Joseph Hotel (Map pp238-9; ☎ 238 1707; sjhiey2002@hotmail.com; Sharia Khaled ibn al-Walid; s/d US$25/30; ✷ ▣) This popular and well-run three-star hotel has been a favourite with small groups for years thanks to its comfortable rooms with satellite TV, air-con and private bathrooms. There is also a (heated) rooftop pool and basement bar. Ask for a Nile view.

Mercure Inn (Map pp238-9; ☎ 237 3321; www .mercure.com; off Sharia al-Karnak; s/d US$55/70; ✷ ▣) Belonging to the French Accor chain, the Mercure Inn has very comfortable, if tackily decorated, rooms, and offers four-star amenities, which include room service, baby-sitting, three restaurants, a bar and a decent-sized swimming pool, for less than most of the other top-end hotels.

New Pola Hotel (Map pp238-9; ☎ 236 5081; www .newpolahotel.com; Sharia Khalid ibn al-Walid; s/d US$45/ 50; ☒ ▣ ▨) Great views and a small rooftop pool make the recently opened New Pola an excellent bargain. The décor is kitsch but the 81 air-con rooms are spotless and come with minibars, satellite TV and private bathrooms. Half also have Nile views. Very good value for money.

New Emilio Hotel (Map pp238-9; ☎ 237 3570; fax 237 0000; Sharia Yousef Hassan; s/d US$20/30; ☒ ▨) A good long-standing midrange hotel, the Emilio has 48 rooms, all with minifridge, satellite TV and 24-hour room service. Other extras include an AstroTurfed roof terrace with plenty of shade and a popular pool, a sauna and some business facilities. Although it suffers slightly from its noisy location, it remains popular and reservations are often needed in winter.

New Radwan Hotel (Map pp238-9; ☎ /fax 238 5501; Sharia Abdel Moneim al-Adasi; s/d E£70/120; ☒ ▨) Easily missed just off Midan al-Mahatta, the New Radwan is an excellent deal with clean comfortable rooms, all with aircon and private bathrooms. There is also a small pool and a garden restaurant. A shame, then, about its noisy location beside a mosque and close to the train station.

Philippe Hotel (Map pp238-9; ☎ /fax 238 0050; Sharia Nefertiti; s/d US$30/40; ☒ ▨) A muchneeded renovation has greatly enhanced the Philippe's rooms, which all have satellite TV, private bathrooms and air-con. Although bland they are comfortable and a great improvement from our last visit. There's also a roof terrace with a decentsized pool. Front rooms are best: most have small balconies and get plenty of light.

Flobater Hotel (Map pp238-9; ☎ 374 223; fax 370 618; off Sharia Khaled ibn al-Walid; s/d E£60/80; ☒) Next to the St Joseph, this family-run hotel has 40 comfortable rooms with fridges, satellite TV, air-con and private bathrooms. There is also a pleasant roof terrace with a pool. Try to get a room with a balcony.

Luxor Wena Hotel (Map pp238-9; ☎ 380 018; fax 380 019; Sharia al-Karnak; s/d US$15/25; ☒ ▨) Once a grand old hotel, then subject to a longrunning court battle, the Wena is frayed at the edges but boasts a great location near Luxor Temple. It sits in a 2-hectare garden and has a variety of restaurants.

Arabesque Hotel (Map pp238-9; ☎ 371 299; fax 372 193; Sharia Mohammed Farid; s/d E£70/100; ☒ ▣)

Close to the main post office, with a rooftop pool and great views over Luxor Temple and the Nile, the Arabesque has a great, if noisy, location. Its dark rooms, all with air-con, and small beds don't quite deliver the goods but it remains a decent option if others are full.

WEST BANK

Nour el-Gurna (Map p248; ☎ 231 1430, 010 129 5812; Gurna; s E£100, d E£120-150, ste E£200) A unique little hotel in a mud-brick house nestled in a palm grove opposite the Antiquities Inspectorate ticket office, Nour el-Gurna has large rooms, each slightly different, with fans, small stereos, locally made furniture and tiled bathrooms. All beds have mosquito nets, which are both practical and decorative. The only complaint is that the traditional cotton mattresses can be hard. Romantic and original, with friendly management and a convenient location, this is one of the nicest hotels in the area and is highly recommended.

Amon Hotel (Map p248; ☎ 231 0912; fax 231 1353; Al-Gezira; s/d in new wing E£100/160, s/d in old wing E£80/120; ☒) It's not hard to see why archaeologists like to stay at the Amon. Small and family-run, it is a comfortable and friendly home away from home, with spotless rooms, a lush garden, extremely helpful staff and home-cooked meals. In the new wing the rooms are large with private bathrooms, ceiling fans, air-con and balconies overlooking the courtyard. In the old wing, some of the small rooms have private bathrooms, and all are air-conditioned. On the top floor are three triple rooms (E£230) with an adjoining terrace and stunning views over the Theban Hills and the East Bank.

Nour el-Balad (Map p248; ☎ 242 6111; Ezbet Bisily; s/d/ste E£120/150/500) A beautiful sister hotel to Nour el-Gurna, Nour el-Balad takes the same traditional-with-a-twist style to the edge of the desert. Upper rooms in the large mud-brick house range from an enormous suite with a stunning view over the desert, to simple singles with woven mats, brass beds and arabesque tiles in bathrooms. Downstairs rooms are small and dark but cosy in winter. All have ceiling fans and are highly recommended. To get there, follow the track behind Medinat Habu for 500m.

Hotel El Fayrouz (Map p248; ☎ 312 709; www.elfay rouz.com; Al-Gezira; s/d E£70/100; ☒ ▣) With eight rooms overlooking fields of wheat and clover, this is a calm place to base yourself for exploring the monuments of the West Bank. German management shows in the simple, nicely decorated rooms, which are spotless and have private bathrooms; some also come with air-conditioning. Meals can be had on the comfortable roof terrace or in the popular garden restaurant.

El Nakhil Hotel (Map p248; ☎ /fax 231 3922; www.luxor-westbank.com; Al-Gezira; s/d US$24/33; ✗) A new hotel nestled in a palm grove (*nakhil* means 'palm tree') at the edge of Al-Gezira, El Nakhil has spotless, well-finished domed rooms, all with private bathrooms and air-con. Family-friendly, with cots available for babies, it also has a room that can cater for disabled guests. With views over the fields and a small restaurant, this is an excellent addition to the growing number of mid-range hotels on the West Bank.

Nile Valley Hotel (Map p248; ☎ 231 1477; www.nilevalley.nl; Al-Gezira; s/d E£75/110; ✗) A large pink block almost exactly in front of the taxi lot, the Dutch-run Nile Valley has small, clean rooms, all with private bathrooms and air-con. Some rooms have Nile views but those overlooking the rear garden are quieter and slightly bigger. Upstairs is a good rooftop bar/restaurant with fantastic views of the Nile and Luxor Temple.

Amenophis Hotel (Map p248; ☎ /fax 231 1228; www.luxor-westbank.com; Kom Lolah; s/d E£85/130; ✗) This quiet hotel, in a large building near the Medinat Habu temple complex, is a good midrange choice, with spotless, comfortable rooms, all with air-con, TV and private bathrooms. The rooftop restaurant has stunning views over the temple and the mountains beyond.

El-Gezira Gardens (Map p248; ☎ 231 2505; Al-Gezira; s/d US$25/35, 2-bed chalet $45; ✗ 🕮) A large motel-like complex of rooms and chalets popular with Germans, this is the only midrange hotel on the West Bank to boast a pool. With tacky décor and poorly finished rooms it will not win any style awards but it is an otherwise decent option located close to the Nile but away from the din of the ferry landing.

Top End

Luxor has many four- and five-star hotels, all, with one notable exception, run by international hotel chains.

EAST BANK

Old Winter Palace Hotel and New Winter Palace Hotel (Map pp238-9; ☎ 238 0422; h1661@accor-hotels.com; Corniche el-Nil; old wing r US$235-1125; new wing r US$175-375; ✗ 🕮 🕮) These hotels stand side by side on the Corniche. Ignore the modernist new section (the rooms are in need of a refit) and head to the old, which was built to attract the aristocracy of Europe and is one of Egypt's most famous historic hotels. An atmospheric Victorian pile, it has high ceilings, fabulous views over the Nile, a large garden with exotic trees and shrubs, a swimming pool, table-tennis tables and a tennis court. Its front terrace is the best place in Luxor to sip a drink and watch the sun setting over the Theban hills.

Mövenpick Jolie Ville (☎ 237 4855; www.moevenpick-hotels.com/hotels/HKLXRHH; Crocodile Island; s/d US$165/210; ✗ 🕮 🕮) Set amid lush gardens on Crocodile Island, 4km south of town, this is a great family hotel with a minizoo and playground in addition to the swimming pool, tennis courts and feluccas. There are 320 comfortable, if architecturally unremarkable, bungalow-style rooms, and a hotel motorboat shuttles guests to and from the centre of town.

Sofitel Karnak (☎ 237 8025; www.sofitel.com; El Zinia Gebly St; r US$120-250; ✗ 🕮 🕮) Quiet and secluded, the Sofitel Karnak is nestled in lush gardens beside the Nile 3km north of the Temples of Karnak. Its Nubian-influenced architecture works well with the palms and bougainvilleas, and it is a tranquil haven after the din of the town. As well as comfortable bungalow-style rooms there is a very pleasant (heated) Nileside pool, tennis and squash courts and a fitness centre, sauna and Jacuzzi. Buses are on hand to shuttle guests into the centre of town.

Sheraton Luxor Resort (☎ 237 4544; www.starwoodhotels.com/sheraton; Sharia Khaled ibn al-Walid; r with garden view US$96, with Nile view US$120; ✗ 🕮 🕮) The Sheraton is a secluded three-storey building set amid lush gardens at the southern end of Sharia Khaled ibn al-Walid – close enough to walk to some restaurants but far enough away to avoid any street noise. Rooms are well appointed and those overlooking the Nile have great views. Try to avoid the garden rooms and plump for those in the main building. Prices do not include breakfast and rates are considerably lower if booked through the Internet.

THE AUTHOR'S CHOICE

Al-Moudira (☎ 012 325 1307; moudirahotel@ yahoo.com; Daba'iyya; r/ste US$200/275; ✗ 🔊 💻 🔊) A stunningly beautiful desert retreat, Al-Moudira is a true luxury hotel, with an individuality that is missing from Egypt's bland five-star chain hotels. Redolent of a Moorish palace, with soaring vaults, pointed arches and enormous domes, its 54 rooms are grouped together around small courtyards; inside, each is decorated with its own hand-painted trompe l'oeil theme and antiques from throughout Egypt. Cushioned benches and comfortable antique chairs invite pashalike lounging and the enormous vaulted bathrooms have the feel of a private *hammam* (bathhouse). Quiet and romantic, with fragrant gardens overlooking the desert mountains south of Thebes, this is by far the best hotel in Luxor, if not the whole of Egypt.

Sonesta St George Hotel (Map pp238-9; ☎ 238 2575; www.sonesta.com/egypt_luxor; Sharia Khaled ibn al-Walid; s/d with Nile view US$120/206, with city view US$103/125; ✗ 🔊 🔊) This 224-room marble-filled hotel has a kitsch value that should not be overlooked, with lots of marble, faux Pharaonic columns and a flamelike fence around the roof. It also has friendly staff, comfortable rooms with great views, a heated swimming pool, a business centre and a good selection of restaurants.

Le Meridien Luxor (Map pp238-9; ☎ 236 6999; www.lemeridien.com; Sharia Khaled ibn al-Walid; s/d US$85/95, with Nile view without breakfast US$100/145; ✗ 🔊 🔊) A squat high-rise on the Nile, Le Meridien has bland architecture with the usual lashings of marble and lack of any real style, but its central location and good restaurants warrant mention here. Rooms are comfortable, with the usual amenities, but outdoor space is limited.

Iberotel Luxor Hotel (Map pp238-9; ☎ 238 0925; h1083@accor-hotels.com; Corniche el-Nil; s/d with Nile view US$87/120, with city view US$78/100; ✗ 🔊 🔊) Formerly the Novotel (and still called that locally), this squat high-rise at the southern tip of the Corniche has an indoor atrium, great Nile views and a floating swimming pool. Rooms are comfortable, if small, and the building interior has the look of a cheap package-holiday hotel, but its location on

the Nile just a short distance from Luxor Temple, is unbeatable.

WEST BANK

Flats in Luxor (Map p248; ☎ 010 356 4540; www.flats inluxor.com; per week Jun-Sep E£1900, Oct-May E£2500; 🔊 💻 🔊) Families or those planning a prolonged stay in Luxor might consider a self-catering option. This new block of well-appointed flats is run by a British-Egyptian couple and located between Al-Gezira and New Gurna. All have three double bedrooms, large sitting/dining areas, satellite TV and fully equipped kitchens. The two upper-floor flats have balconies with views over the hills to the west. There's a roof terrace with pool table and sun-loungers, and a downstairs area with pool and Jacuzzi.

EATING

Most people come to Luxor for monuments, not fine cuisine – which is good because the food is generally mediocre. Outside the hotels few serve alcohol or accept credit card payment; exceptions are noted in the reviews. Unless otherwise noted, restaurants tend to open from about 10am until midnight.

Restaurants

EAST BANK

Oasis Café (Map pp238-9; Sharia Dr Labib Habashi; ☎ 012 336 7121; mains E£10-45; 🕙 10am-10pm; 🔊) Finally Luxor has a restaurant that appreciates décor as much as food. Taking up several rooms of a 1920s building in the centre of town, the Oasis has high ceilings, old tiled floors and traditional-style furniture. With jazz softly playing, watercolours on the walls, smoking and nonsmoking rooms, it feels like an oasis of sophistication compared to the brash tourist restaurants elsewhere in town. The food is good too, with an extensive brunch menu and a regular menu of international dishes, including pastas (E£15 to E£20) and grilled meats (E£30 to E£40). A blackboard lists daily specials. Sandwiches (E£12 to E£18) are hearty and a wide selection of pastries and excellent coffee encourage lingering. An excellent new edition to Luxor's restaurant scene.

Jamboree Restaurant (Map pp238-9; ☎ 235 5827, 012 781 3149; Sharia el-Montazah; dishes E£10-30; 🕙 10.30am-2.30pm for snacks & Oriental dishes, 6-10.30pm for full menu; 🔊) A small British-run restaurant, Jamboree serves international fare in its small, bland dining room or upstairs on a pleasant roof terrace. Lunchtime dishes are limited to good homemade sandwiches and snacks. In the evenings there is a (safe) salad bar (E£14.50) and a full menu with good pasta and meat dishes. There is no liquor licence.

Lotus Restaurant (Map pp238-9; ☎ 238 0419; Sharia As-Souq; mains E£8-30; ⛯) Offering a bird's-eye view of the souq, the 1st-floor Lotus has a mixture of Egyptian and international dishes. There are good Eqyptian starters (E£2 to E£4) and some tasty *tagen*s (stews), and a selection of pastas and steaks.

Dawar al-Umda Restaurant (Map pp238-9; ☎ 237 3321; Sharia al-Karnak; mains E£16-20) Set in the garden of the Mercure Inn, this pleasant outdoor restaurant serves Egyptian specialities, with a good selection of mezze in addition to the usual kebab and *kofta* (mincemeat and spices grilled on a skewer). The Egyptian experience is completed by a belly dancer or folkloric show at least once a week, making it advisable to call ahead for reservations.

Kings Head Pub (Map pp238-9; ☎ 237 1249; Sharia Khaled ibn al-Walid; dishes E£10-30; ⛭ 10am-2am; ⛯) The king may be Akhenaten in a Tudor hat, and the temperature outside may be soaring, but inside the light is dim and the temperature closer to the cool of an English summer day. Somehow this appeals to a wide range of punters, from homesick Brits to curious tourists and those who can't live without their Sky sports. Keeping to the theme, curries (about E£10), chips and (on Sundays) roast beef and Yorkshire pud (E£25) are on offer. Beer is reasonably priced (E£12 for a Stella) and there's an array of cocktails and spirits.

Grand Restaurant & Café (Map pp238-9; ☎ 238 6742; Sharia Khaled ibn al-Walid; mains E£12-25; ⛭ 8am-1am; ⛯) A favourite of tour groups, but nonetheless friendly and a good place to enjoy basic Egyptian food, with a good selection of mezze and salads (E£5) and sandwiches (E£9 to E£15). You can top it off with a *sheesha* (E£5). To avoid the groups, try to get a table on the outdoor terrace.

1886 Restaurant (Map pp238-9; ☎ 380 422; Old Winter Palace Hotel, Corniche el-Nil; set menu E£150; ⛯) The food at the Winter Palace may be good relative to the local restaurant scene but it has never quite matched the style and quality of its own architecture, so eating in its showcase restaurant is not so much a gourmet dining experience as a chance to enjoy the hotel's gracious colonial décor. The set menu is Continental, usually with a strong French emphasis, and the atmosphere is formal in a way that only a grand old hotel can be.

Amoun and Al-Hussein Restaurants (Map pp238-9; Sharia al-Karnak; mains E£7-20) In perennial competition, these two adjacent outdoor restaurants serve similar Egyptian dishes, along with pizzas and soups. The marginally more popular Amoun serves reasonable mezze (E£2.50 to E£7) kebab, chicken, fish and various rice and vegetable dishes at slightly lower prices than the Hussein. Both are popular with tourists.

Chez Omar (Map pp238-9; ☎ 012 282 0282; Midan Hassan; meals E£6-15) This outdoor café is a small oasis of green, with 10 tables under umbrellas. It is a pleasant, if noisy, spot for lunch, with basic Egyptian dishes, salads and french fries. Try the daoud basha (E£8), meatballs served steaming hot in a ceramic dish. Although it has no license, the waiters can usually find a Stella (E£8).

Bombay Restaurant (☎ 010 665 9505; Sharia Khaled ibn al-Walid; dishes E£24-45; ⛭ noon-11.30pm; ⛯) With a new and better location and a revamped menu, the Bombay is no doubt hoping to profit from British tourists' preference for curry. At E£80, the lunchtime set menu for two is good value, offering a good choice of basic curry dishes, along with side dishes like dhal and samosas.

Miyako Restaurant (Map pp238-9; ☎ 238 2575; Sonesta St George Hotel, Sharia Khaled ibn al-Walid; dishes E£35-75; ⛯) A welcome change from the usual fare, Luxor's only Japanese restaurant has teppanyaki tables and a *tatami* room and serves a wide selection of Japanese dishes, including sushi and sashimi.

La Mama (☎ 237 4544; Sheraton Luxor Resort, Sharia Khaled ibn al-Walid; dishes E£12-45) The Italian restaurant on the terrace at the entrance to the Sheraton is a good bet if you've got kids in tow. Apart from the aging pelican that wanders around amusing diners, there's a good selection of pizzas and pastas, all served in clean five-star surroundings.

Oum Hashim Restaurant (Map pp238-9; ☎ 238 6521; Sharia Yousef Hassan; meals E£8-35 ⛯) Good solid Egyptian fare is on offer at this 1st-floor restaurant. Popular with locals for its kebab and *kofta* it is a no-nonsense but clean restaurant that also serves vegetable *tagens* (E£8) and the usual selection of salads and pickles.

7 Days 7 Ways (☎ 236 6264; Sharia Khaled ibn al-Walid; mains E£11-30; ☒) Forget local cuisine; above the Royal Oak Pub, Britannia rules again, with those delightful dishes you thought (hoped?) you'd never see on the banks of the Nile: chip butties (E£11), roast beef and Yorkshire pud (E£29.50, Sundays only) and other stodgy fare. All to be washed down with a cold Stella (E£10.50).

Mish Mish (Map pp238-9; ☎ 238 1756; Sharia Tel-evizyon; meals E£7-18) A long-standing budget-traveller haunt, Mish Mish is showing its age these days. Its prices have jumped too. It's a basic café/restaurant with reasonably priced pizza (E£9 to E£16), salads (E£3 to E£5) and piping hot *tagens* (E£12). There is also fresh fruit juice for E£3.

WEST BANK

Restaurant Mohammed (Map p248; ☎ 231 1014; Gurna; dishes E£12-30) With a shady outdoor terrace and laid-back atmosphere, Mohammed's is the perfect place to recharge batteries in the middle of a day exploring temples and tombs. Attached to owner Mohammed Abdel Lahi's mud-brick house, dishes are cooked by his wife and mother and served by Mohammed himself or his son. There is no menu (you are told what's on offer that day) but you can usually get good, basic Egyptian food, with a variety of home-grown salads, as well as standard chicken or duck and French-fry platters. Stella is available (E£8.50).

Al-Moudira (Map p248; ☎ 012 325 1307; Daba'iyya; dishes E£15-70) In keeping with its décor, Al-Moudira has some of the most sophisticated food in town, with fantastic salads at its poolside restaurant and a mixture of Western and Lebanese cuisine in its sumptuous dining rooms. Whichever you choose, you can be sure the experience will be unforgettable. Call ahead for reservations.

Marsam Hotel (Map p248; ☎ 238 2403; Gurna; lunch E£25, dinner E£20) This hotel near the Antiquities Inspectorate ticket office serves surprisingly good, fresh food in its tree-filled courtyard. Lunch dishes are usually Egyptian specialities, such as stuffed pigeon and lentil soup, while Western-style meals are served in the evenings. Because it is a set menu and the hotel is often full, it is a good idea to call ahead. Beer is not available.

Nour el-Gurna (Map p248; ☎ 231 1430; Gurna; meals E£15-20) Stuffed pigeon, duck and other hearty local dishes are served under a palm-reed shade or in a cool room, depending on the season. Near the Antiquities Inspectorate ticket office, this is a friendly and pleasant place to eat, but alcohol is not available.

Africa Restaurant (Map p248; ☎ 012 365 8722; Al-Gezira; meals E£25) On the right just up the hill from the ferry landing, the Africa Restaurant is a favourite of foreign archaeologists. The food is simple (meat, poultry or fish, accompanied by rice, vegetables and salad) but delicious and is served on a pleasant outdoor terrace. A Stella can usually be conjured up for E£9.

Al-Gezira Hotel (Map p248; ☎ 231 0034; Al-Gezira; dishes E£15-35) This comfortable rooftop restaurant serves Egyptian specialities such as the infamous *molokhiyya* (stewed leaf soup) and *mahshi kurumb* (stuffed cabbage leaves). There are great views over the Nile and the bright lights of Luxor beyond. Beer and wine are available.

Nile Valley Hotel (Map p248; ☎ 231 1477; Al-Gezira; meals E£13-28) A popular rooftop restaurant with a bird's-eye view of the action along the West Bank's waterfront, the Nile Valley has a wide ranging menu of Egyptian and international specialties, but is also a good place to relax with a cold drink and a *sheesha*. On Sunday nights a buffet (E£40) is accompanied by Sufi dancing and local music.

Hatshepsut Restaurant (Map p248; ☎ 231 0469; Gurna; mains E£12-35) This 2nd-floor, shaded, rooftop restaurant is above an alabaster shop and has great views over Hatshepsut's temple and the Theban hills. It serves a mixture of Egyptian and Western dishes. Stick to the Egyptian dishes and head over here in the evenings, when the atmosphere can be good, especially in the cooler months, when Saidi music and dancing takes place.

Tutankhamun Restaurant (Map p248; ☎ 231 0118; Al-Gezira; dishes E£10-25) This small restaurant is on the riverside just south of the local ferry dock. It's run by Aam Mahmoud, a former cook at one of the French archaeological missions in Luxor, who serves up excellent *tagens*, duck à l'orange and other dishes. Unfortunately, the grubby surroundings detract from the food and make one reluctant to gamble with the salads.

Quick Eats

EAST BANK

Sayyida Zeinab (Map pp238-9; Sharia Televizyon; dishes E£2.50-5.50) This tiny but spotless place is one of Luxor's best kushari joints. Takeaway only.

Restaurant Abu'l Hassan el-Shazly (Map pp238-9; Sharia Abdel Moneim al-Adasi; mains E£9-26) A cross between a restaurant and café, Abul Hassan is where locals go for good Egyptian fare such as stuffed pigeon and rice. *Sheeshas* are available for E£2.

Koshari Elzaeem (Map pp238-9; Midan Hussein; dishes E£4-11; ⏰ 24hr) A very popular kushari restaurant that also serves an Egyptian version of spaghetti (E£6 to E£11). There are a few tables, but they fill up fast.

Abu Ashraf (Map pp238-9; ☎ 380 209; Sharia al-Mahatta; dishes E£2-9) This large, popular restaurant and takeaway is just down from the train station. It serves roasted chicken (E£10), pizzas (E£12 to E£18), kushari (E£4 to E£6) and kebabs (E£14).

Salt & Bread Cafeteria (Map pp238-9; Midan al-Mahatta; dishes E£4-10) Quick, cheap meals, including kebab, pigeon, chicken and a variety of omelettes, are served here, although its location next to the train station means that eating meals here can sometimes be noisy.

Self-Catering

Luxor has a number of good bakeries. Try the ones on Sharia Ahmed Orabi, at the beginning of Sharia al-Karnak and on Sharia Gedda (all Map pp238–9).

Fruit & Vegetable Souq (Map pp238-9; Sharia as-Souq) This is the best place for fruit and veg, although the good stuff sells out early in the morning. On either side of the main street are little shops selling produce and groceries throughout the day.

Bakri Supermarket (Map pp238-9; cnr Sharias Medina & Televizyon) A bustling, well-stocked, Western-style store with a good selection of imported products as well as yogurts and cheeses kept in clean, functioning fridges.

Omar (Map pp238-9; Sharia Medina al-Manawwara) A large Western-style minimarket, which has a range of imported goodies.

Al-Ahram Beverages (Map pp238-9; ☎ 237 2445; Sharia Ramses) Al-Ahram Beverages is the Luxor outlet for Egypt's monopoly beer and wine producer.

DRINKING

East Bank

Kings Head Pub (Map pp238-9; ☎ 237 1249; Sharia Khaled ibn al-Walid; 🍺) A relaxed and perennially popular place to have a drink and shoot pool, the Kings Head tries to capture the atmosphere of an English pub without being twee. The laid-back atmosphere also means that women can come here without being harassed.

Nile Terrace Café & Bar (Map pp238-9; ☎ 238 0422; Corniche el-Nil; ⏰ 9am-7pm) The terrace in front of the Old Winter Palace Hotel is the most elegant place in Luxor to watch the sun slowly set over the Theban hills. Starched collars and gin and tonics are the rule here, but there is also ice-cold beer (E£23); or you can order afternoon tea if you prefer.

Metropolitan Café (Map pp238-9; lower level, Corniche el-Nil) A pleasant, popular outdoor café right on the Nile, in front of the Winter Palace Hotel, with a view of the river that is often marred by moored cruise boats. It also serves alcohol and, with its riverside vantage point, is a good place to enjoy a sundowner.

Oum Koulsoum Coffee Shop (Map pp238-9; off Sharia Al-Karnak) An extremely popular *ahwa* (coffeehouse) next to the Nefertiti hotel. Because it caters to tourists as well as locals, women can enjoy a *sheesha* and coffee (E£4) too.

Murphy's Irish Pub (Map pp238-9; ☎ 238 8101; Sharia al-Gawazat; 🍺) With polished wood and a family atmosphere, this pub is a nice place to escape to for a quick, cooling Stella beer or a long evening with friends.

Royal Oak Pub (Map pp238-9; ☎ 236 6264; 2nd fl, Sharia Khaled ibn al-Walid; ⏰ 4pm-2am; 🍺) Yet another attempt to re-create an English pub, complete with bitter on tap, dim light and the ubiquitous Sky TV.

St Joseph Bar (Map pp238-9; St Joseph Hotel, Sharia Khalid ibn al-Wali; ☎ 238 1707) Not an especially exciting venue but popular with those who aren't looking for little England by the Nile. Its popularity is helped by a happy hour that changes depending on the season (call ahead to check), but is currently between 9pm and 10pm, when beer is reduced by 30% and spirits by 50%.

West Bank

There are no real bars on the West Bank; drinking is done at restaurants or not at all.

Ramses Cafeteria (Map p248; Kom Lolah) This friendly outdoor café, in front of Medinat

Habu, is the best place to sip a cold drink after wandering through Ramses III's magnificent temple. The view is superlative and the atmosphere is relaxing.

Ramesseum Rest House (Map p248; beside the Ramesseum, Gurna) A friendly, laid-back place to relax after temple-viewing. In addition to the usual mineral water and soft drinks, Stella is sometimes available

ENTERTAINMENT
East Bank

With tourism booming in Luxor, the town is busy at night. This is not the place to go clubbing, unless you're into dancing to outmoded disco music, but there are some bars with a decent atmosphere. Most of the larger hotels put on a folkloric show several times each week, depending on the season and number of tour groups around.

Dawar al-Umda (Map pp238-9; ☎ 237 3321; Mercure Inn, Sharia al-Karnak) Dawar al-Umda has a popular folkloric show that includes a belly dancer, *rababa* music (named after the instrument that resembles a single-stringed violin) and occasionally a snake charmer. The show does not have a regular schedule, but it usually takes place twice a week in the high season. Call the hotel for information.

Mövenpick Jolie Ville (☎ 237 4855; Crocodile Island; ticket E£150) This folkloric show involves wearing a *galabiyya* (traditional Egyptian man's robe), going on a felucca ride at sunset, being introduced to 'peasants', and then fed and entertained in a tent by the Nile. Call the resort for up-to-date information on the schedule.

If you'd rather move about on the dance floor yourself, the disco at **Tutotel** (Map pp238-9; ☎ 237 7990) is one of the more popular options, while at **Hotel Mercure** (Map pp238-9; ☎ 238 0944; nonguest minimum E£20) the extra charge covers you for watching the belly-dancing show at 11.30pm too.

West Bank

If you want to avoid the bright lights of the town, the West Bank is the place to be. Pharaoh's or Nobi Horse Stables (p271) and QEA (p271) arrange evening desert barbecues for groups of 10 or more and sometimes put on a horse-dancing show.

Hatshepsut Restaurant (Map p248; ☎ 231 0469; Gurna) On Sunday and Wednesday there is a popular belly-dancing and Saidi music

show that usually includes an exhibition of *tahtib* (Saidi stick dancing).

Nile Valley Hotel (Map p248; ☎ 231 1477; Al-Gezira) On Sundays (and occasionally on other days according to demand) you can watch and dance to local musicians on the Nile Valley's pleasant rooftop terrace.

SHOPPING

The whole range of standard Egyptian souvenirs can be bought in Luxor. One exception is alabaster, which is mainly sold on the West Bank. The alabaster is mined about 80km northwest of the Valley of the Kings, and some of the handmade cups, vases and other articles make original souvenirs. Take care when buying, however; the quality can be poor and sometimes what passes for stone is actually wax with stone chips.

The *tagen* (clay pots) that are used in local cooking make a more unusual buy. Extremely practical, they can be used to cook on top of the stove or in the oven and they look good on the table too. Prices start at E£5 for a very small pot and go up to about E£30. They are on sale on the street just beside the police station in Luxor.

Fair Trade Center Luxor Outlet (Map pp238-9; ☎ 238 7015; www.egyptfairtrade.org; Sharia al-Karnak) A nonprofit shop that markets handicrafts from NGO projects throughout Egypt, with a good selection of hand-carved wood and pottery from the nearby villages of Hejaza and Garagos, bead work from Sinai and recycled paper from Cairo. Prices are low and you can be satisfied that you are supporting people in need.

Winter Akhmeem Gallery (Map pp238-9; ☎ 238 0422; Corniche el-Nil) A small shop, beside the staircase to the Old Winter Palace, stuffed with beautiful hand-woven cotton, linen and silk from Akhmin, near Sohag. Prices are steep, averaging E£50 to E£150 per metre, but this is still cheaper than you'd pay for something comparable in most other countries. *Galabiyyas* and shirts can also be made to measure.

GETTING THERE & AWAY
Air

EgyptAir (Map pp238-9; ☎ 238 0581; Corniche el-Nil; ☒ 8am-8pm) operates several daily flights between Cairo, Luxor and Aswan. A one-way ticket to Cairo costs E£714. Tickets to Aswan cost E£360 one way. There are three flights per week to Sharm el-Sheikh (E£537 one way). Flights to Abu Simbel only operate in high season but involve such long waits in Aswan that you're better off arranging a trip from there.

Bus

The bus station has recently been moved to a new location about 1km from the airport, but **Upper Egypt Bus Co** (Map pp238-9; ☎ 232 2218; ticket office, Sharia al-Karnak) tickets can still be bought from the old office in town. A minibus takes passengers to the new station 30 minutes before departure time for E£5. For buses leaving before 9am, passengers have to make their way by private taxi (about E£25). Check with the tourist office to see if this arrangement has changed.

Buses heading to Cairo leave at 7am and 9pm (E£85, 10 to 11 hours). These services are often full so reserve at least a day in advance.

Seven daily buses head to Hurghada (E£25 to E£30, five hours) from 6.30am to 9pm. All stop in Qena (E£5, one to two hours) and Safaga (E£15 to E£20, four to six hours) and go on to Suez (E£46 to E£55, eight to 10 hours). For Quseir and Marsa Alam, change at Safaga. A bus to Sharm el-Sheikh (E£100) and Dahab (E£110, 14 to 16 hours) leaves at 5pm. It is often full so try to reserve in advance.

There are frequent buses to Qena (E£3 to E£5) between 6.30am and 8pm.

Buses travelling to Aswan (E£15, four to five hours) leave at 7.15am, 9.30am and 3.30pm. These are through-services from Qena and Hurghada, so there may not always be seats. The same buses go to Esna (E£5), Edfu (E£10) and Kom Ombo (E£12).

There are buses to Al-Kharga (E£40, three to four hours) on Sunday and Wednesday at 1pm, and Saturday and Tuesday at 7:15am.

Cruise Ship

For information on the 250 cruise boats that ply the Nile between Luxor and Aswan see p286.

Felucca

You can take a felucca from Luxor to Aswan but unless you have a strong wind, it can take days to go more than a few kilometres. For more information, see p287.

POLICE CONVOYS

Getting out of Luxor by road usually involves going in police convoy (see p548). Current convoy times to Hurghada are 8am, 2pm and 6pm. Day trips to Dendara and Abydos leave with the 8am convoy and branch off at Qena with their own escort. There is also a 2pm trip to Dendara. Both return at around 5.30pm.

To Aswan the convoys leave at 7am (stopping at Esna, Kom Ombo and Edfu), 11am (direct) and 3pm (direct). Check these times with the tourist office before travelling.

Vehicles congregate on Sharia Serb (see Map pp238–9) about 30 minutes before the convoy time.

If you are heading further afield by car, you will not fit into the convoy schedule but will still be given a police escort. There are police checkpoints at most municipal boundaries so chances of eluding them are slim. Irritatingly, at each checkpoint your police escort will probably change, involving a delay of a few minutes each time. If possible take the train.

Service Taxi

Foreigners are forbidden from taking service taxis at present. Instead you have to rent the entire vehicle and go in a convoy. The drivers are always ready to bargain for special trips up the Nile to Aswan, stopping at the sights on the way; expect to pay about E£200. To Hurghada, the going rate is about E£300. Make sure you are at the taxi stand 30 minutes before the convoy leaves.

Travellers planning a trip from Luxor to Al-Kharga have to push the police hard if they don't want to go on a long detour to Asyut. Taxis are reluctant to undertake the trip and their current asking price is E£700 for the car (maximum seven people).

Train

Luxor Station (Map pp238-9; ☎ 237 2018; Midan al-Mahatta) has left-luggage facilities, plenty of cardphones and a post office.

The **Abela Egypt Sleeping Train** (☎ 237 2015; www.sleepingtrains.com) goes daily to Cairo at 8.30pm and 9.30pm (single/double including dinner and breakfast US$74/106, nine hours). There are no student discounts; tickets must be paid for in US dollars or euros.

Other trains to Cairo permitted for foreigners are the 981 at 9.15am (1st/2nd class E£62/40, 10 hours), which stops in Balyana (E£16/13, three hours) for those who wish to visit Abydos; 1903 at 9.15pm (1st/2nd class E£67/45, 10 hours); and 980 at 11.10pm (1st/2nd class E£67/45, nine hours). All trains stop in the Nile Valley towns of Qena (1st/2nd class E£15/12), Sohag (E£30/21), Asyut (E£40/26), Minya (E£49/32) and Beni Suef (E£58/36). Student discounts are available on all.

To Aswan (three hours) there are three trains: 996 at 7.15am (1st/2nd class E£30/23); 1902 at 9.30am (1st/2nd class E£30/23); and No 980 at 5pm (1st/2nd class E£26/16). All stop at Esna (1st/2nd class E£14/12), Edfu (E£19/15) and Kom Ombo (E£25/18). Student discounts are available.

There is also a train to Al-Kharga every Thursday at 6am or 7am, depending on the time of year (adult/student E£11/6 in 3rd class only; eight to 10 hours).

GETTING AROUND
To/From the Airport
Luxor airport is 7km east of town. A taxi costs at least E£25 from the centre of town. To get to or from the West Bank costs about E£70. There is no bus between the airport and the town.

Bicycle
A compact town, Luxor lends itself to cycling and distances on the generally flat West Bank are just far enough to give some exercise but not far enough to exhaust (except when the weather is hot). Cycling at night is inadvisable given the local habit of leaving headlights off.

Almost all hotels rent out bikes. Expect to pay from E£10 to E£15 per day and choose carefully – there's nothing worse than getting stuck with a broken chain halfway to the Valley of the Kings. You can take bikes across to the West Bank on the *baladi* ferry (see p270). If you're based on the West Bank, see p270.

Felucca
There is a multitude of feluccas to take you on short trips around Luxor. They leave from various points all along the river. How much you pay depends on your bargaining

---

BROOKE HOSPITAL FOR ANIMALS

Desert rides and horse-drawn carriages are a memorable part of any trip to Egypt but the way some of the animals are treated shocks many visitors. However, there are people working to combat animal cruelty. Although not really a tourist sight, the **Brooke Hospital** (Map pp238-9; ☎ 238 1305; Sharia Muntazha; ⌚ 8am-1.30pm & 5-7pm) is part of a worldwide network of clinics aiming to provide at least minimum care for animals, especially those put to work. It has been operating in Luxor for more than 30 years and welcomes visitors who want to see what is done for the horses that pull the *calèches* through the streets of Luxor. Make sure you read the notice board of dos and don'ts on the treatment of horses, which includes not tipping drivers for pushing the animals into going too fast.

If you are interested in its work, the Brooke Hospital also has branches in **Cairo** (head office ☎ 02-364 9312), Alexandria, Edfu and Aswan.

---

skills, but you're looking at about E£15 to E£20 for an hour of sailing.

Hantour
Also called a *calèche*, horse and carriages cost about E£20 to E£50 per hour depending on your haggling skills (this is where you really need them). Expect to pay about E£10 to get to Karnak.

Pick-up Taxis
Covered pick-up trucks and microbuses are often the quickest and easiest way to get about. To get to the Temples of Karnak, take a microbus from Luxor station or from behind Luxor Temple for 50pt. Other routes run inside the town. For information about West Bank pick-ups, see p270.

Taxi
There are plenty of taxis in Luxor but passengers still have to bargain hard for trips. A short trip around town is likely to cost at least E£10. Taxis can also be hired for day trips around the West Bank; expect to pay E£100 to E£200, depending on the length of the excursion and your bargaining skills.

Cruising the Nile

The ancient Greek traveller and writer Herodotus described Egypt as 'the gift of the Nile', while the ancient Egyptians likened their land to a lotus – the Delta being the flower, the oasis of Al-Fayoum the bud, and the river and its valley the stem. Whichever way you look at it, Egypt *is* the Nile. The river is the lifeblood of the country and the fertile Nile Valley is its main artery.

As the world's longest river, the Nile cuts through an incredible 6680km of Africa as it winds its way north towards the Mediterranean Sea. It begins its journey from two main sources 1500km apart: Lake Victoria in Uganda, from where the White Nile journeys almost 3000km, and Lake Tana in the Ethiopian Highlands, from where the Blue Nile emerges. The two rivers converge at Khartoum in Sudan. They are joined by a single tributary, the Atbara, about 320km north of Khartoum. From there the river flows northwards to the Mediterranean without any other source contributing to the waters.

Although the Nile Basin covers a colossal 3.35 million sq km – an incredible 10% of the African continent – and is shared by 10 countries, Egypt is the main beneficiary of this mighty river. Rain seldom falls in the Nile Valley but until the river was dammed, first by the British in 1902, and then by the Egyptians themselves in 1971, it would break its banks each summer and flood the surrounding land, covering it with a rich layer of silt. As the waters subsided farmers would plant seeds on their newly fertilised land and wait for the crops to grow. As Herodotus put it, the Egyptians 'gather in the fruits of the earth with less labour than any other people'.

HISTORY OF NILE TRAVEL

Until decent roads began to be built in the late 19th century, travel in Egypt meant sailing on the Nile. For millennia the river was Egypt's main transport corridor and information highway, the simplest and quickest way to move cargo, send messages or visit other areas of the country. Away from the river, the desert terrain was difficult to negotiate, slow and dangerous. Such was the ease of boat travel on the Nile that, despite their incredible feats of engineering, the ancient Egyptians didn't have the wheel until about a thousand years after they built the Pyramids. River travel was so central to the Egyptian psyche that it was perfectly natural for the dead to sail to the afterlife, and for the sun god Ra to travel through the sky in a boat.

The earliest boats are thought to have been simple skiffs made of papyrus bun-dles. These would probably have been used for hunting and travelling short distances throughout the Pharaonic period. The ancient Egyptians also had more elaborate wooden boats with multiple sets of oars, a long narrow sail and a steering oar that later evolved into a rudder. The most elaborate surviving example of an ancient boat can be seen at the Solar Barque Museum (p132) at the Pyramids of Giza. Numerous models of simpler boats were found in tombs and can be seen at Cairo's Egyptian Museum (p167).

By the Middle Ages, when Cairo had become Egypt's capital and one of the world's wealthiest trading centres, one Italian traveller estimated that there were as many as 36,000 ships on the Nile. Some were simple, lateen (triangular) sailed cargo boats, given the Italian name felucca; others were elaborate vessels for the rich, the Rolls Royces of their era. These were the dahabiyyas,

---

THE BEST ON THE NILE

When money is no object Enjoying a private cruise on a refurbished dahabiyya (p287).

Economy cruise Taking a felucca trip from Aswan to Edfu (p287).

Nubian treat Sailing to Abu Simbel on the *Kasr Ibrim* (p291).

Nostalgia trip Reliving Agatha Christie's Egypt on the Nile's last steamer, the *Sudan* (p290).

Five-star plutocracy Relaxing in one of the 20 suites on board the *M/S Triton* (p290).

Family fun Combining luxury cruising and sightseeing with kid-friendly cooking on the *Sun Boat III* (p291).

---

described by medieval historians as lavishly decorated, two-masted wooden boats with private cabins and bathrooms. By the time Europeans began travelling here in earnest in the 19th century, the dahabiyya was the preferred mode of transport. A trip from Cairo to Abu Simbel on one of these elegant vessels took the better part of two months, and a large part of the preparations for any trip on the Nile was the renting and kitting out of one's home-away-from-home.

In 1869 Nile travel was changed forever when Thomas Cook, a printer from Britain, brought his first group of tourists to Egypt, accommodating them in two steamers. Package tourism was born and steamers gradually edged out dahabiyyas, making travel on the Nile relatively cheap and accessible for ever-growing numbers of visitors.

Today a trip on the famous river is part of almost every package itinerary to Egypt. From the humble steamer, cruisers have now grown into huge floating hotels. Visitors can fly directly to Upper Egypt from Europe, spend five days on the Nile and be back home again within a week.

ITINERARIES & SITES

With their schedules drawn up months in advance, large cruisers stick to fairly rigid itineraries, particularly on the busy Luxor–Aswan stretch of the Nile. On these trips, generally lasting from three to eight nights, days are spent visiting monuments, relaxing by the pool or enjoying the restaurant offerings. By night there is a variety of entertainment: cocktails, dancing and fancy-dress parties – usually called a 'galabiyya (man's

robe) party', as passengers are encouraged to 'dress like an Egyptian' – are all part of the fun. Actual sailing time is minimal on most of these trips – often as little as four hours each day, depending on the itinerary.

Feluccas and dahabiyyas determine their own schedules and, because they do not need special mooring sites, can stop at small islands or antiquities sites that are skipped by the big cruisers. Using sail-power instead of large engines, a far greater proportion of time is spent sailing. Night-time entertainment is more likely to be star gazing, listening to the sounds of the river, or occasionally music from crew members or villagers.

The stretch of the Nile between Luxor and Aswan has the greatest concentration of

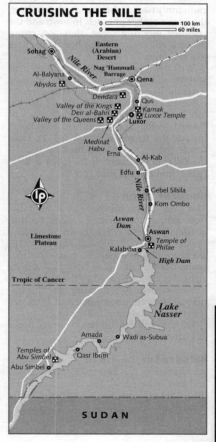

CRUISING THE NILE

0   100 km
0   60 miles

well-preserved monuments in the country, which is why it also has the greatest number of boats and tourists (sailing in both directions). No boats sail north of Abydos, in part because the security forces in northern Upper Egypt are still jittery (see p200). Feluccas and dahabiyyas rarely sail north of Esna because police permits are difficult to get. Dahabiyya operators will bus passengers down to Esna from Luxor. Felucca trips generally start in Aswan and end south of Esna; captains can arrange onward transport to Luxor, but this will cost extra.

The following are the most common stops on cruise itineraries.

Luxor

Almost all boats spend at least one (more commonly two) nights moored here. Given the large number of hotels in town and the crowded mooring scene, those on cruise boats should try to keep on-board time here to a minimum.

With so many ancient sites located in and around Luxor, most cruises can only cover the bare minimum. Most travellers recommend spending an extra day or two before or after the cruise to get a fuller view of the archaeological richness here. Highlights include the **Temples of Karnak** (p242), **Luxor Temple** (p240), the **Valley of the Kings** (p251), the **Valley of the Queens** (p267), **Deir al-Bahri** (p262) and **Medinat Habu** (p269).

NORTH OF LUXOR

The area north of Luxor was excluded from cruiser itineraries for years because of Islamist violence, but the archaeological sites at **Dendara** (p229) and **Abydos** (p226) are beginning to appear on tour schedules again. Usually this means taking a seven- or eight-day cruise, instead of the usual four- or five-day trip. Not all boats offer this option so sites are uncrowded and there are fewer cruisers at mooring docks.

Feluccas and dahabiyyas do not sail north of Luxor.

Between Luxor & Aswan

All cruisers stop at **Esna** (p295), **Edfu** (p297) and **Kom Ombo** (p300). On some cruises, all three sites are visited in a single day. While none of the sites is so large that this is unrealistic, exploring three great temples is a lot to jam into one day and the rushed visit

means that you will be moored longer at Luxor or Aswan.

Dahabiyyas and feluccas take longer to cover the distance between the three temples, usually seeing only one a day. Most dahabiyyas (and some feluccas) also stop at the rarely visited sites of **Al-Kab** (p296) and **Gebel Silsila** (p299). Cruisers do not have moorings here so visitors will likely be limited to your fellow passengers.

Aswan

If you embark at Aswan you will probably spend only one night in the town, but some cruisers stay moored for two nights. Most itineraries include a visit to **Philae** (p319), site of the Temple of Isis, the **High Dam** (p320) and the Northern Quarries, site of the **unfinished obelisk** (p307). Occasionally cruisers offer a felucca ride around **Elephantine Island** (p307) as an excursion. Some also offer an optional half-day tour (generally by plane) to **Abu Simbel** (p328).

Lake Nasser

This lake was created when the High Dam was built near Aswan, and covers the land of Nubia, site of hundreds of tombs, temples and churches (see p322 for details of Nubian history and culture). Many monuments were moved from their original sites prior to the building of the dam and are grouped together at four locations: **Kalabsha** (p325), **Wadi as-Subua** (accessible only by boat; p326), **Amada** (accessible only by boat; p327) and, of course, **Abu Simbel** (p328).

Because there are only six cruisers sailing on Lake Nasser, moorings are never crowded and monuments – with the exception of the Temple of Ramses at Abu Simbel – are not overrun. Itineraries are generally three nights and four days from Aswan to Abu Simbel, or four nights and five days from Abu Simbel to Aswan.

TRAVEL ON THE NILE TODAY

There are hundreds of cruisers travelling the Nile, but they are not the only option for river journeys. Cheaper and more popular with independent travellers are feluccas; these simple sailing boats are an alternative to the crowds and noise of the large boats. For those who want more comfort – and have a larger budget – there are a few beautifully restored dahabiyyas sailing between

Esna and Aswan, offering a return to the days of luxurious, leisurely Nile travel.

Dahabiyyas

The choice between a dahabeeyah and a steamer is like the choice between travelling with post-horses and travelling by rail. The one is expensive, leisurely, delightful; the other is cheap, swift, and comparatively comfortless.

Amelia Edwards,
A Thousand Miles Up the Nile

When the 19th-century traveller Amelia Edwards wrote these lines, package steamer tours were already crowding dahabiyyas off the Nile, and for most of the 20th century dahabiyyas were not seen on the river. But a few smart companies have recognised that some people want to sail in presteamer style – and are prepared to pay for it. The buzz on the Nile is that there will soon be more dahabiyyas spreading their sails but for now this remains an exceptional way to travel. We have listed four boats. All are beautifully appointed, with an antique feel, tasteful décor and double lateen sails. They also have water filters, their own generators and hook-ups to get electricity at certain moorings. Most are privately chartered for honeymooners, extended families or groups of friends. With such small numbers of passengers, this is the most luxurious way to see the monuments without crowds. With flexible itineraries and personalised service, it is also the best way to feel truly independent while travelling in comfort. For the time being, police regulations forbid these boats from sailing between Luxor and Esna. Prices include all meals and transfers to and from airports/train stations and most include the entrance to monuments but you should check when booking your trip. Trips are best arranged before you depart for Egypt.

Assouan (☎ 010 657 8322; www.nourelnil.com; 5-day trip per person approx US$1800) A replica of a 19th-century dahabiyya indistinguishable from the original, the beautifully finished *Assouan* is the largest dahabiyya currently on the Nile. At 37m long and 6.25m wide, it has room for 16 passengers in eight well-appointed cabins with private bathrooms. Because it is newly built, plumbing and water filtration are state of the art. It is also the only dahabiyya that can store power, so

night-lights and toilets can be used without the noise of a generator. Regardless of the modern conveniences, the boat is reminiscent of another, more gracious age of travel. With tailor-made tours, and moorings at small islands and outside villages, this is a unique way to see the Nile.

Vivant Denon (☎ 33-61 015 3789; www.dahabeya .fr.st; per person per week from US$1126, entire boat per week US$6568) Named after an artist who accompanied Napoleon to Egypt, the 30m-long *Vivant Denon* was built in 1889 and has been restored by owner Didier Caille. The boat sails only between October and April and most passengers are French (although English is spoken by Didier and the crew). The emphasis is less on luxury than on simple good taste. Passengers enjoy individually tailored trips that appreciate the beauty of the landscape and the local culture as much as the monuments. It sleeps six.

Neferu-Ra (www.museum-tours.com/tours/neferura .htm; up to 3 people US$3000, each extra person US$1000) Built in 1910 for an Egyptian pasha, the beautifully restored *Neferu-Ra* measures 23m by 4.5m. It sleeps a maximum of five in three single cabins and a double suite. There is also a cosy Victorian salon and a sun deck. The eight-day tour (six nights sailing, one night in a Luxor hotel) takes in the temples at Esna, Edfu and Kom Ombo, as well as Gebel Silsila. A guide is on board to pass passengers around the monuments.

Royal Cleopatra (www.nubiannilecruises.com; d per person, 7-day trip US$1825) The *Royal Cleopatra* is not, strictly speaking, a dahabiyya, but rather a 19m-long *sandale,* a type of modified felucca with two masts that is often used to carry heavy cargo on the Nile. Slightly less picturesque than the other boats listed here, it has nevertheless been beautifully refitted with a bar and living room, two staterooms (these can be configured according to guests' wishes) and private bathrooms. It sleeps up to six and a crew of five, including a resident Egyptologist, looks after your every need. The seven-day tour (the most regimented offering of the four boats listed here) starts at Esna and ends at Aswan. Shorter sailing times are also available.

Feluccas

For many travellers, the only way to see the Nile is from the deck of a felucca. The small size of the boat limits the number of

PLANNING YOUR FELUCCA TRIP

Ensure that your boat is river-worthy Check that the captain has what appears to be a decent, functioning boat, with some blankets and cooking implements, a sunshade and something comfortable to sit on. There should also be a place to lock up valuables. If a different boat is foisted on you at the last minute, be firm in refusing to take it. Likewise with the captain himself – many travellers agree to sail with one man and find themselves with someone else when they get on the boat.

Establish whether the price includes food To be sure you're getting what you paid for, go with whoever does the shopping. Otherwise, set a price for the trip without food and purchase your own.

Agree on the number of passengers beforehand Don't be talked into taking 'a few others on board later downriver', otherwise you'll find yourselves sharing limited supplies of food, water and space.

Decide on the drop-off point before you set sail Although you may think you're going to Edfu, many felucca captains stop 30km short of the town in the villages of Hammam, Faris or Ar-Ramady and arrange for 'special' shared taxis – which take you straight to a hotel of the captain's choice in Luxor for E£10 per person.

Don't hand over your passport Often captains, or more likely middlemen, like to take passports so that they have a couple of passengers 'in the bag'. They then scour around for other people. A photocopy will do for the permit.

Take plenty of bottled water Captains often dip into the Nile for cooking and drinking water.

Bring comfort essentials It can get bitterly cold at night, and the supply of blankets on board won't be enough, so bring a sleeping bag. Insect repellent is a good idea. A hat is essential.

Think ahead Accidents occasionally happen with feluccas. Life jackets are not kept on board, and although nobody will object if you bring your own, you should think twice about taking such a trip if you cannot swim. Packing all your belongings in sealed plastic bags will not only keep them dry, it will help them to float to the surface in the case of an accident. Keeping your important documents on you in a money belt is another common-sense tip.

Take your rubbish with you If you camp overnight on an island or beach, pick up after yourself. After all, nobody wants to spend their trip sitting in a garbage dump.

passengers and means that you have a far more intimate experience of the river and the monuments; the low prices mean that these trips are open to all budgets.

Although it can be difficult to keep small children amused on a sailing boat all day, felucca trips can make great family holidays, especially with older kids. Egyptians love children and the captain and crew will enjoy having them aboard. Just keep in mind that you will have to bring your own life jackets and other safety equipment.

Most felucca trips began at Aswan; the strong northward current means that boats are not marooned if the wind dies. Trips go to Kom Ombo (two days, one night) Edfu (three days, two nights – the most popular option) or Esna (four days, three nights). A typical itinerary is to set sail in the morning and to spend the day heading towards the town of Kom Ombo. Many of the felucca captains are Nubian and will take you for tea in their village along the way. (While you are not expected to pay for this, it is a good idea to have some sweets or pens on hand to give children. Also, women should dress modestly for these excursions.) Nights

are spent on the boat or camping on an island in the Nile. Night-time entertainment ranges from stargazing to partying, depending on you and your fellow passengers. Once you arrive at your destination you can either return to Aswan or head north to Luxor by specially arranged service taxi.

Arranging a felucca trip can seem daunting when you face the legions of touts on Aswan's Corniche. The small hotels can be just as aggressive in trying to rope you in. While it is easier to let the hotels do the organising, remember that they get a percentage of the price, which either comes out of the captain's fee or your food allowance. If you want to be sure of what you're getting it's best to arrange things yourself.

Officially, feluccas can carry a minimum of six passengers and a maximum of eight; it costs E£31 per person to Kom Ombo, E£56.25 to Edfu, E£62.50 to Esna or E£75 to Luxor. On top of this you need to add E£5 per person for police registration (the captain organises the police registration), plus there's the cost of food supplies. You can get boats for less than the official rate, but take care; if it's much cheaper you'll either have a resentful captain and crew, or you'll be eating little more than bread and *fuul* (fava bean paste) for three days.

Finding a good captain is vital, particularly if you are a woman travelling alone or travelling with a group of women. Some women travellers have reported sailing with felucca captains who had groping hands, and there have been some rare reports of assault. Many of the better captains on the river can be found having a *sheesha* (water pipe) in Nileside restaurants such as the Aswan Moon (p315), or near the Panorama restaurant (p315), or on Elephantine Island (p307). If you want help, see Shukri Saad and his assistant Hakeem Hussein at Aswan's tourist office (p304); they can recommend some reputable operators (or at least advise you against some who are shady). They are also the first port of call if you have any problems.

Cruisers

There are over 250 cruisers plying the waters between Aswan and Luxor – so many that there is a moratorium on the launching of new boats (a new boat was launched in 2005, but tourism officials insist that its permit was issued five years ago). Like Egyptian hotels they range from slightly shabby to sumptuous, but almost all have some sort of pool, a large rooftop area for sunbathing and watching the scenery, a restaurant, bar, air-con, TV, minibars and en-suite bathrooms. In general, travelling on one of these floating hotels means entering the package-holiday world that many of our readers try to avoid. But cruisers remain the easiest way to see the Nile in comfort on a mid-range budget and can be ideal for families with children who want to splash in a pool between archaeological visits, or for people who want to combine sightseeing with

---

MEET THE CAPTAIN

Nile cruisers may have state-of-the art navigation systems but nothing can replace years of human experience when sailing on the Nile. A cruiser's captain is more than the crew's boss; he is in charge of the ship's controls and must know every centimetre of the river intimately if he is to safely carry his passengers to their destination.

Most cruiser captains come from Sohag governorate, north of Luxor. They begin their training in childhood; their classroom is a *sandale*, a type of modified felucca with two masts that is often used to carry heavy cargo on the Nile.

Ramadan Gadallah Abdel Latif is captain of the *Jasmin*, a cruiser that runs between Luxor and Aswan. A burly, taciturn man with a thick moustache and the pressed *galabiyya* (man's robe) and spotless white turban of a Saidi (southern Egyptian), he has an air of quiet authority that inspires confidence – a prerequisite when you're keeping a 370m-long ship off sand bars and away from hundreds of other boats.

'I've been on this river since I was six,' he says. 'I love it. I don't have a favourite spot, all of it is beautiful.'

The Nile may be picturesque but it presents special problems for navigation. Although it no longer floods each year, the flow of water is regulated for agricultural purposes, so the depth varies according to the time of year. It is shallowest during the winter months, when sand bars often appear. This is why even the largest boats only have a maximum draught of 1.6m. It's also why captains have to have a sixth sense about where the shallowest spots lie.

'The hardest place to navigate is around Armant [about 40km south of Luxor],' says Captain Ramadan. 'It is very shallow there and there are some sand bars just below the surface. Even though we have a high-tech navigation system, the captain still has to know where the shallow spots are and he controls the propeller.'

The other test of his skill is getting in and out of crowded moorings, particularly at Kom Ombo, where up to 80 boats dock in very close proximity. For Ramadan, 'navigating around the other cruisers here is the most difficult part of the job.'

For these reasons, training is extensive. It takes at least 12 years, several sets of exams and a good dose of natural talent to become the captain of a Nile cruiser. But Ramadan cannot imagine doing anything else. 'It's in my blood,' he shrugs. 'I will be on the Nile until I end my working days.'

CRUISING THE NILE

CRUISE TIPS

When to travel All cruisers (except those on Lake Nasser) must pass through a lock at Esna, and it is closed for two weeks each December and June when water levels in the Nile are lowered for the cleaning of irrigation canals. The exact dates change each year so check with your tour operator or cruise company to avoid having to transfer from Luxor by road.

Where to start Most cruises starting from Luxor are a day longer than those starting from Aswan, partly because they are going against Nile's strong current. If you want to spend longer in Luxor or are concerned about cost, start from Aswan and head north.

Know your boat Ask the name of your boat before you book. If your hotel or travel agency cannot – or will not – tell you, look elsewhere.

Cabin choice Try to avoid the lowest deck. Most of the boats listed here have decent views from all cabins, but the banks of the Nile are high and you want to see as much as possible. Ask for a deck plan when booking.

Sailing time Many Nile cruise passengers are surprised by how little time is actually spent cruising – the boats' large engines cover distances relatively quickly and cruise times are often only four hours per day. Remember that longer cruises, unless they include Abydos and Dendara, are likely to have longer mooring times.

Mooring misery The vast majority of cruisers end up mooring next to each other (the only exception we know of is the *Sudan*, below), so you may have to cross four or five boats to get to your own, or you may find that your large cabin window looks directly onto another ship.

Healthy cruising All cruise boats listed here filter their water but many cruise passengers still get stomach upsets, particularly first-time visitors to Egypt. In general, the more expensive the boat, the better the standard of hygiene. See p553 for more tips.

Safety Issues Check the emergency facilities on your ship before you book. The cruisers listed here have life jackets for all passengers and extensive fire systems.

relaxation. The downside is that monuments are almost always seen with large groups and the itineraries are generally inflexible. Boats are almost always moored together, and the sheer volume of traffic means that generators and air-conditioning units overwhelm the peace of the river. There is also a heavy emphasis on five-star accommodation (although even within this rating there are big variations in standards). The general consensus from our research is that scrimping on cruises means substandard hygiene, no pool, cubby-hole cabins and lots of hidden extras, which makes a felucca trip a far better option. The only way around this is to book an all-inclusive package to Egypt. Not only are the prices usually lower than those listed here but, in the case of cut-price cruises, the agency guarantees the reliability of the boat. See p292 for agencies.

With so many (largely indistinguishable) boats to choose from, the ones we've listed below are noteworthy either for the quality of their facilities or their management. Note that we've listed high-season prices, which include all meals, entrance to monuments and guides. These can vary considerably according to the time of year, the state of tourism, and how you book.

BETWEEN LUXOR & ASWAN

M/S Sudan (www.steam-ship-sudan.com; d per person, 4-night cruise from US$1389) The *Sudan* was built as part of Thomas Cook's steamer fleet in 1885 and was once owned by King Fouad. It was also used as a set in the film *Death on the Nile*. It has been refurbished and offers 23 suites, all with private bathrooms, aircon and small balconies. It's unusual in that it has no pool, but it's also unique because it has character, something sorely missing on most cruisers. Its configuration means it cannot moor to other cruisers, so night-time views are good. Note that the management does not accept children under seven.

M/S Triton (www.capecairo.com/egypt/Nile_cruises/triton.html; per person per night US$360-490) Generally regarded as the plushest boat on the Nile, this large, privately owned vessel has only 20 spacious double rooms, an indoor and outdoor pool, spa, á la carte restaurant and individual stewards for each room. Bookings are offered through a number of upmarket travel agencies, most of them outside Egypt.

M/S Philae (www.oberoihotels.com; s/d/ste 4-night, 5-day cruise US$2400/3000/4000) Managed by Oberoi and designed to evoke a Mississippi paddle boat, the award-winning *Philae* is all wood panelling and antiques. The old-world feel is backed up by state-of-the-art water filtration, a library and all the comforts of a good five-star hotel. This is one of the few boats in which each room has its own balcony. Children are discouraged.

M/S Shehrayar & M/S Shehrazad (www.luxurynile cruisers.com; s/d/ste 4-night, 5-day cruise US$600/760/2000) These identical ships are managed by Oberoi. They're less luxurious than the *Philae* but still well appointed, each with 40 cabins, pools, bars and other five-star amenities. They also have the advantage of the Oberoi's private docks in Aswan and Luxor.

M/S Sun Boat III (www.akegypt.com; per person per night from US$175) Managed by Abercrombie & Kent, *Sun Boat III* carries a maximum of 36 passengers in pampered luxury. This gives the boat a more intimate feeling than many of the behemoths that cruise the river and the company has its own private mooring docks in Luxor, Aswan and Kom Ombo. On-board facilities are excellent and a no-mobile-phone policy is enforced. Children can also take cooking lessons with the chef. Abercrombie & Kent is known for having high-quality Egyptologists accompanying each boat and specialist guides are available on request. The company also operates the M/S *Sun Boat IV*, with excellent facilities and an 80-guest capacity, the *Nile Adventurer*, which can accommodate 68 guests, and the *Nile Explorer*, also capable of carrying 68 guests. Prices for these three boats are about US$104 per person per night.

M/S Moon Goddess (www.sonesta.com/egypt_nile cruise; s/d per night US$192/240) The top boat in the Sonesta's three-boat fleet is the *Moon Goddess*, a large, plush, five-star vessel featuring lots of marble and gilt. Sonesta's sister ships, the M/S *Sun Goddess* and M/S *Nile Goddess*, are similarly appointed but slightly cheaper.

M/S Radamis I & II (www.nile-cruises.net; per person, 3-night, 4-day cruise approx US$326) Owned by the Mövenpick management chain, the *Radamis I & II* are both well-appointed five-star boats with large cabins, panoramic views and excellent facilities.

M/S Beau Soleil (www.beausoleilcruises.com; per person per night from US$80) The five-star *Beau Soleil* is more reasonably priced than many others listed here and recommended for its good service and facilities. The smallest cabins are 15 sq m (large for such a boat) and many of the cabins have their own balconies.

M/S Florence (www.florencesaintmaria.com; per person per night from US$80) Not a beautiful boat compared to some of those listed here, the *Florence* is included because it's one of the more reasonably priced options and comes recommended from a number of sources.

LAKE NASSER

There are six cruise boats currently sailing on Lake Nasser, but two of them stand out above the rest.

Kasr Ibrim & Eugénie (☎ 02-516 9653/4/5; www.kasribrim.com.eg; r per person per night on 3–4-day trip from US$150) Both run by Belle Epoque Travel, these boats were the brainchild of Mustafa al-Guindi, a Cairene of Nubian origin who is almost single-handedly responsible for getting Lake Nasser opened to tourists. The

FISHING ON LAKE NASSER

With few predators apart from the crocodiles that roam the murky waters, the fish living in the silt-rich depths of Lake Nasser are growing to gigantic proportions – the record for a Nile perch is almost 100kg. Not surprisingly, fishing enthusiasts from around the world are lining up to come here and reel in their own record-breaker.

Two companies run fishing trips on Lake Nasser. Both are led by guides with years of experience on the lake and the fish they catch are returned to the waters after weighing. Both also combine their angling with visits to the ancient sites around the lake. The **African Angler** (☎ 097-230 9748; www.african-angler.co.uk) is run by Tim Bailey, formerly a safari guide in Kenya. He runs weekly safaris from September to December and February to June. He also operates through **Abercrombie & Kent** (☎ 02-394 7735) in Cairo and through agencies specialising in fishing throughout Europe and Australia. **Lake Nasser Adventure** (☎ 012 240 5897; www.lakenasseradventure.com) is run by Pascal Artieda, who developed a passion for fishing in Lake Nasser during his three years as manager of the *Eugénie* cruise boat, and his partner Negrashi, a Nubian who has been on the lake for most of his life. As well as fishing on the lake from its comfortable boats, it offers overland safaris in the little-travelled southern part of the Eastern Desert.

boats are stunningly designed: *Eugénie* is modelled on an early-20th-century hunting lodge; *Kasr Ibrim* is all 1930s Art Deco elegance. Each has a pool, *hammam* (bathhouse) and fantastic French cuisine. In addition, passengers are pampered with treats such as evening cocktails and classical music in front of the temples at Abu Simbel.

The other cruise boats on Lake Nasser are neither as plush nor as tasteful, but they are cheaper and easier to book at late notice.

Nubian Sea (☎ 012 322 2065)
Prince Abbas (☎ 097-314 660, 012 220 6747)
Queen Abu Simbel (☎ 097-306 512, 012 224 8658)
Tania (☎ 097-316 393; www.travco-eg.com)

BOOKING A CRUISE

Hundreds of agencies around the world offer Nile cruises, and you'll find that arranging one through them is by far the easiest way to organise your trip. The best deals are from Europe. Avoid booking through small hotels in Egypt; they often send customers on substandard boats and because the hotels are not licensed as travel agencies, you have no recourse if there are problems.

An alternative is to check out museums with large Egyptology departments. London's British Museum, the Smithsonian Institution in Washington, DC and others offer upmarket trips that feature cruises with renowned Egyptologists. Many universities with Egyptology departments run less expensive guided trips that include cruises.

Given the huge number of agencies, we've listed a bare minimum here. More travel agencies can be found on p544.

Egypt

Abercrombie & Kent (☎ 02-574 8334; www.akegypt .com, www.abercrombiekent.com) Offers top-of-the-line, tailor-made cruises and is known for quality guides. Has offices in the UK, the USA and Australia.

Hamis Travel (☎ 02-575 2757; www.hamis-eg.com) Excellent independent travel agency offering a variety of cruises at competitive prices. Also arranges felucca trips.

Thomas Cook (☎ 02-574 3955; www.thomascook egypt.com) The company that started it all. Prices are not low but service is solid and reliable, and on offer is a wide variety of cruise ships for different budgets. There are branches throughout Egypt.

UK

Cox & Kings (☎ 020-7873 5000; www.coxandkings .co.uk) Upmarket travel agency offering a variety of cruises with excellent guides.

Explore WorldWide (☎ 01252-760000; www.explore worldwide.com) Although most Nile trips offered through this company are done on feluccas, a cut-price cruise is part of one Egypt itinerary.

USA

I.Explore (☎ 1-800 439 7567; www.iexplore.national geographic.com) Upmarket educational tours are offered, including cruises accompanied by experts on Egyptian history and culture.

Leisure Connection Tours (☎ 1-800 364 5104; www .lcadventuretravel.com) Reasonably priced adventure tours that include a cut-price Nile cruise, as well as holidays designed specifically for families.

Museum Tours (☎ 1-888 932 2230; www.museum -tours.com) This company works with a number of American museums and Egyptological organisations and offers a variety of all-inclusive educational tours that include cruises, as well as private sailing tours.

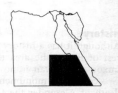

Nile Valley: Esna to Abu Simbel

One after another the great temples next come into view: Kom Ombo dominating a
bend in the river, Edfu still intact on the western bank... There is a monumental stillness in the warm air, an intimation of past existence endlessly preserved...

Alan Moorhead, The Blue Nile *(HarperCollins, 1962)*

Quiet and pastoral, southern Upper Egypt is notable for its well-preserved Graeco-Roman
temples at Esna, Edfu and Kom Ombo, and its lush fields punctuated by villages – it's the
perfect place to glide through on a felucca. Beyond Edfu the ribbon of cultivation on the
Nile's east bank gives way to the Eastern (Arabian) Desert, while at Gebel Silsila, 145km
south of Luxor, the river passes through a gorge, once thought to mark a cataract.

Aswan, the regional capital, is a bustling administrative centre and ancient ivory-trading
post that has a vibrant souq and a laid-back atmosphere that sets it apart from other tourist
centres in Egypt. With a great museum of Nubian culture, ancient remains dating back to
prehistory, beautiful gardens and a unique Nubian-influenced local culture, it is a fascinating
and relaxing place to spend time.

South of Aswan, the Pharaonic dimensions of the High Dam mark the beginning of Lake
Nasser, the world's largest artificial lake. Remarkable monuments that would have been
lost to the lake's waters now stand grouped on its shores and can be visited by boat. The
most spectacular of all is the Great Temple of Ramses II at Abu Simbel; it's one of ancient
Egypt's most awesome structures and a highlight of any visit to Egypt.

HIGHLIGHTS

- Marvel at Ramses II's massive and awe-inspiring tribute to himself, the **Great Temple** (p328)
  at Abu Simbel

- Get some idea of what was lost when the
  High Dam flooded Nubia in the **Nubia
  Museum** (p305) at Aswan

- See one of the last great Pharaonic
  monuments ever built: the imposing
  Temple of Horus (p298) at Edfu

- Uncover fascinating layers of history
  at the ancient settlement of **Abu** (p308)
  on Elephantine Island

- Admire the stark beauty of **Lake Nasser**
  (p325) and visit the unique monuments
  that were saved from its waters

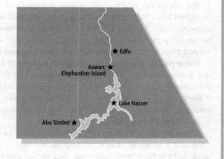

History

Although it has a history as ancient as the rest of Egypt, the area that lies between Luxor and Aswan is now famous for its Graeco-Roman monuments. Following the death of Alexander the Great in 323 BC, his huge empire was divided between his Macedonian generals. For 300 years the Greek-speaking Ptolemies ruled Egypt as pharaohs, respecting the traditions and religion of the Egyptians and setting an example to the Romans who succeeded them.

Their centre of power tied them to Alexandria and the coast, but the Ptolemies also pushed their way south, extending Graeco-Roman power into Nubia (the land that straddled what is now the border between Egypt and Sudan) through their politically sensible policy of assimilation rather than subjugation. They cemented their hold on power in Upper Egypt by erecting temples in honour of the local gods, building them in grand Pharaonic style to appease the priesthood and earn the trust of the people. The riverside temples at Esna, Edfu, Kom Ombo and Philae are all admirable as much for their strategic locations (all either overlook ancient trade routes or were built at key commercial centres) as for their actual artistic or architectural merit.

But Aswan's history dates back far earlier than this. Settlement in the area began on Elephantine Island, in the middle of the Nile, around 3000 BC. Named Abu (Ivory) after the trade that flourished here, it was a natural fortress positioned just north of the First Nile Cataract (one of six sets of rapids between Aswan and Khartoum) and protected by the Nile's rushing waters. When Egypt united in the Old Kingdom (2686–2181 BC), Abu became capital of the first Upper Egyptian nome (province) and developed into a thriving economic and religious centre. Its strategic importance was such that its rulers were known as Keepers of the Gate of the South and were responsible for guarding Egypt's southern flank.

Successive Pharaonic and Ptolemaic leaders took their turn to guard the southern reaches of Egypt from the customary routes of invasion; their fleets patrolled the river as far as the Second Nile Cataract at Wadi Halfa, and their troops penetrated several hundred kilometres into Sudan. Aswan was also, to a certain extent, the Siberia of the Roman Empire – a far-flung garrison where troublesome generals were sent in order to protect the interests of the emperor.

Although Abu maintained its importance until the end of the Graeco-Roman era, settlements began to be built off the island on the east bank of the Nile sometime in the New Kingdom (1550–1069 BC), when documents first mention the Ancient Egyptian word *swenet*, meaning 'trade', a name that later became the Arabic As-Suan, meaning markets. Even today the souq is a lively hub, even if the wares are no longer as exotic as they once were.

In more modern times Aswan once again became an important military post: it was from here that the British launched their attack on the Mahdist rebels in Sudan in 1898.

TRAVELLING IN THE SOUTH

In the aftermath of the 1997 tourist massacre at Luxor, police introduced security measures designed to protect tourists in the heavily travelled area between Luxor and Aswan, and they show no sign of lifting them. For independent travellers this means freedom of movement can be severely curtailed as you are forced to travel in convoy, prevented from taking buses or service taxis and forbidden from wandering about in villages or back lanes.

Some people feel more secure when surrounded by a phalanx of policemen pointing guns at the general populace; others don't, pointing out that the high speeds and dangerous driving in the convoy pose a greater risk to travellers than terrorism. Fortunately, this is Egypt and no rule is hard and fast – sometimes you will be left alone to walk around wherever you want, and see whatever you like; other times you will be politely (or not so politely) escorted to the nearest train station and put on the first train out.

Although there have been no violent incidents in the south since 1997, a bomb in Taba in 2004 and a series of attacks on tourists in Cairo in early 2005 mean that the security forces are unlikely to lighten their heavy-handed tactics any time soon.

Climate

Heading south from Luxor the fertile strip of land on either side of the Nile narrows, and in many places the desert comes almost to its banks. Not surprising, then, that the climate becomes increasingly desertlike as you move south: in winter, the days are warm and dry, with an average temperature of about 26°C, but nights can be cold. In summer, the temperatures hover between 38° and 45°C, making it difficult to do anything outdoors.

Getting There & Away

Constant police checkpoints and an insistence that foreigners travel in convoys make independent road travel in southern Upper Egypt almost impossible (see opposite). The police in Aswan are leery of letting too many foreigners travel on any one bus and can force them off if they deem it necessary. Trains allow more freedom, although strictly speaking there are only three that foreigners are allowed to take. Travel to Abu Simbel has become easier in recent years, with foreigners now being allowed to take buses (although the police still prefer to pack them into convoys), but the plane remains the best, if most expensive, option.

Getting Around

Foreigners may be restricted travelling between towns in the far south of Egypt, but once inside municipal boundaries they are pretty much left alone and can take the same shared taxis as everyone else; outside of Aswan, these are generally pick-up trucks. Fares are usually 25pt or 50pt.

SOUTHERN UPPER EGYPT

ESNA

☎ 095 / pop 71,588

The Graeco-Roman Temple of Khnum is the main attraction of Esna, a busy little farming town on the west bank of the Nile, 54km south of Luxor. Esna should be a pleasant morning excursion from Luxor but because of the convoy system you are only likely to visit if you are en route to Edfu and Kom Ombo, or as part of a cruise itinerary (see p286).

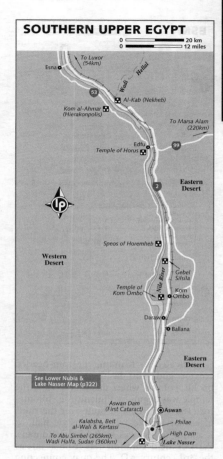

SOUTHERN UPPER EGYPT

The post office and a branch of the Bank of Alexandria are on the street that leads from the canal to the Nile. The **tourist police office** (☎ 240 0686) is in the bazaar near the temple.

Temple of Khnum

All that has been excavated of the **Temple of Khnum** (ticket office at riverside entrance to souq; adult/student E£15/10; ⏱ 6am-4pm Oct-May, to 5pm Jun-Sep) is the hypostyle hall, which sits rather incongruously in its huge excavation pit among the houses and narrow alleyways in the middle of town. Although the temple was built in the Roman Period (30 BC–AD 395), and has been described as 'degenerate', the reliefs are in excellent condition.

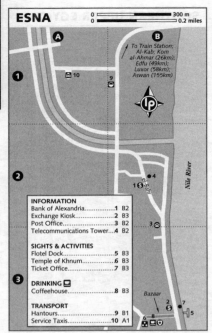

ESNA

0 _____ 300 m
0 _____ 0.2 miles

To Train Station;
Al-Kab; Kom
al-Ahmar (26km);
Edfu (49km);
Luxor (58km);
Aswan (155km)

Nile River

el-Bahr

Bazaar

INFORMATION	
Bank of Alexandria	1 B2
Exchange Kiosk	2 B3
Post Office	3 B2
Telecommunications Tower	4 B2

SIGHTS & ACTIVITIES	
Flotel Dock	5 B3
Temple of Khnum	6 B3
Ticket Office	7 B3

DRINKING	
Coffeehouse	8 B3

TRANSPORT	
Hantours	9 B1
Service Taxis	10 A1

Dedicated to Khnum, the ram-headed creator god who fashioned humankind on his potter's wheel using Nile clay, the temple was begun by Ptolemy VI Philometor (180–145 BC) and built over the ruins of earlier temples. The hypostyle hall, as it stands today, was built by the Romans. Parts of the decoration date from as late as the 3rd century AD. The quay connecting the temple to the Nile was built by Marcus Aurelius (AD 161–80).

Reliefs on the exterior walls have scenes of the pharaoh holding captives by their hair, threatening to strike them. The arms of prisoners are shown being fed to lions.

Inside, the intact roof of the hall is supported by 24 columns that are variously topped with capitals in the form of palm leaves, lotus buds and papyrus fans; some also have bunches of grapes, a distinctive Roman touch. The pillars are decorated with hieroglyphic accounts of temple rituals.

Inside the front corners, beside the smaller doorways, are two hymns to Khnum. The first is a morning hymn to awaken Khnum in his shrine, and the second is a wonderful

'hymn of creation' that acknowledges him as creator of all, even foreigners: 'all are formed on his potter's wheel, their speech different in every region but the lord of the wheel is their father too'.

On the temple's eastern wall are colourful scenes showing the pharaoh catching fish with the gods Horus and Khnum. Some of the royal enemies are trapped in the net with the fish. Next to this the pharaoh is shown presenting the temple to Khnum.

The back wall, to the northeast, is the only remaining part of the original Ptolemaic temple and features reliefs of two Ptolemaic pharaohs, Ptolemy VI Philometor and Ptolemy VIII Euergetes (170–116 BC). A number of Roman emperors are also mentioned near the hall's rear gateway: Septimus Severus, Caracalla, Geta and Decius all have their names inscribed. Above the lintel at the back gateway, Khnum is shown being worshipped as creator by other gods.

Eating & Drinking

Because Esna is so close to Luxor, and the police hurry visitors back into the convoy, few people linger here. There are a few food stands and *ahwas* (coffeehouses) in the souq just before the temple entrance if you're after a cheap snack. Basic food and drinks are also available at the service-taxi station.

Getting There & Away

Trains are a pain because the station is on the opposite (east) bank of the Nile. There are buses to Luxor (E£5, 8.30am, 5.30pm and 8pm) and Aswan (E£10, 8am and 10am), but they generally run on the main north–south road on the east bank and originate elsewhere, stopping only briefly to pick up passengers. Esna's service-taxi station is next to the canal, although arrivals are generally dropped off on the main thoroughfare into town along which *hantour* (horse-drawn carriage) drivers congregate in the hope of picking up a fare. They ask E£5 each way for the five- to 10-minute ride to the temple.

AL-KAB & KOM AL-AHMAR

Between Esna and Edfu are the scattered ruins of two settlements, both dating back over 3000 years, with traces of even earlier habitation.

Al-Kab (adult/student E£30/15), ancient Nekheb, is the site of predynastic and Pharaonic set-

tlements; the remains of the huge mud-
brick walls that once surrounded the ancient
settlement date to the Late Period (747–332
BC). To the north of the walls is an Old Kingdom cemetery and New Kingdom rock-cut
tombs of local governors. The most important of these is the **Tomb of Ahmose**, son of
Ebana (tomb No 2), who took part in the war
to reunite Egypt and drive out the Hyksos,
and left a long, detailed biographical inscription describing his bravery.

Home of Nekhbet (the vulture goddess
of Upper Egypt), Al-Kab has several sandstone temples, most within the enclosure
wall. The first temples existed by the Early
Dynastic Period (c 3100 BC), with later temples built by pharaohs of the Middle Kingdom (2055–1650 BC). However, the remains
seen today are from the New Kingdom
through to the Graeco-Roman Period.

To the north of the town walls are the remains of a small chapel built by Tuthmosis
III (1479–1425 BC), and to the east is a small
Ptolemaic temple partly carved into the rock
face. Some 3.5km further east into the desert
is the small temple of Hathor and Nekhbet
built by Amenhotep III (1390–1352 BC) as
a way station for Nekhbet's cult statue when
she passed through the area. Her protect
ive influence was no doubt appreciated, as
this was one of the supply routes to the gold
mines that gave Egypt much of its wealth.

Across the river is **Kom al-Ahmar**, ancient
Nekhen, home of the falcon god Nekheny, an
early form of Horus. Although little remains of what was Egypt's most important
city in predynastic times, recent excavations have revealed a large settlement (with
Egypt's earliest brewery!) and a cemetery
site dating from around 3400 BC, together
with the site of Egypt's earliest known temple, a large timber-framed structure fronted
by 12m-high imported wood pillars. A century ago, archaeologists discovered within
this sacred enclosure a range of ritual artefacts, including the Narmer Palette and
a superb gold falcon head; both are now in
Cairo's Egyptian Museum.

Close by is Egypt's oldest standing brick
building, the enigmatic mud-brick enclosure
thought to have been built by Khasekhemy
(c 2686 BC). Testament to Nekhen's continued importance during the Dynastic Period,
there is also a series of impressive rock-cut
tombs of New Kingdom dignitaries.

Al-Kab and Kom al-Ahmar are 26km
south of Esna. Convoys do not stop here
and other than sneaking through by dis-
embarking undetected from a bus or hiking
to the sites and taking a chance on finding
a ride when you've finished, there's little
chance of seeing these monuments by land.
The other option is to take a dahabiyya
(houseboat) or felucca from Aswan to Esna.
See p286 for more information.

EDFU
☎ 097 / pop 72,979
The Temple of Horus at Edfu is the most
completely preserved Egyptian temple, and
is definitely worth a visit. One of the last great
Egyptian attempts at monument building

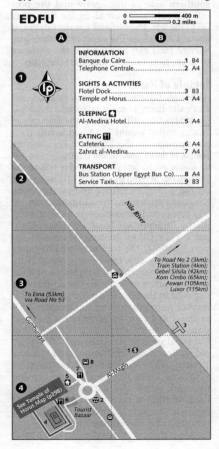

on a grand scale, the temple dominates this west-bank town, 53km south of Esna, although Edfu's more modest structures crowd in on its enclosure wall. Because the town and temple were established on a rise above the broad river valley, they escaped destruction from the disastrous floods that occasionally occurred when Nile waters rose too high.

Modern Edfu, a centre for sugar and pottery, is a very friendly place. Although it is an agricultural town, tourism is the biggest money earner and everyone in the town seems to have a shop in the tourist bazaar, which all visitors must brave in order to reach the temple. Just before the bazaar is the main square, the town's nerve centre. A large, new telephone centrale sits on the southern side of the square and the post office is behind it, just along the first street off to the left. The bus and minibus station is about 100m along the street off to the right. Service taxis can be found at the entrance to town, next to the bridge over the Nile.

Temple of Horus

Although Edfu was a settlement and cemetery site from as early as around 3000 BC (as it was the cult centre of the falcon god Horus and it would have had a cult temple throughout the Dynastic Period), the **Temple of Horus** (adult/student E£50/25; ☯ 6am-4pm Oct-May, to 5pm Jun-Sep) you see today is actually Ptolemaic. Started by Ptolemy III in 237 BC on the site of an earlier and smaller New Kingdom structure, the sandstone temple was completed almost 200 years later in 57 BC by Ptolemy XII Neos Dionysos, Cleopatra VII's father. In conception and design it follows the traditions of Pharaonic architecture, with the same general plan, scale and ornamentation, right down to the Egyptian attire worn by the Greek pharaohs depicted in the temple's reliefs. Although it is much newer than other cult temples, such as those at Luxor or Abydos, its excellent state of preservation helps to fill in a lot of historical gaps; it is, in effect, a 2000-year-old replica of an architectural style that was already archaic during Ptolemaic times.

Excavation of the temple from beneath the sand, rubble and part of the village of Edfu, which had been built on its roof, was begun by Auguste Mariette in the mid-19th century. The impressive entrance to the temple is through a massive 36m-high **pylon**

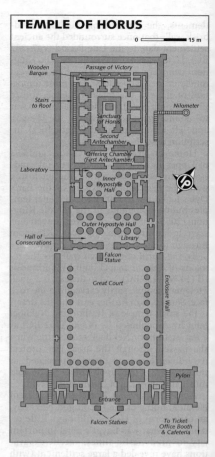

TEMPLE OF HORUS

0 — 15 m

Passage of Victory
Wooden Barque
Stairs to Roof
Nilometer
Sanctuary of Horus
Second Antechamber
Offering Chamber (First Antechamber)
Laboratory
Inner Hypostyle Hall
Outer Hypostyle Hall
Hall of Consecrations
Library
Falcon Statue
Great Court
Enclosure Wall
Pylon
Entrance
Falcon Statues
To Ticket Office Booth & Cafeteria

(gateway) guarded by two huge and splendid granite falcons and decorated with colossal reliefs of Ptolemy XII Neos Dionysos grasping the hair of his enemies, about to smash their skulls in; this is the classic propaganda pose of the all-powerful pharaoh.

Beyond this pylon is the **great court**, where offerings were once made to Horus. The walls are decorated with reliefs, including the 'Feast of the Beautiful Meeting' just inside the entrance, depicting Horus of Edfu and Hathor of Dendara who were brought together each year amid great celebrations.

A second set of Horus statues (in the form of falcons) in black granite once flanked the entrance to the temple's first or **outer hypostyle hall**, but today only one remains. Inside the entrance of the outer hypostyle hall, to the left and right, are two small chambers: the one on the right was the temple **library** where the ritual texts were stored, and the chamber on the left was the **hall of consecrations**, a type of vestry where the priests' freshly laundered robes and ritual vases were kept. The hall itself has 12 columns, and the walls are decorated with reliefs of the temple's founding.

The **inner hypostyle hall** also has 12 columns, and in the top left part of the room is perhaps this temple's most interesting room: the temple **laboratory**. Here, all the necessary perfumes and incense recipes were carefully brewed up and stored, and their ingredients were listed on the walls.

On either side of the hall are doorways that exit into the narrow **Passage of Victory**, which runs between the temple and its massive protective enclosure walls. This narrow ambulatory is decorated with scenes that are of tremendous value to Egyptologists in trying to understand the nature of the ancient temple rituals. Reliefs here show the dramatic reenactment of the battle between Horus and Seth at the annual Festival of Victory. Throughout the conflict, Seth is shown in the form of a hippopotamus, his tiny size rendering him less threatening. At the culmination of the drama the priests are shown cutting up a hippo-shaped cake and eating it to destroy Seth completely.

Back in the inner hypostyle hall, exit through the large central doorway to enter the **offering chamber**, or first antechamber, which has an altar where daily offerings of fruit, flowers, wine, milk and other foods were once left. On the west side are 242 steps leading up to the rooftop, giving a fantastic view of the Nile and the surrounding fields. You may have to pay the guard a bit of baksheesh if you want to go up here.

The second antechamber gives access to the **Sanctuary of Horus**, which still contains the polished-granite shrine that once housed the gold cult statue of Horus. Created during the reign of Nectanebo II (360–343 BC), the statue was reused by the Ptolemies in their newer temple. All around Horus' sanctuary are smaller shrines of other gods, including Hathor, Ra and Osiris, and, at the very back, a modern reproduction of the wooden barque in which Horus' statue would be taken out of the temple in procession during festive occasions.

On the eastern enclosure wall look for the remains of the Nilometer, which measured the level of the river and helped predict the coming harvest. For more on Nilometers and their importance in Ancient Egypt, see the boxed text, p321.

Sleeping & Eating

Al-Medina Hotel (☎ 471 1326; just off Sharia Gumhuriyya; s/d with private bathroom E£40/50) A very basic hotel with threadbare furniture and an erratic hot-water system, Al-Medina is the only option in town. Nevertheless, people do stay here and the large breakfasts are the pride of owner Taha Osman.

As well as the expensive cafeteria in the temple grounds, there are a few kebab places on the square, and **Zahrat al-Medina** (Sharia Gumhuriyya) is a cafeteria that serves basic chicken and vegetable dishes. At all these places you should ask how much dishes cost before you order.

Getting There & Away

Edfu train station is on the east bank of the Nile, about 4km from town. There are frequent trains heading to Luxor and Aswan throughout the day, although most are 2nd and 3rd class only. To get to the town, you must first take a covered pick-up truck to the bridge from the station, then another into town. Each costs 25pt. Alternatively, you can hire an entire pick-up to take you to the main square for about E£5.

Upper Egypt Bus Co (off Sharia Gumhuriyya) operates frequent buses to Luxor (E£10, two hours) and Aswan (E£7, 1½ hours). Marsa Alam buses (E£13, three to four hours) originate in Aswan and pick up passengers at the café by the entrance to the desert road on the east bank at about 7.30am and 8.30am.

The easiest option to visit Edfu is to take a day tour or travel in a private taxi (E£130 to E£150 return) in the 7am daily convoy from Luxor.

GEBEL SILSILA

At Gebel Silsila, about 42km south of Edfu, the Nile narrows considerably to pass between steep sandstone cliffs that are cluttered with ancient rock stelae and graffiti. Known in Pharaonic times as Khenu (Place of Rowing), the gorge also marks the change from limestone to sandstone in the bedrock of Egypt. The local quarries were worked by thousands of men throughout the New Kingdom and Graeco-Roman periods to provide the sandstone used in temple building.

On the west bank of the river is the **Speos of Horemheb**, a rock-hewn chapel dedicated to Pharaoh Horemheb (1323–1295 BC) and seven deities, including the local god Sobek.

At present you can only get to Gebel Silsila if you are on a cruise boat or have a private vehicle. Should the security situation change, you may be able to hire a taxi from Aswan or Kom Ombo to take you there.

KOM OMBO
☎ 097 / pop 80,991
The fertile, irrigated sugar-cane and corn fields around Kom Ombo, 65km south of Edfu, support not only the original community of fellaheen (farmers), but also a large population of Nubians displaced from their own lands by the creation of Lake Nasser. It's a pleasant little place easily accessible en route between Aswan and Luxor. If you're not stopping here on a felucca trip, it's best visited on a day trip from Aswan (40km to the south).

In ancient times Kom Ombo was known as Pa-Sebek (Land of Sobek), after the crocodile god of the region. It became important in Ptolemaic times when its name was changed to Ombos and it was made the capital of the first nome of Upper Egypt during the reign of Ptolemy VI Philometor. Kom Ombo was an important military base and trading centre between Egypt and Nubia, not only for the all-important gold, but also for the African elephants the Ptolemies needed to counteract the Indian elephants used by their long-term rivals the Seleucids, who ruled the largest chunk of Alexander's former empire to the east of Egypt. The main attraction these days, however, is the unique riverside Temple of Kom Ombo, about 4km from the town's centre.

Temple of Kom Ombo
Standing on a promontory at a bend in the Nile, where in ancient times sacred crocodiles basked in the sun on the river bank, the **Temple of Kom Ombo** (adult/student E£30/15; ⌚ 6am-4pm Oct-May, to 5pm Jun-Sep) is more precisely the dual temple of Sobek (local crocodile god) and Haroeris (from *har-wer*, meaning Horus

the Elder). Although there is evidence of earlier Pharaonic structures at the site, the sandstone temple dates from Ptolemaic times; it was part of the ambitious building plans of Ptolemy VI Philometor, though most of its decoration was completed by Cleopatra VII's father, Ptolemy XII Neos Dionysos. The temple's spectacular riverside setting has resulted in the erosion of part of its partly Roman forecourt and outer sections, but most of the complex has survived and is very similar in layout to the other Ptolemaic temples of Edfu and Dendara, albeit smaller. The temple is unusual in that, architecturally, everything is replicated and perfectly symmetrical along the main axis of the temple. There are twin entrances, twin courts, twin colonnades, twin hypostyle halls, twin sanctuaries and, in keeping with the dual nature of the temple, there was probably a twin priesthood. The left (western) side of the temple was dedicated to Haroeris, the right (eastern) half to Sobek.

Entry to the temple is through the damaged gateway built by Ptolemy XII Neos Dionysos. Close to this entrance, to the right of the temple wall, is a small **shrine to Hathor**, now used to store a collection of **mummified crocodiles** and their clay coffins that were dug up from a nearby sacred-animal cemetery; four from the collection are on display. On the opposite side of the compound, to the left (southwest) corner of the temple are the remains of a small **mammisi** (birth house), decorated with reliefs, including one depicting Ptolemy VIII Euergetes in a boat in a reed thicket before the god Min. Beyond this to the north is the deep well that supplied the temple with water, and close by is a small pool in which crocodiles, Sobek's sacred animal, were raised.

Passing into the temple's **forecourt**, where the reliefs are divided east–west between the two gods, there is a double altar in the centre of the court for both gods. Beyond are the two shared hypostyle halls, each with 10 columns, leading into antechambers and then to the unique double-sanctuary arrangement.

Inside the main entrance is a finely executed relief showing Ptolemy XII Neos Dionysos being presented to Haroeris by Isis and the lion-headed goddess Raettawy, with Thoth looking on. On the opposite side of the entrance the unification of Egypt is emphasised in reliefs showing Ptolemy XII

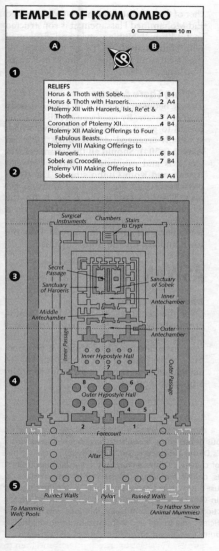

TEMPLE OF KOM OMBO

0   10 m

RELIEFS

Horus & Thoth with Sobek................1 B4
Horus & Thoth with Haroeris................2 A4
Ptolemy XII with Haroeris, Isis, Re'et &
  Thoth................3 A4
Coronation of Ptolemy XII................4 B4
Ptolemy XII Making Offerings to Four
  Fabulous Beasts................5 B4
Ptolemy VIII Making Offerings to
  Haroeris................6 B4
Sobek as Crocodile................7 B4
Ptolemy VIII Making Offerings to
  Sobek................8 A4

Surgical
Instruments   Chambers   Stairs
                          to Crypt

Secret
Passage   Sanctuary
Sanctuary   of Sobek
of Haroeris
                          Inner
Middle   Antechamber
Antechamber
                          Outer
                          Antechamber
Inner Passage

Inner Hypostyle Hall
                          Outer Passage

Outer Hypostyle Hall

Forecourt

Altar

Ruined Walls   Pylon   Ruined Walls

To Mammisi;   To Hathor Shrine
Well; Pools   (Animal Mummies)

Neos Dionysos being crowned by the goddesses Nekhbet (the vulture goddess worshipped at the Upper Egyptian town of Al-Kab) and Wadjet (the snake goddess based at Buto in Lower Egypt). The unification is reinforced with the dual crown of Upper and Lower Egypt worn by the pharaohs, at the front of which Nekhbet and Wadjet, 'the two ladies', have always appeared to protect the pharaoh – as can be seen on Tutankhamun's death mask.

On the north wall of the **inner hypostyle hall** are reliefs showing Haroeris presenting Ptolemy VIII Euergetes with a curved weapon, representing the sword of victory. Behind Ptolemy is his sister-wife and co-ruler Cleopatra II.

From here three **antechambers**, each with double entrances, lead to the **sanctuaries of Sobek and Haroeris**. The now-ruined chambers on either side would have been used to store priests' vestments and liturgical papyri.

The sanctuaries themselves are no longer completely intact, allowing you to see the secret passage between them that enabled the priests to give the gods a 'voice'.

Note the scene on the inside of the left-hand corner of the temple's back wall; usually described as a collection of 'surgical instruments', these could equally well be the implements used during the temple's daily rituals.

Sleeping & Eating

There is nowhere decent to stay in Kom Ombo. On our last visit the only dosshouse in town wouldn't take foreigners. Press on to Luxor or Aswan.

Al-Noba Restaurant (main rd; meals E£5-12) A little way north of the service-taxi station, Al-Noba is the only sit-down eatery in this part of town and it serves chicken, rice and vegetable dishes. Otherwise, there are the usual ta'amiyya and kebab stands.

Snacks can be bought at one of the cafeterias situated on the bank of the Nile between the temple and the boat landing. Of the two, Cafeteria Venus has the best atmosphere, serving burgers, kofta (minced meat on a skewer) and beer in a pleasant garden setting.

Getting There & Away

The easiest way to visit the temple these days is to come in convoy on a tour or by private taxi. A private taxi from Luxor taking in both Edfu and Kom Ombo and returning in the evening costs about E£225 to E£250.

The Luxor–Aswan buses also frequently stop in the town. As you approach Kom Ombo from Aswan, you can ask the driver to drop you off at the road leading to the temple; look for the sign. From here it's about a 2km walk. Should you want to head to the Red Sea from here, the daily bus from Aswan to Marsa Alam (E£15, four to five hours) calls in at around 7.30am.

Trains are another option, but the station is some way from the temple.

To get to the temple from Kom Ombo township, take a covered pick-up (25pt) to the boat landing on the Nile about 800m north of the temple, then walk the remainder of the way. Pick-ups to the boat landing leave from the service-taxi station. A private taxi between the town and temple should cost about E£7 return.

DARAW

The main reason to stop in this otherwise unremarkable village 8km south of Kom Ombo is to see its famous **camel market** *(souq al-gamaal)*. Most of the camels are brought up in caravans from Sudan to just north of Abu Simbel (see below), from where they're trucked to Daraw. The rest walk to the market in smaller groups, entering Egypt at Wadi al-Alagi and making their way through the Eastern Desert.

Camels are sold here each day of the week, but Sunday is when the main caravan of camels (sometimes as many as 2000) that has come up from Abu Simbel is brought to the market.

Also worth seeing is the Nubian house called **Hosh al-Kenzi**. Built in 1912 by the fa-

ther of the current resident, Haj Mohammed Eid Mohammed Hassanein, it is constructed in traditional Nubian style and decorated with Nubian artefacts. To get there, ask for the Dar Rasoul Mosque on Sharia al-Kunuz. The house is clearly visible next door.

Getting There & Away

Trains between Aswan and Luxor usually stop at Daraw. By road you are likely to be forced to go in a convoy to Daraw, which is usually arranged via the tourist office in Aswan (p304). Should all this change, service taxis and minibuses running between Aswan and Kom Ombo stop in Daraw (if passengers indicate that they want to get off). The E£3 fare is the same as for the whole stretch. The camel market is on a large lot 2km from the Luxor–Aswan highway. Turn off at the main road into the town and ask for the 'souk al-gamal'.

ASWAN

☎ 097 / pop 285,403

Over the centuries Aswan, Egypt's southernmost city, has been a garrison town and frontier city; the gateway to Africa and the now-inundated land of Nubia; a prosperous marketplace at the crossroads of the ancient caravan routes; and, more recently, a popular winter resort.

TAKING CAMELS TO MARKET

For hundreds of years camels from Sudan were brought to Egypt in large caravans along the Forty Days Rd (Darb al-Arba'een), the treacherous desert route thought to have been named for the number of days it took to get from Sudan's Darfur province to southern Egypt.

In the centuries following the introduction of camels into the region by the Persians (around the 6th century BC), the animals carried slaves, ostrich feathers, precious stones, animal skins and other goods to Egypt, where they were used by the country's Pharaonic overlords or, in later times, distributed to the great empires in Greece, Persia, Rome and Europe. But by the 18th and 19th centuries, the gradual introduction of steamers and trains in Egypt and Sudan meant that camels were no longer the most efficient way to get goods from south to north. The establishment of air links between the two countries seemed to seal the fate of the caravans as relics of a bygone age.

Camels have continued to come, but not always by the same route. Now, however, they themselves are the cargo. Once they get to Daraw they spend two days in quarantine, where they are inoculated against a number of diseases. After they have been sold, most go on to the camel market in Birqash, about 35km northwest of Cairo, and from there they are sold again.

Some end up doing agricultural work, others are exported to other Middle Eastern countries, but many – if not most – are destined for the dinner tables of poor Egyptians (yes, that cheap kebab does taste a bit strange).

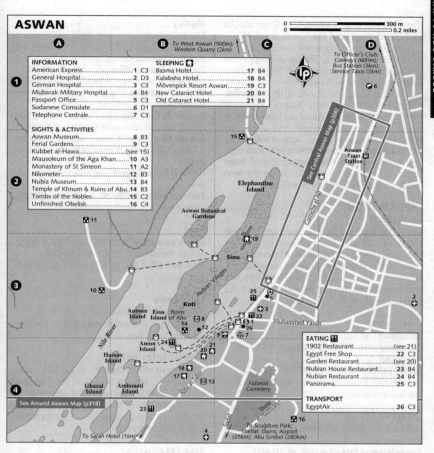

ASWAN

0 _____ 300 m
0 _____ 0.2 miles

To West Bank (500m);
Western Quarry (2km)

To Officer's Club;
Convoys (600m);
Bus Station (3km);
Service Taxis (3km)

INFORMATION		
American Express	1	C3
General Hospital	2	D3
German Hospital	3	C3
Mubarak Military Hospital	4	B4
Passport Office	5	C3
Sudanese Consulate	6	D1
Telephone Centrale	7	C3

SIGHTS & ACTIVITIES		
Aswan Museum	8	B3
Ferial Gardens	9	C3
Kubbet al-Hawa	(see 15)	
Mausoleum of the Aga Khan	10	A3
Monastery of St Simeon	11	A2
Nilometer	12	B3
Nubia Museum	13	B4
Temple of Khnum & Ruins of Abu	14	B3
Tombs of the Nobles	15	C2
Unfinished Obelisk	16	C4

SLEEPING		
Basma Hotel	17	B4
Kalabsha Hotel	18	B4
Mövenpick Resort Aswan	19	C3
New Cataract Hotel	20	B4
Old Cataract Hotel	21	B4

EATING		
1902 Restaurant	(see 21)	
Egypt Free Shop	22	C3
Garden Restaurant	(see 20)	
Nubian House Restaurant	23	B4
Nubian Restaurant	24	B4
Panorama	25	C3

TRANSPORT		
EgyptAir	26	C3

Elephantine
Island

Aswan Botanical
Gardens

Siou

Nubian Villages

Koti

Antoun   Essa   Ruins
Island Island of Abu

Amun
Island

Hassan
Island

Ghazal   Ambonati
Island   Island

See Around Aswan Map (p318)

Fatimid
Cemetery

To Sarah Hotel (1km)

To Sculpture Park;
Shellal; Dams; Airport
(25km); Abu Simbel (280km)

Muhammed Yassin

Aswan
Train
Station

See Central Aswan Map (p306)

Corniche el-Nil

Nile River

Laid-back and pleasant, Aswan is the perfect place for a break from the rigours of travelling in Egypt. The Nile is magically beautiful here as it flows down from the dams and around the giant granite boulders and palm-studded islands that protrude from its waters. Thanks to its long and ancient history, Aswan has fascinating Pharaonic, Graeco-Roman, Coptic, Islamic and modern monuments. It also has the Nubia Museum, superb botanic gardens, the massive High Dam, Lake Nasser and one of the most fascinating souqs outside Cairo. Unlike Luxor, however, Aswan is more than just a tourist town; a governorate capital, it has a large population of educated bureaucrats, a university and other institu-

tions. For all that, it remains relaxed. The Nile dominates the city and many people say they like nothing better than to sit on its banks and watch the feluccas glide by at sunset.

The best time to visit Aswan is in winter, when the days are warm and dry. In summer the temperature hovers between 38°C and 45°C; it's too hot to do anything but sit by a fan and swat flies, or flop into a swimming pool.

ORIENTATION

It's quite easy to find your way around Aswan because there are only three main avenues, and most of the city is along the Nile or parallel to it. The train station is at the northern end of town, only three blocks east of the river and the Corniche el-Nil.

The street running north–south in front of the train station is Sharia as-Souq (also occasionally signposted as Sharia Saad Zaghloul). This is Aswan's market street, where the souq overflows with colourful, tempting and aromatic wares. Running parallel to it is Sharia Abtal at-Tahrir, where you'll find the youth hostel and a few hotels. Most of Aswan's government buildings, banks, travel agencies, restaurants and top-end hotels are on the Corniche, and from there you can see the rock tombs on the west bank, as well as Elephantine Island.

INFORMATION
Bookshops
Only the top-end hotels, such as the New Cataract and the Basma, have bookshops that sell foreign-language material, and these are really only glorified newsstands. If you're after international newspapers and magazines, try the newsstand near the Philae Hotel on the Corniche.

Emergency
Ambulance (☎ 123)
Police (Map p303; ☎ 230 2043; Corniche el-Nil) Near Thomas Cook.
Tourist police (Map p306; ☎ 230 3163, 230 4393; Corniche el-Nil) If possible contact the tourist office first to help with translation.

Internet Access
Internet prices vary between E£6 and E£10 per hour.
Aswan Internet Café (Map p306; ☎ 231 4472; Rowing Club, Corniche el-Nil; ☾ 9am-midnight Sun-Fri)
Aswanet Internet Café (Map p306; ☎ 231 7332; Keylany Hotel, 25 Sharia Keylany; ☾ 9am-11pm) A local Internet service provider, Aswanet has the fastest lines in town.
Rotana Café Net (Map p306; ☎ 232 5798; 2nd fl, Sharia Abtal at-Tahrir; ☾ 24hr)
Tarek for Computer Services (Map p306; ☎ 012 381 7534; Ahmed Maher; ☾ 9am-midnight)

Medical Services
General Hospital (Map p303; ☎ 230 2855, 314 151; Sharia Muhammed Yassin) Only as a last resort.
German Hospital (Map p303; ☎ 231 7176; Corniche el-Nil)
Mubarak Military Hospital (Map p303; ☎ 231 7985, 231 4739; Tariq Sadat) The top hospital in town.

Money
Unless otherwise noted, banking hours are 8.30am to 2pm and 5pm to 8pm from Sunday to Thursday.
American Express office (Map p303; ☎ 230 6983; Corniche el-Nil; ☾ 9am-5pm Sun-Thu, to 2pm Fri & Sat)
Bank of Alexandria (Map p306; Corniche el-Nil) Accepts Eurocheques.
Banque du Caire (Map p306; Corniche el-Nil) Has ATM and will issue cash advances on both Visa and MasterCard.
Banque Misr (Map p306; Corniche el-Nil; ☾ 8am-3pm & 5-8pm) ATM and foreign-exchange booth next to main building.
National Bank of Egypt (Map p306; Corniche el-Nil) ATM.
Thomas Cook (Map p306; ☎ 230 4011; fax 230 6209; Corniche el-Nil; ☾ 8am-2pm & 5-9pm)

Post
Branch post office (Map p306; Sharia Abtal at-Tahrir, opposite Victoria Hotel; ☾ 8am-2pm Sat-Thu)
Main post office (Map p306; Corniche el-Nil; ☾ 8am-2pm Sat-Thu)

Telephone
Telephone centrale (Map p303; Corniche el-Nil; ☾ 24hr) There are also cardphones along the Corniche and at the train station.

Tourist Information
Main tourist office (Map p306; ☎ 231 2811; Midan al-Mahatta; ☾ 8am-3pm & 6-8pm Sat-Thu, 10am-2pm & 6-8pm Fri) Shukri Saad and his assistant, Hakeem Hussein, can usually be found at this office, next to the train station, and they are extremely helpful. They are also the first port of call if you have any problems.

Visa Extensions
Passport office (Map p303; ☎ 231 2238; Corniche el-Nil; ☾ 8.30am-1pm Sat-Thu) For visa extensions go to this office, at the southern end of the Corniche.

SIGHTS
Aswan's sights are spread out, mostly to the south and west of the town. Of those on the east bank, few are within walking distance of the town centre. Those on the west bank involve a short boat trip. The exception to all this is the souq, which bisects the centre of Aswan and is within walking distance of most hotels.

The Town & East Bank
Although the fabulous caravans no longer pass this way, the colour and activity of

Aswan's souq recalls those romantic times. Just wander through the small, narrow alleyways and you'll see, hear, smell and, if you want, taste life as it has been for many centuries in these parts.

At first sight **Sharia as-Souq** appears to be little more than a tourist market: Nubian baskets, T-shirts, perfume, spices, beaded *galabiyyas* (men's robes) and grotesque stuffed crocodiles and desert creatures are all for sale. Unfortunately, the traders have become almost as persistent as those in Luxor, and they can be just as irritating.

But away from the tourist tat, this is very much a living market. Fresh and live produce, including fruit, vegetables, chickens and pigeons, are traded in the street stretching to the south of the Happi Hotel. South of Sharia al-Matar, other items such as clothes and shoes are hawked along with baskets and spices.

Walking along the Corniche and watching the sun set over the desert on the far side of the Nile is another favourite pastime in Aswan. If you want to sit down to watch the sun work its magic, the **Ferial Gardens** (Map p303; admission E£5) at the southern end of the Corniche is a peaceful place.

NUBIA MUSEUM

One of the highlights of a visit to Aswan is the **Nubia Museum** (Map p303; ☎ 231 3826; Abtal at-Tahrir; adult/student E£50/25; ⏱ 9am-1pm & 5-9pm), where the history, art and culture of Nubia from prehistoric times to the present are showcased. It is a very small and belated thanks for the sacrifice made by the Nubian people for the old Aswan Dam (p323). The exhibits are beautifully displayed, and the clearly written explanations take you from 4500 BC through to the present day.

At the entrance to the main exhibition hall is a model of the Nile Valley and the main temple sites. Among the museum highlights are the 6000-year-old painted pottery bowls and a stunning quartzite statue of a 25th-dynasty Kushite priest of Amun. Distinct from the Pharaonic artefacts are the cases filled with objects from burials dating to the Ballana Period (5th to 7th century BC). Examples of weaponry and armour found in Ballana tombs, including a complete set of horse armour displayed on a model horse, show the sophistication of artisanship during this brief ascendancy.

There is also a fascinating display tracing the development of irrigation along the Nile, from the earliest attempts to control the flow of the river, right up to the building of the old Aswan Dam. Detailed displays also explain the massive Unesco project to move Nubia's most important historic monuments away from the rising waters of Lake Nasser following the building of the dam. A model of a Nubian house, complete with old furniture and mannequins wearing traditional silver jewellery, attempts to portray modern Nubian folk culture.

All this is housed in a well-designed modern building, loosely based on traditional Nubian architecture. In the museum garden there is a reconstructed Nubian house (which you can't enter, unfortunately) and a small 'cave' in which prehistoric petroglyphs of giraffes and other wild animals once indigenous to the region have been placed. The site also incorporates an 11th-century Fatimid tomb, as well as a number of other tombs of sheikhs.

The museum entrance is about a five-minute walk from the EgyptAir office on Corniche el-Nil.

FATIMID CEMETERY

Behind the Nubian Museum is the vast **Fatimid Cemetery** (Map p303), a collection of low mud-brick buildings with domed roofs. Many of the graves here are modern, but some of the mausoleums clustered towards the back of the cemetery date from the 9th century. Although the graves are in very bad shape, they show the progression of tomb architecture from simple open enclosures to complex domes built on cubes. In a feature unique to southern Egypt, some of the domes are built on a drum with corners sticking out like horns. Many of the tombs had marble inscriptions attached to them until the late 19th century, when a freak rainstorm caused them to fall off. In a misguided attempt to preserve them, the inscriptions were collected and taken to Cairo without any record of which tomb they were originally attached to. Unfortunately, this means that the dates of the tombs' construction and the names of the deceased are lost forever. A few of the domes towards the outer edges of the cemetery have flags outside them and are in much better shape than the others. These are the graves of local

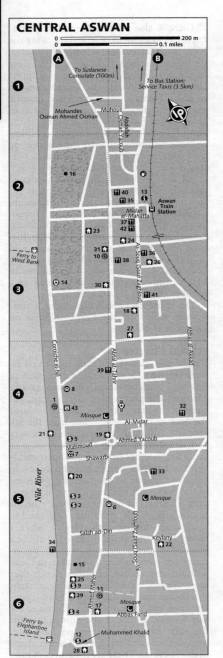

CENTRAL ASWAN

INFORMATION		
Aswan Internet Café	1	A4
Aswanet Internet Café	(see 22)	
Bank of Alexandria	2	A5
Banque du Caire (ATM)	3	A5
Banque du Caire (ATM)	4	A6
Banque Masr (ATM)	5	A4
Branch Post Office	6	B5
Cardphones	7	A5
Main Post Office	8	A4
National Bank of Egypt (ATM)	9	A6
Rotana Café Net	10	A3
Tarek for Computer Services	11	A6
Thomas Cook	12	A6
Tourist Office	13	B2
Tourist Police	14	A3
Travco	15	A6

SIGHTS & ACTIVITIES		
Governorate Building	16	A2

SLEEPING		
Al-Amir Hotel	17	A6
Cleopatra Hotel	18	B3
Happi Hotel	19	A4
Hathor Hotel	20	A5
Isis Hotel	21	A4
Keylany Hotel	22	B5
Marhaba Palace Hotel	23	A2
Marwa Hotel	24	B3
Memnon Hotel	25	A6
Noorhan Hotel	26	B3
Nuba Nile Hotel	(see 40)	
Nubian Oasis Hotel	27	B3
Orchida St George	28	A6
Philae Hotel	29	A6
Ramsis Hotel	30	A3
Yassin Hotel	(see 26)	
Youth Hostel	31	A3

EATING		
Al-Masry Restaurant	32	B4
Al-Sayyida Nefissa	33	B5
Aswan Moon Restaurant	34	A5
Biti Pizza	35	B2
Chef Khalil	36	B3
El Tahrer Pizza	37	B2
Esraa	38	B3
Haramein Foul & Ta'amiyya	39	A4
Koshary Aly Baba Restaurant	40	B2
Madena Restaurant	41	B3
Restaurant Derwash	42	B2

ENTERTAINMENT		
Palace of Culture	43	A4

saints, and sometimes you see Aswanis circumambulating a sarcophagus, praying for the saint's intercession.

The municipality of Aswan has built a large, green metal fence around the Fatimid Cemetery. The main entrance is a five- to 10-minute walk from the roundabout where the road to the airport forks off the Corniche. You can walk right through the cemetery and join the road to the Unfinished Obelisk on the other side; just aim for the four-storey building facing the back of the cemetery. The site's caretaker will often accompany you and show you the best-preserved tombs, for which he should be given a tip of a few pounds.

UNFINISHED OBELISK

Aswan quarries were Egypt's main source of granite, a stone only found in this southerly region. At numerous quarries around here, the ancient Egyptians hacked out most of the hard stone used in their statuary and to embellish temples and pyramids.

In the **Northern Quarries** (Map p318; adult/student E£30/15; 🕑 7am-4pm Oct-May, 8am-6pm Jun-Sep), about 1.5km from town opposite the Fatimid Cemetery, is a huge discarded **obelisk**. Three sides of the shaft, which is nearly 42m long, were completed except for the inscriptions. The completed obelisk would have been, at 1168 tonnes, the single heaviest piece of stone ever fashioned. However, a flaw appeared in the rock. So it lies where the disappointed stonemasons abandoned it, still partly attached to the parent rock, with no indication of what it was intended for.

Due at the time of writing to be unveiled to the public for the first time in 2006 are ancient pictographs of dolphins and ostriches or flamingos. They are thought to have been painted by workers at the quarry and have been off limits until now.

No service taxis run past the site, but you can get one to the junction on Sharia al-Haddadeen and then walk (about 10 minutes). Private taxis will charge about E£10. You can also walk through Fatimid Cemetery to get to it.

SCULPTURE PARK

The little-known **Sculpture Park** (Map p318) houses the sculptures made each spring at Aswan's International Sculpture Symposium. Sculptors from around the world come to Aswan and spend a month creating works on the terrace of the Basma Hotel. Their work is exhibited near the old Southern Quarries. To get here, take the road to Shellal. Instead of turning right towards the ferry to Philae, take the road up the hill. Continue until you reach the top; on the left is the quarry, on the right the sculptures. No service taxis come to the Sculpture Park, so you will have to get a private taxi. Expect to pay about E£10.

The River
ELEPHANTINE ISLAND

For centuries **Elephantine Island** (Map p303) was the centre of life at Aswan. Settlement here began on the southern part of the island in about 3000 BC, but the importance of Abu (as the island was known in ancient times) as a political and economic centre grew strong during the 6th dynasty (2345–2181 BC) and, despite periodic ups and downs, the island retained its importance until the Graeco-Roman period. Its economy flourished with the important trade in ivory as well as the hard stone – especially granite – that was quarried in the area.

As well as being a thriving settlement, Elephantine was the cult centre of the ram-headed god Khnum (creator of humankind and god of the cataracts controlling the Nile's water level), Satis (goddess of Abu and Khnum's wife) and Anukis (their daughter). By the New Kingdom Khnum's importance began to eclipse that of his wife and daughter.

Over time religious edifices took up increasing amounts of the island and other settlements moved either further north on the island or to the east bank. By the end of the Graeco-Roman Period Abu became a temple town, and the establishment of Christianity in the fourth century was the island's *coup de grâce*; worship of the old gods was gradually abandoned and defensive fortifications were moved to Aswan proper.

Nowadays the extensive ruins of Abu take up the southern end of the island and next to them are two lively Nubian villages. Taking up much of the island's northern end is the deluxe and architecturally insensitive Mövenpick resort (with an appalling protrusion resembling an air-traffic control tower). It has its own private ferry and a 3m-high wall around it to keep the tourists in and separate from the local Nubians.

Nubian Villages

Sandwiched between the ruins and the Mövenpick are two colourful Nubian villages, **Siou** and **Koti**. Strolling through their shady alleys is a wonderful way to experience how modern Elephantines live. A north–south path across the middle of the island links the two villages and about halfway along is the Nubian Café, with a shady garden beside a traditional Nubian house.

HENNA TATTOOS

Henna is the natural dye derived from the leaves of the *Lawsonia inermis* shrub, which has been grown in southern Egypt and Nubia for millennia – traces of it have even been found on the nails of mummified pharaohs.

Like their ancestors, Nubian women use henna for their hair and also to decorate their hands and feet prior to getting married. The intricate black designs adorn the skin for a fortnight or so before fading away.

Women visitors who want to get a taste of Nubian culture can have henna 'tattoos' put on their hands (or feet or stomachs) at some of the Nubian villages around Aswan – it looks great and you get to spend time with Nubian women. The Nubian villages on Elephantine Island or in West Aswan, just north of the Tombs of the Nobles, are a good place to try. In Aswan, women also give tattoos at the restaurant **Nubian House** (Map p303; ☎ 232 6226). Tattoos are also on offer in the souq, but check who will apply them – would-be lotharios see this as a great opportunity to get close to a bit of foreign flesh. Men, take note: if you can't resist a henna tattoo, don't risk offending your hosts and asking a woman to apply it. You will have to make do with the guys in the souq.

At all these places you're looking at anywhere between E£15 and E£40 per tattoo, depending on the size and intricacy of the design.

Hamdi, a village elder who can usually be found here, will tell visitors about the local culture and sometimes take them on a tour of the village. Close to the wall separating the Mövenpick from Siou village is Nubian House, another place for tea. This is where you can arrange to have a henna 'tattoo' with local women or hook up with a felucca captain. The house can also arrange Nubian meals and traditional dancing. Women who come here should be respectful of local tradition and wear modest clothes.

Aswan Museum & the Ruins of Abu

The ruins of the original town of Abu and the charming **Aswan Museum** (Map p303; adult/student E£20/10; ☒ 8am-5pm Oct-Apr, 8.30am-6pm May-Sep) lie at the southeastern end of Elephantine island. The older part of the museum building dates back to 1898 and was a rest house for Sir William Willcocks, the architect of the old Aswan Dam. It has been a museum since 1912. The newer extension was added in the early 1990s.

The museum houses a collection of antiquities discovered in Aswan and Nubia. Most of the Nubian artefacts were rescued before the construction of the old Aswan Dam, and many of the best have been moved to the Nubia Museum. However, the museum is worth a visit for the annex, which houses objects found in the excavations on Elephantine. The weapons, pottery, utensils, statues, encased mummies and sarcophagi date from

predynastic to late Roman times, and everything is labelled in Arabic and English. The sarcophagus and mummy of a sacred ram, the animal associated with Khnum, are in a room by themselves to the right of the main entrance, while four mummies can be seen to the left of the entrance.

The lush garden beside the museum leads you to the real highlight of this place, the fascinating **Ruins of Abu**. Excavations began here at the beginning of the 20th century and are still being carried out by Swiss and German teams. Essentially an outdoor museum, it has numbered plaques and reconstructed buildings that lead you through a fascinating history spanning from around 3000 BC to the 14th century AD. The largest structure in the site is the partially reconstructed **Temple of Khnum** (plaque Nos 6, 12 and 13), built in the Old Kingdom but added to and used for over 1500 years before being extensively enlarged and rebuilt in Ptolemaic times. Some other highlights include a small 4th-dynasty **step pyramid**, thought to have been built by Sneferu (2613–2589; father of Khufu of Great Pyramid fame); a tiny **Ptolemaic chapel** (No 15) reconstructed from the Temple of Kalabsha (which is now just south of the High Dam); a reconstructed 18th-dynasty **Satet Temple** (No 2) built by Hatshepsut (1473–1458 BC) and dedicated to the goddess Satis; a **cemetery for sacred rams** (No 11), thought to have been the living embodiment of the god

Khnum; and the ruins of an **Aramaic Jewish colony** dating from the 5th century BC.

Perhaps the most famous and impressive sights are the island's two **Nilometers**. Heavenly portents and priestly prophecies aside, in ancient times the Nilometer gave the only sure indication of the likelihood of a bountiful harvest. When the Nilometer recorded that the level of the river was high, it meant that there would be sufficient water for irrigation vital to a good harvest. It also affected the taxation system: the higher the river, the better the harvest and the more prosperous the fellaheen and merchants – and therefore, the higher the taxes. The **Nilometer of the Temple of Khnum** (No 7) is below the southern balustrade of the Khnum temple terrace. Built in the 26th dynasty, it has stone stairs that lead down into what appears to be a dried up sacred lake but was more likely a basin for measuring the Nile's maximum level. Another stairway, with a scale etched into its wall, leads down to the water from the basin's northern end.

Descending to the water's edge from beneath a sycamore tree near the museum is the **Nilometer of the Satet Temple** (No 10). Built in late Ptolemaic or early Roman times and restored in the 19th century, its staircase is roofed over and niches in the walls would have had oil lamps to provide light. If you look hard as you descend to the river, you can see the names of Roman prefects carved into the left-hand wall.

An excellent guide, *Elephantine: The Ancient Town*, is produced by the German archaeological mission on Elephantine. It explains the long history of Abu and describes in detail the monuments according to their numbered plaques. It is available in English, German and Arabic at the Aswan Museum or, when it is open, at the German excavation house, adjacent to the site.

Getting There & Away

For information on ferries to Elephantine Island, see p311.

ASWAN BOTANICAL GARDENS

To the west of Elephantine are the **Aswan Botanical Gardens** (Map p303; admission E£10; ⏰ 8am-5pm Oct-Apr, to 6pm May-Sep), still often referred to by their old name, Kitchener's Island. The island was given to Lord Horatio Kitchener in the 1890s when he was consul general

---

LOVE ETERNAL

Aswan was the favourite wintering place of Mohammed Shah Aga Khan, the 48th imam (leader) of the Ismaili sect of Islam. When he died in 1957, his widow, the begum (a woman of high rank), oversaw the construction of his domed granite-and-sandstone mausoleum, which can be seen partway up the hill on the west bank opposite Elephantine Island.

The imam's mausoleum is modelled on the Fatimid tombs, and the interior, closed to the public and incorporating a small mosque, is more impressive than the rather severe exterior. The sarcophagus, made from Carrara marble, is inscribed with text from the Quran and stands in a vaulted chamber in the interior courtyard. Until her death in 2000, the begum would place a red rose on her husband's sarcophagus each day. Now she lies inside, reunited with her husband for eternity.

---

of Egypt and commander of the Egyptian army. Indulging his passion for beautiful flowers, Kitchener turned the entire island into a botanical garden in 1928, importing plants from the Far East, India and parts of Africa. Covering 6.8 hectares, it is filled with birds as well as hundreds of species of flora. Unfortunately the gardens are no longer as lush as they once were and some of the plants are beginning to look straggly. Still, they are a pleasant place to have a peaceful stroll except on Fridays, when the place is invaded by picnicking crowds with stereos.

To get to Aswan Botanical Gardens you can incorporate it into a felucca tour or you can take the northernmost ferry to Elephantine and walk through the edge of the village to the other side of the island. You'll find a couple of little feluccas at the western edge of the lush palm gardens. Expect to pay at least E£5 for a one-way trip.

The West Bank

To get to the sights on the West Bank, you can either incorporate them into a felucca tour or you can take a ferry from Elephantine across to the landing for the Monastery of St Simeon. To get to the Tombs of the Nobles, there is a public ferry that leaves from a landing south of the governorate building. See opposite for more details.

MONASTERY OF ST SIMEON

The 7th-century **Monastery of St Simeon** (Map p303; Deir Amba Samaan adult/student E£20/10; 8am-4pm Oct-May, 7am-5pm Jun-Sep) is one of the best preserved of the original Christian strongholds in Egypt. Confusingly, the original monastery foundations were dedicated to a local saint named Hadra, but the monastery survived under the name of St Simeon until Salah ad-Din launched a devastating attack that led to its abandonment in 1173.

Surrounded by desert sands, except for a glimpse of the fertile belt around Aswan in the distance, the monastery has stunning views and bears more resemblance to a fortress than to a religious sanctuary. It once provided accommodation for about 300 resident monks plus a further 100 or so pilgrims. Built on two levels, the lower level of stone and the upper level of mud brick, it was surrounded by 10m-high walls and contained a church, shops, bakeries, offices, a kitchen, dormitories, stables and workshops. Mud-brick architecture buffs will love the long vault in the upper enclosure. Off the vault are the monks' cells with their mastaba (bench) beds. The last room on the right still has graffiti from the Muslim pilgrims who stayed here en route to Mecca.

To get to the monastery from the boat landing, you can either negotiate with the camel drivers (expect to pay about E£30 for an hour; if you want longer, ensure that you agree in advance) or scramble up the desert track (about 25 minutes). Alternatively, you can take the ferry to the Tombs of the Nobles and ride a camel or donkey from there.

TOMBS OF THE NOBLES

The high cliffs opposite Aswan, just north of Kitchener's Island, are honeycombed with the tombs of the princes, nomarchs (governors), keepers of the Gate of the South and other dignitaries of ancient Elephantine. Known as the **Tombs of the Nobles** (Map p303; adult/student E£20/10; 8am-4pm Oct-May, to 5pm Jun-Sep), six of them are open to the public. The tombs date from the Old and Middle Kingdoms and are valuable sources for the early history of Egypt's far south. Most follow a simple plan, with an entrance hall, a pillared room and a corridor leading to

the burial chamber. A set of stairs cutting diagonally across the hill takes you up to the tombs from the ferry landing.

Tombs of Mekhu & Sabni (Nos 25 & 26)

The adjoining tombs of father and son Mekhu (Tomb No 25) and Sabni (Tomb No 26), both overseers of Upper Egypt, date from the extraordinarily long reign of the 6th-dynasty pharaoh Pepi II (2278–2184 BC). Mekhu was given the title 'hereditary prince' by Pepi II and was killed on a military campaign in Nubia. The reliefs in his son's tomb record how Sabni led the army into Nubia to punish the tribe responsible. Sabni recovered his father's body and sent a messenger to the pharaoh in Memphis to inform him that the enemy had been taught a lesson. On his return to Aswan he was met by priests, professional mourners and some of the royal embalmers, all sent by the pharaoh himself to show the importance that was accorded to the keepers of the kingdom's southern frontier. Many of the reliefs in Sabni's tomb still have their original colours and in the chapel, or pillared hall, are some lovely hunting and fishing scenes depicting Sabni and his daughters.

Tomb of Sarenput II (No 31)

Sarenput was the local governor and commander of the frontier garrison of the south under the 12th-dynasty pharaoh Amenemhat II (1922–1878 BC). His is one of the most beautiful and best-preserved tombs, its colours still vivid. A six-pillared entrance chamber leads into a corridor with six niches holding statues of Sarenput. The burial chamber has four columns and a niche with wall paintings showing Sarenput with his wife (on the right) and his mother (on the left). There are paintings depicting Sarenput and his son hunting and fishing.

Tomb of Harkhuf (No 34)

A governor of the south under Pepi II, Harkhuf led three trading expeditions south into Nubia. Although the interior of the tomb is almost without decoration, to the right of the entrance are remarkable hieroglyphic texts about three expeditions made by Harkhuf to Central Africa. Included here is a copy of a letter Harkhuf received from the pharaoh, who was then only a boy of eight. Having heard that Harkhuf had obtained a 'dancing pygmy' on his travels, the young pharaoh was so keen to see the pygmy that he advised Harkhuf to keep a careful watch on him day and night in case he should fall off the boat and into the Nile! 'My majesty desires to see this pygmy more than the gifts of Sinai or of Punt,' Harkhuf writes. Look carefully to see the tiny hieroglyph figure of the pygmy several times in the text.

Tomb of Hekaib (Pepinakht; No 35)

Hekaib, also known as Pepinakht, was the overseer of foreign soldiers during the reign of Pepi II. He was sent to quell rebellions in both Nubia and Palestine, and was even deified after his death as is revealed by the small shrine of Hekaib built on Elephantine Island during the Middle Kingdom (c 1900 BC). His tomb has a columned façade and a large courtyard outside the entrance. There are also some fine reliefs showing fighting bulls and hunting scenes.

Tomb of Sarenput I (No 36)

Sarenput I was the grandfather of Sarenput II and was a regional governor during the 12th-dynasty reign of Sesostris I (1965–1920 BC). His large tomb has a big exterior court and you'll see the remains of six square pillars, each of which is decorated with reliefs. On either side of the entrance Sirenput is shown being followed by his dogs and sandal-bearer, his flower-bearing harem, his wife and his three sons.

KUBBET AL-HAWA

On the hilltop above the Tombs of the Nobles lies Kubbet al-Hawa, a small tomb constructed for a local sheikh. If you climb up to it, you'll be rewarded with fantastic views of the Nile and the surrounding area.

WESTERN QUARRY

In the desert to the west of the Tomb of the Nobles is the ancient **Western Quarry** (Gebel Simaan), where stone for many of ancient Egypt's monuments – possibly including the Colossi of Memnon in Luxor – was quarried. In this bleak and evocative site lies a large **unfinished obelisk**. It was made on the orders of the 19th-dynasty pharaoh Seti I (1294–1279 BC), and was already decorated on three sides of its apex when it was abandoned. The ancient quarry face and marks from where the stone was re-

moved can also be seen nearby, along with the tracks on which the huge blocks were dragged for transportation further afield.

Guides to the quarry can be found at the West Bank ferry landing, in front of the Tombs of the Nobles. Expect to pay at least E£30 to E£50 after bargaining. You go by camel, so allow half an hour each way and take plenty of water. Also, because the site is rarely visited, keep an eye out for snakes.

ACTIVITIES

Feluccas & Ferries

As you will quickly discover if you spend any time near the Nile, feluccas are the traditional canvas-sailed boats of the Nile. The river is at its most picturesque in Aswan, and no visit would be complete without at least an hour spent sailing around the islands in one of these graceful little boats.

In case you've miraculously avoided them, felucca touts hang out on the Corniche. The official government price for hiring a felucca capable of seating up to eight people is E£25 per hour for the boat, but nobody will take you for that price if business is good; if business is slack, you may be able to bargain the price down. A three- or four-hour tour costs at least E£60 to E£80. A two- to three-hour trip down to Seheyl Island costs about E£60.

If you simply want to get from A to B, take the public ferry. For E£1, you can get to Elephantine Island, departing from either the landing opposite the telephone centrale or the one across from Thomas Cook. A ferry to the west bank leaves from a landing south of the governorate building and takes you over to the Tombs of the Nobles, also for E£1. When the river is low the ferry leaves from just north of the tourist-police station.

For details on taking an overnight felucca trip down the Nile, see p287.

Swimming

Aswan is a hot place, and sometimes a swim seems just the way to escape the worst of it. Short of joining the local kids and jumping into the Nile to cool off (which is definitely not advised; see Schistosomiasis, p556), there are a few hotels with swimming pools open to the public, generally from 9am to sunset. The cheapest by far is the small pool at the Cleopatra Hotel (p314), which costs E£10, but it's small and overlooked by other buildings. The Basma Hotel (p315) has a pool that nonguests can use for E£25, while the Mövenpick (p314) and Isis Hotel (p314) charge E£50. Some readers have reported that you can use the New Cataract's (p314) pool for free, as long as you order lunch.

TOURS

Small hotels and travel agencies arrange day tours of the area's major sights. Half-day guided tours usually include the Temple of Isis at Philae, the Unfinished Obelisk and the High Dam, and start at US$27 (per person with three to five people) with Amex or Thomas Cook, including admission to all sites. Bear in mind that while small hotels will offer much cheaper tours, they are not licensed to guide groups. Check with the tourist office if you have any questions.

Travel agencies will also arrange felucca trips to Elephantine and Kitchener's Islands for about E£65 to E£100 per person, based on a group of three to five people.

All travel agencies and some hotels in Aswan offer trips to Abu Simbel. Admission fees are not included in the price of the cheapest trips, so make sure you check when booking. Also, on many cheaper trips the minibuses do not have air-con, which can be extremely uncomfortable in summer, especially if the organisers have packed in too many people (which they often try to do). Most of the larger travel agencies in Aswan send air-con coaches and minibuses to Abu Simbel. Try Thomas Cook, Amex, Travco or one of the other reputable agencies in town. Their bus trips will be a lot more expensive, but you will be comfortable. Thomas Cook charges about E£240 for a seat on its bus, but this doesn't include a guide or admission. By contrast, budget hotels offer tours for about E£60 to E£90, often stopping off at the Unfinished Obelisk and Philae Temple on the return trip. Again, you get no extras and have no protection in case of problems. For more information about getting to Abu Simbel, see p330.

SLEEPING

The hotel scene in Aswan is much less dynamic than that of Luxor. There are few good midrange options and many of the longstanding places seem to be stuck in a time warp regarding décor and service.

Prices vary greatly depending on the season. The high season officially extends from October to April, but its zenith is December and January. In the low season, and even until early November, you'll have no trouble finding a room. We've tried to list high-season rates here. All prices include breakfast and taxes unless otherwise noted.

Budget
HOSTELS
Youth Hostel (Map p306; ☎/fax 230 2235; Sharia Abtal at-Tahrir; dm members/nonmembers E£8.55/10.25, r E£15) Don't be confused with the other hostel next door; there is only one real youth hostel in town – the other is a governorate-run place that is closed to foreigners. The Youth Hostel is in need of a makeover and the (clean) bathrooms show signs of age. Still, for tight budgets, this is not a bad deal. Breakfast is E£6.

HOTELS
If you arrive by train, you'll invariably be met by touts who get commission for taking you to the hotel they work for. This sleazy side of Aswan's budget hotel scene can end up costing you more when you come to pay for your room; ignore them and find your own place to stay.

Keylany Hotel (Map p306; ☎ 231 7332; www.key lanyhotel.com; 25 Sharia Keylany; s/d/t E£50/70/85; ✷ ▣) This remains Aswan's best budget hotel, with friendly management, simple but clean air-conditioned rooms, pine furniture and spotless bathrooms (with proper showers, not just holes in the floor). The roof terrace has no Nile view but has a burlap sunshade and palm furniture, and is a great place to hang out. Highly recommended.

Nuba Nile Hotel (Map p306; ☎ 231 3267; nubanil _hotel@hotmail.com; s/d E£50/70; ✷ ▣) Friendly and spotlessly clean, the family-run Nuba Nile is another good budget option. Rooms vary considerably: some are tiny, others have no windows, but all are comfortable and have private bathrooms, and most have air-conditioning. The convenient location close to the train station and beside a popular *ahwa* is an added bonus.

Hathor Hotel (Map p306; ☎ 231 4580; fax 303 462; Corniche el-Nil; s/d E£33/55; ✷ ▣) With a (small) rooftop pool the Hathor is an excellent deal for the price. The 36 rooms vary in size and can be gloomy, but all are clean and have private bathrooms and most have air-conditioning (which is controlled at the reception). The upstairs terrace has a few poolside chairs and spectacular Nile views.

Memnon Hotel (Map p306; ☎ /fax 230 0483; Corniche el-Nil; s/d E£40/60; ✗ ⓐ) If the Hathor is full, you might consider the Memnon. Easily missed, with an awful entrance on the dusty street behind the Corniche, it has been around for years and has that battered dark furniture that Aswanis seem to love, but the rooms are clean and have air-conditioning and fantastic Nile views. There is a small, slightly murky rooftop pool and roof terrace (without shade).

Happi Hotel (Map p306; ☎ 231 4115; fax 230 7572; Sharia Abtal at-Tahrir; s/d E£60/85; ✗ ⓐ) Turn a blind eye to the gloomy décor and threadbare carpets, and the Happi is not a bad place to stay. The staff can be unresponsive but the rooms are clean and have decent-sized private bathrooms and air-conditioning. Some have Nile views, too. The owner also runs the Cleopatra Hotel, so guests can use the Cleopatra's pool at a discounted price.

Nubian Oasis Hotel (Map p306; ☎ 231 2126; Nubian Oasis_Hotel_Aswan@hotmail.com; 234 Sharia as-Souq; s/d E£20/25; ✗ ⓐ) Just off Sharia as-Souq, this remains one of Aswan's most popular travellers' haunts, although quite why remains a mystery. There's a large lounge area and a pleasant roof garden where Stella (E£7.50) is served. All rooms have private bathrooms and air-conditioning, but the staff can be surly, particularly when they are trying to get you onto one of their tours.

Ramsis Hotel (Map p306; ☎ 230 4000; fax 231 5701; Sharia Abtal at-Tahrir; s/d E£60/100; ✗) A conveniently located high-rise hotel, much like the Cleopatra but cheaper and in better shape. Rooms come with a shower, toilet, colour TV, minifridge and some also have good Nile views. Staff are a bit sleepy but generally pleasant. Not a bad option for the price.

Philae Hotel (Map p306; ☎ 231 2090; fax 232 4089; Corniche el-Nil; s/d Nile view E£60/80, rear view E£50/70; ✗) Rooms on the 1st floor of this longstanding hotel are freshly painted and have new ceramic tile floors (not beautiful, but a huge improvement on the grubby carpets that are so popular in Aswan's budget hotels). Despite this, the newly refurbished bathrooms and the Nile views, the rooms suffer from street noise. Rooms on other

floors were under renovation on our visit but, if finished, could be quieter.

Marwa Hotel (Map p306; ☎ 230 8532; off Sharia Abtal at-Tahrir; per bed in room of 4 E£6) Entered from an alley off Sharia Abtal at-Tahrir, the Marwa has basic rooms with metal beds, fans and shared bathrooms. There are the inevitable Bob Marley pictures on the wall, but it has had a coat of paint since our last visit and the bathrooms are clean, making it a decent place to stay if money is tight. A few rooms have dubious-looking air-con, for which you pay E£2 more. Breakfast is E£2.

Noorhan Hotel (Map p306; ☎ 231 6069; off Sharia as-Souq; s/d E£15/20; ✗ ⓐ) A perennial travellers' haunt with aggressive touts, the Noorhan remains a reasonable cheap option. The rooms have private bathrooms and some have air-conditioning, there is Internet access (E£10 per hour) and Stellas are available (E£8). This hotel is spoilt by the staff aggressively promoting its tours.

Yassin Hotel (Map p306; ☎ 231 7109; s/d E£20/25; ✗) In competition with the neighbouring Noorhan, the Yassin has recently painted, clean rooms, some with private bathrooms. Like the Noorhan, its staff can be pushy, but it remains a good deal if other cheap options are full.

Midrange

Aswan has only a small selection of midrange hotels. There's not much to distinguish those at the bottom end of the scale from the better budget places, so if money's tight look carefully before making a choice.

Marhaba Palace Hotel (Map p306; ☎ 233 0102; marhabaaswan@yahoo.com; Corniche el-Nil; s/d US$50/60 ✗) Given Aswan's dearth of decent midrange hotels, any new place is good news but the Marhaba overshadows the competition. Rooms are small but well appointed, with comfortable beds, tasteful décor, luxurious bathrooms and satellite TV. Bright and welcoming, it overlooks a park on the Corniche and has two restaurants, friendly staff and a roof terrace with excellent Nile views. Recommended.

Sarah Hotel (Map p318; ☎ 232 7234; slasheen@ menanet.net; s/d US$35/50; ✗ ⓐ) If you want peace and quiet, the Sarah is a good choice. Built on a clifftop overlooking the Nile about 2km beyond the Nubia Museum, it is isolated but has fantastic views over the First Cataract and the Western Desert.

The décor is slightly sterile but everything is spotlessly clean, with air-conditioning, satellite TV, friendly staff and a good-sized pool. Try to get a corner room – most have huge balconies. A shuttle bus runs into town every hour.

Isis Hotel (Map p306; ☎ 232 4744; www.pyramisa egypt.com; Corniche el-Nil; s/d US$62/74; 🅧 🅡) The only hotel built right on the riverbank, the 100-room Isis Hotel has a prime location in the centre of town but when we last visited the chalet-style rooms were in need of a coat of paint. In general, though, it remains a good option, with clean, comfortable rooms, a selection of restaurants, a figure-8 shaped pool and good Nile views.

Kalabsha Hotel (Map p303; ☎ 230 2666; fax 230 5974; Sharia Abtal at-Tahrir; s/d excl taxes US$65/85; 🅧 🅡) The four-star Kalabsha Hotel is a large, modernist reminder of Egypt's past flirtation with the Eastern Bloc. It has excellent views of the First Cataract and the west bank. Rooms are in need of a refit but all have air-conditioning and private bathrooms, and there is a good-sized pool, making it a good deal for the price.

Orchida St George (Map p306; ☎ 231 5997; orchida hotel@hotmail.com; Muhammed Khalid; s/d E£80/100; 🅧 🅜) Friendly, helpful staff at this small three-star hotel make up for the tacky décor and odd-shaped rooms. Rooms are clean but differ considerably in size, so try to see several before you commit. Still, with fridges in all rooms, comfortable beds and satellite TV, this isn't too bad for the price.

Cleopatra Hotel (Map p306; ☎ 231 4003; fax 231 4002; Sharia as-Souq; s/d US$48/62; 🅧 🅜 🅡) Away from the bright lobby, the Cleopatra is dark and gloomy, with 109 rooms filled with battered old furniture, ancient air-conditioners and unfriendly staff. Somehow it remains full of groups on cut-price packages, but that may be because the selection of hotels in this price range is so limited. Conveniently located in the centre of town, with a reasonably sized (but overlooked) rooftop pool, this could be much better. Hopefully the opening of the Marhaba Palace will force the management to clean up its act.

Al-Amir Hotel (Map p306; ☎ 231 4732; fax 230 4411; Sharia Abbas Farid; s/d E£90/120; 🅧) A street back from the Corniche, this three-star hotel claims to have Nile views (apparent only if you strain your neck). The kitsch décor sets the tone and betrays a connection with the Gulf (Saudi emblems emblazon the stationery and brochures). The 28 rooms, all with private bathrooms, satellite TV and air-conditioning, are showing their age. Consider only if others are full.

Top End

Aswan has a small but good selection of luxury hotels.

Old Cataract Hotel (Map p303; ☎ 231 6000; www .sofitel.com; Sharia Abtal at-Tahrir; s/d garden view US$175/190, r Nile view US$168-1500; 🅧 🅡) A world-famous grand hotel, the Old Cataract is reminiscent of a bygone age of gracious travel. An impressive Moorish-style building, it is surrounded by gardens on a rise above the river, and has splendid views of the Nile and across the southern tip of Elephantine Island to the mausoleum of the Aga Khan. The hotel's exterior was used in the movie *Death on the Nile*, in part because Agatha Christie wrote part of the novel here. Service here can be erratic and the food doesn't quite match the standard of the architecture, but the atmosphere is unique and the setting unparalleled. Deluxe Nile-view rooms are worth the extra cost, but ask to see several if possible; they differ in size and quality. The hotel is worth visiting just to enjoy a cool cocktail or afternoon tea on the veranda, but expect to be charged E£55 (to be offset against your bar tab) for the privilege.

Mövenpick Resort Aswan (Map p303; ☎ 230 3455; www.moevenpick-aswan.com; Elephantine Island; s/d US$183/286; 🅧 🅡) This famous architectural disaster is under new management. Situated on the northern end of Elephantine Island, it is quiet and tranquil, and renovations planned by Mövenpick should turn it into the relaxing resort that it was meant to be. The large rooms have magnificent views, along with the usual five-star amenities (minibar, very comfortable beds, satellite TV, well-equipped bathrooms), and there is a pool and a spa that does sand treatments for rheumatism. Guests are transported to and from town by a free ferry.

New Cataract Hotel (Map p303; ☎ 231 6002; www .sofitel.com; Sharia Abtal at-Tahrir; s/d city view US$96/124, Nile view US$124/149; 🅧 🅡) If your budget doesn't stretch to the Old Cataract, consider staying at this high-rise lump next door. The rooms are in need of renovation, but those overlooking the Nile have stunning views (try to get one on the upper floors). You must pay an additional E£45 for the obligatory breakfast, and you get access to the Old Cataract's restaurants and facilities.

Basma Hotel (Map p303; ☎ 231 0901; basma@ rocketmail.com; Sharia Abtal at-Tahrir; s/d US$108/141; ☒ ☒ ☐ ☒) Located opposite the Nubia Museum, the Basma has friendly staff, a nice pool and fantastic views over the southern end of Elephantine Island. The good-sized rooms have comfortable beds, satellite TV and other amenities that you expect in this price range, but some are beginning to look a bit shabby. The big letdown here is the food, which is mediocre.

EATING

Restaurants in Aswan don't have the turnover found in many other Egyptian resorts. Few new ones open and old stalwarts don't close, even if they seem to have few customers. Outside the hotels few have liquor licenses and most won't accept credit cards.

Restaurants

1902 Restaurant (Map p303; ☎ 231 6000; Old Cataract Hotel, Sharia Abtal at-Tahrir; set menu per person E£175) Aswan's finest restaurant has a set four-course French-influenced menu that changes daily. Although the atmosphere is formal, the waiting staff is friendly. The quality of food is erratic, but nothing can beat the experience of dining under the restaurant's dome while being serenaded by oud (lute) players. Nonguests of the hotel must call ahead to reserve a table.

Nubian House Restaurant (Map p303; ☎ 232 6226; mains E£7-20) For spectacular views over the First Cataract, this is the place to be. Authentic Nubian food is served, often accompanied by Nubian music (call ahead to see when it's on). There are sunset 'tea' buffets (4pm to 6pm), but they are perfectly happy to let you just sip on a tea and smoke a *sheesha* (water pipe) while taking in the view. Tour groups tend to nab the best tables so see if you can reserve one in advance. To get here, follow the road past the Nubia Museum for about 1km, or 15 minutes. Take a right just past a development of upmarket housing (many still under construction). Take a taxi after sunset; the road is unlit and there is no verge so walking is dangerous.

Panorama (Map p303; ☎ 231 6169; Corniche el-Nil; dishes E£8-15) By the Nile, down from the Corniche, Panorama serves simple Egyptian meals cooked in clay pots and served piping hot, all accompanied by salad, mezze and rice or chips. Alternatively you can plump for the all-day breakfast. It also has a wide selection of herbal and medicinal teas. With its quiet waterside location and pleasant terrace, it is a great place to hang out and watch the Nile flow by.

Aswan Moon Restaurant (Map p306; ☎ 231 6108; Corniche el-Nil; meals E£12-30) A perennially popular hang-out for both locals and tourists, the Aswan Moon has recently stopped serving alcohol, which could lose it much of its clientele. Down on a riverside pontoon, with a laid-back atmosphere and slow but reasonable service, it remains a pleasant place for dinner. The menu is wide ranging, with basic Egyptian and international dishes, including mezze (E£4 to E£9), pizzas, (E£17 to E£23), soups (E£3.50 to E£5) and kebabs (E£20). Our favourite is the *daoud basha* (meatballs in tomato sauce, E£10), served steaming hot in an earthenware dish.

Al-Masry Restaurant (Map p306; ☎ 230 2576; Sharia al-Matar; meals E£8-30) This is one of Aswan's better-known restaurants and is famous for kebabs and *kofta*, but it also serves pigeon and chicken. The meat is excellent and the restaurant's popularity with local families guarantees freshness. Meals are served with bread, salad and tahini.

Chef Khalil (Map p306; ☎ 231 0142; Sharia as-Souq; meals E£25-50) This popular fish restaurant just along from the station serves very fresh fish from Lake Nasser as well as the Red Sea. The fish is sold by weight, and is either grilled, baked or fried, according to your choice, and is served with salad and rice or French fries. It's a small place, but worth the wait if it's full.

Biti Pizza (Map p306; Midan al-Mahatta; dishes E£6-18) Convenient to the station, Biti (bey-ti) is a restaurant and takeaway that serves delicious sweet and savoury *fiteer* (flaky Egyptian pizza), as well as Western-style pizzas. The tuna *fiteer* (E£10) is excellent, as is the fruit-and-nut dessert version (E£9.50). At the moment the English menu only offers Western-style pizzas, which are not as good (or as cheap) as the *fiteer*, but if you insist on these, the waiters should understand.

Madena Restaurant (Map p306; Sharia as-Souq; meals E£20) Small and unpretentious, this no-frills eatery close to the Cleopatra Hotel serves good, basic Egyptian meals at reasonable prices. A decent *kofta* meal, accompanied by bread, rice, salad and tahini, costs E£20. Vegetarian meals cost E£12.

Al-Sayyida Nefissa (Map p306; dishes E£5-30) Tucked away in a side alley off Sharia as-Souq in the heart of the souq, the hard-to-find Al-Sayyida Nefissa currently finds itself beside a building site, making its outdoor tables a bit dusty. But it remains a popular, good-value place serving *kofta*, chicken and stuffed pigeon accompanied by soup, rice, salad, vegetables and bread.

Garden Restaurant (Map p303; ☎ 231 6002; New Cataract Hotel, Sharia Abtal at-Tahrir; meals E£65) This place serves set meals that are billed as Nubian but are in reality Egyptian and Lebanese. Portions are generous, with several dishes of mezze followed by servings of potatoes, rice, chicken, meat and fish cooked in clay pots. The wooden gazebo-type setting is nice if the weather is cool, but it's hot in the summer.

Nubian Restaurant (Map p303; ☎ 230 2465; Essa Island; meals E£35-60) Sitting on a tiny island south of Elephantine Island, the Nubian Restaurant is less about food (which is generally lacklustre) than the after-dinner folkloric show, which some people enjoy but others find tacky. A free boat leaves from opposite EgyptAir.

Restaurant Derwash (Map p306; Midan al-Mahatta; dishes E£6-20) Just off the *midan* (square) opposite the station, this little place has been serving basic kebab and chicken meals, accompanied by rice and vegetables, for years.

Quick Eats

Along Sharia as-Souq is a smorgasbord of small restaurants and cafés in the midst of the lively atmosphere of the souq. There are also plenty of cafés around the train station.

El-Tahrer Pizza (Map p306; Midan al-Mahatta; dishes E£8-15) A popular café that serves pizza and *fiteer* at rock-bottom prices. Also has *sheesha* (E£3) and tea for afterwards.

Haramein Foul & Ta'amiyya (Map p306; Sharia Abtal at-Tahrir; dishes E£1-5) A tiny *fuul* (fava bean paste) and *ta'amiyya* takeaway hidden amongst the low-rise apartment blocks, this is where Aswanis go when they want good *fuul* and *ta'amiyya*.

Koshary Aly Baba Restaurant (Map p306; Sharia Abtal at-Tahrir; dishes E£1-15) A clean and popular

takeaway/restaurant with good *kushari*, as well as shwarma and *kofta*.

Esraa (Map p306; Sharia Abtal at-Tahrir; dishes E£4-12) Another hole-in-the-wall place, this time serving good *kofta* sandwiches at reasonable prices.

Self-Catering

The souq is the best place to head if you want to buy your own food. On the main street, as well as some of the small alleyways, there are small grocery shops that stock canned goods, cheese and UHT milk. Fruit and vegetables are abundant when in season. They are best bought in the morning, when they are fresh.

Egypt Free Shop (Map p303; ☎ 231 4939; Corniche el-Nil; ☺ 9am-2pm & 6-10pm) The only place to buy local beer and wine.

ENTERTAINMENT

Palace of Culture (Map p306; ☎ 231 3390; Corniche el-Nil) Between October and February/March, Aswan's folkloric dance troupe sporadically performs Nubian *tahtib* (stick dancing) and songs depicting village life. If tour groups demand performances and the troupe is not travelling, they begin their performances at around 9pm Saturday to Thursday. The show lasts about two hours and admission is E£10. The centre also sometimes presents other traditional Upper Egyptian and Nubian music performances.

Nubian music is played at the Nubian House Restaurant (p315), although when we visited there was no schedule of performances. Call for details.

Nubian shows are also performed at the Mövenpick Resort and New Cataract hotels, although they sometimes veer into kitsch.

If you are lucky, you may be invited to a Nubian wedding on a weekend night. Foreign guests are deemed auspicious additions to the ceremony, but don't be surprised if you're asked to pay a E£20 'fee' to help defray the huge costs of the band and the food.

Otherwise, strolling along the Corniche, watching the moon rise as you sit at a rooftop terrace and having a beer at one of the floating restaurants is about all that most travellers get up to in Aswan at night. The top-end hotels all have discos and nightclubs, but they're fairly empty.

SHOPPING

Aswan's famous souq may be more touristy than it used to be but it's still a good place to pick up souvenirs and crafts. Colourful Nubian skullcaps are popular and go for about E£5 each. More bulky are the baskets and trays that you can see around town. Prices vary according to size and age; expect to pay about E£60 for an old, medium-sized tray. Small round discs go for around E£15.

The spices and indigo powder prominently displayed are also good buys, and most of the spice shops sell the dried hibiscus used to make the refreshing drink *karkadai*. However, beware of the safflower that is sold as saffron. Aswan is also famous for the quality of its henna powder and its delicious roasted peanuts. The higher grade of the latter go for E£10 a kilogram.

GETTING THERE & AWAY

Air

EgyptAir (Map p303; ☎ 2315000; Corniche el-Nil; ⏰ 8am-8pm) has daily flights from Cairo to Aswan (E£1037 one way, 1¼ hours). The one-way trip to Luxor is E£364 and takes 30 minutes. There are two flights a day to Abu Simbel, leaving at 6.30am and 9am. The round-trip ticket costs E£640, including bus transfers between the airport and the temple site.

Boat

For details about the five-star cruise boats and fishing safaris operating on Lake Nasser, see p291. For details on boat transport to Sudan, see p544.

Bus

The bus station is about 3.5km north of the train station. It costs about E£5 to get there by taxi, or 50pt by service taxi. Buses, service taxis and microbuses are based there.

Upper Egypt Bus Co has three daily buses to Abu Simbel (E£20, four hours, departing 8am, 11.30am and 5pm). Officially only a maximum of four foreigners are allowed per bus but this can stretch to six if you are lucky. Seats cannot be booked in advance, so get to the bus station early to be sure of getting a seat. Take your passport, as there are two checkpoints along the way.

Buses to Luxor (E£15, four to five hours) leave at 6am, 8am, 12.30pm, 2pm, 3.30pm and 5pm, stopping at Kom Ombo (E£3, one hour), Edfu (E£7, two hours) and Esna

---

POLICE CONVOYS

Driving north or south means going in a police convoy. Convoys congregate in front of the Officer's Club, about 1km north of the governorate building on the Corniche. You should get there 15 minutes in advance. There are two daily convoys heading north to Luxor (8am, travelling via Kom Ombo, Edfu and Esna, and 1.30pm, direct to Luxor) and two heading south to Abu Simbel (4am and 11am). The trip to Luxor takes approximately three hours, and 3½ hours to Abu Simbel.

(E£10, three hours). A direct bus to Cairo (E£85, 14 hours) leaves at 3.30pm daily. There are four buses going to Hurghada (E£45, eight hours, 6am, 8am, 3.30pm and 5pm), stopping on the way in Luxor, Qena and Safaga. The 3.30pm service continues on to Suez (E£85, 11 hours) and Cairo. Buses for Marsa Alam (E£20, six hours) leave at 6.30am.

El Gouna Transport also has buses to Abu Simbel at 9am and 4pm. They take four hours and cost E£20.

Service Taxi

Foreigners are forbidden from taking service taxis. If things change (check with the tourist office), service taxis are based next to the bus station, 3.5km north of the train station.

Train

Aswan Train Station (Map p306; ☎ 231 4754) has a number of daily trains running north to Cairo, but only three of them can be used by foreigners. The 981 (6am), 1903 (6pm) and 997 (8pm) all cost the same (1st/2nd class E£81/47, student 1st/2nd class E£55/37, 14 hours). However, if you try climbing aboard another train and buying your ticket on board then usually nobody will stop you. All trains heading north stop at Daraw (1st/2nd class E£11/6, 45 minutes), Kom Ombo (E£15/12, one hour), Edfu (E£19/10, two hours), Esna (E£22/14, 2½ hours) and Luxor (E£26/18, three hours). Student discounts are available on all these trains.

Abela Egypt Sleeping Train (☎ 230 2124; www.sleepingtrains.com) has two daily services to Cairo at 5pm and 6.30pm (single/double cabin US$74/106, 14 hours). There is no student discount. The price includes dinner and breakfast. Tickets must be paid for in US dollars.

GETTING AROUND
To/From the Airport
The airport is 25km southwest of town and the taxi fare between them is about E£25.

Bicycle
Aswan is not a great town for cycling. However, there are a few places at the train-station end of Sharia as-Souq where you can hire bicycles for about E£10 a day.

Taxi
A taxi tour that includes Philae, the High Dam and the Unfinished Obelisk near the Fatimid Cemetery costs around E£40 for five to six people. Taxis can also take you on day trips to Daraw and/or Kom Ombo for about E£100. Remember that you have to join the convoy to do this. A taxi anywhere within the town costs E£5.

Service taxis run along the major roads in Aswan. The fare is 50pt.

AROUND ASWAN

ASWAN DAM
When the British constructed the old Aswan Dam above the First Cataract at the turn of the 20th century it was the largest of its kind in the world. The growing population of Egypt had made it imperative to put more land under cultivation and the only way to achieve this was to regulate the flow of the Nile. The dam was built between 1898 and 1902; it measures 2441m across, and is made almost entirely of local Aswan granite.

Although its height had to be raised twice to meet demand, the dam not only greatly increased the area of cultivable land but also provided the country with most of its hydroelectric power. Now completely surpassed both in function and as a tourist attraction by the High Dam 6km upstream, it is still worth a brief visit, as the area around the First Cataract below it is extremely fertile and picturesque.

The road to the airport and all trips to Abu Simbel by road include a drive across the Aswan Dam.

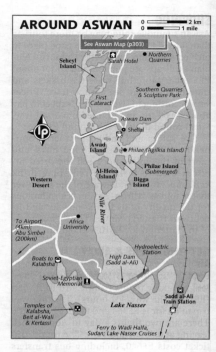

AROUND ASWAN

0 — 2 km
0 — 1 mile

See Aswan Map (p303)

Seheyl Island
Sarah Hotel
Northern Quarries
First Cataract
Southern Quarries & Sculpture Park
Aswan Dam
Shellal
Awad Island
Philae (Agilkia Island)
Philae Island (Submerged)
Al-Heisa Island
Bigga Island
Western Desert
Nile River
To Airport (4km); Abu Simbel (200km)
Africa University
Boats to Kalabsha
Hydroelectric Station
High Dam (Sadd al-Ali)
Soviet-Egyptian Memorial
Sadd al-Ali Train Station
Temples of Kalabsha, Beit al-Wali & Kertassi
Lake Nasser
Ferry to Wadi Halfa, Sudan; Lake Nasser Cruises

SEHEYL ISLAND
The large island just north of the old Aswan Dam, **Seheyl** (adult/child E£50/25; 7am-4pm Oct-Apr, to 5pm May-Sep) was sacred to the goddess Anukis. Prior to the dam's construction, the Nile would rush through the granite boulders that emerged from the riverbed just south of here, forming the First Cataract. Now the waters flow slowly and Seheyl makes an ideal destination for an extended felucca trip. On the island's southern tip is a cliff with more than 200 inscriptions, most dating to the 18th and 19th dynasties. They were inscribed by officials returning from or about to embark upon journeys to Nubia. The most famous is the so-called 'famine stele' that dates from the Ptolemaic period and recounts a terrible seven-year famine that struck Egypt during the reign of the Old Kingdom pharaoh Zoser (2667–2648 BC). According to the stele, Zoser tried to end his country's suffering by making donations to the Temple of Khnum at Elephantine.

Next to the inscriptions is a friendly Nubian village with brightly coloured houses. It is a pleasant place for a stroll.

PHILAE (AGILKIA ISLAND)

The romantic and majestic aura surrounding the **Isis temple complex** (adult/child E£50/30; ⏱ 7am-4pm Oct-May, to 5pm Jun-Sep) on the island of Philae (fee-*li*) has been luring pilgrims for thousands of years. During the 19th century the ruins were one of Egypt's legendary tourist attractions. From the start of the 20th century, Philae and its temples became swamped for six months of every year by the high waters of the reservoir created by the construction of the old Aswan Dam. It seemed that they were destined to be lost forever, and travellers took to rowing boats to glide among the partially submerged columns and peer down through the translucent green to the wondrous sanctuaries of the mighty gods below.

In the 1960s, with the High Dam nearing completion, a rescue of the temple complex was organised by Unesco. The massive complex was disassembled and removed stone by stone from Philae between 1972 and 1980. The temples were reconstructed 20m higher on nearby Agilkia Island, which was even landscaped to resemble the sacred

PHILAE (AGILKIA ISLAND)

0 — 50 m

Gate of Diocletian
Temple of Augustus
Site of Temple of Harnedjotef
Temple of Isis
Church
Gate of Hadrian
Inner Sanctuary of Isis
Osiris Chapel
Second Pylon
Temple of Hathor
Mammisi (Birth House)
Gate of Ptolemy
First Pylon
Kiosk of Trajan
Temple of Imhotep
Outer Temple Court
Temple of Arhesnepher
Hall of Nectanebo
Nile River
Boat Landing

isle of Isis, in positions corresponding as closely as possible to their original layout.

By Roman times, Isis had become the greatest of all the Egyptian gods, worshipped right across the Roman Empire even as far as Britain. Her much older cult rivalled the newfangled cult of Christianity. Indeed, well after Rome and its empire embraced Christianity, Isis was still being worshipped at Philae as late as AD 550, when her temple was closed by the emperor Justinian.

Although Isis worship at Philae dates to around 690 BC at least, the earliest visible remains of the temple date from the reign of Nectanebo I (380–362 BC). Most of the rest was initiated by Ptolemy II Philadelphus and added to for the next 500 years until the reign of Diocletian (AD 284–305). The early Christians also added their bit by transforming the main temple's hypostyle hall into a chapel, building churches and defacing the pagan reliefs. Their inscriptions were then vandalised by the early Muslims.

Touring the Temple

The boat across to the temple leaves you at the base of the **Hall of Nectanebo**, the oldest part of the Philae complex. Heading north, you walk down the **outer temple court**, which has colonnades running along both sides, to the entrance of the Temple of Isis, marked by the 18m-high towers of the **first pylon** with their reliefs of Ptolemy XII Neos Dionysos smiting enemies.

In the central court of the **Temple of Isis** is the *mammisi* dedicated to Horus. Successive pharaohs reinstated their legitimacy as the mortal descendants of Horus by taking part in the *mammisi* rituals, which celebrated the god's birth.

The **second pylon** leads to a 10-columned hypostyle hall and beyond into the **Inner Sanctuary of Isis** where the goddess' gold statue once stood inside a red-granite shrine carved on the orders of Ptolemy VIII Euergetes. Although the stone shrine is now in the British Museum, the stone base that once held the barque in which the statue travelled remains, and is inscribed with the names of Ptolemy III (246–221 BC) and his wife Berenice. A staircase, on the western side, leads up to the **Osiris Chapel**, which is decorated with scenes of mourners; and everywhere there are reliefs of Isis, her husband and son, other deities and, of course, the Ptolemies and Romans who built or contributed to the temple.

On the northern tip of the island are the **Temple of Augustus** and the **Gate of Diocletian**; east of the second pylon is the delightful **Temple of Hathor** decorated with reliefs of musicians (including an ape playing the lute) and Bes, the god of childbirth. South of this is the elegant, unfinished pavilion by the water's edge, known as the **Kiosk of Trajan** (or 'Pharaoh's Bed'), perhaps the most famous of Philae's monuments and frequently painted by Victorian artists. The completed reliefs on the kiosk feature Emperor Trajan making offerings to Isis, Osiris and Horus.

Sound-&-Light Show

Each evening a **sound-and-light show** (admission E£55) is shown at Philae. If you only see one sound-and-light show in Egypt, this should be it. The commentary is still cheesy but wandering through the temple at night is fantastic. In winter (October to May) shows are at 6.30pm, 7.45pm and 9pm; in summer (May to September) they're at 8pm, 9.15pm and 10.30pm; and during Ramadan they're at 7.30pm, 8.45pm and 10pm. Double-check this schedule at the tourist office.

Day	Show 1	Show 2	Show 3
Monday	English	French	-
Tuesday	French	English	French
Wednesday	French	English	French
Thursday	French	Spanish	Italian
Friday	English	French	-
Saturday	English	Arabic	-
Sunday	German	French	-

Getting There & Away

The boat landing for the Philae complex is at Shellal, south of the old Aswan Dam. The only easy way to get there is by taxi or organised trip (arranged by most travel agencies and major hotels in town). The return taxi fare costs about E£30 without bargaining. The official price for a motorboat to the island costs E£25 (day) or E£27 (evening), divided between you if there are eight or fewer passengers. If there are more than eight, each person pays E£3 for the return trip. Fares are paid directly to the boatmen. However, on our last visit the boatmen refused to accept the official rate and were charging E£35 to E£40 during the day.

HIGH DAM

Egypt's contemporary example of construction on a monumental scale contains 18 times the amount of material used in the Great Pyramid of Khufu. When the controversial High Dam (Sadd al-Ali) was completed, the water that collected behind it became Lake Nasser, the world's largest artificial lake.

As early as the 1940s, it was evident that the old Aswan Dam, which only regulated the flow of water, was not big enough to counter the unpredictable annual flooding of the great river. But it wasn't until Gamal Abdel Nasser came to power in 1952 that the plans were drawn up for the new dam, 6km south of the British-built dam. Originally scoffed at as an impossible dream, the building of the dam was fraught with political and engineering difficulties. In 1956, after the USA, the UK and the World Bank suddenly refused the financial backing they had offered for the project, Nasser ordered the nationalisation of the Suez Canal, precipitating the Suez Crisis in which France, the UK and Israel invaded the canal region. They were eventually restrained by the UN. The Soviet Union then offered the necessary funding and expertise, and work began on the High Dam in 1960. It was completed in 1971.

The benefits of building the dam have been enormous. Egypt's area of cultivable land has increased by 30% and the High Dam's hydroelectric station has doubled the country's power supply.

On the other hand, the dam stops the flow of silt that was so critical to the Nile Valley's fertility. The effects of this are being felt all over Egypt. Heavy use of artificial fertilisers has led to increasing salinity of the ground water in agricultural areas. At the Nile's mouth in the Mediterranean, shrimp beds

---

HIGH DAM FACTS

- Length: 3600m
- Width at base: 980m
- Height at highest point: 111m
- Number of workers involved in construction: 35,000
- Number of workers who died during construction: 451

FEAST, FAMINE OR WAR

The fate of Egypt has always been intertwined with the fate of the Nile, and although the river flows through many countries, it is Egypt that has historically gained the most from its beneficence. The ancient Egyptians called their country *Kemet* (Black Land), after the fertile silt that the Nile's receding waters left in their wake. This annual dumping of a thick layer of dark, wet topsoil allowed ancient Egypt's agricultural system to develop and thrive, leading in turn to the accumulation of wealth necessary for such a sophisticated society and culture to flourish. When the floods failed and hunger turned to famine, the entire system broke down. It is no coincidence that consecutive years of inadequate flooding often coincided with the breakdown of central authority or invasion by a foreign power.

Because of this constant threat, the Egyptians developed a highly organised irrigation system to help them deal with unpredictability of the river. Nilometers, usually a series of steps against which the rising water would be gauged, were used to measure the level of the flood, which was crucial for predicting soil fertility and crop yields. Close to Egypt's southern frontier, one of the best surviving examples, the Nilometer at Elephantine (see p309), would be among the first to show evidence of rising water in early June.

When the waters subsided at the end of the summer, land would be surveyed and measured in order to determine the level of tax to be levied. From the earliest times, canals would be dug to help extend the reach of the flood plain, and devices were developed to help move water. These began as simple pots but later the *shadouf,* a long pole with a 'bucket' at one end and counterbalancing weight at the other, and the *saqia,* an animal-powered waterwheel, helped increase the ability to move greater amounts of water and extend the area of cultivable land.

Since the building of the High Dam, Egypt has been freed from the uncertainties of the Nile's annual flood, but the supply of water is still not entirely within its control. At present its use of Nile water is governed by a 1959 treaty with Sudan that essentially divides the flow of the river between the two countries. The eight other countries around the Nile basin claim – not without reason – that this is unfair and are clamouring for a more equitable division of this precious resource. An international initiative to help resolve the issue has been underway since 1999 but Egypt, the largest and most powerful – and the also most Nile-dependent – of the riparian states has so far blocked any changes to the 1959 treaty and has even threatened war if any country violates its terms.

and fishing grounds have disappeared. The now perennially full irrigation canals have led to endemic infection with the bilharzia parasite, which is a huge public health problem. The authorities also face the problem that silt could eventually fill the lake.

Most people get to the High Dam, which is 13km south of Aswan, as part of an organised trip to the sights around Aswan. If you go by taxi, it costs E£5 for entrance onto the dam and into the small pavilion with displays detailing the dimensions and the construction of the dam. If you come by foot from the train station, you'll have to pay 50pt.

Many visitors are disappointed by the visit, expecting more spectacular views, so perhaps you should not hope for too much. Video cameras and zoom lenses cannot be used, although nobody seems to police this.

A stone monument honouring Soviet-Egyptian friendship and cooperation is on the western side of the dam.

Getting There & Away

The quickest way to get to the High Dam is to take a taxi (about E£20). Usually it is combined with a trip to the Temple of Kalabsha, which is about 3km from the western end of the dam and is visible from the dam on the western side of Lake Nasser.

LOWER NUBIA & LAKE NASSER

For countless centuries before the Aswan and High Dams irrevocably changed the topography of the area, the First Cataract at Aswan marked the dividing line between Egypt and its southern neighbour, Nubia, which held the land that lay between Aswan and Khartoum. As the Nile changed here, so too did the territory along its shores. Whereas the land to the north was under continuous cultivation, to the south it was more rugged, with rocky desert cliffs and sand forcing its way down to the water's edge and separating the pockets of agricultural land.

Nowadays all this lies deep under the waters of Lake Nasser. The landscape is dominated by the contrast of smooth desert and calm green-brown water. Apart from the beauty of the lake itself, the main attraction of this region is the temples that were so painstakingly moved away from the floodwaters in the 1960s. See p326 for more about this mammoth cultural rescue mission.

History

The ancient Egyptians called Nubia Ta-Seti (Land of the Bow), after the weapon for which the Nubians were famous. The modern name is thought to come from the ancient Egyptian word *nbw*, meaning 'gold', which was extensively mined in the north-eastern part of the country in Pharaonic and Graeco-Roman times. It is ironic that our name for this now lost land comes from ancient Egyptian, as much of Nubia's long history was dominated by its more powerful northern neighbour. When Egypt was strong it either annexed or aggressively exploited the natural resources of its neighbour; by contrast, times of turmoil in Egypt tended to coincide with periods of indigenous growth and development in Nubia.

There is evidence of settlements in northern Nubia 10,000 years ago. At Nabta

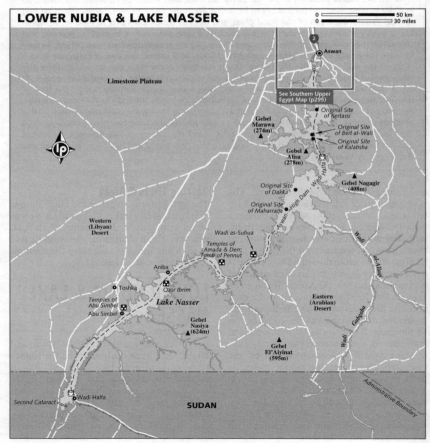

LOWER NUBIA & LAKE NASSER

0   50 km
0   30 miles

Aswan

Limestone Plateau

See Southern Upper
Egypt Map (p295)

*Original Site
of Kertassi*

Gebel
Marawa
(274m) ▲

*Original Site
of Beit al-Wali*

*Original Site
of Kalabsha*

Gebel ▲
Alisa
(278m)

Aswan High Dam – Wadi Halfa

Gebel Nagagir
(408m) ▲

*Original Site
of Dakka*

*Original Site
of Maharraqa*

Western
(Libyan)
Desert

Wadi as-Subua

*Temples of
Amada & Derr;
Tomb of Pennut*

Aniba

Wadi al-Allaqi

Toshka

Qasr Ibrim

*Temples of
Abu Simbel*
Abu Simbel

Lake Nasser

Eastern
(Arabian)
Desert

Gebel
Nasiya
▲(624m)

Wadi Gabgaba

Gebel
El'Aiyinat
(595m) ▲

Administrative Boundary

Second Cataract

Wadi Halfa

SUDAN

Playa, some 100km west of Abu Simbel, archaeologists have recently found evidence of housing, sculpted monoliths and the world's oldest calendar made of small standing stones dating from around 6000 BC. Until 3500 BC it seems that Nubia and southern Egypt developed in roughly similar ways, with the growing domestication of animals, the development of crops and the gradual adoption of permanent settlements. But there were also important differences. Although the two were ethnically linked, the darker-skinned Nubians had more African features than the Egyptians. Furthermore, their language was Nilo-Saharan, while ancient Egyptian was Afro-Asiatic.

With the unification of north and south in around 3100 BC, Egypt developed rapidly. Throughout the Old Kingdom, trading and mining expeditions were sent to extract Nubian mineral wealth, establishing a pattern that was to last nearly 5000 years. When centralised authority collapsed in Egypt during the First Intermediate Period (2181–2055 BC), a new culture began to establish itself in Nubia and relations between the two neighbours appear to have been good. But with the reunification of Egypt at the start of the Middle Kingdom, Lower Nubia (roughly the area between the First and Second Cataracts) was once again annexed as a province and a chain of mud-brick fortresses was built at strategic points along the Nile to safeguard trade.

During the New Kingdom, instead of fortresses the Egyptians built temples in Nubia, dividing the whole of the region into five nomes, ruled on the pharaoh's behalf by his viceroy, who took the title King's Son of Kush (Kush being the southern province of Nubia). Taking advantage of Egypt's political disunity during the Third Intermediate Period (1069–747 BC), the tables were turned and Nubia forged north, ruling Egypt for a century as the 25th Kushite dynasty (747–656 BC). They ruled in the traditional manner as pharaohs, built in the Egyptian style, worshipped Amun and the other gods, and in many ways were more Egyptian than the Egyptians.

The 25th dynasty ended with the Assyrian invasion of Egypt in 671 BC. Over the next several centuries, as Egypt suffered a succession of invasions, Nubia sometimes warred with the conquerors to the north

(as in the case of the Persians) and at other times enjoyed cordial relations (as with the Ptolemies).

Christianity gradually spread to Nubia after the 5th century AD, and by AD 652 the newly Islamised authorities in Egypt made a peace treaty with the Christian kingdoms in Nubia. However, Egyptian attacks on Nubia increased in the 12th and 13th centuries, and in 1315 the last Christian king of Nubia was replaced with a Muslim and most of the population converted to Islam. Once again Lower Nubia reverted to being a transit point between Egypt to the north and Africa to the south. Finally, with the establishment of the Anglo-Egyptian government in Sudan in 1899, a border between Egypt and Sudan was established 40km north of Wadi Halfa and Nubia was divided for the last time.

MODERN NUBIA

Following the completion of the old Aswan Dam in 1902, and again after its height was raised in 1912 and 1934, the water level of the Nile in Lower Nubia gradually rose from 87m to 121m, partially submerging many of the monuments in the area and, by the 1930s, totally flooding a large number of Nubian villages. With their homes flooded, many Nubians moved north into Egypt where, with government help, they bought land and built villages based on their traditional architecture. Most of the Nubian villages close to Aswan, such as Elephantine, West Aswan and Seheyl, are made up of people who moved at this time.

However, the majority of Nubians, assuming that the Nile's new shoreline would not change again, decided to stay in their homeland and build new houses on higher land. The rising waters imposed huge changes on those who stayed: the date plantations that had been central to their economy were destroyed and would take years to replace, so many Nubian men were forced to search for work in the north, leaving the women behind to run the communities.

Less than 30 years later, the building of the High Dam meant that those who had stayed were forced to move again. In the 1960s 50,000 Egyptian Nubians were relocated to government-built villages around Kom Ombo, 50km north of Aswan.

Nubian Culture

There is no doubt that the Nubians have paid an extremely high price for Egypt's greater good. After first losing their homes, and then their homeland, they are now faced with losing their distinctive identity as new generations grow up as Egyptians.

Perhaps because it is so vulnerable, Nubian culture is also very vibrant. Nubian music is famous the world over for its unique sound (see below). This was popularised in the West by musicians such as Hamza ad-Din, whose oud melodies are ethereally beautiful. As well as the oud, two basic instruments give the music its distinctive rhythm and harmony: the *douff*, a wide, shallow drum or tabla that musicians hold in their hands, and the *kisir*, a type of stringed instrument.

Not so well known abroad is Nubia's distinctive architecture. As in Upper Egypt, traditional Nubian houses are made with mud bricks. But here the similarities end. Lower Nubian houses sometimes have domed or vaulted ceilings, and houses from further south usually have a flat split-palm roof. They are plastered or whitewashed and covered with decorations, including ceramic plates. The basic forms of these houses can be seen in the Nubian villages around Aswan and in Ballana, near Kom Ombo.

Nubians also have their own marriage customs. Traditionally wedding festivities lasted up to 15 days but nowadays they are a three-day affair. On the first night, the bride and groom celebrate separately with their respective friends and families. On the second night, the bride takes her party to the groom's home and both groups dance to traditional music until the wee hours. Then the bride returns home and her hands and feet are painted with beautiful designs in henna. The groom will also have his hands and feet covered in henna

NUBIAN MUSIC

It's one of those strange quirks, but it's almost easier to hear and buy Nubian music in the West than it is in Egypt. The city folk of Cairo and Alexandria have an aversion to anything that comes from south of the capital and, with few exceptions, Nubian music is conspicuously absent from national TV and radio. You won't find it in the downtown (Cairo) music shops either. Yet while mainstream Egyptian pop icons such as Amr Diab dream of reaching an audience beyond the Arab world, Nubian artists sell CDs by the rackload in Europe and play to sell-out audiences.

The biggest name is Ali Hassan Kuban, a former tillerman from a small village near Aswan. He grew up playing at weddings and parties, and he made the leap to a global audience after being invited to perform at a Berlin festival in 1989. Until his death in 2001, he toured all over Europe as well as in Japan, Canada and the USA. He has several CDs out on the German record label **Piranha** (www.piranha.de), including *From Nubia to Cairo* and *Walk Like a Nubian*.

What makes Kuban's music appealing to a Western audience is that unlike Arabic music, with its jarring use of quarter tones, the Nubian sound is extremely accessible. It has a rhythmic quality that's almost African, which mixes simple melodies and soulful vocals. It's an incredibly warm sound. This can be heard at its best on a series of CDs by a loose grouping of musicians and vocalists recording under the name Salamat. Look out especially for *Mambo al-Soudani* (again on Piranha).

A slightly different facet of Nubian music is represented by Hamza ad-Din, a Nubian composer born in Wadi Halfa in 1929 and widely respected in the West for his semiclassical compositions written for the oud (lute). Inspired by his Sufi beliefs, Ad-Din's work is extremely haunting, especially *Escalay* (The Waterwheel), which you can find in a recording by the composer himself, or there's an excellent version of it by the Kronos Quartet on their CD *Pieces of Africa*.

Other names to look out for are the now-retired Sayyed Gayer, who sings poems and love songs accompanied only by the *douff* (drum), and Ahmed Monieb and Mohammed Hamam.

The one place in Egypt you might be able to pick up music by some of these artists is in Aswan; there are several music shops in the souq and the sales assistants are happy to pull out their Nubian collections and let you listen. To hear authentic live Nubian music, try to get yourself invited to a Nubian wedding in Aswan. You can also head to Eskaleh in Abu Simbel (p330), where musician Fikry Kachef hosts performances by local musicians.

but without any design. On the third day, the groom and his party walk slowly to the bride's house in a *zaffer* (procession), singing and dancing the whole way. Traditionally the groom will stay at the bride's house for three days before seeing his family. The couple will then set up home.

Getting There & Away

Although all the sites except Qasr Ibrim have roads leading to them, foreigners are currently forbidden to drive to any except Kalabsha, Beit al-Wali and Kertassi. The road to Abu Simbel is open, but foreigners are only allowed to travel in buses or microbuses in a police convoy. Abu Simbel can be reached by plane from Aswan, Luxor or Cairo. For more details on travelling to Abu Simbel, see p330.

For the moment, the rest of the sites can only be reached by boat, which is in any case one of the best ways of seeing Lake Nasser's dramatic monuments. See p286 for details.

LAKE NASSER

Looking out over Lake Nasser's wide expanse of calm green-blue water, it's hard to believe that it is human-made. As the world's largest artificial lake, its statistics are staggering: with an area of 5250 sq km, it stretches 510km in length and between 5km and 35km in width. On average it contains some 135 billion cu metres of water, of which an estimated six billion are lost each year to evaporation. Its maximum capacity is 157 billion cu metres of water. This was reached in 1996 after heavy rains in Ethiopia occasioned the opening of a special spillway at Toshka, about 30km north of Abu Simbel, for the first time since the dam was built. The Egyptian government has since embarked on a controversial project to build a new canal and irrigate thousands of acres in what is now the Nubian Desert between Toshka and the New Valley.

Numbers aside, the contrast between this enormous body of water and the remote desert stretching away on all sides makes Lake Nasser a place of austere beauty. Because the level of the lake fluctuates it has been difficult to build any settlements around its edges. Instead the lake has become a place for migrating birds to rest on their long journeys north and south. Gazelles, foxes and several types of snake

(including the deadly horned viper) live on its shores. Many species of fish live in its waters, including the enormous Nile perch. Crocodiles – some reportedly up to 5m long – and monitor lizards also live in the lake's shallows. The main human presence here, apart from the few tourists who visit, is limited to the 5000 or so fishermen who spend up to six months at a time in small rowing boats, together catching about 50,000 tonnes of small fish each year.

KALABSHA, BEIT AL-WALI & KERTASSI

As a result of the massive Unesco effort, the temples of **Kalabsha**, **Beit al-Wali** and **Kertassi** (admission to all adult/student E£20/10; ☾ 8am-4pm) were transplanted from a now-submerged site about 50km south of Aswan. The new site is on the west bank of Lake Nasser just south of the High Dam.

The **Temple of Kalabsha** was started in the late Ptolemaic period and completed during the reign of Emperor Augustus, between 30 BC and AD 14. It was dedicated to the composite Egyptian-Nubian god Horus-Mandulis and to Isis and Osiris. Later it was used as a church.

In the 1960s and '70s the West German government financed the transfer and reconstruction of the 13,000 blocks of the temple and was presented with the temple's west pylon, which is now in the Berlin Museum. During the rescue operation, evidence was found of even older structures, dating from the times of Amenhotep II (1922–1878 BC) and Ptolemy IX.

An impressive stone causeway leads from the lake up to the first pylon of the temple, beyond which are the colonnaded court and the eight-columned hypostyle hall. Inscriptions on the walls show various emperors or pharaohs in the presence of gods and goddesses. Just beyond the hall are three chambers, with stairs leading from one up to the roof. The view of Lake Nasser and the High Dam, across the capitals of the hall and court, is fantastic. An inner passage, between the temple and the encircling wall, leads to a well-preserved Nilometer.

The **Temple of Beit al-Wali** (House of the Holy Man) was rebuilt with assistance from the US government and was placed just northwest of the Temple of Kalabsha. Most of Beit al-Wali, which was cut into a

SAVING NUBIA'S MONUMENTS

As plans for building the Aswan Dam were drawn up, worldwide attention focused on the antiquities that would be lost by the creation of a huge lake behind the dam. A great many valuable and irreplaceable ancient monuments were doomed by the waters of Lake Nasser.

Between 1960 and 1980 the Unesco-sponsored Nubian Rescue Campaign set out to save as much as they could of this threatened legacy. Expertise and financing was gathered from more than 50 countries, and Egyptian and foreign archaeological teams descended on Nubia. Necropolises were excavated, all portable artefacts and relics were removed to museums and, while some temples disappeared beneath the lake, 14 were salvaged and moved to safety.

Ten of them, including the temple complexes of Philae, Kalabsha and Abu Simbel, were dismantled stone by stone and rebuilt on higher ground. The other four were donated to the countries that contributed to the rescue effort; they include the splendid Temple of Dendur, which has been reconstructed in the Metropolitan Museum of Art in New York.

The preservation of the temples at Abu Simbel, about 200km south of Aswan, must rank as the greatest achievement of the Unesco rescue operation. As the incredible temples were hewn out of solid rock, the modern technology involved in cutting, moving and rebuilding the temples and statues at least paralleled the skill of the ancient artisans who chiselled them out of the cliff face in the first place.

A worldwide appeal for the vital funding and expertise needed to salvage these Abu Simbel monuments was launched in the 1960s. The response was immediately forthcoming and a variety of conservation schemes were put forward. Finally, in 1964 a cofferdam was built to hold back the already encroaching water of the new lake, while Egyptian, Italian, Swedish, German and French archaeological teams began the race to move the massive structures before they were submerged.

At a cost of about US$40 million, the temples were cut up into more than 2000 huge blocks, weighing from 10 to 40 tonnes each, and were reconstructed inside a specially built mountain 210m away from the water and 65m higher than the original site. The temples were carefully oriented to face in the correct direction and the landscape of their original environment was recreated on and around the concrete, dome-shaped mountain.

The project took just over four years. The temples of Abu Simbel were officially reopened in 1968, while the sacred site they had occupied for over 3000 years disappeared beneath Lake Nasser. A plaque to the right of the temple entrance eloquently describes this achievement: 'Through this restoration of the past, we have indeed helped to build the future of mankind'.

---

sandstone cliffside and fronted by a brick pylon, was built by Ramses II and dedicated to Amun-Ra. On the walls of the forecourt are several fine reliefs detailing the pharaoh's victory over the Nubians (on the south wall) and his wars against the Libyans and Syrians (on the north wall). Ramses is gripping the hair of his enemies prior to smashing their brains while women plead for mercy. The most beautiful scenes are those detailing the tribute being paid by the defeated Nubians. The reliefs show Ramses sitting on his throne and receiving, among other things, leopard skins, gold, elephant tusks, feathers, cattle, a monkey and an ostrich.

Just north of the Temple of Kalabsha are the remains of the **Temple of Kertassi**. Two Hathor (or cow-headed) columns, a massive architrave and four columns decorated with intricate capitals are the only pieces that were salvaged from Lake Nasser.

Strewn about the area between these two temples are a jumble of rocks with prehistoric carvings and paintings, some amazingly well preserved, that were salvaged along with the temples.

You'll need a boat to get to the site; motorboats can be found on the western side of the High Dam (see Map p318). It costs about E£25 to hire a boat to take you there and back.

WADI AS-SUBUA

The **temples of Wadi as-Subua** (adult/student E£20/10) were moved to this site, about 4km west of the original Wadi as-Subua (submerged beneath Lake Nasser), by the Department of Antiquities between 1961 and 1965.

Wadi as-Subua means 'Valley of Lions' in Arabic and refers to the avenue of 10 sphinxes that stood in front of the **Temple of Ramses II**. Yet another monument from the reign of the energetic pharaoh, the rear part of the temple was hewn from rock and the front portion was freestanding. At the entrance to the temple itself are the remains of colossal statues of Ramses. The scenes on the pylon show Ramses II (1279–1213 BC) smiting the enemies of Egypt before Amun-Ra. Behind the pylon is a court featuring 10 more statues of the pharaoh, beyond which lies a 12-pillared hall and the sanctuaries, all cut out of the rock face. Although the middle sanctuary was once carved with relief scenes of Ramses making offerings to the temple's gods, it was converted in Christian times into a church and the pagan reliefs plastered over and painted with saints. With part of the plaster having fallen away, Ramses II now appears to be making offerings to St Peter!

About 1km to the north are the remains of the **Temple of Dakka**, begun by the Nubian pharaoh Arkamani (218–200 BC) and continued under Ptolemies VI and VIII and the Romans Augustus and Tiberius. Originally situated 40km north of here, it is dedicated to the god of wisdom, Thoth, and is notable for its 12m-high pylon, which you can climb for great views of the lake and the surrounding temples.

The **Temple of Maharraqa**, the smallest of the three at this site, originally stood 50km north of here near the village of Ofendina. Thought to have been dedicated to Serapis, the Alexandrian god, its decorations were never finished and the walls seem very bare. In the northeast corner of the main hall a spiral staircase leads up to the roof, the only spiral staircase in any ancient Egyptian structure. There is some evidence that the temple was later used as a church, but little of it remains.

AMADA

Situated around 180km south of the High Dam there are two temples and a tomb at **Amada** (adult/student E£20/10).

The **Temple of Amada**, moved about 2.5km from its original location between 1964 and 1975, is the oldest surviving monument on Lake Nasser. It dates from the 18th-dynasty reigns of Tuthmosis III and his son Amen-hotep II, with a hypostyle hall added by his son Tuthmosis IV (1400–1390 BC) and with later Ramessid additions. Dedicated, like many temples in Nubia, to the gods Amun-Ra and Ra-Horakhty, it has some of the finest reliefs of any Nubian monument and contains two important historical inscriptions. The first text is to be found on a stele at the left (north) side of the entrance and describes the unsuccessful Libyan invasion of Egypt in the fourth year (1209 BC) of the pharaoh Merneptah's rule. The second inscription, again carved on a stele, is on the back wall of the sanctuary and dates to the third year of the reign of Amenhotep II (1424 BC). It describes the pharaoh's military campaign in Palestine and details his ruthless killing of prisoners of war. It was no doubt designed to impress upon the Nubians that political opposition to the powerful Egyptians was useless.

On the very top of the temple façade you can see crudely carved camels, thought to have been the work of either Bedouin or travellers during the Middle Ages.

Unlike other Nubian temples, the rock-cut **Temple of Derr** was situated on the river's east bank due to the reversal of the Nile's course in this area. Although the front of the building is damaged, there are some well-preserved reliefs in the pillared hall portraying Ramses II, once again being worshipped as a living god, as at Abu Simbel. In the scenes on either side of the doorway you can see him killing his enemies, accompanied by his famous pet lion. Following cleaning, many of the scenes are once again brightly coloured.

Five minutes' walk from the Temple of Derr is the small rock-cut **Tomb of Pennut**, which was originally situated at Aniba, 40km southwest of Amada. Pennut was the chief administrator of Lower Nubia during the reign of Ramses VI (1143–1136 BC). The tomb consists of a small offering chapel with a niche at the rear; there are still traces of colour on some of its reliefs, which depict events and personalities from Pennut's life, including him being presented with a gift by Ramses VI himself.

QASR IBRIM

The only Nubian monument visible on its original site, Qasr Ibrim sits with water lapping at its edges on what was once the top of a 70m-high cliff about 60km north of Abu Simbel. The unusual name of this fortress is derived from the ancient name, Pedeme, which became Primis in Greek, Phrim in Coptic and finally Ibrim in Arabic (there's no 'p' in Arabic).

Early history of the site is obscure. It's situated at a strategic point overlooking the Nile, and archaeologists have so far found evidence of a fortification dating back to 1000 BC. However, it is possible that there was some sort of garrison at the site as much as 800 years earlier, when the Egyptians built mud-brick fortresses along the Nile to maintain their control over Lower Nubia.

In about 680 BC the 25th-dynasty Nubian pharaoh of Egypt, Taharka (690–664 BC), built a mud-brick temple here and about 700 years later the first fortification wall was built. During Roman times the area appears to have been a bastion of paganism as Christianity spread in Nubia. As many as six temples, including a mud-brick temple to Isis, are thought to have existed on its 2-hectare site. The area finally converted to Christianity more than 200 years after the rest of Egypt and Taharka's temple became a church. By the 13th century Ibrim had become one of Lower Nubia's principal Christian centres and it held out against Islam until the 16th century, when a group of Bosnian mercenaries working for the Ottomans came and occupied the site. They stayed on and married into the local Nubian community, using part of the cathedral as a mosque. Their descendants were driven out by panicked Mamluks fleeing Mohammed Ali's purges in the early 19th century.

Apart from the structural remains, of which an 8th-century sandstone cathedral is the most prominent, many written documents have been found at Qasr Ibrim. At the time of writing extensive archaeological work was being carried out and the site was closed to visitors.

ABU SIMBEL
☎ 097

The village of Abu Simbel lies 280km south of Aswan and only 40km north of the Sudanese border. A small settlement with breeze-block buildings and a few basic workers' cafés, there is little to keep you here other than the colossal temples for which it is famous. Few tourists linger more than a few

hours, although there are five hotels that try to lure visitors for overnight stays.

Information

Abu Simbel Hospital (☎ 499 237; main rd)

Banque du Caire (main rd; ⏱ 8.30am-2pm & 6-8pm Sun-Thu)

Banque Misr (main rd; ⏱ 8.30am-2pm & 6-8pm Sun-Thu)

Main post office (⏱ 8.30am-2.30pm Sat-Mon) On the road to the temples.

National Bank of Egypt (main rd; ⏱ 8.30am-2pm & 6-8pm Sun-Thu)

Telephone centrale (⏱ 24hr) Off the main road.

Tourist police (☎ 400 277/8) On the road to the temples.

Sights & Activities

Overlooking Lake Nasser, the two **temples of Abu Simbel** (adult/student E£70/35; ⏱ 6am-5pm Oct-Apr, to 6pm May-Sep) are reached by a wide divided road or, if you are on a cruise boat, from one of the jetties leading directly into the fenced temple compound.

GREAT TEMPLE OF RAMSES II

While the fate of his colossal statue at the Ramesseum in Luxor (see p266) no doubt gnaws at the spirit of Ramses II, the mere existence, in the 21st century AD, of his great temple at Abu Simbel must make him shake with laughter and shout, 'I told you so'.

Carved out of the mountain on the west bank of the Nile between 1274 and 1244 BC, the temple was dedicated to the gods

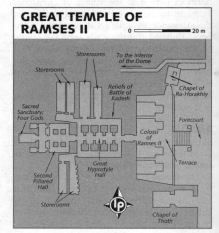

GREAT TEMPLE OF RAMSES II
0 —————— 20 m

Storerooms
To the Interior of the Dome
Storerooms
Reliefs of Battle of Kadesh
Chapel of Ra-Horakhty
Sacred Sanctuary; Four Gods
Forecourt
Colossi of Ramses II
Terrace
Great Hypostyle Hall
Second Pillared Hall
Storerooms
Chapel of Thoth

Ra-Horakhty, Amun and Ptah, and, of course, to the deified pharaoh himself. But primarily, with its four colossal statues of Ramses II addressing the river, it was designed as a show of strength, an awesome sentinel watching over any boats sailing into the pharaoh's lands from the south.

However, over the centuries both the Nile and the desert sands imperceptibly shifted until the temple was lost to human memory. It was rediscovered by chance in 1813 by the Swiss explorer Jean-Louis Burkhardt – only one of the heads was completely showing above the sand, the next head was broken off and, of the remaining two, only the crowns could be seen. There's a superb and often reproduced etching of this scene made by David Roberts, who visited about 25 years after Burkhardt. Sufficient sand was cleared away in 1817 by Giovanni Belzoni for the temple to be entered.

From the temple's forecourt, a short flight of steps leads up to the terrace in front of the massive rock-cut façade, which is about 30m high and 35m wide. Guarding the entrance, the four famous colossal statues of Ramses II sit majestically, staring out across the desert as if looking through time itself. Actually, only three still sit majestically, as the inner left statue collapsed in antiquity and its upper body lies on the ground, left like this when the temple was moved. Each complete statue is more than 20m high and is accompanied by smaller, though much larger than life-size, statues of the pharaoh's mother Queen Tuya, his wife Nefertari and some of their children.

Above the entrance, between the central throned colossi, is the figure of the falcon-headed sun god Ra-Horakhty. Unfortunately, the sun god has been subjected to the trials of time and now lacks part of a leg and foot.

The roof of the large hall is decorated with vultures, which are protective figures symbolising the goddess Nekhbet, and is supported by eight columns, each fronted by a 10m-high statue of Ramses. Reliefs on the walls depict the pharaoh in various battles, trampling over his enemies, victorious as usual. One of the most famous depicts the Battle of Kadesh (c 1274 BC), now in Syria, where the Egyptian army was almost routed by the Hittites. According to his own propaganda, Ramses inspired his demoralised army by his personal courage and the battle turned in their favour. Look for the depiction of this famous battle on the right (northern) wall of the large hall. The Egyptian military camp is walled off by its soldiers' round-topped shields. Also clearly visible is the fortified Hittite town, surrounded by the Orontes River. The scene is dominated by a famous relief of Ramses in his chariot, shooting arrows at his fleeing enemies.

In the next hall, the four-columned vestibule, Ramses and Nefertari are shown in front of the gods and the solar barques that carry the dead to the underworld.

The innermost chamber is the sacred sanctuary, where the four gods of the Great Temple sit on their thrones carved in the back wall and wait for dawn. The temple is aligned in such a way that on 22 February and 22 October every year, the first rays of the rising sun reach across the Nile, penetrate the temple and move along the hypostyle hall, through the vestibule and into the sanctuary, where they illuminate the somewhat mutilated figures of Ra-Horakhty, Ramses II and Amun. Ptah, to the left, is never illuminated. (Until the temples were moved, this phenomenon happened one day earlier.)

TEMPLE OF HATHOR

The other temple at the Abu Simbel complex is the rock-cut Temple of Hathor, dedicated to Queen Nefertari, Ramses' beloved wife. A smaller version of Ramses' own temple, it is fronted by six massive standing statues, each about 10m high. Four of them represent Ramses, the other two represent Nefertari, who is, unusually, portrayed as the same height as her husband (instead of coming up to his knees as most consorts were depicted). The couple is flanked by the smaller figures of the Ramessid princes and princesses.

Inside, the six pillars of the hypostyle hall are crowned with capitals in the bovine shape of Hathor and its walls are adorned with reliefs. They depict Nefertari before Hathor and Mut; the queen honouring her husband; and Ramses, yet again, being valiant and victorious. In the vestibule and adjoining chambers there are colourful scenes of the goddess and her sacred barque. In the sanctuary there is a weathered statue of Hathor as a cow emerging from the rock.

SOUND-&-LIGHT SHOW

A **sound-and-light show** (www.sound-light.egypt.com; admission E£60) is performed each night at 7pm and 8pm in winter (October to May) and 8pm and 9pm in summer (May to September). Headphones are provided allowing visitors to listen to the commentary in various languages. While the text is flowery and forgettable, the laser show projected onto the temples is stunning and well worth the detour.

Sleeping & Eating

Few people linger in Abu Simbel, and hotels are often empty – perhaps that's why they charge those who do stay so much. Keep in mind that prices are usually slashed during the summer months.

Eskaleh (☎ 012 368 0521; fikrykachif@genevalink.com; s US$24-42, d US$36.50-61; 🖳) More a Nubian cultural centre than a hotel, the newly opened Eskaleh is a traditional-style Nubian mud-brick building with five rooms for guests. The brainchild of Fikry Kachif, a Nubian musician and former guide on the *Eugénie* (p291), it features a library of material on Nubian culture, a restaurant/lounge and a roof terrace overlooking the lake. Rooms are simple but comfortable, with well-appointed private bathrooms. Two have their own terraces overlooking the lake. Meals (lunch E£30, dinner E£40) are made with organic produce grown in Fikry's garden. The centre also hosts performances of Nubian music and dance. Internet is available for E£10 per hour.

Seti Abu Simbel (☎ 400 720; www.setifirst.com; s/d US$137/185; 🍴 🖳 🕃) Abu Simbel's only five-star hotel, the Seti has chalet-style rooms overlooking Lake Nasser, all pleasant enough but not worth the prices being charged. The hotel is best booked through its owner, the Cairo-based travel agency **Seti First** (☎ 02-736 9820). Its restaurant offers buffet breakfast (E£42), lunch (E£45) and dinner (E£65).

Abu Simbel Village (☎ /fax 400 092, 012 363 9794; r E£110; 🕃) Abu Simbel's cheapest option, the Abu Simbel Village has basic vaulted rooms based around a concrete courtyard.

Along Abu Simbel's main road is a line-up of cheap cafés. The Nubian Oasis and Wady El Nile are among the most popular but offer little incentive to diners.

Getting There & Away

Foreigners travelling from Aswan to Abu Simbel by road must travel in police convoy. The police have deemed taxis off limits to foreigners, so luxury coach or minibus is your only option. Most people opt for a tour and get the admission and guide included.

You can avoid the convoy by taking a bus. Buses from Abu Simbel to Aswan leave at 7am, 9.30am, 1.30pm, 3pm and 4pm from the Wady El Nile Restaurant on the main street. There is no advanced booking and tickets (E£20) are purchased on board. Note that the official limit is four foreign passengers per bus, although they will generally turn a blind eye to one or two extra.

EgyptAir has flights to Abu Simbel from Aswan; see p317 for flight details.

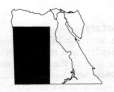

Western Desert

There are deserts and there are deserts. But the Western (or Libyan) Desert, a vast expanse that starts at the western banks of the Nile and continues well into Libya, is the desert of deserts.

Ralph Bagnold, Libyan Sands: Travel in a Dead World *(Hodder & Stoughton, 1935)*

Of all Egypt's natural attractions, the Western Desert is the least visited, much to the joy of people who do make the journey. Covering a total of 2.8 million sq km and bordered by Libya in the west, Sudan in the south and the Mediterranean in the north, the Western Desert is a vast realm of rugged beauty and extreme isolation. It is also one of the few places in Egypt where you can go for days at a time without seeing another person.

Five isolated but thriving oases dot this otherwise uninhabited expanse, strung in a line that seems to run parallel with the Nile: Al-Kharga, Dakhla, Farafra, Bahariyya and, to the northwest of these, Siwa. Herodotus called these settlements the 'Islands of the Blest' and although they have recently received the blessings of tarmac, technology and tourism, they remain remote and need time to get to and to get around. Despite this remoteness, the five oases have long and surprisingly rich histories. Recent research in the area has unearthed a wealth of prehistoric artefacts, pointing to habitation at the very dawn of human history. While much of this research has been conducted in deep, and to most people, inaccessible desert, the oasis towns and villages are dotted with archaeological sites that can be reached by most travellers. Meanwhile, a safari into the open desert beyond is one of the last great adventures to be had in Egypt.

HIGHLIGHTS

- Sleep amid the surreal sculptures rising from the snowlike sands of the **White Desert** (p351)

- See how medieval oasis-dwellers kept sandstorms and marauding tribesmen at bay in **Al-Qasr** (p347)

- Discover how the Romans protected ancient caravan routes at **Qasr ad-Dush** (p341)

- Experience the fascinating culture and seductive oasis beauty of **Siwa Oasis** (p359)

- Soak under the stars in one of the Western Desert's many **natural springs** (p345)

★ Siwa Oasis

★ White Desert

★ Al-Qasr

Qasr ad-Dush ★

History

As with the Sahara and other deserts that stretch across most of northern Africa from the Nile to the Atlantic coast, the Western Desert was once a savanna that supported a variety of wildlife. Giraffes, lions and elephants roamed here in Palaeolithic times, when the landscape is thought to have looked much like the African Sahel. All that you see in the desert, the huge tracts of sand, the vast gravel plains, the fossil beds and limestone rocks, were once the happy hunting grounds that supported nomadic tribes. Gradual climate change, an earlier version of global warming, led to desertification and turned this vast area into the arid expanse we know today. Only depressions in the desert floor now have enough water to support wildlife, agriculture and human settlement.

No-one knows whether the ancient Egyptians knew what had happened to the western grasslands, but they certainly understood the nature of the desert, which they saw as being synonymous with death and exile. This was the realm of Seth, the god of chaos who killed his brother Osiris. Despite their fears, it is believed that they did maintain links with the oases throughout the Pharaonic era although so far, with the exception of Dakhla Oasis, archaeologists have found scant evidence of this before the Third Intermediate Period. But with the accession of a Libyan dynasty (22nd dynasty, 945–715 BC), focus moved to the west and the oases, particularly those with caravan routes to the Nile Valley, grew in importance. Many monuments in Al-Kharga and Bahariyya date from this period.

The Western Desert oases enjoyed a period of great prosperity during Roman times, when new wells and improved irrigation led to a vast increase in the production of wheat and grapes for export to Rome. Prosperity was also encouraged by the presence of provincial army units, usually consisting of non-Romans serving under Roman officers, which protected the oases and trade routes. Garrisoned fortresses can still be seen in the desert around Al-Kharga and Bahariyya, and Roman-era temples and tombs can be seen in all the oases.

When the Romans withdrew from Egypt, the trade routes became unsafe and were often attacked by nomadic tribes. As a result, trade suffered, the oases went into

gradual decline and the population of settlements shrank. By medieval times, raids by nomads were severe enough to bring Mamluk garrisons to many of the oases. The fortified villages built to defend the population can still be seen in Dakhla (Al-Qasr, Balat) and Siwa (Shali).

But even the gradual cessation of attacks and the growing power of the pashas in Cairo during the 19th century could not revive the prosperity of ancient times. Although the oases remained important bulwarks against any threat to Egypt's western flank, the difficulty of travel through the desert meant that the oases remained isolated agricultural communities until the arrival of motor vehicles and paved roads.

The biggest change to the oases after the departure of the Romans occurred in 1958, when President Nasser created the New Valley to relieve population pressure along the Nile. Roads were laid between the previously isolated oases and an administration was established. The New Valley Governorate is the largest in Egypt and one of the least densely populated: although conditions were right for people to migrate to the New Valley, there has never been enough work to attract significant numbers.

Climate

The ideal time to visit the Western Desert is in late autumn or early spring. In summer temperatures can soar as high as 52°C (125°F) and although there is little humidity, the heat can be withering. Winter is very pleasant with average daytime highs of 20°C to 25°C, although it can get very cold (down to 0°C at times) at night. Winds, particularly during April (known as the khamsin), can present great problems for desert travellers.

Long-Range Desert Safaris

Going on safari in the Western Desert can be one of the most magical experiences Egypt has to offer. It can also be one of the most frustrating. Each area has its local guides and experts (see the Tours section of each oasis) but many of them operate on a shoestring and have neither the expertise nor the equipment to pull off a long-range safari. This won't stop many of them from trying to persuade you they can do it. Journeys to the Gilf Kebir (in Egypt's southwest corner), Oweynat (in the extreme south) and the Great Sand Sea need organisation, reliable equipment and plenty of experience. There are risks and people do die in the desert each year. Military permits, which are available locally for short desert treks, must be procured in Cairo for longer trips. For all this, a reliable guide is crucial, even if you intend to drive yourself. Foreigners who've tried to buck the system have found themselves lost or, in extreme cases, have been injured or killed in the minefields that surround most of Egypt's desert frontiers.

The following safari operators are among the more reliable and will treat the desert with the respect it needs.

Egypt Off Road (☎ 010 147 5462; www.egyptoff road.com) Egypt Off Road is one of the most highly recommended desert tour operators in Egypt. Many expat desert rats swear by owner, Peter Gaballa, who taught them how to drive in the desert. Peter is an excellent car mechanic and speaks Arabic, French, English and German fluently. He organises driving lessons in the desert and trips to the Western Desert oases, as well as more serious two-week expeditions to the Gilf Kebir, Uwaynat and the Great Sand Sea. He takes care of all meals, and you have the option of driving your own car, or a rental.

Al-Badawiya (☎ 02-575 8076; www.badawiya.com) The three Ali brothers are Bedouin from Farafra, who began taking foreigners on short desert trips and have now built up a significant business, operating out of their

WESTERN DESERT

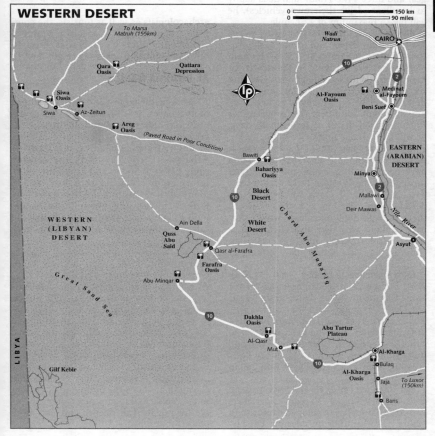

Al-Badawiya Hotel and an office in downtown Cairo. With considerable experience in the Western Desert, they can mount tailored camel or jeep safaris from three to 28 days. They have tents, cooking equipment and bedding. Hamdi Ali is the only brother still working as a guide, so you may find yourself going out with one of their staff.

Amr Shannon (☎ 02-519 6894; ashannon@Internet egypt.com) Artist, desert tracker and *bon vivant* Amr Shannon has been travelling throughout Egypt's deserts for more than 20 years and hosts an occasional series about the desert on Egyptian TV. Along with his wife, who navigates and cooks, he personalises itineraries according to the interests of his clients. Well-equipped with tents, cooking gear and three 4WDs (although he is happy to let clients drive their own vehicles), he will take a maximum of 12 people.

Hisham Nessim (☎ 010 188 1368; www.eg-western desert.com) Rally driver and owner of the Aquasun hotels in Farafra and Sinai, Hisham Nessim has been driving in the desert for many years. With satellite phones, GPS and six 4WDs specially rigged for long-range desert travel, he is prepared to go to all corners of Egypt. He offers five programmes (including self-drive) of seven to 14 days, or will tailor-make tours.

Khalifa Expedition (☎ 02-847 3261; www.khalifa exp.com) Khaled and Rose-Maria Khalifa have been running camel and jeep tours throughout the Western Desert from their base in Bahariyya Oasis for well over a decade. Rose-Maria is a qualified speech therapist and foot masseuse, which perhaps explains why they also offer meditation tours for people more interested in communing with nature than looking at antiquities.

Lama Expeditions (in Frankfurt, Germany ☎ 00-49-69-447 897; www.lama-expedition.de/english) Samir Lama was the undisputed king of the Western Desert explorers and for years organised long-range expeditions. Since his death in January 2004, his wife has continued to run the operation, offering small group tours (maximum of 12) of up to 21 days, crossing from southwest Egypt into Sudan and Libya.

Pan Arab Tours (☎ 02-418 4409; www.moussa.net /pat/safari.htm) With over 30 years' experience, Pan Arab Tours has developed expertise in taking visitors into Egypt's deserts. Used by

---

OASIS SECURITY

At the time of writing, security was very tight across the oases, particularly in Farafra, Al-Kharga and Dakhla. While it was possible in other oases to write a letter absolving the police of responsibility for our security, this was not an option in Al-Kharga, where a detachment of police followed us wherever we went in town and to the outlying sights. We were also given an escort to the edge of the police district. From then on, we were stopped at each checkpoint. Note also that checkpoints at either end of the Luxor–Al-Kharga road close at 4pm prompt. Cars are not allowed through after this time.

---

archaeologists as well as tourists, the company has a number of specially equipped vehicles and offers six itineraries throughout the country, from two to eight days.

AL-KHARGA OASIS
☎ 092

Al-Kharga, the largest and most developed of the oases, is situated in a desert depression 220km long and 40km wide. It grew on the crossing point of a number of desert tracks, including the Darb al-Arba'een (Forty Days Rd), the caravan route between Sudan and Egypt (for more information see the boxed text, p337). Many of the ruins that dot the desert here were fortresses or lookout towers, some built as late as the 1890s by the British, to safeguard the lucrative route and the 'back door' into Egypt.

The chief town is Al-Kharga, which is 233km from Asyut. When the New Valley Governorate was created in the late 1950s, Al-Kharga, being nearest to the Nile Valley, was chosen as its capital. The anticipated influx of people from the Nile was to be supported by land reclamation and intensive agriculture. Although the actual population has never matched government projections, the environmental drawbacks to the reclamation schemes have become increasingly apparent. Most obvious and alarming has been the drying up of ancient wells. People looking for new water sources are having to drill deeper and use more powerful pumps.

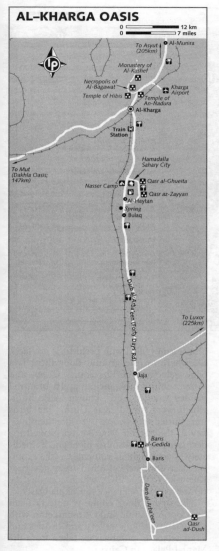

AL-KHARGA OASIS

0 _____ 12 km
0 _____ 7 miles

To Asyut (205km)
Al-Munira
Monastery of Al-Kashef
Necropolis of Al-Bagawat
Kharga Airport
Temple of Hibis
Temple of An-Nadura
Al-Kharga
Train Station
Hamadalla Sahary City
To Mut (Dakhla Oasis; 147km)
Nasser Camp
Qasr al-Ghueita
Qasr az-Zayyan
Al-Haytan
Spring
Bulaq
Darb al-Arba'ien (Forty Days Rd)
To Luxor (225km)
Jaja
Baris al-Gedida
Baris
Darb al-Arba'ien
Qasr ad-Dush

Al-Kharga

If your idea of an oasis is all palm trees and camels, then Al-Kharga, the largest town in the Western Desert, will come as a surprise. While some of the other oasis towns have retained their original character, Al-Kharga has turned its back on the past in an attempt to reflect the dreams of Egyp-

tian urban planners. The town can appear uninteresting at first sight and it's unlikely you'll want to spend much time here. But its broad streets and lush gardens do give it charm, and there is a good museum, a small but lively souq and some fascinating ancient sites nearby, many of which date from the Graeco-Roman period. Although there is no record of trouble in the oasis, at the time of our visit foreigners were being given police escorts around town and to nearby sights.

WESTERN DESERT

ORIENTATION

The bus station is in the southeast of Al-Kharga, near the souq and what's left of the old centre, and it's a fair hike to most of the hotels. If you're coming from Dakhla, decide where you want to stay before arriving – you may want to be let off at Sharia al-Adel rather than having to trudge all the way back again.

The main north–south road is Sharia Gamal Abdel Nasser. Many government offices, banks and hotels are either on or just off this thoroughfare.

INFORMATION

Emergency
Ambulance (☎ 123)
Tourist police (Map p336; ☎ 792 1673; Sharia Gamal Abdel Nasser)

Internet Access
Governorate Information Support Centre (Map p336; ☎ 792 6973; Governorate Bldg, Sharia Gamal Abdel Nasser; ⏱ 8am-3pm & 6-12pm Sat-Thu) Free access.
Nasat Internet Café (Map p336; ☎ 793 0722; off Midan Sho'ala; per hr E£20; ⏱ 8am-2pm & 4-11pm)

Medical Services
General Hospital (Map p336; ☎ 792 0777; Sharia Basateen)

Money
Banque du Caire (Map p336; off Sharia Gamal Abdel Nasser) Very slow service, but there is an ATM.
Banque Misr (Map p336; Dakhla rd)

Post & Telephone
As elsewhere in Egypt, private telephone shops are opening all over Al-Kharga.
Main post office (Map p336; Sharia Abdel Moniem Riad; ⏱ 8am-2.30pm Sat-Thu)
Telephone centrale (Map p336; Sharia al-Gomhuriyya; ⏱ 24hr)

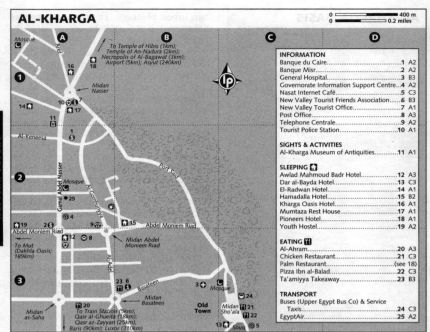

AL-KHARGA

Tourist Information

New Valley Tourist Friends Association (Map p336; ☎ 792 1451; Midan Basateen; ⏱ 5-10pm Sat-Thu) A source of friendly advice.

New Valley Tourist Office (Map p336; ☎ 792 1206; fax 792 1205; Midan Nasser; ⏱ 8.30am-3pm Sat-Thu) Tourism Manager Ibrahim Hassan and his crew are very helpful and have information for Al-Kharga, Dakhla and Farafra Oases. If you don't manage to get to the office during daytime opening, it is worth checking to see if someone is working in the evening.

SIGHTS
Al-Kharga Museum of Antiquities

Down the road from the tourist office, the two-storey **Al-Kharga Museum of Antiquities** (Map p336; Sharia Gamal Abdel Nasser; adult/student E£20/10; ⏱ 8am-5pm) houses archaeological exhibits from various ancient sites around Al-Kharga and Dakhla Oases. On the ground floor, in the room to the right of the entrance hall, is a particularly good selection of well-displayed prehistoric objects. Sponsored by the Canadian-led archaeological mission in Dakhla Oasis, it traces the prehistory of the oases in both English and Arabic and has four vitrines filled with prehistoric artefacts. Elsewhere on the ground floor there is a wide selection of Pharaonic, Greek and Roman antiquities, including 10 beautiful painted wooden birds, known as Ba Birds, which were found near Dush. The birds were buried with people to ensure their journey to the afterlife (the Ba represented the deceased's soul). Another highlight, immediately to your right as you enter, is the exquisite false door stele of 6th-dynasty governor Khent-ka (c 2700 BC), which contains the earliest known reference to Dakhla Oasis.

The upper floor contains objects from the Coptic, Islamic and Ottoman eras, with some fascinating jewellery and textiles and a fair selection of tableware taken from the Manial Palace in Cairo.

Temple of Hibis

The ancient town of Hebet ('the Plough', now corrupted into Hibis) was the capital of the oasis in antiquity, but all that remains is the **Temple of Hibis** (Map p335; adult/student E£16/8; ⏱ 8am-5pm Oct-Apr, 8am-6pm May-Sep) that once stood at its centre. It's the largest of the Al-Kharga temples and was dedicated to Amun. Built using the local limestone, it was begun during the reign of the 25th dynasty, although the decoration was not completed until the reign of the Persian king Darius I, some 200 years later. A **colonnade** was added a century later by Nectanebo II and there were further additions by the Ptolemies. An **avenue of sphinxes** leads to a series of gateways, the colonnade of Nectanebo and then a **court**, a **hypostyle hall** and an **inner sanctuary**. Among the reliefs in the hypostyle hall is one showing the pharaoh offering lettuce to the fertility god Min, and another of the god Seth battling with the evil serpent Apophis, an archetype of the St George and dragon motif. Among the graffiti left by 19th-century European travellers is a lengthy inscription from 1818 by Frederic Cailliaud, who claimed to have been the first European to see the temple.

The temple was cleared of sand and the mud-brick buildings inside by the Metropolitan Museum of Art between 1909 and 1910, but is currently enshrouded in scaffolding while a massive restoration/reconstruction is carried out to protect it from rising ground water. It's 2km north of town just to the left of, and visible from, the main road. If it's too hot to walk from the town, pick-ups (50pt) heading to Mounira pass this way. Be sure to tell the driver that you want to get off at al ma'abad (the temple).

Temple of An-Nadura

Located on a hill off the main road at the north end of town, the **Temple of An-Nadura** (Map p335) also doubled as a fortified lookout. It was built during the reign of Roman emperor Antoninus Pius (138–161) to protect the oasis. Inside are the remains of a sandstone temple, with hieroglyphic inscriptions. It was later used as a fortress by the Ottomans.

Entry to the temple is free. You can't miss the ruins, perched on a rise off to the right of the main road, shortly before the Temple of Hibis becomes visible. Follow the road to the right for 500m and scramble up the potsherd-strewn hill. Although the temple is ruined, it has sweeping views of the desert and oasis, and is a great place to watch the sunset.

Necropolis of Al-Bagawat

About 1km north of the Temple of Hibis, the **Necropolis of Al-Bagawat** (Map p335; adult/student E£20/10; 8am-5pm Oct-Apr, 8am-6pm May-Sep) is one of the earliest surviving Christian cemeteries in the world. If you're on foot, you can cut across the desert from the main road when you see the necropolis to your left. By car, you'll have to drive 1km or so up the road to the entrance. Most of the 263 mud-brick tombs appear to date from the 4th to the 6th centuries AD, although this is still being debated. The majority of

---

THE WAY TO DUSTY DEATH

Al-Kharga Oasis sits atop what was once the only major African north–south trade route that cut through Egypt's Western Desert: the notorious Darb al-Arba'een, or Forty Days Rd. A 1721km track linking Fasher in Sudan's Darfur Province with Asyut in the Nile Valley, this was one of Africa's great caravan trails, bringing the riches of Sudan – gold, ivory, skins, ostrich feathers and especially slaves – north to the Nile Valley and beyond to the Mediterranean. It's thought to date back to the Old Kingdom, and the richness of the merchandise transported along this bleak track was such that protecting it was a priority. The Romans invested heavily here, building a series of fortresses – such as Dush, the Monastery of Al-Kashef and Qasr al-Ghueita – to tax the caravans and try to foil the frequent raids by desert tribesmen and, on occasion, Nubians.

Despite the dangers, Darb al-Arba'een flourished until well into the Islamic era, by which time it was Egypt's main source of slaves. Untold numbers of tragic human cargo died of starvation and thirst on the journey north. According to 19th-century European travellers, slavers travelled in the intense summer heat, preferring to expose their merchandise to dehydration on what British geographer GW Murray (author of the 1967 *Dare Me to the Desert*) called 'the way of dusty death', rather than risk the possibility of bronchitis and pneumonia from the cold winter winds.

Despite repeated attempts by the British to suppress the trade, slaves were brought north until Darfur became part of Sudan at the beginning of the 20th century. The Darb al-Arba'een withered and today its route has been all but lost.

these traditional domed Coptic tombs are undecorated inside, but a few have interesting murals of biblical scenes. One of the guardians will be anxious to guide you and will show you inside some of the more colourful tombs. He should be tipped (E£3 to E£5) for his help. The so-called **Chapel of Peace** has figures of the apostles on the squinches of the domes, just visible through the Greek graffiti. The **Chapel of the Exodus**, one of the oldest tombs, also has the best-preserved paintings: the dome has been decorated with two registers of Old Testament stories, including Moses leading the children of Israel out of Egypt. The graffiti dates back to the 9th century. Also worth seeing are the large family tomb (No 25), which has a mural of Abraham sacrificing Isaac and a dome decorated with birds, and a small tomb known as the **Chapel of the Grapes** (Anaeed al-Ainab) after the images of grapevines that cover the walls.

Monastery of Al-Kashef

Dominating the cliffs to the north of Bagawat is the ruined **Monastery of Al-Kashef** (Deir al-Kashef; Map p335), named after Mustafa al-Kashef, the tax collector. To get there, walk or drive on the left-hand track from the ticket office at the Necropolis of Al-Bagawat. The track snakes behind the hill on which the cemetery is built. After about 1km you will come upon the imposing mud-brick ruins. Strategically placed to overlook what was once one of the most important crossroads of the Western Desert, the point where the Darb al-Ghabari from Dakhla crossed the Darb al-Arba'een, the magnificent remains date back to the early Christian era, although the site was occupied as early as the Middle Kingdom. Once five storeys high, much of it has collapsed but you can see the tops of the arched corridors that crisscrossed the building. Mustafa al-Kashef was governor here during the Mamluk period. On the plain below are other ruins, including a small church with some barely visible wall paintings on the west wall and the remains of the tiny cells where the monks once slept.

TOURS

Unlike the other oases, Al-Kharga has few outfits offering desert trips, although at the time of our visit there was talk of two new agencies opening in the near future. The Hamadalla Hotel and its sister hotel, Hamadalla Sahary City, both run day trips that involve some off-road driving, but there is a dearth of overnight trips on offer. For more information on longer desert trips, see Long-Range Desert Safaris on p332 or the Tours section of the other oases.

SLEEPING
Hotels

None of Al-Kharga's limited selection of hotels is outstanding, but there is a variety and, as they seem to be half empty most of the time, it isn't usually a problem to find a room.

Pioneers Hotel (Map p336; ☎ 792 7982; www.solymar-hotels.com; Sharia Gamal Abdel Nasser; s/d half board E£530/701; ✷ ▢ ▣) Pioneers was the first and is still one of only a handful of luxury hotels in the Western Desert. And while its salmon-pink, low-rise architecture looks like it has escaped from one of the tackier Red Sea resorts, the hotel offers a level of comfort and a range of facilities that were until recently unimaginable in the oases, including a swimming pool that is open to nonresidents when it's quiet. It is also the only place in Al-Kharga where you can count on getting alcohol. The Sol Y Mar management also runs Nasser Camp (opposite).

Kharga Oasis Hotel (Map p336; ☎ 792 1500; Midan Nasser; s/d E£63/88, with air-con E£70/95; ✷) Another modern homage to concrete, the 1960s Kharga Oasis was undergoing a thorough refit at the time of writing. A favourite stopping-off point for desert adventurers, it offers simple but comfortable midpriced rooms, a friendly welcome and a lush palm-filled garden and terrace.

Dar al-Bayda Hotel (Map p336; ☎ 792 1717; Midan Sho'ala; s/d/tr E£25/30/40, with private bathroom E£30/35/45) A shabby budget place just to the left off Midan Sho'ala, where the buses and service taxis are based, so it's handy for late arrival or early departure. Most rooms have fans, but can be noisy. There is a restaurant on top.

Youth Hostel (Map p336; ☎ 792 2640; Sharia Abdel Moniem Riad; dm E£6) Although inconveniently located at the eastern end of town, the Youth Hostel is very clean. Each dorm has its own bathroom.

Hamadalla Hotel (Map p336; ☎ 792 0638; fax 792 5017; off Sharia Abdel Moniem Riad; s/d E£53/75; ✷) A midrange hotel popular with overland tour groups, Hamadalla has rooms that are clean, but dark and gloomy. There are a number of different room configurations, so ask to see a few.

Awlad Mahmoud Badr Hotel (Map p336; ☎ 792 2689; Sharia Gamal Abdel Nasser; s/d E£15/20, with private bathroom E£20/30) A small, family-run budget place at the southern end of Al-Kharga's main drag. Rooms can be stuffy but are reasonably clean.

Mumtaza Rest House (Map p336; ☎ 792 1206; fax 792 1205; Sharia Gamal Abdel Nasser; dm E£20; ✷) This is the best of several government rest houses in Al-Kharga, a concrete development of six rooms immediately behind the tourist office. Reservations are made through the tourist authorities.

El-Radwan Hotel (Map p336; ☎ 792 1716, 012 747 2087; beside the Town Hall, off Sharia Gamal Abdel Nasser; s/d E£50/80; ✷) There's a good welcome at the Radwan, which is well-located for the Antiquities Museum and the tourist office. The rooms are well-kept and off the main road. The hotel can also arrange lunch and dinner (E£15).

Hamadalla Sahary City (Map p335; ☎ 798 2240, 012 747 2097; Kharga–Dush rd; s/d E£85/110; ✷) 15km from Al-Kharga town and near Qasr al-Ghueita, Hamadalla Sahary City has clean, comfortable rooms with private bathrooms, clustered together in groups of three or four. The brightly coloured walled compound has expanses of ceramic tile and something of an urban feel, despite being surrounded by desert. This is one of the oasis's best midpriced options if you don't mind the location.

Camping

Given the vast expanses of empty desert surrounding Al-Kharga, it seems unlikely that anyone would want to camp in the town, which explains the lack of choice.

Kharga Oasis Hotel (Map p336; ☎ 792 1500; Midan Nasser; per person E£7) If you must sleep under canvas, this is the only place in town to do it (once its restoration is complete). You can use the hotel's toilet and shower facilities. But be warned, the palm-filled garden has proved to be an ideal breeding ground for mosquitoes.

Nasser Camp (Map p335; ☎ 792 7982; fax 792 7983; Kharga–Dush rd; canvas tents per person E£12, bungalows per person E£50) Just south of Qasr al-Ghueita, 20km south of Al-Kharga, this camp site is owned by Pioneers Hotel in Al-Kharga. Tents and overpriced, stuffy prefab bungalows are set in a straggling garden beside a spring.

EATING

Western-style restaurants are few and far between in Al-Kharga and the best places to eat here are the hotels. Your only other options are the small *fuul* and *ta'amiyya* places scattered around Midan Sho'ala and Sharia al-Adel. There's a cheap chicken place a few doors down from the bus station on Midan Sho'ala. There's also a *ta'amiyya* takeaway joint on Sharia al-Adel near Midan Basateen.

Palm Restaurant (Map p336; ☎ 792 7982; fax 792 7983; Pioneers Hotel, Sharia Gamal Abdel Nasser; buffet dinner E£74) If there is a group staying here, dinner tends to be a buffet; otherwise the restaurant offers an à la carte selection of continental dishes. Although none of the cooking here is very inspiring, this is one of the best dining experiences to be had in Al-Kharga. The bar is well stocked but expensive.

Pizza Ibn al-Balad (Map p336; Midan Sho'ala; pizzas E£6-20) This bustling, clean takeaway is one of the most popular places to eat, with a wide selection of *fiteer* (Egyptian pancake/pizza).

Hamadalla Hotel (Map p336; ☎ 792 0638; off Sharia Abdel Moniem Riad; set lunch & dinner E£20) Not the best culinary option in town, but included here because of the limited choices available. On the positive side, the staff is very friendly and there's a bar where you may find beer.

Kharga Oasis Hotel (Map p336; ☎ 792 1500; Midan Nasser; lunch E£25, dinner E£28) As so often in the oases, the set menu includes soup followed by chicken or grilled meat with vegetables and rice. You may also find beer.

Al-Ahram (Map p336; Waha Hotel, Sharia an-Nabawi; meals E£8-20) This small, friendly place serves roast chicken and *kofta* (spiced minced meat on a skewer) accompanied by basic salads and vegetable dishes.

GETTING THERE & AWAY
Air

The airport is 5km north of town, but at the time of writing there were no civil flights into the oasis, although EgyptAir has plans to relaunch a Cairo–Al-Kharga–Luxor–Cairo service.

Bus

Upper Egypt Bus Co (Map p336; ☎ 792 0838; Midan Sho'ala) operates buses to Cairo at 7am (E£30, nine to 10 hours), 9.30pm (E£33, seven to eight hours) and 11pm (E£38, seven to eight hours). The 7am goes via Asyut and takes the Nile Valley agricultural road, lengthening the trip but allowing stops in Minya or Beni Suef.

There are several buses to Asyut (E£9 to E£10, three to four hours) leaving at 6am, 7am, 11am and 9pm. The 8.30am and 11.30am services originate in Dakhla.

Buses to Luxor (E£40, three to four hours) leave on Sunday and Wednesday at 7am and Saturday and Tuesday at 1pm. Buses to Dakhla (E£6 to E£9, two hours) leave daily at 11am, 2pm, 11pm, 1am and 3am.

There are local buses to Baris (E£2, one hour) at 7am and 2pm.

Minibuses to Asyut and Dakhla cost E£9 and leave from the bus station.

Service Taxi

The **service-taxi station** (Map p336; Midan Sho'ala) is next to the bus station. Most of the vehicles are microbuses but there are also a few Peugeot station wagons. Destinations include Asyut (E£10, three to four hours) and Dakhla (E£10, three hours).

Taxi

Thanks to the new road, special taxis can get you to Luxor (via Jaja) in three hours, but it will set you back E£300. Cairo (six to seven hours) costs E£500 for the car (maximum seven people).

Train

Al-Kharga's train station, on the road south to Baris, reflects government ambitions for the place, but the service doesn't live up to the dream: there is one weekly departure, on Friday at 7.30am (E£11/10.25 for 2nd/3rd class). The ticket office reckons on eight to 10 hours, but be prepared for up to 12 to cover the 477km to Luxor. It is worth turning up early. To get to the station, take any micro or bus heading for Baris. A taxi will cost E£10.

GETTING AROUND

Microbuses (50pt) run along the main streets of Al-Kharga, especially Sharia Gamal Abdel Nasser. Outside the town, covered pick-up trucks go to the villages along the road south

to Baris. Expect to pay E£1.50 to E£2, depending on the length of the journey.

South to Baris

A good asphalt road heads south of Al-Kharga to Baris, the southernmost town in the Western Desert. As you follow the road there are a number of easily accessible sites.

QASR AL-GHUEITA & QASR AZ-ZAYYAN

It is easy to see why the Romans chose this site, some 18km south of Al-Kharga, for **Qasr al-Ghueita** (Map p335; adult/student E£16/8; ☺ 8am-5pm Oct-Apr, 8am-6pm May-Sep). The imposing Roman fortress, built from mud brick, has survived millennia and still dominates the road to Baris. The massive outer walls enclose a 25th-dynasty sandstone temple, dedicated to the Theban triad Amun, Mut and Khons. Additions were made by Darius I and several Ptolemies. In later centuries, the fortress served as an outer wall for a village. The temple has been cleared and restored since then, but some houses survive along the outer wall. Within the hypostyle hall, a series of reliefs show Hapy, the potbellied Nile god, holding symbols of the nomes (provinces) of Upper Egypt.

The fortress's name translates as Fortress of the Small Garden, which seems an unlikely name for a place surrounded by desert. But in antiquity, Qasr al-Ghueita was the centre of a fertile agricultural community, renowned for its grapes: tomb inscriptions in Thebes mention the quality of the Ghueita grapes. The foundations and other remains of this once-thriving ancient community can be seen outside the fortress walls.

An asphalt road leads 2km to the temple from the main road. About 7km further south are the remains of **Qasr az-Zayyan** (Map p335; adult/student E£16/8; ☺ 8am-5pm Oct-Apr, 8am-6pm May-Sep), another temple inside a fortress. Close to a modern village, it doesn't have the remote feel of the other temple-fortresses in the area, but it is still worth a visit.

If you don't have a vehicle you can get to the temples by taking a bus heading for Baris (see left) or a covered pick-up going to Bulaq (E£1). Ask the driver to let you off at the asphalt road leading to the temples. There is an asphalt road linking the two, but 7km is a long hike if you're on foot. If you are planning to walk between the sites, be sure to take plenty of water.

BARIS

Baris, 90km south of Al-Kharga, was once one of the most important trading centres along the Darb al-Arba'een, but there is little now to remind you of that in what is the fourth town of the New Valley Governorate. Other than a few kiosks selling *fuul* and *ta'amiyya* there is little of note apart from the mud-brick houses of **Baris al-Gedida** (Map p335), about 2km north of the original town. Hassan Fathy, Egypt's most influential modern architect, intended Baris al-Gedida to be a model for other new settlements. He designed the houses using traditional materials and structures, and made good use of space. When work stopped at the outbreak of the Six Day War of 1967, only two houses and some public spaces, including the market place, had been completed. Work was never resumed and the village is now abandoned.

About 13km to the southeast of Baris is **Qasr ad-Dush** (Map p335; adult/student E£16/8; 8am-5pm Oct-Apr, 8am-6pm May-Sep), an imposing Roman temple-fortress completed around AD 177 on the site of the ancient town of Kysis. Dush was a border town, one of the southern gateways to Egypt. It was an important stopping point on the Darb al-Arba'een and may also have been used to guard the Darb al-Dush, an east–west track to the Esna and Edfu temples in the Nile Valley. As a result it was solidly built and heavily garrisoned. Standing on a hill, with 6m-high walls, it dominates the landscape. Four or five more storeys lie underground. The sandstone temple abutting the eastern side of the fortress is dedicated to Isis and Serapis, and was built by Domitian in the 1st century AD. Trajan added a court in AD 117 and Hadrian also contributed some sections. The gold decorations that once covered parts of the temple and earned it renown have long gone, but there is still some decoration on the inner stone walls.

Some European travellers who visited Qasr ad-Dush in the 19th century left their names inscribed for posterity, and these can still be seen in the gateway, next to the original inscriptions of Roman emperors. The temple now stands alone in a dramatic landscape, but it was once the centre of a thriving community and, as you walk down the hill, you can see the outlines of Kysis, whose inhabitants lived off the caravan trade. It is hard to imagine that the arid desert landscape was once fertile enough to sustain the substantial production needed to feed such a community but at Kysis' peak, agricultural production was high.

Baris is not a good place to stay the night, and you're better off staying in, or closer to, Al-Kharga.

Getting There & Away

There are buses between Al-Kharga and Baris (E£3, two daily), leaving from Al-Kharga at 7am and 2pm, and Baris at 6am and noon. The frequent microbuses and pick-up trucks are a more convenient option between Al-Kharga and Baris, and cost about E£3. To cover the 15km between Qasr ad-Dush and Baris, negotiate a special ride with a covered pick-up, usually available for E£20 to E£30, depending on the waiting time.

DAKHLA OASIS
☎ 092

If the concrete and modernity of Al-Kharga was a disappointment, then Dakhla, some 189km to the west, is sure to please. As the name of its main town, Mut (the god Amun's consort) suggests, the oasis was settled back in Pharaonic times. In fact recent research has shown that the oasis was inhabited in prehistory. In Neolithic times Dakhla was the site of a huge lake and rock paintings show that elephants, buffaloes and ostriches wandered along its shores. As the lake dried up, the human population is thought to have migrated eastwards to become some of the earliest settlers in the Nile Valley. Remains of this ancient past are being excavated throughout the oasis, improving our knowledge of its economic and political links with Pharaonic Egypt.

The oasis today is a joyful vision, with its palm groves, orchards and fields appearing out of the harsh desert. Picturesque mud-brick villages, many built upon much older settlements, sit among lush greenery. The oasis is home to about 100,000 people, most of whom are still involved in agriculture, growing rice, wheat, mangoes, oranges, olives and dates. Apricots, which are dried to be sold during Ramadan, are also grown. Unlike Al-Kharga and other places in the Nile Valley, Dakhla has maintained many of its craft traditions and is famous for its baskets woven from straw and palm fronds.

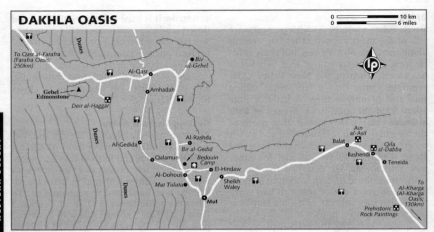

DAKHLA OASIS

Mut, the largest town in the oasis, makes the

Mut

Mut, the largest town in the oasis, makes the most convenient base for travellers. Much of it is a typical modernist Egyptian town, with concrete architecture ill-suited to the climate. But its wide boulevards, the low-rise development and the proximity of the palm groves all help to give it some charm, while the remains of the ruined old town show how Mut must have once looked.

INFORMATION

Emergency
Ambulance (☎ 123)
Police station (☎ 782 0664; cnr Midan at-Tahrir & Sharia 10th of Ramadan)
Tourist police (☎ 782 1687; Sharia 10th of Ramadan)

Internet Access
There are no Internet cafés in Dakhla but the following have terminals of varying speeds that can be used for E£10 to E£15 per hour:
Abu Mohamed Restaurant (☎ 782 1431; Sharia as-Sawra al-Khadra; ✆ 7am-midnight)
Anwar Hotel (☎ 782 0070; Sharia Basateen) The Anwar had the newest computer equipment at the time of our visit.
Fursan Hotel (☎ 782 1343; Sharia al-Wadi)
Mebarez Hotel (☎ 782 1524; Sharia as-Sawra al-Khadra)

Medical Services
General Hospital (☎ 782 1555; off Sharia 10th of Ramadan)

Money
Banque Misr (Sharia al-Wadi; ✆ 8.30am-2pm Sun-Thu) Exchanges cash and travellers cheques.

Post & Telephone
Branch post office (Sharia as-Salam; ✆ 8am-2pm Sat-Thu)
Main post office (Midan al-Gamaa; ✆ 8am-2pm Sat-Thu)
Telephone centrale (Sharia as-Salam; ✆ 24hr)

Tourist Information
Branch tourist office (☎ 782 0407; Midan al-Gamaa; ✆ 8am-3pm) Tourist-office director Omar Ahmad is a mine of knowledge about the oases and is very obliging. He flits between the main office and this branch office (in the same building as the Government Rest House). If you have an urgent problem out of hours, he can also be contacted at home (☎ 782 0782).
Main tourist office (☎ 782 1685; Sharia as-Sawra al-Khadra; ✆ 8am-3pm & some evenings)

SIGHTS & ACTIVITIES
Ethnographic Museum
Dakhla's wonderful **Ethnographic Museum** (Sharia as-Salam; admission E£2; ✆ 8am-2pm Sat-Thu), attached to Dar al-Wafdeen Government Hotel, is only opened on request: ask at either of the tourist offices or at the **Cultural Palace** (☎ 782 1311; Sharia al-Wadi), where the museum's manager, Ibrahim Kamel, can be found. The museum is laid out as a traditional home, with different areas for men, women and visitors. Displays of clothing, baskets, jewellery and other domestic items give an insight into oasis life.

Old Town of Mut

For much of its existence, the villagers of old Mut lived with the threat of raiding Bedouin. This, together with the need to keep out the heat and wind, explains why most houses have no outside windows. The high wall was built in the 1890s as a defence against the Mahdists from Sudan. Often ignored by passing travellers, the labyrinth of mud-brick houses and lanes that wind up the slopes of the hill is definitely worth exploring. From the top of the hill, at the **citadel** (the original town centre), there are great views of the new town and the desert cliffs and dunes that surround it. Parts of the old town are now under excavation and the discoveries will soon be on view to visitors.

TOURS

Like every other oasis, Dakhla has its share of would-be desert guides. Most hotels and restaurants will offer to take you on a trek around the area. A typical day trip around Dakhla includes visits to Qalamun and Al-Gedida, a drive through the dunes, visits to a spring and a tour of Al-Qasr, for up to E£100 per person, usually for no more than six people. An overnight trip around the same area, with Bedouin music, will cost about E£400 per person, including food. The owners of the Bedouin Camp (right) are camel experts and can arrange long and short trips into the desert around Dakhla. You're looking at about E£150 to E£200 per person per day, which includes a guide, all meals and bedding. Before committing to anything, check the price with the tourist office, who will also be able to confirm whether the person taking you has the necessary permits, especially important if you want to go further afield – Dakhla is one of the closest oases to the Gilf Kebir but permits to go there are only issued from Cairo. For more information about desert safaris, see p332.

SLEEPING
Hotels

Mut has a good selection of hotels, although most are in the budget category and even the more expensive places tend to be small and friendly, which can go some way towards making up for a lack of amenities. Some hotels offer half board, which includes breakfast and dinner.

Mut Inn (792 7982; www.solymar-hotels.com; Mut Talata Springs; s/d US$50/78;) The only three-star in town, Mut Inn is operated by Sol y Mar, which also runs the Pioneers Hotel in Al-Kharga. It has six chalets, six lodge rooms with fans, a five-room villa and a restaurant. The décor is kitsch and rooms hugely overpriced, but this is a comfortable hotel with a pleasant deep pool fed by warm water from the adjacent spring.

El Ngoom Hotel (782 0014; fax 782 3084; north of Sharia as-Sawra al-Khadra; s/d E£40/50, with air-con E£50/57;) On a quiet street behind the tourist office and near a selection of restaurants, this friendly hotel has a range of clean rooms with bathroom and some with air-con and TV. One of our favourite hotels in Dakhla.

Mebarez Hotel (/fax 782 1524; Sharia as-Sawra al-Khadra; s/d E£35/50, with private bathroom E£50/60;) Safari groups and other groups doing an oases tour like to use this hotel, where the rooms are reasonably comfortable with clean shared facilities, but where the staff can be surly.

Fursan Hotel (782 1343; fax 782 2870; Sharia al-Wadi; s/d E£16.50/25, s/d with private bathroom E£25/45, d with air-con E£55;) A modern white building on the edge of the old city, the Fursan has friendly management and simple but comfortable rooms, though the bathrooms could be cleaner. It also has an outdoor cafeteria where meals are available for around E£15 to E£20. Breakfast costs E£5.

Bedouin Camp (785 0480; bedouincamp@hotmail.com; Al-Dohous; d E£60, huts per person E£20) Al Hag Abdel Hameed comes from a family of Bedouin who settled in the area a generation ago. He and his camp have come a long way since then. Some of the original reed huts remain but most rooms are in new concrete clusters that were just being finished at the time of our visit. Meals used to be served in a large sitting area with rugs and cushions, but a new restaurant is also under construction (meals E£45). Check prices in advance as they do have a tendency to change. The nearby spring looks inviting but may stain clothes.

Bedouin Oasis Village (782 0070, 012 531 9355; s/d E£30/50, with private bathroom E£50/60;) On a rise above the main street into town, this newcomer has well-designed traditional buildings (only right, given that it is opposite the architectural school), with plenty of domes and vaults. The restaurant/café has wonderful views of town.

WESTERN DESERT

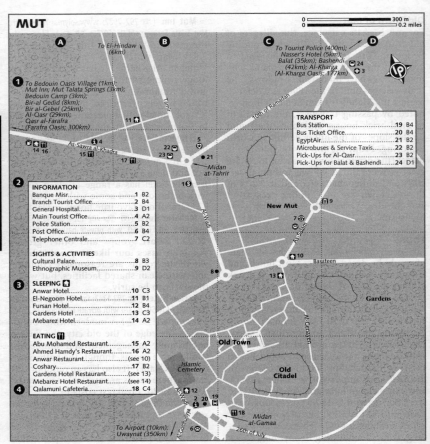

MUT

Gardens Hotel (☎ 782 1577; Sharia al-Genayen; s/d E£19/24, with shower E£18/23) Low prices and a good location help keep rooms full at this popular budget hotel. The downside is that shared bathrooms can be pretty dire and single women may feel uncomfortable with the stares from the many Egyptian men who stay here. Breakfast is extra and the hotel rents bicycles for E£10 per hour.

Anwar Hotel (☎ 782 0070; Sharia Basateen; s/d/tr with fan E£15/20/45, with air-con E£20/30/50; ✕ 🖳) The Anwar family run this hotel with clean but scruffy rooms above their restaurant of the same name. Some have complained about noise from the nearby mosque.

Nasser's Hotel (☎ 782 2727, 010 682 6467; Sheikh Waley; r per person E£20; 🖳) While his broth-

ers Abu Mohamed and Ahmed Hamdy run two of Dakhla's better restaurants, Nasser has gone into the hotel and tour business. His hotel has grown from simple mud-brick buildings into a labyrinth of stark two- and three-bed rooms with shared bathrooms. A murky-looking pool has been added on a terrace. Nasser also runs desert trips with car or camel. Look for the signposts about 5km from Mut on the road to Al-Kharga Oasis. The hotel is about 400m off the main road on the left-hand side.

Camping
You should be able to camp near the dunes west of Mut or in Al-Qasr, on a plateau

just north of town, where the night sky is a spectacular field of stars, but check first with the tourist office in Mut.

EATING

There is no fancy dining in Mut, but there is some good, fresh food to be had in some restaurants, most of which serve pretty much the same selection of chicken/kebab and rice meals.

Anwar Restaurant (☎ 782 0070; Sharia Basateen; meals E£2-15) A popular café/restaurant located below the hotel of the same name, Anwar serves up *ta'amiyya* and *fuul*, in addition to the more substantial chicken and rice combo, and is popular with locals.

Ahmed Hamdy's Restaurant (☎ 782 0767; Sharia as-Sawra al-Khadra; meals E£2-15) On the main road into town, Ahmed Hamdy's popular place serves delicious chicken, kebabs, vegetables and a few other small dishes inside or on his terrace. The freshly squeezed lime juice is excellent and you can request beer and *sheesha* (water pipe).

Abu Mohamed Restaurant (☎ 782 1431; Sharia as-Sawra al-Khadra; meals E£3-25; 🖳) Abu Mohamed, brother of Ahmed Hamdy, cooks and serves in this simple roadside restaurant. His set meal includes good vegetables with kebab or pigeon (you need to order ahead for this) and ends with homemade *basbousa* (a sticky dessert). Vegetarians are welcome, and cold beer is served. Something of an entrepreneur (he already has Internet and bike hire), Abu Mohamed has plans to rent rooms upstairs.

Gardens Hotel Restaurant (☎ 782 1577; Sharia al-Genayen; dishes E£5-12) Gardens serves a range of meat dishes, rice, omelettes and salad, plus a very tasty mixed vegetable dish baked in an earthenware pot. Prices are low, but it's best to eat here in the evening when the head chef is around.

Mebarez Hotel Restaurant (☎ 782 1524; Sharia as-Sawra al-Khadra; meals E£16-20; 🗷) This place serves similar food to the others but it's slightly higher quality. Beer is also served.

Qalamuni Cafeteria (Midan al-Gamaa; dishes E£2-10) Another basic cafeteria, Qalamuni has a reasonable choice of *fuul*, *ta'amiyya* and vegetable dishes.

Al-Wadi Fiteer (Sharia as-Sawra al-Khadra; meals E£5; 🗷) An extremely popular *fiteer* place past the tourist office, heading towards Midan at-Tahrir.

Coshary (Sharia as-Sawra al-Khadra; meals E£2) One of Egypt's offerings to world cuisine – pasta, rice, lentils, onions and more. Open for lunch and dinner, you can take away or eat in.

GETTING THERE & AWAY

Bus

Upper Egypt Bus Co (☎ 782 1538; Midan al-Gamaa) runs at 7pm and 8.30pm to Cairo (E£50 to E£55, eight to 10 hours) via Al-Kharga Oasis (E£10, one to two hours) and Asyut (E£20, four to five hours). Other services to Al-Kharga leave at 6am, 8.30am and 10pm. You can also go to Cairo (E£50) via Farafra Oasis (E£20, 4½ hours) and Bahariyya Oasis (E£35, seven hours) at 6am and 6pm.

Service Taxi

Peugeots and microbuses leave from the station on Sharia as-Sawra al-Khadra, and cost E£10 to Al-Kharga, E£20 to either Farafra or Asyut and around E£60 to Cairo. All services depart when full from near the new mosque.

GETTING AROUND

Abu Mohamed Restaurant and Gardens Hotel rent out bicycles for E£10 per hour.

Most places in Dakhla are linked by pick-up, but working out where they all go can be difficult and they can be ridiculously crowded. Those heading to Al-Qasr (75pt) depart from near the police station. You can take pick-ups to Balat and Bashendi from in front of the hospital for E£1. It may prove easier on occasion to bargain for a 'special' pick-up.

Around Mut

HOT SPRINGS

There are several hot sulphur pools around the town of Mut, but the easiest to reach is the official tourist spring 3km down the road to Al-Qasr. Called **Mut Inn** (Mut Three), the spring is the site of a small hotel (p343), so unless you stay there, you have to dip in the very exposed 1.5m-deep pool just outside the hotel's pink walls. The pool's rust-coloured water may not look inviting (and can stain clothes) but it is both hot and relaxing.

Bir al-Gedid (New Spring) is, as its name suggests, the latest artesian well to be dug. It is a short distance from the Bedouin

SPRING ETIQUETTE

- If locals are bathing, wait until they are finished before entering the water.

- During the day, women should wear a long baggy T-shirt over their bathing suit, although in some places even this may not be appropriate.

- To locals, a woman bathing alone is about as subtle as standing naked on Bawiti's main drag; don't do it.

Camp (p343). **Bir al-Gebel** (Mountain Spring) has been turned into a day-trip destination where blaring music and hundreds of school children can overwhelm the desert ambience. At night, however, it is quiet and the stars are overhead. A sign marks the turn-off about 20km north of Mut, from where it's about another 5km to the spring.

SAND DUNES & CAMEL RIDES
A few kilometres out past the bus station you can have a roll around in sand dunes which, while not the most spectacular in the desert, are easy to reach for people without their own transport. Other dunes can be seen to the right of the airport road. Almost every hotel and restaurant in Mut offers day trips that include sand dunes. Sunset camel rides out to the dunes can also be arranged – see Tours on p343.

ROCK CARVINGS
About 45km southeast of Mut heading to Al-Kharga, at a bend on the southwest side of the road beyond Teneida, Dakhla's cultivated land ends at the feet of some strange rock formations. This was the crossroads of two important caravan routes, the Darb al-Ghabari between Dakhla and Al-Kharga and another, now lost, track that linked the village of Teneida with the Darb al-Arba'een to the south. Carved into the soft rock are **prehistoric rock carvings**, showing camels and tribal markings. Long visited by desert travellers, some of whom left their names carved in the rock, it has recently suffered from the attentions of less scrupulous travellers who have all but ruined most of these images by carving their own graffiti into the rock. If you must visit, be sure not to add to this vandalism.

BALAT
About 35km east of Mut on the road to Al-Kharga, Balat has retained much of its medieval Islamic character. There has been a town on this site since the Old Kingdom, when it had strong trading links with Kush (Nubia), but what you see now is medieval or later. Balat is a living monument to the possibilities of Sudanic-style mud architecture, a place of covered streets, moulded benches, smoothly rounded walls and tiny doors, designed to keep houses cool (and confuse invaders). To get to Balat, a pick-up from near the hospital in Mut will cost E£1.

You will need your own vehicle to explore a couple of nearby sites that date back to Pharaonic times. **Ain al-Asil**, or the Spring of the Origin, is an Old Kingdom settlement. The oasis expert Ahmed Fakry, who excavated here in the 1970s and found remains of a large fortress and possibly a canal, believed it was once the capital of the oasis. The site is thought to have been abandoned in Ptolemaic times. Ain al-Asil is about 2km down a track that leads north off the main road 200m east of Balat.

About 1.5km past Ain al-Asil is **Qila al-Dabba** (admission E£20; ⏱ officially 8am-5pm Oct-Apr, 8am-6pm May-Sep, but you may need to find the guardian in the nearby buildings), Balat's ancient necropolis. The five mastabas here, the largest of which stands over 10m high, resemble those at Saqqara and appear to date back to the 6th dynasty. Four are ruined, but one has been restored and is now open to the public. Originally all five would have been clad in fine limestone. Three have been identified by the French archaeologists working here as belonging to Old Kingdom governors of the oasis, evidence of Dakhla's importance to the centre of power in the Nile Valley. You might need a torch (flashlight) to see inside.

BASHENDI
This small village to the north of the main Dakhla–Al-Kharga road takes its name from Pasha Hindi, the medieval sheikh buried here. As with most villages in the vicinity, it appears to be built over a far older settlement. Some historians believe that the distinctive design of the village houses, with their square pillars and balconies, is based on Pharaonic design. The main reason to come here, though, is to see the collection of Roman tombs that lie in

---

THE LONG DRY WALK

Teneida, the easternmost village in the Dakhla Oasis, has existed since ancient times, but its modern fame comes from the part it played in one of last century's most incredible desert journeys. When the Italians took over Kufra Oasis (now in Libya) in 1930, some of the nomads of the area preferred to risk death in the desert rather than be subjected to foreign rule. With no time for real preparation, a group of about 500 men, women and children set out on a risky 322km journey across the Great Sand Sea and the Gilf Kebir to Uwaynat. They arrived only to find that there had been no rain for years. Without food for themselves or their camels many gave themselves up for dead. Others, without knowing the area, wandered in the direction of Dakhla. By chance, a British patrol found the emaciated group that remained in Uwaynat and managed to save most of them. After 21 days, three of the men who'd left Uwaynat staggered into Teneida and a rescue operation was mounted to find the remainder of the refugees wandering in the desert. According to a report in the *Times* of London in May 1931, some 300 nomads reached Dakhla after covering a staggering 676km of desert on foot without water. The newspaper described it as an epic journey that few have managed throughout the long history of desert travel.

---

the desert behind the village, two of which are of particular interest.

The **Tomb of Pasha Hindi** is covered by an Islamic-era dome, which sits over a Roman structure, clearly visible from the inside of the building. Locals make pilgrimages to pray for the saint's intercession. Nearby is the sandstone **Tomb of Kitines** (admission to both tombs E£16; ☯ 8am-5pm Oct-Apr, 8am-6pm May-Sep), which was occupied by Sanussi soldiers during WWI and by a village family after that. Nevertheless, some funerary reliefs have survived and show the 2nd-century AD notable meeting the gods Min, Seth and Shu.

AL-QASR

On the edge of lush vegetation at the foot of high limestone cliffs lies the extraordinary medieval/Ottoman town of Al-Qasr, a charming place that provides a glimpse of how other oasis towns looked before the New Valley development projects transformed the area. Several hundred people still live in the town that not so long ago was home to several thousand.

Sights

The Supreme Council for Antiquities has taken responsibility for the town, but because people still live there, are unable to enclose the site or charge an entrance fee. Visitors are expected to go with one of the Antiquities guards (who will want a 'donation' of up to E£10).

As so often in Egypt, the town is built on ancient foundations. The gateway of a temple to Thoth (buried) is now the front of a private house, and inscribed blocks from the temple have been used in other local buildings, although most of what you can see dates to the Ottoman period (1516–1798). The size of the houses and the surviving fragments of decoration suggest a puzzling level of wealth. It is hoped that documents discovered among the ruins will explain why the Ottomans gave it such importance.

The architecture has retained much of its ancient character. The narrow covered streets remain cool in the hot summer and also serve to protect their inhabitants, to some extent, from desert sandstorms. Entrances to old houses can be clearly seen and some are marked by beautiful lintels – acacia beams situated above the door, and carved with the names of the carpenter and the owner of the house, the date and a verse from the Quran. There are 37 lintels in the village, the earliest of which dates to the early-16th century. One of the finest is above the **Tomb of Sheikh Nasr ad-Din** inside the old mosque, which is marked by a 12th-century mud-brick minaret (it was rebuilt in the 19th century). Adjoining it is **Nasr ad-Din Mosque**, with a 21m-high minaret. The Supreme Council for Antiquities has renovated several buildings, including one that appears to have been a **madrassa**, a school where Islamic law was taught, which doubled as a town hall and courthouse: prisoners were tied to a stake near the entrance. A sign here claims the madrassa to be an Ayyubid structure, but although the design is Ayyubid, there is no proof that it wasn't built much later.

Also of interest is the restored **House of Abu Nafir**. A dramatic pointed arch at the entrance frames a huge studded wooden door. Built of mud brick, but on a grander scale than the surrounding houses, it incorporates huge blocks from an earlier structure, most of them decorated with hieroglyphic reliefs. Other buildings in the vicinity also have a few reused ancient stones, and local legend says that a temple, probably dating back to Ptolemaic times, once stood here.

Other buildings include the **pottery factory** and a huge old **corn mill**. You can still see people making mud bricks in the time-honoured way, as well as men working an antique bellows in a tiny foundry. The newest attraction is the **Ethnographic Museum** (admission E£3; ⏰ 9am-sunset). Occupying Sherif Ahmed's house, dating back to 1785, the museum's everyday objects try to give life to the empty buildings around them.

Heading back to Mut from Al-Qasr, take the secondary road for a change of scenery. You can visit several **tombs** (admission E£10) near the ruined village of Amhadah, dating from the 2nd century. About 15km further towards Mut is the Mamluk village of **Qalamun**, with both Ottoman and modern houses built of mud. There are good views of the country from the cemetery.

Sleeping

Al-Qasr Hotel (☎ 787 6013; dm E£10) This hotel, the nearest accommodation, is run by the very friendly Mohamed. Sitting above Mohamed's coffeehouse, on the main road near the old town, the hotel has four big, screened rooms with narrow balconies. Shared bathrooms are clean and, contrary to the norm, have hot water only. For E£3, you can also sleep on a mattress on the roof. The ground-floor coffeehouse and restaurant serves good basic fare like chicken, rice, *fuul* and salad. Breakfast costs E£3. Mohamed also rents bikes for E£5 a day.

Desert Lodge (☎ 772 7061/2, in Cairo 02-690 5240; www.desertlodge.net; s/d/tr half board US$95/160/225; ✖ 🖳) The best accommodation in Dakhla also has the best view of Al-Qasr. This lodge has 32 large rooms in traditionally designed clusters with views over the old town and surrounding desert. The restaurant is adequate, and there is a bar and many of the services you would expect for the price.

Beir Elgabal Camp (☎ 787 6600; elgabalcamp@ hotmail.com; s/d/tr E£15/35/50; 🖳) Located 4km from the turn-off on the Mut road, this place has clean, plain rooms and a pool fed by a spring, in an idyllic position at the base of the mountain.

Getting There & Away

Pick-ups to Al-Qasr from near the police station in Mut cost 75pt.

DEIR AL-HAGGAR

Deir al-Haggar is signposted about 7km west of Al-Qasr, at the checkpoint on the road to Farafra Oasis. From the turn-off it's another 5km to the restored Roman **sandstone temple** (admission E£20; ⏰ 8am-sunset). Dedicated to the Theban triad of Amun, Mut and Khons, as well as Horus (who can be seen with a falcon's head), it was built between the reigns of Nero (AD 54–68) and Domitian (AD 81–96). The cartouches of Nero, Vespasian and Titus (Domitian's father and elder brother respectively) can be seen in the hypostyle hall, which has also been inscribed by almost every 19th-century explorer who passed through the oasis. If you look carefully in the adjacent Porch of Titus you can see the names of the entire expedition of Gerhard Rohlfs, the 19th-century desert explorer. Also visible are the names of Edmonstone, Drovetti and Houghton, all famous desert travellers.

The temple has been enclosed by a wall to help prevent wind and sand erosion, and at the entrance is a display room outlining its history and the restoration process.

FARAFRA OASIS
☎ 092

The most remote and smallest of the New Valley oases, Farafra was also one of the most exposed: if trouble came from the west, as it often did in antiquity and after in the shape of the Libyans, then this was where it arrived. As a result, there are many people of Libyan descent and many Bedouin too. Because of this, and because of the reduced state of the main town, Farafra can be a difficult place to understand.

There were only eight flowing springs in the oasis in 1960, but now there are more than 100, many sunk in the mid-1960s as part of the government's programme to revitalise the region. Not all of them are open

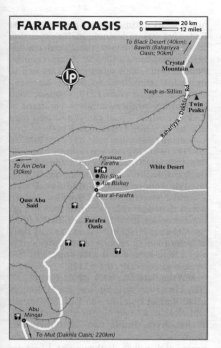

FARAFRA OASIS

0 —— 20 km
0 —— 12 miles

To Black Desert (40km);
Bawiti (Bahariyya
Oasis; 90km)

Crystal
Mountain

Naqb as-Sillim

Bahariyya-Dakhla Rd

Twin
Peaks

To Ain Della
(30km)

Aquasun
Farafra

Bir Sitta

Ain Bishay

Qasr al-Farafra

White Desert

Quss Abu
Said

Farafra
Oasis

Abu
Minqar

To Mut (Dakhla Oasis; 220km)

to travellers but some can be visited. These springs have provided the means by which the oasis's agriculture has been revived and there is now a good trade in olives and olive oil, dates, apricots, guava, figs, oranges, apples and sunflowers. For the majority of travellers now, Farafra Oasis is most likely to be a stepping stone to the glorious White Desert.

Qasr al-Farafra

The first European to visit Farafra, in 1819, mentioned that the qasr (fortress), was uninhabited and that villagers lived around it. This process has continued: the **fortress** (Map p350) has now all but disappeared and most people in this, the oasis's main town, have moved even further away from the mound on which it was built. Some small mud-brick houses remain, their doorways still secured with medieval peg locks, and some of the walls are painted with verses of the Quran and murals of ships and planes – references to the haj (pilgrimage to Mecca) made by their inhabitants. But apart from the sense of abandonment and calm (and

the well-kept gardens), there isn't much to detain you in town.

INFORMATION
For tourist information, contact the tourist office in Mut (p342).

Hospital (Map p350; ☎ 751 0047; main Bahariyya-Dakhla rd) For emergencies only.

Main post office (Map p350; off main Bahariyya-Dakhla rd; ☒ 8.30am-2.30pm)

Police (Map p350; ☎ 751 0070; main Bahariyya-Dakhla rd)

Telephone centrale (off main Bahariyya-Dakhla rd; ☒ 24hr)

SIGHTS & ACTIVITIES
Badr's Museum
Badr Abdel Moghny is a self-taught artist whose gift to his town has become its only sight. **Badr's Museum** (Map p350; ☎ 751 0091, 012 170 4710; donation E£5; ☒ 8.30am-sunset) is worth seeing for the energy and enthusiasm that he puts into his work, much of which records oasis life and is a protest at the use of concrete in the oasis. His distinctive style of painting and sculpture in mud, stone and sand has won him foreign admirers; he exhibited successfully in Europe in the early 1990s and later in Cairo. His museum's latest addition is a desert garden.

Bir Sitta
A popular stop is **Bir Sitta** (Well No Six; Map p349), a sulphurous hot spring 6km northwest of Qasr al-Farafra. Water gushes into a Jacuzzi-sized concrete pool and then spills out into a larger tank. This is a good place for a night-time soak under the stars.

Ain Bishay
This Roman spring bubbles forth on a hillock on the northwest edge of town. It has been developed into an irrigated grove of date palms together with citrus, olives, apricots and carob trees, and is a cool haven amid the arid landscape. Several families tend the crops here; you should seek someone out and ask permission before wandering around.

TOURS
Farafra is nearer to the White Desert than Bahariyya and yet, perhaps because of its size, there is a very limited choice of serious desert outfits. Al-Waha Hotel offers trips around Farafra and the White Desert

for around E£400 per vehicle for an overnight stay, including food, but check the vehicle before you go. Both Al-Badawiya and Aquasun are more expensive, but are well equipped for long-range desert travel as well as trips closer to home – for more information on them and other long-range safari operators, see p332.

SLEEPING

Al-Badawiya Safari & Hotel (Map p350; ☎ 751 0060, 012 214 8343; www.badawiya.com; s/d/tr with private bathroom US$20/29/35; ✳ 🖳 🐹) We hear mixed opinions about the Al-Badawiya on the Bahariyya–Dakhla road, but there is no escaping the dynamism of the Ali brothers, who dominate Farafra tourism with their

QASR AL-FARAFRA

INFORMATION	
Hospital.................................1	B2
Police...................................2	B4
Post Office.............................3	B3
Telephone Centrale....................4	B3

SIGHTS & ACTIVITIES	
Badr's Museum.........................5	B3
Hot Spring.............................6	A3
Old Fort...............................7	A3

SLEEPING 🏠	
Al-Badawiya Safari & Hotel............8	B2
Al-Waha Hotel.........................9	B3

EATING 🍴	
Al-Badawiyya Restaurant..............10	B3
Al-Tamawy Restaurant.................11	B4
Hussein's Restaurant.................12	B4
Shops, Bakery & Coffee Shop..........13	B4

hotel, safari outfit and new restaurant. The Badawiya was undergoing major expansion at the time of our visit, the 25 older mudbrick rooms being joined by 15 larger rooms. Popular with small safari groups as well as individual travellers, so worth reserving ahead. Breakfast costs E£17. Owners, Saad Ali and his brother Hamdy – Farafrans of Bedouin origin – lead camel and jeep trips into the Western Desert (see p333).

Aquasun Farafra (Map p349; ☎ 012 211 8632, 010 635 7340, 02-337 2898; www.eg-westerndesert.com; Bir Sitta; s/d/tr E£120/170/270, half board US$40; ✳ 🐹) Built beside Bir Sitta, Aquasun has 21 chalet-style rooms built in traditional style around a peaceful garden. Each has its own porch thatched with palm fronds, and piping-hot water from Bir Sitta fills the hotel pool. Owner Hisham Nessim has had years of hotel-owning experience in Sinai and is also a long-time desert-safari operator (for more on his safaris, see p334).

Al-Waha Hotel (Map p350; ☎ 751 0040, 012 720 0387; hamdyhamouda@hotmail.com; d/tr E£30/45) A small budget hotel beside Badr's Museum and close to a bustling café/restaurant, Al-Waha offers simple two- and three-bed rooms and clean shared bathrooms. New rooms with private bathroom and fans are under construction.

EATING

Eating choices are limited in Farafra. There are some shops and a bakery at the southern end of the main road. Alcohol is not served all year round, as no one in the town is allowed to buy it, but some places may stock it when things are busy.

Al-Badawiya Safari & Hotel (Map p350; ☎ 751 0060, 012 214 8343; meals E£17-50) Al-Badawiya's pleasant vaulted restaurant serves freshly made if rather expensive dishes including pasta and simple three-course meals, using organic vegetables from its own farm. It may also serve beer and wine.

Aquasun Farafra (Map p349; ☎ 012 225 9660; meals E£12-30) Fresh organic ingredients are used in Aquasun's restaurant, and dishes are a choice of the usual Western and Egyptian staples. May serve beer and wine.

Zwanda (Map p350; ☎ 751 0011) The Ali brothers' latest development was still not open at the time of our visit, but the former Hotel Zwanda was being refashioned into the Al-Badawiya Restaurant and café. Beside food, drinks and Internet, they have plans for a handicraft shop and safari supply store.

Al-Tamawy Restaurant (Map p350; dishes E£2-10) A cafeteria on the main road, Al-Tamawy has basic food on offer along with the usual tea, coffee and *sheesha*.

Hussein's Restaurant (Map p350; dishes E£5-9) A simple shack on the main street by the fountain, with tables outside and a grill on which Hussein cooks chicken.

SHOPPING

It's a family affair. In the summer, Dr Socks takes wool from the neck and lower back of camels, spins it and knits. His sister makes sweaters, his uncle blankets, while he and his mother get on with the socks and scarves. He and his wares can usually be found at the Al-Badawiya Safari & Hotel. Count on E£10 to E£30 for socks, and up to E£400 for a blanket.

GETTING THERE & AWAY

There are buses from Farafra to Cairo (E£40, eight to 10 hours) via Bahariyya (E£15, three to four hours) at 10am and 10pm. Buses from Farafra to Dakhla (E£15, four to five hours) originate in Cairo and leave between 1pm and 2pm and between 1am and 2am.

Buses stop at Al-Tamawy Restaurant, the petrol station and at Al-Badawiya. Tickets are bought from the conductor. As usual, you should check the latest schedules for all these buses.

Microbuses to Dakhla (E£15, four to five hours) also leave from in front of Al-

Tamawy Restaurant whenever they have a full load. There's not a lot of traffic between the two oases, however, and you're better off going early in the morning. The same goes for microbuses to Bahariyya (E£15, three hours). A service taxi to Dakhla costs E£15, to Al-Kharga E£10.

FARAFRA TO BAHARIYYA OASIS

The desert between the Farafra and Bahariyya Oases offers some of the most varied and amazing terrain in the Western Desert. From the snowlike ergs of the White Desert to the Black Desert's eerie black cones, the landscape never disappoints. Because the major sights are relatively easy to access the area is a favourite destination for safari outfits in Qasr al-Farafra and Bawiti.

White Desert

The White Desert (Sahra al-Beida) is an otherworldly region of blindingly white rock formations worn by the elements into strange and suggestive shapes. About 20km northeast of Farafra you can see the first formations on the east side of the road. A few kilometres further you reach the edge of the 300-sq-km White Desert Protectorate. As you approach the outcroppings they take on surreal forms – you can make out ostriches, camels, hawks and other bizarre shapes. In a country with fewer natural than artificial sights, these are a national monument on a par with the Grand Canyon in the USA. They are best viewed at sunrise or sunset, when the sun turns the white

---

FOREVER WHITE

Even in Egypt, where spectacles are to be found around almost every bend, the White Desert is a showstopper. Its unique formations, wedged so unexpectedly between the lushness of Farafra Oasis and the menacing shades of the Black Desert, never fails to amaze visitors. But it is in danger of becoming a victim of its own popularity as more and more people choose to make the journey. On busy nights, the horizon can be filled with the lights of camp fires, the still night rippled with the sound of drums and singing. Daylight reveals burned out camp fires, discarded refuse and, most depressing, tyre tracks over the white rocks. The fragile white chalk formations are now threatened and although the area has been designated a protectorate, there is not enough funding to pay for adequate protection. There are signs that the people who depend on the desert most – tour operators in Bahariyya and Farafra – might begin to take steps to protect their livelihood: the Badawiya Safari & Hotel in Farafra offers free week-long trips in the summer to volunteers prepared to help clean up the desert. If you are going to visit – and we are not suggesting you don't – consider going by foot or camel, be sure to leave nothing behind and, if you are driving, discourage your guide from driving over the rocks.

into chalk pink and orange – rather like a Salvador Dali painting – or under a full moon, which gives the landscape an eerie arctic, whipped-cream appearance. The sand around the outcroppings is littered with quartz and different varieties of deep-black iron pyrites, as well as small fossils (which should be left in the desert).

On the other side of the road, away from the wind-eroded shapes, there are small canyons formed by white, clifflike chalk monoliths called inselbergs. Less dramatic than other areas, they are nevertheless beautiful and eerie to walk around. The shade and privacy they provide also makes them good camping spots.

About 50km north of here, on the southeast side of the road, are two flat-topped mountains known as the **Twin Peaks**, one of the key navigation points for travellers. They are surrounded by small rounded, bowl-like hills and are a favourite destination of local tour operators. Just beyond here, the road climbs a steep escarpment known as **Naqb as-Sillim** (Pass of the Stairs), the main pass that leads into and out of the Farafra depression and marks the end of the White Desert.

A few kilometres further along, the desert floor becomes littered with quartz crystals. A closer look at the rock formations here reveal them to be largely made of crystal, too. The most famous of these formations is the **Crystal Mountain**, actually a large rock made entirely of quartz crystal. It sits right beside the main road some 24km north of Naqb as-Sillim, and is easily recognisable by the large hole through its middle.

Ain Della

About 120km from Farafra, surrounded by cliffs on the north and east and dunes to the south and west, lies Ain Della, or Spring of the Shade. The contrasting tawny hues of the landscape here give it a softness that is very beautiful. But Ain Della is more than a picturesque water hole. Lying within 200km of the three major oases of Siwa, Bahariyya and Farafra, it has been a strategic and extremely important source of water for desert travellers since ancient times. Most famously, the army of the Persian conqueror Cambyses is thought by many to have disappeared in the dunes near here on its ill-fated journey to destroy

the Temple of the Oracle in Siwa Oasis around 525 BC (see p362). During WWII the British Army's Long Range Desert Group stored fuel and supplies here and used it as a jumping-off place for their raids behind German and Italian lines.

Ain Della's position is still considered vital to controlling vast swathes of the Western Desert: it is from here that Egyptian army patrols search the desert for drugs and arms smugglers. As a result, anyone coming here must have a military permit (obtained through desert guides; see p332, p357 or p349).

Black Desert

About 50km south of Bawiti, the desert floor turns from beige to black. This is the beginning of the Black Desert (in Arabic, *Sahara Suda*), formed by the erosion of the mountains, which have spread a layer of black powder and rubble over the ground. It ends with small, black, volcano-shaped mountains, part of a fault that runs through Bahariyya Oasis. The Black Desert is a favourite off-road destination for tours running out of Bahariyya as there are a number of sights here. **Gebel Gala Siwa** is a pyramid-shaped mountain that was formerly a lookout post for caravans coming from Siwa. **Gebel az-Zuqaq** is a mountain known for the red, yellow and orange streaks in its limestone base. There is an easily climbed path leading to the top. Located about 10km south of Bawiti is the domed **Tomb of René Michel**; Michel was a Swiss man who retired to Bahariyya in 1981 and was the first to take tourists on safaris in the surrounding desert. He died in 1986.

Getting There & Away

Ordinary vehicles are able to drive the first kilometre or so off the road into the White or Black Deserts, but only 4WD vehicles can advance deeper into either area. Some travellers simply get off the bus and take themselves into the White Desert – but be very sure that you have adequate supplies, and remember that traffic in either direction is rarely heavy. Venturing to Ain Della is more of an expedition, and needs a guide and permits.

There are plenty of safari outfits that can take you around these sights. See p349 and p357 for listings.

BAHARIYYA OASIS

☎ 02

Bahariyya is the closest of the New Valley oases to Cairo, some 365km away, and it makes a great introduction to life in the desert. Situated in a fertile, 2000-sq-km depression, it has been a major agricultural centre since at least the Middle Kingdom, when Bahariyya was famous for its wine, which was sold along the Nile and even in Rome. Linked to the Nile Valley, Fayoum Oasis and Siwa by a number of caravan routes, Bahariyya thrived until the 4th century AD and was famed for its wheat and grape production. With the decline of Roman power and the subsequent breakdown of security, large swathes of agri- cultural land returned to desert. In recent years, archaeological excavations have begun to uncover the oasis's rich archaeological heritage and a number of sites have been opened to visitors.

Bawiti

Bawiti, the main town of the oasis, can come as a surprise: its main street looks much like many other low-rise concrete places in Egypt and touts selling hotel rooms and tours can be aggressive when the Cairo bus arrives. But there are pleasures to be had, both in the quieter areas off the main street, where many people still live in traditional mud-brick houses, and in several little villages spread throughout the palm-covered oasis. On the western, older side of town, houses are surrounded by lush palm plantations, watered by mineral-rich springs, some of them ancient. It is easy to imagine that these tranquil gardens have changed little since Roman times.

INFORMATION

There are no Internet cafés in Bawiti but a couple of kiosks around the Popular Restaurant have slow-speed terminals that can be used for E£10 to E£15 per hour.

Hospital (☎ 847 2390) Head to Cairo except in dire emergency.

National Bank for Development (☖ 9am-2pm Sun-Thu) Changes cash only. No ATM.

Old Oasis Hotel (☎ 847 3028) Offers Internet access.

Tourist office (☎ 847 3835; ☖ 8am-2pm & 7-9pm Sat-Thu) Run by the friendly Muhammed Abd El-Kader (☎ 012 373 6567; Mohamed_kader26@hotmail.com).

Tourist police (☎ 847 3900; Sharia Masr)

SIGHTS & ACTIVITIES

Until recently, Bawiti was a quiet town dependent on agriculture, but it's getting a new lease of life as more people head to the desert or come to see the Golden Mummies. The area's antiquities (Tomb of Alexander, Chapel of Ain al-Muftella) have been spruced up and, in some cases (Qarat Qasr Salim) reopened to the public.

Surrounding the town are mud-brick villages and palm gardens, many fed by springs that are ideal for a night-time soak. Further afield lies some spectacular desert scenery; Black Desert, Gebel Dist and Gebel Maghrafa can be seen on a day trip or on an overnight safari.

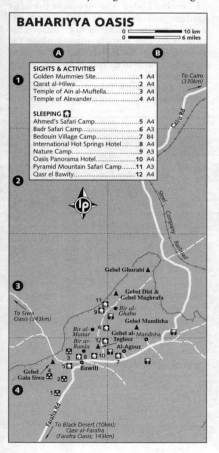

BAHARIYYA OASIS

0   10 km
0   6 miles

SIGHTS & ACTIVITIES
Golden Mummies Site.....................1 A4
Qarat al-Hilwa..............................2 A4
Temple of Ain al-Muftella...............3 A4
Temple of Alexander......................4 A4

SLEEPING
Ahmed's Safari Camp.....................5 A4
Badr Safari Camp...........................6 A3
Bedouin Village Camp.....................7 B4
International Hot Springs Hotel........8 A3
Nature Camp.................................9 A3
Oasis Panorama Hotel...................10 A4
Pyramid Mountain Safari Camp......11 A3
Qasr el Bawity............................12 A4

To Cairo (330km)

Cairo Rd

Steel Company Railroad

Gebel Ghurabi

Gebel Dist & Gebel Maghrafa

Bir al-Ghaba

Gebel Mandisha

To Siwa Oasis (343km)

Bir al-Mattar
Bir ar-Ramla
Gebel al-Mandisha
Ingleez
Al-Agouz

Gebel Gala Siwa

Bawiti

To Black Desert (10km); Qasr al-Farafra (Farafra Oasis) (143km)

Farafra Rd

WESTERN DESERT

Museum (al-Mathaf)

Since the discovery of the 'golden mummies' in the 1990s (see opposite), growing interest in Bahariyya's ancient past has led to the opening of a new **museum** (Sharia al-Mathaf; ticket office is the hut 50m from the museum towards Sharia Masr; 8am-2pm). The building resembles a concrete bunker, but don't let that put you off. This is where the mummies rest. Some of the 10 mummies on show are richly decorated and while the motifs are formulaic and the work second rate, the painted faces show a move away from stylised Pharaonic mummy decoration towards Fayoum portraiture (see p191). Underneath the beautiful wrappings, the work of the embalmers appears to have been sloppy: in some cases the bodies decayed before the embalming began, which suggests that these mummies mark the beginning of the end of mummification. Nevertheless, they are an eloquent reminder of Bahariyya's antiquity.

Oasis Heritage Museum

You can't miss Mahmoud Eed's **Oasis Heritage Museum** (847 3666; Sharia al-Masr; admission E£5; no set opening times), about 1km from the police station on the road to Cairo: it is announced by massive clay camels looking onto the street. Inspired by Badr's Museum in Farafra (p349), its creator wishes to capture, in clay, scenes from traditional village life, among them men playing *siga* (a game played in the dirt with clay balls or seeds) and a barber/doctor at work. There is also a display of old oasis dresses and jewellery.

Hot & Cold Springs

The closest springs to central Bawiti are the so-called Roman springs, known as **Al-Beshmo**, about a 10-minute walk from the Popular Restaurant, down beside the Al-Beshmo Lodge. The view over the oasis gardens and the desert beyond is wonderful, but the spring is not suitable for swimming. An equally useless place for swimming is **Bir al-Muftella**, about 3km from the centre of town. It's an interesting walk out through the town, but don't go for the water alone. Take the Siwa road and keep asking. If you pass a big, white conical

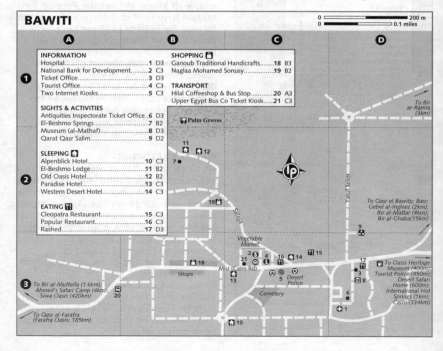

BAWITI

0   200 m
0   0.1 miles

INFORMATION
Hospital.....................................1 D3
National Bank for Development........2 C3
Ticket Office...............................3 D3
Tourist Office..............................4 C3
Two Internet Kiosks......................5 C3

SIGHTS & ACTIVITIES
Antiquities Inspectorate Ticket Office..6 D3
El-Beshmo Springs.......................7 B2
Museum (al-Mathaf).....................8 D3
Qarat Qasr Salim..........................9 D2

SLEEPING
Alpenblick Hotel...........................10 C3
El-Beshmo Lodge.........................11 B2
Old Oasis Hotel...........................12 B2
Paradise Hotel.............................13 C3
Western Desert Hotel....................14 C3

EATING
Cleopatra Restaurant....................15 C3
Popular Restaurant.......................16 C3
Rashed.....................................17 D3

SHOPPING
Ganoub Traditional Handicrafts.......18 B3
Naglaa Mohamed Sonusy...............19 B2

TRANSPORT
Hilal Coffeeshop & Bus Stop...........20 A3
Upper Egypt Bus Co Ticket Kiosk.....21 C3

Palm Groves

To Bir ar-Ramla (3km)

To Qasr el Bawity; Basr; Gebel al-Ingleez (2km); Bir al-Mattar (4km); Bir al-Ghaba (15km)

Vegetable Market

Yusuf Selim

Sabaa

Misr (Cairo Rd)

Shops

Desert Police

Cemetery

To Bir al-Muftella (1.6km); Ahmed's Safari Camp (4km); Siwa Oasis (420km)

To Qasr al-Farafra (Farafra Oasis; 185km)

To Oasis Heritage Museum (400m); Tourist Police (450m); Desert Safari Home (600m); International Hot Springs (1km); Cairo (334km)

BAHARIYYA'S GOLDEN PAST

Put it down to the donkey: until 1996, no-one had any idea of the extent of Bahariyya's glorious past. Then a donkey stumbled on a hole near the temple of Alexander the Great and its rider saw the face of a golden mummy peering through the sand. Since then Dr Zahi Hawass, head of the Supreme Council of Antiquities, and his team have done extensive research in a cemetery that stretches over 3 sq km. Radar has revealed more than 10,000 mummies, and excavation has revealed over 230 of them in what has come to be called the Valley of the Golden Mummies.

These silent witnesses of a bygone age could shed new light on life in this part of Egypt during the Graeco-Roman period, a 600-year interlude marking the transition between the Pharaonic and Christian eras. Bahariyya was then a thriving oasis, and with its rich, fertile land, watered by natural springs, was a famous producer of wheat and wine. Greek and, later, Roman families set up home here and became a kind of expatriate elite.

Research has shown that after a brief decline when Ptolemies and Romans fought for control of the oasis, Roman administrators embarked on a major public works programme, expanding irrigation systems, digging wells, restoring aqueducts and building roads. Thousands of mud-brick buildings sprang up throughout the oasis. Bahariyya became a major source of grain for the empire and was home to a large garrison of troops; its wealth grew proportionately.

How this affected life for ordinary oasis dwellers remains a mystery, but it is likely that their lot was harsh. Rome imposed heavy taxes on noncitizens. One study has found that the life expectancy for Egyptians decreased to between 22 and 25 during the Roman period. Whether Bahariyya's residents fared any better than Nile Valley dwellers is a question that experts are hoping to answer by examining the mummified remains found here.

structure (a sheikh's tomb) on your right, you will know you're on the right track.

The hot sulphurous spring of **Bir ar-Ramla** is very hot (45°C) and you may feel a bit exposed to the donkey traffic passing to and fro. Women should stay well covered. It's about a 3km walk north from the centre of the town.

One of the most satisfying springs to visit is **Bir al-Ghaba**, about 15km northeast of Bawiti. There is nothing quite like a moonlit hot bath on the edge of the desert.

At **Bir al-Mattar**, 7km northeast of Bawiti, cold springs pour into a viaduct, then down into a concrete pool where you can splash around during the hot summer months. As with all the springs the mineral content is high and the water can stain clothing.

Qarat Qasr Salim

This small mound, amid the houses of Bawiti, is likely to have been built upon centuries of debris. There are two 26th-dynasty tombs here. Both were robbed in antiquity and reused as collective burial sites in Roman times. The rock-cut **Tomb of Zed-Amun-ef-ankh** is a fascinating glimpse of Bahariyya in its heyday. It appears that Zed-Amun-ef-ankh was not a government official but given the richness of the tomb paintings, he was clearly a rich and important man in ancient Bahariyya. Researchers assume he was a trader, perhaps a wine merchant or landowner making money out of Bahariyya's thriving wine-export business. Unusually, his tomb contains only one chamber, with four circular (as opposed to the usual square) pillars and seven squat false doors.

Next to it lies the **Tomb of Bannentiu**, his son. Consisting of a four-columned burial chamber with an inner sanctuary, it is covered in fine reliefs depicting Bannentiu in various positions with the gods. The most interesting pictures flank the entrance to the burial chamber. On one side, the journey of the moon is shown, with the moon, in the form of the god Khons, depicted as a source of life and flanked by goddesses Isis and Nephthys. The other side of the entrance is decorated with the journey of the sun.

SLEEPING

Unlike most places in the New Valley, there is a good selection of budget and midpriced hotels in Bawiti and elsewhere in Bahariyya Oasis, although nothing so far for the luxury traveller. For hotels outside the town of Bawiti, see p359.

Budget

It makes sense to sort out accommodation in Bawiti before you arrive, especially in high season. If you don't, be warned that because touts from budget hotels are so aggressive, a tourist policeman now meets buses and escorts new arrivals to the Bawiti tourist office. Once there, the tourist office manager, Mohamed Abd El-Kader, helps visitors choose a hotel, has a list of up-to-date prices and ensures that transportation is arranged.

Desert Safari Home (☎ 847 1321, 012 731 3908; khozamteego33@hotmail.com; s/d E£10/20, with private bathroom E£35/50, d with air-con E£75; ⛽) The 27-room Desert Safari Home is a friendly base in Bawiti, although the location, off the main road at the entrance to town, makes it a long walk to the centre. Rooms are simple but clean and owner Badry Khozam makes a good host. The restaurant serves the usual full dinner for £15 and there is beer. Badry also runs a thriving safari business.

Paradise Hotel (☎ 847 2600; Sharia Misr; s/d E£7.50/15) Recent redecoration has stopped us condemning the Paradise outright, but this is a very basic place in the centre of town. The eight rooms have shared bathrooms, cotton mattresses and filing cabinets for bedside tables. Breakfast on the small vine-covered terrace is an extra E£2.

Alpenblick Hotel (☎ 847 2184, 010 441 9934; ALPENBLICK@hotmail.com; off Sharia Misr; d/tr E£60/80, with private bathroom & air-con E£100/120; ⛽) Another place that has recently been expanded and redecorated, this is one of Bawiti's original hotels, conveniently located and with a range of rooms.

YOUR TICKET TO ANTIQUITIES

In a move to make their lives easier, Bahariyya's authorities have decided to issue a one-day ticket that gives entry to five of the oasis's ancient sites: the museum, the tomb of Zed-Amun-ef-ankh, the tomb of Bannentiu, the Bir al Muftella and the temple of Alexander the Great. Tickets (adult E£30, student E£15) are available at the at the **ticket office** (⏰ 8.30am-4pm) of the new antiquities museum. This is annoying as most visitors either don't have the time or the desire to see all the sights the oasis has to offer, yet have to pay for them.

Midrange & Top End

El-Beshmo Lodge (☎ /fax 847 2177; www.beshmo lodge.com; by El-Beshmo spring; s/d/tr E£90/130/150; ⛽ ⛽) Another old-timer, El-Beshmo Lodge sits beside the spring of the same name (the small pool is filled with spring water). The 25 comfortable rooms here are simply furnished, most with their own bathroom. There is also a good café-restaurant serving meals, tea, coffee and *sheesha* in a pleasant atmosphere. All this, plus obliging and friendly staff.

Old Oasis Hotel (☎ 847 3028, 012 232 4425; www .oldoasissafari.4t.com; by El-Beshmo spring; s/d E£70/120 ⛽ ⛽ ⛽) Saleh Abdallah, one of the original partners in El-Beshmo, has set up on his own hotel on the adjacent plot. The Old Oasis sits above a beautiful garden of palm and olive trees and has 13 simple rooms (more were being built at the time of our visit). A large pool gets steaming hot water from the nearby spring; the runoff waters the hotel garden. A good restaurant serves full meals (dinner E£30).

Western Desert Hotel (☎ 847 1600; westerndesert hotel@hotmail.com; off Sharia Misr; s/d US$17/25; ⛽ ⛽) A new hotel right in the middle of town, opposite Popular Restaurant, the 17 rooms are clean, simple and good value. You pay the same price with or without air-con, so it's worth booking ahead and specifying. The Western Desert is well-placed for late or early bus rides.

EATING

Popular Restaurant (meals E£15-20; ⏰ 5.30am-10pm) Popular by name, popular by nature. Just off the main road in Bawiti, this small roadside restaurant is the chosen stopping-off point for many people passing through Bawiti. The irrepressible Bayoumi serves the usual selection of chicken, soup, rice and vegetable dishes, most of it delicious. There's cold beer too. Prices can vary, so check carefully before ordering.

Rashed (meals E£12-15) More a cafeteria than a restaurant, Rashed serves hot and cold drinks and *sheeshas* (E£2) as well as simple meals of rice, chicken or meat, and vegetables. It's near the petrol station.

Cleopatra Restaurant (meals E£3-12; ⏰ 6am-10pm) A simple, popular place with two big tables and cave-like décor. Mohamed runs a small operation serving excellent chicken, *fuul, ta'amiyya* and eggs.

TOURS

There is fierce competition throughout the oases – and even in Cairo – for tour business, but it is particularly fierce in Bahariyya, where every hotel offers tours, as do a number of young men who have taken out bank loans to pay for their cars. The advice of Mohamed Abd El-Kader in the tourist office is only to go with a driver approved by your hotel or the tourist office – others may be cheaper, but you will have no comeback if something goes wrong. And things do go wrong: there were at least seven serious incidents involving Bahariyya drivers in 2005, and at least one foreigner died.

A typical itinerary will take you to the sights in and around Bahariyya (Temple of Alexander, Ain el-Muftella, Gebel Dist and Maghrafa) then out through the Black Desert, with a stop at the Crystal Mountain and then into the White Desert.

To give an idea of prices, a one-night camping trip into the White Desert will cost E£150 to E£400 per day. If you're travelling into the remote corners of the desert, you'll be looking at E£550 to E£650 per day. One of the variables is how much of the distance is covered off-road (which uses more fuel and is more wearing on the cars).

Before signing up, check vehicles to make sure they're roadworthy, confirm how much food and drink is supplied (and what this will be), ask how long the operators have been conducting safaris, confirm start and end times (some operators start late in the afternoon and return early in the morning but charge for full days) and try to talk with travellers who have just returned from a trip to get their feedback.

If you're planning on exploring remote parts of the desert such as the Gilf Kebir, Oweynat or the Great Sand Sea it is absolutely imperative that you go with an outfit that supplies new 4WDs (travelling in convoy), GPS, satellite phones and experienced Bedouin guides. You'll need an official permit for the Great Sand Sea (US$100, takes 14 days to process).

If you are at all unsure of arrangements, check with Mohamed Abd El-Kader. And be sure to inspect the car, its spare tyres, water and communications before leaving.

SHOPPING

Considering that there is a living craft tradition in the oases, Bawiti makes for disappointing shopping. There are several handicraft shops, but most sell things made elsewhere.

Ganoub Traditional Handicrafts (Sharia Misr; ☾ closed Tue) A tasteful little shop with the best selection of crafts in Bawiti, brought from all over Egypt, including camel-wool blankets and traditional oasis robes. Also has a small selection of books on the desert as well as postcards.

Naglaa Mohamed Sonusy (☎ 847 2101, 012 429 5299; on the way to El-Beshmo spring) Naglaa is a self-taught artist from the oasis who has taken a room near her home to sell her work. While her style won't suit everyone, there is no denying her enthusiasm and her understanding of oasis life.

GETTING THERE & AWAY

Bus

Upper Egypt Bus Co (☎ 847 3610; Sharia Misr; ☾ roughly 9am-1pm & 7-11pm) runs buses to Cairo (E£20, three to four hours, four daily) at 7am, 11.30am, 3pm and about midnight. The 7am and 3pm buses originate in Dakhla and stop at the Hilal Coffeeshop at the western end of town, as well as at the ticket office.

If you're heading to Farafra (E£15, one to two hours) and Dakhla (E£30, four to five hours), you can pick up one of the buses from Cairo that are supposed to leave Bahariyya at 11.30am, 1pm and 11.30pm. Passengers are usually dropped off at Popular Restaurant before the bus continues down the street to one of the coffeehouses at the western end of town, where it stops for about 30 minutes.

Only some bus tickets can be booked from the Bawiti ticket kiosk, at the Upper Egypt Bus Co office. As most of the buses don't originate here, you either have to book in Cairo or take your chances on standing. Ticket-office opening hours are erratic. The tourist office has up-to-date information.

Service Taxi

Microbus service taxis run from Bawiti to Moneeb (near the bus station) in Cairo whenever they have enough customers.

A seat costs about E£20. A microbus to Farafra (they're not very frequent) will cost E£14. Tickets can be bought opposite the desert police station or, again, ask at Popular Restaurant.

There are no service taxis to Siwa, although this may change when the new road opens. You should be able to hire one on a private basis for E£800 to E£1500.

Around Bawiti
SIGHTS
Temple of Alexander
Southwest of Bawiti, just beyond Ahmed's Safari Camp, is the only place in Egypt where Alexander the Great's image and cartouche have been found (although since they were uncovered by archaeologists in the late 1930s they have been worn away by the wind). Alexander was known to have visited Siwa, but there is no evidence to suggest that he passed through Bahariyya, so his representation here is puzzling. The temple has suffered from corrosive desert winds and an insensitive restoration that has left few clues of its original splendour.

Temple of Ain al-Muftella
Slightly south of the spring here are four 26th-dynasty chapels that together form the **Temple of Ain al-Muftella**. The bulk of the building was ordered by 26th-dynasty high priest Zed-Khonsu-ef-ankh, whose tomb was recently discovered under some houses in Bawiti (but is still closed to the public). The layout here is unusual because it doesn't conform to any known temple plan. Archaeologists suspect that the chapels could have been built during the New Kingdom and then significantly expanded during the Late Period and added to during Greek and Roman times. All have been extensively restored and have been given wooden roofs to protect them from the elements. The walls are patchily covered with reliefs that are similar in style to contemporary Theban temples.

Qarat al-Hilwa
This sandstone ridge is about 3km south of Bawiti, northwest of the road to Farafra. In the New Kingdom this was a necropolis, a burial place of successive governors who, as representatives of the pharaoh, were the most powerful figures in the oasis. The 18th-dynasty **Tomb of Amenhotep Huy** is the only

inscribed tomb left in the necropolis and, as the oldest tomb found in the oasis, is an important source of information about Bahariyya's ancient past. The tomb plan mimics those of Nile Valley New Kingdom tombs, with an entrance hall that was originally supported by two columns, a second chamber with four column bases and three burial chambers cut into the tomb walls. The sunken reliefs here have faded but they show scenes of Amenhotep's dreams for the afterlife: banquet tables groaning with fruit, cakes, flowers and casks of wine. It also shows him making offerings to the gods. On the eastern wall are scenes showing corn and wine being gathered for tribute to the pharaoh.

Other Sights in Bahariyya Oasis
There are a number of other sights in Bahariyya that are included as part of a tour by the many safari operators in Bawiti. Most can also be done on foot if the weather is cool.

Gebel Mandisha is a ridge capped with black dolomite and basalt that runs for 4km behind the village of the same name, just west of Bawiti.

Clearly visible from the road to Cairo, flat-topped **Gebel al-Ingleez**, also known as the Black Mountain, takes its name from the remains of a WWI lookout post. From here Captain Williams, a British officer, monitored the movements of Libyan Senussi tribesmen. To get here from Bawiti, go out along the road to Cairo and turn off onto the track heading to Bir al-Ghaba and the Government Rest House at Bir al-Mattar. Keep the mountain in sight and follow village tracks out to it. The walk takes about an hour.

Gebel Dist is a pyramid-shaped mountain that can be seen from most of the oasis. A local landmark, it is famous for its fossils. Dinosaur bones were found here in the early part of the 20th century, disproving the previously held theory that dinosaurs only lived in North America. In a strange twist of fate, the remains were destroyed by WWII Allied bombs while in storage in Germany. In 2001 researchers from the University of Pennsylvania found the remains of another huge dinosaur, the Paralititan stromeri. The discovery of this giant herbivore, which the team deduced was standing on the edge of a tidal channel when it died 94 million years ago, makes it likely that Bahariyya was once a swamp similar to the Florida everglades.

The U Penn team has also found fossils of fish, turtles and crocodiles in the vicinity. They continue to dig here. About 100m away is **Gebel Maghrafa**, or Mountain of the Ladle.

SLEEPING & EATING
Budget

Nature Camp (☎ 012 337 5097, in Cairo 02-347 3643; naturecamps@hotmail.com; Bir al-Ghaba; r per person E£35) On the edge of the cultivated land, at the foot of Gebel Dist, Nature Camp sets new standards for environmentally concerned, budget accommodation in the oasis. The peaceful cluster of candle-lit huts looks out onto the desert beside Bir al-Ghaba. The food is very good (meals E£25) and the owner, Ashraf Lotfe, is a skilled desert hand. There are three rooms with bathroom (E£55 per person), and staff will drive you the 17km into Bawiti if you arrive without transport.

Pyramid Mountain Safari Camp (☎ 847 2184, 010 441 9934; Bir al-Ghaba; huts per person incl transport E£50) Anyone can camp at Bir al-Ghaba, but the Alpenblick Hotel has gone one step further and built Pyramid Mountain right beside the well. There are 15 huts with mattresses. Call ahead to check on the food arrangements. Alpenblick arrange musical evenings if there are enough willing guests.

Bedouin Village Camp (☎/fax 847 6811; www .sadiq1.20m.com; Al-Agouz; s/d E£30/60) A Bedouin-themed camp with small shabby rooms circled around a central thatched area. The bathrooms are not clean but the place is about to get a facelift. The atmosphere is friendly and owner Abdelsadiq Elbadrmani, an accomplished Bedouin musician, provides the evening entertainment.

Badr Safari Camp (Gebel al-Ingleez; huts E£15) A couple of kilometres from town, and a half-hour walk from Gebel al-Ingleez, Badr's has a handful of two-bed huts with tables and chairs outside. Hot water and electricity don't always work.

Midrange & Top End

Ahmed's Safari Camp (☎/fax 847 2090; ahmed_saf ari@hotmail.com; tent or reed huts per person E£10, d E£50-80; ☒ ☐ ☒) About 4km west of the centre, near the Siwa road, Ahmed's is an old favourite among travellers and trans-Africa groups, although the growing number of hotels in Bawiti is providing competition and rooms here are being upgraded (prices too). There are cool, pleasant, domed double

rooms or basic ones (three of which have air-con, the rest have fans); you can sleep under the stars on the roof (E£5). Basic meals (E£55) and beer are available, which is just as well because it's a long walk to town if you have no transport. There's a hot spring a few steps from the hotel.

International Hot Springs Hotel (☎ 847 2322; www.whitedeserttours.com; s/d/tr half board per person US$38/30/25) About 1km outside town on the road to Cairo, this German-run three-star spa resort has forgettable architecture but its 36 rooms and eight chalets are extremely comfortable, built around a hot spring and set in a delightful garden. As well as a deep pool of therapeutic spring water there's a gym, sauna and a good restaurant. Owner Peter Wirth is an old Western Desert hand and organises recommended trips throughout the area.

Oasis Panorama Hotel (☎ 847 2894; www.oasis panorama.com; Cairo rd; s/d/tr E£170/200/240, with air-con E£190/240/300; ☒) This crescent-shaped hotel on a piece of featureless, windswept desert is a joint Egyptian-Dutch venture with tacky décor but 32 comfortable, well-maintained rooms. In conjunction with the Dutch tour operator Desert Tours, the hotel offers a good selection of desert trips.

Qasr el Bawity Hotel & Restaurant (☎ 847 1880, Cairo office 02-753 8108; www.qasrelbawity.com; half board s/d $55/66, ste s/d $99/132) The Qasr el Bawity opened at the end of 2005 and offers some of the best accommodation in Bahariyya. The hotel has been built with care for aesthetics and environmental concerns – no steel or concrete was used. The site, on the side of a hill, has good views over the oasis and desert. The swimming pool is filled with spring water.

SIWA OASIS
☎ 046

Alexander the Great never explained his motives for going to the lush oasis of Siwa, deep in the Western Desert, but nowadays it seems quite obvious why one would want to make the long journey by road: Siwa is simply one of the most picturesque and idyllic places in Egypt. If you are in search of somewhere peaceful, isolated and unique, then you need look no further. Against the awesome backdrop of eroded sandstone hills and a sea of sand dunes, the oasis of Siwa appears like the proverbial mirage. Its

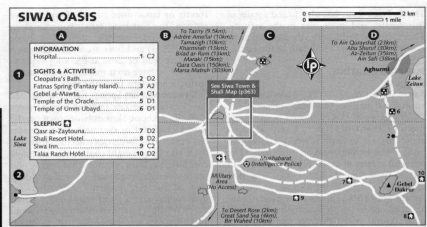

SIWA OASIS

0 - 2 km
0 - 1 mile

To Taziry (9.5km);
Adrére Amellal (10km);
Tamazigh (10km);
Kharmisah (13km);
Bilad ar-Rum (13km);
Maraki (15km);
Qara Oasis (150km);
Marsa Matruh (303km)

To Ain Qurayshat (23km);
Abu Shuruf (30km);
Az-Zeitun (35km);
Ain Safi (38km)

Aghurmi

Lake Zeitun

See Siwa Town & Shali Map (p363)

Lake Siwa

Mukhabarat
(Intelligence Police)

Military Area
(No Access)

To Desert Rose (2km);
Great Sand Sea (4km);
Bir Wahed (10km)

Gebel Dakrur

WESTERN DESERT

abundant gardens are irrigated by natural springs and support hundreds of thousands of olive and fruit trees and palms, which produce the sweetest dates in Egypt and give shade to the mud-brick villages. At the edge of the oasis are the sand dunes of the Great Grand Sea and beyond it the Sahara, connecting Siwa with deepest Africa.

Siwa is actually a small archipelago of oases, situated 305km southwest of Marsa Matruh and 550km west of Cairo, very close to the Libyan border. It sits in a depression 12m below sea level, 80km long and ranging from 9km to 28km in width. The oasis was on the ancient date caravan route that travelled via Qara, Qattara and Kerdassa (near Cairo) and ended at Memphis, but for centuries only caravan traders and the odd pilgrim on his way to the famed Oracle of Amun ventured here. Islam and Arabic eventually did reach this far into the desert, but Siwa's solitary location and strong traditions have ensured that the predominantly Berber-speaking inhabitants have preserved their particular character and many of their customs.

But Siwa is changing fast and many inhabitants are worried that the Egyptian state's attempts to 'develop' the oasis, together with the effects of settlers from the Nile Valley and of fast-growing tourism, will all but wipe out their culture and transform the landscape. So far they have been successful in ensuring that most tourism projects are small-scale and that the airport is not opened to commercial flights. So for now, like Alexander the Great, one still has to make that long journey overland across the desert.

History

Siwa has a long and ancient past, but little is known of its earliest inhabitants. Flints discovered in the oasis prove that it was inhabited in Palaeolithic and Neolithic times, but beyond that Siwa's early history remains shrouded in mystery.

The oldest monuments in the oasis, including the Temple of the Oracle, date from the 26th dynasty, when Egypt was invaded by Assyrians. Siwa's Oracle of Amun (p362) was already famous then, and Egyptologists suspect that it dates back to the earlier 21st dynasty, when the Amun priesthood and oracles became prominent throughout Egypt.

Such was the fame of Siwa's oracle that it threatened the Persians, who invaded Egypt in 525 BC and ended the 26th dynasty. One of the Western Desert's most persistent and romantic legends, which comes down from Herodotus, is the tale of Persian King Cambyses, who sent an army of 50,000 men to destroy the oracle and its priests after it predicted his tragic end. According to the legend, Cambyses's army was swallowed up in a sandstorm and never reached its destination. This only helped increase the prestige of the oracle and reinforce the political power of the Amun priesthood. For centuries, travellers have looked for remains of the lost army and their fabulous treasure and archaeologists are still looking today, but so far no trace has been found.

The oracle's power, and with it Siwa's fame, grew throughout the antique world. The young conqueror Alexander the Great led a small party on an eight-day journey across the desert in 331 BC. It is believed that the priests of Amun, the supreme god of the Egyptian pantheon and later associated with the Greek god Zeus, declared him to be a son of the god. On coins minted after this, Alexander was often portrayed with the ram's horns associated with Amun. Ptolemaic leaders, anxious to prove their credentials, also made the trek. The tombs at Gebel al-Mawta (p363) are testament to the prosperity of the oasis during this period.

The end of Roman rule, the collapse of the trade route and the gradual decline in the influence of oracles all contributed to Siwa's slide into obscurity. While Christianity spread through most of Egypt, there is no evidence that it ever reached Siwa and priests continued to worship Amun here until the 6th century AD. The Muslim conquerors, who crossed the desert in 708, were defeated several times by the Siwans walled in their fortress. There was a cost to this isolation: it is said that by 1203 the population had declined to just 40 men, who moved from Aghurmi to found the new fortress-town of Shali. They gradually built up wealth trading their date and olive crops along the Nile Valley, and with Libyan Fezzan and the Bedouin.

European travellers arrived at the end of the 18th century – WG Browne in 1792 and Frederick Hornemann in 1798 – but most were met with a hostile reception and several narrowly escaped with their lives. The Siwans thus gained a reputation for being fiercely independent and hostile to non-Muslim outsiders. Throughout the 19th century, the Egyptian government also had problems trying to gain the loyalty of the oasis. Siwa played a cameo role in WWII, when the British and Italian/German forces chased each other in and out of Siwa and Jaghbub, 120km west in Libya, until Rommel turned his attention elsewhere. By then the Siwans were fully incorporated into Egypt, but the oasis remained isolated until the asphalt road connected it to Marsa Matruh in the 1980s. As a result, Siwans still speak their own distinct Berber dialect and have a

RESPECTING LOCAL TRADITION

Siwans are very proud of their traditions, which are part of what makes the place so special. They are particularly sensitive where women are concerned. The least visitors can do to help preserve Siwa's culture is to respect local sensibilities and act accordingly. Modest dress is appreciated and women travellers in particular should make sure they cover their upper arms and their legs, and wear baggy T-shirts over bathing suits when taking a dip in any of the numerous springs. Do not, as the tourist office puts it, show 'displays of affection' in public.

Much attention has been paid to Siwa's tradition of male homosexuality and the oasis has been listed in several gay directories as a likely place to find some action. Siwa's reputation for homosexuality, or 'male marriage' as it has been called, is said to have developed during the time when families lived inside the Shali walls and young men slept out in the gardens to protect the crops. It is certainly frowned upon now and most Siwi men are not amused at being propositioned by passing foreigners.

strong local culture, quite distinct from the rest of Egypt. The oasis is now home to 25,000 Siwans and just over 1000 Egyptians.

Information

EMERGENCY
Police (Map p363; ☎ 460 1008; post office bldg, Siwa Town)

INTERNET ACCESS
El Negma Internet Centre (Map p363; ☎ 460 0761; 59 central market sq, Siwa Town; ☺ 9am-midnight; per hr E£10) This is the best and fastest place in town with two computer terminals.

Siwa Information Center and Bookshop (Map p363; ☎ 460 0489; behind the King Fuad Mosque, Siwa Town; ☺ 10am-10pm; per hr E£10)

Siwa Oasis Net (Map p363; ☎ 460 2049; central market sq, Siwa Town; ☺ 10am-2.30pm & 6-11pm)

MEDICAL SERVICES
Hospital (Map p360; ☎ 460 2019; Sadat St, Siwa Town) Only for emergencies.

Pharmacy Al-Ansar (Map p363; ☎ 460 1310; central market sq & Sharia Sadat, Siwa Town; ☺ 8am-2pm & 4pm-2am)

MONEY

Banque du Caire (Map p363; next to the police station, Siwa Town; 8.30am-2pm & 5-8pm) Has an ATM where you can theoretically take out a maximum of E£1000 a day, but it doesn't always work.

PERMITS

A permit is needed to venture off the beaten track from Siwa, but this can be arranged at the tourist office by your guide. Mahdi Hweiti at the Siwa tourist office will arrange permissions quite quickly (but not on Fridays), at the fixed rate of US$10 (payable in US dollars or euros) and an extra E£11 for the local Mukhabarat (Intelligence Police) office. The same rate applies for the permit to travel from Siwa to Bahariyya. You will need your passport.

POST & TELEPHONE

Main post office (Map p363; behind Arous Al-Waha Hotel, Siwa Town; 8am-2pm Sat-Thu)

Telephone centrale (Map p363; Siwa Town; 24hr) Located at the beginning of Matruh road.

TOURIST INFORMATION

Tourist office (Map p363; ☎ 460 1338; mahdi _hweiti@yahoo.com; Siwa Town; 9am-5pm, but often until 10pm Sat-Thu) The office is at the beginning of Marsa Matruh road. The very helpful and knowledgeable Mahdi Hweiti has plenty of information about travelling in the oases and can help to arrange trips to some of the surrounding villages or in the desert. Mahdi can also be reached on his mobile (☎ 010 546 1992). In the evening, you can watch an interesting documentary about Siwa in English, French or German.

Sights & Activities

Strolling around the palm gardens, sitting on a terrace and watching Siwans go about their business, chatting to fellow travellers and going on desert trips are just some of the delights of Siwa. No hurry, the mood is easy and relaxed; 'sit back and see what happens' seems to be the motto. A day on a bicycle will set the right pace and take you to most of the town's sights, which include a good ethnographic museum and the old town of Shali, as well as the ancient remains at Aghurmi and the Gebel al-Mawta. Day trips by jeep to the surrounding villages, the desert or to Bir Wahed, a cold freshwater lake and a hot spring in the dunes can easily be arranged. Or you can go further and arrange an overnight safari into the Great Sand Sea.

SIWA TOWN

Siwa is a pleasant little town centred around a market square, where the roads lead off into the palm groves. No longer as sleepy as it used to be, new hotels are sprouting like mushrooms and there is now even a bank and a few Internet cafés. The few sights are near the centre of the town. Around the corner from the local council offices is the small **House of Siwa Museum** (Map p363; adult/student E£10/5; 10am-noon Sat-Wed), which contains a modest display of traditional clothing, jewellery and crafts typical of the oasis. It was inspired by a Canadian diplomat who feared that Siwan culture and its mud-brick houses would disappear in a flood of concrete and modernity. You can also arrange to see the museum through the tourist office.

The centre of the town is dominated by the spectacular organic shapes of the remains of the 13th-century mud-brick **fortress of Shali** (Map p363). Built from a material known locally as kershef (large chunks of salt from the lake just outside town, mixed with rock and plastered in local clay), the labyrinthine buildings were originally four- or five-storeys high and housed hundreds of people. For centuries, few outsiders were admitted inside – and even fewer came back out again to tell the tale. But three days of rain in 1926 caused more damage than any invader had managed and, over the last decades, inhabitants moved to newer and more comfortable houses with running water and electricity. Now only a few buildings around the edges are occupied or used for storage, including the **mosque** (Map p363) with its old, chimney-shaped minaret.

With each rainfall more of these buildings disintegrate. However Siwans are beginning to recognise the uniqueness of their heritage, as well as the need to preserve it, in part encouraged by the environmentalist owner of the Shali Lodge and the Adrère Amellal Hotel (p367), who is restoring several rooms in Shali. These should be available for rent in 2006. Wandering around the old town is fascinating and provides a great vantage point to watch the sunset.

AGHURMI

Before Shali was founded in the 13th century, Siwa's main settlement was at Aghurmi, 4km east of the present town of Siwa. It was here that in 331 BC Alexan-

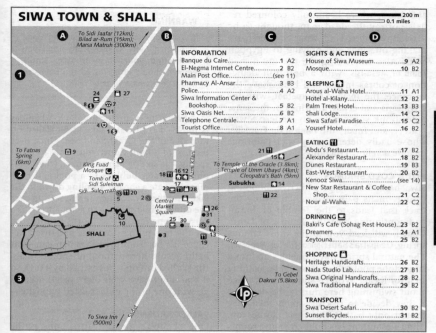

SIWA TOWN & SHALI

0 — 200 m
0 — 0.1 miles

To Sidi Jaafar (12km);
Bilad ar-Rum (15km);
Marsa Matruh (300km)

INFORMATION
Banque du Caire.............................1 A2
El-Negma Internet Centre............2 B2
Main Post Office.....................(see 11)
Pharmacy Al-Ansar........................3 B3
Police...4 A2
Siwa Information Center &
　Bookshop.....................................5 B2
Siwa Oasis Net...............................6 B2
Telephone Centrale.......................7 A1
Tourist Office.................................8 A1

SIGHTS & ACTIVITIES
House of Siwa Museum..................9 A2
Mosque...10 B2

SLEEPING
Arous al-Waha Hotel...................11 A1
Hotel al-Kilany............................12 B2
Palm Trees Hotel.........................13 B3
Shali Lodge..................................14 C2
Siwa Safari Paradise....................15 C2
Yousef Hotel................................16 B2

EATING
Abdu's Restaurant.......................17 B2
Alexander Restaurant..................18 B2
Dunes Restaurant........................19 B3
East-West Restaurant..................20 B2
Kenooz Siwa........................(see 14)
New Star Restaurant & Coffee
　Shop...21 C2
Nour al-Waha...............................22 C2

DRINKING
Bakri's Cafe (Sohag Rest House)..23 B2
Dreamers......................................24 A1
Zeytouna......................................25 B2

SHOPPING
Heritage Handicrafts...................26 B2
Nada Studio Lab..........................27 B1
Siwa Original Handicrafts............28 B2
Siwa Traditional Handicraft.........29 B2

TRANSPORT
Siwa Desert Safari........................30 B2
Sunset Bicycles............................31 B2

To Fatnas
Spring
(6km)

King Fuad
Mosque
Tomb of
Sidi Suleiman

Sidi Suleyman

Central
Market
Square

To Temple of the Oracle (3.8km);
Temple of Umm Ubayd (4km);
Cleopatra's Bath (5km)

Subukha

Torrar

To Gebel
Dakrur (5.8km)

SHALI

To Siwa Inn
(500m)

WESTERN DESERT

---

der the Great consulted the oracle (p360) at the 26th-dynasty **Temple of the Oracle** (Map p360; adult/student E£20/10; ☺ 9am-4pm). Built in the 6th century BC, probably on top of an earlier temple, it was dedicated to Amun (occasionally referred to as Zeus or Jupiter Ammon). One of the most revered oracles in the ancient Mediterranean, its power was such that kings sent armies to destroy it.

Today the Temple of the Oracle sits in the northwest corner of the ruins of Aghurmi village (look for the signs), approached through the village gate. Treasure hunters have clearly been at work here. The buttressed temple was poorly restored in the 1970s, but it remains an evocative site, steeped in history, surrounded by the ruins of Aghurmi and commanding stunning views across the oasis.

About 200m further along the track stands the remains of the almost totally ruined **Temple of Umm Ubayd** (Map p360), also dedicated to Amun. This was originally connected to the Temple of the Oracle by a causeway and was used during oracle rituals. Nineteenth-century travellers saw more

of it than we can: an Ottoman governor in need of building material blew up the temple in 1896 and only part of a wall covered with inscriptions now survives. However, earlier drawings have revealed that the original structure was built by Nectanebo II during the 30th dynasty.

GEBEL AL-MAWTA
A small hill at the northern end of town, **Gebel al-Mawta** (Map p360; adult/student E£20/10; ☺ 9am-4pm) – whose name means Mountain of the Dead – is honeycombed with rock tombs, most dating back to the 26th-dynasty, Ptolemaic and Roman times. Only 1km from the centre of town, the tombs were used by the Siwans as shelters when the Italians bombed the oasis during WWII. Many new tombs were discovered at this time but were not properly excavated. In his book *Siwa Oasis*, Ahmed Fakhry recalls British soldiers paying Siwan families a few piastres to cut away large chunks of tomb paintings to keep as souvenirs.

Despite the damage, some tomb paintings have survived. The best are in the **Tomb**

of Si Amun, where beautifully coloured reliefs portray the dead man, thought to be a wealthy Greek landowner or merchant, making offerings and praying to Egyptian gods. Also interesting are the unfinished **Tomb of Mesu-Isis**, with a beautiful depiction of cobras in red and blue above the entrance; the **Tomb of Niperpathot**, with inscriptions and crude drawings in the same reddish ink you can see on modern Siwan pottery; and finally the **Tomb of the Crocodile**, whose badly deteriorating wall paintings include a yellow crocodile.

HOT & COLD SPRINGS

Siwa has no shortage of active, bubbling springs in its palm groves. Following the track that leads to the Temple of Amun and continuing past the Temple of Umm Ubayd, will lead you to the most famous spring, **Cleopatra's Bath** (Spring of the Sun; Map p360). The natural spring water bubbles up into a large stone pool, which is a popular bathing spot for locals. Women should think twice about swimming here during the day, and if they decide to risk the stares then they should only bathe with their clothes on. Abdu Restaurant has built changing rooms and a sitting area beside the pool but the place is often locked. Ancient travellers, including Herodotus, believed that the bubbles were a result of the water changing temperature over the course of the day, cooler in the day and hotter at night.

There's a similar but slightly more secluded pool at **Fatnas Spring** (Map p360), the small island in the salty Birket Siwa (Lake Siwa) accessible across a narrow causeway. The pool, about 6km from Siwa town, is in an idyllic setting amid palm trees and lush greenery. Although it is a safer place for a swim than Cleopatra's Bath, women should not swim alone and, again, should leave their bikinis for the Red Sea beaches. There's a small café among the palms, which is good for sitting and puffing on a *sheesha* or drinking a cold beer, but a ministry of agriculture project to try and improve the lake's drainage has left the 'island' high and dry, so that the café now looks out over salty mudflats rather than water. To get there, go past the council building and take the road to the left at the first fork. Continue around the base of Shali. At the next intersection, a sign points the way.

> **WARNING**
>
> To oasis dwellers, a woman walking alone in palm gardens is provocative and you could find yourself in trouble. Single women should either avoid the palms or find a companion to stroll with.

A favourite excursion among local guides is the cold freshwater lake at **Bir Wahed** on the edge of the Great Sand Sea. Once over the top of a high dune, you come to a hot spring, the size of a large Jacuzzi, where sulphurous water bubbles in a pool and runs off to irrigate a garden. Cooling down in the lake, and then watching the sun setting over the dunes while soaking in a hot spring, is a surreal experience. The thorns in this rose are the mosquitoes that bite at sunset. Because it's far from town, women can wear bathing suits here without offending locals. Bir Wahed can only be reached by 4WD, so if you don't have your own, you'll need to go with one of the guides listed opposite.

PALM GARDENS

One of Siwa's greatest attractions is the oasis itself, which boasts more than 300,000 palm trees, 70,000 olive trees and a great many fruit orchards. The vegetation is sustained by more than 300 freshwater springs and streams, and the area attracts an amazing variety of bird life, including quail and falcons.

GEBEL DAKRUR

About 4km from town, this mountain is a popular place with rheumatism sufferers. From July to September people flock here to be plopped into a bath of very hot sand for 20 minutes at a time, and then extracted and given hot tea. Local doctors claim that five to seven days of this treatment can cure rheumatism and arthritis. The mountain also supplies the oasis with the reddish-brown pigment used to decorate Siwan pottery. Siwans believe that the mountain is haunted and claim that afrit or spirits can be heard singing in the gardens at night. The area now has several peaceful hotels.

OUTLYING VILLAGES

There are a few interesting villages to the northwest of the main town of Siwa.

Kharmisah and **Bilad ar-Rum** (City of the Romans) are 15km from town and can be reached by local bus. They are Berber villages, and the latter has about 100 tombs cut into the rock of the nearby hills.

About 2km west of here is **Maraqi**, where Lianna Souvaltzis, a Greek archaeologist, claimed in 1995 to have found the tomb of Alexander the Great. Her findings proved controversial and the Egyptian authorities revoked her permit and closed the site.

There are more springs to the east of Siwa. **Ain Qurayshat** is 27km out from the town and **Abu Shuruf**, a clean spring said by locals to have healing properties, is 7km further east from Ain Qurayshat at the next palm thicket. The clear water here is about 3m deep and spills into Lake Zeitun, another huge saltwater lake. Another 5km brings you to **Az-Zeitun**, an abandoned mudbrick village, beaten by the sand and wind, which sits alone on the sandy plain. Hundreds of Roman-era tombs have been discovered about 2km beyond Az-Zeitun and are currently under excavation, although little of interest has so far been found.

From Az-Zeitun, another 3km brings you to **Ain Safi**, the last human vestige before the overwhelming wall of desert dunes that stretch for hundreds of kilometres, all the way south to the Al-Kharga Oasis. Some 30 Bedouin families live at Ain Safi.

To visit the sights east of Siwa you'll need your own sturdy vehicle. Mahdi Hweiti from the tourist office, and almost every restaurant and hotel in town, organises trips.

Tours

Almost all restaurants and hotels in Siwa offer tours, ranging from half a day in the desert around Siwa Town to a full five- or six-day safari. The tourist office can be a great help in organising trips around the oasis. Abdallah Baghi at the Siwa Original Handicrafts shop, next door to Abdu's Restaurant, is also very helpful. All desert trips require permits, which cost US$10 plus E£10.50 and are usually obtained by your guide from the tourist office. Prices and itineraries vary, but one of the most popular trips takes you to the desert hot spring at Bir Wahed, on the edge of the Great Sand Sea. Here you can have a simple meal or tea, then move on to the nearby spring-fed lake, where, in the summer, you can take a dip. Usually you will

do a spot of dune driving, stop at fossil sites and see some fantastic desert vistas before returning to Siwa. This half-day trip costs about E£50 to E£70 per person.

Other popular half-day itineraries include a tour of the springs Ain Qurayshat, Abu Shuruf, Az-Zeitun and Ain Safi (E£40 per person); a tour of Siwa Town and its environs (Temple of the Oracle, Gebel al-Mawta, Cleopatra's Bath, Shali and Fatnas; E£30). Overnight trips vary in length according to destination but a popular one-night trip is to Qara Oasis (E£300 to E£500 per vehicle, depending on whether asphalt or desert track is taken). Most trips are done by 4WD, so ensure that the vehicle is roadworthy before you set out, and as with any desert trip, ensure you have enough water.

Camels were recently introduced to the oasis, only to do desert trips. Sherif Fahmy of the **Talaa Ranch** (Map p360; ☎ 010 588 6003; talaranchsiwa@hotmail.com; Gebel ad-Dakrour) can arrange camel tours to watch the sunset from the sand dunes or a longer desert safari. Abdul at **Shali Camel Safaris Ranch** (☎ 010 194 1653; Market Sq) also organises camel tours with all meals included. Costs are one day and one night E£150 per person, two days and one night E£250 per person and one day until sunset E£100 per person.

Festivals & Events

Gebel Dakrur is the scene of the annual **Siyaha festival**. For three days around the October full moon, thousands of Siwans gather to celebrate the date harvest, renewing friendships and settling any quarrels that might have broken out over the previous year. All Siwans, no matter what their financial or social standing, eat together at a huge feast after the noon prayer each day during the festival. The festival is intertwined with Sufism, and each evening, hundreds of men form a circle and join together in a *zikr*, a long session of dancing, swaying and singing repetitive songs in praise of God. Siwan women do not attend the festivities, although girls up to about the age of 12 are present until sunset. Each year hundreds of non-Siwans, Egyptians and foreigners, attend the festival.

Once a year, just after the corn harvest in the late summer, the small tomb shrine of Sidi Suleiman, behind the King Fuad mosque in the centre of Siwa Town, is the scene of a *moulid* (religious festival), known in Siwi as the **Moulid at-Tagmigra**. Banners announce the *moulid*, and *zikrs* are performed outside the tomb.

Occasionally on Thursday nights, after the evening prayer, local Sufis of the Arusiya order gather near the tomb for a *zikr* and they don't mind the odd foreigner watching.

Sleeping

Siwa's hotel selection is expanding fast and the choice of accommodation is better than in the other oases. Stiff competition among the cheaper options means that the standard of budget hotels is higher here, too. Hotels offering half board include breakfast and dinner in the price.

As with most places in Egypt, the police here are jittery about people camping close to town. If you really want to avoid other people, you're best off organising a trip to the desert with one of the many local operators (see p365).

SIWA TOWN

Shali Lodge (Map p363; ☎ 460 1299; info@eqi.com.eg; Sharia Subukha; s/d E£200/250; ▨) This tiny, beautiful mud-brick hotel, owned by environmentalist Mounir Neamatallah, nestles in a lush palm grove about 300m from the main square. The palms are a feature of the building wherever possible and the seven large, extremely comfortable rooms are arranged courtyard style around a small (but currently empty) stone-lined pool. Tasteful and quiet, this is how small hotels should be.

Palm Trees Hotel (Map p363; ☎ 460 1703; salahali2@yahoo.com; Sharia Torrar, just off the main square; s/d E£15/25, d with private bathroom E£35) This popular budget hotel has reasonably clean rooms with screened windows, fans and balconies. The bathrooms, however, are pretty dirty and mosquitoes are plentiful. The shady, tranquil garden with date-palm furniture is delightful, and the roof terrace has great views, but single women may not feel comfortable staying here. Breakfast costs E£5.

Arous al-Waha Hotel (Map p363; ☎ /fax 460 0027; opposite the tourist office, at the beginning of the Matruh road; s/d E£45/64) The 20-room Arous al-Waha, near the main mosque, is one of the oldest hotels in town. A former government rest house, the rooms are clean and spacious, if utilitarian, and the management is friendly and helpful.

Hotel al-Kilany (Map p363; ☎ 460 1052, 010 646 3721; zaitsafari@yahoo.com; central market sq; s/d E£50, with breakfast E£60/70) A modern hotel in a good location, the Kilany has 10 sparkling rooms with very clean bathrooms, hot and cold water, and a friendly management.

Yousef Hotel (Map p363; ☎ 460 0678; central market sq; dm E£8d with/without private bathroom E£24/16) A popular backpacker haunt, Yousef has four floors of rooms, some dorm-style. The top floor has doubles with attached bathrooms. All rooms have fans, the beds are reasonably comfortable and the showers hot. The marketplace location means that it can be noisy.

Siwa Safari Paradise (Map p363; ☎ 460 1590; www.siwaparadise.com; s/d bungalow half board US$35/49, with air-con US$39/55; ▨ ▨) A real three-star resort hotel that mainly attracts northern Europeans looking to get a suntan by the natural spring pool. The decoration is quite tacky but the rooms are cool and comfortable, so it is not a bad option if other recommended hotels are full.

Siwa Inn (Map p360; ☎ 460 2287; s/d E£110/165; ▨) A small hotel on the edge of the desert just outside of town, Siwa Inn has 10 simple but comfortable rooms, its own organic garden and mineral spring pool. It is not as aesthetically pleasing as Shali Lodge, but makes a good alternative.

Desert Rose (☎ 012 440 8164; s/d E£50/75; ▨) Overlooking the dunes that stretch out to the southeast of Siwa, this is a welcoming and cosy little hotel with simply decorated, spotless rooms without electricity. Breakfast is E£10. Guests can prepare their own meals in the kitchen or eat food prepared by the staff. Extremely good value, it has its own pool of natural spring water and a roof terrace for sunset watching. The silence is only disturbed by the barking of dogs.

SIDI JAAFAR

Taziry (☎ 010 644 5881, 010 112 2519; Taziry@hotmail.com; Gaary; s/d with breakfast E£250/350, 4-course dinner E£50; ▨) Taziry means moon in Siwi, and this lovely hotel was designed and built by its friendly owners, an artist and an engineer, both from Alexandria. The large rooms are decorated with local crafts and Bedouin rugs, and have their own bathroom. Tranquil and laid-back, with no electricity and a natural spring pool overlooking the lake, it is a great place to unwind and experience Siwa's magic.

THE AUTHOR'S CHOICE

Adrére Amellal (in Cairo ☎ 02-736 7879; info@eqi.com.eg; Sidi Jaafar, White Mountain; s/d incl all meals, drinks & desert excursions US$200/400; 🔊) Backed by the dramatic White Mountain (called Adrére Amellal in Siwi), a huge white limestone crag, this true desert retreat is set in its own oasis and has stunning views over the salt lake of Birket Siwa and the dunes of the Great Sand Sea beyond. It is a unique place, built in kershef (mixture of salt from the lake, rock and clay), using revived traditional building techniques, and simply decorated. You can enjoy the architecture and the landscape in blissful peace far from the modern world as mobile phones are banned outside the rooms and there is no electricity: the garden and common area are lit by torches, the rooms by candlelight. It offers the ultimate spartan chic, as gourmet dinners are eaten under the stars or in salt-encrusted chambers. The swimming pool is an ancient stone natural spring. The owner, environmentalist Mounir Naematalla, claims that the site is mystical and after spending time there you may come to agree with him. With simple but beautiful rooms and suites, innovative food that uses produce from its own organic garden and the feel-good factor of environmentally sound luxury, it has featured in countless travel and style magazines and is one of the best and most innovative places to stay in the country. If you don't have your own transport, the reservations staff in Cairo can help with travel arrangements.

Tamazigh (in Cairo ☎ 02-736 7879; info@eqi.com.eg; Sidi Jaafar, White Mountain; 🔊) A more intimate and more luxurious version of the Adrére Amellal and just around the corner from it, this gorgeous large villa in traditional kershef has only eight very spacious rooms. Food is served in several dining rooms and there is a large spring-fed swimming pool set in a lush garden. Some rooms are made entirely out of salt, including the beds and bedside tables. The price was not yet fixed at time of writing.

GEBEL AD-DAKROUR

Talaa Ranch Hotel (Map p360; ☎ 010 588 6003; talaranch@hotmail.com; d with breakfast E£380, 4-course dinner E£57) This newcomer offers a very different experience of Siwa with six stylish and comfortable rooms on the edge of the desert, all with bathroom. This place is as relaxing as things get, totally quiet, with the camels, the desert and the wind as the only distractions. Sherif can organise camel trips or safaris for guests, while his wonderful wife, Siham, prepares excellent Oriental food, served in a Bedouin tent.

Siwa Shali Resort (Map p360; ☎ 010 111 9730; www.siwashaliresort.com; s/d half board US$45/65; 🍽 🔊) A new resort built in traditional style with a 500m long spring-fed swimming pool running between the 100 rooms. Facilities include air-con, satellite TV, fridge and locally made palm frond furniture. The stylish main restaurant offers buffet-style meals, and a more intimate mud-brick restaurant

is under construction. A Bedouin tent offers coffee, tea and *sheesha*s. This is a far cry from Siwa Town but a relaxing albeit rather sterile environment all the same.

Qasr az-Zaytouna (Map p360; ☎/fax 460 0037, 012 107 4126; d E£100, s/d with private bathroom E£120/150) Simple but clean rooms with fans, set in a large and very quiet garden. The rooms on the 1st floor have great views over the garden. The hotel is run by a German/Siwan couple.

Eating

There are a handful of restaurants and cafés in Siwa, most of which cater exclusively to tourists. With the exception of the delicious restaurant at the Adrére Amellal, and the home-cooked food at places like Taziry and Talaa Ranch, which is for residents only, most restaurants in Siwa offer a fairly similar menu of simple dishes, and the service and quality often vary from day to day.

Kenooz Siwa (Map p363; ☎ 460 1299; Sharia Subukha; dishes E£8-35) This café/restaurant on the roof terrace of the Shali Lodge is a great place to hang out with a mint tea or a cold drink, although the quality of the food, once the best in town, seems to have deteriorated dramatically recently.

Nour al-Waha (Map p363; ☎ 460 0293; Sharia Subukha; dishes E£5-20) A popular hangout in a palm grove opposite Shali Lodge, Nour al-Waha has shady tables, plenty of tea and games on hand for those who just want to while away the day in the shade. The food is a mixture of Egyptian and Western and while it couldn't be called gourmet, it is generally fresh and good. At night *sheeshas* are available at E£7, and sometimes there is live music.

Abdu's Restaurant (Map p363; ☎ 460 1243; central market sq; dishes E£5-25; 🕒 8.30am-midnight) Abdu's, the longest-running restaurant in town, is across the road from Yousef Hotel. An ever-popular hub, it remains one of the best eating options in town, serving a large menu of breakfast, pasta, traditional dishes, vegetable stews, couscous and roasted chickens.

Dunes Restaurant (Map p363; ☎ 010 653 0372; Sharia Torrar; dishes E£8-25) With tables set under the palm trees and a large menu covering everything from herbal tea to couscous, Dunes is just another a place to hang out and relax. The usual traveller stalwarts (pancakes and smoothies) can be found here, as well as local specialities such as stuffed pigeon (by special order). *Sheeshas* are de rigueur and the owner can arrange special evenings with traditional Siwan music.

Alexander Restaurant (Map p363; off central market sq; dishes E£5-15) With a similar winning formula to Abdu's, Alexander serves the usual budget-restaurant fare, with pizzas, veggie stews, very good chicken and, innovatively for Siwa, curries. Service can be very slow, but what's the hurry? You're in Siwa!

East-West Restaurant (Map p363; dishes E£4-12) Another restaurant in the Abdu's/Alexander style, just off the main square; it's not as popular as the others, but serves pretty much the same quality of food.

New Star Restaurant & Coffee Shop (Map p363; ☎ 460 0293; Sharia Subukha; dishes E£5-20) Large restaurant set in a beautiful palm grove, almost opposite the Siwa Safari Paradise, serving the usual oasis staples. The small shop on the premises sells interesting traditional clothes and crafts.

Drinking

All of the restaurants listed under Eating also serve as cafés but there are several others around town that do not serve food. Most are no-name places where Siwi men gather to watch TV and chat, but no alcohol is served. The only places to get a beer or other local alcohol for residents is at the Adrére Amellal, at the cafeteria at Fatnas Spring (p364) and at the bar of the Trariyen

Tourist Village, 5km out of town on the Matruh road.

Zeytouna (Map p363; central market sq) Popular café on the main square, with a palm-beamed ceiling and a chilled atmosphere.

Bakri's Cafe (Map p363; Sohag Rest House, central market sq) A long-standing favourite, where *sheesha* and backgammon dominate.

Dreamers (Map p363; opposite the Arous al-Waha Hotel) Lively café open late where you can smoke a *sheesha* on an old-fashioned sofa while watching TV with locals, or drink a juice listening to reggae music.

Shopping

There has been an explosion of craft shops around Siwa town in recent years, all competing for the lucrative tourist trade and selling new versions, some better than others, of old Siwan baskets, jewellery, pottery and the blue shawls worn by the local women (see the boxed text, opposite). Most sell similar things but compare prices and goods at Heritage Handicrafts (Map p363), on Siwa Town's main square, and the no-name stand just off the main square on the road towards Cleopatra Hotel. Siwa Original Handicrafts (Map p363), next to Abdu's Restaurant, has set prices, which can make things easier. Owners Abdallah Baghi and his cousin Suleiman have also saved some old pieces in an effort to conserve at least part of Siwa's unique cultural heritage. They will allow you to look through them, but they're not for sale. Suleiman's brother Ali Abd Allah has the best handicrafts shop in Siwa, the **Siwa Traditional Handicraft** (Map p363; ☎ 460 1063, 010 304 1191), around the corner on the main market square. He sells better quality stuff, much cleaner than elsewhere, at fixed prices. His wife designs some clothes herself. Embroidered black Siwan scarfs go for E£250 to E£300.

Siwa is also known for its dates and olives, available in shops around the main market square. Usually someone will open a jar so you can try the olives to find the variety you like. Everyone has a favourite brand of dates; Jawhara are particularly good.

Camera film and batteries can be bought at Nada Studio Lab (Map p363), just past the telephone centrale on the main road out of Siwa Town. The lab can also print from digital cameras.

SIWAN CRAFTS

Siwa's rich culture is easily identified these days by the abundance of traditional crafts that are still made for local use as well as for tourists. Unfortunately, an estimated 98% of the older artefacts – among them jewellery, wooden chests and other family heirlooms – have become collectors' items and, over the years, have been sold to collectors from around the world. These pieces of Siwan heritage may be lost, but young Siwan craftsmen are slowly starting to make these pieces again.

Siwans love to adorn themselves and they are second only to the Nubians in their quest for the biggest and most ornate pieces of jewellery to be found in Egypt. Siwan women only wear the heavy silver jewellery on special occasions these days, but several interesting pieces are still made. New rings and bracelets with traditional designs can be bought at craft shops for E£80 to E£250.

Siwan wedding dresses are famous for their red, orange, green and black embroidery, which is often embellished with shells and beads. The black silk *asherah nazitaf* and the white cotton *ahserah namilal* dresses can both be found on the local market and can cost anywhere from E£250 to E£500. The scarves with this embroidery go for E£200 to E£300.

Baskets woven from date-palm fronds are still made here by women and girls. You can spot old baskets by their finer workmanship and the use of silk or leather instead of polyester and vinyl. The *tarkamt*, a woven plate that features a red leather centre, is traditionally used for serving sweets and sells for E£20 to E£60, depending on the size. The largest basket is the *tghara*, which is used for storing bread. You can buy one for E£150 to E£400. Smaller baskets include the *aqarush* and the red-and-green silk-tasselled *nedibash*, which start at E£20 and go up in price according to size.

Local clays are mixed with straw and coloured with pigment from Gebel Dakrur to make pottery water jugs, drinking cups and incense burners. The *maklay*, a round-bottomed cup, and the *adjra*, used for washing hands, are among the most popular buys, as are *timjamait*, or incense burners. The smaller ones can be bought for about E£10.

Getting There & Away

BUS

There's no bus station in Siwa. When you arrive, you'll be let off the bus in the central market square. To purchase tickets to Marsa Matruh or Alexandria you'll need to visit the West Delta Bus Company (WDBC) office at the southern end of town, near the Sports Centre. To get there walk down Sharia Sadat past the mosque and the Cleopatra Hotel. The road divides just past the mosque; take the right fork and you'll soon come to a residential block of apartments on the right-hand side of the street that's part of a housing estate. Look for the ground-floor window with a blue shutter – this is the ticket office. It's sensible to buy your ticket ahead of time, as buses are often full. You can board from here, or from the central market square.

There are three daily buses to Alexandria (E£27, eight hours), stopping at Marsa Matruh (E£12, four hours). These leave at 7am, 10am and 10pm. The 7am and 10am buses connect with buses to Cairo

at Marsa Matruh (1½ hour transit). There is an additional daily service to Marsa Matruh at 1pm.

Microbuses going to Marsa Matruh leave from the main square near the King Fuad Mosque. They are more frequent but not as comfortable as the WDBC bus. Tickets cost the same.

SERVICE TAXI

There is no service-taxi station, but those making the trip to Marsa Matruh (E£12) leave from the area in front of Abdu's Restaurant. The taxis (mostly microbuses) tend to leave in the early morning or after sunset, but ask around to confirm this.

A new road linking the oases of Siwa and Bahariyya is under construction and should be finished in 2006. The old road, which passes through some stunning desert landscapes, is asphalted, but is in very bad shape and a permit (see p362) is needed to drive along it. There are no buses or service taxis on this route, but some Siwan drivers are willing to make the 10-hour trip for about E£900 to E£1500 per car. If you do go, ensure that the vehicle is a roadworthy 4WD and that you have food and water.

TO/FROM LIBYA

Siwans visit their families in Libya and vice versa, but at the time of writing it is still illegal to cross into Libya and go on to the town of Jaghbub, about 120km away, unless you travel via Sallum (see p408). Although the border is only 50km away it is reportedly mined, so things are unlikely to change soon.

Getting Around

BICYCLE

Bicycles are one of the best ways to get around and can be rented from several sources, including most hotels, Sunset Bicycles on the main square, and a number of other shops dotted around the town centre. The going rate is about E£10 per day.

DONKEY CART

Donkey carts, or *careta*s, are a much used mode of transport for Siwans and can be a more amusing, if slower, way to get around than bicycles or cars. Some of the boys who drive the carts speak some English. Expect to pay about E£25 for half a day or E£5 for a short trip.

MOTORCYCLE

Imagine the peace of the quiet town being shattered by the revving of motorbikes or quad bikes in the desert. Enterprising locals are offering them for rent (E£250 per day), as does **Siwa Desert Safari** (Map p363; ☎ 012 418 0292; central market sq), but check with the tourist office before signing up – at the time of writing they still had no permits for them.

SERVICE TAXI

Pick-up trucks serve as communal taxis linking Siwa Town with the surrounding villages. To get to Bilad ar-Rum costs E£1 each way; closer destinations are 50pt. If you want to get to more remote sites, Mahdi Hweiti at the tourist office or any of the restaurants will be able to help. Prices depend on haggling skills, the duration of the trip and the distance to be covered.

DUNES FOR BEGINNERS

Formal classification of the types of sand dune was made in the 1970s, when scientists could examine photographs of dune fields taken on an early space mission. They identified five types of dune, four of which are found in Egypt.

Parallel Straight Dunes

Called *seif* or sword in Arabic because they resemble the blades of curved Arab swords, these dunes are formed by wind and are primarily found in the Great Sand Sea and the northern Western Desert. Usually on the move, they will even fall down an escarpment, reforming at its base.

Parallel Wavy (or Barchan) Dunes

These are crescent-shaped dunes, with a slip face on one side. They are as wide as they are long and are usually found in straight lines with flat corridors between them. Usually on the move, they can travel as far as 19m in one year. They are predominant in the Al-Kharga and Dakhla Oases and are also found in the Great Sand Sea.

Star Dunes

Created by wind blowing in different directions, these dunes are usually found alone. Instead of moving, they tend to build up within a circle. They are rare in Egypt.

Crescent (or Whaleback) Dunes

These are hill-like dunes formed when a series of smaller dunes collide and piggyback one another. Distinctive, with sides pointing in different directions, they can be seen in the area between the Al-Kharga and Dakhla Oases.

BEYOND SIWA
Qara Oasis

About 120km east of Siwa, near the Qattara Depression, is another oasis, Qara. The remote oasis is home to 317 Berbers who, like the Siwans, built their fortress-like town on top of a mountain. According to legend, the harsh environment and scarce resources in the area meant that whenever a child was born in Qara an older person would have to leave in order to keep the population at a sustainable level. Whether or not this is true, it is no longer practised, although the Qarans remain small in number and their life is harsh. Unlike in Siwa, the old fortress is still inhabited, but an increasing number of new concrete houses are being built down below. To get there, take the narrow asphalt road that branches off the Siwa–Marsa Matruh road at the rest house, 150km from Siwa. You can either rent a pick-up to take you there for about E£400 or talk to the many people in town offering desert safaris. For more information see p365.

Great Sand Sea

One of the world's largest dune fields, the Great Sand Sea straddles Egypt and Libya, stretching over 800km south to the Gilf Kebir. There are 18 sand seas around the world, four of them in North Africa. The Great Sand Sea begins south of the Mediterranean coast. A branch splits off in Libya, south of Siwa, forming the Calanscio Sand Sea; the rest carries on southeast within Egypt. Sitting on a rise in the desert floor and covering a colossal 72,000 sq km, it contains some of the largest recorded dunes in the world, including one that is 140km long. Crescent, *seif* (sword) and parallel wavy dunes are found here (see opposite), some of which are on the move while others remain in place. Undulating and beautiful, the dunes are treacherous and have challenged desert travellers for hundreds of years. The Persian king Cambyses is thought to have lost an army here, while the WWII British Long Range Desert Group spent months trying to find a way through the impenetrable sands to launch surprise attacks on the German army. Aerial surveys and expeditions have helped the charting of this vast expanse, but it remains one of the least-explored areas on earth.

The Great Sand Sea is not a place to go wandering on a whim, and you will need military permits as well as good preparation. Guides will take you to the edges of the Great Sand Sea from Siwa and most of the safari outfits listed in Long-Range Desert Safaris, p332, will take you on expeditions that skirt the area. Remember that you don't need to penetrate far into the desert in order to feel the isolation, beauty and enormous scale of this amazing landscape.

WESTERN DESERT

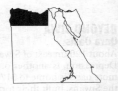

Alexandria & the Mediterranean Coast

For thousands of years, two things stood out along Egypt's north coast and were used as markers by Mediterranean sailors: the branch of the Nile that runs into the Mediterranean near the town of Rosetta, staining the blue sea brown, and the teeming city of Alexandria, once the shining gem of the Hellenistic world. Alexander's ancient capital has lived in Cairo's shadow almost continuously since the Arab invasion nearly 1400 years ago. But recently the city has had a good shake-up, courtesy of an enlightened and free-spending governor and the high-profile activities of a bunch of foreign archaeologists whose underwater discoveries have helped keep the city in the news.

East of Alexandria, the Nile Delta contains some of the world's most fertile farmland. But to the west, the desert runs right up to the coast. Traditionally this western strip of coast served as grazing land for nomadic herders and a lonely highway for traders. It was also a route favoured by invading armies, from the ancient Libyans to the Italians and Germans in WWII who were memorably turned back at the railway halt of El Alamein. The events of that key battle are commemorated at a museum and by the sombre ranked headstones and crosses of several large cemeteries. The area between Alexandria and the cemeteries is fast being developed into huge beach resorts, most of which are intended to appeal to Egyptian holidaymakers.

The attractions begin to thin beyond El Alamein – a handful of former Bedouin settlements, a few beach resorts, the odd dazzling patch of white sand and turquoise water – until 290km west of Alexandria, when the road reaches Marsa Matruh. The only town of any size west of Alexandria, Matruh slumbers for two-thirds of the year, but it stirs to life during the summer when it becomes a popular retreat for Egyptians. Most foreigners use it for little more than a brief stop or to change buses en route to the oasis of Siwa, four hours' drive to the southwest. Few travellers continue further west along the coast, where the road leads only to Salloum, the remote border post with Libya.

HIGHLIGHTS

- Eat the catch of the Mediterranean at an **open-air street restaurant** (p393) in Anfushi, or at the **Fish Market** (p393) overlooking the Eastern Harbour in Alexandria
- Kick-start the day with a black coffee at one of the city's wonderful **period cafés** (p394)
- Admire the beautiful Tanagra ladies at the **Graeco-Roman Museum** (p379)
- Visit the Ottoman houses of **Rosetta** (p399) and take a boat trip to the mouth of the Nile
- Visit the small but spectacular **Agiba Beach** (p406) near Marsa Matruh; outside the summer season it's the dictionary definition of idyllic

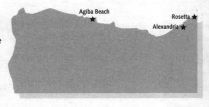

ALEXANDRIA

☎ 03 / pop 3.8 million

Alexandria (Al-Iskendariyya) is often said to be the greatest historical city with the least to show. It was founded by Alexander the Great, yet it bears no trace of the conquering hero. It is the site of one of the wonders of the ancient world, but you have to know where to look to find a surviving ancient monument. It was ruled by Cleopatra and was the rival of Rome, but has now become a provincial city, large on humanity but somehow short on prestige. But times they are changin'! Since the arrival of a dynamic new city governor in the late 1990s, a huge sum of money has been spent on the place: buildings have been spruced up, trees have been planted and public spaces, including the Corniche along the seafront, have been beautified. The high-profile opening of the Bibliotheca Alexandrina (p386) and a new Alexandria National Museum (p381), together with the restoration of the city's major museums and opera house, are some of the more successful efforts to put Alexandria back on the cultural map.

The last few years have seen something of a cultural renaissance as young Alexandrian writers and artists have found their voices. This has been matched by a renewed energy for cultural projects from the city's cultural centres and the opening of more avant-garde venues such as the Garage (p396). And at the same time Alexandrians, particularly the younger generation, seem to have given up their evening walk along the sea for a stroll through one of the vast, new suburban shopping malls.

In spite of these changes, Alexandria remains a city haunted by the nuances and shades of its past, with plenty to be enjoyed if you're prepared to invest some time. Come up here to kick back for a couple of days, to rub shoulders with a young, energetic crowd and to hang out in the atmospheric old watering holes, to eat fish and to lose yourself in nostalgic meanderings.

HISTORY

Alexandria's history is the bridging link between the pharaohs and Islam. The city gave rise to the last great Pharaonic dynasty (the Ptolemies), provided the entry into Egypt for the Romans and nurtured early Christianity before rapidly fading into near obscurity when Islam's invading armies passed it by to set up camp on a site along the Nile that later become Cairo.

The city began with the conquests of Alexander the Great. Arriving from Sinai and having had his right to rule Egypt confirmed by the priests of Memphis, the Macedonian general followed the Nile down to the Mediterranean. There, on the shores of the familiar sea, he chose a fishing village as the site for a new city that he hoped would become a bridge between the old Pharaonic world and the new world of the Greeks. The foundations were laid in 331 BC. Almost immediately Alexander departed for Siwa to consult the oracle, before marching for Persia. His conquering army went as far as India, where he died just two years later. His body was returned to Egypt for burial. When the priests at Memphis refused to bury him, the Greek pharaoh was buried in Alexandria, the city he had conceived as the cultural and political centre of his empire.

Alexander had left one of his generals, Ptolemy, to oversee the development of the new city and the viceroy continued this work after Alexander's death. Under Ptolemy's direction Alexandria was filled with architecture every bit as impressive as that of Rome or Athens. To create a sense of continuity between his rule and that of the Pharaonic dynasties, Ptolemy made Alexandria look at least superficially Egyptian by adorning the city with sphinxes, obelisks and statues scavenged from the old sites of Memphis and Heliopolis. The city developed into a major port and became an important halt on the trade routes between Europe and Asia. The ensuing economic wealth was matched by its intellectual standing. Its famed library is said to have contained up to 700,000 volumes, and stimulated some of the great advances of the age: this was where Herophilus discovered that the head, not the heart, is the seat of thought; Euclid developed geometry; Aristarchus discovered that the earth revolves around the sun; and Erastothenes calculated the earth's circumference. A grand tower, the Pharos, one of the Seven Wonders of the ancient world, was built on an island just offshore and acted as both a beacon to guide ships entering the booming harbour and, at a deeper level, as an ostentatious symbol of the city's greatness.

During the reign of its most famous regent, Cleopatra, Alexandria rivalled Rome in everything but military power – a situation that Rome found intolerable and was eventually forced to act upon. Under Roman control, Alexandria remained the capital of Egypt but during the 4th century AD civil war, famine and disease ravaged the city's populace and it never regained its former glory. Alexandria's decline was sealed when the conquering Muslim armies swept into Egypt in the 7th century. The Arab general Amr ibn al-As was still impressed by the city – he left a detailed description of its broad marble-lined streets, its many baths and theatres – but was instructed to ignore the Mediterranean city in favour of a new capital further south on the Nile.

Alexandria went into slow decline all through the Middle Ages and was even superseded in importance as a seaport by the nearby town of Rosetta. Over the centuries, its monuments were destroyed by earthquakes and their ruins quarried for building materials, so much so that one of the greatest cities of the classical world was reduced to little more than a fishing village (now Anfushi) on the peninsula between two harbours, with a population of less than 10,000.

The turning point in Alexandria's fortunes came with Napoleon's invasion of 1798; recognising the city's strategic importance, he initiated its revival. During the subsequent reign of the Egyptian reformist Mohammed Ali, a new town was built on the top of the old one, its role in Egypt's trade guaranteed by the digging of a canal that linked the city with the Nile. Alexandria once more became one of the Mediterranean's busiest ports and attracted a cosmopolitan mix of people, among them wealthy Turkish-Egyptian traders, Jews, Greeks, Italians and others from around the Mediterranean. Multicultural, sitting on the foundations of antiquity, perfectly placed on the overland route between Europe and the East, and growing wealthy from trade, Alexandria took on an almost mythical quality and served as the muse for a new string of poets, writers and intellectu-

ALEXANDRIA & THE MEDITERRANEAN COAST

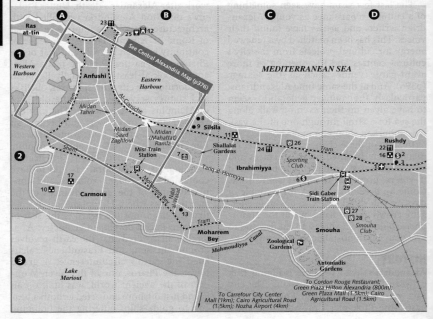

als. But the wave of anticolonial, pro-Arab sentiment that swept Gamal Abdel Nasser to power in 1952 also spelled the end for Alexandria's cosmopolitan communities. Those foreigners who didn't stream out of the country in the wake of King Farouk's yacht found themselves forced out a few years later, in the wake of the Suez crisis, when Nasser confiscated many foreign properties and nationalised many foreign-owned businesses.

Since that time the character of the city has changed completely. In the 1940s some 40% of the city's population were foreigners, while today most are native Egyptians. And where there were 300,000 residents in the 1940s, Alexandria is now home to nearly four million, a figure swelled by the steady drift of people from the country to the city.

ORIENTATION

Squeezed between the Mediterranean and Lake Maryout, nearly 20km long from east to west and only about 3km wide, Alexandria is a true waterfront city. Downtown,

the centre of the city arcs around the Eastern Harbour, almost closed by two spindly promontories. The city's main tram station, Mahattat Ramla (Ramla Station) on Midan Ramla, where most lines terminate, is considered the epicentre of the city. Two of downtown's main shopping streets, Sharia Saad Zaghloul and Sharia Safiyya Zaghloul, run off this square. Just west of the tram station is the larger and more formal square, Midan Saad Zaghloul, with a popular garden facing the seafront. Around these two *midans*, and in the streets to the south and west, are the central shopping area, the tourist office, airline offices, restaurants and most of the cheaper hotels.

To the west of this central area are the older quarters of the city, notably Anfushi, and further on the city's best beaches at the more upmarket resort town of Agami. Heading east, a succession of newer districts stretch right along the coast to the upmarket residential area of Rushdy and, further on, to Montazah, with its palace and gardens, which marks the eastern limits of the city.

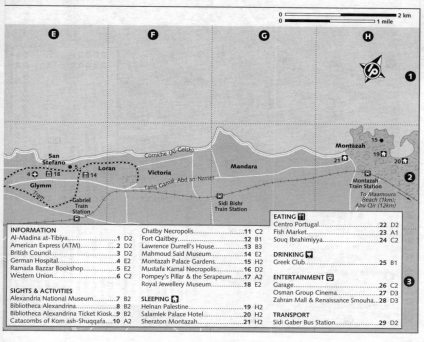

CENTRAL ALEXANDRIA

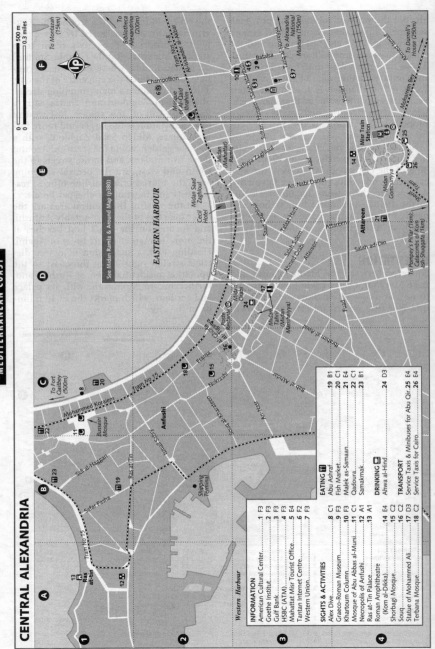

ALEXANDRIA & THE MEDITERRANEAN COAST

500 m
0.3 miles

EASTERN HARBOUR

See Midan Ramla & Around Map (p380)

Western Harbour

INFORMATION
American Cultural Center............1 F3
Goethe Institut...........................2 F3
Gulf Bank...................................3 F3
HSBC (ATM)...............................4 F3
Mahattat Misr Tourist Office........5 E4
Tantan Internet Centre...............6 F2
Western Union............................7 F3

SIGHTS & ACTIVITIES
Alex Dive....................................8 C1
Graeco-Roman Museum..............9 F3
Khartoum Column......................10 F3
Mosque of Abu Abbas al-Mursi...11 C1
Necropolis of Anfushi.................12 A1
Ras at-Tin Palace........................13 A1
Roman Amphitheatre
(Kom al-Dikka).......................14 E4
Shorbagi Mosque.......................15 C2
Souq...16 C2
Statue of Mohammed Ali............17 D3
Terbana Mosque........................18 C2

EATING 🍴
Abu Ashraf................................19 B1
Fish Market...............................20 C1
Malek as-Samaan.......................21 E4
Qadoura....................................22 C1
Samakmak..................................23 B1

DRINKING 🍷
Ahwa al-Hind.............................24 D3

TRANSPORT
Service Taxis & Minibuses for Abu Qir.25 E4
Service Taxis for Cairo...............26 E4

INFORMATION

Bookshops

Al-Ahram (Map p380; ☎ 487 4000; cnr Tariq al-Horreyya & Talaat Harb; 9am-4pm Sat-Thu, 9am-1.30pm Sun)
Dar al-Mustaqbal Bookshop (Map p380; ☎ 487 2452; 32 Sharia Safiyya Zaghloul; ⏰ 9am-4pm Sat-Thu, 9am-1pm Sun)
Ramada Bazaar Bookshop (Map pp374-5; ☎ 549 0935; Ramada Renaissance Hotel, 54 Sharia al-Geish, Sidi Bishr; ⏰ 9am-midnight)

Cultural Centres

Most of the city's cultural centres operate libraries and organise occasional films, lectures, exhibitions and performances – see the local press for notices of what's on. It's a good idea to take along your passport as you may have to show it before entering.
Alexandria Centre of Arts (Map p380; ☎ 495 6633; 1 Tariq al-Horreyya; ⏰ 10am-10pm Sat-Thu) This very active cultural centre, housed in a whitewashed villa, hosts contemporary arts exhibitions, poetry readings and free concerts in its theatre (8.30pm twice weekly, days vary). There is also an art studio, library and cinema (free films 6pm each Sunday) on the 1st floor. Programmes are available in English.
American Cultural Center (Map p376; ☎ 486 1009; www.usembassy.egnet.net; 3 Sharia al-Pharaana, Azarita; ⏰ 10am-4pm Sun-Thu)
British Council (Map pp374-5; ☎ 545 6512; www2.britishcouncil.org/egypt.htm; 11 Sharia Mahmoud Abu al-Ela, Kafr Abdu, Rushdy; ⏰ 10am-8pm Mon-Thu, 1-8pm Fri-Sun)

French Cultural Centre (Map p380; ☎ 391 8952; www.alexfrance.org.eg; 30 Sharia an-Nabi Daniel; ⏰ 9am-noon, 5-7.30pm Sun-Thu)
Goethe Institut (Map p376; ☎ 487 9870; www.goethe.de/alexandria; 10 Sharia al-Batalsa, Bab Sharqi; ⏰ 9am-2pm Sun, 9am-1pm Mon-Thu)

Internet Access

The Internet-café business is booming in Alex and there are now Internet cafés all over downtown and in the main shopping malls. Here are but a few.
Alex Gateway (☎ 522 1310; 450 Tariq al-Horreyya; per hr E£3; ⏰ 24hr)
Cyber Club (Map p380; ☎ 480 9308; cnr Sharia al-Bursa al-Qadima & Sharia Polanski; per hr E£2; ⏰ 9am-2am)
Global Net (Map p380; ☎ 495 8981; 29 Sharia an-Nabi Daniel; per hr E£10; ⏰ 11am-11pm Sat-Thu, 3-11pm Fri)
Mougy Internet Cafe (Map p380; ☎ 487 5675; 18 Sharia Kulliyet at-Tib; per hr E£3; ⏰ 8am-1am Sat-Thu, 3pm-1am Fri)
Tantan Internet Centre (Map p376; ☎ 485 7353; 18 Sharia Dr Ahmed Badawy; per hr E£2; ⏰ 10am-1am)
Zawiya Internet Cafe (Map p380; ☎ 484 8014; Sharia Dr Hassan Fadaly, off Sharia Safiyya Zaghloul; per hr E£4; ⏰ 11am-11pm)

Medical Services

HOSPITALS

Al-Madina at-Tibiya (Map pp374-5; ☎ 543 2150/7402; Sharia Ahmed Shawky, Rushdy) Well-equipped private hospital, accustomed to dealing with foreign patients.

ALEXANDRIA IN...

Two days

Start your day with breakfast at the **Trianon** (p395), then walk over to the **Graeco-Roman Museum** (p379), a great introduction to the city's unique mix of ancient Egyptian, Greek and Roman influences. From there, visit the **Alexandria National Museum** (p381). Have lunch at the lively **Coffee Roastery** (p394) and watch the young Alexandrians at play. In the afternoon visit **Kom al-Dikka** (p381) and admire its mosaics. Return to the Corniche and stroll along the sea, or take a taxi to **Fort Qaitbey** (p385). Watch the sunset over the glittering sea and have a cold beer at the **Greek Club** (p395), before heading for dinner at the **Fish Market** (p393) along the Corniche or one of the more popular street fish restaurants in **Anfushi** (p393).

On your second day, visit the **Bibliotheca Alexandrina** (p386), a suitably literary start to the **walking tour** (p388) in literary Alexandria. Go for a swim on one of the beaches then have dinner at the **Cap d'Or** (p395).

Four Days

Follow the two-day itinerary, then add a day trip to **Rosetta** (p399) and the mouth of the Nile and on the fourth day head to **El Alamein** (p402) and spend the afternoon on the beach in **Sidi Abdel Rahman** (p404).

German Hospital (Map pp374-5; ☎ 585 7681/2/3; 56 Sharia Abdel Salaam Aarafa, Glymm) Next to the Al-Obeedi Hospital. Well-equipped and staffed by highly qualified doctors. It also has a private day clinic with specialised doctors for nonemergency patients.

PHARMACIES

There's no shortage of pharmacies around the Midan Ramla area, with two or three well-stocked places at the northern end of Sharia Safiyya Zaghloul. There's usually someone available who speaks English.

Khalil Pharmacy (Map p380; ☎ 480 6710; Sharia Al Ghorfa at-Tigariya, off Midan Saad Zaghloul; ⏰ 9am-10pm Mon-Sat, 10am-10pm Sun) Well-stocked pharmacy.

Money

For changing cash or cashing travellers cheques, the simplest option is to use one of the many exchange bureaux on the side streets between Midan Ramla and the Corniche. There are also dozens of currency exchange offices along Sharia Talaat Harb.

ATMS

There are many ATMs in downtown Alexandria and in the large shopping malls, particularly on Sharia Salah Salem and Talaat Harb, the city's banking district. You can also find one at the Metropole Hotel on Midan Ramla, and at the following banks.

American Express (Map pp374-5; ☎ 541 0177; fax 545 7363; 34 Sharia al-Moaskar ar-Romani, Rushdy; ⏰ 9am-5pm) This office is also a travel agency. Note that it's quite some distance from the centre, out near Sidi Gaber train station, and a real drag to get to.

Banque du Caire Sharia Salah Salem (Map p380; 5 Sharia Salah Salem); Sharia Sisostris (Map p380; cnr Sharia Sisostris & Talaat Harb)

Gulf Bank (Map p380; 80 Sharia Sultan Hussein)

HSBC (Map p380; 47 Sharia Sultan Hussein)

MIBank (Map p380; 45 Sharia Safiyya Zaghloul)

Thomas Cook (Map p380; ☎ 484 7830; fax 483 4073; 15 Midan Saad Zaghloul; ⏰ 8am-5pm)

MONEY TRANSFER

If you need to have money wired to you, Western Union has two offices in town.

Western Union Tariq al-Horeyya (Map p376; ☎ 420 1148; 281 Tariq al-Horreyya); Tariq al-Horeyya (Map pp374-5; ☎ 492 0900; 73 Tariq al-Horreyya)

Post

The main post office (al-Busta) is just east of Midan Orabi, and several other branches are dotted around the city. The most convenient branches are on Midan Ramla and Sharia al-Ghorfa at-Tigariya.

To pick up poste restante, which is unreliable, go to the mail-sorting centre one block east of Midan Orabi and a block north of Midan Tahrir. It's a decrepit little stone building opposite a new 15-storey high-rise.

DHL (Map p380; 9 Sharia Salah Salem; ☎ 424 0001; ⏰ 9am-4.30pm Sat-Thu)

Express Mail Service (EMS; ⏰ 8.30am-3pm Sat-Thu) At the post offices mentioned.

Main post office (Map p380; ⏰ 8.30am-3pm Sat-Thu) Two blocks east of Midan Orabi.

Poste restante (Map p376; mail-sorting centre, Sharia Sahafa; ⏰ 6.30am-6pm Sat-Thu) Mail is usually held for three weeks.

Telephone

Menatel cardphones can be found all over the city, although the policy of placing them on street corners (or streets, for that matter) can make it hard to hear and be heard.

The main telephone centrale (Map p380) is on Midan Ramla, just by the newspaper sellers.

Tourist Information

Mahattat Misr tourist office (Map p376; ☎ 492 5985; Misr station, platform 1; ⏰ 8am-8pm)

Main tourist office (Map p380; ☎ 485 1556; Midan Saad Zaghloul; ⏰ 8.30am-6pm, 9am-4pm during Ramadan)

Tourist police (Map p380; ☎ 483 3378) Upstairs from the main tourist office.

Visa Extensions

The **passport office** (Map p380; ☎ 482 7873; 25 Sharia Talaat Harb; ⏰ 8.30am-2pm Sat-Thu, 9-11am Sat & Sun, 10am-2pm Fri) is the place for visa extensions. You need to provide one passport-size photo and a photocopy of the relevant pages of your passport (available from the machines out front), as well as the passport itself. Note that visa extension applications are only accepted until noon.

SIGHTS

The sights of Alexandria are spread right across the city. Midan Ramla, the heart of the 19th-century city, is the place to start from. Beginning here it's possible to walk to the Graeco-Roman Museum, the Alexandria National Museum, the Roman Amphitheatre at Kom al-Dikka and then on to Pompey's Pillar and the Catacombs of Kom ash-Shuqqafa all within the space of a day. You could happily spend a second day scooting along the seafront Corniche in a succession of taxis (or use the local trams) to see Fort Qaitbey, the Bibliotheca Alexandrina and then further east to the Royal Jewellery Museum, Mahmoud Said Museum and perhaps Montazah.

Ancient Alexandria

Ancient Alexandria is almost as intangible to us as Atlantis. It's a place of legendary status connected to half-remembered tales of Cleopatra, the Seven Wonders of the World and the great library. It borders on the mythological. The odd column or two, some catacombs and a few sculptures in the city's museums are the most accessible hints that it might once all have been real. But thanks to ongoing archaeological research, more and more evidence is being unearthed to give physical shape to the ancient city. Much remains inaccessible – the Alexandria of Cleopatra's time lies buried 6m down. But every now and then the city gives up more of its secrets, as happened in 1997 when a road-building crew stumbled across a honeycomb of Graeco-Roman tombs. In recent years underwater archaeology has also thrown up some dramatic finds (see p385).

But in spite of these finds, Alexandria remains a city for nostalgics, because only with a good dose of imagination can one come closer to understanding the city's glorious past. The modern city, built directly on top of the ancient city, often follows the ancient street pattern. So, for instance, the street now known as Tariq al-Horreyya was the ancient Canopic Way, extending from the city's Gate of the Sun in the east to the Gate of the Moon in the west. Two thousand years ago, Sharia an-Nabi Daniel was called the Street of the Soma. Standing at the intersection of Sharia an-Nabi Daniel and Tariq al-Horreyya, you find yourself at the crossroads at the heart of the ancient city. This, according to the 1st century AD geographer Strabo, was where Alexander's tomb once stood. Archaeologists have long speculated on the tomb's current whereabouts. Heinrich Schliemann, who came to Alexandria in 1888 after rediscovering the ruins of Troy, believed that the tomb lay beneath the modern and fairly unnoteworthy **Mosque of An-Nabi Daniel** (Map p380), on the east side of the street. Since then, some scholars, amateur archaeologists and many romantics have believed, hoped and dreamed that Schliemann was right. Trial excavations raised the temperature of this debate when they revealed that the mosque does indeed rest on the site of a 4th-century Roman temple, but religious authorities have placed a halt on any further digging. Since then, some respected archaeologists have turned their attention elsewhere by relocating the crossroads referred to by Strabo further to the east, arguing that by the time Strabo visited the city, the centre had moved east. The most likely location is now believed to be the intersection of Tariq al-Horreyya and a street known as R1, which runs through the middle of the Chatby necropolis (p387). Here, where there are extensive Greek graveyards, archaeologists have discovered an impressive alabaster antechamber, which would originally have led to a massive tumulus tomb. The belief among archaeologists at work in Alexandria today is that the founder's tomb lies in Chatby, a matter of metres from the last resting place of the city's greatest poet, Constantine Cavafy. Pending further discoveries, the best of Alexandria's treasures are on display at the city's Graeco-Roman Museum.

GRAECO-ROMAN MUSEUM

The dusty but wonderful **Graeco-Roman Museum** (Map p376; ☎ 486 5820; 5 Al-Mathaf ar-Romani; adult/student E£30/15; ☺ 9am-4pm) has one of the most extensive collections of Graeco-Roman art in the world, with over 40,000 objects. At the time of writing some parts of the museum were still undergoing restoration, with a few empty rooms and empty cases, but most of the work seems to have been completed. However, some rooms were still not numbered.

The room not to miss is the **Tanagra room**, where a large collection of fine realistic terracotta statuettes (tanagra) from the Hellenistic period are displayed. In another room the city's founder, Alexander, is represented by three different carved heads. These are overlooked by an impressive wall-hung mosaic from the Delta region, and dating from about 100 years after Alexander (3rd century BC), portraying Berenice, wife of Ptolemy III. Equally impressive in this room is the giant Apis bull in basalt

MIDAN RAMLA & AROUND

INFORMATION
Al-Ahram Bookshop.....................1 C6
Alexandria Centre of Arts...........2 C6
Arab Bank (ATM).........................3 B5
Banque du Caire..........................4 B6
Banque du Caire (ATM)..............5 B5
Banque Misr (ATM)....................6 B5
Banque Misr (ATM)....................7 B6
Cyber Club..................................8 B5
Dar al-Mustaqbal Bookshop.......9 D5
DHL...10 A5
EAB Bank (ATM)........................11 A5
EgyptAir.....................................12 D3
French Consulate.......................13 A4
French Cultural Centre..............14 B4
Global Net.................................15 C6
HSBC ATM.................................16 C5
Khalil Pharmacy.........................17 B4
Main Post Office........................18 A4
Main Tourist Office....................19 B4
Mena Tours...........................(see 33)
MIBank (ATM)...........................20 D5
Mougy Internet Café..................21 D4
Passport Office..........................22 B5
Telephone Centrale....................23 A5
Thomas Cook.............................24 D3

Tourist Police.......................(see 19)
Zawiya Internet Cafe.................25 C4

SIGHTS & ACTIVITIES
Attareen Antique Market...........26 B6
Banque Misr Building.................27 B5
Cavafy Museum..........................28 C5
Mosque of An-Nabi Daniel.........29 C6
Pastroudis..................................30 D6
Pharmacie Suisse.......................31 C3
Synagogue.................................32 C4

SLEEPING
Cecil Hotel................................33 B4
Hotel Acropole..........................34 B4
Hotel Crillon.............................35 B4
Hotel Union...............................36 B4
Hyde Park Hotel........................37 D3
Metropole Hotel........................38 C4
Nile Excelsior Hotel...................39 A4
Windsor Palace Hotel................40 B4

EATING
Al-Shark...................................41 A4
Beer Shop.................................42 B4
China House........................(see 33)

Elite..43 D5
Mohammed Ahmed...................44 C4

DRINKING
Athineos....................................45 C3
Bistrot.......................................46 C6
Brazilian Coffee Store................47 C4
Brazilian Coffee Store................48 B5
Cap d'Or...................................49 A5
Coffee Roastery.........................50 D5
Delices.......................................51 C4
Sofianopoulo Coffee Store.........52 A5
Spitfire......................................53 A4
Sultan Hussein...........................54 D5
Trianon.....................................55 C4

ENTERTAINMENT
Alexandria Opera House.............56 C5
Amir Cinema.............................57 D6
Cinema Metro............................58 D5
Royal Renaissance.....................59 C5

TRANSPORT
No 1 Minibus to Sidi Gaber........60 C4
West Delta
  Booking Office.........................61 B4

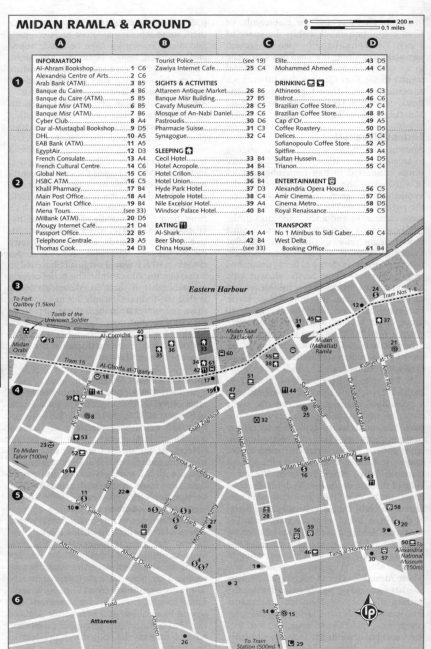

from the time of Hadrian, found at the Serapeum, and two carvings of the god Serapis – one in wood, the other in marble. Serapis is a wholly Alexandrian creation, a divinity part Egyptian (the husband of Isis) and part Greek, with echoes of Zeus and Poseidon. Ptolemy I promoted him as a way of bringing together his Egyptian and Greek subjects in shared worship. It worked, and the museum is full of images of the god (the Apis bull is Serapis in another guise).

Room 9 contains a mummified crocodile, which would have been carried in processions devoted to the god Sobek. Facing the mummy is a carved wooden door from a temple discovered in Al-Fayoum; the temple has now been rebuilt in the museum's garden.

Room 12 has more examples of the melding of Greek and Egyptian culture; in this case pink granite statues of Egypt's Greek-Ptolemaic kings are shown wearing Pharaonic dress and crowns, an attempt to legitimise them as the heirs of the pharaohs. The fine statue at the centre of the room is of the Roman emperor Marcus Aurelius, who spent the winter of AD 175–176 in Alexandria and whose wife had died on the crossing from Rome. It was found during the digging of the foundations for the Said Darwish theatre, just off Tariq al-Horreyya.

In **Room 18**, the fourth cabinet on the left contains just about the only historical depictions of the Pharos in Alexandria; these come in the shape of several terracotta lanterns dating back to the 3rd-century BC and shaped according to the three stages of the tower (see p386).

In the **coin room** (Room 24) there are several coins from Alexander's time, displaying a portrait of the Macedonian (panels 36 to 43) and several bearing profiles of Cleopatra VII (panel 88) – the Cleopatra of Shakespearian and Hollywood fame, though it has to be said that she looks more Virginia Woolf than Elizabeth Taylor.

For anyone with more than just a passing interest we recommend that you pick up the well-illustrated *A Short Guide to the Graeco-Roman Museum* by the French archaeologist Jean-Yves Empereur, who has done so much to reveal the ancient city. It should be available at the museum bookshop.

ALEXANDRIA NATIONAL MUSEUM

The most recent museum to open in town, the **Alexandria National Museum** (Map pp374-5; ☎ 483 5519; 110 Tariq al-Horreyya; adult/student E£30/15; ⏱ 9am-4pm) relates the city's individual history from antiquity until the modern period. Housed in a beautifully restored Italianate villa, the well-displayed and labelled items, which have been selected from other museums in Alex, are arranged chronologically over three floors.

The ground floor is dedicated to the Graeco-Roman period, where the highlights include a sphinx and other sculptures found during underwater excavations at Abu Qir, and an eclectic granite Pharaonic-style statue of the Roman emperor Caracalla. Also look out for the beautiful statue of a Ptolemaic queen with Egyptian looks and a Hellenistic body. The basement covers the Pharaonic period, with finds from all over Egypt, including an unusual New Kingdom pottery jar with the god Bes and the head of Queen Hatshepsut in painted limestone. The top floor displays artefacts from Islamic and modern periods, with some jewellery from the Royal Jewellery Museum (p387). Well-written panels on the walls provide useful insights into the life, art and beliefs of the Alexandrians through the centuries.

ROMAN AMPHITHEATRE (KOM AL-DIKKA)

The 13 white-marble terraces of the only **Roman Amphitheatre** (Map p376; ☎ 486 5106; Sharia Yousef, off Midan Gomhuriyya; adult/student E£15/10; ⏱ 9am-5pm) in Egypt were discovered when foundations were being laid for a new apartment building on a city-centre site known as Kom al-Dikka, or Mound of Rubble. Although the scale is unprepossessing, the terraces, which are arranged in a semicircle around the arena, remain excellently preserved. A significant area around the amphitheatre has been kept clear and excavation has now shifted to the north, where a team is working to expose the remains of Roman-era baths and a villa, where large floor mosaics have been uncovered and restored. A nine-panel mosaic masterpiece depicts several colourful birds. This 'villa of the birds' is open to the public but to see it you will need to buy another ticket (adult/student E£10/5) at the main ticket office.

ALEXANDRIA & THE MEDITERRANEAN COAST

POMPEY'S PILLAR & THE SERAPEUM

The massive 30m-high pink granite column, known as **Pompey's Pillar** (Map pp374-5; ☎ 484 5800; Carmous; adult/student E£10/5; ☺ 9am-4pm), looms over the debris of the glorious ancient settlement of Rhakotis, the original settlement from which Alexandria grew. For centuries the column has been one of the city's prime sights, a single shaft of tapered Aswan granite, 2.7m at its base and capped by a fine Corinthian capital. The column was given its name by travellers who remembered the murder of the Roman general Pompey by Cleopatra's brother. But a large inscription on the base (presumably once covered with rubble) announces that it was erected in AD 291 to support a statue of the emperor Diocletian.

The column rises out of the disappointing ruins of the **Serapeum**, which cover the acropolis. In ancient times the temple, not the column, would have caught the eye. When completed, it had 100 steps leading past the living quarters of the priests to the great temple of Serapis, the man-made god of Alexandria (see p381). Also here was the 'sister library', the second great library of Alexandria, which was said to have contained some 700,000 papyrus rolls, mostly copies of texts held in the Mouseion library. The difference between this and the Mouseion library is that these rolls could be consulted by anyone using the temple. As a result, Rhakotis was one of the most important intellectual and religious centres in the Mediterranean. But in AD 391, Christians launched a final assault on pagan intellectuals and destroyed the Serapeum and its library, leaving only the pillar standing. The site is now little more than a mound of rubble pocked by trenches and holes with a few sphinxes (originally from Heliopolis), a surviving Nilometer and the pillar, which is in fact the only ancient monument remaining whole and standing today in Alexandria.

To reach the pillar, walk west from Midan Gomhuriyya (the train station square), following the tram tracks along Sharia Sherif and turning left where they do. This will bring you into a busy market street. The entrance to the Serapeum is 300m ahead on the right. In all it's a walk of about 1.5km.

CATACOMBS OF KOM ASH-SHUQQAFA

About five minutes' walk south of Pompey's Pillar is **Kom ash-Shuqqafa** (Map p383; ☎ 484 5800; Carmous; adult/student E£20/10; ☺ 9am-5pm). Follow the wall around to the right after leaving the Serapeum and keep straight on. The entrance to the catacombs is on the left about 150m beyond the small square.

These catacombs are the largest known Roman burial site in Egypt and were discovered accidentally in 1900 when a donkey disappeared through the ground. They consist of three tiers of tombs and chambers cut out of the rock to a depth of about 35m. The bottom level, some 20m below street level, is flooded and inaccessible but the areas that can be visited are impressive and reveal the unique fusion of Pharaonic and Greek that became the city's hallmark.

Enter by descending the spiral staircase cut into a circular shaft; the bodies of the dead would have been lowered on ropes down the centre of the shaft. The staircase leads off to a **rotunda** with a central well piercing down into the gloom of the flooded lower level. When the catacombs were originally constructed in the 2nd century AD, probably as a family crypt, the rotunda would have led to the triclinium (to your left) and principal tomb chamber (straight ahead) only. But over the 300 years the tomb was in use, more chambers were hacked out until it had developed into a complex that could accommodate more than 300 corpses.

The **triclinium** is a banqueting hall where grieving relatives paid their last respects with a funeral feast. Mourners, who returned to feast after 40 days and again on each anniversary, reclined on the raised benches at the centre of the room around a low table. Tableware and wine jars were found when the chamber was excavated.

Back in the rotunda, head down the stairs to the **principal tomb**, the centrepiece of the catacombs, like a miniature funerary temple, where an antechamber with columns and pediment leads through to an inner sanctum. The typical Alexandrian-style decoration shows a weird synthesis of ancient Egyptian, Greek and Roman funerary iconography. For instance, the doorway to the inner chamber is flanked by figures representing Anubis, the Egyptian god of the dead, but dressed as a Roman legionary and with a serpent's tail representative of

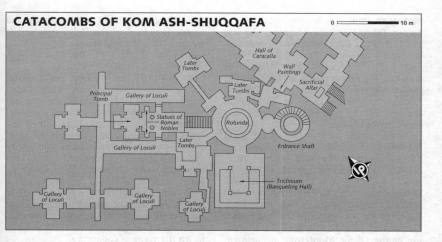

CATACOMBS OF KOM ASH-SHUQQAFA   0 |━━━| 10 m

ALEXANDRIA & THE
MEDITERRANEAN COAST

Agathos Daimon, a Greek divinity. No-one knows who was buried here, but some think it might be the noble Roman couple shown standing in the niches in the antechamber.

From the antechamber a couple of short passages lead to a large U-shaped chamber lined with loculi – the holes in which the bodies were placed. After the body (or bodies, as many of the loculi held more than one) had been placed inside, the small chamber was then sealed with a plaster slab.

Back up in the rotunda, four other passageways lead off to small clusters of tombs. One of these gives access to an entirely different complex, known as the **Tomb of Caracalla**. This had its own staircase access (long-since caved in) and has been joined to Kom ash-Shuqqafa, which it predates, by the efforts of tomb robbers who hacked a new passageway. Beside the hole in the wall (and repeated in adjoining niches), a double-register painting shows the mummification of Osiris and the kidnapping of Persephone by Hades, ancient Egyptian and Greek funerary myths that held out the hope of salvation through death.

For further information Jean-Yves Empereur's *A Short Guide to the Catacombs of Kom el Shoqafa* has some great photos and very readable text.

Central Alexandria

'Like Cannes with acne' was Michael Palin's verdict on Alexandria's looping seafront **Corniche** (in his book of the TV series *Around the World in 80 Days*). Right in the middle of the sweeping Corniche overlooking the Eastern Harbour is the legendary **Cecil Hotel** (Map p380) overlooking Midan Saad Zaghloul. Built in 1930, it's an Alexandrian institution and a memorial to the city's *belle époque,* when guests included Somerset Maugham, Noel Coward and Winston Churchill, and the British Secret Service operated out of a suite on the first floor. The hotel was eternalised in Lawrence Durrell's *Alexandria Quartet.*

The area around Midan Ramla is full of snapshots of the city's cosmopolitan past – take a look in the **Pharmacie Suisse** (Map p380) with its beautiful dark wood and glass cabinets painted with skull and crossbones and the warning '*substances toxique'.* Next door is **Athenios,** a once-grand tearoom formerly frequented by Greek girls and besuited Egyptian pashas.

Midan Ramla was roughly the site of the Caesareum, a large sanctuary and temple initiated by Cleopatra in honour of the deified Julius Caesar, and continued by Augustus, the first Roman ruler of Egypt. Two great obelisks brought up from Heliopolis marked the entrance to the sacred site. Long after the Caesareum disappeared the obelisks remained standing, until the 19th century when Mohammed Ali gave them away. They now grace London's Victoria Embankment and New York's Central Park.

ALEXANDRIA & THE MEDITERRANEAN COAST

MIDAN TAHRIR

Midan Tahrir (Liberation Square) was laid out in 1830 as the centrepiece of Mohammed Ali's new-look, Europeanised Alexandria. The impressive **statue** (Map p376) standing high on a plinth at the centre of the *midan* represents Mohammed Ali on horseback. A recent clean up accentuates the fine architecture of the square's surrounding buildings.

At the eastern end of the square stood the Bourse, Alexandria's Cotton Exchange, burned down in the food riots of 1977. Nearby in a peaceful garden stands the Anglican church of St Mark, with its banners and memorials to British residents and soldiers. Midan Orabi, which runs from Tahrir to the sea, was once the fine French Gardens. A passage into the grand building of the Okelle Monferrato department store on the corner of both squares leads to a wonderful Alexandrian café where men play dominoes and smoke water pipes.

At the southwestern end of the square the battered, grand architecture switches scale to something more intimate as you enter the city's **souq district** (Map p376). Two main streets head into the market: to the left is Sharia Nokrashi, and to the right, Sharia Fransa. Nokrashi, which runs for about a kilometre, is one long, heaving bustle of fruit, vegetables, fish and meat stalls, bakeries, cafés and sundry shops selling every imaginable household item. Fransa begins with cloth, clothes and all things connected with dressmaking. The tight weave of covered alleys running off to the west are collectively known as Zinqat as-Sittat, or 'the alley of the women'. Here you'll find buttons, braid, baubles, bangles, beads and much more, from junk jewellery to enormous padded bras. Beyond the haberdashery there are the gold and silver dealers, then herbalists and spice vendors.

ANFUSHI

The beautiful little **Terbana Mosque** (Map p376) stands at the junction of Sharia Fransa and Souq al-Kharateen. All this quarter, known as Gumruk, stands on land that was underwater in the Middle Ages. The late-17th-century builders managed to incorporate bits of ancient Alexandria in the mosque's structure, reusing two classical columns to support the minaret. The red-and-black painted brickwork on the façade is typical of the Delta style architecture. The **Shorbagi Mosque** (Map p376), nearby on Sharia Nokrashi, is also built with salvaged remnants of antiquity.

At this point, you're deep into Anfushi, the old Turkish part of town. While Midan Ramla and the Midan Tahrir area were developed along the lines of a European model in the 19th century, Anfushi remained untouched, an indigenous quarter standing in counterpoint to the new cosmopolitan city and considered a bit beyond the pale. This is where writer Lawrence Durrell's characters came in search of prostitutes and a bit of rough trade. Today it remains one of the poorest parts of the city, where a huge number of people live squeezed into old, decaying buildings, many of which seem to be on the verge of collapsing.

Continuing on Sharia Fransa north of Sharia Ras at-Tin, the street narrows before opening suddenly into a *midan* dominated by the large, white **Mosque of Abu Abbas al-Mursi** (Map p376). Built in 1943 on the site of an earlier mosque that covered the tomb of a 13th-century Muslim saint, this is a modern but impressive example of Islamic architecture. On feast days and during Ramadan, this is the place to come as thousands converge here for the night-time festivities.

From the mosque, Fort Qaitbey, seen across the water, is just over 1km along the curving Corniche. Alternatively, if you're keen on tombs, there's the **Necropolis of Anfushi** (Map p376; ☎ 486 5820; Sharia Ras at-Tin; adult/student E£12/6; ☼ 9am-4pm), five tombs dating back to the 2nd and 1st centuries BC, 1km to the west. The two principal tombs contain some faded wall decoration, some intended to imitate marble and alabaster. And although they're not as eloquent as the catacombs of Kom ash-Shuqqafa, the Anfushi tombs also speak of the way the Greeks of Alexandria assimilated Egyptian beliefs into their funerary practices. Just beyond the tombs is the 19th-century **Ras at-Tin Palace** (Map p376), the centre of power each summer during the first half of the 19th century, when Mohammed Ali was in residence. From here, King Farouk boarded his yacht and left Egypt after abdicating on 26 July 1956. It is now closed to the public.

Fort Qaitbey

The Eastern Harbour is dominated by the fairy-tale **Fort Qaitbey** (Map pp374-5; ☎ 486 5106; Eastern Harbour; adult/student E£20/10; ⌚ 9am-4pm winter, 9am-6pm summer). Built on a narrow peninsula by the Mamluk sultan Qaitbey in AD 1480, it sits on the remains of the legendary Pharos lighthouse (p386).

The lighthouse, which had been in use for some 17 centuries, was finally destroyed by an earthquake and was in ruins for over 100 years when Qaitbey ordered the fortification of the city's harbour. Naturally, material from the old Pharos was reused, and if you get close to the outer walls you can pick out some great pillars of red granite which in all likelihood came from the ancient lighthouse. Other parts of the ancient building are scattered around the nearby seabed.

The fort has recently been renovated and is now open to the public. It makes for a pleasant walk and the view back across the harbour is spectacular, with a foreground of colourful bobbing fishing boats and, in the distance, the sunlike disk of the new library. There's also a lively fish market nearby.

Count on anywhere between 30 and 45 minutes to walk along the Corniche to the fort from Midan Ramla. Otherwise take a yellow tram 15 from Midan Ramla for 25pt

NAUTICAL ARCHAEOLOGY

Alexandria has sunk 6m to 8m since antiquity, so most of what remains of the ancient city is now hidden beneath the modern city or the waters of the Mediterranean. On land, much has been destroyed as the city has grown; the only archaeological remains preserved since the 1960s are at Kom al-Dikka (p381). Rescue archaeologists like Jean-Yves Empereur, who has been working in the city for over 25 years, are allowed to excavate before a new building, tunnel or road project goes ahead, but they are usually only given a few weeks, or months at the most, and so they fight a constant battle with the developers and are always short of time.

But underwater the story is different. Underwater archaeology has media appeal and, therefore, has attracted greater interest. Each year, excavations reveal more finds from the Ptolemaic period. High-profile discoveries such as those that made the news in the late '90s are rare, but shipwrecks and parts of ancient Alexandria are increasingly being located and mapped. Eventually all the submerged towns along the Mediterranean coast will be mapped, but so far exploration is concentrated around the fortress of Qaitbey where the Pharos (see p386) is believed to have stood, the southeastern part of the Eastern Harbour where parts of the submerged Ptolemaic royal quarter were found, and Abu Qir (p398) where remains of the two sunken cities of Herakleion and Menouthis were found.

The Qaitbey dive has recorded hundreds of objects including sphinx bodies (their heads tugged off by the motion of the sea), columns and capitals, and fragments of obelisks. Divers have also discovered giant granite blocks, some of them broken as if by a fall from a great height – more circumstantial evidence for the likely end of the Pharos.

In the royal-quarter area a French-Egyptian diving team has discovered platforms, pavements and red granite columns that they speculate were part of a former palace ('Cleopatra's Palace', as it is being called), as well as remains of a 5th-century wooden pier and a remarkably complete shipwreck that has been carbon dated to between 90 BC and AD 130. In October 1998, in front of a crowd of international journalists and cameramen, archaeologists raised a beautiful black granite statue of a priest of Isis holding the Canopic emblem of Osiris, followed by a diorite sphinx adorned with the face of what's thought to be Ptolemy XII, father of Cleopatra.

The most recent excavations in Abu Qir have revealed L'Orient (Napoleon's flagship that sunk in 1798), the city of Menouthis with a harbour, houses, temples, statues and gold jewellery, and another city believed to be Herakleion or Thonis, a port that guarded the Canopic branch of the Nile.

At the moment some recovered treasures can be seen in the city's museum, and there are plans for the world's first underwater museum. But the best way of seeing what's in the water is to dive on the submerged harbour sites. Contact the small independent agency **Alex Dive** (Map p376; ☎ 483 2042, 010 666 6514; www.alexandria-dive.com). You'll find its office in the grounds of the Grand Café/Tikka Grill/Fish Market complex on the Corniche near Fort Qaitbey.

THE PHAROS

The Egyptian coast was a nightmare for ancient sailors, the flat featureless shoreline making it hard to steer away from hidden rocks and sand banks. To encourage more trade to his port city, Ptolemy I ordered a great tower to be built, one that could be seen by sailors long before they reached the coast. After 12 years of construction, the tower, or Pharos, was finally inaugurated in 283 BC. The structure was added to until it acquired such massive proportions and was of such a unique design that ancient scholars regarded it as one of the Seven Wonders of the World.

In its original form the Pharos was a simple marker, probably topped with a statue, as was common at the time. The tower became a lighthouse, so historians believe, in the 1st century AD, when the Romans added a beacon, probably in the form of an oil-fed flame that was reflected by sheets of polished bronze. Some excellent descriptions of the Pharos exist from as late as the 12th century. It had a square base, an octagonal central section and a round top (which is the form seen in early minarets, leading some historians to speculate that the Pharos was the original inspiration for this Islamic structure). Contemporary images of the Pharos still exist, most notably in a mosaic in St Mark's Basilica in Venice and in a church in eastern Libya, and in two terracotta representations in Alexandria's Graeco-Roman Museum.

In all, the Pharos withstood winds, floods and the occasional tidal wave for 17 centuries. However, in the year 1303 a violent earthquake rattled the entire eastern Mediterranean, from Egypt to Greece, and the Pharos was finally toppled. A century later the sultan Qaitbey quarried the ruins for the fortress that still stands on the site.

or flag down any of the microbuses barrelling along the Corniche. A taxi should cost E£4.

Eastern Suburbs

BIBLIOTHECA ALEXANDRINA

A mammoth piece of late-20th-century architecture, the Alexandrian library, known as the **Bibliotheca Alexandrina** (Map pp374-5; ☎ 483 9999; www.bibalex.org; Corniche al-Bahr, Chatby; adult/student E£10/5; ⏰ 11am-7pm Sun-Thu, 3-7pm Fri & Sat, closed Tue), was officially opened in 2002. Inspired by the great ancient library, the project was an attempt to put the city back on the world cultural map. The original was founded by the first Ptolemy in the late 3rd century BC, shortly after the city itself. Agents were sent across the Greek world to search out important texts for the new project, which eventually housed as many as three quarters of a million texts and became one of the greatest of all classical institutions, providing the environment for some of the major advances in ancient learning.

The impressive building housing the modern library was designed as a gigantic angled discus embedded in the ground – a second sun rising out of the Mediterranean. The ancient wealth of learning is lyrically evoked on the curved exterior walls, which are carved with giant letters, pictograms, hieroglyphs and symbols from every known alphabet. In keeping with its declared intention of be-

coming 'the world's window on Egypt and Egypt's window on the world', the new library has room for eight million books in its vast rotunda space. The complex has become one of Egypt's major cultural venues and a stage for many international performers.

The permanent **Impressions of Alexandria** exhibit, tracing the history of the city through drawings, maps and early photographs, is definitely worth a visit. Also included in the ticket price is a guided tour in several languages introducing visitors to the history of the ancient library and explaining the concept and significance of this modern one. **Culturama** (☎ 483 9999, ext 1574; admission free; ⏰ shows in French 12.30pm, in English 1.30pm Sun, Mon, Wed & Thu) is an interactive show on nine screens lasting 15 to 30 minutes, portraying Egypt's history. Adjacent rooms hold the **Manuscript Museum** (adult/student E£20/10), containing ancient manuscripts and antiquarian books (so badly lit that it's almost impossible to make out what you're looking at) and a temporary art exhibition space. In the library's basement is the **Antiquities Museum** (adult/student E£20/10), containing overspill from the Graeco-Roman Museum, including a fine Roman mosaic of a dog discovered when the foundations of the library were dug. There's also a bookshop in the foyer, a conference centre with exhibition halls and a **Planetarium** (☎ 483 9999, ext 1464; admission E£10-25 depending on show schedule; ☾ shows Wed-Mon), which is a separate, spherical structure on the outside plaza and looks like nothing so much as the Death Star from *Star Wars*.

Ticketing is unnecessarily confusing. The day ticket for the library itself is bought from a **kiosk** (Map pp374–5) on Sharia Port Said, a few minutes' walk up the street near the Hassan Rasen tram stop. This is also the place for tickets to the manuscript collection and for checking in *all* bags. Tickets for the Antiquities Museum are bought from a different kiosk, which is across the piazza from the library entrance. Tickets for the Planetarium are bought at the door, where show times are posted.

The Bibiliotheca also marks the starting point for a leisurely stroll through the literary city of the early 20th century: see p388.

NECROPOLI
The **Chatby necropolis** (Map pp374-5; Sharia Port Said, Chatby; adult/student E£10/5; ☾ 9am-4pm) is considered to be the oldest necropolis in Alexandria. Discovered in 1904, the burials here date from the 4th century BC, soon after the city's founding, and belong to the first generations of Alexandrians. Appropriately, if current archaeological thinking is correct, Alexander the Great may also have been interred here. Further east, opposite American Express is the **Mustafa Kamal necropolis** (Map pp374-5; Sharia al-Moaskar ar-Romani, Rushdy; adult/student E£12/6; ☾ 9am-4pm). Two of the four tombs are in excellent condition, and interesting for the Doric columns at their centre.

Bus 218 from Midan Ramla will drop you near the Chatby necropolis. To get to the Mustafa Kamal necropolis, take tram 1 or 2 to the Mustafa Kamal as-Sughayyer stop and walk east a couple of blocks to Sharia Al-Moaskar ar-Romani. Turn left here (towards the sea) and walk a couple more blocks. The necropolis is on the left.

ROYAL JEWELLERY MUSEUM
It is hard, in a country with such a long line of monarchs, to make a name for yourself, but Farouk, the last king of Egypt, succeeded. Renowned for extravagance, excess and a love of gambling, he once lost US$150,000 in a single sitting at the gaming tables. This at a time when the majority of his subjects struggled in poverty. He appears to have

been a womaniser too, and society hostesses reputedly hid their daughters when the king appeared at their parties. The 1952 Revolution would no doubt have happened without him, but his decadence only hastened the demise of the house of Mohammed Ali. The **Royal Jewellery Museum** (Map pp374-5; ☎ 582 8348; 27 Sharia Ahmed Yehia Pasha, Glymm; adult/student E£35/20; ☾ 9am-4pm) is a testament to royal excess. It houses a glitzy collection of personal and family heirlooms. Aside from the standard (medals, jewels, etc), exhibits include diamond-encrusted garden tools, jewelled watches with hand-painted miniature portraits and a golden chess set. The collection is housed in a lovely villa formerly belonging to the family of Farida, Farouk's first queen. It retains some wonderfully eclectic décor: one corridor is lined with a series of floor-to-ceiling painted-glass windows depicting a bright parade of waltzing courtesans, while the ceilings reach the height of kitsch with pink cherubs on cotton-wool clouds.

To get to the museum take tram 2 from Midan Ramla and get off at the Qasr as-Safa stop, beside the Faculty of Fine Arts, then look for the big white villa surrounded by a high wall. The museum was closed for renovation at our last visit, but was due to reopen in late 2005. Check with the tourist office that it has reopened before trekking out here.

MAHMOUD SAID MUSEUM
He might be little known outside his home country, but Mahmoud Said (1897–1964) was one of Egypt's finest 20th century artists. He was a judge by profession and painted only as a sideline, but he became a key member of an influential group of sophisticates who devoted themselves through the 1920s and '30s to forging an Egyptian artistic identity. Said's work has echoes of the past (some of his portraits bear resemblance to the Graeco-Roman Fayoum Portraits, see p191) but he also blended European and American influences and experimented with techniques such as cubism and social realism. The **Mahmoud Said Museum** (Map pp374-5; ☎ 582 1688; 6 Sharia Mohammed Said Pasha, Gianaclis; adult/student E£10/5; ☾ 9am-1.30pm, 5-9pm Sat-Thu) presents about 40 of his works housed in the beautiful Italianate villa in which he once lived. He seems to have been most successful with his nudes, honey-toned, earthy women depicted against richly coloured backgrounds.

LAWRENCE DURRELL'S HOUSE

Committed fans of the *Alexandria Quartet* might like to search out the Villa Ambron in Moharrem Bey where Durrell lived during the last two years of the war and wrote (not the *Quartet*, which came later, but poetry and *Prospero's Cell*). He wrote in the top room of an octagonal tower in the garden. 'I sit in my tower and listen to ideas moving around inside, aqueous and dim like fishes,' he wrote in a letter to his friend Diana Gould in 1944. Gilda Ambron, whose name appeared in the *Quartet's* 'Balthazar', painted with her mother in a studio in the garden, which she also shared with their neighbour Clea Badaro, who provided inspiration for the character of Clea in the *Quartet*. Sadly the **house** (Map pp374–5) has deteriorated badly over the past couple of decades. But don't mistake this for neglect. It's now owned by a development company. The law forbids them from tearing it down, but they have built ugly apartment buildings in the garden and removed most of the villa's interior features which will hasten its collapse. The villa may have disappeared by the time you read this, but if you are in for a pilgrimage anyway, from Misr train station walk southeast down Sharia Moharrem Bey. At the little square at the end, turn left on Sharia Nabil al-Wakad. Sharia Maamoun is a couple of hundred metres along on the right. The Villa Ambron was No 19.

Also included in the collection are works by two of his contemporaries, Saif and Adham Wanli. There is also a small Museum of Modern Art in the basement. To get here, take tram 2 from Midan Ramla to the San Stefano stop – a ride of about 20 minutes – then cross the tracks and go up the steps to the raised road. Go right, and Sharia Mohammed Said Pasha is a short distance along on the left.

MONTAZAH PALACE GARDENS

Khedive Abbas Hilmy (1892–1914) built Montazah as his summer palace, a refuge when Cairo became too hot. Sited on a rocky bluff overlooking the sea, it's designed in a pseudo-Moorish style, which has been given a definite Florentine twist with the addition of a tower modelled on one at the Palazzo Vecchio. Now used by Egypt's president, the palace is off limits to the public but the surrounding lush groves and **gardens** (Map pp374-5; admission E£5), planted with pine and palms, are accessible and they are a favourite place for courting or picnicking locals. There's also an attractive sandy cove with a semiprivate beach (E£10 to use it, although it's not particularly clean), and an eccentric Victorian-style bridge running out to a small island. If you ignore the fast-food restaurants, it makes a pleasant escape from the city centre's traffic and concrete. A second royal residence, known as the Salamlek and built in an Austrian style, has now been converted into a luxury hotel (see p392).

The simplest way to get there is to stand on the Corniche or on Tariq al-Horreyya and flag down a microbus; when it slows, shout 'Montazah' and if it's going that way (and most of them are) it'll stop and you can jump in. Most of these services originate at Midan al-Gomhuriyya, the square in front of the train station, so you could also catch one from there.

Beaches

There are a plenty of public and paying beaches along Alexandria's waterfront, but the ones between the Eastern Harbour and Montazah are often crowded and very grubby. **Mamoura**, about 1km east of Montazah, is slightly better – it even has a few small waves rolling in. The local authorities are trying to keep this beach suburb exclusive by charging everyone who enters the Mamoura area a fee of E£5, payable at the toll booth as you drive in off Sharia Abu Qir; there's then a further fee of E£10 to get onto the sand. Women should note that even here modesty still prevails and we recommend covering up when swimming – wear a baggy T-shirt and shorts over your swimsuit. To get here jump in an Abu Qir–bound microbus at Midan al-Gomhuriyya and make sure that the driver knows you want Mamoura.

WALKING TOUR

Many a traveller arrives at Misr train station with a copy of Lawrence Durrell's *Alexandria Quartet* in hand for the simple reason that Alexandria is better known for its literature and writers than for any stone-built monument or tourist site. So it seems appropriate to start walking at the **Bibliotheca Alexandrina** (**1**; p386) and to stroll around the downtown Alexandria evoked by Durrell, EM Forster and the Alexandrian-Greek poet Constantine Cavafy.

After visiting the library stroll west along the Corniche towards Midan Ramla. Durrell, Forster and Cavafy were all somehow haunted by the city. Born of Greek parents, Cavafy (1863–1933) lived all but a few of his 70 years in Alexandria. In some poems he resurrects events and figures from the Ptolemaic era and classical Greece, in others he captures fragments of the city through its routines or chance encounters. He was born into one of the city's wealthiest families, but a reversal of fortune forced him to earn money and he spent most of his working life

WALK FACTS

Start Bibliotheca Alexandrina
Finish Pastroudis
Distance Just over 2km
Duration About two hours

as a clerk for the Ministry of Public Works, in an office above the **Trianon** (**2**; p395) at the western end of Midan Ramla. The place still possesses a wonderfully grand Art Deco dining room with fabulous murals (it's currently unused and you need to ask to see it) but the tearoom is as good a place as any for a morning coffee with a shot of period charm. When Durrell was posted to Alex in October 1942, he took a room at the **Cecil Hotel** (**3**; p391) on Midan Saad Zaghloul, still an icon, but now much altered and missing most of its early-20th-century elegance.

A short walk south, passing the Brazilian Coffee Store, crossing Sharia Saad Zaghloul and turning into Sharia an-Nabi Daniel, you'll find Alexandria's chief **synagogue** (**4**). It was built over a century ago to serve a thriving, wealthy, cosmopolitan Jewish community of about 15,000. Since the wars with Israel and the 1956 Suez crisis, that community has dwindled so that now when the synagogue opens each Shabbat, they rarely have the necessary 10 men to hold a service. But the fabulous Italian-built structure with its pink marble pillars is a reminder of the

ALEXANDRIA & THE
MEDITERRANEAN COAST

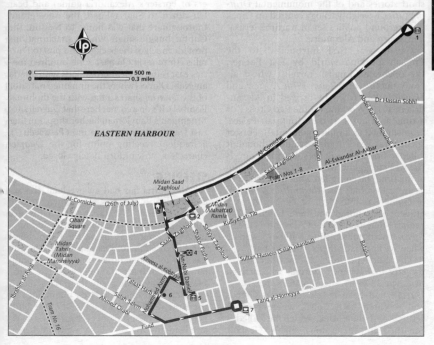

community's former wealth. Casual visitors are not usually admitted.

Just south of the synagogue, turn left off Sharia an-Nabi Daniel, on the side street leading to the former rue Lepsius (now Sharia Sharm ash-Sheikh), where for the last 25 years of his life, Cavafy lived in a 2nd-floor apartment above a ground-floor brothel. With a Greek church (St Saba Church) around the corner and a hospital opposite, Cavafy thought this the ideal place to live; somewhere that could cater for the flesh, provide forgiveness for sins and a place in which to die. The flat is now preserved as the **Cavafy Museum** (5; ☎ 486 1598; 4 Sharia Sharm ash-Sheikh; admission E£8; ☺ 10am-4pm Tue-Sun) with two of the six rooms arranged as Cavafy kept them. When Durrell returned for the BBC in 1978, he admitted he found it 'rather sacrilegious to sit at the actual desk of the old poet'. Editions of the poet's publications and photocopies of his manuscripts, notebooks and correspondence have been spread out on tables in other rooms. There's also a small exhibit devoted to fellow Alexandrian-Greek writer Stratis Tsirkas, author of poems and short stories and of the monumental *Drifting Cities*, a weighty trilogy centred on Greek underground politics set in wartime Jerusalem, Cairo and Alexandria.

Cavafy was first introduced to the English-speaking world by EM Forster, the celebrated English novelist who'd already published *A Room With A View* and *Howards End* when he arrived in Alexandria in 1916. Working for the Red Cross (for a time as a nurse at the Montazah Palace, requisitioned as a military hospital), Forster spent three years in the city and although it failed to find a place in his subsequent novels (he was struggling with *A Passage To India* at the time) he compiled what he referred to as an 'anti-guide'. His *Alexandria: A History & Guide* was intended, he explained, as a guidebook to things not there, based on the premise that 'the sights of Alexandria are in themselves not interesting, but they fascinate when we approach them from the past'.

The guide provided an introduction to the city to Lawrence Durrell, who arrived in Egypt 22 years after Forster's departure. Durrell had been evacuated from Greece and resented both Cairo, where he first settled, and then Alex, which he called a 'smashed up broken down shabby Neapol-

itan town'. But as visitors discover today, first impressions are misleading and between 1941 and 1945 Durrell found great distraction in the slightly unreal air of decadence and promiscuity engendered by the uncertainties and transience stemming from the ongoing desert war. He also found inspiration. On arrival he wrote that 'if one could write a single line of anything that had a human smell to it here, one would be a genius'. After his departure, he did just that.

From the Cavafy Museum head west along Sharia Kineesa al-Kobtiyya, taking the first left into Sharia Mohammed Azmy; at the top of this street on the left is the wonderful **Banque Misr Building (6)**, the former Banco di Roma. It's a working bank so you can stick your nose in and take a look at the church-like interior with its high-backed benches, Gothic arches and stained glass. It's absolutely beautiful. Just around the corner, at 2 Rue Tousoum Pasha (formerly No 1), is the building where in 1942 Lawrence Durrell worked at the British Information Office.

Continue south to the junction with Salah Salem (the address of the original publishers of Forster's Alexandria guide) and bear left down to Sharia Fuad, the once-grand thoroughfare that was home to Nessim, the Coptic businessman whose machinations provide much of the background plot to Durrell's *Alexandria Quartet*. One hundred metres east is the ancient crossroads with Sharia an-Nabi Daniel (where the unnamed narrator of the *Quartet* shares a flat with the diplomat Pombal). It's on a corner here that Durrell sites Mnemjian's Babylonian barber shop. Further east was the tearoom/restaurant **Pastroudis (7)**, a frequent meeting point for the *Quartet* characters, now unfortunately closed.

SLEEPING

As Alexandria has had an overhaul, the accommodation scene is also slowly getting better. Several five-star hotel chains are building new hotels in the city, including a luxurious Four Seasons on the Corniche at San Stefano, due to open late 2006. The city has few midrange hotels, and options jump straight from budget to high end. The cheapies are really quite seedy these days, and if you don't like the standards maintained at the Hotel Union, by far the best of the budget options, then the only recourse is a massive leap into the US$100-a-night bracket.

The summer months of June to September are the high season in Alexandria, when half of Cairo seems to decamp here to escape the heat in the capital. They mainly occupy the masses of holiday apartments that line the Corniche in the eastern suburbs, but at the peak of the season, in August, you may have difficulty finding a hotel room even at some of the budget places.

Budget

Quite a few of the budget hotels front at least partly onto the Corniche, so don't settle for a room that doesn't have a sea view – one of the pleasures about staying in Alex is pushing open the shutters in the morning to get a face full of the Eastern Harbour and a blast of air off the Mediterranean.

Hotel Union (Map p380; ☎ 480 7312; 5th fl, 164 Sharia 26th of July; s/d E£57/87, with private bathroom E£63/93) The Union is by far the best budget option in town; breakfast is served in a simple but nice room overlooking the Mediterranean. The smallish rooms are ultraclean with sparkling tiled bathrooms, some have air-con and some have a balcony overlooking the bay. The staff are friendly and helpful. Reservations are essential.

Hotel Crillon (Map p380; ☎ 480 0330; 3rd fl, 5 Sharia Adib Ishaq; s/d E£60/90) Two blocks west from the Cecil, the Crillon is not a bad second choice if the Union is full. The staff are attentive, rooms are clean and bed sheets are changed every day. Some rooms have polished wooden floors and French windows that open onto balconies with that great harbour view. We particularly love the pre-Revolutionary reception/lounge area. Note that you can pay for either a room with a bathroom or a room with a sea view; you can't get both, and the price is the same for either option.

Hotel Acropole (Map p380; ☎ 480 5980; 1 Sharia Gamal ad-Din Yassin; s/d E£35-55, with private bathroom E£65/75) The Acropole is very run down these days and the rooms are quite shabby, although the management remains friendly and makes some effort. Some rooms have a side glimpse of the harbour, others have a good view over Midan Saad Zaghloul. Tram noises ('bucking, clicking' as Durrell described it) also included.

Hyde Park Hotel (Map p380; ☎ 487 5666; 11 Sharia Amin Fikry; s/d E£35/45, d with private bathroom E£55) While it's too far back from the harbour to benefit properly from the sea,

THE AUTHOR'S CHOICE

Cecil Hotel (Map p380; ☎ 487 7173; www.sofitel .com; 16 Midan Saad Zaghloul; s/d US$120/156, with sea view US$143/190) Alexandria's legendary hotel, now managed by the international Sofitel chain, has been refitted several times over the last couple of decades but unfortunately not for the better. The rooms are fully equipped but quite gloomy and service is slow, while the grand lobby and famous bar (now relocated to the first floor) lack the lustre they once had – Justine (as described in Durrell's *Alexandria Quartet*) is no longer likely to swing through these doors. To that extent the Cecil very much reflects the city in which it stands, where the past has to be imagined. There are consolations and the sweeping views over the Eastern Harbour are unbeatable, although nostalgia comes at a price! The Chinese restaurant (China House, p392) on the top floor is the best in town, but a little expensive for what it is.

some rooms look down on all the activity around Midan Ramla (the view from room 44 is especially good).

Nile Excelsior Hotel (Map p380; ☎ 480 799; nile hotel@hotmail.com; 16 Sharia al-Bursa al-Qadima; s/d/tr with private bathroom E£50/80/100; ⊠) Very central hotel in the same street as the Spitfire Bar (handy for a nightcap). The stairs up to the hotel are rather dirty and uninviting, but the small rooms have high ceilings and are clean and comfortable. No sea views.

Top End

Metropole Hotel (Map p380; ☎ 486 1467; www.paradise innegypt.com; 52 Sharia Saad Zaghloul; s US$77-114, d US$109-132; ⊠ ▣) The Metropole has a great central location with most rooms overlooking the squares of Midan Ramla or Midan Saad Zaghloul and the Mediterranean. It's a classy old joint, entirely renovated in the 1990s to earn itself a four-star rating. The lobby is rather overdone, but high-ceilinged rooms are more tasteful and with loads of character, while the staff are meticulously polite. A best available rate is given when asked.

Windsor Palace Hotel (Map p380; ☎ 480 8123; www.paradiseinnegypt.com; Sharia ash-Shohada; s US$100-135, d US$120-155; ⊠ ▣) Regular visitors to Alexandria swear by this Alexandria institution on the Corniche overlooking the Med. Built in 1907, the Windsor was bought by Paradise Inn in the late 1990s, after their success with the Metropole, and given a much-needed smartening up. Thankfully the wonderful old elevators and grand lobby have been retained, and the characterful rooms are comfortable and clean. More expensive rooms have excellent sea views.

Green Plaza Hilton Alexandria (☎ 420 9120; www.hilton.com; Green Plaza Shopping Mall, 14th of May Bridge, Smouha; s/d/tr US$98/148/198; ✗ 🖳 🖳) One of Alexandria's most luxurious hotels, this Hilton has large rooms equipped with all mod cons, a good business centre and is close to Nozha Airport. The Green Plaza Mall with its plethora of shops, restaurants, and a cinema is a favourite hang-out for Alexandrian families. But the hotel is far from the city centre (a 20-minute taxi ride), and rooms overlooking the mall are quite dark and noisy.

Salamlek Palace Hotel (Map pp374-5; ☎ 547 7999; www.sangiovanni.com; Montazah Palace Gardens; d US$200; ✗) This former royal hunting lodge, built by Khedive Abbas II for his Austrian mistress, is next door to the presidential summer palace in the Montazah Gardens. The building looks like a rich Viennese pastry, but rooms are opulently furnished in swanky period style. The hotel boasts a casino and two quality restaurants (ties required for male diners). The park setting is fantastic but, again, the big drawback is the distance from the city centre (a 30- to 45-minute drive), and rather stiff and at times painfully slow service.

Helnan Palestine (Map pp374-5; 547 4033; www .helnan.com; Montazah Palace Gardens; s/d US$295/330; ✗ 🖳) This popular hotel in the middle of the Montazah Gardens is in a heavy 1970s block, but the views over the little private bay are gorgeous and rooms are very quiet. The great distance from the hotel to the city centre (a 30- to 45-minute drive) is a drawback if you want to visit the city's sights, but a plus if you want to swim in the Med.

Sheraton Montazah (Map pp374-5; ☎ 548 0550; fax 540 1331; Corniche, Montazah; d US$180; ✗ 🖳) An ugly modern building on the noisy corner of the Corniche, just opposite the Montazah Gardens. Rooms are comfortable and the facilities are good, but the location is terrible.

EATING

The old and once-grand restaurants, such as Pastroudis and the Union, have long closed, leaving downtown Alex something of a culinary wilderness. Much of the better, often Western-style cooking is now to be found in upmarket hotels and noisy shopping malls where Alexandrians love to hang out. Still, one of the delights to be had in old Alexandria is to eat the freshest catch from the Mediterranean in one of the seafood restaurants overlooking the Eastern Harbour. Most of these restaurants don't serve alcohol, the exception being the Fish Market. Equally enjoyable is to stroll around the city centre, where you can sit in one of city's many cafés – old glory or MTV generation – and watch Alexandrians at play. Quite a few good restaurants are in the coastal suburb of Agami, where Cairenes often come to spend the weekend, or in Abu Qir. Unless otherwise stated, restaurants are open from around 11am to midnight.

Restaurants

CENTRAL ALEXANDRIA

China House (Map p380; ☎ 487 7173; Cecil Hotel, 16 Midan Saad Zaghloul; meals E£25-55; ✆ 11am-11.30pm) With great views over the Eastern Harbour, this is Alexandria's best Chinese restaurant, although admittedly there is little competition. Chicken dumplings are excellent as is the grilled beef with garlic, but save room for the desserts.

Elite (Map p380; ☎ 486 3592; 43 Sharia Safiyya Zaghloul; dishes E£4.50-30; ✆ 9am-midnight) Near the Cinema Metro, this is one of those Alexandrian time-warp affairs. Faintly resembling an old US diner, it seems sealed in a 1950s bubble, now slowly but surely sliding towards a total standstill. The menu, displayed outside beside the door, runs from spaghetti bolognese to grilled meats. Best stick to the simple things.

Malek as-Samaan (Map p376; ☎ 390 0698; off Sharia Attareen; two birds E£25; ✆ 8pm-3am) Just south of the junction with Sharia Yousef, by day this is a small courtyard clothes market, by night an open-air restaurant serving just one dish: quail. Diners sit under an awning on a rough dirt floor and tuck into grilled or stuffed birds served with rice and salad. A bit hard to find, but look for a painted sign with a small bird.

ANFUSHI

For some authentic Alexandrian flavour and atmosphere head for the simple good-value, streetside restaurants in Anfushi's *baladi* (working-class) district. Sharia Safar Pasha is lined with a dozen places where the fires are crackling and flaming under the grills barbecuing meat and fish. Most of these places do not serve alcohol. You could chance a table at any of them and probably come away satisfied but those mentioned below are the ones that have impressed us.

Abu Ashraf (Map p376; ☎ 481 6597; 28 Sharia Safar Pasha, Bahari; dishes E£30-50; ⏱ 24hr) One of this street's fish specialists. Make your selection from the day's catch then take a seat under the green awning and watch it being cooked. Sea bass stuffed with garlic and herbs is a speciality as is the creamy shrimp *kishk* or casserole. Price is determined by weight and type of fish, ranging from grey mullet at E£35 per kilo to jumbo prawns at E£130.

Fish Market (Map p376; ☎ 480 5119; on the Corniche beside the Kashafa Club, Bahari; dishes E£40-60; ⏱ noon-2am) The most upmarket fish restaurant in town, with great views over the Eastern Harbour. Fish or seafood is selected from a large and usually very fresh display, and cooked to perfection in the way you desire. Service is swift, the salads are great and the bonus is that you can eat your seafood accompanied by a glass of icy-cold Egyptian white wine.

Samakmak (Map p376; ☎ 481 1560; 42 Qasr Ras at-Tin; dishes E£40-60) Owned by Zizi Salem, the retired queen of the Alexandrian belly-dancing scene, Samakmak is definitely one step up from the other fish eateries in the neighbourhood. The fish is as fresh as elsewhere, but customers flock to this place for its specials, including crayfish, excellent crab *tagen* (stew cooked in a deep clay pot) and a great spaghetti with clams.

RUSHDY

Centro de Portugal (Map pp374-5; ☎ 542 7599; 42 Sharia Abd al-Kader, off Sharia Kafr Abduh; entrance E£10, dishes E£40-55; ⏱ 6pm-1am) The Portuguese Club is a favourite with the local expat community, a place where American petrol workers get together over a beer or game of snooker. The atmosphere inside can be too noisy 'male plural', but the Portuguese Club serves the best steak and fries in town, as well as other international cuisine, and the garden is very pleasant. Thursday night is disco night upstairs.

SMOUHA

Cordon Rouge (☎ 420 8666; Green Plaza Mall, 14th of May Bridge; dishes E£45-90; ⏱ noon-2am) Lively bar/restaurant in a contemporary setting, popular with Alexandrians and expats who gather at the bar to drink and chat to the cool barman, or to eat at the Mediterranean style restaurant. The international menu focusses on salads, pastas and grills.

AGAMI

Most restaurants and bars in this coastal resort only open in summer, when crowds of wealthy Cairenes open their summer villas, but these two remain year-round.

Christina (☎ 433 2014; 1Bis Champs Elysees, Biancchi; dishes E£25-60; ⏱ 7.30pm-midnight) Christina is an Agami institution, in an old villa, off the beaten track but definitely worth a little search. The food, like the décor, is very French-Mediterranean, and the atmosphere is like Christina and her husband Ismail, totally laid back. Regular guests might play the piano or bass guitar in the dining room.

Seagull (☎ 445 5575; beginning of the Agami rd at Al-Max; dishes E£45-90; ⏱ 10am-midnight) The Seagull is another landmark: a mock castle built on the spot where Napoleon Bonaparte landed in 1798. The décor may be pleasantly over the top, but the deliciously prepared fish comes fresh from the sea, and the fruit and vegetables directly from the restaurant's own farm. This is a great place to take the kids too as the garden is full of animals, including ponies to ride, and there is a play area.

THE AUTHOR'S CHOICE

Qadoura (Map p376; ☎ 480 0405; 33 Sharia Bairam at-Tonsi; ⏱ 9am-3am) Pronounced 'Adora', this is one of Alexandria's most authentic fish restaurants. Pick your fish from a huge ice-packed selection, which usually includes sea bass, red and grey mullet, bluefish, sole, squid, crab and shrimp, and often a lot more. Food is served at tables in the narrow street. A selection of mezze is served with all orders (don't hope for a menu or alcohol). Most fish is around E£55 per kilo, prawns E£90 per kilo.

Quick Eats

The place for cheap eats is the area where Sharia Safiyya Zaghloul meets Midan Ramla, and along Sharia Shakor Pasha, one street over to the west. There are plenty of little *fuul* and *ta'amiyya* places here as well as sandwich shops.

Mohammed Ahmed (Map p380; ☎ 483 3576; 17 Sharia Shakor Pasha; dishes E£2-5) The king of *fuul* and *ta'amiyya* has a widespread reputation and Alexandrians queue here day and night to fill that gap in their stomachs. Mohammed Ahmed even has a menu in English, which, in addition to sandwiches, includes other staples such as omelettes and fried cheese, as well as all the usual salad and dip accompaniments. Sit in or takeaway.

Al-Shark (Map p380; Sharia al-Bursa al-Qadima, opposite Nile Excelsior Hotel; main courses E£3.40-15.50) Extremely popular Egyptian restaurant with traditional dishes such as Egyptian baked macaroni, rice with gizzards, *fatta* with mutton and grilled kebab by the kilo. Simple surroundings and quick service. Takeaway and sit down area.

Self-Catering

For fruit and vegetables, either head for Souq Nokrashi on the street of the same name just west off Midan Tahrir, or the Souq Ibrahimiyya (Map pp374–5), which is a couple of stops east of Midan Ramla on any tram – get off at the Al-Moaskar stop. These two areas are also good for *ba'al*s (grocers) where you can get cheese, olives, yogurt, bread and the like. Takeaway beer is available in the centre at a dedicated Stella shop just off Midan Saad Zaghloul, below Hotel Acropole. The newly opened Alexandria City Centre Mall, on the Cairo road, has a large Carrefour supermarket, but it is way out of the centre.

DRINKING
Cafés

Different worlds came together, mingled and mixed in Alexandria in the first half of the 20th century and nowhere were they more evident than in the cafés. Here the city's famous literary figures met, chatted, searched for love and conjured the city they could not quite grasp. Many of these cafés, including the most famous of them all, Pastroudis, have now closed, but a few remain where time has somehow stood still.

The elegant Trianon has spawned a chain with several branches across town, but the beautiful original one in Midan Saad Zaghloul remains a favourite. Note that these old haunts are definitely worth a visit for nostalgic purposes, historical associations and grand décor, but not necessarily for the food or drink. Alexandrians now prefer modern Western-style cafés such as the Coffee Roastery or the many café terraces in the Green Plaza Mall or other malls.

Athineos (Map p380; ☎ 487 7173; 21 Midan Saad Zaghloul, opposite Ramla Station) Athineos lives off nostalgia. The café part on the Midan Ramla side still seems to have its original '40s fittings and period character, and a loyal following of old men drinking tea. The entrance on the lower seaside floor leads to a tacky restaurant with tasteless décor and an uninspiring menu. Lots of history here, but the food is hard to stomach and the service is pretty desperate.

Bistrot (Map p380; ☎ 486 9061; 6 Sharia Fuad) A modern venue with decent coffee, fresh juices, good pastas, salads and sandwiches, and a pastry corner for breakfast. The décor is simple but has character and there is a terrace in the shade for alfresco lunches – it's often busy with flirty young couples imagining their future together.

Brazilian Coffee Store (Map p380; Sharia Saad Zaghloul) Another old haunt and a perfect place for a kick-start espresso, knocked back at the counter (no seats). A favourite with local businessmen, and now very old Greek men. There's another branch on Sharia Salah Salem (with seats).

Cilantro (☎ 546 0828; at the end of Sharia Kafr Abduh, Roushdy; ☯ 10am-12.30am) Great coffee and cappuccino with real croissants, and comfy leather armchairs. Equally good salads and sandwiches are served later in the day.

Coffee Roastery (Map p380; ☎ 483 4363; 48 Sharia Fuad; ☯ 7am-2am) This Western-style café/restaurant does great coffee, milk shakes, fresh juices and a large sandwich, snack and lunch menu. This is the trendy place to hang out, and it teems with gorgeous young 'Justines', hip Alexandrians, students and young families, who meet here to the background of MTV on a large screen. Swinging music all day and a very happening atmosphere.

Delicies (Map p380; 46 Sharia Saad Zaghloul; ☯ from 7am) Just a few steps west of Midan Ramla, this enormous old tearoom full of old atmosphere does a decent breakfast, and tea with cakes in the afternoon.

Sofianopoulo Coffee Store (Map p380; Sharia Saad Zaghloul) At the western end of the street, Sofianopoulo is a gorgeous store that would be in a museum anywhere else in the world. The coffee shop is dominated by huge silver coffee grinders and cases and sacks of shiny, dark aromatic beans. Beautiful to look at and excellent espresso too, but no seating.

Trianon (Map p380; 56 Midan Saad Zaghloul; ⏰ from 7am) Facing Midan Ramla, Trianon was a favourite of the Greek poet Cavafy, who worked in offices above. It's still popular and a good place for a Continental-style breakfast, but the adjoining restaurant has seen better days: the food tastes like it was prepared the day before and the service is shambolic.

Ahwas

Alexandria has nothing like the density of *ahwa*s (coffeehouses) found in Cairo, but during the summer the whole 20km length of the Corniche from Ras at-Tin to Montazah becomes one great strung-out coffeehouse. Generally speaking though, these are not the greatest places – they're catering for a passing holiday trade and so they tend to overcharge.

Sultan Hussein (Map p380; cnr Sharias Safiyya Zaghloul & Sultan Hussein) Our favourite Alexandrian *ahwa* is a good, no-nonsense place with excellent *sheesha* (water pipe). It's popular with chess players and has a separate family area where women can sit unharassed.

Ahwa al-Hind (Map p376; Midan Tahrir) You have to squeeze through a passageway almost closed by clothes stalls to find this *ahwa* in the central courtyard of the big, battered old building on the corner where Midan Orabi meets Midan Tahrir. It's scruffy (hygiene isn't high on the agenda) but the setting is atmospheric and it's the perfect place to while away a hot afternoon or lazy evening.

Bars

Sixty years ago – pre-Revolution – Alexandria was thriving with Greek tavernas and divey little watering holes. Sadly, today only a few fine places survive.

Greek Club (Club Nautique Hellenique; Map pp374-5; ☎ 554 4512; Sharia Qasr Qaytbay, Anfushi; ⏰ noon-11pm) The Greek Club is the perfect place for a sunset drink, inside its large newly restored

---

THE AUTHOR'S CHOICE

Cap d'Or (Map p380; 4 Sharia Adib; ⏰ noon-2am) The Cap d'Or, just off Sharia Saad Zaghloul, is a great place to relax, and one of the only surviving typical Alexandrian bars. With beer flowing generously, stained-glass windows, a long, high marble-topped bar, plenty of ancient memorabilia decorating the walls and crackling tapes of old French *chanson* or Egyptian hits, it feels very much like an Andalusian tapas bar. Crowds come to drink cold Stella beer with excellent hotpots of calamari, shrimp or fish, or just to hang out at the bar with a beer and listen to the often present oud (lute) player, who, like the poets of the ancient city, sings his songs of love, longing and nostalgia for things lost.

---

rooms or, even better, on the wide terrace catching the afternoon breeze or watching the lights on this legendary bay. The beers are cold and the atmosphere is perfectly Mediterranean. The new menu had not been fixed at the time of writing, but is likely to include lots of grilled fish and squid.

Spitfire (Map p380; 7 rue de L'Ancienne Bourse; ⏰ noon-1am) Just north of Sharia Saad Zaghloul, Spitfire feels almost like a Bangkok bar – but without the women, of course. It has a reputation as a sailors' hang-out and the walls are plastered with shipping line stickers, rock-and-roll memorabilia and photos of drunk regulars, but it's a great place for an evening out in one of the world's great harbours, listening to American rock and roll from the '70s.

Elite (Map p380; ☎ 486 3592; 43 Sharia Safiyya Zaghloul; ⏰ 9am-midnight) You can also have a cheap beer without having to eat at this place, which has the appeal of large windows so you can street-watch over your Stella.

ENTERTAINMENT

Alexandria's cultural life has never really recovered from the exodus of Europeans and Jews in the 1940s and '50s, but in recent years things have started to change for the better. Since the opening of the Bibliotheca Alexandrina, Alexandria is once again trying to compete with Cairo, the selfish proprietor of Egyptian arts. The Alexandria Centre of the Arts is very active, there are new galleries in town, and new cinemas at the shopping malls. Also new on the scene is the beautifully restored Alexandria Opera House (formerly the Sayyid Darwish Theatre).

Cinemas

The following cinemas regularly screen English-language films.

Amir Cinema (Map p380; ☎ 391 7972; 42 Tariq al-Horreyya) A refitted grand old place now with six screens, screening almost exclusively Hollywood products.

Cinema Metro (Map p380; ☎ 487 0432; 26 Sharia Safiyya Zaghloul) In central Alexandria, this beautiful old place has been very well looked after – pity the movies it screens are often so bad.

Green Plaza Mall Cineplex (☎ 420 9155; 14th of May Bridge) This large cinema, part of the buzzing Green Plaza Mall complex, has six screens all showing first-run American blockbusters. A taxi out here will cost about E£6 to E£10 and take 25 minutes from the city centre.

Osman Group Cinema (Map pp374–5; ☎ 424 5897; Smouha Mall) A good cinema in the central court of the Smouha Mall, next to the Zahran Mall in Smouha. A taxi from the centre will cost about E£5 to E£7 and take 15 to 20 minutes.

Renaissance City Center (☎ 397 0156; Carrefour City Center Mall, beginning of the Cairo Desert rd) The newest cinemas in town with seven excellent screens. Very popular with Alexandrian youth who come to see the Hollywood blockbusters. A taxi from the centre will cost about E£7 to E£10 and take 20 to 25 minutes

Royal Renaissance (Map p380; ☎ 485 5727; 20 Tariq al-Horreyya) The old cinema beside the Alexandria Opera House was recently upgraded. Two of its three screens are usually devoted to English-language programming.

Music, Theatre & Dance

The Elite restaurant (p392) usually posts notices advertising anything that's happening; alternatively, see *Egypt Today*. Also, check the French Cultural Centre (p377) as it organises quite a few performances.

Bibliotheca Alexandrina (Map pp374–5; ☎ 483 9999; www.bibalex.org; Corniche al-Bahr, Chatby) The Bibliotheca is the most important cultural venue in town now, hosting major music festivals, international concerts and performances.

Alexandria Centre of Arts (Map p380; ☎ 495 6633; 1 Tariq al-Horreyya) This place hosts twice-

weekly concerts, but there is little going on in the way of theatre or music.

Garage (tfetouh@yatfund.org; Jesuit Centre, Sharia Bur Said, Sidi Gaber) The renovated garage of the Jesuit Centre and maintained by the Young Arab Theatre Fund, Garage is definitely a breath of fresh air on the city's cultural scene, presenting new performances by local and international youth theatre groups.

SHOPPING

There's a souq just west of Midan Tahrir, and Sharias Safiyya Zaghloul and Saad Zaghloul are lined with an assortment of old fashioned and more trendy clothes shops and shoe stores, but overall the city centre is not a great place to shop. Alexandrians have only recently discovered the joys of shopping malls, but there is no stopping them now. They seem to love them and malls are going up all over the city, particularly in the more spacious suburbs. Malls are there for shopping, but also for entertainment, cafés, *ahwa*s and restaurants. Last but not least, younger Alexandrians have found them great places to meet the opposite sex, the latest pick-up accessory being a Bluetooth phone.

City Center Mall (beginning of the Cairo Desert rd) a 20-minute drive south of the city, this is one of the largest malls, with the massive French superstore, Carrefour. It sells everything from groceries to TVs.

Green Plaza Mall (14th of May Bridge, Smouha) Slightly older but still a big hit with locals is Green Plaza Mall, out beyond the suburb of Smouha on the Agricultural Rd to Cairo. It is as kitsch as things get, a local shopping version of Disneyland, with shops and shops and shops plus an extremely noisy funfair, a snooker hall, a bowling alley, a food court, a cineplex, a Hilton hotel and a 'Roman temple' housing a conference and marriage centre.

Antique collectors might have some fun strolling through the confusion of backstreets and alleys of the Attareen district. When Alexandria's European high society was forced en masse to make a hasty departure from Egypt following the Revolution in 1952, they largely went without their personal belongings – much of what they left has over the years found its way into the Attareen Antique Market (Map p380). These days there are fewer and fewer wonderful finds, and none of them are bargains. After all, dealers know to recognise quality from when the going was good and their bedtime reading may well include Christie's and Sotheby's catalogues.

GETTING THERE & AWAY
Air
There are direct international flights from Alexandria to London (British Mediterranean), Athens (Olympic Airways) and Frankfurt (Lufthansa), and to Saudi Arabia and Dubai (EgyptAir). Alexandria's airport Burg al-Arab (☎ 425 0527) is 60km west of the city. The 555 air-con airport bus (E£6 one way plus E£1 per bag, one hour) leaves from in front of the Cecil Hotel on Midan Saad Zaghloul two hours before all departures. A taxi should cost no more that E£80.

There's a second smaller airport at Nouzha (☎ 427 1036), much closer to the city where some EgyptAir (Map380; ☎ 487 3357, 486 5937; 19 Midan Saad Zaghloul; ✆ 8am-8pm) and other flights land. Catch the 711 or 703 minibus (50pt) from Midan Orabi or Ramla. A taxi should cost no more than E£10.

Boat
Passenger boats used to sail regularly out of Alexandria, but cheap airfares have taken the trade and the last boats quit in 1997. This situation is not expected to change.

Bus
Long-distance buses all leave from one garage behind Sidi Gaber train station; the 1 minibus from outside the Cecil Hotel connects it with the city centre. (If you get dropped off at the front of the train station you need to take the underpass to the platform on the far side of the tracks, then down another flight of steps to get out.)

The main companies operating from here are Superjet (☎ 429 8566), whose ticket office and bays are almost immediately out the back of Misr train station, and West Delta

(☎ 363 9658), which is about 100m to the east. Between these two offices are several little cabins beside the road for the East Delta and Upper Egypt bus ticket offices.

West Delta also has a city centre booking office (Map p380; ☎ 480 9685; Midan Saad Zaghloul; ✆ 10am-3pm) close to the main tourist office.

CAIRO
Superjet has buses to Cairo (also stopping at Cairo airport) every 30 minutes from 5.30am to 10pm, plus a further service at 1am. The trip takes 2½ hours and costs E£23 in the morning, E£25 in the afternoon. The fare to Cairo airport is E£28, or E£34 on the 1am bus. West Delta also has buses to Cairo every 30 minutes between 5am and 2am (5.30am to 1am from October to April) and charges E£19 to E£23 in the morning, E£19 to E£30 in the afternoon, and E£28 to E£33 to the airport. The Superjet buses are a bit bigger and more modern.

NORTH COAST & SIWA
West Delta has buses to Marsa Matruh (E£15 to E£33, four hours, around 20 daily) between 9am and 1.30am. Almost all of these buses continue on to Sallum (E£23, nine hours) on the border with Libya. Three services go on to Siwa (E£27, nine hours) at 8.30am, 11am and 2pm. Otherwise just take any Marsa Matruh bus and change there.

Most of the Matruh buses stop in El Alamein (E£10, one hour), and will stop at Sidi Abdel Rahman (E£6) if you want to get off.

Superjet runs buses to Marsa Matruh (E£25) only during the summer months of June to September, departing at 7.15am and 4pm daily.

SINAI
Superjet has a daily 7.30pm service to Sharm el-Sheikh (E£80, seven hours); West Delta has one at 9pm (E£65).

SUEZ CANAL & RED SEA COAST
Superjet has five services daily to Port Said (E£22 to E£28, four hours) between 6am and 7pm, and two daily services to Hurghada (E£70, nine hours) at 8.30am and 6.30pm. West Delta has several services a day to Port Said (E£20 to E£25), three to Ismailia (E£22) at 7am, 9am, 2.30pm, and three to Suez (E£25) at 6.30am, 9am, 2.30pm and 5pm. The Upper Egypt Bus Company also

has three daily Hurghada buses (E£55) that continue on down to Port Safaga (E£60).

INTERNATIONAL BUSES

For information on international services from Alexandria, see p541.

Service Taxi

Service taxis for Abu Qir depart from outside Misr station; all others go from the *Al-mo'af al-gedid* (new garage) out at Moharrem Bay. Minibuses shuttle there from in front of the railway station. Fares are between E£15 and E£18 to Cairo or Marsa Matruh, depending on who you ask. To more local destinations, some sample fares are Zagazig E£10, Tanta E£8, Mansura E£10 and Abu Qir E£1.

Train

There are two train stations in Alexandria. The main terminal is **Mahattat Misr** (Cairo Station; Map p376; ☎ 392 5985), about one mile south of Midan Ramla. **Mahattat Sidi Gaber** (Sidi Gaber Station; Map pp374-5; ☎ 426 3953) serves the eastern suburbs. Trains from Cairo stop at Sidi Gaber first, but the only reason to get off there is if you are staying in that part of town, if you need to make an immediate transfer to a bus, or to purchase a bus ticket (the long-distance bus station is just south of the railway platforms).

At Mahattat Misr, 1st- and 2nd-class aircon tickets must be bought from the ticket office next to the tourist information booth; 3rd-class and 2nd-class ordinary tickets are purchased from the front hall. Cairo-bound trains leave from here at least hourly, from 4.30am to 10pm, stopping five minutes later at Sidi Gaber station. The best trains, the Turbini and Espani, don't stop again until 2½ hours later when they arrive in Cairo. They depart Misr at 7am, 8am, 2pm, 3pm, 4.45pm, 7pm and 10.20pm. Tickets for 1st-/2nd-class air-con cost E£34/25.

The next-best trains, the Faransawi, stop at Damanhur, Tanta and Benha taking three hours to get to Cairo; they depart at 6am, 10am, 11am, 1pm, 3.30pm, 4.45pm, 5pm and 8pm and cost E£28/18 in 1st/2nd class.

From June to September one train a day leaves Alexandria for Marsa Matruh (about six hours) at 6.45am; 1st/2nd class costs E£37/23. However the bus service on this route is a much better option, faster and more comfortable.

GETTING AROUND
Bus & Minibus

As a visitor to Alexandria, you won't use the buses at all – the trams and microbuses are a much better way of getting around.

Taxi

You can expect to pay for taxis in Alexandria what you would pay in Cairo. A short trip, say from Midan Ramla to Misr station, will cost E£5; from the city centre to Fort Qaitbey E£5; from the city centre to the Royal Jewellery Museum or Mahmoud Said Museum E£5; from the city centre to Montazah or Maamoura E£10.

Train

About the only conceivable, but not recommended service you might use in Alexandria is the very slow 3rd-class train from Misr station to Abu Qir. It stops, among many other places, at Sidi Gaber, Montazah and Maamoura, but only serious train buffs would consider taking it. The fare is 50pt.

Tram

Tram is the best way to travel in Alex. Mahattat Ramla is the main tram station and from here lime-yellow coloured trams go west. The 14 goes to Misr station and Moharrem Bey, and the 15 goes past the Mosque of Abu Abbas al-Mursi and Fort Qaitbey to Ras at-Tin.

The blue coloured trams travel east: the 1 to Sidi Gaber, Rushdy and Victoria; the 2 to Sidi Gaber and Victoria via Rushdy; 8 to San Stefano via the Sporting Club; 25 from Ras at-Tin to Sidi Gaber via Midan Ramla.

Some trams have two or three carriages, in which case one of them is reserved for women. It causes considerable amusement when a poor unsuspecting foreigner gets in the wrong carriage. The standard fare is 25pt.

AROUND ALEXANDRIA

ABU QIR

This coastal town, 24km east of central Alexandria, is historically important for three major 18th-century battles between the French and English. During the so-called Battle of the Nile in 1798, Admiral Nelson surprised and destroyed the French fleet in the bay at Abu Qir. Although Napoleon still controlled Egypt, his contact with France by sea was effectively severed. The British landed 18,000 Turkish soldiers at Abu Qir in 1799, but the French force of 10,000 men, mostly cavalry led personally by Napoleon, forced the Turks back into the sea, drowning at least 5000 of them. In 1801 however the French lost a further battle with the British troops at the same place and the French expeditionary corps was then forced out of Egypt.

Recent underwater excavation (see p385) has revealed two sunken cities believed to be the legendary Herakleion and Menouthis, with several treasures, some of which are now on display at the Alexandria National Museum (p381). The beach however is rubbish-strewn so the main reason to head in this direction is for lunch at one of the fish restaurants, particularly at the **Zephyrion** (☎ 562 1319; seafront Abu Qir; dishes E£25-90; ⏱ 11.30am-11pm), Greek for 'sea breeze'. This old Greek fish taverna was founded in 1929. The excellent fish and seafood is served on the sweeping blue and white terrace that overlooks the bay. There is no wine list but you can bring your own and they will open it for you without complaint.

There are plenty of buses from central Alexandria to Abu Qir every day (including the 260 and 261 and minibus 729 from Midan Orabi), but it's probably easier to take a microbus 728 from in front of Misr station, or 729 from Midan Orabi, for 60pt. Remember Abu Qir is pronounced 'Abu Ear'.

ABU MINA

St Mina is said to have fallen victim to anti-Christian feeling in the Roman Empire of the early 4th century. Born in West Africa, he did a stint in the Roman army before deserting and finally being tortured and beheaded for his faith. He was buried at a place near the present site of Abu Mina, which eventually became a place of pilgrimage. Churches and even a basilica were built, and all subsequently destroyed. In the 14th century, a Mamluk army supposedly rediscovered the site and the bones of St Mina, which could not be burned (proving to the Mamluks that they belonged to a saint).

A German team has been working at Abu Mina since 1969 (excavations have uncovered the early medieval Church of the Martyr, where St Mina's remains are believed to be buried), and although there are grand plans for a museum and archaeological park, at present the site is not open to visitors.

ROSETTA (AR-RASHID)

Rosetta, also known by its Arabic name of Ar-Rashid, is 65km east of Alexandria, where the western branch of the Nile empties into the Mediterranean, some 6680km from its source at Lake Victoria.

The town is most famous as the discovery place of the stone stele that provided the key to deciphering hieroglyphics (see p401). But during the 17th and 18th centuries, this was also Egypt's most vital port. Founded in the 9th century, Rosetta thrived as Alexandria declined, and faded again when Alexandria staged its comeback in the 19th century. Today it is a quaint provincial town, mostly sustained by fishing and dates. Everyone knows each other and there are still more donkey carts and horse and traps than cars on the streets. A visit to its restored old merchant houses, combined with a boat trip on the Nile, makes Rosetta a nice day trip away from Alexandria. The Nile here is particularly beautiful, wide and full, with boat builders along the Rosetta Corniche and loads of palms on the far bank.

Sights

Rosetta's main attractions are its fine old **Ottoman-era merchants' houses**. These are built in a distinctive Delta style of small flat bricks painted alternately red and black. They tend to be three storeys high with each of the upper floors sticking out slightly from the one below it, and there's a lot of jutting *mashrabiyyas* – the intricately assembled wooden screens that serve for windows. The houses are beautiful and there are at least 22 of them, including the **houses of Abou Houm, Al-Baqawali, Bassiouni, Al-Gamal, Al-Qanadili, Asfur, Kohiya, Moharrem** and **Tabaq**. There are also 12 mosques within a square 500m, though not all are open to the public. Most have either been restored or are undergoing restoration

ALEXANDRIA & THE MEDITERRANEAN COAST

WARNING

Do not visit Rosetta within days of any significant rain – the town's streets are not sealed and after a downpour the whole place becomes one big mud bath.

ROSETTA (AR-RASHID)

0 ————— 100 m
0 ————— 0.1 mile

INFORMATION	
Tourist Office	1 D1

SIGHTS & ACTIVITIES

Abou Houm House	2 B3
Al-Baqrawali House	3 C3
Bassiouni House	4 A3
Beit Killi Museum	5 C1
House of Abu Shaheen	6 B2
House of Al-Gamal	7 B3
House of Al-Mizuni	8 B2
House of Al-Qanadili	9 B2
House of Al-Toqatli	10 B3
House of Amasyali	11 B2
House of Asfur	12 B1
Kohiya House	13 A3
Moharrem House	14 B3
Mosque of Sheikh Ali al-Mahalli	15 C1
Ramadan House	16 B3
Tabaq House	17 B2

TRANSPORT

Boat Docks	18 D1
Service Taxis	19 A3

ALEXANDRIA & THE MEDITERRANEAN COAST

work, and about eight are currently open to the public. Tickets can be bought at the **tourist office** (☎ 045-293 0125) opposite the **Beit Killi museum**, on the main square, off the Corniche an-Nil. The museum was closed for restoration at the time of writing, but due to reopen in 2006. A ticket to the few open monuments in the centre of town costs E£12 for adults and E£6 for students. A separate ticket to the Fort of Qaitbey and another separate ticket to at-Tahona Mill, Al-Mayzuni House and Hammam Azouz, slightly out of the centre, both cost E£12 for adults and E£6 for students. Most houses have a similar layout, so whichever one is open when you visit will be quite similar to the description of the Ramadan House.

RAMADAN HOUSE

One of the most impressive of all Rosetta's fine buildings is the **Ramadan House**, part of the grouping immediately west of the *midan* where the service taxis and minibuses pull up. It was closed for restoration at the time of writing, but should reopen in 2006. Although it's devoid of furniture

and totally bare – as are all the buildings – it is still possible to get a very clear idea of how the house worked. A series of rough stone chambers make up the ground floor, and these would have been used for storage. The 1st floor is for the men; one of the rooms here is a reception room, overlooked by a screened wooden gallery, behind which the women would have sat, obscured from view. The stair to the gallery is hidden behind a false cupboard. As you go up the main staircase to the 2nd floor, notice at foot level that there is a little revolving turntable, designed so that women could serve tea and coffee without being seen.

The first thing you encounter on entering the women's apartments on the upper floor, off to the left, is the kitchen, identifiable as such by the huge flue. Notice how light it is up here and how airy, thanks to the *mashrabiyya* screens, which allow cooling breezes to circulate around the house.

On the uppermost floor there's a tiny *hammam* (public bath) with a domed ceiling into which pieces of coloured glass would have been set.

THE ROSETTA STONE

Now a crowd-pulling exhibit at the British Museum in London, the Rosetta Stone is the most significant find in the history of Egyptology. Unearthed in 1799 by a French soldier doing his duty improving the defences of Fort St Julien near Rosetta, the stone is the lower half of a large dark granitic stele. It records a decree issued by the priests of Memphis on 27 March 196 BC, the anniversary of the coronation of Ptolemy V (205–180 BC), and it announces their decision to honour the 13-year-old king with his own cult in return for tax exemptions and other perks. In order to be understood by Egyptians, Greeks and others then living in the country, the decree was written in the three scripts current at the time – hieroglyphic, demotic (a cursive form of hieroglyphs) and Greek, a language that most European scholars would have read fluently. The trilingual inscription was set up in a temple beside a statue of the king. At the time of its rediscovery, much was known about ancient Egypt, but scholars had still not managed to decipher hieroglyphs. It was quickly realised that these three scripts would make it possible to compare identical texts and therefore to crack the code and recover the lost world of the ancient Egyptians.

When the British defeated Napoleon's army in 1801, they wrote a clause in the surrender document insisting that antiquities be handed to the victors, the Rosetta Stone being foremost among them. The French made a cast and the original was shipped to London, where an Englishman, Thomas Young, established the direction in which the hieroglyphs should be read, and recognised that hieroglyphs enclosed within oval rings (cartouches) were the names of royalty.

But in 1822, before Young was able to devise a system for reading the mysterious script, a Frenchman, Jean François Champollion, recognised that signs could be alphabetic, syllabic or determinative, and established that the hieroglyphs inscribed on the Rosetta Stone were actually a translation from the Greek, and not the other way around. This allowed him to establish a complete list of signs with their Greek equivalents His obsessive work not only solved the mystery of Pharaonic script but also contributed significantly to a modern understanding of ancient Egypt.

OTHER HOUSES

On leaving the Ramadan House head downhill and take the second left into Sharia Amasyali; there are more fine houses along this street and in the alleyways that lead off it. The **House of Al-Toqatli** (second street on the right), though closed to the public, has an interesting façade.

Back on Sharia Amasyali, you pass three more houses, all closed to the public, before reaching the splendid **House of Amasyali**, which has possibly the best façade of all, with beautiful small lantern lights and vast expanses of *mashrabiyya*. It has a painted ceiling with an Islamic motif in one of the ground-floor rooms, and some fine woodwork inlaid with mother-of-pearl on the upper floors. It was closed for restoration at the time of writing, but said to reopen in 2006, together with several other houses in town.

Next door to the Amasyali house, the **House of Abu Shaheen** incorporates a reconstructed mill on the ground floor. Out back in the courtyard, the roof of the stables is supported by granite columns with Graeco-Roman capitals. Nearby, the large and still-functioning 18th-century **Mosque of Sheikh Ali al-Mahalli** contains 99 columns recycled from Roman and Mamluk monuments.

At the time of writing, the only Rosetta house open to the public was the four-storey **House of Al-Mizuni**. To get there from the mosque turn right onto the market street, then left on Sharia Souk al-Hudar and after 150m right again. The French General Mineau lived here after he married Zubayda al-Bawab, the daughter of a rich local merchant.

Hammam Azouz, a 19th-century bathhouse with a fine marble interior, is just out of the centre.

The **Fort of Qaitbey** was built in 1479, just before the sultan's fort in Alexandria, to guard the mouth of the Nile. Boats make the tour to the mouth of the Nile, 5km upriver for E£50 per person (1½ hours).

Getting There & Away

Although buses and trains operate between Alexandria and Rosetta, the easiest way to make the trip is by service taxi (E£5,

ALEXANDRIA & THE MEDITERRANEAN COAST

one hour) from Midan al-Gomhuriyya in Alexandria. Alternatively take a minibus from Alexandria's Misr station to Abu Qir (60pt). Ask to be dropped at the Rosetta minibus stand (E£2.50, 45 minutes) near Abu Qir. Coming back, it's possible to get a minibus (E£3.50) from Rosetta straight to central Alexandria (they travel the length of the Corniche, passing Midan Saad Zaghloul). If you are several, you can share a private taxi from Alexandria to Rosetta, which should cost E£100 to E£120 including waiting time.

MEDITERRANEAN COAST

Almost the entire stretch of coastline west of Alexandria up to Sidi Abdel Rahman has been developed and is covered by very large concrete tourist villages. Most cater for wealthy Cairenes who come to escape the unbearably hot summers in the city, although the hundreds of identical bungalows seem so densely packed together that it almost feels as if they are recreating Cairo's overcrowded streets by the sea. Several of these resorts were recently in the news for providing very popular women-only beaches, where Cairene and Alexandrian professionals, among others, can lie on the beach in bikinis, attended by female staff and entertained by female DJs.

EL ALAMEIN
☎ 046

The small coastal village of El Alamein, 105km west of Alexandria, is most famous as the scene of a decisive Allied victory over the Axis powers during WWII.

In June 1942 the German general Erwin Rommel, nicknamed the 'Desert Fox', launched an offensive from Tobruk, Libya, in an attempt to push his troops and 500 tanks all the way through the Allied lines to Alexandria and the strategically important Suez Canal. It was not the first attempt in what had been two years of seesaw battles, but this time the Axis forces were confident of a breakthrough. However, the Allies, under the command of General Bernard Montgomery, stopped their advance with a line of defence stretching southward from El Alamein to the Qattara Depression. On 23 October 1942 Montgomery's 8th Army swooped down from Alexandria with a thousand tanks, and within two weeks routed the combined German and Italian forces, driving Rommel and what was left of his Afrika Korps back to Tunis.

More than 80,000 soldiers were killed or wounded at El Alamein and in the subsequent battles for control of North Africa. The thousands of graves in the three massive war cemeteries in the vicinity of the town are a bleak reminder of the losses.

The town's museum and the Commonwealth cemetery are actually along a side road that leaves the main highway at the

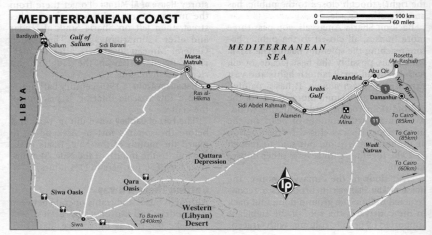

MEDITERRANEAN COAST

Greek war memorial and rejoins it again after passing right through the town. Should you need to make a phone call there's a centrale a little way beyond the museum.

Though it's possible to stay overnight nearby in Sidi Abdel Rahman, El Alamein is best visited as a day trip from Alexandria; there really isn't much here that would detain any but the most enthusiastic of military historians for more than a few hours.

Sights

COMMONWEALTH WAR CEMETERY

On the eastern side of town, the Commonwealth War Cemetery is a haunting place where more than 7000 tombstones cover a slope overlooking the desert battlefield of El Alamein. Soldiers from the UK, Australia, New Zealand, France, Greece, South Africa, East and West Africa, Malaysia and India who fought for the Allied cause lie here. The cemetery is maintained by the War Graves Commission, and admission is free. Outside, a small separate memorial commemorates the Australian contingent and a little further east is another memorial for the Greeks.

GERMAN & ITALIAN WAR MEMORIALS

About 7km west of El Alamein, what looks like a hermetically sealed sandstone fortress appears on a bluff overlooking the sea. Inside this silent but unmistakable reminder of war lie the tombs of German servicemen and, in the centre, a memorial obelisk.

About 4km further on, the Italian memorial has a tall, slender tower as its focal point. Before reaching the German memorial, you may notice on the left side of the road what appears to be a glorified milestone. On it is inscribed in Italian *Mancò la fortuna, non il valore* – 'We were short on luck, not on bravery'.

WAR MUSEUM

There is a good collection of memorabilia, uniforms and pictorial material of each country involved in the Battle of El Alamein and the North African campaigns at the **War Museum** (☎ 410 0031/0021; adult/student E£10/5; ☼ 9am-4pm). Maps and explanations of various phases of the campaign in Arabic, English, German and Italian complement the exhibits, and there's a 30-minute Italian-made documentary that you can watch. A collection of tanks, artillery and hardware from the fields of battle is displayed outside the museum.

Sleeping & Eating

The Al-Amana Hotel almost opposite the museum has a small cafeteria where you can get a greasy omelette, a drink and some biscuits but nothing more. They have a few very spartan bedrooms, only used as an emergency by drivers to the nearby beach resorts. The closest viable place to stay or eat is the El Alamein Hotel at Sidi Abdel Rahman (p404), 23km west of El Alamein town. Another 12km further west, the Mövenpick El Alamein Resort & Spa is a new development for European package holidaymakers. It may be possible to camp on the beaches nearby, but you'll have to hunt around for the police and attempt to get a *tasreeh* (permit).

Getting There & Away

The easiest option is to organise a car and English-speaking driver through **Mena Tours** (Map p380; ☎ 480 9676, fax 486 5827; ☼ 9am-6pm Sat-Thu), based next to the Cecil Hotel in Alexandria. This will cost approximately E£350. A private taxi will charge between E£150 and E£200 to take you to the museum, ferry you around the cemeteries and bring you back to Alexandria.

Alternatively, catch any of the Marsa Matruh buses from Sidi Gaber in Alexandria (see p397). You'll be dropped on the main road about 200m down the hill from the museum.

Service taxis leave from the lot in front of Alexandria's Misr station and cost about E£5 to E£8. More often than not they are of the microbus variety. You can pick up one of these from El Alamein to get back to Alexandria or to head further west to Sidi Abdel Rahman. Some have found the return trip to Alexandria more of a challenge. You'll need to flag down the minivan by the side of the highway. Sometimes it will go all the way to Moharrem Bey, but other times it will stop in an outlying suburb and you'll need to find another minivan to take you into town.

Charter flights have just started operating from the UK and Germany to El Alamein airport in combination with a week stay at the Mövenpick El-Alamein Resort & Spa.

SIDI ABDEL RAHMAN

☎ 046

The fine, white sandy beach and sparkling turquoise water of the Mediterranean make this stunning place, 23km west of El Alamein, a rare and as yet unspoilt coastal beauty spot, even though the resort has recently been enlarged. It can't be too long before it is joined by the resorts all the way west from Alexandria, particularly since international charter flights from Europe started arriving at El Alamein airport.

Bedouins occasionally congregate in a small village about 3km in from the beach. They belong to the Awlad Ali tribe, who came into the region several hundred years ago from Libyan Cyrenaica and subdued the smaller local tribes of the Morabiteen. There are now five main tribes subdivided into clans, each of which has several thousand members. The Egyptian government has been attempting to settle these nomads, so nowadays most Bedouin have forsaken their tents and herd their sheep and goats from the immobility of government-built stone and concrete houses.

The beach, the Bedouins and an expensive hotel are about all there is to Sidi Abdel Rahman.

Sleeping

El Alamein Hotel (☎ 468 0140; s/d US$111/160) This small resort tends to be both fully booked and fully functioning all summer, but can be quite desolate for the rest of the year. The food is OK, though not great, but the views over the clear turquoise waters are magnificent. About 3km west, a turn-off leads to Hanna Beach (Shaat al-Hanna), where during summer you might find a few tents set up for passers-by. You may be able to camp further along the beach, but again, technically, you will still need a permit.

Mövenpick El Alamein Resort & Spa (☎ 419 0060; www.moevenpick-elalamein.com; 140km from Alexandria on the Matruh rd, Ghazala Bay, s/d US$90/120) Another 12km further west, this large new resort caters for European package tourists who fly in on charters. The large comfortable rooms have views over the azure waters of the sea and the large swimming pool. Also on offer are a spa, fitness centre, indoor swimming pool and several restaurants, but there is nowhere else to go near the hotel. Check their website for promotional offers,

particularly in summer. At the time of publication, this place was about to change its name to Charm Hotel Grande, but contact details remained the same.

Getting There & Away

The same buses that can drop you at El Alamein en route to or from Marsa Matruh can also drop you here. They generally stop for a break just after the Hanna Beach turn-off. There are service taxis operating between El Alamein and Sidi Abdel Rahman and to places further west, but nothing much happens after early afternoon.

MARSA MATRUH

☎ 046

The large waterfront town of Marsa Matruh, built around a bay of stunning turquoise waters and white, sandy beaches, is a very popular summer destination with Egyptians. This popularity is a problem: as a result, the place is completely overrun in summer and most of the beaches – particularly those close to town – are pandemonium. Away from the sand, the town can seem rather dull and unattractive, but a new governor is making great efforts to clean up the seafront and the Corniche. Outside the summer season, this is little more than a sleepy provincial town where Bedouin and Libyans come to stock up on goods. While this means empty expanses of gleaming white beach for travellers, it also means that many of the town's hotels and restaurants are closed. Few foreign tourists stay here, except to break the journey to Siwa.

Orientation

The two key streets in Marsa Matruh are the Corniche (al-Corniche), which runs all the way around the waterfront, and Sharia Iskendariyya, which runs perpendicular to the Corniche, towards the hill behind the town. The more expensive hotels are along the Corniche, while most others are near Sharia Iskendariyya, along with most of the restaurants and shops.

Information

There are several exchange bureaux on Sharia al-Galaa.

Banque Misr (Sharia al-Galaa; ⏰ 9am-2.30pm & 6.30-8pm Sun-Thu) ATM.

Main post office (Sharia ash-Shaati; ☒ 8.30am-2.30pm Sun-Fri)

Military Hospital (☎ 493 5286; Sharia al-Galaa)

National Bank of Egypt (off Sharia al-Matar; ☒ 9am-2pm & 6-9pm Sun-Thu)

Passport office (☎ 493 5351; off Sharia Iskendariyya; ☒ 8.30am-2pm & 6-9pm Jun-Sep, 5-8pm Oct-May)

Telephone centrale (Sharia ash-Shaati; ☒ 24hr)

Tourist office (☎ 493 1841; cnr Sharia Omar Mukhtar & al-Corniche; ☒ 8.30am-2.30pm)

Tourist police (☎ 493 5575; al-Corniche)

Sights & Activities

ROMMEL'S MUSEUM & BEACH

Set in the caves Rommel is said to have used as his headquarters during part of the El Alamein campaign, the rather poor **Rom-** mel's Museum (admission E£10; ☒ 8am-5pm) contains a few photos, a bust of the Desert Fox, some ageing German, Italian and British military maps and what is purported to be Rommel's greatcoat. The museum is about 3km east of the town centre, out by the beach of the same name. The turn-off to the museum and beach is signposted.

Rommel's Beach, a little east of the museum, is supposedly where the field marshal took time off from tanks and troops to have his daily swim. It would have been a good choice and is now popular with holidaying Egyptians in summer; women will feel uncomfortable bathing here. To get here you can walk around the little bay, hire a bike or take a taxi (E£5) from Marsa Matruh.

MARSA MATRUH

0   300 m
0   0.2 miles

INFORMATION	
Banque Misr (ATM)	1 C3
EgyptAir	2 B3
Exchange Bureaux	3 C2
Main Post Office	4 C2
National Bank of Egypt	5 B2
Passport Office	6 C4
Telephone Centrale	7 C2
Tourist Office	8 C2
Tourist Police	9 C2

SLEEPING	
Arous al-Bahr Hotel	10 B2
Ghazala Hotel	11 C3
Hotel Beau Site	12 A2
Hotel Hamada	13 C3
Negresco Hotel	14 A2
Riviera Palace Hotel	15 C2
Rommel House Hotel	16 D2

EATING	
Abdu Kofta	17 D3
Abu Rabie	18 C4
Asmak Hammo al-Temsah	19 C3
Beau Site Restaurant	(see 12)
Kebab Restaurant	20 C3
Panyotis Greek Restaurant	21 C3
Pizza Gaby	22 A2

MEDITERRANEAN SEA

Beach

Beach (Lido)

To Ar-Radir Hotel (3km); Rommel's Museum (3km); Rommel's Beach (3km)

Awam Mosque

Al-Corniche

Ash-Shaati

To Cleopatra's Beach (14km); San Giovanni Cleopatra Hotel (14km); Shaati al-Gharam (17km); Agiba Beach (24km)

Al-Matar

Al-Galaa

To Military Hospital (200m)

Tahrir

To Sidi Barani (135km); Sallum (Libyan Border; 225km); Siwa (305km)

Fruit & Vegetable Market

Alam ar-Rum

Cleopatra

Pick-ups to the Bus Station

Train Station

To Bus Station; Service Taxis (1.5km); Alexandria (275km)

OTHER BEACHES

The luminescence of the water along this stretch of the coast would be even more striking if the town and its hotels were not here. But further away the water is just as nice and you can still find a few places where the developers have not yet started work. During the hot summer months women cannot bathe in swimsuits, unless they can handle being the object of intense harassment and ogling. The exception is the private beach at Hotel Beau Site, although even here most Egyptian women remain fully dressed and in the shade.

If you do manage to get into the turquoise waters, offshore lies the wreck of a German submarine, and sunken Roman galleys reputedly rest in deeper waters off to the east.

The **Lido**, the main beach in town, is no longer an attractive swimming spot.

The next choice is either **Cleopatra's Beach** or **Shaati al-Gharam** (Lovers' Beach), which are about 14km and 17km respectively west of town. The rock formations here are certainly worth a look and you can wade to Cleopatra's Bath, a natural pool where legend has imagined the great queen and Mark Antony enjoying a swim. In summer several boats leave from near Hotel Beau Site to go across the bay to Cleopatra's Beach and Shaati al-Gharam. Taxis will charge about E£70 to bring you here and to wait while you enjoy the beach.

Agiba means 'miracle' in Arabic and **Agiba Beach**, about 24km west of Marsa Matruh, is just that. It is a small but spectacular cove, accessible only via a path leading down from the cliff top. There is a café nearby (open in summer only) where you can get light refreshments. Again, it is absolutely packed in summer.

Sleeping

The accommodation situation in Marsa Matruh is pretty bad. With the exception of the Beau Site and the new San Giovanni Cleopatra, the hotels are generally sad and overpriced, but demand for rooms over summer is such that hoteliers really don't need to try very hard. We list a few of the better, more central options.

Prices vary greatly from winter to summer, and substantial discounts are sometimes available until mid-June. If only one price is given (the summer price), a lower price will be available or should be bargained for. Hotels with half board include accommodation, breakfast and dinner.

BUDGET

Ghazala Hotel (☎ 493 3519; Sharia Alam ar-Rum; dm E£15) The entry to this backpackers' haven is hidden between two shops, but it remains the most popular budget option in town. The accommodation is very basic but clean, and some rooms have balconies. The shared bathrooms are reasonably clean but have no hot water.

Radi Hotel (☎ 493 4827/8; al-Corniche; s/d half board Jun-Sep US$35/55, Oct-May s/d US$10) This three-star hotel overlooking Rommel Beach has spacious air-con rooms with private bathrooms and satellite TV. It is block-booked in the summer with Cairenes, when half board is obligatory.

Arous al-Bahr Hotel (☎ 493 4420; fax 493 4419; al-Corniche; s/d half board Jun-Sep E£45/55, Oct-May E£28/38) A dull and unattractive hotel whose cheap rooms have very little character, though the private bathrooms are clean and some rooms have balconies.

Hotel Hamada (☎ 493 3300; Sharia Tahrir; s/d with shared bathroom E£20/25) Located right in the centre of town, the Hamada is a basic budget option with reasonably clean rooms and friendly staff.

MIDRANGE

There are hotels dotted along the waterfront and in the town centre. Those on the Corniche have good views but little else in the way of amenities; the others are closer to the few shops and restaurants.

Rommel House Hotel (☎ 493 5466; fax 493 2485; Sharia al-Galaa; s/d half board Jun-Sep E£80/130, Oct-May E£50/65; ✷) This is a reasonable, long-standing hotel with private bathroom, TV and refrigerator.

Riviera Palace Hotel (☎ 493 3045; fax 493 0004; Sharia Iskendariyya; s/d half board US$30/50; ✷) A decent hotel with very little character but with clean spacious rooms, some of which have views over the sea. During the summer season though the hotel is usually prebooked by Cairenes who come every year.

Negresco Hotel (☎ 493 4491/2; fax 493 3960; al-Corniche; s/d half board Jun-Sep E£180/270, Oct-May E£80/120) While a bit on the expensive side, the Negresco has spotless rooms, decent facilities and a little more character than most.

TOP END

Hotel Beau Site (☎ 493 2066; www.BeauSiteHotel .com; al-Corniche; s/d US$54/73; ✷ ▢) This is the best option in Matruh town, particularly if you choose the slightly more expensive 'luxury' rooms on the beach, with air-con and satellite TV. The Beau Site boasts the only private beach in the centre, and has several good restaurants in the complex.

San Giovanni Cleopatra (☎ 494 7600; www.san giovanni.com; near Cleopatra Beach, 14km west of Matruh; s/d Jun-Sep US$110/150, Oct-May US$75/110) The most recent arrival is the town's only five-star beach resort, part of the San Giovanni chain. Designed to imitate an overgrown Italianate villa, its 67 spacious rooms overlook the private beach and swimming pool. The hotel also offers a range of beach activities, a health club and video games for the kids. The hotel boats make trips to nearby beaches.

Eating

The dining situation in Matruh is nothing to write home about. In winter you may have a hard time finding something to eat, although Abdu Kofta is open all year round.

RESTAURANTS

Beau Site Restaurant (☎ 493 8555; Hotel Beau Site; al-Corniche; dishes E£10-90; ✷) The Beau Site is famous for its food (although admittedly it is not hard to shine in Marsa Matruh). Meals are a mixture of Egyptian and standard Mediterranean, with an emphasis on fish.

Asmak Hammo al-Temsah (Sharia Tahrir; dishes E£5-30) A modest restaurant where the locals go for fish, served with rice and mezze. Fish is sold by weight and cooked according to your choice. Try the blackened fish, which is rolled in a salty spice mixture that forms a crust on the grill, leaving the inside tender and juicy.

Panyotis Greek Restaurant (Sharia Iskendariyya; dishes E£5-20) Matruh's oldest restaurant rests a little on its laurels, but it is still OK. Fish and seafood are accompanied by tahini and salads and, a rarity in town, a cold beer.

Abdu Kofta (☎ 012 314 4989; Sharia Gamal Abd an-Nasser, off Sharia at-Tahrir; dishes E£5-60; ✷) Ask anyone from Matruh what the best restaurant in town is and they will invariably name Abdu Kofta. In the clean and cool 1st-floor room, it serves kofta or grilled meat by the weight served with good mezze and salads. No alcohol.

QUICK EATS

Kebab Restaurant (Sharia al-Galaa; dishes E£3-15) Serves kebab sandwiches as well as *fiteer*, the Egyptian pizza.

Abu Rabie (Sharia Iskendariyya; dishes E£3-15) A plain but good takeaway with *fuul* and *ta'amiyya*, salads as well as fried *gambari* (shrimp) and *kalamaari* (squid).

Pizza Gaby (al-Corniche; pizzas E£10-20; ☾ Jun-Sep) The pizzas are edible, better than most pizzas in town, but this is not a very attractive spot to linger.

Getting There & Away

AIR

EgyptAir (☎ 493 4398; Sharia al-Matar) has twice-weekly flights between Cairo and Marsa Matruh from June to September. Tickets are about E£520 one way.

BUS

Matruh's bus station is 2km out of town on the main coastal highway. Expect to pay about E£7 for a taxi from the town centre. The following bus companies are located at the bus station and share an office.

Superjet (☎ 490 5079) has two services a day June to September. Buses to Alexandria (E£24, 4½ hours) leave at 2.30pm and to Cairo (E£30 to E£42, five hours) at 3pm.

West Delta Bus Co (☎ 490 5079) has hourly services to Alexandria from 7am to 2am (E£20 to E£26, four hours). Buses to Cairo (E£35 to E£40, five hours) leave at 7.30am, noon and 3.30pm in winter; from June to September they leave hourly from 7.30am to midnight. Buses to Sallum (E£10, four hours) run from 6am to midnight.

Buses to Siwa (E£12, four hours) leave at 7am, 1.30pm, 4pm and 7.30pm.

SERVICE TAXI

The service taxi lot is beside the bus station, 2km out of town. Service taxis to Siwa cost E£15, if there are enough passengers. Other fares include El Alamein (E£10), Alexandria (E£15), Cairo (E£25 to E£30), Sallum (E£12) and Sidi Barani (E£12).

TRAIN

Between June and September there is a daily luxury sleeper train between Cairo and Marsa Matruh. Trains leave Matruh at 11pm and arrive in Cairo at 6am. Tickets are E£225 per person in a double cabin,

E£356 single. Reservations can be made at the station in **Matruh** (☎ 493 3036) or in **Cairo** (☎ 02-738 3682/4).

Otherwise, avoid the rails. Even the stationmaster at Marsa Matruh calls the trains 'horrible'.

Getting Around

Until recently the taxi service of choice in Matruh was the *Careta,* or donkey cart, but these have now been abolished in favour of real taxis. Private taxis or pick-ups can be hired for the day, but you must negotiate and bargain aggressively, especially in the summer. Expect to pay from E£80 to E£150, depending on the distance travelled.

SIDI BARANI
☎ 046

About 135km west of Marsa Matruh on the way to Libya is this small but busy Bedouin town. It serves a bit of a food and petrol to traffic coming from Libya, but that's about it. There's a small hotel and a few unsanitary places to eat.

SALLUM
☎ 46

Nestled at the foot of Gebel as-Sallum, on the gulf of the same name, Sallum (pronounced sa-*loom*) is in the proverbial middle of nowhere. This was the ancient Roman port of Baranis, and there are still a few Roman wells in the area. It is also a Bedouin trading post. The town sees very few Western travellers, so the hassling is minimal. There is a post office here but the branch of the National Bank of Egypt was closed at the time of writing.

The sea here, as along the rest of this stretch of coast, is crystal clear and turquoise, but there are several good reasons not to go to the beach, one being the rubbish dumped on the sand. If you go to se-

---

> **LIBYA BORDER CROSSING**
>
> The border crossing point of Amsaad, just north of Halfaya Pass, is 12km west of Sallum. For details see p542.

---

cluded spots further from the centre, you will need to be sure that it is not government property. Finally, being on the beach without a permit after about 5pm can get you into trouble.

On the eastern entrance to the town there is a WWII Commonwealth War Cemetery, a much more modest version of the one at El Alamein.

Sleeping & Eating

If you can, you will want to avoid staying in Sallum, but if you have no choice the **Hotel al-Ahram** (☎ 480 0148; s/d E£14/21) is the best of an unattractive bunch. The rooms are very spartan and when there is water, it's cold. There are a couple of *lokandas* (basic, cheap places to doss) with their names in Arabic only, of which the Sirt Hotel is the better one. There are no banks open and no exchange office in Sallum, although some hotels may agree to exchange money.

At the border, 12km further on, is Hotel at-Ta'un (signed in Arabic only). There are two modest *fuul* stands around, but check on the price first as it may be higher for the lone foreigner passing by.

Getting There & Away

There are buses and the odd service taxi leaving from Alexandria (p397) and Marsa Matruh (p407).

From Sallum, buses for Marsa Matruh (E£12, four hours) depart hourly between 7am and 2am; some of these continue on to Alexandria (E£23, eight hours). A service taxi to Marsa Matruh will cost about E£15.

Suez Canal

The Suez Canal slices through the desert sands of the Isthmus of Suez, separating mainland Egypt from the Sinai Peninsula, and Africa from Asia. In addition to being one of the world's most famous artificial waterways, it's also one of the busiest, with around 20,000 ships yearly plying its 163km length as they make their way between the Mediterranean and Red Seas.

The three cities that sit along its western banks, Port Said, Ismailia and Suez, emerged largely as colonial creations as the canal grew in prominence. They were on the front line during the wars with Israel and suffered greatly from bombardments. Yet, their 19th-century beginnings still show in the wide, leafy boulevards and graceful colonial architecture that line their picturesque town centres and set them apart from the rest of Egypt.

If you have the time and the inclination to step off Egypt's more trodden trails, the canal's urban trio offers an altogether distinctive experience – an intriguing combination of *belle époque* architecture, modern shipping infrastructure and port-city energy – and makes an agreeable contrast with other areas of the country.

The mainstay of the area's economy, the Suez Canal is surprisingly narrow up close, which makes the colossal cargo ships gliding through its waters seem even larger when seen from its banks. Viewed from afar, they appear to be ploughing through the desert, a surreal and unforgettable sight that puts a new slant on the oft-used phrase 'ships of the desert'.

HIGHLIGHTS

- Watch supertankers appear to glide through the desert as they make their way through the **Suez Canal** (p411), one of the world's most famous waterways
- Stroll along the waterfront in **Port Said** (p413), and take in its graceful 19th-century architecture and port-city bustle
- Wander through **Ismailia's** (p416) old European quarter and into Egypt's colonial past
- Take the **free ferry** (p414) from Port Said to Port Fuad to get a brief taste of life on the canal
- Relax for an afternoon at the **Mercure Forsan Island's beach** (p418) in Ismailia

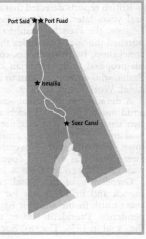

Port Said ★★ Port Fuad

★ Ismailia

★ Suez Canal

History

The Suez Canal – one of the greatest feats of modern engineering – represents the culmination of centuries of effort to enhance trade and expand the empires of Egypt by connecting the Red Sea with the Mediterranean Sea.

Construction of the first recorded canal was begun by Pharaoh Nekau II between 610 and 595 BC. The canal stretched from the Nile Delta town of Bubastis, near present-day Zagazig, to the Red Sea via the Bitter Lakes. After reputedly causing the death of more than 100,000 workers, construction of the canal was abandoned. The project was picked up again and completed about a century later under Darius, one of Egypt's Persian rulers. The canal was improved by the Romans under Trajan, but over the next several centuries it was either neglected and left to silt up, or dredged for limited use depending on the available resources. The canal was again briefly restored in AD 649 for a period of 20 years by Amr ibn al-As, the Arab conqueror of Egypt.

Following the French invasion in 1798, the importance of some sort of sea route south to Asia was again recognised. For the first time, digging a canal directly from the Mediterranean Sea to the Red Sea, across the comparatively narrow Isthmus of Suez, was considered. The idea was abandoned, however, when Napoleon's engineers mistakenly calculated that there was a 10m difference between the two sea levels.

British reports detected that mistake several years later, but it was Ferdinand de Lesseps, the French consul to Egypt, who pursued the Suez Canal idea through to its conclusion. In 1854, de Lesseps presented his proposal to the Egyptian khedive Said Pasha, who authorised him to excavate the canal. Work began in 1859.

A decade later the canal was completed amid much fanfare and celebration. When two small fleets, one originating in Port Said and the other in Suez, met at the new town of Ismailia on 16 November 1869, the Suez Canal was declared open and Africa was officially severed from Asia.

Ownership of the canal remained in French and British hands for the next 86 years until, in the wake of Egyptian independence, President Nasser nationalised the canal in 1956. The two European pow-

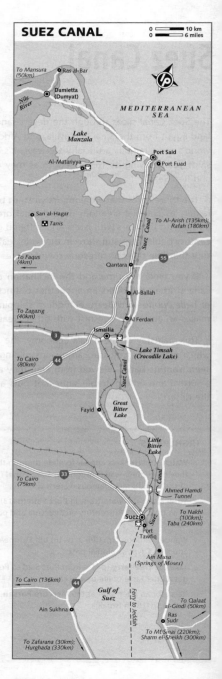

ers, in conjunction with Israel, invaded Egypt in an ungallant attempt to retake the waterway by force. In what came to be known as the 'Suez Crisis', they were forced to retreat in the face of widespread international condemnation.

Today, the Suez Canal remains one of the world's most heavily used shipping lanes and toll revenues represent one of the largest contributors to the Egyptian state coffers.

Getting There & Around
Most visitors travel to the Suez Canal area by road. There are also train links, albeit very slow, between Cairo and the three main canal towns. Suez is connected by ferry with Jeddah (Saudi Arabia) – see p543 for information – and Port Said is a common stop for cruise liners from elsewhere in the Mediterranean basin. Once in the region, bus is the best way to get around, with frequent and straightforward connections between major towns.

PORT SAID
☎ 066 / pop 540,000
Port Said's main attraction, and the reason for its establishment on the Mediterranean, is the Suez Canal, and the sight of enormous ships and tankers lining up to pass through the canal's northern entrance is a highlight for most visitors. Thanks to its duty-free status it is the most flourishing of all the canal cities, with good shopping and vaguely New Orleans overtones.

Port Said was founded in 1859 by its namesake, the khedive Said Pasha, when excavation for the Suez Canal began. Much of the city is an island, created by filling in part of Lake Manzala, to the west, with sand from the canal site. Upon completion of the canal 10 years later, Port Said was the scene of the opening ceremony for the festivities that followed, touted in the international press as 'the party of the century'.

The city continued to grow until 1956, when much of it was bombed during the Suez Crisis. It suffered again during the 1967 and 1973 wars with Israel. Damage from the wars can still be seen, but most of the city has been rebuilt, and it exudes a bustling, prosperous air.

Port Said is also a popular summer resort, and beach bungalows line the coast along its northern edge.

Orientation
Port Said is connected to the mainland by a bridge to the south and a causeway to the west. There is also a ferry between Port Said and its sister town of Port Fuad on the opposite side of the canal.

Most banks and important services are on Sharia Palestine, which runs along the canal, or on Sharia al-Gomhuriyya, two blocks inland.

Information
CUSTOMS
Port Said was declared a duty-free port in 1976. In theory, everyone must pass through customs when entering and leaving the city, though in practice this is seldom enforced. Be sure to have your passport with you, and if you are given the choice of declaring cameras and electronic goods on entering, then do so. For major purchases, it's also worth checking in the shop whether or not duty must be paid. Also note that duty-free in Egypt doesn't necessarily mean that all items are tax free.

EMERGENCY
Tourist police (☎ /fax 322 8570; post office bldg, off Sharia al-Gomhuriyya) Near Ferial Gardens.

INTERNET ACCESS
Compunet (per hr E£3; ☺ 9am-midnight) Next to Ferial Gardens.
Net Café & Ice (Sharia Palestine; per hr E£6; ☺ 1pm-1am) Diagonally opposite the lighthouse.

MEDICAL SERVICES
Delafrant Hospital (☎ 322 3663; Sharia Orabi)
Public Hospital (☎ 322 0694; Sharia Safiyya Zaghloul)

MONEY
There are ATMs scattered around town, including at the **National Bank of Abu Dhabi** (Sharia Palestine), and at Banque du Caire and Banque Misr, both on Sharia al-Gomhuriyya. Other banks:
American Express Bank (Sharia Palestine; ☺ 9am-2pm & 6.30-8pm Sun-Thu) Has services for American Express card holders and an ATM.
Bank of Alexandria (Sharia al-Gomhuriyya; ☺ 8.30am-2pm & 6-8pm Sun-Thu)
National Bank of Egypt (Sharia al-Gomhuriyya; ☺ 9am-2pm & 6.30-8pm Sat-Thu)
Thomas Cook (☎ 322 7559; 43 Sharia al-Gomhuriyya; ☺ 8am-4.30pm)

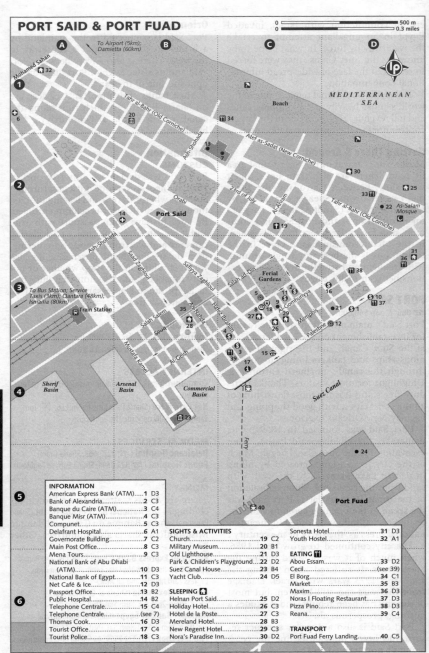

PORT SAID & PORT FUAD

SUEZ CANAL

INFORMATION
American Express Bank (ATM)....**1** D3
Bank of Alexandria....................**2** C3
Banque du Caire (ATM)..............**3** C4
Banque Misr (ATM)...................**4** C3
Compunet................................**5** C3
Delafrant Hospital.....................**6** A1
Governorate Building.................**7** C2
Main Post Office.......................**8** C3
Mena Tours.............................**9** C3
National Bank of Abu Dhabi
(ATM)................................**10** D3
National Bank of Egypt.............**11** C3
Net Café & Ice.........................**12** D3
Passport Office........................**13** B2
Public Hospital........................**14** B2
Telephone Centrale...................**15** C4
Telephone Centrale.............(see **7**)
Thomas Cook..........................**16** D3
Tourist Office...........................**17** C3
Tourist Police...........................**18** C3

SIGHTS & ACTIVITIES
Church...................................**19** C2
Military Museum.......................**20** B1
Old Lighthouse.........................**21** D3
Park & Children's Playground.....**22** D2
Suez Canal House......................**23** B4
Yacht Club..............................**24** D5

SLEEPING
Helnan Port Said......................**25** D2
Holiday Hotel...........................**26** C3
Hotel de la Poste......................**27** C3
Mereland Hotel........................**28** B3
New Regent Hotel.....................**29** C3
Nora's Paradise Inn..................**30** D2

Sonesta Hotel..........................**31** D3
Youth Hostel...........................**32** A1

EATING
Abou Essam............................**33** D2
Cecil.................................(see **39**)
El Borg..................................**34** C1
Market..................................**35** B3
Maxim...................................**36** D3
Nora I Floating Restaurant.........**37** D3
Pizza Pino...............................**38** D3
Reana...................................**39** C4

TRANSPORT
Port Fuad Ferry Landing............**40** C5

POST
Main post office (Sharia al-Geish; ⊗ 8.30am-2.30pm Sat-Thu) Near Ferial Gardens.

TELEPHONE
Telephone centrale (Sharia Palestine; ⊗ 24hr)
Telephone centrale (Governorate Bldg, Sharia 23rd of July; ⊗ 24hr)

TOURIST INFORMATION
Tourist office (☎ 323 5289; 8 Sharia Palestine; ⊗ 9am-6pm Sat-Thu) Very efficient and helpful.

VISA EXTENSIONS
Passport office (4th fl, left wing, window 7, Governorate Bldg, Sharia 23rd of July; ⊗ 8am-2pm Sat-Thu)

Sights & Activities
SUEZ CANAL HOUSE
If you've ever seen a picture of Port Said, it was probably of the striking green domes of the Suez Canal House. One of the best views of the Suez Canal used to be from this white-columned building, southwest of the ferry terminal, which was built in time for the inauguration of the canal in 1869. It is off-limits to visitors.

TOWN CENTRE
The heart of Port Said is along the canal edge, on and around Sharia Palestine. Here, the waterfront is lined with late-19th-century five-storey buildings complete with wooden balconies, louvered doors and high verandas in grand *belle époque* style. Take a stroll down Sharia Memphis, in particular, with its old Woolworth's building

---

LIBERTY ON THE CANAL
New York's Statue of Liberty was originally designed to stand in Port Said at the entrance to the Suez Canal. Inspired by the colossal statues at Abu Simbel, French sculptor Frédéric-Auguste Bartholdi formulated the idea of a huge statue of a woman bearing a torch. She was to represent progress – 'Egypt carrying the light of Asia', to use Bartholdi's own words. The idea was ultimately abandoned due to the cost, and the 'Light of Asia', which had developed from one of Bartholdi's models, was sent to New York, where she became Lady Liberty.

(now a souvenir emporium), and around the streets just north of the Commercial Basin. There are some wonderfully odd colonial remnants, such as the old Postes Françaises; a sign for the ship chandlers of the pre-Soviet 'volunteer Russian fleet' and another for the Bible Society. Northeast of here, on Sharia 23rd of July, is the Italian consulate building, erected in the 1930s and adorned with an engraved piece of the propaganda of Fascist dictator Benito Mussolini: 'Rome – once again at the heart of an Empire'. Several blocks inland, on and around Sharia Salah Salem, is an impressive collection of churches, including the Coptic Orthodox church of St Bishoi of the Virgin and the Franciscan compound.

At the very northern end of Sharia Palestine, near the Sonesta Hotel, is a large stone plinth that once held a statue of Ferdinand de Lesseps, until it was torn down in 1956 with the nationalisation of the Suez Canal. Although the statue was restored at the expense of the French government in the early 1990s, it has yet to be re-erected.

There are children's **playgrounds** dotted around town, including in the small park on the southwestern side of the New Corniche, diagonally opposite the Helnan Port Said.

MILITARY MUSEUM
The compact **Military Museum** (☎ 322 4657; Sharia 23rd of July; admission E£5; ⊗ 9am-4pm Sat-Thu) houses relics from the 1956 Suez Crisis and the 1967 and 1973 wars with Israel. Among other things, you can see captured US tanks with the Star of David painted on them, a few unexploded bombs and various other reminders of recent wars, as well as a small display relating to ancient Pharaonic and Islamic conflicts.

PORT FUAD
Across the canal from Port Said is the genteel suburb of Port Fuad, founded in 1925. The streets near its quay invite a stroll, with their sprawling residences, lush gardens and sloping tiled roofs recalling the one-time European presence. Port Fuad – specifically, its **yacht club** – is also the place to go to find a passage or work on a vessel plying the canal, as the captains are sometimes looking for crew members. Free ferries from Port Said to Port Fuad offer impressive views of the canal, and leave

CRUISING THE CANAL

Although hundreds of ships pass through the Suez Canal each week, canal enthusiasts who want to do the same will find that it's not that easy. Organised trips don't exist, and the police do not allow private boats to cruise the canal for security reasons.

The easiest way to get a fleeting taste of life on the canal is to take the free ferry over to Port Fuad from in front of the tourist office on Sharia Palestine in Port Said. Otherwise, you can try the sporadically functioning *Noras I* Floating Restaurant, also in Port Said, at the northernmost end of the canal. When it is operating it offers a one-hour tour of the canal for E£17.50 per person, which includes a soft drink. Theoretically, departures occur daily at 3.30pm and 9.30pm, but as this book was being researched, the boat was indefinitely out of service.

In Suez, the best bet is to enjoy the canal from the windows of the restaurant on the top floor of the Red Sea Hotel, or while strolling along the waterside promenade paralleling the street behind the Saudi Arabian consulate.

If you do manage to get on some sort of vessel, remember that taking photographs is generally prohibited, as there is a strong military presence all along the canal.

about every 10 minutes throughout the day from the terminal at the southwestern end of Sharia Palestine.

Sleeping

In the early 20th century, Port Said boasted one of the most famous hotels in the country – the mammoth, seven-storey Eastern Exchange, which stood roughly opposite where Banque du Caire is today. But that was in the days when passenger liners regularly docked at the port, and the town was a global transit point. Today, the offerings are much more modest, catering primarily to business travellers and summer holidaymakers.

BUDGET

Hotel de la Poste (☎ /fax 322 4048, 322 8898; 42 Sharia al-Gomhuriyya; s/d/tr E£39/49/55.50) This faded classic still manages to maintain a hint of its original charm, and is Port Said's best budget option. Some rooms have a small balcony, and others have TV and fridge. Downstairs is a small restaurant.

Youth Hostel (☎ 322 8702; Sharia Mohamed Sahan; dm E£8.25) This is the cheapest place to stay in Port Said. It has basic bunk beds, with 20 beds per room, and is tolerable enough, apart from its highly inconvenient location behind the stadium and well away from the town centre. On the plus side, there's a public beach within easy walking distance.

Mereland Hotel (☎ 322 7020, 332 1570; s/d E£15/20, with private bathroom E£25/30) This tatty hotel, in a small lane between Sharia Saad Zaghloul and Sharia an-Nahda, has definitely

seen better days, but its rooms are large and the price is among the lowest you'll find. Breakfast costs extra.

MIDRANGE

New Regent Hotel (☎ 323 5000, 322 3802; fax 322 4891; off Sharia al-Gomhuriyya; s/d E£198/270; 🌂) This smart three-star hotel has a convenient location in a lane, two blocks in from the canal, and small, spotless rooms with TV.

Nora's Paradise Inn (☎ 333 1911/2; pst@sedapnet .org.eg; Sharia Atef as-Sadat; 2-/3-bedroom apt E£247/302; 🌂) Comprising clean, modern apartments (all with kitchenette) it's in a compound of high-rise blocks just in from the sea and just west of the Helnan Port Said hotel, and is not to be confused with the neighbouring Nora's Beach Hotel.

Holiday Hotel (☎ 322 0711, 322 1160; fax 322 0710; 23 Sharia al-Gomhuriyya; s/d E£261/320; 🌂) A large modern block on the main street, the Holiday has a café on the ground floor, and simple but decent rooms with TV and minifridge.

TOP END

Helnan Port Said (☎ 332 0890; www.helnan.com; Sharia Atef as-Sadat; s/d US$70/120; 🌂 🖥 🏊) Overlooking the Mediterranean at the north end of town is the Helnan, Port Said's main five-star hotel. It has well-appointed rooms, views over the end of the canal and the Mediterranean, and a restaurant.

Sonesta Hotel (☎ 332 5511; www.sonesta.com /egypt_portsaid; Sharia Palestine; s/d US$110/140; 🌂 🏊) This modest but pleasant four-star hotel is conveniently located just southeast of the Helnan, and overlooks the canal. It has efficient staff and all the usual amenities, plus a play area for children.

Eating

Port Said has a good selection of eateries, especially seafood restaurants. Most are open from about 1pm until 1am.

Abou Essam (☎ 323 2776; Sharia Atef as-Sadat; meals E£20-30; ✖) This bright, modern place is diagonally opposite the Port Said Helnan. It has a serve-yourself salad bar featuring tahini, *baba ghanoug* and other local delicacies, plus a good selection of grilled or fried fish, pasta and meat.

El Borg (☎ 332 3442; Sharia Atef as-Sadat; dishes E£12-30; ✆ 10am-3am) A local favourite, with an Arabic-only menu, and serve-yourself seafood grills.

Pizza Pino (☎ 323 9949; Sharia al-Gomhuriyya; pizzas E£11-20, dishes E£25-65) A pleasant local version of a Pizza Express, the popular Pizza Pino serves up pizza and pasta in smart, attractive surroundings.

Maxim (☎ 323 8628; 1st fl, Sonesta Shopping Centre, Sharia Palestine; dishes E£25-85; ✖) This upmarket seafood restaurant near the waterfront offers a good menu selection and views over the canal that compensate for its otherwise bland ambience.

Noras I Floating Restaurant (☎ 332 6804; Sharia Palestine; ✖) The boat was indefinitely out of service when this book was researched, but when operational, it can be chartered from its canal mooring at the northern end of Sharia Palestine for a 1¼-hour tour of the canal, during which a predominantly seafood lunch or dinner is served.

Reana (Sharia al-Gomhuriyya; dishes E£15-35; ✖) This place offers reasonable attempts at Chinese or Korean dishes with a seafood slant. Below is the Cecil bar for a pre- or postdinner Stella.

For fruit and vegetables, try the lively market on Sharia Souq, three blocks north of Sharia al-Gomhuriyya.

Shopping

Almost anything can be bought in Port Said, with cheap electronics and designer jeans among the biggest-selling items, although an increasing number of upmarket boutiques are also springing up. The best deals are on and around Sharia al-Gomhuriyya; for slicker outlets, head to the

northeastern end of Sharia al-Gomhuriyya, near Sharia 23rd of July.

Getting There & Away
BOAT

Numerous five-star cruise ships ply the waters between Port Said and Limassol (Cyprus), with most sailing between April and October; see p542 for details. A good local contact for information on prices and schedules is **Mena Tours** (☎ 322 5742, 323 3376; Sharia al-Gomhuriyya).

BUS

The bus station is about 3km from the town centre at the beginning of the road to Cairo (about E£3 to E£5 in a taxi).

Superjet (☎ 372 1779) has hourly buses to Cairo (E£17, three hours) from 7am until about 8pm, and a bus to Alexandria (E£22, four hours) at 4.30pm daily. Bookings are advisable.

East Delta Bus Co (☎ 372 9883) also has hourly buses to Cairo (E£13.50 to E£16, three hours) from 6am to 10pm daily. Buses to Alexandria (E£20 to E£22, four hours) leave at 7am, 11am, 3.30pm and 7pm. Buses to Ismailia (E£4 to E£5.50, one to 1½ hours) depart hourly between 6am and 7pm. Buses to Suez (E£10.50, 2½ to three hours) depart at 10am and 3.30pm. There is a daily bus to Hurghada at 5pm. For Al-Arish on the Sinai Peninsula, the only option is service taxi.

SERVICE TAXI

Service taxis have an area in the bus station (about E£3 to E£5 in a taxi, ask for '*al-mahattat servees*'). Sample destinations and fares include: Cairo (E£15), Ismailia (E£7), Qantara (E£5) and Suez (E£10).

TRAIN

The five daily trains to Cairo via Ismailia are slow (five hours), and not recommended. They run at 5.30am, 9.45am, 1pm, 5.30pm and 7.30pm. There are no 1st-class services. Fares are E£15/7/3.25 for 2nd-class air-con/ 2nd-class ordinary/3rd class .

There are an additional five trains that travel daily to Ismailia only (E£7/3/1.25).

Getting Around
HANTOUR

The most enjoyable way to tour Port Said, especially around sunset, is by *hantour* (horse-drawn carriage). *Hantour*s can be found along all the main streets, and cost about E£10 per hour after some bargaining.

MICROBUS

Microbuses run along main arteries such as Sharia Orabi and Sharia ash-Shohada, and cost 50pt for a short ride.

TAXI

There are plenty of blue-and-white taxis around Port Said. Fares for short trips within the town centre average E£1 to E£3.

QANTARA

The only reason to visit the town of Qantara, 50km south of Port Said, is to cross to the east side of the canal. The canal itself is spanned by the enormous Mubarak Peace Suspension Bridge – built with Japanese assistance in an effort to boost links with North Sinai – and the bridge crossing offers some impressive views. Most of Qantara was destroyed during the 1973 war with Israel, and some of the town's buildings are still scarred with bullet holes. Buses to Al-Arish usually stop in Qantara.

ISMAILIA

☎ 064 / pop 860,000

Ismailia's picturesque town centre – with its elegant colonial streets, expansive lawns and late-19th-century villas – makes an agreeable day excursion from Cairo or a worthwhile overnight stop if you are travelling around the canal area.

Ismailia was founded by and named after Pasha Ismail, who was khedive of Egypt in the 1860s while the Suez Canal was being built. Ferdinand de Lesseps, the director of the Suez Canal Company, lived in the city until the canal was completed.

As you experience the architecture and shady lanes in the city centre, it's interesting to see how Ismailia grew in the image of the British and French masters who had ensconced themselves in Egypt in the 19th century and first half of the 20th century.

Orientation

The heart of Ismailia (from a visitor's perspective) and the area most worth exploring is the old European quarter around Sharia Thawra and the peaceful central square, Midan al-Gomhuriyya. Sharia Thawra (for-

merly known as Sharia Sultan Hussein) runs south from the train line to the placid Sweetwater Canal, with Midan al-Gomhuriyya several blocks to the west. The road running parallel to the Sweetwater Canal is known by three names: Mohammed Ali Quay, the Promenade and Sharia Salah Salem. North of the train line is a dusty, chaotic area of fast-growing urban sprawl.

Information

INTERNET ACCESS

Rodu Internet Café (Sharia Thawra; per hr E£1.50; ⏱ 10am-8pm) Tucked into a small alley next to the FedEx office.

Speednet (cnr Sharia at-Tahrir & Sharia Abu Bakr as-Sadiq; per hr E£1.5; ⏱ 10am-1am) Near Midan Orabi.

MEDICAL SERVICES

Hospital (☎ 337 3902/3; Sharia Mustashfa)

MONEY

Bank of Alexandria (Midan Orabi; ⏱ 9am-2pm & 6-8pm Sun-Thu)

Banque du Caire (Sharia Hassan Nadh; ⏱ 9am-3pm Sun-Thu) ATM.

POST

Main post office (Sharia el-Horreyya; ⏱ 8.30am-2.30pm Sat-Thu)

TELEPHONE

Telephone centrale (Midan Orabi; ⏱ 24hr)

TOURIST INFORMATION

Tourist office (☎ 332 1078; 1st fl, New Governorate Bldg, Sharia Tugary, Sheikh Zayeed area; ⏱ 8.30am-3pm Sat-Thu) About 1.5km north of Midan Orabi.

Tourist police (☎ 333 2910; tourist village, beach area)

VISA EXTENSIONS

Passport office (☎ 391 4559; Midan al-Gomhuriyya; ⏱ 8am-2pm Sat-Thu)

Sights & Activities

ISMAILIA MUSEUM

More than 4000 objects from Pharaonic and Graeco-Roman times are housed at the small but interesting **Ismailia Museum** (☎ 391 2749; Mohammed Ali Quay; adult/child E£6/3; ⏱ 8am-4pm, closed for Friday midday prayers), on the eastern edge of town. There are statues, scarabs, stelae and records of the first canal, built between the Bitter Lakes and Bubastis by the Persian ruler Darius. The highlight of the collection

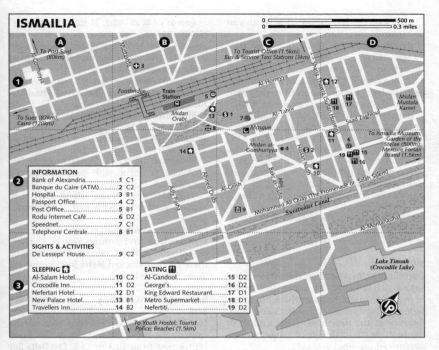

ISMAILIA

0 — 500 m
0 — 0.3 miles

To Port Said (80km)

To Tourist Office (1.5km); Bus & Service Taxi Stations (3km)

Footbridge Train Station

Midan Orabi

Al-Horreyya

Al-Tahrir

Mosque

Midan al Gomhuriyya

To Suez (87km); Cairo (120km)

Midan Mustafa Kamel

To Ismailia Museum, Garden of the Stelae; Mercure Forsan Island (1.5km)

Mohammed Ali Quay (The Promenade or Salah Salem)

Sweetwater Canal

Al-Montanashat

Lake Timsah (Crocodile Lake)

To Youth Hostel; Tourist Police; Beaches (1.5km)

INFORMATION
Bank of Alexandria...................1 C1
Banque du Caire (ATM)............2 C2
Hospital....................................3 B1
Passport Office.........................4 C2
Post Office................................5 B1
Rodu Internet Café...................6 D2
Speednet...................................7 C1
Telephone Centrale...................8 B1

SIGHTS & ACTIVITIES
De Lesseps' House.....................9 C2

SLEEPING
Al-Salam Hotel........................10 C2
Crocodile Inn..........................11 D1
Nefertari Hotel........................12 D1
New Palace Hotel....................13 B1
Travellers Inn..........................14 B2

EATING
Al-Gandool...............................15 D2
George's...................................16 D2
King Edward Restaurant..........17 D1
Metro Supermarket..................18 D1
Nefertiti...................................19 D2

is a 4th-century AD mosaic depicting characters from Greek and Roman mythology. At the top Phaedra is sending a love letter to her stepson Hippolytus, while below, Dionysus, the god of wine, tags along on a chariot driven by Eros. The bottom section recounts the virtues of Hercules, demigod and son of Jupiter.

GARDEN OF THE STELAE
Just southwest of the museum is a garden containing a rather forlorn little sphinx from the time of Ramses II. You need permission from the museum to visit the garden, but you are able to see the unremarkable statue from the street. The attractive grounds of the majestic residence between the garden and the museum belong to the head of the Suez Canal Authority, and are off limits to the public.

DE LESSEPS' HOUSE
The residence of the one-time French consul to Egypt used to be open to the public. Now you can see the interior only if you're a VIP of some sort, as these days it serves

as a private guesthouse for important visitors of the Suez Canal Authority. Inside the grounds is de Lesseps' private carriage encased in glass. His bedroom looks as if it has hardly been touched; old photos, books and various utensils are scattered around the desk by his bed and on the floor. The house is on Mohammed Ali Quay near the corner of Sharia Ahmed Orabi.

BEACHES
There are several beaches around Lake Timsah, on the southeastern edge of town, though the better ones are owned by the various clubs dotting the shore, so you'll need to pay to use them (on average about E£20). The public beaches charge between E£3 and E£5.

Sleeping
BUDGET
Youth Hostel (☎ 392 2850; Lake Timsah; dm/d/tr E£15.25/54/81) This hostel has clean rooms – all with private bathrooms – plus views and its own beach. Prices are discounted by E£2 per person with a HI/YHA membership

card. It's on the lake, about 2km southwest of Midan al-Gomhuriyya.

New Palace Hotel (☎ 391 7761; Midan Orabi; s/d E£60/120) A drab place with reasonable though somewhat overpriced rooms – all with air-con and TV – and a central location near the train station. Apart from the youth hostel, it's the best budget choice in town.

Nefertari Hotel (☎ 391 2822; 41 Sharia Thawra; s/d E£40/50) The faded Nefertari has few attractions, other than the price. It's in the town centre, south of the railway tracks. Not recommended for women travellers.

Travellers Inn (☎ 392 3304; Sharia Ahmed Orabi; r per person with/without bathroom E£20/10) This strictly shoestring place is one of the cheapest options in town. Its musty rooms and grubby bathrooms are somewhat compensated for by a convenient location just west of Midan al-Gomhuriyya.

MIDRANGE

Crocodile Inn (☎ 391 2555; cnr Sharias Thawra & Saad Zaghloul; s/d E£80/120; ✷) This five-storey place in the town centre has a spiffy, modern exterior, and spartan, reasonably clean rooms. Because of the dearth of competition, it's the best choice in this price range, though overpriced for what you get.

Al-Salam Hotel (☎ 391 4401; 9 Sharia al-Geish; d E£95; ✷) The Al-Salam was closed for renovation when we visited, but once reopened, it promises to be one of the better places in the town centre, with reasonably comfortable rooms and a quiet location near the canal.

TOP END

Mercure Forsan Island (☎ 391 6316, 391 8040, 02-525 3419; www.accor.com; Gezirat Forsan; s/d/chalet US$120/133/376; ✷ ▨) About 1.6km southeast of the old centre of town, the four-star Mercure is the only hotel in Ismailia that can be described as appealing. It sits on its own on a small island on the eastern edge of town, overlooking a tranquil beach with a few palm trees, and makes a relaxing overnight getaway. The pool costs E£15 Monday to Thursday, and E£25 Friday to Sunday (including towel hire) for nonguests.

Eating & Drinking

Nefertiti (☎ 391 0494; Sharia Thawra; dishes E£15-50; ✷) This cosy little place has a bright interior, red-checked table cloths, fresh seafood and other meals, and a bar.

George's (☎ 391 8327; 11 Sharia Thawra; dishes E£20-60; ✷) The classic George's has been around since 1950, but is quite faded these days. Its large menu features fried calamari and other seafood and meat dishes of varying quality, but the cosy British pub–style ambience compensates for any shortfalls in the cuisine. There's also a bar.

King Edward Restaurant (☎ 392 3611; 171 Sharia at-Tahrir; dishes E£7-30; ✷) Another faded classic, with a modest selection of meat and fish dishes and an unappealing ambience.

Al-Gandool (☎ 392 8251; Sharia Thawra; dishes E£5-15) A local favourite, with reasonably priced mixed grills, fish and pasta.

The Mercure Forsan Island (left) has a good restaurant with a popular buffet lunch.

Takeaway and budget places are concentrated on and around Sharia Thawra, and around Midan Orabi. For self-caterers, there's a well-stocked **Metro Supermarket** (cnr Sharias Thawra & at-Tahrir).

Getting There & Away

BUS

Ismailia's bus station is about 3km northwest of the old quarter; taxis to the town centre cost from E£3 to E£5. **East Delta Bus Co** (☎ 332 1513) has buses to Cairo (E£8, 2½ hours) every half hour between 6am and 8pm. Buses to Alexandria (E£25, five hours) leave at 7am, 10.30am and 2.30pm. Buses to Port Said (E£4 to E£5.50, two hours) and Suez (E£5, 1½ hours) depart every hour from 7am to 6pm.

There are also hourly buses to Al-Arish (E£10, three to four hours) between 8.30am and 5.30pm. Buses to Sharm el-Sheikh (E£30, six hours) leave frequently throughout the morning, starting at 6.30am. Afternoon and evening departures include those at noon, 2.30pm, 5.30pm, 10pm and 11pm, with the 2.30pm and 11pm services going on to Dahab (E£43, eight hours).

SERVICE TAXI

These depart from the bus station. Destinations include Suez (E£5), Port Said (E£5), Zagazig (E£5), Cairo (E£10) and Al-Arish (E£10).

TRAIN

Trains in the canal zone are slow and inefficient. If you must use them, trains to

Cairo (eight daily, four to five hours) cost E£11/6/2.50 in 2nd-class air-con/2nd-class ordinary/3rd class.

To Port Said, there are six trains per day (E£7/3/1.25 in 2nd-class air-con/2nd-class ordinary/3rd class, 1½ hours). There are also frequent trains to Suez (E£1.50 in 3rd class only).

Getting Around

MICROBUS
Microbuses ply the main arteries of the city. Fares average 50pt.

TAXI
There are plenty of taxis around town. Short trips cost E£1 to E£3; between town and the beaches expect to pay E£5.

SUEZ
☎ 062 / pop 500,000

Balmy, bustling Suez sprawls around the shores of the gulf where the Red Sea meets the southern entrance of the Suez Canal. It was heavily damaged during the 1967 and 1973 wars with Israel, although little evidence of the devastation remains. The rebuilt main streets, however, are mostly a façade hiding a maze of ramshackle backstreet neighbourhoods. A memorial on Sharia al-Galaa commemorates both wars.

The town itself is divided between Suez proper and Port Tawfiq. The latter is at the mouth of the canal, and is an ideal place for watching the ships go by. It also has several streets with gracious old colonial buildings that managed to escape the bombing. Joining Port Tawfiq with town is Sharia al-Geish, a wide thoroughfare that cuts through an industrial area before leading through the heart of Suez. Here, you'll find a few staid old buildings and a surprising number of colonial-era churches crowded among a proliferation of sombre high-rises.

Suez' main attractions are the canal and the city's agreeable, down-to-earth ambience, which is especially noticeable if you're coming from one of the resort areas elsewhere in the country. It is also a major transit point – not only for the great tankers, cargo vessels and private yachts en route to or from the Mediterranean, but also for thousands of Muslim faithful who pass through each year on their way to Saudi Arabia for the haj.

Information
General Hospital (☎ 333 1190; Sharia al-Baladiya)
Main post office (Sharia Hoda Shaarawi; ☯ 8.30am-2.30pm Sat-Thu)
Port Tawfiq post office (Sharia al-Marwa; ☯ 8.30am-2.30pm Sat-Thu) Next to the tourist office.
Telephone centrale (Sharia Saad Zaghloul; ☯ 24hr)

EMBASSIES & CONSULATES
Saudi Arabian consulate (☎ 333 4017/8; Sharia al-Geish, Port Tawfiq; ☯ 9am-3pm Sat-Thu) Mainly processes work and haj visas; allow up to one month for transit or tourist visas. The best bet is to go through Mena Tours (below), which will simplify the lengthy process and make sure you have the correct documents in advance.

INTERNET ACCESS
CACE (Sharia al-Geish, Suez; per hr E£2; ☯ 9am-8pm) Near Midan Nesima, with another branch next to Green House Hotel.
Net Café (Sharia al-Geish, Suez; per hr E£2; ☯ 9am-10pm) In Renaissance Cinema, next to Green House Hotel.

MONEY
Bank of Alexandria (off Sharia al-Geish; ☯ 9am-2pm Sun-Thu)
Banque Misr (Sharia al-Geish; ☯ 9am-2pm Sun-Thu)
Commercial International Bank (Sharia al-Geish; ☯ 9am-2pm Sun-Thu) ATM.
National Bank of Egypt (Sharia Saad Zaghloul; ☯ 9am-2pm Sun-Thu) ATM.

TOURIST INFORMATION
Tourist office (☎ 333 1141; Sharia al-Marwa, Port Tawfiq; ☯ 8am-8pm Sat-Thu, 8am-3pm Fri)
Tourist police (Sharia al-Marwa, Port Tawfiq) Next to the tourist office.

TRAVEL AGENCIES
Mena Tours (☎ 322 8821, 322 0269, 010 516 9841; Sharia al-Marwa; ☯ 9am-3pm Sat-Thu) On the waterfront in Port Tawfiq, diagonally behind the Saudi Arabian consulate. Arrange transit and tourist visas for Saudi Arabia here.

VISA EXTENSIONS
Passport office (Sharia al-Horreyya; ☯ 8.30am-3pm) Issues visa extensions.

Sleeping

BUDGET
During the month of the haj, budget places fill up with passengers travelling to and from Saudi Arabia by sea. For the rest of the year, you should have no problem finding a room.

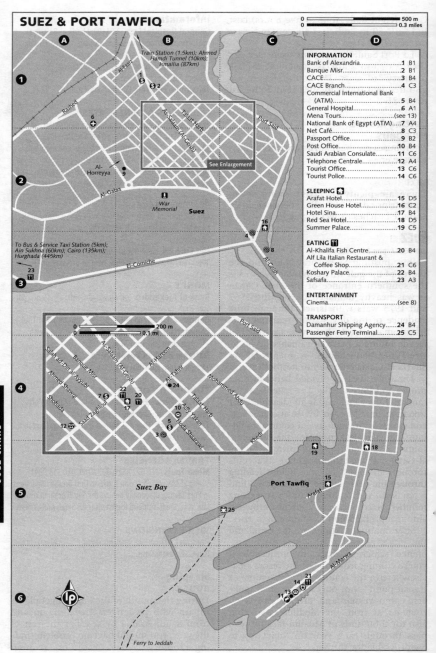

SUEZ & PORT TAWFIQ

INFORMATION
Bank of Alexandria..........................1 B1
Banque Misr..................................2 B1
CACE..3 B4
CACE Branch..................................4 C3
Commercial International Bank
(ATM)...5 B4
General Hospital..............................6 A1
Mena Tours..............................(see 13)
National Bank of Egypt (ATM).......7 A4
Net Café..8 C3
Passport Office...............................9 B2
Post Office...................................10 B4
Saudi Arabian Consulate...............11 C6
Telephone Centrale.......................12 A4
Tourist Office...............................13 C6
Tourist Police...............................14 C6

SLEEPING
Arafat Hotel................................15 D5
Green House Hotel........................16 C2
Hotel Sina...................................17 B4
Red Sea Hotel..............................18 D5
Summer Palace.............................19 C5

EATING
Al-Khalifa Fish Centre....................20 B4
Alf Lila Italian Restaurant &
Coffee Shop...............................21 C6
Koshary Palace.............................22 B4
Safsafa.......................................23 A3

ENTERTAINMENT
Cinema....................................(see 8)

TRANSPORT
Damanhur Shipping Agency..........24 B4
Passenger Ferry Terminal...............25 C5

Arafat Hotel (☎ 333 8355; Sharia Arafat, Port Tawfiq; s/d E£27/34, with bathroom E£33/43) This small hotel is the only budget option near the port. It's on a small side street off Sharia al-Geish, with tidy but musty rooms with fans, and no meals.

Hotel Sina (☎ 333 4181; 21 Sharia Banque Misr, Suez; s/d E£23/35, d/tr with bathroom E£45/52; ✷) This faded place is one of the better options if you want to be based in the town centre. It has reasonable rooms with ceiling fans, and is not recommended for women travellers. Breakfast is not included.

MIDRANGE & TOP END
Red Sea Hotel (☎ 333 4302; www.redseahotel.com; 13 Sharia Riad, Port Tawfiq; s/d from E£272/332; ✷) This is the city's premier establishment, with small but comfortable rooms and a good restaurant. Watch for the hotel's large white-and-red sign poking out above the rooftops near the yacht club in Port Tawfiq.

Green House Hotel (☎ 333 1553/4; greenhouse-suez@hotmail.com; Sharia al-Geish, Suez; s/d US$53/66; ✷ ✷) This large hotel is in a relatively quiet location at the southern edge of town. It has views of the canal, comfortable rooms with minifridges and balconies, a garden and a bar.

Summer Palace (☎ 322 1287; fax 332 6615; Port Tawfiq; s/d E£291/372; ✷ ✷) The bright orange Summer Palace has a decent location with gulf views, a restaurant and a tranquil waterfront bar, but bland and overpriced motel-style rooms. Its seawater pool costs E£10 if you're not a hotel guest.

Eating & Drinking
For inexpensive favourites like *ta'amiyya* and *shwarma,* take a wander around the streets bounded by Sharia Talaat Harb, Sharia Abdel as-Sarawat, Sharia Banque Misr and Sharia Khedr. There are also a few juice stalls, and plenty of cafés and coffeehouses in this area.

Red Sea Hotel (☎ 333 4302; www.redseahotel.com; 13 Sharia Riad, Port Tawfiq; mains E£25-40) The 6th-floor restaurant at the Red Sea Hotel has a tranquil ambience, tasty seafood meals, plus an assortment of other offerings, and wonderful views over the canal.

Safsafa Seafood Restaurant (☎ 366 0474; Corniche; dishes E£10-50) A new place with a good selection of pastas and seafood grills.

Al-Khalifa Fish Centre (☎ 333 7303; Sharia al-Geish, Suez; dishes E£20-50) Tucked away on the edge of Midan Nesima in the congested town centre, this no-frills place sells the day's catch by weight; pick your fish, then wait for it to be grilled.

Koshary Palace (Sharia Saad Zaghloul, Suez; meals E£1.50-5) Clean and friendly, with lots of local flavour and good *kushari* in your choice of sizes. It's just around the corner from the Al-Khalifa Fish Centre.

Alf Lila Italian Restaurant & Coffee Shop (Sharia al-Marwa; dishes E£5-25) One of several cafés in Port Tawfiq, and a decent spot to while away a few hours sipping a drink or puffing on a *sheesha* while watching ships on the canal.

Getting There & Away
BOAT
It's possible to travel by boat from Suez to Jeddah (Saudi Arabia), from where you can arrange onward boat travel to Port Sudan (Sudan); see p543 for details. Tickets to Jeddah can be booked through Mena Tours (p419). You'll need to already have your visa in order to purchase a ticket, and it's impossible to get a ticket during the haj.

Sometimes you can find passage on private yachts to destinations such as India, South Africa and even Australia. A good contact for arranging this is Mohammed Moseilhy at the **Damanhur Shipping Agency** (☎ 333 0418; 012 798 6338; Sharia at-Tahrir).

BUS
The bus station is located 5km out of town along the road to Cairo. **Upper Egypt Bus Co** (☎ 356 4258) has buses to Cairo (E£8, two hours) every 15 to 30 minutes from 6am to 9pm daily. Buses to Hurghada (E£33 to E£40, four to five hours) leave almost hourly between 5am and 11pm. There are buses to Luxor (E£46 to E£55, eight to 10 hours) via Safaga (E£35 to E£43) and Qena (E£43 to E£50) at 8am, 2pm and 8pm. Buses to Aswan (E£54 to E£62, 11 to 12 hours) leave at 5am, 11am and 5pm. Buses to Quseir (E£35, seven hours) leave at 9am, 11.30am and 3pm.

East Delta Bus Co (☎ 356 4853) has buses to Sharm el-Sheikh (E£30, five to six hours) departing at 8.30am, 11am, 1.30pm, 3pm, 4.30pm, 5.15pm and 6pm. There is a bus at 11am to Dahab (E£35, five hours), and at 2pm to St Katherine (E£25). Buses to Taba and Nuweiba (both E£35) leave at 3pm and 5pm.

Buses to Ismailia (E£5, 1½ hours) depart every half hour from 6am to 4pm. Departures to Port Said (E£10.50, 2½ to three hours) are daily at 7am, 9am, 11am, 12.15pm and 3.30pm.

SERVICE TAXI

Service taxis leave from beside the new bus station to many of the destinations that are also serviced by buses and trains, including Cairo (E£7), Ismailia (E£5), Port Said (E£10) and Hurghada (E£30). The only place in Sinai that service taxis go is Al-Tor (E£15).

With a group of seven people you can hire a 'special' taxi to get you to various other destinations, including St Katherine's Monastery (E£225 per vehicle), and the Red Sea monasteries (E£350, return).

TRAIN

Six very slow and uncomfortable Cairo-bound trains depart Suez daily, beginning at 5.30am (E£3.50/1.25 in 2nd/3rd class, three hours) and going only as far as Ain Shams, 10km northeast of central Cairo. There are eight very slow trains to Ismailia (E£1.50 in 3rd class only, three hours).

Getting Around
MICROBUS

There are regular microbus services along Sharia as-Salaam to Port Tawfiq. They will pick up or drop off anywhere along the route and cost 50pt.

TAXI

Taxis (painted blue) are easy to find almost everywhere. Expect to pay from about E£5 between the bus station and town, about E£10 between the bus station and Port Tawfiq, and about E£3 between Suez and Port Tawfiq.

Red Sea Coast

Egypt's Red Sea Coast stretches for more than 800km – from the port city of Suez in the north to the dusty trading outpost of Shalatein in the south, near the disputed border with Sudan. Famed for its brilliant turquoise waters, splendid coral and exotic creatures of the deep, the coast attracts thousands of tourists annually. It's Egypt's most rapidly developing area, with more hotels and resorts constructed here in recent years than anywhere else in the country. Inland – in the desert tracts fringing the sea, but far removed from the coastal tourism scene – are Christianity's two oldest monasteries, plus traces of Pharaonic, Roman and other settlements dotting the silent expanses of the Eastern Desert.

Unfortunately, the massive growth along the coast has resulted in significant environmental damage. An estimated 60% to 80% of the coral reefs around the premier resort town of Hurghada have been damaged due to illegal landfill operations and irresponsible reef use. In some places the coast has simply eroded away due to the construction of solid concrete jetties that have altered the natural shoreline. Though environmental laws have made many of these practices illegal, there appears to be little effort to contain the speculative boom based on the area's future as a major source of tourist growth. Half-finished resorts dot the coastline into the far south and environmentalists fear that here, too, the marine life will soon start to fade.

In the short term, diving and sunbathing along the coast are likely to remain the main attractions for most visitors. Yet exploring the Eastern Desert – with its monasteries, wadis, intriguing tribal cultures and ancient rock art – offers an alluring, adventurous and increasingly popular alternative.

HIGHLIGHTS

- Plunge in amongst the Red Sea's spectacular **reefs** and abundant **marine life** (p431)
- Discover Christian monasticism's centuries-old roots at the **monasteries of St Anthony** and **St Paul** (p425)
- Experience sunset and sunrise amidst the rugged mountains and wadis of the **Eastern Desert** (p444)
- Wander along the picturesque waterfront of sleepy **Al-Quseir** (p442)
- Catch a glimpse of life and trade millennia ago with visits to old gold and mineral **mines**, the **ruins** of Pharaonic and Roman settlements and **ancient rock art sites** (p444) around Hurghada, Safaga and Marsa Alam

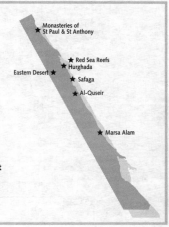

Monasteries of St Paul & St Anthony ★

★ Red Sea Reefs
★ Hurghada
Eastern Desert ★
★ Safaga
★ Al-Quseir

★ Marsa Alam

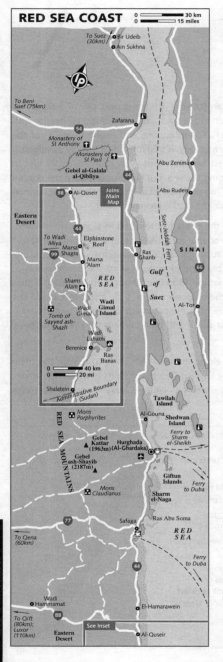

AIN SUKHNA
☎ 062

Ain Sukhna (Hot Spring) – an area, rather than a town – is the site of springs originating from within Gebel Ataka, the northernmost mountain in the Eastern Desert. Although not one of Egypt's stellar destinations, the coastline is attractive, edged by low hills sloping down to the beach. If you can ignore the industrial area to the north, it makes an agreeable outing from Cairo, or an overnight getaway for those who don't have time to visit points further south.

Sleeping & Eating

While there's no budget accommodation, the resorts sometimes offer good-value specials midweek and in the low season.

Palmera Beach Resort (☎ 341 0816; fax 341 0825; s/d US$29/38; ✗ ▨) This resort has a pleasant setting overlooking the water, rows of thatched beach umbrellas and all the standard amenities. It's about 20km north of the main Ain Sukhna junction.

Swiss Inn (☎ 325 0100; www.swissinn.net/stella/; s/d US$90/115; ✗ ▨ ▢ ▨) This five-star place, in the sprawling Stella di Mare resort complex along the main road, offers Ain Sukhna's most luxurious accommodation. There are comfortable rooms and several good restaurants, an attractive beach, a children's play area and a very large pool. Coming from Cairo via the Katameya/Ain Sukhna road, take a left (north) at the Ain Sukhna junction; the hotel is located about 5km up, and about 2km north of the port.

Also recommended:

Planhotel (☎ 325 0200; www.planhotel.ch/stella; s/d half board E£480/550; ✗ ▨ ▢ ▨) A reliable four-star place in the Stella di Mare complex, set in landscaped grounds somewhat back from the beach and sharing many facilities with the neighbouring Swiss Inn.

Ramada El Sokhna Resort (☎ 329 0500, 02-262 8939; s/d E£550/730, midweek E£480/650; ✗ ▨) Whitewashed blocks of rooms are clustered around a large pool and overlook a small patch of sand. It's about 35km south of the Katameya road junction.

All of the resorts have restaurants, and there are roadside KFC and Pizza King outlets near the main police checkpoint.

Getting There & Away

With public transport, the best connections are via Suez, from where there are buses almost hourly (E£5, one hour), most continuing on to Hurghada. Once in Ain Sukhna, however, there's no public transport, other than what you can arrange at your hotel. Driving from Cairo, you can go via Suez, or take the faster Ain Sukhna/Katameya toll road that branches off Cairo's Ring Rd just north of Ma'adi (110km, E£5).

ZAFARANA

The dusty junction town of Zafarana is of note solely as the gateway for visits to the isolated Coptic monasteries of St Anthony and St Paul in the mountains overlooking the Gulf of Suez. Other than its two hotels, there are no tourist facilities.

The four-star **Zafarana Resort** (☎ 010 519 2292, 02-418 5672, 418 6703; reservation@pharaohotels .com; s/d half board E£210/300; ☒ ☒) is on a pleasant stretch of sand just off the coastal road, about 13km south of the main Zafarana junction. Rooms are in long blocks, some with views of the water, and there's a restaurant with buffets and à la carte meals.

At the **Sahara Inn Motel** (s/d E£60/80, with air-con E£ 100/120; ☒), the rooms are grim and very basic, but the roadside restaurant – with inexpensive, filling meals – does a brisk business catering to travellers en route to/from Hurghada and other points south.

Zafarana is 62km south of Ain Sukhna and 150km east of Beni Suef on the Nile. Any bus running between Cairo or Suez and Hurghada will drop you here, though you'll need to pay the full fare. There's also one bus daily to and from Beni Suef, departing Zafarana from the main junction about 11.30am and Beni Suef at about 8am (E£20, three to four hours). For information on transport to the monasteries, see p427.

RED SEA MONASTERIES

The Coptic monasteries of St Anthony and St Paul are Egypt's and Christianity's oldest monasteries, and are among Coptic Egypt's holiest sites. If you're at all interested in the country's long Christian history, both make fascinating and inspiring visits.

Information

Both monasteries are open daily throughout the year (St Anthony's from 7am to 5pm, St Paul's from 8am to 3pm), except during Advent and Lent, when they can only be visited on Friday, Saturday and Sunday. During Holy Week they are closed completely to visitors. For inquiries or to confirm visiting times, contact the monasteries' Cairo headquarters: **St Paul's** (☎ 02-590 0218; 26 Al-Keneesa al-Morcosia) or **St Anthony's** (☎ 02-590 6025; 26 Al-Keneesa al-Morcosia), located off Clot Bey, south of Midan Ramses in Cairo.

Monastery of St Anthony

The establishment of the religious community of St Anthony's, hidden in the barren cliffs of the Eastern Desert, marks the beginning of the Christian monastic tradition. The monastery traces its origins to the 4th century AD, when monks began to settle at the foot of Gebel al-Galala al-Qibliya, where their spiritual leader, Anthony (see p426), lived. Over the next few centuries, the community moved from being a loosely organised grouping of hermits to a somewhat more communal existence in which the monks continued to live anchoritic lives, but in cells grouped together inside a walled compound. In the 8th and 9th centuries the monastery suffered Bedouin raids, followed in the 11th century by attacks from irate Muslims and in the 15th century a revolt by bloodthirsty servants that resulted in the massacre of the monks. The small mudbrick **citadel** into which they would retreat during attacks can still be seen, although visitors are not usually admitted. It's also possible to see the large basket and wooden winch that were the only means of getting into the monastery in times of attack.

Today the monastery is a large complex surrounded by high walls (it's possible to walk along the top of some sections), with several churches and chapels, a bakery, a lush garden and a spring. The source of the latter, deep beneath the desert mountains, produces 100 cu metres of water daily, allowing the monks to cultivate olive and date trees and a few crops. The oldest part of the monastery is the **Church of St Anthony**, built over the saint's tomb and containing one of Egypt's most significant collections of Coptic wall paintings. Painted in secco (whereby paint is applied to dry plaster), most date back to the early 13th century, with a few possibly much older. Stripped of the dirt and grime of centuries, the paintings are clear and bright, and demonstrate how medieval Coptic art was connected to the arts of the wider Byzantine and Islamic eastern Mediterranean. The monks who live here, following centuries-old traditions and the examples set by St Anthony, St Paul and their followers 16 centuries ago, have dedicated their lives to seeking God in the stillness and isolation of the desert, in a life centred completely around prayer.

Perched about 300m – or 1158 wooden steps – above the monastery on a nearby cliff is the **Cave of St Anthony**, where Anthony spent the final 40 years of his life. The climb up is hot and steep, and takes about half an hour if you're reasonably fit. At the top is a small clearing (now littered with the graffiti of countless pilgrims) with wide vistas over the hills and valley below. In the cave itself – which is for the svelte and nonclaustrophobic only, as you need to squeeze through a narrow tunnel to get inside – there is a small chapel with an altar, and a tiny recessed area where Anthony lived. Bring a torch along to illuminate the interior.

There is usually an English-speaking monk on hand to give tours of the monastery (free, but a donation is expected). The monastery bookstore has a good selection of materials on Coptic Christianity.

Monastery of St Paul

St Paul's monastery dates to the 4th century, when it began as a grouping of hermitages in the cliffs of Gebel al-Galala al-Qibliya around the site where St Paul had his hermitage. Paul, who was born into a wealthy family in Alexandria in the mid-3rd century, had fled to the Eastern Desert to escape Roman persecution. He lived alone in a cave here for over 90 years, finding bodily sustenance in a nearby spring and palm tree. According to tradition, in AD 343 the then 90-year-old St Anthony – following a vision he had of Paul – made the difficult trek through the mountains to visit him and, after Paul's death, buried him.

The heart of the monastery complex is the **Church of St Paul**, which was built in and around the cave where Paul lived. It's cluttered with altars, candles, ostrich eggs (the symbol of the Resurrection) and murals representing saints and biblical stories. The **fortress** above the church was where the monks retreated during Bedouin raids.

St Paul's monastery is quieter and much more low key than St Anthony's, and is often bypassed in favour of its larger neighbour. Yet, if you can manage to miss the frequent arrivals of pilgrimage buses from Cairo, a visit is well worthwhile, and gives a glimpse into the life of silence, prayer and asceticism that has flowered here in the Eastern Desert for almost two millennia. Visitors are welcome, and there is usually an English-speaking monk available to give a guided tour (free, but donation appreciated).

THE FATHER OF MONASTICISM

Although St Paul is honoured as the earliest Christian hermit, it is St Anthony who is considered to be the Father of Monasticism. Anthony was born around AD 251, the son of a provincial landowner from a small Upper Egyptian town near Beni Suef. Orphaned with his sister at the age of 18, he was already more interested in the spiritual than the temporal, and soon gave away his share of the inheritance to the poor. After studying with a local holy man, Anthony went into the Eastern Desert, living in a cave and seeking solitude and spiritual salvation. However, word of his holiness soon spread, and flocks of disciples arrived, seeking to imitate his ascetic existence.

After a brief spell in Alexandria ministering to Christians imprisoned under Emperor Maximinus Daia in the early 4th century, Anthony returned to the desert. Once again, he was pursued by eager followers. Eventually, after fleeing even further into the desert in search of solitude, he established himself in a cave on a remote mountain. His disciples formed a loose community at its base, and thus was born the first Christian monastery.

The number of Anthony's followers grew rapidly, and within decades of his death, travellers reported how every town in Egypt was surrounded by hermitages. Soon the whole Byzantine Empire was alive with monastic fervour, which by the next century had spread throughout Italy and France.

It is ironic that for all his influence, Anthony spent his life seeking to escape others. When he died at the advanced age of 105, his wish was finally respected and the location of his grave kept secret for generations.

Hiking Between the Monasteries

It is possible to hike between the two monasteries along a trail across the top of the plateau. However, hiking this rugged area, commonly known as 'Devil's Country', is only for the fit and experienced and should be done with a guide. In 2001 a lone tourist attempting the walk died of thirst after losing his way, so it is not a trip to undertake lightly. Those who have made the hike recommend starting from St Paul's. The hike (about 30km) is possible in one long day, but better broken up into two.

Sleeping & Eating

There is no accommodation for the general public at either monastery, although the guards at St Paul's will usually allow you to pitch a tent outside the main monastery gate. The monastery guesthouses are reserved for pilgrimage groups.

Both monasteries have canteens that sell snacks, drinks and simple meals.

Getting There & Away

St Anthony's and St Paul's monasteries are only about 25km apart, but thanks to the cliffs and plateau of Gebel al-Galala al-Qibliya (which lies between 900m and 1300m above sea level) the distance between them by road is around 85km.

Buses running between Cairo or Suez and Hurghada will drop you at Zafarana, but direct access to the monasteries is limited to private vehicles and tour buses from Cairo or Hurghada.

To get to St Anthony's start from the main Zafarana junction and follow the road west to Beni Suef for 37km to the monastery turn-off. From here, it's 17km further south along an unsurfaced but good road through the desert to St Anthony's. The bus between Zafarana and Beni Suef (see p425) will drop you at the turn-off, from where the only option is walking or hitching (and you'll need to wait until the next day for a bus from the turn-off back to Zafarana or on to Beni Suef). If you do decide to hike in from the main road (which isn't the best idea), don't go alone, and be sure you're properly equipped, especially with water, as it's a long, hot, dry and isolated stretch.

The turn-off for St Paul's is about 27km south of the Zafarana lighthouse along the road to Hurghada (watch for a small sign-post). Once at the turn-off, it's then 10km further along a good tarmac road to the main gate of the monastery, and about 3km further to the monastery itself. Buses running between Suez and Hurghada will drop you along the main road at the turn-off, from where the only options are walking or hitching.

If you don't have your own vehicle, the easiest way is to join a tour from Cairo or Hurghada (most midrange and top-end hotels organise these) or hire a taxi from Suez. It's also often possible to join a pilgrimage group from Cairo; the best way to arrange this is by inquiring at local Coptic churches. There is also a pick-up owner in Zafarana (best contacted through the manager of Sahara Inn, p425) with whom you can sometimes arrange transport to the monasteries, though there are no guarantees the driver will be around when you are hoping to visit. If you find him, expect to pay from about E£120 return, including a reasonable waiting time.

AL-GOUNA
☎ 065

This self-contained resort town, built by one of Egypt's biggest tycoons, is frequented by Egypt's rich and famous, as well as by Westerners on package tours. Among other attractions, it boasts several hotels, an airport, a hospital and decompression chamber, an open-air amphitheatre, a golf course, a brewery and several outdoor shopping centres, and is a popular venue for concerts and sporting events. There are also lots of activities for children. If you're looking for a place to laze on a beach surrounded by Western amenities and cushioned from the colour and bustle of Egyptian town life, and if you don't mind a homogenised, vacation-community ambience, you'll likely enjoy Al-Gouna.

In the signposted and central 'downtown' area, there's a cluster of ATMs and banks, a **tourist information centre** (www.elgouna.com; ☽ 10am-1pm & 3-10pm), bike rental shops, an **Internet café** (per hr E£10; ☽ 10am-2pm & 4-10pm), several dive centres, a supermarket, a pharmacy and various eateries and hotels. Also here is the **Al-Gouna museum** (admission E£5; ☽ 10am-2pm & 6-10pm), though its collection is almost exclusively reproductions, and your time is better spent at the beach.

Sleeping

Dawar al-Umda (☎ 354 5060; www.sultandawar-el gouna.com; Kafr Al-Gouna; s/d US$94/125; ☒ ☒ ☒) This intimate and tastefully decorated four-star was designed by Rami el-Dahan, who was clearly influenced by the work of Hassan Fathy, one of Egypt's most famous architects. It's squeezed in among several other buildings in the heart of downtown Al-Gouna, with cosy, well-appointed rooms and a convenient lagoonside location (though there's no beach).

Sheraton Miramar (☎ 354 5606; www.starwood hotels.com/sheraton; Al-Gouna; s/d half board US$142/221; ☒ ☒ ☒ ☒) A five-star, pastel-coloured, postmodern desert fantasy, the Sheraton was designed by well-known architect Michael Graves, with all the luxury features you'd expect, as well as a series of small beaches and access to Al-Gouna's other amenities. It is also participating in a pilot programme to develop environmentally friendly practices in hotels on the Red Sea.

Also recommended:

Three Corners Rihana Resort (☎ 358 0025; www .threecorners.com; s/d full board US$78/125; ☒ ☒) A comfortable four-star establishment popular with package tours and families, and with the advantage of being slightly removed from the main downtown area.

Panorama Bungalows Resort (☎ 358 0053, 02-273 9400; www.panoramabungalows.com; s/d bungalow half board US$120/150; ☒ ☒) A large, bland complex with a collection of closely set bungalows, including some completely surrounded by the lagoon. There's a golf course next door and a small beach.

Getting There & Away

Al-Gouna is situated along the main highway about 20km north of Hurghada. There are twice-weekly flights on **Orascom Aviation** (☎ 358 0211, 02-305 2401) between Al-Gouna and Luxor, departing Al-Gouna at 6am and returning by evening. Orascom Aviation also has twice-weekly flights between Cairo and Al-Gouna.

El-Gouna Transport buses travel three times daily between Cairo, Al-Gouna and Hurghada (E£55, five hours), best booked a day in advance. The ticket office and bus stop in Al-Gouna is on the main plaza in downtown Al-Gouna, opposite the tourist information centre.

Orascom Limousine (☎ 358 0061), near the bus stand, can help with car rentals, both self-drive and chauffeured.

HURGHADA

☎ 065

Once an isolated and modest fishing village, Hurghada (or, as it's called in Arabic, Al-Ghardaka) has metamorphosed into a sprawling collection of more than 100 hotels, and is today Egypt's most popular resort destination.

Despite its popularity, much of the town is a construction site. For more than 20km to the south, a dense band of concrete in the form of four- and five-star resorts has created the kind of disaster that you can also see in southern Europe, and the reefs close to shore have been degraded by uncontrolled development. Even the government concedes that it has made planning mistakes here.

On the positive side, Hurghada is an Egyptian town with a diversity missing from the airbrushed resort of Sharm el-Sheikh. Diving is good here, particularly for beginners, although most of the best sites can only be reached by boat. Hurghada is also convenient if you want to combine a diving holiday with a visit to Luxor and other Nile Valley sites. If you're seeking sun and sand, and don't mind a packaged feel, Hurghada is for you. For something more scenic or rugged, head further south or go to Dahab (p492).

Orientation

Hurghada is split into three main areas. To the north is Ad-Dahar, where most budget accommodation is located. This is also the most 'Egyptian' part of town, with lively backstreet neighbourhoods and a bustling souq. The main inland artery through Ad-Dahar is Sharia an-Nasr.

Separated from Ad-Dahar by a sandy mountain called Gebel al-Afish is the fast-growing and congested Sigala area, where resort hotels jostle for sea frontage, while smaller two- and three-star establishments and dozens of restaurants fill the spaces inland. This is also where you'll find the port for ferries to Sharm el-Sheikh and Duba. Sigala's main thoroughfare is Sharia Sheraton.

South of Sigala, lining the coastal road and increasingly some inland arteries as well, is the resort strip. Here you'll find an ever-lengthening row of mostly upmarket hotels, small shopping malls and the half-finished shells of future pleasure domes.

HURGHADA COAST

0 _____ 2 km
0 _____ 1 mile

To Zafarana
(245km);
Suez (445km)

Ad-Dahar

See Ad-Dahar
Map (pp434-5)

HURGHADA
(Al-Ghadarka)

To Airport
(500m)

Resort Strip

Sigala

RED
SEA

See Sigala Map (p437)

Ferries to
Sharm el-Sheikh;
Duba

To Makadi Bay;
Travco (35km);

Sharm el-Naga
(40km);
Soma Bay
(42km);
Safaga (45km);
Al-Quseir
(135km)

To Oberoi Sahl
Hasheesh (4km)

INFORMATION
As-Salam Hospital...**1** B1
Banque Misr (ATM)..**2** A4
Bulls Internet Café...(see 21)
Café Online..**3** A4
HSBC (ATM)...**4** A3
Naval Hyperbaric & Emergency Medical Center.....**5** B2
Thomas Cook..**6** A4
Tourist Office..**7** A4
Tourist Police..**8** A4

SIGHTS & ACTIVITIES
Divers Lodge & InterContinental Hotel............**9** A5
Jasmine Diving Centre.....................................(see 18)
Magawish Tourist Village..............................**10** A5
Red Sea Scuba Schools & Emperor Divers.........(see 14)
Sindbad Submarine & Sindbad Beach Resort.......**11** A4
Sub Aqua Diving...(see 20)

SLEEPING
Fantasia..(see 24)
Giftun Beach Resort..**12** A4
Hilton Hurghada Plaza....................................**13** A1
Hilton Hurghada Resort..................................**14** A5
Hor Palace..**15** A4
Hurghada Marriott Beach Resort...................**16** B3
Iberotel Arabella...**17** B2
Jasmine Village...**18** A6
Sindbad Al-Mashrabiya...................................**19** A3
Sofitel..**20** A5

EATING
Bordiehn's..(see 17)
Bulls Steakhouse..**21** A3
Da Nanni...**22** B3
European Bakery..(see 21)
Felfela Restaurant..**23** B3

DRINKING
Hilton Pub..(see 14)

ENTERTAINMENT
Alf Layla wa Layla...**24** A6
Black Out Disco...**25** A6
Calypso...**26** B3
Hard Rock Café..**27** A4

TRANSPORT
EgyptAir..**28** A4
El-Gouna Transport...**29** A1

Information
EMERGENCY
Air ambulance (☎ 010 154 1978)
Ambulance (☎ 354 6490, 123)
Police (Map p437; ☎ 354 6303/6; Sharia Shedwan, Sigala)
Tourist police Ad-Dahar (Map pp434-5; ☎ 344 4774; Sharia Al-Tahrir); Resort Strip (Map p429; ☎ 344 4773/4; next to the tourist office)

INTERNET ACCESS
There are Internet cafés all over town and in many hotels, most charging between E£4 and E£16 per hour.

RED SEA COAST

Bulls Internet Café (Map p429; Bulls Steakhouse, Sharia Sheraton, Resort Strip; 6am-midnight;) Free Internet access with a meal.

Café Online (Map p429; Resort Strip; per hr E£16; 10.15am-11.15pm;) Has a juice bar.

El Baroudy Internet (Map pp434-5; Sharia Sheikh Sabak, Ad-Dahar; per hr E£4; 24hr;)

Golden Net (Map pp434-5; Sharia Sayyed al-Qorayem, Ad-Dahar; per hr E£4; 24hr;)

Speed.Net (Map p437; Sharia Al-Hadaba, Sigala; per hr E£10; 10am-midnight;) Next to Zak Royal Wings Hotel.

MEDICAL SERVICES

Al-Gouna Hospital (358 0011; Al-Gouna)

Al-Saffa Hospital (Map pp434-5; 3546 965; Sharia an-Nasr, Ad-Dahar)

As-Salam Hospital (Map p429; 354 8785/6/7; Corniche) Just north of Iberotel Arabella.

Decompression Chambers Al-Gouna (358 0011, 012 218 7550; Al-Gouna); Naval Hyperbaric & Emergency Medical Center (Map p429; 344 9150, 354 8450; Corniche, near Iberotel Arabella)

Public Hospital (Map pp434-5; 354 6740; Sharia Mustashfa, Ad-Dahar)

MONEY

ATMs are all over town, including at the following locations:

Banque Misr Ad-Dahar (Map pp434-5; Sharia an-Nasr; 8.30am-2pm & 6-9pm Sat-Thu); Resort Strip (Map p429)

HSBC (Map p429; opposite Sindbad Beach Resort, Resort Strip)

Le Pacha Resort (Map p437; Sharia Sheraton, Sigala)

National Bank of Egypt (Map pp434-5; Sharia an-Nasr, Ad-Dahar; 8.30am-2pm & 6-9pm Sat-Thu)

Triton Empire Beach (Map pp434-5; Sharia Sayed al-Qorayem, Ad-Dahar)

Other money outlets:

Thomas Cook Ad-Dahar (Map pp434-5; 354 1870/1; Sharia an-Nasr; 9am-2pm & 6-10pm); Sigala (Map p437; 344 3338; Sharia Sheraton; 9am-3pm & 4-10pm); Resort Strip (Map p429; 344 6830; 9am-5pm)

Western Union (Map p437; 344 2771, 19190; Sharia Sheraton, Sigala; 8.30am-10pm Sat-Thu, 3-10pm Fri)

POST

Main post office (Map pp434-5; Sharia an-Nasr, Ad-Dahar; 8.30am-2.30pm Sat-Thu)

TELEPHONE

Telephone centrales Ad-Dahar (Map pp434-5; Sharia an-Nasr; 24hr); Port area (Map p437; Midan Shedwan; 24hr); Sigala (Map p437; Sharia Sheraton; 24hr)

TOURIST INFORMATION

Tourist office (Map p429; 344 4420; Resort Strip; 9am-8pm Sat-Thu, 2-10pm Fri)

TRAVEL AGENCIES

Abanoub Travel (Map p437; 344 2843; abanoubt@ menanet.net; 2nd fl, Cotton House Bldg, Sigala)

Thomas Cook (344 3338; www.thomascookegypt .com); Ad-Dahar (Map pp434-5; Sharia an-Nasr; 9am-2pm & 6-10pm); Sigala (Map p437; Sharia Sheraton; 9am-3pm & 4-10pm); Resort Strip (Map p429; 9am-5pm)

Travco (359 0111; www.travco-eg.com) Located in Makadi Bay, 35km south of Hurghada.

VISA EXTENSIONS

Passport & Immigration Office (Map pp434-5; Sharia an-Nasr, Ad-Dahar; 8am-2pm Sat-Thu) For visa extensions and re-entry visas.

Dangers & Annoyances

Although Hurghada is a resort, many of the workers here come from the conservative towns of Upper Egypt. To avoid hassle, women should dress modestly when walking around town, especially in the souq area of Ad-Dahar.

Sights & Activities

AQUARIUM

If you don't want to put your head under the water, you can still get an idea of some of the life in the Red Sea's waters at the **aquarium** (Map pp434-5; 354 8557; Corniche, Ad-Dahar; admission E£5; 9am-10pm). It's just north of the public hospital in Ad-Dahar and has a reasonable, if somewhat neglected selection of fish and other marine creatures.

RUINS

About 50km northwest of Hurghada is the old Roman mining centre of **Mons Porphyrites**; see p445.

BEACHES & POOLS

Although many of Hurghada's beaches are bare and stark, developers have snapped up almost every available spot. Apart from the not-so-appealing **public beach** (Map p437; Sigala; 8am-sunset), the main option for enjoying sand and sea is to go to one of the resorts, most of which charge nonguests between E£20 and E£60 for beach access. The best are those away from town, including **Magawish Tourist Village** (Map p429; ☎ 344 2621; Resort Strip), with one of the best stretches of sand; and **Jasmine Village** (Map p429; ☎ 344 7442; Resort Strip), with a small reef that allows you to combine snorkelling with sunbathing.

Other options include **Papas Beach Club** (Map p437; www.papasbar.com; Sigala; admission E£20; ✆ 9am-4am), where you can spend the day lazing under a palm shade listening to laid-back sounds; and the highly popular **Liquid Lounge** (Map p437; www.papasbar.com; Sharia Sheraton, Sigala; minimum food/beverage charge E£25; ✆ 9am-3am), a very chilled out beach bar/restaurant, with hammocks and floor pillows.

SNORKELLING

Although there is some easily accessible coral at the southern end of the resort strip, the best reefs are offshore, and the only way to see them is to take a boat and join a snorkelling or diving excursion for at least one day.

Among the most popular sites are the Giftun Islands, part of the Red Sea Protectorate with restricted access. On the larger island, a day resort called **Mahmya** (☎ 344 9736; www .mahmya.com; per day US$62) runs trips departing from the Sheraton Marina at 9am and returning by 4.30pm. These give you the run of the island's pristine beaches, an hour-long

guided snorkelling trip and buffet lunch. All garbage and waste water is removed from the island by specially equipped boats. Many of the better dive clubs also arrange day excursions for snorkellers and by going with one of them you're almost assured of environmental reef protection practices being observed. See p458 for club listings. Overnight trips are also possible. However, carefully choose the captain and crew, as groups of women may face unwanted advances or worse from their male 'guides'.

For all excursions, shop around a bit. Relying on your hotel (and many of the smaller hotels work hard to get you to join the trips for which they get a commission) may not be the best way to do things, as several travellers have complained of not getting everything they thought they would. For any boat excursion, take your passport with you, as you'll need to show it at the port.

OTHER WATER SPORTS

Most of the larger resorts have a full range of water sports. Well-known **windsurfing** places include Triton Empire Beach hotel (p433), Jasmine Village (p435) and Giftun Beach Resort (p433). Keep in mind that construction along the coast has affected

---

RESCUING THE RED SEA

Conservationists estimate that more than 1000 pleasure boats and almost as many fishing boats ply the waters between Hurghada and the many reefs situated within an hour of the town. Until recently, there was nothing to stop captains from anchoring to the coral, or snorkellers and divers breaking off a colourful chunk to take home. But due largely to the efforts of the Hurghada Environmental Protection & Conservation Association (Hepca) and the Egyptian National Parks Office in Hurghada, the Red Sea's reefs are at last being protected.

Set up in 1992 by 15 of the town's larger, more reputable dive companies, Hepca's programme to conserve the Red Sea's reefs includes public-awareness campaigns, direct community action and lobbying of the Egyptian government to introduce appropriate laws. Thanks to these efforts, the whole coast south of Suez Governorate is now known as the Red Sea Protectorate. Over 570 mooring buoys have been set up at popular dive sites around Hurghada and further south, enabling boat captains to drop anchor on a buoy rather than on the coral itself, and marine rangers from the Egyptian National Parks Office police the waters.

The Egyptian National Parks Office is also trying to establish new dive sites to ease the pressure on existing sites, as well as trying to reduce the number of new boats licensed in the Red Sea. Finally, a symbolic 'reef conservation tax' of E£1 has been introduced and is payable by anyone using the reefs for diving, snorkelling or any other boating activities. It is designed to make the public aware that the reefs and offshore islands are now protected areas, rather than simply a source of revenue.

For more information on safe diving practices or about how you can help **Hepca** (Map p437; ☎ 344 6674; www.hepca.com; off Corniche, Sigala) in its efforts to protect the Red Sea's reefs, check the organisation's website or call in between 9am and 5pm Saturday to Thursday.

the wind here, so if you're a windsurfing buff, you're better off in Sinai or around Safaga.

Paragliding, paraskiing and water skiing are also available at some resorts, and several places, including **Colona Divers** (www .colonawatersports.com), at Magawish Tourist Village, also offer kite surfing.

UNDERWATER PHOTOGRAPHY

Focus (Map p437; ☎ 344 4675; www.redsea-images.com; Sharia Sheraton, Sigala; ✆ 9am-10pm) rents underwater cameras, produces videos and offers photography courses.

Tours

Tours to almost anywhere in Egypt can be organised from Hurghada, including whirlwind one-day jaunts to Cairo (from E£250), slightly more leisurely two-day tours for about E£500 and one-day excursions to Luxor from around E£250. More feasible are some of the desert jeep safaris, which usually include visits to either Mons Porphyrites (p445) or Mons Claudianus (p444), and which start at about E£150. Other possibilities include a full-day excursion to the monasteries of St Paul and St Anthony; half-day desert safaris, including a one-hour camel trek; and evening excursions into the desert, including a sunset drive, camel ride and BBQ dinner. To arrange any of these, contact any of the larger hotels or a travel agency (see p430). A minimum number of people is needed for most trips, so it's best to inquire several days in advance.

A ride in the yellow **Sindbad Submarine** (Map p429; ☎ 344 4688; www.sindbad-group.com; Sindbad Beach Resort; adult/child US$25/50) – which takes up to 46 people to a depth of 22m – is one way to plumb the depths of the Red Sea while staying dry. Although it's billed as a two-hour trip, an hour of this is spent on a boat travelling between Sindbad Beach Resort and the site where the submarine is moored. Bookings can be made at any hotel or travel agency, or at the Sindbad Beach Resort. Glass-bottom boats can also be easily organised with most larger hotels from about E£40 per hour.

Sleeping

Hurghada has the greatest selection of accommodation outside of Cairo, spanning most budgets, but there's a heavy emphasis on midrange and top-end resorts. As supply outstrips demand, prices can often be negotiated.

BUDGET
Ad-Dahar

Most budget hotels are in Ad-Dahar and not far from the sea, though the water is rarely within sight.

Al-Arosa Hotel (Map p434-5; ☎ 354 8434; elarosa hotel@yahoo.com; off Corniche; s/d with private bathroom E£100/150; ✆ ✆) Al-Arosa overlooks the sea in the distance from the inland side of the Corniche. Rooms are faded but spotless and all have air-con, TV, phone and seafacing balconies. The pool is indoors and guests have free access to the beach at the nearby Geisum Village. Advance bookings recommended.

Snafer Hotel (Map pp434-5; ☎ /fax 354 0260; off Sharia Sayyed al-Qorayem; s/d E£55/85; ✆) A friendly place with clean, large, good-value rooms. All have minifridge and some have a balcony and views to the water.

Four Seasons (Map p434-5; ☎ /fax 354 5456; fourseasonshurghada@hotmail.com; off Sharia Sayyed al-Qorayem; s/d with private bathroom E£40/60; ✆) This small, friendly hotel is popular and often full. Its simple rooms have hot water and most also have air-con. Guests can use the beach at the Geisum Village hotel.

Happy Land Hotel (Map pp434-5; ☎ 354 7373; Sharia Sheikh Sebak; s/d with private bathroom E£40/70) Clean and well run, all the rooms have phones and a fan. The location near the souq means it can be noisy at night.

Pharaohs Hotel (Map pp434-5; ☎ 354 7577; off Sharia Sayyed al-Qorayem; d E£30, with private bathroom E£40) This hotel has large carpeted no-frills rooms (with fan) that are dark, but clean and a good deal for the price. There's no food.

St George Hotel (Map p434-5; ☎ 354 8246; off Sharia Sheikh Sebak; s/d E£30/40, with private bathroom E£35/50) Run by a Coptic family, the St George has dark and somewhat musty but clean rooms, which can be noisy because of the adjacent souq. It's a reliable choice for solo women shoestring travellers. Breakfast costs E£7.

California Hotel (Map pp434-5; ☎ 012 246 3605; off Sharia Sayyed al-Qorayem; s/d E£25/35) Cramped and rather grubby rooms are compensated for by a friendly ambience and a rooftop terrace with sea views.

Shakespears Hotel (Map pp434-5; Sharia Sayyed al-Qorayem; d E£35, with private bathroom E£45) Spacious but dingy doubles with fans. Ask to see a few rooms to compare, as some are much better than others. There's no breakfast.

Other recommendations:

Seaview Hotel (Map pp434-5; ☎ 354 5959, 012 224 7415; Corniche; s/d E£75/100; ✷) Spotless, sterile and efficiently run. It's about 2km north of the Hilton on the opposite side of the road.

Gobal Hotel (Map pp434-5; ☎ 354 6623; Sharia Sheikh Sabak; s/d/tr E£30/40/50) Clean rooms with fan and shared bathroom.

Sigala
Sigala is congested and noisy, though it makes a convenient base if you want to be near the nightlife.

White Albatross (Map p437; ☎ /fax 344 2519; walbatros53@hotmail.com; Sharia Sheraton; s/d E£100/170; ✷) This is a 40-room family-owned hotel with clean rooms – some with street-facing balconies – and beach use at the Aloha Resort (E£15), about 1km away.

MIDRANGE
Ad-Dahar
There are a few decent midrange options in Ad-Dahar, many of them beachfront resorts that have lowered their rates due to competition from the newer, better-appointed places to the south.

Triton Empire Beach (Map pp434-5; ☎ 354 7816; www.threecorners.com; Sharia Sayyed al-Qorayem; s/d US$35/50; ✷ ✷) This large place is a reasonable three-star choice with grassy grounds and a central seaside location. It's primarily used by package tours.

Triton Empire Inn (Map pp434-5; ☎ 354 9200; www.threecorners.com; Sharia Sayyed al-Qorayem; ✷) Under the same management as the Triton Empire Beach, but more intimate, with a shady side-street entrance and good rooms. At the time of writing it was being rented in its entirety, but once in business again will be one of the better options in this range, likely priced similarly to Triton Empire Beach.

Geisum Village (Map pp434-5; ☎ 354 6692; Corniche; s/d half board E£150/280; ✷ ✷) A large compound, and one of the cheapest of the beachfront places.

Sand Beach (Map pp434-5; ☎ 354 7992; www.sandbeachhurghada.com; Corniche; s/d half board US$40/60; ✷ ✷) A large establishment favoured by Russian groups, with its own beach and diving centre and the usual amenities.

Sigala
Most of Sigala's midrange places are clustered on or near Sharia Sheraton.

Zak Royal Wings Hotel (Map p437; ☎ 344 6012; www.zakhotel.com; Sharia al-Hadaba; s/d US$21/32; ✷ ✷) A small, good-value place next to Papas Bar, with clean rooms – all with TVs and phones – clustered around a pool.

Sea Garden (Map p437; ☎ 344 7493; www.seagarden.com.eg; off Sharia Sheraton; s/d US$50/62; ✷) Also good value, this high-rise block is off Sharia Sheraton, en route to Papas Beach Club.

Le Pacha Resort (Map p437; ☎ 344 4150; www.lepacharesort.com; Sharia Sheraton; s/d all-inclusive US$70/120; ✷ ▢ ✷) Le Pacha is a large place in the centre of Sigala with its own small beach and a shopping mall.

Roma Hotel (Map p437; ☎ 344 8140/1; www.roma-hurghada.com; Sharia Sheraton; s/d US$90/120; ✷ ✷) A somewhat hulking midrange hotel near the cluster at the end of Sharia Sheraton with its own beach and views of the sea in the distance.

Other recommendations:

Eiffel Hotel (Map p437; ☎ 344 4570; fax 344 4572; off Sharia Sheraton; s/d E£100/140; ✷) A large block of a place offering reasonably comfortable rooms with TV. It's popular with Eastern European tour groups, and guests can use the adjacent public beach.

Andrea's Hotel (Map p437; ☎ 344 3388; www.andreashotel.com; Sharia al-Hadaba; s/d US$22/36; ✷ ✷) Just up from Roma Hotel, this is a functional place with standard rooms and an unappealing cement-ringed pool, lacking any touch of greenery.

Al-Tabia Hotel (Map p437; ☎ 344 2350; fax 442 351; Sharia al-Hadaba; s/d E£110/170; ✷ ✷) Next door to Andrea's, with a somewhat kitsch exterior and a similarly unappealing pool.

Resort Strip
Most hotels along Hurghada's resort strip are in the top price bracket, but you can still find some less-expensive places catering to Eastern European groups or travellers on all-inclusive packages from Europe.

Giftun Beach Resort (Map p429; ☎ 346 3040; www.giftunbeachresort.com; s/d all-inclusive US$52/81; ✷ ▢ ✷) A good place, with pleasant chalet-style rooms, a popular diving centre and excellent windsurfing facilities (from E£25 per hour).

Sindbad Al-Mashrabiya (Map p429; ☎ 344 3330/2; www.sindbad-group.com; s/d half board US$60/90; ✷ ✷) Run by Sindbad, a local hotel operator, Sindbad Al Mashrabiya has its own beach, several

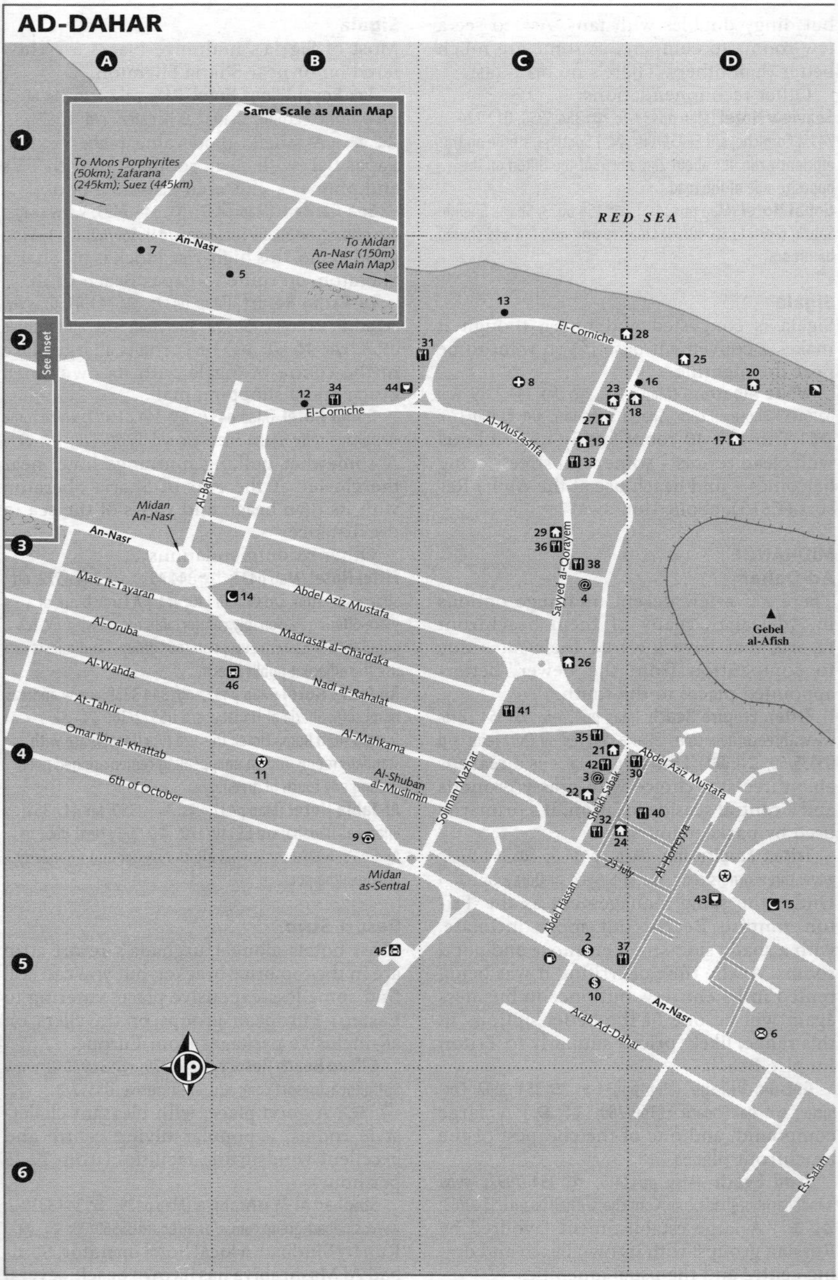
AD-DAHAR
A
B
C
D
1
2
3
4
5
6
Same Scale as Main Map
To Mons Porphyrites (50km); Zafarana (245km); Suez (445km)
An-Nasr
To Midan An-Nasr (150m) (see Main Map)
See Inset
RED SEA
El-Corniche
Al-Mustashfa
Al-Bahr
Midan An-Nasr
An-Nasr
Masr It-Tayaran
Al-Oruba
Al-Wahda
At-Tahrir
Omar ibn al-Khattab
6th of October
Abdel Aziz Mustafa
Madrasat al-Ghardaka
Nadi al-Rahalat
Al-Mahkama
Al-Shuban al-Muslimin
Soliman Mazhar
Sayyed al-Qorayem
Sheikh Sabak
23 July
Al-Horreyya
Abdel Hassan
Arab Ad-Dahar
Es-Salam
Midan as-Sentral
Gebel al-Afish

INFORMATION
Al-Saffa Hospital.....................................**1** F6
ATM..(see 28)
Banque Misr (ATM).............................**2** C5
El Baroudy Internet.............................**3** C4
Golden Net...**4** C3
Governorate Building..........................**5** B2
Main Post Office.................................**6** D5
National Bank of Egypt (ATM)...(see 2)
Passport & Immigration Office........**7** A2
Public Hospital...................................**8** C2
Telephone Centrale............................**9** B4
Thomas Cook....................................**10** C5
Tourist Police...................................**11** B4

SIGHTS & ACTIVITIES
Aquanaut Red Sea & Shedwan Hotel.**12** B2
Aquarium..**13** C2
Easy Divers.................................(see 28)
Main Mosque....................................**14** B3
Mosque..**15** D5
Subex..**16** D2

SLEEPING 🏠
Al-Arousa Hotel.................................**17** D2
California Hotel.................................**18** D2
Four Seasons....................................**19** C3
Geisum Village..................................**20** D2
Gobal Hotel......................................**21** C4
Happy Land Hotel..............................**22** C4
Pharaohs Hotel..................................**23** C4
St George Hotel.................................**24** C4
Sand Beach.......................................**25** D2
Shakespears Hotel.............................**26** C4
Snafer Hotel.....................................**27** C2
Triton Empire Beach..........................**28** C2
Triton Empire Inn..............................**29** C3

EATING 🍴
Abu Ashara.......................................**30** D4
Cafe Cheers......................................**31** C2
Chez Pascal.................................(see 29)
La Torta..**32** C4
Lo Scarabeo......................................**33** C3
Mandarine Lebanese Restaurant.......**34** B2
Pizza Tarboush..................................**35** C4
Portofino..**36** C3
Red Sea I..**37** C5
Red Sea II...**38** C3
Seaview Hotel...................................**39** F2
Souq..**40** D4
Taibeen..**41** C4
Young Kang......................................**42** C4

DRINKING 🍷
Beer & Wine Shop.............................**43** D5
Jukebox..**44** B2
Papas II......................................(see 44)

TRANSPORT
Service Taxi......................................**45** B5
Superjet Bus Station..........................**46** B4
Upper Egypt Bus Co..........................**47** E6

restaurants and bars, and a windsurfing and diving centre.

Jasmine Village (Map p429; ☎ 346 0460; jasmine@tut2000.com; s/d all-inclusive US$52/84; 🍴 🏊) One of Hurghada's older establishments, with 400-plus bungalow-style rooms catering mainly to Eastern European groups. There is disabled access, a playground and a full water-sports centre, which includes a reputable diving club and windsurfing facilities.

Other recommendations:

Fantasia (Map p429; ☎ 346 4601; www.hotel1001.de; s/d US$72/102) If you can't get enough of the Disneyesque atmosphere at Alf Layla wa Layla (p438), this comfortable hotel – in the centre of the Alf Layla wa Layla compound – is the place to stay. Breakfast costs E£35 extra.

Hor Palace (Map p429; ☎ 346 5301; www.horpalace hotel.com; s/d half board US$30/50; 🍴 🏊) Another of Hurghada's older establishments, with its somewhat drab interior compensated for by a beach and competitive prices.

TOP END

With the exception of Cairo, Hurghada has the greatest concentration of four- and five-star hotels and resorts in Egypt, though most are geared to package tours. Most places are on the resort strip, but there are also some along the beach between Ad-Dahar and Sigala. Note that travel agencies in Europe and Cairo can offer often-significant reductions if you book in advance, and that prices fluctuate according to the season and state of the tourism industry.

Oberoi Sahl Hasheesh (☎ 344 0777; www.oberoi hotels.com; Sahl Hasheesh; ste from US$310; ☒ 🍴 🖥 🏊) Peaceful, exclusive and beautiful, the Oberoi features stunning suites decorated in minimalist Moorish style, complete with sunken marble baths, walled private courtyards – some with pools – and panoramic sea views. Other attractions include a small spa, tennis courts and a house reef. It is one of the most luxurious destinations on the Red Sea.

Sofitel (Map p429; ☎ 346 4641; www.sofitel.com; Resort Strip; s/d half board US$100/150; ☒ 🍴 🖥 🏊) Another exclusive spot, with 300-plus rooms clustered into 12 Arabesque-style blocks. It offers a full range of water sports and has a 700m-wide beach, as well as a kids club, jogging track, tennis and squash courts and several restaurants and bars.

Iberotel Arabella (Map p429; ☎ 354 5087, 354 5090; www.iberotel-eg.com/arabella; Corniche; s/d half board US$63/90; 🍴 🖥 🏊) A good-value place with a warren of tasteful, whitewashed domes on a nice stretch of beach between Sigala and Ad-Dahar.

Hurghada Marriott Beach Resort (Map p429; ☎ 344 6950; http://marriott.com; Resort Strip; s/d US$90/110; ✗ ✗ 🖳 🖳) This six-storey luxury hotel is very conveniently located near the beginning of the resort strip, and has a small beach, a pool and all the amenities you'd expect.

Hilton Hurghada Resort (Map p429; ☎ 346 5036; www.hilton.com; Corniche; s/d US$58/70; ✗ ✗ 🖳 🖳) The Hilton lacks the aesthetic appeal of some of the other resorts, but is nonetheless quite comfortable, with a good dive centre and a lively bar and nightlife.

Hilton Hurghada Plaza (Map p429; ☎ 354 9745; www.hilton.com; Corniche; s/d US$63/83; ✗ 🖳 🖳 🖳) A plush five-star place close to the centre of town with a good dive centre and comfortable rooms.

Eating

With its diverse population and large pool of tourists, Hurghada has a good variety of restaurants.

BUDGET
Ad-Dahar

Ad-Dahar has dozens of inexpensive local-style eateries, and several Western-style ones as well.

Pizza Tarboush (Map pp434–5; ☎ 354 8456; Sharia Abdel Aziz Mustafa; pizzas E£10-20) This popular takeaway pizzeria on the edge of the souq has a variety of topping choices and a few chairs on the sidewalk for those who want to dine in.

Taibeen (Map pp434–5; ☎ 354 7260; Sharia Soliman Mazhar; dishes E£3-15) Good kebab and *kofta* (mincemeat and spices grilled on a skewer), to take away or eat in.

La Torta (Map pp434–5; Sharia Sheikh Sabak; pastries E£1-5) A tiny café serving filter coffee and a small selection of pastries at six small tables.

Café Cheers (Map pp434–5; Corniche; dishes E£8-25) This tiny 24-hour café/bar serves sandwiches, pizzas and burgers as well as cold beer.

For self-caterers, there are dozens of supermarkets, including the well-stocked **Abu Ashara** (Map pp434–5; Sharia Abdel Aziz Mustafa), just down from Pizza Tarboush. The nearby souq (Map pp434–5) is the best place for fruit and vegetables.

Sigala

Most of Sigala's cheapest eateries are at the northern end of Sharia Sheraton, around Midan Sigala.

Abu Khadigah (Map p437; ☎ 344 3768; Sharia Sheraton; meals E£3-15) This no-frills place is known for its *kofta*s, stuffed cabbage leaves and other Egyptian staples. It's patronised by an intriguing mix of workers and local businessmen, as well as the odd tourist.

Hefny Seafood Restaurant (Map p437; Sharia Shedwan; meals E£15-40; ✗) A basic but good seafood restaurant where the fish is sold by weight and served with salads and rice.

Abu Ashara (Map p437; Sharia Sheraton) A well-stocked supermarket.

MIDRANGE
Ad-Dahar

There are a number of midpriced restaurants in Ad-Dahar, most centred on the souq.

Bordiehn's (Map p429; ☎ 354 5087; Iberotel Arabella, btwn Ad-Dahar & Sigala; dishes E£15-75; ✗) Bordiehn's mall-like surroundings and loud background music are compensated for by a wide selection of international dishes made with an emphasis on fresh ingredients, and delicious desserts.

Portofino (Map pp434–5; ☎ 354 6250; Sharia Say-yed al-Qorayem; dishes E£25-40; ✗) This long-standing restaurant serves good-value Italian cuisine, plus some Egyptian dishes as well.

Chez Pascal (Map pp434–5; ☎ 354 9200; Sharia Sayyed al-Qorayem; meals E£20-50; ✗) A clean, bright place with pizza and international fare served in friendly surroundings.

Mandarine Lebanese Restaurant (Map pp434–5; ☎ 354 7007; Corniche; dishes E£30-70) Tasty Lebanese cuisine and outdoor seating.

Young Kang (Map pp434–5; ☎ 012 422 9327; Sharia Sheikh Sabak; dishes E£25-35; ✗) This small and unassuming place does a surprisingly good far-Eastern cuisine, including a tasty rendition of fried rice and sweet-and-sour chicken.

Lo Scarabeo (Map pp434–5; ☎ 012 364 6927; Sharia Sayyed el-Qorayem; dishes E£10-50) Good pastas and pizzas, huge salads and delicious bread served in a simple setting.

Red Sea I (Map pp434–5; ☎ 354 9630; off Sharia an-Nasr; dishes E£20-60; ✗) and its sister restaurant, **Red Sea II** (Map pp434–5; ☎ 354 9630; Sharia Sayyed al-Qorayem; meals E£20-60) offer a wide selection of seafood, plus Egyptian dishes and pizza, steaks, poultry and pleasant rooftop seating.

Sigala & Resort Strip

Sigala – and increasingly the northern end of the Resort Strip as well – has the greatest variety of restaurants in town, with new ones opening all the time. Following is just a small sampling.

Felfela Restaurant (Map p429; ☎ 344 2410/1; Sharia Sheraton; dishes E£10-60; ☺ 8.30am-midnight) Sitting on a gentle bend in the coastline and overlooking the turquoise sea, this branch of the Felfela chain wins a prize for vistas, which you can enjoy while dining on serviceable Egyptian classics at reasonable prices. If you're on a tight budget, be prepared for the extra charges (like bread, E£1 per piece).

Da Nanni (Map p429; ☎ 344 7018; Sharia al-Hadaba; meals E£20-75) Some of the best pizza in town,

plus good pastas, steaks and other meals. It's at La Perla Hotel, on the northern end of the Resort Strip.

Rossi Restaurant (Map p437; ☎ 344 7676; Sharia Sheraton; mains E£17-50) This popular hang-out for divers and expats serves a variety of pizza toppings on crispy crusts, and pasta dishes. The service is laid-back and women on their own can relax without being hassled.

Liquid Lounge (Map p437; www.papasbar.com; Sharia Sheraton; meals E£25-40; ☺ 9am-3am) A laid-back and very hip beach bar serving lunches and dinner, including a 'liquid lunch' special – main dish plus drink – for E£30.

Il Forno (Map p437; ☎ 010 177 4001; Sharia Sheraton; dishes E£25-80) Good Italian food in a quiet setting.

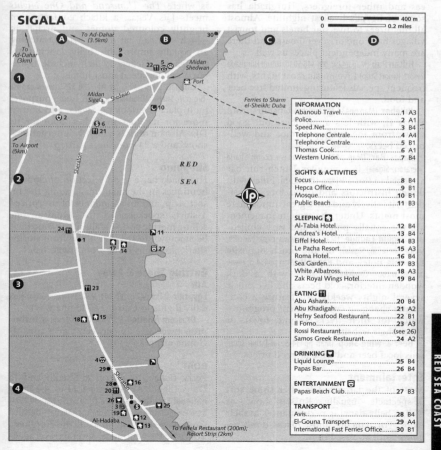

SIGALA

0   400 m
0   0.2 miles

To Ad-Dahar (3.5km)
To Ad-Dahar (3km)
Midan Shedwan
Midan Sigala
Sheratan
Shedwan
Port
Ferries to Sharm el-Sheikh; Duba
To Airport (5km)
RED SEA
Sheratan
Al-Hadaba
To Felfela Restaurant (200m); Resort Strip (2km)

INFORMATION	
Abanoub Travel	1 A3
Police	2 A1
Speed.Net	3 B4
Telephone Centrale	4 A4
Telephone Centrale	5 B1
Thomas Cook	6 A1
Western Union	7 B4

SIGHTS & ACTIVITIES	
Focus	8 B4
Hepca Office	9 B1
Mosque	10 B1
Public Beach	11 B3

SLEEPING	
Al-Tabia Hotel	12 B4
Andrea's Hotel	13 B4
Eiffel Hotel	14 B3
Le Pacha Resort	15 A3
Roma Hotel	16 B4
Sea Garden	17 B3
White Albatross	18 A3
Zak Royal Wings Hotel	19 B4

EATING	
Abu Ashara	20 B4
Abu Khadigah	21 A2
Hefny Seafood Restaurant	22 B1
Il Forno	23 A3
Rossi Restaurant	(see 26)
Samos Greek Restaurant	24 A2

DRINKING	
Liquid Lounge	25 B4
Papas Bar	26 B4

ENTERTAINMENT	
Papas Beach Club	27 B3

TRANSPORT	
Avis	28 B4
El-Gouna Transport	29 A4
International Fast Ferries Office	30 B1

RED SEA COAST

Bulls Steakhouse (Map p429; ☎ 344 4414; Resort Strip; dishes E£10-30; ☒) A popular steakhouse with a good selection of international dishes, plus some Chinese food. It's diagonally opposite the Marriott Beach Resort.

Samos Greek Restaurant (Map p437; Sharia Sheraton; meals E£20-40; ☒) A long-standing place in the centre of Sigala catering to tourists and serving the usual salads, moussaka and souvlakia.

European Bakery (Map p429; Sharia Sheraton, Resort Strip; dishes E£2-20) European-style bread and pies, and reasonably priced sandwiches.

Drinking

Thanks to its large community of resident dive instructors, tour guides, hotel employees and other foreigners, Hurghada has some of Egypt's liveliest nightlife. Almost all the three- to five-star hotels and tourist villages have one or several bars, and there are many independent places as well.

Hilton Pub (Map p429; ☎ 346 5036; Hilton Hurghada Resort, Resort Strip) Live music most nights, with frequent specials featuring limited free beer and food.

Jukebox (Map pp434-5; Corniche) Upstairs from Papas II, with less atmosphere but good views from the rooftop terrace and well-priced beers.

Papas Bar (Map p437; www.papasbar.com; Sharia Sheraton, Sigala) is a popular Dutch-run bar attached to Rossi Pizza in Sigala. Filled with diving instructors and other foreign residents, it is lively and has a great atmosphere most nights. Under the same management are the equally popular and very chilled-out **Liquid Lounge** (Map p437; www.papasbar.com; Sharia Sheraton, Sigala), on the beach opposite El-Tabia hotel, and **Papas II** (Map pp434-5; www .papasbar.com; Corniche, Ad-Dahar), with a dark wooden interior, cold beers and live music several nights weekly. All feature a constantly changing entertainment program – watch for their flyers around town, or check their website.

Beer & Wine Shop (Map pp434-5; Ad-Dahar souq) sells local beer and wine at good prices.

Entertainment

Most of the large hotels offer some sort of spectacle – usually a Russian show – as well as belly-dancing performances in their clubs. For dancing, most places don't get going until at least 11pm.

Papas Beach Club (Map p437; www.papasbar.com; Sigala; admission E£50; ☒ 10pm-4am) A popular beach club that brings DJs from Europe and has regular parties. Food and drink are included in the cover charge.

Black Out Disco (Map p429; ☎ 346 0460; alibaba@ tut2000.com; Ali Baba Palace, Resort Strip; admission Wed-Mon E£30, Tue E£60) One of the most popular dance spots in town, with Ibiza-style foam nights on Tuesday and free drinks on Friday.

Hard Rock Café (Map p429; ☎ 346 5179, 346 5168/ 9; Resort Strip; ☒ noon to 4am) In the centre of the Resort Strip, with dancing from midnight until the wee hours.

Alf Layla wa Layla (Map p429; ☎ 346 4601; Safaga rd; dinner US$15, show US$25; ☒ 9.30-11.30pm) This is where *The Thousand and One Nights* meets Las Vegas: a kitsch confection of brightly coloured domes and arches in which you can eat dinner while watching an equally improbable belly-dancing extravaganza. Tickets (which include transport) are on sale at most hotels.

Calypso (Map p429; ☎ 012 280 1251; www.calypso -hrg.com; Sharia al-Hadaba, Sigala) A huge, purpose-built place overlooking Sigala, and known more for its Russian 'ladies' than for its DJs. Also on offer is a nightly 'international show' and a 24-hour beer garden.

Shopping

Hurghada has a good selection of clothing boutiques in the small malls along the resort strip, and an abundance of overpriced T-shirts, snorkels and fins. Avoid anyone selling marine curios; stalls in the souq have been known to sell everything from stuffed sharks to lamps made from triggerfish.

Getting There & Away

AIR

EgyptAir (Map p429; ☎ 344 3592/3; Resort Strip) has daily flights to Cairo (E£740 one way).

Orascom Aviation (☎ 358 0211) flies a turbo-prop twice weekly between Cairo and Al-Gouna airport.

BOAT

Ferry tickets to Sharm el-Sheikh and to Duba (Saudi Arabia) are sold at the **International Fast Ferries office** (Map p437; ☎ 344 7571/ 2; www.intlfastferries.com; Corniche, Sigala) behind Fantasia restaurant, opposite the Hurghada Touristic Port entrance. Several travel agencies in town, including Thomas Cook (p430) are also ticket agents. See p543 for details on the ferry to Duba. The ferry to Sharm el-Sheikh departs Hurghada at 5am Monday and at 8am on Tuesday, Thursday and Saturday (E£250/US$40 one way, 90 minutes). The rate of the dollar against the Egyptian pound and the whim of the ferry officials determine which currency you'll need to use for the Sharm ferry ticket. Come prepared with dollars, as they're not available at banks in Hurghada, but be prepared to convert them to pounds. Note that departure times of the Sharm el-Sheikh ferry don't correspond with bus arrivals from Luxor, so you'll need to spend at least part of a night in Hurghada.

The ferry is often cancelled during winter because of windy conditions, stranding travellers in Hurghada. For this reason, it's a good idea not to buy tickets in Luxor beforehand (trying to get refunds is difficult if not impossible) and to get them at the port on arrival instead. If the ferry is likely to be cancelled for a few days, you can then make alternative arrangements to get to Sharm by bus or service taxi.

BUS
Superjet (Map pp434-5; ☎ 354 4722; Sharia al-Oruba, Ad-Dahar) has daily buses to Cairo (E£57 to E£60, six hours) departing at noon, 2pm, 5pm and midnight. A 2.30pm service also goes to Alexandria (E£83, nine to 10 hours).

Upper Egypt Bus Co (Map pp434-5; ☎ 354 7582; off Sharia an-Nasr, Ad-Dahar) has 10 daily buses to Cairo (E£55, six to seven hours) about every two hours from 10am to 1.30am. If you want an earlier connection to Cairo, you'll have to take your chances on getting a place on the 6am bus from Safaga, which reaches Hurghada about 7am. The 7.30pm Cairo bus goes on to Alexandria (E£75, at least nine hours). Buses for Suez (E£35, five hours) leave almost hourly between 10am and 4pm, then at 5.30pm, 7pm, 11pm and 2am. There are daily buses to Luxor (E£30, five hours), via Safaga (E£5) and Qena (E£15), leaving at 10am, 1pm, 7pm, 10.30pm, 12.30am 1am, 3am and 4am. The 10am, 1pm, 10.30pm and midnight services go on to Aswan (E£45, eight hours). There is an occasional service to Luxor at 7.30pm. Services to Quseir (E£20, three hours), Marsa Alam (E£30, five hours) and Shalatein (E£50, nine hours) leave at

1am, 3am (terminating in Marsa Alam), 5am and 8pm.

Confirm these schedules at the bus station, as changes are likely, and try to book ahead for long-distance journeys such as to Luxor and Cairo.

El-Gouna Transport (☎ 354 1561; Sharia an-Nasr, Ad-Dahar) has daily buses to Cairo (E£40 to E£55), departing at 9am, 1pm, 2.30pm, 4pm, 6pm 9pm, midnight, 1am, 2am and 3am, all leaving from the centrale in Ad-Dahar.

SERVICE TAXI
The **service taxi station** (Map pp434-5; off Sharia an-Nasr, Ad-Dahar) has taxis to Cairo (E£35 per person, six hours), Safaga (E£3, 45 minutes), Al-Quseir (E£10, two hours), Qena (E£12, three hours), Marsa Alam (E£20, four hours) and Suez (E£27, 3½ to four hours). They cannot take you to Luxor or Aswan except on a private basis in a police convoy. With bargaining, it costs about E£200 per vehicle (up to seven passengers) to Luxor.

Getting Around
TO/FROM THE AIRPORT
The airport is close to the resort strip. A taxi to downtown Ad-Dahar will cost between E£10 and E£25.

CAR
There are numerous car rental agencies along Sharia Sheraton in Sigala, including **Avis** (Map p437 ☎ 344 7400).

MICROBUS
Microbuses run through the day from central Ad-Dahar south to the InterContinental

---

POLICE CONVOYS
Whether you're going by taxi or private car, if you're heading across to the Nile Valley you'll be forced to go in a police convoy (see p548). They depart from the police checkpoint at the northern edge of Safaga near the start of the Qena road at 7am, 9am and 4pm, but confirm these times with the tourist office. There are also convoys to Cairo, departing from the police checkpoint at the Al-Gouna turn-off (20km north of Hurghada) at 2.30am, 11am and 5pm, though convoy travel on the Cairo road is often not enforced.

hotel on the resort strip (E£1), and along Sharia an-Nasr and other major routes. Short rides cost 25pt to 50pt.

El-Gouna Transport (Map p437; ☎ 354 1561) operates a more comfortable route (E£5) between Al-Gouna, Ad-Dahar and the end of Sharia Sheraton in Sigala about every half hour, beginning at 9am. You can flag the bus down at any point along the way and pay on board.

TAXI

Taxis from Ad-Dahar to the start of the resort strip (around the Marriott hotel) charge about E£15. Travelling from the bus station to the centre of Ad-Dahar, expect to pay between E£5 and E£10.

AROUND HURGHADA
Resorts

The Hurghada–Safaga coast is dotted with resorts offering less crowded alternatives to the more hectic scene in Hurghada.

Sharm el-Naga Resort (☎ 010 111 2942, in Cairo 02-793 1166; www.sharmelnaga.com; s/d half board US$42/65; ⌘) This low-key, good-value resort is set on a small bay about 40km south of Hurghada. It has a good reef for divers and snorkellers (both of which are possible from shore), a dive centre, a covered restaurant serving à la carte lunches, a beach bar for keeping thirst at bay while you sunbathe and a children's play area. While it is popular as a day excursion from Hurghada (per person entry US$10), it's also possible to spend the night in pleasant beach-facing bungalows with bathroom. For dive centre details, see p460.

Soma Bay Sheraton (☎ 354 5845; www.sheraton -somabay.com; s/d half board US$230/337; ⌘ ⌘ ⌘ ⌘) This 298-room resort is part of the Ras Abu Soma 'resort cluster' – one of a number of self-contained tourist centres being built along the coast south of Hurghada along the lines of Al-Gouna (see p427). Among other amenities, the resort (www.somabay .com) boasts a golf course, several hotels and tennis courts. The Sheraton itself, which is built in pseudo-Pharaonic style, has well-appointed rooms, including some with disabled access, plus several plush, beach-facing suites. It was also a pioneering member of a Red Sea sustainable tourism initiative targeted at helping hotels become environmentally friendly. The hotel is at Ras Abu Soma, just south of Sharm el-Naga; airport transfers can be arranged.

Makadi Bay Le Meridien (☎ 359 0590; www .makadibay.lemeridien.com; s/d US$120/140; ⌘ ⌘ ⌘ ⌘) This vast, plush complex is about 35km south of Hurghada. In addition to its huge pool, it has golf, horse riding and an array of diving and desert excursions.

SAFAGA
☎ 065

Safaga (sometimes referred to as Port Safaga) is a rough-and-ready port town that keeps itself in existence through the export of phosphates from local mines. It's also a major local terminal for the ferry to Saudi Arabia, and during the Haj thousands of pilgrims from the Nile Valley embark here on their voyages to Mecca.

Despite the turquoise waters and the reefs that lie offshore, the town itself is unattractive, barely stretching beyond a few flyblown streets off a main thoroughfare. Unless you're into windsurfing (which is top notch here) or diving (which is better elsewhere), and are thus staying at one of the beach hotels along the resort strip at the northern end of the bay, it is hardly worth a stop. This is particularly true if you're on a budget, as cheap accommodation is geared to truck drivers, not tourists.

Orientation & Information

Safaga is a long town, stretched out over about 5km, and centred around Sharia al-Gomhuriyya, the main road running parallel to the waterfront. The bus station is near the southern end of town. Heading north there is a motley collection of small, cheap eateries, and beyond these the **post office** (⏱ 8.30am-2.30pm Sat-Thu). About 1.5km north of the bus station is the service taxi station, followed by the port entrance (for ferries to Saudi Arabia). Just up from here is the main **telephone centrale** (⏱ 24hr) and next to this are branches of **Banque Misr** (⏱ 8.30am-2pm Sun-Thu) and **Banque du Caire** (⏱ 8.30am-2pm Sun-Thu), with several ATMs nearby. At the far-northern end of town, near the roundabout with the large dolphin sculptures, a road branches northeast off Sharia al-Gomhuriyya leading to the northern resort strip. Microbuses run along Sharia al-Gomhuriyya for 25pt, and between town and the northern resorts.

Sights & Activities

The old Roman settlement of **Mons Claudianus** lies about 40km from Safaga along the Qena road; see p444.

Safaga is a famously windy place, with a fairly steady stream from the north, and most of the resort hotels have **windsurfing** centres, plus kite surfing and other sports.

Sleeping & Eating

Holiday Inn Resort Safaga Palace (☎ 326 0100, 325 2821; www.ichotelsgroup.com; Resort Strip; s/d half board US$94/125; ✗ ✗ 🖳 🖳) This large complex on the northern resort strip compensates for its lack of ambience with good facilities, including a large pool, a beach, well-appointed rooms, good water-sport facilities, a play area for children and an ATM.

Shams Safaga (☎ 325 1781; info@shamshotels.com; Resort Strip; s/d half board US$75/100; ✗ 🖳) This bland but reliable hotel has pleasant rooms (either chalet-style or in a central block) and a full range of water sports, including kite surfing, and a good windsurfing centre.

Lotus Bay Beach Resort (☎ 02-748 2639; www.lotusbay.com; Resort Strip; s/d half board US$54/72; ✗ 🖳) A moderately sized hotel with appealing gardens, pleasant rooms (ask for one as close to the beach as possible), tennis courts and windsurfing and other water sports.

Nemo Dive Club & Hotel (☎ 325 6888; www.nemodive.com; Corniche; s/d US$30/45; ✗) This high-rise hotel at the northern end of town is primarily for divers, though they'll also take in the stray traveller. Downstairs is a popular bar.

Qasr el-Nakhil Hotel (☎ 325 4691; Hurghada-Safaga rd; d with fan/air-con E£40/60; ✗) Clean no-frills rooms and reasonable prices make this the best of the budget places. It's along the main road at the northern end of town, near the Bank of Alexandria.

At the northern end of town, just south of the dolphin roundabout are several inexpensive eateries, including a branch of the chain **First Cook** (dishes E£5-15) with Egyptian fast food. A step up is **Pizzeria Ali Baba** (☎ 325 0253; Hurghada-Safaga rd; dishes E£20-55), with good pizzas and seafood grills. **Rausha Seafood Restaurant** (☎ 325 1650, 010 612 3851; Sharia Al-Maglis; dishes E£20-65) has tasty seafood grills; advance bookings are required. It's off the main road near the hospital.

Getting There & Away

BOAT

The only passenger boat from Safaga is the slow ferry to Duba; see p543.

BUS

Safaga is located along the main highway, 53km south of Hurghada. There are seven buses daily to Cairo (E£35 to E£47, about eight hours), with the first departure at 6am. Some stop in Suez, and there are also direct Suez services (E£22 to E£30, five to six hours) about every two hours, all of which also stop in Hurghada (E£5, one hour). Buses to Al-Quseir (E£5, two hours) depart at 2am, 6am, 4pm, 7pm and 9pm, with all except the 4pm continuing to Marsa Alam (E£15, three to four hours). Buses to Qena depart about every two to three hours (E£12 to E£15), with many originating in Hurghada. Daily departures to Luxor (E£25) and Aswan (E£27 to E£35) are at 2am (Luxor only), 10am, 2.30pm (Luxor only), 4.30pm and 11.30pm.

SERVICE TAXI

There are three main routes. Getting to or from Hurghada takes about 40 minutes and costs E£5. The trip to Al-Quseir (try asking early in the morning) costs E£7, and to Marsa Alam it's E£20. To Cairo it costs E£40. Because of the convoy system (see p439), you can only get to the Nile Valley (ie Qena, Luxor and Aswan) by hiring the entire taxi. Expect to pay about E£250 and be prepared to haggle.

AL-QUSEIR
☎ 065

Al-Quseir lies on the coast 85km south of Safaga and about 160km east of Qift on the Nile. Its history stretches back to Pharaonic times, when it was the launching point for boats sailing to Punt. Although the ancient port – about 8km north of present-day Al-Quseir – is now silted up, the 'modern' town is just as interesting. Until the 10th century, it was one of the most important ports on the Red Sea and a major exit point for pilgrims travelling to Mecca. It was also a thriving centre of trade and export between the Nile Valley and the Red Sea and beyond. Even in decline it remained a major settlement, and was sufficiently important for the Ottomans to fortify it in the 16th century. Later the British beat the French for control of Al-Quseir, and for a time it was the main import channel for the spice trade from India to Britain. The opening of the Suez Canal in 1869 put an end to all this, and the town's decline accelerated, with only a brief burst of prosperity as a phosphate-processing centre in the early decades of the 20th century.

Today Al-Quseir's long history and sleepy present lend it a charm absent from Egypt's other Red Sea towns. Its centre is dominated by an Ottoman fortress, and old coral-block buildings with wooden balconies line the waterfront. Mixed among these are domed tombs of various saints – mostly pious pilgrims who died en route to or from Mecca.

Information

Hot Line Internet Café (Sharia Port Said; per hr E£10; 9am-3am)

Main post office (Sharia al-Sheikh Abdel Ghafaar; 8.30am-2pm Sat-Thu)

National Bank of Egypt (Safaga rd; 8.30am-2pm Sun-Thu) No ATM (yet).

Quseir Hospital (☎ 333 0077; Safaga rd) Head to Hurghada if possible.

Telephone centrale (Sharia al-Maghreb; 24hr)

Tourist information (Sharia al-Gomhuriyya) Scheduled to open soon, in a booth in front of the fortress.

Tourist police (☎ 335 0024; Safaga rd)

Sights

The 16th-century Ottoman **fortress** (admission E£5; 9am-5pm) is the town's most important historical building. It was modified by the French, and some 6000 British cannonballs rained upon it during a heated battle in the 19th century. The British then added a fortified gate to make sure nobody else could take it away from them. The fortress has been partially restored and it now houses a visitors' centre with small displays on local history.

Just across from the fortress is the 19th-century **shrine** of a Yemeni sheikh, Abdel Ghaffaar al-Yemeni, with the old gravestone in a niche in the wall.

A few blocks south along the waterfront is the picturesque **police station**, originally an Ottoman diwan (council chamber) and

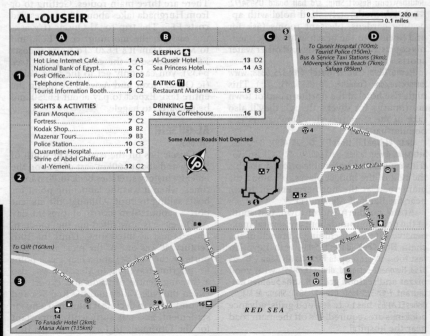

AL-QUSEIR

0 — 200 m
0 — 0.1 miles

INFORMATION
Hot Line Internet Café..............1 A3
National Bank of Egypt..............2 C1
Post Office................................3 D2
Telephone Centrale....................4 C2
Tourist Information Booth...........5 C2

SIGHTS & ACTIVITIES
Faran Mosque...........................6 D3
Fortress...................................7 C2
Kodak Shop..............................8 B2
Mazenar Tours..........................9 B3
Police Station..........................10 C3
Quarantine Hospital.................11 C3
Shrine of Abdel Ghaffaar
    al-Yemeni...........................12 C2

SLEEPING
Al-Quseir Hotel........................13 D2
Sea Princess Hotel....................14 A3

EATING
Restaurant Marianne.................15 B3

DRINKING
Sahraya Coffeehouse.................16 B3

To Quseir Hospital (100m);
Tourist Police (150m);
Bus & Service Taxi Stations (3km);
Mövenpick Sirena Beach (7km);
Safaga (85km)

Al-Maghreb

Al-Sheikh Abdel Ghafaar

Some Minor Roads Not Depicted

To Qift (160km)

Al-Oruba

Al-Gomhuriyya

Al-Wehda

Um Sabr

Orabi

Al-Nemr

Al-Shohda

Port Said

Port Said

To Fanadir Hotel (2km);
Marsa Alam (135km)

RED SEA

RED SEA COAST

later the town hall. Photos aren't permitted,
and it's not open to the public.

Behind here is another fortresslike
building, formerly a quarantine hospital
built during the reign of the Ottoman sultan Selim II. Just next to this is the **Faran
Mosque**, dating to 1704. Running between
the waterside Sharia Port Said and the
main street, Sharia Al-Gomhuriyya, are
numerous small lanes good for wandering
around to get a glimpse of local life. One of
them, Sharia Um Sabr, has been restored;
it's best reached from a turn-off on Sharia
Al-Gomhuriyya, opposite the Kodak shop.

Activities

Diving and excursions into the Eastern
Desert can be arranged with **Mazenar Tours**
(☎ 333 5247, 012 265 5044; rockyvalleycamp@yahoo.dk;
Sharia Port Said) along the waterfront. They also
run the Rocky Valley Diving Camp, 14km
north of Quseir along the main road, with
simple, thatched bungalows and a resident
dive outfitter.

Sleeping

Al-Quseir Hotel (☎ 333 2301; Sharia Port Said; s/d
E£112/157; 🐕) This charming hotel has six
simple but spacious rooms in a renovated
1920s merchant's house on the seafront.
With its original narrow wooden staircase,
high wooden ceilings and latticework on the
windows, it's full of atmosphere, and staying
here is a pleasure. Bathrooms are shared between three rooms, but are large and clean.
There are also good views from the seafront
rooms, and a tiny restaurant serving breakfast (included in the room price) and other
meals on order.

Mövenpick Sirena Beach (☎ 333 2100; www
.movenpick-quseir.com; r from US$200; 🐕 🖥 🍸) This

low-set, domed ensemble 7km north of the
town centre is top of the line in Al-Quseir,
and one of the best resorts along the coast.
Its amenities include excellent food and
the usual five-star facilities, a Subex diving centre, quiet evenings and a refreshing
absence of the glitz so common in other
resort hotels. Management is known for its
environmentally conscious approach and
will ask guests to leave the water if it finds
them breaking off coral on the hotel's reef.
Recommended if you're seeking comfort
and relaxation in a beautiful setting.

Fanadir Hotel (☎ 333 1414; hotel@fanadirhotel
.com; s/d E£160/320; 🐕 🍸) This pleasant place,
about 2km south of central Al-Quseir along
the Marsa Alam road, had just changed
hands as this book was researched, and was
in the process of getting a complete facelift.
Named after a rocky islet just to the south,
it has 55 adjoining domed bungalows, plus
two large villas, and good sea views.

Sea Princess Hotel (☎ 333 1880; Sharia al-Gomhuriyya; s/tw/tr E£27/44/67) This is the only shoestring
choice in town, with a large, bright lobby,
cubiclelike rooms and marginal shared bathrooms. Breakfast costs E£5 extra.

Eating & Drinking

Dining options in Al-Quseir are limited.
There are the usual *ta'amiyya* and fish
joints around the seafront and the bus station. The best place to have a cup of coffee
is at the **Sahraya Coffeehouse** (Sharia Port Said) on
the waterfront, which also serves snacks.
Diagonally opposite is **Restaurant Marianne**
(☎ 333 4386; Sharia Port Said; dishes E£15-50) with
grilled fish and other simple but filling
meals. Other than that, the **Fanadir** (☎ 333
1414; hotel@fanadirhotel.com; dishes E£20-45) and the
Mövenpick Serena Beach (☎ 333 2100; www.moven
pick-quseir.com; dishes E£30-90, buffet E£180) both
have good restaurants open to nonguests.

Getting There & Away

The bus and service-taxi stations are next
to each other about 1.5km northwest of the
Safaga road, and about 3km from the telephone centrale (E£2 to E£3 in a taxi).

BUS

Buses run to Cairo (E£57, 11 hours) via Safaga (E£5, two hours) and Hurghada (E£15,
three hours) departing at 6am, 7.30am, 9am,
7pm and 8.30pm. The 6am bus also stops at

Suez. Buses to Marsa Alam (E£5, two hours) are at 5am, 9am 7pm and 8pm, continuing to Shalatein. To Qena, there are five buses daily (E£10, five hours) via Qift.

SERVICE TAXI

Sample fares include Cairo E£43, Suez E£30, Qena E£20, Hurghada E£10 and Safaga E£6. As in Hurghada and Safaga you have to hire the entire taxi for the trip to Luxor, Qena or Aswan (all routes via Safaga). Expect to pay from E£250 after negotiating.

Getting Around
MICROBUS

Microbuses go along Sharia al-Gomhuriyya, from the roundabout near Sea Princess Ho-

tel north to the administrative buildings on the road to Safaga, with some also going to the bus and service-taxi stations. Fares are between 50pt and E£1, depending on the distance travelled.

MARSA ALAM
☎ 065

The small town of Marsa Alam lies along a rugged stretch of coast that has rapidly increased in popularity in recent years as a diving and adventure destination. It's of appeal primarily to those seeking to avoid the crowds on reefs further north or those wanting to explore the Eastern Desert. The area has also been targeted as the site of the massive new Port Ghalib marina and resort

---

EASTERN DESERT

The Eastern Desert – a vast, desolate area rimmed by the Red Sea Mountains to the east and the Nile Valley in the west – was once crisscrossed by ancient trade routes and dotted with settlements that played vital roles in the development of many of the region's greatest civilisations. Today the desert's rugged expanses are filled with fascinating footprints of this history, including rock inscriptions, ancient gold and mineral mines, wells and watchtowers, and religious shrines and buildings.

One of the most impressive collections of **rock inscriptions**, many of which date to prehistoric times, is found in the barren tracts fringing the Marsa Alam–Edfu road, beginning close to Marsa Alam, where the smooth, grey rock was perfect for carving. They include hunting scenes with dogs chasing ostriches, depictions of giraffes and cattle and hieroglyphic accounts of trade expeditions.

In the remote **Wadi Miya**, west of Marsa Alam, in what was likely an ancient mine works, are the remains of a temple said to be built by Seti I. **Wadi Sikait**, about 80km southwest of Marsa Alam, was an emerald-mining centre at least as early as the Ptolemaic period. It provided emeralds that were used throughout the ancient world and was the exclusive source of emeralds for the Roman Empire.

The high, smooth walls of **Wadi Hammamat**, about halfway along the road connecting Al-Quseir to the town of Qift, display a remarkable collection of graffiti dating from Pharaonic times down to Egypt's 20th-century King Farouk. The road through the wadi runs along an ancient trade route, and remains of old wells and other evidence of the area's long history can also be seen. In Graeco-Roman times, watchtowers were built along the trail at short enough intervals for signals to be visible, and many of them are still intact on the barren hilltops on either side of the road.

Starkly beautiful **Wadi Gimal**, which extends inland for about 85km from its coastal opening south of Marsa Alam, is home to a rich variety of birdlife, gazelles and stands of mangrove. In ancient times, the surrounding area was the source of emerald, gold and other minerals used in Pharaonic and Roman civilisations. Together with tiny Wadi Gimal Island, just offshore from the wadi's delta area, Wadi Gimal has been given protected status and targeted for development as an ecotourism destination. Because of its long history and abundance of historical monuments, the area has also been proposed as a Unesco World Heritage site.

About 40km along the Safaga–Qena road, a signposted track breaks off northwest towards **Mons Claudianus**, an old Roman granite quarry/fortress complex, and one of the largest of the Roman settlements dotting the Eastern Desert. This stark and remote place was the end of the line for Roman prisoners brought to hack the granite out of the barren mountains, and was a hardship post for the soldiers sent to guard them. It was more a concentration camp than a

complex being constructed near Marsa Alam airport which, once opened, will give tourism in the region an entirely different profile.

Despite its current remote location, the area around Marsa Alam has an ancient history. Gold and emeralds were once mined in the barren, mineral-rich mountains just inland, and the road leading from Marsa Alam west to Edfu in the Nile Valley follows an ancient route that was originally built by Ptolemy II. Today phosphate mining is the area's main industry, although it is fast being overtaken by tourism.

Orientation & Information

Marsa Alam itself little more than a T-junction where the road from Edfu meets the coastal road. Just south of the junction is a modest collection of shops, a pharmacy, a telephone centrale and a bustling market. The coast to the south and north is sprinkled with resorts.

EMERGENCY

Air ambulance (☎ 010 154 1978)
Decompression chamber (☎ 012 218 7550, 019 510 0262, emergency VHF code16; Marsa Shagra) Twenty-four km north of Marsa Alam.
Tourist police (☎ 375 0000; Quaraya Hotel, coastal rd)

Sights & Activities

Diving and desert excursions are the main activities around Marsa Alam. For more on diving – which is primarily for experienced

---

quarry; you can still see the remains of the tiny cells that these unfortunates inhabited. There is also an immense cracked pillar, left where it fell 2000 years ago, a small temple and some other ruins. Once the granite was mined, it was carved and transported more than 200km across the desert to the Nile, from where it then was taken to the Mediterranean and the heart of the empire. The site is about 25km north of the turn-off along deteriorated tarmac.

Mons Porphyrites – about 40km northwest of Hurghada – is the site of ancient porphyry quarries worked by the Romans. The precious white-and-purple crystalline stone was mined and then transported across the desert along the Via Porphyrites to the Nile for use in sarcophagi, columns and other decorative work elsewhere in the Roman world. The quarries were under the direct control of the imperial family in Rome, which had encampments, workshops and even temples built for the workers and engineers here. Evidence of this quarry town can still be seen, although not much of it is standing. A road leading to the site branches off the main road about 20km north of Hurghada.

In addition to the many traces of Pharaonic and other ancient civilisations, the Eastern Desert is also home to numerous Islamic tombs and shrines. One of the best known is the **tomb of Sayyed al-Shazli**, a 13th-century sheikh who is revered as one of the more important Sufi leaders. His followers believe that he wanted to die in a place where nobody had ever sinned. Evidently such a place was difficult to find, as the site was a journey of several days from either the Nile Valley or the coast. Al-Shazli's tomb – which lies about 145km southwest of Marsa Alam at Wadi Humaysara – was restored under the orders of King Farouk in 1947, and there is now an asphalt road leading to it. His *moulid* (religious festival), on the 15th of the Muslim month of Shawal, is attended by thousands of Sufis.

Trips to many of these and other places of interest in the desert can be organised with **Red Sea Desert Adventures** (☎ 012 399 3860; www.redseadesertadventures.com; Marsa Shagra), a highly recommended safari outfit run by Dutch geologist Karin Van Opstal and her Austrian partner, offering tailor-made walking, camel and jeep safaris throughout the area. Van Opstal has lived in Marsa Alam for over a decade and is an authority on the local Ababda tribesmen, with whom she works closely. Camel safaris cost approximately US$100 per person per day; other prices are available on their website. In order that the necessary permits can be organised for multiday desert safaris, try to book at least one month in advance. Visits to Mons Claudianus and Mons Porphyrites can also be arranged with major hotels in Hurghada, or with any of the larger hotels along Safaga's resort strip.

If you're contemplating exploring independently, keep in mind that none of the roads crossing the desert can be freely travelled – some are completely closed to foreigners, and others require a convoy – and all the sites require a guide.

divers only – see p455. For more on desert safaris, see p432.

Sleeping

There is nowhere to stay in Marsa Alam village itself. But north and south along the coast is an ever-growing number of four- and five-star resorts with all the amenities, plus a handful of simple, diver-oriented 'ecolodges' or diving camps. These usually consist of no-frills reed or stone bungalows, sometimes with en suite bathrooms, generator-provided electricity, and a common area. They are run together with a dive centre, and offer a rugged alternative to the resort scene for backpackers or backpackers-at-heart. In addition to diving, most places can also arrange desert excursions. If you're travelling during the winter and planning to stay in a tent or hut at an ecolodge, ask if they provide blankets; if not, it's a good idea to bring a sleeping bag along for warmth.

ECOLODGES

Shagara Eco-Lodge (☎ 02-337 1833; www.redsea -divingsafari.com; Marsa Shagra; d in tents/huts/chalets full board US$88/100/125) This simple place owned by Hossam Helmi – lawyer, committed environmentalist and diving enthusiast – was one of the first ecolodges along the southern Red Sea coast, and remains the best. It offers simple but spotless and comfortable accommodation in a choice of two-bed tents, stone huts sharing bathroom facilities or en suite stone chalets – all designed to be as kind to the environment as possible – plus first-rate diving. Nondivers in search of beautiful vistas and tranquillity are welcome, too. It's along the main road, 24km north of Marsa Alam.

The same owner also runs a similar camp with the same prices at Marsa Nakari, 18km south of Marsa Alam, plus a camp with 25 tents and 16 stone chalets in **Wadi Lahami** (d in tents/chalets full board US$88/125), a remote mangrove bay just north of Ras Banas, near Berenice and 120km south of Marsa Alam. There are live-aboards based in each of the three camps used for offshore diving. With his legal qualifications, Helmi has also developed a sideline in underwater weddings.

HOTELS & RESORTS

Shams Alam (☎ 02-417 0046; www.shamshotels.com /alam.htm; s/d half board US$58/90; ✷ ✷) This

pleasant resort, 42km south of Marsa Alam, specialises in diving trips to local and less-frequented southern reefs. There are 160 comfortable rooms in domed and vaulted two-storey chalets, most of which overlook the beach, plus good snorkelling.

Kahramana Beach Resort (☎ 02-748 0883; www .kahramanaresort.com; s/d half board US$88/125; ✷ ✷) The large Kahramana, 26km north of Marsa Alam at Marsa Shagra, has attached chalets in shades of ochre set around an attractive beach, a good Italian restaurant and a diving centre.

El-Nabaa Resort (☎ 012 235 3475; www.elnabaa .com; s/d half board tents US$25/45, huts US$49/78, hotel US$74/118) About 30km north of Marsa Alam, El-Nabaa is a wide bay with a laid-back three-star resort consisting of 40 tents, 10 huts and a 50-room hotel. The tents are closely spaced, but comfortable and better value than the huts, which are rather optimistically referred to as 'bungalows', and are overpriced. If you're into surfing, it's a reasonable place to hang out for a few days.

Also recommended:

Zabargad Hotel (☎ 010 528 9231; www.orca.de; d half board about US$125; ✷ ✷) A pleasant three-star place with a down-to-earth ambience and 55 attached rooms, all facing the water. Caters primarily to those on all-inclusive dive packages booked from Germany. The hotel is about 115km south of Marsa Alam in the Hamata area (about 25km north of Berenice), and near Fury Shoal.

Lahami Bay Beach Resort (☎ 195 100 354/355; info@lahamibay.com; d half board US$138; ✷ ✷) Another German-run four-star establishment with a dive centre (☎ 195 100 356; www.oceanpro-diveteam.com). It's about 7km south of Zabargad Hotel and 123km south of Marsa Alam, and is currently the most southerly resort on the Egyptian Red Sea.

Sol y Mar Solaya (☎ 375 0015; www.solymar-hotels .com; s/d all-inclusive US$140/190; ✗ ✷ ▯ ✷) A vast, plush place at Coraya Bay, about 75km north of Marsa Alam and about 5km from the airport.

Abo Nawas Resort (☎ 012 243 9951; www.abonawas resort.com; s/d half board US$75/125; ✷ ▯ ✷) Another large complex 22km north of Marsa Alam, with its own mini shopping arcade. It has several handicapped-accessible rooms and bathrooms, and wheelchair-friendly ramps.

Eating

In town there are a couple of cafés at the junction where you can find ta'amiyya and similar fare, and there is a small supermarket with a modest selection of basics. The only other option is the cafeteria next to the service station, where the choice of food is limited to stale sandwiches, packet soups and frozen hamburgers. All the resorts and lodges have restaurants and half- or full-board packages.

Getting There & Away

AIR

The **Marsa Alam International Airport** (www.marsa -alam-airport.com) is 67km north of Marsa Alam along the Al-Quseir road. There is no public transport, so you'll need to arrange a transfer in advance with your hotel. Egypt-Air has indefinitely suspended its flights to/from Cairo, and the airport is currently used only by charters.

BUS

There is no bus station in Marsa Alam. For transport to Shalatein, wait at the coffee shop next to the police post at the entrance to Marsa Alam. For transport to the Nile Valley, wait at the petrol station in Marsa Alam, or at the T-junction about 1km further along on the Edfu road. Buses from Shalatein pass Marsa Alam en route to Aswan (E£15, six hours), via Edfu (E£12,

four hours) at around 7am and 9am daily. Buses to Shalatein (E£20, four hours) come from Hurghada and depart Marsa Alam at around 5am, 7am, noon and 8.30pm.

There are four daily buses to Al-Quseir (E£5, two hours) and Hurghada (E£20, five hours), departing at 5am, 12.30pm, 2.30pm and 5pm. To Cairo direct, the fare is E£80 (11 to 12 hours).

BERENICE

The military centre and small port of Berenice, 150km south of Marsa Alam, was founded in 275 BC by Ptolemy II Philadelphus. From about the 3rd through the 5th century AD, it was one of the most important harbours and trading posts on the Red Sea coast, and is mentioned in the 1st-century AD mariner's chronicle, *Periplus of the Erythraean Sea*. The ruins of the ancient town, including ruins of the **Temple of Serapis** are located just south of the present-day village, and have been the subject of ongoing archaeological investigations. About 100km to the northwest are ruins of the old Roman settlement of Sikait, that was once at the centre of major emerald-mining operations in the region. Today the main activity is at Ras Banas peninsula – jutting into the

---

NOMADS OF THE EASTERN DESERT

Although the desert of the southern Red Sea may seem empty and inhospitable (except possibly to tourism developers), the area has been home to nomadic Ababda and Besharin tribes for millennia. Members of the Beja, a nomadic tribe of African origin, they are thought to be descendents of the Blemmyes, the fierce tribesmen mentioned by classical geographers. Until well into the 20th century the extent of the territory in which they roamed was almost exactly as described by the Romans, with whom they were constantly at war, some 2000 years earlier. Expert camel herders, their nomadic lifestyle hardly changed until the waters of Lake Nasser rose and destroyed their traditional grazing lands. While most Besharin, many of whom do not speak Arabic, live in Sudan, most of the Arabic-speaking Ababda are settled in communities in the Nile Valley between Aswan and Luxor. A small number continue to live in their ancestral territory, concentrated in the area from Marsa Alam to Wadi Gimal, as well as on the eastern shores of Lake Nasser.

With the rapid expansion of tourism along the southern Red Sea, long-standing Ababda lifestyles have become increasingly threatened. Tourism has begun to replace livestock and camels as the main source of livelihood, and many Ababda men now work as guards or labourers on the resorts springing up around Marsa Alam, while others have started working with travel companies, offering camel safaris to tourists. And increasingly, semisettled village life is replacing a proud nomadic past. If you spend time in the region, however, you'll still likely see the traditional Ababda hut, lined inside with thick, hand-woven blankets, or hear Ababda music, with its rhythmic clapping and drumming and heavy use of the five-stringed lyrelike *tamboura*. At the centre of Ababda social life is *jibena* – heavily sweetened coffee prepared from fresh-roasted beans in a small earthenware flask heated directly in the coals.

sea just northeast of Berenice – which is an important military base. Because of this, and because of the region's proximity to the Sudanese border, independent visits are not permitted. You'll need a permit, and can expect a police escort. There is no tourist accommodation.

SHALATEIN

This dusty outpost 90km south of Berenice marks the administrative boundary between Egypt and Sudan. Egypt considers the political boundary to be another 175km southeast, beyond the town of Halayeb, a once-important Red Sea port that has long since fallen into obscurity. Now a trading post, Shalatein's colourful camel market is a major stop on the camel-trading route from the Sudan that for many of the camels finishes in the Birqash camel market outside of Cairo (p193). Amid the dust and the vendors, Rashaida tribesmen in their lavender *galabiyya*s mix with

Ababda, Besharin and other peoples from southern Egypt and northern Sudan. Some top-notch dive sites are also located in this area, and dive companies from further north are increasingly organising boat safaris to the region.

Because of Shalatein's proximity to the border, independent visitors are discouraged, and the area is sporadically closed to foreigners completely. If you are travelling on your own, expect to be questioned by the tourist police, and to be accompanied by an escort if you succeed in getting to Shalatein. There is no official accommodation, and camping needs to be cleared with the police.

Buses depart Shalatein for Hurghada (E£50, nine hours) via Marsa Alam (E£20, four hours) at 7am, 3pm and 5pm. **Red Sea Desert Adventures** (☎ 012 399 3860; www.redsea desertadventures.com; Marsa Shagra) organises half-day excursions to the camel market from various points along the coast.

Diving the Red Sea

Plunge into the Red Sea's clear depths and you'll find yourself surrounded by one of nature's most magnificent sights, with coral mountains rising from the sea bed, shallow reefs swarming with brightly coloured fish, sheer drop-offs disappearing into unplumbed depths and coral-encrusted shipwrecks, all bathed in an ethereal blue hue. In 1989 a panel of scientists and conservationists selected the northern portion of this 1800km-long body as one of the Seven Underwater Wonders of the World, and since then it has become one of the world's most popular diving destinations, with thousands of visitors each year.

Diving tends to be concentrated at the northern end of the Egyptian Red Sea, although increasing numbers of advanced divers are pushing further south. The most popular sites are around the southern tip of the Sinai Peninsula, most famously the thin strip of land that juts out into the sea and forms Ras Mohammed National Park – the jewel in the Red Sea's crown. Another major diving area is in the Strait of Tiran, which forms the narrow entrance to the Gulf of Aqaba. The currents sweeping through the deep channel allow coral to grow prolifically, attracting abundant marine life. The reefs further north along the shores of the Gulf of Aqaba are also popular. On the western side of the Sinai Peninsula lie the Straits of Gubal, a series of coral pinnacles just beneath the surface of the sea, famous for snagging ships trying to navigate north to the Suez Canal. This is where the majority of Egypt's shipwrecks, including the famous vessel *The Thistlegorm*, lie.

Heading south, the best reefs are found around the many offshore islands. Although most reefs near Hurghada have been damaged by uncontrolled tourist development, there is a plethora of pristine dive sites further south. Some can be reached from shore or on day trips, while others are best accessed via live-aboard dive safari arrangements.

HIGHLIGHTS

- Marvel at the coral and teeming fish life in magnificent **Ras Mohammed National Park** (p453)

- Explore the remains of **The Thistlegorm** (p454), bombed in WWII, rediscovered by Jacques Cousteau and now a highly sought-after wreck-dive

- Combine diving and Bedouin culture in a **camel/dive safari** (p459) from Dahab

- Visit the **Southern (Far) Islands** (p456), south of Berenice, where the reefs are stunning, the coral lush, pelagic fish plentiful and the diving highly challenging

- Spend your days sailing from one remote site to the next on a **live-aboard dive safari** (p459)

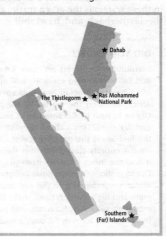

★ Dahab

The Thistlegorm ★ ★ Ras Mohammed National Park

Southern (Far) Islands ★

MARINE LIFE

The Red Sea is teeming with more than 1000 species of marine life and is an amazing spectacle of colour and form. Reef sharks, turtles, stingrays, dolphins, corals, sponges, sea cucumbers and a multitude of molluscs all thrive in these waters.

Coral is what makes a reef and, though thought for centuries to be some form of flowering plant, it is in fact an animal. Both hard and soft corals exist, their common denominator being that they are made up of polyps – tiny cylinders ringed by waving tentacles that sting their prey and draw it into their stomach. During the day corals retract into their tube, only displaying their real colours at night.

Most of the bewildering variety of fish species in the Red Sea – including many that are found nowhere else – are closely associated with the coral reef, and live and breed in the reefs or nearby sea-grass beds. These include groper, wrasse, parrotfish and snapper. Others, such as shark and barracuda, live in open waters and usually only venture into the reefs to feed or breed.

When snorkelling or diving, the sharks you're most likely to encounter include white- or black-tipped reef sharks. Tiger sharks, as well as the enormous, plankton-eating whale sharks, are generally found only in deeper waters. Shark attacks in the Red Sea are extremely rare, and there are no sea snakes here.

The most common type of turtle found in these waters is the green turtle, although the leatherback and hawksbill are occa-

sionally sighted. Turtles are protected in Egypt but, although they're not deliberately hunted, they are sometimes caught in nets and end up on menus in restaurants in Cairo and along the coasts.

As intriguing as they may seem, there are some creatures that should be avoided, especially moray eels, sea urchins, fire coral, blowfish, triggerfish, feathery lionfish, turkeyfish, stonefish, and, needless to say, sharks. Familiarise yourself with pictures of these creatures before snorkelling or diving. Single-page colour guides to the Red Sea's common marine hazards can be bought in hotel bookshops around diving areas. Providing you don't touch things, stand on the reef or attempt to feed a moray eel, you shouldn't have too many worries.

DIVE SITES

Following are brief descriptions of some of the Red Sea's more popular diving destinations, listed from north to south. Several websites also have good descriptive listings, including www.redseavdc.com (see p461). In general, sites in the far south are for experienced divers only. Elsewhere, you'll find a mix, with something to suit all levels. We've given a general indication of difficulty where this is straightforward, but you should seek the advice of your dive guide when deciding where to go, and remember that strong currents or winds can make an otherwise fairly tame site dangerous or undiveable.

Dahab Area
BELLS WALL
Rich coral and marine life, including large fish and rays; best suited for experienced divers. It is just north of The Blue Hole, which is reached through a small chute.

THE BLUE HOLE
An 80m-deep pool in the reef, just a few metres offshore. It's an infamous deep dive which has claimed many lives due to nitrogen narcosis or improper use of equipment (which isn't difficult at such a depth), and should only be attempted by experienced divers.

THE CANYON
A popular dive, but often harrowing for an inexperienced diver. From the shore, snor-

---

DID YOU KNOW?

Surrounded by desert on three sides, the Red Sea was formed some 40 million years ago when the Arabian Peninsula split from Africa, allowing the waters of the Indian Ocean to rush in. Bordered at its southern end by the 25km Bab al-Mandab Strait, the Red Sea is the only tropical sea that is almost entirely closed. No river flows into it and the influx of water from the Indian Ocean is slight. These unique geographical features, combined with the arid desert climate and high temperatures, make the sea extremely salty. It is also windy – on average the sea is flat for only 50 days a year.

kel along the reef before diving, past a wall of coral, to the edge of The Canyon and into a cavern under the sea bed. The cavern was formed by volcanic activity millions of years ago, and hard and soft corals proliferate.

EEL GARDEN

A popular snorkelling spot that's also good for learner divers, with a reef visited by barracuda, rays and turtles. It's 15 minutes' walk north of the lighthouse area in Assalah.

REEF PROTECTION

The Red Sea's natural wonders are just as magnificent as the splendours of Egypt's Pharaonic heritage, and appear all the more stunning when contrasted with their barren desert backdrop. However, care is needed if the delicate world of coral reefs and fish is not to be permanently damaged. Almost the entire Egyptian coastline in the Gulf of Aqaba is now a protectorate, as is the Red Sea coast from Hurghada south to Sudan. Divers and snorkellers should heed the requests of instructors *not* to touch or tread on coral (if you kill the coral, you'll eventually kill or chase away the fish, too).

It's also worth remembering that paying baksheesh to do something you shouldn't be doing, such as breaking off a bit of coral, is illegal and you can be prosecuted. The Egyptian National Parks Office has begun cracking down on offenders and checking bags at the country's exit points. You can be fined, and in some cases forbidden to dive here again.

Overall, the paramount guideline for preserving the ecology and beauty of reefs is to *take nothing with you, leave nothing behind*. Other considerations:

■ Don't collect, remove or damage any material, living or dead, such as coral, shells, fish, plants or any other marine souvenirs. This also includes anything from marine archaeological sites (mainly shipwrecks), which are protected by Egyptian law.

■ Don't touch, kneel on or kick coral, and don't walk or anchor on any reef area. Coral are delicate creatures that are damaged when touched. Try to time snorkelling with the high tide, so that you can swim, rather than walk, over the living reef to get to a good drop-off.

■ Don't feed fish, pick up and play with sea creatures, or otherwise disturb any part of the reef community.

■ Don't fish or spearfish. If you see others doing so, report them to the Egyptian National Parks Office.

■ Don't wear gloves (though as you're not touching marine life, you won't need them anyway). The wearing of gloves is banned in Ras Mohammed National Park and around the southern islands, but some dive clubs are lax in enforcing this rule.

■ Be conscious of your fins, and don't stir up sand. Even without contact, the surge created from heavy fin-strokes near the reef can damage delicate organisms. When treading water in shallow reef areas, take care not to kick up clouds of sand, as settling sand can smother delicate reef organisms.

■ Maintain proper buoyancy control. Major damage can be done by divers descending too fast and colliding with the reef. Because the Red Sea is so salty you'll need to add extra weight to overcome the increased buoyancy. Make sure you are correctly weighted and that your weight belt is positioned so that you stay horizontal. If you haven't dived for a while, have a practice dive in a pool before taking to the reef. Be aware that buoyancy can change over the period of an extended trip: initially you may breathe hard and need more weight; a few days later you may breathe more easily and need less weight.

■ Take great care in underwater caves. Spend as little time within them as possible as your air bubbles may be caught within the roof and thereby leave previously submerged organisms high and dry. Taking turns to inspect the interior of a small cave will lessen the chances of damaging contact.

■ Ensure that you take home all your rubbish. Plastics in particular are a serious threat to marine life. Turtles can mistake plastic for jellyfish and eat it.

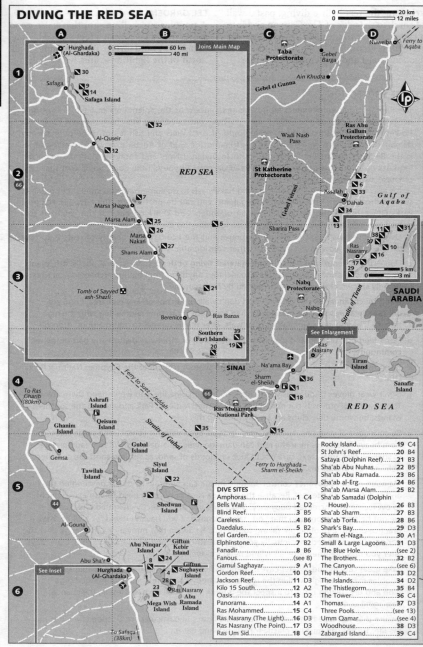

DIVING THE RED SEA

DIVE SITES

Amphoras........................1	C4
Bells Wall.......................2	D2
Blind Reef.......................3	B5
Careless.........................4	B6
Daedalus........................5	B2
Eel Garden......................6	D2
Elphinstone.....................7	B2
Fanadir..........................8	B6
Fanous.....................(see 8)	
Gamul Saghayar..............9	A1
Gordon Reef..................10	D3
Jackson Reef..................11	D3
Kilo 15 South.................12	A2
Oasis...........................13	D2
Panorama.....................14	A1
Ras Mohammed..............15	C4
Ras Nasrany (The Light)....16	D3
Ras Nasrany (The Point)...17	D3
Ras Um Sid....................18	C4

Rocky Island..................19	C4
St John's Reef................20	B4
Sataya (Dolphin Reef).....21	B3
Sha'ab Abu Nuhas..........22	B5
Sha'ab Abu Ramada........23	B6
Sha'ab al-Erg................24	B6
Sha'ab Marsa Alam.........25	B2
Sha'ab Samadai (Dolphin	
House).......................26	B3
Sha'ab Sharm................27	B3
Sha'ab Torfa..................28	B6
Shark's Bay...................29	D3
Sharm el-Naga...............30	A1
Small & Large Lagoons.....31	D3
The Blue Hole..........(see 2)	
The Brothers.................32	B2
The Canyon.............(see 6)	
The Huts......................33	D2
The Islands...................34	D2
The Thistlegorm............35	B4
The Tower....................36	C4
Thomas.......................37	D3
Three Pools...........(see 13)	
Umm Qamar.............(see 4)	
Woodhouse..................38	D3
Zabargad Island............39	C4

THE HUTS

Also known as Abu Talha; huge corals in the shallows, with rich marine life and unusual formations. The site is good for all levels, and is often combined with a drift dive to Abu Helal, 4km north of Dahab.

THE ISLANDS

This collection of colourful coral pinnacles is just south of Dahab before the lagoon, and offers beautiful table corals and abundant fish.

OASIS

A secluded spot excellent for a variety of marine life, 8km south of Dahab and named for the cluster of palm trees on the shore. Nearby are the **Three Pools**.

Sharm el-Sheikh & Na'ama Bay Area

RAS NASRANY

This small cape has two notable sites – The Light and The Point – featuring attractions such as 40m drop-offs and an abundance of reef and pelagic fish.

SMALL & LARGE LAGOONS

Just off the northwest tip of Tiran Island, these lagoons feature a shallow reef and the wreck of the *Sangria*, and the Large Lagoon has reef and sand fish. Due to strong currents, the site is best for more experienced divers. There's a mooring so that boats don't have to drop anchor onto the reef.

JACKSON REEF

Midway between Tiran Island and the mainland, this reef is home to sharks and large pelagic fish, and features a 70m drop-off. However, currents here are dangerous, and this site should only be explored by experienced divers.

GORDON REEF

Close to Ras Nasrany and a popular site with experienced divers. In addition to sharks and open-water fish, there's a wreck on the reef. The nearby **Thomas** and **Woodhouse** reefs also have some excellent diving, but strong currents mean that they, too, are for advanced divers only.

SHARK'S BAY

A good shore-entry dive for beginners, but with attractions for more advanced divers as well, including a sloping reef and a deep canyon offshore. Famous for manta rays.

THE TOWER

South of Na'ama Bay, this is a remarkable wall dropping 60m into the depths just offshore. Among other amazing underwater life it is frequented by sea horses and ghost-pipe fish, and its deep colours are ideal for photography. Suitable for all levels.

AMPHORAS

Also known as Mercury. The waters here harbour the wreck of a Turkish galleon, and evidence of its cargo of mercury can still be seen among the coral. Other dives between here and Ras Um Sid include **Turtle Bay**, **Paradise** and **Fiasco**.

RAS UM SID

A prime dive site with a deep, sloping wall, and easy access near the lighthouse. The beautiful coral garden boasts an abundance of colourful fan coral and a great variety of fish. Because the small beach here is divided between a number of hotels, non-guest divers and snorkellers must use the access path to the left of the lighthouse.

Ras Mohammed National Park Area

RAS MOHAMMED

Without doubt, one of the best dive sites in the world, with superb and extensive corals and an unparalleled diversity of fish and other marine life. Among the 1000-plus fish species found here are white-tip reef sharks and an abundance of angel, butterfly and other colourful reef fish. Other highlights include over 200 hard coral species, about 120 soft coral species and excellent visibility. In an attempt to protect the park area, the number of boats that can bring in divers is subject to limits, and water access is restricted to designated areas, which means you'll have to organise dives here through the dive clubs. There are 20 dive sites within the park, including the challenging and world-renowned Shark Reef, with an astounding variety and number of pelagics and reef fish; the much easier Eel Garden (with eels, of course); and Shark Observatory, where – in addition to sharks and many pelagics – you may also find sea turtles. For detailed site descriptions and ratings of the park sites, check out the very informative www.rasmohamed.com. Also in the area is the shipwrecked *Yolanda* (at 10m to 15m), with its cargo of hundreds of toilet bowls now scattered on the ocean floor, and the wreck of the *Dunraven,* a British vessel that went down in 1876 on a voyage from Bombay to Newcastle in England. Many dive clubs combine diving this wreck with that of *The Thistlegorm,* which lies outside the marine park boundaries, to the northwest. When you're diving in the park, note that there are designated access points to reduce damage to reefs.

THE THISTLEGORM

This British warship sank with a full consignment of armaments and supplies, including tanks, jeeps and guns, after being bombed during WWII. It was discovered by Jacques Cousteau in the 1950s, who kept its location secret, and only rediscovered in 1993, when some divers stumbled upon it, laying at a depth of 17m to 35m to the northwest of Ras Mohammed. It's now *the* wreck to explore in the Red Sea, although it has been stripped of much of its wartime memorabilia. *The Thistlegorm* is best dived on an overnight trip, as it takes 3½ hours each way from Sharm el-Sheikh by boat. It is often too rough to dive here.

SHA'AB ABU NUHAS

This group of small, submerged islands at the southern entrance to the Straits of Gubal has snagged more ships than any other reef group since the opening of the Suez Canal in 1869. One of the most famous wrecks in this marine graveyard is the *Carnatic,* which went down in 1879 and, with its rotting wooden beams, is now almost a reef in itself. It's a popular dive site, together with the nearby wrecks of two Greek cargo ships, the *Giannus D* and the *Chrisoula K,* both of which sank in the early 1980s. The three are about 45 minutes by boat from the point of Ras Mohammed, but can also be visited from Hurghada, about two hours away.

Hurghada & Safaga

The reefs close to Hurghada have been much destroyed by the recent unfettered touristic development. Experienced divers now generally prefer sites further afield, often sailing at least two hours from Hurghada, or opting for dive clubs further down the coast. On a positive note, conservation measures are finally being implemented, spearheaded by groups such as Hepca (p431), and there is a chance that the situation around Hurghada will begin to improve. For now, some of the best sites in the Hurghada-Safaga area include the following.

SHEDWAN ISLAND

This 25km-long island has long, sheer walls that attract sharks and other pelagic fish. At its northern end is **Blind Reef**, another deep wall. Accessible by boat from Hurghada.

SHA'AB AL-ERG

A horseshoe-shaped reef with a shallow lagoon about 1½ hours north of Hurghada. It's famous for dolphins and manta rays, and you may sometimes find reef white-tips.

FANADIR

A popular reef close to Hurghada. Coral gardens lead to a ledge that drops off into the depths. The site teems with many different fish species, but is known especially for stonefish and scorpionfish. It's also frequented by dolphins.

FANOUS

These two reefs, Fanous East and Fanous West, 45 minutes from Hurghada, are known for dolphins and occasional rare-fish sightings, as well as beautiful coral pinnacles.

UMM QAMAR

A long, thin reef about 1½ hours north of Hurghada, with a vertical wall plunging down on the east side. Three coral towers just off the wall are swathed in beautiful purple soft coral and surrounded by glassfish.

CARELESS

A midsea reef 5km north of the Giftun Islands, best suited for experienced divers, and often off limits because of strong, unpredictable currents. It's famous for its two ergs on a plateau leading to a spectacular drop-off. The ergs are surrounded by a forest of coral around which swim swarms of fish, including a group of moray eels.

GIFTUN ISLANDS

The islands of Giftun Kebir and Giftun Sughayer (Big Giftun and Little Giftun) are a short boat ride from Hurghada, and are popular dive destinations. They are surrounded by a number of spectacular reefs teeming with marine life, including Hamda, Banana Reef, Sha'ab Sabrina and Erg Somaya. In the strait between the Giftun Islands is **Sha'ab Torfa**, a long crescent reef teeming with fish, including clownfish.

SHA'AB ABU RAMADA
About 11km southeast of Hurghada, and nicknamed the Aquarium because of its enormous schools of fish.

GAMUL SUGHAYAR
Only 15 minutes from Safaga, and the second in a chain of reefs stretching north from Safaga Island. Diveable in any weather and famous for its abundant marine life, including a hollow pillar of coral with gorgonian inside.

PANORAMA
This site surrounds a small island with a beacon just over one hour outside Safaga. There's a plateau at 15m to 25m which leads down to a dramatic drop-off. Large fish abound, and you can see turtles, schools of barracuda, and various species of sharks, rays and dolphins.

South Coast
As tourist development expands southwards, so too does diving, although this part of the coast remains remote, with most diving done from live-aboards. Many of the sites are difficult to dive because of high winds and strong currents, and thus suited for experienced divers only. But the reefs are spectacular and the fish, especially pelagics, copious. Some of the best-known sites:

KILO 15 SOUTH
This reef lies 15km south of Al-Quseir, and is accessed through a smooth tunnel from 5m to 7m, leading to a canyonlike passage between steep vertical walls. It boasts many hard coral species, and is frequented by sharks, including reef white-tips and guitar sharks.

ELPHINSTONE
A long, fingerlike reef opposite Marsa Shagra, about 20km north of Marsa Alam. The steep reef walls are covered with soft corals, and the strong currents and rich fish life

make it ideal for sharks, with seven species reportedly frequenting its waters. Legend has it that a large arch in the reef, between 50m and 70m down, contains the sarcophagus of an unknown pharaoh. Adding to the mystery, divers have reported seeing a coral-encrusted rectangular shape at about 60m.

SHA'AB MARSA ALAM
A large reef adjacent to Marsa Alam, with rich coral gardens, and schools of snapper, jacks, goat fish and banners.

SHA'AB SAMADAI (DOLPHIN HOUSE)
A horseshoe-shaped reef about 18km south of Marsa Alam at Marsa Nakari. The reef is wrapped around a shallow lagoon which is home to a school of spinner dolphins. There are beautiful corals along its outer walls, and a large group of pinnacles (rich with reef fish) rises from its western tip.

SHA'AB SHARM (GOTA SHARM)
This large, kidney-shaped offshore reef just south of Sha'ab Samadai has steep walls hosting rich corals. Currents are strong, but fish life is excellent, with hammerheads, barracuda, groper, snapper and yellowmouth moray eels.

DAEDALUS
A large reef (topped with a lighthouse) 60km from shore, with steep walls covered in a profusion of corals. Strong currents make diving here tricky, but perseverance pays off, with large pelagics and an impressive variety of fish among the rewards.

SATAYA (DOLPHIN REEF)
Located bout 28km north of Ras Banas, the horseshoe-shaped Dolphin is the main reef of Fury Shoal. It has steep walls leading down to a sandy slope scattered with coral heads. In addition to a great variety of corals, especially in the uppermost 10m, there is also abundant fish life, including dolphins and several species of shark.

ST JOHN'S REEF
A large, beautiful reef close to the Sudanese border. Consisting of different islets and coral reefs, it is filled with rich pelagic fish life and hard coral. Difficult to reach and often impossible to dive because of high winds and currents, but worth the trouble.

Southern (Far) Islands

Dotting Egypt's southernmost waters are four islands – the **Brothers** (Big Brother and Little Brother), east of Al-Quseir, plus **Zabargad** and **Rocky**, both southeast of Berenice – that are considered to offer some of the best diving in the Red Sea, and are coveted and highly challenging destinations for experienced divers. Access is strictly regulated, and divers must have completed a minimum of 50 dives before entering. Night diving or landing on the islands is prohibited and national park rules apply, so fishing, spear fishing and the use of gloves are banned. Permission must be given for each trip and a park ranger will often accompany boats to ensure that the rules are being enforced and to monitor the site. In order to carry divers, boats must have special safety equipment, which national-park and Red Sea governorate officials inspect before each trip.

If you've been offered a trip to these remote areas, it's worth checking in with one of the organisations mentioned on right to see that the boat is licensed. If you are caught on an unlicensed boat you could have your own equipment or belongings confiscated and find yourself in custody. Even if you do make it to the islands, strong currents and choppy seas often mean it's not possible to get in the water. But if you do, you'll be rewarded by spectacular and rarely visited reefs and amazing marine life. As veterans of these islands will tell you, once you've dived there nothing else will compare.

BIG BROTHER

The most northerly of the two 'brothers', Big Brother has a small lighthouse and two wrecks lying on its walls, one a freighter and the other an Italian ship called the *Aida II*. Currents are strong, and the soft corals are amazing. Other marine life is also rich, and large pelagics are frequently sighted.

LITTLE BROTHER

This small island has a long reef protruding from its northern end. Sharks cruise here in the strong current. Elsewhere there are huge fan corals, caves and overhangs. Pelagic fish throng the waters to the southeast, including thresher sharks, silver tips, hammerheads and grey reef sharks.

ZABARGAD ISLAND

This large mountain emerging from the sea has snagged at least two ships. It's surrounded by a lagoon (which is circled by a reef), and offers rich coral and marine life.

ROCKY ISLAND

A small, rocky protrusion just south of Zabargad. Attractions include steep walls, strong currents and incredibly rich offerings of reef fish, soft corals and pelagics.

DIVING TOURS

While it's quite possible to book yourself a basic package to Sinai or Hurghada and sort out your own diving arrangements with a local company when you get there (see below), there are numerous agencies that specialise in Red Sea diving holidays and can save you some time if your stay in Egypt is limited. A small sampling:

Crusader Travel (in UK ☎ 020-8744 0474; www.divers .co.uk) Diving packages in the Red Sea, including diving for the disabled.

Explorers Tours (in UK ☎ 0845-644 7090; www.explorers .co.uk) Diving packages and live-aboards around Sharm el-Sheik, Dahab and elsewhere in the northern Red Sea.

Oonasdivers (in UK ☎ 01323-648924; www.oonasdivers .com) Diving tours based at Na'ama Bay, Red Sea diving safaris from the Marsa Alam region and live-aboard trips.

Scubasnacks Diving Safaris (in UK ☎ 0870-746 1266; www.scuba-diving.safaris.co.uk) A full range of live-aboard safaris covering northern and southern Red Sea dive sites.

DIVE CLUBS

As Egypt's Red Sea and Sinai coasts continue to develop, the number of dive clubs is mushrooming. Almost all of the large resorts have a dive centre. There are also smaller places – some long-standing, others fly-by-night outfits cashing in on the area's popularity among divers. Given the huge choice, there is something to suit everyone. Some clubs are laid-back and informal, others are slick and structured. When deciding which one to use, the main considerations should be the club's attention to safety and its sensitivity to environmental issues.

Safety Concerns

There is no government regulatory body responsible for overseeing dive clubs in Egypt, although two nongovernmental organisations – the **Red Sea Association for**

WHERE TO GO?

With so many dive clubs and reefs to choose from, it's difficult to know where to base yourself. Here are our tips:

- for postdiving nightlife and a good mix of sites: Sharm el-Sheikh, followed by Hurghada
- for Western amenities with a remote outpost ambience and the chance for desert excursions: Marsa Alam
- for combining diving with Bedouin culture: Dahab
- for guaranteed underwater magnificence and a good collection of wrecks: Ras Mohammed National Park area
- for on-the-edge diving away from the crowds: the far south (advanced divers only).

Diving & Watersports (RSADW; ☎ 065-344 4802; association@redseaexperience.com), for the area from Al-Gouna south to the Sudanese border, and the **South Sinai Association for Diving & Marine Activities** (SSDM; ☎ 069-366 0418; www .southsinai.org), for all of southern Sinai – are increasingly taking on this function. All dive guides must have a valid ID card from one of these entities, and in the southern Sinai, all dive centres and live-aboards must be members of the SSDM. However, accidents still occasionally happen as a result of neglect and negligence. Before making any choices, carefully check out the club you're considering. Confirm with the relevant organisation that a club or guide is registered. Other guidelines:

- Take your time when choosing clubs and dive sites, and don't let yourself be pressured into accepting something, or someone, you're not comfortable with.
- Don't choose a club based solely on cost. Safety should be the paramount concern; if a dive outfit cuts corners to keep prices low, you could be in danger.
- If you haven't dived for more than three months, take a check-out dive. This is for your own safety (and is required by many operators), and the cost is usually applied towards later dives.
- If you're taking lessons, ensure that the instructor speaks your language well.

If you can't understand them, request another.
- Check that all equipment is clean and stored away from the sun, and check all hoses, mouthpieces and valves for cuts and leakage.
- Confirm that wet suits are in good condition. Some divers have reported getting hypothermia because of dry, cracked suits.
- Check that there is oxygen on the dive boat in case of accidents.
- If you're in Sinai, ask if the club donates US$1 per diver each day to the decompression chamber; this is often a reflection of the club's safety consciousness.

The RSADW also has the following rules in place for its jurisdictional area:

- For live-aboard diving, there should be a diver-guide ratio of one guide to every 12 divers (or every eight divers in marine park areas). For non-live-aboard diving, there should be a minimum of one guide per every 12 certified divers (with 25 dives or more), or per every eight beginner divers.
- Divers on live-aboards entering marine park areas must have a minimum of 50 logged dives, as well as insurance coverage. (Outside marine park areas, there is no minimum number of logged dives.)

Diving Courses

Most dive clubs in Egypt offer **PADI** (www .padi.com) certification, although you'll also find **NAUI** (www.naui.org), **SSI** (www.divessi.com), **CMAS** (www.cmas2000.org), **BSAC** (www.bsac.com) and several others. Prices vary but not greatly. PADI open-water dive courses, which usually take five (intensive) days, cost between US$250 and US$370. When comparing prices, check to see whether the certification fee and books are included. Note that while you can generally make arrangements with individual operators to pay in Egyptian pounds, all dive clubs quote their prices in US dollars or euros, and usually expect payment this way as well.

Beginner courses are designed to drum into you things that have to become second nature when you're underwater. They usually consist of classroom work, where you learn the principles and basic knowledge needed to dive, followed by training in a

confined body of water, such as a pool, before heading out to the open sea. If you've
never dived before and want to give it a try
before you commit yourself, all dive clubs
offer introductory dives for between US$40
and US$50, including equipment.

In addition to basic certification, most of
the well-established clubs on the coast also
offer a variety of more advanced courses, and
some also offer professional-level courses
or training in technical diving. Expect to
pay from about US$200 for an advanced
open-water course, about US$100 for a one-
day Medic First Aid course and from about
US$550 for a dive-master course.

Equipment

All operators rent scuba and snorkelling
equipment, usually at competitive prices.
While some divers prefer to bring their
own masks, snorkels and fins, and some
like to have their own regulator, these are
all also available for rent. Masks and snorkels average about US$4 and US$1 per day
respectively, while full scuba-equipment
rental costs about US$20 to US$35 per day.

Despite the intense desert heat of the
Egyptian coast, the waters of the Red Sea
are surprisingly cool and you'll need some
sort of wet suit for diving, even in summer. In winter you may even need a dry
suit. Again, although many people like to
bring their own, these are all available for
between US$6 and US$20 per day, depending on the type and size.

Trips

Before agreeing to dive with a club, be sure
you know where they are going to take you.
Apart from seeing the best coral, it's important to ensure that you are experienced
enough for the site. Sometimes dive centres
will put a novice on a boat going to reefs
that demand a high level of expertise. A
reputable dive club should not do this but
if you feel unsure of yourself or have any
doubts, ask to go somewhere else.

If you're going to Ras Mohammed or the
Nabq Protectorate (p492), bring your passport, and remember that you may have to
pay park fees in addition to the cost of the
dive. There are also often supplementary
charges for going to wrecks in the Straits of
Gubal; for example, US$15 to US$20 extra
for a dive at the *Dunraven*, and from US$75

to US$100 for a day trip from Sharm el-
Sheikh to *The Thistlegorm*, depending on
whether food is included.

Many clubs organise dive safaris to remote sites ranging from one night to two
weeks. The cost of these live-aboard dive
safaris (also known as marine safaris) varies
according to the boat and the destination,
with the more remote sites in the far south
generally the most expensive. While you
won't see much of terrestrial Egypt, they
allow you to access a greater range of dive
sites, including many more distant destinations that are too far to explore as day
trips. There is a wide choice of live-aboards,
especially around Hurghada, and although
you can negotiate directly with captains,
arrangements are usually made through
dive clubs, many of which have at least one
or two boats of their own. Ask to see the
boat before agreeing to sail on it. Also, if a
trip is very cheap, check whether or not the
cost of diving and food are included.

Clubs

SHARM EL-SHEIKH & NA'AMA BAY AREA

There are dozens of dive clubs to choose
from; the following is just a small sampling
of the more reputable ones, all in Na'ama
Bay except Shark's Bay Diving Club.

Anemone Dive Centre (Map p486; ☎ 069-360 0999;
anemone@sinainet.com.eg; Sharm-Na'ama Bay rd, Na'ama
Bay) PADI, SSI. Laid-back and longstanding Bedouin-owned
centre next to the Pigeon House hotel.

Camel Dive Club (Map p486; ☎ 069-360 0700; www
.cameldive.com; Camel Hotel, King of Bahrain St, Na'ama
Bay) PADI, BSAC. A highly respected club owned by
longtime Sinai diver Hisham Gabr. It also has facilities for
disabled divers, and an attached hotel.

Divers International (Map p486; ☎ 069-360 0865;
www.diversintl.com; Sharm-Na'ama Bay rd, Na'ama Bay)
PADI. Large diving outfit offering a wide range of courses
and dive excursions.

Emperor Divers (Map p486; ☎ 069-360 1734; www
.emperordivers.com; Sharm-Na'ama Bay rd, Na'ama
Bay) PADI. A branch of the five-star outfit with offices
next to the Rosetta Hotel. A PADI open-water certificate
costs US$406 and there are courses that teach breathing
underwater to children as young as eight.

Oonas Dive Centre (Map p486; ☎ 069-360 0581;
www.oonasdivers.com; Na'ama Bay) PADI. At the northeastern end of Na'ama Bay. This is a popular centre and,
for those undertaking a course, it offers reasonably cheap
(by Sharm el-Sheikh standards) accommodation: air-con
singles/doubles cost US$50/75, including breakfast. Oper-

ates dive camps in the far south of the Red Sea with Red Sea Diving Safari (see p460).

Red Sea Diving College (Map p486; ☎ 069-360 0145; www.redseacollege.com; Na'ama Bay) PADI. Courses only, in conjunction with Scuba Pro International, which provides highly respected diving curricula. It's at the southern end of Na'ama Bay's pedestrian promenade.

Shark's Bay Diving Club (☎ 069-360 0942; www .sharksbay.com; Shark's Bay) PADI, SSI. Also known as Umbarak, Shark's Bay is a Bedouin-run centre with years of experience and its own house reef.

Sinai Divers (Map p486; ☎ 069-360 0697; www.sinai divers.com; Na'ama Bay) PADI, SSI, CMAS, TDI. One of Sharm el-Sheikh's most established dive centres, based at the Ghazala Hotel, with branches in Dahab.

Subex (Map p486; ☎ 069-360 0122; www.subex.org; Na'ama Bay) CMAS, SSI. Swiss-based dive club at the Mövenpick Hotel with years of experience in the Red Sea.

DAHAB

Dahab's main attractions as a diving destination include very good local reefs, and the chance to do a camel/dive safari. Most of these are day or overnight trips involving a jaunt by jeep and camel along the desert coastline to a remote offshore dive site, and they're ideal for combining desert travel with underwater adventure. There are currently at least 40 dive clubs in Dahab, although not all of them have good safety records. Following are some of the most reliable:

Desert Divers (Map p494; ☎ 069-364 0500; www .desert-divers.com; Masbat) PADI. A popular place offering a range of diving courses, plus camel/dive safaris, yoga classes and more.

Fantasea Dive Centre (Map p494; ☎ 069-364 0483; www.fantaseadiving.net; Masbat) PADI, TDI. This long-standing Australian-Egyptian-owned five-star PADI centre at the northern end of Masbat gets consistently good reviews. In addition to a wide array of courses, it offers one-day camel/dive safaris from US$88.

Fish & Friends (Map p494; ☎ 069-364 0720; www .fishandfriends.com; Masbat) PADI. A small British-Egyptian-run diving centre offering dive safaris and open-water courses. Environmentally conscious and well managed. It's next to next to Ali Baba Hotel.

Inmo (Map p494; ☎ 069-364 0370; www.inmodivers.de; Inmo Hotel, Mashraba) PADI. Run by Mohammed and Ingrid al-Kabany, this family-friendly outfit was one of the first dive clubs to start operating in Dahab. It has an attractive domed complex, with hotel accommodation and restaurant, and offers the full range of diving services. Its three-day camel/dive safari goes to dive sites south of Dahab and starts at US$144 per day.

Nesima Dive Centre (Map p494; ☎ 069-364 0320; www.nesima-resort.com; Nesima Hotel, Mashraba) PADI. A well-managed and reputable club owned by local environmental activist and veteran diver Sherif Ebeid. Also has a hotel attached (see p497). One-day camel/dive safaris begin at US$100.

Orca Dive Club (Map p494; ☎ /fax 069-364 0020; Masbat) PADI, TDI. A well-established outfit just north of Bamboo House Hotel that offers technical instruction, as well as the usual introductory courses. It's managed by an ex-merchant marine officer, Wael Derballa, and supports local Bedouin through its camel/dive safaris (minimum three persons required).

Sunsplash (Map p494; ☎ 069-364 0932; www.sun splash-divers.com; Mashraba) PADI. A small but long-standing German-run diving centre at the southern end of Mashraba, Sunsplash offers the usual courses as well as camel/dive safaris with local Bedouin. It also has its own accommodation attached to the centre.

NUWEIBA

With its less developed hotel scene and relative paucity of rich reefs nearby, Nuweiba has fewer dive centres than other resort towns.

Diving Camp Nuweiba (Map p501 ☎ 012 249 6002; www.scuba-college.com) PADI. At Nuweiba Village hotel in the centre of Nuweiba, with the usual array of instruction in various languages. PADI open-water courses for beginners cost US$310, excluding the manual, log books and certificate.

Emperor Divers (☎ 069-352 0321; www.emperor divers.com) PADI. Situated at the Hilton Nuweiba Coral Resort, this place is part of the multibranch Emperor empire, offering five-star PADI service. Open-water courses cost US$370. Branches elsewhere include those in Hurghada, Dahab, Sharm el-Sheikh and Marsa Alam.

HURGHADA & RED SEA COAST

Because the offshore reefs of Hurghada are not as rich as they once were, this is the place for live-aboards, which take in sites ranging from the relatively close Shedwan Island to the distant shores south of Marsa Alam. There are over 100 dive centres to choose from; the following is only a small sample.

Aquanaut Red Sea (Map pp434-5; ☎ 065-354 9891; www.aquanaut.net; Corniche, Ad-Dahar, Hurghada) PADI, CMAS, VDTL. Founding member of the Hurghada Quality Dive Club, a group of clubs that tries to maintain basic standards of safety and service. This club, based at the Shedwan Hotel, has multilingual staff and two custom-built live-aboards.

Barakuda Diving Centre (☎ 065-325 3911, 065-326 0049; www.barakuda-diving.com; Resort Strip, Safaga) PADI, SSI, CMAS. Based at the Lotus Bay Beach Resort,

Barakuda offers an array of courses and promotes reef protection.

Divers Lodge (Map p429; ☎ 065-346 5100; www .divers-lodge.com; Resort Strip, Hurghada) PADI, BSAC, TDI. Based at the InterContinental, with a branch in Al-Gouna; offers a choice of live-aboards as well as training.

Easy Divers (Map pp434-5; ☎ 065-354 7816; www.easy divers-redsea.com; Corniche, Ad-Dahar, Hurghada) PADI, SSI, BSAC, TDI. Based at the Triton Empire Beach hotel, British-managed Easy Divers offers instruction to all levels of divers, and is active in Hepca, the local environmental NGO (see the boxed text, p431). There is also a branch in Al-Gouna (☎ 065-358 0027).

Jasmin Diving Centre (Map p429; ☎ 065-346 0475; www.jasmin-diving.com; Resort Strip, Hurghada) PADI, SSI. At Jasmine Village, this is another member of the Hurghada Quality Dive Club. Runs dive safaris from its own live-aboards.

Red Sea Diving Safari (in Cairo ☎ 02-337 1833, 02-337 9942; www.redsea-divingsafari.com; Marsa Shagra) PADI. Run by environmentalist and longtime diver Hossam Hassan. Hassan pioneered diving in the Red Sea's deep south, and has years of experience here. He runs three dive camps, at Marsa Shagra, Marsa Nakari and Wadi Lahami (see p446), with live-aboards based in each of the three for offshore diving. Trips can also be booked through Oonas Dive Centre (p458).

Red Sea Scuba Schools/Emperor Divers (Map p429; ☎ 065-344 4854; www.emperordivers.com; Resort Strip, Hurghada) PADI. At the Hilton Hurghada Resort. A highly reputable dive school with various branches, including in Sharm el-Sheikh, Dahab and Nuweiba.

Sharm el-Naga Dive Center (Map p452 ☎ 010 111 2942; www.sharmelnaga.com; Sharm el-Naga) PADI, CMAS. Dutch-managed diving centre on a secluded bay between Hurghada and Safaga at Sharm el-Naga on the Safaga road; gives instruction in six languages. There is no-frills accommodation on the beach; also offers safaris.

Sub Aqua (Map p429; ☎ 065-346 4101; www.subaqua -diveteam.de; Resort Strip, Hurghada) PADI, SSI, CMAS. Branch of Diveteam Sub Aqua at the Sofitel Hotel, which specialises in diving around the world.

Subex (www.subex.org) Hurghada (Map pp434-5; ☎ 065-354 7593; Ad-Dahar); Al-Quseir (☎ 065-333 2100; Sirena Beach) CMAS, SSI. A well-known Swiss outfit, based near California Hotel in Hurgada.

TIPS FOR SAFE DIVING IN THE RED SEA

Once you've chosen your club, arranged your equipment and learned about reef-protection measures, the main thing left to remember is to use common sense.

Most diving fatalities are caused by divers forgetting some of the basic rules. In Dahab, where the majority of accidents have occurred, drink and drugs have often played a starring role in these tragic and largely avoidable deaths. Many of those who lose their lives are experienced divers who should have known better than to go beyond safety limits or dive under the influence. Others are divers who were not experienced enough for the situations they found themselves in – next time you complain about having to take a test dive, remember that dive clubs have a good reason to be cautious.

The following are a few common-sense tips for safe diving:

- Don't drink and dive. Alcohol dehydrates, especially in a dry climate such as Egypt's, and increases your susceptibility to decompression sickness.
- Be sure you are healthy and feel comfortable diving. If you are taking prescription drugs, inform your medical examiner that you intend to be diving. Sometimes diving can affect your metabolism and your dosage might need to be changed.
- Dive within your scope of experience. The Red Sea's clear waters and high visibility often lull divers into going too deep. The depth limit for sports divers is 30m. Stick to it.
- Do not fly within 24 hours of diving. You also shouldn't climb above 300m, so don't plan a trip to St Katherine's Monastery or into the Eastern Desert mountains for the day after a dive.
- Make sure you can recognise your boat from in the water. Some dive sites get crowded and boats can look similar from underneath. It's not unknown for divers to get left behind because they didn't realise that their boat had left without them.
- Be aware that underwater conditions vary tremendously from site to site, and that both daily and seasonal weather and current changes can significantly alter any site and dive conditions. These differences influence not only which sites you can dive on any particular day, but the way you'll need to dress for a dive and the necessary dive techniques.
- Be insured. If something happens to you, treatment in the decompression chamber can cost as much as US$6000. The most reputable clubs will make

insurance a condition for diving with them. If you hadn't planned to dive before arriving in Egypt, many of the better clubs can provide insurance.

Emergency Information

Note, the VHF emergency channel is 16. In addition to the following listings, a decompression chamber run by **DECO International** (www.deco-international.com) is scheduled to open soon in Dahab, to be located near the CIB bank at Blue Hole Plaza.

El Gouna Hospital & Hyperbaric Centre (☎ 065-358 0011, 012 218 7550, 012 219 0383; Al-Gouna)

Marsa Shagra Decompression Chamber (☎ 012 218 7550, satellite 0195-100 262; Marsa Shagra) Located 24km north of Marsa Alam.

Naval Hyperbaric & Emergency Medical Center (Map p429; ☎ 065-344 9150, 065-354 8450; Corniche, Hurghada) Has two decompression chambers.

Safaga General Hospital & Decompression Chamber (☎ 012 218 7550)

Sharm el-Sheikh Hyberbaric Medical Center (Map p470; ☎ 069-366 0922/3, 24hr emergency 012 212 4292; hyper_med_center@sinainet.com.eg; Sharm el-Sheikh; ⏰ 10.30am-6pm) Run by Dr Adel Taher and Dr Ahmed Sakr. Highly recommended.

Sharm el-Sheikh International Hospital (Map p470; ☎ 069-366 0893/4/5; Sharm-Na'ama Bay Rd, Sharm el-Sheikh) A computerised hyperbaric chamber at the pyramid-shaped hospital.

The following are hyperbaric specialists:
Dr Adel Taher (☎ 012 212 4292; Sharm el-Sheikh)
Dr Hanaa Nessim (☎ 012 219 0383; Hurghada)
Dr Hossam Nasef (☎ 012 218 7550; Hurghada)

LITERATURE

Lonely Planet's *Diving & Snorkeling the Red Sea* is a full-colour guide that includes detailed descriptions of more than 80 dive sites in Egypt.

Red Sea Diver's Guide from Sharm El Sheikh to Hurghada by Shlomo and Roni Cohen has excellent maps and descriptions of sites around Ras Mohammed, the Straits of Gubal and Hurghada.

Sinai Dive Guide by Pete Harrison has detailed maps and explanations of the main Red Sea sites. Also good is *Sharm el-Sheikh Diving Guide* by Alberto Siliotti, with maps and ratings of numerous sites around Sharm el-Sheikh and Ras Mohammed National Park. *Red Sea Diving Guide* by Andrea Ghisotti and Alessandro Carletti

covers Egyptian sites, as well as others in Sudan, Israel and Eritrea.

The Red Sea: Underwater Paradise by Angelo Mojetta is one of the better glossy coffee-table books with beautiful photos of the flora and fauna of Egypt's reefs.

The Official HEPCA Dive Guide, produced by the Hurghada Environmental Protection & Conservation Association (Hepca), details 46 sites with artists' drawings and a small fish index. Proceeds from the sale of this guide go towards maintaining mooring buoys on the Red Sea. For more on Hepca, see the boxed text, p431.

INTERNET & OTHER RESOURCES

Many dive-centre websites have information about reefs and diving conditions. In addition, consult the following:

GoRedSea.com (www.goredsea.com) A growing index of dive centres and live-aboards as well as links to jobs on offer for divers, and other information on the Red Sea.

H2O Magazine (www.h2o-mag.com) The website of the quarterly publication of the Red Sea Association for Diving and Watersports, with articles and updates on diving in the region.

Man & the Environment (MATE; ☎ 069-364 1091; www.mate-dahab.com) Environmental resource centre in Dahab where divers can learn more about the area's reefs and how to protect them. It also helps organise trash dives in an effort to keep garbage off the reefs.

Ras Mohamed (www.rasmohamed.com) A comprehensive site on Ras Mohamed National Park, including good background information on local corals and other marine life.

Red Sea Association for Diving & Watersports (RSADW; ☎ 065-344 4802; www.redseaexperience.com; Hurghada) This NGO – concerned about the unregulated nature of diving the Red Sea – is scheduled to launch its website soon. Among its goals are raising the quality of dive centres and other water sports throughout the Red Sea governorate with measures such as standardised testing and identity cards for all dive masters, and a rating system for dive centres. It encourages feedback from visiting divers about their experiences. For more detail on safety concerns, see p456.

Red Sea Virtual Dive Center (www.redseavdc.com) Detailed descriptions of more than 73 dive sites.

Red-Sea.com (www.red-sea.com) Similar to GoRedSea.com.

Reef Check (www.reefcheck.org) A membership organisation working to save coral reefs in the Red Sea and elsewhere in the world.

South Sinai Association for Diving & Marine Activities (SSDM; ☎ 069-366 0418; www.southsinai .org) An entity similar to the Red Sea Association for Diving and Watersports.

Sinai

Here, not for the first time, I fell deeply in love with the landscape…I longed to reach out and stroke the great gaunt flanks of the mountain falling away into bewildering foot-hills and plains of dazzling sand. Africa and Asia might watch with jealous eyes, I heeded them not.

GW Murray, Dare Me to the Desert *(London: George Allen & Unwin, 1967)*

Sinai, a region of stark beauty, has been a place of refuge, conflict and curiosity for thousands of years. Wedged between Africa and Asia, it is an intercontinental crossroads *par excellence* – prophets, nomads, exiles and conquerors have all left their footprints here.

Sinai's northern coast is bordered by the Mediterranean Sea, and its southern peninsula by the Red Sea Gulfs of Aqaba to the east and Suez to the west. Row upon row of barren, red-brown mountains fill the southern interior, surrounded by relentlessly dry desert plains that metamorphose into many-hued panoramas under the rays of the morning and evening sun. From the palm-lined coast, the dunes and the swamps of the north to the white-sand beaches and stunning coral reefs fringing the Red Sea, Sinai abounds with contrasts.

Most visitors head to the resorts, of which there are hundreds – most are amenable enough places for sea-and-sand holidays. But if you get past the glitz, Sinai's stunning desert and marine environments offer much more. Among the highlights are snorkelling or diving amid teeming coral reefs, close-up encounters with traditional Bedouin culture and following pilgrims' roads to biblical sites. Whatever your preference, Sinai will undoubtedly be one of the most memorable parts of your Egyptian travels.

HIGHLIGHTS

- Climb **Mt Sinai** (p510), with its magnificent panoramas and long religious history
- Experience life with the Bedouin on a trek through the rugged **Sinai desert** (p512)
- Combine desert and undersea adventures on a **camel/dive safari** (p495)
- Marvel at the corals and teeming fish life of **Ras Mohammed National Park** (p468)
- Follow the footsteps of centuries of pilgrims on a visit to **St Katherine's Monastery** (p508)

Sinai Desert ★

Mt Sinai; St Katherine's Monastery ★

Ras Mohammed National Park ★

History

Some 40 million years ago the African and Arabian continental plates began to move apart, creating the relatively shallow (95m deep) Gulf of Suez and the much deeper (1800m) Gulf of Aqaba. The Gulf of Aqaba, which varies from 14km to 25km in width, is part of a rift (a crack in the earth's top layer) that extends 6000km from the Dead Sea, on the border between Israel and Jordan, through the Red Sea, Ethiopia and Kenya down to Mozambique in southern Africa.

In Pharaonic times the quarries of Sinai provided great quantities of turquoise, gold and copper. The importance of this 'Land of Turquoise' also made it the goal of empire builders and the setting for countless wars. As a link between Asia and Africa, it was of strategic value; many armies marched along its northern coast to or from what is now Israel and the Palestinian Territories.

For many people, Sinai is first and foremost the 'great and terrible wilderness' of the Bible, across which the Israelites journeyed in search of the Promised Land, having been delivered from the Egyptian army by the celebrated parting of the Red Sea that allowed the 'Children of Israel' to safely gain access to the dry land of Sinai. It was here that God is said to have first spoken to Moses from a burning bush and it was at the summit of Mt Sinai that God delivered his Ten Commandments to Moses:

Tell the children of Israel; Ye have seen what I did unto the Egyptians... If ye will obey my voice and keep my covenant, then ye shall be a peculiar treasure unto me above all people: for all the earth is mine. And ye shall be unto me a kingdom of priests, and a holy nation.

And Mount Sinai was altogether in smoke, because the Lord descended upon it in fire; and the whole mount quaked greatly... And the Lord came down upon Mount Sinai...and called Moses up to the top of the mount... And God spoke all these words, saying, I am the Lord thy God, which have brought thee out of the land of Egypt, out of the house of bondage. Thou shalt have no other gods before me.

Exodus 19:4–6; 19:18–20:3

Early in the Christian era Sinai was a place for Christian Egyptians to escape Roman persecution. Monasticism is thought to have begun here as early as the 3rd century AD, with most hermits settling in the caves of Wadi Feiran, on the assumption that the nearby Gebel Serbal was in fact the 'Mountain of God'. By the time the Emperor Justinian founded a monastery at the foot of Mt Sinai (Gebel Musa) in the 6th century, it had been decided that this was the mountain on which God had spoken. For centuries thereafter, the peninsula was a place of pilgrimage. It later became one of the routes taken to Mecca by Muslim pilgrims. Until recently the majority of its inhabitants were Bedouin, the only people capable of surviving in the peninsula's harsh environment.

In recent years Sinai has become the focus of development and 'reconstruction' in much the same way that the New Valley in the Western Desert was during the 1970s and 1980s, when landless fellaheen (peasant farmers) from an overcrowded Nile Valley were encouraged to move to the oases. The government has built a new pipeline, called the Al-Salam Canal, to bring fresh water from the Suez Canal to various areas of North Sinai targeted for resettlement. Agriculture is to be expanded dramatically, roads are being paved and desalination plants are being installed in coastal towns.

Tourism, too, has brought great changes, especially around the Gulf of Aqaba. Surveys estimate that the southern tourist town of Sharm el-Sheikh has seen an eightfold population increase in the past 15 years, and the small villages of Dahab and Nuweiba have grown into sprawling beachfront tourist towns. The Bedouin, the traditional inhabitants of Sinai, are now a minority in their native land. Marginalised by Cairo-based tour operators and a suspicious and aggressive police force, they have little means to resist all this change.

Climate

Sinai's climate is extreme: on one hand it can get very hot, so remember always to carry water, use copious amounts of sunblock and wear sensible clothes to avoid sunburn (wearing a T-shirt while snorkelling is advisable), as well as a hat or scarf. On the other hand, while summer temperatures can climb to 50°C, it gets very cold at night

SINAI

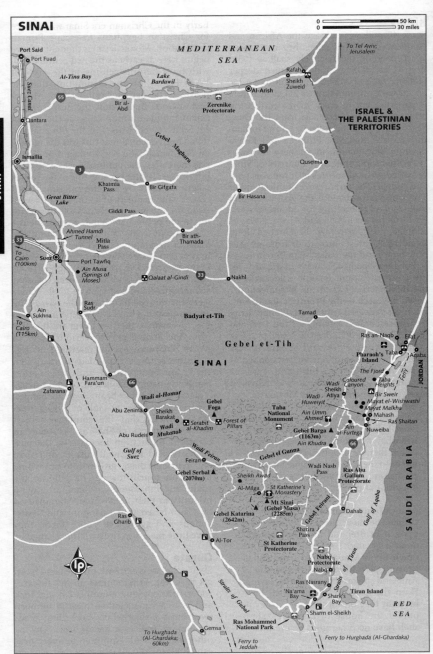

and the mountains can be freezing during the day; come prepared with warm clothing, especially if you'll be trekking, or climbing Mt Sinai. Camping out in winter requires a warm sleeping bag and good jacket – snow is frequent at this time of year.

Dangers & Annoyances

While G-strings and topless sunbathing seem to be *de rigueur* for some tourist groups in Sharm el-Sheikh, women should be aware that Egypt is a conservative country and tourists have been assaulted in Sinai. While rape is rare, it does occur, so don't sunbathe alone in an isolated location. And keep in mind that as well as offending the local people, topless sunbathing is illegal (in Sinai, as in the rest of Egypt).

Activities

Although Sinai's waters are famous for their diving opportunities, they are becoming increasingly well known for other water sports as well. For those wary of donning oxygen tanks and descending into the depths, many of the area's spectacular reefs can be enjoyed while snorkelling. All major tourist centres also offer glass-bottom boats for those who want to see the reefs but don't want to get wet. Banana boats and parasailing are also on offer.

With the steady winds that blow down both sides of the Sinai Peninsula, the parts of Sinai's coast that have not been developed offer excellent windsurfing. One of the most famous places for those in the know is Moon Beach resort (p467) at Ras Sudr on the Gulf of Suez, where the British magazine *Boards* tests equipment each year. Dahab (p492) is also famous for its offshore winds. See the relevant sections for hotels offering windsurfing.

Getting There & Away

Sinai's international air hub is at Sharm el-Sheikh, which receives regular charters from Europe, as well as local flights. There is also an international airport in Taba, though it currently receives only occasional charter flights. For overland travel, the peninsula is linked to the mainland by the Ahmed Hamdi Tunnel, and by the Mubarak Peace Suspension Bridge, both of which connect to main arteries to Cairo.

PROTECTING SINAI'S FRAGILE ECOSYSTEMS

Although much of Sinai is hot, dry desert, it is full of life. Craggy mountains are sliced by dry gravel wadis in which sprout the odd acacia tree or clump of gnarled tamarisk, while a surprisingly rich variety of plants tenuously cling to the loose, sandy flanks of coastal dunes. Once every few years, when storm clouds gather over the mountains and dump water onto this parched landscape, the entire scene is transformed into a sea of greenery as seeds that have lain dormant burst into life. For Sinai's wildlife, such as the gazelle and rock hyrax (as well as for the goats herded by local Bedouin), these rare occasions are times of plenty.

Yet these fragile ecosystems – which depend on a delicate balance of conditions for their survival – have come under increasing threat from the rapid onslaught of tourism. Until relatively recently, the only people to wander through this region were Bedouin on camels. Now adventure seekers in ever-multiplying numbers are ploughing their way through in 4WDs and quads (four-wheeled motorcycles) in search of pristine spots, and in so doing, churning up the soil, uprooting plants and contributing to erosion.

In order to minimise the environmental damage, the government has banned vehicles from going off road in certain areas, including Ras Mohammed National Park and the protected areas of Nabq, Ras Abu Gallum and Taba. Yet enforcement in Sinai's vast wilderness areas is difficult, and while rangers do patrol protectorates, a large part of the responsibility is left with visitors to follow the rules. To do your part, try not to be persuaded by over-eager guides wanting to show you something that's off the beaten track. If you really want to explore the region in depth, do it in the age-old fashion, going on foot or by camel. Also be aware of rubbish, which has become an increasingly serious threat to Sinai's ecosystems. Dive clubs in Dahab and Sharm el-Sheikh organise regular trash dives, and always find more than they can collect. Carry out all your litter with you, and dispose of it thoughtfully. And wherever you visit, treat Sinai's ecosystems – both those above and those below the sea – with care.

SINAI

The 1.6km-long tunnel, which goes under the Suez Canal near Suez, was completed in 1982 and named after a martyr of the 1973 war. It is open 24 hours. There are frequent buses connecting Cairo and other destinations with all major towns on the Sinai Peninsula. A railway has been built to part of North Sinai but there are no passenger services.

Getting Around

Because of Sinai's rugged landscape, paved roads link only the permanent settlements, and public transport is not as regular as elsewhere in Egypt. You can get to all major destinations by bus, but in many cases there are only a couple of connections a day – and sometimes only one. Service taxis are a popular means of transport in northern Sinai (primarily along the route connecting Rafah and Al-Arish with Suez and Cairo). Elsewhere on the peninsula, with the exception of the coastal route to Al-Tor, it's only possible to arrange a service taxi by bargaining and paying far more than would be the case over similar distances elsewhere in Egypt.

If you are driving yourself, exercise caution. Stick to tracks when going off the road, as there are still mines left over from the wars with Israel. When at the wheel in winter, remember that it rains with some frequency in Sinai, and flash floods often wash out paved roads, particularly around Wadi Feiran. Bus drivers are a good source of information on trouble spots.

COAST

AIN MUSA

Ain Musa (Springs of Moses) is said to be the place where Moses and the Israelites camped after crossing into Sinai, and where Moses – on discovering that the water was too bitter to drink – took the advice of God and threw a special tree into the springs, miraculously sweetening the water. Only one of the 12 original springs still exists, now filled with litter and surrounded by a stand of date palms.

The site is about 25km south of the Ahmed Hamdi Tunnel, just off the main road and signposted only in Arabic. It is watched over by an officer from the antiquities department, together with a very eager guide. Camping at the site is possible in theory, but unappealing due to the litter, the proximity of the roadway and a nearby settlement. There's also no drinkable water (as the spring water is too brackish, with no sign of Moses' special tree). It's best to visit with your own vehicle, or on a tour organised through one of the hotels in Ras Sudr. All buses heading south pass by here and will drop you off, though it can be difficult to find onward transport.

RAS SUDR

☎ 069

Ras Sudr, or Sudr, is a small and peppy town about 60km south of the Ahmed Hamdi Tunnel. Although originally developed around one of Egypt's largest oil refineries, its coastline and proximity to Cairo have spurred its transition into a resort area. However, there are few reefs, and apart from catering to those who appreciate the excellent windsurfing opportunities, the coastline is primarily a destination for Cairene families with time-share villa arrangements. If you're looking for a place to break the journey between Cairo and points further south, or are a windsurfer and want to take advantage of the area's uninterrupted winds blowing at mostly force five or six, Ras Sudr makes a reasonable stopping point. If you're after a day or overnight getaway, the closer and less blustery beaches around Ain Sukhna are a better bet.

The town centre – which lies just off the main highway – boasts several small restaurants, a post office and telephone centrale, a bank and various small shops. Well away from here, to the south and north, are a handful of resorts interspersed with blocks of holiday villas.

Sleeping & Eating

La Hacienda Beach Resort (in Cairo ☎ 02-418 6667, 010 117 7200,; info@lahaciendaresort.com; s/d half board US$50/80; ✕ ⛱) A new place about 35km south of Ras Sudr on the main highway and well-signposted, with Mediterranean-style décor, bright, pleasant rooms and a (soon-to-open) windsurfing centre.

Moon Beach (☎ 340 1500/1/2, in Cairo ☎ 02-336 5103; www.moonbeachretreat.com; s/d half board US$60/90; ✕) This three-star hotel, on a quiet beach just off the main coastal road and marked with a small signpost, has beachfront bungalows with balconies and fridges, plus excellent windsurfing and kitesurfing. While overpriced for the facilities on offer, special deals are available to windsurfers who book from outside Egypt (in UK ☎ 01580-753824). Day use of the beach costs E£45/15 per person with/without lunch.

Away from the resorts, the main dining options are a handful of small restaurants clustered around the main junction. One of the better ones is the undistinguished **Sheikh Zeen** (Ras Sudr town; dishes E£10-25), with tasty seafood grills.

Getting There & Away

East Delta has its terminal along the main road about 500m south of the main junction. Buses to Cairo (E£25, two to three hours) depart at 7.30am, 2pm and 4pm. A taxi from the bus station in Ras Sudr to Moon Beach or La Hacienda Beach Resort costs about E£25 to E£30.

HAMMAM FARA'UN

Hammam Fara'un (Pharaoh's Bath) is the site of hot springs which are used by local Bedouin as a cure for rheumatism. The springs are in a cave beside the beach, but are too hot for all but the most dedicated hot-tub fans, and the litter-strewn beach makes swimming in the warm surrounding sea uninviting. Women who decide to brave the waters should avoid swimming in anything more daring than leggings and a baggy T-shirt. There's nowhere to stay near the springs.

Hammam Fara'un is about 50km south of Ras Sudr, and signposted only in Arabic. It's best to visit with your own transport, or on a visit organised by Moon Beach resort (left) or one of the other Ras Sudr hotels. Sinai buses to/from Cairo and Suez can drop you at the turn-off, from where it's about 2km further to the beach; getting an onward lift can be difficult.

AL-TOR
☎ 069

Al-Tor, also known as Tur Sinai, is the administrative capital of the South Sinai Governorate. It has been a significant port since ancient times, and also served as a gateway for many of the early Christians who ultimately settled around Wadi Feiran and further east towards St Katherine's Monastery. Today there's little in Al-Tor but government buildings and a windy Corniche bisected by a broad central avenue bordered by apartment blocks. If you're staying at any of South Sinai's resorts, this is the closest place where you can extend your visa; which can be done at the town's Mogamma, the large administrative building on the main road in the town centre.

More enjoyably, Al-Tor has stiff and constant breezes similar to those buffeting the coastline further north around Ras Sudr, and is trying to build up a name for itself as a windsurfing destination. About 5km from town are some hot springs known as **Hammam Musa** (admission E£20), which tradition holds to have been one of the possible stopping points used by Moses and the Israelites on their journey through Sinai. It's possible to bathe in the springs, and there are some paved walkways, a changing area and a small café.

National Bank of Egypt has a branch with an ATM; it's in the town centre near the post office.

Moses Bay Hotel (☎ 377 4343; www.mosesbayetur .com; d half board US$37.50; ✕ ⛱) This place – about 3km from town on the beach – is the focal point of windsurfing in Al-Tor, and the nicest spot to stay in the area. It has its own stretch of sand, pleasant rooms, a restaurant and a wind- and kitesurfing centre.

Delmon Hotel (☎ 377 1060; Sharia Manshiyya; s/d with private bathroom E£60/90; ✕) The most appealing place to stay in the town centre, with helpful staff and reasonable rooms. It's one

HISTORY'S FOOTPRINTS

Sinai's rugged expanses are dotted with traces of early settlements and pilgrimage routes. One of the most impressive sites is **Serabit al-Khadim**, a ruined Pharaonic temple surrounded by ancient turquoise mines and starkly beautiful landscapes. Despite the remoteness of the location, turquoise was mined here as far back as the Old Kingdom. The temple itself dates back to the 12th dynasty and is dedicated to the goddess Hathor; beside it is a New Kingdom shrine to Sopdu, god of the Eastern Desert. Throughout the temple's many courts, inscriptions list the temple's benefactors, including Hatshepsut (1473–1458 BC) and Tuthmosis III (1479–1425 BC). It is thought to have been abandoned during the reign of Ramses VII.

Serabit al-Khadim can be reached via an unsignposted track just south of the coastal settlement of Abu Zenima or, more interestingly, from a track branching north off the road running east through Wadi Feiran via **Wadi Mukattab** (Valley of Inscriptions), which itself is well worth a visit. Here Sinai's largest collection of rock inscriptions and stelae, some dating back to the 3rd dynasty, give further evidence of ancient turquoise mining activities. Unfortunately many of the workings and stelae were damaged when the British unsuccessfully tried to revive the mines in 1901.

Heading inland from Serabit al-Khadim, another track takes you through the colourful wadis of **Gebel Foga** to the cliffs that edge Gebel et-Tih and the **Forest of Pillars**, a naturally occurring phenomenon accessible with 4WD and camel via a long track.

All of these destinations require guides and a 4WD. The most straightforward way to visit is to arrange a jeep trip with Moon Beach resort (p467), or with an outfit in Na'ama Bay. If you are travelling in your own vehicle, you can head into the village of **Sheikh Barakat** and get a guide: coming from Ras Sudr, follow the marked track that leads off into the desert, just south of Abu Zenima, for about 39km. When you see a white dome on your right, take the track to your left. After about 3km you'll come to Sheikh Barakat, where you can camp (the closest hotels are in Al-Tor and Ras Sudr), and organise a guide to take you the remaining 7km to the trail leading up to Serabit al-Khadim. At the end of this you'll need to park your vehicle and climb for about an hour. The track up the mountain is steep at times and involves a bit of scrambling, but can be handled by anyone who is reasonably fit. Coming from Wadi Feiran, you can negotiate for a guide in the village of Feiran.

block in from the Corniche, and southwest of the Coptic church (a major landmark).

East Delta has its station along the main road at the northern edge of town opposite the hospital, and about 700m from the Delmon Hotel. Buses depart from 7am onwards throughout the day to Sharm el-Sheikh (E£12, 1½ hours), and at 10.15am, 11.45am, 1.45pm and 4.15pm to Cairo (five to six hours). From the bus station, you can hire a pick-up for E£10 to take you to Moses Bay Hotel, or arrange transport directly with the hotel.

RAS MOHAMMED NATIONAL PARK

About 20km west of Sharm el-Sheikh on the road from Al-Tor lies the headland of **Ras Mohammed National Park** (admission per person US$5, per vehicle additional US$5; ☉ 8am-5pm), named by local fishermen for a cliff that resembles a man's profile. The waters surrounding the peninsula are considered the

jewel in the crown of the Red Sea. The park is inundated with more than 50,000 visitors annually, enticed by the prospect of marvelling at some of the world's most spectacular coral-reef ecosystems, including a profusion of coral species and teeming marine life. The most ancient are fossil reefs dating back some two million years. Because they are similar in composition and structure to present-day reefs, they are an invaluable source of scientific information about changing sea levels and past climatic conditions. Most, if not all, of the Red Sea's 1000 species of fish can be seen in the park's waters, including large pelagics such as sharks, making the area a mecca for divers. Because many of the reefs can easily be reached from the shore, Ras Mohammed is also ideal for snorkelling.

Ras Mohammed was declared a marine reserve in 1983 and became Egypt's first national park in 1989. It occupies a total of

480 sq km of land and sea, including the desert in and around the *ras* (headland), Tiran Island and the shoreline between Sharm el-Sheikh harbour and Nabq Protectorate. At the time of its declaration, the park was the subject of controversy, but since then has proved its value in preventing the area's fragile environment from being destroyed by the sort of development that has transformed the Sharm el-Sheikh coast. Hotels are not permitted, only 12% of the park is accessible to visitors and limits are applied to the number of dive boats allowed.

You'll need your passport to enter the park. Visitors on Sinai-only permits cannot go to Ras Mohammed as it is beyond the Sharm el-Sheikh boundary, but should not have any problem on boat dive trips. Check with the dive clubs if you have any doubts. For more on dive sites in the park, see p453.

Activities

The entrance to the park is about 20km from the reefs. A **visitors' centre** (☺ 10am-sunset Sat-Thu) with a restaurant is clearly marked to the left of the main access road in an

area known as Marsa Ghoslane. Videos are shown here, and you may be able to pick up a booklet highlighting local fauna. The park is laid out with colour-coded trails and clearly marked pictograms of what each site offers. At the park's laboratory, a pink trail leads to **Khashaba Beach** and a camping area. Yellow arrows lead to the sandy beaches and calm waters of **Marsa Bareika**, excellent for snorkelling and safe for children. Blue arrows take you to **Main Beach**, which gets crowded with day visitors but remains one of the best places to see vertical coral walls. Brown arrows lead to **Aqaba Beaches**, which border the **Eel Garden**, named after a colony of garden eels 20m down. This is a great area for snorkelling in calm weather. Just beyond here, orange arrows lead to **Shark Observatory**, a cliff-top area where you can sometimes see sharks as they feed off Ras Mohammed's rich offerings. The red arrows lead to **Yolanda Bay**, another beach with good snorkelling and diving, and green arrows lead to the **Mangrove Channel** and **Hidden Bay** (both well-suited for bird watching) and to **Old Quay**, a spectacular vertical reef teeming

SINAI

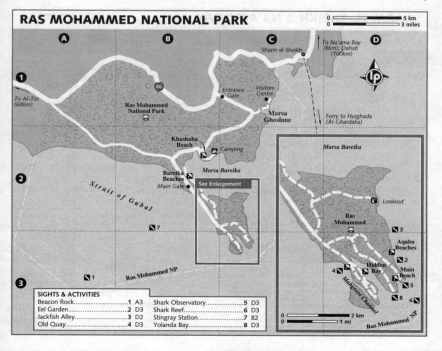

RAS MOHAMMED NATIONAL PARK

0 — 5 km
0 — 3 miles

To Al-Tor (68km)

66

Ras Mohammed National Park

To Na'ama Bay (8km); Dahab (100km)

Sharm el-Sheikh

Entrance Gate

Visitors Centre

Marsa Ghoslane

Khashaba Beach

Camping

Bareika Beaches

Marsa Bareika

Main Gate

See Enlargement

Strait of Gubal

7

1

Ras Mohammed NP

Ferry to Hurghada (Al-Ghardaka)

Marsa Bareika

Lookout

Ras Mohammed

3

Aqaba Beaches

4

Hidden Bay

Main Beach

5

8   6

Mangrove Channel

0 — 2 km
0 — 1 mi

Ras Mohammed NP

with fish and accessible to snorkellers as well as divers. Offshore, some of the most popular dive sites include **Jackfish Alley**, **Shark Reef**, **Stingray Station** and **Beacon Rock**.

Sleeping

Camping is permitted in designated areas, with permits (per person US$5) available from the entrance gate. You'll need to bring all supplies with you; the nearest shops are in Sharm el-Sheikh. If you camp, respect the environment and clean up. In particular, don't bury toilet paper or garbage, as the relentless winds here mean that nothing stays under the sand for long. Camp rules are enforced by rangers and if you're caught violating them you may be prosecuted.

Getting There & Around

If you don't have a car, you can hire a taxi from Sharm el-Sheikh to bring you here, but expect to pay at least E£150 for the day. If you don't mind company, the easiest option is to join one of the many day tours by jeep or bus from Sharm el-Sheikh and Na'ama Bay, most of which will drop you

at the beaches and snorkelling sites. Expect to pay from E£150. Alternatively, divers are often brought in by boat from tourist centres elsewhere on the Red Sea.

To move around the park you'll need a vehicle. Access is restricted to certain parts of the park and, for conservation reasons, it's forbidden to leave the official tracks.

SHARM EL-SHEIKH & NA'AMA BAY
☎ 069

The southern coast of the Gulf of Aqaba, between Tiran Island and Ras Mohammed National Park, features some of the world's most brilliant and amazing underwater scenery. The crystal-clear waters, rare and lovely reefs and an incredible variety of exotic fish darting in and out of the colourful coral have made this a snorkelling and scuba-diving paradise, attracting visitors from all over the globe.

Unfortunately, the resort of Sharm el-Sheikh, comprising two adjacent bays – Na'ama Bay and Sharm al-Maya – does not reflect this underwater beauty. Na'ama Bay – the focus of all the action – is a string of

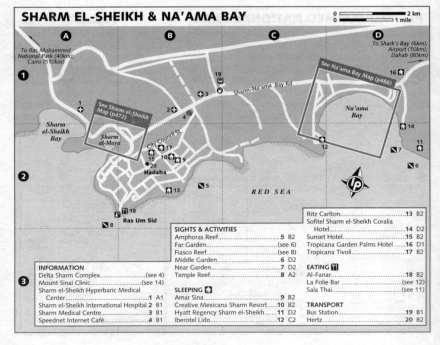

SHARM EL-SHEIKH & NA'AMA BAY

SIGHTS & ACTIVITIES	
Amphoras Reef	5 B2
Far Garden	(see 6)
Fiasco Reef	(see 8)
Middle Garden	6 D2
Near Garden	7 D2
Temple Reef	8 A2

SLEEPING 🏠	
Amar Sina	9 B2
Creative Mexicana Sharm Resort	10 B2
Hyatt Regency Sharm el-Sheikh	11 D2
Iberotel Lido	12 C2

INFORMATION	
Delta Sharm Complex	(see 4)
Mount Sinai Clinic	(see 14)
Sharm el-Sheikh Hyperbaric Medical	
Center	1 A1
Sharm el-Sheikh International Hospital	2 B1
Sharm Medical Centre	3 B1
Speednet Internet Café	4 B1

Ritz Carlton	13 B2
Sofitel Sharm el-Sheikh Coralia	
Hotel	14 D2
Sunset Hotel	15 B2
Tropicana Garden Palms Hotel	16 D1
Tropicana Tivoli	17 B2

EATING 🍴	
Al-Fanar	18 B2
La Folie Bar	(see 12)
Sala Thai	(see 11)

TRANSPORT	
Bus Station	19 B1
Hertz	20 B2

resorts that has grown from virtually nothing in the early 1980s to a Las Vegas–style strip with all the charm of a shopping mall, and the surrounding areas are not much better.

If you're interested in exploring Egypt's underwater treasures, a visit here is a must. Sharm's charms are also appreciated by many Cairo dwellers – Egyptians and foreign residents alike – for its clean air, sea vistas and relaxed ambience. However, if your time in Egypt is limited and you're primarily interested in discovering local culture or finding scenic beaches, Sinai's other resorts make better destinations.

In July 2005 three terrorist bombs exploded in Sharm el-Sheikh, killing 63 people and injuring over 100. The worst damage was in the Sharm Old Market area (see right) and near the Ghazala Hotel in Na'ama Bay. In the wake of the bombings, the Egyptian government increased security at all Sharm el-Sheikh hotels and began building a fence around the town. The government has also been working to revive tourism to the city with incentives ranging from discounted flight prices to free concerts. As this book went to press, reconstruction of the affected establishments was proceeding apace and temporarily plummeting tourist numbers were again on the upswing, although scars remain.

Orientation

Most midrange and top-end resorts are clustered along or just inland from the beach at Na'ama Bay. If you enjoy being in the centre of the action and don't mind the crush of pedestrians, central Na'ama Bay – consisting of a beachfront promenade and a pedestrians-only area lined with hotels, restaurants and shops – is the most convenient base. The further away from this central strip you go, the quieter things become: most of the resorts lining the coast north of Na'ama Bay are comparatively tranquil upscale retreats with their own patch of sand and easy taxi access to the central area. While there are a few inexpensive hotels in Na'ama Bay, if you're on a tight budget, it's generally better to head further north to Shark's Bay (see p489) or, better still, to leave Sharm completely and head to Dahab.

Sharm al-Maya, located about 6km west of Na'ama Bay, centres on a large, walled

market area known as Sharm Old Market, with a selection of inexpensive eateries. A large section of the Old Market area was heavily damaged in the tragic bombings of July 2005, and is currently being rebuilt. On the southwestern edge of Sharm al-Maya is the port. Spread out on a cliff top above Sharm al-Maya is the administrative area of Hadaba, which is rimmed by a barren network of long, treeless avenues lined with primarily midrange resorts. These are targeted at travellers flying in directly from Europe, and are connected to the beach via shuttle bus. To the southeast of the administrative area is Ras Um Sid, with an agreeable stretch of coastline, a lighthouse and a row of upmarket hotels.

Information

BOOKSHOPS

Hilton Fayrouz Village and the Mövenpick Hotel have a selection of glossy guides to Egypt and diving in the Red Sea. International newspapers are sold at kiosks along the beach strip in Na'ama Bay.

Al-Ahram Bookshop (Map p486; Sharm-Na'ama Bay rd, Na'ama Bay; 🕙 10am-1.30pm & 6-8pm) Sharm el-Sheikh's best-stocked bookshop, with a reasonable selection of books and magazines. It's just west of Avis.

EMERGENCY

Ambulance (☎ 123)

Tourist police Hadaba (Map p472; ☎ 366 0311); Na'ama Bay (Map p486; ☎ 360 0554, 366 0675; booth next to Marina Sharm Hotel)

INTERNET ACCESS

Many hotels have Internet access, and there are Internet cafés dotted around town. In Na'ama Bay, most charge E£20 per hour, though it's sometimes possible to negotiate a lower rate. The cheapest connections (E£5 per hour) are in or near downtown Sharm.

Al-Awamy Internet Cafe (Map p472; Sharm Old Market, Sharm el-Sheikh; per hr E£5; 🕙 24hr)

Felicita.Net (Map p486; Na'ama Bay; per hr E£20; 🕙 24hr) Above the Egyptian-American Bank.

Naama Internet (Map p486; Na'ama Centre, Na'ama Bay; per hr E£20; 🕙 noon-3am)

Speednet Internet Café (Map p470; Sharm-Na'ama Bay rd, Sharm el-Sheikh; per hr E£5; 🕙 24hr) In the Delta Sharm complex.

Yes Business Centre (Map p486; Na'ama Bay; per hr E£12; 🕙 11am-1am) Between Mall 7 and Avis car rental.

SINAI

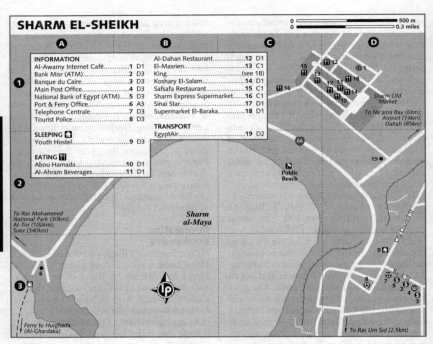

SHARM EL-SHEIKH

INFORMATION		
Al-Awamy Internet Café	1	D1
Bank Misr (ATM)	2	D3
Banque du Caire	3	D3
Main Post Office	4	D3
National Bank of Egypt (ATM)	5	D3
Port & Ferry Office	6	A3
Telephone Centrale	7	D3
Tourist Police	8	D3

SLEEPING		
Youth Hostel	9	D3

EATING		
Abou Hamada	10	D1
Al-Ahram Beverages	11	D1

Al-Dahan Restaurant	12	D1
El-Masrien	13	C1
King	(see 18)	
Koshary El-Salam	14	D1
Safsafa Restaurant	15	C1
Sharm Express Supermarket	16	C1
Sinai Star	17	D1
Supermarket El-Baraka	18	D1

TRANSPORT		
EgyptAir	19	D2

Sharm Old Market

To Na'ama Bay (6km); Airport (14km); Dahab (85km)

Public Beach

Sharm al-Maya

To Ras Mohammed National Park (30km); Al-Tor (100km); Suez (340km)

Bank St

City Council St

Ferry to Hurghada (Al-Ghardaka)

To Ras Um Sid (2.5km)

MEDICAL SERVICES

There are two decompression chambers in Sharm; see p461.

Mount Sinai Clinic (☎ 012 218 9889); Mövenpick Hotel (Map p486; Na'ama Bay); Sofitel Sharm el-Sheikh Coralia Hotel (Map p470; Na'ama Bay) Specialises in diving-related medical problems as well as ordinary ailments.

Omar & Omar Pharmacy (Map p486; ☎ 360 0960; King of Bahrain St, Na'ama Bay; ☒ 24hr) At Shamandura Supermarket, opposite Falcon Hotel.

Sharm el-Sheikh Hyberbaric Medical Center (Map p470; ☎ 366 0922/3, 012 212 4292; hyper_med _center@sinainet.com.eg; Sharm el-Sheikh)

Sharm el-Sheikh International Hospital (Map p470; ☎ 366 0893/4/5; Sharm-Na'ama Bay rd, Sharm el-Sheikh)

Sharm Medical Center (Map p470; ☎ 366 1744; Sharm-Na'ama Bay rd, Sharm el-Sheikh; ☒ 24hr) Next to the bus station.

MONEY

You will find ATMs every few metres in Na'ama Bay, including several in Na'ama Centre (Map p486), as well as ATMs in the lobbies of most larger hotels. Otherwise, all the major banks have branches in Hadaba.

Banque du Caire (Map p472; Hadaba; ☒ 8.30am-2pm Sun-Thu)

Banque Misr Hadaba (Map p472; Bank St; ☒ 8.30am-2pm & 5-8pm Sun-Thu) Na'ama Bay (Map p486; King of Bahrain St) ATM.

Commercial International Bank (Map p486; Na'ama Center, Na'ama Bay; ☒ 9am-1pm & 6-10pm Sat-Thu, 10-11am Fri)

Egyptian American Bank (Map p486; ☎ 360 1423; Na'ama Bay; ☒ 8.30am-2pm Mon-Thu) American Express agent; diagonally opposite Cataract Resort.

National Bank of Egypt Hadaba (Map p472; Bank St; ☒ 8.30am-2pm & 6-9pm Sat-Thu, 9am-1pm & 6-9pm Fri); Na'ama Bay (Map p486; Na'ama Centre; ☒ 6pm-1am) ATM.

Thomas Cook (Map p486; ☎ 360 1808; Gafy Mall Sharm-Na'ama Bay rd, Na'ama Bay; ☒ 9am-2pm & 6-10pm) Just west of Sinai Star Hotel.

Western Union (Map p486; ☎ 364 0466; Rosetta Hotel, Na'ama Bay; ☒ 8.30am-2pm & 6-10pm Sat-Thu, 3-10pm Fri)

POST

Main post office (Map p472; Bank St, Hadaba; ☒ 8.30am-2.30pm Sat-Thu)

(Continued on page 485)

BRETT SHEARER

Shifting sands near Siwa Oasis (p359)

Western Desert (p331) between Siwa and Bahariyya Oasis

JOHN ELK III

Dune, Dakhla Oasis (p341)

WILL SALTER

CHRIS BAR

Rock formation in the White Desert (p351), near Farafra

SARA-JANE CLELAND

Young boy, Siwa Oasis (p359)

Badr's Museum (p349), Farafra

JONH EL

Siwa Oasis (p359)

Clay images of village life, Oasis Heritage Museum (p354), Bawiti

Local woman, Dakhla Oasis (p341)

Rocky outcrops, White Desert (p351)

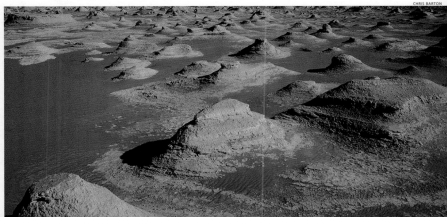

Fruit and vegetable stand, Siwa Oasis (p359)

Boy, Dakhla Oasis (p341)

Sunset, Western Desert (p331)

JOHN ELK III

Road from Siwa to Bahariyya, Western Desert (p331)

DAVID ELSE

Date palms, Western Desert
(p331)

Boy on horse, Siwa Oasis (p359)

BECCA POSTERINO

Fortress of Shali (p362), Siwa Oasis

Traditional door, Dakhla Oasis
(p341)

Monastery of St Simeon (p310), Aswan

Baron's Palace (Qasr al-Baron; p135), Heliopolis, Cairo

EDDIE GERALD

Necropolis of al-Bagawat (p337), Al-Kharga

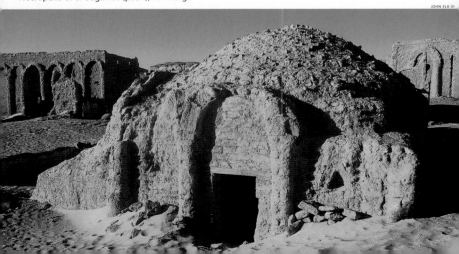

JOHN ELK III

Dahab (p492), Sinai Peninsula

BRETT SHEARER

MARK DAFFEY

Ras Um Sid, Sharm el-Sheikh (p470)

Rocky Island (p456), Red Sea

CASEY & ASTRID WITTE MAH

MARK WEBSTER

Diver on reef wall, Thomas Reef (p453), Red Sea

School of fish, Ras Mohammed National Park (p453)

DAVE LEVITT

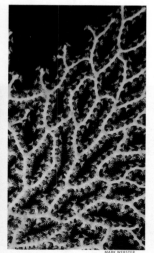

MARK WEBSTER

Yellow Gorgonian coral, Ras
Mohammed National Park (p453)

JOHN ELK III

Highway, Sinai (p462)

Climbing Mt Sinai (p510), Sinai

MARK DAFFEY

View of Sinai from Mt Sinai (p509)

CHRIS BA

JOHN BORTHWICK

St Katherine's Monastery (p508) at the foot of Mt Sinai, Sinai

JOHN BORTHWICK

Church at St Katherine's Monastery (p508)

St Katherine's Monastery (p508), Sinai

ANDREW BURKE

484

Sunset over Aswan (p302)

Field of sugar cane and wheat,
Luxor (p233)

Sunrise, Mt Sinai (p509), Sinai

(Continued from page 472)

TELEPHONE

There are several cardphones in Na'ama Bay, including one at the Shamandura Supermarket (Map p486) and at least two on the beachfront promenade, one of them in front of the Red Sea Diving College (Map p486). Cards can be bought everywhere, but watch out for overcharging by shopkeepers. There are also several call centres where you can dial internationally for between E£4 and E£7 per minute.

Telephone centrale (Map p472; Bank St, Hadaba; ⏰ 24hr).

Activities

DIVING

The clear, turquoise depths surrounding Sharm el-Sheikh are the area's major draw, and there are dozens of dive clubs catering to visitors from around the world. (Note that all diving here must be arranged through a dive club.) Long-time favourites include **Camel Dive Club** (Map p486; ☎ 360 0700; www.camel dive.com; Camel Hotel, King of Bahrain St, Na'ama Bay), **Subex** (Map p486; ☎ 360 0122; www.subex.org; Na'ama Bay) and **Sinai Divers** (Map p486; ☎ 360 0697; www .sinaidivers.com; Na'ama Bay). For further details of these and others, see p458.

SNORKELLING

Together with diving, snorkelling in the waters around Sharm el-Sheikh is excellent. While there are some easily accessed reefs in central Na'ama Bay, it's better to make your way to the more impressive **Near** and **Middle Gardens**, or the even more beautiful **Far Garden**. The Near Garden is around the point at the northern end of the bay just below the Sofitel hotel, and the Middle and Far Gardens are below the Hyatt Regency. All can be reached on foot, or you can take a boat organised by one of the diving centres; bring plenty of drinking water and sunblock along.

Another prime spot for snorkelling is **Ras Um Sid Reef**, near the lighthouse at Sharm el-Sheikh, which is known for its fan corals and plethora of fish, although the small beach is parcelled up between several resorts and can get quite crowded. The area near the lighthouse itself is part of Al-Fanar restaurant (p489), and beach entry costs E£40. Apart from Ras Um Sid Reef, the popular **Temple** and **Fiasco Reefs** are within easy swim-

ming distance, and while they're primarily dive destinations, snorkellers can still get a taste of their flora and fauna. Beside the Ritz Carlton Hotel is **Amphoras Reef**, another popular snorkelling spot. On the road to the airport, **Shark's Bay** (p489) also has a good reef that is frequented by large rays in springtime. Tickets for beach use cost E£15, and are issued at the camps on the left side of the beach. For more on local dive sites, see p453.

It's possible to get to more distant sites by joining a dive boat, which can be arranged at most local dive clubs; expect to pay between US$25 and US$50 for a day trip. Many of the clubs also do snorkelling trips to Ras Mohammed National Park, with prices starting at about US$50. While there is some excellent snorkelling in the park, be sure that you'll be taken to a suitable site, as some dive destinations are not always ideal for snorkellers, and some areas have strong currents that are not for the faint-hearted.

Most dive clubs rent masks, snorkels and fins. Remember that the same reef-protection rules apply to snorkellers as to divers. As snorkellers tend to stick to shallower waters, their fins often do more damage to reefs than those of divers, so take care to keep your distance from the corals. See p451 for more on reef-protection measures.

OTHER WATER SPORTS

Most major hotels offer a range of other water sports, including sailing lessons, windsurfing, parasailing, pedalos, glass-bottom boats and banana boats. Most hotels also have beach access – either their own stretch of waterfront, or by agreement with another resort. Check when booking, as the beaches of some hotels are fairly distant (up to 10km) from the hotel itself, and can only be accessed via shuttle. There is also a narrow stretch of public beach diagonally opposite Hilton Fayrouz Village on Na'ama Bay, but it is so crowded with rental chairs that it is difficult to see the sand. Keep in mind that it's illegal to swim off Na'ama Bay after 11pm, and that despite all the development, the beaches and waters of Na'ama Bay are part of the Ras Mohammed National Park and its regulations apply here.

In Sharm al-Maya there is also a stretch of public beach. However, there's no reef, and women swimming here are likely to be ogled by young Egyptian men.

SINAI

CAMEL RIDES

Camel rides to 'traditional Bedouin villages' can be easily arranged with most hotels, but it's usually a better and more authentic experience if you can negotiate treks directly with the Bedouin in Dahab or Nuweiba. If you decide to try one from Sharm, expect to pay between US$40 to US$60, and to find yourself in the midst of a large group.

HORSE RIDING

Several top-end hotels, including **Sofitel Sharm el-Sheikh Coralia Hotel** (Map p470; ☎ 360 0081; www.sofitel.com; Na'ama Bay), offer horse riding from about US$20 per hour.

Tours

Almost all travel agencies and large hotels organise jeep or bus trips to St Katherine's Monastery (p508), and to desert attractions such as the Coloured Canyon (p502). However, most of the guides are Nile Valley dwellers, not Bedouin, and the groups are often large. Better, more sensitive trips can be arranged from Dahab, Nuweiba or Al-Milga (Katreen) village.

Sleeping

SHARM EL-SHEIKH

Budget

If you're on a budget there's little choice in the vicinity of Sharm el-Sheikh; the best bets are the camps at Shark's Bay (p489).

Youth Hostel (Map p472; ☎ /fax 366 0317; City Council St, Hadaba; members/nonmembers per person with bathroom E£25/56; 🖭) The main attraction of Sharm el-Sheikh's Youth Hostel is that it's the cheapest place to stay in the area. Rooms – all doubles or triples – are soulless but quite decent for the price. It's up on the hill in Hadaba, near the police station and mosque and away from the beach, though frequent microbuses pass by out front that can take you to Na'ama Bay or Ras Um Sid.

Midrange

A cluster of midrange hotels has sprung up in the area rimming Hadaba. While lacking ambience – most hotels are spread along or near a wide concrete strip – prices are more reasonable than on the waterfront, and most places have shuttle buses to take guests to the beach at Ras Um Sid or to Na'ama Bay.

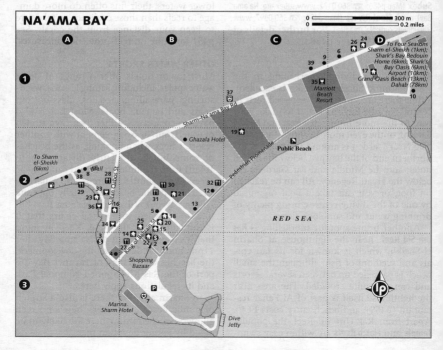

Amar Sina (Map p470; ☎ 366 2222/9; www.minaseg ypt.com; Hadaba; s/d US$45/60; ✗ ⬛ ⬜ ⬛) This popular hotel features domes and brick architecture, and has beach space at Ras Um Sid.

Tropicana Tivoli (Map p470; ☎ 366 1384; www .tropicanahotels.com; Hadaba; s/d US$35/40; ✗ ⬛) A good option for families, with simple but clean rooms with kitchenettes, and beach use at Ras Um Sid.

Sunset Hotel (Map p470; ☎ 366 1673/4; www .hai-partner.com; Hadaba; s/d US$30/40; ✗ ⬛) This three-star hotel has good-value rooms and use of the beach at Ras Um Sid.

Creative Mexicana Sharm Resort (Map p470; ☎ 366 1490, in Cairo ☎ 02-257 7029; www.creative mexicana.com; Hadaba; s/d half board US$75/100; ✗ ✗ ⬛ ⬛) A bright, pleasant place just up the road from Amar Sina hotel, with rooms around a pool-courtyard area.

Top End

Ritz Carlton (Map p470; ☎ 366 1919; www.ritzcarlton .com; Ras Um Sid; r from US$220; ✗ ⬛ ⬛) This luxurious property boasts attractive, well-appointed rooms, large grounds overlooking the water and a child-friendly atmosphere.

NA'AMA BAY
Budget

Pigeon House (Map p486; ☎ 360 0996; fax 360 0995; Sharm-Na'ama Bay rd; s/d E£75/95, with private bathroom &

air-con E£120/170; ✗ ⬜) Rooms here are somewhat faded, but they're good value for the price (which is among the cheapest you'll find in Sharm el-Sheikh), and it's one of the few budget places in Na'ama Bay. It's an easy 10-minute walk to central Na'ama Bay.

Ocean Bay Hotel (Map p486; ☎ 360 1012; s/d US$35/50; ✗ ⬛) A bland but clean and well-located hotel within easy walking distance of Na'ama Bay's beachfront promenade.

Camel Dive Club (Map p486; ☎ 360 0700; www .cameldive.com; King of Bahrain St; dm from US$26) and **Oonas Dive Centre** (Map p486; ☎ 360 0581; www.oonasdivers.com; s/d US$50/75; ✗) also offer cheap(ish) accommodation for people taking their diving courses.

Midrange

Beachfront hotels in Na'ama Bay are generally expensive. For a better deal, choose one that's set back a bit; most of them have beach access.

Camel Hotel (Map p486; ☎ 360 0700; www.camel dive.com; King of Bahrain St, s/d street view US$103/126, pool view US$120/143; ✗ ⬛ ⬛) This small and well-appointed four-star hotel is attached to a dive centre of the same name in the heart of Na'ama Bay. It is efficiently run and quiet, despite its proximity to nightlife, and offers five rooms specially equipped for guests in wheelchairs. All rooms have a

---

INFORMATION
Al-Ahram Bookshop	.................1 A2
Banque Misr (ATM)	...............2 B3
Cardphone	................(see 5)
Commercial International Bank	..(see 4)
Egyptian American Bank	...........3 A3
Felicita.Net	.................(see 3)
Mount Sinai Clinic	.................(see 21)
Na'ama Centre	.................4 A3
Naama Internet	.................(see 4)
National Bank of Egypt (ATM)	................(see 4)
Omar & Omar Pharmacy	..........5 B2
Shamandura Supermarket	.......(see 4)
Thomas Cook	.................6 D1
Tourist Police	.................7 B3
Western Union	................(see 37)
Yes Business Centre	.................8 A2

SIGHTS & ACTIVITIES
Anemone Dive Centre	..........(see 24)
Camel Dive Club	..............(see 14)
Divers International	...............9 C1
Emperor Divers	.................(see 37)
Oonas Dive Centre	...............10 D1
Red Sea Diving College	.............11 B3
Sinai Divers	.................12 B2
Subex	.................13 B2

SLEEPING
Camel Hotel	.................14 B3
Cataract Layalina Resort	...........15 B2
Cataract Resort	.................16 A2
Days Inn Gafy	.................17 D1
Falcon Hotel	.................18 B3
Hilton Fayrouz Village	.............19 C2
Kanabesh Hotel	.................20 B2
Mövenpick Hotel	...............21 B2
Naama Bay Hotel	...............(see 36)
New Tiran Hotel	.................22 B3
Ocean Bay Hotel	...............23 A2
Pigeon House	.................24 D1
Sanafir Hotel	.................25 B2
Sinai Star Hotel	.................26 D1

EATING
Abou es-Sid	.................(see 34)
Al-Nile Market	.................(see 38)
Andrea's	.................(see 3)
Da Franco Pizza & Takeaway	..(see 32)
El-Fawanes Restaurant	.............27 B3
Gado	.................28 A2
Kokai	.................(see 32)
La Rustichella	.................29 A2
Mashy Café	.................(see 25)
Mövenpick Jolie-Ville Bakery	....30 B2
Na'ama Beach Market	.............31 B2

DRINKING
Portofino	.................(see 38)
Safsafa	.................(see 4)
Tam Tam Oriental Café	...........32 B2
Tandoori	.................(see 14)
Bacchus	.................33 A2
Camel Roof Bar	.................(see 14)
Hard Rock Café	.................34 A2
Harry's Pub	.................35 C1
Little Buddha	.................36 B2
Mexicana Bar	.................(see 36)
Pirates' Bar	.................(see 19)

ENTERTAINMENT
Black House Disco	...............37 C1
Bus Stop	.................(see 25)
Mövenpick's Casino Royale	....(see 21)
Pacha	.................(see 25)
Rosetta Hotel	.................(see 37)

SHOPPING
Gafy Mall	.................(see 6)

TRANSPORT
Avis	.................38 A2
Mena Tours	.................39 C1
Sixt Car Rental	.................(see 19)

minifridge, and there's a popular bar and two restaurants. Rates are discounted if you book in advance by email, which can be done via the website. Breakfast costs extra.

Tropicana Garden Palms Hotel (Map p470; ☎ 360 1290/1; www.tropicanahotels.com; Sharm-Na'ama Bay rd; s/d all-inclusive US$80/90; ✂ 🖳 🐾) An appealing place with attractive grounds, two pools, views to the mountains and a children's play area. It's on the inland side of the main road in Na'ama Bay, several kilometres east of the central strip, and offers an hourly shuttle service to the beach at Shark's Bay.

Sanafir Hotel (Map p486; ☎ 360 0197; reservation@ sanafirhotel.com; King of Bahrain St; s/d US$108/134; ✂ 🖳 🐾) The nerve centre of Na'ama Bay, the Sanafir was one of the first hotels to be built here. In recent years it has expanded its food and entertainment offerings at the expense of its hotel guests. But the older rooms with their domed ceilings and built-in beds are pleasant, if noisy due to nightly partying at Bus Stop (see p491). Breakfast costs extra.

Falcon Hotel (Map p486; ☎ 360 0827/8; King of Bahrain St; s/d US$56/88; ✂ 🐾) This conveniently located Swiss-run place has small but spotless rooms around a bougainvillea-draped courtyard, and a small pool.

New Tiran Hotel (Map p486; ☎ 360 0225; newtiran@ access.com.eg; King of Bahrain St; s/d US$60/70; ✂ 🐾) Another centrally located hotel, with 48 rooms around a pleasant pool-courtyard area. All rooms have minifridge, and there's beach access. For more quiet, ask for a room away from the street.

Sinai Star Hotel (Map p486; ☎ 360 0652; www .tropicanahotels.com; Sharm-Na'ama Bay rd; s/d US$45/65; ✂ 🖳 🐾) A plain but well-run three star set back from the road behind Na'ama Bay, and under the management of the Tropicana chain. For some sun and sand, a shuttle bus runs about four times daily to/from Grand Oasis beach near the airport.

Also recommended:

Kanabesh Hotel (Map p486; ☎ 360 0184; kanabesh@ access.com.eg; King of Bahrain St; s/d US$56/68; ✂ 🐾) Central and pleasant, with a variety of rooms, including some split-levels.

Days Inn Gafy (Map p486; ☎ 360 0210; www.daysinn .com; Sharm-Na'ama Bay rd; s/d half board US$80/100; ✂ 🐾) A bland but comfortable hotel just opposite Pigeon House Hotel, on the beach side of the road, with mandatory half board.

Naama Bay Hotel (Map p486; ☎ 360 0570; www .naamabayhotel.com; s/d US$90/130; ✂ ✂ 🖳 🐾)

This large, multistorey complex is in the heart of Na'ama Bay, with a gelato shop, its own beach and several wheelchair-accessible rooms.

Cataract Resort (Map p486; ☎ 360 1820/8/9; www .cataracthotels.com; Sultan Qabos St; s/d US$110/140; ✂ 🐾) More of the same; under the same management as Cataract Layalina Resort.

Cataract Layalina Resort (Map p486; ☎ 360 1820/8/9; King of Bahrain St) Just around the corner from the similarly priced Cataract Resort.

Top End

The entire coast from Na'ama Bay northwards towards the airport has been the target of a massive construction boom in recent years, and Sharm is now home to a large number of five-star resorts. Despite the luxury names, most are geared to visitors on all-in tours, and prices are considerably cheaper if booked from outside Egypt or as part of a package.

Sofitel Sharm el-Sheikh Coralia Hotel (Map p470; ☎ 360 0081; www.sofitel.com; s/d US$194/212; ✂ 🖳 🐾) Dominating the bay's northern cliffs, this whitewashed hotel terraces down towards the sea. The vaguely Moorish-looking rooms have wooden furniture and stunning views over the bay, as do some of the bars and restaurants. There's also a wonderful and very large pool and a children's play area.

Hyatt Regency Sharm el-Sheikh (Map p470; ☎ 360 1234; www.sharm.hyatt.com; s/d from US$195/226; ✂ 🖳 🐾) Luxury perched above the rich corals of the Near Garden reef, with lashings of marble, large rooms, great sea views and a pool with a water slide. It also has several bars and restaurants.

Hilton Fayrouz Village (Map p486; ☎ 360 0137; www.hiltonworldresorts.com; s/d from US$100/125; ✂ 🖳 🐾) This sprawl of deluxe air-con bungalows along the promenade is well located and somehow feels a little more intimate than some of its giant neighbours. As you'd expect of a Hilton, it has the usual pools, restaurants and beach facilities, and an appealing grassy lawn.

Other recommendations:

Iberotel Lido (Map p470; ☎ 360 2603/4; www .iberotel-eg.com; s/d US$75/100; 🖳 🐾) A small and good-value hotel in a central yet tranquil setting at the southern end of Na'ama Bay.

Mövenpick Hotel (Map p486; ☎ 360 0100; www .moevenpick-hotels.com; s/d from US$135/160; ✂ ✂ 🖳 🐾) A vast, sprawling and very comfortable albeit rather centreless place along the Na'ama Bay waterfront with extensive facilities, including a fitness centre and a casino.

SHARK'S BAY

The Shark's Bay area, about 6km northeast of Na'ama Bay along the road to the airport and easily reachable by taxi, was once home to a quiet Bedouin village. Over the past decade it has been developed with amazing rapidity, and now a row of exclusive luxury hotels lines the coast. The only exceptions are two camps on a placid cove that are good choices for budget travellers, and more tranquil than the alternatives in town. Between the two camps is a tiny market area with Internet access and a small supermarket selling a decent supply of basics. If you're staying at one of the top-end resorts, your every whim will be catered for on their grounds.

Budget

Shark's Bay Bedouin Home (☎ 360 0942; www .sharksbay.com; sea-view huts with fan & shared bathroom s/d/tr US$15/19/22.50, with air-con & private bathroom US$25/37.50/49; ✷) This long-standing Bedouin-owned camp – also known as Shark's Bay Umbi – has a relaxing ambience, simple but clean huts with shared bathrooms up on the cliff, and pricier huts down below with air-con and bathroom. There's also the Bedouin-style tented Shark's Bay Umbi Restaurant (mains E£20 to E£35) overlooking the water.

Shark's Bay Oasis (☎ 360 0450; sharksbayoasis@ hotmail.com; huts s/d US$15/19, bungalow US$25/37.50; ✷) Next door to Shark's Bay Bedouin Home, with similar facilities, including bungalows with air-con and bathroom up on the cliff overlooking the water, and no-frills huts down below.

To reach both camps, just tell the taxi driver 'Shark's Bay Bedouin'; expect to pay about E£25 from Na'ama Bay and E£50 from the port at Sharm. If you're driving, take the airport road from town to a right-hand turn-off for the Savoy and Conrad Concorde hotels, follow this road for 400m to the right-hand turn-off for Gardenia Plaza, then turn and continue 2km further to Shark's Bay.

Top-End

Four Seasons Sharm el-Sheikh (☎ 360 3555; www .fourseasons.com/sharmelsheikh; s/d sea view US$487/548; ✕ ✷ ⬛ ⬤) A tasteful Arabesque-style re-

sort has wonderful views over the Strait of Tiran, nicely decorated suite-sized rooms, palm-ringed courtyards and excellent facilities, including a spa.

Eating

SHARM EL-SHEIKH

Except as noted, all listings here are in the Sharm Old Market area of Sharm el-Sheikh. Small, friendly, local-style restaurants predominate, but the food is good and the service usually efficient.

Restaurants

Al-Fanar (Map p470; ☎ 366 2218; www.elfanar.net; Ras Um Sid; dishes E£40-130; ◔ 10am-10.30pm) This upscale place has an excellent seafront location at the base of the lighthouse, cosy alcoves, Bedouin-influenced décor, indoor and outdoor dining and a large Italian menu. The views over the water are marvellous, the food – especially the thin-crust pizza – is well prepared and tasty, and the beers and wine are well chilled.

Abou Hamada (Map p472; ☎ 366 3016; mains E£25-35) This down-to-earth place serves delicious seafood; try the mixed grill with mezze, or the grilled catch of the day.

Sinai Star (Map p472; ☎ 366 0323; dishes E£20-45) Another no-nonsense place serving up tasty seafood meals. It doesn't have beer, but will bring you some from the Al-Ahram Beverages shop next door.

Safsafa Restaurant (Map p472; ☎ 366 0474; dishes E£20-50; ✷) A small establishment offering some of the freshest fish in Sharm. Try the calamari and rice, with tahini and *baba ghanoug* (puree of grilled aubergines with tahini and olive oil). Whole fish is priced between E£40 and E£50 per kilo. No alcohol is served.

Al-Dahan Restaurant (Map p472; ☎ 366 0840; meals E£15-50) Small 'Oriental' restaurant serving Egyptian/Middle Eastern food, with the emphasis on mezze and meat.

El-Masrien (Map p472; ☎ 366 2904; dishes E£5-25) A small local-style place with grills and *kofta* (mincemeat and spices grilled on a skewer).

Quick Eats

King (Map p472; dishes E£2-7; ◔ from 7am) A clean and popular *fuul* (fava bean paste) and *ta'amiyya* takeaway in the centre of the market, with a range of snacks and the additional advantage of being open early in the morning.

Koshary El-Salam (Map p472; dishes E£2-5; ☺ from 8am) Another local favourite, with heaping bowls of kushari in your choice of size.

Self-Catering

There are several small but well-stocked supermarkets in Sharm Old Market, including Supermarket El-Baraka next to the King restaurant, and the large Sharm Express Supermarket just outside the market gates along the road towards Ras Mohammed. Beer and wine can be bought at **Al-Ahram Beverages** (Map p472; ☎ 366 3133), next to Sinai Star restaurant.

NA'AMA BAY

Na'ama Bay has a large selection of eateries, and it's easy to while away a few hours each evening walking along the beachfront promenade and sampling different places – although it takes some searching to find real standouts.

Restaurants

Little Buddha (Map p486; ☎ 360 1030; www.littlebuddha sharm.com; Naama Bay Hotel; mains E£25-95; ☒) Currently one of the places to go in Sharm, featuring Asian fusion cuisine, an excellent sushi bar and a hugely popular bar-lounge area that stays open until 3am.

Tam Tam Oriental Café (Map p486; ☎ 360 0150; Ghazala Hotel; dishes E£20-60) This somewhat overpriced but popular Egyptian restaurant is along the waterside promenade in front of Ghazala Hotel. It's a laid-back place where you can delve into a range of Egyptian fare, including mezze, kushari and roast pigeon, while relaxing on cushions overlooking the beach or puffing on a *sheesha* (water pipe).

Tandoori (Map p486; ☎ 360 0700, ext 329; Camel Hotel, King of Bahrain St; dishes E£25-100; ☺ 6.30-11.30pm) This small place in the courtyard of the Camel Hotel has what many consider to be Sharm's best Indian food, including a selection of tandoori dishes and an excellent *dhal makhani* (dish of black lentils and red kidney beans). Advance bookings highly recommended.

Sala Thai (Map p470; ☎ 360 1234; Hyatt Regency Sharm el-Sheikh; dishes E£40-120; ☒) Delicious Thai food and pleasing aesthetics with teak décor and an outdoor terrace overlooking the sea.

Safsafa (Map p486; Na'ama Centre; dishes E£25-50; ☒) An upmarket branch of the original Sharm el-Sheikh favourite, Safsafa offers a wide range of seafood dishes, including pizzas. The only drawback is its stale location in a mall.

El-Fawanes Restaurant (Map p486; King of Bahrain St; mains E£40-80) Tasty Lebanese food and a pleasant upstairs terrace dining area.

Portofino (Map p486; ☎ 360 1591; Sharm-Na'ama Bay rd; mains E£60-80; ☒) Delicious Italian food in a quiet, candlelit setting. It's next to Avis car rental.

La Rustichella (Map p486; ☎ 360 1154; pizza E£25-40, mains E£40-75; ☒) More Italian cuisine, featuring seafood dishes and a mellow atmosphere. They have various specials, including a lunchtime offer from noon to 4pm with pizza or pasta plus ice cream for E£38, and an evening two-/three-course meal for E£44/E£60 between 4pm and 7pm.

Mashy Café (Map p486; ☎ 360 0197; Sanafir Hotel; dishes E£35-75) A decent Lebanese restaurant on the pavement outside Sanafir Hotel.

Andrea's (Map p486; ☎ 360 0972; opposite Hard Rock Café; dishes E£20-40) Reasonably priced and reasonably tasty Egyptian food from a Cairo-based chain served in an outdoor restaurant in the centre of the action.

Also recommended:

Da Franco Pizza & Takeaway (Map p486; ☎ 360 0150; Ghazala Hotel; dishes E£25-110) Very tasty pizza, pasta and other Italian cuisine in a waterfront setting.

Kokai (Map p486; ☎ 360 0150; Ghazala Hotel; dishes E£55-70) Primarily Japanese cuisine served in a waterfront setting.

Abou es-Sid (Map p486; ☎ 360 3910; next to Hard Rock Café; ☒) A branch of the Cairo favourite, featuring *molokhiyya* (stewed leaf soup) and other Egyptian cuisine.

Quick Eats

Gado (Map p486; Sultan Qabos St; dishes E£2-10; ☺ 24hr) A *fuul* and *ta'amiyya* place that's clean and deservedly popular. It has indoor and outdoor seating, and is one of the few places that's open early.

Self-Catering

There are numerous supermarkets in central Na'ama Bay, including **Al-Nile Market** (Map p486; next to Avis; ☺ 24hr), and **Na'ama Beach Market** (Map p486; ☺ 9am-2am) opposite the **Mövenpick Jolie-Ville Bakery** (Map p486; Mövenpick Hotel; ☺ 11am-11pm), which is a good place for fresh rolls and pastries.

Drinking

Sharm el-Sheikh has one of Egypt's liveliest bar scenes. Many places have early evening happy hours, and some of the dive schools along the beach have small bars too; watch for specials advertised along the promenade.

Al-Fanar (Map p470; ☎ 366 2218; www.elfanar .net; Ras Um Sid) Superb views, drinks every evening, and a popular open-air party (admission US$25) on Wednesday night from 11.30pm. There's no entry charge if you have dinner at the restaurant.

Hard Rock Café (Map p486; Sultan Qabos St, Na'ama Bay) A late-night disco-bar with dancing, and one of Sharm's most popular nightspots. Dancing starts at midnight and goes on until late.

Camel Roof Bar (Map p486; ☎ 360 0700; Camel Hotel, Na'ama Bay) A favourite among dive instructors and an optimal place to start off the evening in the centre of things.

Pirates' Bar (Map p486; ☎ 360 0137; Hilton Fayrouz Village, Na'ama Bay) A cosy, pub-style bar where divers congregate for an early evening drink or bar meal. Happy hour is from 5.30pm to 7.30pm.

Harry's Pub (Map p486; ☎ 360 0190; Marriott Beach Resort, Na'ama Bay) This expensive pseudo-English pub has a large selection of beers on tap and occasional special nights with unlimited draught beer at a very reasonable price.

Little Buddha (Map p486; ☎ 360 1030; www.little buddhasharm.com; Na'ama Bay Hotel, Na'ama Bay) A large circular place with dim lights, big, cushiony chairs and mellow ambience. Things start to get going after 11pm, once the kitchen has closed.

Mexicana Bar (Map p486; ☎ 360 0570; Na'ama Bay Hotel, Na'ama Bay) A small and sometimes happening place close to the promenade.

La Folie Bar (Map p470; ☎ 360 2603; Iberotel Lido, Na'ama Bay; ⏲ 2pm-2am) For a more sedate start to your evening, head to this quiet, pleasant bar on the water overlooking the bright lights of Na'ama Bay.

Bacchus (Map p486; ☎ 360 3948; Sultan Qabos St, Na'ama Bay; ⏲ 9am-4am) This place sells beer and wine to go at a considerable mark-up.

Entertainment

A young resident population and large number of relatively wealthy tourists make Sharm el-Sheikh's entertainment scene just as lively as its bar scene. Dancing gets going around midnight and ends at dawn.

Pacha (Map p486; ☎ 012 399 5020; www.pacha sharm.com; Sanafir Hotel, King of Bahrain St, Na'ama Bay; admission E£100, except Thu E£175; ⏲ 10pm-4am)

The Sanafir is the hub of Sharm's nightlife, with Pacha its most popular venue. There's a daily discotheque (with 'VIP' seating in the adjoining Bus Stop pub), and Thursday nights in particular see the crowd go wild. Owner Adli Mestakawi also holds Echo Temple Concerts in the desert outside Sharm on Fridays during the high season (E£145), bringing big name singers to play to audiences of thousands under the stars. Watch for Pacha's advertising around town to see what is playing.

Black House Disco (Map p486; ☎ 360 1888; Rosetta Hotel, Na'ama Bay; ⏲ 11pm-4am) A popular place with a good DJ that makes an amenable change of pace from Pacha.

Mövenpick's Casino Royale (Map p486; ☎ 360 0100; Mövenpick Hotel, Na'ama Bay; ⏲ 9pm-4am) One of several casinos where visitors (no Egyptians allowed) can gamble away their dollars and yen (no Egyptian pounds).

Getting There & Away
AIR
EgyptAir (Map p472; ☎ 366 1056/8/9; Sharm al-Maya; ⏲ 9am-9pm) has daily flights to Cairo (one way E£739), and twice-weekly flights to Luxor (E£535). Charter flights from various European cities run year-round.

BOAT
Tickets for the high-speed ferry to Hurghada from Sharm el-Sheikh (US$40, 90 minutes) can be bought from various travel agencies in town, including **Mena Tours** (Map p486; ☎ 260 0190; Marriott Beach Resort, inland side of Sharm-Na'ama Bay rd, Na'ama Bay). They are also sold at the ferry office at the port on days that the ferry runs, beginning at 4pm (two hours before departure time). Boats leave from the port west of Sharm al-Maya at 6pm on Saturday, Monday, Tuesday and Thursday; you must be at the port with your passport one hour before departure. The boat can also take vehicles (from E£150, depending on engine size). For more on the ferry, see p438.

BUS
The bus station (Map p470) is along the Sharm–Na'ama Bay road behind the Mobil station. Seats on buses to Cairo should be reserved in advance. Buy tickets from the following bus companies at the station.

Superjet (☎ 366 1622, in Cairo ☎ 02-290 9017) runs buses to Cairo (E£68, six hours) at noon, 1pm, 3pm, 5pm and 11pm, with the 3pm bus continuing on to Alexandria (E£88, nine hours).

East Delta Bus Co (☎ 366 0660) has buses to Cairo (E£55 to E£65, six to eight hours) at 7am, 10am, 11am, noon, 1pm, 2.30pm, 4.30pm and 5.30pm. There are daily buses to Suez (E£30, five hours) at 7am, 9am and 10am; to Dahab (E£11, 1¼ hours) and Nuweiba (E£21.50, three hours) at 9am, 2.30pm and 5pm; and to Taba (E£26.50, 4½ hours) at 9am. A bus to St Katherine's departs at 7.30am (E£28, 3½ hours), and a direct bus to Luxor (E£95, 12 to 15 hours) via Hurghada leaves at 6pm.

Getting Around
TO/FROM THE AIRPORT
Sharm el-Sheikh International Airport is about 10km north of Na'ama Bay at Ras Nasrany; taxis charge E£20 to E£25.

BICYCLE
Standard and cross-country bicycles can be hired from stands along the promenade in Na'ama Bay from E£25 per day.

CAR
Car-rental agencies in Na'ama Bay include **Avis** (Map p486; ☎ 360 2400, 360 0979; Sharm-Na'ama Bay rd, Na'ama Bay), just west of Mall 7; **Hertz** (Map p472; ☎ 366 2299; Bank St, Hadaba) and **Sixt Car Rental** (Map p486; ☎ 360 0137; Hilton Fayrouz Village). All charge about US$80 for a basic saloon, and US$120 and up for a roomier 4WD. Unlimited kilometre arrangements generally require a minimum three- to four-day rental.

MICROBUS & TAXI
Toyota pick-ups and minibuses regularly ply the stretch between central Na'ama Bay and Sharm el-Sheikh. The going fare is E£2, though foreigners are often charged E£5. Taxis charge a minimum of E£10 between the two centres, and between Hadaba and Na'ama Bay, and from E£5 within Na'ama Bay. Many of the hotels above Ras Um Sid have their own shuttles to Na'ama Bay.

The usual warnings about hitching apply, and women should avoid it completely.

NABQ
Thirty-five kilometres north of Sharm el-Sheikh is Nabq, the largest coastal protectorate on the Gulf of Aqaba. It is named after

an oasis that lies within its boundaries, and straddles 600 sq km of land and sea between the Strait of Tiran and Dahab. Nabq's main attraction is its **mangrove forest**, which is along the shoreline at the mouth of Wadi Kid, and is the most northerly mangrove stand in the world. Mangrove root systems filter most of the salt from sea water and help to stabilise shorelines, while also providing an important habitat for birds and fish. Just inland from the mangrove forest are the dunes of Wadi Kid, which are home to one of the Middle East's largest stands of **arak bushes** (arak twigs were traditionally used by Bedouin to clean teeth). Gazelles, rock hyraxes and Nubian ibexes can be seen in the protectorate, and it is home to two villages of Bedouin from the Mizena tribe. Offshore there are rich reefs with easy access, although visibility can be poor because of sediment from the mangroves.

Because it is less frequently visited than Ras Mohammed, Nabq is a good place to see Sinai as it was before the arrival of mass tourism. There is a **visitors' centre** (admission US$5; ☾ 8am-5pm), several hiking trails, clearly marked snorkelling spots and designated camping areas.

To visit Nabq, you'll need a vehicle or will have to join a tour from one of the resorts. Most of the dive centres in Dahab offer dive safaris to Nabq, some by camel, and **Abanoub Travel** (☎ 352 0201; abanoubt@menanet.net; Mizena) in Nuweiba can also organise visits. If you drive, remember that vehicles are strictly forbidden to leave the tracks. The visitors' centre is off the road leading from Sharm el-Sheikh past the airport and Ras Nasrany.

DAHAB
☎ 069
With its golden beaches, rugged mountain backdrop and smooth fusion of hippie mellowness and resort chic, Dahab has become one of Sinai's most popular coastal destinations. Unlike most of Egypt's other resorts, it's also a place where individual travellers are still the rule rather than the exception, and it offers a wide array of accommodation and diversions catering to all tastes and budgets.

Dahab (the name means 'gold' in Arabic, after the area's sandy coastline) long had a reputation as the Koh Samui of the Middle East. But in recent years it has grown up and while the banana fritters remain, they now coexist with Internet cafés, Italian restaurants and upscale hotels. The once chilled-out beachfront area of Assalah is now lined by a paved path, and you're just as likely to see New Age families strolling along as tie-dyed beatniks.

The town makes a convenient base for diving and desert trips, and if you find the ambience doesn't suit, the more homogenised attractions of Sharm el-Sheikh are an easy 85km bus ride further south.

Orientation

There are two parts to Dahab: the small and newer area of Dahab City, with a smattering of resort hotels, the bus station, post and phone offices and a bank; and Assalah, which is north along the beach, and was originally a Bedouin village. Assalah is divided into Masbat and Mashraba. Masbat starts roughly at the lighthouse at the northern end of Assalah and is made up of a stretch of 'camps', hotels and laid-back restaurants among the palm trees, as well as a busy little bazaar. To the south, starting roughly at the ruins (currently off limits as an excavation site), is the slightly more staid Mashraba, named after the freshwater springs that apparently exist around the beach. In the centre of Masbat, just north of Red Sea Relax Terrace Restaurant, is a bridge, which makes a convenient landmark and is a good place to find taxis.

Information

EMERGENCY
Police (☎ 364 0213/5; Masbat) Near Ghazala Supermarket.
Tourist police (☎ 364 0188; Dahab City)

INTERNET ACCESS
Most of the many cafés in Dahab charge E£5 per hour.
Download.Net (per hr E£4; Sharia Al-Mashraba, Mashraba; ☽ 24hr) Next to Nesima Resort.
Felopater Internet Cafe (per hr E£5); Masbat (100m south of police station on beachside promenade; ☽ 10am-midnight); Mashraba (Sharia Al-Mashraba, just north of Nesima Resort; ☽ 24hr)

MEDICAL SERVICES
Dahab Hospital (☎ 364 0208; Dahab City)
Dr Sherif Salah (☎ 012 220 8484) Local doctor recommended by most hotels; office at the Hilton Dahab Resort.

MONEY
Banque du Caire (Sharia Al-Mashraba, Mashraba; ☽ 9am-2pm & 6-9pm Sat-Thu, 9-11am & 6-9pm Fri) Near Inmo Divers.
Commercial International Bank ATM (Blue Hole Plaza) About 1.5km northeast of the Hilton, between the resort strip and Mashraba.
National Bank of Egypt Assalah (just north of Shark Club Restaurant; ☽ 9am-10pm); Dahab City (☽ 9am-2.30pm & 6-8pm Sun-Thu); Swiss Inn Golden Beach Resort (Resort Strip; ☽ 9am-1pm) The Dahab City and Assalah branches each have an ATM.
Western Union (☎ 364 0466; just north of Bamboo House Hotel, Masbat; ☽ 8.30am-2pm & 6-10pm Sat-Thu, 3-10pm Fri)

POST
Main post office (Dahab City; ☽ 8.30am-2.30pm) Post boxes are also outside Ghazala Supermarket, Masbat, and next to Red Sea Relax Terrace Restaurant, Masbat.

TELEPHONE
In addition to the telephone centrale and cardphones, you will find numerous call centres along the beachfront in Assalah where you can dial internationally for E£7 per minute.
Call centre (Masbat; per min E£7; ☽ 10am-3pm & 6-9pm Sat-Thu, 3-9pm Fri) Just north of Western Union.
Telephone centrale (Dahab City; ☽ 24hr) There are cardphones throughout Assalah. Cards are sold at the Ghazala Supermarket and at most small shops.

Activities

DIVING
Other than just lounging around, diving is the most popular activity in Dahab. There are several dozen dive clubs, offering a full range of diving possibilities. Two favourites are **Fantasea Dive Centre** (☎ /fax 364 0483; www .fantaseadiving.net) and **Fish & Friends** (☎ 364 0720; www.fishandfriends.com). Choose your club carefully, as some places have less than stellar reputations when it comes to safety standards (see p459 for recommendations).

SNORKELLING
The reefs off Assalah are often strewn with litter, but if you can ignore this, the reef at the northern end of Mashraba has table corals and impressive fish life. Also worthwhile are the reefs off the southern end of Mashraba, just before the lagoon; **Lighthouse Reef**, a sheltered snorkelling site at the northern tip of Assalah; and the popular **Eel Garden**,

SINAI

SINAI

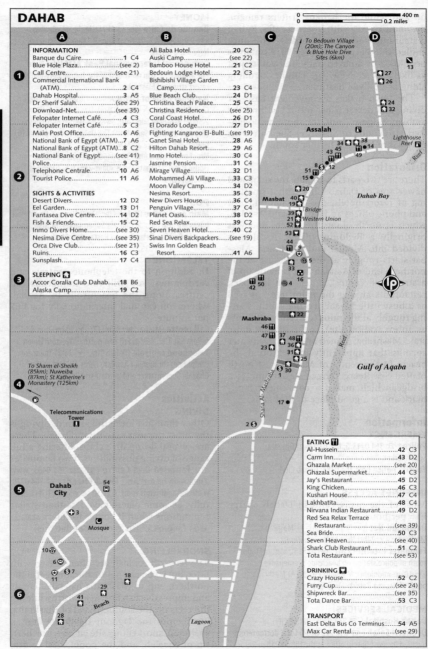

DAHAB

0 ————— 400 m
0 ————— 0.2 miles

INFORMATION
Banque du Caire..........................1 C4
Blue Hole Plaza........................(see 2)
Call Centre.............................(see 21)
Commercial International Bank
  (ATM)....................................2 C4
Dahab Hospital.............................3 A5
Dr Sherif Salah.......................(see 29)
Download-Net............................(see 35)
Felopater Internet Café...................4 C3
Felopater Internet Café...................5 C3
Main Post Office..........................6 A6
National Bank of Egypt (ATM)..............7 A6
National Bank of Egypt (ATM)..............8 C2
National Bank of Egypt.................(see 41)
Police.....................................9 C3
Telephone Centrale.......................10 A6
Tourist Police...........................11 A6

SIGHTS & ACTIVITIES
Desert Divers.............................12 D2
Eel Garden................................13 D1
Fantasea Dive Centre......................14 D2
Fish & Friends............................15 C2
Inmo Divers Home......................(see 30)
Nesima Dive Centre....................(see 35)
Orca Dive Club........................(see 21)
Ruins.....................................16 C3
Sunsplash.................................17 C4

SLEEPING 🛏
Accor Coralia Club Dahab.................18 B6
Alaska Camp...............................19 C2

Ali Baba Hotel............................20 C2
Auski Camp............................(see 22)
Bamboo House Hotel........................21 C2
Bedouin Lodge Hotel......................22 C3
Bishibishi Village Garden
  Camp....................................23 C4
Blue Beach Club..........................24 D1
Christina Beach Palace...................25 C4
Christina Residence...................(see 25)
Coral Coast Hotel........................26 D1
El Dorado Lodge..........................27 D1
Fighting Kangaroo El-Bulti...........(see 19)
Ganet Sinai Hotel........................28 A6
Hilton Dahab Resort......................29 A6
Inmo Hotel................................30 C4
Jasmine Pension..........................31 C4
Mirage Village...........................32 D1
Mohammed Ali Village.....................33 C3
Moon Valley Camp.........................34 D2
Nesima Resort............................35 C3
New Divers House.........................36 C4
Penguin Village..........................37 C4
Planet Oasis.............................38 D2
Red Sea Relax............................39 C4
Seven Heaven Hotel.......................40 C2
Sinai Divers Backpackers..............(see 19)
Swiss Inn Golden Beach
  Resort..................................41 A6

To Bedouin Village
(20m); The Canyon
& Blue Hole Dive
Sites (6km)

Assalah

Lighthouse
Reef

Reef

Masbat

Dahab Bay

Bridge
Western Union

Mashraba

Red

Gulf of Aqaba

To Sharm el-Sheikh
(85km); Nuweiba
(87km); St Katherine's
Monastery (125km)

Telecommunications
Tower

Dahab
City

Mosque

Sharia Al-Mashraba

EATING 🍴
Al-Hussein...............................42 C3
Carm Inn.................................43 D2
Ghazala Market.......................(see 20)
Ghazala Supermarket......................44 C3
Jay's Restaurant.........................45 D2
King Chicken.............................46 C3
Kushari House............................47 C4
Lakhbatita...............................48 C4
Nirvana Indian Restaurant................49 D2
Red Sea Relax Terrace
  Restaurant..........................(see 39)
Sea Bride................................50 C3
Seven Heaven.........................(see 40)
Shark Club Restaurant....................51 C2
Tota Restaurant......................(see 53)

DRINKING 🍸
Crazy House..............................52 C2
Furry Cup............................(see 24)
Shipwreck Bar........................(see 35)
Tota Dance Bar...........................53 C3

TRANSPORT
East Delta Bus Co Terminus...............54 A5
Max Car Rental.......................(see 29)

Beach

Lagoon

just north of Assalah, where a colony of eels lives on the sandy sea bed. About 6km further north are the **Canyon** and **Blue Hole** dive sites. Despite their intimidating reputation as danger zones for careless divers, the tops of the reefs are teeming with life, making them fine snorkelling destinations when the sea is calm. It's easy to find half-day tours to both sites, but watch for hidden 'extras' such as overpriced drinks and gear-minding fees at some of the cafés around the Blue Hole. Many dive centres also organise dive safaris to the Ras Abu Gallum and Nabq Protectorates (p499 and p492 respectively). Although most cater to divers, some will also take snorkellers along.

You can hire snorkelling gear from all the dive centres and many other places in Masbat for about E£25 to E£40 per day. Keep in mind that some of the reefs have unexpected currents. After watching a dramatic rescue at a reef close to Eel Garden, one reader discovered that several people had drowned there.

OTHER WATER SPORTS
Pedalos and kayaks can be rented at the northern end of Masbat and at the holiday villages on the lagoon. Windsurfing is another popular pastime. Hilton Dahab Resort and Swiss Inn Golden Beach Resort have windsurfing centres, and the bay there is excellent for it. Windsurfers can also be rented at the northern end of Dahab Bay, although the wind tends to be gusty here. Kitesurfing is also starting to take off in Dahab, although offshore winds limit the areas where it can be done.

There's no beach to speak of in Assalah itself; instead the rocky coastline leads straight out onto the reef. For the golden sands after which Dahab was named, you'll need to head down to the lagoon area where the resorts are clustered.

CAMEL & JEEP TREKS
Treks to Sinai's interior or to Ras Abu Gallum are easy to arrange in Dahab. When choosing who to go with, try to find a Bedouin – or at least someone who works with Bedouin – because many are excluded from the tourist industry, which tends to be dominated by migrants from the Nile Valley. Camel drivers congregate along the waterfront in the village. Register with the police

before beginning the trek, and don't pay the camel driver until you return to the village. **Centre for Sinai** (☎ 364 0702; www.centre4sinai.com .eg) is one outfit that tries to promote knowledge of the local culture as well as showing visitors the sights and is a good place to look for guides. **Man & the Environment Dahab** (MATE; ☎ 364 1091; www.mate-dahab.com) is an environmental education centre that helps arrange treks with Bedouin guides. **Nesima Dive Centre** (☎ 364 0320; Nesima Resort, Mashraba) and **Orca Dive Club** (☎ /fax 364 0020) also use local guides for their excursions. All of the hotels, dive centres and travel agencies also offer trips to the Coloured Canyon (p502) and Ras Abu Gallum (p499). Itineraries are generally custom-designed but expect to pay from E£40 per person (with a minimum of four people) for a morning jeep trip to the Blue Hole or from E£70 for an evening trip into the mountains with dinner at a Bedouin camp. Camel trips are more expensive – from about E£300 per person per day for a three-day trek, including all food and water.

HORSE RIDING
If you want to go riding, just wait on the beach in Mashraba for one of the Bedouin who walk up and down with horses for hire. Rates start at about E£20 per hour. You can also ask around the camps. **Blue Beach Club** (☎ 364 0411; reservations@bluebeachclub.com; Assalah) can arrange horses for E£80 per hour, and it's also possible to organise horse riding at the **Accor Coralia Club Dahab** (☎ 364 0301; www .accorhotel.com; Resort Strip).

Sleeping
BUDGET
Most budget travellers head straight for the camps of Assalah. The cheapest ones are generally compounds with spartan stone, cement or reed huts, usually with two or three mattresses tossed on the floor, and communal bathroom facilities. Some have attractive waterfront areas with cushioned seating shaded by palm groves, and many also have pricier rooms with private bathrooms.

When choosing a place remember that concrete huts with iron roofs are hotter than those made of reeds, but the latter may be less secure; ask for a padlock. Also check that there's electricity and running water – some places have hot water – as well as decent mattresses, fly screens and fans. The following list is a small sampling of what is available. Prices at most places can be negotiated during the low season.

Penguin Village (☎ 364 1047; www.penguindivers .com; Mashraba; s/d E£60/80, with air-con E£75/100, with sea view E£80/120; ✖ ⬛) This agreeable place – these days more a hotel than a camp – sits behind a cluster of palms in a relatively quiet setting on the waterfront in Mashraba. It has a whitewashed block of simple, clean rooms – all with bathroom – and staff can help you organise jeep and camel safaris. Breakfast isn't included in the room price.

Sunsplash (☎ 364 0932; www.sunsplash-divers.com; Mashraba; bungalow E£40, s/d with private bathroom E£60/120; ✖) A friendly German-run dive centre set on its own at the southern end of Mashraba, with a quiet beachfront location and your choice of bungalows or simple but comfortable rooms. All are spotless, and there's a pleasant restaurant and a beachside lounging area. Breakfast isn't included in the price.

Seven Heaven Hotel (☎ 364 0080; www.7heaven hotel.com; Masbat; huts d E£10, d with air-con E£50-60; ✖) This deservedly popular camp has wooden huts around a small courtyard, a range of rooms (the upstairs ones cost more), a rooftop where you can set out a mattress for E£4 and a dive centre. Breakfast costs extra.

Alaska Camp (☎ 364 1004; www.dahabescape.com; Masbat; huts E£20, d with bathroom & fan/air-con E£40/60; ✖) Good, no-frills and centrally located, with a choice of double huts or simple rooms with bathroom and either a fan or air-con. It's also the base of Sinai Divers Backpackers; try ☎ 012 396 6397 or backpackers@sinai divers.com for more information.

Auski Camp (☎ 364 0474; auskicamp@hotmail.com; Mashraba; s/d E£20/25, with private bathroom E£50/60) This popular camp has simple rooms, hot water and beach access. It's run with the neighbouring Bedouin Lodge Hotel.

Bedouin Lodge Hotel (☎ 364 0317; www.bedouin divers.com; Mashraba; s/d from E£60/70; ✖) This place offers more upscale rooms than Auski Camp – all with private bathroom and some with views of the water – and has a dive centre. The compound is at the southern end of the boardwalk.

Mirage Village (☎ 364 0341; www.mirage.com.eg; Assalah; s/d US$19/25; ✖) Pleasant rooms – all with fly screens and bathroom – around a courtyard, plus a cushioned waterside seating area and a restaurant. Breakfast costs extra. It's just north of the lighthouse area and a good choice if you're looking for the laid-back ambience of a camp, but with some comforts.

Mohammed Ali Village (☎ 364 0380; www.club-red .com; Masbat; d with fan/air-con/sea view E£50/80/150; ✖) In the centre of Assalah, this popular place is the largest and longest running of the camps, though its huts are long since gone, replaced by clean but often noisy rooms.

Bishibishi Village Garden Camp (☎ 364 0727; kingjimmy99@hotmail.com; Sharia Al-Mashraba, Mashraba; s/d with fan E£30/35, with private bathroom & air-con from E£50/60; ✖) A very basic camp set back from the sea on the street parallel to the waterfront. All accommodation comes with towel and toilet paper, and there's a Bedouin-style seating area around a fire pit. Breakfast isn't offered.

Moon Valley Camp (☎ 010 647 2881; moonvalley@ hotmail.com; Masbat; dm E£10, r with fan & private bath-room E£25) One of the older camps, with small rooms with fan and hot water. It's in the thick of things along the restaurant strip, and sometimes noisy at night.

Fighting Kangaroo El-Bulti (☎ 012 359 8741; Masbat; d with/without bathroom E£60/40, with bathroom & air-con E£90; ✖) A quiet, homey place with rather dark rooms set around a tiny garden. They're made more appealing by the fact that they're among the cheapest rooms with private bathroom that you'll find in town. Management can also help you organise reasonably priced jeep safaris.

Planet Oasis (☎ 364 1324; www.planetdivers.com; Masbat; d US$22-32; ✖) A new place near the lighthouse with simple, clean rooms and a breezy terrace.

Jasmine Pension (☎ 364 0852; www.jasminepen sion.com; Mashraba; d E£60, with sea view & air-con E£100; ✖) Small, bland rooms and a beachside restaurant. It's on the seafront at the southern end of Mashraba. Breakfast isn't available.

MIDRANGE

Many camps have moved upmarket in recent years, and Dahab now has a good selection of midrange hotels.

Inmo Hotel (☎ 364 0370; www.inmodivers.de; Mashraba; s/d 'backpacker' US$18/25, d US$45, with air-con, private bathroom & balcony US$58; ✖ ✖) With colourful rooms, domed ceilings and attractive furniture, this well-run, family-friendly hotel mainly caters to people on diving packages from Europe, especially Germany, although it does take in stray travellers if there's room. Rooms have a fan, most have a bathroom, some have air-con and the best ones have balconies overlooking the beach. There are a few mountain bikes for guests to use and child care can be arranged, as can camel/dive safaris.

Christina Beach Palace & Christina Residence (Beach Palace ☎ 364 0390, Residence ☎ 364 0406; www .christinahotels.com; Mashraba; Beach Palace s/d E£265/340, Residence s/d E£120/160; ✷ ▣) These small Swiss-run hotels – Christina Beach Palace is on the beach, and Christina Residence is just inland – have spotless rooms and a convenient location. Some rooms have small balconies, some have air-conditioning, and there's a pleasant restaurant. The same management team runs both.

Nesima Resort (☎ 364 0320; www.nesima-resort .com; Mashraba; s/d US$62/81; ✷ ▣) Overlooking the beach in Mashraba, this centrally located but calm hotel has pleasing stone and wood overtones, and simple but comfortable domed rooms with minifridge. The rooms don't have sea views, but the small pool overlooks the beach and there's a restaurant and a popular happy hour (see p498).

Ali Baba Hotel (☎ 364 0504; www.alibabahotel .net; Masbat; r/ste US$31/41; ✷ ▣) A good-value hotel in the heart of Assalah with large, attractive rooms, some with sea views and small balconies. Breakfast isn't included in the room price. Next door are a small bakery and a 24-hour supermarket.

Bamboo House Hotel (☎ 364 0263; bamboohouse hotel@hotmail.com; Masbat; d with private bathroom, with/without seaview E£175/140; ✷) Large, bright rooms with TV and minibar and large bathrooms. It's just before the bridge.

Red Sea Relax (☎ 364 1309; www.red-sea-relax .com; Masbat; dm US$12, d with fan/air-con/sea view US$32/35/38; ✷ ▣) Formerly Hotel Neptune Beach, this place is well located just before the bridge, and has clean, comfortable rooms, a rooftop terrace and a dive centre.

Blue Beach Club (☎ 364 0411; reservations@blue beachclub.com; Assalah; d US$35; ✷) Sea views over a windy stretch of beach at the northern end of Assalah, and comfortable rooms.

New Divers House (☎ /fax 364 0451; divershouse@ gmx.de; Mashraba; s/d from US$12/19; ✷) A small hotel on the waterfront with agreeable rooms and close proximity to beachfront restaurants. Gives preferential treatment to divers.

Other recommendations:

Coral Coast Hotel (☎ 364 1195; www.thecoralcoast .com; s/d/tr US$40/50/60; ✷) A relaxed place overlooking Eel Garden, a few minutes' walk from the action of Assalah. It has pleasant rooms and sea views.

Ganet Sinai Hotel (☎ 364 0440; www.ganetsinai.com; Resort Strip; s/d/tr US$45/60/75; ✷ ▣) Bland but reasonable chalet-style rooms overlooking the bay near Dahab City. There is also a beach and a windsurfing centre.

El Dorado Lodge (☎ 364 1027; www.eldoradodahab .com; s/d with fan US$25/31, with private bathroom US$38/44; ✷) An attractive Italian-run place with small but spotless rooms with mosquito nets and tiny windows, a restaurant (meals E£20-40) and air-con in the summer months. It's on the seafront just north of Coral Coast Hotel.

TOP END
Most of Dahab's higher-priced accommodation is set off on its own along the beach near Dahab City.

Hilton Dahab Resort (☎ 364 0310; www.hilton.com; Resort Strip; s/d from US$76/101; ✷ ▣ ▣) The five-star Hilton has comfortable rooms in white-washed, domed two-storey villas set amid lush gardens. There are two pools, a beach, a play area for children and a full range of water sports, including a dive centre run by Sinai Divers (www.sinaidivers.com).

Swiss Inn Golden Beach Resort (☎ 364 0054; www.swissinn.net/dahab/; Resort Strip; s/d half board US$72/106; ✷ ▣) This family-friendly four-star resort has well-appointed rooms, including some with sea views, and a pleasantly low-key ambience, as well as a poolside café and a windsurfing centre.

Accor Coralia Club Dahab (☎ 364 0301; www .accorhotel.com; Resort Strip; s/d half board from US$56/75; ✷ ▣) Overall good value, with bright, pleasant rooms, a dive centre and an attractive stretch of beach.

Eating
The waterfront in Assalah is lined with restaurants, some of which are quite good, and most of which are similarly priced (with main dishes averaging E£25 to E£40). Seafood is on almost all menus, together with a good selection of pizza, pasta, meat and vegetarian dishes, and many seafront places have Bedouin-style beachfront seating areas where you can relax on cushions while gazing out over the sparkling waters of the Gulf of Aqaba.

Seven Heaven (☎ 364 0080; Masbat; meals E£10-25) The restaurant at this popular guesthouse has the best-value spaghetti bolognaise in town, with large, tasty portions for E£10 to E£15.

Carm Inn (☎ 364 1300; Masbat; dishes E£25-65) This waterfront place is a favourite of local dive instructors, with a varied menu of Western, Indian and Indonesian dishes served in mellow surroundings with a hint of the South Pacific. The chef uses fresh ingredients and the results are delicious.

Jay's Restaurant (☎ 364 1228; 010 188 8907; Masbat; dishes E£7-10; ☯ 11am-3pm & 5-10pm) Another perennial favourite, with a mixture of Egyptian and Western fare, including a few vegetarian dishes, at very reasonable prices. The menu changes weekly, and dishes such as coconut rice and curried vegetables make a welcome change from the usual offerings. No alcohol is served. It's just north of Carm Inn.

Shark Club Restaurant (Masbat; dishes E£10-35; ☯ dinner only) A local dive instructors' favourite, with a wide choice of main courses, including a daily vegetarian special. No alcohol is served, but you can bring your own, and there's a rooftop terrace.

Red Sea Relax Terrace Restaurant (☎ 364 0262; Masbat; dishes E£15-50) Chinese cuisine in an open-air setting with views over the passing scene on the waterfront.

Nirvana Indian Restaurant (☎ 364 1261; Masbat; dishes E£20-50) Dahab's best Indian food, including an impressive vegetarian selection. They also have a few inexpensive rooms (see www.nirvanadivers.com).

Jasmine Pension (☎ 364 0852; Mashraba; dishes E£25-50) Pleasant beachside seating and delicious meals, including grilled fish, pasta and pizzas and milkshakes.

Lakhbatita (☎ 364 1306; Mashraba; dishes E£30-100) This eccentric beachfront establishment at the southern end of Mashraba is decorated with old Egyptian furniture that looks like it hasn't seen a dusting in years. The food includes Egyptian dishes, seafood and Italian cuisine, and is generally delicious.

Tota Restaurant (☎ 364 0014; Masbat; dishes E£20-60) This unmissable boat-shaped place in the heart of Assalah is primarily a bar (see right), but it serves Italian cuisine as well, including tasty soup with garlic bread, large pizzas (a bit light on toppings) and a range of other meals and desserts.

For cheaper fare, head into the back streets, where you can get a large bowl of kushari at **Kushari House** (Sharia Al-Mashraba; meals E£3-5); half a chicken with rice and all the trimmings at **King Chicken** (Sharia Al-Mashraba; meal E£12) or **Al-Hussein** (meal E£11), just around the corner; or fresh, pick-it-yourself seafood at the popular **Sea Bride** (meals E£25-35), two doors down from Al-Hussein.

For self-caterers, there are numerous supermarkets dotted around Assalah, including **Ghazala Market** (Masbat; ☯ 24hr) near Ali Baba Hotel, and **Ghazala Supermarket** (Masbat; ☯ 8am-2am), near the main junction at the southern end of Masbat.

Drinking

In comparison with Sharm el-Sheikh and Hurghada, Dahab is fairly quiet at night. However, it has a good selection of lively bars, some of which turn into discos if the atmosphere is right.

Furry Cup (☎ 364 0411; Blue Beach Club, Assalah) One of the most popular spots in town, and the bar of choice for many of Dahab's diving instructors, with cushioned chairs, a lively atmosphere and good music. Happy hour is daily from 6pm to 8pm.

Shipwreck Bar (☎ 364 0320; Nesima Resort, Mashraba) A rooftop bar with great views over the sea, and happy hours daily from 7pm to 8pm and again from 10.30pm to 11.30pm.

Tota Dance Bar (☎ 364 0014; Masbat) A popular nautically themed drinking spot that sometimes turns into an impromptu disco. The top deck is a good place to watch the sunset while sipping a cold beer, especially during the 5pm to 7pm happy hour.

Crazy House (Masbat) Beers are cheap and there's a billiard table.

Outside Assalah, the main (only) place to find bars and nightlife is at the resort hotels.

Getting There & Away

BUS

East Delta Bus Co (☎ 364 1808; Dahab City), with its new station in Dahab City, well southwest of the centre of action, has buses to Sharm el-Sheikh (E£12 to E£18, 1½ hours) departing at 8am, 8.30am, 10am, 11.30am, 12.30pm, 2.30pm, 4pm, 5.30pm, 8.30pm and 10pm. Buses to Nuweiba (E£11, one hour) leave at 8.30am and 10.30am, with the 10.30am bus continuing on to Taba (E£22, two hours). There is a 9.30am bus to St Katherine (E£16, 2½ hours). Buses heading to Cairo (E£62 to E£75, nine hours) depart at 8.30am, 12.30pm,

2.30pm and 7.30pm. Buses for Suez (E£35 to E£47, 6½ hours) depart at 8am and 4pm. There is also a daily direct bus to Luxor (E£110, 15 to 18 hours) departing at 4pm, which while long, is a faster and less expensive option than going via Hurghada on a combination of bus and ferry. Most hotels and camps can arrange your bus tickets for you, plus transport to the station, for about E£10 to E£15 extra.

SERVICE TAXI

Service taxis are generally more expensive than buses, and as travellers are a captive market, there's usually not much room for negotiation. Per person rates (multiply these by seven to charter an entire taxi) average about E£30 to St Katherine and E£15 to Nuweiba or Sharm el-Sheikh.

Getting Around

Pick-ups and minibuses go up and down the main street in Assalah and, less frequently, around the resort strip. The usual fare is E£1 for around town, and E£1.50 if you find one doing the entire stretch between Assalah and Dahab City. In addition to a handful of taxis, a minibus usually meets incoming buses at East Delta's Dahab City terminus and goes up to Assalah. Departing Assalah, you'll need to rely on taxis to get to the bus station (E£5).

Max Car Rental (☎ 364 0310; maxrent@max.com.eg) has a branch at the Hilton Dahab Resort.

RAS ABU GALLUM PROTECTORATE

The starkly beautiful Ras Abu Gallum Protectorate covers 400 sq km of coastline between Dahab and Nuweiba, mixing high

SINAI

SINAI'S BEDOUIN

Sinai's rugged tracts are home to the Bedouin (desert dwellers), most of whom live in the north of the peninsula. The Bedouin – whose numbers are variously estimated to be between 80,000 and 300,000 – belong to 14 distinct tribes, most with ties to Bedouin in the Negev, Jordan and northern Saudi Arabia, and each with their own customs and culture. The Sukwarka, who live along the northern coast near Al-Arish, are the largest tribe. Others include the Tarabin, who have territory in both northern and southern Sinai; the Tyaha in the centre of the peninsula who, together with the Tarabin, trace their roots to Palestine; and the Haweitat, centred in an area southeast of Suez, and originally from the Hejaz in Saudi Arabia.

The seven Bedouin tribes in southern Sinai are known collectively as the Towara or 'Arabs of Al-Tor', the provincial capital. Of these southern Bedouin, the first to settle in Sinai were the Aleiqat and the Suwalha, who arrived soon after the Muslim conquest of Egypt. The largest southern tribe is the Mizena, who are concentrated along the coast between Sharm el-Sheikh and Nuweiba. Members of the tiny Jabaliyya tribe, centred in the mountains around St Katherine, are descendants of Macedonians sent by the Emperor Justinian to build and protect the monastery in the 6th century.

Thanks to centuries of living in the harsh conditions of Sinai, the Bedouin have developed a sophisticated understanding of their environment. Strict laws and traditions govern the use of precious resources. Water use is closely regulated and vegetation carefully conserved, as revealed in the Bedouin adage, 'killing a tree is like killing a soul'. Local life centres around clans and their sheikhs (leaders), and loyalty and hospitality – essential for surviving in the desert – are paramount. Tea is traditionally taken in rounds of three, and traditional dwellings are tents made of woven goat hair, sometimes mixed with sheep wool. Women's black veils and robes are often elaborately embroidered, with red signifying that they are married, and blue unmarried.

Despite their long history and immense knowledge of the peninsula, Sinai's original inhabitants are often left behind in the race to build up the coast. They are sometimes viewed with distrust because of their ties to tribes in neighbouring countries, especially Israel & the Palestinian Territories, and their strong traditions, respect for their environment, and proud nomadic past are often given short shrift by Nile Valley dwellers, many of whom treat the peninsula as a gold mine to be exploited. With their coastal landholdings sold out from under them by the state, their fishing grounds polluted by uncontrolled development and their nomadic past often turned into a caricature of packaged camel rides and desert dinners, the Bedouin have become increasingly marginalised in their own land.

SINAI

coastal mountains, narrow valleys, sand dunes and fine gravel beaches with several excellent diving and snorkelling sites. Scientists describe the area as a 'floristic frontier', in which Mediterranean conditions are influenced by a tropical climate. This, together with its 165 plant species (including 44 that are found nowhere else in Sinai) and wealth of mammals and reptiles, gives it great environmental importance and makes it a fascinating place to visit. As in nearby Nabq, Bedouin of the Mizena tribe live within the protectorate confines, fishing here as they have done for centuries (although this is now regulated by the protectorate). There is a designated camping area and several walking trails, and you can hire Bedouin guides and camels through the ranger house at the edge of **Wadi Rasasah**. Otherwise, there are no facilities, and no visitors' centre. Popular destinations within the protectorate include **Bir el-Oghda**, a now-deserted Bedouin village, and **Bir Sugheir**, a water source at the edge of the protectorate.

Dive centres and travel agencies in Nuweiba and Dahab offer camel and jeep excursions to Abu Gallum, often as part of a diving safari. Abanoub Travel (p502) is also a good contact for arranging a visit. If you are driving, remember that all vehicles should stick to the tracks. The entry track off the main highway is unsignposted. The protectorate can also be reached by hiking in from north of the Blue Hole near Dahab.

NUWEIBA
☎ 069

Turquoise waters edged by fine, sandy beaches and rimmed on both sides by barren, rugged mountain chains give Nuweiba one of the most attractive settings among Sinai's resort towns. However, its centre-less layout (stretched randomly over about 15km), its lack of ambience and its comparatively low-key diving scene mean that it has never managed to attract the cult following of nearby Dahab or the massive development of Sharm el-Sheikh. Yet the lack of crowds gives Nuweiba its own appeal, and the town makes a reasonable stop if you're working your way up or down the coast. Nuweiba is also a good place to organise jeep and camel safaris into the interior.

During the Israeli occupation, Nuweiba was the site of a large moshav (farming settlement), which has since been converted into a residence for Egyptian government officials. In the 1990s Israelis formed the bulk of the tourist trade, but the vagaries of the regional political situation over the past decade and the fallout from the Iraq war have forced many new tourism projects to a halt, and left the coastline north to Taba littered with the shells of half-built resorts.

Orientation
Nuweiba is divided into three parts. To the south is the port, with a bus station, banks and a couple of scruffy hotels. About 8km further north is Nuweiba City, a small but spread-out settlement with a variety of accommodation options, a small bazaar and several cheap places to eat. About a 10-minute walk north along the beach is Tarabin, Nuweiba's equivalent of Dahab's Assalah area, though it's a bit of a ghost town these days, with an unbroken stretch of bamboo-and-concrete huts, small hotels and souvenir shops lining the shoreline.

Information
EMERGENCY
Tourist police Nuweiba City (☎ 350 0231; near Nuweiba Village hotel); Nuweiba Port (☎ 350 0401)

INTERNET ACCESS
Al-Mostakbal Internet Café (☎ 350 0090; Nuweiba City; per hr E£6; ☯ 9am-3am)

MEDICAL SERVICES
Nuweiba Hospital (☎ 350 0302; Nuweiba City) Just off the main highway to Dahab, and to be avoided except in the direst emergencies.

MONEY
Neither of the banks at the port will handle Jordanian dinars.
Banque du Caire (Nuweiba Port; ☯ 9am-2pm Sun-Thu) Has an ATM.
Banque Misr (Nuweiba Port; ☯ 8.30am-2pm Sun-Thu) ATM.
National Bank of Egypt Nuweiba Port (☯ 8.30am-2pm Sun-Thu) ATM; Nuweiba Village (☯ 9am-1pm & 7-9pm Sat-Thu, 9-11am Fri) ATM.

POST
Branch post office (Nuweiba Port; ☯ 8.30am-2.30pm Sun-Thu)
Main post office (Nuweiba City; ☯ 8.30am-2.30pm Sun-Thu)

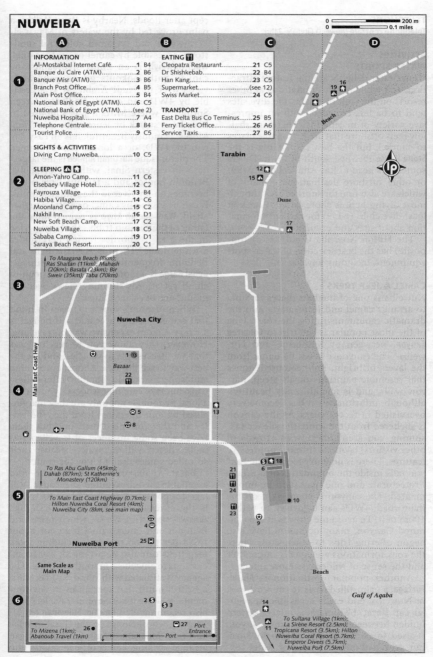

NUWEIBA

0 —————— 200 m
0 —————— 0.1 miles

INFORMATION	
Al-Mostakbal Internet Café	1 B4
Banque du Caire (ATM)	2 B6
Banque Misr (ATM)	3 B6
Branch Post Office	4 B5
Main Post Office	5 B4
National Bank of Egypt (ATM)	6 C5
National Bank of Egypt (ATM)	(see 2)
Nuweiba Hospital	7 A4
Telephone Centrale	8 B4
Tourist Police	9 C5

SIGHTS & ACTIVITIES	
Diving Camp Nuweiba	10 C5

SLEEPING	
Amon-Yahro Camp	11 C6
Elsebaey Village Hotel	12 C2
Fayrouza Village	13 B4
Habiba Village	14 C6
Moonland Camp	15 C2
Nakhil Inn	16 D1
New Soft Beach Camp	17 C2
Nuweiba Village	18 C5
Sababa Camp	19 D1
Saraya Beach Resort	20 C1

EATING	
Cleopatra Restaurant	21 C5
Dr Shishkebab	22 B4
Han Kang	23 C5
Supermarket	(see 12)
Swiss Market	24 C5

TRANSPORT	
East Delta Bus Co Terminus	25 B5
Ferry Ticket Office	26 A6
Service Taxis	27 B6

Tarabin

Beach

Dune

SINAI

Nuweiba City

Main East Coast Hwy

Bazaar

To Maagana Beach (8km);
Ras Shaitan (11km); Mahash
(20km); Basata (23km); Bir
Sweir (35km); Taba (70km)

To Ras Abu Gallum (45km);
Dahab (87km); St Katherine's
Monastery (120km)

To Main East Coast Highway (0.7km);
Hilton Nuweiba Coral Resort (4km);
Nuweiba City (8km, see main map)

Nuweiba Port

Same Scale as
Main Map

To Mizena (1km);
Abanoub Travel (1km)

Port
Entrance

Port

Beach

Gulf of Aqaba

To Sultana Village (1km);
La Sirène Resort (2.5km);
Tropicana Resort (3.5km); Hilton
Nuweiba Coral Resort (5.7km);
Emperor Dives (5.7km);
Nuweiba Port (7.5km)

SINAI

TELEPHONE
Telephone centrale (Nuweiba City; ☺ 24hr)

Activities

WATER SPORTS

Underwater delights are the feature attraction, and while not as dramatic as at other resorts on the Gulf of Aqaba, the dive sites tend to be less crowded, with an impressive variety of marine life. There are shallow reefs offshore that are reasonable places to snorkel, but the best snorkelling is the **Stone House** reef just south of town. Divers sometimes head to Ras Abu Gallum (p499) or other offshore destinations – many of which are also fine for snorkellers – though most diving here is shore based. Check at local dive clubs (p459) for further information about sites and excursions.

The Hilton Nuweiba Coral Resort (opposite) has the best selection of water-sport equipment, including kayaks.

CAMEL & JEEP TREKS

Nuweiba is one of the best places in Sinai to arrange camel and jeep safaris into the dramatic mountains lining the coast. One of the most popular is the trip to **Coloured Canyon**, between St Katherine and Nuweiba. The canyon derives its name from the layers of bright, multicoloured stones that resemble paintings on its steep, narrow walls, and is magnificently beautiful, although unfortunately it has become very overvisited in recent years. As the canyon is sheltered from the wind, the silence (assuming you aren't there with crowds of other visitors) is one of its most impressive features. There is no entry fee, but the canyon falls inside the boundaries of the Taba Protectorate and one may soon be implemented. The canyon is about 5km off the main road; 4WDs can be driven to within 100m of it. To avoid the crowds at the Coloured Canyon, many operators have also begun offering trips to other sites, where the rock formations are equally impressive and the sense of wilderness more intact.

Another popular destination is **Ain al-Furtega**, a palm-filled oasis 16km northwest of Nuweiba, and easily accessible by regular car. **Mayat el-Wishwashi** is a large cistern hidden between two boulders in a canyon. It used to be the largest cistern in Sinai, but now has only a trickle of water, ex-

cept after floods. Nearby is **Mayat Malkha**, a palm grove fed by the waters of Mayat el-Wishwashi and set amid colourful sandstone, accessible by camel or on foot only. **Wadi Huweiyit** is an impressive sandstone canyon with lookouts giving panoramic views over to Saudi Arabia. It is accessible by 4WD and camel. **Ain Hudra** (Green Spring) is where Miriam was supposed to have been struck by leprosy for criticising Moses. Famously beautiful, it is an easy day trip by 4WD, or a longer trip by camel. The picturesque **Ain Umm Ahmed** is the largest oasis in eastern Sinai, with lots of palms, Bedouin houses and a famous stream that becomes an icy river in the winter months. It can be visited by camel or 4WD. Further afield, **Wadi Sheikh Atiya** is named after the father of the Tarabin tribe – the largest tribe in the area – who lies buried here under a white dome. There is an oasis here and Bedouin frequently come on pilgrimage. **Gebel Barga** is a mountain that is difficult to climb yet affords stunning views over the mountains of eastern Sinai.

When planning your trip, keep in mind that camels are a slower and – if budget is a worry – more expensive way of travelling. However, they allow you to reach places that are inaccessible to vehicles, and are the best way to see the area. Almost every camp and supermarket in Tarabin offers these trips, but take care that whoever you pick is a local Bedouin – not only are they marginalised by tour operators from the Nile Valley and therefore need the work, but there have been some instances of travellers lost in the desert without water because their so-called guides didn't know the routes.

Basata (p506) is a good place to find a reliable Bedouin guide. Fayrouza Village (opposite) is another place to try, as is the efficient **Abanoub Travel** (☎ 352 0201; abanoubt@menanet.net; Mizena), which uses local Bedouin and offers camel treks for about US$4 per person per day, including food. Jeep treks can also be arranged, as can excursions to anywhere in southern Sinai. The agency is affiliated with Wind, Sand & Stars, a British outfit that specialises in environmentally aware treks. Several travellers have also recommended **Ibrahim Suleyman** (☎ 012 795 2402), who belongs to the Tarabin tribe and runs Maagana Camp (p505), and can arrange walking, camel or jeep safaris into the surrounding area. Expect to pay about E£150 per person for a guided camel trek.

Remember also that most areas listed here are within the confines of either the St Katherine or Taba Protectorates, so their rules apply (see p513).

Sleeping

The hotels near the port are poor value and not recommended. It's better to head up to the camps of Tarabin or the hotels of Nuweiba City.

NUWEIBA CITY

This stretch of Nuweiba is the town's tourist hub, with a collection of mostly midrange hotels, plus a few quiet backpackers camps.

Hotels

Nuweiba City's hotels are quite widely spaced; if you need to get between them you'll need a car or taxi.

Nuweiba Village (☎ 350 0401; www.nuweibaresort .com; s/d from US$40/50, huts s/d US$15/20; ✖ ▢ ▩) This good place has a long stretch of beach, a dive centre and other water sports. The main hotel area consists of a collection of attached bungalow-style rooms looking over a central garden area, all with satellite TV and the usual amenities. Nearby on the beach in front of the dive centre is a collection of closely spaced wooden huts with shared facilities for those on a budget (breakfast costs extra). It's at the southern end of Nuweiba City off the main coastal road.

Tropicana Resort (☎ 352 1056; www.tropicana hotels.com; s/d half board from US$40/60; ✖ ▩) This whitewashed four-star hotel is good value, with comfortable rooms, a pool and a great stretch of sandy beach. It's south of Nuweiba Village hotel along the coastal road.

Hilton Nuweiba Coral Resort (☎ 352 0320; www .hiltonworldresorts.com; Nuweiba Port; s/d half board from US$79/95; ✖ ▢ ▩) This large resort boasts lush, appealing gardens, a good beach, a play area for children and excellent water sports. It's about 2.5km south of Tropicana Resort, and about 4km via road before the port area.

Other recommendations:

La Sirène Resort (☎ 350 0701; fax 350 0702; s/d from US$45/50; ✖) A large compound with whitewashed rooms with TV and some with a small terrace, plus a beachside restaurant and a dive centre. It's about 3km past

the southern edge of Nuweiba City, and about 1.5km north of Tropicana Resort.

Sultana Village (☎ 350 0490; www.sinai4you /sultana; s/d US$30/40; ✖) A reasonable midrange hotel, with accommodation in small, spartan stone huts on the beach and an open-air restaurant.

Camps

Nuweiba City's camps are a good alternative if you're travelling on a budget but want more tranquillity and space than you'll find in Tarabin.

Fayrouza Village (☎ 350 1133; fayrouza@sinai4you .com; s/d US$10/14) This comfortable place is well located on the beach at the edge of Nuweiba City and in front of a reef, with simple but spotless huts, all with fan, electricity, window screens and good beds. The shared bathrooms have hot water, and the restaurant serves up filling, tasty meals. Excellent all-round budget value. They can also help you organise reasonably priced camel and jeep safaris to surrounding attractions. If you're arriving in Nuweiba by bus, ask them to drop you at the hospital, from where it's a 10-minute walk down to Fayrouza.

Amon-Yahro Camp (☎ 350 0555; www.amonyahro .net; per person E£20) A good, simple camp with huts on raised concrete platforms overlooking the beach. All have electricity and bathrooms, and there's a restaurant.

Habiba Village (☎ 350 0770; www.sinai4you /habiba; huts US$21, with private bathroom & air-con US$65) This small hotel has a selection of double huts and overpriced air-con rooms, and a beachfront restaurant. If you're after quiet, it may not be the best choice, as many of the rooms are near the restaurant area.

TARABIN

Tarabin has been badly hit by the lack of Israeli tourists since the outbreak of the Palestinian intifada (the Palestinian uprising against Israeli authorities in the West Bank, Gaza and East Jerusalem that began in December 1987 and is ongoing) and is very quiet these days, although it continues to attract a trickle of visitors. While many of the original camps have either closed or gone upscale, it's still possible to find a mattress in a bamboo or concrete hut at one of the camps for E£10, or less in the off season. If you enjoy the laid-back, Bohemian scene but want more comforts, there are also several hotels. Almost all the camps have attached cafés selling food and drinks and a few are run by Sudanese, with their own special low-key touch. The main part of Tarabin stretches over about 1.5km, and it's easy to walk from one place to another along the sandy, pedestrians-only seafront road.

Hotels

Nakhil Inn (☎ 350 0879; www.nakhil-inn.com; s/d US$40/50; 🌣) This good-value hotel is at the northern end of Tarabin. Rooms are spacious and well appointed, all with satellite TV. Staff are helpful, and the hotel has its own beach.

Elsebaey Village Hotel (☎ 350 0373; d E£30, with private bathroom & air-con E£60; 🌣) This small hotel in the heart of Tarabin has a range of simple tiled rooms, a rooftop bar, a restaurant and a small supermarket.

Camps

Listings here are from south to north.

New Soft Beach Camp (☎ 010 364 7586; www .softbeachcamp.com; s/d E£15/20; 🖳) This camp has one of the best settings, at the quieter end of Tarabin near the dunes, with the usual simple huts, communal outdoor showers that are generally reliable (except when the garden is being watered) and a decent restaurant.

Moonland Camp (☎ 350 1229; 2- to 3-person huts E£10) Another decent choice, though the compound is somewhat closed in and set back from the beach. Accommodation is in a collection of huts, all with fan, and there's hot water in the communal showers. It's a few minutes' walk north of Soft Beach at the southern end of Tarabin.

Saraya Beach Resort (☎ 350 1230; huts per person with/without air-con E£20/15, 4-person r with bathroom & air-con E£150; 🌣) A popular and well-run place with a choice of double or triple huts, or a block of rooms. It's north of Moonland in the heart of Tarabin.

Sababa Camp (☎ 012 462 2871; sababa_sinai@hot mail.com; huts E£15) Small, clean huts with lots of thatch, set around a tiny walled garden.

Eating

At the port there is a cluster of *fuul* and *ta'amiyya* places in the area behind the National Bank of Egypt and before the ticket office for Aqaba ferries. The selection is much better in and around Nuweiba City, where you have a choice of several small eateries or the hotel restaurants.

Dr Shishkebab (☎ 350 0273; Bazaar Nuweiba City; dishes E£10-50; 🕒 7am-11pm) This popular place offers a generous spread of *ta'amiyya*, salad, fried aubergine and hummus with all meals; the *daoud basha* (meatballs in a rich tomato sauce) and rice is particularly tasty. Although famous for meat dishes, it also serves cheap vegetarian meals and breakfasts.

Han Kang (☎ 350 0970; Nuweiba City; dishes E£20-50) This small, spotless restaurant, just down from and opposite Nuweiba Village hotel, has friendly proprietors and surprisingly good Chinese and Korean cuisine.

Cleopatra Restaurant (☎ 350 0503; Nuweiba City; dishes E£15-60) One of a row of restaurants opposite the Nuweiba Village hotel, this place features fish meals, Egyptian mezze and pizza.

Habiba Camp (☎ 350 0770; Nuweiba City; buffet E£50) A good all-you-can-eat lunchtime buffet, if you don't mind the crowds of tour groups that inundate the restaurant from late morning onwards.

Swiss Market (☎ 350 1140) Self-caterers can try this market next to Cleopatra Restaurant. It has a selection of basics, and an owner who can help with information on the area or arranging taxis and excursions.

There are also several small supermarkets in Tarabin, including one just up from Elsebaey Village Hotel.

Getting There & Away

BOAT

For information about ferries and speedboats to Aqaba in Jordan, see p543. Tickets must be paid for in dollars, which you'll need to have with you as they're not available from any of the banks in Nuweiba. If you're planning to travel this route during the haj (pilgrimage to Mecca), the boats fill up, so buy your ticket as far in advance as possible. Tickets are sold at the yellow building near the port: walk south from the bus station, go right after the National Bank of Egypt, continue one long block, and you'll see the ticket office ahead to your left.

BUS

East Delta Bus Co (☎ 352 0371; Nuweiba Port) has buses to Cairo (E£55, seven to eight hours) leaving at 9am, 11am and 3pm and going via Taba (E£11, one hour); and to Sharm el-Sheikh (E£21, three hours) via Dahab (E£11, one hour) at 6.30am, 8.30am, 10am and 4pm. There is a bus to Suez (E£30, four hours) at 6.30am, and an inconvenient connection from Nuweiba to St Katherine via Dahab departing at 8.30am (E£21).

SERVICE TAXI

There is a service-taxi station by the port, but unless you get there when the ferry has arrived from Aqaba, you'll have to wait a long time for the car to fill up. Per person fares (multiply by seven for the entire car) average about E£30 to Sharm el-Sheikh, E£15 to Dahab and E£60 to Cairo (usually changing vehicles in Suez). It's also possible to find service taxis at the outskirts of Tarabin that will take you directly out on the road north towards Taba or south to Dahab, St Katherine's Monastery or Sharm el-Sheikh.

Getting Around

Since Nuweiba is so spread out, taxis are expensive. Expect to pay E£10 to E£20 for a taxi from the port/bus station to Nuweiba City, depending on your destination and negotiating powers, and from E£5 for the few kilometres between Tarabin and Nuweiba City. If you're arriving in Nuweiba by bus, you can usually ask to be dropped at the hospital, from where you can walk to Fayrouza Village and nearby camps/hotels.

NUWEIBA TO TABA

☎ 069

The stunning coastline between Nuweiba and Taba is fringed by aqua waters and rimmed by chains of low, barren mountains. While there are a few pristine spots left, much of it is lined by a string of 'tourist villages' in various stages of completion, interspersed with simple beach camps consisting of reed huts and an eating area. Many of these camps sprung up when the local Bedouin were forced off their land to make way for hotel and resort development, and as a result have developed into what the Ministry of Tourism terms 'clusters'. From the road it's often difficult to distinguish where one camp cluster ends and another begins, but it doesn't really matter as most offer similar facilities in a very laid-back ambience. At most places, there's nothing much to do other than relax on the sands while gazing out at the turquoise panoramas stretching out before you, or – if you're feeling energetic – organise camel and jeep safaris to the interior.

Business, which traditionally has come primarily from visiting Israelis, has suffered greatly with the political turns of recent years, and you'll frequently have much of the beach to yourself. Unless otherwise noted, all the camps charge between E£10 and E£20 per person in a very basic hut with mattresses on the floor and shared facilities. The only way to reach them is by service taxi or bus. Buses will drop you at any of the places, although you'll probably have to pay the full Nuweiba–Taba fare (E£12, or E£70 from Cairo). When you're ready to leave, staff will help you hail a bus from the road. The closest places to change money, or to stock up if you want to self-cater, are Taba and Nuweiba.

Maagana Beach

This stretch of sand is the closest to Nuweiba. While the site is unappealing – it's close to the road and exposed to the wind – the **Maagana** (☎ 012 795 2402) is a decent base for organising camel safaris and jeep trips. In addition to simple huts, there's a restaurant and helpful Bedouin staff.

Ras Shaitan

This rocky point (its name translates as Satan's Head) jutting into the gulf 3km north of Maagana Beach came tragically into the world spotlight in 2004 when it was targeted as part of the same series of terrorist bombings that also hit the Taba Hilton. Since then the pace of life has returned to normal, and it's one of the most popular beach areas on the Taba–Nuweiba strip.

The peaceful and popular **Ayyash Camp** (☎ 012 760 4668; huts per person E£20), owned by a local Bedouin, has a placid setting on a wide stretch of sand, Bedouin tents and simple huts with shared facilities and no electricity.

Castle Beach (☎ 012 739 8495; d E£80; 🕸) is a pleasant place just north of Ayyash Camp near the *ras* (headland), and one of the few midrange camps. Accommodation is in comfortable bungalows, and there's a beachside restaurant. Camel and jeep treks can be organised for a minimum of four people. Breakfast costs extra.

Mahash

Continuing northwards, the next cluster of camps is in the Mahash area, about 20km north of Nuweiba on an attractive stretch of beach.

Basata means 'simplicity' in Arabic, and **Basata** (☎ 350 0480/1; www.basata.com; Nuweiba-Taba rd; camping per person US$7, huts per person US$12, 3-person chalet US$58), a clean, ecologically minded and hugely popular travellers' settlement, reflects its name. Owner Sherif Ghamrawy's concern for the environment is reflected in the philosophy of the hotel, which has organically grown produce and recycling for rubbish. There are simple huts sharing facilities, pleasant chalets with electricity and private bathroom, a large camping area, a kitchen (where you can self-cater or arrange to have prepared meals), a bakery and ablution blocks. Any cooking ingredients you could want are available, the ambience is very laid-back and family friendly with a New Age twist, and TVs and music are prohibited. For diversion, there's snorkelling in the bay (no diving allowed). Basata is about 25km north of Nuweiba; advance bookings are recommended. Staff can help you arrange a taxi to/from Cairo (about E£100 per person).

The pleasant three-star **Bawaki Beach Hotel** (☎ 350 0470; www.bawaki.com; s/d US$35/45; ⊠) sits on its own about 20km north of Nuweiba overlooking some good snorkelling sites. Accommodation is in pleasant octagonal bungalows and staff can help sort you out with camel and jeep safaris.

Club Aquasun (☎ 350 1208; www.clubaquasun.com; Nuweiba-Taba rd; d half board US$55; ⊠) is a 75-room domed hotel/resort about 30km north of Nuweiba set on a good 2km beach with a house reef, comfortable rooms and a restaurant. Camel and jeep safaris to the interior can be arranged.

Just beyond Club Aquasun and under the same management, **Aquasun Ghazaly** (d huts/r half board US$35/55) has a choice of simple beach huts or rooms, a laid-back beach bar and a dive centre.

Sally Land Tourist Village (☎ 353 0380; fax 353 0381; Nuweiba-Taba rd; s/d half board US$44/57; ⊠) is a two-star village just north of Aquasun without the atmosphere of Basata, but with reasonable rooms, a bar and a restaurant.

About 22km from Nuweiba near Aquasun, **Ananda Camp** (☎ 012 356 1742; huts s/d E£20/30) is a simple, clean and quiet Bedouin-owned place, with simple but pleasant huts and a beachfront dining area.

Ibrahim Camp (☎ 012 724 3817, 010 163 9444; huts s/d E£20/40) is another simple Bedouin-owned camp, about 7km south of Ananda Camp.

Bir Sweir

Further north is Bir Sweir, a particularly lovely stretch of sand with a long row of camps – many now closed – with names such as Sayal, Nirvana and Lama Beach. They charge the usual E£15 to E£20 per person in a hut, and most have no electricity. Camps that are open include Trankila (just north of Sally Land), Sayal (4km south of Trankila) and Antica Beach.

Taba Heights

North of Bir Sweir and about 20km south of Taba is the massive new **Taba Heights development** (www.tabaheights.com), one of the lynchpins in Egyptian efforts to create a 'Red Sea Riviera'. When complete it will house several luxury hotels, a casino, numerous shops, bars, restaurants, a medical clinic and extensive water-sports facilities. For now, much of the area is still under construction, although a few resorts are open.

The **Hyatt Regency** (☎ 358 0234; www.taba .hyatt.com; r from US$115; ⊠ ⊠ ⌨ ⛱ ⛲) is a tasteful desert-pastel hotel designed by the American designer and architect Michael Graves. Nestled beside the mountains close to the beach, it has excellent facilities, including lush gardens, several pools, a large health centre and extensive water sports.

Less of an architectural treat than the Hyatt but still a reasonable five-star resort, **Taba Heights Marriott Beach Resort** (☎ 358 0100; www.marriott.com/tcpeg; s/d US$80/100; ⊠ ⊠ ⌨ ⛲) offers a full spa, pools, a business centre and extremely comfortable rooms.

Pharaoh's Island

About 7km south of Taba and 250m off the Egyptian coast, is **Pharaoh's Island** (Gezirat Fara'un; adult/child E£20/10; ⏰ 9am-5pm), a tiny islet in turquoise waters, dominated by the much-restored Castle of Salah ad-Din. The castle is actually a fortress built by the Crusaders in 1115, but captured and expanded by Saladin in 1170 as a bulwark against feared Crusader penetration south from Palestine. At the height of Crusader successes, it was feared they might attempt to head for the holy cities of Mecca and Medina. Some of the modern restoration is incongruous (concrete was not a prime building material in Saladin's time), but the island is a pleasant place for a half-day trip, with limpid and enticing waters and coral for snorkelling at the island's southern end. There is also a café serving soft drinks, and a restaurant is planned.

The only boat to the island runs from Salah ad-Din Hotel, on the coast just opposite. It was indefinitely out of service when this book was researched, but usually costs US$4 return. Tickets are available from the hotel reception, and tickets for the island are available on landing.

Opposite Pharaoh's Island, the three-star **Salah ad-Din Hotel** (☎ 353 0340/2; tabarsrt@gega .net; s/d half board US$60/89; ✿) has 120 low-key rooms that are pleasant enough but overpriced, a restaurant and superb views.

TABA
☎ 069

Until 1989 Taba – a few hundred metres of beach and a handful of hotels and cafés on the Israel-Egypt border – was a minor point of contention between the two countries. After several years of formal arbitration, the land was returned to Egypt. Since 1982, when the rest of Sinai was returned by Israel, Taba has served as a busy transit point. The border is open 24 hours daily; for more information see p541.

There is a **post & telephone office** (⌚ 24hr) in the town, along with the Taba Emergency Centre hospital, a bakery and an EgyptAir office (near Taba Hilton; it's often closed and there's currently no flights). Just inside the border are an ATM and several foreign-exchange booths. Cash and travellers cheques can also be exchanged at the Taba Hilton.

Sleeping & Eating
Taba Hilton Nelson Village (☎ 353 0140; www.hilton .com; Taba Beach; s/d US$70/90; ✿ ✿) The Hilton gained worldwide attention and sympathy in 2004 when much of it was destroyed in a terrorist car-bomb attack and many guests and employees were killed. Since then it has been rapidly rebuilding and now offers a good selection of rooms in its Nelson Village compound, set in lush grounds overlooking the turquoise waters of the Gulf of Aqaba.

Tobya Boutique Hotel (☎ 353 0275; www.tobya boutiquehotel.com; s/d US$55/80; ✿) This small, attractive hotel is on the inland side of the road about 2km south of the Hilton. It has pleasant, good-value rooms, a 24-hour restaurant, a bar and a pretty beach.

Castle Zaman (☎ 350 1234, 012 214 0591; www .castlezaman.com; meals from E£110, minimum charge

per person E£40; full castle rental per night from US$1000; ⌚ from 10am; ✿) This atmospheric stone castle on a cliff with views over the gulf has the best cuisine along this stretch of coast, featuring huge portions of items such as a full racks of grilled ribs. There's also a bar, a pool, a small private beach and a couple of rooms (available only to those who want to rent the castle out in its entirety). It's a good idea to call in advance to confirm opening times, as the castle is sometimes booked for weddings or other events. Otherwise, it is open to anyone, though the facilities aren't suitable for young children. Meals should also be booked in advance.

Getting There & Away
AIR
EgyptAir has suspended its domestic flights to/from Taba, although they still maintain an office near the Taba Hilton. The airport is at Ras an-Naqb, 38km from Taba town.

BUS
East Delta Bus Co (☎ 353 0250) has its station along the main road about 800m south of the border. Buses to Nuweiba (E£12, one hour) leave at 7am, 9am and 3pm, with the 7am bus continuing to St Katherine (E£26, four hours). There's also a bus from Cairo to Nuweiba that passes Taba about noon. Departures to Cairo (E£55 to E£60, six to seven hours) are at 10.30am, 12.30pm and 4.30pm, and to Suez at 7.15am (E£35, four hours). Buses to Dahab (E£21, 2½ hours) and Sharm el-Sheikh (E£26, 3½ hours) leave at 7am (terminating in Dahab), 9am and 3pm (both continuing to Sharm el-Sheikh).

Getting Around
CAR
Max Car Rental (☎ 353 0333; tabareservation@max .com.eg; ⌚ 6am-8pm) is just before the border post, opposite the Taba Hilton.

SERVICE TAXI
Taxis and minibuses wait by the border for passengers. If business is slack you may have a long wait for the vehicle to fill up – or you can pay the equivalent of all seven fares and leave immediately. Per person fares are about E£12 to Nuweiba, E£30 to Dahab and E£45 to Sharm el-Sheikh or St Katherine's, and E£55 to Cairo. Your bargaining power increases if the bus is not too far off.

SINAI

INTERIOR

Sinai's rugged interior, with barren mountains, wind-sculpted canyons and wadis that burst into life with even the shortest rains, is a region of breathtaking natural beauty. The rocks and desert landscapes turn shades of pink, ochre and velvet black as the sun rises and falls, and what little vegetation there is appears to grow magically out of the rock. Bedouin still wander through the wilderness and camels are the best way to travel, with much of the terrain too rocky even for a 4WD. Over the past several millennia, some of human history's most significant events have played out against this isolated backdrop and today the region remains sacred to the all the world's major monotheistic religions.

ST KATHERINE'S MONASTERY & MT SINAI

☎ 069

St Katherine's Monastery

Tucked into a barren valley at the foot of Mt Sinai, the ancient **St Katherine's Monastery** (in Cairo ☎ 02-482 8513; sinai@tedata.net.eg; admission free; ⏰ 9am-noon Mon-Thu & Sat, except religious holidays) has been a place of pilgrimage since the 4th century. It traces its founding to about 330 AD, when the Roman empress Helena had a small chapel and a fortified refuge for local hermits built beside what was believed to be the burning bush from which God spoke to Moses. In the 6th century Emperor Justinian ordered a fortress to be constructed around the original chapel, together with a basilica and a monastery, to provide a secure home for the monastic community that had grown here and as a refuge for the Christians of southern Sinai. Since then the monastery has been visited by pilgrims from throughout the world, many of whom braved extraordinarily difficult and dangerous journeys to reach the remote and isolated site. Today St Katherine's is considered one of the oldest continually functioning monastic communities in the world, and its chapel is one of early Christianity's only surviving churches.

The monastery – which, together which the surrounding area, has been declared a Unesco World Heritage site – is named after St Katherine, the legendary martyr of Alexandria, who was tortured on a spiked wheel and then beheaded for her faith. Tradition holds that her body was transported by angels away from the torture device (which spun out of control and killed the pagan onlookers) and onto the slopes of Egypt's highest mountain peak. The peak, which lies about 6km south of Mt Sinai, subsequently became known as Gebel Katarina. Katherine's body was subsequently 'found' about 300 years later by monks from the monastery in a state of perfect preservation.

Today a Tarmac access road has removed the hazards that used to accompany a trip to the monastery, and both the monastery and the mountain are routinely packed with tour buses and people. It is especially full early in the morning, although somehow the monastery's interior tranquillity manages to make itself felt despite the crowds. When you visit, remember that this is still a functioning monastery and dress conservatively.

Although much of the monastery is closed to the public, it is possible to enter the ornately decorated 6th-century **Church of the Transfiguration**, with its nave flanked by massive marble columns and walls covered in richly gilded icons and paintings. At the church's eastern end, a gilded 17th-century iconostasis separates the nave from the sanctuary and the apse, where St Katherine's remains are interred (off limits to most visitors). High in the apse above the altar is one of the monastery's most stunning artistic treasures, a 6th-century mosaic of the biblical account of the transfiguration of Christ, although it can be difficult to see past the chandeliers and the iconostasis.

To the left of and below the altar is the monastery's holiest area, the **Chapel of the Burning Bush**. Access is restricted, but it's possible to see what is thought to be a descendant of the original **burning bush** in the monastery compound. According to the monks, this bush was transplanted from the nearby chapel in the 10th century, and continues to thrive centuries later. Near the burning bush is the **Well of Moses**, a natural spring that is supposed to give marital happiness to those who drink from it. Above the well is the superb **Monastery Museum** (adult/child under 12/student E£25/free/10) – also known as the Sacred Sacristy – which has recently been magnificently restored. It has displays (labelled in Arabic and English)

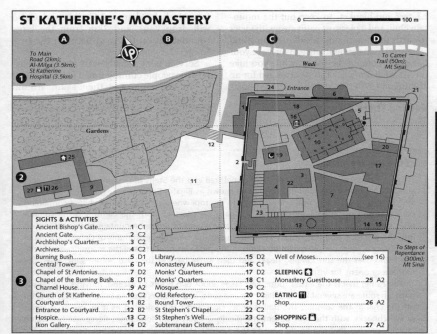

ST KATHERINE'S MONASTERY

0 — 100 m

To Main
Road (2km);
Al-Milga (3.5km);
St Katherine
Hospital (3.5km)

Wadi

To Camel
Trail (50m);
Mt Sinai

Gardens

Entrance

To Steps of
Repentance
(300m);
Mt Sinai

SIGHTS & ACTIVITIES
Ancient Bishop's Gate	1	C1
Ancient Gate	2	C2
Archbishop's Quarters	3	C2
Archives	4	C2
Burning Bush	5	D1
Central Tower	6	D1
Chapel of St Antonius	7	D2
Chapel of the Burning Bush	8	D1
Charnel House	9	A2
Church of St Katherine	10	C2
Courtyard	11	B2
Entrance to Courtyard	12	B2
Hospice	13	C2
Ikon Gallery	14	D2
Library	15	D2
Monastery Museum	16	C1
Monks' Quarters	17	D2
Monks' Quarters	18	C1
Mosque	19	C2
Old Refectory	20	D2
Round Tower	21	D1
St Stephen's Chapel	22	C2
St Stephen's Well	23	C2
Subterranean Cistern	24	C1
Well of Moses	(see 16)	
SLEEPING		
Monastery Guesthouse	25	A2
EATING		
Shop	26	A2
SHOPPING		
Shop	27	A2

SINAI

of many of the monastery's artistic treasures, including some of the spectacular Byzantine-era icons from its world-famous collection, numerous precious chalices and gold and silver crosses, and a priceless collection of ancient manuscripts and illuminated Bibles from the monastery's **library**. Admission fees and gift-shop purchases can also be paid in dollars or euros.

Outside the monastery walls is a gift shop selling replicas of icons and other religious items (with branches in the museum and inside the monastery compound just near the entrance), and a café that has an array of cold drinks and snacks. The least crowded days for visiting the monastery are generally Tuesday and Wednesday, while Saturday and Monday tend to be the most crowded.

Mt Sinai

Rising up out of the desert and jutting above the other peaks surrounding the monastery is the towering 2285m Mt Sinai, which is known locally as Gebel Musa, and is not to be confused with the far lower

mountain directly up the valley behind the monastery. Although some archaeologists and historians dispute Mt Sinai's biblical claim to fame, it is revered by Christians, Muslims and Jews, all of whom believe that God delivered his Ten Commandments to Moses at its summit. The mountain is easy and beautiful to climb, and – except at the summit, where you'll invariably be overwhelmed with crowds of other visitors – it offers a taste of the serenity and magnificence of southern Sinai's high mountain region. For those visiting as part of a pilgrimage it also offers a moving glimpse into biblical times. For details of the climb, see p510.

Sleeping

In addition to the Monastery Guesthouse, there are several hotels and guesthouses in Al-Milga (Katreen) village, 3.5km from the monastery; see p511 for listings.

Monastery Guesthouse (☎ 347 0353; fax 347 0543; St Katherine's Monastery; dm per person half board US$20; s/d/tr with private bathroom & half board US$32/54/69) This simple, good guesthouse just next to the monastery has comfortable rooms with heaters and blankets to keep out the mountain chill, and a pleasant patio area with views towards the mountains. Meals are filling and tasty, and management will let you leave your baggage in one of the rooms while you hike up Mt Sinai. Lunches can be arranged for an additional US$4 per person.

Getting There & Away

The monastery is about 3.5km from the village of Al-Milga (which is where buses from Dahab, Sharm el-Sheikh and Cairo will drop you), and 2km from the large roundabout on the road between the two. See p513.

Service taxis usually wait at the monastery for people coming down from Mt Sinai in the morning, and then again around midday when visiting hours end. A lift to the village costs E£10 to E£15. Plan on paying about E£30/45 per person to Dahab/Sharm el-Sheikh.

CLIMBING MT SINAI

There are two well-defined routes – the camel trail and the Steps of Repentance – which meet about 300m below the summit at a plateau known as Elijah's Basin. Here, everyone must take a steep series of 750 rocky and uneven steps to the top, where there is a small chapel containing paintings and ornaments, although it is usually kept locked. Both the climb and the summit offer spectacular views of nearby plunging valleys and of jagged mountain chains rolling off into the distance, and it is usually possible to see the even higher summit of Gebel Katarina in the distance. Most people make the climb in the predawn hours to see the magnificence of the sun rising over the surrounding peaks and then arrive back at the base before 9am, when the monastery opens for visitors.

The camel trail is the easier route, and takes about two hours to ascend, moving at a steady pace. En route are several kiosks selling tea and soda, and vendors renting blankets (E£5) to ward off the chill at the summit. The trail is wide, clear and gently sloping as it moves up a series of switchbacks, with the only potential difficulty – apart from sometimes fierce winds – being gravelly patches that can be slippery on the descent. Most people walk up, but it's also possible to hire a camel at the base, just behind the monastery, to take you all or part of the way to where the camel trail meets the steps. If you decide to try a camel, it's easier on the anatomy to ride up the mountain, rather than down.

The alternative path to the summit, the taxing 3750 Steps of Repentance, was laid by one monk as a form of penance. The steps – 3000 up to Elijah's basin, and then the final 750 to the summit – are made of roughly hewn rock and are steep and uneven in many places, requiring strong knees and concentration in placing your feet. If you want to try both routes, it's best to take the path on the way up and the steps – which afford impressive views of the monastery – on the way back down.

During the summer try to avoid the heat by beginning your hike by 3am. Although stone signs have been placed on the trail as guides, it can be a bit difficult in parts and a torch (flashlight) is essential. The start of the camel trail is reached by walking along the northern wall of the monastery past the end of the compound. The Steps of Repentance begin outside the southeastern corner of the compound.

Due to the sanctity of the area and the tremendous pressure that large groups place on the environment, the Egyptian National Parks Office has instituted various regulations. Apart from the basic trekkers' code (see p513), if you spend the night on the mountain, you are asked to sleep below the summit at the small Elijah's Basin plateau. Here you'll find several composting toilets and a 500-year-old cypress tree, marking the spot where the prophet Elijah heard the voice of God. Bring sufficient food and water, warm clothes and a sleeping bag, as there is no space to pitch a tent. It gets cold and windy, even in summer, and in winter light snows are common. As late as mid-May, be prepared to share the summit with up to several hundred other visitors, some carrying stereos, others Bibles and hymn books. With the music and singing, and people nudging each other for space, it can be difficult to actually sleep, especially in the small hours before sunrise. For more tranquillity, the dawn views are just as impressive from the upper reaches of the camel path, shortly before it joins the Steps of Repentance.

Many hotels and camps in Dahab, Nuweiba and Sharm el-Sheikh, as well as travel agencies in Cairo, also organise trips to the monastery and Mt Sinai.

AROUND ST KATHERINE'S MONASTERY
Al-Milga
☎ 069

This small village, set in the midst of the mountainous desert landscape 3.5km from the monastery, is also called Katreen and is known as the 'Meeting Place' by local Jabaliyya Bedouin. It has a range of hotels and basic facilities, and is a good place to base yourself if you're interested in hiking in southern Sinai.

There are two main roads running through town, with the midrange hotels lining one of them, and the Fox of the Desert and Safary Moonland guesthouses along the other. They meet at the main roundabout, near which you'll find the post office, bank and bus stand.

INFORMATION
Banque Misr (beside petrol station; ☯ 10am-1pm & 5-8pm Sat-Thu) Cash advances on Visa and MasterCard.
Police (☎ 347 0046; beside the monastery visitors' centre)
St Katherine Hospital (☎ 347 0263) Very basic care only.
Telephone centrale (beside the bakery; ☯ 24hr)

SLEEPING
Budget
Al-Milga has three good budget camps.

El-Malga Bedouin Camp (☎ 010 641 3575; fax 347 0042; sheikhmousa@yahoo.com; camping per tent E£10, dm/d E£10/30; ▯) This place has simple, clean rooms with sleeping mats (most rooms have four mats, and one has eight), and shared bathrooms with hot water. It's next to the mountain trekking office and an easy 500m walk from the bus stand. It's run by Sheikh Mousa, who can also help you organise mountain trekking (see p512). Free coffee and tea are included in the room price, and cooking facilities and a laundry service are available.

Fox of the Desert Camp (☎ 347 0344; faragfox 2003@yahoo.com; camping per person E£5, dm/d E£10/40) Another relaxed budget camp with simple, clean facilities; run by local Bedouin, Soliman and Farag al-Gebaly. It's on the road behind the Catherine Plaza Hotel

about 200m from the main roundabout. The owners can also arrange desert safaris from about E£75 per person per day, with a minimum of three people.

Safary Moonland Hotel & Camp (☎ 347 0085, 010 658 9550; mnland2002@yahoo.com; s/d/tr E£25/50/60) This friendly, Jabaliyya-run budget hotel/ camp just up from Fox of the Desert Camp has basic but clean rooms with fans and shared bathrooms. More upscale rooms with private shower are set to open soon (double about E£100), as well as a hostel (about E£10 per person).

Midrange
St Catherine's Tourist Village (☎ 347 0333; fax 347 0325; s/d/tr half board from US$40/70/90; ☒) This four-star establishment is Al-Milga's plushest accommodation, with pleasant stone bungalow-style rooms that blend in with the surrounding landscape. It's along the same road as Daniela Village hotel, about 500m past the hospital and about 2km from the bus station.

Daniela Village (☎ /fax 347 0379, in Cairo ☎ 02-748 2671; s/d half board US$53/78; ☒) This reasonable three-star hotel has stone-clad prefab huts and a bar. It's diagonally opposite the hospital and about 1.5km from the bus station.

Catherine Plaza Hotel (☎ 347 0293; fax 347 0292; s/d US$30/40; ☒ ☒) Just down from Daniela Village (and after Al-Wadi al-Mouquduss hotel), this is another three-star hotel with bland but reasonable-value rooms and a small pool.

Al-Wadi al-Mouquduss (☎ /fax 347 0225; s/d E£120/ 170; ☒) A nondescript two-star hotel next to Daniela Village. Breakfast costs E£10 extra.

Al-Karm Ecolodge (☎ 347 0032; www.stkparks.gov .eg; Sheikh Awaad; camping/r per person E£25/75) Well outside Al-Milga – but a fine, albeit rugged, base for immersing yourself in the beauty of southern Sinai – is the Bedouin-owned Al-Karm Ecolodge, in a remote wadi near the small settlement of Sheikh Awaad. It offers simple rooms, solar-heated shared showers, a kitchen and tranquillity; bring your own bedding. To get here, follow the track from Tarfa village, about 20km from St Katherine on Wadi Feiran road. If you aren't with a local, call the protectorate for directions, and they can arrange for someone to meet you. Once at the lodge, the local Bedouin can help you arrange hiking and camel treks.

EATING

In Al-Milga there's a bakery opposite the mosque and several well-stocked supermarkets in the shopping arcade. Just behind the bakery are a few simple restaurants. Other than these, the only option is to eat at one of the hotels.

Katrien Rest House (☎ 347 0374; dishes E£2-15) This popular Bedouin-owned restaurant serves filling chicken, rice and vegetable meals either inside or on a veranda. It's behind the mosque and next to the bakery.

Kafeteria Ikhlas (☎ 347 0455; dishes E£5-15) Next door to Katrien Rest House, this simple and friendly restaurant has carpets and low tables under palm fronds, and serves hearty breakfasts and chicken, rice and vegetable meals.

SHOPPING

Fan Sina (⏱ 9am-3pm Sat-Thu) This cooperative owned and managed by Bedouin women sells locally made beadwork and other good-quality crafts at very reasonable prices. At

---

TREKKING AROUND ST KATHERINE'S MONASTERY

St Katherine's Monastery lies in the heart of South Sinai's high mountain region, and the surrounding area is ideal for trekking for anyone with a rugged and adventurous bent. Treks range from half a day to a week or more, and can be done either on camel or on foot. Even if you decide to walk, you'll need at least one camel for your food and luggage.

One of the most common circuits goes to the **Galt al-Azraq** (Blue Pools) and takes three to four days. The trail leaves Al-Milga via the man-made **Abu Giffa Pass** and goes through **Wadi Tubug**, taking a detour around **Wadi Shagg**, where there are springs, water holes and lush, walled gardens (bustans). The walk then goes through the picturesque **Wadi Zuweitin** (Valley of the Olives), with ancient olive trees said by local Bedouin to have been planted by the founder of the Jebaliyya tribe. The first night is often spent here, and there is a small stone hut in which hikers can sometimes sleep. The hike continues through **Wadi Gibal**, through high passes and along the valleys of **Farsh Asara** and **Farsh Arnab**. Many hikers then climb either **Ras Abu Alda** or **Gebel Abu Gasba** before heading to the spring of **Ain Nagila** and the ruins of a Byzantine monastery at **Bab ad-Dunya** (Gate of the World). On the third day the trail leads to the crystal-clear, icy waters of the **Galt al-Azraq**, a deep, dramatic pool in the rock, before continuing on the fourth day through more dramatic wadis to a camel pass on **Gebel Abbas Basha**. A one-hour hike up a fairly easy but steep path leads to a ruined palace built by the 19th-century viceroy Abbas Hilmi I, with stunning views from the summit (2304m). The trail then goes back to Wadi Zuweitin and retraces its way to Al-Milga.

Other destinations include **Sheikh Awad**, with a Sheikh's tomb and Bedouin settlement; the **Nugra Waterfall**, a difficult to reach, rain-fed cascade about 20m high, which is reached through a winding canyon called **Wadi Nugra**; and **Naqb al-Faria'**, a camel path with rock inscriptions. A shorter trip is the hike to the top of **Gebel Katarina**, Egypt's highest peak at 2642m. It takes about five hours to reach the summit along a straightforward but taxing trail. The views from the top are breathtaking, and the panorama can even include the mountains of Saudi Arabia on a clear day. The **Blue Valley**, given its name after a Belgian artist painted the rocks here blue some years ago, is another popular day trip.

All treks must be done with a Bedouin guide and most are arranged through **Sheikh Musa** (☎ 010 641 3575; fax 069-347 0042; sheikhmousa@yahoo.com; Mountain Tours Office, Al-Milga), a member of the local Jabaliyya tribe. He will take your passport, register you with the police and arrange a guide for about E£50 per day. Another E£50 goes to Sheikh Musa and camels cost from E£50 per day each. He can also provide food and utensils at a negotiable price, usually around E£30 to E£50 per day. You can also buy firewood here (sold by the protectorate to discourage destruction of the few trees in the mountains). Guides can also be arranged at Fox of the Desert Camp (p511) or at Sheikh Hamed, near the turn-off to Nuweiba.

Whoever you go with, make sure you bring water-purification tablets, unless you want to rely on the mountain springs. You'll also need comfortable walking boots, a hat and sunglasses, sunblock, a warm jacket, a good sleeping bag and toilet paper. Keep in mind that it can get very cold at night – frost, and even snow, are common in the winter.

SINAI

ST KATHERINE PROTECTORATE

The 4350-sq-km **St Katherine Protectorate** (admission US$3) was created in 1996 to counteract the detrimental effects of rapidly increasing tourism on St Katherine's Monastery and the surrounding mountains. In addition to the area's unique high-altitude desert ecosystem, it protects a wealth of historical sites sacred to the world's three main monotheistic religions, and the core part around the monastery has been declared a Unesco World Heritage site. In order to limit the impact of tourists upon this special place, the following Trekkers' Code is now in force:

■ Respect the area's religious and historical importance and the local Bedouin culture and traditions.

■ Carry your litter out with you, bury your bodily waste and burn your toilet paper.

■ Do not contaminate or overuse water sources.

The following acts are illegal:

■ removing any object, including rocks, plants and animals

■ disturbing or harming animals or birds

■ cutting or uprooting plants

■ writing, painting or carving graffiti.

To allow the local population to benefit from tourism, visitors are also requested to hire a local Bedouin guide. The protectorate has published informative guides to four 'interpretive trails' established in the area, including one for Mt Sinai. These booklets take you through each trail, explaining flora and fauna as well as sites of historical and religious significance, and are available from the **St Katherine Protectorate Office** (☎ 347 0032; www.stkparks.gov.eg), near St Catherine's Tourist Village hotel at the entrance to Al-Milga. This is also where you'll need to pay your entry fee.

the time of writing it was in the process of relocating to a building directly opposite Safary Moonland camp.

GETTING THERE & AWAY

Bus

East Delta Bus Co (☎ 347 0250) has its station and ticket office on the main road near the post office. There is a daily bus to Cairo (E£47, six to seven hours) at 6am, via Wadi Feiran and Suez (E£35, four hours), and another to Dahab at 1pm (E£16, two hours), where you can get onward connections to Nuweiba and Taba. For Sharm el-Sheikh, Hurghada and Luxor, it's necessary to change buses in Dahab. East Delta buses from Cairo to St Katherine's depart Turgoman Garage at 10.30am (and about noon from Al-Maza).

Service Taxi

Taxis travel in and out of Al-Milga village irregularly and infrequently, butz there are plenty available if you are willing to pay for the extra places to fill the vehicle (up to seven people). Per person fares are E£30/45

to Dahab/Sharm el-Sheikh. To Cairo, expect to pay about E£400 per vehicle.

WADI FEIRAN

This long valley serves as the main drainage route for the entire high mountain region into the Gulf of Suez. Sinai's largest oasis, it is lush and very beautiful, containing more than 12,000 date palms, and Bedouin from all Sinai's tribes. Stone walls surround the date palms and the *bustans,* and the rocky mountains on each side of the wadi have subtly different colours that stand out at sunrise and sunset, making the landscape even more dramatic.

Feiran also has biblical significance. It is believed to be the place where Moses struck a rock with his staff, bringing forth water, and later became the first Christian stronghold in Sinai. An extensively rebuilt early Christian convent remains from this time, although you need permission from St Katherine's Monastery if you want to visit.

The valley is also an ideal spot from which to trek into the surrounding mountains. To the south, the 2070m **Gebel Serbal** (believed by early Christians to have been the real Mt Sinai) is a challenging six-hour hike along a track also known as **Sikket ar-Reshshah**. Those who persevere are rewarded with fantastic panoramic views. You must be accompanied by a Bedouin guide for all hikes. This is most easily arranged in Al-Milga, near St Katherine's Monastery (see p511).

QALAAT AL-GINDI & NAKHL

In the centre of Sinai, about 80km southeast of the Ahmed Hamdi Tunnel, is Qalaat al-Gindi, which features the 800-year-old **Fortress of Saladin** (Salah ad-Din). In the 12th century Muslims from Africa and the Mediterranean streamed across Sinai on their way to Mecca. The three caravan routes they followed all converged at Qalaat al-Gindi, prompting Saladin to build a fortress here to protect the pilgrims making their haj. He also planned to use the fort, which is still largely intact, as a base from which to launch attacks on the Crusaders, who had advanced as far as Jerusalem. As it turned out, Saladin managed to evict the Crusaders from the Holy City even before the completion of his fortress.

Qalaat al-Gindi is well off the beaten track and seldom visited. From the coast, you must turn off at Ras Sudr and follow the unsignposted road from there. As there is no public transport, you'll need to either have your own vehicle or hire a taxi. You're required to be accompanied by a guide, best arranged through one of Ras Sudr's hotels.

Continuing north from Qalaat al-Gindi for about 20km you'll reach the turn-off for Nakhl, another 60km east. This little community sits almost in the centre of the Sinai Peninsula, surrounded by a vast wilderness. It boasts a petrol station, a surprisingly well-stocked supermarket and a bakery. A road leads north from here to Al-Arish, but foreigners are forbidden to use it.

NORTHERN SINAI

Rarely visited by tourists, Northern Sinai has a barren desert interior, much of which is off limits to foreigners, and a palm-fringed Mediterranean coast backed by soft white sands sculpted into low dunes. As a crossroad between Asia and Africa, the coastal highway follows what must be one of history's oldest march routes, and was known in ancient times as the Way of Horus. It was used by the pharaohs to penetrate into what is now Israel & the Palestinian Territories and then on to Jordan and Syria, and by the Persians, Greeks, Crusaders, Arab Muslims and many others coming the other way. Egypt's Copts believe that the infant Jesus also passed along this route with his parents during their flight into Egypt.

Today Northern Sinai is inhabited mostly by Bedouin, many of whom have developed small farms close to the coast. The area is also the target of an ambitious government programme to reclaim 160,000 hectares of desert which will support the transfer of some three million Nile Valley dwellers. A large canal bringing recycled drainage water and Nile water has already been built, but for now the Bedouin remain the majority.

AL-ARISH

☎ 068 / pop 40,000

Much of the north coast of Sinai between Port Fuad and Al-Arish is dominated by the swampy lagoon of Lake Bardawil, separated from the Mediterranean by a limestone ridge. East of Lake Bardawil is Al-Arish, the capital of North Sinai Governorate and the only major town in the region. It boasts a long, palm-fringed beach with small surf, a collection of holiday villages and chalets and a peppy town centre bustling with Bedouin traders. The town comes alive during the height of summer, when vacationing Cairenes arrive en masse. Otherwise, it's rarely visited. In the winter months, the waterside areas resemble a ghost town, and you'll likely have the wind-swept beach to yourself.

Orientation

The main coastal road, Sharia Fuad Zikry, forms a T-junction with Sharia 23rd of July, which runs a couple of kilometres south (changing name to Sharia Tahrir on the way) to the main market area.

Information

EMERGENCY

Ambulance (☎ 123)

Tourist police (☎ 336 1016; Sharia Fuad Zikry) Offers little information and opening hours are erratic.

INTERNET ACCESS
El Basha.Net (per hr E£2; ☾ 11am-3am) Just off Midan Al-Gamma at the southern edge of town, signposted on the 2nd storey of a small, white building.

MEDICAL SERVICES
Mubarak Military Hospital (☎ 332 4018; near Governorate Bldg, Rafah Rd)
Public Hospital (☎ 336 0010; Sharia Fuad Zikry) To be avoided except in the direst emergencies.

MONEY
Bank of Alexandria (Sharia 23rd of July; ☾ 8.30am-2pm & 6-8pm Sun-Thu))
Banque du Caire (Sharia 23rd of July; ☾ 8.30am-2.30pm Sun-Thu)
Banque Misr (off Sharia Tahrir; ☾ 9am-2.30pm & 6-8pm Sun-Thu)
National Bank of Egypt (Sharia Tahrir; ☾ 9am-2.30pm Sun-Thu) Has an ATM.

POST
Main post office (off Sharia Tahrir; ☾ 8.30am-2.30pm Sat-Thu)

TELEPHONE
Telephone centrale (off Sharia Tahrir; ☾ 24hr)

TOURIST INFORMATION
Tourist office (☎ 336 3743; Sharia Fuad Zikry; ☾ 9am-2pm Sat-Thu)

Sights & Activities
Stretched along the Mediterranean coast from the eastern edge of Lake Bardawil until about 25km east of Al-Arish is the 220-sq-km **Zerenike Protectorate** (admission US$3; ☾ sunrise-sunset), a haven for migrating birds and a good destination for nature-lovers. The entrance to the protectorate – which was established by the Egyptian National Parks Office in 1985 – is about 35km east of Al-Arish. Inside the gates there is a **visitors' centre** (☾ 9am-5pm Sat-Thu) with a cafeteria and information about some of the species of birds that stop here as they migrate between Europe and Africa. There's also a simple **dormitory** (☎ 010 544 2641; per person US$10) and **camping** (per person US$5). For both, you'll need to bring all food and drink with you; basic cooking facilities are available on site.

The small **Sinai Heritage Museum** (Coast Rd; admission E£1, camera/video E£5/25; ☾ 9.30am-2pm Sat-Thu), on the outskirts of Al-Arish along the coastal road to Rafah, was established

several years ago to inform people about life in Sinai. Displays include Bedouin tools, handicrafts, clothing and traditional medicines, with the odd English explanation.

Much livelier is the **Bedouin market** (☾ 9am-2pm Thu), held at the southern edge of town near the main market (it's signposted in Arabic as Souq al-Hamis). It's fascinating to watch as Bedouin come in from the desert in pick-up trucks or occasionally on camels, with the veiled women trading silver, beadwork and embroidered dresses, while the men sell camel saddles. Sometimes you can see the women buying gold after having sold their own handiwork. While some of the crafts are of high quality, you'll need to bargain hard to get these, as the savvy women usually save their best wares for middlemen buying for Cairo shops.

Al-Arish's other attraction is its long **beach**. With its parade of palms, fine white sand, clean water and the occasional small wave, it is one of the better Mediterranean spots in Egypt, and wonderfully peaceful in the off season. Note that women may feel uncomfortable swimming here unless they're in the confines of the El-Arish Resort. There is a beach curfew after dark, though it is only sporadically enforced.

Sleeping
Al-Arish has a dwindling selection of accommodation. Solo women travellers will likely not feel comfortable at any of the budget places, with the possible exception of the Hotel Sinai Sun.

BUDGET
Hotel Sinai Sun (☎ /fax 336 1855, 336 3855; Sharia 23rd of July; s/d/tr from E£60/70/80; ☒) The rooms at this ageing but respectable hotel are quite faded, but linens are clean, and overall it's a reasonable deal for the price. Most rooms have TV and phone. Breakfast costs extra.

Mecca Hotel (☎ /fax 335 2632; Sharia As-Salam; s/d E£38/50) Despite lacking a beachfront location, the high-rise Mecca is a decent choice, with spartan rooms with fan and hot water, and a small restaurant. It's about two blocks southeast of Sharia Fuad Zikry.

Moon Light Hotel (Sharia Fuad Zikry; s/d from E£25/40) This tiny hotel on the beach has reasonable rooms in small, detached chalets. Those closest to the water cost slightly more. Breakfast costs extra.

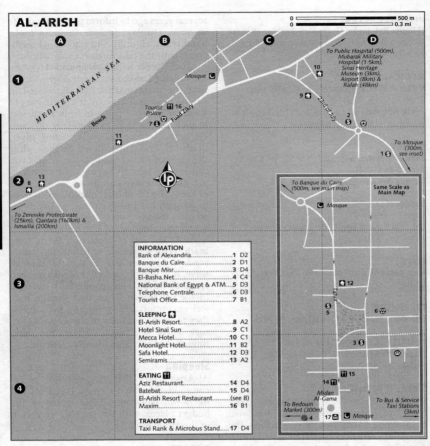

INFORMATION
Bank of Alexandria.................1 D2
Banque du Caire.....................2 D1
Banque Misr.............................3 D4
El-Basha.Net............................4 C4
National Bank of Egypt & ATM....5 D3
Telephone Centrale.................6 D3
Tourist Office...........................7 B1

SLEEPING
El-Arish Resort.........................8 A2
Hotel Sinai Sun.......................9 C1
Mecca Hotel...........................10 C1
Moonlight Hotel.....................11 B2
Safa Hotel...............................12 D3
Semiramis...............................13 A2

EATING
Aziz Restaurant......................14 D4
Batebat...................................15 D4
El-Arish Resort Restaurant.........(see 8)
Maxim....................................16 B1

TRANSPORT
Taxi Rank & Microbus Stand.....17 D4

Safa Hotel (☎ 335 3798; Sharia Tahrir; s/d E£20/30) Safa is the main budget choice if you want to be near the town centre. Rooms are small and run-down, but reasonably clean, and have private bathroom and fan. There's also a rooftop terrace from where you can almost see the water in the distance. It's tucked away on a tiny side street just off Sharia Tahrir.

MIDRANGE & TOP END
El-Arish Resort (☎ 335 1321; Sharia Fuad Zikry; s/d US$60/80; ✷ ⌘) This faded but pleasant five-star establishment (formerly the Oberoi) is well located on a long, breezy stretch of beach. All rooms have sea views, balconies and the usual amenities, and you

can fall asleep to the sounds of the surf. There's a restaurant and two large swimming pools, which are only filled during the summer months.

Semiramis (☎ /fax 336 4167/8; Sharia Fuad Zikry; s/d from US$30/40; ✷ ⌘) The Semiramis takes a distant second place to the El-Arish Resort, its neighbour to the west, though rooms are quite decent for the price. Ask for one near the water; those in the compound across the street aren't worth considering.

Eating
Dining options in Al-Arish are limited to the hotel restaurants and simple *kofta* places where no alcohol is served.

El-Arish Resort restaurant (☎ 335 1321; Sharia Fuad Zikry; dishes E£25-75; ✗) Offering good value, this is the best of the hotel restaurants, with tasty lentil soup and a range of continental dishes.

Aziz Restaurant (☎ 335 4345; Sharia Tahrir; dishes E£5-25) This is the best in the budget range, with filling meals of *fuul* and *ta'amiyya* as well as grilled chicken, *kofta*, rice and spaghetti. It has an atmospheric Bedouin-style inner room, and with advance notice the owner can prepare multicourse meals for you featuring local specialities; agree on the price in advance. Aziz is also open for breakfast.

Maxim (☎ 334 0850; dishes E£20-50) This seafood restaurant, set among the palms on the beach, serves grilled fish and other delicacies, but is open in summer only.

Batebat (Sharia Tahrir; dishes E£5-10) A popular *fuul* and *ta'amiyya* place, diagonally opposite Aziz Restaurant.

Getting There & Away

The main bus and service-taxi stations are next to each other, about 3km southeast of the town centre (about E£2 in a taxi).

BUS

Superjet has buses to and from Cairo (E£21 to E£25.50, five hours) departing in each direction at 8am and 4pm. Similarly priced **East Delta Bus Co** (☎ 332 5931) has buses to Cairo departing at 8am, 4pm and 5pm (E£18 to E£25), and departures to Ismailia (E£10, three to four hours) at 7am,

10.30am, 11.30am, 1pm, 2pm, 3pm and 4pm. For Suez, change in Ismailia.

SERVICE TAXI

Service taxis from Al-Arish to Cairo cost around E£15 per person. Service taxis to Qantara cost E£7, to Ismailia E£8, and to the border (or vice versa) for anywhere between E£10 and E£20.

Getting Around

The main taxi rank and microbus stand is at Midan Al-Gama, near the market at the southern end of town. Microbuses shuttle regularly between here and the beach for 25pt.

RAFAH

☎ 068

This coastal town, 48km north of Al-Arish, marks the border with the Gaza Strip and Israel. Despite its warm Mediterranean location, it has no hotels (the nearest one is in Sheikh Zuweid, 17km west), and little to offer tourists, although its distinctly Palestinian feel is intriguing if you won't have a chance to travel further east. The town centre – which has a post office and a branch of the National Bank of Egypt – is about 4km north of the main road and border crossing.

Several service taxis run daily between the Rafah border crossing and Al-Arish for about E£5. From the border crossing it's easy to find transport to the town centre. For border-crossing details and warnings see p541.

Directory

CONTENTS

ACCOMMODATION

Egypt offers visitors the full spectrum of accommodation: hotels, flotels (Nile cruisers), pensions, youth hostels, a few camping grounds and even the odd ecofriendly resort.

In midrange and top-end hotels, rates often go up by around 10% during peak times, including the two big feasts (Eid al-Fitr and Eid al-Adha; see p529), New Year (20 December to 5 January) and sometimes for the summer season (approximately 1 July to 15 September).

Just because a hotel has its rates displayed it doesn't mean they are untouchable. In off-peak seasons haggling will often get you significant discounts, even in midrange places.

PRACTICALITIES

- *Egyptian Gazette* (50pt) is Egypt's flimsy and embarrassingly bad daily English-language newspaper. *Al-Ahram Weekly* (E£1) appears every Thursday and does a much better job of keeping English-readers informed of what's going on. There's an on-line version at www.ahram.org.eg/weekly. *Egypt Today* (E£12) is an ad-saturated general-interest glossy with good listings.

- You can pick up the BBC World Service on various radio frequencies, including 1323AM in Alexandria, the Europe short-wave schedule in Cairo and the Middle East short-wave schedule in Upper Egypt. See www.bbc.co.uk /worldservice for details. In Cairo, 95FM broadcasts on 557kHz between 7am and midnight daily, including news in English at 7.30am, 2.30pm and 8pm. Nile FM (104.2kHz) is an English-language music station broadcasting out of Cairo.

- Satellite dishes are common in Egypt, and international English-language news services such as CNN and BBC World can be accessed in hotel rooms throughout the country.

- Electrical current is 220V AC, 50Hz in most parts of the country. Exceptions are Alexandria, and Heliopolis and Ma'adi in Cairo, which have currents of 110V AC, 50Hz. Wall sockets are the round, two-pin European type.

- Egypt uses the metric system for weights and measures.

Prices cited in this book are for rooms in the high season and include taxes. Breakfast is included in the price unless indicated otherwise in the review. Some places offer half board (two meals), full board (three meals) or all-inclusive rates that usually include most drinks as well as some activities. We have defined budget hotels as any that charge up to E£100 (US$17) for a double

room, midrange as any that charge between E£100 and E£580 (US$17 to US$100)
and top end as those that charge E£580
(US$100) or more for a room.

Hotels rated three-star and up generally
require payment in US dollars. They are increasingly accepting credit-card payments
but you shouldn't take this for granted.

Camping
Officially, camping is allowed at only a few
places around Egypt, such as at Harraniyya
near Giza in Cairo, Luxor, Aswan, Farafra and Ras Mohammed National Park. A
few private hotels around the country also
allow campers to set up in their backyards,
such as at Abu Simbel, Al-Kharga, Nuweiba, Basata, Qena and Abydos. Facilities
in most of these places, including official
sites, are extremely basic. In Sinai the most
popular budget choices are beach-side
camps – all have electricity and 24-hour
hot water unless noted in our reviews.
You'll find these listed under the Budget
heading rather than a Camping heading.

Hostels
Egypt has 15 hostels recognised by **Hostelling
International** (HI; www.hihostels.com): in Cairo,
Alexandria, Al-Fayoum, Aswan, Asyut, Da-
manhur, Hurghada, Ismailia, Luxor, Marsa
Matruh, Port Said, Sharm el-Sheikh, Sohag,
Suez and Tanta. They generally range in
price from E£8 to E£14 for a dorm bed.
In some cases the price includes breakfast.
Having an HI card is not absolutely necessary as nonmembers are admitted, but a
card will save you between E£2 and E£4,
depending on the hostel. The hostels tend
to be noisy, crowded and often a bit grimy.
In some there are rooms for mixed couples
or families, but on the whole the sexes are
segregated. Reservations are not usually
needed. Most of the time you'll be much
better off staying at a budget hotel instead.

The offices of the **Egyptian Youth Hostels
Association** (☎ 02-794 0527; fax 795 0329; 1 Sharia Ibrahimy, Garden City, Cairo) can give you the latest
information.

Hotels
BUDGET
The two-, one- and no-star hotels form the
budget group. Often the ratings mean nothing at all, as a hotel without a star can be as

good as a two-star hotel, only cheaper. Luck
of the draw often applies – you can spend
as little as E£25 a night for a clean single room with hot water; or E£80 or more
for a dirty double room without a shower.
Generally, the prices quoted include taxes;
quite often they also include breakfast – but
don't harbour any great expectations about
this, as it is often a couple of pieces of bread,
a frozen patty of butter, a serving of jam,
and tea or coffee.

Competition among the budget hotels
in cities such as Cairo and Luxor is fierce,
which is good news for travellers as it leads
to an overall improvement in standards
and services offered. Increasingly, hotels
are offering rooms with private bathrooms
and air-con (this costs an extra E£20 or so),
improving the quality of their breakfasts
and providing welcoming lounges with satellite TV and backgammon boards.

Some hotels will tell you they have hot
water when they don't. They may not even
have warm water. Turn the tap on and check,
or look for an electric water heater when
inspecting the bathroom. If there's no plug
in your bathroom sink and you forgot to
bring your own, then try using the lid of a
Baraka mineral-water bottle – according to
one cluey traveller, they fit 90% of the time.

Many budget establishments economise
on sheets. If you aren't carrying your own
sleeping sheet, just ask for clean sheets –
most hotels will oblige. Toilet paper is usually supplied, but you'll often need to bring
your own soap.

MIDRANGE
Egypt has a great range of budget and
top-end hotels, but midrange options
are surprisingly limited. This is particularly so in Cairo and Alexandria, where
foreign investment is channelled into top-
end accommodation. In these cities local
establishments often pitch themselves as
midrange establishments but end up offering no-star facilities at three-star rates.
Also, beware the extras: sometimes you'll
be charged extra for the fridge, air-con and
satellite TV in your room – before agreeing to take the room, always confirm what
the quoted cost actually covers. This is
particularly important when it comes to
taxes, which are as high as 24% in many
midrange and top-end establishments.

DIRECTORY

TOP END

Visitors are spoilt for choice when it comes to top-end hotels in Egypt. While prices and amenities are usually up to international standards, in some instances service and food can fall short.

ACTIVITIES

The heat and predominantly desert landscape greatly limit the types of activities available in Egypt, but following is a brief listing of some of the possibilities.

Bird-Watching

Egypt is an ornithologist's delight. The country boasts several excellent bird-watching areas holding a plethora of birds, both native and migrant (p79). Prime among these areas is Lake Qarun, in the Al-Fayoum region, where species range from the spoonbill to the marsh sandpiper. The saltwater lagoons in the northern Delta and the Zerenike Protectorate on Lake Bardawil in northern Sinai are home to the greater flamingo, white pelican and spoonbill (all winter visitors). It's also possible to see huge flocks of pelicans around the small lakes near Abu Simbel in southern Egypt. In the desert you may see – or hear – eagle owls. In spring the cliffs at Ain Sukhna on the Red Sea coast offer opportunities for viewing eagles, vultures and other birds of prey.

'Nature Notes' in *Egypt Today* is a great monthly wildlife column. *A Photographic Guide to Birds of Egypt and the Middle East* by Richard Porter and David Cottridge (E£40) and *Common Birds of Egypt* by Bertel Bruun and Sherif Baha el Din (E£35) are

good illustrated references published by the American University in Cairo Press. Both are available in Egypt. Or visit the website of the Egyptian birding community, www.birdingegypt.com, which lists top birding sites, rarities reports and travel tips.

Cycling

High temperatures, a limited road network and some fairly dull landscape mean that Egypt is not the ideal place for cycle touring, but see p545 for ideas on making the best of what there is. There's a club, **Cairo Cyclists** (☎ 02-519 6078), that meets at 7am on Friday and Saturday at the front gate of the Cairo American College on Midan Digla in Ma'adi, a southern suburb of Cairo. The club organises long-distance rides.

Desert Safaris

For desert safaris the options are the Western Desert, with its fantastic sand landscapes, weirdly eroded rocks and Roman ruins, or the more rugged, rocky surrounds of Sinai. Western Desert trips can be arranged cheaply in the oases (particularly Farafra) or, more expensively (involving 4WDs), in Cairo; for details see p332.

Sinai safaris are perhaps easier to arrange. These typically involve a day or two (with overnight camping) trekking through desert canyons on foot, by camel or in a jeep. These expeditions can be organised on the ground at one of the south Sinai resorts such as Sharm el-Sheikh, Dahab or Nuweiba, but the best place to organise them is the small town of Al-Milga, near St Katherine's Monastery (p508). Alternatively, you can book a complete holiday with a specialised Sinai outfit such as Wind, Sand & Stars (p545).

A growing number of travellers are choosing to combine an Eastern Desert safari with a diving holiday by visiting Marsa Alam on the Red Sea coast. See p444 for more details.

Diving & Snorkelling

Many visitors to Egypt rarely have their heads above water. No wonder, as some of the best diving in the world is to be found along the Red Sea coast (for more information see p449). The best diving is along the southern stretch towards the border with Sudan and along the southern coast of the Sinai Peninsula. Away from the resort at-

TIPS FOR WOMEN TRAVELLERS

- Wear a wedding ring. Generally, Egyptian men seem to have more respect for a married woman.
- If you are travelling with a man, it is better to say you're married rather than 'just friends'.
- Avoid direct eye contact with an Egyptian man unless you know him well; dark sunglasses could help.
- Try not to respond to an obnoxious comment from a man – act as if you didn't hear it.
- Be careful in crowds and other situations where you are crammed between people as it is not unusual for crude things to happen behind you.
- On public transport, sit next to a woman if possible. This is not difficult on the Cairo metro where the first compartment is reserved for women only.
- If you're in the countryside (off the beaten track) be extra conservative in what you wear.
- Keep your distance. Remember that even innocent, friendly talk can be misconstrued as flirtation by men unused to close interaction with women. Ditto for any physical contact.
- If you need help for any reason (directions etc), ask a woman first.
- Be wary when horse or camel riding, especially at touristy places. It's not unknown for a guy to ride close to you and grab your horse, among other things. Riding with an unknown man on a horse or camel should be avoided.
- Egypt is not the place for acquiring a full suntan. Only on private beaches in the top-end resorts along the Red Sea and in southern Sinai are you likely to feel comfortable stripping down to a bikini. Along the Mediterranean coast and in oasis pools, you'll have to swim in shorts and a T-shirt at the very minimum, and even then you'll attract a flock of male onlookers. Egyptian women rarely go swimming at public beaches; when they do, they swim fully clothed, scarf and all.
- You may find it handy to learn the Arabic for 'don't touch me' (la' tilmasni). Also worth memorising are ihtirim nafsak (literally 'behave yourself') or haasib eedak (watch your hand). Swearing at would-be Romeos will only make matters worse.
- Being befriended by an Egyptian woman is a great way to learn more about life in Egypt and, at the same time, have someone totally nonthreatening to guide you around. Getting to know an Egyptian woman is, however, easier said than done. All we can say is seize on whatever opportunities you get.

although, as with anything forbidden, it still happens. Nevertheless, it is the exception rather than the rule – and that goes for men as well as women. For women, however, the issue is potentially far more serious. With the possible exception of the upper classes, women are expected to be virgins when they marry and a family's reputation can rest upon this point. In such a context the restrictions placed on a girl – no matter how onerous they may seem to a Westerner – are to protect her and her reputation from the potentially disastrous attentions of men.

The presence of foreign women presents, in the eyes of some Egyptian men, a chance to get around these norms with ease and without consequences. This belief is reinforced by

distorted impressions gained from Western TV and by the inappropriate clothing worn by some female tourists. As a woman traveller you may receive some verbal harassment at the very least. Serious physical harassment and rape do occasionally occur, but more rarely than in most Western countries.

What to Wear

Away from the Sinai and Red Sea beaches, Egyptians are quite conservative about dress. As with anywhere, take your cues from those around you: if you're in a rural area and all the women are in long, concealing dresses, you should be conservatively dressed. If you're going out to a hip Cairo nightspot, you're likely to see middle- and upper-class Egyptian girls in the briefest designer gear and can dress accordingly – just don't walk there.

It is particularly important to cover up when visiting mosques and churches – you'll find that carrying a shawl to use as a head covering will come in very useful, particularly when visiting areas such as Islamic and Old Cairo.

Unfortunately, although dressing conservatively should reduce the incidence of harassment, it by no means guarantees you'll be left alone.

WORK

More than 40,000 foreigners live and work in Egypt. It is possible to find work with one of the many foreign companies, especially if you begin your research before you leave home. *Cairo: A Practical Guide,* edited by Claire E Francy and published by the American University in Cairo Press (E£60), has lots of information about working in Cairo. Once you have an employer, securing a work permit through an Egyptian consulate or from the Ministry of the Interior (if you are in Egypt) should not be difficult.

If you are looking for casual work to extend your stay in Cairo then teaching English at a 'cowboy school' (see right) is probably the easiest way. It's sometimes possible to find other types of work in resorts. Dahab in particular has a relatively large number of travellers who find short-term work as bartenders or administrators in the many hotels and dive centres that dot the beach. There are also a few enterprising travellers who've financed their stay by setting up shop as masseurs, acupuncturists and herbalists.

Away from the beaches, some of the larger hotels in Luxor and Aswan occasionally take on foreigners as entertainment directors, but many of the large chains have their own staff sent in from abroad.

Dive Instructors

If you are a dive master or diving instructor you can find work in Egypt's diving resorts fairly easily. As many divers fund their travels through such work the turnover is high and you're likely to find an opening if you can hang around for a couple of weeks. Owners say that apart from the basic diving

qualifications, they look for languages and an ability to get along with people. If you're interested in a job, a dive centre will usually take you along on a few dive trips to assess your diving skills and to see how you interact with others before offering you work.

English Tutoring

The most easily available work for native or fluent English-speakers is teaching the language to the locals. The best places to do this are reputable schools such as the ILI in Cairo (see p523). However, all of these places require qualifications and the minimum requirement is a Certificate in English Language Teaching to Adults (Celta). The ILI runs several one-month intensive Celta courses each year and sometimes employs course graduates.

If you have no qualifications or experience, you could try one of the 'cowboy schools' such as central Cairo's **International Living Language Institute** (ILLI; 34 Talaat Harb, Cairo), which is on the top floor above El-Abd bakery. These are fly-by-night places (that said, the ILLI has been around for nearly 20 years) that take on unqualified staff and work them hard for little financial return. But they do pay enough to allow you to stay on and maybe earn enough to take the Celta and gravitate to better-paid employment.

Film & TV Extras

Europeans are often in demand to appear as background decoration in local TV commercials, dramas or even films. The work is far from glamorous and involves hanging around all day when often you're only required for five minutes of shooting. Still, it pays about E£50 per session. Notices for persons wanted are sometimes posted at the hostels in the Tawfiqiyya Souq in Cairo or, more commonly, middlemen will tell you. They haunt Ash-Shams coffeehouse (see p154) off Tawfiqiyya Souq.

Newspapers & Magazines

A source of work for English-speakers with a good sense of grammar is in copy-editing for one of Cairo's many English-language publications. *Cairo* magazine, *Egyptian Gazette* and *Al-Ahram Weekly* are probably the best places to inquire. The pay is nothing terrific.

Transport

GETTING THERE & AWAY

If you're heading to Egypt from Europe, the easiest way to get there is to fly direct. If you're coming from any other continent, it can sometimes be cheaper to fly first to Europe and then make your way to Egypt. And of course there are also the overland combinations of bus, taxi and ferry from other African and Middle Eastern countries to consider.

ENTERING THE COUNTRY

If you enter the country via Cairo airport, there are a few formalities. After walking past the dusty-looking duty-free shops you'll come to a row of exchange booths, including a Thomas Cook booth. If you haven't organised a visa, you'll need to pay US$15 or €15 here to receive a visa stamp (see p535). You then fill in one of the pink immigration forms available on the benches in front of the immigration officials before queuing to be processed. The whole process takes around 20 minutes.

WARNING – THINGS CHANGE

The information contained in this chapter is particularly vulnerable to change: prices for international travel are volatile, routes are introduced and cancelled, schedules change, special deals come and go, and rules and visa requirements are amended. Airlines and governments seem to take pleasure in making price structures and regulations as complicated as possible. You should check directly with the airline or your travel agency to make sure you understand how a fare (and ticket you may buy) works. In addition, the travel industry is highly competitive and there are many lurks and perks.

The upshot of this is that you should get opinions, quotes and advice from as many airlines and travel agencies as possible before parting with your hard-earned cash. The details given in this chapter should be regarded as pointers and are not a substitute for your own careful, up-to-date research.

Entering overland is more arduous as baggage checks are routine and there are departure and entry taxes to be paid.

Passport

Your passport should be valid for at least three months from the date of entry into the country.

AIR
Airports & Airlines

Egypt has quite a few airports, but only seven of these are official international ports of entry: Cairo, Alexandria, Luxor, Aswan, Hurghada, Sharm el-Sheikh and Marsa Alam. Most air travellers enter Egypt through Cairo, Alexandria or Sharm el-Sheikh. The other airports tend to be used by charter and package-deal flights only. The small airport near St Katherine's in Sinai is also sometimes used by international charters.

Egypt's international and national carrier is **EgyptAir** (MS; national call centre ☎ 0900 70000;

www.egyptair.com.eg; ☺ 8am-8pm). The airline's hub is Cairo International Airport. Egypt-Air's service isn't particularly good and its fleet is in need of an upgrade. You'll do better flying with a different airline. For details of its offices in Egypt, see Getting There & Away sections of destination chapters throughout the book.

Air tickets bought in Egypt are subject to hefty government taxes, which make them extremely expensive. Always try to fly in on a return or onward ticket.

For airport details, see the To/From the Airport information in the Getting Around section of destination chapters throughout the book.

Airlines that fly to/from Egypt include the following:

Air France (AF; in Cairo ☎ 02-575 8899; 2 Midan Talaat Harb, Downtown; www.airfrance.com) Hub: Charles de Gaulle Airport, Paris.

Alitalia (AZ; in Cairo ☎ 02-578 5823; Nile Hilton, 1113 Corniche el-Nil, Downtown; www.alitalia.it) Hub: Fiumicino, Rome.

British Airways (BA; www.britishairways.com) Cairo (☎ 02-578 0741-6; 1 Sharia Abdel Salam Aref, Midan Tahrir, Downtown); Cairo Airport ☎ (02-690 1690) Hub: Heathrow Airport, London.

El Al Israel Airlines (LY; in Cairo ☎ 02-736 1620; 5 Sharia al-Maqrizi, Zamalek; www.elal.com) Hub: Ben-Gurion Airport, Tel Aviv.

Emirates Airlines (EK; www.emirates.com) Cairo (☎ 02-336 1555; 18 Sharia Wizeraat El Zeraah, Mohandiseen); Cairo Airport (☎ 02-418 0305) Hub: Dubai International Airport, UAE.

KLM (KL; www.klm.ae) Cairo (☎ 02-580 5700; 11 Sharia Qasr el-Nil, Downtown); Cairo Airport (☎ 02-418 2386) Hub: Amsterdam International Airport.

Lufthansa (LH; in Cairo ☎ 02-739 8339; 6 Midan Sheikh al-Marsafy, Zamalek; www.lufthansa.com) Hub: Munchen Airport, Frankfurt.

Malaysia Airlines (MH) Cairo (☎ 02-576 6777; Nile Hilton, 1113 Corniche el-Nil, Downtown); Cairo Airport (☎ 02-266 3146) Hub: Kuala Lumpur International Airport.

DEPARTURE TAX

If you're leaving Egypt by air your departure tax will usually have been prepaid with your ticket. If you're departing by land, you'll need to pay E£2 (travellers who entered Egypt on a Sinai-only visa are exempt).

Middle East Airlines (ME; in Cairo ☎ 02-574 3422; 12 Sharia Qasr el-Nil, Downtown; www.mea.com.lb) Hub: Beirut International Airport.

Olympic Airways (OA; in Cairo ☎ 02-393 1277; www.olympic-airways.gr) Hub: Eleftherios Venizelos International Airport.

Royal Jordanian (RJ; in Cairo ☎ 02-575 0905; 6 Sharia Qasr el-Nil, Downtown; www.rja.com.jo) Hub: Amman International Airport.

Singapore Airlines (SQ; in Cairo ☎ 02-575 0276; Nile Hilton, 1113 Corniche el-Nil, Downtown; www.singapore airlines.com) Hub: Changi Airport, Singapore.

Syrian Arab Airlines (RB; in Cairo ☎ 02-392 8284/5; 25 Sharia Talaat Harb, Downtown www.syrianair.com) Also known as Syrianair; Hub: Damascus Airport.

Tickets

Most tickets are sold for flights in and out of Cairo, but sometimes it is possible to get cheaper deals to the airports serving resorts such as Sharm el-Sheikh. While you could use Sharm as a starting point for travelling around the country, it is a good six-hour bus ride from Cairo (where you'll need to go for connections to the rest of the country) and the loss of time may outweigh any potential savings in money.

Australia & New Zealand

The best way to get to Egypt is to fly to Singapore and/or Dubai, and then go on to Cairo. Singapore Airlines and Emirates Airlines fly out of Melbourne and Sydney and follow this route.

Two well-known agencies for air fares are **STA Travel** (☎ 1300 733 035; www.statravel.com .au) and **Flight Centre** (☎ 133 133; www.flightcentre .com.au).

Emirates Airlines flies from New Zealand to Dubai via Australia, and then on to Egypt. **STA Travel** (☎ 0508 782 872; www.statravel .co.nz) and **Flight Centre** (☎ 0800 243 544; www .flightcentre.co.nz) have branches throughout the country.

Canada

Canadian discount air-ticket sellers are known as consolidators. Their air fares tend to be about 10% higher than those sold in the USA. The *Globe & Mail, Toronto Star, Montreal Gazette* and *Vancouver Sun* carry travel agency ads and are a good place to look for cheap fares.

Travel CUTS (☎ 800-667 2887; www.travelcuts.com) is Canada's national student travel agency.

For online bookings try www.expedia.ca and www.travelocity.ca.

Mainland Europe

Innumerable airlines fly direct from their European hubs to Cairo. See p539 for a list.

UK

British Airways and EgyptAir offer direct flights from London to Cairo, and many other airlines fly via their European hubs.

Soliman Travel (☎ flights 020-7370 5159, tours 020-7244 6855; www.solimantravel.com) is a long-established Egypt specialist. Its prices are very competitive. Another good specialist often able to secure the cheapest fares is **Egypt On The Go** (☎ 020-8993 9993).

Popular travel agencies in the UK include **STA Travel** (☎ 020-7361 6142; www.statravel.co.uk) and **Trailfinders** (☎ 020-7938 3939; www.trailfinders .co.uk). For online bookings try www.travel bag.co.uk or www.ebookers.com.

USA

Discount travel agencies in the USA are also known as consolidators. San Francisco is the ticket-consolidator capital of the USA, although some good deals can be found in Los Angeles, New York and other big cities. Consolidators can be found through the Yellow Pages or the major daily newspapers. The *New York Times*, *Los Angeles Times*, *Chicago Tribune* and *San Francisco Examiner* all produce weekly travel sections in which you will find a number of travel agency ads.

Ticket Planet (www.ticketplanet.com) is a leading ticket consolidator in the USA. **STA Travel** (☎ 800-777 0112; www.statravel.com) has offices in most major cities.

The cheapest way from the USA to the Middle East and Africa is usually a return flight to London and a cheap fare from there. EgyptAir flies direct from New York and Los Angeles to Cairo. A round-the-world (RTW) ticket including a stopover in Cairo is also a possibility.

LAND

Egypt has land borders with Israel & the Palestinian Territories, Libya and Sudan, but for Sudan there is no open crossing point. The only way to travel between Egypt and Sudan is to fly or take the Wadi Halfa ferry (see p544). Though Jordan and Egypt do not share a land border, it is easy

to travel between the two countries by bus and car ferry across the Gulf of Aqaba.

Note that most international bus and ferry tickets must be paid for in US dollars.

Israel & the Palestinian Territories

The two official borders with Israel & the Palestinian Territories are Rafah and Taba.

RAFAH

At the time of research, the Rafah border crossing, which services a direct route from Cairo to Tel Aviv through the Gaza Strip, was closed to individual travellers. Responsibility for policing the border was relinquished by the Israelis after their withdrawal from Gaza in September 2005, and the border is now jointly policed by the Palestinian Authority and the Egyptian Government. At the time of writing, there were problems with border security – large groups of Palestinians illegally crossed into Egypt to shop and visit extended family as soon as the security handover took place, greatly upsetting the Egyptians. As a result, the situation is unsettled and foreigners are unlikely to be able to use the border crossing in the near future.

TABA

Taba is in the extreme east of Sinai, at the point where Egypt, Israel & the Palestinian Territories and Jordan almost come together. It's just a few kilometres from Eilat (Israel & the Palestinian Territories) and Aqaba (Jordan).

Egypt to Israel & the Palestinian Territories

The border crossing at Taba is used for the majority of travel between Egypt and Israel & the Palestinian Territories. Travellers make their way to Taba from destinations across Egypt and then walk across the border, which is open 24 hours, into Israel & the Palestinian Territories. An Israeli visa is not required for most nationalities. Once the border is crossed, taxis or buses (city bus E£15) can be taken the 4km to Eilat, from where there are frequent buses onward to Jerusalem and Tel Aviv. Keep in mind that there are no buses operating in Israel & the Palestinian Territories on Friday evenings or before sundown Saturday, the Jewish holy day of Shabbat.

Israel & the Palestinian Territories to Egypt

You must have a visa in advance unless your visit is limited to eastern Sinai or you have prearranged your entry with an Egyptian tour operator (see p535). If you don't have a visa there is an **Egyptian embassy** (☎ 03-546 4151; Rehov Basel 54, Tel Aviv; ☒ applications 9-11am Sun-Thu) in Tel Aviv and a **consulate** (☎ 972-637 6882; fax 972-637 1026; 68 Afrouni St; ☒ 9-11am Sun-Thu) in Eilat. An Egyptian visa sourced through either of these offices will cost 65NIS for US and German citizens and 100NIS for everyone else. Deliver your passport, application and one passport-sized photo during opening hours in the morning and you'll be able to pick up the visa around 2pm on the same day.

At the **border crossing** (☎ 08-637 2104, 08-636 0999) you'll need to pay a 68NIS fee to leave Israel & the Palestinian Territories. Once you've crossed the border you'll need to pay an Egyptian entry tax of E£30 at a booth about 1km south of the border on the main road. Alternatively, you can pick up a free Sinai-only entry permit (see p536).

Vehicles can be brought into Egypt from Eilat (you will pay around 32NIS on the Israel & the Palestinian Territories side and E£180 on the Egyptian side), but no private vehicles are permitted to cross at Taba *from* Egypt to Israel & the Palestinian Territories.

Bus

At the time of research **Misr Travel** (☎ 02-335 5470; Cairo Sheraton, Midan al-Galaa, Doqqi) and **Mazada Tours** (☎ 972 3 544 4454; www.mazada.co.il; 141 ibn Guirol St, Tel Aviv) were both running an express service (US$55, 12 to 14 hours) leaving the Cairo Sheraton Hotel on Sunday, Monday and Thursday at 9am, travelling via Taba to Tel Aviv and then heading on to Jerusalem. Contact the companies for details.

Three East Delta Bus Co buses run daily to Taba from Cairo's Turgoman Garage at 6.30am (E£55), 9.30am (E£55) and 10.15pm (E£75), a journey of around seven hours. If you're at one of the south Sinai resorts, such as Dahab, Nuweiba or Sharm el-Sheikh, there are plenty of buses heading north up the coast or you can jump in a service taxi if no other means are available.

Jordan

BUS

There's a twice-weekly Superjet service to Amman (US$70) leaving Cairo's Al-Mazah Garage on Sunday and Thursday at 5am. There is also a daily East Delta Bus Co service from here to Aqaba (US$41) at 8pm.

From Alexandria, there's one daily Superjet service to Amman (US$72) at 4pm and one service to Aqaba (US$34) at 6pm.

These services use the ferry between Nuweiba and Aqaba, so you will be liable for the port tax and the cost of a ferry ticket.

Libya

The border crossing point of Amsaad, just north of Halfaya Pass, is 12km west of Sallum. Service taxis run up the mountain between the town and the Egyptian side of the crossing for E£5. Once you've walked through passport control and customs, you can get a Libyan service taxi on to Al-Burdi for about LD1. From there, buses run to Tobruk and Benghazi.

Note, it is still not possible to get a Libyan visa at the border, but check with the Libyan embassy in Cairo (p526) as the regulations do seem to be becoming more user-friendly. It is also not possible to get an Egyptian visa at the border, but this may also change in the near future. Departure tax from Egypt is E£20; there is no Libyan departure tax.

BUS

From Cairo, one daily Superjet service leaves the Al-Mazah Garage near the airport at 7.30am going to Benghazi (E£140). East Delta Bus Co services also travel to Benghazi (E£114), leaving on Sunday, Tuesday, Wednesday and Friday at 8am. East Delta Bus Co services leave on Monday, Wednesday, Thursday and Saturday at 8am travelling to Tripoli (E£255).

East Delta Bus Co runs daily buses from Alexandria to Benghazi (E£115, 17 hours) and Tripoli (E£235, 24 hours) departing at midnight. Superjet has services to Benghazi (E£125, 17 hours) at 8.30am and to Tripoli (E£250, 24 hours) at 1am, 3am, 5am and 10am on Sunday, Tuesday and Thursday.

SEA & LAKE

Cyprus

From Port Said, boats to Limassol in Cyprus depart twice weekly from May to November. A ticket costs US$120 one way. For information and tickets, visit one of the many shipping agents in town. These include **Canal Tours** (☎ 066-332 1874, 012 798 6338; canaltours@bec.com.eg; 12 Sharia Palestine, Port Said; ✆ 8am-3pm & 7pm-midnight), a few blocks up from the tourist office. Note that some nationalities (mainly those from the subcontinent) must be in possession of a valid visa for Cyprus to be allowed on to the boats.

Europe
Mena Tours (☎ 066-322 5742, 066-323 3376; Sharia al-Gomhuriyya, Port Said) acts as the agency for the limited passenger-ship services that operate between Port Said and various Mediterranean destinations, including Beirut (Lebanon) and Antalya (Turkey). At the time of research no passenger boats were operating between Egyptian ports and any ports in Europe.

Israel & the Palestinian Territories
There's been talk about resuming the boat service from Port Said to Haifa in Israel & the Palestinian Territories; ask Canal Tours (see p544) for the latest information.

Jordan
There's an excellent fast-ferry service between Nuweiba in Egypt and Aqaba in Jordan leaving Nuweiba at 2pm and only taking one hour. One-way tickets cost US$55 for adults, US$39 for children three to 12 years old. You must be at the port two hours before departure so as to go through the shambolic departure formalities in the main ferry terminal building.

Tickets must be paid for in US dollars (note that these are not always available at the banks in Nuweiba) and can be purchased on the day of departure only at the **ticket office** (✆ 9am), in a small building near the port. To find it turn right when you exit the bus station, walking towards the water, and turn right again after the National Bank of Egypt. Continue one long block, and you'll see the sand-coloured ticket office building ahead to your left. The office stops selling tickets approximately one hour before the ferry leaves.

There's also a slow ferry (adult/child US$41/29, 2½hrs) leaving at noon daily.

No student discounts are available on these ferry services.

Note that boats are always full during the haj, and you'll need to purchase your ticket through a travel agent a long way in advance.

Free Jordanian visas can be obtained on the ferry if you have an EU, US, Canadian, Australian or New Zealand passport. Fill out a green form on board, give it and your passport to the immigration officers and – hey presto – your passport and visa are collected when you pass through Jordanian immigration at Aqaba. Other nationalities will need to organise a visa in advance.

Saudi Arabia
Telestar Tours runs an irregular service on its *El-Salaam* ferry between Suez and Jeddah (about 36 hours). Tickets (one way) cost E£300 for deck class, E£400 for 3rd class, E£500 for 2nd class and E£600 for 1st class (or the US dollar equivalent). The ferry carries cars. Once in Jeddah, you can arrange an onward ticket to Port Sudan. Note that getting a berth during the Haj is virtually impossible. **Mena Tours** (☎ 062-322 8821, 062-322 0269, 010 516 9841; Sharia Al-Marwa; ✆ 9am-3pm Sat-Thu) in Suez can organise tickets.

There is a daily fast ferry between Hurghada and Duba (three hours) on Tuesday, Friday and Sunday at 9am. It returns from Duba at 4pm on the same days. Tickets cost E£300/200 per adult/child one way. You must be at the port three hours before departure. For information, contact an agent for **International Fast Ferries Co** (☎ 065-344 7571; www.internationalfastferries.com) or inquire at the Hurghada port.

Another, much slower, ferry travels to Duba from Safaga on the Red Sea coast at 11pm daily, returning at 4pm. It takes about nine hours and costs E£210/185/150/125 in 1st/2nd/3rd/deck class. Vehicles cost US$100 to US$125 (or the equivalent in Egyptian pounds). Tickets are issued at **Sherif Tours** (☎ 065-252 685; Safaga port; ✆ 24hr).

You will not be allowed to board any of these services unless you have a valid Saudi visa in your passport.

PORT TAX

All Egyptian international ferries charge an E£50 port tax per person on top of the ticket price.

TRANSPORT

Sudan

VIA WADI HALFA

The **Nile River Valley Transport Corporation** Aswan (☎ 097-303 348; in the shopping arcade behind the tourist police office; ☺ 8am-2pm Sat-Thu); Cairo (☎ 02-575 9058; next to the 3rd-class ticket window at Ramses Station) runs one passenger ferry per week from Aswan to Wadi Halfa. One-way tickets cost E£383.50 for 1st class with bed in a cabin, E£236.50 for an airline seat and E£164.50 for deck class. At the time of research the ferry was departing on Monday at around noon. Tickets are also issued on Monday at the company's **office** (☎ 097-480 567) in Aswan Port. No tickets will be issued, nor will you be able to board the ferry, unless you have a valid Sudanese visa in your passport. Tea, soft drinks and snacks are available on board.

The trip takes between 16 and 24 hours (usually closer to 24). Passengers should arrive at about 8.30am to allow time to clear customs and fight for a decent seat. Some of the Sudanese immigration formalities are carried out on the boat; they'll ask for a yellow-fever certificate. The return trip departs Wadi Halfa on Wednesday.

The Nile Navigation Company attaches a pontoon to the ferry whenever it is needed. Prices are E£370 for a motorcycle and E£2455 for a car or 4WD. Drivers and passengers travel inside the ferry, for which they must also buy tickets. If you are taking a vehicle, you must have the usual *carnet de passage en douane* and allow plenty of time for customs procedures.

VIA THE RED SEA

At present there are no scheduled ships heading from Egypt to Port Sudan. You can get a boat from Suez to Jeddah and then from Jeddah to Port Sudan, but your transit visa will only be issued if you ensure that the ship leaves the same day that you arrive from Suez. For more information call **Mena-Tours** (☎ 062-228 821) in Suez and see p543.

Other Destinations

It's sometimes possible to find passage on private yachts from Suez to destinations such as India, South Africa and even Australia. Mohamed Moseilhy at **Canal Tours** (☎ 066-332 1874, 012 798 6338; canaltours@bec.com.eg; 12 Sharia Palestine, Suez; ☺ 8am-3pm & 7pm-midnight) is a good contact if you are keen to investigate this.

TOURS

There are any number of tour possibilities to Egypt, and there is a plethora of agencies dealing with everything from overland safaris to Nile cruises (see p285) or diving trips (see p456). The programmes on such trips are usually fairly tight, leaving little room for roaming on your own, but the advantages are that many of the time-consuming hassles, such as waiting for public transport and finding accommodation each night, are taken care of, therefore maximising time for exploring and sightseeing. There's also the security that comes with being in a group, which allows you to do things like camping out in the desert or exploring off-the-beaten-track activities that might be unsafe for individuals or couples.

It pays to shop around. When considering a tour, ask what the price includes. Flights? Visa fees? Site-admission fees? Food? Some companies include these in their prices, while others don't, so you need to be aware of what you're paying for when you compare prices.

Adventure & Overland Safaris

In this kind of tour you travel in a specially adapted 'overland truck' with anywhere from 16 to 24 other passengers and your group leader-cum-driver/navigator/nurse/mechanic/guide/fixer/entertainer. Accommodation is usually a mix of camping and budget hotels. Food is bought along the way and the group cooks and eats together. You are expected to muck in.

African Trails (☎ 020-7706 7384; www.africantrails .co.uk) Offers a three-week Istanbul to Cairo trip, a five-week 'Middle East Trail' trip and a two-week Egypt tour. Offices in the UK, Australia, New Zealand and Europe.

Dragoman (☎ 870-499 4475; www.dragoman.co.uk) A UK-based overland specialist with numerous itineraries through North Africa and the Middle East.

Other Tours

Following is a list of specialist operators that organise Egypt packages tailored for independently minded travellers looking for more than just two weeks in the sun.

AUSTRALIA

Intrepid Travel (☎ 03-8602 0500; www.intrepidtravel .com) Highly regarded small group tours with an emphasis on responsible tourism. Also has a London office.

Peregrine Adventures (☎ 03-9663 8611; www .peregrineadventures.com) An agent for the UK's Dragoman, Exodus and the Imaginative Traveller.

EGYPT

Egypt Panorama Tours (☎ 02-359 0200; www.ep tours.com; 4 Rd 79, Ma'adi, Cairo) One of the best and most reputable agencies in Egypt; accepts bookings from overseas.

Experience Egypt (☎ 02-302 8364; www.experience -egypt.com; 42 Sharia Abu el-Mahassen el-Shazly, Mohandiseen, Cairo) Part of Lady Egypt Tours. Organises small group tours of Sinai, Alexandria and the Nile Valley that are marketed in the UK and Canada.

UK

Bales Tours (☎ 0870 752 0780; www.balesworldwide .com) Bales Tours runs upmarket tours utilising five-star accommodation.

Egypt On The Go (☎ 020-7371 1113; www.egypton thego.com) Tours of Egypt and PADI diving-course holidays. Also has an Australian office.

Exodus (☎ 0870 240 5550; www.exodus.co.uk) Includes Nile cruises and tours around Sinai and through the Western Desert.

Explore Worldwide (☎ 0800 227 8747; www.explore worldwide.com) A variety of short and long itineraries.

Hayes & Jarvis (☎ 0870 366 1636; www.hayes-jarvis .com) A respected Egypt specialist.

Imaginative Traveller (☎ 0800 316 2717; www .imaginative-traveller.com) Small group tours.

Voyages Jules Vernes (☎ 0845 166 7003; www.vjv .co.uk) Top-class tour operator.

Wind, Sand & Stars (☎ 020-7359 7551; www.wind sandstars.co.uk) A Sinai specialist that organises trips involving climbing and walking, desert camping, bird-watching and snorkelling.

USA & CANADA

Abercrombie & Kent (☎ 1800 554 7016; www.aber crombiekent.com) Classy packages using top-end hotels, domestic flights and its own custom-built Nile cruisers. Has offices worldwide, including in Cairo.

Bestway Tours & Safaris (☎ 604-264 7378; www .bestway.com) Canadian company offering small group tours. These include a tour from Siwa to Ghadames in Libya and one visiting Egypt, Israel & the Palestinian Territories and Jordan.

GETTING AROUND

Egypt has a very extensive public and private transport system. You can travel just about anywhere in Egypt relatively cheaply.

AIR

EgyptAir is the main domestic carrier. **Air Sinai** (Map pp94-5; ☎ 02-577 2949; Nile Hilton, 1113 Corniche el-Nil, Cairo), which to all intents and purposes is EgyptAir by another name, is just about the only other operator. Fares are expensive and there are no student discounts. Travellers flying the international sectors of their journey with EgyptAir should receive a 50% discount on internal flights. Check with your travel agency at the time of booking.

During the high season (October to April), many flights are full so it's wise to book as far in advance as possible. Due to volatile exchange rates, these fares are likely to increase; check with the airline for the latest figures. The return cost is always double the one-way cost.

From	To	One way
Aswan	Abu Simbel	E£320
Cairo	Aswan	E£1037
	Hurghada	E£740
	Luxor	E£714
	Sharm el-Sheikh	E£733
Luxor	Aswan	E£364
	Sharm el-Sheikh	E£537

For EgyptAir contact details see the Getting There & Away section of individual cities and towns.

BICYCLE

You meet very few cyclists touring Egypt. There's no reason why it shouldn't be possible, particularly in Sinai and along the Nile Valley. The major problem would be the heat, which is at its worst from June to August. May to mid-June and September to October would be the best times for two-wheel touring, and even then, it would be necessary to make an early morning start and be finished by early afternoon.

Carrying a full kit with you is recommended, as spares are hard to come by, although in a pinch Egyptians are excellent 'bush mechanics'.

Members of **Cairo Cyclists** (☎ 02-519 6078) reckon the best place in Cairo for repairs is Ghoukho Trading & Supplies near St Mark's Cathedral, 800m south of Midan Ramses. It's quite hard to find, so be prepared to ask for directions.

TRANSPORT

TRANSPORT

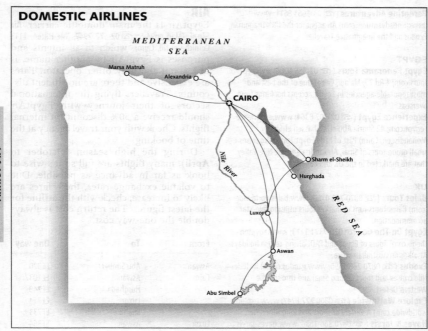

DOMESTIC AIRLINES

If you are considering cycling Egypt but have a few pressing questions that first need answering, one place to go is the Thorn Tree on Lonely Planet's website (www.lonelyplanet.com). Post your query on the Activities branch and there's a strong likelihood somebody will respond with the information that you're looking for.

Alternatively, you could contact the **Cyclists' Touring Club** (CTC; ☎ 01483-417 217; www.ctc .org.uk), a UK-based organisation that, among other things, produces information sheets on cycling in different parts of the world. At the time of research it had a dossier on Egypt. The club also publishes a good, glossy bimonthly magazine that always carries one or two travel-type cycling pieces.

BOAT

For Nile cruises and felucca trips see the Cruising the Nile chapter on p285.

BUS

Buses service just about every city, town and village in Egypt. Ticket prices are generally comparable with the cost of 2nd-class train tickets. Intercity buses, especially on shorter runs and in Upper Egypt, tend to become crowded, and even if you are lucky enough to get a seat in the first place, you'll probably end up with something or somebody on your lap. The prices of tickets for buses on the same route will usually vary according to whether or not they have air-con and video, how old the bus is and how long it takes to make the journey – the more you pay, the more comfort you travel in and the quicker you get to your destination.

Relatively comfortable, air-con 'deluxe' buses travel between Cairo, Alexandria, Ismailia, Port Said, Suez, St Katherine's Monastery, Sharm el-Sheikh, Hurghada and Luxor. Tickets cost a bit more than those for standard buses, but they're still cheap. The best of the deluxe bus companies is Superjet – try to travel with them whenever possible.

The bulk of buses servicing other routes are uncomfortable, dirty and noisy. Arabic videos, pop music or Quranic dirges are played at ear-splittingly loud levels – it's a good idea to take earplugs. You might also find a sweater or scarf handy on overnight buses as the air-con brings the temperature way down.

These days most buses have a strict no-smoking rule. On some trips passengers are offered water (no charge, but remember that it's from the tap) and on the deluxe or VIP services snacks and tea are sometimes offered (beware: these are not included in the price of the ticket). These buses also sometimes have toilets on board, but these are often filthy – you're usually better off waiting for the designated toilet stop en route.

Tickets can be bought at bus stations or often on the bus. Hang on to your ticket until you get off, as inspectors almost always board to check fares. You should also always carry your passport, as buses are often stopped at military checkpoints for random identity checks. This is particularly common on the bus between Aswan and Abu Simbel, and all Sinai buses.

It is advisable to book tickets in advance, at least on very popular routes (such as from Cairo to Sinai) and those with few buses running (from Cairo to the Western Desert). International Student Identification Cards (ISIC) now get passengers discounts on some bus routes, so always remember to ask. Where you are allowed to buy tickets on the bus, you generally end up standing if you don't have an assigned seat with a booked ticket. On short runs there are no bookings and it's a case of first on, best seated.

CAR & MOTORCYCLE

Driving in Cairo is a crazy affair, so think seriously before you decide to rent a car there. Driving in other parts of the country, at least in daylight, isn't so bad (though you should avoid intercity driving at night). And having a car – or better still a 4WD – opens up entire areas of the country where public transport is nonexistent.

A motorcycle would be an ideal way to travel around Egypt. The only snag is that you have to bring your own and the red tape involved is extensive. Ask your country's automobile association and Egyptian embassy about regulations.

TRANSPORT

ROAD DISTANCES (KM)

	Al-Arish	Al-Fayoum	Alexandria	Aswan	Asyut	Beni Suef	Cairo	Giza	Hurghada	Ismailia	Luxor	Marsa Matruh	Minya	Port Said	Sharm el-Sheikh	Suez
Al-Arish	---															
Al-Fayoum	431	---														
Alexandria	451	327	---													
Aswan	1238	822	1133	---												
Asyut	712	296	607	526	---											
Beni Suef	453	37	346	785	259	---										
Cairo	325	106	220	913	387	128	---									
Giza	333	98	228	903	377	118	8	---								
Hurghada	668	636	754	496	478	532	530	538	---							
Ismailia	185	246	266	1053	527	268	140	148	483	---						
Luxor	955	608	919	209	322	571	699	689	287	770	---					
Marsa Matruh	741	617	290	1423	897	638	510	518	1040	556	1209	---				
Minya	579	163	473	659	133	126	254	244	611	394	455	764	---			
Port Said	200	331	354	1138	612	353	225	233	563	85	850	644	479	---		
Sharm el-Sheikh	638	610	710	1279	909	632	504	512	783	444	1070	1000	758	529	---	
Suez	287	273	354	1047	521	262	134	142	395	88	682	644	388	168	388	---

Petrol and diesel are readily available and very cheap (18pt a litre). Lead-free is only available at a handful of pumps in Cairo (mainly in Mohandiseen, Zamalek and Ma'adi) and Alexandria. When travelling out of Cairo, remember that petrol stations are not always that plentiful; when you see one, fill up.

Bringing Your Own Vehicle

If you're bringing a car or motorcycle into the country, you'll need the vehicle's registration papers, liability insurance and an International Driving Permit in addition to your domestic licence. You will also need multiple copies of a *carnet de passage en douane*, which is effectively a passport for the vehicle, and acts as a temporary waiver of import duty. The carnet may also need to list any expensive spares that you're planning to carry with you, such as a gearbox. If you're driving a car, you'll also need a fire extinguisher. Contact your local automobile association for details about all documentation.

At the Egyptian border, you'll be issued with a licence valid for three months (less if your visa is valid for less time). You can renew the licence every three months for a maximum of two years but you'll have to pay a varying fee each time. There is an E£1032 customs charge (also valid for three months) and you must pay E£210 for number-plate insurance (keep your receipt and you'll be refunded E£20 for the plates when you leave the country). The COMESA Yellow Card is not accepted for insurance.

The Egyptians themselves give conflicting advice on whether or not diesel-powered vehicles may enter the country. People wishing to bring in 4WDs should check at an Egyptian embassy, as the rules governing these vehicles are contentious. For further information try contacting the **Automobile & Touring Club of Egypt** (☎ 02-574 3355; 10 Qasr el-Nil, Cairo; ⏰ 9am-1.30pm Sat-Thu).

If you plan to take your own vehicle, check in advance which spares are likely to be available. You may have trouble finding some parts for your car.

THE CURSE OF THE CONVOYS

If you're planning on travelling by road in the Nile Valley or along parts of the Red Sea coast you have no choice but to do so in a police-escorted convoy. A legacy of the Islamist insurgency of the 1990s, which reached its apogee with the 1997 terrorist attack at the Temple of Hatshepsut in Luxor, the convoy system was introduced by the Egyptian government so as to give foreign tourists a sense of personal security when travelling through the Nile Valley and across to Hurghada. Fast forward to 2006, and what the government is providing for these valuable tourists is just one enormous pain in the neck. Put simply, the convoys are a farce, with their only real purpose being to provide much-needed duties for the country's large and underemployed tourist police force.

Take the daily convoy from Aswan to Abu Simbel, for instance, which comprises a long line of coaches, minibuses and taxis all driving dangerously fast on poor roads at the same time of every morning of every day of every week. All this convoy does is ensure that any would-be terrorists will know exactly when and where large groups of foreign tourists can be targeted – it's almost as if the government wants to provide sitting ducks. The few police who do accompany the convoys are inadequately armed and spend all of their time proving their machismo by driving faster than the average Formula One competitor, in turn forcing every driver in the convoy to drive in the same irresponsible way. It's like the Wacky Races, with minibuses overtaking coaches and the occasional clapped out Peugeot trying to assert itself by dodging dangerously between the bigger vehicles. And having braved the convoy, its frustratingly rigid schedule means that all tourists only get two hours or so at one of the most significant sites in Egypt.

The convoys between Luxor and Aswan and Luxor and Hurghada are equally ridiculous, and are also frustrating in that they end up dictating whole itineraries – most only leave a couple of times per day, and don't allow stops at major sites in the afternoon (no doubt so the tourist police can knock off work early; see also the boxed text, p200). This results in many tourists missing sites such as Abydos altogether purely because the convoy won't stop en route. Appalling.

We say it's high time that this curse is lifted.

Driving Licence

Drivers with non-Egyptian licences need an International Driving Permit to drive in Egypt. Ensure that you keep this with you at all times while you are driving – if you cannot supply it when stopped a hefty fine will be levied and you may have to leave your vehicle with the police until you can produce your licence. Likewise, ensure that you always have all car registration papers with you while driving.

Hire

Several car rental agencies have offices in Egypt, including Avis, Hertz, Thrifty, Europcar and Budget. See p165 for details of car-hire firms in Cairo. Their rates match international charges and finding a cheap deal with local agencies is virtually impossible. No matter which company you go with, make sure you read the fine print.

An International Driving Permit is required and you can be hit with a heavy fine if you're caught renting a car without one. Drivers should be over the age of 25.

If you choose to hire a car, rates are around US$50 a day for a small Toyota (100km included, $0.25 per km after this) to US$90 a day for a Cherokee 4WD ($0.40 for extra km). This doesn't include taxes. Prices generally include insurance and the first 100km, but check this before signing. Remember that taxes of up to 17% (depending on where you are) will be added to your bill. It's usually possible to pay with travellers cheques or by credit card.

Some companies, such as Europcar, offer the option of one-way rentals from, for example, Cairo to Sharm el-Sheikh. It's also possible to hire a car plus a driver for those who don't feel like tackling Egyptian roads.

Road Rules

Driving is on the right-hand side. The official speed limit outside towns is 90km/h (though it is often less in some areas) and 100km/h on four-lane highways such as the one between Cairo and Alexandria. If you're caught speeding the police confiscate your licence and you have to go to the traffic headquarters in the area to get it back – a lengthy and laborious process. A few roads, such as the Cairo-Alexandria Desert Hwy, the Cairo–Fayoum road and the road

through the Ahmed Hamdi Tunnel (which goes under the Suez Canal near Suez) are subject to tolls of about E£1.50.

Many roads have checkpoints where police often ask for identity papers, so make sure you've got your passport and driving licence on hand or you may be liable for a US$100 on-the-spot fine.

Although city driving may seem chaotic, there is one cardinal rule: whoever is in front has the right of way – even if a car is only 1cm ahead of you and cuts across your path suddenly, you'll be liable if you hit it.

When driving through the countryside, keep in mind that children and adults are liable to wander into your path, even on main roads. Drive very carefully and use your horn liberally – hitting someone, even if it was their own fault, can sometimes result in the driver being attacked by angry villagers. If you do have an accident, get to the nearest police station as quickly as possible and report what happened.

HITCHING

Hitching is never entirely safe in any country in the world, and it is not recommended. Travellers who decide to hitch should understand that they are taking a small but potentially serious risk. People who do choose to hitch will be safer if they travel in pairs and let someone know where they are planning to go. Women must never hitch on their own here, as the general assumption about such behaviour is that only prostitutes would do such a thing.

LOCAL TRANSPORT

As well as the local transport options described here, some cities and towns have their own – most are variations on the pony-and-trap theme.

Bus & Minibus

Cairo and Alexandria are the only cities with their own bus systems. Taking a bus in either place is an experience far beyond simply getting from A to B. Firstly there's getting on. Egyptians stampede buses, charging the entrance before the thing has even slowed. Hand-to-hand combat ensues as they run alongside trying to leap aboard. If you wait for the bus to stop, the pushing and shoving to get on is worse. Often several passengers don't quite manage to get on and they make their journey hanging off the back doorway, clinging perilously to the frame or to someone with a firmer hold.

The scene inside the bus in this case usually resembles a Guinness World Record attempt on the greatest number of people in a fixed space. At some point during the trip, a man will somehow manage to squeeze his way through to sell you your ticket.

The buses rarely completely stop to let you off. You stand in the doorway, wait for the opportune moment and launch yourself onto the road.

Taking a minibus is an easier option. Passengers are not allowed to stand (although this rule is frequently overlooked), and each minibus leaves as soon as every seat is taken.

Metro
Cairo is the only city in Egypt with a metro system (for more details see p165).

Microbus
Privately owned and usually unmarked microbuses shuttle around all the larger cities. For the average traveller they can be difficult to use, as it is unclear where most of them go; however, quite often there's a small boy hanging out of the doorway yelling the destination. In Cairo, you might have occasion to use a microbus to get out to the Pyramids, while in Alexandria they shuttle the length of Tariq al-Horreyya and the Corniche to Montazah, and in Sharm el-Sheikh they carry passengers between Old Sharm, Na'ama Bay and Shark's Bay. Most of the smaller cities and towns have similar microbuses doing set runs around town.

Pick-Up
As well as servicing routes between smaller towns, covered pick-up trucks are sometimes used within towns as local taxis. This is especially so in some of the oases towns, on Luxor's West Bank and in smaller places along the Nile. Should you end up in one of these, there are a couple of ways you can indicate to the driver when you want to get out: if you are lucky enough to have a seat, pound on the floor with your foot; alternatively ask one of the front passengers to hammer on the window behind the driver; or, lastly, use the buzzer that you'll occasionally find rigged up.

Taxi
There are taxis in most cities in Egypt; in Cairo they're all black and white, while in Alexandria they're black and orange. Almost every second car is a taxi and they are by far the most convenient way of getting about. Stand at the side of the road, stick your hand out and shout your destination at any cab passing in the right direction. It doesn't matter if there is already someone inside because taxis are shared. When a taxi stops, restate where you want to go and if the driver's amenable, hop in.

Do not ask 'how much?' The etiquette is that you get in knowing what to pay and when you arrive, you get out and hand the money through the window. Make sure that you have the correct money (hoard E£1 bills) because getting change out of drivers is like having your teeth pulled. If a driver suspects that you don't know what the correct fare is then you're fair game for fleecing. If once you get in the taxi the driver starts talking money then just state a fair price (we give examples of correct fares throughout this book) and if it's not accepted, get out and find another car.

Often when it comes to paying, a driver will demand more money and may yell. Don't be intimidated and don't be drawn into an argument. As long as you know you're not underpaying (and the fares in this book are generous), just walk away. It's all bluster and the driver is playing on the fact that you're a *khwaga* (foreigner) and don't know better.

Tram
Cairo and Alexandria are the only two cities in the country with tram systems. While Alexandria still has a fairly extensive and efficient network, Cairo now only has a handful of lines. See p166 for more details.

MICROBUS
A slightly bigger version of the service taxi, the *meecrobus* is a Toyota van that would normally take about 12 people but in Egypt takes as many as 22. These run on the same principle as service taxis and cost about the same, but operate on fewer routes.

> **'TAXI!'**
>
> Taxis are at once a blessing and a curse. They're a remarkably convenient and easily afford-able way of getting around the city but they can also be a frequent source of unpleasantness when it comes to paying the fare. The problem comes with the unmetered system of payment, which can lead to discontent. Passengers frequently feel that they've been taken advantage of (which they often have), while drivers are occasionally genuinely aggrieved by what they see as underpayment. So why don't the drivers use the meter? Because they were all calibrated at a time when petrol was ludicrously cheap. That time has long passed and any driver relying on his meter would now be out of pocket every time he came to fill up.
>
> Taxi driving is far from being a lucrative profession. Of the more than 60,000 taxis on the road in Cairo it would be a safe bet to assume none of the drivers are yet millionaires. Average earnings after fuel has been paid are about E£8 per hour. Consider too, that many drivers don't even own their car and have to hand over part of their earnings as 'rent'.
>
> Which isn't to say that next time you flag a taxi for a short hop across town and the driver hisses '10 pounds' that you should smile and say 'OK', but maybe you can see that from a certain point of view, it was worth his while trying. After all, if you can afford to make it all the way to Egypt, you can probably afford to pay a bit more than the going rate for a taxi and so make the taxi driver's hard slog of a life just that tiny bit easier.

PICK-UP

Toyota and Chevrolet pick-up trucks cover a lot of the routes between smaller towns and villages off the main roads. The general rule is to get 12 inside the covered rear of the truck, often with an assortment of goods squeezed in on the floor. After that, it's a matter of how many can and want to scramble on to the roof or hang off at the rear.

SERVICE TAXI

Travelling by *servees* is one of the fastest ways to go from city to city. Service taxis are generally big Peugeot 504 cars that run intercity routes. Drivers congregate near bus and train stations and tout for passengers by shouting their destination. When the car's full, it's off. A driver won't leave before his car is full unless you and/or the other passengers want to pay for all of the seats. Fares are usually cheaper than either the buses or trains and there are no set departure times, you just turn up and find a car. The drawbacks are that with six or seven squeezed in, journeys tend to be a bit uncomfortable and there's little room for baggage. Try and grab a window seat if at all possible. Service-taxi rides can also be a little hairy at times – the drivers tend to be overconfident and often tired from long shifts on the road. Accidents involving service taxis are all too common and for this reason using them is not recommended unless as a last resort.

TRAIN

Although trains travel along more than 5000km of track to almost every major city and town in Egypt, the system is badly in need of modernisation (it's a relict of the British occupation). Most services are grimy and battered and are a poor second option to the deluxe bus. The exceptions are the *Turbini* and *Espani* services to Alexandria and the tourist and sleeping trains down to Luxor and Aswan – on these routes the train is the preferred option over the bus.

If you have an International Student Identification Card (ISIC) discounts of about 33% are granted on all fares except those for the sleeping-car services. It is possible to travel from Cairo to Aswan for only a few pounds if you have an ISIC and are willing to suffer in the 3rd-class cars.

Classes & Services

Trains with sleeping cars (wagons-lit) are the most comfortable and among the fastest in Egypt. The cars, which are run by Abela Egypt, are the same as those used by trains in Europe. At least one sleeping train travels between Alexandria, Cairo, Luxor and Aswan every day. For details see the Getting There & Away sections of those cities.

The Abela sleeping trains are 1st class only and must be booked in advance. Compartments come with a seat that converts

TRANSPORT

into a bed, a fold-down bunk (clean linen, pillows and blankets) and a small basin with running water. Beds are quite short, and tall people may spend an uncomfortable night as a result. It's worth requesting a middle compartment, as those at the ends of the carriages are near the toilets and can be noisy. Shared toilets are generally clean and have toilet paper. Aircraft-style dinners and breakfasts are served in the compartments, but you shouldn't expect a gourmet experience. Drinks (including alcohol) are served by the steward. A beer costs E£15, tea is E£2.25, mineral water is E£3.75 and a small wine is E£31.50. It's worth taking mineral water with you (to clean teeth and to drink).

Regular night trains with and without sleeper compartments and meals included

leave for Luxor and Aswan every day and cost much less than the sleeping trains. Reservations must be made in advance at Ramses Station in Cairo. Unless you specify otherwise, you'll be issued with a ticket that includes meals on board. You may want to flout the rules and bring your own food. Both 1st- and 2nd-class compartments have air-con and they can get chilly at night; have something warm to put on.

Non-air-con trains are next down the scale. Classes are divided into 2nd-class ordinary, which generally has padded seats, and 3rd class, where seating is of the wooden bench variety. These trains are generally filthy, tend to spend a lot of time at a lot of stations and can be subject to interminable delays.

Health Dr Caroline Evans

Prevention is the key to staying healthy while travelling in Egypt. Infectious diseases can and do occur here, but these are usually associated with poor living conditions and poverty, and can be avoided with a few precautions. The most common reason for travellers needing medical help is as a result of accidents – cars are not always well maintained and poorly lit roads are littered with potholes. Medical facilities can be excellent in large cities, but may be more basic in other areas.

BEFORE YOU GO

A little planning before departure, particularly for pre-existing illnesses, will save you a lot of trouble later. See your dentist before a long trip; carry a spare pair of contact lenses and glasses (take your optical prescription with you); and carry a first-aid kit.

It's tempting to leave it to the last minute – don't! Many vaccines don't ensure immunity for two weeks, so visit a doctor four to eight weeks before departure. Ask your doctor for an International Certificate of Vaccination (also known as the yellow booklet), which lists all the vaccinations you've received. This is mandatory for countries that require proof of yellow fever vaccination, but it's a good idea to carry it wherever you travel.

Travellers can register with the **International Association for Medical Advice to Travellers** (IAMAT; www.iamat.org). Their website can help travellers to find a doctor with recognised training. Those heading off to very remote areas may like to do a first-aid course (Red Cross and St John Ambulance can help) or attend a remote medicine first-aid course such as that offered by the **Royal Geographical Society** (www.rgs.org).

Bring your medications in their original, clearly labelled, containers. A signed, dated letter from your physician describing your medical conditions and medications, including generic names, is also a good idea. If carrying syringes or needles, be sure to have a physician's letter documenting their medical necessity.

INSURANCE

Find out in advance if your insurance plan will make payments directly to providers or reimburse you later for overseas health expenditures (in many countries doctors expect payment in cash); it's also worth ensuring your travel insurance will cover repatriation home or to better medical facilities elsewhere. Your insurance company may be able to locate the nearest source of medical help, or you can ask at your hotel. In an emergency contact your embassy or consulate. Your travel insurance will not usually cover you for anything other than emergency dental treatment. Not all insurance covers emergency aeromedical evacuation home or to a hospital in a major city, which may be the only way to get medical attention for a serious emergency.

RECOMMENDED VACCINATIONS

The World Health Organization (WHO) recommends that all travellers, regardless of the region they are travelling in, should be covered for diphtheria, tetanus, measles, mumps, rubella and polio, as well as hepatitis B. While making travel preparations, take the opportunity to ensure that all of your routine vaccination cover is complete.

HEALTH

The consequences of these diseases can be very severe and outbreaks do occur in the Middle East.

MEDICAL CHECKLIST
Following is a list of other items you should consider packing in your medical kit.

- Antibiotics (if travelling off the beaten track)
- Antidiarrhoeal drugs (eg loperamide)
- Acetaminophen/paracetamol (Tylenol) or aspirin
- Anti-inflammatory drugs (eg ibuprofen)
- Antihistamines (for hay fever and allergic reactions)
- Antibacterial ointment (eg Bactroban) for cuts and abrasions
- Steroid cream or cortisone (for allergic rashes)
- Bandages, gauze, gauze rolls
- Adhesive or paper tape
- Scissors, safety pins, tweezers
- Thermometer
- Pocket knife
- DEET-containing insect repellent for the skin
- Permethrin-containing insect spray for clothing, tents, and bed nets
- Sun block
- Oral rehydration salts
- Iodine tablets (for water purification)
- Syringes and sterile needles (if travelling to remote areas)

INTERNET RESOURCES
There is a wealth of travel health advice on the Internet. For further information, the **Lonely Planet** (www.lonelyplanet.com) website is a good place to start. **The World Health Organization** (www.who.int/ith/) publishes a superb book, *International Travel and Health,* which is revised annually and is available online at no cost. Another website of general interest is **MD Travel Health** (www.mdtravelhealth.com), which

---

TRAVEL HEALTH WEBSITES

It's usually a good idea to consult your government's travel-health website before departure, if one is available.

Australia (www.dfat.gov.au/travel)
Canada (www.travelhealth.gc.ca)
UK (www.doh.gov.uk/travel advice)
United States (www.cdc.gov/travel)

---

provides complete travel health recommendations for every country, updated daily, also at no cost. The **Centers for Disease Control and Prevention website** (www.cdc.gov) is a useful source of travellers' health information.

FURTHER READING
Lonely Planet's *Healthy Travel* is packed with useful information including pretrip planning, emergency first aid, immunisation and disease information, as well as what to do if you get sick on the road. Other recommended references include *Traveller's Health* by Dr Richard Dawood (Oxford University Press), *International Travel Health Guide* by Stuart R Rose, MD (Travel Medicine Inc) and *The Travellers' Good Health Guide* by Ted Lankester (Sheldon Press), an especially useful health guide for volunteers and long-term expatriates working in the Middle East.

IN TRANSIT

DEEP VEIN THROMBOSIS (DVT)
Deep vein thrombosis occurs when blood clots form in the legs during plane flights, chiefly because of prolonged immobility. The longer the flight, the greater the risk. Though most blood clots are reabsorbed uneventfully, some may break off and travel through the blood vessels to the lungs, where they may cause life-threatening complications.

The chief symptom of deep vein thrombosis is swelling or pain of the foot, ankle or calf, usually but not always on just one side. When a blood clot travels to the lungs, it may cause chest pain and difficulty breathing. Travellers with any of these symptoms should immediately seek medical attention.

To prevent the development of deep vein thrombosis on long flights you should walk about the cabin, perform isometric compressions of the leg muscles (ie contract the leg muscles while sitting), drink plenty of fluids, and avoid alcohol and tobacco.

JET LAG & MOTION SICKNESS
Jet lag is common when crossing more than five time zones; it results in insomnia, fatigue, malaise or nausea. To avoid jet lag try drinking plenty of fluids (nonalcoholic) and eating light meals. Upon arrival, seek

exposure to natural sunlight and readjust your schedule (for meals, sleep etc) as soon as possible.

Antihistamines such as dimenhydrinate (Dramamine) and meclizine (Antivert, Bonine) are usually the first choice for treating motion sickness. Their main side-effect is drowsiness. A herbal alternative is ginger, which works like a charm for some people.

IN EGYPT

AVAILABILITY & COST OF HEALTH CARE

The health care systems in Egypt are varied. Care can be excellent in private hospitals and those associated with universities, but patchier elsewhere. Reciprocal payment arrangements with other countries rarely exist and you should be prepared to pay for all medical and dental treatment.

Medical care is not always readily available outside major cities. Medicine, and even sterile dressings or intravenous fluids, may need to be bought from a pharmacy. Nursing care may be limited or rudimentary as this is something families and friends are expected to provide. The travel assistance provided by your insurance may be able to locate the nearest source of medical help, otherwise ask at your hotel. In an emergency contact your embassy or consulate.

Standards of dental care are variable and there is an increased risk of hepatitis B and HIV transmission via poorly sterilised equipment. And keep in mind that your travel insurance will not usually cover you for anything other than emergency dental treatment.

For minor illnesses such as diarrhoea, pharmacists, who are well qualified, can often provide valuable advice and sell over-the-counter medication. They can also advise whether more specialised help is needed.

INFECTIOUS DISEASES

The following diseases are all present in Egypt.

Diphtheria

Spread through close respiratory contact, diphtheria causes a high temperature and severe sore throat. Sometimes a membrane forms across the throat requiring a tracheostomy to prevent suffocation. Vaccination is recommended for those who are likely to be in close contact with the local population in infected areas. The vaccine is given as an injection alone or with tetanus, and lasts 10 years.

Hepatitis A

This is spread through contaminated food (particularly shellfish) and water. It causes jaundice, and although it is rarely fatal, can cause prolonged lethargy and delayed recovery. Symptoms include dark urine, a yellow colour to the whites of the eyes, fever and abdominal pain. Hepatitis Avaccine (Avaxim, VAQTA, Havrix) is given as an injection: a single dose will give protection for up to a year, while a booster 12 months later will provide a subsequent 10 years of protection. Hepatitis A and typhoid vaccines can also be given as a single-dose vaccine (hepatyrix or viatim).

Hepatitis B

Hepatitis B is transmitted by infected blood, contaminated needles and sexual intercourse. It can cause jaundice, and affects the liver, occasionally causing liver failure. All travellers should make this a routine vaccination. (Many countries now give hepatitis B vaccination as part of routine childhood vaccination.) The vaccine is given singly, or at the same time as the hepatitis A vaccine (hepatyrix). A course will give protection for at least five years. It can be given over four weeks, or six months.

HIV

HIV is spread via infected blood and blood products, sexual intercourse with an infected partner and from an infected mother to her newborn child. It can be spread through 'blood to blood' contacts such as contaminated instruments during medical, dental, acupuncture and body-piercing procedures and sharing used intravenous needles.

Malaria

Malaria is found in certain parts of some of the oases; risk varies seasonally. Risk of malaria in most cities is minimal, but check with your doctor if you are considering travelling to any rural areas. It is important to take antimalarial tablets if the risk is significant. For up-to-date information about the risk of contracting malaria, contact your local travel health clinic.

Anyone who has travelled in a country where malaria is present should be aware of the symptoms of malaria. It is possible to contract malaria from a single bite from an infected mosquito. Malaria almost always starts with marked shivering, fever and sweating. Muscle pains, headache and vomiting are common. Symptoms may occur anywhere from a few days to three weeks after the infected mosquito bite. The illness can start while you are taking preventative tablets if they are not fully effective, and may also occur after you have finished taking your tablets.

Poliomyelitis

This generally spreads through contaminated food and water. It is one of the vaccines given in childhood and should be boosted every 10 years, either orally (a drop on the tongue) or as an injection. Polio may be carried asymptomatically, but it can cause a transient fever and, in rare cases, potentially permanent muscle weakness or paralysis.

Rabies

Rabies spreads through bites or licks on broken skin from an infected animal. Rabies is fatal. Animal handlers should be vaccinated, as should those travelling to remote areas where a reliable source of postbite vaccine isn't available within 24 hours. Three injections are needed over a month. If you have not been vaccinated you will need a course of five injections starting within 24 hours or as soon as possible after the injury. Vaccination does not provide you with immunity, it merely buys you more time to seek appropriate medical help.

Rift Valley Fever

This haemorrhagic fever is spread through blood to blood products, including those from infected animals. It causes a flulike illness with fever, joint pains and occasionally more serious complications. Complete recovery is possible.

Schistosomiasis

Otherwise known as bilharzia, this is spread by the freshwater snail. It causes infection of the bowel and bladder, often with bleeding. It is caused by a fluke and is contracted through the skin from water contaminated with human urine or faeces. The Nile is known to be full of bilharzia, but paddling or swimming in *any* suspect freshwater lakes or slow-running rivers should be avoided. Possible symptoms include a transient fever and rash, and advanced cases of bilharzia may cause blood in the stool or in the urine, however there may be no symptoms. A blood test can detect antibodies if you have been exposed and treatment is then possible in specialist travel or infectious-disease clinics.

Tuberculosis

Also known as TB, this is spread through close respiratory contact and occasionally through infected milk or milk products. BCG vaccine is recommended for those likely to be mixing closely with the local population. It is more important for those visiting family or planning on a long stay, and those employed as teachers and health-care workers. TB can be asymptomatic, although symptoms can include cough, weight loss or fever, months or even years after exposure. An x-ray is the best way to confirm if you have TB. BCG gives a moderate degree of protection against TB. It causes a small permanent scar at the site of injection, and is usually only given in specialised chest clinics. As it's a live vaccine it should not be given to pregnant women or immuno-compromised individuals. The BCG vaccine is not available in all countries.

Typhoid

This is spread through food or water that has been contaminated by infected human faeces. The first symptom is usually fever or a pink rash on the abdomen. Septicaemia (blood poisoning) may also occur. Typhoid vaccine (typhim Vi, typherix) will give protection for three years. In some countries, the oral vaccine Vivotif is also available.

Yellow Fever

This vaccination isn't required for the Middle East. However, the mosquito that spreads yellow fever has been known to be present in some parts of the Middle East. It is important to consult your local travel health clinic as part of your predeparture plans, for the latest details. For this reason, any travellers from a yellow-fever endemic area will need to show proof of vaccination against yellow fever before entry. This normally means if arriving directly from an infected country or if the traveller has been in an infected country during the last 10 days. We would recommend however that travellers carry a certificate if they have been in an infected country during the previous month, to avoid any possible difficulties with immigration. There is always the possibility that a traveller without an up-to-date certificate will be vaccinated and detained in isolation at the port of arrival for up to 10 days, or even repatriated. The yellow-fever vaccination must be given at a designated clinic. It is valid for 10 years. It is a live vaccine and must not be given to immuno-compromised or pregnant travellers.

In Cairo, you can obtain a yellow-fever vaccine at the medical clinic in Terminal 1 of Cairo airport (approximately E£60). Note that you must show proof of having a yellow-fever vaccination before being allowed entry to or from Sudan.

TRAVELLER'S DIARRHOEA

To prevent diarrhoea, avoid tap water unless it has been boiled, filtered or chemically disinfected (iodine tablets). Eat only fresh fruits or vegetables if cooked or if you have peeled them yourself, and avoid dairy products that might contain unpasteurised milk. Buffet meals are risky. Food should be piping hot; meals freshly cooked in front of you in a busy restaurant are more likely to be safe.

If you develop diarrhoea, be sure to drink plenty of fluids, preferably an oral rehydration solution containing lots of salt and sugar. A few loose stools don't require treatment but, if you start having more than four or five stools a day, you should start taking an antibiotic (usually a quinolone drug) and an antidiarrhoeal agent (such as loperamide). If diarrhoea is bloody, persists for more than 72 hours, is accompanied by fever, shaking chills or severe abdominal pain you should seek medical attention.

ENVIRONMENTAL HAZARDS
Heat Illness

Heat exhaustion occurs following heavy sweating and excessive fluid loss with inadequate replacement of fluids and salt. It is particularly common in hot climates, if you take unaccustomed exercise before full ac-

climatisation. Symptoms include headache, dizziness and tiredness. You're already dehydrated by the time you feel thirsty – aim to drink sufficient water so that you produce pale, diluted urine. Treatment consists of fluid replacement with water or fruit juice or both, and cooling by cold water and fans. The treatment of the salt-loss component consists of taking in salty fluids such as soup or broth, and adding a little more table salt to foods than usual.

Heat stroke is much more serious. This occurs when the body's heat-regulating mechanism breaks down. Excessive rise in body temperature leads to sweating ceasing, irrational and hyperactive behaviour and eventually loss of consciousness and death. Rapid cooling by spraying the body with water and fanning is an ideal treatment. Emergency fluid and electrolyte replacement by intravenous drip is usually also required.

Insect Bites & Stings

Mosquitoes may not carry malaria but can cause irritation and infected bites. They also spread dengue fever. Using DEET-based insect repellents will prevent bites.

Bees and wasps only cause real problems to those with a severe allergy (anaphylaxis). If you have a severe allergy to bee or wasp stings you should carry an adrenaline injection or similar.

Sandflies are located around the Mediterranean beaches. They usually only cause a nasty itchy bite but can carry a rare skin disorder called cutaneous leishmaniasis. Bites may be prevented by using DEET-based repellents.

Scorpions are frequently found in arid or dry climates. They can cause a painful bite which is rarely life threatening.

Bed bugs are often found in hostels and cheap hotels. They lead to very itchy lumpy bites. Spraying the mattress with an appropriate insect killer will do a good job of getting rid of them.

Scabies are also frequently found in cheap accommodation. These tiny mites live in the skin, particularly between the fingers. They cause an intensely itchy rash. Scabies is easily treated with lotion available from pharmacies; people who you come into contact with also need treating to avoid spreading scabies between asymptomatic carriers.

Snake Bites

Do not walk barefoot or stick your hand into holes or cracks. Half of those bitten by venomous snakes are not actually injected with poison (envenomed). If bitten by a snake, do not panic. Immobilise the bitten limb with a splint (eg a stick) and apply a bandage over the site and firm pressure, similar to a bandage over a sprain. Do not apply a tourniquet, or cut or suck the bite. Get the victim to medical help as soon as possible so that antivenin can be given if necessary.

Water

Tap water is not safe to drink throughout Egypt. Stick to bottled water or boil water for 10 minutes, use water-purification tablets or a filter. Do not drink water from rivers or lakes, as this may contain bacteria or viruses that can cause diarrhoea or vomiting.

TRAVELLING WITH CHILDREN

All travellers with children should know how to treat minor ailments and when to seek medical treatment. Make sure the children are up to date with routine vaccinations, and discuss possible travel vaccines well before departure as some vaccines are not suitable for children aged under one year old.

In hot, moist climates any wound or break in the skin may lead to infection. The area should be cleaned and then kept dry and clean. Remember to avoid contaminated food and water. If your child is vomiting or experiencing diarrhoea, lost fluid and salts must be replaced. It may be helpful to take rehydration powders with you, to be reconstituted with boiled water. Ask your doctor about this.

Children should be encouraged to avoid dogs or other mammals because of the risk of rabies and other diseases. Any bite, scratch or lick from a warm-blooded, furry animal should immediately be thoroughly cleaned. If there is any possibility that the animal is infected with rabies, immediate medical assistance should be sought.

WOMEN'S HEALTH

Emotional stress, exhaustion and travelling through different time zones can all contribute to an upset in the menstrual pattern. If using oral contraceptives, remember some antibiotics, diarrhoea and vomiting can stop the pill from working and lead to the risk of pregnancy – remember to take condoms with you just in case. Condoms should be kept in a cool dry place or they may crack and perish.

Emergency contraception is most effective if taken within 24 hours after unprotected sex. The International Planned Parent Federation (www.ippf.org) can advise about the availability of contraception in different countries. Tampons and sanitary towels are not always available outside major cities in the Middle East.

Travelling during pregnancy is usually possible but there are important things to consider. Have a medical check-up before embarking on your trip. The most risky times for travel are during the first 12 weeks of pregnancy, when miscarriage is most likely, and after 30 weeks, when complications such as high blood pressure and premature delivery can occur. Most airlines will not accept a traveller after 28 to 32 weeks of pregnancy, and long-haul flights in the later stages can be very uncomfortable. Antenatal facilities vary greatly between countries in the Middle East and you should think carefully before travelling to a country with poor medical facilities or where there are major cultural and language differences from home. Taking written records of the pregnancy, including details of your blood group, is likely to be helpful if you need medical attention while in a foreign country. Try to find an insurance policy that covers pregnancy, delivery and postnatal care, but remember that insurance policies are only as good as the facilities available.

Language

CONTENTS

Arabic is the official language of Egypt. However, the Arabic spoken on the streets differs greatly from the standard Arabic written in newspapers and spoken on the radio (which is known as Modern Standard Arabic or MSA). MSA is the written and spoken lingua franca that is common to all Arabic-speaking countries.

Egyptian Colloquial Arabic (ECA) is fun, but difficult to learn. It's basically a dialect of the standard language, but so different in many respects as to be virtually another language. As with most dialects, it's the everyday language that differs the most from that of Egypt's other Arabic-speaking neighbours. More specialised or educated language tends to be pretty much the same across the Arab world, although pronunciation may vary considerably. An Arab from, say, Jordan or Iraq will have no problem having a chat about politics or literature with an Egyptian, but might have more trouble making themselves understood in a Cairo bakery.

There is no official written form of the Egyptian Arabic dialect, although there is no practical reason for this – Nobel Prize–winning author Naguib Mahfouz has no trouble writing out whole passages using predominantly Egyptian (or Cairene) slang. For some reason though, foreigners who specifically want to learn Egyptian Arabic instead of MSA are told that it can't be written in script, and are then presented with one system or other of transliteration – none of them totally satisfactory. If you're getting a headache now, you'll have some idea of why few non-Arabs and non-Muslims embark on the study of the language.

Nevertheless, if you take the time to learn even a handful of words and phrases, you'll discover and experience much more while travelling through the country. If you'd like a more comprehensive guide to the language, pick up a copy of Lonely Planet's *Egyptian Arabic Phrasebook*, which includes script for Egyptian Arabic (not MSA) throughout.

Arabic uses masculine and femine forms, which are indicated in this language guide by (m) and (f) respectively, or separated by a slash (m/f) if both forms are given.

TRANSLITERATION

Converting what for most outsiders is just a bunch of squiggles into meaningful words (ie those written using the Roman alphabet) is a tricky business – in fact, no satisfactory system of transliteration has been established, and probably never will be. For this book, an attempt has been made to standardise some spellings of place names and the like.

There is only one article in Arabic: *al* (the). It's also sometimes written as 'il' or 'el' and sometimes modifies to reflect the first consonant of the following noun, eg in Saladin's name, *Salah ad-Din* (righteousness of the faith), the 'al' has been modified to 'ad' before the 'd' of 'Din'. The article *el* is used only in a few instances in this book, such as well-known places (El Alamein, Sharm el-Sheikh) or where locals have used it in restaurant and hotel names.

The whole business of transliteration is fraught with pitfalls, and in a way there are no truly 'correct' systems. The locals themselves can only guess at how to make the conversion – often with amusing results. The fact that French and English have had a big

THE STANDARD ARABIC ALPHABET

Final	Medial	Initial	Alone	Transliteration	Pronunciation
ﺎ			ﺍ	ā/aa	as in 'father'/as the long 'a' in 'ma'am'
ﺐ	ﺒ	ﺑ	ﺏ	b	as in 'bet'
ﺖ	ﺘ	ﺗ	ﺕ	t	as in 'ten'
ﺚ	ﺜ	ﺛ	ﺙ	th	as in 'thin'
ﺞ	ﺠ	ﺟ	ﺝ	g	as in 'go'
ﺢ	ﺤ	ﺣ	ﺡ	H	a strongly whispered 'h', like a sigh of relief
ﺦ	ﺨ	ﺧ	ﺥ	kh	as the 'ch' in Scottish *loch*
ﺪ			ﺩ	d	as in 'dim'
ﺬ			ﺫ	dh	as the 'th' in 'this'
ﺮ			ﺭ	r	a rolled 'r', as in the Spanish word *caro*
ﺰ			ﺯ	z	as in 'zip'
ﺲ	ﺴ	ﺳ	ﺱ	s	as in 'so', never as in 'wisdom'
ﺶ	ﺸ	ﺷ	ﺵ	sh	as in 'ship'
ﺺ	ﺼ	ﺻ	ﺹ	ş	emphatic 's'
ﺾ	ﻀ	ﺿ	ﺽ	ḍ	emphatic 'd'
ﻂ	ﻄ	ﻃ	ﻁ	ţ	emphatic 't'
ﻆ	ﻈ	ﻇ	ﻅ	ẓ	emphatic 'z'
ﻊ	ﻌ	ﻋ	ﻉ	'	the Arabic letter *'ayn*; pronounce as a glottal stop – like the closing of the throat before saying 'Oh-oh!' (see p561)
ﻎ	ﻐ	ﻏ	ﻍ	gh	a guttural sound like Parisian 'r'
ﻒ	ﻔ	ﻓ	ﻑ	f	as in 'far'
ﻖ	ﻘ	ﻗ	ﻕ	q	a strongly guttural 'k' sound; in Egyptian Arabic often pronounced as a glottal stop
ﻚ	ﻜ	ﻛ	ﻙ	k	as in 'king'
ﻞ	ﻠ	ﻟ	ﻝ	l	as in 'lamb'
ﻢ	ﻤ	ﻣ	ﻡ	m	as in 'me'
ﻦ	ﻨ	ﻧ	ﻥ	n	as in 'name'
ﻪ	ﻬ	ﻫ	ﻩ	h	as in 'ham'
ﻮ			ﻭ	w	as in 'wet'; or
				oo	long, as in 'food'; or
				ow	as in 'how'
ﻲ	ﻴ	ﻳ	ﻱ	y	as in 'yes'; or
				ee	as the 'e' in 'ear', only softer; or
				ai/ay	as in 'aisle'/as the 'ay' in 'day'

Vowels Not all Arabic vowel sounds are represented in the alphabet. For more information on the vowel sounds used in this language guide, see p561.

Emphatic Consonants To simplify the transliteration system used in this book, the emphatic consonants have not been included.

influence (though the latter has all but conquered the former in modern Egypt) has led to all sorts of interesting ideas on transliteration. Egypt's high rate of illiteracy doesn't help either. Don't be taken aback if you start noticing half a dozen different spellings for the same thing.

For some reason, the letters **q** and **k** have caused enormous problems, and have been interchanged willy-nilly in transliteration. For a long time, Iraq (which in Arabic is spelled with what can only be described in English using its nearest equivalent: 'q') was written, even by scholars, as 'Irak'. Other examples of an Arabic **q** receiving such treatment are souq (market), often written 'souk'; qasr (castle), sometimes written 'kasr'; and the Cairo suburb of Doqqi, often written 'Dokki', although the Egyptian habit of swallowing 'q' and pronouncing the place name 'Do'i' is a dead giveaway. It's a bit like spelling English 'as she is spoke' – imagine the results if Australians, Americans, Scots and Londoners were all given free rein to write as they pronounce!

PRONUNCIATION

Pronunciation of Arabic can be somewhat tongue-tying for someone unfamiliar with the intonation and combination of sounds. Pronounce the transliterated words and phrases slowly and clearly.

The following guide should help, but it isn't complete because the myriad rules governing pronunciation and vowel use are too extensive to be covered here.

Vowels

a	as in 'had' (sometimes very short)
aa	like the long 'a' sound in 'ma'am'
ā	as the 'a' in 'father'
e	as in 'bet' (sometimes very short)
ee	as in 'beer', only softer
i	as in 'hit'
o	as in 'hot'
ō	as the 'o' in 'four'
oo	as in 'food'
u	as in 'put'

Diphthongs

ow	as in 'how'
ai	as in 'aisle'
ay	as in 'day'

Consonants

Pronunciation of all Arabic consonants is covered in the alphabet table on p560. Note that when double consonants occur in transliterations, each consonant is pronounced. For example, il-Hammām (bathhouse) is pronounced 'il-ham-maam'.

Other Sounds

Arabic has two sounds that are very tricky for non-Arabs to produce: the 'ayn and the glottal stop. The letter 'ayn represents a sound with no English equivalent that comes even close – it is similar to the glottal stop (which is not actually represented in the alphabet) but the muscles at the back of the throat are gagged more forcefully and air is allowed to escape, creating a sound that has been described as reminiscent of someone being strangled! In many transliteration systems 'ayn is represented by an opening quotation mark, and the glottal stop by a closing quotation mark. To make the transliterations in this language guide (and throughout the rest of the book) easier to use, we have not distinguished between the glottal stop and the 'ayn, using the closing quotation mark to represent both sounds. You'll find that Arab speakers will still understand you.

ACCOMMODATION

I'm looking for a ...	a·na ba·*dow*·war *'a*·la ...
pension	ban·syon
hotel	fun·du'
youth hostel	bait sha·*bāb*

Where can I find a cheap hotel?
a·*la'*·ee fun·du' ra·*khees* fayn?
What is the address?
il *'un·waan* ey?
Could you write the address, please?
mum·kin tik·tib/tik·ti·bee il' un·waan min fad·lak? (m/f)
Do you have rooms available?
'an·dak/'an·dik ghu·raf fad·ya? (m/f)

I'd like (a) ...	a·na 'aiz/'ai·za ... (m/f)
I'd like to book (a) ...	'aiz aH·gaz ... low sa·maHt (m)
	'ai·za aH·gaz ... low sa·maH·tee (f)
bed	si·reer
single room	ghur·fa li waa·Hid
double room	ghur·fa bi si·reer muz·dow·ag
room with two beds	ghur·fa bi si·reer·ain

room with a bathroom	ghur·fa bi Ham·mām khās
room with air-con/fan	ghur·fa bi tak·yeef/mar·wa·Ha
bed in a dorm	ghur·fa mush·ta·ri·ka

in the name of ...	bi 'ism ...
date	ta·reekh
from (date) to (date)	min yom (...) li yom (...)
credit card ...	kre·dit kard ...
number	ra·qm
expiry date	ta·reekh al·'in·ti·ha'

How much is it ...?	bi·kam ...?
per night	li lai·la waa·Hid·a
per person	lil fard

Do you have any cheaper rooms?
fee ghu·raf ar·khas?
May I see it?
mum·kin a·shuf·ha?
Where is the bathroom?
fayn il Ham·mām?
I'm/We're leaving today.
(a·na Ham·shi/iH·na Ha·nim·shi) inn·har·da.

CONVERSATION & ESSENTIALS

Arabic is more formal than English, especially with greetings; thus even the simplest greetings, such as 'hello', vary according to when and how they're used. In addition, each greeting requires a certain response that varies according to whether it is being said to a male, female or group of people.

Hello.	sa·lām 'a·lay·kum
(response)	wa 'a·lay·kum es sa·lām
Hello/Welcome.	ah·lan wa sah·lan
(response)	ah·lan beek (to a man)
	ah·lan bee·kee (to a woman)
	ah·lan bee·kum (to a group)
Good morning.	sa·bāH al·khayr
(response)	sa·bāH an·noor
Good evening.	mi·sa' al·khayr
(response)	mi·sa' an·noor
Good night.	tis·baH 'a·la khayr (to a man)
	tis·baH·ee 'a·la khayr (to a woman)
	tis·baH·u 'a·la khayr (to a group)
(response)	wen·ta bi·khayr (to a man)
	wen·tee bi·khayr (to a woman)
	wen·too bi·khayr (to a group)
Goodbye.	ma'·as sa·laa·ma
Yes.	ai·wa (or na·'am – more formal)
No.	la'

Please.
min fad·lak/fad·lik/fad·lu·kum (to man/woman/group; used when asking for something in a shop)
low sa·maHt/sa·maH·tee/sa·maH·tu (to man/woman/group; similar, but more formal)
tfad·dal/tfad·da·lee/tfad·da·loo (to man/woman/group; used when offering something or inviting someone)
it·fad·dal/it·fad·da·lee/it·fad·da·loo (to man/woman/group; similar, or can mean 'Please, go ahead and do something)

Thank you (very much).
shu·kran (ga·zee·lan)
Excuse me.
'an iz·nak, es·maH·lee (to man)
'an iz·nik, es·ma·Hee·lee (to woman)
'an iz·nu·kum, es·ma·Hoo·lee (to group)
That's fine/You're welcome.
'af·wan (or al·'aff·u)

Sorry. (ie forgive me)	'as·sif
What's your name?	is·ma key? (to man)
	is·mi key? (to woman)
My name is ...	is·mee ...
Pleased to meet you.	ta·shar·raf·na (pol)
(when first meeting)	fur·sa sa·'eed·a (inf)
How are you?	iz·zay·yak? (to a man)
	iz·zay·yik? (to a woman)
	iz·za·yu·kum? (to a group)
I'm fine.	kway·yis il·Ham·du lil·lah (to a man)
	kway·yi·sa il·Ham·du lil·lah (to a woman)
	kway·seen il·Ham·du lil·lah (to a group)

(On their own, kwayyis/a/een literally mean 'good' or 'fine', but they are rarely heard alone in response to 'How are you?')

Where are you from?	en·ta/en·tee min·ain? (m/f)
I'm from ...	a·na min ...
I like/don't like ...	a·na ba·Hibb/ma·ba·Hib·bish
Just a minute.	da·'ee·'a waa·Hid·a

A useful word to know is imshee, which means 'Go away'. Use this at the Pyramids or at other tourist sites when you are being besieged by children. Don't use it on adults; instead, just say, la' shukran (No thanks).

DIRECTIONS

| Where is ...? | fayn ...? |
| Go straight ahead. | 'a·la tool |

SIGNS

Entrance	مدخل
Exit	خروج
Open	مفتوح
Closed	مغلق
Prohibited	ممنوع
Information	معلومات
Hospital	مستشفى
Police	شرطة
Men's Toilet	حمام للرجال
Women's Toilet	حمام للنساء

Turn left.	How·id shi·*māl*
Turn right.	How·id yi·*meen*
at the (next) corner	'al·al nas·ya (il·li gai·ya)
at the traffic lights	'and il i·*shā*·ra
behind	wa·ra
in front of	'ud·*daam*
far (from)	ba·*'eed* ('an)
near (to)	'u·ra·yib (min)
opposite	'u·*sād*

here	hi·na
there	hi·*naak*
this address	al·'an·waan da
north	shi·*maal*
south	ga·*noob*
east	shark
west	gharb

beach	al blaaj/ash·*shā*·ti
bridge	ku·bri
castle	al·a·a
my hotel	il fun·duq be·taa·'ee
island	ga·zee·ra
main square	al·mai·daan ar·ra·'ee·si
mosque	al·gaa·me'
museum	al·mat·Haf
old city	al·me·dee·na al·'a·dee·ma
palace	al·'asr
pyramids	ah·ra·*māt*
The Pyramids (of Giza)	al·ah·*rām*
ruins	a·*sār*
sea	baHr
square	mi·*daan*
street	ash·shaa·ri'
tower	burg
university	al·ga·m'a
village	al·qar·ya

HEALTH

I'm ill.	a·na 'ai·yaan/a (m/f)
My friend is ill.	sa·dee·qi 'ai·yaan
It hurts here.	bi·yuw·ga·'ni hi·na

I'm ...	'an·dee ...
asthmatic	az·mit ra·boo
diabetic	is suk·kar
epileptic	sa·ra'

I'm allergic ...	'an·dee Ha·sa·siy·ya ...
to antibiotics	min mu·*dād* Hai·o·wi
to aspirin	min as·bi·reen
to penicillin	min bi·ni·si·*leen*
to bees	min naHl
to nuts	min mu·*kas*·sar·āt

antiseptic	mu·*tah*·hir
aspirin	as·bir·een
condoms	'aa·zil za·ka·ry (ka·boot, slang)
contraceptive	wa·sā·'il man·a' il Haml
diarrhoea	is·haal
fever	su·khoo·na
headache	su·*dā*'
hospital	mus·*tash*·fa
medicine	dow·a
pharmacy	ag·za·khaa·na or sai·da·liy·ya
pregnant	Haa·mel
prescription	ro·shet·ta
sanitary napkins	fu·wat sa·Hiy·ya
stomachache	wa·ga' fil *bātn*
sunblock cream	kreym di dish·shams
tampons	tam·bax

EMERGENCIES

Help!	el·Ha'·nee!
There's been an accident.	fee Had·sa!
I'm lost.	a·na tā·yih/tāy·ha (m/f)
Go away!	im·shee!
Call a doctor!	i·tas·sal bi·dok·toor! (m)
	i·tas·sal·ee bi·dok·toor! (f)
Call the police!	i·tas·sal bil·bo·lees!
I've been robbed.	a·na it·sa·ra't
Where are the toilets?	fayn at·twa·let?

LANGUAGE DIFFICULTIES

Do you speak English?
en·ta bi·tit·kal·lim in·glee·zee? (to a man)
en·tee bi·tit·kal·li·mee in·glee·zee? (to a woman)
Does anyone here speak English?
fee Hadd bi·yit·kal·lim in·glee·zee?
How do you say ... in Egyptian Arabic?
iz·zai a·'ool ... bil 'a·ra·bee?
What does ... mean?
ya'·ni ... ey?
I understand.
a·na faa·hem/fah·ma (m/f)

I don't understand.
   a·na mish *faa*·hem/*fah*·ma (m/f)
Please write it down.
   mum·kin tik·*ti*·buh/tik·*ti*·beeh? (m/f)
Can you show me (on the map)?
   mum·kin ti·war·*ree*·ni ('*al*·al kha·*ree*·ta)?

NUMBERS

Arabic numerals are simple to learn and, unlike the written language, run from left to right. Pay attention to the order of the words in numbers from 21 to 99. When followed by a noun, the pronunciation of *miyya* changes to *meet* for the numbers 100 and 300–900, and the noun is always used in its singular form.

0	sifr	•
1	*waa*·Hid	١
2	it·*nayn*	٢
3	ta·*laa*·ta	٣
4	ar·*ba*·a	٤
5	*kham*·sa	٥
6	*sit*·ta	٦
7	*sa*·b'a	٧
8	ta·*man*·ya	٨
9	*ti*·s'a	٩
10	'*ash*·a·ra	١•
11	Hid·'*ash*·ar	١١
12	it·*n'ash*·ar	١٢
13	ta·lat·*t'ash*·ar	١٣
14	ar·ba·'·*t'ash*·ar	١٤
15	kha·mas·*t'ash*·ar	١٥
16	sit·*t'ash*·ar	١٦
17	sa·ba·'·*t'ash*·ar	١٧
18	ta·man·*t'ash*·ar	١٨
19	ti·sa·'·*t'ash*·ar	١٩
20	'*ish*·reen	٢•
21	*waa*·Hid wi '*ish*·reen	٢١
22	it·*nayn* wi '*ish*·reen	٢٢
30	ta·la·*teen*	٣•
40	ar·ba·'*een*	٤•
50	kham·*seen*	٥•
60	sit·*teen*	٦•
70	sab·'*een*	٧•
80	ta·ma·*neen*	٨•
90	tisa·'*een*	٩•
100	*miy*·ya (*meet* before a noun)	١••
200	mi·*tayn*	٢••
1000	'alf	١•••
2000	'alf·*ayn*	٢•••

How many?   kam *waa*·Hid?

PAPERWORK

name	ism
nationality	gin·*siy*·ya
date/place of birth	ta·*reekh*/ma·*Hal* il mi·*laad*
sex (gender)	gins
passport	bas·*boor* or gow·*aaz* is sa·far
visa	ta'·*shee*·ra

QUESTION WORDS

Who?	meen?
What?	ey?
When?	*im*·ta?
Where?	fayn?
How?	iz·*zay*?
Which?	ayy?

SHOPPING & SERVICES

I'd like to buy ...	'*aiz*/'*ai*·za ash·*ti*·ri ... (m/f)
How much is it?	bi·*kam* da?
I don't like it.	mish '·a·*gib*·ni
May I look at it?	*mum*·kin a·*shoo*·fu?
I'm just looking.	bat·*far*·rag bas
It's cheap.	da ra·*khees*
It's too expensive.	da *ghaa*·lee '*ow*·ee
No more than ...	mish *ak*·tār min ...
I'll take it.	'·a·*khud*·ha
Can you give me ...?	*mum*·kin tid·*dee*·ni ...?
a discount	takh·*feed*
a good price	sa'r *kway*·yis
Do you accept ...?	bi·*ta*·khud ...? (m)
	bi·*ta*·khu·dee ...? (f)
credit cards	*kre*·dit kard
traveller cheques	sheek si·*yaa*·Hi
more	*ak*·tar
less	a'·all
smaller	as·ghar
bigger	*ak*·bar
I'm looking for ...	*a*·na ba·*dow*·war '*a*·la
a bank	bank
the bazaar/market	as·*sooq*
the city centre	wust al·*ba*·lad
the (...) embassy	as·si·*fā*·ra (...)
the post office	al·*boos*·ta/*mak*·tab al·ba·*reed*
the telephone centre	sen·*traal* it·te·li·fo·*naat*
the tourist office	*mak*·tab as·si·*yaa*·Ha
I want to change ...	*a*·na '*aiz*/'*ai*·za u·sar·*raf* ... (m/f)
money	fu·*loos*
travellers cheques	shee·*kaat* si·ya·*Hiy*·ya

TIME & DATES

What time is it?	*saa·'a kam?*
It's (8) o'clock.	*saa'a (ta·man·ya)*
in the morning	*sa·ba·Han*
in the afternoon	*ba'·d id duhr*
in the evening	*bil layl*
today	*inn·har·da*
tomorrow	*bo·kra*
yesterday	*im·be·riH*
day	*yom*
month	*shahr*
week	*us·bu·'a*
year	*sa·na*
early	*ba·dree*
late	*mit·'akh·ar*
daily	*kull yom*

Monday	(yom) al·it·*nayn*
Tuesday	(yom) at·ta·*laat*
Wednesday	(yom) al·*ar*·ba'a
Thursday	(yom) al·kha·*mees*
Friday	(yom) al·*gu*·m'a
Saturday	(yom) as·sabt
Sunday	(yom) al·Hadd

January	*ya·nay·ir*
February	*fi·bra·yir*
March	*maa·ris*
April	*ab·reel*
May	*ma·yu*
June	*yun·yu*
July	*yul·yu*
August	*a·ghus·tus*
September	*sib·tim·bir*
October	*'uk·too·bir*
November	*nu·fim·bir*
December	*di·sim·bir*

TRANSPORT
Public Transport

When does the ... leave/arrive?	*im·ta qi·yaam/wu·suul ...?*
boat	*al·mar·kib*
bus	*al·o·to·bees*
ferry	*ma'a·diy·ya*
plane	*al·tay·yā·ra*
train	*al·'atr*

I'd like a ... ticket.	*'ayz/'ayz·a ... taz·kar·it* (m/f)
one-way	*zi·haab*
return	*'ow·da*
1st-class	*da·ra·ga oo·la*
2nd-class	*da·ra·ga tan·ya*

I want to go to ...	*a·na 'aiz/'ai·za a·rooH ...* (m/f)
The train has been cancelled/delayed.	*il·'atr it·'akh·khar/it·la·gha*
Which bus goes to ...?	*o·to·bees nim·ra kam ye·rooH ...?*
Does this bus go to ...?	*al·o·to·bees da ye·rooH ...?*
Please tell me when we arrive in ...	*min fad·lak, 'ul·lee em·ta Ha·noo·sel ...*
What is the fare to ...?	*bi·kam at·taz·ka·ra li ...?*
Stop here, please.	*wa·'if hi·na, min fad·lak*
Wait!	*is·tan·na!*

the first	*il aw·wil/oo·la* (m/f)
the last	*il aa·khir*
the next	*il·li gayy*
airport	*ma·tār*
bus station	*ma·Hat·tat a·lo·to·bees*
bus stop	*maw·'if a·lo·to·bees*
city	*al·me·dee·na*
platform number	*ra·seef nim·ra*
station	*al·ma·Hat·ta*
ticket office	*mak·tab at·ta·zaa·ker*
timetable	*gad·wal*
train station	*ma·Hat·tat al·'atr*

Private Transport

I'd like to hire	*'aiz/'ai·za a·'ag·gār ...* (m/f)
a/an ...	
car	*say·yā·ra/'a·ra·biy·ya*
4WD	*'a·ra·biy·yet gharz/jeep*
motorbike	*mu·tu·sikl*
bicycle	*'a·ga·la*
camel	*ga·mal*
donkey	*Hu·mār*
horse	*Hu·sān*

Is this the road to ...?	*i·ta·ree' da yi·was·sil li ...?*
(How long) Can I park here?	*mum·kin ar·kin hi·na (ad·di ay)?*
Where do I pay?	*ad·fa'a fayn?*
I need a mechanic.	*miH·taag/miH·taa·ga me·ka·nee·ki* (m/f)
The car/motorbike has broken down (at ...)	*il 'a·ra·biy·ya/mu·tu·sikl 'i·til 'and ...*
The car/motorbike won't start.	*il 'a·ra·biy·ya/mu·tu·sikl mish bit·door*

I have a flat tyre.
il ka·*witsh* nay·im
I've run out of petrol.
il ben·*zeen* khi·lis
I've had an accident.
kaan '*an*·dee *Had*·sa
Where's a service station?
fayn ma·*Hat*·tet ben·*zeen*?
Please fill it up.
faw·*wil*·ha, low sa·*maHt*
I'd like (30) litres.
'aiz/'*ai*·za (ta·la·*teen*) litr (m/f)

diesel	so·*lār*
leaded petrol	ta·ma·*neen* (regular)
	ti·sa·'*een* (super)
unleaded petrol	min ghair ru·*sās* or
	kham·sa wa ti·sa·'*een*

TRAVEL WITH CHILDREN

Is there a/an ...?	fee ...?
I need a/an	'aiz/'*ai*·za ... (m/f)
car baby seat	*kur*·si 'a·ra·*biy*·ya li tifl
child-minding service	*khid*·mat ra'·*ai*·it tifl
children's menu	me·*nai* lil at·*fāl*
nappies/diapers	*bam*·bers (brand name)
formula (milk)	*la*·ban mu·*ga*·faf lil *bay*·bi
(English-speaking) babysitter	*ga*·lis·at at·*fāl* (bi·tit·*kall*·im in·*glee*·zee)
highchair	*kur*·si lil at·*fāl*
potty	as·*riy*·ya

Do you mind if I breastfeed here?
mum·kin a·*rad*·da·'a *hi*·na?
Are children allowed?
mas·mooH bis·ti·*Haab* il at·*fāl*?

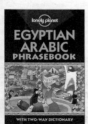

Also available from Lonely Planet:
Egyptian Arabic Phrasebook

Glossary

For a glossary of Pharaonic terms, see p62, and for food and drink terms, see p89.

abd – servant of
abeyya – woman's gown
abu – father, saint
ahwa – coffee, coffeehouse
ain – well, spring

ba'al – grocer
bab – gate or door
baksheesh – alms, tip
baladi – local, rural
bawwab – doorman
beit – house
bey – term of respect
bir – spring, well
burg – tower
bustan – walled garden

calèche – horse-drawn carriage
caravanserai – merchants' inn
careta – donkey cart

dahabiyya – houseboat
darb – track, street
deir – monastery, convent
domina – dominoes

effendi – gentleman
eid – Islamic feast
emir – Islamic ruler, military commander or governor; literally, prince

fellah – (plural: fellaheen) peasant farmer or agricultural worker who makes up the majority of Egypt's population; fellaheen literally means ploughman or tiller of the soil
filoos – money

galabiyya – man's full-length robe
gebel – mountain
gezira – island
ghawazee – cast of dancers who travelled with story-tellers and poets; they performed publicly or for hire
guinay – pound (currency)

haikal – altar area
haj – pilgrimage to Mecca; all Muslims should make the journey at least once in their lifetime

haji – a man who has made the *haj* to Mecca (female: hajia)
hammam – bathhouse
hantour – horse-drawn carriage
haram – anything forbidden by Islamic law
hegab – woman's headscarf
Hejira – Islamic calendar; Mohammed's flight from Mecca to Medina in AD 622

ibn – son of
iconostasis – screen with doors and icons set in tiers, used in Eastern Christian churches
iftar – breaking the fast after sundown during the month of *Ramadan*
iwan – vaulted hall, opening into a central court in a *madrassa* or a mosque

al-jeel – a type of music characterised by a hand-clapping rhythm overlaid with a catchy vocal; literally 'the generation'

kershef – building material made of large chunks of salt mixed with rock and plastered in local clay
khamsin – a dry, hot wind from the Western Desert
khan – another name for a *caravanserai*
khanqah – *Sufi* monastery
khedive – Egyptian viceroy under Ottoman suzerainty
khwaga – foreigner
kineesa – church
kuttab – Quranic school

leila kebira – 'big night'; climax of a *moulid*
lokanda – basic, cheap place to doss

ma'abad – temple
madrassa – school, especially one associated with a mosque
mahattat – station
makwagee – laundry man
malqaf – angled wind catchers on the roof that direct the prevailing northerly breezes down into the building
maristan – hospital
mashrabiyya – ornate carved wooden panel or screen; a feature of Islamic architecture
mastaba – mud-brick structure in the shape of a bench above tombs that was the basis for later pyramids; Arabic word for 'bench'
matar – airport
mawladiyya – people who provide the infrastructure for *moulids*
midan – town or city square

mihrab – niche in the wall of a mosque that indicates the direction of Mecca

minbar – pulpit in a mosque

Misr – Egypt (also means Cairo)

moulid – religious festival

muezzin – mosque official who calls the faithful to prayer

mufti – Muslim legal expert or leader of the religious community

mugzzabin – *Sufi* followers who participate in *zikrs*

muqarnas – stalactite-like stone carving used to decorate doorways and window recesses

nahr – river

nai – reed pipe

oud – a type of lute

piastre – Egyptian currency; one Egyptian pound consists of 100 piastres

qa'a – reception room

qala'a – fortress

qasa'id – long poems

qasr – castle or palace

Ramadan – ninth month of the lunar Islamic calendar during which Muslims fast from sunrise to sunset

ras – headland

sabil – public drinking fountain

sakia – water wheel

sandale – modified felucca

servees – service taxi

shaabi – music of the working class

shadouf – water wheel used for irrigation purposes

sharia – road or street

sharm – bay

sheesha – water pipe

siga – a game played in the dirt with clay balls or seeds

souq – market

speos – rock-cut tomb or chapel

Sufi – follower of any of the Islamic mystical orders that emphasise dancing, chanting and trances in order to attain unity with God

tabla – small hand-held drum

tahtib – male dance performed with wooden staves

tarboosh – the hat known elsewhere as a fez

tasreeh – permit for camping

towla – backgammon

ulema – group of Muslim scholars or religious leaders; a member of this group

umm – mother of

wadi – desert watercourse, dry except in the rainy season

waha – oasis

wikala – another name for a *caravanserai*

zikr – long sessions of dancing, chanting and swaying usually carried out by *Sufi mugzzabin* to achieve oneness with God

Behind the Scenes

THIS BOOK

This eighth edition of *Egypt* was commissioned in Lonely Planet's Melbourne office and researched and written by Virginia Maxwell (coordinating author), Mary Fitzpatrick, Siona Jenkins and Anthony Sattin. Dr Joann Fletcher wrote the Pharaonic Egypt chapter and reviewed the book's other pharaonic content, as she has done for the past two editions. The Health chapter was adapted from material written by Dr Caroline Evans. The 7th edition of *Egypt* was researched and written by Andrew Humphreys, Gadi Farfour, Siona Jenkins and Anthony Sattin, and the 6th edition by Andrew Humphreys, Gadi Farfour and Siona Jenkins.

THANKS from the Authors

Virginia Maxwell In Egypt, many thanks to Hisham Youssif of the Berlin Hotel in Cairo, Caroline Evanoff, Mourad Gamil Abd Rabu from the Tourist Office in Luxor and Salah Muhammad from Noga Tours in Cairo. Thanks also go to my fellow authors Mary Fitzpatrick, Siona Jenkins and Anthony Sattin. All generously shared their knowledge and great love of Egypt. Discoveries on the road were shared with my favourite travelling companions, Max and Peter. Max would like to thank Nobi and his family in Luxor for a great day, Rami for use of the MP3 player at Saqqara and Mohammed for an exciting trip through the Western Desert. In Melbourne, thanks to Lonely Planet commissioning editors Lynne Preston and Kerryn Burgess, managing cartographer Shahara Ahmed and cartographer Mandy Sierp.

Siona Jenkins The Egyptian reputation for kindness and hospitality is well-founded and having a baby in tow made the help even more appreciated. Thanks to Karima Khalil and Max Rodenbeck for a place to relax in Cairo and a crucial car seat, Muhammed Mustafa for logistical help, Mohamed for driving and babysitting in Luxor, Osama Abd el Hafiz and Mourad Gamil in Luxor's tourist office for patiently answering last minute questions and Hakeem Hussein and Shukry Saad for help in Aswan. Final thanks to Leo and James for helping me find time to write and to Keira for being so good natured as she was bounced around Upper Egypt in often extreme heat.

Anthony Sattin As ever, many people made the travel and research both easier and more enjoyable, among them my partner Sylvie Franquet, Colin Clement, Abdallah Baghi, Mounir Neamatalla, Mahdi Hweiti, Peter Gaballa, Muhammad Abd el-Kadir, Ashraf Lotfi, Pascal Quint, Saad and Hamdi Ali, Wael Abed, Omar Ahmad, Ibrahim Hassan, Ibrahim Mohamed, Misr Limousine and Avis Cairo. Thanks also to all at Lonely Planet, especially commissioning editors Lynne Preston, Stefanie Di Trocchio and Kerryn Burgess, coordinating author Virginia Maxwell and map guru Shahara Ahmed. Final thanks to the concerned security forces who watched me wherever I went in the country.

CREDITS

Commissioning Editors Kerryn Burgess, Lynne Preston
Coordinating Editor Kate Whitfield
Coordinating Cartographers Simon Tillema, Kusnandar

THE LONELY PLANET STORY

The story begins with a classic travel adventure: Tony and Maureen Wheeler's 1972 journey across Europe and Asia to Australia. There was no useful information about the overland trail then, so Tony and Maureen published the first Lonely Planet guidebook to meet a growing need.

From a kitchen table, Lonely Planet has grown to become the largest independent travel publisher in the world, with offices in Melbourne (Australia), Oakland (USA) and London (UK). Today Lonely Planet guidebooks cover the globe. There is an ever-growing list of books and information in a variety of media. Some things haven't changed. The main aim is still to make it possible for adventurous travellers to get out there – to explore and better understand the world.

At Lonely Planet we believe travellers can make a positive contribution to the countries they visit – if they respect their host communities and spend their money wisely. Every year 5% of company profit is donated to charities around the world.

Coordinating Layout Designer Katie Thuy Bui
Managing Cartographer Shahara Ahmed
Assisting Editors Dianne Schallmeiner, Nigel Chin, Lutie Clark, Charlotte Orr, Louisa Syme, Sasha Baskett, Lauren Rollheiser, Helen Koehne, Kate McLeod, Brooke Lyons
Assisting Cartographers Sophie Reed, Katie Cason, Jacqueline Nguyen
Assisting Layout Designer Wibowo Rusli
Cover Designer Pepi Bluck
Colour Designer Carol Jackson
Indexers Kate Whitfield, Kate McLeod
Project Manager Fabrice Rocher
Language Content Coordinator Quentin Frayne

Thanks to Glenn Beanland, David Burnett, Stefanie Di Trocchio, Yvonne Bischofberger, Melanie Dankel, Sally Darmody, Brigitte Ellemor, James Hardy, Adriana Mammarella, Wayne Murphy, Darren O'Connell, Malisa Plesa, Diana Saad, Suzannah Shwer, Amanda Sierp, Celia Wood

THANKS from Lonely Planet
Many thanks to the hundreds of travellers who used the last edition and wrote to us with helpful hints, useful advice and interesting anecdotes.

A Peter Abdon, Elise Ackerman, Peter Adamson, Carina Aeppli, Jorge Alves, Kristof Ampe, Isabell Andreasson, Cameron Anley, Georgios Axarlis, Mehdi Azam **B** Tom Baecker, Inti Bakker, Tim Barber, Ann Barrett, Filip Bartczak, Kirsten Bel, Caroline Bell, Jeltsje Benedictus, Giorgio Biscari, Claudine Bonder, Alison Bonner, Kim Boreham, David Bos, Cliff Bott, Carol Brazier, Yasmin Brennan, Lindsay Brett, Ken Brown, Richard Brown, Toby Brown, Michael Bucksmith, Ivette Buere, John Bushby **C** Paul Cammaert, Pa Carlier, Niall Carter, Rachel Carter, Desideria Cavina, Chris Chan, Andre Chappot, Mark & Claire Charlwood, Amanda Chase, Yasmin Chaudhry, Angela Cheadle, Bei Chen, Karen Cheung, Kate Chisholm, Debora Chobanian, Umberto Ciccarelli, Lynne Collings, John Collins, Edward Comfort, Debra Conkey, Pinky Contractor, Kay Louise Cook, Simon Cooke, Daniel Cooper, Jeff Cords, Neil Cornick, Will Cottrell, Joanne Crawford, Tara Cujovic **D** Sion Davies, Richard Dawson, Mike Day, Scott Day, Jenny de Booy, Jan Peter de Grauw, Jonas de Jong, Marielle de Sain, Maria de With, Levente Deák, Anthony Dean, Julie Dean, Paul Dehaan, Damjan Demsar, Amir Dessouki, Drew Dilkens, Melanie Dohoda, Jeffrey Dorfman, Tonia Dunnette **E** Hugh Edwards, Alvis Eglitis, Albrecht Eisen, Bassam Suhail El Nayeef, Samira El-Majzoub, Jake England, Massimo Evangelisti **F** Romy Farrelly, Allen Fisher, Mark Fissel, Dan Forrester, Lauren Foster, Helena Frontil **G** Emily Gale, Christina Galic, Nicole Gallahar, Andreas Gasser, Ziegler Georg, Heinz Gerber, David Gerrard, Andrew Gibbs, Gawaine Glasby, Florian Goessmann, Geir Gogstad, Maelle Goldberg, Neil Goldsmith, Mikael Grahn, Monica Gupta **H** Abby Hales, Darren Hales, Jenny Hall, Aimee Harlan, Andy Harley, Leanne Harlick, S Harrall, Chris Havre, Roger Hennekens, Judith Henson, Rune Henvig, Derek Hoffman, John Hogan, Tamer Hossien, Michael Houston, Robyn Howard, Frank Hsin, Yu Ching Hsu, Simon Hudson, Karen Hunnisett, Graham Hurst, Michelle Hutton **I** Alene Ivey **J** Tan Janice, Rok Jarc, Guan Jiaxin, Benny Jonason, Eschauzier Jonathan, Yvette Jones, Boris Josipovic, Matthias Junken **K** Mona Karlsson, Vit Karvay, Karen Kavas, Jim Kennedy, Gareth Key, Lisa Keys, Gil Kezwer, Bob Kieckhefer, Gregor Kier, Alexander King, Sandra Knight, Ingrid Kottke, Owen Kruger, Joshua Kuswadi, Joanna Kyffin **L** Alejandro Laborda Vicuña, Susannah Lancashire, Ines Lawicki, Karen Lawson, Steve Lazatin, Ana Lazic, Cyrex Lee, Mike Lee, Vicki Lee, Ulla Lehtonen, Ivor Leonard, John Lloyd **M** Lizzie Mace, Liz Mair, Michael Malone, Jason C Maloney, Edward Marshall, Cindy McCallum, Stevan McCallum, Roy C Merano, Nikola Milcic, Andrew Miller, Brian Milloy, Mike Mimirinis, Aykut Misirligil, Hiroko Miyokawa, Tammy Moharram, Hugh Mongey, Melanie Monroe, Dore J Montes, Ruben Mooijman, John Morrison, Alison Mountain, Veronika Mueller, April Mulqueen, Kim Munro, Ross Murrell **N** Severin Nawrockyj, Raquel Neto, Joy Neugebauer, Stefan Neuman, Melanie Nicholls, Dan Norman, Sandi Notredame **O** Delwyn Ogden, Simon Ohmsen, Daniel O'Kelly, Staffan Olofsson, Heather Osborn, Patrick Ostyn, Peter Ottis **P** Alexander Page, Madolene Page-Wood, Sarah Park, Sam Pearse, Catherine Peppers, Palfi Peter, Hoang Phan, Julie Picard, Eckhard Piegsa, Nicola Pierce, Marcela Pinzon Mejia, Jure Plahutnik, Anne Podt, Liam Pounder, Rita Powell, Jose Pozuelo, Roxanne Pritchard, Nina Prochazka **Q** Mark Quandt, Brendan Quirk **R** Jakub Radocha, Claire Ranyard, Michael Raue, Adi Raveh, Carole Rawlinson, Charlotte Rawlinson, Samantha & Adnan Reguieg, Stephan Rey, Katherine Richards, Paul Richardson, Clive Robson,

Cheryl Rogers, Michael Romig, Karen Rose, Anne Rothwell, Alma Roussy, Keith Rowlands, Anil Rupani **S** Adrian Sackson, Marcin Sadurski, Marianne Sahli, Mohamed Salah, Anne Sauer, Adrian Sayers, Louis J Scerri, Greg Schachtman, Karen & Thomas Schembri, Lyons Sean, Kodzo Selormey, Craig Shaw, Jo Shaw, Farne Sinclair, Jennifer Slater, Ann Smith, Diana Smith, Kelly Smith, Pablo Soledad, Niloo Soleimani, Carmencita Soriano, Sarah Stead, Anna Stevens, Peter Stibal **T** Naureen Tadros, Adam Tang, Garry Tarapaski, Helena Telfer, Joanna Then, Raphael Thies, James Thomson, Darja Tjioe, Janina Torkar, Paul Troon, Hau Yen Tsen, Laurence Tuckwood, Alan Tulla, Tomaz Tusar, Warren Tute, Deborah Tyler **U** Tania Utley **V** Kristjan Väärt, Tuma Valerio Secondo, Juha Valimaki, Jurge van de Peppel, Guido van Garsse, Michelle Vanny, Helen Vaux, Xavier Vilalta, Milena Vojtech, Eric Volkman, Joachim von Loeben **W** Robbert Wagemaker, Tony Wagman, Sandra Waterhouse, Mike, Joanna, Ben & Amy Watson, Robyn Webb, David Webster, Goh Wee, Tao Wei, Patrick Werr, Deirdre Whelan, Frances Wiig, Ian Wikarski, Samantha Wildeman, Hilary Wise, Wim Woittiez, Brad Woodcock, Marshall Woodworth, Julie Wyss **Y** Deirdre Yapp, Evangeline Yeun, Colin Youl, Hyangwoon Young, Martin Yoxall **Z** Libor Zidek

ACKNOWLEDGMENTS

Many thanks to the following for the use of their content: Globe on back cover © Mountain High Maps 1993 Digital Wisdom, Inc.

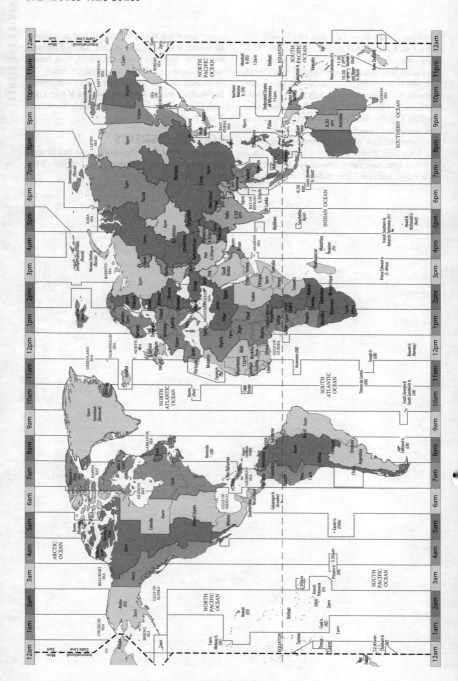

Index

Index

INDEX

MAP LEGEND

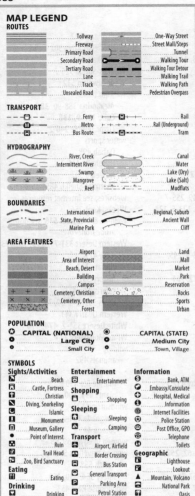

ROUTES

	Tollway		One-Way Street
	Freeway		Street Mall/Steps
	Primary Road		Tunnel
	Secondary Road		Walking Tour
	Tertiary Road		Walking Tour Detour
	Lane		Walking Trail
	Track		Walking Path
	Unsealed Road		Pedestrian Overpass

TRANSPORT

	Ferry		Rail
	Metro		Rail (Underground)
	Bus Route		Tram

HYDROGRAPHY

	River, Creek		Canal
	Intermittent River		Water
	Swamp		Lake (Dry)
	Mangrove		Lake (Salt)
	Reef		Mudflats

BOUNDARIES

	International		Regional, Suburb
	State, Provincial		Ancient Wall
	Marine Park		Cliff

AREA FEATURES

	Airport		Land
	Area of Interest		Mall
	Beach, Desert		Market
	Building		Park
	Campus		Reservation
	Cemetery, Christian		Rocks
	Cemetery, Other		Sports
	Forest		Urban

POPULATION

⊕	**CAPITAL (NATIONAL)**	◉	**CAPITAL (STATE)**
●	**Large City**	◉	**Medium City**
●	Small City	●	Town, Village

SYMBOLS

Sights/Activities
- Beach
- Castle, Fortress
- Christian
- Diving, Snorkeling
- Islamic
- Monument
- Museum, Gallery
- Point of Interest
- Ruin
- Trail Head
- Zoo, Bird Sanctuary

Eating
- Eating

Drinking
- Drinking
- Café

Entertainment
- Entertainment

Shopping
- Shopping

Sleeping
- Sleeping
- Camping

Transport
- Airport, Airfield
- Border Crossing
- Bus Station
- General Transport
- Parking Area
- Petrol Station
- Taxi Rank

Information
- Bank, ATM
- Embassy/Consulate
- Hospital, Medical
- Information
- Internet Facilities
- Police Station
- Post Office, GPO
- Telephone
- Toilets

Geographic
- Lighthouse
- Lookout
- Mountain, Volcano
- National Park
- Oasis
- River Flow

LONELY PLANET OFFICES

Australia
Head Office
Locked Bag 1, Footscray, Victoria 3011
☎ 03 8379 8000, fax 03 8379 8111
talk2us@lonelyplanet.com.au

USA
150 Linden St, Oakland, CA 94607
☎ 510 893 8555, toll free 800 275 8555
fax 510 893 8572
info@lonelyplanet.com

UK
72–82 Rosebery Ave,
Clerkenwell, London EC1R 4RW
☎ 020 7841 9000, fax 020 7841 9001
go@lonelyplanet.co.uk

Published by Lonely Planet Publications Pty Ltd
ABN 36 005 607 983

© Lonely Planet Publications Pty Ltd 2006

© photographers as indicated 2006

Cover photographs: Egyptian playing football at the Pyramids Egypt, Hugh Sitton/Alamy (front); Camel handler, Birqash market, Cairo, Sara-Jane Cleland/Lonely Planet Images (back). Pharaonic Egypt illustrations by Yukiyoshi Kamimura. Many of the images in this guide are available for licensing from Lonely Planet Images: www.lonelyplanetimages.com.

Printed through The Bookmaker International Ltd.
Printed in China